Kleppner's ADVERTISING PROCEDURE

Sixteenth Edition

W. Ronald Lane
University of Georgia

Karen Whitehill King
University of Georgia

J. Thomas Russell
Piedmont College

PEARSON

Prentice
Hall

Upper Saddle River, New Jersey 07458

Library of Congress Cataloging-in-Publication Data

Lane, W. Ronald
  Kleppner's advertising procedure / W. Ronald Lane, Karen King, J. Thomas Russell.—
16th ed.
    p. cm.
  Includes bibliographical references and index.
  ISBN 0-13-140412-1
    1. Advertising. I. King, Karen. II. Russell, Thomas, 1941- III. Kleppner, Otto, 1899-
Advertising procedure. IV. Title.
  HF5823.K45 2004
  659.1—dc22

                                                                        2004044713

Acquisitions Editor: Wendy Craven
VP/Editorial Director: Jeff Shelstad
Assistant Editor: Melissa Pellerano
Editorial Assistant: Rebecca Cummings
AVP/Executive Marketing Manager: Michelle O'Brien
Marketing Assistant: Nicole Macciavelli
Senior Managing Editor (Production): Judy Leale
Production Editor: Theresa Festa
Permissions Coordinator: Charles Morris
Permission Researcher: Keri Jean Miksza
Manufacturing Buyer: Diane Peirano
Design Director: Maria Lange
Art Director: Jill Little
Interior Design: Carmen DiBartolomeo
Illustrator (Interior): ElectraGraphics, Inc.
Cover Photo: Pete McArthur
Director, Image Resource Center: Melinda Reo
Manager, Rights and Permissions: Zina Arabia
Manager, Visual Research: Beth Brenzel
Manager, Cover Visual Research & Permissions: Karen Sanatar
Image Permission Coordinator: Cynthia Vincenti
Photo Researcher: Melinda Alexander
Manager, Print Production: Christy Mahon
Composition/Full-Service Project Management: Carlisle Communications, Ltd.
Printer/Binder: R.R. Donnelley & Sons/Phoenix Color Corporation

Credits and acknowledgments borrowed from other sources and reproduced, with permission, in this textbook appear on appropriate page within text.

Pearson Education LTD.
Pearson Education Singapore, Pte. Ltd
Pearson Education, Canada, Ltd
Pearson Education–Japan

Pearson Education Australia PTY, Limited
Pearson Education North Asia Ltd
Pearson Educación de Mexico, S.A. de C.V.
Pearson Education Malaysia, Pte. Ltd

10 9 8 7 6 5 4 3 2
ISBN 0-13-140412-1

To Sheri and Jeff for tolerating the lack of attention, and to Sarah, "We're going to Disney World!" — **Ron Lane**

To Dan, Lauren, and Tommy for their love, encouragement and support. You are the best! — **Karen King**

To Tommy, Elizabeth, and Sam — **Tom Russell**

BRIEF CONTENTS

CONTENTS

PREFACE

he sixteenth edition of *Kleppner's Advertising Procedure* combines the tradition of providing basic coverage of the fields of advertising and promotion with an in-depth description of the fast-changing environment in which modern marketing operates. The text offers a comprehensive, yet clear, discussion of the trends in marketing communication. Among the primary goals of the current edition is to provide students with an appreciation of the developments in communication technology, marketing research, as well as the ramifications of consolidation and globalization on the practice of advertising and promotion.

While this text retains the basic organization of previous editions, it has undergone the most extensive revision in its history. New cases, examples, and exhibits as well as viewpoints from some of the industry's leading practitioners will offer students and instructors an appreciation of the complex and fast-changing world of advertising and promotion. To better meet the needs of today's busy classrooms and provide greater clarity, this edition has been slightly streamlined without sacrificing the key concepts and in-depth coverage that has made this text a bestseller.

This text presents ideas and issues in a context where students see the variables and options that marketers must deal with to solve problems. In a complex, global economy, there is rarely a single right or wrong answer. Students are introduced to the cultural, psychological, sociological, and economic factors that determine the proper role of advertising, and they learn that advertising and promotion do not function in a void—that the successful practitioner must be able to comprehend complex information from a number of disciplines. The primary goal of the sixteenth edition is to introduce students to the many aspects of advertising and promotion. However, just as importantly, *Kleppner's Advertising Procedure* attempts to convey the enthusiasm and enjoyment that the field offers. The sixteenth edition is intended for students majoring in advertising, studying advertising as part of a related discipline or those who will use the information as informed consumers.

KLEPPNER VIEWPOINT 3.1

BRAD MAJORS

CEO, SOCOH Marketing LLC

Brand Development Demystified

here is a lot of talk about "branding" or "brand development" these days, as if it is the next "new thing" in marketing and sales. "Brand development" is not a new phenomenon. It has been around for at least 100 years.

Any marketer or ad agency worth its salt practices "brand development" every time they perform any marketing function. The history of advertising in America is, essentially, the history of branding. That is what good advertising (and the other communication disciplines) does—create good and consistent reputations for products or services and this consistent imagery is what converts a product into a "brand."

I say "consistent" because one of the greatest sins of marketing these days (especially for smaller businesses) is a lack of "integrated marketing." By this I mean that there may be mixed messages (from media advertising, public relations, the Web site, package copy, or whatever) that go out to consumers from a brand. And with these inconsistent messages comes an inconsistent image for the

Brad Majors

ORGANIZATION AND WHAT'S NEW

Above all, the current edition emphasizes the importance of the consumer. In an environment that is moving towards two-way communications and audience control of the communication channel, it is imperative that advertisers be able to deal with a marketing system controlled by the customer. Concepts such as "permission marketing" are no longer interesting ideas, but instead are the core of successful marketing and promotion. The sixteenth edition is organized as follows:

PART I

The authors take a consumer-centric approach throughout the text beginning with Part I in which the historical roots of advertising are discussed.

■ **Chapter 1** offers an overview of how advertising and marketing developed as part of the larger society. Rather than a stale listing of names and dates, the chapter brings the personalities who created the modern American marketing system to life.

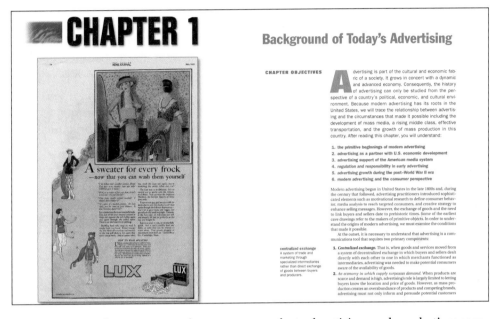

■ **Chapter 2** demonstrates the many ways that advertising and marketing communications are used by advertisers as small as the neighborhood retailer and as large as global multinational corporations.

PART II

The second part of the text focuses on advertising planning and brand research.

■ **Chapter 3** introduces the concept of the product life cycle and the strategies needed to keep brands vital in a changing marketplace.

■ **Chapter 4** looks at means for advertisers to determine their prime prospects and better understand consumers.

PART III

The third part of the text discusses the organization of the advertising from both the advertisers and agency perspectives.

■ **Chapters 5 and 6** explore how the advertising and management function have become more complex. Today, advertising is more likely to be integrated into a total marketing communication program resulting in management and relationship changes from the past.

PART IV

Part IV of the sixteenth edition examines the various advertising media vehicles or consumer contact points available to advertisers.

■ **Chapter 7** explores the media planning function and the role of the media planner in delivering advertising messages to consumers.

■ **Chapters 8 to 14** is where specific media types are discussed individually, but with a priority of linking these media in a manner that demonstrates the complementary way each supports the others. This section also addresses the communication strengths and weaknesses of each medium and how these media are converging as consumers embrace new technology and media companies merge to form large multimedia conglomerates.

PART V

Discussion of the creative function begins in this section of the text. While advertising is largely identified with the finished advertisements and commercials, creative ideas usually are the result of research that offers insight into consumer, product selection, and media preferences.

■ **Chapters 15 to 22** outline the many steps of planning, research and production necessary to bring rough ideas to fruition as a finished ad. Contrary to popular opinion, great advertising is rarely a result of spontaneous brilliance, but rather is the byproduct of hours of hard work and study.

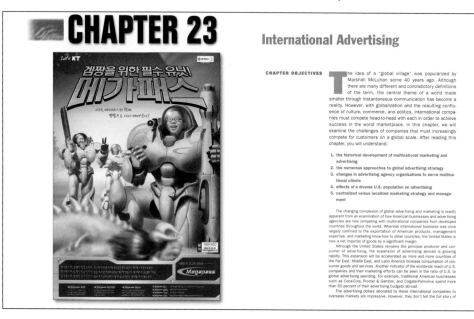

■ **Chapter 23** covers the current state of international advertising with the broader context of a shrinking world. While the United States continues to be the major player in international commerce, it no longer dominates the global economy as it did in much of the last century. Today, the United States is more of a partner and participant in international business than an overwhelming force. Not only has the production of large segments of product categories such as textiles, electronics, and automobiles moved to foreign countries, but advertising and promotional expertise is also likely to be found abroad.

■ **Chapter 24** features a new discussion of legal, regulatory, and ethical considerations as they impact advertising and promotion. It now offers an integrated discussion of the host of controls, both internal and external, in which the modern advertising practitioner operates. As we enter a period of unprecedented scrutiny of all aspects of business, it is incumbent for advertisers to examine their activities in light of public perception of what is right for consumers as well as for the companies they serve. More and more the public is demanding that advertisers be sensitive to the societal and cultural dimensions in the messages they distribute. For their part, advertisers are finding that doing what is right is also good business.

A Prentice Hall
EXCLUSIVE!

PARTNERS IN ADVERTISING: ADCRITIC.COM AND PRENTICE HALL

Prentice Hall and AdAge are working together so instructors and students can access today's leading commercials and commentary from advertising experts. For a deeply discounted rate, students can receive 16-week-access to a special **adcritic.com** site that also includes AdAge's *Encyclopedia of Advertising* archive of articles. Visit www.prenhall.com/adcritic for a tour.

Note: An adcritic.com student access code can be obtained only when shrink-wrapped with a Prentice Hall text. We strongly advise instructors specify this value-package with their bookstore in advance.

TEACHING RESOURCES

Many of the following supplements can also be downloaded via our password-protected Instructor's Resource Center. Visit www.prenhall.com/marketing and go to the catalog page for this text.

Printed Instructor's Manual (0-13-140414-8) Contains chapter objectives, chapter overview, detailed chapter outlines, answers to review questions, class projects and exercises, Internet exercises, and term projects.

Printed Test Item File (0-13-140413-X) Contains over 2,600 multiple-choice, true-false, matching, completion, and essay questions. These questions are also available preloaded in our TestGenEQ test generating software, which can be downloaded via our Instructor's Resource Center or accessed on the Instructor's Resource CD-ROM.

PowerPoints Includes chapter outline, images from in and out of the book, discussion questions, and Web links. These slides are delivered on the Instructor's Resource CD-ROM.

Instructor's Resource CD-ROM (0-13-140416-4) Provides the above mentioned supplements on one CD for convenient access. It also includes our easy-to-use TestGenEQ test generating software preloaded with all questions from the Test Item File and .jpeg files of most images from the text.

Video Segments (0-13-182821-5) We are pleased to offer a VHS video library of 8 to 10 minute video segments that were all filmed in 2002 and 2003. A video teaching guide is also available to instructors via our online Instructor's Resource Center.

Companion Website Located at www.prenhall.com/russell this site includes student self-study quizzes and text glossary.

ACKNOWLEDGMENTS

Over the years, *Kleppner's Advertising Procedure* has benefited from the advice and expertise of hundreds of professional advertisers. Media Planners, account executives, creative personnel and brand managers at numerous companies have combined their knowledge to offer students the latest information about the changing fields of advertising and promotion. Although the authors are solely responsible for the content of the text, we are indebted to the following people who have offered their counsel in the sixteenth edition of the text.

THANK YOU TO OUR CONTRIBUTORS:

Jeff Asken, Intel Corporation, Santa Clara

Sheri Bevil, Bevil Advertising and Designs, Atlanta

David Botsford, The Botsford Group, Atlanta

Jason Boyd, Grady College, The University of Georgia

Wendy Brown, Bright Ideas Group, Macon

Mary Beth Burner, Cooking Light/Southern Progress

Kelly Caffarelli, Home Depot, Atlanta

Steve Cararelli, Office of the Treasury, State of Georgia

Tom Carroll, VitroRobertson, San Diego

Frank Compton, Sawyer Riley Compton, Atlanta

Scott Crawford, Howard, Merrell & Partners, Raleigh

Sylvia Fox, Sawyer Riley Compton, Atlanta

Valerie Graves, Uniworld Group, New York

Bruce Hall, Howard, Merrell & Partners, Raleigh

Kathy Haskins, Bright Ideas Group, Macon

Ron Huey, Huey/Poprocki/Atlanta

Sarah Hughes, Sawyer Riley Compton, Atlanta

Tiffany Johns, Audium Records, Nashville

Susan Kahrs, Grady College, The University of Georgia

Gilad Kat, AC&W (Grey Tel Aviv, Israel)

Mark Kooyman, Venture Brands, Atlanta

Jason Kreher, Messner Vetere Burger McNamee Schmetter/Euro RSCG, New York

Steven Lang, Southern Broadcasting Corp., Athens, GA

Donna LeBlond, Grady College, The University of Georgia

Thomas Lentz, Broyhill Furniture Industries, Lenoir, N.C.

Amy Looken, McRae Communications, Atlanta

Brad Majors, Socoh Marketing, Greenville, S.C.

Craig McAnsh, The Convex Group, Atlanta

Charlie McQuilkin, Young & Rubicam/San Francisco

Page Miller, New Business Development, The Kaplan Thaler Group, New York

Richard Nelson, Techsonic Industries, Alpharetta, GA

Chris Oberholtzer, Comcast, Atlanta

Charles M. Penuel, Georgia Higher Education Savings Plan

Suzanne Piel, McCann-Erickson, New York

John Robertson, VitroRobertson, San Diego

Chang Hwan Shin, KT Korea

Andrea Shuff, VitroRobertson, San Diego

Swann Seiler, Savannah Electric, Savannah

Alana Stephenson, Luckie & Company, Birmingham

Andrea Vassallo, Element 79 Partners, Chicago

HyunJae Yu, Grady College, The University of Georgia

AND REVIEWERS:

Suzanne Benet, Grand Valley State University

Molly Blume, Bellevue Community College

Paula Bobrowski, SUNY Oswego

Roy Busby, University of North Texas

Chris Cakebread, Boston University

George Coakley, San Jose State University

Sandie Ferriter, Harford Community College

Jamie Fullerton, Oklahoma State University

Jennifer Gregan-Paxton, University of Delaware

Larry Londre, University of Southern California - Northride

Beth Mott-Stenerson, New Mexico State University

Barbara Mueller, San Diego State University

Robert O'Gara, Point Park College

Allen Smith, Florida Atlantic University

John Wardrip, University South Carolina

Roger Watson, Ohio University

Sherri Weiss, San Francisco State University

Gary B. Wilcox, University Texas

Jill Witter, Northwood University

James Zarnowski, University of Cincinnati

About THE AUTHORS

OTTO KLEPPNER
(1899-1982)

A graduate of New York University, Otto Kleppner started out in advertising as a copywriter. After several such jobs, he became advertising manager at Prentice Hall, where he began to think that he, too, "could write a book." Some years later, he also thought that he could run his own advertising agency, and both ideas materialized eminently. His highly successful agency handled advertising for leading accounts (Dewar's Scotch Whisky, I. W. Harper Bourbon and other Schenley brands, Saab Cars, Doubleday Book Clubs, and others). His book became a bible for advertising students, and his writings have been published in eight languages.

Active in the American Association of Advertising Agencies, Mr. Kleppner served as a director, a member of the Control Committee, chairman of the Committee of Government, Public and Educator Relations, and a governor of the New York Council. He was awarded the Nichols Cup (now the Crain Cup) for distinguished service to the teaching of advertising.

W. RONALD LANE

Ron has worked in most aspects of advertising. He began in advertising and promotion for a drug manufacturer. Ron has worked in creative and account services for clients including Coca-Cola, National Broiler Council, Minute-Maid, and Callaway Gardens Country Store.

He is a professor of advertising at the University of Georgia and has served as advertising manager of the *Journal of Advertising.* He was coordinator of the Institute of Advanced Advertising Studies sponsored by the American Association of Advertising Agencies for six years. He is also a partner in SLRS Communications, an advertising-marketing agency.

Currently, Ron is a member of the American Advertising Federation's (AAF) Academic Division, Executive Committee. He has been the AAF Academic Division Chair and served as a member of the AAF Board of Directors, Council of Governors, and Executive Committee. He has

(L to R) W. Ronald Lane, Karen Whitehill King, J. Thomas Russell

been an ADDY Awards judge numerous times and has been a member of the Advertising Age Creative Workshop faculty. He is a member of the Atlanta Advertising Club, American Academy of Advertising, American Marketing Association, and the ACEJMC Accrediting Council.

KAREN WHITEHILL KING

Karen King is a professor of advertising and the Head of the Department of Advertising and Public Relations in the Grady College of Journalism and Mass Communication at the University of Georgia. She received her Ph.D. in communications from the University of Illinois. While on the faculty at UGA, she has been a visiting communication researcher at the Centers for Disease Control and Prevention in Atlanta, working on their AIDS public service campaign, and a visiting professor at Lintas in New York.

Karen's research interests include advertising industry issues and health communication. She has published her research in leading academic journals including: *Journal of Advertising, Journal of Advertising Research, Journal of Public Policy and Marketing, Journal of Current Issues and Research in Advertising, Journalism and Mass Communication Quarterly, Journal of Newspaper Research, Journal of Health Care Marketing* and *Journalism, and Mass Communication Educator.* She was the editor of the *1994 Proceedings of the American Academy of Advertising Conference* and she co-authored a textbook supplement, *Media Buying Simulation.*

Prior to joining the Grady College, Karen was a research supervisor and a media planner/buyer at FCB Chicago. Her clients included Kraft, Coors, Sears, Sunbeam, and International Harvester. In 1999, Karen was named the Donald G. Hileman Educator of the Year by the American Advertising Federation's Seventh District for her work with the UGA Ad Club and its AAF campaign competition team.

J. THOMAS RUSSELL

Thomas Russell is Phil Landrum Professor of Communications. He also is Dean Emeritus of the College of Journalism and Mass Communication at the University of Georgia. Tom received his Ph.D. in communications from the University of Illinois and has taught and conducted research in a number of areas of advertising and marketing. He was formerly editor of the *Journal of Advertising.*

In addition to his academic endeavor, Tom has worked as a retail copywriter as well as been a principal in his own advertising agency. He is a member of a number of academic, professional, and civic organizations. He also has served as a judge and faculty member for the Institute of Advanced Advertising Studies sponsored by the American Association of Advertising Agencies.

The Place of Advertising

PART ONE

CHAPTER 1

Background of Today's Advertising

Advertising is part of the cultural and economic fabric of a society. It grows in concert with a dynamic and advanced economy. Consequently, the history of advertising can only be studied from the perspective of a country's political, economic, and cultural environment. Because modern advertising has its roots in the United States, we will trace the relationship between advertising and the circumstances that made it possible including the development of mass media, a rising middle class, effective transportation, and the growth of mass production in this country. After reading this chapter, you will understand:

1. the primitive beginnings of modern advertising
2. advertising as a partner with U.S. economic development
3. advertising support of the American media system
4. regulation and responsibility in early advertising
5. advertising growth during the post–World War II era
6. modern advertising and the consumer perspective

Modern advertising began in United States in the late 1800s and, during the century that followed, advertising practitioners introduced sophisticated elements such as motivational research to define consumer behavior, media analysis to reach targeted consumers, and creative strategy to enhance selling messages. However, the exchange of goods and the need to link buyers and sellers date to prehistoric times. Some of the earliest cave drawings refer to the makers of primitive objects. In order to understand the origins of modern advertising, we must examine the conditions that made it possible.

At the outset, it is necessary to understand that advertising is a communications tool that requires two primary components:

centralized exchange
A system of trade and marketing through specialized intermediaries rather than direct exchange of goods between buyers and producers.

1. *Centralized exchange.* That is, when goods and services moved from a system of decentralized exchange in which buyers and sellers dealt directly with each other to one in which merchants functioned as intermediaries, advertising was needed to make potential consumers aware of the availability of goods.

2. *An economy in which supply surpasses demand.* When products are scarce and demand is high, advertising's role is largely limited to letting buyers know the location and price of goods. However, as mass production creates an overabundance of products and competing brands, advertising must not only inform and persuade potential customers

that these products exist but also give consumers reasons to purchase one brand or product category over those of competitors. "Societies of scarcity . . . need not advertise anything. Their people sign up to buy a car, wait three years or more and then gladly take whatever is assigned them. Their people line up to buy bread; they cannot shop among enriched and homogenized and white and pumpernickel and rye."[1]

While centralized exchange and excess supply were necessary ingredients for advertising, a number of other factors came together in the 50 years after the Civil War to create the foundations for this multibillion-dollar industry. The first was the beginning of the fulfillment of democratic ideals. Although eighteenth-century America had far to go before basic rights such as women's suffrage and full citizenship for Americans of African descent were a reality, public education was creating a literate population and interest in the political process created both a need and support for newspapers and magazines.

Second, advertising prospered as the industrial revolution swept across the United States during the latter part of the nineteenth century. Mass production allowed not only the efficient manufacturing of a multitude of goods, but also this same technological expertise created the high-speed presses that enabled the publishing of mass circulation magazines and newspapers that carried the advertising that provided their financial foundations. Just as importantly, the growth of these industrial empires created the need for skilled workers who earned higher wages and moved from the farm to urban centers.

The efficiencies of mass production allowed manufacturers to produce many more goods than could be sold on a local or regional basis. The introduction of the railroad not only created unity among a formerly divided country but also created a means of national distribution for the products of a growing manufacturing sector. The railroad, combined with instant telegraph communication, connected the country economically and culturally. However, it wasn't until the introduction of national brands that advertising and marketing began to fulfill their promise.

National brands, supported by a coast-to-coast system of railroad distribution and national magazines to advertise them, provided the impetus for a sophisticated advertising and marketing structure based on product differentiation and consumer loyalty to those brands. Nationally branded goods changed the relationship between buyers and sellers from one of commodity goods to that of a marketing system based on consistent product quality and identification and gave manufacturers leverage over retailers that would continue for the next 100 years until the rise of mega-retailers during the 1990s.

The introduction of national brands and the advertising and distribution systems to sell and market them cannot be underestimated. Although advertising did not create a centralized, efficient system of national marketing, it did provide one of the primary ingredients to make such a strategy practical. Entrepreneurs rushed to benefit from the advantages of being the first in the marketplace with branded goods. Quaker Oats cereal is generally considered to be the first national marketer, but men such as Daniel Gerber, Dr. William Scholl, Gail Borden, Richard Sears, and Frederick Maytag have all left their legacies through the brands they established. A Kodak camera ad (see Exhibit 1.1) published in 1889 demonstrates a sophisticated approach to advertising including testimonials from satisfied customers.

The convergence of the availability of branded products, the ability to provide national distribution, and a growing middle class as buyers for these products had evolved sufficiently by 1920 to support the creation of an advertising industry that demonstrated most of the basic functions found among modern agencies and corporate advertising departments today.

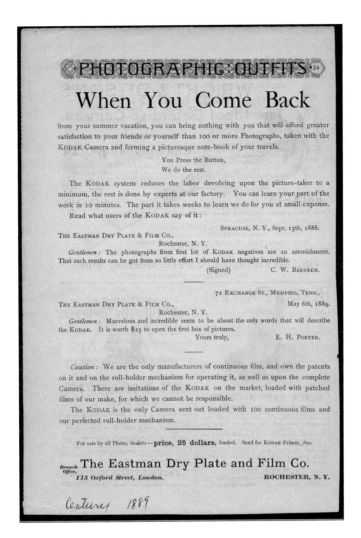

ADVERTISING'S MODERN ERA: RESEARCH AND RESPONSIBILITY

The two elements missing in most advertising during the early years of the twentieth century were:

1. an ethical framework for creating promotional messages
2. valid and reliable research to measure advertising effects

At first glance, these may seem to be unrelated concerns. However, from a philosophical perspective they are very much related. Advertising was part of a rising democratic movement with foundations in Europe's eighteenth-century Age of Enlightenment where, for the first time, a philosophy was introduced that held the individual was fully capable of discerning truth from falsehood, and in a truly open marketplace of ideas, falsehoods would be identified and rejected as part of some natural process. In such an environment, there would be little need for regulation of information. Furthermore, research to find underlying consumer motivations would be of scant value in influencing totally "rational" buyers.

However, the outrageous claims of many nineteenth-century advertisers, especially those hawking patent medicines, and an emerging emphasis on advertising claims that addressed psychological motivations rather than product characteristics soon led to a call for consumer protection. Many of the most zealous proponents of advertising regulation were as extreme in their criticism of advertising as the fraudulent advertisers themselves. These critics continued their condemnations of advertising throughout most of the twentieth century. Promoting false fears of the power of techniques such as subliminal advertising and motivational research, a host of advertising commentators demanded that both advertising research and the messages that resulted from it be curtailed or greatly limited.

There is no question that advertising excesses of the early 1900s needed to be addressed by strong legislation. It was just as obvious that advertising research held little danger of mind control, subliminal or otherwise, for the average consumer. If anything, most of the early research was almost laughable in its lack of sophistication. For example, "Several agencies boasted of . . . research into consumer attitudes in the late 1920s, but their crude, slapdash methods made these 'surveys' of questionable value in providing accurate feedback. One agency reported that it could obtain quick, inexpensive results . . . by having all members of the staff send questionnaires to their friends."[2]

Despite the rather primitive research methods of the period, a few advertising executives such as Claude Hopkins were conducting direct mail and coupon response research in the 1920s to gather information about effective advertising messages. Pond's was among a few enlightened advertisers that were analyzing audience response to advertising (see Exhibit 1.2). However, it would not be until the 1950s that advertising research gained widespread acceptance.

EXHIBIT 1.2

Courtesy of Unilever. From John W. Hartman Center for Sales, Advertising & Marketing History; Duke University Rare Book, Manuscript, and Special Collections Library; http://scriptorium.lib.duke.edu/eaa/.

BEGINNINGS

The urge to advertise seems to be a part of human nature, evidenced since ancient times. Of the 5,000-year recorded history of advertising right up to our present television satellite age, the part that is most significant begins when the United States emerged as a great manufacturing nation about 100 years ago. The early history of advertising, however, is far too fascinating to pass by without a glance.

It is not surprising that the people who gave the world the Tower of Babel also left the earliest known evidence of advertising. A Babylonian clay tablet of about 3000 B.C. bears inscriptions for an ointment dealer, a scribe, and a shoemaker. Papyri exhumed from the ruins of Thebes show that the ancient Egyptians had a better medium on which to write their messages. (Alas, the announcements preserved in papyrus offer rewards for the return of runaway slaves.) The Greeks were among those who relied on town criers to chant the arrival of ships with cargoes of wines, spices, and metals. Often a crier was accompanied by a musician who kept him in the right key. Town criers later became the earliest medium for public announcements in many European countries, and they continued to be used for centuries. (At this point, we must digress to tell about a promotion idea used by innkeepers in France around A.D. 1100 to tout their fine wines: They would have the town crier blow a horn, gather a group, and offer samples!)

Roman merchants, too, had a sense of advertising. The ruins of Pompeii contain signs in stone or terra-cotta, advertising what the shops were selling: a row of hams for a butcher shop, a cow for a dairy, a boot for a shoemaker. The Pompeiians also knew the art of telling their story to the public by means of painted wall signs.

Outdoor advertising has proved to be one of the most enduring forms of advertising. It survived the decline of the Roman empire to become the decorative art of European inns in the seventeenth and eighteenth centuries. That was still an age of widespread illiteracy, so inns vied with one another in creating attractive signs that all could recognize. This accounts for the charming names of old inns, especially in England, such as the Three Squirrels, the Man in the Moon, and the Hole in the Wall (see Exhibit 1.3). In 1614, England passed a law, probably the earliest on advertising, that prohibited signs from extending more than 8 feet out from a building. (Longer signs pulled down too many house fronts.) Another law required signs to be high enough to give clearance to an armored man on horseback. In 1740, the first printed outdoor poster (referred to as a "**hoarding**") appeared in London.

We begin our discussion of the foundations of modern advertising by examining its history, which we will divide into four broad periods:

I. The *premarketing era.* From the start of product exchange in prehistoric times to the middle of the seventeenth century, buyers and sellers communicated in very primitive ways. For most of this period "media" such as clay tablets, town criers, and tavern signs were the best ways to reach potential prospects for a product or service. Only in the latter decades of the period did primitive printing appear as the forerunner of modern mass media.

II. The *mass communication era.* From the 1700s to the early decades of the 1900s, advertisers were increasingly able to reach larger and larger segments of the population. Mass newspapers first appeared in the 1830s, quickly followed by a number of national magazines. By the 1920s, radio had ushered in the broadcast era when advertising was delivered free to virtually every American household.

III. The *research era.* During the last 50 years, advertisers have used ever more sophisticated techniques for identifying and reaching narrowly targeted audiences with messages prepared specifically for each group or individual (in the case of direct mail). Early research was based on general information about the age, sex, and geographic location of consumers. Today, advertising

hoarding
First printed outdoor signs—the forerunner of modern outdoor advertising.

premarketing era
The period from prehistoric times to the eighteenth century. During this time, buyers and sellers communicated in very primitive ways.

mass communication era
From the 1700s to the early decades of this century, advertisers were able to reach large segments of the population through the mass media.

research era
In recent years advertisers increasingly have been able to identify narrowly defined audience segments through sophisticated research methods.

EXHIBIT **1.3**

Signs outside seventeenth-century inns.

Hog in Armour

Three Squirrels

King's Porter and Dwarf

Harrow and Doublet

The Ape

Hole in the Wall
"A Guide for Malt Worms"

Barley Mow

Bull and Mouth

Man in the Moon

Goose and Gridiron

interactive era
Communication will increasingly be controlled by consumers who will determine when and where they can be reached with promotional messages.

research deals with much more detailed information about the lifestyles and motivations of consumers. Rather than who we are, advertising research is studying the motivations behind our purchase behavior.

IV. The *interactive era.* A fourth era, which we are just embarking on, is one of interactive communication. As advertisers begin to understand their customers on a one-to-one basis, they are starting to use this information to reach buyers with customized information. Soon consumers will use communication on an interactive basis. Rather than mass media sending one-way messages to the audience, the audience will control when and where they will give permission for the media to reach them. Obviously, the change from media to consumer control of the communication channel will have major implications for both the mass media and advertising.

As we begin our discussion of the development of advertising, we must keep in mind the interrelationships among marketing, the general business climate, and social mores and conventions, as well as public attitudes toward advertising. As advertising has become an integral part of our economy, advertising practitioners have come under closer public scrutiny and must work within a complex legal and regulatory framework. Perhaps the most important change in the business climate during the last 20 years has been the growing sense of social responsibility within the advertising community. Many advertising practices that were routine a century ago are universally condemned by the industry today. Advertisers realize that public trust is a key to successful advertising. Throughout the remainder of this chapter, we will discuss the forces that have shaped contemporary advertising.

THE MOVE TO CREATIVITY IN ADVERTISING

As we mentioned earlier, the original advertising companies were really no more than space brokers. However, by 1900, both agencies and their clients were placing major emphasis on persuading consumers through creative advertising messages. Several factors caused this move to more creative and persuasive advertising messages during the early decades of the twentieth century:

1. By 1900, the industrial output of products had reached a point where serious brand competition was taking place in a number of product categories such as soap and food. The movement from commodity products to branded goods was well established.
2. Innovative marketers such as John Wannamaker of Wannamaker Department Store in New York City saw the need to sell products on the basis of style and luxury rather than simple utility. He hired John Powers, considered by many to be the first true copywriter. By the turn of the century agencies were emphasizing their creative expertise as they moved toward providing full-service advertising to their clients (see Exhibit 1.4).
3. Advertising was beginning to draw from social science research to determine the most effective means of reaching consumers. In 1921, J. Walter Thompson hired John Watson from Harvard. Watson, the "father of **behavioral research**," was one of the earliest researchers to study the underlying motivations of consumer purchasing.

behavioral research
Market research that attempts to determine the underlying nature of purchase behavior.

4. Building on the work of Watson and others, Alfred Sloan, Jr., made General Motors (GM) the preeminent car maker by surpassing his major rival Henry Ford. Sloan viewed the automobile as a symbol of status and GM advertising sought to transform Ford's idea of the car as low-cost transportation to one in which consumers were encouraged to trade up to buy the newest tailfins and other cosmetic changes as automobiles introduced model changes from year to year. Sloan is credited with introducing the idea of planned obsolescence in which products would be discarded not because of a loss of utility but because of a loss of status.

By the 1950s, virtually all national companies had accepted the concept that it was the brand more than real product superiority that would determine which firms would be successful. "If sales were not dependent either upon ever lower

prices or real technological improvements but on status perceptions, artificial needs and superficial change, then focusing on the brand, rather than individual products, might prove the best way for a marketer to achieve lasting profitability. Products, after all, had life cycles and died. Brands, properly managed, could last forever."[3]

THE DEVELOPMENT OF PRINT MEDIA

Although product availability and compelling selling messages are certainly necessary components for the growth of advertising, neither can be successful without a readily available means of reaching consumers and prospects with the messages and communicating the availability of goods and services. The early history of advertising cannot be separated from early print media that carried its messages. From our discussion, it will become obvious that the relationship between advertising and the mass media is a symbiotic link with growing media circulations allowing advertisers to reach more and more buyers and increasing advertising dollars enabling the media to prospect in an environment largely free from government regulation.

The Newspaper as an Advertising Medium

Newspapers have historically been the primary medium for information and commerce. It has only been in the last century that other communication media have challenged the preeminent position of newspapers. As early as 59 B.C., the Romans posted daily government-published news sheets known as *acta diurna* and the forerunners of modern want ads were **siquis,** which were notices posted by early clergy seeking positions. The name comes from the Latin *si quis* ("if anyone"), which was the way the notices usually began. The name **siquis** continued, although soon these notices covered a variety of subjects, including lost-and-found objects, runaway apprentices, and so on, much in the mode of many modern classified ads.[4]

Johann Gutenberg's invention of moveable type eventually opened the door to more formal publications. The first English newspaper, *The Oxford Gazette*, was published in 1665. The first colonial newspaper, Benjamin Harris's *Publick Occurrences*, was published in Boston in 1690 and it was promptly banned by the governor after one issue. The first American newspaper to carry advertising was the *Boston Newsletter*, published in 1704. Soon newspapers were common throughout the colonies and by 1800 every major city in the United States had several daily or weekly publications.

With the introduction of Richard Hoe's rotary press during the 1830s, Benjamin Day's *The New York Sun* ushered in the era of the so-called **penny press,** which provided inexpensive newspapers to the general population. For the first time, both readers and advertisers had extensive access to inexpensive newspapers. By 1900, newspapers such as the *New York World* and the *Chicago Tribune* had circulations of more than 500,000. These high circulation publications and many more like them were supported by advertisers seeking more and more buyers for their goods. The newspapers of the era established the model for financial support from advertising that continues for the majority of media to the present.

siquis
Handwritten posters in sixteenth- and seventeenth-century England—forerunners of modern advertising.

penny press
Forerunner of the mass newspaper in the United States that first appeared in the 1830s.

Magazines

The earliest colonial magazines gave little promise that they would grow into a major mass medium. The first magazine in America was published by William Bradford in 1741. Aptly named the *American Magazine*, it lasted all of three issues. Its major competitor, Benjamin Franklin's *General Magazine*, started in the same year, died a quiet death after only six issues.

Despite the barriers to financial success for magazines, a number of publications emerged during the latter part of the eighteenth century. By 1800 there were more than 100 magazines serving an educated and wealthy elite with articles and essays on matters of literary, political, or religious interest. Unlike newspapers, magazines were national or regional in scope and, therefore, poor transportation and high cost further prohibited the rapid growth of magazines. Although legislation providing low-cost distribution for magazines had passed Congress as early as 1794, it wasn't until the Postal Act of 1879 that magazines enjoyed significant discounts in mailing costs.

Despite the hurdles for magazines, publications such as *Harper's Monthly*, *Atlantic Monthly*, and *Century* were widely read and some, such as *The Saturday Evening Post*, provided content of a more popular nature. However, the editorial and advertising foundations of the modern consumer magazines didn't take shape until the latter part of the nineteenth century. Using the business plan developed by Benjamin Day and other publishers of penny newspapers and supporting a populist agenda, many magazines of the day began to speak to the concerns of the American family with articles on health, fashion, and food. In addition, some of the major writers of the time such as Mark Twain and Sir Arthur Conan Doyle were frequent contributors to these magazines. Unlike their newspaper counterparts, these magazines had a national audience with influence beyond the borders of a particular city.

In many respects, the magazine was a unifying means of communication and, serving as a slower version of the telegraph, gave the far-flung country a sense of common purpose after the Civil War. "The magazine was a vehicle which could present simultaneously identical facts, uniformly treated, in every locality. Men and women, North, South, East, and West, could read and judge the same materials, instead of forming their beliefs and reaching their decisions on the basis of varied accounts published in different sections and often distorted by regional prejudice."[5]

By the turn of the century, *Ladies Home Journal* passed a milestone with 1 million circulation and other major magazines of the day such as *Munsey's* and *McClure's* had circulations of more than a half million. Many of the major publishers of the day also embarked on campaigns to address the abuses of patent medicine advertising as well as social reforms in industries such as meatpacking and industrial monopolies.

Advertising support for these publications came from manufacturers that were enjoying success with the distribution of national brands such as Quaker Oats and Uneeda Biscuit. It was very common for magazines of the time to carry 100 pages or more of advertising. For advertisers, magazines provided the only means of reaching buyers throughout the country. Advertising was crucial to the success of most magazines, since subscription prices covered little of the total costs of publishing with the shortfall being made up from advertising buying the huge audiences attracted to these low-cost magazines. By 1920, high-quality color advertisements were commonplace in most major publications (see Exhibit 1.5).

By 1923 when Henry Luce and Briton Hadden founded *Time*, magazines were the preeminent medium for national advertisers. They offered national circulation, both editorial and advertising credibility, color availability, and an extremely low-cost means of reaching millions of readers.

Mass Production Matures

mass production
A manufacturing technique utilizing specialization and interchangeable parts to achieve production efficiencies.

By the mid–1700s, primitive forms of **mass production** were being introduced into English textile industries. In America, the manufacture of firearms during the Revolutionary War was one of the earliest examples of production using interchangeable parts. By the end of the Civil War, American industry was rapidly adopting many of the techniques of mass production as factories produced an array of goods such as textiles, furniture, and even food. For example, by the 1850s, Gail Borden was selling purified, airtight sealed milk from his Connecticut plant.

Although the beginnings of mass production in this country were impressive, it was the introduction of the automobile that created the foundations of American industry. Innovators such as Henry Leland, who built the first Cadillac, Louis Chevrolet, Albert Champion, Walter Chrysler, and John and Horace Dodge all contributed to the growth of the automotive industry. However, it was Henry Ford and his Model T selling for less than $600 that put a car within the reach of the ordinary family. With its 1908 introduction, Ford sold 10,000 cars and by 1913 sales passed 250,000. Ford was a visionary who saw that mass production was based on high volume, affordable price, and mass selling through advertising. Throughout the early 1900s, American industry was quick to adapt to the successful formula of Henry Ford.

The Advertising Agency

Volney Palmer is generally given credit for starting the first advertising agency in 1841. In reality, he was little more than a space broker, buying bulk newspaper space at a discount and selling it to individual advertisers at a profit. In 1869 George Rowell published *Rowell's American Newspaper Directory*, which provided newspaper circulation estimates and started the movement toward published rate cards and verified circulation.

By the end of the nineteenth century, major agencies such as J. Walter Thompson, N. W. Ayer & Sons, and Batten and Company (the forerunner of BBDO) were providing creative services, media placement, and basic research and developing the functions of the full-service agencies of the future. In 1917, the **American Association of Advertising Agencies (AAAA, 4As)** was founded with 111 charter members. Today, the 4As has more than 500 member agencies that place approximately 75 percent of all advertising dollars. By the 1930s agencies such as McCann-Erickson and J. Walter Thompson had established overseas offices to begin the movement to global advertising. Marion Harper, a legendary advertising innovator, founded the Interpublic Group in 1954, which sought to provide a holding company for separate agencies that could then serve competing accounts. By 1960, Interpublic not only controlled a number of agencies but also owned subsidiaries that conducted research, provided television production, and handled the public relations needs of clients. At the time, *Advertising Age* wrote that Harper's plan "may be a wholly new tactic for the agency business."[6] Certainly, Interpublic represented the first formal move to integrated marketing by a major advertising company. We devote Chapter 5 to the role of the advertising agency.

American Association of Advertising Agencies (AAAA, 4As)
The national organization of advertising agencies.

AMERICA ENTERS THE TWENTIETH CENTURY

The nineteenth-century development of American industry, advertising, and society in general was impressive by virtually any standard. In that short 100 years, the country saw a movement to urbanization, the abolition of the blight of slavery, railroads and instantaneous communication spanning the continent, and the emergence of the United States as a world power. However, all the changes during the period were not positive. In the decades after the Civil War, a moral business atmosphere emerged that reflected laissez-faire policies in the extreme. The administration of Ulysses S. Grant (1869–1877) is still considered one of the most corrupt in American history. By the dawn of the twentieth century, the excesses of big business and the advertising that contributed to the environment of immorality reached a stage when both the public and Congress demanded stricter regulation of advertising and other business practices.

The Pure Food and Drug Act (1906)

Concerns about public safety in the food supply dates to colonial times. However, it wasn't until after the Civil War that serious efforts were mounted for national legislation to protect consumers. As Americans moved from farms to cities, for the first time a majority of people were dependent on others for their food. While mass production was bringing a host of economically priced products to American consumers, many food and drug products were notably lacking in purity and often placed the health of consumer in jeopardy.

Furthermore, the advertising claims for these products were often outrageous (see Exhibit 1.6). A number of media had taken up the challenge of exposing the problem. Some, such as the *New York Herald Tribune* and the *Ladies Home Journal* restricted or completely banned medical advertising. These media were joined by industry leaders such as H. J. Heinz who made food safety a primary attribute of all his products. He was among the first to sell products in clear glass jars to demonstrate to buyers that they were buying untainted food. By 1906 public opinion had reached the point that Congress moved to protect public health with passage of the **Pure Food and Drug Act.** President Theodore Roosevelt signed the act on June 30, 1906.

Although the 1906 act did much to protect the public health, it failed to address a number of important issues. For example, product content information on labels had to be truthful, but there was no requirement that such labels had to be used. In addition, false claims for patent medicines were outlawed, but enforcement required that the government had to prove that the manufacturer intended to swindle buyers. In other words, if defendants asserted that they believed the claims, no matter how absurd, there was little the government could do.

The modern era of food and drug enforcement began with passage of the Federal Food, Drug, and Cosmetic Act, which was signed by President Franklin Roosevelt on June 25, 1938. Among the several provisions of the 1938 act, drug manufacturers were required to provide scientific proof of new product safety and proof of fraud was no longer required to stop false claims for drugs. Since that time, a number of amendments including those dealing with pesticide, food additives, and color additives have continued to strengthen the role of the Food and Drug Administration (FDA) in production and labeling of food, drug, and cosmetic products.[7]

The Federal Trade Commission Act (1914)

The **Federal Trade Commission's (FTC)** original mandate was to protect one business owner from the unscrupulous practices of another. In 1914 when the Federal

Pure Food and Drug Act
Passed in 1906 by Legislation, it was one of the earliest attempts by the federal government to protect consumers.

Federal Trade Commission (FTC)
The agency of the federal government empowered to prevent unfair competition and to prevent fraudulent, misleading, or deceptive advertising in interstate commerce.

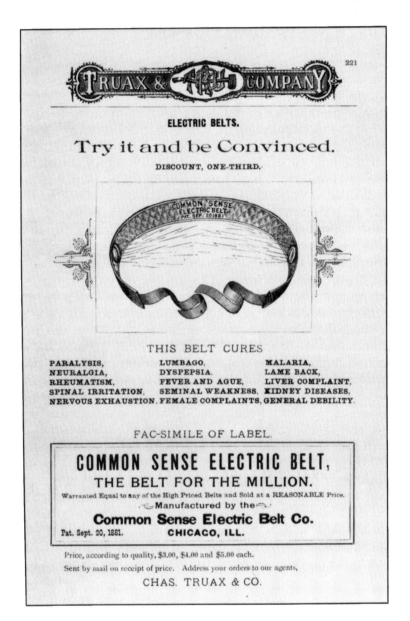

EXHIBIT 1.6

One of the more restrained ads in the patent-medicine category. Electricity, the new, magic power of the 1890s, was offered in a curative belt.

Trade Commission Act was passed, Congress and the public were increasingly alarmed over antitrust violations by big business. It was clear by the early 1900s that the antitrust actions of John D. Rockefeller and other business titans would soon drive their competitors into bankruptcy and create monopolies in vital industries such as oil and steel. Basically, the law said that unfair business practices were now illegal and would no longer be tolerated.

In 1938, the Wheeler-Lea Act extended the FTC's original mission to offer protection to consumers as well as businesses. By combining both business and consumer protection activities, the FTC "seeks to ensure that the nation's markets function competitively, and are vigorous, efficient, and free of undue restrictions. The Commission also works to enhance the smooth operation of the marketplace by eliminating acts or practices that are unfair or deceptive."[8] Today, the FTC is the primary federal enforcement agency to ensure that advertising claims and sales practices meet reasonable standards for honesty and truthfulness.

In Chapter 24, we will discuss in detail not only the role of the FTC but also other regulatory and legal bodies that are concerned with truthful advertising. In addition, the advertising industry's self-regulatory mechanisms will be examined as well as a number of criticisms of advertising's social effects will be addressed.

ADVERTISING COMES OF AGE

During the early years of the twentieth century, there emerged a class of advertising executives who recognized that the industry had to do more to ensure legitimate advertising and to earn the confidence of the public. They gathered with like-minded peers in their communities to form advertising clubs.

These clubs subsequently became the Associated Advertising Clubs of the World (now the American Advertising Federation). In 1911, they launched a campaign to promote truth in advertising. In 1916, they formed vigilance committees that developed into today's **Council of Better Business Bureaus,** which continues to deal with many problems of unfair and deceptive business practices. In 1971, the bureaus became a part of the National Advertising Review Council, an all-industry effort at curbing misleading advertising. The main constituency of the American Advertising Federation continues to be the local advertising clubs. On its board are also officers of the other advertising associations.

Council of Better Business Bureaus
National organization that coordinates a number of local and national initiatives to protect consumers.

In 1910, the Association of National Advertising Managers was born. It is now known as the Association of National Advertisers (ANA) and has about 500 members, including most major national advertisers. Its purpose is to improve the effectiveness of advertising from the viewpoint of the advertiser. In 1917, the American Association of Advertising Agencies was formed to improve the effectiveness of advertising and the advertising agency operation. More than 75 percent of all national advertising is currently placed by its members, both large and small.

In 1911, *Printers' Ink*, the leading advertising trade paper of the day, prepared a model statute for state regulation of advertising, designed to "punish untrue, deceptive or misleading advertising." The ***Printers' Ink*** **Model Statute** has been adopted in its original or modified form by a number of states, where it is still operative.

***Printers' Ink* Model Statute (1911)**
The act directed at fraudulent advertising, prepared and sponsored by *Printers' Ink,* which was the pioneer advertising magazine.

Up to 1914, many publishers routinely exaggerated their circulation claims. In the absence of reliable figures, advertisers had no way of verifying what they got for their money. However, in that year, a group of advertisers, agencies, and publishers established an independent auditing organization, the **Audit Bureau of Circulations (ABC),** which conducts its own audits and issues its own reports of circulation. Most major publications belong to the ABC, and an ABC circulation statement is highly regarded in media circles. As advertising has become international, similar auditing organizations are operating throughout the world. In June 1916, President Woodrow Wilson, addressing the Associated Advertising Clubs of the World convention in Philadelphia, was the first president to give public recognition to the importance of advertising. Advertising had come of age!

Audit Bureau of Circulations (ABC)
The organization sponsored by publishers, agencies, and advertisers for securing accurate circulation statements.

Advertising in World War I

World War I marked the first time that advertising was used as an instrument of direct social action. Advertising agencies turned from selling consumer goods to arousing patriotic sentiment, selling government bonds, encouraging conservation, and promoting a number of other war-related activities. One of the largest agencies of the era, N. W. Ayer & Sons, prepared and placed ads for the first three Liberty Loan drives and donated much of its commission to the drive.[9]

Soon these efforts by individual agencies were coordinated by the Division of Advertising of the Committee of Public Information, a World War I government propaganda office. This wartime experience convinced people that advertising could be a useful tool in communicating ideas as well as in selling products.

The 1920s

The 1920s began with a minidepression and ended with a crash. When World War I ended, makers of army trucks were able to convert quickly to commercial trucks.

Firestone spent $2 million advertising "Ship by Truck." With the industry profiting by the good roads that had been built, truck production jumped from 92,000 in 1916 to 322,000 in 1920. Door-to-door delivery from manufacturer to retailer spurred the growth of chain stores, which led, in turn, to supermarkets and self-service stores.

The passenger car business also boomed, and new products appeared in profusion: electric refrigerators, washing machines, electric shavers, and, most incredible of all, the radio. Installment selling made hard goods available to all. And all the products needed advertising.

Introduction of Radio Radio was invented by Guglielmo Marconi in 1895 as the first practical system of wireless communication. In the early years, radio was viewed as a means of maritime communication using Morse code and, with the first voice transmission in 1906, as a diversion for hobbyists. Prior to 1920, few investors saw any commercial potential for the medium. KDKA, the first commercial station, was established in Pittsburgh by Westinghouse to provide programming to buyers of its radio sets.

The modern era of radio communication is traced to the broadcast of the Harding–Cox presidential election results in 1920. Soon radio was broadcasting sporting events such as the 1921 heavyweight title fight between Jack Dempsey and Georges Carpentier and various local entertainment shows.[10] By 1922 there were more than 500 licensed stations on the air, but fewer than 2 million homes owned radio sets (see Exhibit 1.7). By the mid–1920s the emphasis was shifting away from local radio to networks where several stations could simultaneously broadcast programs. In 1926, the Radio Corporation of America (RCA) established two NBC networks with 24 stations and a year later William Paley founded CBS with 16 stations.

The depression of the 1930s had a positive impact on the number of radio listeners. The cost of radio sets became more affordable and the medium provided free entertainment in a period of economic hardship. Regular programming featuring news, drama, and comedy was becoming standard at both the local and network levels. Radio came under government regulation with formation of the Federal Communication Commission (FCC) in 1934. By 1939 there were 1,464 stations in the United States and by the end of World War II, 95 percent of households owned at least one radio.[11] Today, Americans average more than five radio sets per household and it is difficult to find an automobile or workplace without at least one set. From its noncommercial beginnings, radio advertisers now spend approximately $18 billion annually.

The Great Depression of the 1930s

The rapid growth of advertising was temporarily slowed by the Great Depression beginning with the stock market crash of 1929 and continuing through much of the 1930s. The crash had a shattering effect on our entire economy: Millions of people were thrown out of work; business failures were widespread; banks were closing all over the country. Breadlines and high unemployment eventually moved the government to establish the Works Progress Administration (WPA) to put people to work on public service projects. However, even this extraordinary step offered only partial relief to a country in crisis.

Some of the major causes for the depression, that is, excess industrial capacity, heavy consumer debt, and declining price levels, combined to discourage consumer spending and manufacturing output with a resulting negative impact on advertising. Although radio advertising experienced modest gains during the period, as a whole it was a time of catastrophe for advertising, businesses, and society in general. With the start of World War II, the economy recovered. However,

EXHIBIT 1.7

Source: From John W. Hartman Center for Sales, Advertising & Marketing History; Duke University Rare Book, Manuscript, and Special Collections Library; http://scriptorium.lib.duke.edu/eaa/.

wartime restrictions on consumer goods would not permit a rejuvenation of advertising until after the war.

Advertising During World War II

In many respects, business and advertising returned to the practices learned during World War I. As production turned to war goods, virtually all civilian material was rationed or in short supply. Although most consumer goods were not available, many companies continued to advertise to keep their brand names before the public as they looked to a future of peacetime normalcy. Most advertising was created to encourage Americans to cooperate in the war effort through conservation and volunteerism.

However, the government needed the public to do more than simply adhere to the letter of rationing regulations. "Food, clothing and a variety of essential items were to be used wisely. Avoiding purchasing items through a black market and acting in the interest of the greater community were strongly encouraged, both to hold down inflation and to ensure that scarce items would be available for everyone."[12] The majority of these advertising messages were sponsored by the government, but many private companies also joined in helping disseminate similar information (see Exhibit 1.8).

EXHIBIT **1.8**

Courtesy Narragansett Electric, a National Grid Company. From John W. Hartman Center for Sales, Advertising & Marketing History; Duke University Rare Book, Manuscript, and Special Collections Library; http://scriptorium.lib.duke.edu/eaa/.

THE WAR ADVERTISING COUNCIL

In November 1941, at a meeting of advertising executives, James Webb Young of the J. Walter Thompson advertising agency suggested the idea that ". . . a greater use of advertising for social, political and philanthropic purposes will help immeasurably to remove the distaste for advertising that now exists."[13] With the Japanese attack on Pearl Harbor three weeks later, the advertising industry began this mission with the beginning of World War II.

With the support and cooperation of the government, the **War Advertising Council** was formed in 1942. The first campaign from the Council was developed by J. Walter Thompson to encourage women to enter the workforce. The "Rosie the Riveter" campaign successfully overcame prejudices toward women in the workforce and added significantly to a labor pool depleted by wartime service. Among the many themes and projects promoted by the Council were conservation of items such fuel, fat, and tires, planting victory gardens, buying war bonds, promoting rationing, encouraging communications from home to our troops, and reminding Americans not to reveal sensitive information (see Exhibit 1.9). War bond sales efforts that resulted in the selling of $35 billion worth of bonds and a Victory Garden initiative that encouraged the planting of some 50 million gardens were among the most successful wartime campaigns of the Council.

War Advertising Council Founded in 1942 to promote World War II mobilization, it later evolved into the Advertising Council.

EXHIBIT 1.9

Courtesy of The Advertising Council, Inc.

Advertising Council
A non-profit network of agencies, media, and advertisers dedicated to promoting social programs through advertising.

Advertising's success during the war moved President Franklin Roosevelt to urge peacetime continuance of the organization as the **Advertising Council.** Today, the Council annually produces more than 35 campaigns ranging from environmental issues, educational concerns, family preservation, and anti-drinking promotions. Each year member advertising agencies create campaigns on a pro bono basis and media outlets donate more than $1 billion in time and space for Council messages. During the last 25 years, Council campaigns have been instrumental in addressing crucial issues to Americans. In doing so, it has created a number of slogans and characters that have become advertising icons such as Smokey the Bear and McGruff the Crime Dog.

Advertising After World War II to 1975: The Word Was Growth

Advertising, like every aspect of American society, took a backseat to the war during the early 1940s. The advertising that did run was largely confined to reminding the public of trademarks and logos in anticipation of the end of the war. Even institutional advertising (e.g., "Lucky Strike Green Has Gone to War") had a wartime or patriotic theme.

With the end of World War II, advertising and consumer goods began to reach out to a public ready to get on with their lives and spend, spend, spend. With "the end of the war pent-up demand led to an unprecedented acceleration in the rate of growth of advertising media investment—so much so that ad media volume by 1950 was almost three times what it had been only ten years earlier!"[14]

By 1950 Americans were living better than at any time in their history. Moreover, it is doubtful that any nation had ever experienced the same rate of economic expansion as the United States did during the decade after World War II. Consumer goods purchases grew at an unprecedented rate and advertising was the fuel that fed this consumer buying spree.

In 1947 America discovered television and began a love affair that continues to the present. From its crude beginnings in a few major markets, television set ownership grew from less than 10 percent household penetration in 1950 to more than 90 percent in 1960. At the same time, television's share of total advertising expenditures increased 400 percent from 4 to 17 percent. As millions of viewers gave up playing bridge, going to the movies, and even talking to each other to tune in to Milton Berle and *The $64,000 Question*, national advertising dollars poured into television.

By the 1960s, television had forever changed both magazines and radio as advertising media. Television also had major influences on both sports and politics. In its insatiable appetite for programming, television brought thousands of hours of sports into the living room. It was the lure of television dollars that created the American Football League and the American Basketball Association and it allowed even mediocre players to become millionaires.

But perhaps television of the period had its greatest impact on politics. As television's popularity continued to grow, it soon became apparent to politicians that the same formula used so successfully in selling soap and cigarettes might be adapted to selling candidates. Rosser Reeves is generally credited with introducing the 60-second commercial to American politics during the 1960 election campaign of Dwight Eisenhower. In a series of commercials, Reeves converted the reserved, rather stiff and awkward candidate into the personable "Man from Abilene." For better or worse, politics would never be the same again.

The Figures Also Said Growth Between 1950 and 1973, the population of the United States increased by 38 percent, while disposable personal income increased by 327 percent. New housing starts went up by 47 percent, energy consumption by 121 percent, college enrollments by 136 percent, automobile registrations by 151 percent, telephones in use by 221 percent, number of outboard motors sold by 242 percent, retail sales by 250 percent, families owning two or more cars by 300 percent, frozen-food production by 655 percent, number of airline passengers by 963 percent, homes with dishwashers by 1,043 percent, and homes with room air conditioners by 3,662 percent.

Advertising not only contributed to the growth but also was part of it, rising from an expenditure of $5,780 million in 1950 to $28,320 million in 1975—a growth of 490 percent. There were many developments in advertising during this time:

- In 1956, the Department of Justice ruled that advertising agencies could negotiate fees with clients rather than adhere to the 15 percent commission that had been required on all media placed. This encouraged the growth of specialized companies, such as independent media-buying services, creative-only agencies, and in-house agencies owned by advertisers.
- The voice of the consumer became more powerful.
- Congress passed an act limiting outdoor advertising along interstate highways. Cigarette advertising was banned from television.

- The FTC introduced corrective advertising by those who had made false or misleading claims. Comparison advertising (mentioning competitors by name) was deemed an acceptable form of advertising.

- The magazine-publishing world saw the disappearance of the old dinosaurs— *The Saturday Evening Post, Collier's,* and *Women's Home Companion.* There was no vacuum at the newsstand, however, for there was an immediate upsurge in magazines devoted to special interests.

- Newspapers felt the effect of the shift of metropolitan populations to the suburbs. Freestanding inserts became an important part of newspaper billings.

- Radio took a dive when television came along. The story of how it came out of that drastic decline is a good example of turning disadvantages into advantages.

- Direct-response advertising soared from $900 million in 1950 to $8 billion in 1980, reflecting the growth of direct marketing.

- The two biggest developments to emerge were television and electronic data processing. Television changed life in America as well as the world of advertising. Data-processing systems brought before the eyes of management a wealth of organized information. This, together with syndicated research services, revolutionized the entire marketing process and the advertising-media operation.

Advertising in the Fragmented 1980s

As we have seen in this chapter, advertising is a volatile business. It must constantly adapt to changes in business conditions, technology, and the social and cultural environment. In some cases, it has a role in causing these changes; in others, it simply follows. The decade of the 1980s was a period of significant transformations in American society, and certainly advertising was affected by many of these changes.

Let's briefly discuss some of the major developments during this period:

1. *New technology.* Changes in technology and diversification of the communication system had profound effects on advertising during this period. Cable television, home video recorders, a proliferation of specialized magazines, the success of direct mail and home shopping techniques, and the growth of sales promotion changed the practice of advertising in fundamental ways. The advertising practitioners of today are much more likely than their predecessors to be marketing generalists, competent in evaluating research and understanding the psychology of consumer behavior as well as executing advertising.

audience fragmentation
The segmenting of mass-media audiences into smaller groups because of diversity of media outlets.

2. ***Audience fragmentation.*** The 1980s may have marked the end of the traditional mass market. Advertisers no longer identified customers by households but rather by demographics and the number of heavy users of specific products within various audience segments. Television went from a medium of three channels to one of a 100-plus options; newspapers, rather than appealing to a single homogeneous readership, are positioned more as cafeterias where readers choose only what they want to read; and the VCR, DVR, and home computer now allow the audience to control the flow of information, entertainment, and advertising.

3. *Consolidation.* Paradoxically, as media and audiences proliferated, ownership of brands, ad agencies, and media was consolidated among a few giant companies. Firms such as Procter & Gamble, American Home Products, and General Electric provided corporate umbrellas for dozens, even hundreds, of separate brands. With their billion-dollar-plus budgets, they exercised significant lever-

age over the total advertising enterprise including the advertising agencies vying for their accounts and the media carrying their messages.

Like their clients, ad agencies also merged into so-called mega-agencies or holding companies designed to offer greater service to these giant conglomerates usually on a global basis. Often as not, these agency mergers led to as many headaches as benefits, starting with awkward client conflicts. Like both corporations and agencies, media increasingly came under the control of fewer and fewer communication companies. The Turner empire of cable networks, Time Warner's ownership of a bewildering array of media, and Gannett's interest in everything from newspapers to TV production were only a few examples of the changing media landscape during the 1980s.

4. *Credit.* Perhaps the greatest long-term legacy of the 1980s was the "buy now, pay later" mentality that pervaded every facet of American life from the federal government to the individual household budget. The leveraged buyouts of corporate America and the overuse of consumer credit created an atmosphere in which living within one's income was an illusion. By the late 1990s, when companies and consumers began the slow process of paying for the excesses of the past decade, advertising was often the first victim of any cutbacks. Media saw advertising revenues fall; advertising was harder to sell even with deep discounts; merchants began to deal with a reluctant consumer more interested in deals than fancy advertising; and some of the most famous names in American business faced serious trouble, if not outright bankruptcy.

America Becomes a Service Economy

Earlier in the chapter, we discussed the numerous changes in nineteenth-century American society that transformed the country from the Jeffersonian ideal of a rural nation to an urbanized country where manufacturing ran the economic engine.[15] During the last 50 years, another equally momentous conversion of the American economy has taken place. A nation, once respected around the world for its technical and production expertise, has been transformed into one focused on the providing of services. This conversion was underscored in 2001 when Wal-Mart became the largest company in the United States, replacing General Motors and Exxon Mobil for the top spot. It was the first time in history that a service company held the number-one position.

While Wal-Mart, barely 40 years old, is a phenomenon by any standard, the movement to a service-oriented society is a longtime trend. As recently, as 1955, the *Fortune* 500 was dominated by companies such as Western Electric, Corn Products Refining, U.S. Plywood, and Shoe Corporation of America. As household income increased, the percentage spent on basics declined and there were greater opportunities to indulge in travel, movies, and more expensive houses. Today, manufacturing, with a significantly smaller workforce, accounts for the same dollar share of the economy as it did in 1955. Technology and production efficiency have allowed manufacturers to replace marginal workers and marginal operations. In their place is a sophisticated workforce of engineers and computer specialists.

As Harvard economist Claudia Goldin points out, the twentieth-century move to a service economy is the continuation of a process that began in the 1800s when numerous small town mills and slaughterhouses were replaced by men such as Pillsbury, Armour, and Swift whose large operations soon made these small operations obsolete.[16] Wal-Mart did the same to many mom-and-pop stores. In fact, manufacturing's share of employment peaked in 1953 when 35 percent of the workforce was employed in producing goods. Over the last five decades, the industrial share of workers has steadily declined. The U.S. Bureau of Labor Statistics predicts that by 2010, service employment will outpace manufacturing by a five-to-one margin.

Advertising and the Twenty-First Century

As previously discussed in this chapter, during the early 1900s businesses and advertisers attempted to gain the trust of an American public that viewed both as adversaries. During the latter part of the twentieth century, the United States became a nation built on mass production and the delivery of affordable brands and services to an increasingly affluent population. In the first decade of the twenty-first century, many businesses are once again trying to rebuild a trust that has been lost in the wake of accounting scandals, Internet scams, and stock manipulations.

In addition to the "trust factor," Americans are coping with issues of international terrorism that have tragically invaded our shores and an economy marked by long-term recession. In this environment, advertising has a challenge as great as any it has faced in the last century. On the one hand, it needs to be sensitive to the feelings of a population that is seeking security and a return to familiar routines, but at the same time it needs to aggressively promote goods and services to increase spending by both consumers and businesses. Predicting the future in a period of such flux is indeed difficult. However, let's briefly examine several of the trends that may define advertising in coming years.

First, the tone of advertising will change, at least in the short term. It is obvious that the events of 9/11 have fundamentally altered the way that Americans approach many issues, including appropriate advertising messages. Advertisers now must walk a fine line between sensitivity and exploitation in the minds of consumers. As one advertising executive observed, "The note you hit may send a reverberating screech across your product or service. If consumers suspect that you are trying to manipulate them for financial gain during a time of national tragedy, not only will they shun your brand in the short term, they will likely eschew you in the long term as well."[17]

During the last decade, media companies have trumpeted the cause of consolidation and convergence. The proponents of convergence predicted great advantages for huge companies blending technologies such as television, cable, and the computer to create Internet interactivity with the technical speed of cable and the sight, sound, and motion of television. According to its proponents, convergence was going to offer advertisers the ability to reach audiences on a one-to-one basis with individualized commercial messages tailored specifically for their needs.

Clearly, the consolidation of media is a reality. Led by Time Warner, four companies accounted for more than $10 billion in advertising revenue and another eight totaled between $5–10 billion. However, many of the most optimistic predictions of cross-media advertising have not come to fruition. In some cases, the companies themselves have divisions that have historically been in competition and their corporate cultures have yet to deal with either the technology or the management of these enterprises. For example, how do top executives of these mega-corporations deal with the problem of their recording divisions being at odds with their online counterparts over downloading music from the Web? Or how do they corporately reconcile between their program production studios negotiating fees with cable and network entities under the same ownership seeking the lowest possible costs?

Another unresolved issue is gaining acceptance from the advertising community for these integrated media companies. For example, it is obviously to the advantage of Time Warner to sell an advertising package of *Sports Illustrated, Sports Illustrated for Kids,* signage at Turner Field and a special promotion with the Atlanta Braves (the company owns both the stadium and the team), and banners on Internet sports services. On the other hand, individual advertisers may want to buy *Sports Illustrated* but see better value in buying spots for *Monday Night Football* on Disney-owned ABC, and the Fox Sports Internet owned by News Corp. There is no question that integration and convergence of media and advertising content will come. The form it will take and the scope of these changes have yet to be determined.

Related to the idea of convergence is another characteristic of advertising in the coming century—*permission marketing*. The term refers to the fact that when consumers control communication channels, they determine which messages, including advertising, they will receive. As technology improves and the techniques of target marketing become even more sophisticated, we will see audiences assume greater control over the communication process. Rather than listeners or readers having to accept whatever advertising accompanies their favorite medium, in the future the audience will determine what messages they receive. In this environment, advertising becomes an invited guest rather than an intrusion. Permission marketing has major implications for advertising since, presumably, permission is granted because the advertiser has a product or service that either has solved a consumer's problems in the past or has the potential to do so in the future.

With the advent of permission marketing, companies will find that strong brands are more important than ever. After all, we don't invite strangers into our house and, likewise, unknown brands will find it difficult to get an invitation. It will be harder to develop new markets by sheer weight of advertising and we will probably see more brand extensions in the future to take advantage of established brand names. On the other hand, smaller companies with superior products may find that customized communication may make entry to the market possible at a lower cost than they might pay using traditional mass media outlets.

Another area of concern for advertisers in coming years will be globalization and diversity. One only has to look at the population projections for Latin America, the Far East, and Africa to see the potential for sales of virtually any goods but particularly consumer products. The smallest increase in the market share of Coca-Cola, Tide detergent, Huggies diapers, Gerber Baby Food, or Charmin toilet tissue in India or China would create a profit windfall for these brands.

Understanding the language, culture, economy, and political environment of countries throughout the world is already a prerequisite for most marketing executives. It will become even more important as new areas of the globe are opened to foreign investment. Multinational marketers will find that a locally oriented strategy for global marketing is essential. Corporations such as Coca-Cola, Sony, Ford, and Procter & Gamble will continue to increase their expansion into every part of the world. However, global strategies will increasingly be geared to each country or region.

An advertiser does not have to go abroad to see the necessity for marketing plans that consider a diversified marketplace. Marketing executives and advertisers must realize that in our own country Hispanic, Asian American, and African American consumers are part of the fabric of our society and they must be reached through messages that are sensitive to their needs. This sensitivity means supporting minority media owners with advertising dollars, hiring a diverse workforce in the advertising industry, creating advertising and commercials that fairly reflect the various ethnic and cultural groups within this country and, when appropriate, developing products specifically for these markets. In Chapter 24, we will discuss the globalization of advertising as well as the need for greater sensitivity to the issue of diversity in domestic advertising.

SUMMARY

The history of advertising can only be studied within the context of the social and economic development of a country. In the United States, advertising prospered because of a unique environment that included a democratic government, unfettered business institutions, sophisticated technology, a free media, and a receptive culture. The move from an agrarian to an urban, industrialized society brought with it unprecedented specialization. However, the efficiencies of mass production and specialization could only be achieved with effective use of mass advertising and promotion.

As we write this text, advertising is undergoing fundamental changes. For example, the development of e-commerce, or Internet selling, has not had the immediate effects on marketing, promotion, and selling that its most enthusiastic proponents predicted a few years ago. However, the notion of reaching consumers on a more personal basis is having major impact on the way we communicate with consumers. We are beginning to look at consumers as individuals as opposed to large groups of buyers. This approach is moving firms to adopt more personalized and localized product offering and advertising campaigns.

As audiences take greater control of communication channels, advertisers will need to view themselves as invited guests rather than opportunistic intruders. Likewise, advertisers will have to adapt creative messages to the specific needs of smaller groups of homogeneous consumers. The Internet will be only one piece of the marketing puzzle. Marketers will have to coordinate a host of available communication and distribution channels to reach evermore demanding buyers. Traditional retailers will increasingly utilize direct-selling techniques such as the Internet while e-commerce companies and cataloguers will establish retail outlets to serve specific segments of their prime prospects.

In this uncertain advertising atmosphere, it is clear that the next decade will bring fundamental changes to marketing and mass communication not seen since the advent of high-speed presses and the introduction of broadcasting. Nevertheless, it is difficult to determine exactly when and in what form this new marketing and media revolution will take place. In this text, we try to explain the current practices of advertising while offering insights in this fast-changing field.

 **REVIEW**

1. Advertising operates most effectively in an economic environment where supply exceeds demand. Why?

2. How did branded goods contribute to the growth of national advertising and, in turn, how did advertising make widely sold brands possible?

3. Discuss the four major historical eras of advertising development.

4. Discuss the evolution of the modern advertising agency from Volney Palmer to Marion Harper.

5. What is the relationship between the growth of creative advertising and product differentiation?

6. What were the primary reasons for passage of the Federal Trade Commission Act of 1914?

7. How did the introduction of radio change advertising?

8. Discuss the role of the War Advertising Council.

9. What effect have the following trends had on advertising?
   a. new technology
   b. audience fragmentation
   c. business and media consolidation
   d. easily obtainable consumer credit

 **TAKE IT TO THE WEB**

The John W. Hartman Center for Sales, Advertising, and Marketing History is housed in Duke University's Rare Book, Manuscript, and Special Collections Library (**http://scriptorium.lib.duke.edu/hartman/brochure.html**). Compare early advertisements with modern ones for similar products and brands.

Review how the topics of the Ad Council (**www.adcouncil.org**) have changed over the last 50 years. Pay particular attention to the advertisements produced during the years of the War Advertising Council when most consumer products were unavailable or in short supply.

The history of the Federal Food and Drug Administration (**www.fda.gov/opacom/ backgrounders/miles.html**) provides a useful insight into the development of consumer protection in the United States.

CHAPTER 2

YOUR PASSION IS OUR OBSESSION. Whether in tight sand or thick Bermuda, nowhere is feel more important than your wedge game. And nothing feels quite like the Mizuno RAW Black Ox™. Its finish helps maximize spin for pinpoint accuracy, while its lie responsive sole lets you to hit the ball from virtually any lie.

Mizuno®
SERIOUS PERFORMANCE

Roles of Advertising

Advertising, like all forms of mass communication, has undergone dramatic changes during the last decade. Although it continues to be a primary tool for marketing communication, the forces of technological change and business consolidation have had significant effects on the practice and execution of advertising. Regardless of the revolutionary changes in mass communication, advertising's primary role continues to be to convey information about products, services, or ideas to a targeted audience.

In coming years, the media that carry advertising will doubtlessly continue to change and specific advertising executions will become more targeted as we become better able to identify and reach small groups of customers or even individual buyers. However, the basic communication goals of good advertising will remain constant whether it is used by companies to reach customers on a global basis or around the corner. After reading this chapter, you will understand:

1. **measuring advertising as a marketing communication tool**
2. **advertising as only one element in the marketing mix**
3. **the core mission of advertising**
4. **communicating to both consumers and businesses**
5. **advertising of ideas and nonprofit organizations**

ADVERTISING AND THE CHANGING COMMUNICATION ENVIRONMENT

In recent years, one of the major concerns of marketers has been the role of communication convergence on the process of reaching consumers in the most effective way. The term **convergence** means coming together or intersecting different components of some related system. In mass communication, the term has come to refer to three distinct though related areas:

1. *Technological convergence.* For example, listening to radio programs over your home computer or watching movies through a VCR connected to your television set.
2. *Business convergence.* Usually referred to as consolidation, one of the dominant trends of modern business is the merging of company after

convergence
The blending of various facets of marketing functions and communication technology to create more efficient and expanded synergies.

company, including, as we will discuss later in the text, advertising agencies and media companies.

3. *Content convergence.* Content is the primary expense of most communication companies. Whether it is a network showing reruns to amortize its investment in its shows or an advertising agency using clip art or sharing footage with its global partners, companies try to stretch the use of communication content.

As we discuss the functions and procedures of modern advertising, we will see that the forces of convergence and consolidation and striving for cost efficiencies are dominant themes in virtually every advertising, promotion, and marketing decision.

Advertising as a Communication Tool

Advertising is among the most flexible and adaptive elements of marketing communication. It is used for a number of purposes by industrial giants, nonprofit organizations, and the smallest retail establishments. No matter what the goal of a specific advertising strategy, the key to success depends on planning in a number of areas. The idea that great advertising flows from spontaneous ideas apart from planning and research is a myth that few businesses can afford to embrace.

Advertisers must address a number of factors before the first headline is written or the first commercial scene is shot. The first step in the planning process is a thorough knowledge of the marketing plan that will incorporate the strategy. Advertising objectives must be viewed from a *communications* perspective; advertising rarely can accomplish tasks that are not related to communication. When we stray from this fundamental concept, we are placing unrealistic burdens on advertising and setting ourselves up for failure.

Because advertising objectives must complement the marketing plan, let's look at the primary factors in a typical marketing plan. As we do, consider those aspects that can be addressed by marketing communication and in what ways communication could complement the implementation of the plan:[1]

1. *Overall goal(s) of the plan.* Usually, marketing goals are expressed in financial terms such as expected sales revenues at the end of the first year or percent increases over previous years.

2. *Marketing objectives.* Here the objective and rationale of the plan are stated. For example, we may want to show a significant increase in market share relative to specific competitors.

3. *Marketing strategy.* The strategy outlines the steps to achieve our goals and objectives. We might suggest a greater investment in advertising or promotion or a switch in distribution outlets. The strategy offers only a general overview of primary marketing considerations.

4. *Situational analysis.* This analysis is a statement of the product benefits and the pertinent data available concerning sales trends, competitive environment, and industry forecasts.

5. *Problems and opportunities.* At this point, we outline the major problems and opportunities facing the brand. For example, a manufacturer of lawn tools found that it was losing sales because its competitors had signed exclusive contracts with major retail chains. However, the company soon found that there were numerous opportunities to sell through local, independent retailers that did not have access to several brands sold exclusively through chains.

6. *Financial plan.* The financial plan is an outline of the expected profit or loss that will be experienced over various time frames. It is here that the company projects the extent of investments that have to be made before a product shows a profit. As we have seen in recent years, a number of e-commerce companies grossly underestimated the extent of this investment and potential profitability.

7. *Research.* Ideally, a company wants to answer questions from available data, but sometimes the marketing plan suggests that primary research is needed. In these cases, a research plan must be suggested. In any case, the research section should include how the plan will be evaluated on the basis of measurable results.

With the marketing plan providing our blueprint, we begin to plan our advertising to accomplish the communication tasks specific to brand and company objectives.

A. *Prospect identification.* The guiding principle of the advertising plan is a detailed identification of a company's prime prospects. As we will discuss in Chapter 4, identifying prime prospects entails both who they are (e.g., basic demographic data) and also the social, cultural, and psychological characteristics that determine purchase behavior and those messages that will influence that behavior.

B. *Consumer motivations.* Accurate insight about our core consumers will greatly enhance our chances of success as we move to determine the role that advertising can play in channeling consumer needs, wants, and aspirations into purchases of general product categories and, more importantly, specific brands of goods and services.

C. *Advertising execution.* Once we identify the role of advertising within the context of the marketing program, our next step is to develop messages that effectively set our brand apart from its competitors (see Exhibit 2.1). What we generally refer

EXHIBIT 2.1

Effective advertising solves specific problems for targeted consumers.

Courtesy of McRae Communications and Techsonic Industries, Inc./Hummingbird.

to as advertising creativity (see Chapter 16) is most often a result of having a sales message flow logically from prospect identification and prospect motivation to attention-grabbing communication.

D. *Media planning.* Our next decision is media placement. Advertising does not communicate in a void; rather it benefits from a synergism between message and medium. An effective television product demonstration will usually be unsuitable for radio and a long copy, descriptive magazine advertisement would probably be impractical in a 30-second television commercial format. Media selection must provide an efficient means of reaching potential consumers (e.g., radio for teens) *and* provide a communication channel that is suitable for the message being conveyed.

E. *The advertising budget.* Finally, we will find that budgetary considerations are constant limiting factors for virtually all advertising plans. Advertising is not cheap and there will rarely be enough funds to accomplish all the tasks we wish to execute. Most marketers use past performance and budgets as a starting benchmark and then adjust future budgets based on factors such as inflation, changes in market share, product innovations, competitive environment, and the general state of the economic environment.

For the remainder of this chapter, we will examine the many aspects of advertising and the planning and executions that result in success or failure for the companies that advertise.

ADVERTISING AND PROFITABILITY

Although advertising alone rarely creates sales, like any marketing function, it must demonstrate a contribution to profits. Generally, this contribution is expressed as **return on investment (ROI),** which measures revenues against expenditure of resources.[2]

The measure of advertising's contribution to profitability can be shown in three steps:

1. *Advertising and brand awareness.* Research suggests if not causality, then a strong relationship exists between brand awareness and market share (see Exhibit 2.2).

return on investment (ROI)

One measure of the efficiency of a company is the rate of return (profits) achieved by a certain level of investment on various business functions including advertising.

EXHIBIT 2.2

The relationship between brand awareness and market share is strong.

Courtesy of *Cahners Advertising Research Report,* No. 2000.6, p. 2.

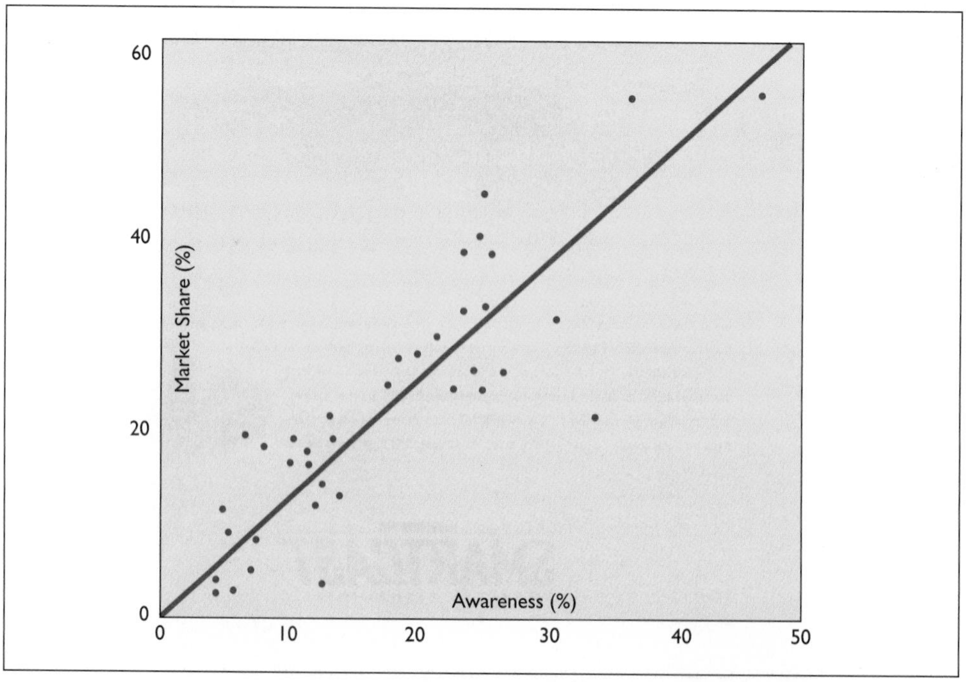

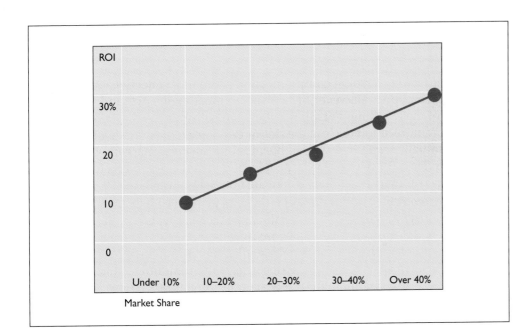

EXHIBIT 2.3

The relationship between market share and pretax ROI.

Courtesy of *Cahners Advertising Research Report*, No. 2000.6, p. 3.

Perhaps the most significant role that advertising plays is its contribution to the creation of brand awareness. Generally, studies show that the more businesses spend on advertising and promotion as a percentage of sales, the higher are the levels of brand awareness.

2. *Market share and return on investment.* The market share for a brand has been shown to be one of the primary contributors to ROI (see Exhibit 2.3). Businesses demonstrating high levels of market share benefit from economies of scale in production, marketing, and so forth, which has the effect of increasing profitability. By producing and marketing greater product volume, these businesses tend to be more efficient and have lower costs. The conversion of brand awareness into market share and, finally, into profitability is shown in Exhibit 2.4.

Clearly, this process is not a guarantee of success. The quality of advertising, continuing product development, and the entry of competitors into a market will all have an effect on profitability. However, regardless of the market circumstances, maintaining high brand awareness through advertising and promotion demands continuing attention from top management.

INTEGRATED MARKETING

Marketing consists of four primary elements: product, price, distribution, and communication. These are the primary elements in what is known as the

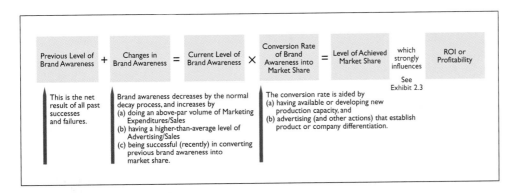

EXHIBIT 2.4

How brand awareness aids profitability (the sequence of events).

Courtesy of *Cahners Advertising Research Report*, No. 2000.6, p. 6.

marketing mix
Combination of marketing functions, including advertising, used to sell a product.

sales promotion
(1) Sales activities that supplement both personal selling and marketing, coordinate the two, and help to make them effective. For example, displays are sales promotions. (2) More loosely, the combination of personal selling, advertising, and all supplementary selling activities.

public relations
Communication with various internal and external publics to create an image for a product or corporation.

marketing mix.[3] Marketing communication is further divided into four primary categories:

1. *Personal selling.* Personal communication is the most effective means of persuading someone. However, it is also the most expensive and impractical means of mass selling. Personal selling is most often used as a follow-up to mass communication to close the sale or develop a long-term relationship that will eventually result in a sale. In business-to-business marketing this means opening doors for personal salespeople, and in consumer marketing it means steering customers to retailers where the final sale takes place.

2. *Sales promotion.* Sales promotion is an extra incentive for a customer to make an immediate purchase. It is by far the most inclusive category of promotional spending. Sales promotion may consist of a special sales price, a cents-off coupon, a colorful point-of-purchase display, or a chance to win a trip to Hawaii in a sweepstakes. The largest category of promotions, those directed to the distribution channel, are rarely seen by consumers. These promotions, known as trade promotions, are used to persuade retailers and wholesalers to carry a brand or give a specific brand some advantage, such as favorable shelf space. One of the fears, especially during recessionary periods, is that an overuse of short-term promotions such as coupons and various trade deals will not only cut into profits but also harm long-term brand equity by placing a major emphasis on price. Marketers are well aware of the potential downside of promotional offers and the most astute companies incorporate strong brand messages in their promotions. By doing so, they ensure that promotions remain short-term sales incentives rather than having consumers rely on them for their primary purchase decision making. In the past a number of promotional offers such as automobile rebates and disposal diaper coupons created price competition within these product categories that caused some erosion in brand loyalty and profitability.

3. *Public relations.* According to the Public Relations Society of America, "**Public relations** helps an organization and its publics adapt mutually to each other." For many years, public relations and propaganda were considered almost synonymous. Thomas Paine, the Revolutionary War firebrand and author of *Common Sense,* may have been America's first public relations practitioner. However, only in recent years has public relations been fully integrated into the marketing communication plans of most companies.

   The key to effective public relations is that it must convey a story—the best public relations is news. When Gillette introduced its Mach 3 razor in 1998, ads showing the design innovation and obvious product benefits generated 1.6 billion impressions. Likewise, the Segway personal transformation device had news coverage estimated to be worth $80 million. Although these are unusual cases, public relations has been effective in keeping old brands viable through programs such as the Pillsbury Bake-Off, and numerous product extensions such as Crest Whitestrips have also benefited from public relations.[4]

   Public relations and advertising are rarely competitors. Rather, they work in concert to get the brand message to as many prospects as possible. Because public relations is usually seen as news, it has credibility that is lacking in most advertising. On the other hand, even a unique product is news for only a short period of time. When media mogul Ted Turner began Ted's Montana Grill, which featured bison burgers, the introduction was communicated entirely through public relations. However, it was the plan all along to shift into advertising once the chain achieved a level of awareness through public relations.[5] Ted's Montana Grill's promotion strategy was based on the fact that the media will not continue to carry stories about a product indefinitely. Furthermore, unlike advertising, a public relations message is ultimately controlled by the media. The media make decisions concerning when, where, and if a particular product story will be carried. It is the elements of message control and credibility that most distinguish public relations and advertising.

4. *Advertising.* **Advertising** is a message paid for by an identified sponsor and usually delivered through some medium of mass communication. Advertising is persuasive communication. It is not neutral; it is not unbiased; it says: "I am going to sell you a product or an idea." Throughout the remainder of this text, we will not only be discussing the principles of advertising but also how advertising interacts with other forms of marketing communication.

advertising
Advertising consists of paid notices from identified sponsors normally offered through communication media.

During the early development of modern marketing and advertising, each of these marketing communication components was regarded as more or less discrete functions. Each had its own manager, and coordination of the functions was not always as rigorous as it should have been. This lack of overall coordination led many companies to address their customers with many different and sometimes confusing and contradictory messages. However, in recent years, companies have begun to move toward a consolidation of all areas of the marketing function, especially marketing communication.

For example, the term *speaking with one voice* entered the marketing lexicon as companies demanded that all communication from their letterheads to product packaging demonstrated a consistent look and message. This movement to organize the total communication program is known as **integrated marketing communication (IMC).** A primary implication of this integrated approach is less concern with how a message is delivered (e.g., advertising, public relations, etc.) and more emphasis on the effectiveness of the total marketing communication plan. In advertising jargon, expenditures in traditional advertising media are known as **above-the-line spending.** Spending for public relations, sales promotion, and most other promotional vehicles is known as **below-the-line expenses.** During most of the twentieth century, above-the-line expenses accounted for the biggest share of the promotional spending for most major companies.

integrated marketing communication (IMC)
The joint planning, execution, and coordination of all areas of marketing communication.

above-the-line expenses
These usually include advertising in traditional media. In recent years, the development of the Internet and interactive media have blurred this line.

Today, major marketers are much more interested in the efficiency and benefits of their total marketing communication program than concerned with the specific means of achieving these results. "Whatever the disciplines used . . . they all must work together to give a unified message to consumers. It is relationships with consumers that matter, and these are built by ideas that transcend individual media."[6]

below-the-line expenses
These refer to promotions other than advertising such as public relations. Typically, they are more difficult to measure than above the line expenses.

One study conducted in the five largest advertising markets (the United States, Japan, Germany, the United Kingdom, and France) showed that by 2002 advertising accounted for only 44.4 percent of marketing communication expenditures, a drop of one percentage point from 2001. While public relations expenditures remained flat and sales promotion decreased slightly, interactive marketing including Internet advertising and Web-based marketing increased almost 15 percent during the same period.[7]

The reasons for the move to IMC are numerous and complex. However, there are three primary factors that are driving these changes:

1. *The multifaceted consumer.* Americans are more diverse than ever before. Not only are we culturally and racially diverse, but also we exhibit much different lifestyles than those of earlier generations. For example, the 9-to-5 workday is a thing of the past. For example, at 5 A.M. there are 12 million television viewers, an increase of almost one-third since 1999. Local news is on the air earlier to serve these early birds and advertisers have enthusiastically reached out to these mostly affluent households.[8]

2. *Demands for promotional efficiency.* The recession of the early 2000s required companies to demand that their promotional dollars and the agencies that

spend them demonstrate a return on their investment. Companies know that they are dealing with consumers who have become jaded by the unrelenting bombardment of advertising messages. These companies are experimenting with a combination of nontraditional means of reaching prospects. As one marketing executive observed, firms must deliver "messages to consumers in the medium of their choice and a medium that they'll respond to."[9] In addition, as companies such as Home Depot expand their business into service and installation, it is imperative that they keep the brand focus to consumers (see Exhibit 2.5).

3. *Revolutionary communications technology.* "In the 1990s, satellite and broadband technology allowed Hollywood to deliver a smorgasbord of niche programming to viewers, widening the gap from the days when most owners of television sets sat down in their living rooms at the same time to watch 'I Love Lucy.'"[10] New technology is both a blessing and a curse to the twenty-first-century marketer. On the one hand, there are numerous opportunities to use event sponsorships, such as NASCAR and rock concerts, product placement in major movies and television shows, and a host of content-specific, targeted media. By the same token, new technology such as DVR has given audiences

EXHIBIT 2.5

A single brand message has been imperative as Home Depot expands into service, installation, and other areas to benefit its consumers.

Courtesy of Homer TLC, Inc., Copyright 2003.

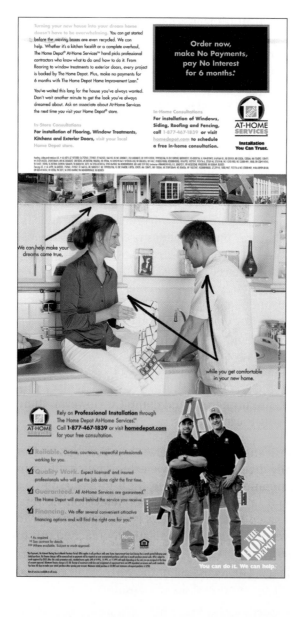

unprecedented control over the communication channel. With this shift in control, advertisers will have to be less intrusive and more in tune with their audience's core needs for products and services. To compete in this sales environment, companies find that they must routinely use techniques as varied as product sampling and one-to-one Internet messages to reach core prospects.

As integration of the various promotional functions becomes more typical, the advertising professional of the future will be required to make decisions about the role that both advertising and other promotional tools will play in any particular campaign. This assessment will include an evaluation of marketing goals and strategies, identification of prime prospects, product characteristics, and the budget available for all areas of the communication mix. Although the benefits of IMC are apparent, the implementation of the strategy can be extremely difficult, especially for multibrand companies with numerous target customers. In later chapters, we will discuss in more detail the execution of IMC.

ADVERTISING AS AN INSTITUTION

For the past 100 years, advertising has been a major element in the growth of mass marketing and the resulting economic expansion of U.S. business. Even critics of advertising acknowledge that it is a significant force in persuading consumers to purchase a host of products and services. The very pervasiveness of advertising and its perceived power have moved many scholars to examine the role of advertising as a fundamental institution in American society.

These studies have viewed advertising from two broad perspectives: (1) its economic role and (2) its social and cultural role in communicating not only product information but also social values. A review of the literature concerning advertising leads to the conclusion that the economic role of advertising is viewed in a much more positive fashion than its social and cultural roles. That is, the basic economic functions of advertising to disseminate product information that allows consumers to know that products exist, give consumers information about competing brands, and permit consumers to make intelligent choices among product options are accepted by most observers.

However, advertising effects beyond these strictly utilitarian or economic functions are viewed with suspicion in many quarters. Increasingly, critics and advertisers alike are examining advertising messages from a social perspective. As one advertising executive remarked, "What is *truthful* is determined clearly by the law. . . . What is *right* is no less important. Advertising is a powerful communicator of values. It cannot be expected to lead social change, but it must be sensitive to changing values in our society. Advertising does not exist in an amoral environment."[11] Issues such as the inclusion and portrayal of women, ethnic groups, and the elderly in adverting are among the issues contemporary advertising must confront that were minor considerations in the past.

In the summer of 2002, the National Council of Women's Organizations (NCWO) criticized Augusta Nation Golf Club for not allowing women members. Sponsors of the Master's Golf Tournament, such as Coca-Cola, became one of the primary focuses of NCWO's campaign. It was a case in which, in the opinion of NCWO, advertising was a contributor to what it saw as a social issue, even though the sponsors of the golf tournament were not involved in the selection of club members.

The Master's incident and numerous other similar examples point out that advertising is regarded by many as an institution that communicates social as well as economic messages even when the social aspects of advertising are both unintended and undesirable from the advertiser's perspective.

The majority of both practitioners and consumers accept the fact that advertising has an ethical and moral responsibility to provide product information that is both truthful and socially appropriate. On the other hand, it is obvious that consumers make purchase decisions on the basis of psychological and social factors as well as strictly utilitarian considerations. People buy Cadillacs instead of Chevrolets, not just for basic differences in transportation needs but also because the Cadillac brand satisfies a need for prestige, social status, and a number of other psychological factors. It can be argued that advertising creates these wants (as opposed to needs). But, in fact, advertising mirrors the society in which it functions while over time it probably contributes to subtle changes in the mores and behavior of the public that is exposed to it.

Advertising's role as an institution has been studied by both critics and proponents. These perspectives about the roles of advertising generally fall into one of the following three categories.

What Advertising Does for Consumers

As we discussed earlier, modern marketing strategy focuses on the consumer as the core element for effective advertising. With this in mind, it is appropriate to examine

EXHIBIT 2.6 a & b

Callaway Gardens sells its vacation resort with a humorous attention-getting approach to differentiate it from the many other options available to customers.

Courtesy of Sawyer Riley Compton and Callaway Gardens.

SHE SAYS "I LOVE YOU."

YOU SAY "THANKS."

Why do you need 40 acres of flowers?

🌿 Callaway Gardens

For reservations call 1.800.CALLAWAY or visit callawaygardens.com.

the role that advertising plays in benefiting individual consumers. Advertising's primary function for consumers is providing information about products and services that they otherwise would not have heard about. Advertising aids the consumer in making the best decision about the products that will solve some problem.

"'Different strokes for different folks' is the underlying logic of market segmentation. The fact is that different types of people . . . prefer different types of goods and services (defined by attributes such as quantity, price and style)."[12] With the advent of specialized media that can reach narrowly segmented audiences, advertising has an expanded ability to provide even better information to selected consumers about specialized product categories. Effective advertising creatively suggests different options for consumers (see Exhibit 2.6 a & b).

Closely related to the concept of consumer information is the idea that advertising promotes greater choice for the consumer. Effective communication provides a means for new products to enter the marketplace and, therefore, increases the number of products available to consumers. In the future, as technology and interactive media increase the practicality for consumer feedback, buyers will have even greater input into the marketing process. The prevailing consumer focus that creates an environment where products are designed for the consumer rather than forcing consumers to accept what is available will be greatly enhanced during the next decade.

YOU SAID "YES, SIR."

YOU SHOULD HAVE SAID "YES, MA'AM."

Why do you need 40 acres of flowers?

🌹 Callaway Gardens

For reservations call 1.800.CALLAWAY or visit callawaygardens.com.

What Advertising Does for Business

One of the myths perpetrated by advertising critics is that there is an adversarial relationship between businesses selling goods and consumers buying them with each side trying to "beat" the other in a game of commercial exchange. If the marketing concept has taught us anything, it is that the long-term success of a business is built on a positive and mutually beneficial relationship with its consumers. This relationship can only be maintained if consumers perceive value in the goods they purchase and the business enjoys a reasonable profit for its efforts.

Just as mass production provides economies of scale in production, advertising provides similar efficiencies in communicating to mass audiences. Despite the coming of specialized media reaching smaller and smaller audience segments, there remains a demand for mass advertising to promote widely distributed products and services. Without advertising, many businesses would not be able to bring new products to the attention of enough consumers fast enough to make the enormous cost of creating, developing, manufacturing, and distributing these products practical. In other words, advertising is both a tool and requirement of an abundant economy. For businesses, one of the primary roles of advertising is contributing in launching new products, increasing the sale of existing brands, and maintaining the sale of mature brands.

What Advertising Does for Society

Advertising, like most institutions, plays both a micro and macro role. As we have seen, on a micro level, individual consumers and businesses gain a benefit from advertising, but does advertising provide a more general benefit to society as a whole? More than 30 years ago, in testimony before the FTC, an advertising executive laid out the case for advertising's contribution to society. He stated the case for advertising:

> Business, by creating what the public wants and delivering it at prices more and more people can afford, builds prosperity and a stronger economy. . . . Advertising is both the sparkplug and the lubricant of the economy which creates consumer wealth.[13]

This viewpoint is obviously from the industry's perspective. However, the intended result of most advertising is to contribute to the profitable sale of products and a continuing economic expansion that presumably is a benefit for society as a whole. In addition to its economic role, advertising revenues support a diverse and independent press system protected from government and special interest control.

While advertising continues to function as an important economic force, recent years have seen a growing emphasis concerning advertising's responsibility as a mirror and monitor of society.

> Even as it reinforces social norms that exist in the outside world, advertising grapples with controversies over the norms that govern it. Among the issues that are hotly debated are *what* should be advertised, *who* should be allowed to advertise their services, *which groups* should be permitted to use the power of advertising to promote their own views on social issues, and *what techniques* stretch the limits of social tolerance.[14]

Clearly, there are numerous opinions regarding the proper role of advertising as it relates to the overall social good. However, there is little question that advertisers have a new and different responsibility to society in the way they sell their products and services. New technology and sophisticated research methods have only increased the importance of issues such as consumer privacy and the potentially intrusive nature of advertising.

ADVERTISING TO DIVERSE PUBLICS

When we consider advertising, most of us think primarily of messages sent to consumers or, in the case of business-to-business advertising, to the various components of the distribution channel such as wholesalers or retailers. However, most advertising, regardless of its intended recipients, communicates a message to various groups and individuals, who in turn interpret this message in the context of their own interests.

When designing an advertisement or advertising campaign, firms must consider the many publics that will be reached by their messages and take into account the perception that each of these groups will have of the advertising. Often an advertising campaign is intended to carry out several functions at once. A single advertisement might be directed to a number of publics:

1. *The **distribution channel.*** With the growth of huge national retailers such as Wal-Mart and Kmart, national advertisers often use consumer advertising to demonstrate to retailers that they are offering brands with high consumer demand and ones they are willing to support with significant advertising dollars at the consumer level.

2. *Employees.* With companies operating in a recessionary environment, it is more important than ever to build loyalty and teamwork among employees. A company's consumer advertising is a means of instilling pride and loyalty in its employees. Sometimes this is done overtly by mentioning the quality workmanship that goes into a product or featuring company employees in advertising. More often, the message to employees is less overt but nevertheless is an important function of advertising. In any case, advertising as a form of internal communication is increasingly recognized as ". . . a management priority where leaders recognize that a real competitive advantage can be gained through an engaged, motivated, knowledgeable, and respected work force."[15]

3. *Customers.* Present customers are a vital audience for any advertising. Current customers can be encouraged to use more of a product and not consider a competitor as well as reinforce previous purchases of the product.

4. *Potential customers.* As we discussed earlier, one of the primary objectives of advertising is to create awareness among those who are unfamiliar with a brand. Obviously, a person who doesn't know about a product will not buy it. For most products, advertising provides the lifeblood for continued success by encouraging prospects to become customers.

5. *Stockholders.* Most large national companies are publicly held and depend on stockholders as a major source of operating revenue. Studies have shown that high brand awareness and a company's positive reputation are contributing factors to keeping stock prices higher than might otherwise be the case. In the fall of 2002, when Red Lobster seafood restaurants dropped its "Go Overboard" advertising campaign, one of the reasons cited was that it wanted a more unifying theme that would appeal to the equity market and improve the stock price of Darden Restaurants, the chain's parent company.[16]

6. *The community at large.* Many companies operate local plants throughout the country. Advertising is often used to influence public opinion so that when the inevitable disputes about local tax assessments, excessive noise, or zoning ordinances arise, the company is viewed as a good neighbor.

Too often advertisers take a short-term, narrow view of advertising. These companies view advertising from the perspective of the immediate (and intended) communication effects on the primary market for their products. However, advertising functions within a matrix of political, legal, economic, and cultural environments.

distribution channel
The various intermediaries, such as retailers, that control the flow of goods from manufacturers to consumers.

Within each of these categories are interested parties who are judging companies and their products by the advertising messages they disseminate. It is important to consider the entire range of publics when developing a particular advertisement, commercial, or advertising campaign.

THE COMPONENTS OF ADVERTISING STRATEGY

In this section, we will deal with some of the specific components of advertising strategy. Companies, even those marketing similar products, often demonstrate markedly different approaches to advertising. Advertising should be designed to reach those consumers who are interested in the particular product features and benefits that a company can offer. The most successful advertisements are those messages that are unique to each brand and product category and, consequently, create a differentiated position for a specific brand. However, even with a unique advertising approach, there are basic considerations that virtually all advertising must consider in building brands. In this section, we will discuss some of the primary elements of successful advertising. In subsequent chapters, we will examine the various executions of these basic principles that set one brand apart from its competitors.

EXHIBIT 2.7 a & b

Gaining awareness with interesting graphics is a first step in successful advertising.

Courtesy of McRae Communications and Pathway Communities.

Brand Name

A **brand name** that customers recognize and respect is one of the most valued assets of a company. One of the principle uses of advertising is to enhance brand identification in the minds of consumers with an umbrella theme and benefit (see Exhibit 2.7 a & b). Research shows that brand usage is driven by adverting exposure and the resulting brand awareness. In fact, for many products, their brand name alone is as important as any physical features of the products. For example, the primary difference between McDonald's and the thousands of other fast-food restaurants that compete for consumers' dollars is the name.

A recent study by the Grocery Manufacturers of America found that a familiar brand name was either the first or second most important reason respondents gave for buying a product. The same survey found that 76 percent of grocery shoppers would go to another store to find the brand that they wanted.[17] Another study by ACNielsen determined that 19 brand names, led by Coca-Cola with a value of $15 billion, are worth more than $2 billion each.[18]

Although high brand recognition is important for any product, it is especially crucial for product categories that have little inherent product differentiation. That is, soft drinks, beer, cigarettes, and similar products are easily duplicated by competitors from a functional standpoint. What these competitors cannot duplicate are

brand name
The written or spoken part of a trademark, in contrast to the pictorial mark; a trademark word.

All That's Missing Is You.

Neighbors are cheering at match point on the tennis courts. Friends are putting for birdie on the championship 18-hole golf course. Families are playing at the pools and lazy river. And boaters are casting off at the pristine 100-acre stocked lake. It's all here. Exciting amenities. Peaceful parks and trails. A variety of homes wired for advanced technology by some of the area's best builders. Plus a location that's convenient to Newnan, Atlanta, and Hartsfield International Airport. So come and visit SummerGrove today. Because once you're here, this award winning community won't be missing a thing.

SUMMER GROVE
AT NEWNAN

Homes from the $130s to $700s • 770-252-9000 • summergrove.com • Information Center open Daily 11-6, Sunday 1-6
I-85 South to Exit 47 (Newnan). Left on Hwy. 34, one mile. Turn right on Shenandoah Blvd. Continue 1¼ miles to SummerGrove. Follow signs to Information Center.

the years of successful brand building, primarily through advertising, that the parent companies have invested in their brands.

Branding is entering a new phase as companies face some of the most fierce competition in recent history. Obviously, high-profile brands are a major resource for companies in such an environment. They are such a benefit that companies are tempted to move into extensive brand extension as they attempt to efficiently and profitably introduce new products. Just as Coke stands out from competitors, Vanilla Coke will have quicker product acceptance than Vanilla Brand X. The problem faced by contemporary marketers is to determine when excessive brand extension begins to harm core brands that, in some cases, have been nurtured for a century or more.

"If you chase two rabbits, both will escape."

Anonymous

Brand extensions are sometimes like the hunter chasing two rabbits. Companies want to keep their core audience while using the brand to increase sales with other versions of the product. Soft drinks and automobiles have been among the most persistent users of **brand extensions.** As established brands such as Coke Classic and Pepsi demonstrate flat sales trends, the companies have moved to give sales a boost by introducing numerous products under some version of the core brand. In the three years from 2000 to 2002, Coke and Pepsi together introduced more than 13 new beverages. Many, such as Pepsi Blue, Pepsi Twist, and Diet Coke with Lemon, used the core brand name. In other cases, products were brought to market under different names, such as Sierra Mist (Pepsi) and Red Flash (Coke).

brand extensions
These are new product introductions under an existing brand to take advantage of existing brand equity.

The determination to use a brand extension or introduce an entirely new product is not a trivial decision. Major soft-drink makers know that many of these brands will not be successful. A major consideration is whether or not a failure will hurt the entire product line in the minds of consumers. "There's also the danger of cannibalizing sales of existing brands when new products are pushed hard. . . . Companies also run the risk of confusing consumers by introducing too many products."[19]

An overriding problem of brand extensions is that successful brands have defined a special niche in the minds of consumers. When companies attempt to significantly enlarge the scope of these brand positions, it leads consumers to question the values and benefits of the brand. At the same time, many successful brands reach a point of saturation among their core consumers and see some form of brand extension, either through new products or different advertising positioning, as the only way to expand their markets.

Victoria's Secret was just such a retailer facing the problem of expanding its market. Famous for sexy lingerie, the company had positioned the brand with celebrity models and an aura of sophistication and a fanciful lifestyle. However, despite the high awareness of the Victoria's Secret brand, the reality is that almost 80 percent of bra purchases are modest styles that are comfortable and durable. The store launched a "Body by Victoria" line of simple bras and also extended its line of items such as linen and cotton pajamas.

So far the strategy has worked. Women seem to see this extension as an addition to the product line rather than a move away from the sexy items that originally built the brand. However, as one marketing executive noted, "They are really at risk of harming the core brand that they've built by simply extending it to cover a broad array of products."[20] Nevertheless, given the reality of the marketplace, Victoria's Secret had little choice in making such a decision.

Brand extensions in lingerie and soft drinks are one thing, but the risk inherent in line extensions in product categories such as luxury cars is much greater. Yet, in the last several years, virtually all the major luxury car makers have moved into less expensive lines. The Mercedes 230 coup, the BMW Mini, and the Cadillac CTS are only a few of the examples of luxury car makers moving into the $30,000 or less price range. With some exceptions, the move to lower-priced vehicles has been successful for these luxury brands. But remember that brand equity is a long-term concept. It took decades for Mercedes and BMW to achieve preeminence among upscale buyers. The question is whether these affluent customers will continue to see the same prestige and value in an $80,000 Mercedes when the same brand can be purchased for $30,000. As one marketing executive observed about automobile brand extensions, "Yes, this brand extension thing is a tricky business. Yes, it is hard to mix two different customer bases."[21]

At the other end of the brand extension spectrum is Volkswagen's attempt to enter the luxury market with the introduction of the Phaeton, selling for up to $85,000. Comparing the challenges of Mercedes and Volkswagen, an advertising executive observed, "It is harder to convince consumers to pay a lot of money for a model with a mass market badge on it than for a luxury car marketer to tempt a customer with a less expensive model."[22] Clearly, the marketing problems facing Mercedes and Volkswagen are different. However, both companies face a similar problem of how to move brands to a different position in consumers' minds without harming the core brand.

The examples of Coke and Pepsi, Victoria's Secret, and Mercedes and Volkswagen have in common that in each case the companies have moved ahead with aggressive brand extensions of their core brand. Of course, not all companies elect the extension strategy. Major companies entering the natural food category have found that they can build sales more easily by distancing themselves from their mass market brands. For example, many niche food products have determined that corporate identity is not as important as an organic designation to health food consumers.

Over the past decade a number of major companies have bought organic or health food companies. In almost every case, the companies have continued to market these products under their original names. In fact, more and more formerly niche brands such as Cascadian Farm cereal (General Mills), Kashi cereals (Kellogg), Boca Burger vegetarian burgers (Kraft Foods), and Red Dog beer (Miller Brewing Company) are owned by *Fortune* 500 companies. To some, for a company such as General Mills ". . . to keep its legendary logo off of a cereal box defies all conventional marketing wisdom. But these new cereals aren't aimed at the conventional market. They're organic, and organic-food buyers tend to eschew conglomerates' famous brands."[23]

From these examples, we can see that there is no single brand strategy that is right for every company. However, regardless of the approach, building brand value or equity is one of the most important elements of advertising. Whether introducing a new product or maintaining the vitality of a mature one, brand identity is crucial to a product's success. Products are concrete objects; brands, on the other hand, represent attitudes and feelings about products. Branding allows companies to favorably position products and companies by creating unique identities. Brand identity is increasing in importance as companies try to differentiate their products in increasingly crowded fields.

The importance of brand image is so critical that few companies fail to include brand enhancement as a primary role of their advertising strategy. Companies know that brand image must be continually protected. For example, the problems that Coca-Cola faced with product recalls in Belgium, replacement of its CEO after only two years, and declines in profits and stock prices all contributed to a temporary erosion of brand equity. For Coca-Cola and other businesses, the development, protection, and maintenance of brand value will continue to be one of the driving forces in modern advertising.

A GOOD PRODUCT THAT MEETS A PERCEIVED NEED

In a highly competitive environment it is more critical than ever for companies to offer consumers quality products that meet their needs in an affordable manner. There are simply too many options for consumers to settle for brands that fail to provide the benefits they are seeking. As we mentioned earlier, the heart of the marketing concept is a management strategy that places the consumer at the center of the planning process starting with product design.

When evaluating the marketing potential for innovative products or product line expansions, firms often have to determine the social and psychological tendencies of their prospects before moving ahead. The most successful marketing plan starts with an imaginative way of looking at consumer problems and how to solve them.

For example, makers of major home appliances such as refrigerators, stoves, and washers and dryers are facing a significant problem. For the first time in several years, shipments of all types of appliances have decreased significantly. Even microwave oven sales fell some 5 percent in 2002 compared to a year earlier. Manufacturers are faced with selling mature product lines with an effective life of a decade or longer. As the economic downturn of the early 2002s took place, many consumers were unwilling to replace appliances on a discretionary basis.

When Whirlpool Corporation began studying the problem, it found that the 18–24-year-old market was the least likely to own appliances, especially washers and dryers. The company found that space, money, and time were among the major obstacles to purchase. Many in that age group were college students living in dorms or cramped quarters and others were sharing small apartments with roommates.

Whirlpool is addressing the problem with an experimental line of small appliances designed for this younger market. They include small portable refrigerators in silver with orange trim and a companion microwave. The company also is testing small washing machines with a single off/on button and no washing cycles. Also in the line is a battery-operated dryer large enough for a couple of pairs of jeans and small enough to fit on a dresser.[24]

The research by Whirlpool underscores the idea that successful products usually follow the identification of specific consumer problems. The idea that advertising can sell products for which there is no inherent demand—and it was never true—is certainly a myth in today's marketplace.

Of course, attempting to determine the needs of consumers and actually doing so are two different things. For one thing, consumers may know their problems but not be able to enunciate the type of products that would solve these problems. This is particularly true of yet to be marketed pioneering products. For example, before the invention of the microwave oven, consumers couldn't say they wanted a device that would stir up water molecules and provide a hot dinner in minutes. They could say that when they were tired and hungry they didn't want to wait 45 minutes for a conventional oven.[25]

Furthermore, as we have discussed, individual brands rarely appeal to all consumers within a product category. Therefore, target marketing is an essential foundation in product innovation. The most successful products normally appeal to consumers with specific characteristics and not, coincidentally, to consumers with distinctive interests related to these characteristics. For example, a toothpaste with a "whitening" position would be of limited appeal to consumers seeking cavity protection.

In assessing what constitutes a good product, we must also take into account changes in public perception of particular product categories. For years, fast-food chains, snack makers, and soft-drink companies prospered with a formula of convenience and inexpensive and readily available products with little attention to issues such as nutrition, calories, or fat content. However, in recent years numerous voices from public interest groups to the U.S. Surgeon General have come out against unhealthy eating habits represented by these foods. Chains such as McDonald's, KFC, Wendy's, and Burger King have even faced lawsuits accusing them of contributing to obesity and other health problems.[26]

As these companies react to changing consumer preferences, we will see that the definition of good products has been modified significantly in both product development and advertising and promotional messages. For example, Subway, the pioneer among chains in promoting healthy eating, developed a major campaign to encourage better eating habits among teens. Likewise, Pepsi, Coke, and Frito-Lay have all promoted greater physical activity among children and teens.[27] These promotions are combined with significant offerings of products such as Tostitos Organic and Lay's Natural designed for the health-conscious consumer. At the same time, fast-food chains such as McDonald's have introduced salads and other "healthy" alternatives to their traditional menus.

It is not unusual for products to face changing preferences in the marketplace. The astute marketer is able to predict and adapt to these shifts in consumer attitudes. However, regardless of changing consumer tastes in products, there is always a basic expectation of quality in the products and services that are purchased. Even the most established companies and brands will experience consumer wrath when they ignore quality issues. During the 1990s, Ford built a loyal following with the slogan "Quality is Job 1" and a quality control program to back it up. However, in the last several years, Ford experienced consistent quality control problems that in 2001 landed it in last place in a J.D. Powers and Associates quality survey. Because the Powers survey is regarded as an industry standard, it represented a major blow to Ford. In 2002, Ford instituted a rigorous testing program across its product line that involved both management and line workers. As one automotive writer observed, "Ford's turnaround is predicated on fixing quality problems."[28]

A key ingredient in determining product success is reliable research. Companies constantly employ a host of research techniques to discover the most appealing products, advertising and promotional messages that will be most interesting to target prospects, and even information about pricing and distribution preferences. However, over the years, researchers have discovered that consumers have a difficult time relating various elements of what makes a good product. For example, survey respondents may say that they want an array of product features, but deciding the priority of these features and a price that they would be willing to pay for them is a much more difficult problem.

Over the last 20 years, a research technique known as **conjoint analysis** has been developed to address the numerous ways a consumer considers a product. "The rationale underlying the technique is that consumers weigh all the many elements of a product or service—such as price, ingredients, packaging, technical specifications, and on and on—when choosing, say, a sweater, airline ticket, stereo system."[29] Consumers may prefer a particular airline, but scheduling (one stop versus nonstop) or bargain pricing may move them to another normally less preferred carrier.

conjoint analysis
A research technique designed to determine what consumers perceive as a product's most important benefits.

Conjoint analysis considers the many individual elements that together determine consumer preference. By placing a value on these elements it offers insight into the way consumers actually weigh considerations in making purchases. Done correctly, conjoint analysis can prevent costly mistakes when companies emphasize product characteristics that are of little value to consumers. By the same token, the technique allows product designers and marketers alike to concentrate on those factors that determine what is a "good product" in the minds of target prospects.

As we have seen in these examples, the key to successful advertising begins with product development from the consumer's perspective. Product quality and consumer research go hand in hand. Product development is largely dependent on consumer research to determine the most important attributes consumers are looking for in a product. Likewise, research is crucial in prioritizing the qualities that are most important in influencing purchase decisions. Every product is unique. A brand's position in the product life cycle, quality perceptions by consumers, distribution channels, and a number of other factors will determine specific marketing and advertising strategies that contribute to the long-term success of a brand.

Unfortunately, even the most focused and marketing-oriented company cannot guarantee success for all its products. The estimates for new product failures run as high as 90 percent. Behind each of these failures is a company that took a wrong turn. Sometimes the error was at the very beginning by overestimating consumer demand; sometimes a good product idea is wrecked by inferior quality or service; sometimes an indifferent or untrained sales staff is the culprit; and sometimes unrealistic or poorly executed advertising must take the blame. Regardless of the reason for the failure of a particular product, some marketing mistake almost always plays a role.

The concept of matching product quality with consumer demand is fundamental to advertising and marketing success.

Sales, Revenues, and Profit Potential

The most clever advertisement or the most humorous, memorable television commercial is totally worthless unless it contributes directly to company or brand profitability. Too often, unsophisticated executives emphasize sales and revenue goals to the detriment of profits. In competitive product categories, there is a temptation to take extraordinary steps to keep market share at the expense of profits. Throughout the late 1990s, Energizer and Rayovac batteries engaged in advertising and price promotions featuring Michael Jordan as the Rayovac spokesperson and the Energizer Bunny. In the end, the brands did little to increase total battery demand but planted a "price versus brand" mentality in the minds of many consumers.

Unilever, one of the world's largest makers of laundry products, announced in 2002 that it was going to forgo continuing share of market battles with Procter & Gamble in favor of placing a priority on profits. This emphasis on profits led to a decrease in promotional spending for brands such as All and Wisk. Likewise, Dial and Colgate-Palmolive have shown a management focus on profits while conceding that the strategy may mean a loss of market share to competing brands.

Increasing profits is a major challenge for mature brands. As we saw in the case of soft drinks, product extensions and new offerings are a strategy used by many companies in this situation. Usually, the extensions are variations on a core product. For example, Kraft Foods markets more than 500 cheese products and holds 40 percent of the U.S. cheese market with $6 billion in sales. Kraft continues to introduce new cheese products such as Rip-Ums cheese sticks. In addition, Kraft seeks to reposition cheese products to different market segments. For teens and children, Kraft makes its products entertaining with cartoon character packaging. It also is aggressively marketing cheese as a tasteful and convenient way to ensure that daily levels of calcium are achieved.[30] Companies such as Kraft know that continuing line extension and product development is necessary for maintaining annual sales increases. At the same time, such extensive product development and marketing is risky from a profit standpoint.

Sometimes the search for profits leads companies into unfamiliar territory. For retailers, extension often means cultivating partnerships with other companies to use valuable retail space and increase profits. In recent years, banks have found that grocery stores are an ideal method of servicing present customers and opening new accounts. Grocers increase profitability from fees paid by the banks as well as impulse purchases from bank customers. Similarly, FedEx has opened a number of stations in Kinko copy centers, and Reebok displays its shoes in music stores such as Wherehouse and FYE. McDonald's, with more than 13,000 U.S. stores, recently has begun to explore a number of partnership possibilities with, for example, banking, toy, and video companies. McDonald's goal is to make its vast real estate holdings and customer base more profitable than is feasible in a saturated burger market.[31]

The quest for profits also has led to some changes in the way product development is viewed by major companies. Manufacturers of soaps, detergents, cosmetics, and a host of other household products view product research and development (R&D) as the lifeblood of these firms. At Procter & Gamble, scientists annually receive as many as 400 patents for their work. For such companies, these patents have long represented a point of pride. Yet, the R&D departments at many companies operated largely as independent units without specific coordination from either marketing or sales departments.

However, just as the demand for profits and accountability has resulted in more creative management decisions, such as cross-product partnerships, it also has led to a review of the relationships between research and marketing. At Unilever, in a major restructuring, marketing and research were brought under a common brand development umbrella to better utilize research as an applied tool to solve marketing problems. As P&G President and CEO A. G. Lafley commented, "No consumer, or customer, or employee or shareholder cares about how many patents we have . . . What they care about is how many truly valuable branded products and services we can commercialize."[32]

One of the significant changes in marketing during the last decade has been an emphasis on profit-based accountability in all areas of advertising and promotion. Advertising agencies are being compensated on how their work contributes to a client's bottom line, not whether they produce award-winning ads. Media buys are evaluated from the perspective of their return on investment (see Exhibit 2.8). At the corporate levels all marketing and promotional functions are being given much greater scrutiny than ever before and are increasingly being judged on a profitability basis.

This move to more precisely measure the contributions of advertising has led to a broader view of what advertising can and should accomplish. For example, advertisers are focusing on the role of advertising in *maintaining* sales and market share as a goal of equal importance to increasing sales. It is difficult to measure the value of advertising in terms of sales not lost versus sales gained. However, given the cost

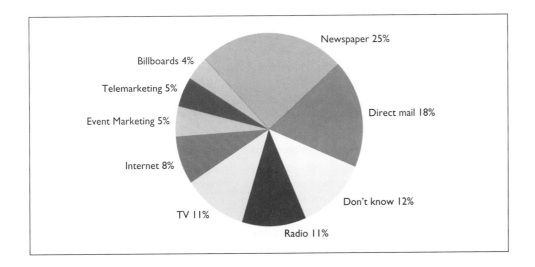

EXHIBIT 2.8

Getting the Highest Return

Dealers were also asked, "Which medium provides you with the highest ROI?" Return on investment is a major consideration for any advertising expenditure.

Source: Copyright Crain Communications. Reprinted with permission. *Advertising Age,* 27 May 2002, 45.

involved in finding new customers versus keeping present ones, the overall contributions to profitability may actually be greater in the former case.

The emphasis on profitability and accountability has largely eliminated the mistakes made by viewing sales and revenues as substitutes for profits. A review of the last decade demonstrates that some of the largest companies in America (in terms of sales volume) experienced the largest financial losses. Anyone can devise a marketing plan that will result in greater sales if profits are not considered.

Product Timing

product life cycle
The process of a brand moving from introductions, maturity, and, eventually, either adaptation or demise.

Because timing is a critical element in advertising, it is a significant consideration in numerous marketing and promotional decisions. Some of these decisions involve broad strategy assessments. For example, the level of maturity of a brand is a critical timing issue in future marketing and advertising decisions. Advertising functions differently at various stages of the **product life cycle.** During the introduction and growth phase of a product, businesses advertise to establish a beachhead against competition and gain a level of consumer awareness. As products enter more mature stages of development, advertising strategies take longer perspectives and their goals are likely to be involved in brand equity and a longer horizon for sales development. With this in mind, businesses constantly evaluate their brands based, in part, on the maturity of the brands.

The product life cycle is especially critical for new product categories. For example, banks have tried to encourage customers to use online financial services for more than two decades. Yet, this segment still constitutes a minor percentage of total banking transactions. However, as the population becomes more computer literate and consumers are more comfortable with online financial security measures, online banking will be more widely accepted. Twenty years ago, no amount of advertising could overcome the fact that the timing was not right for general adoption of online banking.

Products can rarely be forced on consumers before they are ready to accept them. Sometimes the catalyst for product acceptance is price. When the cost of videocassette recorders (VCRs) was reduced to approximately $300, consumer demand skyrocketed. Broadband technology is another example of consumers adopting a product category more slowly than marketers had predicted. In the late 1990s, many experts thought that the appeal of digital television with Internet and interactive capability, video-on-demand, and access to an unlimited amount of information and entertainment transmitted instantaneously would put a system into virtually every household by the early 2000s. However, like home computers in the 1980s, household penetration of broadband systems has fallen far below these optimistic estimates. There is little doubt that broadband technology will be the standard sometime in the future. The key from a marketing perspective is predicting when that future will occur and investing accordingly.

Timing also is a major factor in the everyday function of advertising. Agency media planners deal with timing issues every day. Should television commercials be placed in prime time? Daytime? Late night? Should they be 30-second or one-minute commercials? Should newspaper advertisements run on weekends or in midweek? Are magazine advertisements more effective in monthly or weekly publications, and in either case, what is the most effective placement schedule? Every issue? Every fourth issue? Timing, in all its variations, is one of the most important decisions in advertising.

Changing the normal buying season for a product category can be extremely profitable. For example, over the years, marketers have found that seasonal products such as soft drinks and soup can effectively expand the life of a product from a niche category to one with year-round potential. In fact, off-timing from competitive advertising patterns is a method of differentiation if consumers will purchase during nontraditional periods. Still, it is rare for any product category to have consistent sales throughout the year and advertisers are taking a major risk when they run counter to established consumer buying patterns and preferences.

In other cases, product timing is a matter of changes in lifestyles that move categories from niche products to the mainstream. For example, during the next 20 years, the United States will see growing numbers of singles, elderly, and various ethnic minorities. These changes will have an impact on all consumer markets but especially on the food industry. More meals will be eaten out of the home, there will be a demand for smaller packages, consumers will purchase more health-oriented foods, and manufacturers will offer much more diversity in food in both the restaurant and grocery store categories. We will see formerly niche products entering the mainstream. For example, sports drinks such as Gatorade are already showing up in vending machines, and salsa has replaced ketchup as the condiment of choice.

Product Differentiation

Marketing success depends on a product that meets a perceived consumer need with benefits that are not available from other brands or product categories at a price compatible with these benefits. Put more simply, consumers are looking for products that provide a clear and relevant differentiation from competing brands. A storm strikes and you need a flashlight, the battery is dead or dying. Excalibur Electronic, addressing the problem, has marketed the "Forever Flashlight." Its flashlight uses a light-emitting diode and never requires a new bulb. In addition, the flashlight is powered by shaking it. Twenty seconds of shaking produces five minutes of light.[33] Whether the Forever Flashlight will be a success remains to be seen, but without question the company has created a real consumer product with unique benefits.

In the contemporary marketing environment, one of the major challenges for businesses is to separate their products from competitors in the minds of consumers. The key for advertising is to find relevant differences among often similar brands. The primary element in successful **product differentiation** is consumers' perception that it solves a problem better than other options. If consumers *perceive* a company's product as being differentiated from competitors' products, then it is.

product differentiation
Unique product attributes that set off one brand from another.

Remember that just being different is not enough. It is not even sufficient that consumers perceive that the product is different. The key is that prospects see a brand as differentiated in a manner that is important to their particular circumstance. The growth of drive-in windows at fast-food chains is ample evidence that we are a society on the go with little time for sit-down meals. While the drive-in window solved one problem, it didn't address the dilemma of what to do with the food once you get it. A burger, fries, and shake are not conducive to freeway driving. Enter the one-handed meal. Fast-food establishments now offer wraps and other convenience foods for drivers.

Not to be outdone, several major food companies have entered the convenience market with an array of products. Campbell Soup has introduced "Soup at Hand" in sippy containers. Coke and Pepsi have both marketed fortified drinks as breakfast replacements for those who eat on the drive to work. Hershey has introduced Portable Pudding in tubes that can be eaten with one hand. Kraft entered the one-handed market with a cupholder-contoured snack pack featuring mini versions of its cookies and crackers.[34] Going back to our discussion of the marketing concept, successful products generally start with the identification of a consumer problem. The most successful products are those that are able to discern these problems first and address them with unique solutions.

One of the most important elements of differentiation is keeping an open mind about how to achieve it. If a product is a bundle of benefits, we must look at the entire bundle when searching for a meaningful differentiation. Minute Rice introduced a package with a built-in pour spout; General Motors introduced the notion of zero financing for its cars and trucks; and Subway offers a free sandwich with every eight purchases. None of these companies made any changes to their product lines, but they established a meaningful differentiation among competing brands. The idea of product differentiation must take into account the full spectrum of the marketing mix. Price, promotion, place, and product all offer potential opportunities for meaningful differentiation.

A marketing executive outlined the five primary factors that create strong brands:[35]

1. *High involvement.* Product categories such as credit cards and automobiles are used often and have the potential to develop strong brands that build a bond and loyalty with customers.

2. *Product quality.* The most creative advertising cannot overcome the disappointment of a bad product experience. To a degree, great advertising can worsen the products of an inferior brand by creating unrealistic expectations. Advertising can create initial trials for a product, but it can never overcome a bad experience with a product.

3. *Brand longevity.* Strong brands are rarely created overnight. Consumer brand loyalty is established by consistent performance and quality that demonstrate a genuine advantage over other marketplace options.

4. *Advertising and market communication.* Powerful brands are not reluctant to communicate their benefits to consumers. Successful brands are usually those that not only embody relevant consumer benefits but also have a strong marketing communication program that makes consumers aware of these benefits. Strong brands are not bashful.

5. *Brand personality.* Prosperous brands have a personality—a distinctive, well-defined identity in the consumer's mind.

Another marketer commented, "Corporate and brand images are a matter of economics. Consumers are drowning in product alternatives and media messages. Powerful images are essential to success in the American culture. These images have clear meanings. They reflect positive values. It's a matter of common sense. Consumers turn to familiar and comprehensible images. They reject images that are unrecognizable or incomprehensive."[36]

A recurring theme in all these observations is that brands must be focused on important consumer benefits and the core message of the brand's personality must be continually communicated to consumers. One of the primary consequences of the abundance of brand extensions and expansion of product lines is that consumers find it difficult to identify with the central values of a company or brand. In announcing a return to a more limited product line, the chairman of RadioShack said, "RadioShack tried to be too many things to too many people, straying from its roots as a neighborhood store for inexpensive essentials such as cables and adapters. We became nothing more than a small generalist. For us to be a generalist, we'd get eaten alive."[37]

Before we leave the topic of product differentiation, we should mention two important elements involved in the process. First, as companies set about to differentiate their brands, they should remember that product differentiation is also a means of target marketing. As they make their brands essential to a specific market segment, they often simultaneously surrender those consumers looking for features not emphasized in their brands to other manufacturers. Before embarking on a specific product differentiation strategy, companies must make sure that their brand position is important to enough prospects so that they will be able to sustain a profitable niche.

Finally, firms have a special responsibility as they embark on a strategy of brand differentiation. Advertisers have an obligation to promote meaningful product differences. Much of the criticism of modern advertising is that it tries to make obscure and inconsequential product variations important. There is no question that some advertising promotes inconsequential product features. However, the best and most successful products demonstrate obvious differences from their competitors.

Price

Pricing strategy is a necessary ingredient in the marketing process. A company has a number of options when it comes to whether or not to advertise, to use a particular distribution system, or to offer warranty and service guarantees. However, each product must have a price. Sometimes, as in the case of automobiles, price is negotiated, but in most cases manufacturers and retailers give a fixed price for their goods and services. Obviously, the cost of producing and marketing a product has to play a role in pricing strategy, but the role of pricing is much more complicated than simply covering costs and providing a reasonable profit. We cannot separate consumer perceptions of the value of a product from the price they are willing to pay. In many instances, the value of a brand has little to do with its objective worth. In fact, a primary function of advertising is to create, or enhance, a positive gap between the price of a product and the value the average consumer ascribes to the product. The greater this **value gap,** the more insulated the product is from competitive price competition. The concept of the value gap underscores the notion that price alone is not a particularly safe means of establishing a long-term, competitive advantage.

value gap
The perceived difference between the price of a product and the value ascribed to it by consumers.

Conventional wisdom often cites low price as the best method of increasing a customer base and establishing a brand. In this case, conventional wisdom is often wrong. Peter Murane, a marketing consultant, points out that when price becomes the central focus of a brand's selling proposition, it risks having consumers see the brand as a commodity rather than having intrinsic value.[38] There are a few price leaders, such as Wal-Mart and Southwest Airlines, but even in those cases the companies combine other values and benefits with price. Wal-Mart built a distribution infrastructure that made it all but impossible for other discounters to compete. Southwest combined a reputation for on-time arrivals and excellent service in areas such as baggage handling to best its larger competitors.

At the other extreme, we see industries such as wireless telephones in which number of discounted minutes is the primary reason for choosing a carrier. Likewise, many upscale retailers panicked during the Christmas shopping seasons in 2001 and 2002 and offered as much as 70 percent discount on some merchandise. After two years of discounting, consumers, as we would expect, sat back and waited for the next deal. A recent survey (see Exhibit 2.9) indicated that for many customers price has become the primary motivation for choosing a retailer. It is significant that store name and reputation (the brand) are a distant consideration in making a shopping decision.

We can cite a number of examples in which a specific brand, or even an entire product category, has engaged in price competition to the point that consumers began to devalue all brands in a category. For example, during the late 1990s, a number of hotel chains began to offer discounted rates online through third-party brokers such as Expedia.com and Hotels.com. Originally, the hotels looked on these services as a method of filling room vacancies among a small group of bargain hunters.

However, the use of these discounters has broadened to include business travelers with hotels finding they are often selling discounted rooms to upscale customers. In 2000, online brokers booked $4 billion in room rentals; by 2006, it is projected that they will gross more than $15 billion. Once brand equity has been damaged, it is very difficult to reverse the trend. The discounters almost overnight have transformed the

EXHIBIT **2.9**

Dollars over Design

A store's reputation pales next to the price of its wares. Retailing is increasingly becoming a price-driven industry.

Source: Copyright Crain Communications. Reprinted with permission. Alice Z. Cuneo, "Retailers grasping for right mix," *Advertising Age,* 11 March 2002, S-4.

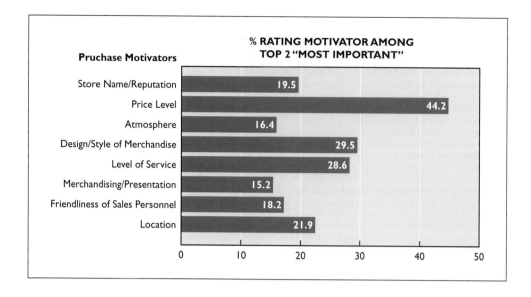

% RATING MOTIVATOR AMONG TOP 2 "MOST IMPORTANT"

Pruchase Motivators

Store Name/Reputation	19.5
Price Level	44.2
Atmosphere	16.4
Design/Style of Merchandise	29.5
Level of Service	28.6
Merchandising/Presentation	15.2
Friendliness of Sales Personnel	18.2
Location	21.9

way travelers book hotels. One online executive commented, "[Online discounters] . . . are completely disrupting the price integrity of hotels."[39] Once price becomes the primary motivation for bookings, deals replace brand name as a deciding factor as to where to stay.

We should make it clear that we are not disparaging a low-price strategy as a legitimate marketing tool and advertising strategy. It can be an important element in the marketing process. Depending on the product category, pricing strategy can be both a means of market entry for new products and a means of product differentiation for mature products. A new product can gain immediate visibility with a price advantage. For example, KIA cars owe much of their initial success to their low price. Likewise, for both new and mature products, price is an important point of differentiation.

Pricing strategy is often used as a means of temporary inventory control. End-of-season sales at the retail level are an obvious means of clearing out merchandise from Christmas cards and wrapping paper in January to swimsuits in September. Many marketers have long used a strategy known as **yield management** to even out supply and demand. Hotels offer special weekend rates to offset the loss of business travelers. Car rental companies offer specials based on seasonal demand and telephone companies cut long-distance rates on weekends and evenings as a form of yield management.

Pricing is one of the most studied areas of marketing and advertising. Proper pricing strategy is necessary for profitability and the continued existence of a business. However, it is a rare circumstance when a brand enjoys long-term success with a low-price strategy in the absence of some other brand value positioning. Price also plays a major role in advertising strategy. It is very difficult for an advertising creative plan to ignore the basic price/value perception held by a target audience. The pricing strategy for a brand determines to a significant degree the type of marketing strategy that can be used and the success that advertising will have in promoting and selling a specific brand.

yield management
A product pricing strategy to control supply and demand.

VARIATIONS IN THE IMPORTANCE OF ADVERTISING

The role of advertising has unique elements for each company. Advertising investments fall along a continuum from the rare company that uses none to the equally unusual business that spends its entire marketing communication budget in advertising. Even among heavy advertisers, the advertising-to-sales ratios demonstrate huge variance.

The reality is that most firms use advertising in concert with a number of other promotional activities. Advertising is given more or less emphasis depending on a number of factors such as the maturity of a product line, the importance of trade promotion and sales promotion in a product category, and the degree of competition. For example, sellers of air conditioners and heating equipment spend less than 2 percent of their revenues on advertising, whereas beverage manufacturers and amusement parks spend more than 10 percent.[40]

As we mentioned earlier, businesses are more interested in marketing communication synergism than ever before. Marketers are continually looking for the proper mix of marketing communication techniques that will best reach their prime prospects. The determining factors that move a company or product category to a particular communication option are both diverse and complex. However, a number of factors will determine the degree to which advertising is used. Among the more important ones are:[41]

1. The faster a market is growing, the higher the advertising expenditures as a share of total market sales will be. Businesses in growing markets take advantage of these opportunities by spending significantly more on advertising than businesses in stagnant markets.

2. Advertising expenditures as a share of sales tend to be higher when production capacity is low. During periods of high demand, the ratio of advertising to sales is lower than when there is low demand for a product category. The rate of advertising also tends to be related to the number of competitors in a shrinking market. For example, soft-drink companies spend a great deal on advertising because there is so much brand switching as opposed to market expansion.

3. Products with lengthy purchase cycles tend to have higher advertising-to-sales ratios. Basically, companies that produce big-ticket items that are infrequently bought, such as automobiles and household appliances, must keep their brands before consumers even though the purchase cycle is very long. Often media advertising is supplemented by direct-response advertising to people who have owned a car for three or four years in an attempt to anticipate their next purchase cycle.

4. The earlier a product is in the life cycle, the higher are advertising-to-sales ratios. Advertising is higher in the introductory and growth stages of development as the process of building brand awareness and equity demands high promotional expenditures. When Unilever wanted to relaunch its Robusto! brand of Ragu pasta sauce in 2002, it increased the brand's adverting budget 10 times over the year before.[42] The company will probably not sustain that level of advertising, but the investment was needed to give the brand a one-time kick start.

5. The higher the perceived product quality of a brand in a product category, the higher the expenditure of advertising to sales. Competing brands with perceived lower product quality often depend on price and cost-cutting promotions as primary sales tool. Product quality must be continually promoted through advertising to maintain brand equity.

6. Businesses with major new competition have higher advertising expenditures. As we discussed previously, when new competitors come into the marketplace, they usually spend heavily on advertising. Established brands are forced to meet this competitive spending to protect their product franchise.

This list is not intended to include all the factors that might determine the advertising expenditures in a specific marketing communication plan. However, it does demonstrate the many variables that must be considered when a business is deciding the role that advertising will play.

Companies, even those with similar product lines, not only use different levels of advertising as part of their marketing communication mix, but they also demonstrate vastly different types of advertising. For example, Lowe's building supply stores, a company that is expanding into a number of markets, spends almost 7 percent of its advertising budget on outdoor advertising while Home Depot, with more stores and fewer new markets, spends less than one-half of 1 percent in outdoor. Even brands such as Lincoln and Cadillac, competing for very similar buyers, show major differences in their advertising media expenditure. Whereas Lincoln spends 21 percent of its advertising budget in magazines, Cadillac allocates almost 50 percent less, preferring to allocate one-third more to network television than Lincoln.[43]

The allocation of advertising dollars is a continually changing dynamic of marketing management. Advertising's role in the marketing process is determined by a number of constantly changing factors. Sometimes changes in advertising's role are made simply to avoid audience wearout after being exposed to the same marketing communication mix over a long period of time. However, most often advertising is evaluated according to some specific change in the marketing environment.

ADVERTISING AND THE MARKETING CHANNEL

One of the most important aspects of marketing is the development of the marketing channel (see Exhibit 2.10). The marketing channel creates efficiencies through specialization in the movement of goods from producers to ultimate consumers. Most of the advertising that we see every day is called consumer advertising because it is directed to end-of-channel customers. However, advertising also plays a major role in moving products through the various levels of production and distribution known as the marketing channel.

For most of the last century, the fundamentals of the marketing channel remained unchanged. Each product and service developed certain distribution methods of reaching consumers that were largely unchanged over time. However, in the last decade, new technology has started to change even longtime relationships among various elements of the marketing channel. For example, travel agents have seen their business drop as more and more travelers go directly to airlines and hotels to book their trips. Digital cameras have greatly reduced the demand for film processors and the drugstores and other outlets that function as their distribution channel. The ability to download music has had a well-publicized effect on the profits of recording companies, but the local music store has a major stake in this battle. As we discuss the distribution channel, we should be aware of the significant changes that the future will bring to these marketing relationships.

At each level of the channel, marketing decisions must be made about the most effective type of marketing communication to employ. Marketing decisions are not made in a void and decisions in one area of marketing and promotion have an immediate and direct effect on others. For example, when a choice is made to expand a company's personal sales force, a concurrent decision is being made about the availability of funds for advertising, or sales promotion, or public relations.

EXHIBIT 2.10

Industrial advertising often includes a means of interactive communication for prime prospects.

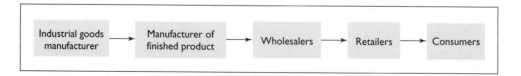

Marketing decisions not only determine the role of advertising and its budget but also often play a major part in decisions concerning media choices. For example, a strategy to use a coupon promotion will probably dictate a print media strategy. A decision to demonstrate product features may mean that television will get the call. A complex sales message may take us to magazines and a localized advertising strategy may move our message into newspapers.

In the remainder of this chapter, we will examine some of the ways advertising functions in various industries and stages of the marketing channel. Although you are most familiar with consumer advertising, it is only one of a number of categories that are used to bring products to market. Regardless of its audience, effective advertising must be successful on two levels: (1) communicating and (2) carrying out marketing goals.

Perhaps the easiest way to evaluate advertising's role in the marketing process is evaluate the *directness* of the intended communication effect and the anticipated *time* over which that effect is supposed to function. In other words, how much of the total selling job should be accomplished by advertising and over what time frame will that task be accomplished?

Advertising designed to produce an immediate response in the form of product purchase is called *direct-action, short-term* advertising. Most retail advertising falls into this category. An ad that runs in the newspaper this morning should sell some jeans this afternoon. Advertising used as a direct-sales tool but designed to operate over a longer time frame is called *direct-action, long-term* advertising. This advertising category is used with high-ticket items (washers and tires) in which the purchase decision is a result of many factors and the purchase cycle is relatively long.

Another category of advertising includes those advertisements that are used as an indirect sales tool. Such indirect advertising is intended to affect the sales of a product only over the long term, usually by promoting general attributes of the manufacturer rather than specific product characteristics. Included in this category are most institutional or public relations advertising. The exception would be remedial public relations advertising designed to overcome some immediate negative publicity concerning product safety, labor problems, and so on.

The aim of most advertising is to move a product or service through the various levels of the marketing channel. The objectives and execution of advertising will change from level to level. The intended target audience will result in markedly different advertising strategies. In the following sections we examine several categories of advertising to both consumers and businesses.

ADVERTISING TO THE CONSUMER

National Advertising Although we normally associate national advertising with giant brands such as Tide, Chevrolet, and Nike, the term is not limited to those products that are only sold nationwide. The term **national advertising** has a special nongeographic meaning in advertising: It refers to advertising by the owner of a trademarked product (brand) or service sold through different distributors or stores, wherever they may be.

Traditionally, national advertising has been the most general in terms of product information. Because retailers often have varying policies and business practices, information concerning price, retail availability, and even service and installation is often omitted from national advertising or mentioned only in general terms. However, the need to communicate more closely with targeted consumers has caused national advertising to take on a more personalized tone during the last decade.

Beginning in the late 1980s, many national advertisers began to target their advertising on a geographic basis—first regionally and, increasingly, on a market-

national advertising
Advertising by a marketer of a trademarked product or service sold through different outlets, in contrast to local advertising.

by-market basis. More recently, with a combination of better consumer research and advances in technology, national advertisers have begun to identify and reach more narrowly defined market segments and, in some cases, individual consumers. In coming years, growth of Internet advertising in concert with scanner research at the retail level will allow national advertisers to offer specifically tailored messages to consumers based on individual lifestyle and product usage characteristics. However, in the near term, national advertising will continue to emphasize brand introductions of new products and greater brand loyalty for established products.

Retail (Local) Advertising Retail is the workhorse of the advertising world. It usually combines aspects of hard-sell messages with institutional advertising. On the one hand, retailers must compete in an extremely competitive business environment to move large volumes of merchandise. At the same time, their advertising must enhance their image among customers. **Retail advertising** often includes price information, service and return policies, store locations, and hours of operation—information that national advertisers usually cannot provide.

retail advertising
Advertising by a merchant who sells directly to the consumer.

Retail marketing and advertising have changed dramatically in recent years. During the last two decades, the retail environment has been dominated by a few large chains such as Home Depot, Target, and Wal-Mart. These huge retailers offer an array of merchandise from clothing to tires and from prescription drugs to sporting goods. It is estimated that more than 55 percent of Americans shop at a mass retailer weekly and, of that number, 39 percent go to Wal-Mart.[44] It has become so important for manufacturers to gain entry to these mega-stores that vendors provide a number of product, merchandising, and promotional services specific to each retailer. For example, some products are manufactured to an individual retailer's specifications and both in-store promotions and advertising may be unique to a particular chain.

End-Product Advertising What do products such as Intel computer chips, Lycra, and Nutrasweet have in common? They are rarely purchased directly by consumers. Instead, they are bought as an ingredient in other products. The promotion of such products is called *end-product advertising* (or *branded ingredient advertising*). **End-product advertising** is most commonly used by manufacturers of ingredients used in consumer products. Successful end-product advertising builds consumer demand for an ingredient that will help in the sale of a product. The knowledge that consumer demand exists will encourage companies to use these ingredients in their consumer products.

end-product advertising
Building consumer demand by promoting ingredients in a product. For example, Teflon and Nutrasweet.

End-product advertising began in the 1940s when DuPont began promoting its Teflon nonstick coatings. Soon consumers began to associate Teflon with a special benefit in cookware and merchandise with the Teflon seal was marketed at a premium price and quickly built a loyal following among buyers.

After 50 years of selling Lexan, a polycarbonate plastic, General Electric (GE) recently embarked on a program of ingredient branding. Lexan is used in products as diverse as space helmets worn by astronauts and NASCAR drivers to cooking utensils and the colorful iMac computer cases. GE has partnered with a number of manufacturers such as Eddie Bauer, chef Wolfgang Puck, and KBC racing helmets to introduce the ingredient to the public.[45]

Despite the obvious benefits to the manufacturer, building demand through end-product advertising is not easy. It took Intel almost five years before computer buyers started actively seeking out the Intel brand when shopping for a computer. Regardless of the superiority of an ingredient, consumers must be convinced that it adds a significant benefit to the final product. The selling task is made even more difficult by the fact that such ingredients usually are not obvious in the product and, therefore, extensive advertising is required to make consumers aware of their advantages. Successful end-product advertisements are those that create meaning-ful differentiation for consumer purchase decisions. End-product advertising is a small part of total advertising, but it is extremely important in a number of product categories.

Direct-Response Advertising   Direct marketing and **direct-response advertising** are not new. In this country, Ben Franklin is credited with the first direct-sales cata-log, published in 1744 to sell scientific and academic books. The modern era of direct selling was ushered in with the publication of the Montgomery Ward catalog in 1872. While it has grown steadily throughout the last 50 years, the twenty-first century will be the era of direct-response marketing.

Currently, direct-response expenditures are more than $200 billion with almost one-quarter invested in direct mail. Predictions are that direct response will con-tinue to see significant increases in the foreseeable future (see Exhibit 2.11). Not only will new technology, such as the Internet and interactive television, provide a cata-lyst for future growth, but also traditional media advertisers will increasingly adopt direct-response techniques. Often companies promote 800-numbers not only to sell a product directly to consumers but also to allow customers to obtain information such as the location of local retailers or more detailed information about an item. In addition, cable television shopping channels and videocassettes give consumers the opportunity to see merchandise "live" before ordering it from their living rooms. The future holds great promise for various forms of interactive media that will provide even more innovative ways of communicating with prospects.

Direct selling will be an increasingly popular method of reaching consumers during the coming decade. One of the reasons for the growing use of direct response is its flexibility. For example, it can be used to solicit a direct order through a catalog or direct-mail piece; it can generate leads for personal salespersons or follow-up promotions; and it can be used to build store traffic for retailers such as automobile dealers with the final sale completed at the store location. Direct response also lends itself to various media. For a number of years, telemarketing has been the leader in generating direct-response sales, followed by direct mail, television, and newspapers. However, with the recently established federal "no-call list," telemarketers expect a significant decline in their revenues.

ADVERTISING TO BUSINESS AND PROFESSIONS

Business-to-business (B2B or B-T-B) is one of the fastest-growing categories of advertising. The average person doesn't see a very important portion of advertising, because it is aimed at retail stores, doctors, home builders, wholesalers, and others who operate at various stages of the marketing channel.

direct-response advertising
Any form of advertising done in direct marketing. Uses all types of media: direct mail, TV, magazines, newspapers, radio. Term replaces mail-order advertising. See direct marketing.

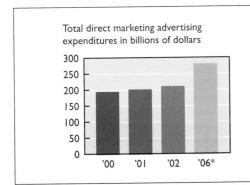
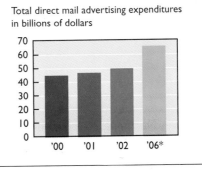

EXHIBIT 2.11

Direct marketing advertising expenditures will continue to grow at a significant rate throughout the decade.

Source: Copyright Crain Communications. Reprinted with permission. Cara B. DiPasquale, "Direct marketing: A tale of rapid recovery," *Advertising Age*, 9 September 2002, 10.

B2B marketing requires a much different strategy than consumer advertising. The marketing communication strategies for B2B advertisers are unlike the basic media and promotional plans for consumer advertising. Although business publications remain a primary tool of B2B marketing, personal selling, telemarketing, and the Internet occupy a much higher share of expenditures compared to consumer advertising.

Another major difference between B2B and consumer advertising is the type of messages used in each. Although all advertising has to gain the audience's interest and attention, B2B tends to be factually oriented with few of the emotional appeals found in consumer advertising. B2B messages are addressed not only to specific industries but also often to particular job classifications within these industries. In addition, B2B advertising appeals are very profit oriented. How a product will eliminate downtime, decrease customer complaints, save time and money, and contribute to the overall efficiency of a business are among the primary themes of B2B marketing.

B2B advertising also has to consider major differences in the buying process compared to consumer purchase behavior. Consumer purchases tend to be fairly straightforward. There may be some external influences on the purchase decision, such as children determining a family's fast-food or cereal preferences, but these casual relationships have little similarity with the formal purchasing models used in many B2B buys. For example:[46]

1. *Purchase collaboration.* Major B2B purchase decisions are often made by a committee or a group of decision makers. In many cases, a number of people from different departments within a company have input into the final decision. These people may have different perspectives and backgrounds and the B2B seller must account for the various interests among decision makers in making the sale.

2. *Purchase cycles.* In the B2B environment, impulse buying is almost unheard of. In the B2B purchase process, most companies have formal procedures that must be followed before major acquisitions can be made. These buying cycles can last from weeks to months, especially in the case of significant capital expenditures. During these long-term purchase cycles, advertising is usually supplemented heavily with personal selling and direct-response techniques.

3. *Purchase scale.* Typically, the number of sales opportunities are much less than in consumer purchasing. For this reason, the average time and expense of making a B2B sale are significantly higher than in consumer advertising. Also many of the measures of audience reach such as CPM are often immaterial in B2B. Whereas consumer advertisers generally measure advertising in terms of target audience reach and frequency, B2B measures are much more sales oriented.

CATEGORIES OF BUSINESS ADVERTISING

Trade Advertising Manufacturers use trade advertising to promote their products to wholesalers and retailers. **Trade advertising** emphasizes product profitability and the consumer advertising support retailers will receive from manufacturers. In addition, trade advertising promotes products and services that retailers need to operate their businesses. Advertising for shelving, cleaning services, and cash registers is part of trade advertising.

Trade advertising has several objectives:

1. *Gain additional distribution.* Manufacturers are interested in increasing the number of retail outlets that carry their brands.

trade advertising
Advertising directed to the wholesale or retail merchants or sales agencies through whom the product is sold.

2. *Increase trade support.* Manufacturers compete for shelf space and dealer support with countless other brands. Trade advertising can encourage retailers to give prominent position to products or to use a manufacturer's point-of-purchase material.

3. *Announce consumer promotions.* Many trade advertisements offer a schedule of future consumer promotions and demonstrate to retailers that manufacturers are supporting brands with their advertising.

There are approximately 9,000 trade publications—several for virtually every category of retail business. The average consumer probably has not heard of most of these publications, but trade journals such as *Progressive Grocer* and *Drug Topics* play an important role in the advertising plans of most national advertisers.

Industrial Advertising   A manufacturer is a buyer of machinery, equipment, raw materials, and components used in producing the goods it sells. Companies selling to manufacturers most often address their advertising to them in appropriate industry publications, direct mail, telemarketing, and personal selling. This method is quite unlike consumer advertising and is referred to as **industrial advertising.** Industrial advertising is directed at a very specialized and relatively small audience.

> **industrial advertising**
> Addressed to manufacturers who buy machinery, equipment, raw materials, and the components needed to produce goods they sell.

Industrial advertising rarely seeks to sell a product directly. The purchase of industrial equipment is usually a complex process that includes a number of decision makers. Often industrial advertising is a means of introducing a product or gaining brand name awareness to make it easier for follow-ups from company sales representatives to close a sale.

Professional Advertising   The primary difference between **professional advertising** and other trade advertising is the degree of control exercised by professionals over the purchase decision of their clients. Whereas a grocery store encourages consumer purchases of certain goods by the brands it stocks, people can go to another store with more variety, lower prices, or better-quality merchandise. On the other hand, a person rarely will change doctors because a physician doesn't prescribe a certain brand of drugs, change banks because the bank orders checks for its customers from a particular printer, or choose an architect based on how designs are reproduced.

> **professional advertising**
> Directed at those in professions such as medicine, law, or architecture, who are in a position to recommend the use of a particular product or service to their clients.

Corporate (or Institutional) Advertising   While **institutional advertising** remains a long-term image-building technique, in recent years it has taken on a decided sales orientation in terms of the audiences reached and intent of communication. Like any advertising, corporate advertising reaches an identified target audience with a specific objective. Among the groups most often targeted for corporate advertising are ultimate customers, stockholders, the financial community, government leaders, and employees. Frequently cited objectives of corporate advertising are:

> **institutional advertising**
> Advertising done by an organization speaking of its work views, and problems as a whole, to gain public goodwill and support rather than to sell a specific product. Sometimes called public-relations advertising.

■ To establish a public identity.

■ To overcome negative attitudes toward a company.

■ To explain a company's diverse missions.

■ To boost corporate identity and image.

■ To overcome a negative image.

■ To gain awareness with target audiences for later sales.

■ To associate a company with some worthwhile project.

These are only a few examples of possible corporate advertising objectives. The competitive environment of recent years has brought about dramatic changes in corporate advertising.

NONPRODUCT ADVERTISING

Idea Advertising It is not surprising that the same marketing techniques so successful in selling products would be used to promote ideas. We are living in a period of conflicting ideas and special interest groups. Marketing concepts and advertising have become important elements in swaying public opinion. As we saw in Chapter 1, advertising propaganda is not a new phenomenon. What is new is the number of public interest groups using advertising and the sophistication of the communication techniques being employed. In recent years, issues such as gun control, abortion, animal rights, and the environment have been debated in mass advertising.

idea advertising
Advertising used to promote an idea or cause rather than to sell a product or service.

Idea advertising is often controversial. Apart from the emotionalism of many of the topics being espoused, there are critics who think that advertising messages are too short and superficial to fully debate many of these issues. Proponents counter that advertising is the only practical way to get their messages before a mass audience.

They point out that idea advertising may be the most practical means for these groups to use their First Amendment privileges. Regardless of one's position on idea advertising, the increasing ability of media to narrowly target audiences, by ideology as well as product preference, will make this type of advertising more prevalent in the future.

service advertising
Advertising that promotes a service rather than a product.

Service Advertising We are becoming a nation of specialists with more and more Americans seeking advice and services for everything from financial planning to child care. Because services are basically people enterprises, **service advertising** almost always has a strong institutional component. Often service companies keep the same slogan, theme, or identifying mark over long periods of time to increase consumer awareness. Because service industries are so similar (and often legally regulated), it is difficult to develop a distinct differentiation among competitors. Banks and insurance companies have a particularly difficult time in establishing an effective identity.

Fundamentals of good advertising are the same regardless of whether a product or service is being promoted. However, many marketing experts point out that differences between the two categories require some care in the manner in which service messages are handled. Some basic principles of service advertising include:

1. *Feature tangibles.* Because service advertising cannot feature a product, it should be personalized in some way. For example, service advertisements often use testimonials. Service messages should show the benefits of the service, such as an on-time plane trip that results in closing a deal or a contented older couple as a result of good investment advice by their broker.
2. *Feature employees.* Because the value of a service largely depends on the quality of a firm's employees, it is important to make them feel an important part of the company and develop trust with customers. Often service messages feature real employees in their advertisements. This approach has the advantage of personalizing the service to customers and building employee morale.
3. *Stress quality.* Because the quality and performance of services are more difficult to measure than products, advertisements should emphasize consistency and high levels of competency. Hospitals use phrases such as "caring," "professional," and "convenient," in their advertising.

GOVERNMENT ADVERTISING

As we discussed in Chapter 1, all levels of government in this country have created various forms of propaganda and public policy messages since the earliest days of our founding. However, in the last 20 years, the growth of government services and

It all starts with an education.

Higher education is the gateway to a child's future. It opens minds, which leads to endless opportunities. And even if your child receives a HOPE Scholarship or other forms of financial aid when the time comes, saving for college now will be a key step in providing flexibility down the road.

Now, thanks to a program offered by the State of Georgia — the **Georgia Higher Education Savings Plan** — you have a smart and flexible way to help save for future higher education expenses.

The Georgia Higher Education Savings Plan offers significant tax advantages, a choice of investment options, and the flexibility to use your savings at any eligible educational institution in the U.S. or abroad.

It's easy to enroll.

Visit us at www.GAcollegesavings.com or call toll free 877 424-4377 and we'll send you all the details about the Plan, along with the materials to get started. Our telephone consultants are available **from 8a.m.–11p.m.**, Eastern Time, Monday–Friday, to answer your questions.

If you are not a Georgia resident or if you have taxable income in another state, consider whether that other state offers a 529 plan with favorable state income tax or other benefits not available if you invest in the Georgia 529 Plan.

The *Program Disclosure Booklet* should be read carefully before opening an account. The state of Georgia, its agencies, TFI, Teachers Insurance and Annuity Association of America (TIAA), located in New York, NY, and its affiliates do not insure any account or guarantee its principal or investment return (except for the guarantee of TIAA-CREF Life Insurance Company to the Board of Directors of the Georgia Higher Education Savings Plan under the Guaranteed Option). Account value will fluctuate based upon a number of factors, including general financial market conditions. Investments are made through Teachers Personal Investors Services, Inc. as distributor.

TIAA CREF

Ge⬤rgia
Higher Education Savings Plan

EXHIBIT 2.12

Georgia Higher Education Savings Plan

Government agencies and other nonprofits are increasingly using advertising to reach prospects for their programs and services.

Courtesy of the Georgia Higher Education Savings Plan.

programs has resulted in a greater use of traditional advertising by government agencies. The federal government spends millions of dollars each year promoting an array of agencies including the volunteer armed forces, consumer protection programs, and environment and health initiatives. State governmental agencies also have seen the advantage of advertising in reaching the citizens with beneficial services such as savings plans for higher education (see Exhibit 2.12).

SUMMARY

The roles of advertising are many, varied, and ever changing. The options open to advertisers have never been greater and the costs of errors are significantly magnified compared to only a few years ago. With fragmented audiences and media, higher costs of reaching prospects, and the challenges of effectively using new media technology, the demands on advertisers and their agencies have never been greater. However, regardless of the changes in the advertising process, two fundamentals for successful advertising will remain constant:

1. Effective advertising can only function within the context of an organized marketing plan.

2. Advertising is a marketing communication tool and rarely will be successful if directed at noncommunication problems. It is difficult, if not impossible, for advertising to overcome deficiencies in the core marketing program.

An effective advertising plan is an extension of the marketing goals of a firm. Advertising, typically is asked to help develop or maintain product awareness, build company and brand image, and provide product information that differentiates one brand from another. The execution of advertising will vary by the stage in the trade channel to which it is directed (e.g., retail, consumer, industrial, or professional). Furthermore, it can adapt to the primary product benefits and express them in a number of ways (e.g., testimonials, demonstrations, or long copy). Advertising also is modified according to budgetary considerations as well as the corporate philosophy concerning the value of advertising within the marketing plan.

It is clear that advertising is only one of a number of possible sales tools. The advertising executive of the future will be a marketing communicator who is able to utilize an array of marketing communication elements including promotion, public relations, and person selling in a coordinated fashion to bring synergy and unity to the overall corporate message.

Although major changes in advertising are on the horizon, the key to its success will continue to be the ability to develop an interesting message that will reach potential customers in an appropriate environment at the most opportune time. Planning is the foundation for successful advertising. During the remainder of the text, we will discuss the techniques of advertising against a backdrop of marketing, research, and planning.

 **REVIEW**

1. Discuss the three primary types of convergence that have had an effect on advertising.

2. Discuss the major elements of a typical marketing plan and those factors that are most important to advertising.

3. Briefly describe the major advantages and disadvantages of the four components of marketing communication.

4. What is advertising's role in building brand equity?

5. How does product differentiation relate to target marketing and audience segmentation?

6. What are some of the reasons that advertising plays a different role in the marketing of similar products?

7. Discuss some of the primary differences between national and retail advertising.

8. Why have direct-response advertising techniques become so popular in recent years?

9. Compare and contrast trade and consumer advertising in terms of audiences, media, and promotional techniques.

 **TAKE IT TO THE WEB**

The Public Relations Society of America (**http://www.prsa.org/**) is the leading professional organization dedicated to the improvement of the field. Note the far reaching programs of the society and how they interact with both marketing and advertising.

The American Association of Advertising Agencies (**http://www.aaaa.org/**) provides a great deal of information about the current practice of advertising. What are some of the major primary topics of interest to the association and it agency members?

One of the keys to successful advertising is the ability to integrate all aspects of the marketing communication program. How do various advertisers use IMC to reach all their diverse target markets (**http://marketing.about.com/**)?

Planning The Advertising

PART TWO

FIRIONA VIE from "EverQuest ®" courtesy Sony Online Entertainment Inc. Visit www.everquest.com.

intel®

The Advertising Spiral and Brand Planning

CHAPTER OBJECTIVES

One of the critical aspects of marketing communications decision making is developing a strategy. It has been said that strategy is everything. After reading this chapter, you will understand:

1. the importance of understanding the product life cycle
2. the relationship of the advertising spiral
3. the birth and basics of branding
4. brands and integrated marketing
5. brand equity
6. strategic planning methods

If you read the trade press, you will find a lot written about brands. Advertisers and their agencies don't agree on a lot of issues; but almost everyone agrees that brands are a company's most valuable assets. In most cases we recognize that consumers have the power today. They're more sophisticated than ever before about marketing efforts. Yet, consumers' brand confidence is confused by the deluge of brand names, subbrands, and minibrands directed at them. At the same time manufacturers are having trouble finding substantial and long-term ways of differentiating their products and services. It is a complex environment. If companies or brands set up false or unachievable objectives, they are likely to have failures. How do you differentiate your product and manage and protect your most important asset—your brand? How do you know what kind of strategic message is needed? How do you manage advertising or branding for success?

In this age of enormous and fundamental changes in the marketplace, new emphasis is being placed on ways to integrate brand communications (also called integrated marketing communication), build brand equity, and build better strategies for marketing products. It doesn't matter what the product category is—marketing is marketing. Great importance is placed on the development of a product and its marketing objectives as part of a brand's strategic plan prior to creating ads. Here we examine several aspects important to creating the strategic plan and their advertising implications. Despite many marketing practices being challenged today, one of the constants is the need to have a clear understanding of the product and consumer wants and needs when making strategic advertising decisions.

Think about the many stages in life. We are born; we grow up, mature, grow old, and at some point expire. You have already gone through a number of stages of development in your life with more to come. Products also pass through a number of stages. The developmental stage of a product determines the advertising message. As products pass through a number of stages—from introduction to dominance to ultimate demise—the manner in

EXHIBIT **3.1**

Primary Stages of the Life-Cycle Model

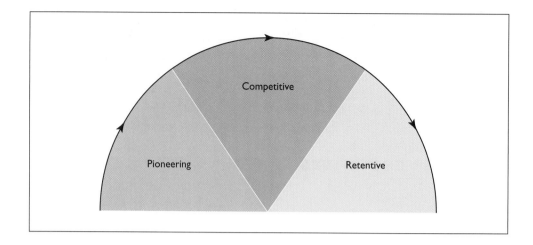

which advertising presents the product to consumers depends largely on the degree of acceptance the product has earned with consumers. The degree of acceptance can be identified as the product passes through its life cycle. It is this degree of acceptance that determines the advertising stage of the product. The life-cycle model discussed in this chapter consists of three primary stages (see Exhibit 3.1):

- Pioneering stage
- Competitive stage
- Retentive stage

The nature and extent of each stage are discussed in the next sections.

PIONEERING STAGE

Over the past 25 years, almost 60 percent of the companies appearing on the *Fortune* 500 list have been replaced by new companies. These new companies' success is because they have created new markets or reinvented existing ones. One way of accomplishing this is to create new products or new product categories. Companies like Procter & Gamble (P&G) have grown because of their ability to launch new products and create new product categories successfully. P&G introduced Tide in 1941. It also introduced a new product category—the disposable diaper or Pampers—in 1961, which became a billion-dollar product. In 1986, P&G introduced the first shampoo-conditioner combination. It also introduced the successful Swiffer mop.[1] Recently P&G introduced a product called Dryel. It too created a new consumer category—home dry cleaning. P&G projects Dryel sales of $500 million, making it as big as Downy or Bounce. But selling a new kind of home dry-cleaning product is not like selling the newest version of Tide; it's much harder. P&G had to convince consumers that they need a kind of product they've never heard of. P&G's thinking is that Dryel is cheaper than professional dry cleaning. It works, but will consumers think it fits their needs? Take a look at Dryel the next time you are in the supermarket.

When manufacturers create revolutionary new products, they may think consumers will flock to buy them. Many times manufacturers have trouble accepting the fact that despite all the money spent in developing and then promoting their product, consumers pay little or no attention to it. There are no guarantees that consumers will see a need for the product. It may never have occurred to consumers that they need or want the product, and as a result they don't feel compelled to buy it. Until people appreciate the fact that they need it, a product is in the **pioneering stage.**

Advertising in the pioneering stage introduces an idea that makes previous conceptions appear antiquated. It must show that methods once accepted as the only

pioneering stage
The advertising stage of a product in which the need for such a product is not recognized and must be established or in which the need has been established but the success of a commodity in filling those requirements has to be established. See competitive stage, retentive stage.

ones possible have been improved and that the limitations long tolerated as normal have now been overcome. It may be difficult to believe, but consumers didn't rush out to buy the first deodorants. Many consumers who were concerned with body odor simply used baking soda under their arms. So we can't take for granted that consumers will change their habits. Advertising in this stage must do more than simply present a product—it must implant a new custom, change habits, develop new usage, or cultivate new standards of living. In short, advertising in the pioneering stage of a product's life cycle must educate the consumer to the new product or service.

In 1973, Fleischmann's introduced Egg Beaters, a frozen egg alternative made from real eggs but without the yolk. The company had to convince consumers they needed an egg alternative. It had to convert egg eaters into Egg Beaters customers. Its market was concerned about the high cholesterol and fat of egg yolks. Fleischmann's had to change attitudes and habits to be successful. By accomplishing this, it became the dominating force in this new product segment. In the early 1990s, Egg Beaters tried to expand the market with an ad campaign built around the theme "When the Recipe Calls for Eggs" (see Exhibit 3.2). These ads tried to sell Egg Beaters as a substitute in cooking "because you're using the healthiest part of real eggs. No cholesterol. No fat." Do you and your family use Egg Beaters or egg substitutes?

EXHIBIT 3.2

Egg Beaters expands the market by trying to get the consumer to substitute Egg Beaters for eggs in cooking.

Courtesy of © ConAgra Brands, Inc. EGG BEATERS is a trademark of ConAgra Brands, Inc. All rights reserved.

The purposes of the pioneering stage of a product's life cycle, reduced to its simplest terms, are:

- to educate consumers about the new product or service
- to show that people have a need they did not appreciate before and that the advertised product fulfills that need; and
- to show that a product now exists that is actually capable of meeting a need that already had been recognized but could not have been fulfilled before

Pioneering advertising generally stresses what the product can do, offer, or provide that could not have been done, offered, or provided by any product before.

A true pioneering product offers more than a minor improvement. It is important for the advertiser to remember that what determines the stage of the advertising is consumer perception of the product. In the pioneering stage, the consumer is trying to answer the question "What is the product for?" It does not really matter what the manufacturer thinks. Does the consumer think the improved changes in the product are significant? Or, does the product really offer a better way of doing things?

Often the copy focuses on the generic aspect of the product category in an attempt to educate or inform the consumer. In the late 1980s, Interplak introduced a revolutionary new home dental product—an automatic instrument that removed plaque using two rows of counterrotating oscillating brushes. Interplak had to convince consumers that this product cleaned teeth better than any kind of toothbrush—electric or otherwise (see Exhibit 3.3). This was no easy task because the product cost about $100 at introduction. The pioneering Interplak ads suggested that "Plaque is the real villain in oral hygiene. If not removed daily, its bacterial film can lead to early gum disease and tooth decay. But clinical studies have shown that manual brushing removes only some of the plaque buildup." Twenty

EXHIBIT 3.3

INTERPLAK introduces a new kind of home dental care.

Courtesy of Bausch & Lomb, QualCare Division.

years later Interplak is still trying to get the average household to try its product. And, of course, there is a new generation of less expensive toothbrushes using the same idea.

Consumer acceptance and understanding may take a long period of time—a few months, a number of years, or perhaps never. Yahoo! was introduced in 1994 as the first search engine. Both eBay and Amazon.com were introduced in 1995 as the first auction site and online bookstore. Priceline.com came along in 1998 selling airline tickets on the Internet with a "name-your-own-price" selling system. These selling concepts became accepted rather rapidly considering they were new business and technology types. Of course, they were enhanced by all the attention to the Web and their leadership.

Snapple was created in 1972 as an all-natural juice drink line to be sold primarily in health food stores. It didn't become a national beverage company until 1992. Originally few consumers were interested in natural beverages and the idea took time to grow. Today almost everyone buys bottled water products like Aquafina or Disani. This concept wasn't accepted overnight either. But once it was accepted by many consumers along came products like Propel offering enhanced water with vitamins and/or flavors. Manufacturers may produce a product that does something many consumers instantly desire—a DVD player/recorder, a cellular phone, a laptop computer, or a PDA (personal data assistant). For these products, advertising will not exhort consumers to raise their standards of acceptance but rather will aim at convincing them that they can now accomplish something they couldn't before, through the use of the new product. For instance, the cellular phone industry told businesswomen that the cellular phone could not only keep them in touch with their clients but also can be used as a security device—especially if they had car trouble or were threatened in some way. Now it is more a matter of deciding on design, color, or size, and other features, than if they should own one. For many people today, a cell phone is one of life's necessities.

Usually during the early introduction of a new product, heavy advertising and promotional expenses are required to create awareness and acquaint the target with the product's benefits. To expand, the manufacturer must gain new distribution, generate consumer trial, and increase geographical markets. The product in the pioneering stage is not usually profitable. In other words, there can be a number of factors involved in the acceptance and purchase. According to a U.S. study by Ernst & Young, there is a 67 percent failure rate among the truly new products that create a new product category.[2]

Purell Instant Hand Sanitizer was introduced in 1997 with a $15 million ad budget. Instant hand sanitizers require no soap, water, or towels and claim to be effective against 99.9 percent of all common germs. This was a new concept for consumers who may have used antibacterial soaps to kill germs. Purell was earlier marketed to only health care and food service workers, but the company wanted to grow the consumer market. When a new pain product called Aleve, containing naproxen, was introduced, it created a new category in a very mature analgesic market. Consumers had many analgesic choices to fight pain: Aspirin was the first major product (i.e., Bayer) to fight pain, then came aspirin compounds (Anacin, BC tablets, among others), then acetaminophen (Tylenol), then ibuprofen (Advil, Nuprin), and then naproxen. Aleve's advertising support for the introduction was about $50 million. As you can see, pioneering advertisers incur heavy expenses in the process of educating the public about the advantages of a new type of product. If the advertiser has some success with the new idea, one or more competitors will quickly jump into the market and try to grab share from the pioneer.

Usually the main advantage of being a pioneer is that you become the leader with a substantial head start over others. So a pioneering effort can secure customers before the competition can even get started. "When you're the market leader," says Ivan Seidenberg, Verizon CEO, "part of your responsibility is to reinvent the market."[3]

THE COMPETITIVE STAGE

Once a pioneering product becomes accepted by consumers, there is going to be competition. The consumer now knows what the product is and how it can be used. At this point, the main question the consumer asks is, "Which brand shall I buy?" When this happens, the product has entered the **competitive stage,** and the advertising for it is referred to as competitive advertising. (Note that this is a restrictive meaning of the term, not to be confused with the broader meaning that all ads are competitive with each other.)

In the short term, the pioneer usually has an advantage of leadership that can give dominance in the market. Snapple was the dominant leader in ready-to-drink iced tea, but Pepsi and Coke quickly became aggressive with their versions of ready-to-drink iced tea to get a piece of the action. Generally, in the early competitive stage, the combined impact of many competitors, each spending to gain a substantial market position, creates significant growth for the whole product category. If the pioneer can maintain market share in this category during the initial period of competitors' growth, it can more than make up for the earlier expense associated with its pioneering efforts.

Among the many everyday products in the competitive stages are deodorants, soaps, toothpaste, cars, detergents, headache remedies, shaving creams, shampoos, televisions, DVD players, cat food, computers, and packaged foods. The purpose of competitive stage advertising is to communicate the product's position or differentiate it to the consumer; the advertising features the differences of the product.

Competitive slogans and headlines include the following:

The dawn of a new PC era. The 64-bit processor.

Apple computers

The most coverage worldwide.

AT&T Wireless

**Tungsten: A strong, dense metal used in the production of missles.
And drop shots too.**

Prince tennis racquets

**The smell of home cooking can now waft through the house four times
faster.**

Kenmore speedcook oven

How to tell a pair of quality sunglasses from high-priced junk.

Costa Del Mar

Leaves other wipes in the dust.

Orange Glo polishing cloths

Now there is a solution to the soap opera of shaving.

Schick Intuition razor

These one-liners don't educate you as to the product category advantages; they are taken for granted. Instead, each headline and the copy that follows set out to tell you why you should select that particular brand. VitroRoberston, San Diego, cre-

---

competitive stage
The advertising stage a product reaches when its general usefulness is recognized but its superiority over similar brands has to be established in order to gain preference. See pioneering stage, retentive stage.

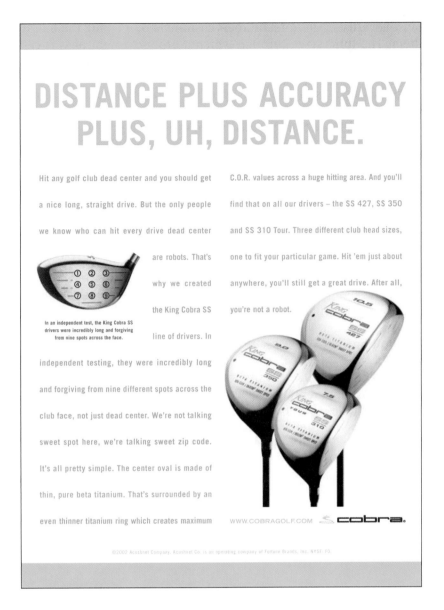

ated an ad for Cobra Golf (see Exhibit 3.4) that said,"Distance Plus Accuracy Plus, Uh, Distance." The copy stated, "Hit any golf ball dead center and you should get a nice long, straight drive. But the only people we know who can hit every drive dead center are robots. That's why we created the King Cobra S5 line of drivers. In independent testing, they were incredibly long and forgiving from nine different spots across the club face, not just dead center. . . . After all, you're not a robot." The copy then told how the club is made to deliver its benefit.

THE RETENTIVE STAGE

Products reaching maturity and wide-scale acceptance may enter the **retentive stage,** or reminder stage, of advertising.

If a product is accepted and used by consumers, there may not be a need for competitive advertising. At this point, everybody knows about this product and likes or dislikes it—why advertise? The chief goal of advertising may be to hold on to those customers. Over the years, many manufacturers of successful products have stopped advertising and have seen the public quickly forget about them.

retentive stage
The third advertising stage of a product, reached when its general usefulness is widely known, its individual qualities are thoroughly appreciated, and it is satisfied to retain its patronage merely on the strength of its past reputation. See pioneering state, competitive stage.

Most advertisers try to retain their customers by keeping the brand name before them. The third stage through which a product might pass is called reminder advertising—it simply reminds consumers that the brand exists. This kind of advertising is usually highly visual and is basically name advertising, meaning the ad gives little reason to buy the product. Most reminder ads look like posters—they have a dominant illustration of the product and a few words. Generally, there is little or no body copy because there is no need to give consumers this kind of information.

Few products are entirely in the reminder stage. There usually are other products in the pioneering and competitive stages challenging their leadership position. In fact, if your product is truly all alone in the retentive stage, that may be cause for alarm. It may mean the product category is in decline, and the competition sees little future in challenging you for consumers.

The advertiser's goal in the retentive stage is to maintain market share and ward off consumer trial of other products. Products in the retentive stage do not necessarily cut back on their advertising expenditures, but they adopt different marketing and promotional strategies than those used in the pioneering and competitive stages. When a brand is used by a large portion of the market, its advertising is intended to keep present customers and increase the total market, on the assumption that the most prominent brand will get the largest share of the increase.

Generally, products in the retentive stage are at their most profitable levels because developmental costs have been amortized, distribution channels established, and sales contacts made. The development of advertising and promotion may often be routine at this stage. Obviously, companies like to maintain their products in the retentive stage as long as possible.

THE ADVERTISING SPIRAL

The advertising spiral (see Exhibit 3.5) is an expanded version of the advertising stages of products just discussed. The spiral provides a point of reference for determining which stage or stages a product has reached at a given time in a given market and what the thrust of the advertising message should be. This can be important information for deciding on strategy and giving the creative team a clear

EXHIBIT **3.5**

The Advertising Spiral

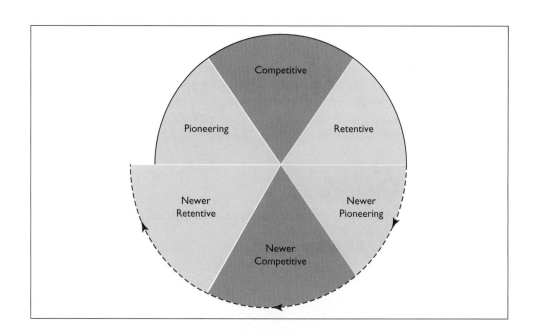

perspective on what information they need to communicate to prospects. In many respects, the advertising spiral parallels the life cycle of the product.

Comparison of Stages

Naturally, there are fewer products in the pioneering stage than in the competitive stage. The development of new types of products or categories does not take place frequently. Most advertising is for products in the competitive stage. As already pointed out, such advertising often introduces features of a new product that is in the pioneering stage and gets the spotlight for a period of time.

In using the advertising spiral, we deal with one group of consumers at a time. The advertising depends on the attitude of that group toward the product. A product in the competitive stage may have to use pioneering advertising aimed at other groups of consumers to expand its markets. Thus, pioneering and competitive advertising could be going on simultaneously. Each series of ads, or each part of one ad, will be aimed at a different audience for this same product.

Products in the retentive stage usually get the least amount of advertising. This stage, however, represents a critical moment in the life cycle of a product when important management decisions must be made. Hence, it is important to create effective advertising in this stage.

Product in Competitive Stage, Improvement in Pioneering Stage It is not unusual for a new brand to enter the competitive stage without doing any pioneering advertising. A new product entering an established product category must hit the ground running to differentiate itself from the competition. Every new brand thus enjoys whatever pioneering advertising has already been done in the product category. Marketers obviously see the value of new products, as 31,432 new consumer packaged goods were introduced in 2000, according to Productscan Online. That's nearly twice the amount introduced in 1992. New brands entering an existing category experience a 50 percent failure rate and, perhaps most surprising, an 84 percent failure rate among brand extensions. Ernst & Young cited a fundamental lack of competitive differentiation as the reason for line extension failure.[4]

Let's think about one of your favorite products—deodorants. In 2002, manufacturers placed 150 new deodorant and antiperspirant products on store shelves, according to market researcher Mintel International Group Ltd. In 2000, there were only 20 new products in the category introduced. Unilever brought its Axe line of full-body deodorant sprays from Europe in 2002, sparking competitive sales in the category to quadruple in 12 months, according to A.C. Nielsen. New formulas hit the market in all forms—gels, creams, sticks, and sprays. Manufacturers rushed to differentiate new products. Procter & Gamble created a "soft solid" that came out as a gritty mush squished through a mesh that then melted on the skin. Herbal Care introduced a deodorant with "anti-irritant and antioxidant" properties, aimed particularly at women sensitive because of shaving. Manufacturers are turning to technology to get at the cause of odor. Gillette and Unilever have introduced "odor-blocking technology" in some of their brands as they try to starve the odor causing bacteria. Take a look at the deodorant section the next time you're in a mass discounter, grocery store, or drugstore. See how manufacturers are attempting to differentiate their products. Gillette makes over 60 varieties of antiperspirant and deodorant across five brands appealing to the different needs of consumer targets.[5] As you can see, simply selling deodorant is very complex and competitive. Most new deodorants have to start in the competitive stage even when they are attempting to create a new subcategory.

Change is a continuum: As long as the operation of a competitive product does not change, the product continues to be in the competitive stage, despite any pioneering improvements. Once the principle of its operation changes, however, the product itself enters the pioneering stage. Think about the change from the needle record player to compact disc technology. When a product begins to move into more than one stage, the changes are not always easy to categorize.

Whenever a brand in the competitive stage is revitalized with a new feature aimed at differentiating it, pioneering advertising may be needed to make consumers appreciate the new feature. Recently, Toyota introduced a new Prius sedan using electric power steering and sensors that help guide the car when it reverses into a parking space.

Scramblers and Better'n Eggs, Healthy Choice eggs, and Simply Eggs created nonfrozen egg substitutes to compete with Egg Beaters' frozen product. Egg Beaters developed a refrigerated version to go with its frozen product. Exhibit 3.6 shows a television commercial that tells consumers they can find Egg Beaters in either the frozen food section or the egg section of their grocery. Was this new Egg Beaters in the competitive stage, the pioneering stage, or both?

EXHIBIT 3.6

Egg Beaters expanded beyond the freezer with its refrigerated version. Advertisements told consumers where in the store they could find the product.

Courtesy of © ConAgra Brands, Inc. EGG BEATERS is a trademark of ConAgra Brands, Inc. All rights reserved.

Gillette has been a master of creating new products with new features in its razors. They don't always come easily. Gillette spent more than $750 million in development of Mach 3 razors.[6] That's quite an investment by the marketer.

The Retentive Stage

The life of a product does not cease when it reaches the retentive stage. In fact, it may then be at the height of its popularity, and its manufacturer may feel it can just coast along. But a product can coast for only a short time before declining. No business can rely only on its old customers over a period of time and survive.

As noted earlier, the retentive stage is the most profitable one for the product. But all good things must come to an end. A manufacturer has a choice between two strategies when the product nears the end of the retentive stage.

In the first strategy, the manufacturer determines that the product has outlived its effective market life and should be allowed to die. In most cases, the product is not immediately pulled from the market. Rather, the manufacturer simply quits advertising it and withdraws other types of support. During this period, the product gradually loses market share but remains profitable because expenses have been sharply curtailed. This strategy is the one typically presented in textbook descriptions of the product life cycle, but it is not necessarily the one that corresponds to actual product development.

The problem with the typical life-cycle model in Exhibit 3.7 is that it portrays an inevitable decline in the product life cycle, whereas most long-term products go through a number of cycles of varying peaks and duration before they are finally taken off the market. The advertising spiral depicted in Exhibit 3.5 shows these cycles. The advertising spiral—the second strategy for a product nearing the end of the retentive stage—does not accept the fact that a product must decline. Instead, it seeks to expand the market into a newer pioneering stage. General Mills' CEO's advice is, "Do not believe in the product life cycle. Innovate constantly." Tide detergent was introduced in 1946. Since then, Tide has gone through more than 60 product upgrades.

As a product approaches the retentive stage, management must make some important decisions:

■   Can it make some significant improvements in the present product so that it virtually represents a new type of product or category (e.g., Clorox Cleaner)?

■   Is there a possibility for line extensions (e.g., Diet Coke)?

As we have seen, the life cycle of a product can be affected by many conditions. If, however, the product is to continue to be marketed, its own advertising stage should be identified before its advertising goals are set.

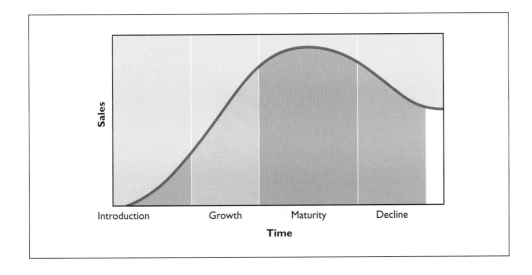

EXHIBIT 3.7

A Typical Life-Cycle Model

The three basic stages of the spiral (pioneering, competitive, and retentive) are straightforward and easy to understand. However, the stages in the bottom half (newer pioneering, newer competitive, and newer retentive) are trickier. To continue to market an established product successfully and profitably, creative marketing is necessary.

The newer pioneering stage attempts to get more people to use the product. Basically, there are two ways to enter this new stage. The first is by-product modification. This can be minor, such as adding a new ingredient to a detergent or a deodorant to a bar of soap, or—in the other direction—taking caffeine or sodium out of a soft drink or fat out of a food product. Alternatively, it may entail a complete overhaul of a product, such as a radical model change for an automobile. In some cases, advertising alone may be enough to get consumers to look at the product in a new light.

Advertisers cannot afford to simply rely on old customers because they die off, are lured away by the competition, or change their lifestyles. Smart advertisers will initiate a change in direction of their advertising when their product is enjoying great success. They will show new ways of using the product and give reasons for using it more often. For instance, if you are a successful soup company and your customers are eating your canned soup with every meal, you have reached a saturation point. How can you increase sales? Simply by encouraging people to use soup in new ways. You create recipe advertising that shows new food dishes and casseroles that require several cans of your product. You now have your customers eating your soup as soup, along with making casseroles with your soup. Of course, this means more sales and a new way of thinking about soup. That's exactly what Egg Beaters did once the manufacturer got consumers to switch from eggs to Egg Beaters for breakfast. Then the company tried to get cooks to use Egg Beaters in their next recipe and emphasize taste.

New Pioneering Stage and Beyond

A product entering the new pioneering stage is actually in different stages in different markets. Longtime consumers will perceive the product to be in the competitive or retentive stage. New consumers will perceive it as being a pioneer. At this point, the advertising spiral will have entered still another cycle (see Exhibit 3.8), which we will call the newest pioneering stage, where the focus is on getting more people to use this

EXHIBIT **3.8**

Expanded Advertising Spiral

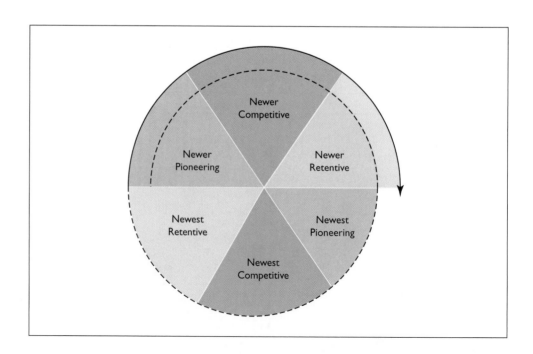

type of product. Today Egg Beaters still advertises, "They taste like real eggs, because they are real eggs." The copy adds, "Look for Garden Vegetable and Southwestern with real vegetables and special seasonings." The new "Garden Vegetable" adds a blend of green and red peppers, onions, celery, and seasonings, whereas the "Southwestern" adds red and green peppers, onions, chilies, and southwestern spices for burritos and omelets. It is also now part of ConAgra Foods (see Exhibit 3.9).

The product in this stage is faced with new problems and opportunities. Can you convince segments of your market not using your product that they should? Obviously, you have to understand why consumers were not interested in the product earlier. Creative marketing and a flexible product help this process.

McDonald's, Nike, Jell-O, Pepsi-Cola, Mountain Dew, Budweiser, Disney, ESPN, and Gillette are a few of the brands that reached the retentive stage and began to look for ways to move beyond it. All of these companies moved into new pioneering with product innovations. Hence, products such as Diet Coke, Cherry Coke, Diet

EXHIBIT 3.9

Courtesy of © ConAgra Brands, Inc. EGG BEATERS is a trademark of ConAgra Brands, Inc. All rights reserved.

Pepsi, Pepsi One, Diet Mountain Dew, and Bud Light were born. New pioneering can be the result of reworking the original product or a line extension—with a new formula and name—that is related to the original version of the product.

Creating product innovation does not always translate into brand share. Royal Crown Cola has been an industry innovator—first with national distribution of soft drinks in cans (1954), a low-calorie diet cola (1962), a caffeine-free diet cola (1980), and a sodium-free diet cola (1983).[7] It had the innovation but didn't effectively manage its advertising against the larger companies of Coca-Cola and Pepsi, nor did it effectively communicate with consumers.

Since its launch in April 2001, sales of Kellogg's Special K Red Berries have been so strong the company asked grocers not to promote it because the company couldn't keep up with the demand. According to Information Resources Inc., a Chicago market research firm, two years after its introduction, during an eight week period during March and April, sales rose over 21 percent versus the previous year, while overall cereal sales sagged 0.7 percent. Targeting the improved product by new pioneering advertising increased the total brand's performance in the marketplace. J.M. Smucker Company tested a frozen peanut butter and jelly sandwich to the tune of $20 million in sales. It was a convenient way for Mom to send the kids to school with a sandwich that thaws out about lunchtime. That's innovation.

As with the pioneering stage, once an established product in the competitive stage begins to innovate successfully in a newer pioneering stage, competition isn't far behind. In January 2003, General Mills answered by adding freeze-dried berries to its Cheerios, the nation's top-selling cereal brand, creating Cheerios Berry Burst cereals. Initially, Cheerios Berry Burst jumped to a 2 percent share of the total cereal market in its first month. Other cereal manufacturers like Post and McKee Foods followed with berry entries of their own.[8]

The idea for Special K Red Berries grew out of Kellogg's European operations, where French focus groups told the cereal maker they craved fruit on their flakes. Because there wasn't a mass market for freeze-dried berries in Europe, Kellogg's uses a produce broker to match Polish berry growers with European freeze-dry coffee producers. In 1999, Kellogg's Special K Red berries, which included strawberries, raspberries, and cherries, launched in France and the United Kingdom and took off like a rocket, according to Jeff Montie, vice president of innovation in Europe for Kellogg's.

The advertising focus in the newer pioneering stage must be on getting consumers to understand what the product is about. Advertising in the newer competitive stage aims at getting more people to buy the brand. Moving through these stages—newer pioneering, newer competitive, newer retentive—is not easy. It requires the manufacturer to develop either product innovations or advertising positioning strategies that make the product different in consumers' eyes. Also, as we move to the newer stages of the spiral, there are usually fewer prospects for the product. Therefore, a company must become most efficient at targeting smaller groups of prospects. H.J. Heinz Co. introduced EZ Squirt, a line of colored, vitamin C fortified ketchup in packaging especially designed for kids. EZ Squirt was developed from insight that kids under 12 are the biggest ketchup consumers. The advertising promoted the green-colored ketchup variety plus the product's easy-to-grip, squeezable bottles with a cap that allows kids to control the ketchup stream for drawing.[9]

Since Bayer introduced and sold the first aspirin product in the late 1800s (first in powder form, then in 1915, as a tablet), it has become both a medical and marketing marvel. Its new pioneering stages have been endless. It has been sold for headaches, toothaches, muscle aches, back pain, and more recently to stave off first and repeat heart attacks. The Food and Drug Administration recently officially approved new uses, recommending aspirin for the prevention of heart problems, angina (severe chest pain), and stroke. In 2003, research showed daily aspirin use significantly reduced incidence of colorectal tumors. Another study among postmenopausal women suggested the use of aspirin may reduce their risk of developing breast cancer by 21 percent. Each time a new use for the product is found, a new advertising campaign promotes the product to an appropriate group of consumers.

Just take the statement of Emory University professor and cardiologist, John Douglas. "Aspirin is the standard treatment for any person who has coronary heart disease," he said. "It should be standard therapy for anyone who's had a heart attack, has angina or cornary atherosclerosis—hardening of the arteries." Such comments are a marketer's dream. Obviously, most products aren't as versatile as this miracle product. But if marketers can find new uses for their products, then a new stage of pioneering advertising may result.[10]

New Pioneering It is easy to understand the need for pioneering advertising when a new wrinkle in a product category is created. Just think of all the new technology advances over the past few years. Think of the recent changes in cell phone uses beyond talking. It has become an entertainment medium offering photos, games, music, and information. In these cases, a marketer must simply educate consumers what the product will do for them. And think of the impact of Apples' iPod and iTunes. Many consumers are eagerly waiting for the advances in this product category.

As another example, look at the evolution of Procter & Gamble's Crest toothpaste.

Crest was launched in 1955.

Crest gets American Dental Association Approval in 1960.

Crest gel was introduced in 1980.

Crest Tartar Control introduced in 1985.

Crest Sparkle for Kids launched in 1988.

Crest Multicare introduced in 1996.

The Advertising Spiral as a Management Decision Tool

A product may try to hold on to its consumers in one competitive area while it seeks new markets with pioneering advertising aimed at other groups. We must remember that products do not move through each stage at the same speed. In some instances, a product may go quickly from one stage in one cycle to a newer stage in another cycle. This change may also be a matter of corporate strategy. A company may believe it can obtain a greater share of business at less cost by utilizing pioneering advertising that promotes new uses for the product. It is possible that the same results could be obtained by continuing to battle at a small profit margin in a highly competitive market. A retentive advertiser may suddenly find its market slipping and plunge into a new competitive war without any new pioneering work. Like a compass, the spiral indicates direction; it does not dictate management decisions.

Before attempting to create new ideas for advertising a product, the advertiser should use the spiral to answer the following questions:

- In which stage is the product?
- Should we use pioneering advertising to attract new users to this type of product?
- Should we work harder at competitive advertising to obtain a larger share of the existing market?
- What portion of our advertising should be pioneering? What portion competitive?
- Are we simply coasting in the retentive stage? If so, should we be more aggressive?

So far we've shown how the life cycle of a product or brand may be affected by many conditions. If the brand is to continue to be marketed, its advertising stage must be identified before its advertising goals can be set. Next, we examine how to expand on what we have learned to develop a strategic plan for a brand.

Building Strong Brands and Equity

Brands are the most valuable assets a marketer has (and we'll remind you of this more than once), so we need to understand a little about them. The product is *not* the brand. A product is manufactured, a brand is created. A product may change over time, but the brand remains. A brand exists only through communication. Landor Associates' Antonio Marazza said, "A brand represents the most powerful link between the offer and consumer. What else is a brand if not what consumers (or more generally, stakeholders) perceive it to be? Familiarity, image and trust drive a brands' reason to be and thus they are the building blocks of its capacity to generate value. It follows that to value a brand, you have to investigate not only within the company walls (or accounts), but above all else the mind of the consumer, where the real value of the brand resides." Landor's brand pioneer Walter Landor argued that "products are made in the factory, but brands are created in the mind."[11]

Every product, service, or company with a recognized brand name stands for something slightly different from anything else in the same product category. If the difference is a desirable one and is known and understood by consumers, the brand will be the category leader. Today, more than ever before, the perception of a quality difference is essential for survival in the marketplace.[12]

brand
A name, term, sign, design, or a unifying combination of them, intended to identify and distinguish the product or service from competing products or services.

The Origin of Branding In the mid-1880s, there were no **brands** and little quality control by manufacturers. Wholesalers held power over both manufacturers and retailers. Manufacturers had to offer the best deals to wholesalers to get their products distributed. This created a squeeze of profits. As a result of this profit squeeze, some manufacturers decided to differentiate their products from the competition. They gave their products names, obtained patents to protect their exclusivity, and used advertising to take the news about them to customers over the heads of the wholesalers and retailers. Thus, the concept of branding was born. Among the early brands still viable today are Levi's (1873), Maxwell House Coffee (1873), Budweiser (1876), Ivory (1879), Coca-Cola (1886), Campbell Soup (1893), and Hershey's Chocolate (1900).[13] In 1923, a study showed that brands with "mental dominance" with consumers included Ivory (soaps), Gold Medal (flour), Coca-Cola (soft drinks), B.V.D. (underwear), Kellogg's Cornflakes (breakfast food), Ford (automobiles), Del Monte (canned fruit), and Goodyear (tires). Today, we have a whole new generation of brands fighting for value and a permanent place in consumers' lives, including TiVo, Starbucks, Panera, America Online, Swiffer, eBay, ThermaCare, Febreze, Amazon.com, and others.

Branding as a Financial Decision

Howard, Merrell & Partners of Raleigh, an IPG unit, introduces itself to clients by saying, "Branding isn't an advertising decision. It's a financial decision. We have learned that creating brand leverage is about dealing correctly with strategic issues and financial commitments at the top management level—then taking the risks necessary to deliver category-dominating creative. It is about risk management. It is about a deep understanding of a brand's one-on-one relationship with people, considered in the context of a macro-competitive environment. We believe that perhaps our most important role is assisting our client partners to achieve the alignment needed to reinforce brand values at all points of human contact. . . ."[14] HM&P builds the SAS brand, "We're an equal opportunity knowledge provider. We don't care where your data comes from" (see Exhibit 3.10).

Consumer Environment

The brand environment has changed because the consumer has changed. Today, consumers set the terms of their marketplace relationships because they have more access to information than ever before, and marketers seek to meet terms set by con-

We're an equal opportunity knowledge provider. We don't care where your data comes from.

You've got the operational data. The transactional data. And, now, a boatload of e-commerce data. What you don't have is a reliable way to quickly bring it all together. And learn something from it. Fortunately, we do. SAS' Intelligent Warehousing Solutions enable you to integrate all of your company's data, regardless of its source or platform. Then mine the data to reveal previously unknown patterns in customer behavior, employee productivity, even supplier relationships. Providing you with insights that can have a real impact on your business performance. To learn more about how we can help you identify new opportunities—and give you the confidence to act on them—call us up at 1-800-727-0025. Or stop by www.sas.com.

The Power to Know   §sas.

EXHIBIT 3.10

SAS Intelligent Warehousing Solutions enable you to integrate all your company's data, regardless of the platform.

Courtesy of Howard, Merrell & Partners and SAS.

sumers. Consumers are likely to look at product information on the Web prior to making major purchases. Advertisers talk in terms of person-to-person. Database marketers talk in terms of customer satisfaction. Information specialists talk in terms of smart systems. This is a new era for brands. It is about consumers telling marketers what they want and marketers responding. It is about interactive, continuous, real-time dialogue replacing traditional models of advertising and consumer communication. Yet consumers have consistently said year after year in Yankelovich's MONITOR research that once they find a brand they like, "it is difficult to get them to change."[15]

Habit is a marketer's biggest challenge. People's past experiences with a brand are consistently the most important factors in their future choices. Despite all the talk about quality, past experiences followed by price, quality, and recommendations from other people lead the reasons people buy a brand. These factors haven't significantly changed over the past two decades; however, price has become more important. Yes, psychological motivations are important, but a brand's most powerful advantage is rooted in the human tendency to form habits and stick to routines. Most people will buy the same brand over and over again if it continues to satisfy their needs.

For marketers to succeed, they must answer three questions: Who buys the brand? What do they want from it? Why do they keep coming back? According to the Roper Organization, many people buy familiar brands even if they believe the product does not have an actual advantage. Only half of Americans think that a specific brand of mayonnaise is different or better than others and worth a higher price. However, 62 percent know what brand of mayonnaise they want when they walk into the store. Another 22 percent look around for the best price on a well-known brand. Brand behavior is complex. Not everyone is brand conscious, and not all brand-conscious people are truly brand driven.[16] Private-label store brands from Publix, CVS, Wal-Mart, and Target are gaining credibility in terms of quality,

KLEPPNER VIEWPOINT

BRAD MAJORS

CEO, SOCOH Marketing LLC

Brand Development Demystified

There is a lot of talk about "branding" or "brand development" these days, as if it is the next "new thing" in marketing and sales. "Brand development" is not a new phenomenon. It has been around for at least 100 years.

Any marketer or ad agency worth its salt practices "brand development" every time they perform any marketing function. The history of advertising in America is, essentially, the history of branding. That is what good advertising (and the other communication disciplines) does—create good and consistent reputations for products or services and this consistent imagery is what converts a product into a "brand."

I say "consistent" because one of the greatest sins of marketing these days (especially for smaller businesses) is a lack of "integrated marketing." By this I mean that there may be mixed messages (from media advertising, public relations, the Web site, package copy, or whatever) that go out to consumers from a brand. And with these inconsistent messages comes an inconsistent image for

Brad Majors

price, and market share. Once these were looked at as generic brands, but they are a force for national brands to deal with.

Marketers need to be aware that as consumers' needs change, their purchase behaviors also may change. It is not unusual for needs to change when a life stage changes. For example, a couple may trade in their sports car for a van or SUV when they have a child. A recently divorced parent may be forced to change buying patterns due to less income. Interestingly, 40 percent of the people who move to a new address change their toothpaste. Yes, we need to understand consumers and their relationship to brands. Technology companies live in an even faster changing world. Their products change quickly and often live in a compressed life cycle. Technology changes and consumer needs change just as quickly.

Brands and Integrated Communication

In the past, many marketing functions—advertising, promotion, packaging, direct marketing, public relations, events—were created and managed independently in most organizations. The economic pressures facing companies today have created the need to manage these activities more efficiently and to ensure they all reinforce each other. Today a brand's equity is best strengthened through the integrated use of all marketing communication tools. It is imperative to project a single, cohesive brand image into the marketplace and into the consumer's mind. The result has been what is labeled integrated marketing communications.

Integrated communications refers to all the messages directed to a consumer on behalf of the brand: media advertising, promotion, public relations, direct response, events, packaging, Web, and so forth. Each message must be integrated the brand. Developing integrated marketing communications is one of the most important activities that can be done to enhance the value of a client's brand. It is nearly impossible to build a brand with inconsistencies in your marketing communications mix.

Business schools teach "the Marketing Mix," which is pretty basic stuff, but bear with me. This Marketing Mix includes the Four P's of marketing: the Product itself (and its structural packaging), the Price of the product, the Place (of distribution) where the product can be purchased, and the Promotion of the product. Interestingly, the fourth P, Promotion, is simply the communication of aspects of the first three P's.

What else is critical to the sale other than what the product does, how much it costs, and where you can get it? Only one more "element" I can think of.

Enter the "Fifth P," which isn't discussed in B-School textbooks, but I doubt the idea is mine alone. What does the Fifth P stand for? The Prospect. The person who is going to buy this product or service, based on perceived needs and wants.

If the Fourth P, Promotion, connects Product, Price, and Place, it also performs another valuable function. Good Promotion, be it in the form of media advertising, packaging graphics, public relations, or in-store merchandising, also has the responsibility of connecting the Prospect to the Product, its Price, and the Place it can be found. In essence, the product is just a collection of features and attributes until the Prospect arrives on the scene. When the Prospect's needs and wants begin to surface, so do the brand's marketing possibilities.

As the Prospect evaluates all the information he or she knows about the product (what it does, what it costs, where it can be purchased), a relationship may begin to form. However, this will only happen if the brand imagery has been consistently presented. This relationship is based on how the Prospect feels the product (or service) will meet his or her needs and wants. I call this "personal relevance." How does the Prospect relate emotionally to those rational product attributes? This "personal relevance" is not a new concept in marketing either. Marketers have been trying to figure out how to achieve the emotional bond between Prospect and brand since the 1920s when Motivational Research was first used by ad agencies. And we are still trying to crack the code on why consumers make the brand choices they make.

A final comment in the Brand Development Demystification process: Sometimes the term *brand development* can suggest some type of inexpensive shortcut in marketing. I have spoken with entrepreneurs who wanted to do "brand development" because they didn't have money for advertising. Sorry, it doesn't really work that way. While media advertising may not be the only way to promote your brand, developing a brand takes time and money. Strong brands do not come cheaply. Fortunately, if the "brand development" process is successful, that investment will pay out big as you go down the marketing road. ■ ■ ■

or dovetailed in order to support all the other messages or impressions about the brand. If this process is successful, it will build a brand's equity by communicating the same brand message to consumers.

Charlie Wrench of Landor Associates, a branding company, said, "Brand integration doesn't mean ensuring that your logo and end line are always the same. It doesn't mean persuading half a dozen agencies to work together. It is a result, not a process. When customers have a coherent experience whenever and wherever they come across your brand you have achieved integration." The capacity to integrate depends more on the quality of the idea than the degree of insistence. Your positioning is your authority, not your position. Before you demand that your partners work more closely together, check that the idea they are to work on is genuinely powerful, differentiating, and relevant. Ensure that it can be expressed in a few clear statements and grasped in a single thought.[17] Ideas that can be captured in a nutshell can be more easily understood.

There are those who say integration has been around for decades and decades, but it wasn't as important an issue as it is today.

During the 1980s, too many marketers milked their brands for short-term profits instead of protecting and nurturing their brands. In the 1990s, brand building became fashionable again. Today marketers realize the brand is their most important asset. Because integrated programs and brand building are so important, we discuss a system of integrated communications that builds brand equity. The most important factor in determining the actual value of a brand is its equity in the market. We can define **brand equity** as the value of how people such as consumers, distributors, and salespeople think and feel about a brand relative to its competition.

Let us look at how Young & Rubicam assesses brand equity's value.

brand equity
The value of how such people as consumers, distributors, and salespeople think and feel about a brand relative to its competition over a period of time.

89

Young & Rubicam's Brand Asset Valuator (BAV)

It is important to assess a brand's stature among consumers. Young & Rubicam (Y&R) created a study aid to evaluate a brand's value called the brand asset valuator (BAV), which explains the strengths and weaknesses of brands on measures of stature and vitality. It believes the relationship between these two factors tells the true story about the health of brand equity and can help diagnose problems and solutions.

Brand asset valuator demonstrates that brands are built in a very specific progression of four primary consumer perceptions: differentiation, relevance, esteem, and knowledge.

- Differentiation is the basis for choice: the essence of the brand, source of margin.
- Relevance relates to usage and subsumes the five P's of marketing related to sales.
- Esteem deals with consumer respect, regard, and reputation and relates to the fulfillment of perceived consumer promise.
- Knowledge is the culmination of brand building efforts and relates to consumer experiences.

A brand's vitality lies in a combination of differentiation and relevance. A brand must be distinct, or it simply isn't a brand. But the fact that a brand is highly differentiated doesn't necessarily mean consumers have the desire or means to buy it. Unless a brand is also relevant, the consumer has no reason to select it. The lack of relevance is the reason so many fads come and go.

The two components of brand stature are esteem and familiarity, that is, whether people know and understand your brand and whether they like it. A brand that more consumers know than like is a clear warning signal. Similarly, a brand that is held in high esteem but ranks lower in familiarity suggests that increasing awareness is an appropriate objective.

BAV measures brands in 32 countries. Its research shows that brand development across cultures is more complicated than simply using one voice everywhere. Sharon Slade of Marketing Corporation of America says, "Where many people go wrong is to assume there is one answer to evaluating brand equity. Having worked across a variety of categories, I can tell you that you need a variety of tools in your tool box. One of the keys to understanding brand equity is to recognize that there are differences between product categories. People buy computers differently from the way they buy soft drinks. Their relationship to that category is different, so the way you diagnose the health of a brand will be different as well."[18]

From this discussion, you should be getting the sense that developing advertising strategy and building brand equity deal with many complex issues. Despite being a little deep, this discussion has given you a feel for the many issues and terms advertising practitioners face daily. Despite this complexity, the development of advertising isn't brain surgery. It is understanding all the ramifications in the market and the consumer's mind, so we can integrate communication and build brand equity better.

Brand Equity and Developing Integrated Marketing Communications Strategic Plans

Before you start to think about creating ads for a brand, you need a strategic plan. Before you can develop a strategy, you need an understanding of the marketing situation and a clear understanding of the brand's equity. There are four logical steps in this process resulting in the creative brief or plan:

1. Brand equity audit analysis
2. Strategic options and recommendations
3. Brand equity research
4. Creative brief

Of course, these generally would be followed by evaluation or assessment of some nature. An outline of a strategic planning process is presented next to give you insight into what is required. Some of the concepts and terms are discussed in more detail throughout the text.

Brand Equity Audit Analysis

There are a number of areas to examine in the first step, brand equity audit analysis. For instance, the context of the market, strengths and weaknesses, consumer attitude descriptions, and competitive strategies and tactics are of importance here.

Market Context We begin by examining the existing situation of both the market and the consumer. What we are looking for are clues and factors that positively or negatively affect brand equity. The whole purpose is to set the scene. The types of questions that are asked include the following:

- What is our market and with whom do we compete?
- What are other brands and product categories?
- What makes the market tick?
- How is the market structured?
- Is the market segmented? If so, how? What segment are we in?
- What is the status of store and generic brands?
- Are products highly differentiated?
- What kind of person buys products in this category?
- In the minds of these consumers, what drives the market or holds it back (needs, obstacles, and so forth)? What are the key motivators?
- Do consumers perceive the brands as very much alike or different?
- Is the product bought on impulse?
- How interested are consumers in the product?
- Do consumers tend to be brand loyal?

These questions should help us understand the status and role of brands in a given market. For example, when the market is made up of a few brands, the consumer will likely be more brand sensitive than if the market is split up into many brands.

We must look at the market from varying angles and select only the relevant ones, so that we can set the scene for understanding and building brand equity. The Ritz-Carlton has a unique quality brand image (see Exhibit 3.11).

Brand Equity Weaknesses and Strengths Now we have a better understanding of the market context and are ready to examine the current brand equity—how strong or weak consumer bias is toward our brand relative to other brands. The following is a list of weakness and strength indicators often used.

- Brand awareness—top of mind is best
- Market share, price elasticity, share of voice, and similar factors
- Brand sensitivity—the relative importance of the brand to other factors involved in the purchase, such as price, pack size, model
- Consistency of the brand's communication over time
- Image attribute ratings or ranking attributes
- Distribution, pricing, product quality, and product information
- Brand loyalty—the strength of a brand lies in the customers who buy it as a brand rather than just as a product

Once the key weakness and strength indicators have been identified, they are used for future tracking purposes.

EXHIBIT 3.11

The Ritz-Carlton is a special brand.

Courtesy of Sawyer Riley Compton and The Ritz-Carlton.

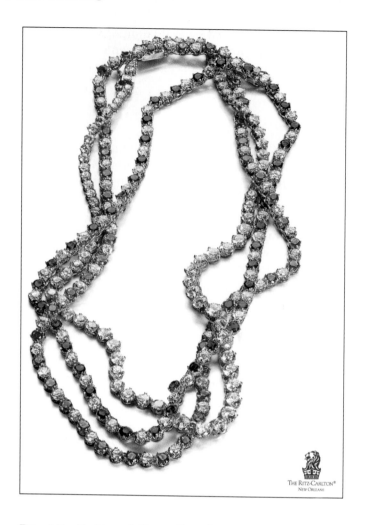

THE RITZ-CARLTON®
NEW ORLEANS

market
A group of people who can be identified by some common characteristic, interest, or problem; use a certain product to advantage; afford to buy it; and be reached through some medium.

Brand Equity Descriptions Now that we understand the **market** in which our brand operates and have a clear understanding of the strengths and weaknesses of our brand equity, we need to identify and describe consumers' thoughts and feelings that result in their bias toward our brand relative to other brands. This personal relationship between the consumer and the brand provides the most meaningful description of brand equity. To accomplish this, we need to analyze from two points of view.

First, we need to review all the available research to get as close a feeling as possible on how consumers view the brand and how they feel about it. Second, we must analyze in depth our brand's and its competitors' communications over a period of time. It is from these communications that most of the consumer's feelings (emotional elements) and opinions (rational elements) about the brand are derived (see Exhibit 3.12).

A brand equity description for the Golf GTI automobile might be as follows:

Emotional Elements	**Rational Elements**
My little sports car	Inexpensive
Sets me free	High gas mileage
It makes me feel and look good	Retains value
Simple	Durable
It's there when I want it	Dependable
I'm in control	Handles well
	Easy to park—small

Competitive Strategies and Tactics This area of the audit is designed to provide a clear summary of the current communication strategies and tactics of our brand

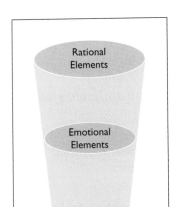

EXHIBIT **3.12**

The Basic Elements of a Brand.

and of key competitors. It should include an analysis of all integrated communications in relation to brand equity. Is the strategy designed to reinforce current brand equity? Who is the target audience? Are there different target audiences? What are the themes and executional approach? How are the marketing funds being spent (e.g., consumer pull versus trade push, advertising, promotions, direct marketing, others)? An assessment of problems and opportunities is also in order here.

Strategic Options and Recommendations   The second step draws on the conclusions from the analysis to develop a viable recommendation plan. The strategic options include:

■ *Communication objectives.* What is the primary goal the message aims to achieve?
■ *Audience.* To whom are we speaking?
■ *Source of business.* Where are the customers going to come from—brand(s) or product categories?
■ *Brand positioning and benefits.* How are we to position the brand, and what are the benefits that will build brand equity?
■ *Marketing mix.* What is the recommended mix of advertising, public relations, promotion, direct response, and so on?
■ *Rationale.* How does the recommended strategy relate to, and what effect is it expected to have on, brand equity?

Brand Equity Research

The third step is where we do the proprietary, qualitative research. It is exploratory and task oriented. Here we need to determine which element(s) of brand equity must be created, altered, or reinforced to achieve our recommended strategy and how far we can stretch each of these components without risking the brand's credibility. This may give us a revised list of rational and emotional elements that describe how we want consumers to think and feel about our brand in the future.

Creative Brief

The final step is a written creative brief (or work plan) for all communications. We synthesize all the information and understanding into an action plan for the development of all communications for the brand: advertising, public relations, promotion, and so forth.

The creative strategy (brief or work plan) is a short statement that clearly defines our audience, how consumers think or feel and behave, what the communication is intended to achieve, and the promise that will create a bond between the consumer and the brand. A typical strategy would include the following:

- *Key observations*—the most important market/consumer factor that dictates the strategy
- *Communication objective*—the primary goal the advertising/communication aims to achieve
- *Consumer insight*—the consumer "hot button" our communication will trigger
- *Promise*—what the brand should represent in the consumer's mind; what the brand is promising the consumer
- *Support*—the reason the promise is true
- *Audience*—to whom we are speaking and how they feel about the brand
  There may be a need for an additional element:
- *Mandatories*—items used as compulsory constraints for example, a specific legal requirement or corporate policy that impacts the direction of the strategy

Other Examples of Strategic Planning

It is important to understand that there isn't just one approach to developing an integrated strategic plan for a brand. The basic steps are similar, but each agency approaches the process with a little different wrinkle. Let us take a look at the basics of a couple of other strategic planning approaches.

Avrett, Free & Ginsberg's Planning Cycle   Avrett, Free & Ginsberg (AFG) uses a seven-step planning cycle that helps create strategic advertising. It uses the discipline of account planning at each stage of developing strategy. Briefly, the framework for its strategic planning cycle (see Exhibit 3.13) involves the following steps:

1. *Brand/market status.* AFG evaluates where the brand is in its marketplace and determines strengths, weaknesses, opportunities, and threats.
2. *Brand mission.* After determining brand status, AFG proposes and agrees on brand goals, that is, where it can take the brand.
3. *Strategic development.* Here AFG explores various options to determine which of several strategies will empower the brand to achieve the mission. AFG uses a process called needs mapping (see Exhibit 3.14). The basic principle is that people respond or bond to products based on a wide range of psychological and rational needs. This process is loosely based on Maslow's hierarchy of needs.

EXHIBIT **3.13**

AFG Planning Cycle

Courtesy of Avrett, Free & Ginsberg.

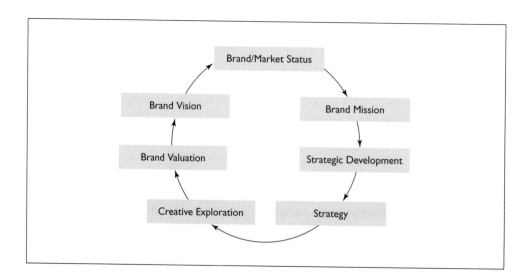

EXHIBIT **3.14**

An Example of AFG's Need-Mapping Process.

Courtesy of Avrett, Free & Ginsberg.

STRATEGIC DEVELOPMENT

MODERN

Extremism

Leading Edge

Expressive Individuality

Self-Actualization

Leadership

Stimulating Experimentation

"Going for It"

Active Sociability

Smart Sociability

Display

SPECIAL

EVERYDAY

Statement

Enhanced Quality

Intimate Sociability

Established Superiority

Heritage

Security

TRADITIONAL

4. *Strategy.* AFG formulates a tight strategy to be used in developing a fully integrated marketing communication program.

5. *Creative exploration.* AFG develops, explores, and evaluates a range of executions to ensure that it maximizes the relevancy, distinctiveness, and persuasiveness of the strategy and final execution.

6. *Brand valuation.* AFG tracks marketplace performance and progress because it believes it must be accountable for the results its work generates. AFG constantly fine-tunes and improves communications in response to changing market conditions.

7. *Brand vision.* In building equities for a brand through effective communications, AFG plots long-range expansion plans for the base brand. AFG determines if the emerging brand equities can be line extended or translated to serve needs in other related categories.

These seven steps are constantly pursued in the evaluation of a brand's life cycle to ensure long-term growth and brand equity.

Another View of the Planning Process Below are some of the typical steps agencies and clients take in the planning process.

1. *Current Brand Status.* Here there is an attempt to evaluate the brands overall appeal. The brand is examined in the contexts marketplace, consumers' view, in relation to its competitors. It answers: Where do we stand in the marketplace? What are our real competitors? What is the consumer attitude towards our brand? The category? Who are they?

2. *Brand Insights.* The agency may use a series of tools designed to help it develop insights to better understand the consumer's view. For example, it may attempt to capture the words that best describe the brand, the target audience, and the relationship between the two. This may include determining the key attributes, benefits, personality, and answering: "How does it (brand) make you feel?," and "What

does it (brand) say about you?" This is where (SWOT) strengths, opportunities, weaknesses, and threats are determined.

3. *Brand Vision.* The strategic planners look for the consumer's hot button to identify the most powerful connection between the brand and the consumer. This is the bridge between the insight of planning and the magic of creative innovation.

4. *Bid Idea.* The next step is identifying the Big Idea, the creative expression of the Brand Vision. The Big Idea for branding becomes the foundation of all communication briefs. A communication plan is built on this idea. This plan is designed to reach the consumer target at a point where and when the consumer will be most receptive to the message.

5. *Evaluation.* An essential aspect of communications planning is accountability. The agency and client need to determine how well the objectives have been met, and how to improve the communication the next time. Agencies may use their own proprietary tools to evaluate and learn from its performance, or they may use outside sources to accomplish this measurement.

Today, almost every agency has its own version of strategic brand building and understanding the consumer. After all, they have to differentiate themselves to attract clients, The word "disruption" and the TBWA agency have become synonymous with one another. Disruption helps TBWA define brands for its clients. Their process challenges the underlying conventions that shape communication and marketing on every level in an attempt to break the status quo. Euro RSCG Worldwide looks at the marketer's need for ideas that apply to their business strategy. This strategic integration goes beyond advertising into such areas as "buzz" or word-of-mouth that transfers brand information through social networks. Their buzz doesn't concentrate on the traditional trendsetters of society, but a group defined as trend spreaders. So when we talk about a strategic approach it may include approaching the brand problem or solution from a different direction.

In short, the consumer (target) has to be an important part of the strategic planning process. How the advertiser engages consumers is critical to the process. In the past, marketers spoke and consumers listened. Today's consumers are proactive and speak loudly and marketers have learned they need to listen. You can't plan integrated communications effectively without understanding the target more wisely than ever before.

Ogilvy & Mather As Shelly Lazarus, CEO and chairman of Ogilvy says, "At Ogilvy, we take a holistic look at communications and use what is necessary from each of the disciples (advertising, web, PR, promotion, direct marketing, etc.) to build a brand." Ogilvy calls this 360 Degree Branding. Under 360, every point of contact builds the brand. Every communication from any discipline reflects the same insight. All media contributes to a campaign as a whole.

What Great Brands Do

Scott Bedbury, former senior vice president of marketing at Starbucks Coffee, said, "I walked through a hardware store last night and I came across 50 brands I didn't know existed. They may be great products, but they're not great brands." Scott should know brands. He's the man who gave the world "Just Do It," Nike's branding campaign. A few of Bedbury's brand-building principles are examined here:[19]

■ *A great brand is in it for the long haul.* For decades there were brands based on solid value propositions—they had established their worth in the consumers' minds. Then, in the 1980s and 1990s, companies focused on short-term eco-

KLEPPNER VIEWPOINT

MARK KOOYMAN

EVP, Brand Strategy, BaylessCronin

The Marketing Challenge Ahead

The challenge facing marketers today is not the creation of dynamic advertising, but rather the creation of a dynamic brand essence. Consumers today have more touch-points with brands than ever before. PC's and DSL have literally brought the shopping experience itself into the bedroom of the home. And the brand experience as we have historically defined it transcends above and beyond the actual use and interface of the product itself.

Brands like Apple, Nike, Starbucks, Mercedes, HBO, Cartoon Network, Southwest Airlines, Abercrombie & Fitch, Absolut, TiVo, Altoids, and eBay have netted more than the purchase transaction, but instead a marriage with their customers' bodies, minds, and spirits.

To deliver the dynamics of the brand essence requires moving beyond the attributes and benefits of a brand and digging deeper into the emotional ignition points of the experience it provides. To build the programs to do this requires brand teams to think on broad levels. The traditional disciplines of business like marketing, financial, sales, and distribution need to be married with nontraditional studies like anthropology, sociology, psychology, and neurology that bring into the fold the dynamics of how consumers think and interact with others.

Marketing communications functions as the invitation to the brand experience. It essentially delivers a taste of the brand that invites the audience into the adventure of a relationship.

For example, Apple ran a television spot during the Super Bowl that literally used a spear to launch the dynamics of its brand. The ad only ran once. Today, Apple owns a

Mark Kooyman

brand essence that is conveyed at every point of contact from brand name to retail to direct computer interface to online assistance to new gadgets that can link up to the computer base. And Apple has achieved success with a brand essence that is conveyed through graphics, language use, and design that ignites the emotional chords of individual identity and simplicity in a climate of mass automation and high technology. Apple is a statement of who the owner is beyond the mechanics of the computer. ■ ■ ■

nomic returns and diminished long-term brand-building programs. As a result, there were a lot of products with very little differentiation. Today a great brand is a necessity, not a luxury. By using a long-term approach, a great brand can travel worldwide, speak to multiple consumer segments simultaneously, and create economies of scale, by which you can earn solid margins over the long term.

■ *A great brand can be anything.* Some categories lend themselves to branding better than others, but anything is brandable. For example, Starbucks focuses on how coffee has woven itself into the fabric of people's lives, and that's an opportunity for emotional leverage. Almost any product offers an opportunity to create a frame of mind that is unique. Do you know what Intel computer processors do, how they work, or why they are superior to their competitor? All most people know is that they want to own a computer with "Intel Inside."

- *A great brand knows itself.* The real starting point is to go out to consumers and find out what they like or dislike about this brand and what they associate as the very core of the brand concept. To keep a brand alive over the long haul, to keep it vital, you have got to do something new, something unexpected. It has to relate to the brand's core position.

- *A great brand invents or reinvents an entire category.* The common ground that you find among brands such as Disney, Apple, Nike, and Starbucks is that these companies made it an explicit goal to be the protagonists for each of their entire categories. Disney is the protagonist for fun family entertainment and family values. A great brand raises the bar—it adds a greater sense of purpose to the experience.

- *A great brand taps into emotions.* The common ground among companies that have built great brands is not just performance. They realize consumers live in an emotional world. Emotions drive most, if not all, of our decisions. It is an emotional connection that transcends the product. And transcending the product is the brand.

- *A great brand is a story that's never completely told.* A brand is a metaphorical story that is evolving all the time. This connects with something very deep. People have always needed to make sense of things at a higher level. Levi's has a story that goes all the way back to the gold rush. It has photos of miners wearing Levi's dungarees. Stories create connections for people. Stories create the emotional context people need to locate themselves in a larger experience.

- *A great brand is relevant.* A lot of brands are trying to position themselves as "cool," but most of them fail. The larger idea is to be relevant. It meets what people want; it performs the way people want it to. In the past couple of decades a lot of brands promised consumers things they couldn't deliver. Consumers are looking for something that has lasting value. There is a quest for quality, not quantity.

SUMMARY

Products pass through a number of stages from introduction to ultimate demise, known as the product life cycle. Advertising plays a different role in each stage of product development. Until consumers appreciate the fact that they need a product, that product is in the pioneering stage of advertising. In the competitive stage, an advertiser tries to differentiate its product from that of the competition. The retentive stage calls for reminder advertising.

A product's age has little to do with the stage it is in at any given time. Rather, consumer attitude or perception determines the stage of a product. As consumer perception changes, moving it from one stage to another, the advertising message should also change. In fact, the advertising may be in more than one stage at any given time. Creative marketing may propel a product through new pioneering, new competitive, and new retentive stages. And it is even possible for a product to continue on into the newest pioneering, newest competitive, and newest retentive stages. As a product ages, so do its users, which is why no product can survive without attracting new customers. Long-term success depends on keeping current customers while constantly attracting new ones.

In the mid-1880s there were no brands. Manufacturers differentiated their products and gave them names as the concept of branding was born. Brands are now among the most valuable assets a marketer owns. The product is not the brand. A product is manufactured; a brand is created and is made up of both rational and emotional elements. In today's marketing environment, it is essential that every communication reinforces brand personality in the same manner: advertising, public relations, promotion, packaging, direct marketing, and so forth. The most important factor in determining the actual value of a brand is its equity in the market: how consumers think and feel about the brand.

Avrett, Free & Ginsberg (AFG) use a seven-step planning cycle that helps create strategic advertising. They use the discipline of account planning at each stage of developing a campaign: Brand/marketing status, Brand mission, strategic development, creative exploitation, brand valuation, and brand vision.

 ## REVIEW

1. Briefly identify each stage in the first half of the advertising spiral.

2. What determines the stage of a product?

3. What is the essence of the advertising message in each stage of the spiral?

4. What is brand equity?

5. What are the elements of the creative brief?

6. What are the key elements in the AFG planning cycle?

 ## TAKE IT TO THE WEB

Tabasco Sauce was created by the McIlhenny Company, which was founded in 1868. Visit **www.tabasco.com** and decide in which stage of the product life cycle Tabasco Sauce currently resides. What are the strengths, weaknesses, opportunities, and threats facing the brand?

Walt Disney and The Walt Disney Company have long been associated with family fun and magical vacations. How does Disney Online (**www.disney.com**) work to create an emotional connection with consumers via the interactive Web site? Why is an emotional connection with a product an important part of building brand strength?

Manning Selvage & Lee is an example of a global public relations firm. Visit the Web site (**www.mslpr.com**) and learn about Brand Vision – MS&L's program designed to come up with a brand strategy and improve market share. How is Brand Vision executed, and how are results measured?

Paper Mate has been producing pens, pencils, and correction products for over 50 years. On the Paper Mate Web site (**www.papermate.com**) see how the company is able to promote new writing products in the pioneering stage while continuing to generate interest in products that have been around for several years.

CHAPTER 4

my reflection.

i admit it.
sometimes, when i run by a window, i turn around and look at it.
not to admire myself, and how i look.
but just to nod at the person running, 'cause i know i'll see them tomorrow.

The GEL-Cumulus™ II gives your feet all the cushi[...]
durable enough to help you train in comfort day aft[...]

Target Marketing

n Chapter 3 we examined the brand in the context of its market and consumers. In the creative brief we were asked, "Whom are we speaking to?" Here we speak to answering your options and understanding changes taking place in society and their impact on business. After reading this chapter, you will understand:

1. **defining prime prospects**
2. **importance of target marketing information**
3. **marketing concept**
4. **planning the advertising**
5. **niche marketing and positioning**
6. **beyond demographics: psychographics**

Who do we think is going to buy our product? Men? Women? Teenagers? College students? Men and women? Seniors? 25- to 49-year-olds? Primarily Hispanics? To whom are we going to aim our advertising? Is it going to be profitable? What is our rationale for selecting this target? Have there been any changes in this target? There are a lot of questions to be answered. We need a lot of answers. In the process, does that mean we don't aim at everybody who has money? We know that won't work—that's a shotgun approach. We need to be focused and direct, like a rifle shot, to hit our target.

The monolithic mass market of the mid-twentieth century has long been laid to rest, and smaller mass markets have taken its place. VitroRobertson, San Diego, created the Yamaha WaveRunner ad (see Exhibit 4.1) targeting prospects. It says, "Horsepower only matters if you have someplace to go." Its copy includes, "115 horsepower. Where will it take you?" What kind of prospect do you perceive the ad is trying to reach?

Marketing Generalization A word of caution: Marketers have a tendency to generalize. We talk about baby boomers, seniors, generations X, Y, and Z, or limit discussions to demographics (age, income, sex) as if each is a uniform group of people who live, think, and act exactly the same. Do all 20-year-old women think and act alike? Do all Hispanics? Virtually no generalization encompasses an entire consumer segment, especially age groups. If we stop to think about it, we know better than to generalize. Consider that seniors or matures can be wealthy or not, love the outdoors or not, be inclined to travel or be homebodies, own a vacation home or live in a mobile home. The same considerations apply to virtually each of these catch-all categories. Of course, these groupings or segments can be very useful in assessing potential markets; after all, they do have group behavior and lifestyle commonalities. These segments should be

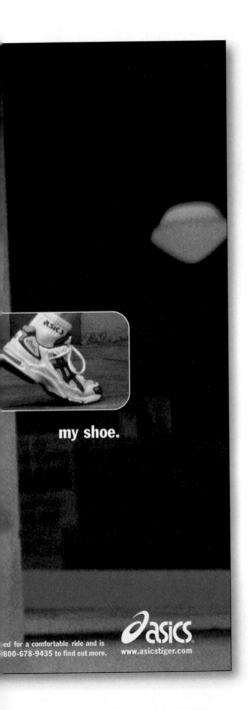

my shoe.

101

EXHIBIT 4.1

Who is Yamaha WaveRunner trying to reach with this ad?

Courtesy of VitroRobertson, Inc. and Yamaha Watercraft and Robert Holland, photographer.

considered, but remember they stereotype groups of people. We all know that all Russians drink vodka, Germans drink beer, and the French drink wine, right? Or that all Southerners eat grits? It is okay to start with a premise in narrowing to one of these groups, but it is important to dig deeper.

One of the cardinal rules in marketing has always been to know your market. That doesn't mean segmenting young and old or rich and poor. It means defining your target in as much detail as circumstances allow and necessity requires. There is a reason that reliable market research looks at multiple factors such as age, gender, income, net worth, ethnicity, geography, lifestyle, and family status. It is very appropriate to use "families" as a partial descriptor of a given market, as long as it doesn't become a synonym for the market itself.[1] Now that we have sent up a red flag, let us look at some factors and segments used in target marketing. When possible, today's marketing aims at the individual and not at the mass market.

Once you ask the obvious questions, you must determine which answers are critical to your decision making. Do you need more information to reach your prospects successfully? Do you understand their problems? Have you thought about what you want people to think and feel about your brand as a result of being exposed to your advertising?

DEFINING PRIME PROSPECTS

One of the decisions critical to success is defining prime prospects so you do not waste time and money advertising your product to people unlikely to buy it or people you can't make a profit by attracting. This search for the best prospects among all consumers is called **target marketing.**

The process of finding prime prospects can be very complex because there are numerous ways of looking at consumers, many different kinds of information to

target marketing
Identifying and communicating with groups of prime prospects.

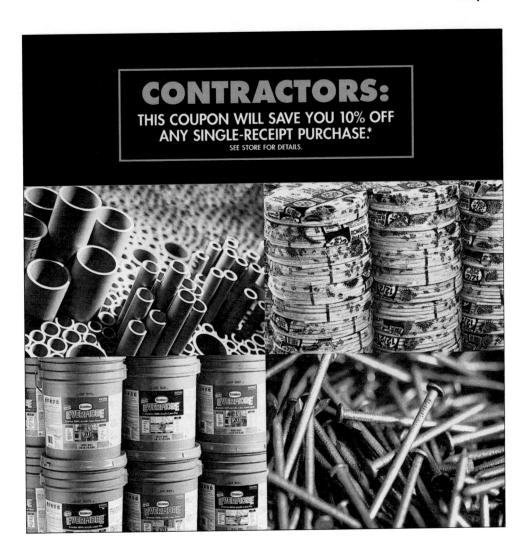

EXHIBIT **4.2**
Home Depot targets building contractors through highly targeted direct mail.
Courtesy of Homer TLC, Inc. © 2003.

consider, and a constantly changing consumer environment. Home Depot targets building contractors (as well as consumers) through highly targeted direct mail (see Exhibit 4.2).

Where Do We Start?

Different agencies and companies approach the process a little differently, as we saw in the last chapter, but all have to answer the same important questions before advertising can be created. Brand equity research, for instance, seeks to answer a number of questions and examine the existing state of the brand in the context of market and consumers. Today, marketers have a host of informational sources to help plan integrated marketing programs aimed at individual users or groups. Let us look at some of the information sources and trends in America and their implications for advertising planning.

Census Data

Marketing executives must adapt to a constantly changing environment, especially shifts in demographics and lifestyles. Census data offer marketers a wealth of information about people and how they live in the United States. Much of the database is online. The Topologically Integrated Geographic Encoding and Referencing system, known as TIGER, is one of the more sophisticated tools. This coding of the country's natural, political, and statistical boundaries includes every street, road, and subdivision. TIGER provides the data for computer maps to plan sales territories and pinpoint direct-marketing prospects. This information can be linked to a number of relevant characteristics, such as age, income, and race. Custom research companies using these data have developed software for marketers to access geodemographic databases.

Now advertisers have a number of geodemographic sources that claim unprecedented precision and details about consumers and their purchasing behavior based on their home addresses. These services using 2000 Census data clusters promise advertisers that classifying geodemographics has grown from an art to a science. Each service organizes America's households into 40 to 70 number-coded nicknames (Blue Bloods, Trailblazers, Penny Pinchers, Shotguns, and Pickups) to identify lifestyle segmentation. Claritas' PRIZM, for example, steps beyond ZIP code + 4 level of detail, a geographical area that encompasses 10 to 12 households, as opposed to Blocks, which have 340 households, and ZIP codes, which include 3,600 households. These companies can zero in on smaller segments of the population than was previously possible. They also overlay precise demographic information with consumer behavior information giving advertisers a better consumer picture. Depending on the level of information, these geodemographic services can cost an advertiser from $500 to $100,000. Some of these services described here will be discussed later in the text:[2]

- Aciom: has a life stage–driven, household-level, consumer segmentation system representing approximately 110 million U.S. households.
- Claritas: by segmenting customers using demographic and behavioral traits, it can identify who the best customers are, what they are like, and where to find them.
- ESRI: provides a demographic and lifestyle picture of neighborhoods, enabling businesses to profile their best customers.
- Experian: a global segmentation product accessing resources including automotive, retail, and catalog transactional information, household demographics, and so on.
- Mapinfo: ties location to behaviors and characteristics of the population helping advertisers make decisions about market and product potential and store placement.

Population

The Census Bureau reported that the U.S. population grew 2.5 percent to 288.4 million from 2000 to 2002. Hispanics accounted for half the increase. We'll talk about the significance of that increase shortly. In the United States, marketers have always had to deal with population growth and shifts that influence advertisers' markets in some way. Obviously, we need to know who is out there in the marketplace. How many of them? Where and how do they live? What do they need? What are their buying patterns? We can't easily reach people if we don't know where they are. But population is more than simple numbers of people. Society tends to group people by age, ethnicity, generation, or some other factor. For instance, *American Demographics* breaks down the generations living in 2000: GI Generation, 71 plus years old (9.1%); Depression, 61–70 years old (6.5%); War Babies, 55–60 years old (5.7%); Baby Boomers, 36–54 years old (28.2%); Generation X, 22–34 years old (16.4); Generation Y, 6–23 years old (25.8); and Millennials, 0–5 years old (8.3%).[3] How they think, act, and spend influences marketers. An advertiser must understand these people beyond the numbers.

The U.S. Census Bureau data projections indicate that by the year 2025, 70 percent of the growth will take place in the South and West. By 2025, there will be moderate growth for New York, New Jersey, Pennsylvania, Ohio, and Michigan. California will double its population from the year 1990 to 2040. But that is only part of the story. California gained 1.3 million immigrants while losing 1.5 million natives to surrounding states. So numbers alone don't tell the picture. But the numbers themselves indicate change.

Selected Census State Population Projections*

	2000	2025
California	32,423	41,480
Texas	20,119	27,183
New York	18,146	19,830
Florida	15,233	20,710
Pennsylvania	12,202	12,683
Illinois	12,051	13,440
Ohio	11,319	11,744
Michigan	9,679	10,078
Georgia	7,875	9,869
North Carolina	7,777	9,349
Colorado	4,168	5,188
Oregon	3,397	4,349
West Virginia	1,841	1,845
Montana	950	1,121
North Dakota	662	729
Wyoming	525	694

*Data in millions
Source: U.S. Census Bureau projections.

Changes Coming

American Demographics says the population for the next quarter century will be larger, older, and more diverse, one with many opportunities and challenges for business. Of course, it is difficult to accurately predict the future. The demographics are easy because they are alive today. Speculation about the social and cultural—and even political aspects—is not so clear. By 2025, the U.S. population is expected to exceed 350 million—a 25 percent increase. As this population grows, niche markets may become unwieldy for businesses to target with a single strategy. The niche market of today may become a mass market in its own right, segmented not only by nationality but also by spending behavior and other psychographic characteristics. This trend is called "beehiving" says, Vickie Abrahamson of Iconoculture, a trend consulting firm. Beehiving is the growth of tight-knit, alternative communities sharing common values and passions. Abrahamson says, "Marketers must tap in to beehive rituals, customs and language to build trust and patronage."[4]

The biggest growth over the next 25 years will be in the 65 and older set. The baby boomers will double the size of that group compared to today. In addition to being focused on youth, marketers will also pay more attention outside the youth market. A recent Pepsi commercial showing a teenage boy in the middle of a mosh pit at a rock concert discovers his father rocking nearby. The Pepsi generation is becoming multigenerational. The clue in the future will be how to establish brands that attract older consumers without alienating younger ones.

We are not going to attempt to cover all the demographics that may be important, but these items should give you something to think about. Keep in mind that these may or may not be important to a specific marketing situation. It is imperative to get a handle on what data are important.

Multicultural Overview

The multicultural market is growing in importance to marketers. Defining it appears to be a problem for some. "We tend to forget that a culture means a culture, not necessarily a different language," says Lynn Adrian-Hsing, Asian segments marketing manager-multicultural marketing integration at Bank of America.[5] She encourages advertisers to "think outside the traditional 'multicultural box'" to include gay and lesbian consumers, seniors and gen Xers and Yers. "These are cultural markets, not ethnic." Recently, Bank of America placed 25 percent of its advertising budget to win business from African Americans, Hispanics, and Asian Americans. The campaign's objective was to add mortgages and about a million new checking accounts over a 12-month period. Citigroup and J.P. Morgan Chase are other banking corporations that tailor campaigns to specific ethnic groups. The 2000 Census indicated that African, Americans, Hispanics, and Asian Americans comprised roughly 30 percent of the total U.S. population. If a marketer included gays and lesbians in the population mix, they would account for another 20 million potential consumers.[6]

Today's multicultural marketing has evolved since the term *minority marketing* was used to describe targeting African Americans during the 1960s. As marketers included Hispanic American efforts, it was called *ethnic marketing*. Today many marketers prefer the term *multicultural marketing* because it encompasses not only a range of ethnicities but also lifestyle-related targets such as the gay and lesbian markets.

Selected Demographic Snapshots

African Americans The Census Bureau's statistical profile of African Americans released in 2003 indicated a population of 36.6 million. The black population is younger and faster growing than the white population. The median income of all black families was $25,970 compared to that of white families at $45,020. However, married-couple black families' median income was similar to the income of white families, at $49,752 versus $59,025. Between 2001 and 2010, there will be a slight decline in black students in schools aged 5 to 9, and a decrease of 9 percent for children aged 10 to 14. Census data indicate 55.3 percent of African Americans live in the South, 18.1 percent live in the Northeast, 18.1 percent live in the Midwest, and about only 8.6 percent live in the West.

An analysis of the 2000 Census reveals the importance of the rising black middle class. It indicates that nearly 30 percent of African American households have achieved middle- and upper-income status. *American Demographics* reports that in areas such as Middlesex, New Jersey, and Nassau-Suffolk, New York, home of many commuting New Yorkers, and in San Jose and Orange County, California, home of suburbanizing Los Angelinos, more than half of all black households earn more than $50,000 a year. The number of African American college graduates has increased significantly over the

EXHIBIT 4.3

Ford targets minorities directly.

Courtesy of UniWorld Group, Inc. and Ford Motor Company.

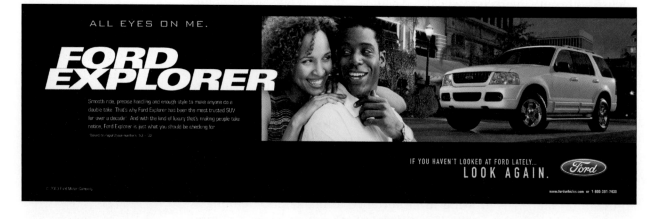

ALL EYES ON ME.

FORD EXPLORER

Smooth ride, precise handling and enough style to make anyone do a double take. That's why Ford Explorer has been the most trusted SUV for over a decade. And with the kind of luxury that's making people take notice, Ford Explorer is just what you should be checking for.

IF YOU HAVEN'T LOOKED AT FORD LATELY...
LOOK AGAIN.   *Ford*

www.fordvehicles.com or 1-800-301-7430

past two decades adding to the middle-class impact. Today there is a greater tendency for Gen X and Gen Y blacks to graduate from college and enter professional careers. How do advertisers reach them effectively as they become more mobile across the nation? "A number of marketers still tend to think African-Americans are darker versions of white people, that they don't have to do anything different to reach them," says Howard Buford, CEO of Prime Access, a multicultural agency.[7]

Hispanics Hispanics outnumbered blacks as the nation's largest minority in 2003 for the first time with 38.8 million reported. In 1995, there were about 26.5 million Hispanics in the United States, or 10 percent of the population. In perspective, this market is comparable to the entire population of Canada. By 2010, the Hispanic population is projected to increase to 50 million. Keep in mind there isn't a single Hispanic market because of cultural differences from their countries of origin. The latest census report indicated that among the Hispanic population 66 percent were of Mexican origin, 14.3 percent were Central and South American, 8.6 percent were Puerto Rican, 3.7 percent were of Cuban origin, and 6.5 were from other Hispanic origins. Latinos (interchangeable term used by the Census Bureau) reside nearly equally in the West, South, and Northeast. Cubans reside mostly in the South, and Puerto Ricans live mostly in the Northeast. Educational attainment varies among Latinos 25 years and older. For example, those receiving bachelor's degrees include 18.6 percent Cubans, 17.3 percent Central and South Americans, and 19.7 for other Hispanics to 7.6 percent for Mexicans. Remember our warning about generalizations. Their buying power was estimated to reach $630 billion in 2002. In general, Hispanics lag behind African Americans in education; however, the 2000 Census indicated they accounted for 9.3 percent of the 15.3 million college students enrolled in the United States. Sixty-five percent of Hispanic households have children present compared to 48 percent non-Hispanic households.

Asians and Pacific Islanders In 2002, the census reported 12.5 million Asians and Pacific Islanders live in the United States, representing 4.4 percent of the population. Of the total, 51 percent live in the West, 19 percent live in the South, 12 percent live in the Midwest, and 19 percent live in the Northeast with 95 percent living in metropolitan areas. In 2002, Asians were younger than non-Hispanic whites: 26 percent of Asians were under 18, compared with 23 percent of non-Hispanic whites. A high value is placed on education: 51 percent of Asian men and 44 percent of Asian women earned at least a bachelor's degree compared to 32 percent of men and 27 percent of non-Hispanic whites. A glance at income in 2001 indicates 40 percent of all Asian families had incomes of $75,000 or more, compared with 35 percent of non-Hispanic whites. However, 17 percent had incomes less than $25,000, compared with 15 percent of non-Hispanic whites. There are separate communities to consider: Japanese Americans, Chinese Americans, Filipino Americans, Korean Americans, Vietnamese Americans, Asian Indians, and others differing in culture, language, and history. Each factor drives what will be the most effective channel for reaching these consumers. The percentage increase in Asian children rises faster than Hispanics; ages 5 to 9 will increase by 22 percent by 2010, and those aged 10 to 14 will increase by 31 percent.[8]

"The Asian market will become increasingly more important over the next decade," says Bank of America's Ms. Adrian-Hsing, especially for high-end products. "It is slowly being discovered that this is an extremely wealthy, extremely affluent segment that is relatively untapped."[9]

Gilbert Davila, vice president-multicultural market for The Walt Disney Co., puts all of this into a marketing perspective, saying, "Multicultural marketing is not a fad. When you take a look at everything that's happening, at all the projections from the census, America is only going to become increasingly diverse, which will

EXHIBIT **4.4**

This restaurant chain's catering division attempts to reach people interested in catering services.

Courtesy of Bevil Advertising, Inc., and Folks.

place more challenges on companies to figure out how to better market, be more relevant and target these constituencies."[10]

Other Target Influences

As you can see, there is a lot of information for marketers to digest. There are many additional factors a marketer can examine that might influence basic marketing decisions. For example, Home Depot may target women, do-it-yourselfers, contractors, and gardeners, requiring an understanding of many groups and lifestyles. Exhibit 4.4 shows Folk's restaurant aiming for people interested in a "Southern food experience" in catering, which can include consumer groups or businesses. Again, we'll sample some of the typical information available to marketers.

Household Income The Bureau of Labor Statistics' Consumer Expenditure Survey produces annual estimates of household spending on hundreds of items, cross-tabulated by demographic characteristics. As with most data, you need to use these data wisely. In addition to looking at household income, advertisers often look at disposable and discretionary income. Disposable income is after-tax income. Discretionary income is the amount of money consumers have after paying taxes and buying necessities such as food and housing.

In September 2000, the Census Bureau reported that the typical U.S. household had a median income of $40,816 in 1999. Women's median earning was $26,324 and men's $36,476. Marketers have to look carefully at the numbers. For example, the Census Bureau reported household non-Hispanic white, $44,366, black $27,910, Asian/Pacific Islander $51,205, and Hispanic 30,735. In the Northeast it was $41,984 and in the Midwest, $42,679; metro areas had a household median income of $42,785 against nonmetro's $33,021; Alaska was reported at $51,046, Maryland $50,630, Michigan $40,066, Louisiana $32,218, Mississippi $30,628, and West Virginia $28,420. The largest income growth was among blacks and Asian/Pacific Islanders. As you can see, marketers need to look beyond the basic numbers to get a better picture if household income is a factor in developing targets. Looking at gender, race, geography, age, and education will paint a different picture.

Spending *American Demographics* found that the average U.S. metropolitan household devotes 16 percent of its spending for shelter, 17 percent for transportation, 14 percent for food, 6 percent for utilities, 6 percent for apparel, 5 percent for entertainment, 3 percent for household operations, and 11 percent for personal insurance. Spending patterns depend strongly on the unique age and income characteristics of individual markets.[11] Many products and services depend on disposable income of consumers for their existence.

Marrieds The U.S. Census Bureau reported in 1999 that 110.6 million Americans aged 18 and over were married. That is 56 percent of the adult population. The report indicates the median age for men at first marriage was 26.7, compared to 26.1 in 1976. For women it was 25.0, the highest median age for first marriage. Some 19.4 million adults are currently divorced. There were 1,348,000 interracial married couples. Nearly 6 percent of all children under 18 live with grandparents. Clearly, this decline has had social and marketing ramifications.

Birthrate To marketers, the number of births in a given year can be important in projecting market size. The birthrate in the United States has been in decline for decades. In 1960, the rate was 23.7 per 1,000 population, and it was 13.9 per thousand in 2002, the lowest since government records have been kept. There were 4,019,280 recorded births in America in 2002. Just think of the significance to companies selling baby items. If marketers marry knowledge of fluctuations in the birthrate with an understanding of how consumers tend to act at different stages of their lives, they can get a rough picture of the market challenges that lie in the future.

In recent years there were slightly fewer than 4 million babies a year born; about one-third of children in 1997 were ethnic minorities, and roughly 62 percent of married mothers with preschoolers were in the workforce (in 1965 only 23 percent of married mothers worked).

Aging In 2003, one in eight Americans were 65 years or older. It is estimated that by 2020, one in every six Americans will be 65 plus. Census estimates indicate that the seniors segment of the population will more than double by 2050. This will have a significant implication for both marketers and society as a whole.

Women According to the U.S. Department of Education, in every state, every income bracket, every racial and ethnic group, and most industrialized Western nations, women earn an average 57 percent of all bachelor's degrees and 58 percent of all master's degrees in the U.S. alone.[12]

Women comprise 51.4 percent of the U.S. population and purchase or influence 85 percent of all products (see Exhibit 4.5). The demands on marketers will increase as women increase their wealth, education, and longevity. For decades marketers have known women drive all the obvious categories of food, beauty, and household products. Today they also make 80 percent of all health care choices and 65 percent of new car purchases, and comprise 50 percent of the traveling population. Mary Lou Quinlan in her book, *Just Ask a Woman,* tries to answer a number of questions marketers have tried to answer in their products, marketing, and advertising. Why do women want to be special? What does that mean? Do they want different products than men? Do they want marketers to feminize advertising?[13] And, of course, are there major differences among African American, Hispanic, Asian, Italian, Greek, and other women? Or does everybody think the same? It is another example of having to really understand the target because numbers don't always tell the whole story.

Single-Person Households For the first time in history, there are now more people living alone in single-person households than there are traditional families of husband, wife, and child. In the latest census data there were about 27.2 million single-person households versus about 16.6 million three-person family households.

EXHIBIT 4.5

The Macon Mall knows women are its primary market. They sell lifestyle and fashion.

Courtesy of Bright Ideas Group, Inc., and Colonial Mall Macon.

According to the 2001 Consumer Expenditure Survey, these singles spend 153 percent more per person on rent than those who live in households of two people or more. What sets singles apart from the rest of the population is their singular focus on themselves. For the last three decades the home-alone household has been increasing, accounting for 26 percent of U.S. households. A quarter of single-person households are made up of young people under 35 years of age who have never been married, many of them "financially independent singles" who are postponing marriage. The rest of the demographic is made up of older singles in their middle and senior years. Across the board, members of single-person households tend to defy stereotypes that have become way out of date. The targeting of singles has only just begun to emerge in a number of areas such as food and household products such as toilet cleaners that once were the sole domain of housewives. It is a good market for affluent products because of the attitude that "if I really want something, price is not an object."[14] The people who choose to live alone are creating their own communities without regret or unwanted claims made on their lives.

Marketers need to realize that despite the potential of this group, like the others we have discussed, it is not a homogenous target audience. For example, Looking Glass, Inc., lists eight of its 30-plus key consumer segments that are likely to live as one-person households. Among them are upscale mature women (56 percent of the segment lives alone), working-class women (63 percent), fit and stylish students (52 percent), well-to-do gentlemen (76 percent), and working-class men (78 percent).[15]

GENERATIONAL MARKETING

The consumer society is really a twentieth-century phenomenon, and for the past century or so, many businesses have made decisions based on the assumptions that one generation will grow up and make the same kinds of choices made by the group that went before them at the same stages of life.

Modern marketing's definition of *generation* is composed of two disparate parts. First, there's the traditional definition used by demographers as the number of people in any age group and what that portends about the size and shape of tomorrow's markets. Second, there's the issue of shared attitudes, a common history, and formative experiences. Both definitions are important to marketers of life. Most agree a *generation* usually is defined as 30 years and extends past a single decade. Demographers are beginning to agree that Gen Xers were born between 1964 and 1984.

Marketers think experiences bind people that are born in continuous years into *cohorts*—a group of individuals who have a demographic statistic in common. Demographers like to package things in a way that's easy to measure, and date of birth is the easiest way to define generations. Generational marketing people take the statistical analysis of births and overlay major world events that occurred during a generation's formative years to construct a picture of a generation's personality.[15] Knowing how many babies are born and then tracing the numbers through different stages of their lives give marketers a rough idea of the challenges and opportunities over 10, 20, and even 30 years.

Researchers have concentrated on four generations mentioned earlier (Matures, Boomers, and Generations X and Y), and are beginning to learn about the Millennials (Gen. Z). There are distinct differences in how each generation thinks and buys.

The values of Matures are close to what are considered classic American values: They favor a kind of Puritan work ethic, with plenty of self-sacrifice, teamwork, conformity for the common good, and so forth.

The Boomers, on the other hand, are self-assured and self-absorbed. They are much better educated than any generation before them, and they are aware of this. They think they are more sophisticated and believe they know better than their predecessors. They are very self-conscious about changing the world and fixing things.

Generation X Generation Xers were born in the post–Baby Boom with the leading edge approaching their early-forties; currently, about 44 percent are married, and almost half are parents. This generation was a long time media whipping post, once decried as overeducated slackers. Recent Yankelovich Partners research finds Xers to be self-reliant, entrepreneurial, techno focused, media savvy, socially tolerant, and slowly, but surely, parents. Growing up with skyrocketing divorce rates and with less than family stability, Gen Xers have been more cautious about entering the life stage of family formation. As a result, today's Xers are reinventing the traditionalism they are bringing to family life. Generation X is not a life stage; it is a birth group ultimately moving through life stages.

Research indicates they are much more likely than their Boomer counterparts were some 20 years ago to want to return to traditional standards across a number of domains, especially family life. Their homes will be practical and utilitarian; pragmatic concerns outweigh "home as a showplace" considerations. For instance, the kitchen will be more about convenience. The dining room is a victim of Xer lifestyle components: fast-paced lives, multitasking (consuming food and media at the same time), and the proliferation of "home meal replacement" options. There will be a trend toward "great rooms" that can be used for many purposes. Marketers have begun shifting their views as these changing self-concepts evolve from care-free kids to obligation-bound parents. A recent ad campaign cleverly highlighted markers of this life stage transition, focusing on events such as the first time a man is called "sir," and the first time one doesn't get carded at a bar; the ad touts sporty cars that will "make the other soccer moms talk." Regardless of the specifics, the bottom line is that a generation moving to a new life stage is always a catalyst for social change.[17]

Gen Y (Echo Boomers)   Although demographers debate cutoff dates, most calculations place Gen Y (also called Echo Boomers) as those born from 1979 to 1995. By 2010, the 12 to 19 age group will have expanded to a historic peak of 35 million. Baby Boomers number 77 million, and Gen Xers are estimated to be about 40 million. However, they outspend all previous generations. According to *USA Today*, they're techno-savvy, coddled, optimistic, prone to abrupt shifts in taste, and tough to pigeonhole. Take music for example: Boomers, embroiled in civil rights battles, antiwar protests, and sexual liberation, launched a rock revolution in the sixties. Gen X, mired in a depressed economy, turned to angry, brooding grunge. Gen Y, marinating in financial fitness, fancies peppy rock.[18]

Generation Y is the first generation to come along that's big enough to hurt a Boomer brand simply by giving it a cold shoulder. This generation is more racially diverse: One in three is not Caucasian. Marketers will have to learn to think like they do—and not like the Boomer parents.[19]

Toyota, whose Camry and other models are popular among older buyers, is looking ahead to the next generation of potential customers. Recently, Toyota introduced its inexpensive boxy Scion line to appeal to buyers in their twenties. It appears to be working. The average buyer's age for Toyota is 47, and the Toyota Scion's average buyer is significantly lower at 39. The Scion is riding the California youth car fad known as "JDM," short for Japanese Domestic Market. Originally, the term referred to car-customization parts only available in Japan. The JDM look is in as the clever look for those who want to move to something new. All automobile producers understand that if they misfire with Generation Y, they will miss the largest cohort of consumers to come along since the post–World War II baby boom.[20] Toyota realizes that its average customer is among the oldest in the industry.

Generation Z   Generation Z will come from a wider mix of backgrounds and will bring different experiences for marketers to understand. By 2010, marketers will have to start all over again to figure out how to impress this new generation.

Why is all of this important to advertising people?

No company provides a better object lesson in the importance of staying relevant than Levi Strauss & Co., one of America's great brands. Levi's lost more than half its share of the American jeans market during the 1990s, and its sales fell 28 percent between 1996 and 1999 alone. According to John Hancock Financial's CEO, David D'Alessandro, Levi's failed to invest in Gen X and the Echo Boom. It didn't catch on to the fact that kids no longer wore the tight-legged jeans. It didn't offer this target anything of value to distinguish them from the previous generation.[21] Without an accurate view of generations, you are likely to misinterpret what you see in the marketplace. In Exhibit 4.6, Asics "My reflection. My shoe." ad says, "I admit it. Sometimes when I run by a window I turn around and look at it. Not to admire myself. And how I look. But just to nod at the person running 'cause I know I'll see them tomorrow." Certainly, this ad is talking directly to the target. Marketers need to know all about generations. The consumer marketplace is no longer the homo-

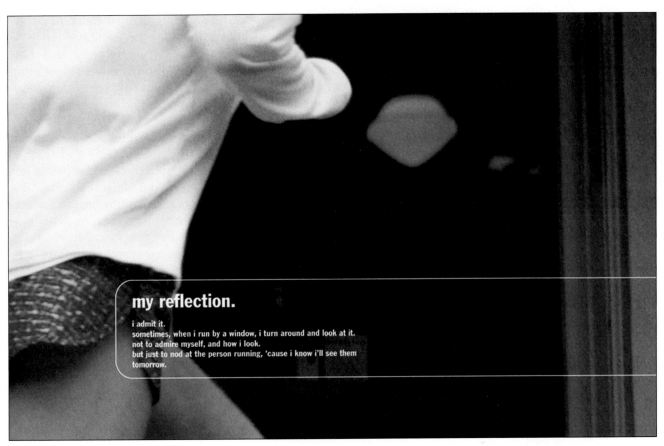

my reflection.

i admit it.
sometimes, when i run by a window, i turn around and look at it.
not to admire myself, and how i look.
but just to nod at the person running, 'cause i know i'll see them
tomorrow.

EXHIBIT 4.6

Asics talks directly to a target's lifestyle.

Courtesy of VitroRobertson, Inc., Asics, and James Schwartz, photographer.

geneous marketplace of the 1950s and early 1960s that was dominated by Matures. The Xers' view of convenience has moved from the Matures' "do it quickly" and the Boomers' "do it efficiently" to their own "eliminate the task."[22]

Marketing Concept and Targeting

We've already said you cannot operate in every market and satisfy every consumer need. Companies generally find that it is necessary to divide the market into major market segments, evaluate them, and then target those segments it can best serve. This focus on specific groups of buyers is called market segmentation. It is an extension of the **marketing concept,** defined by Philip Kotler, that achieving organizational goals depends on determining the needs and wants of target markets and delivering the desired satisfactions more effectively and efficiently than competitors. This idea has been stated as "find a need and fill it" or "make what you sell instead of trying to sell what you can make." Advertisers have expressed this concept in colorful ways; for example, Burger King said, "Have It Your Way," and United Airlines said, "You're the Boss."[23]

marketing concept
A management orientation that views the needs of consumers as primary to the success of a firm.

The old marketing concept—the management philosophy first articulated in the 1950s—is a relic of an earlier period of economic history. Most of its assumptions are no longer appropriate in the competitive global markets of today. The world is rapidly moving toward a pattern of economic activity based on long-term relationships and partnerships among economic factors in the loose coalition frameworks of network organizations. The concept of customer value is at the heart of the new marketing concept and must be the central element of all business strategy.

As we look at the differences, the old marketing concept had the objective of making a sale, whereas under the new marketing concept, the objective is to develop a customer relationship in which the sale is only the beginning. Under both marketing concepts, market segmentation, marketing targeting, and positioning are essential requirements for effective strategic planning. In the new marketing concept, the focus is sharpened by adding the idea of the value proposition.[24]

Market-driven companies need to understand how customer needs and company capabilities converge to form the customer's definition of value. This is more than a philosophy; it is a way of doing business. It includes customer orientation, market intelligence, distinctive competencies, value delivery, market targeting and the value proposition, customer-defined total quality management, profitability rather than sales volume, relationship management, continuous improvement, and a customer-focused organizational structure.[25]

Marketing databases are helping companies deliver one-to-one relationships not previously available. They include comprehensive data about individual customers' and prospects' sales histories, as well as demographics and psychographics. Interest by marketers has changed from simply getting people to switch brands to figuring ways to keep from losing current customers by continually trying to meet their needs.

Radio frequency identification (RFID) tags are a new type of bar code with tremendous data implications for tracking products and understanding how they are used by consumers. An RFID tag is a small strip of plastic containing a computer chip and radio antenna. The chip holds up to 96 characters and identifies the article to which it is attached. The antenna sends information to a receiver, which transfers the information to a computer for tracking analysis. It is a very advanced bar code. The long-term implication is enormous because the tag might tell companies what is being bought and where the product goes once bought. Down the road, stores may be able to track products beyond store shelves—perhaps learning which clothes you wear to work, which you wear to party, and where your clothes go.[26] The world of marketing is constantly changing.

What Is a Product?

Let us define a product as a bundle of ingredients put together for sale as something useful to a consumer. You don't go into a store to buy SD alcohol 40-B, butane, hydrofluorocarbon 152A, fragrance, isopropyle myristate, and so on. Many guys do, however, go into a store and buy AXE deodorant body spray. It is more than a physical object. It represents a bundle of satisfactions—a product that helps fight body odor all over.

Some of these satisfactions are purely functional—a watch to tell time or a car for transportation. Some of the satisfactions are psychological—a car may represent status and a watch may represent a piece of beautiful jewelry. Different people have different ideas about which satisfactions are important. Products are often designed with satisfactions to match the interests of a particular group of consumers. We are also judged in large measure by our physical possessions—think of your attitude toward Mercedes, BMW, Jaguar, and so on. The products that we purchase say something about us and group us with people who seek similar satisfactions from life and products. As we match people and benefits, we create product loyalty that insulates us against competitive attack.

The yearly 25,000-plus new products have a difficult time finding a place in the market. The manufacturer must be selective in defining the most profitable market segments because the cost of introducing a new product can be expensive. New products need to be well thought out and a key is to innovate brands that are sustainable. One such failure in the soft-drink industry is Surge, Coke's much-hyped rival to Mountain Dew. Surge was introduced in 1997, and sales soared to 70 million cases. In 2003, Surge had almost faded out of the U.S. market. There are numerous ways to estimate the chances of getting a heavy user of another brand to try a new brand. One technique is to define market segments according to their brand loyalty and preference for national over private brands. Studies of packaged goods brand loyalty found six such segments:[27]

1. *National-brand loyal.* Members of this segment buy primarily a single national brand at its regular price.

2. *National-brand deal.* This segment is similar to the national-brand-loyal segment, except that most of its purchases are made on deal (that is, the consumer is loyal to only national brands but chooses the least expensive one). To buy the preferred national brand on deal, the consumer engages in considerable store switching.

3. *Private-label loyal.* Consumers in this segment primarily buy the private label offered by the store in which they shop (for example, CVS, Wal-Mart, Target, Publix, and other store brands).

4. *Private-label deal.* This segment shops at many stores and buys the private label of each store, usually on a deal.

5. *National-brand switcher.* Members of this segment tend not to buy private labels. Instead, they switch regularly among the various national brands on the market.

6. *Private-label switcher.* This segment is similar to the private-label-deal segment, except that the members are not very deal prone and purchase the private labels at their regular price.

Price, product distribution, and promotion also affect the share of market coming from each competing brand. However, a new national brand would expect to gain most of its initial sales from segments 2 and 5, whereas segments 1 and 3 would normally be poor prospects to try a new brand. There are many factors to consider. But remember today a camera is not just a camera; markets change with the product, and products change with the market.

Of course, a product might actually be a service as with Paragon Home Inspections (see Exhibit 4.7).

What Is a Market?

All advertising and marketing people could easily answer this question, but you might get different answers, depending on their perspectives. For our purposes, a *market* can be defined as a group of people who can be identified by some common characteristic, interest, or problem; who could use our product to advantage; who could afford to buy it; and who can be reached through some medium.

Markets can be defined differently and broadly or narrowly. Examples of potential markets are weight watchers, golfers, mothers of young children, singles, matures, newly marrieds, skiers, tennis players, Hispanic teens, do-it-yourselfers, runners, seniors, and tourists. The *majority fallacy* is a term applied to the assumption, once frequently made, that every product should be aimed at, and acceptable to, a majority of all consumers. Research tells us that brands aimed at the majority of consumers in a given market will tend to have rather similar characteristics and will neglect an opportunity to serve the needs of consumer minorities. Take, for example, chocolate cake mixes. A good-sized group of consumers would prefer a light chocolate cake or a very dark chocolate cake, but the majority choice is a medium chocolate cake. So although several initial cake mix products would do best to market a medium chocolate cake to appeal to the broadest group of consumers, later entrants might gain a larger share by supplying the smaller but significant group with its preference.

What Is Competition?

How would you define Sierra Mist's competition? Sprite? 7UP? Mountain Dew? Bottled water? Iced tea? Starbucks' Frappuccino? It could be one or all of these products. A major purpose of target marketing is to position a brand effectively within a product category (soft drinks) or subcategory (lemon lime). We are speaking of competition in the broadest sense to include all the forces that are inhibiting the sales of a product. They may be products in the same subclass as your product,

or in the same product class, or forces outside the category of your product. Think of the toothpaste choices—brighteners, abrasives, fresh breath, fluorides, pastes, gels, peroxides, and so on. Look in the analgesic section of your supermarket. You will find many brands competing for your attention: Bayer, Aleve, Advil, Tylenol, Aspirin-Free Anacin, Empirin, Vanquish, Motrin IB, Goody's, BC, Excedrin IB, and the list goes on. Why does one consumer choose one brand and another consumer something else? How does one even get on the shelf to compete? These are very important questions to the makers of these products.

Our list of analgesics includes products in different subcategories: Bayer, Tylenol, Aleve, and Advil are each in different analgesic categories, such as aspirin, acetaminophen, naproxen, and ibuprofen. Advil and Nuprin are in the same subcategory. Does that mean they compete with only themselves? The answer is generally no. Many consumers don't even consider the subclasses; they only think in terms of pain relief. If consumers are considering only the benefits of an ibuprofen, then the answer is yes. Advil, Motrin IB, and Excedrin IB would all compete. The point is that advertisers and marketers need to try to find the answers as to which products in what categories compete for the consumer's attention and dollar. It may sound confusing because you don't know the category, but the seasoned marketer for these products knows its category and the products and the reasons people buy.

Marketers for all kinds of products and services must answer: Who are our competitors? What are their brands? What are other product categories? Are there many brands or only a few? Which are strong? Which are vulnerable? What impact, if any, do store brands and generics have? Are there any strong, long-established brands, or is the market volatile?

PLANNING THE ADVERTISING

Market Segmentation

Most would agree that one size doesn't fit all in the marketplace. Marketers can't efficiently reach every person who has a dollar to spend. It is about maximizing your potential in the marketplace by targeting your product to certain segments of the population with similar behaviors, such as people your age, gender, and with a similar lifestyle. From a communication standpoint, it is usually more difficult than you would imagine. You must understand each segment's cultural nuances and choose the right message, so you don't stereotype the service or product you're selling as one designed only for them. It has been said," If you try to talk to everyone, you'll end up talking to nobody." The division of an entire market of consumers into groups whose similarity makes them a market for products servicing their special needs is called **market segmentation.**

This classifying of consumers is generally one of the tasks of a marketing plan's **situation analysis** section, which consists of four components: a description of the current situation, an analysis of strengths, weaknesses, opportunities, and threats (SWOT), major issues, and assumptions about the future. This Ritz-Carlton ad reeks upscale in its appeal (see Exhibit 4.8). It certainly isn't aiming at the Motel 6 consumer.

market segmentation
The division of an entire market of consumers into groups whose similarity makes them a market for products serving their special needs.

situation analysis
The part of the advertising plan that answers the questions: Where are we today and how did we get here? It deals with the past and present.

EXHIBIT 4.8

The Ritz-Carlton reeks of quality as it "Raises your expectations of the hereafter."

Courtesy of Sawyer Riley Compton and The Ritz-Carlton.

Raises your expectations of the hereafter.

For reservations, call 1-800-241-3333 or visit www.ritzcarlton.com.   THE RITZ-CARLTON®

Typically the process runs through a number of steps:

Segment your market.

Target a segment.

Position your product for that segment.

Communicate your positioning.

There are a number of factors to be considered in planning advertising to take advantage of market segmentation. The first step is to determine the variable to use for dividing a market. In addition to demographics, the major means of market segmentation are geographical, product user, and lifestyle segmentation. It is common for marketers to combine more than one segmentation variable than in seeking their target. Of course, the segment has to be large enough in size to justify the marketing effort.

Geographical Segmentation Geographical segmentation, the oldest form of segmentation, designates customers by geographical area. It dates back to earlier days when distribution was the primary concern of manufacturers. Today geomarketing is of particular importance to media planners in deciding on national, regional, and local ad campaigns. It is only recently that geomarketing has been elevated to a marketing discipline the way demographics was in the 1950s and psychographics was in the 1970s. In this instance, consumers haven't changed but marketers' awareness of regional and global marketing has. Geodemographical marketing is just another way of segmenting the market for companies in search of growth.

There has been a "data explosion" on local markets. Some of the information comes from an abundant number of research services for use on merchandising and buying decisions. Many retail companies such as supermarkets practice micromarketing—treating each individual store as its own market and trading area. Often this approach translates into different ads for different markets. When thinking about geographical segmentation, advertisers have a number of categories to explore:

census trace data	areas of dominant influence (ADI)
ZIP codes	states
counties	census regions
metropolitan statistical areas	total United States

Companies that lack national distribution may consider geographical segmentation. Pro Balanced dog food is distributed primarily in the South but has to compete against national brands to survive. There are many local or regional brands that must be successful in their geographical areas to survive. Cheerwine is a cherry cola–like soft drink that is strong in its home area but would have problems in areas where its history and tradition were unknown. In the past, Cheerwine used a slogan that said, "It's a Carolina Thing." In this example, geographical segmentation is a distribution strategy rather than a promotional one.

It is not unusual for national companies to divide their advertising and marketing efforts into regional units to respond better to the competition. McDonald's uses a major advertising agency to handle its national advertising and numerous (generally smaller) agencies to handle franchise and regional efforts supplementing the national effort. Of course, we didn't mention their multicultural agencies that serve minority marketing. When McDonald's launched "i'm lovin' it," a global ad campaign using Justin Timberlake, they used a German agency. This gives McDonald's the ability to react to the marketplace by cities, regions, or individual stores as well as globally.

Product User Segmentation **Product user segmentation** is a strategy based on the amount and/or consumption patterns of a brand or category. The advertiser is interested in product usage rather than consumer characteristics. As a practical matter, most user segmentation methods are combined with demographic or lifestyle consumer identification. Here the advertiser is interested in market segments with the highest sales potential. Typically, a market segment is first divided into all users and then subdivided into heavy, medium, light users, and nonusers of the product. For example, let us look at the frequency of weekly use of fast foods:

Frequency	Adults	Men	Women
Heavy (4 plus visits)	11.4%	14.8%	8.3%
Medium (1–3 visits)	44.9	46.5	43.3
Light (less than weekly)	22.8	20.6	24.8

The definition of usage varies with the product category. For example, heavy fast-food use may be defined as four or more times per week; heavy luxury-restaurant use as once a week; and heavy seafood-restaurant use as once a week. As you can see, product user segmentation can get quite complex, but these kinds of data allow marketers to use a rifle instead of a shotgun.

Lifestyle Segmentation **Lifestyle segmentation** makes the assumption that if you live a certain way, so do your neighbors and, therefore, any smart marketer would want to target clusters filled with these clones. Lifestyle clusters are more accurate characterizations of people than any single variable would be.

The concept of lifestyle segmentation is a viable one; however, researchers are having to adjust to a sea of changes taking place among America's shopping public. For example, old attitudes toward work and leisure or fitness don't fit today's realities. As a result, segmentation researchers are changing how they view many of the new lifestyle characteristics driving this new era.[28]

Marketers have used specialized segmentation techniques to find the most fruitful target audiences since PRIZM (Potential Rating Index for ZIP Markets) in 1974 grouped people who had similar demographics and lifestyles into neighborhood clusters on the theory that "birds of a feather, flock together." A number of similar programs have popped up since—such as CACI's Acorn and SRI's VALS (**Values and Lifestyle System**)—all based on the premise that people in the same ZIP code or neighborhood tend to buy the same products. Each research company has its own terminology for the various clusters it identifies. Recently Yankelovich Partners Inc. developed a psychographic segmentation system called Monitor Mindbase. Its premise is the idea of segmenting individuals by values, attitudes, and mind-sets rather than by geography, demographics, and consumption patterns. It segments people into categories of consumers with varying degrees of materialism, ambition, orientation to family life, cynicism, openness to technology, and other elements.[29]

SummerGrove homes (see Exhibit 4.9) range from $130s to $700s and is convenient to Atlanta and the airport. If you can afford them, those are good attributes, but copywriter Amy Lokken knew the lifestyle appeal is the 18-hole championship golf course, the 100-acre lake filled with fish, acres of parks and paths, and a lazy river. The copy concludes, "Because once you're here, this award winning community won't be missing a thing."

Researchers Kevin Clancy and Robert Shulman argue that "off-the-shelf segmentation studies cannot be as good as customized segmentation done with a specific product or service in mind. VALS will help break up the world into pieces, but the pieces may or may not have any relevance for any one brand."[30]

product user segmentation
Identifying consumers by the amount of product usage.

Lifestyle segmentation
Identifying consumers by combining several demographics and lifestyles.

Values and Lifestyle System (VALS)
Developed by SRI International to cluster consumers according to several variables in order to predict consumer behavior.

One approach to determining lifestyle characteristics is to identify consumers' activities, interests, and opinions (AIO). Typical AIO measures are:

- *Activities:* hobbies or leisure-time preferences, community involvement, and preferences for social events
- *Interests:* family orientation, sports interest, and media usage
- *Opinions:* political preferences and views on various social issues.

Benefits and Attitude Segmentation Not everyone wants the same thing from a product. There isn't just a single toothpaste, because some people are interested in taste, or fresh breath, or whiteness of their teeth, or decay prevention, or tartar control for gums, or value, and so on. The objective here is to cluster people into groups based on what they want in a product.

Segmentation Risks Although segmentation is very important to successful advertising, it isn't without risks. One problem is that once the outer limits of the niche are reached, sales growth will be limited unless the company can expand beyond its niche. By too narrowly defining a market—that is, by excessive segmenting—a marketer can become inefficient in media buying, creating different ads, and obtaining alternative distribution channels. A few years ago, Taco Bell was the first fast-food chain to target people with its Value Menu. It was so successful that most other fast-food companies followed with their own Value Menus. As a result of this competition, the pool of value-conscious consumers was split among numerous companies, diluting the profit.

Target Market Sacrifice

Consultant Jack Trout says that staying focused on one target segment in a category enables you to be different by becoming the preferred product by the segment: Pepsi for the younger generation, Corvette for the generation that wants to be young, Corona beer for the yuppies on their way up, Porsche for the yuppies who have made it. When you chase after another target segment, chances are you'll chase away your original customer. Whatever you do, you should not get greedy but stay true to your product type, your attribute, or your segment.[31]

Niche marketing can serve at least two purposes. It can gain a product entry into a larger market by attacking a small part of it not being served by the competition. It can also cater to latent needs that existing products do not adequately satisfy.

Niche Marketing

Niches usually are smaller groups of consumers with more narrowly defined needs or unique combinations. But **niche marketing** is not another buzzword for marketing segmentation, says Alvin Achenbaum.[32] It is essentially a flanking strategy, the essence of which is to engage competitors in those product markets where they are weak or, preferably, have little or no presence. The guiding principle of niche marketing is to pit your strength against the competitor's weakness. No-frill motels did not exist for many years, but they were logical means of competing against other motel segments. Red Roof Inn opened its motels with an ad claiming "Sleep Cheap," and positioned itself to value consumers not wanting to pay high prices for a place to sleep. Later they even made fun of hotels placing a chocolate mint on your pillow for an extra $30 or $40. Today, most major hotel chains have moved into that niche with their own no-frills express motels.

niche marketing
A combination of product and target market strategy. It is a flanking strategy that focuses on niches or comparatively narrow windows of opportunity within a broad product market or industry. Its guiding principle is to pit your strength against their weakness.

Heart Attack Niche Niche marketers may create a specific product through variations of their product to meet a specific niche's needs. For example, Bayer aspirin created an adult low-strength tablet for aspirin regimen users. Research indicated that second heart attacks were greatly reduced by simply taking an aspirin daily. The only problem was that regular use of aspirin by some people resulted in stomach problems. A regular aspirin tablet consisted of 325 milligrams. The doctor-recommended daily therapy for patients having suffered an initial heart attack was 81 milligrams. Adults started taking children's aspirin, which was 81 milligrams, to prevent stomach problems and yet get the advantage of heart attack protection. As a result of this consumer action, Bayer introduced Bayer enteric aspirin, which was 81 milligrams and protects the stomach.

Brand marketers seeking new niche opportunities should pay attention to marketing basics: changing shopping trends, demographics, marketing strategy, and delivery on commitments.[33]

Each niche offers challenges for advertisers. When trying to develop niche marketing to Asians, understanding of cultural and language issues is required, as we have indicated.

Companies can build growth out of finding small niches to serve consumers' needs. For example, Kimberly-Clark launched Huggies Pull-Ups training pants in 1989. In 1994, it launched Goodnites for older children who wet the bed. In 1997, it introduced Huggies Little Swimmers designed to survive swimming. The niche for

This so-called miracle drug has been marked for many niche uses over the product's life including the "heart niche."

Huggies Little Swimmers is a very narrow category segment. Originally, Procter & Gamble said the training pants niche was too small, but it has grown to a $400 million segment within the disposable diaper category.[34]

An Example of Narrow Segmentation: Bobos

In segmentation, marketers may slice the population very narrowly to find very specific groups. One example of such segmentation is *Bobos,* which is short for Bourgeois Bohemian. David Brooks coined this term in 2000 in his book, *Bobos in Paradise.* Professor Richard Florida writes about them in *The Rise of the Creative Class.* In defining Bobos, these creative people seem to have combined the countercultural 1960s and the achieving 1980s into one social ethos. This group is 38 million strong and is comprised of people working in a range of fields from science to entertainment, but all are employed to create new ideas, new technology, and new content. Typically, these people don't work 9-to-5 jobs, since they are working on projects with deadlines. Generally, age isn't a defining factor and they are highly educated. Doug Cameron, strategist at Amalgamated ad agency, says that Bobos go for the functionally extreme. He says that rather than buying any refrigerator, they'll buy an $8,000 Sub Zero. Most Bobos' income exceeds $75,000 annually, but many earn above $150,000. They tend to cluster in communities with certain characteristics and share common consumption habits. The group favors brands such as Jet Blue Airways, Volkswagen, and Apple computers. Cameron says the top 10 Bobo markets include San Francisco, Seattle, Boston, Austin, San Diego, Washington, DC, Chapel Hill–Raleigh–Durham, New York, Minneapolis, and Denver.[34] One method marketers use to find Bobos is by looking at educational levels and Starbucks per capita, culled from the census data.

POSITIONING

Positioning has to be done with a target in mind. You position a product in the mind of a specific prospect. **Positioning** is another term for fitting the product into the lifestyle of the buyer. It refers to segmenting a market by either or both of two ways: (1) creating a product to meet the needs of a specialized group, and/or (2) identifying and advertising a feature of an existing product that meets the needs of a specialized group.

Estrovite vitamins recognized a potential problem among women on birth control pills and created a product positioned to fulfill that need. The headline read, "Your birth control pills could be robbing you of essential vitamins and minerals." The copy explained why.

Sometimes products don't quite work out in testing. The original Nyquil was created as a superior daytime cough suppressant. It had a slight flaw. The product made people drowsy. In an attempt to regain product development costs, the side effect of drowsiness was transformed into a powerful positioning strategy. It became "the nighttime, coughing, sniffling, sneezing so you can rest" medicine. As a result, Nyquil created a new category resulting in the ownership of the nighttime cold remedy market.

The purpose of positioning is giving a product a meaning that distinguishes it from other products and induces people to want to buy it. Positioning is what you do to the mind of the consumer. Specifically, you position the product in the mind of the prospect. You want your positioning to be in harmony with the lifestyles and values we have discussed. It is necessary to understand what motivates people to buy in the product category—what explains their behavior. It is also necessary to understand the degree to which the product satisfies the target's needs.[35] One automobile may be positioned as a sports car, another as a luxury sports car, another as the safest family car, and still another as a high-performance vehicle.

It is possible for some products to successfully hold different positions at the same time. Arm & Hammer baking soda has been positioned as a deodorizer for refrigerators, an antacid, a freezer deodorizer, and a bath skin cleanser without losing its original market as a cooking ingredient.

You might try to get the following reactions from consumers to a new line of frozen entrees that are low in calories, sodium, and fat, and have larger servings than the competition's. Before seeing your advertising, the consumer thinks:

> I like the convenience and taste of today's frozen foods but I don't usually get enough of the main course to eat. I would like to try a brand that gives me plenty to eat but is still light and healthy—and, most important, it has to taste great.

After being exposed to your advertising, the consumer thinks:

> I may buy Ru's Frozen Food entrees. They taste great and I get plenty to eat, and they are still low enough in calories that I don't feel I'm overeating. They're better for me because they have less sodium and fat than others. Also, there is enough variety so that I can eat the foods I like without getting bored by the same old thing.

HOW TO APPROACH A POSITIONING PROBLEM

As you would expect, not all products lend themselves to the type of positioning discussed here. The advertiser must be careful not to damage current product image by changing appeals and prematurely expanding into new markets. Jack Trout and

positioning
Segmenting a market by creating a product to meet the needs of a select group or by using a distinctive advertising appeal to meet the needs of a specialized group, without making changes in the physical product.

Al Ries, who have written about positioning for several decades, say that the advertiser who is thinking about positioning should ask the following questions:[37]

- What position, if any, do we already own in the prospect's mind?
- What position do we want to own?
- What companies must be outgunned if we are to establish that position?
- Do we have enough marketing money to occupy and hold that position?
- Do we have the guts to stick with one consistent positioning concept?
- Does our creative approach match our positioning strategy?

According to David Aaker, the most used positioning strategy is to associate an object with a product attribute or characteristic (see Exhibit 4.10). Developing such associations is effective because when the attribute is meaningful, the association can directly translate into reasons to buy the brand. Crest toothpaste became the leader by building a strong association with cavity control in part created by an endorsement of the American Dental Association. BMW has talked about performance with its tag line: "The Ultimate Driving Machine." Mercedes: "The Ultimate Engineered Car." Hyundai: "Cars That Make Sense." The positioning problem is usually finding an attribute important to a major segment and not already claimed by a competitor.[37] Philip Kotler says many companies advertise a major single benefit position, for example, best quality, best performance, most durable, fastest, least expensive, and so on. In automobiles Mercedes owns the "most prestigious" position, BMW the "best driving performance," Hyundai owns the "least expensive," and Volvo owns the "safest." They also claim to be one of the most durable.[39]

Following up on this, David Martin, founder of the Marin agency, says to think about Volvo for a minute. What is its core identity? Which benefits stand out and should be featured? What is the emotion the target feels from the brand? Would you agree with Volvo being the "safest" car? The car handles well, has speed and styling, with many-built in safety features that include sturdy construction. Reassurance — appeal to the basic instinct of fear. *I feel better because my daughter drives a Volvo.* Martin also says if you do your homework on the brand you may be able to fill in the following blanks for developing a brand positioning statement.[40]

To the (target market), (brand name here), is the brand of (frame of reference) with (benefits and attributes) that (sustainable and emotional point of difference).

Or, To the *car owner, Volvo* is the brand of *automobile* with *all the style, power, and comfort you want* that is *built to be safe.*

POSITIONING EXAMPLES

- Dove soap is the moisturizing beauty bar.
- Allstate insurance is the good hands people.
- Cheer is the detergent for all temperatures.
- Intel is the computer inside.
- Ace hardware is the helpful place.
- Bloomingdale's is like no other store in the world.
- Milk-Bone dog biscuits clean teeth and freshen breath.

Some marketers frequently alter a brand's positioning for the sake of change. This is especially unfortunate for those brands that are firmly entrenched and successful because their reason for being is widely accepted. In the past, a number of positioning statements were successful but were dropped; "Good to the Last Drop," "Pepperidge Farm Remembers," and "Two Mints in One" are examples. These campaigns were revised long after they were discontinued because they truly represented the consumer end benefit and character of the brand.[41]

Profile of the Market

Up to this point, we have discussed market segments. Now we examine the overall **market profile** for a product. First, we determine the overall usage of the product type. This is usually defined in terms of dollars, sales, number of units sold, or percentage of households that use such a product. Then we determine if the category is growing, stagnant, or declining. We compare our share of the market to the competition. Next we ask what the market share trends have been over the past several years. Finally, we want to know the chief product advantage featured by each brand.

When you look at market share, beware as to whether you are looking at a brand's share or a company's share. For example, in the soft-drink market in late

market profile
A demographic and psychographic description of the people or the households of a product's market. It may also include economic and retailing information about a territory.

August 2003, convenience store share indicated Coke Classic had a 15.7 percent share, Pepsi-Cola a 15.3 percent share, and Mountain Dew was third with 12.4 percent. But the share drops when we get to the fourth brand, Dr Pepper, with a 7.9 percent share. These were followed by Diet Coke with 6.7 percent, Diet Pepsi with 5.3 percent, and Sprite with 4.8 percent. A surprise new brand, Mountain Dew LiveWire, had a 2.5 percent share, but this was due to the heavy introduction of the brand, which hasn't maintained the sales. Rounding out the top 10 were Diet Mountain Dew (2.0 percent share) and Diet Dr Pepper (1.7 percent share). A marketer with a leading share in a product category and a marketer with a very small share will probably approach advertising in very different ways.[42]

Despite a $500 million marketing launch in 2001, which was more than the entire product category spent in 2002, Microsoft's Xbox two years later had only a 24 percent share of the video console market. Sony held a 54 percent share of the market.

It is important for the advertiser to know not only the characteristics of the product's market but also similar information about media alternatives. Most major newspapers, magazines, and broadcast media provide demographic and product user data for numerous product categories. Database marketing is giving the marketer an abundance of information on which to base integrated promotional decisions.

PROFILE OF THE BUYER

Earlier in this chapter we highlighted ethnic groups (Hispanics, African Americans, and Asians) that were largely ignored by advertisers in the past, but their increasing numbers demand attention in today's marketplace. The Xers, Boomers, teenagers, college students, and the 50-plus markets are all studied by smart advertisers to understand their potential for specific products and services. As indicated, these groups of consumers are not necessarily easy to understand or reach with effective integrated programs. Not all Boomers act the same, and all Gen Yers don't respond to messages in the same manner.

Advertisers have to look at demographics and lifestyles, for starters, to understand any market.

Teens have been called the most active target in the world. As a group they spend over $175 billion on themselves. Their disposable income keeps growing. A 2003 study indicated that males spend $71 a week and females almost $62. Among teens ages 13 to 18, 82 percent have computers, 62 percent have video consoles, and 49 percent have cell phones. Growing up with the Internet, cell phones, and other new information receptacles, teens are multitaskers assimilating multiple marketing communications simultaneously. It goes without saying that the Internet is a vital part of the teen marketing mix. Marketers believe it is necessary to create product interaction rather than regular product advertising. "You have to figure out a way to permeate the teen lifestyle without being gratuitous," says Chip Lange, vice president of marketing. Mountain Dew teamed up with Microsoft Xbox to create the Dew Den at the Mall of America allowing gamers to try the latest games and compete in Xbox tournaments. "Gaming as a lifestyle is so relevant. It is about the same thing Dew is: pushing the limits, being over-the-top, irreverent," says Mt. Dew's brand director. The company spent over $60 million on media advertising in 2002.[43] It never takes a marketing step without talking to its target first. Teens are a fickle, seemingly sophisticated, fast-moving market.

Demography is the study of vital economic and sociological statistics about people. In advertising, demographic reports refer to those facts relevant to a per-

Demographic		Regular		Diet	
		Cola	Other	Cola	Other
Total	181	60.3	43.3	42.2	29.2
Sex:	Male	65.5	46.1	38.6	27.8
	Female	55.5	40.5	45.6	30.4
Age:	18–24	72.5	50.4	32.7	24.4
	25–34	67.6	48.8	42.5	30.1
	35–44	62.6	45.1	45.2	29.3
	45–64	55.9	39.2	42.6	29.2
	65+	46.3	34.5	41.2	29.2
Region:	Northeast	59.8	45.3	37.6	27.7
	South	65.0	42.2	41.8	26.9
	West	57.2	43.4	42.2	31.5
Race:	White	58.9	41.1	43.5	29.1
	Black	69.3	55.4	35.7	27.2

EXHIBIT 4.11

Selected Demographics of Regular and Diet Soft Drink Average Weekly Consumption for Specific Types (in percentages)

Courtesy of Radio Advertising Bureau.

son's use of a product. Exhibit 4.11 presents a snippet of average weekly regular and diet soft-drink demographics.

The selected soft-drink demographics probably offer few surprises to you. However, be sure to examine the differences in regular and diet consumption between males and females, or between consumers ages 18 to 24 and older, and compare regional differences for starters. You can begin to understand how demographic differences could be important factors in advertising strategy and expenditure decisions.

Heavy Users

Take any product category and you will find that a small percentage of users is responsible for a disproportionately large share of sales. The principle of heavy usage is sometimes referred to as the 80/20 rule—that is, 80 percent of the units sold are purchased by only 20 percent of the consumers. Few products meet this exactly, but Kraft's Miracle Whip comes fairly close. And the most avid Miracle Whip customers live in the Midwest. So Kraft knows who buys the most and where they live. Of course, the exact figure varies with each product and product category, but the 80/20 rule is representative of most product sales. In the case of Diet Coke, 8 percent of the households account for 84 percent of the volume—rather significant information. Keeping that small segment loyal to Diet Coke is smart marketing, pure and simple. Heavy users are identified not only by who they are but also by when they buy and where they are located. Of course, another issue for marketers is not only how to reach these consumers but also what to say or do once they make contact.

The following table shows that the heavy users of brand X are women aged 55 and older. In addition, the most effective selling is done from January through June in the East Central and Pacific regions. Obviously, heavy users are an important part of the market; however, they are also the group most advertisers are trying to target and, therefore, the competition can be fierce and expensive. Some advertisers find that aiming for a less lucrative segment—medium or light users—may offer more reasonable expectations. A marketer cannot just assume the best prospects are 18- to 49-year-old women, heavy users, or people similar to current customers. Instead, marketers need to carefully study their target audience in great depth. In defining their market, then, they must determine who the heavy users are and identify their similarities, which would define the marketing goal.

Users of Brand X

1. Target Audience: Current Consumers

Women	Pop. (%)	Consumption (%)	Index (100 = national average)
18–24	17.5	5.0	29
25–34	21.9	10.1	46
35–54	30.1	24.0	80
55+	30.5	61.0	200
Total	100.0	100.0	

2. Geography: Current Sales

Area	Pop. (%)	Consumption (%)	Index
Northeast	24	22	92
East Central	15	18	120
West Central	17	16	94
South	27	24	89
Pacific	17	20	118
Total	100	200	

3. Seasonality

Period	Jan.–Mar.	Apr.–Jun.	Jul.–Sept.	Oct.–Nov.
Consumption (%)	30	36	20	14
Index	120	144	80	—

BEYOND DEMOGRAPHICS: PSYCHOGRAPHICS

When driving through any suburban area past modest-sized yards of middle-class homes, one is struck first by their similarity. But a harder look is more illuminating, for behind the similarities lie differences that reflect the interests, personalities, and family situations of those who live in such homes. One yard has been transformed into a carefully manicured garden. Another includes some shrubs and bushes, but most of the yard serves as a relaxation area, with outdoor barbecue equipment and the like. A third yard is almost entirely a playground, with swings, trapezes, and slides. A swimming pool occupies almost all the space in another yard. A tennis court occupies yet another. Still another has simply been allowed to go to seed and is overgrown and untended by its obviously indoor-oriented owners.

Although the neighborhood consists of homes of similar style, age, and value, the people are not all the same. If you want to advertise to this neighborhood, you would be speaking to people with different interests and different tastes. There may be a big difference in the nature and extent of purchases between any two groups of buyers that have the same demographic characteristics. The attempt to explain the significance of such differences has led to an inquiry beyond demographics into psychographics. **Psychographics**—studying lifestyles—sharpens the search for prospects beyond demographic data. It has been said that lifestyle information gives the soul of the person. Good creative people can devise copy that appeals to a specific segment's lifestyle interest. The media are then selected, and advertising is directed to that special target group or groups. Put very simply, lifestyle information gives the soul of a person; demographics alone gives only a skeleton and not a whole person.

psychographics
A description of a market based on factors such as attitudes, opinions, interests, perceptions, and lifestyles of consumers comprising that market.

Target Audience: Beyond Demographics

Let us look at an example of a travel advertiser's defined target. This profile is based on the advertiser's research that helped define those people most likely to visit the area.

Research indicated that the basic demographic guideline for the consumer target is households with a combined household income of $35,000 or more. Households with less than $35,000 simply do not have the discretionary income necessary for vacation travel.

The other qualifiers in defining a consumer **target audience** are lifestyle and geography:

Primary vacation travelers—vacation travelers who take a one-week plus vacation during the primary season (summer).

Weekend travelers—those people living in states within close proximity who can be attracted during the fall, winter, and spring seasons.

Mature market (50-plus)—people who have both the discretionary income and available time to travel.

Business travelers—businesspeople coming to an area on business who can be encouraged to either extend their stay for pleasure travel purposes or to bring their spouse and family along.

International travelers—Canada provides an enormous influx of visitors. Also, the increasing number of international flights to and from the area provide increasing opportunities.

What is the target for the Callaway Gardens tourism ad in Exhibit 4.12?

target audience
That group that composes the present and potential prospects for a product or service.

Psychographic Research

Today there is much more refined information available. Agency research information includes syndicated research from outside sources, client's research, and the agency's own resources. Syndicated research services specialize in different types of information on what types of products people buy and which brands, who buys them and their demographic and psychographic distinctions, a comparison of heavy and light users, how people react to products and to ads, and people's styles of buying and what media reach them.

Lifestyle categories are numerous. Data categories are available through syndicated research to advertisers and their agencies to help them select the target market. This information is available on a market-by-market basis defining both demographic and lifestyle information. Some of the categories indicating the percentage of household activities include:

- Credit card usage for travel and entertainment, bank cards, gas and department store usage
- Good life activities, which include such activities as attending cultural or arts events, foreign travel, gourmet cooking and fine food interests, stock investments, antique interest, wines
- High-tech activities and usage, which involve home computers, watching cable TV, DVD recording and viewing, photography interests
- Sports and leisure activities by households, which include bicycling, boating, golf, bowling, tennis, jogging
- Outdoor activities, which include the number of households in a specific market involved in camping, fishing, motorcycling, environmental interests
- Domestic activities such as gardening, Bible and devotional reading, coin collecting, pets, sewing, crafts, reading

EXHIBIT 4.12

Why does someone need to visit a Garden resort of 40 acres of flowers?

Courtesy of Sawyer Riley Compton and Callaway Gardens.

SHE ASKS,

"HAVE I GAINED WEIGHT?"

YOU HESITATE.

Why do you need 40 acres of flowers?

❧ Callaway Gardens

For reservations call 1.800.CALLAWAY or visit callawaygardens.com.

Test Marketing

Although extremely helpful, psychographic research cannot replace market testing as the ultimate guide to successful advertising and marketing. Manufacturers seldom introduce new products without doing some prior testing. This kind of testing helps determine if consumers will really purchase a product or react to specific advertising and promotional activities.

It is difficult to say which cities are best for testing. Ira Weinblatt, a Saatchi & Saatchi senior vice president, says, "You can't say one place represents everything because there are so many different lifestyles." Some cities are historically popular for test marketing. The Midwest has been popular because, geographically, it is the heartland of America. Each test market represents a kind of microcosm of America. Saatchi & Saatchi ranks the top-performing test markets. To make the list:

A city's demographics must fall within 20 percent of the national average.

The city should be somewhat isolated.

Local media should be relatively inexpensive.

Greater Goldsboro, North Carolina

Legendary Treasures

Rumor has it that Andy Griffith was a high school teacher in the sleepy little town of Goldsboro before he moved on to "keep the peace" in Mayberry.

Folks still talk about Sherman's invasion of Goldsboro during the War Between the States.

Local legend suggests that barbecue was born here. And...mystery still shrouds the towering, majestic Cliffs of the Neuse River, known around these parts as North Carolina's natural wonder.

Pull up a chair and listen to our legends, but let me warn you. If you don't like long civil war stories, lip-smacking barbecue and lots of interesting characters, you might not like what you hear.

Greater Goldsboro
NORTH CAROLINA

EXHIBIT 4.13

The Greater Goldsboro Travel and Tourism Department touts the nature of the area, people, and its barbecue.

Courtesy of Bright Ideas Group, Inc. and The Greater Goldsboro Travel and Tourism Department.

Citizens should not be extremely loyal to any particular brand.

Supermarkets should be impartial enough to give new products good display on their shelves.

Milwaukee, one of the test market cities that historically makes the list, is popular because the newspapers offer marketers the flexibility to split production runs. This allows advertisers to test up to four ads at a time and to experiment with run-of-the-paper color or freestanding inserts. Typically, researchers examine purchases for a number of weeks before ads run, during the period of the test, and afterward.

The perils of introducing a product nationally without test marketing include failure. This can be extremely expensive, and most marketers are not willing to take that risk without some type of testing. In the late nineties Pepsi-Cola took its lemon-lime Storm into 11 test markets over two years without success. Pepsi also tested a lemon-lime cola called Pepsi Twist in mid-2000. The test was in Minneapolis and San Antonio using television and FSI (freestanding inserts) support. What makes Twist an interesting product is the fact that it was viewed as a possible in-and-out seasonal product and continues to be a niche product today. Pepsi replaced Storm with caffeine-free Sierra Mist, which is now available nationally.

KLEPPNER VIEWPOINT 4.1

BY MICHAEL MARTIN

Director of Marketing Programs
Employease

Using the Net to Target Customers

We're a different kind of company. Before we talk about how we do marketing, I'll tell you what we are about. Based in Atlanta, Employease is an Internet provider of human resources benefits and payroll solutions. Employease takes full advantage of the Internet's power to facilitate communication and connectivity between employers, employees, managers, benefits carriers, and service providers. For example, our clients view their employees' work-related data to process hirings, promotions, and terminations with HR approval. Similarly, employees enroll in benefits programs and update contact information online. HR manages and reports on data while controlling all access. Employease helps over 1,000 customers reduce administrative costs, improve service to employees and, most importantly, increase focus on strategic HR.

Our first marketing effort sent out e-mails soliciting business, with little response. We went back and tweaked the message and received over 1,500 replies in several hours—that's direct response.

What we do here is different from what the industry has traditionally done in marketing to prospects. My previous agency and corporate advertising and marketing jobs required that we plan marketing programs well in advance of implementation. Of course, we then had to produce the materials and deliver them to the appropriate targets. Once you had one of your marketing programs operating you could easily justify the program, but it was difficult to adjust an ongoing program. You just didn't have a lot of marketing flexibility.

Today, my job is to develop campaigns that create interest in our products and drive sales. Most of our programs are electronically focused using e-mail, online seminars, and reference forums.

One of the most cost-effective tools we use is online seminars. They are similar to a talk-radio show where you

Michael Martin

can listen to a live interview with one of our customers and then ask questions yourself. It is similar to the testimonial copy technique. The listener can find out what our customer's situation was before we were hired and how we solved their problems. It really works well.

The technology offers solutions more effectively than many of the practices in the past, where you rented a hotel or resort meeting room, flew in special entertainment, and spent lots of money. Today our clients can simply go to our Web site, saving time and travel. This is a new way of doing business-to-business marketing. It is evidence that we're in a changing world.

In my job I have to rely on my past experiences and gut, but I have to test and monitor everything I do. As with any marketing communication, you must know your target's issues so you can understand their needs. ■ ■ ■

 **SUMMARY**

The accurate identification of current and prospective users of a product will often mean the difference between success and failure. The targeting of advertising to these prospects in an efficient media plan with appropriate creativity is critical.

This chapter has concentrated on fundamentals: Who are the prospects? What is a market? What about competition? Positioning? Numerous methods of examining segmentation and other important considerations in planning integrated marketing programs have been discussed. Understanding these basic concerns through research is part of the process. Research is the key to successful target marketing. Market research to define prime market segments, product research to meet the needs of these segments, and advertising research to devise the most appropriate messages are mandatory for the success of a firm in a competitive environment. Also, we need to be familiar with the multitude of research services providing data for aiding our planning.

Ads are aimed at consumers with a rifle instead of a shotgun approach. It is becoming easier to tailor messages through a variety of special interest media vehicles.

Advertisers place more importance on lifestyle characteristics than on demographic factors. Advertisers recognize that purchase behavior is the result of a number of complex psychological and sociological factors that cannot be explained by a superficial list of age, sex, income, or occupational characteristics.

Finally, we need to keep abreast of changes in population and better understand such important segments as Hispanics, Asians, and African Americans as well as generational groups. This kind of knowledge will lead to better communications and targeting. We need to know more than simply numbers and location. We need to understand consumer lifestyles, identities, and motivations.

 ## REVIEW

1. What is target marketing?

2. What is market segmentation?

3. What is multicultural marketing?

4. What is positioning?

5. What is the 80/20 rule as it relates to target marketing?

 ## TAKE IT TO THE WEB

Visit the Pringles potato chip Web site (**www.pringles.com**) and determine what type of consumer the Web site is attempting to attract. Consider that although children may be the primary targets, they may not have the purchasing power to buy the product. How does the Web site appeal to more than one target market?

The United States Census Bureau records health, housing, income, poverty, population statistics, and more. How can information from the Census Bureau (**www.census.gov**) help you to make an informed marketing decision?

Can you think of an example of how a marketer has worked to create a variation on a product in order to attract different consumers? Wendy's fast-food chain is working to attract members of the Hispanic community by offering a version of the Web site in Spanish (**www.wendys.com**).

Compare and contrast how Duke University (**www.duke.edu**), a private college, and the University of Virginia (**www.virginia.edu**), a public college, recruit high school students via their Web sites. Are the two schools attempting to attract the same type of student?

Managing The Advertising

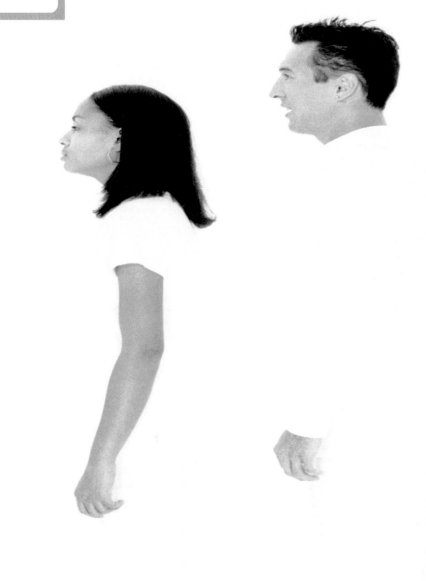

PART THREE

CHAPTER 5

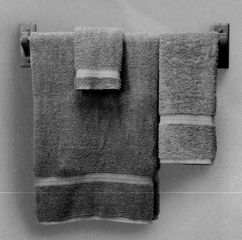

STUFFING THESE UNDER A DRAFTY DOOR IS NOT THE ANSWER. EVEN IF IT'S A CHEAP ONE YOU "BORROWED" FROM A HOTEL.

THERE'S A BETTER WAY TO CUT YOUR ELECTRIC COSTS.

FILL IN THE CRACKS

Nooks and crannies...Those gaps around doors and windows, loose fitting ducts, patches of missing insulation - all these let precious hot air out, causing more work for your heating system. Seal up your house. Purchase weather stripping, seal duct openings, and add an extra layer of insulation. The less your heating system has to work, the more money you'll have working for you. For more energy saving tips, visit www.savannahelectric.com.

SAVANNAH ELECTRIC

A SOUTHERN COMPANY

The Advertising Agency, Media Services, and Other Services

CHAPTER OBJECTIVES

Advertising agencies create most national and international advertising. The agency role and relationships are changing. After reading this chapter, you will understand:

1. the agency
2. the history of the agency business
3. the full-service agency
4. global advertising agencies
5. agency and client relationships
6. forms of agency compensation
7. other advertising services

Despite the pressures for advertising agencies to be more responsive to client needs, they continue to be the most significant companies in the development of advertising and marketing, not only in the United States but globally as well. During a time when every business is being reinvented, agencies are grappling with a number of issues: media unbundling, compensation, client loyalty, short-term pressures on the bottom line, lean structures, reorganization, and how to deal with media fragmentation and make integrated communication really work the way it was envisioned.

The changes in corporations have pressured agencies to become stronger partners in reaching advertisers' marketing and sales goals. Agencies have undergone their own reengineering, adapting to the environment in which they operate and to the clients they serve. Not only have agencies changed their structures, but also many have gobbled up specialty firms such as health care, online, mail-order, and promotion companies and other units involved in integrated communication. Make no mistake about it—it's not business as usual. Roles and relationships are changing. "We've been here before," says Keith Reinhard, chairman of DDB Worldwide, of the challenges presented to the ad industry by new technologies like the Internet. "You have to focus on human beings. You can't forget that you're trying to reach someone who has age-old desires to be noticed, admired, and loved."[1]

THE AGENCY

An advertising agency, as defined by the American Association of Advertising Agencies, is an independent business, composed of creative and business people, who develop, prepare, and place advertising in advertising media for sellers seeking to find customers for their goods or services. Exhibit 5.1 is an example of an agency promoting its point of view on a number of marketing issues. The objective is to drive the respondent to its Web site for more in-depth information. Socoh Group's CEO Brad P. Majors

EXHIBIT 5.1

"Socoh tried to drive prospective clients to its Web site to get Socoh's marketing point of view."

Courtesy Socoh Marketing LLC.

says, "Know-how is the result of personal experience applied to scholarly knowledge." At the Web site, Socoh talks about its marketing experience with major clients.

According to the U.S. Census Bureau, there are more than 10,000 agencies in operation in this country. The *Standard Directory of Advertising Agencies* (also known as the *Agency Red Book*) lists over 8,000 agency profiles, including full-service agencies, house agencies, media-buying services, sales promotion agencies, cyberagencies, and public relations firms. The *Adweek Agency Directory* lists more than 6,400 agencies, PR firms and media-buying services, plus 26,000 personnel listings. There are about 2,000 agencies listed in the New York Yellow Pages alone. Unfortunately, there isn't a single printed or online directory listing every agency throughout the country.

The majority of agencies are small one- to ten-person shops (we talk about size and services later in this chapter). You will see ads for many specialized products and services throughout this text—from consumer, dot-com, industrial products, and services to pro-bono causes—in which the agency had to become an expert in marketing as well as writing the ad.

Huey/Paprocki develops ads for the Atlanta History Center, which means it must understand the exhibits and scope out key prospects. Exhibit 5.2 attracts people to see Colonial Williamsburg furniture.

HOW AGENCIES DEVELOPED

Before we discuss present-day agencies further, let us take a look at how advertising agencies got started and how they developed into worldwide organizations that play such a prominent role in the marketing and advertising process.

The Early Age (Colonial Times to 1917)

It is not generally known that the first Americans to act as advertising agents were colonial postmasters:

> In many localities advertisements for Colonial papers might be left at the post offices. William Bradford, publisher of the first Colonial weekly in New York, made an arrangement with Richard Nichols, postmaster in 1727, whereby the latter accepted advertisements for the *New York Gazette* at regular rates.[2]

Space Salesmen Volney B. Palmer is the first person known to have worked on a commission basis. In the 1840s, he solicited ads for newspapers that had difficulty getting out-of-town advertising. Palmer contacted publishers and offered to get them business for a 50 percent commission, but he often settled for less. There was no such thing as a rate card in those days. A first demand for $500 by the papers might be reduced, before the bargain was struck, to $50. (Today we call that negotiation.) Palmer opened offices in Philadelphia, New York, and Boston. Soon there were more agents, offering various deals.

Space Wholesalers During the 1850s in Philadelphia, George P. Rowell bought large blocks of space for cash (most welcome) from publishers at very low rates, less agents' commissions. He would sell the space in small "squares"—one column wide—at his own retail rate. Rowell next contracted with 100 newspapers to buy one column of space a month and sold the space in his total list at a fixed rate per line for the whole list: "an inch of space a month in one hundred papers for one hundred dollars." Selling by list became widespread. Each wholesaler's list was his private stock in trade. (This was the original media package deal.)

The First Rate Directory In 1869 Rowell shocked the advertising world by publishing a directory of newspapers with their card rates and his own estimates of their circulation. Other agents accused him of giving away their trade secrets; publishers howled too because his estimates of circulation were lower than their claims. Nevertheless, Rowell persisted in offering advertisers an estimate of space costs based on those published rates for whatever markets they wanted. This was the beginning of the media estimate.

The Agency Becomes a Creative Center In the early 1870s, writer Charles Austin Bates began writing ads and selling his services to whoever wanted them, whether advertisers or agents. Among his employees were Earnest Elmo Calkins and Ralph Holden, who in the 1890s founded their own agency, famous for 50 years under the name of Calkins and Holden. These men did more than write ads. They brought together planning, copy, and art, showing the way to combine all three into effective advertising. Not only was their agency one of the most successful agencies for half a century, but also the influence of their work helped to establish the advertising agency as the creative center for advertising ideas. Many of the names on the list of firms advertising in 1890 (see Chapter 1) are still familiar today; their longevity can be attributed to the effectiveness of that generation of agency people who developed the new power of advertising agency services. The business had changed from one of salesmen going out to sell advertising space to one of agencies that created the plan, the ideas, the copy, and the artwork, produced the plates, and then placed the advertising in publications from which they received a commission.

To this day, the unique contribution to business for which agencies are most respected is their ability to create effective ads.

Agency–Client Relationship Established In 1875, Francis Ayer established N. W. Ayer & Son (one of the larger advertising agencies today). Ayer proposed to bill advertisers for what he actually paid the publishers (that is, the rate paid the publisher less the commission), adding a fixed charge in lieu of a commission. In exchange, advertisers would agree to place all their advertising through Ayer's agents. This innovation established the relationship of advertisers as clients of agencies rather than as customers who might give their business to various salespeople, never knowing whether they were paying the best price.

The Curtis No-Rebating Rule In 1891, the Curtis Publishing Company announced that it would pay commissions to agencies only if they agreed to collect the full price from advertisers, a rule later adopted by the Magazine Publishers of America. This was the forerunner of no-rebating agreements, which were an important part of the agency business for more than 50 years. (Agency commissions, however, ranged from 10 to 25 percent in both magazines and newspapers.)

Standard Commissions for Recognized Agencies Established In 1917, newspaper publishers, through their associations, set 15 percent as the standard agency commission, a percentage that remains in effect for all media to this day (except local advertising, for which the media deal directly with the stores and pay no commission). The commission would be granted, however, only to agencies that the publishers' associations "recognized." One of the important conditions for recognition was an agency's agreement to charge the client the full rate (no rebating). Other criteria for recognition were that the agency must have business to place, must have shown competence in handling advertising, and must be financially sound. These three conditions are still in effect. Anyone may claim to be an agency, but only agencies that are recognized are allowed to charge a commission.

Today's agencies still receive commissions from the media for space they buy for clients. However, artwork and the cost of production are generally billed by the agency to the advertiser, plus a service charge—usually 17.65 percent of the net, which is equivalent to 15 percent of the gross. By preagreement, a charge is made for other services.

The American Association of Advertising Agencies Founded in 1917, the **American Association of Advertising Agencies** (sometimes known as AAAA or 4As), is the national trade association representing the advertising agency business in the United States. Its membership produces approximately 75 percent of the total advertising volume placed by agencies nationwide. Although virtually all of the large, multinational agencies are members of the AAAA, more than 60 percent of their membership bills less than $10 million per year. It is a management-oriented association that offers its members the broadest possible services, expertise, and information regarding the advertising agency business. The typical AAAA agency has been a member for more than 20 years.

> **American Association of Advertising Agencies (AAAA, 4As)**
> The national organization of advertising agencies.

The No-Rebate Age (1918–1956)

The events of this era that left their mark on today's agency world are summarized here.

Radio One of the main events of 1925 was the notorious Scopes trial, and the main advent was radio. They did a lot for each other. Radio dramatized evolution-on-trial in Tennessee; it brought the issue of teaching scientific evolution home to Americans and it brought people closer to their radios. Tuning in to radio soon became a major part of American life, especially during the Great Depression and World War II. Radio established itself as a prime news vehicle. It also gave advertising a vital new medium and helped pull agencies through those troubled years. A number of agencies handled the entire production of a radio program as well as its commercials. By 1942, agencies were billing more for radio advertising ($188 million) than they were for newspaper advertising ($144 million). The radio boom lasted until television came along.

Television Television became popular after 1952, when nationwide network broadcasts began. Between 1950 and 1956, television was the fastest-growing medium. It became the major medium for many agencies. National advertisers spent more on television than they did on any other medium. TV expenditures grew from $171 million in 1950 to $1,225 million in 1956.

Electronic Data Processing The computer entered advertising through the accounting department. By 1956, it was already changing the lives of the media department, the marketing department, and the research department—all having grown in competence with the increasing number of syndicated research services. Agencies prided themselves on their research knowledge and were spending hundreds of thousands of dollars for research every year to service their clients better.

Business was good, and American consumers were attaining a better standard of living than they had ever enjoyed. The period from 1950 to 1956 proved to be the beginning of the biggest boom advertising ever had. Total expenditures jumped from

$4.5 billion in 1950 to $9.9 billion in 1956. More than 60 percent of this spending was national advertising placed by advertising agencies. And the agency business was good, too.

The Age of Negotiation (1956–1990)

Consent Decrees In 1956, a change occurred in the advertiser–agency relationship. The U.S. Department of Justice held that the no-rebating provision between media associations and agencies limited the ability to negotiate between buyer and seller and, therefore, was in restraint of trade and in violation of antitrust laws. Consent decrees to stop no-rebating provisions were entered into by all media associations on behalf of their members.

Although the Justice Department's ruling in no way affected the 15 percent that commission agencies were accustomed to getting from the media, it opened the way to review the total compensation an agency should receive for its services, with the 15 percent commission a basic part of the negotiations. Later we look at the effects this has had on the agency–client relationship.

The Reengineering Age (1990–2000)

Mergers During the 1980s many corporations merged, creating giant corporations. To be more competitive, agencies followed suit, many merging because of financial pressures to serve larger clients.

Integrated Services The 1990s was about agencies reevaluating how they operate. *Integrated services* has been a buzzword relating to efforts to coordinate a client's entire marketing mix, including public relations, promotion, direct marketing, package design, and so on. Some agencies have expanded their communication services to clients by expanding departments or buying or creating subsidiary companies that enable them to offer sales promotion, public relations, direct marketing, logo and packaging design, and even television programming. One of the reasons is financial—clients have been moving dollars from advertising to promotion, and clients want their communications integrated. Agencies are trying to change to supply those needs.

Media Consolidation (Since 2000)

Agency holding companies created mega-media agencies' profit centers to attract global clients in an effort to become more efficient and cost-effective. As a result, many clients unbundled their media from their agencies and gave them to a single-media agency to buy and place.

THE FULL-SERVICE AGENCY

full-service agency
One that handles planning, creation, production, and placement of advertising for advertising clients. May also handle sales promotion and other related services as needed by client.

In the simplest terms, the **full-service agency** offers clients all the services necessary to handle the total advertising function—planning, creation, production, placement, and evaluation. Many have expanded this to include the management of all integrated marketing communications. Today, integrated marketing makes it possible to manage the product's message through a variety of disciplines—advertising, promotion, direct marketing, public relations, and so forth—with a tight strategic marketing focus so that the brand image is reinforced every time the consumer is exposed to a communication.

Many agencies have concluded that the next generation of advertising will require a new concept of the role and responsibilities of an advertising agency. A new mission will demand a different organization. As we have said, many agencies have undergone a restructuring or reengineering in recent years. Most believe that brand building is impossible without creative, persuasive advertising, which is with few exceptions the most potent component in the marketing communication mix. Despite the restructuring, most marketers will find familiar unit names: account management, creative, media, research or account planning, and administration. But many of these agencies have changed how they operationalize the work. It still isn't brain surgery, but it does require a managed process.

First, there isn't a universal model, but let us take a look at the functions full-service agencies perform. When a new account or a new product is assigned to a full-service agency, work on it will generally proceed along the following lines.

Diagnosing the Marketing and Brand Problem

The process begins with the collection of all that you know about the product category, the brand, and its competitors. Research takes the lead, looking at consumer attitudes to develop penetrating insights into the prospects and defining the brand's core: Who are the prime prospects? Where are they? What are their demographics and psychographic characteristics? How does the product fit into their lifestyles? How do they regard this type of product, this particular brand, and competitive products? What one benefit do consumers seek from this product and this particular brand? In what distinctive way can the product solve the prime prospects' problems? What media will best reach your market? Some ad agencies sell their research capability to attract clients. An agency self-ad said, " . . . It's understandable that when you advertise, you tend to do it from your own perspective . . . we don't promote who you think you want to be. We explore through research who consumers will let you become. Then we apply that knowledge to the most important part of any communication plan, the ad itself."

Setting Objectives and Developing Strategy

Using the answers to these questions, a strategy is formulated that positions the product in relation to the prime-prospect customer and emphasizes the attribute that will appeal to the prime prospect. Account management is responsible for leading this phase. Here you define what is to be accomplished strategically, such as intensifying brand imagery and recapturing prior users, and plan how to carry it out. These strategic dialogues involve teams of account, creative, media, and research people. Socoh Marketing's self-promotion (see Exhibit 5.3) is aimed at marketing professional services. Socoh feels these services are complex to sell (physician groups, accounting firms, engineering firms, financial institutions, law offices, etc.) and, therefore, require different objectives and strategies than consumer product companies.

Creating the Communication

Once the overall strategy is determined, you decide on the creative strategy, write copy, and prepare rough layouts and storyboards. In advertising, the creative impulse is always disciplined—an imaginative and persuasive expression of the selling strategy and the character of the brand.

The Media Plan You define media strategy, checking objectives to ensure that they parallel your marketing objectives. Then you select media. All traditional and nontraditional options are explored, the goal being to avoid mere execution and add value instead. Media schedules are prepared with costs. At this stage, you seek to coordinate all elements of the marketing communication mix to ensure maximum exposure. Media leads the process by developing an environment that multiplies the impact of the creative team. This step may be implemented by the agency or an independent media agency or buying service.

PS2B
Professional Services-to-Businesses

Marketing professional services to businesses is a complex task. You're talking to multiple decision-makers, each with their own concerns, which tends to complicate the selection process.

Furthermore, professional services are highly specialized and intangible. This makes it difficult for prospects to assess the value of what you're offering them.

When you market your services, you make a promise. How does your prospect know you'll keep it?

SOCOH
MARKETING LLC

EXHIBIT 5.3

Socoh Marketing tells prospects that marketing professional services to businesses is complex.

Courtesy of Socoh Marketing LLC.

The Total Plan You present roughs of the copy, layouts, and production costs, along with the media schedules and costs—all leading to the total cost.

Evaluation Plan The evaluation step in the process is both the end and the beginning. It is the moment of reckoning for the creative work, based on the objectives set in the beginning, and provides the evidence needed to refine and advance future efforts. As such, it is an accountable system.

Notify Trade of Forthcoming Campaign

For many product categories you would inform dealers and retailers of the campaign details early enough so that they can get ready to take advantage of the ad campaign.

Billing and Payments

When ads are run, you take care of billing the client and paying the bills to the media and production vendors. As an example of the billing procedure, let us say that through your agency an advertiser has ordered an ad in *Leisure Gourmet* magazine for one page costing $10,000. When the ad appears, the bill your agency gets from the publisher will read something like this:

1 page, August *Leisure Gourmet* magazine	$10,000
Agency commission @ 15% (cash discount omitted for convenience)	1,500
Balance Due	$ 8,500

Your agency will then bill the advertiser for $10,000, retain the $1,500 as compensation, and pay the publisher $8,500.

The agency commission applies only to the cost of space or time. In addition, as mentioned earlier, your agency will send the advertiser a bill for production costs for such items as the following:

finished artwork	reproduction prints/films
typography (typesetting)	recording studios
photography	broadcast production
printing collateral	

The items are billed at actual cost plus a service charge, usually 17.65 percent (which is equivalent to 15 percent of the net).

THE TRADITIONAL AGENCY ORGANIZATION

In this section, we first examine the traditional approach to the full-service agency structure, and then we look at the reengineering of this process.

Advertising agencies come in all sizes and shapes. The largest employ hundreds of people and bill thousands of millions of dollars every year. The smallest are one- or two-person operations (usually a creative person and an account manager). As they grow, they generally must add to their organizational structure to handle all the functions of a full-service agency.

All agencies do not structure themselves in exactly the same manner. For discussion purposes, we have chosen a typical organizational structure under the command of major executives: the vice presidents of (1) the creative department, (2) account services, (3) marketing services, and (4) management and finance (see Exhibit 5.5). We discuss briefly how each department is organized.

Creative Department

Ken Roman, former chairman of Ogilvy & Mather Worldwide, says, "Agencies are generally hired on the basis of their creative abilities—the promise that they can create campaigns that will build business for the client." Every agency that exists is concerned with creating good advertising.[3] Yet, only a small number of agencies are known for their creative work. Later in Chapter 16, Frank Compton takes a look at defining the requirements to creating more than fundamentally basic ads. In almost every agency, the agency creative director is almost a mythical, often legendary creature positioned near the top of the agency totem pole. The creative director is considered to be responsible for the care and feeding of its most prized possession—the creative product. Today, more than ever before, success is measured by the client's results. The creative director is expected to have an opinion on everything from sales promotion to public relations. In addition to den mother, psychologist, cheerleader, arbiter of taste, basketball coach, team player, historian, jack-of-all-trades, showman, social convener, architect, designer, and Renaissance person, today's more evolved species is also required to be a strategist, businessperson, planner, financier, and new product developer. Bill Westbrook, on taking over as creative head of Fallon McElligott, stressed the importance of strategy: "If it's not a great strategy, it isn't a great campaign." Lee Chow, chairman and chief creative officer of TBWA/Chiat Day, says, "Managing an integrated campaign is different from doing just ads, as creative directors we've become joined at the hip with account planners."[4]

At first, all writers and artists will work right under one creative director; but as the business grows, various creative directors will take over the writing and art activities of different brands. A traffic department will be set up to keep the work flowing on schedule.

The print production director and the TV manager also report to the creative director, who is ultimately responsible for the finished product—ads and commercials.

KLEPPNER VIEWPOINT

JOHN ROBERTSON

Founder, Co-Creative Director
VitroRobertson

Taking Responsibility

We believe that when a group of people get together and decide to open an advertising agency, that decision carries with it a group of responsibilities.

The agencies that, over the long term, neglect those responsibilities will struggle and make foolish compromises and allow their creative product to erode until those agencies themselves erode.

The agencies that never lose sight of those responsibilities and that try to live up to them every day are the agencies that will be respected and do outstanding work and will prosper in even the most competitive of environments.

At least that's our theory. Here are the responsibilities we try to live up to.

Our Responsibilities to Consumers:

We have a responsibility to show them a good time. They have better things to do than to pay attention to advertising messages. We'll reward them for their time by making it an interesting, entertaining experience.

We have a responsibility to tell them what they want or need to know. We won't be all style and no substance. We won't waste their time.

We will be nice. We won't be obnoxious, rude, or inappropriate in our advertising. If they like the advertising, they'll like the company. And, if they like the company, they'll want to do business with it.

John Robertson

Our Responsibilities to Clients:

We will listen. Carefully. We will never forget that they know a lot more about their business, their customers, and their market than we do. Our job is to pay attention and make sure that they don't get caught up in too much "inside-out" thinking.

We will NOT do everything we're told. We will make it our responsibility to bring them ideas they didn't ask for and to keep solving problems in new and different ways.

Account Services

The vice president in charge of account services is responsible for the relationship between the agency and the client and is indeed a person of two worlds: the client's business and advertising. This vice president must be knowledgeable about the client's business, profit goals, marketing problems, and advertising objectives. He or she is responsible for helping to formulate the basic advertising strategy recommended by the agency, for seeing that the proposed advertising prepared by the agency is on target, and for presenting the total proposal—media schedules, budget, and rough ads or storyboards—to the client for approval. Then comes the task of making sure that the agency produces the work to the client's satisfaction.

As the business grows and takes on many clients, an account supervisor will appoint account executives to serve as the individual contacts with the various accounts. Account executives must be skillful at both communications and

EXHIBIT 5.4

Courtesy of VitroRobertson, Inc., Yamaha Watercraft and Robert Holland, photographer.

We will argue for what we believe in, but we won't be jerks about it. There are enough jerks in the world already. In addition to being nice to the consumer, we will be nice to them, too.

We think they deserve our full attention and our best thinking.

Perhaps most importantly, we'll respect their product and their brand. We'll treat it very carefully, because we know how much it's worth.

When we went into business more than 10 years ago, this was what we believed in. And we still do today. ▪ ▪ ▪

follow-up. Their biggest contribution is keeping the agency ahead of its client's needs. But the account supervisor will continue the overall review of account handling, maintaining contacts with a counterpart at the client's office (see Exhibit 5.6).

Marketing Services

The vice president in charge of marketing services is responsible for media planning and buying, for research, and for sales promotion. The marketing vice president will appoint a media director, who is responsible for the philosophy and planning of the use of media, for the selection of specific media, and for buying space and time. As the agency grows, there will be a staff of media buyers, grouped according to media (print, TV, or radio), accounts, or territory. The media staff will include an estimating department and an ordering department, as well as a department to handle residual payments due to performers. The

EXHIBIT **5.5**

Organization of a Typical Full-Service Agency

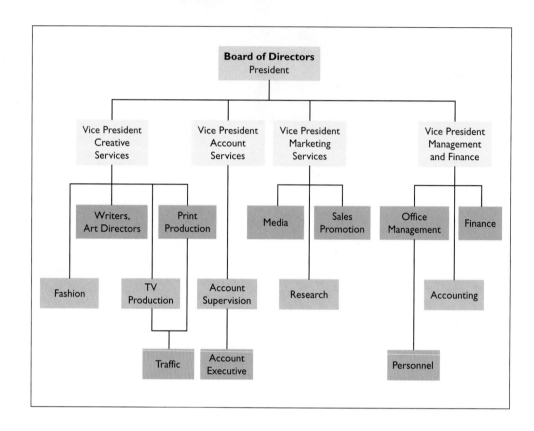

media head may use independent media services, especially in the purchase of TV and radio time.

The research director will help define marketing and copy goals. Agencies usually use outside research organizations for fieldwork, but in some agencies, research and media planning are coordinated under one person. The division of work among the executives may vary with the agency.

The sales promotion director takes care of premiums, coupons, and other dealer aids and promotions.

Management and Finance

Like all businesses, an advertising agency needs an administrative head to take charge of financial and accounting control, office management, and personnel (including trainees).

THE CONTINUING EVOLUTION OF THE AGENCY

Once clients sought the agency powerhouse talents of Leo Burnett, Bill Bernbach, David Ogilvy, Rosser Reeves, Howard Gossage, and Mary Wells. Then agencies were less driven by famous individuals, and more often driven by a collection of bright talent. There has always been some sort of agency evolution taking place. In the 1980s agencies followed the trend of clients and merged to be more financially competitive. With these mergers came restructuring. Each agency restructured its operation to meet its clients' needs. The 1990s brought a major reengineering to the very core of many agencies, as they changed their structure to better serve the integrated needs of clients but no longer called themselves "advertising agencies." For example, J. Walter Thompson says it is a "brand communication company." What that means is it has key integrated services and com-

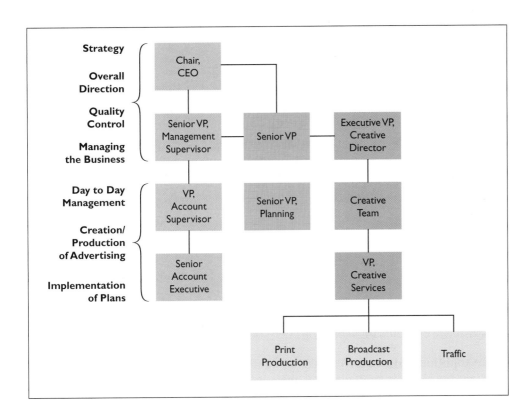

EXHIBIT **5.6**

Typical Team Responsibilities

In some agencies, the account planner works directly with creative to provide research and consumer viewpoints.

panion companies offering marketing expertise beyond traditional advertising and marketing.

Traditionally, agencies were trusted partners in the stewardship of the brand. They would be key in developing products, serving as marketing and media experts and visionaries. Today, most major corporate marketing departments have the ability to manage these functions. Many agencies feel they are treated more like vendor-order takers than partners as clients seek solutions from any place, once the exclusive territory of agencies. Some clients treat them as an expense rather than as trusted partners.

Under the traditional structure, an account person may meet regularly with creative people to discuss strategy and ad copy, or with media people to review scheduling, or separately with the public relations person. In some cases, there might be a meeting in which specific players in the process meet to discuss a problem or progress. In most reengineered operations, on the other hand, the key people on the team meet on a regular basis so that everyone knows what is going on in every aspect of the account. Richard Riley says the account circle at Sawyer Riley Compton meets every Monday morning to review the week's work—and meets again when necessary. This means the sales promotion person knows about the public relations work, and the art director knows about media planning. If necessary, the client participates in the review. Exhibit 5.7 shows the players on a typical account circle team. One of the pluses in this process is that everyone on the team—senior or junior staffer—understands every function in the process and how his or her work relates to everyone else's work. In theory, a client could call anyone on the team to get an answer.

A few years ago, Jay Chiat, a pioneer in agency reengineering, said:

We believe the hierarchical structure [of the traditional agency], if not obsolete at present, is on its way. The traditional pyramid is about personal power and focuses on how to run a business. Therefore most

EXHIBIT **5.7**

**Sawyer Riley Compton
Account Circle Approach**

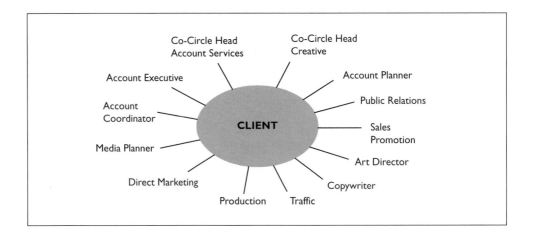

decisions are about the organization's needs, concentrating on fiscal and administrative issues. An agency is a service organization whose sole existence depends on satisfying client needs.[5]

In traditional agencies, senior managers spend 15 to 20 percent of their time on client business. In reengineered agencies, they spend about 60 percent of their time in the trenches working on client business. Middle managers in reengineered agencies act as coaches, team leaders, and quality control managers. One of the significant changes is that creative staff, account managers, and media planners must work together as a team—a team of people working together to rapidly solve problems. Most agency reengineers say their teams consist of 8 to 12 people, although Sawyer Riley Compton uses teams called account circles of about 20 (see Exhibit 5.8). Most agencies' reengineered structure is somewhat similar to traditional structure. It is how business works that is different. People don't do their thing in isolation; they approach problem solving together. The team concept often helps younger people because it allows them to work side by side with senior people.

As with any new management trend, traditional agencies will copy and modify those reengineering structures that have been successful to meet their specific needs. There is little doubt that the agency structure in the future will not be a copy of today's.

Agency Size

Some agencies are run by one or two people, others by hundreds or thousands. There has always been an argument that large agencies offer more services and expensive star-talent. The negative is they generally charge more and aren't very flexible because of their size. Small agencies promote that small-to-medium clients can be serviced by the agency's senior management and creative.

Brad Majors, president of Socoh, who has worked for agencies of all sizes, offers these thoughts about size of agency:

- Large/public agencies will, more than ever, be confined to large, multinational accounts. It will be nearly impossible for them to profitably service smaller clients. And since there will continue to be large multinational clients (with growth primarily from the acquisitions of smaller competitors' brands), there should be room for the larger agencies to profitably handle them.

- Medium-sized agencies, which have been the greatest source of creativity historically, will exist but will remain in the state of flux we see today and have seen for 20 years. As they grow, they will have the resources to hire strong talent. Much of this talent, without the cumbrances of public ownership, will continue to produce provocative work. As the work is noticed and clients and prospects become more interested, these medium-sized agencies will become attractive to larger agencies as an acquisition target. As the principals of the agency age, an immediate cash-rich buyout may seem more attractive than a deal with the next generation of the agency's management. Thus, the newly acquired agency will not be medium sized any longer but will become only a part of the larger whole. Once acquired, it will be important for them to remain in the niche prescribed for them by the parent agency.

■ Interestingly, smaller agencies will not only exist but also will thrive, if managed prudently. Historically, small agencies have either fared very well or gone under. To some extent, small agency success has been determined by how strong the agency's financial management was. Managing cash flow and account receivables has been a critical issue for most small agencies and it will continue to be so. But given the instability expected in medium-sized agencies, there should be great opportunities for smaller agencies that combine a marketing-driven creative product with sound financial management.

COMPETING ACCOUNTS

The client–agency relationship is a professional one. It may involve new product strategies, new promotions, sales data, profit or loss information, and new marketing strategies—information that is sensitive and confidential. As a result, most clients will not generally approve of an agency's handling companies or products in direct competition; Coca-Cola isn't going to allow its agencies to handle Pepsi products. In some cases, agencies will handle accounts for the same type of product or service if they do not compete directly—for example, banks that do not compete in the same market. Many agency–client conflicts result from mergers in which one merger partner handles an account for a product that competes with a product being handled by the other merger partner. When agencies consider merging, the first question is, "Will any of our accounts conflict?" There are a number of large national agencies with independent offices around the country that hope clients will not view the same type of account in another office as a conflict.

CLIENT–AGENCY RELATIONSHIP LENGTH

Clients generally retain agencies as long as the relationship seems to be working. However, most contracts allow for a 90-day cancellation by either party if the relationship goes sour. At the same time, agencies can resign an account if they differ with the client's goals and the account isn't profitable. American Association of Advertising Agencies research has indicated that the average tenure of client–agency relationships has declined from 7.2 years to 5.3 years since 1984. Yet today, some clients have been with their agencies for decades. For example, GE (1920), Hormel Foods (1931), DaimlerChrysler (1926), and Campbell Soup (1954) have been clients of BBDO Worldwide for many years.

AGENCY OF RECORD

The agency-of-record relationship offers marketers an advertising team to work solely on their brand, creating a stable of experts in that particular industry. Global agencies claim they are capable of providing multiple services to a client, which enables marketers to respond quickly to changes in the global business environment.[6]

In some instances, large advertisers may employ a number of agencies to handle their advertising for various divisions and products. To coordinate the total media buy and the programming of products in a network buy, the advertiser will appoint one agency as the agency of record. This lead agency will make the corporate contracts under which other agencies will issue their orders, keep a record of all the advertising placed, and communicate management's decisions on the allot-

ADVANTAGE POINT

Element 79 Partners

Element 79 Partners was officially and unprecedentedly launched in late February 2002. It was, and remains, the largest advertising agency start-up in the industry's history. A unit of Omnicom Group, Inc., Element 79 was begun with an initial client roster of world-class brands including, among others, Gatorade, Cap 'N Crunch Cereal, Aunt Jemima, Quaker Oatmeal, Propel Fitness Water, Tropicana, Dole, Life Cereal, Quaker Chewy Granola Bars, Aquafina bottled water, and Crisp 'Ums. Since its launch, the agency has added Cracker Jack, Rice-A-Roni, Supercuts, and Lowe's Home Improvement Centers as clients.

Just as Element 79 helps its clients establish and build strong brands, it also works hard to create and nurture its own agency brand. The name, Element 79, stands for gold as gold is the 79th element on the periodic table. The agency's logo is AU^{79}, which is the periodic table's symbol for gold. Gold is also symbolic of the building blocks on which Element 79's brand identity is based. The firm's essence and character are deeply rooted in the "golden rule," — which, in turn, serves to remind all employees how they should treat clients and each other.

Courtesy of Element 79 Partners and The Gatorade Company.

Additionally, the gold metaphor speaks to the ultimate mission of the company, which is to drive clients' business and, in turn, put some "gold" in agency pockets. Finally, gold underscores the intense emphasis on quality the company places on its ideas and finished work as everyone is always held to the highest "gold standards."

With approximately 130 employees, Element 79 is one of the most efficient agencies in its industry. It accomplishes this by ensuring that it has very senior, experienced people leading each of its accounts. These senior agency people mirror the involvement of key decision makers at the client, which allows better decisions to be made faster and more easily. While efficient, Element 79 has also proven itself to be one of the industry's most effective agencies. In its first two years, the firm has won five Effies, the industry's highest honor for effective business-building advertising. No other agency has won more Effies per employee than Element 79. Additionally, Element 79 created and ran one of the industry's most talked about and admired commercials in the 2003 Super Bowl. Its "23 vs. 39" commercial for Gatorade featured basketball legend Michael Jordan, playing one-on-one with a younger version of himself. ■ ■ ■

ment of time and space in a schedule. Recently on the McDonald's fast-food account, DDB Needham was considered the lead agency, with about 66 percent of the business, and Leo Burnett handles about 33 percent. For this service, the other agencies pay a small part of their commissions (usually 15 percent of 15 percent) to the agency of record.

AGENCY MULTIPLE OFFICES

Many major agencies have offices in cities throughout the United States. Foote, Cone & Belding is typical, with major offices in New York, Chicago, and San Francisco. J. Walter Thompson operates agencies in Toronto, Montreal, and Vancouver in Canada. In the United States it has offices in Atlanta, Chicago, Denver, Detroit, Houston, Los Angeles, Miami, Minneapolis, and Seattle with its headquarters in New York. It also has a number of JWT Specialized Communication offices in a number of other cities, as well as other offices throughout the world. BBDO has regional headquarters in Atlanta, Chicago, Detroit, Miami, Minneapolis, and Los Angeles in addition to its New York worldwide headquarters. For the most part, each office functions as an autonomous agency that serves different clients and is able to draw on the talents and services of the other offices. As a rule, these offices don't normally work on the same project for the same client. Whereas the parent organizations are busily marketing themselves as global networks, each local office fiercely tries to protect its unique culture. As Foote, Cone & Belding's CEO puts it, "We have a very New York agency; a very Chicago agency; and a very San Francisco agency. When agencies succeed in putting two or more offices together on a project, a New York office is usually involved." This most commonly occurs on the media side. In fact, some offices will make media buys in their region of the country for all of the agency's offices. BBDO's chairman says, "It's no secret that BBDO in Los Angeles is our best agency in terms of print creative. Why shouldn't we make that expertise available to clients from other offices?"[7] It may be said that because each office handles different kinds of accounts, each office probably has different specialties that could be leveraged on behalf of all clients. But, as a general rule, each office works primarily on its own accounts.

A few agencies recently created new West Coast offices to take advantage of the many talents that exist there. These offices are evolving as creative idea centers to help clients in any of the agency brand's offices develop stronger creative products.

GLOBAL AGENCIES AND GLOBAL MARKETS

Globalization has become a necessary part of business and advertising. The demands on marketers to survive in a global economy place pressures on large- and medium-sized agencies to become global partners. It is more than simply a language problem. Companies and agencies need to learn cultural and market patterns and understand consumers from a global perspective. Someone trying to sell burgers, fries, and soft drinks outside of the United States may think there is no competition because there are no other burger outlets. The local version of fast food may not include hamburgers at all; the real competition may be a rice shop or a tacqueria.

Unless marketers understand competing sources for that same dollar, they won't be successful.[8] It can be complex. Many small-to-medium agencies that don't have the resources for international offices have made affiliations with agencies or independent agency networks throughout the world to service clients and give advice. If an agency doesn't have the resources to help clients engage in international marketing, then the client is likely to turn to other agencies that do have the resources and knowledge, or the client may seek a local agency in the country where it is doing business. Major agencies have been global in nature for decades, if not longer, to service their clients' international needs.

J. Walter Thompson opened its first office outside the United States in 1891 in London. It now has 315 offices in 90 countries. Following is a list of its non–North American offices.

JWT Global Agency Network

Latin America	Asia Pacific	Europe	Africa	Middle East
Argentina	Australia	Austria	Ghana	Egypt
Bolivia	Bangladesh	Belgium	Ivory Coast	Israel
Brazil	China	Bosnia-Herzegovina	Kenya	Jordan
Chile	Hong Kong	Bulgaria	Mozambique	Kuwait
Colombia	India	Croatia	South Africa	Lebanon
Costa Rica	Indonesia	Czech Republic	Zimbabwe	Morocco
Dominican Republic	Japan	Denmark		Saudi Arabia
Ecuador	Korea	Estonia		Syria
El Salvador	Malaysia	Finland		UAE
Guatemala	Nepal	France		
Honduras	New Zealand	Germany		
Mexico	Pakistan	Greece		
Nicaragua	Philippines	Hungary		
Panama	Singapore	Ireland		
Paraguay	Sri Lanka	Italy		
Peru	Taiwan	Latvia		
Puerto Rico	Thailand	Macedonia		
Uruguay	Vietnam	Netherlands		
Venezuela		Norway		
		Poland		
		Portugal		
		Romania		
		Russia		
		Slovenia		
		Spain		
		Switzerland		
		Turkey		
		Ukraine		
		United Kingdom		
		Yugoslavia		

JWT Worldwide has a system to manage a client's global business that includes the following:

1. *Global teams.* JWT can help clients achieve their communications objectives virtually anywhere in the world.
2. *Director-in-charge system.* JWT uses an account director, who is the director-in-charge (DIC) on a global scale. These people operate as heads of an "agency within the agency," working with all offices to service global clients. The DICs work closely with their regional directors, local office CEOs, and account directors in each country to make sure the agency's network comes together seamlessly to execute a multinational advertiser's global communications efforts to build its business.
3. *Regional directors.* JWT regional directors have the responsibility for a specific group of countries. The CEOs of JWT's offices in that region report to the regional director.
4. *Global directors.* Each worldwide client is represented by a global business director, who sits on the JWT worldwide executive group. The DIC reports to the global business director, whose role is to ensure that the full resources of the JWT global network are brought to bear in servicing multinational accounts.

WWP, the parent of JWT, sponsors BrandZ, a research study that interviews some 70,000 people around the world. This study asks consumers questions in 50 categories to understand how consumers view 3,500 brands. These insights are available to JWT clients.

Most global agencies have similar operations as JWT. For instance, DDB has 221 offices in 72 countries. BBDO has 345 offices in 76 countries. Lowe & Partners Worldwide has 180 offices in over 80 countries. McCann Erickson Worldwide has offices in over 130 countries. Sometimes agency offices are opened in a country because a client wants to do business there.

In Chapter 24, we deal extensively with international operations.

Global Ad Centers The leading international advertising centers ranked in terms of local advertising billings are New York and Tokyo—fighting neck and neck for world leadership. Other major advertising centers include London, Paris, Chicago, Los Angeles, Detroit, San Francisco, Minneapolis, Frankfurt, São Paulo, Düsseldorf, Madrid, and Seoul. Almost every country has an advertising agency center. Exhibit 5.9 shows a Korean utility ad. For U.S. agencies, setting up a foreign office can be very complex. Each country is a different market, with its own language, buying habits, ways of living, mores, business methods, marketing traditions, and laws. So instead of trying to organize new agencies with American personnel, most U.S. agencies purchase a majority or minority interest in a successful foreign agency. They usually have a top management person as head of an overseas office. Key members of the international offices regularly meet for intensive seminars on the

EXHIBIT 5.9

The Korean Telecom ad's banner says, "Congratulations Megapass! Investment from foreign customers!" The bottom copy says, "Thank you for contracts! Three million customers! Megapass Summer special event."

Courtesy of Korean Telecom and Chang Hwan Shin.

philosophy and operation of the agency and share success stories. Remember, good marketing ideas can come from any place. The United States doesn't have a lock on great ideas.

Global Efficiencies Cost efficiencies in production of global advertising motivate advertisers to seek a single world execution. A single execution also helps build the same global brand equity. However, "every international brand starts out as a successful local brand . . . reproduced many times."[9] Being a global advertiser and having one global campaign sounds easy. But it is not. Despite being a global advertiser for many decades, it was only in 1992 that Coca-Cola launched its first global advertising campaign with all the ads being similar in each country. Exhibit 5.10 shows an ad developed by Coca-Cola Company–Japan. A brand and its advertising must be presented in relevant and meaningful ways in the context of local environments, or consumers won't care. As many experienced multinational marketers know, for any given brand, advertising that elicits the same response from consumers across borders matters much more than running the same advertising across borders. That may mean using the same brand concept or advertising concept and similar production format across borders, but the executions need to be customized to local markets so the consumers can relate to and empathize with the advertising. Simply translating American ads into foreign languages has proved dangerous. Perdue's (Chicken) Spanish translation of "It takes a tough man to make a tender chicken," actually said, "It takes a sexually excited man to make a chick affectionate." Language can be a barrier as with "Come alive with the Pepsi Generation," translated in Chinese as "Pepsi brings your ancestors back from the grave."

Global Marketing Companies are continually attempting to become more globally integrated. Sometimes these efforts don't work as smoothly as the company wishes. Coke's Chairman-CEO Douglas Draft gave a "Think local, act local" edict to solve some of the company's marketing problems. Success often stems from a

EXHIBIT 5.10

Coca-Cola (Japan) Co. Ltd tries to create a dialogue with young consumers in an attempt to develop a lasting relationship between the brand and the reader.

Courtesy of Coca-Cola (Japan) Company, Limited.

product or positioning that is relevant to consumer needs, which often vary by culture. Although cultures and habits vary, people's emotions are remarkably similar. People are very much alike in their attitudes regarding love, hate, fear, greed, envy, joy, patriotism, material comforts, and family. Ogilvy & Mather has found that strategies can and do move worldwide, but it is usually best to create advertising locally from a worldwide plan and strategy. Each country must agree to create advertising on the approved strategy to maintain the desire brand image. If there is a local reason to vary strategy, it should be worked out in advance. For smaller companies, the promise of global branding has been a bumpy road. Global players face a common problem—virtually every global strategy now has a full complement of strong multinational and regional competitors. The promise of managing marketing from a single headquarters hasn't worked the way it was planned.[10] Jerry Judge, CEO of Lowe Worldwide says, "There really isn't much global marketing. There are companies that market globally." According to Ken Kaess, president and CEO of DDB Worldwide, "The benefit is consistency of product image or message, which is particularly true of service marketers like American Express, McDonald's, or Exxon Mobil. They have the same core values around the world."[11]

It is only logical that multinational clients want their agencies to know how to develop great advertising campaigns that can run across all the principal markets of the world. As the chairperson of Leo Burnett International said, "As the world gets smaller, there needs to be brand consistency so people don't get confused as they move from market [country] to market."[12] The result of this need is pressure on U.S. agencies to produce, place, and research global advertising.

AGENCY NETWORKS

Many small- and medium-sized agencies that have working agreements with each other to help with information gathering from different markets and sharing are called agency networks. Usually there is only one network member in each market or region. Agency networks provide information and financial skills to enhance agency operations.

The Mega-Agency Holding Companies

Marion Harper set out his holding company vision for Interpublic Group of companies in 1960. He understood that once an agency reached a certain size, account conflicts hindered the agency's growth. His solution was to create an organization that would own individual agencies that could handle competing brands. Each of these agencies would operate freely and independently. The definition still holds true today, by and large, but not quite as Harper envisioned. There are still account conflict problems. And how is the integration of these agency brands working? Do clients really prefer one-stop shopping? Some of the holding companies are selling integrated services to a number of clients successfully.[13]

Mega-agency holding companies have networks of their agencies and support companies around the world to serve clients. The modern version of the mega-agency holding company started in 1986, when a small London agency, Saatchi & Saatchi PLC, systematically grew over a two-year period to become a mega-agency network with capitalized billings of more than $13.5 billion. This was a significant change in the advertising business as it became the world's largest advertising organization for a brief period and truly changed global advertising. Today, the largest organizations are WWP Group (London), Omnicom Group (New York), Dentsu (Tokyo), and Publicis Groupe (Paris). These and other mega-agency organizations own many advertising agencies throughout the world. Some of the holdings of the Omnicom Group, founded in 1986, are listed here:

Omnicom's Three Global Advertising Agency Networks

BBDO Worldwide, Inc., New York

TBWA Worldwide, New York

DDB Worldwide, New York

Leading U.S.-Based National Agencies

Arnell Group, New York

Element 79 Partners, Chicago

Goodby, Silverstein & Partners, San Francisco

GSD&M, Austin

Martin/Williams Advertising, Minneapolis

Merkley Newman Harty/Partners, New York

Zimmerman Partners, Fort Lauderdale

Omnicom Media Group

OMD Worldwide Media, New York

PhD Network, London

Diversified Agency Services (100 companies)

(Public Relations/Public Affairs)

Fleishman-Hillard

Ketchum

Porter Novelli International

Brodeur Worldwide

(Promotional Marketing/Direct Marketing)

Tracy Locke Partnership

Alcone Marketing Group

Integer Group

Rapp Collins Worldwide

Mega-agencies offer several advantages to their clients other than sheer size. Among the most important are a greater reservoir of talent and an ability to shift portions of accounts from one agency to another without going through the time-consuming, and often confusing, agency review. (Coca-Cola has switched assignments for its brands among several Interpublic Group of Cos. agencies and given new product assignments to others.) There are also some disadvantages for clients, the most important of which is conflicts with competing accounts.

Size, in itself, doesn't have significant advantages or disadvantages in developing the ads themselves. All agencies—large or small—consist of small units or teams that work on an assigned account or group of accounts. The ability of the team and the dedication to creative and professional excellence are dictated by the talent and innovative abilities of individuals, not the size of their company. Obviously, size and structure of an agency will attract or repel clients, depending on what level and quality of services they are seeking. The agency business is simply mirroring business in general by diversifying, economizing, and becoming more efficient and profitable.

Publicis Groupe Chairman-CEO Maurice Levy recently said he didn't think the holding-company-as-superagency model worked, so Publicis Groupe changed to give its agency networks a distinct identity. "Each has its own individual character that is not artificial," he said. Mr. Levy described the Leo Burnett network as the agency strongly associated to heartland American brands such as McDonald's Corp. and the U.S. Army, whereas Saatchi has an edgier British origin and is known as an ideas company. Publicis is differentiated by its French origin and strong integrated approach to communication.[14]

Despite using agency holding companies, not all advertisers think they are perfect partners. C. J. Fraleigh, General Motors' executive director for corporate advertising and marketing, has called agency holding companies "flabby" organizations that have become "more revenue models than consumer-solution models."[15]

OTHER ADVERTISING SERVICES

New services are continually springing up in competition with advertising agencies. Each new service is designed to serve clients' needs a little differently. This competition has impacted agency structure and operations.

Talent and Production Agencies Creating Creative

A relatively new resource for clients is the melding of talent sources to develop ad concepts. Creative Artists Agency (CAA), a production and talent agency involving entertainment stars, writers, directors, and others, made inroads with Coca-Cola in 1991, as a working partner with Coke's advertising agencies, in some cases independently developing advertising concepts and commercials. The 1993 Coke-guzzling polar bears were created by both Coke's agency and CAA. A number of other talent agencies have had working agreements with marketers and their advertising agencies to provide creative and talent services. After creating underwhelming creative for Coke, the creative duties returned to their agency. Today, CAA has restructured and is responsible for bringing Coke and Fox together with the producer of *American Idol*. As a result, the soft drink got aboard the show's first season. "The receptivity to *American Idol* was far more overwhelming than we expected," said David Raines, vice president of integrated communications at Coca-Cola. "Consumers liked it. It facilitated social connection, access to behind-the-scenes. It was fun, relevant and somewhat organic—it didn't feel forced. It provided branded experience rather than brand exposure."[16] Some industry insiders believe such talent agency relationships can add another dimension to the advertising agency and client resources.

Agency holding company WWP's Mediaedge bought a stake in The Leverage Group, an entertainment company. Omnicom Group bought Davie Brown entertainment consultancy, and other agency holding companies are including more Hollywood assets to offer clients.

Independent Creative Services

Some advertisers seek top creative talent on a freelance, per-job basis. Many creative people do freelance work in their off-hours. Some make it a full-time job and open their own creative shop or creative boutique. In general, the creative boutique has no media department, no researchers, and no account executives. Its purpose is strictly to develop creative ideas for its clients.

À La Carte Agency

Today, many agencies offer for a fee just the part of their total services that advertisers want. The à la carte arrangement is used mostly for creative services and for media planning and placement. Many agencies have spun off their media departments into independent divisions to seek clients interested only in media handling. Handling only the media portion of an account typically brings commissions that range from 3 to 5 percent.

In-House Agency

When advertisers found that all the services an agency could offer could be purchased on a piecemeal basis, they began setting up their own internal agencies, referred to as in-house agencies. The **in-house agency** can employ a creative service to originate advertising for a fee or markup. It can buy the space or time itself or employ a media-buying service to buy time or space and place the ads. As a rule, the in-house agency is an administrative center that gathers and directs varying outside services for its operation and has a minimum staff.

in-house agency
An arrangement whereby the advertiser handles the total agency function by buying individually, on a fee basis, the needed services (for example, creative, media services, and placement) under the direction of an assigned advertising director.

Folks, Inc., an Atlanta restaurant company, had an agency. Then it created an in-house agency, which developed all creative concepts, copy, layout ideas, radio scripts, and so forth. It used art studios and graphic computer services to produce the finished art and used broadcast production companies for its broadcasts. It brought all print media in-house and used a media-buying service to place its broadcast buys. It also developed all direct mail, store marketing, public relations, and promotion. Recently Folks found a need for strategic marketing services and hired Cole Henderson & Drake advertising to assist in strategic development for one of its restaurant concepts. The agency then created advertisements, produced advertising, and bought media. When the agency contract expired, the company turned to its former marketing director's company, Sheri Bevil, now CEO of Bevil Advertising, for its marketing communication. Exhibit 5.11A is a promotional ad for Folks Southern Kitchen and Exhibit 5.11B is an example of collateral later developed by Bevil.

When Tom Lentz came to head Broyhill Furniture's marketing, he soon found that this account wasn't big enough to demand attention from larger national agencies, and the turnover of personnel in smaller-to-medium agencies often made it difficult to work with knowledgeable people. They were always having to educate account people about the furniture business. Broyhill solved its problem by building a strong in-house agency. In-house agencies are generally created to save money or give advertisers more control over every aspect of their business. Many industrial companies have highly technical products that constantly undergo technological changes and advances; it may well be more efficient to have in-house technical people prepare ads. This saves endless briefings that would be necessary if outside industrial writers were used. When the companies place their ads, they use an agency of their choice at a negotiated commission.

Rolodex Agency

An agency run by several advertising specialists, usually account and/or creative people, that has no basic staff is called a Rolodex agency. It hires specialists—in marketing, media planning, creative strategy, writing, and art direction, for example—who work on a project basis. The concept is similar to hiring freelance creative people to

EXHIBIT **5.11a**

This FSI shows the nature of restaurant marketing being similar to retail advertising— selling price and a deal.

Courtesy of Bevil Advertising and Folks.

execute ads, except that the experts are hired as needed. The Rolodex agency claims to be able to give advertisers expertise that small full-service agencies cannot match.

Media-Buying Services

The mid-1990s saw major changes in the way advertisers handle their media. Some major advertisers chose to unbundle media or give their media buys to independent media-buying services or other agencies to try to gain buying efficiencies. At the same time, agencies reinvented their media operations to remain competitive with the growing number of media-buying services, and developing them as a stand-alone profit center. Many of the large agencies have made their media services independent of other agency services to better compete.

We've already talked about agencies spinning off their media departments into separate and independent planning and buying companies. For example, J. Walter Thompson and Ogilvy, two global agencies owned by the same parent, followed the

trend of creating joint media alliances. They formed MindShare, a mega-media planning and buying agency to serve advertisers better. MindShare's Kristen Kyle says, "Technology is opening many doors to reach people through new media. Omnicom holding company created a mega-media agency, OMD Worldwide Media, from their BBDO, TBWA Worldwide, and DDB Worldwide agencies. It is simply big business."

In order to be more efficient and deal with this new terrain, many agencies are spinning off their media departments. There are four main reasons for these newly formed media agencies: First, media agencies are stronger, with better resources to explore new areas within media; second, the fragmentation of target audiences and media vehicles has made media more important than ever before; third, it has the potential to be a major profit center. If the agency loses the creative responsibilities of a client, the media agency could continue serving the client because it is separate. Finally, the reciprocal action allows media agencies to acquire accounts that work with other parent agencies for their creative work.[17] One of the reasons for the consolidation is the fact that mega-advertisers have consolidated their multiple accounts to obtain better rates in their media buying.

In 2003, Coca-Cola shifted its U.S. media planning and buying to one media agency, Starcom MediaVest Group.

Coke's domestic media buying and planning had been handled previously by Universal McCann and Starcom MediaVest. The accounts are worth about $350 million. Coke said the changes were spurred by an ongoing integration of Coke's three big North American units: Coca-Cola North America, Coca-Cola Fountain, and Minute Maid. Starcom MediaVest is part of Publicis Groupe, which is based in Paris.[18]

In-House Media Services

A few large advertisers have taken the media-buying function in-house so they will have more control over the buying operation. However, this doesn't appear to be a trend. It is more likely that advertisers will keep a seasoned media consultant on staff to ride herd on their agency or media service's performance.

FORMS OF AGENCY COMPENSATION

Historically, agency compensation has been fairly standardized since the 1930s. An agency received a commission from the media for advertising placed by the agency. The commission would cover the agency's copywriting and account services charges. This method of compensation has been unsatisfactory during recent years due to the changing nature of business. The straight 15 percent remains, but in some instances there are fixed commissions less than 15 percent (some large advertisers have negotiated a rate closer to 10 percent), sliding scales based on client expenditures, flat-fee arrangements agreed on by clients and agency, performance-based systems, and labor-based fee-plus-profit arrangements. In other words, compensation arrangements now take many forms. Despite this change, there are only two basic forms of advertising agency compensation: commissions and fees.

- *Media commissions.* The traditional 15 percent commission remains a form of agency income, especially for modestly budgeted accounts. Clients and agency may agree to a relationship in which the rate is fixed at less than 15 percent. This generally applies to large-budget accounts—the larger the budget, the lower the rate for the agency. With a sliding-scale commission agreement, the agency receives a fixed commission based on a certain expenditure. After that level of spending, the commission is reduced (there may be a 14 percent commission for the first $20 million spent by the client and a 7 percent commission on the next $15 million). Media payment is complicated by the independent media agency arrangements, but most of these negotiated contracts are similar to the foregoing. The combinations are endless.

- *Production commissions or markups.* As indicated earlier, agencies subcontract production work (all outside purchases such as type, photography, or illustrators) and charge the client the cost plus a commission—17.65 percent is the norm (see Exhibit 5.12).

- *Fee arrangements.* At times, the 15 percent commission is not enough for agencies to make a fair profit. For example, it may cost an agency more to serve a small client than a large one. The agency and client may negotiate a fee arrangement. In some cases it is a commission plus a fee. There are a number of options: A cost-based fee includes the agency's cost for servicing the account plus a markup, a cost-plus fee covers the agency cost and a fixed profit; a fixed fee is an agreed-upon payment based on the type of work being done (for example, copywriting at hourly fixed rates, artwork charges based on the salary of the

EXHIBIT 5.12

This is typical of direct-mail collateral that would be marked up 17.5 percent by an agency or created in-house by a client.

Courtesy of Homer TLC, Inc., © 2003.

involved personnel); and a sliding fee is based on a number of agreed-upon parameters. Again, there are many possibilities based on agency and client needs.

■ *Performance fees.* A predetermined performance goal may determine the compensation fee. For example, ad recall scores, unit sales, or market share may determine the level of compensation. If the agency meets the goals, compensation may be at the 15 percent level; if it exceeds them, a bonus could give the agency a 20 percent level. If it fails to meet the goals, compensation could be much less than 15 percent.

In 2002, the American Association of Advertising Agencies and the Association of National Advertisers, Inc., released a joint position paper outlining a set of guidelines covering compensation agreements between agencies and advertisers. The Guidelines for Effective Advertiser/Agency Compensation Agreements is divided into two sections: "Guiding Principles" and "Best and Worst Practices."

Many marketers have replaced the traditional commission system of paying media commissions with performance-based compensation. Agency payments are calculated on predetermined, measurable goals like growth in sales, increasing awareness of a brand, or gaining broad distribution for a new product. In some agreements compensation is determined by sales objectives, with agencies being paid more if a brand's sales increase and less if sales decline. All Coca-Cola agencies are on fees plus bonuses. This payment system allows the agencies not to worry if Coke cuts its advertising budget; it is designed to give the agency the best return on investment they can get. An example of a commission plus a fee is described in the following agency contract copy:

Internal creative services provided by [agency] shall be applied against the monthly agency fee at the prevailing hourly rates [as distinguished from services bought outside our organization]. Such services include preparation of print, radio, television production, storyboards, special comprehensive layouts, booklets, catalogues, direct mail, sales representations, extraordinary research, package design, collateral materials, etc.

Schedule of Agency	Hourly Rates
Creative director	$150
Copywriter	120
Art director	120
Production supervisor	95
Computer design	150
Type and composition	130
Computer artwork	130
Research/planning	130

Most agencies aim for a 20 percent profit on each account to cover personnel and overhead costs plus a profit. The president of Campbell-Mithun-Esty says, "There's a broad acceptance among clients that it's in their best interest that their account be profitable for their agency. The smarter client understands that's what gets it the best people on their account. That's what gets it the best service."[19]

An advertising management consultant suggests the key flaw of compensation based on the price of traditional media is the lack of a consistent relationship between income generated and the cost of providing services required by the clients. This will continue to be a problem as new media techniques are developed. He suggests agencies align their compensation with their roles as salespeople, not buyers of media, and to link agency profit goals to agreed-upon performance standards.[20]

OTHER SERVICES

Barter

barter
Acquisition of broadcast time by an advertiser or an agency in exchange for operating capital or merchandise. No cash is involved.

One way for an advertiser or agency to buy media below the rate card price, especially in radio or television, is **barter.** The Atlanta Convention and Visitors Bureau (ACVB) bartered for commercial time from television and broadcast stations to advertise the city's accommodations, restaurants, and attractions. Its agency offered hotel rooms, tickets to local attractions, and meals at Atlanta area restaurants. The ACVB was able to turn a $165,000 budget into $1.5 million in promotions. A typical prize would be a three-day trip to Atlanta for a family of four with tickets to four attractions, according to Bill Howard of the ACVB. He said more than 900 packages were offered in exchange for airtime.[21]

Barter houses often become brokers or wholesalers of broadcast time. They build inventories of time accumulated in various barter deals. These inventories are called time banks, which are made available to advertisers or agencies seeking to stretch their broadcast dollars.

One of the drawbacks of barter is that the weaker stations in a market are more apt to use it the most. Some stations will not accept barter business from advertisers already on the air in the market. Generally, the airtime is poor time, although it is generally a good value at the low rate paid.

Research Services

The advertiser, the agency, or an independent research firm can conduct any needed original research. Large agencies may have substantial in-house research departments. In some, the research title has been replaced by the account planner. Account planning has a crucial role during strategy development, driving it from the consumer's point of view. The account planners are responsible for all research, including quantitative research (usage and attitude studies, tracking studies, ad testing, and sales data) as well as qualitative research (talking face-to-face to their target). On the other hand, many smaller agencies offer little in-house research staffing, although many agencies have moved to add account planners.

In addition to the syndicated research previously discussed, which regularly reports the latest findings on buyers of a product—who and where they are, how they live and buy, and what media they read, watch, and listen to—these research companies offer many custom-made research reports to advertisers and their agencies, answering their questions about their own products and advertising. Studies cover such subjects as advertising effectiveness, advertising testing, customer satisfaction, concept and product testing, premium or package design testing, image and positioning, brand equity measurement, market segmentation, strategic research, media preferences, purchasing patterns, and similar problems affecting product and advertising decisions.

A fascinating variety of techniques is available to gather such information, including consumer field surveys (using personal or telephone interviews or self-administered questionnaires), focus groups, consumer panels, continuous tracking studies, cable testing of commercials, image studies, electronic questionnaires, opinion surveys, shopping center intercepts, and media-mix tests. (Research techniques are discussed in Chapter 15.) Regardless of the technique used in collecting data for a research report, its real value lies in the creative interpretation and use made of its findings.

Managing Integrated Brands

A brand needs a single architect, someone who will implement and coordinate a cohesive strategy across multiple media and markets. According to David Aaker, the advertising agency is often a strong candidate for this role.[22] It regularly develops brand strategy and gains insights due to exposure to different brand contexts. An advertising agency inherently provides a strong link between strategy and executions because both functions are housed under the same roof. Strategy development in an agency is more likely to include issues of implementation. On the downside, many agencies still have a bias toward media advertising, and their experience at managing event sponsorships, direct marketing, or interactive advertising may be limited.

The challenge for today's agency is to be able to develop an integrated program that accesses and employs a wide range of communication vehicles. There are several approaches to managing this.

Agency Conglomerate   Many agencies have approached the integrated communication program by acquiring companies with complementary capabilities. The usual mix includes promotions, corporate design, direct marketing, marketing research, package design, public relations, trade shows, and even event marketing. The hope is that advertisers will buy one-stop coordinated communications. The general consensus is that this approach doesn't work well because the units that make up the conglomerate often don't blend well with each other and are rivals for the advertiser's budget, and each unit within the conglomerate isn't necessarily best suited to solve the problem at hand.

In-House Generalist Agency Another option is to expand the agency's capabilities to include such functions as promotions and public relations. Brand teams spanning communication vehicles can then deal with the coordination issue. Hal Riney & Partners exemplified this approach with its set of promotional programs designed for Saturn. Riney was named guardian of the Saturn brand and created ads, promotions, and a Web site, and even helped design a retail concept. This approach works if the agency has the talent to handle the new services or has the clients or revenues to support such a diverse staff.

Service Cluster A service cluster team is a group of people drawn together from all the agency affiliate organizations. Strategically, the cluster's purpose is to service client needs, and the cluster has the flexibility to change with the needs of the client. A key characteristic of the service-cluster team is that it focuses on creating ideas rather than ads.

Communication Integrator In this approach the agency draws from sources outside the agency and integrates these services for the brands.

Brand Strategy In-House

Many advertisers choose not to rely on the agency at all for managing brand strategy. Their view may be that agencies may be great at creating ads, but brand strategy may be better planned by the brand management team. If outside help is needed, their view may be that the agency may not be the best source—particularly if it has limited research resources. Some clients have found it beneficial to employ a team of specialized communication firms that each are the best in what they do. The advertiser may develop specialized expertise—including research, media buying, and strategy consulting.

 **SUMMARY**

The advertising agency is in a period of transition. It is being reevaluated and reengineered to be more responsive to clients' needs.

A full-service agency works on many aspects of a client's marketing problems: strategy, creative response, media planning, and trade campaigns. Many agencies are organized into four divisions: account services, marketing services, creative services, and management and finance. Some agencies have a domestic network of offices or affiliates to service their large accounts better. The growing importance of global marketing to some clients has led agencies to expand internationally. Clients usually pay agencies by commission, fees, or a combination of the two.

Other types of advertising services beside the traditional advertising agency include in-house agencies, à la carte agencies, creative boutiques, Rolodex agencies, and media-buying services. Agencies usually cannot and will not handle two accounts that compete in the same market.

REVIEW

1. What is a full-service agency?

2. Give an example of a global agency network.

3. What is an agency of record?

 **TAKE IT TO THE WEB**

Foote Cone & Belding (**www.fcb.com**) and Grey Global Group (**www.greyglobalgroup. com**) are both worldwide advertising agencies. Compare the ways in which the two agencies manage global advertising.

Ogilvy & Mather is an example of a global advertising and public relations firm. Visit the Ogilvy & Mather Web site (**www.ogilvy.com**) for a look at how the agency–client relationship is developed and maintained through the Customer Relationship Management system and its trademarked Customer Ownership approach.

The American Association of Advertising Agencies (**www.aaaa.org**) is the national trade organization that represents advertising agencies in the United States. Look over both the standards of practice and creative code for the organization.

Visit the Web site of J. Walter Thompson (**www.jwtworld.com**) and review how research is handled. What is the Current Brand Situation approach?

CHAPTER 6

Look, ma. No wires.

None on the sensor. None on the display. No wires anywhere to tangle up a fun day of fishing. Simply attach the Remote Sonar Sensor™ to your line and cast. Then watch as it wirelessly transmits real-time views of fish, bottom, and structure right to the innovative Wristmount display. The action is always easy to see, whether you're fishing or just scouting an area. Plus, you can quickly switch from one location to the next since there's nothing to carry. So strap on a SMARTCAST™ Wristmount display and go anywhere! Because a fishfinder shouldn't tie you down. It should set you free.

HUMMINBIRD.
SMARTCAST™
WIRELESS FISHFINDERS

humminbird.com

The Advertiser's Marketing/Advertising Operation

CHAPTER OBJECTIVES

We often hear someone say that "the world is changing." It is, and marketers fight constantly to deal with these changes. During about a 25-year period, some 60 percent of the companies listed in the *Fortune* 500 were replaced by other more successful companies. Today marketers understand the need to change as the world around the consumer seems to constantly change. Many companies have restructured their marketing operations to be more competitive in an attempt to make all of their consumer communication efforts speak with one voice. Here we learn about some fundamentals about marketing structure in a time of change. After reading this chapter, you will understand:

1. **the marketing service system**
2. **integrated marketing brand management**
3. **how advertising budgets are set**
4. **advertising goals versus marketing goals**
5. **agency–client relationships**

Today everyone wants to be more efficient and competitive. For some marketers it is simply a case of survival. Advertising is a tool used by marketers who must always remember that advertising is a business. It has a structure and an organization, and must be managed, just like any business. Advertising is a financial investment in the brand or company. The advertising and marketing departments control the dollars and decide on the need for an advertising agency or, in some cases, multiple agencies for different products. At times they may hire an agency to handle only creative or to place the ads in the media. They may choose to use freelancers or creative boutiques or to use a media-buying service or combine their media-buying strength for all their products with one agency. They may decide to staff an in-house agency to develop ads, as discussed in Chapter 5. It is their ball game. They call the shots.

Traditionally, all advertising functions are funneled through the advertising department, which is headed by an advertising manager or the director in who operates under a marketing director. Broadly speaking, the ad manager controls the entire advertising strategy and operation: budgeting, monitoring the creation and production of the advertising, research, planning the media schedule, and keeping expenditures in line. As the business grows and new lines of products are added, *assistant advertising managers,* usually known as *product advertising managers,* are appointed to handle the advertising for different brands of the company, working under the supervision of the advertising manager. To give you a better perspective of the scope of brands to be managed, Frito-Lay lists 56 brands on its Web site including Lay's potato chips, Smith's potato chips, Walker's potato chips, Miss Vickie's potato chips, and Wotsits corn snacks. Procter & Gamble has almost 300 brands (e.g., Crest, CoverGirl, Tide, Bounty, Clairol, Head & Shoulders, Ivory, Pampers, Vicks, etc.) in 22 product categories. Unilever has some 200 brands in a number of categories with the following examples:

Category	Sample Brands
Dressings	Bertolli, Hellmann's
Savoury	Knorr, Ragu, Lawry's
Frozen food	Birds Eye, Igloo
Ice cream	Bryers
Tea	Lipton
Spreads	"I Can't Believe It's Not Butter"
Household care	Domestos
Laundry	Snuggle, Ala
Deodorant	Axe, Rexona, Impulse
Hair care	Thermasilk, Organics
Skin care	Dove, Vaseline, Pond's
Health and wellness	Slim-Fast
Oral care	Signal, Close-Up
Prestige fragrance	Calvin Klein

Because companies vary in size and structure, it only makes sense that advertising and marketing staffs also differ from organization to organization. They may have a large department controlling all marketing activities, or they may have limited personnel in marketing, or they may rely on operation managers or the president to make the marketing decisions. Before we complicate the process of integrated marketing structure, let us examine the typical structure.

MARKETING SERVICES SYSTEM

With increasing structural and organizational changes in business, the results are being felt in the advertising and marketing function. The advertising department structure—the traditional system—worked well for most companies. Exhibit 6.1 illustrates this organizational structure.

EXHIBIT **6.1**

Simple organization chart for advertising department

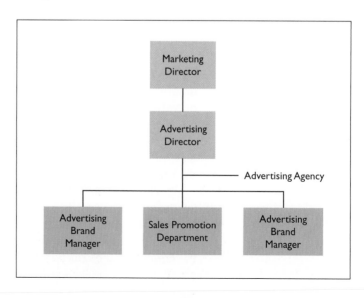

Procter & Gamble (P&G) was founded by William Procter and James Gamble in 1837 as a maker of soap and candles. It launched Tide in 1946 and won the American Dental Association's approval for Crest as an effective cavity fighter in 1960; Pampers, the first disposable diaper, was created in 1961. The first shampoo-conditioner was P&G's Pert Plus. P&G is known as a marketing innovator. It even invented the soap opera, a perfect consumer-sales vehicle. P&G has long been known as the world's finest marketing training ground.

In 1931, P&G developed a new organizational structure to solve its growing brands and marketing problems. The idea of brand management—setting up marketing teams for each brand and urging them to compete against each other—was the birth of the marketing services system. It became the model for handling brands. This concept has been widely adopted, especially in the packaged goods fields and by a number of service-oriented companies. Under this concept, each brand manager is, in essence, president of his or her own corporation-within-the-corporation. The brand manager is charged with developing, manufacturing, marketing, promoting, integrating, and selling the brand.

The marketing services system has two parts (see Exhibit 6.2). One is the marketing activity, which begins with the product manager assigned to different brands. The other part is a structure of marketing services, which represents all the technical talent involved in implementing a marketing plan, including creative services, promotion services, media services, advertising controls, and marketing research services. All of these services are available to the product manager, as is the help from the advertising agency assigned to that manager's brand. The product manager can bring together the agency personnel and his or her counterpart in the marketing services division, giving the company the benefit of the best thinking of both groups—internal and external. Each group has a group product manager, who supervises the individual product managers.

The **product manager** is responsible for planning strategy and objectives, obtaining relevant brand information, managing budget and controls, and getting agency recommendations, and is the primary liaison between the marketing department and all other departments. The product manager's plans must be approved by the group product manager, who then submits the plans for approval of the vice president for marketing and finally of the executive vice president.

The advertising department is a branch of the marketing services division. The vice president for advertising, responsible for the review and evaluation of brand media plans, attends all creative presentations to act as an adviser and consultant on all aspects of advertising. The vice president for advertising reports to the senior vice president, director of marketing.

Under this system, the advertising does not all come through one huge funnel, with one person in charge of all brands. The advantage to the corporation is that each brand gets the full marketing attention of its own group, and all brands get the full benefit of all the company's special marketing services and the accumulated corporate wisdom. The more important the decision, the higher up the ladder it goes for final approval (see Exhibit 6.3).

Large companies with many categories of products, such as Unilever and Procter & Gamble, can have another layer of management called the **category manager.** All disciplines—research, manufacturing, engineering, sales, advertising, and so on—report to the category manager. The category manager follows the product line he or she is in charge of and decides how to coordinate each brand in that line. The category manager decides how to position brands in each category.

In 2003, Procter & Gamble restructured its 3,400 global marketers, restoring a level that had been eliminated a decade earlier. It reclassified about half of its global marketing directors to associate marketing directors. Brand managers now report to either a marketing director or an associate director. Now senior brand managers who get promoted will become associate directors instead of directors. Jim Stengel Global

product manager
In package goods, the person responsible for the profitability of a product (brand) or product line, including advertising decisions. Also called a brand manager.

category manager
A relatively new corporate position, this manager is responsible for all aspects of the brands in a specific product category for a company including research, manufacturing, sales, and advertising. Each product's advertising manager reports to the category manager. Example: Procter & Gamble's Tide and Cheer detergent report to a single category manager.

EXHIBIT **6.2**

A large company with a marketing services division may be organized into (a) a marketing department; and (b) a marketing services department, where specialists in creative, media, and research advise product managers and consult with counterparts in the agency.

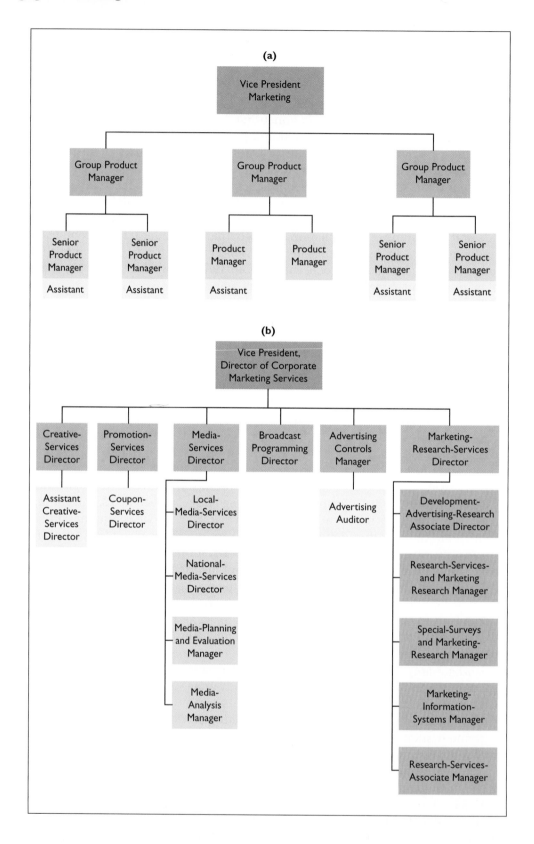

Marketing Officer, says managers will stay in their position longer under the new system, giving them a broader experience with sales teams and research and development and other areas. Under the new system a product's general manager is likely to remain in that position for five years. Brand managers' tenure in a position would be about three years, and assistant brand managers jobs' would last about two and a half years. The P&G restructuring was an attempt to streamline the marketing organization.[1]

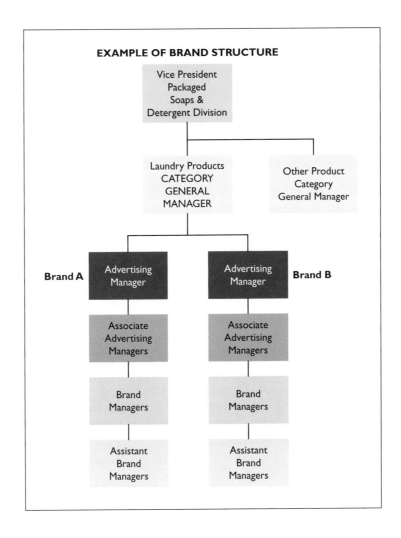

EXAMPLE OF BRAND STRUCTURE

EXHIBIT **6.3**
The category manager is responsible for all aspects of the brands in his or her category. Each product's advertising manager reports to the category manager.

INTEGRATED MARKETING BRAND MANAGEMENT

Previously, we discussed integrated marketing, or one-voice marketing, from the agency perspective. There has been debate about whether agencies can effectively implement this concept because of their structure. One of the major problems is that agencies are set up as separate profit centers, which results in competition among their own units for a strong bottom-line showing.

Research involving marketing executives indicates that integration of advertising, promotion, public relations, and all other forms of marketing communications is the most important factor influencing how strategies will be set. Larry Light, the former chairman of the international division of Bates Worldwide, says, "The reason integrated marketing is important is consumers integrate your messages whether you like it or not. The messages cannot be kept separate. All marketing is integrated in the mind of consumers. Your only choice is how that message is integrated."[2]

An integrated marketing communication (IMC) study report found that "organizations are taking charge of the integration process themselves rather than looking to ad agencies or other suppliers to provide the integration." Professor William Swain says, "While there is some agreement that corporations are better equipped than their agencies to oversee IMC, there is no universal agreement where within the organization IMC leadership does or should reside."[3] Hy Haberson of True North Advertising Group, Toronto, is a little more blunt, "The single most critical issue is the recognition that traditional ad agencies are not staffed properly to foster this type of integrated thinking. The second reason agencies fail to properly provide integrated marketing services is that most only concern themselves with communicating to the end customer/consumer. They are myopic in considering non-advertising marketing tactics (sales/training materials, POS displays, sales incentive programs, etc.)."[4] Of course, he feels his agency delivers in these areas. As you can see, how to organize and handle IMC is still controversial.

Integrated Functions

Integrated marketing communication can function in the marketing services system if there is management of this process among all the departments involved—advertising, sales promotion, public relations, and other existing departments. Some organizations call the process integrated brand communication (IBC). Radical organizational changes don't seem to work well with regard to implementation. Many organizations have found that integrated functions become evolutionary. However, there are marketers who feel that this kind of management isn't practical because the resistance to change by managers is just too great. Don Schultz, author of *Integrated Marketing Communications,* suggests that reengineering the communications function and structure within the company is sometimes necessary. He suggests the following functions:

1. Start with the customer or prospect and work back toward the brand or organization. That's the outside-in approach. Most organizations are structured to deliver inside-out communications, which allows the budget cycle to dictate when communications can be delivered.

2. Good communications require knowledge of customers and prospects. Without specific customer information, the marketing organization will continue to send out the wrong message and information to the wrong people at the wrong time at an exorbitant cost.

3. A database is critical to carry out the IMC communication task.

4. Brand contacts—all the ways the customer comes in contact with the organization—are the proper way to think about communications programs. This goes beyond traditional media. It includes managing the impact and influence of packaging, employees, in-store displays, sales literature, and even the design of the product so that the brand clearly or concisely communicates with the right person, at the right time, in the right way, with the right message or incentive through the right delivery channel.

There are three forms of adaptation to integrated marketing within corporate structures:[5]

- *Marcom (marketing communications) manager.* Adapting a business-to-business organizational structure called marcom management centralizes all the communication activities under one person or office (see Exhibit 6.4). Under this structure, all communication is centralized. Product managers request communication programs for their products through a marcom manager. The manager develops the strategy and then directs the communication programs either internally or externally.

- *Restructured brand management approach.* This approach reduces the layers previously involved in the process. All sales and marketing activities for the brand, category, or organization are reduced to three groups, all reporting to the CEO, and all are on the same organizational level. They are marketing services/communications (MSC), marketing operations, and sales. Marketing operations is responsible for developing and delivering the product to the MSC, which works with sales to develop and implement all sales and marketing programs (including advertising).

- *Communications manager.* This approach names a communication manager who is responsible for approving or coordinating all communications programs for the entire organization. The various brands develop their own communica-

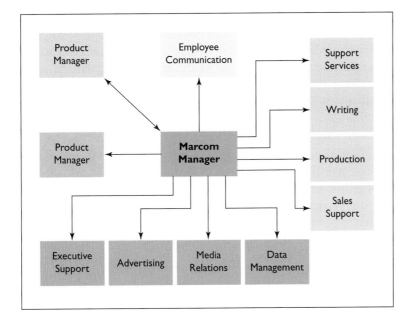

EXHIBIT **6.4**
Marcom management centralizes all the communication activities under one person or office.

tion programs as they have traditionally done. These plans go to the communications manager, who is responsible for coordinating, consolidating, and integrating the programs, messages, and media for the organization (see Exhibit 6.5).

IMC Focus

Using IMC to coordinate all messages a company communicates through advertising, direct marketing, public relations, promotion, and so on helps to create a unified image and support relationship building with customers. The key, however, is to determine exactly what your IMC strategy should achieve.

One of the first steps is to identify the specific target (such as users or influencers) and understand what each needs from your IMC campaign. To sharpen the focus, concentrate on one or two goals to avoid stretching the strategy or budget. Three such possible goals are the following:[6]

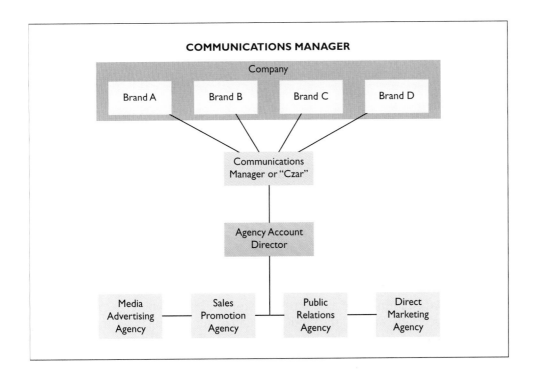

EXHIBIT **6.5**
The communications manager approves or coordinates all communications programs for the entire organization.

■ *Build brand equity.* By using IMC to reinforce your brand's unique value and identity, you increase awareness and encourage stronger preference among customers and prospects. The business-to-business ads for Scotchgard, the stain protector, are aimed at the textile and garment industry, for example, stating the product keeps apparel in good shape by adding stain-shedding qualities.

■ *Provide information.* Business customers need a lot of information. Differentiate products or features if applicable.

■ *Communicate differentiation/positioning.* What does the product stand for and how is it better than the competitors' products? IMC helps convey your most significant points. For instance, a UPS ad stressed the range of guaranteed "urgent delivery" choices. These choices differentiated it from its competition while positioning it as being able to meet virtually any deadline.

Another View

Al Ries takes issue with the term *marcom,* saying, "The name encourages advertising people to go in the wrong direction. Advertising is not communication; advertising is positioning. What the best advertising does, however, is to establish and reinforce a position in the prospect's mind." That's the primary function of a marketing organization according to Ries. Of course, this thought is from one of the people who created the concept of positioning decades ago. He makes a point:[7]

"Better ingredients, better pizza," says Papa John's.

As a result of this positioning, Papa John's has become the third-largest pizza chain in America. Ries asks, "Do you know what the better ingredients are? Do you know that Papa John's uses fresh crushed tomatoes, real mozzarella cheese and distilled water in the preparation of its pizzas? Most people don't. Does it matter? Probably not. Better ingredients, better pizza is enough to position Papa John's a step above Pizza Hut and Domino's."

Despite the structural quibbling among advertisers and agencies, in general, the concept of IMC itself has become a fundamental goal of most marketers and ad agencies.

New Corporate Attitude

There has been a recent trend among leading marketers to dump their marginal brands and focus on the top performers in their portfolios. Global giant Unilever marketed some 1,600 brands during the mid-1990s. Today it has culled its brands to only some 200. Many of the major marketers have developed a philosophy that a brand must be one of the top three brands in their category to get marketing support.[8] As a result, many marketers are selling or spinning off divisions or brands that haven't lived up to expectations in their categories. This trend is a move by marketers to focus on their core brands and an unwillingness to support those that don't offer large-scale manufacturing, distribution, and advertising synergies. Tom Lawson of Arnold Communications says, "Second-tier brands become milked by their owners, then they stop being brands and become products."[9]

Better Advertising Expenditure Expectations

John Wanamaker, founder of a department store in Philadelphia, is credited with saying, "I am certain that half the money I spend in advertising is wasted. The trouble is, I do not know which half." That uneasy sense of mystery has undergirded the growth of modern marketing according to consultants at Booz Allen Hamilton (who many times are in competition with advertising agencies). As a result, companies rely on imperfect metrics and anecdotes to guide their marketing programs to answer questions such as: What works best—sustained brand advertising or targeted retail promotion. Is likeable media advertising a more effective vehicle than hard-sell direct marketing?

The consultants claim companies can know how and where to apply marketing expenditures to achieve significant and lasting lifts in a product's or service's profitability. They call it ROI (return on investment) marketing, which is the application of modern measurement technologies and contemporary organization design to understand, quantify, and optimize marketing spending. ROI marketing is not a fix but a philosophy.[10] Today organizations view how they allocate and use marketing communication expenditures differently. Each tries to solve their interpretation of how to become more efficient and not waste half their money, as Wanamaker was convinced was happening to his company.

SETTING THE BUDGET

Trying to get beyond Wanamaker's perception of what works and what doesn't, we generally agree advertising is supposed to accomplish some objective. It is a business decision. The Folks catering ad (see Exhibit 6.6) is trying to get product trial by

EXHIBIT 6.6

Folks catering reduces potential customer risk by absorbing part of the price, making the product a strong value.

Courtesy of Bevil Advertising and Folks.

EXHIBIT **6.7**

Savannah Electric invests in educating and demonstrating it is a good citizen.

Courtesy of Savannah Electric, A Southern Company.

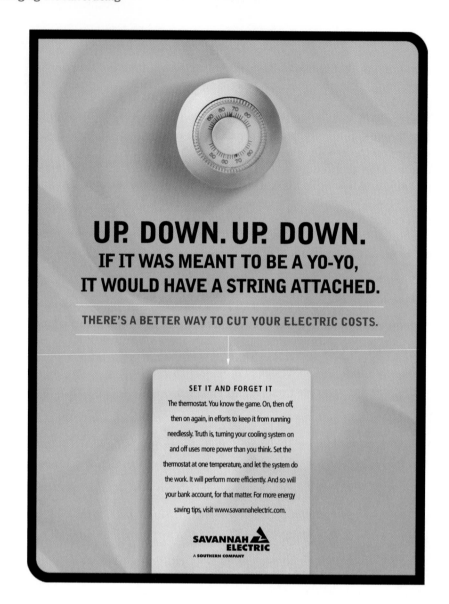

reducing the risk in an extremely competitive market and category. It will be able to measure the number of coupons. On the opposite end of the spectrum is Savannah Electric (see Exhibit 6.7). Despite being a public utility, it would say it has competition from other energy sources. Its objective is to provide a service to its customers and be a good citizen. Both advertisers expect a return for their investment despite the fact that they are totally different kinds of advertisers, each with a different reason for being.

What is an investment in an ad or campaign supposed to accomplish? Launch a new product? Increase a brand's awareness level? Neutralize the competition's advertising? Educate? Increase sales? A key question is how much money it will take to accomplish the objective. Even if we have been successful with the product, do we know whether we are spending too much on advertising—or not enough? Despite all the technology available to help us to determine how much should be spent, the final decision is a judgment call by corporate management. The person responsible for the budget decision varies across companies and according to objectives. In general, a Gallagher Report says, the vice president of marketing and the vice president of advertising are the people most responsible for setting the ad budget (see Exhibit 6.8). Two-thirds of advertising budgets are submitted for approval in September or October; almost 80 percent are approved during the period of September to November. As you might expect for such an important decision, most presidents or chief operating officers strongly influence the approval process.

Who Prepares Clients' Ad Budgets[a]		Who Approves Client's Ad Budgets[a]	
VP Marketing	63.2%	President or CEO	68.5%
VP Advertising	31.6	VP Marketing	37.3
Ad manager	22.2	Executive VP	20.9
Brand manager	16.3	Division manager	17.2
Ad agency	21.7	VP Advertising	14.4
Sales promotion	5.6	Treasurer or controller	8.6

[a]Totals more than 100% due to multiple responses.

EXHIBIT 6.8

Source: *26th Gallagher Report Consumer Advertising Survey.*

Budgets are usually drawn up using one of four approaches: percentage of sales, payout plan, competitive budgeting, and the task method.

Percentage of Sales

The percentage of sales method simply means the advertising budget is based on a percentage of the company's sales. For instance, a family restaurant chain might budget 5 percent of its sales for advertising. A company using this method to determine its advertising budget will not spend beyond its means because the ad budget will increase only when sales increase. If sales decrease, so will its advertising; however, if competitive pressures are severe, it may have to maintain or increase the budget to retain market share, even though there is no prospect of increased profit. This method can actually reverse the assumed cause-and-effect relationship between advertising and sales. That is, because the budgeting is based either on the previous year's sales—usually with some percentage of increase added—or next year's anticipated sales, then it can be said that the sales are causing the advertising rather than advertising causing the sales.

A Gallagher Report indicates that about 9 percent of companies surveyed take a percentage of last year's sales.[11] Roughly 35 percent use a percentage of anticipated sales, 30 percent combine needed tasks with a percentage of anticipated sales, 13 percent outline needed tasks and fund them, 13 percent set arbitrary amounts based on the general fiscal outlook of the company, and 9 percent calculate an average between last year's actual sales and anticipated sales for the coming year. In any method, a change in sales changes the amount of advertising expenditure.

Payout Plan

The payout plan looks at advertising as an investment rather than as an expenditure. It recognizes that it may take several years before the company can recover start-up costs and begin taking profits.

Exhibits 6.9 and 6.10 are examples of typical payout plans. Let us go briefly through Exhibit 6.9, a payout plan for a new fast-food operation. In the first year of operation, the company spent the entire gross profits ($15,274,000) on advertising. In addition, the company invested $10,300,000 in store development for a first-year operating loss.

In the second year, the company again invested gross profits ($48,122,000) in advertising and carried over the $10,300,000 debt from the first year. By the third year, sales had increased to the point where advertising as a percentage of gross sales had dropped to 13 percent, or $46,312,000, leaving a profit of $35,625,000. After covering the first-year debt of $10,300,000, the payout was $25,625,000.

If the company had demanded a 10 percent profit in the first year (0.10 × $84,854,000 = $8,485,400), it would have had to curtail advertising drastically, reduce corporate store investment, or do some combination of both. In that case, the company would have made a profit the first year but risked future profits and perhaps its own long-term survival.

EXHIBIT **6.9**

Fast-Food Payout Plan
Investment Introduction—
36-Month Payout

Systemwide Payout (Fiscal Years 1, 2, 3)

		Year 1		Year 2		Year 3
Sales		$84,854,000		$218,737,000		$356,248,000
Food cost	34%	28,850,000	34%	74,371,000	34%	121,124,000
Paper cost	5	4,245,000	5	10,937,000	5	17,812,000
Labor	22	18,668,000	20	43,747,000	20	71,250,000
Overhead	21	17,819,000	19	41,560,000	18	64,125,000
Total op. exp.	82	69,580,000	78	170,615,000	77	274,511,000
Gross profit	18	15,274,000	22	48,122,000	25	81,937,000
Advertising/Promo		$15,274,000		$48,122,000	13	$46,312,000
Store profit		0		0	10	35,625,000
Corp. invest.		10,300,000		0		0
Corp. profit		(10,300,000)		0		35,625,000
Cumulative		(10,300,000)		(10,300,000)		25,625,000

Competitive Budgeting

Another approach to budgeting is to base it on the competitive spending environment. In competitive budgeting, the level of spending relates to the percentage of sales and other factors: whether the advertiser is on the offensive or defensive, media strategies chosen (for example, desire to dominate a medium), or answers to questions such as, "Is it a new brand or an existing one?" The problem here is that competition dictates the spending allocation (and competing companies may have different marketing objectives).

The Task Method

The task method of budgeting is possibly the most difficult to implement, but it may also be the most logical budgeting method. The method calls for marketing and advertising managers to determine what task or objective the advertising will fulfill over the budgetary period and then calls for a determination of how much money will be needed to complete the task. Under this method, the company sets a specific sales target for a given time to attain a given goal. Then it decides to spend whatever money is necessary to meet that quota. The task method might be called the "let's spend all we can afford" approach, especially when launching a new product. Many big businesses today started that way. Many businesses that are not here today did too.

EXHIBIT **6.10**

Package Goods Product
Payout Plan

Investment Introduction—36 Month Payout

	Year 1	Year 2	Year 3	3-Year Total	Year 4
Size of market (MM cases)	8	10	11		12
Share goal:					
Average	12%	25%	30%		30%
Year end	20	30	30		30
Consumer movement (MM Cases)	1.0	2.5	3.3	6.8	3.6
Pipeline (MM Cases)	.3	.2	.1	.6	—
Total shipments (MM Cases)	1.3	2.7	3.4	7.4	3.6
Factory income (@ $9)	$11.7	$24.3	$30.6	$66.6	$32.4
Less costs (@ $5)	6.5	13.5	17.0	37.0	18.0
Available P/A (@ $4)	$5.2	$10.8	$13.6	$29.6	$14.4
Spending (normal $2)	$12.8	$10.0	$6.8	$29.6	$7.2
Advertising	10.5	8.5	5.4	24.4	5.7
Promotion	2.3	1.5	1.4	5.2	1.5
Profit (Loss):					
Annual	($7.6)	$0.8	$6.8	—	$7.2
Cumulative	($7.6)	($6.8)	—	—	$7.2

The approach can be complex. It involves several important considerations: brand loyalty factors, geographic factors, and product penetration. Advertisers who use this method need accurate and reliable research, experience, and models for setting goals and measuring results.

The task method is used most widely in a highly competitive environment. Budgets are under constant scrutiny in relation to sales and usually are formally reviewed every quarter. Moreover, they are subject to cancellation at any time (except for noncancelable commitments) because sales have not met a minimum quota, money is being shifted to a more promising brand, or management wants to hold back money to make a better showing on its next quarterly statement.

No one approach to budgeting is always best for all companies.

THE CHANGING MARKETING ENVIRONMENT

Marketers are in an irreversible restructuring in the way businesses operate—one that may require a major rethinking of the agency–client relationship in today's environment. The retail universe has consolidated, and the media universe has shattered. It is harder for an advertiser to reach mass numbers of consumers. They now have 500 channels to reach their targets instead of a handful using similar budgets. In 1995 it took three television spots to reach 80 percent of the women. Five years later it took 97 spots to reach the same group. Some companies are calling for radical changes in the way they do business.

Recently, Coca-Cola Company chief Steve Heyer challenged marketers, media moguls, and agency heads to rethink the core assumptions. He said that the Coca-Cola Company was thinking about marketing in a radically new way. Coke will accelerate the convergence of Madison and Vine (advertising community with the creative Hollywood entertainment community)—a convergence of the trinity in brand building—content, media, and marketing. "Imagine if we used our collective toolkit to create an ever-expanding variety of interactions for people that—over time—built a relationship, an ongoing series of transactions, that is unique, differentiated and deeper . . . improving everyone's economics and reversing the buyer-seller, zero-sum game," Heyer said.[12] Advertising agency TBWA Worldwide had similar views a couple of years earlier when it established TBWA/Connect to blend knowledge of consumers' touch points with the new science of media consumption and influence. TBWA also believed that integration is no longer enough to help companies compete. Its goal was not about taking one discipline and extending into other channels but about how to connect big ideas across all channels of communication. Additionally, the shortage of content for media channels represents a new set of opportunities for clients to market their brands. These views indicate marketers are looking for new marketing and communication formulas.

Some of the factors driving the change at companies include the following:[13]

- *Fragmented consumer target.* Consumer groups are more fragmented than ever before by demographics, age, ethnicity, family type, geographic location, and media usage.

- *Parity performance.* The importance of value, convenience, and service in influencing preference is increasing, and the impact of low-priced, satisfactorily performing private brands is growing.

- *Cost control.* Marketers must remain price competitive and must develop new strategies for offsetting internal cost increases.

- *Erosion of advertising effectiveness.* Advertisers have settled for advertising that doesn't present a compelling basis for consumer preference and fails to effectively reinforce relevant brand equity in other marketing activities.

- *Strengthened retailer influence.* Retailers are equipped with detailed data on consumer purchase behavior, which give them leverage against marketers.

Launching new products. Developing new strategies for established brands.

Both require MARKETING KNOW-HOW.

Socoh℠ Marketing has one seasoned executive who has:

- Developed new products for Lipton, Swedish Match, and Dow
- Launched new products for Nestlé/Carnation, JVC, Gillette, Reckitt Benckiser, and Johnson & Johnson
- Revitalized established brands for Gillette, Nestlé/Carnation, and Hiram Walker

(And then there's the day-to-day marketing of world-renowned brands for Sara Lee, DuPont, Gallo, Pinkerton Security Services, DowBrands, Jimmy Dean Foods, and Mead Paper.)

Small Business can trust the marketing resource that Big Business has trusted.

SOCOH MARKETING LLC

EXHIBIT 6.11

Socoh tells potential clients about the breadth of its personnel's experience in managing new and established products.

Courtesy of Socoh Marketing LLC.

Agencies understand that companies are concerned about matching the right advertising agency and/or promotion agencies, public relations firms, and so on to help manage and promote their brands. Socoh Marketing's self-promotion (see Exhibit 6.11) talks about staff experience developing and launching new products for a number of companies (Lipton, Dow, JVC, Gillette, Nestlé/Carnation, and others) and developing new strategies for established brands.

MANAGING BRANDS

Retailer Control

There is no doubt about who controls shelf space and entry into supermarkets, discounters, and mass merchandise stores today. It is the mass channel, not the mass media, that is demanding most of the marketing dollars. It is estimated that almost 60 percent of the manufacturers' marketing budgets goes to the retailer in the form of trade spending (ads in shoppers, displays, etc). Wal-Mart alone is driving a number of product categories. In household staples (toothpaste, shampoos, paper towels, etc.) it controls about 30 percent of the U.S. market. It controls 28 percent of Dial's total sales, 24 percent of Del Monte foods, and 23 percent of Clorox and Revlon's sales.[14] As the world's largest company with over 4,750 stores and 138 million weekly shoppers, Wal-Mart controls who and what is on the shelves. The manufacturer is somewhat at the mercy of retailers like Wal-Mart, Target, Home Depot, Lowe's, Kohl's, Kroger, and others. Category managers must understand the needs of these retailers as well as they do the needs of consumers. They must be sure that their promotions are integrated into the retailer's total marketing program. Retailers like Wal-Mart favor strong consumer brands that are supported through consumer advertising.

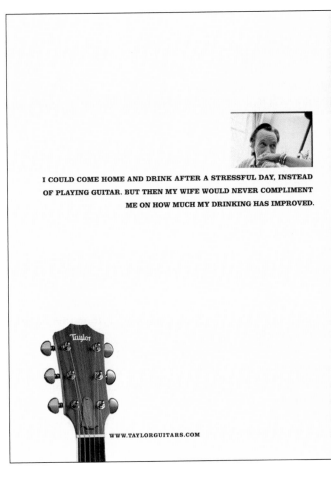

I COULD COME HOME AND DRINK AFTER A STRESSFUL DAY, INSTEAD
OF PLAYING GUITAR. BUT THEN MY WIFE WOULD NEVER COMPLIMENT
ME ON HOW MUCH MY DRINKING HAS IMPROVED.

WWW.TAYLORGUITARS.COM

EXHIBIT 6.12

Agency and client use a little humor as they speak to potential users.

Courtesy of VitroRobertson, Inc., Taylor Guitars and Marge Casey, photographer.

Slotting Allowances

Every square foot of a supermarket costs money and needs to pay for itself by moving products and brands quickly. There is only so much shelf space for the category manager to obtain from grocers. Because grocers control the space, many charge slotting allowances for shelf space. This admission fee, which comes primarily from the marketer's trade promotion funds, ensures space for a period of about three to six months. Supermarkets use the slotting allowance to pay for slow-moving products and for administrative overhead for placing a new product into their system, including warehouse space, computer input, communications to individual stores about the product's availability, and the redesign of shelf space. The frozen-food section has only a finite amount of space and almost always demands slotting allowances. Yet, the largest retailer, Wal-Mart, doesn't charge manufacturer's slotting fees but instead usually negotiates a number of cost requirements.[15]

Experimentation and Risk

Today marketers are forced to find the right formula and be innovative in marketing new and established products. IBM's Marianne Caponetta tells agencies seeking her business, "Demonstrate you understand my business, my issues and have a compelling point of view."[16] VitroRobertson has helped Taylor Guitars find the formula for success. The ad in Exhibit 6.12 says, "I could come home and drink after a stressful day, instead of playing guitar. But then my wife would never compliment me on how much my drinking has improved." Both agency and client understand the user and use a little humor to interest them.

"We believe in this age of increased clutter, the only risk is not to take a risk. If your gut doesn't bubble up with an instinct that isn't just right about an idea, then you should think about something else." This kind of thinking makes Kerri Martin most creative peoples' dream client. She is the "guardian of brand soul," or marketing communications manager for BMW of North America's Mini brand. She led the marketing team responsible for the 2002 hugely successful launch campaign for the Mini brand.[17]

The discussion of risk is not new with agency people. Years ago, Bill Borders of Borders, Perrin & Norrander, said, "Risk taking is the lifeblood of an agency." However, a former director of creative at Pepsi-Cola says, "The problem with most clients is that they are not willing to join the agency in the risk. Through the years Pepsi-Cola has told BBDO to take the risk. If you miss, we understand that not everything is going to be a home run. But it could be a single. Occasionally, we have burned the film knowing that we tried and it just didn't work."[18] Unfortunately, most clients can't find the courage to join Pepsi in taking chances or risk to seek cutting-edge advertising.

Bob Moore, creative director of Fallon, Minneapolis, says, "I am a believer that you have to do strong ads that stand out. A lot of times that leads you to something that is different. By its very nature, different is going to lead you to something risky. What's risky gets people talking. You can do work that feels good, but no one notices it. It is like wallpaper. That's far riskier."[19]

Many clients are looking for ad home runs to drive their brands. But in many cases a marketing executive is in power an average of 18 months on a brand. They only care about what's happening now, many critics say. The brand management system attempts to prevent failure by relying strongly on research and testing. The brand managers are promoted if they don't make mistakes as well as if they hit a home run. This creates brand managers who play it safe and won't take risks. Some companies are extending how long brand managers stay on a particular assignment. Advertising never pays for itself in the short term. Promotions always do. Yet, some marketers are calling for change and risk beyond the creative ad idea (as did Coca-Cola's CEO mentioned earlier) in the way the industry looks at things. Mark Kaline, global media manager at Ford, says, "The most effective way to cope with change is to help create it. We cannot be afraid to take risk." He said, "We're willing to invest in the right ideas—from brand inspired merchandise to product tie-ins with movies to corporate sponsorships of landmark events or TV shows."[20]

Some advertisers are integrating technology in their strategy in nontraditional ways. In 2000, Volvo launched the S60 completely online without any traditional advertising media support for the first three months. Some companies are willing to experiment and take risk. "How does the Internet fit into our marketing plan?" is a frequent question. Will text messages and video give us an advantage? Tech-savvy youth's 24/7 use of cell phones has spurred the marketing use of short messaging service (SMS), which lets mobile phone users transmit text messages—over 400 billion global messages.[21] Marketing applications are becoming more common. SMS is proving to be an excellent means of communicating brand values, says CEO of Enpocket. Already the technology is changing from SMS marketing to MMS-multimedia messaging service, which allows more complex transmissions that incorporate audio and video images with traditional text messages.

AGENCY–CLIENT RELATIONSHIPS

It has been said that agency–client relationships are much like interpersonal relationships: If you don't like each other, you move apart. If you like each other, you gravitate toward each other and great stuff gets produced. The agency should be trusted as an employee—it is in business with the client. The relationship between the agency and the client is a partnership. A self-promotion from Ames Scullin O'Haire agency said,

> There was a time when ad agencies were partners, not vendors. They were trusted, not suspected. They added value, not expenses. Then agencies got greedy. In pursuit of hefty fees, ad agencies began to pay more attention to their own business than their clients'. Merger mania began as conglomerates gobbled agencies like Pac Man with the munchies. Soon agencies became little more than order-takers. Ironically, today clients pay consultants tens of millions for marketing advice while beating up their ad agencies over courier charges. Where's the love, babe, where's the love?
> We're Ames Scullin O'Haire, an ad agency built around you.

Some would say they are close to the heart of the problem.

In 2003, Continental Consulting Group reported that many clients are not satisfied with their advertising agencies, claiming their shops are understaffed, overcompensated, and not as creative as agencies were two decades ago. The report also complained that there is less experienced account management personnel and weak strategic thinking. Clients responded that the quality of agency staffers is less than it was five years ago, and more than half said the person heading their account is less experienced than an account manager would have been five or ten years ago. Some 81 percent of those surveyed felt agency people are stretched too thin.

Erwin Ephron, principle of Ephron Consultancy, believes a real look at the survey shows agency compensation has decreased dramatically over the past decade. His view is that agencies are underpaid but admits the truth is between his view and the survey results.[22]

Also in 2003, Nancy Salz Consulting found that advertisers and agencies agreed that costs to develop ads would decline if they could work together more productively. And both sides agreed that the major reasons for higher ad development cost could be found with advertisers rather than agencies. Among the problems both cited were too many rounds of creative revisions, too many approval levels for creative changes, and too many disagreements about strategy as well as creative elements of the ads.[23]

Agencies have always prided themselves on selling the creative product; however, many people feel today's agencies are not producing the strongest creative product. Some clients hire ad agencies because they believe they can help them persuade customers to do or think something. Clients may select an agency based on the agency's ability to be persuasive. The real task for the agency is to become a persuasion partner.

When advertisers develop a new product or become disenchanted with their existing advertising, they will conduct advertising reviews in which their current agency and others can compete for the account. This review process may take several months. The advertiser will evaluate which agencies it wants to participate in the review. Keep in mind that there are agencies that specialize in certain types of accounts.

With competitive pressures mounting, companies are more enamored with brand strategies and solutions—whether they are "advertising" driven or not—than with creative work. As a result, companies seek solutions from a coterie of other advisers, not exclusively from ad agencies. Today, agencies are again trying to find their place at the table. Many are changing their direction or focus: "Clients don't care where good ideas come from," says WPP Group Chief Executive Martin Sorrells. Agencies seek to be full-service partners, as opposed to being vendors, where clients go for any and all business solutions.[24]

KLEPPNER VIEWPOINT

THOMAS N. LENTZ

**Vice President Advertising and
Marketing Services**
Broyhill Furniture Industries, Inc.

The Best of Both Worlds—An In-House Agency

I began my advertising career on a July morning in 1979 when I entered 380 Madison Avenue (Wow! Madison Avenue), stepped off the elevator on the 18th floor, and stared at "Ogilvy & Mather" in shiny chrome letters on a fire truck red wall (Wow! Ogilvy & Mather—home of the advertising industry's David). Here I was—a rookie assistant account executive at *Ogilvy & Mather* on the Owens-Corning Corporation account. I expected to continue my career as an agency "account management guy" for many years. However, after starting a family some nine years later, my wife and I realized the benefits of being closer to our families and out of the rigors of New York commuting. So I looked for advertising opportunities nearer our Carolina roots.

This search led me to Broyhill Furniture Industries, Inc., one of the world's largest manufacturers of residential furniture and one of the best known brands among consumers. The CEO interviewing me was looking for someone who knew nothing about furniture (he wanted fresh ideas) but had lots of experience with consumer marketing. My years on packaged goods accounts such as Procter & Gamble, Lever Brothers, Colgate-Palmolive, Bristol-Myers, and General Foods would come in handy. This seemed like the perfect fit for Broyhill and me.

Suddenly I'm *The Client*—no more agency guy for me. Now I would have an agency at my beck and call—or so I thought. Ironically, this former agency account manager does not use an agency for the advertising needs of Broyhill. In place of an advertising agency we have assembled a top-notch in-house agency staff. This staff handles all our agency needs from creative development to media negotiations/planning to public relations to production and traffic. Why? Because we have found that agencies do not make our lives easier—listen up all you potential agency folks.

*Thomas N. Lentz, Vice President,
Advertising and Marketing Services, Broyhill
Furniture Industries, Inc.*

As a big New York agency account manager I was trained to be a strategic partner with our clients and to constantly bring "added value" to their business. Of course, my former agencies created, produced, and placed great advertising, but we understood the client's business so well we could make strategic recommendations, suggest new product ideas, or create innovative promotions all designed to grow their business and gain market share. The health of their business was paramount to the agency.

Agency Search Consultants

A continuing trend is clients hiring consultants to help them seek out the best agency to handle their accounts (this is a similar process to companies hiring headhunters to find executives or other employees). An estimated 60 percent of recent account reviews for major advertisers involved consultants, whose job is to

For Broyhill, agency relationships did not work. Agencies never really learned the nuances of the furniture business. They never understood the difference between branding and retail advertising—and the fact that Broyhill needed to be both. How to represent furniture to the consumer is more important than how clever the headline needed to be. Agencies approached furniture advertising as if the consumer was bored with furniture and needed to be entertained by advertising. Quite the contrary, buying furniture and creating beautiful rooms is one category many consumers love. They are very similar to car consumers. They want to see lots of products and understand many of the features and benefits of these products. Consumers buy home shelter magazines to read the furniture ads just as women buy beauty magazines to peruse the beauty products advertised. There is even an entire cable network dedicated to the home, yet agencies think we need to be "creative." As a result, you could barely see the furniture in their ads.

Why have we chosen to go the in-house agency route? *These regional agencies just didn't get it.* The agencies did not study our business thoroughly enough to learn all the complexities of retail buyers, retail floor sales associates, distribution issues, and management idiosyncrasies. It seems that too many of today's agencies are staffed with account management types that do not know their client's business well enough to guide the creatives—people who often seem more interested in developing advertising they personally like and hope will win awards. Speaking of awards, in 1984 Benton & Bowles had a Clio-winning Scope mouthwash commercial in a test market. This award-winning commercial that everyone loved was tested against a "hidden-camera testimonial" campaign straight out of the sixties. Guess which campaign took Scope to #1 in the mouthwash category? *The testimonial.* We all wanted the clever, creative, award-winning campaign to be more effective, but consumers spoke with their pocketbooks.

An in-house agency staff often truly understands all the brand's marketplace dynamics better than an agency. With today's incredible computer technology and many young, creative people available, Broyhill has solved its advertising and marketing needs by building a small agency that lives and breathes furniture—and understands what the consumer wants in advertising. Our magazine advertising has consistently ranked #1 or #2 in Starch Readership

EXHIBIT 6.13

Everything old is new again.

Courtesy of Thomas N. Lentz, Vice President, Advertising and Marketing Services, Broyhill Furniture Industries, Inc.

research. Focus groups have given our ads high marks in providing consumers the information they need. And as for awards—the ring of the cash register brings smiles and satisfaction to our marketing services staff.

An in-house advertising operation or an outside agency? To be successful both have to understand the client's business extremely well. But today I see more and more companies developing in-house agency capabilities. For many of us an in-house agency offers much of the same satisfaction as an advertising agency with the insight of the client. In many ways it's the best of both worlds—at least it has been for me. ■ ■ ■

do the initial screening, manage the search process, and in some cases negotiate compensation agreements. This may cost a client between $35,000 and $100,000. In the past, clients relied more heavily on their own marketing departments to conduct searches. Consultants have been hired more in recent years because fewer clients find they are qualified to do it themselves and because there have been so many changes in the agency landscape, according to an agency principal.[25]

The consultant has been characterized as a "marriage broker" between client and agency.

Some industry observers believe there are currently more reviews of their agencies by marketers than in recent years. Part of this is a result of the restructuring of businesses. When marketing departments get restructured and people change jobs, there is a tendency to start from scratch and this includes reviewing or changing advertising agencies. In addition, one of the driving forces on account reviews is pressure on advertisers' marketing departments to sell more units and a fixation on quarterly financial results. That position deemphasizes the importance of long-standing relationships and puts the spotlight on how well agencies can deliver quick fixes to sales problems. Because marketers have already done as much downsizing as practical, increases now have to be achieved through "real unit growth."[26] This creates pressure on both clients and agencies.

Selecting an Agency

Choosing an agency can be a complicated matter. Do you need a full-service agency, one with integrated services, one with strong media departments, or a specialized agency? After deciding whether you want a large, medium, or small, specialized, full-service, domestic, or global agency, the following points may help you in evaluating specific agencies:

1. Determine what types of service you need from an agency and then list them in order of their importance to you. For instance, (a) marketing expertise in strategy, planning, and execution; (b) creative performance in TV, print, radio, or outdoor; (c) media knowledge and clout; (d) sales promotion and/or trade relations help; (e) public relations and corporate- or image-building ability; (f) market research strength; (g) fashion or beauty sense; (h) agency size; or (i) location in relation to your office. Your special needs will dictate others.

2. Establish a five-point scale to rate each agency's attributes. A typical five-point scale would be (1) outstanding, (2) very good, (3) good, (4) satisfactory, and (5) unsatisfactory. Of course, you should give different values or weights to the more important agency attributes.

3. Check published sources and select a group of agencies that seem to fit your requirements. Use your own knowledge or the knowledge of your industry peers to find agencies responsible for successful campaigns or products that have most impressed you. Published sources include the annual issue of *Advertising Age*, which lists agencies and their accounts by agency size, and the "Red Book" (*Standard Advertising Register*), which lists agencies and accounts both alphabetically and geographically. In case of further doubt, contact the American Association of Advertising Agencies, New York, for a roster of members. Of course, you can do this online.

4. Check whether there are any apparent conflicts with accounts already at the agency. When agencies consider a new account, that is the first question they ask (along with the amount of the potential billings).

5. Now start preliminary discussions with the agencies that rate best on your initial evaluation. This can be started with a letter asking if they are interested or a telephone call to set up an appointment for them to visit you or for you to visit the agency. Start at the top. Call the president or the operating head of the agency or office in your area, who will appoint someone to follow up on the opportunity you are offering.

6. Reduce your original list of potential agencies after the first contact. A manageable number is usually no more than three.

7. Again prepare an evaluation list for rating the agencies on the same five-point scale. This list will be a lot more specific. It should cover personnel. Who will supervise your account and how will the account be staffed? Who are the creative people who will work on your business? Similarly, who will service your needs in media, production (TV) research, and sales promotion, and how will they do it? What is the agency's track record in getting and holding on to business and in keeping personnel teams together? What is the agency's record with media, with payments? Make sure again to assign a weighted value to each service aspect. If TV is most important to you and public relations the least important, be sure to reflect this in your evaluation.

8. Discuss financial arrangements. Will your account be a straight 15 percent commission account, a fee account, or a combination of both? What services will the commission or fee cover, and what additional charges will the agency demand? How will new product work be handled from both a financial and an organizational point of view? What peripheral service does the agency offer, and for how much?

9. Do you feel comfortable with the agency?

10. If your company is an international one, can the agency handle all of your non-domestic business, and if so, how will they do it?

Client Requirements

The amount of work an agency does for a client may vary significantly. Agencies may produce only a few ads for a client during a year, which isn't taxing on their creative and management abilities. At SLRS Advertising, only four trade print ads were created for Segil Carpets during an entire year (see Exhibit 6.14). On the other hand, Ogilvy & Mather creates about 6,000 jobs for IBM around the world, creating work for the company's software, services, and systems that requires excellent creative and management skills.

Using Multiple Agencies

Many clients are now hiring several agencies and giving them different assignments for the same product. In some cases, this is changing the agency–client relationship by treating agencies as vendors and not as full marketing partners. One of the reasons for this change is that new marketing executives are under pressures from their CEOs. The message is, "I don't care about your situation. I need an idea and people who are passionate about my business."

In the 1950s, the agency–client relationship was defined in *The Encyclopedia of Advertising*:

> An advertising agency is an organization which provides advertising, merchandising and other services and counsel related to the sale of a client's goods or services. It is understood that the client agrees not to engage a second agency to handle part of the advertising of the product *without the consent of the first agency.*

Over a decade ago, Coca-Cola decided that its agency of many years wasn't creating enough big ideas. As a result, it took the freelance route for a while and then hired about 40 agencies and boutiques over time to create ads. Coke's contention was: *We know and understand our strategy better than our agencies do. So their job is to do the best execution of the strategy they can.*

A number of major marketers use multiple agencies. Many use a major global agency, plus a number of smaller creative shops. For example, when Coca-Cola's

Sprite brand started losing ground to Pepsi's Sierra Mist lemon-lime soda, Coca-Cola asked four creative boutiques about creative ideas in addition to its main agency Ogilvy & Mather. Traditionally, a marketer used one agency per brand.

Earlier in 2003, Coke bypassed its agency, Interpublic Group's McCann Erickson, and named Berlin Cameron/Red Cell, a WPP-owned smaller creative agency, as the U.S. creative agency for Coke Classic. However, Coca-Cola remained a McCann client. This may be a permanent trend; struggling with the economy many marketers are seeking "ideas" to improve its competitive positions as well as saving money from many sources. For example, Sun Microsystems dropped its global agency J. Walter Thompson in 2003, which had created its advertising. Sun turned to five smaller agencies for its creative. Dropping its agency of record status, Sun no longer paid an annual fee to J. Walter Thompson (as goes to the agency of record) but continued to compensate the agency on the basis of specific assignments. The business of marketing communication has gotten more complex, like most other aspects of business.

What's fueling this boom in clients using more than one agency is the same thing that fostered the recent reverse trends in consolidations: Marketers want a creative edge and are changing the nature of their agency relationships. In the end, successful advertising has more to do with the quality of the advertiser's agency relationship than with the quantity of such relationships. Big advertisers from AT&T to Sears have trusted their brand images to teams of agencies. "The size of our business is such that it demands the expertise and attention of a number of agencies," said the national director of marketing communications at AT&T. "There are so many projects and assignments to be handled that one agency couldn't do it all. But using multiple agencies puts the onus on us to make sure all the messages are coordinated and represent one consistent voice coming from the company." These needs are different from a client having one agency partner to handle everything.[27]

The ad business is famously cyclical, so it remains to be seen whether this multiple-agency trend is a permanent shift or a temporary blip. Right now, advertisers are looking for the best custom-made solutions to their marketing problems.

The Creative Digital Library

Global clients and major advertising agencies build creative digital libraries for agencies in different parts of the globe to use. For example, McDonald's digital commercial archive holds commercials from the chain's advertising since 1967 that may be used by local co-ops and agencies. It is a password-only system, so consumers or competition can't access the files. Most archives include still graphic assets, such as logos, product shots, text custom ads, point-of-purchase displays, and other print material. Over the years, McDonald's has produced more than 50,000 global commercials. Agencies like Intel's Euro RSCG MVBMS store digital commercials and print materials in their creative library, which is similar to McDonald's library. It allows for integration of visuals to all agencies around the globe working on the account. Exhibit 6.15 is an example of an Intel "Education" that would be in its library.

APPRAISING NATIONAL ADVERTISING

The big questions that national advertising and marketing management must answer are: How well is our advertising working? How well is our investment paying off? How do you measure national advertising, whose results cannot be traced as easily as those of direct-response advertising?

Advertising Goals Versus Marketing Goals

The answer is not simple. Much of the discussion on the subject centers around a report Russell H. Colley prepared for the Association of National Advertisers (ANA) which is the industry's premier trade association dedicated exclusively to marketing and brand building. Representing over 300 companies with 8,000 brands that collectively spend over $100 billion in marketing communications and advertising, the association's members market products and services to consumers and businesses.[28] The thesis of this study is that it is virtually impossible to measure the results of advertising unless and until the specific results sought by advertising have been defined. When asked exactly what their advertising is supposed to do, most companies have a ready answer: increase their dollar sales or increase their share of the market. However, these are not advertising goals, Colley holds; they are total **marketing goals.**

marketing goals
The overall objectives that a company wishes to accomplish through its marketing program.

advertising goal
The communication objectives designed to accomplish certain tasks within the total marketing program.

National advertising alone cannot accomplish this task. It should be used as part of the total marketing effort. The first step in appraising the results of advertising, therefore, is to define specifically what the company expects to accomplish through advertising. The Colley report defines an **advertising goal** as "a specific communications task, to be accomplished among a defined audience to a given degree in a given period of time."

As an example, the report cites the case of a branded detergent. The marketing goal is to increase market share from 10 to 15 percent, and the advertising goal is set as increasing, among the 50 million housewives who own automatic washers, the number who identify brand X as a low-sudsing detergent that gets clothes clean. This represents a specific communications task that can be performed by advertising independently of other marketing forces.

The Colley report speaks of a marketing-communication spectrum ranging from unawareness of the product to comprehension to conviction to action.

According to this view, the way to appraise advertising is through its effectiveness in the communication spectrum, leading to sales.

Researchers disagree on whether the effectiveness of national advertising—or, for that matter, of any advertising—should be judged by a communication yardstick rather than by sales. As a matter of fact, in Chapter 15 we discuss whether an ad's effectiveness should be measured by some research testing score.

CHANGES IN MARKETING

Clearly, we are in the midst of a revolution. This period of change has been compared to the French and Russian revolutions. The truth is we are in the midst of several revolutions at once, including globalization, technology, management, and uncertain economy. We are in competition with everyone, everywhere in the world. Computers and electronics have altered the way we do everything. Word processing replaced the typewriter, ATM machines have replaced bank tellers, and voice mail and e-mail have given us the ability to communicate 24 hours a day. Today's management buzzwords are reengineering, downsizing, and eliminating hierarchy. Small, flexible organizations have the advantage in today's world. Finally, we are undergoing a revolution in our business structure.

The Traditional Five Ps of Marketing

The traditional five Ps of marketing consist of the elements product, price, place, packaging, and promotion (which includes positioning, advertising, sales promotion, public relations, and so forth). With a strategy in each of these areas, a person can put together an effective marketing plan. In the packaged goods category, the general belief is that promotion accounts for about 90 percent of the marketing equation. Each product category may be different, as seen with automobiles, where price and product are key, with promotion being a small percentage. So the advertiser must understand what is important.

The New Five Ps of Marketing

TBWA/Chiat/Day's Tom Patty says the old five Ps served us well in a world dominated by stability and a growing economy with much less competitive pressures than we have today. Patty's new five Ps are aimed at helping us succeed in a world where chaos has replaced stability, where the fast-growing economy has slowed, and where global competition demands even greater levels of effectiveness and efficiency. The new five Ps are more abstract and conceptual than the traditional ones. They include paradox, perspective, paradigm, persuasion, and passion.[29]

Paradox A paradox is a statement or proposition that, on the face of it, seems self-contradictory. Example: "All cars are the same; all cars are different." The paradox always contains within it an opportunity. An advertiser must exploit the differentiation. Miller used the paradox of "lite" beer to help focus on the dual benefits of the lite paradox, "Tastes Great, Less Filling." Everyone knows what a sports car is, but Nissan created a new category of sports cars in which it was first—the four-door sports car. To master the paradox, you first have to find or identify this opportunity and then exploit the changes. One way to create this unique identity is to be the first

ADVANTAGE POINT

Propel Fitness Water
A Product Story

EXHIBIT 6.16

TV frame from "Drip" commercial.

Courtesy of Element 79 Partners and The Gatorade Company.

As thirst experts with more than 35 years of research, The Gatorade Company understood the hydration needs of active people. Gatorade Thirst Quencher is the nation's leading sports drink. The company saw a need for fitness water and created a new product, Propel Fitness Water, which became the enhanced water market leader, the fastest-growing segment of the beverage category. Propel is a lightly flavored alternative to plain water with just 10 calories per eight-ounce serving and essential vitamins.

Since its national launch in 2002, Propel Fitness Water has achieved numerous distinctions, including becoming the number-one enhanced water on the market. Marie Devlin, director of marketing for Propel, said, "Propel has exceeded expectations because active people understand Propel was created by the hydration experts at Gatorade, they love the great flavor of the product, and they connect very strongly to our advertising," she added.

The eye-catching "Drip" campaign for Propel, introduced in 2002 as part of the brand's national launch, showcased people who "drip" from a Propel bottle and spring into exercise and fitness activity as the drop hits the surface. In a later set of ads, "Surfaces," which included both print and TV executions, various active people once again drip from a Propel bottle, but this time the individuals included a basketball player, tennis player, volleyball player, and kickboxer splashing directly onto their respective courts or surfaces. In an innovative twist, a rock climber who drips out of the bottle attempts to climb back up and scale her surface—the bottle itself. The innovative campaign was developed by Element 79 Partners in Chicago (see profile in Chapter 5).

"'Drip' was a major factor behind the extraordinary national launch of Propel," said Dennis Ryan, chief creative officer for Element 79 Partners. "Our challenge in evolving the campaign was to take the brand's powerful visual metaphor of athletes born from water and reinvigorate it without reinventing it, which we achieved in a very compelling way." A variety of print ads accompanied the 30-second commercials, appearing in a number of magazines including *Self, Shape, Fitness, Men's Fitness,* and *Men's Health.*

To further build on its success, Propel introduced two new flavors in 2003 as additions to its previous four-flavor lineup: Peach and Kiwi-Strawberry. In addition to the advertising, the brand continued to be supported by a fully integrated marketing campaign, including sampling, public relations, and point-of-sale and in-store merchandising. Visit www.propelwater.com. ■ ■ ■

in something. For years, advertising told us that trucks are tough and rugged and durable, whereas cars are comfortable, luxurious, and safe. The new Dodge Ram exploits the paradox of combining many car-type features with the rugged look and performance of a Mack truck.

Perspective Perspective is the ability to see things in relationship to each other. The manufacturer's perspective isn't the proper perspective. Advertisers must look at every issue—whether it's a product issue, a pricing issue, or a distribution issue—from the consumer perspective. The only perspective is the consumer's perspective. Here several questions that need answers: What consumer need does my product or service satisfy? How does it satisfy this need differently and better than competitors? Similarly, as it relates to advertising, are we in the advertising business or are we in the persuasion business? We should be in the business of persuading consumers to think or to do something.

Paradigm Here we need a pattern example, a model way of doing things. We need to understand that we may not need to do business the "old" way. Certainly, the marketing bundle of Saturn reflects a new automotive paradigm. Instead of believing that product and price are the main ingredients of the marketing equation, Saturn believes that the major components are issues such as the experience of buying and owning a Saturn. They place much less emphasis on the product and much greater emphasis on the experiential component. There are also different advertising paradigms. In the model advertising paradigm, advertising has a simple task: "Show the product and communicate the product features and benefits." A very different paradigm is called the brand advertising paradigm, for which Saturn again is a good example. In this paradigm the task is to communicate who and what you are.

Persuasion Here we attempt to induce someone to do or think something. All marketing and sales jobs are in the business of persuasion. The advertising agency's role is to help the client persuade potential consumer audiences either to do or to think something. To be persuasive, you have to understand three essential components: the credibility of the speaker, the content of the message, and the involvement of the audience. This is a problem for advertisers. According to Yankelovich Monitor, only 8 percent of people believe advertising. Credibility and trust are emotional, not rational. You can't make someone trust you. You have to earn it over time. The Honda brand has credibility. Consequently, the advertising tends to be simple and sparse. For a brand with less credibility you need to provide more content, more information to be persuasive. The content includes the position of the brand. It needs to address the consumer need or desire this product satisfies. Remember, consumers do not buy products; they buy solutions to their problems. They buy holes, not drill bits; they buy hope, not perfume. The third and final element in any attempt to persuade is that you must understand the motivation of your customer so you can create an emotional connection with them. You also need to select the right persuasion tool. For example, if the brand has a credibility problem, the most persuasive tool might be public relations, although it is more difficult to control the content of the message in public relations. In advertising, you get complete control of content.

Passion Passion is an aim or object pursued with zeal or enthusiasm. We no longer have products for the masses. Instead, products are designed for specific needs and wants. Marketers are moving into a new paradigm in which advertising creates exciting, stimulating dialogues with consumers designed not just to make a sale but also to create a relationship. In this new marketing environment, you need passion.

 ## SUMMARY

Procter & Gamble first developed the marketing service system. Today it has two parts: (1) brand management, under a brand manager, who is assigned a brand, and (2) marketing services, comprised of the technical talent involved in implementing the marketing plan, including creative services, promotion services, media services, advertising controls, and marketing research.

As companies consider implementing integrated marketing communications into their firms, there are three basic structures available: a centralized communication function under a marcom manager, a restructured brand manager approach, and the structure involving a communication manager who is responsible for approving and coordinating all communication programs.

Advertising budgets are usually drawn up using the task method, the payout plan, competitive budgeting, and the most commonly used percent-of-sales method.

Advertisers are seeing the advantage of allowing their agencies more creative freedom and encouraging them to take more creative risk as long as it is on strategy. As Bill Borders said, "Risk taking is the lifeblood of an agency."

Agency search consultants are sometimes hired to help find the best agency for their company. The consultant has been characterized as a marriage broker between client and agency. Many clients hire several agencies for multiple products or for the same product. Many senior company marketing executives are in their positions an average of 18 months.

The traditional five Ps of marketing consist of product, price, place, packaging, and promotion. Tom Patty says the new five Ps are paradox, perspective, paradigm, persuasion, and passion.

 ## REVIEW

1. In how many product categories do Procter & Gamble products compete?

2. What is the marketing services system?

3. What is a category manager?

4. What are the major methods of developing an advertising budget?

5. Who in the corporation prepares most of the advertising budgets?

6. What is a slotting allowance?

 ## TAKE IT TO THE WEB

The John Deere tractor company has been in operation since 1837. Visit **www.johndeere.com** and see how John Deere has used the Web site in conjunction with traditional forms of advertising to promote their products.

How does a global advertising firm such as DDB Worldwide attempt to measure the results of advertising (**www.dddb.com**)? Check out the measurement tools that DDB employs to help them along the way.

Imagine you own and run a small business out of your home in the suburbs of Chicago. Where would you search online to find the best advertising agency to represent your business? What type of service are you looking for? What concerns would you need to address before hiring an agency?

The Volvo Group has successfully persuaded consumers that Volvo is the safest car they can drive. Visit their Web site (**www.volvo.com**) to see how Volvo works to maintain their credibility in terms of safety. What type of emotional connection has Volvo been able to establish?

Media

PART FOUR

CHAPTER 7

41.8 se
was all it t
Kelly Gilh
he had to
Taylor gui
He just sto
and played
another 25
so he woul
like some
of trust fu
or somethi

Basic Media Strategy

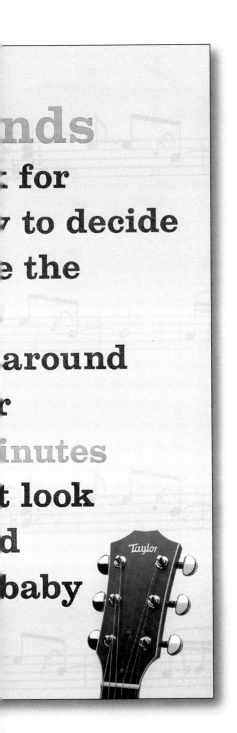

CHAPTER OBJECTIVES

The demand for efficiency, effectiveness, and creativity in the media-planning process has never been greater. The steady increase in the number of media and promotional options and unprecedented audience fragmentation have combined to create uncertainty for both advertisers and media executives. After reading this chapter, you will understand:

1. **the basic functions of the media planner**
2. **the role of media in the total advertising function**
3. **characteristics of the major media categories**
4. **relationships between media planning and target marketing**

The media function, whether executed by an advertising agency, an independent media-buying and planning firm, or a company's in-house media department, is becoming increasingly complex. Let's begin our discussion by examining the primary characteristics of the media function.

ORGANIZATION OF THE MEDIA FUNCTION

1. *Media planner.* The role of the **media planner** is to supervise all areas of the advertising campaign as it relates to the media function. Contemporary media planners have added the role of marketing specialist to their other duties. The media environment is changing so rapidly that it is part of the media planner's job to anticipate future trends in communications and keep agency management and clients abreast of major changes. In such an atmosphere, media planners have come to occupy a pivotal position in the advertising process.

2. *Media research.* The media research department coordinates both primary and secondary research data and functions as a support group for media planners. Often the media research department is responsible for gauging and anticipating future trends in media. Sometimes the media research department is also responsible for estimating the likely audience for new magazines or television programs.

3. *Media buying.* The media-buying department executes the overall media plan. **Media buyers** select and negotiate specific media placements and they are responsible for monitoring postplacement executions. Depending on the size of a media unit, there may be separate groups for broadcast and print or even local and national broadcast. Recently, some media departments have established units to research and buy Internet advertising or to construct client Web sites.

media planner
Media planners are responsible for the overall strategy of the media.

media buyers
Execute and monitor the media schedule developed by media planners.

Few areas of marketing and advertising have experienced the change demonstrated by media planning in the last decade. The media function has been driven by changes in the number of media options as well as by the increasing expenditures in media and the financial risk associated with media-buying mistakes. When a medium-sized company invests as much as $2.4 million in a single Super Bowl spot, careers may ride on the outcome!

In 2002, total advertising expenditures were over $236 billion, according to advertising forecasting guru Robert Coen of Universal McCann.[1] Projections for 2004 have advertising spending at over $266 billion.[2] The media planner of 2010 will be dealing with media outlets that probably don't exist today. Yet, these planners will have to provide clients with buying rationales, budget efficiencies, and measurable audience delivery in this unbelievably complicated environment.

THE NEW MEDIA FUNCTION

As the media adapt to new technology and methods of planning, there are a number of trends that set the tone for these changes and provide an assessment of the future of media planning and buying. Among the most important are convergence, interactivity, creativity, and optimizers.

Convergence

convergence
The blending of various facets of marketing functions and communication technology to create more efficient and expanded synergies.

One of the primary trends of the next five years will be media **convergence.** Simply stated, convergence is the blending of distribution, content, and/or hardware from a number of media companies to create a new or significantly expanded communication system. Examples of convergence are numerous—telephone companies offering cable service, cable companies offering Internet connections, or NBC and Microsoft combining to create MSNBC. These types of collaborations are important for the businesses involved and may even expand promotional opportunities for advertisers. However, the audience is more interested in convergences such as WebTV, in which the home television becomes a computer link, or online services selling that combines catalog merchandise, TV-like product demonstrations, and immediate buying capabilities.

Consumers will continue to see numerous types of convergence. For example, when ESPN publishes a magazine or CNN (owned by Time Warner) partners with *Sports Illustrated* (another Time Warner property) to create a popular Web site, CNN/SI.com, the media that are created are the result of convergence. Most experts predict that marketing, media content, and technological convergences are in their embryonic state. Although we are not certain where it will lead in the next 20 years, convergence is certainly a trend of the present and even more so of the future.

Interactivity

As briefly discussed in Chapter 2, the future of advertising will be controlled to a great extent by the audience. Technology will allow consumers to deal directly with marketers for their entertainment, purchases, and other services, bypassing traditional media and marketing channels. The system will allow buyers and sellers to deal on a one-to-one basis with communication and products tailored to the interests of specific households and individuals.

Companies such as Sony anticipate "being able to use the Web and broadband to sell directly to consumers and supplant broadcasters and cable TV systems and record stores and video-rental outlets as the primary purveyor of Sony's movies and music."[3] In many cases, technological capabilities will probably outpace consumer utilization of these services. However, interactive media are dramatically changing marketing even in their infant stage.

for his first studio album on this imprint, *Population Me*, starred in a major feature film with Harrison Ford (*Hollywood Homicide*), and collaborated with Modern Foods for what became one of Wal-Mart's best-selling food lines, Dwight Yoakam's Bakersfield Biscuits. Each of these endeavors gave me a lot to draw from in composing the campaign for the *Population Me* release in June 2003. The uniting element was obviously Dwight, but this thing could get really random really quickly if I was not careful. I sought to touch all of my bases while generating synergy for Dwight and his many pursuits.

After strategizing with the various pieces of Dwight's many career interests, a plan was developed to include *everything*. Not an easy task, but one that was made manageable by Dwight's across-the-board appeal. Our push was first focused on the music industry. A single and video from the album was released to radio and television in May, rolling off the presses with the pre-movie buzz. When CMA Fan Fair kicked off in Nashville, we feted radio broadcasters to a catered breakfast courtesy of Dwight's Bakersfield Biscuits. Found at each place setting was a cache of movie swag (baseball caps, t-shirts, koozies, water bottles, and even snap bracelets). To build presence and awareness of the new music release and Dwight's role in *Hollywood Homicide*, we partnered up with Columbia Pictures and gave radio stations the opportunity to conduct listener contests awarding exclusive movie screenings. And, most importantly, we introduced industry movers and shakers to *Population Me*, Dwight's new studio album, challenging them to "make it the soundtrack of their summer."

With the industry pulled in, we doubled up our efforts to influence consumers via press and marketing. Dwight was a true sport working in a very busy press schedule while touring. He was in his element as a creative force, piggybacking interviews and press for both the film and movie release. He took a seat for couch time on *The Tonight Show* with Jay Leno and then seamlessly transitioned over to the performance stage where a full orchestral string section accompanied him in a stirring performance of the current radio single. Consumer ads were found in publications that ranged from the rootsy music magazine *No Depression* to the glitzy *Hollywood Reporter*. And there were loads of viral e-mail campaigns, street team actions, fan club participation, and product placements.

Is it brain surgery? No, entertainment marketing is just taking advantage of opportunities and creating situations. It is changing ahead of the times and bringing the entertainment-consuming public along for the ride. Entertainment marketing is the most fun you can have and still get paid. It is simply cutting a wide, enthusiastic trail across varied terrain and aiming for more hits than misses. Selling entertainment is like a huge fishing expedition where the goal is the whole ocean. You can only catch the entire ocean by targeting the right spots and digging deep. My personal philosophy is that by casting the net wide enough I can hook the whole ocean. But like P. T. Barnum said, "Never attempt to catch a whale with a minnow." I always aim to develop a multilevel marketing plan that borders on sensory overload.

In a perfect world it all works well. In that perfect world, on any given Friday night, my consumers are clad in my artist's latest fashion statement. They are subconsciously aware of my artist's music in the background, while talking about the latest video premiering on MTV. They are on their way downtown in a subway car papered with my artist's likeness. And when they reach their stop, they exit in front of Madison Square Garden where my artist is playing to a sold-out crowd of brand new fans. They present their tickets (won via a radio contest) and embark on a multimedia extravaganza, starring my artist and benefiting the charity that he has founded. And in that perfect world I'm at the show, too. You might not see me. I do try to blend in. I'm there taking lots of notes, sizing up the players, asking questions, and taking care of the VIP guests. And I am looking out at the crowd from backstage, what I consider to be the very best seat in the house.
Courtesy of Tiffany Johns. ▪ ▪ ▪

---

nies was that their media experts could obtain better commercial rates rather than through full-service agencies, which often concentrated on creative services.

Although major advertising agencies took exception to this claim, the idea of breaking out the media function as a separate business has become an important trend during the last decade. With the new focus on the media function there are two major areas of disagreement:

■ *Where media planning (as contrasted with media buying) should take place.* Some independent media firms have control of the overall media function including both negotiation and buying. In other cases, firms only execute the media plan provided by an agency or client. Many argue that by divorcing planning strategy from buying tactics you lose much of the efficiencies promised by the new emphasis on media.

■ *Degree of coordination between creative and media strategy.* According to Donny Deutsch, chairman and CEO of Deutsch advertising agency, "Having media under one roof is a real advantage to us. Under one roof, literally sitting next door to our chief media officer—our brilliant thinker—media planner and buyer—is our head of account planning, our creative people, what-not. It's completely one profit center, completely de-siloed." This view is not shared by other media directors. According to Jack Klues, CEO of Starcom MediaVest group, the unbundled media operation of Leo Burnett advertising, "I've lived for twentysomething years in a media environment where we were at the bottom of the agency food chain. I'm a better partner to my creative-agency brethern because I run my own business versus having to work my way through some agency food chain where I'm driving profits in and can't get money back to reinvest in my product. . . . I don't dismiss the benefits of physical proximity, but I would argue that your media director has the same access to resources, intellectual capital, financial capital, and can be as good as an outside strategic media partner. I would argue that just because he sits near you doesn't make him the peer of a more unbundled operation."[5]

The concept of a totally unbundled media department is a core issue for many agencies. Historically, advertising agencies have promoted themselves to prospective clients on the basis that they could offer a complete menu of advertising services. Creative strategy and execution, account management and interface with a client's marketing department, and media research, planning, and placement could all be handled within a single agency. Up until the late 1980s, most agency reputations were determined by creative expertise and the number of award-winning advertisements and commercials they produced. Media departments (and the few independent media-buying firms that existed) were generally regarded as ancillary functions to the creative departments.

However, a number of factors changed the role of media and eventually led to the era of unbundling.

1. *Integrated marketing.* As clients began to view advertising as only one element in a complex marketing communication program, they began to see that advertising agencies were not the only source of communication expertise. To gain specialization in diverse areas, large companies often hired public relations firms, sales promotion agencies, and direct-response companies, in addition to their advertising agencies. As clients became comfortable dealing with a number of communication agencies, it was natural that they would look to specialization within the advertising function—such as unbundled media-buying companies.

2. *Cost factors.* As the cost of media time and space escalated, clients gave more attention to the media-buying function. Clients were demanding greater cost efficiencies, better identification of narrowly defined target markets, and accountability of media expenditures.

   The primary problem of achieving media cost efficiencies is that the goal of low cost is largely contradictory to the current move toward specialized media. Up until a few years ago, advertisers were faced with a limited number of media choices. In an environment controlled by a few mass circulation magazines, dominance by three major networks, and largely monopolistic daily newspapers, advertisers sought to reach as many people as possible, even when the strategy carried high waste circulation. In today's world of fragmented media with much smaller but homogeneous audiences, advertisers are routinely paying much more for each person reached than only a few years ago.

3. *Globalization.* As clients began to market throughout the world, the expertise and demands on agency media departments grew exponentially. Major clients recognized that without strategic media planning, global brands could not

achieve worldwide recognition and dominance no matter how well the creative function was executed.

4. *Complexity of the media function.* Media planning has moved light years from the days of dominance by mass circulation media. Large corporations such as General Motors and Procter & Gamble have invested advertising dollars in a diversified media schedule including the Internet, numerous niche cable networks, and prototype interactive media on an experimental basis. In addition, companies are demanding that this advertising be monitored and coordinated with event marketing opportunities, sales promotion, and public relations. Often there is a significant role for media planning in the execution of these programs. This type of expertise requires a much greater level of knowledge and specialization than can be provided by a traditional media department.

5. *Profitability.* In addition to the benefits that unbundling accrues to clients, it also has added a profit center for the agencies engaging in it. Now agencies can compete for clients' media accounts even when another agency handles the creative side. Unbundled companies such as Mediaedge:cia, Starcom, and ZenithOptimedia are playing a significant role in the media plans of major advertisers (see Exhibit 7.1). Only a few years ago, the clients being served by these independent media buyers would have been handled by full-service agencies such as Young & Rubicam, Foote Cone & Belding, and Leo Burnett, all of which have unbundled their media department.

Unbundling has given media executives a greater role in the overall planning of advertising strategy. It also has highlighted the importance of media as part of the advertising mix. It is obvious that, in a world of fragmented audiences and niche media, media decisions will continue to occupy a primary position in advertising

EXHIBIT 7.1

World's Top Media Specialist Cos. Recma's ranking by worldwide billings in 2002

Source: Copyright Crain Communications. Reprinted with permission. *Advertising Age*, 21 April 2003, S–12.

Rank				Worldwide Billings
2002	2001	Media Specialist Company	Headquarters	2002
1	3	Starcom MediaVest Worldwide	Chicago	$18.40
2	4	MindShare Worldwide	New York	18.00
3	2	OMD Worldwide	New York	17.90
4	1	Initiative Media Worldwide	New York	16.85
5	5	Carat	London	16.65
6	6	ZenithOptimedia Group	London	16.15
7	7	Universal McCann	New York	14.95
8	8	Mediaedge:cia Worldwide	London	13.55
9	9	MediaCom	New York	12.35
10	10	MPG	New York	8.55

Recma's ranking by U.S. billings in 2002

Rank				U.S. Billings
2002	2001	Media Specialist Company	Headquarters	2002
1	1	Starcom MediaVest Worldwide	Chicago	$10.85
2	3	MindShare Worldwide	New York	8.65
3	2	Initiative Media Worldwide	New York	8.40
4	4	OMD Worldwide	New York	7.75
5	5	Universal McCann	New York	7.10
6	6	ZenithOptimedia Group	London	7.00
7	7	Mediaedge:cia Worldwide	London	4.66
8	9	MediaCom	New York	4.20
9	8	Carat North America	New York	4.32
10	10	PHD	New York	3.67

planning. Advertisers increasingly realize the wasted effort and money in delivering even the most creative messages to the wrong audience.

BASIC MEDIA STRATEGY

Traditionally, media planners have used a **building block strategy** to develop a media schedule. Keeping in mind cost efficiencies, they start with the medium that reaches the most prospects and work down to those that reach the smallest portion of the audience. In the past, the first or second "blocks" were relatively easy to determine. Most national advertisers used network television or magazines as the dominant medium. The media planner then considered other vehicles to reach smaller audience segments.

As mentioned earlier, the media options available to supplement an advertiser's primary vehicles have grown dramatically. The introduction of vehicles such as the Internet, video catalogs, and interactive television have brought major changes to the job of the media planner. They also have created new ways to view the media function and media buying. Media planners are forced to go beyond costs in developing plans. When dealing with these specialized media, planners must consider factors such as additional weight against prime prospects, ability to deliver a communication message in a unique manner, and the prestige of a medium that may outweigh low audience delivery. More and more media planners are examining qualitative factors of the media such as the communication interactions between the audience and the individual media.

Historically, the advertising process began with development of broad marketing and advertising strategies, moved to creative execution, and finally to media placement, which was often viewed as nothing more than a channel for creative messages. Today, that notion is changing in some fundamental ways:

1. *Core values of media.* Media planners are increasingly working with the creative team to understand the qualitative core values of each medium. These core values interact with advertising messages to enhance or diminish the advertising.

    For example, magazines are about information, television scores better as an emotional medium, and direct mail is about personalization. "If the brand message is in conflict with these values, the advertising won't be credible . . . it simply won't connect to an audience. . . . A thoughtful, introspective-seeming brand . . . might be difficult to sell on a billboard drivers pass going 60 miles an hour, even if they are the right audience for that brand."[6]

    The experienced media buyer must be able to look beyond personal media preferences and determine the media vehicles that will best reach prospects. It may be that a network television spot is needed or the best ad placement may be a stock car carrying a sponsor's logo. In any case, media planners must be able to step away from their personal biases and put themselves in the place of a client's prime prospects.

2. *Fading distinctions among media.* Technology is changing the fundamental relationships among media, audiences, and advertisers and creating an environment where distinctions among media are fading. For example, is the delivery of newspaper content over a computer still a "print" medium? Likewise, are text messages available through television still "broadcast" signals?

    In this new environment, media planners must be creative in the utilization of media vehicles and look less at the distribution system and more at the audiences and communication effectiveness. Even the traditional organizations of agency media departments will have to be realigned to comply with changing media technology.

3. *Media accountability.* Changes in media buying and scheduling are putting pressure on media planners to become more knowledgeable in areas that were

not part of their responsibility only a few years ago. In the near future, job functions such as media planner and media buyer may be replaced by more inclusive titles such as marketing communication specialist. The change in terminology is more than semantic; rather, it more accurately reflects both the job function and the expectations for the advertising media executive of the future.

Research has shown that networks also have distinctive brand identities that appeal to certain demographic and buyer categories. High brand identification for a network does not always translate into short-term viewership. For example, the top two "brands" among television networks are The Discovery Channel and The Weather Channel, but neither averages 1 percent of the viewing audience. However, it bodes well for these networks as audience fragmentation drives more and more viewers to niche vehicles.

Another factor in network branding, just as in the case of products, is that differentiation is not enough. There also is a question of affinity for certain networks. In one study, respondents were asked to identify what types of people are users of certain media. They were then asked about the types of people with whom they wanted to associate. By correlating the two scores, media planners can see which media have the highest affinity and those programs and networks with which advertisers and consumers would most want to have their products associated.[7]

Ultimately, advertising accountability means that businesses want to be able to link their advertising to specific sales of their brands. As noted earlier, it is difficult to determine exactly what contribution advertising makes to total sales, much less how it influences a single buyer or group of buyers. There are software programs available that try to make this link. Scanner data from the checkout counter are used to attempt to relate television viewing and purchase behavior to estimate the sales volume produced by viewers of specific shows.

The need to find ways to better link advertising and sales becomes even more important as technology continues to change the nature of both mass media and advertising. Many advertisers predict that in the near future we will not be dealing with distinct media vehicles. Rather, through the use of in-home fiber optics, there will be a convergence of media into a single multimedia source where telephones, interactive computers, movies-on-demand, and laser printers make obsolete the traditional media categories. Consumers will have much greater control over communication outlets, selecting only those entertainment, information, and advertising messages they want. Waste circulation will be limited because, by definition, self-selected communication will only go to prospects. The organizations we view as media today will be information sources, and the carriers of this information will be limited to a few cable outlets, telephone companies, or other common carriers.

Media Characteristics

Before a media strategy can be planned and implemented, we must have a basic knowledge of the characteristics and functions (both editorial and advertising) of the major media. Faced with a multitude of media choices, one of the most important attributes of a media planner is an open mind. From established media such as network television to the newly emerging Internet, media planners must be able to sort those media that best fit the marketing and promotional goals of individual clients.

We must remember that advertising budgets are not growing as fast as the increase in media options, so hard budget choices are the rule of the day for agencies and their clients. "In broad terms, we cannot sell more cars, sneakers or boxes of cereal to . . . people as a result of new technology. To fund these new media efforts, marketing executives will need to take a fresh look at the macro-level allocation of budgets as new media forms begin to take on some of the blended attributes of traditional advertising media, promotion, and direct marketing."[8] Future chapters will discuss the various strengths and weaknesses of media vehicles from an advertising perspective.

PUTTING IT ALL TOGETHER: THE MEDIA PLAN

Knowing the characteristics of the various media is only a necessary first step. Not having a plan to organize media buys into a meaningful whole is analogous to trying to speak a language knowing many words but without grammar to make sense of it. Media planners must be able to use the distinctive attributes of each medium as part of a sophisticated analysis that leads to a complete media plan for an advertising campaign. Although there is no standard format, we will offer a brief outline of a typical plan and then discuss in detail some of the most important elements:

A TYPICAL MEDIA PLAN

I.   Marketing Analysis
   A. Fundamental marketing strategy
        1. Sales, share of market, and profitability goals
             a. Demographics characteristics
             b. Lifestyle characteristics
             c. Geographic location
             d. Level of product usage
   B. Product benefits and differentiating characteristics
   C. Pricing strategy
   D. Competitive environment
        1. Number and competitive market share of product category firms
        2. Regulatory and economic situation facing product category
II. Advertising Analysis
   A. Fundamental advertising strategy
        1. Product awareness goals
        2. Target audience(s) advertising weight
   B. Budget
        1. Allocation to marketing communication mix
        2. Allocation by media category
        3. Allocation by media vehicle
III. Media Strategy
   A. Match media vehicles (*Time, Monday Night Football,* country music radio, etc.) with target audience media preferences
   B. Creative and communication considerations
        1. Need for product demonstration
        2. Need for complex message
        3. Daypart and/or seasonal requirements
        4. Media compatibility with message themes and competitive considerations
IV. Media Scheduling
   A. Print insertion dates and production requirements
   B. Broadcast allocations and availabilities
   C. Budget allocation each medium (magazines) and media vehicle (*Sports Illustrated*)
   D. CPM estimates (by total audience, prime prospects, etc.)
V.   Justification and Summary
   A. Statement of ad goals in terms of measurable results
   B. Research plan to measure achievement of ad goals
   C. Contingencies for media schedule adjustments

No two media plans will have exactly the same components nor will they give the same weight to those media that they include. However, the following section discusses those elements that are found in virtually every plan.

Target Audience

As we have discovered, a **media plan** encompasses a number of factors involving both marketing strategy and advertising tactics. However, none is more crucial to the ultimate success of an advertising campaign than the proper identification of the prime target market(s) for a brand. If errors are made at this stage of the advertising process, it is virtually impossible for the advertising program to be successfully executed. The foundation of media planning is the identification of prime prospect segments within the audience of various media. More often than not, this process is aimed not only at finding demographic niches but also is directed at identifying consumer needs and the product benefits that meet these needs.

> **media plan**
> The complete analysis and execution of the media component of a campaign.

Throughout the media-planning operation, buyers and planners must keep their focus on the total picture of consumer, product, and benefit rather than considering only reaching the target market at the lowest cost. In recent years, the process of evaluating media's contribution to the advertising message (in addition to the message itself) has become a major research track. Advertising researchers are constantly seeking more sophisticated tools to get a clear picture of consumers and the ways in which they interact with media and advertising messages.

In viewing these interactions, media planners are looking at cost efficiencies in more sophisticated ways than in previous years. At a minimum, this broader approach to cost efficiency requires that media plans maximize delivery of prospects as opposed to people or households. Until recently, media planners tended to concentrate on overall audience delivery by various media. The hope was that by reaching the greatest audience at the lowest cost, the media schedule would also reach a fair share of prospects. This strategy worked in a day of mass circulation magazines and network television domination of the airwaves. The most common measure of efficiency during that period was the **cost per thousand (CPM).** We will start with a definition of the CPM as we begin our discussion of the relationship between cost and targeting prospects.

> **cost per thousand (CPM)**
> A method of comparing the cost for media of different circulations. Also weighted or demographic cost per thousand calculates the CPM using only that portion of a medium's audience falling into a prime-prospect category.

The CPM is a means of comparing media costs among vehicles with different circulations. The formula is stated:

$$CPM = \frac{Ad\ cost \times 1,000}{circulation}$$

If we assume that *Family Circle* magazine has a circulation of 4.6 million and a four-color page rate of $223,410, then its CPM is calculated:

$$Family\ Circle\ CPM = \frac{223,410 \times 1,000}{4,6000,000} = \$48.57$$

Obviously, no medium provides an audience in which every member is of equal benefit to a specific advertiser, that is, with zero waste circulation. Let's assume that our client is a diaper manufacturer and only wants to reach women with children 2 years old or younger. In order to measure *Family Circle's* efficiency in reaching this audience, we might use some variation of the weighted or demographic CPM. Let's look at an example of the weighted CPM.

In this case, we find that of *Family Circle's* 4.6 million readers, 920,000 have children under age 2. Now we calculate the CPM weighted to consider only our target audience rather than the total circulation of the magazine.

Therefore:

$$\text{Weighted CPM} = \frac{223,410 \times 1,000}{920,000} = \$242.84$$

You will recall that in Chapter 4 we discussed a number of different means of identifying target markets. In the preceding weighted CPM example, a media planner can substitute any number of lifestyle, product user, or psychographic data for the demographic category we used in the *Family Circle* example. It is important to note that CPM figures are important only as comparisons with those of other media. *Family Circle*'s CPM of $48.57 is of interest only to the extent that it might be compared to another magazine with a CPM of $36.90.

Media planners are constantly attempting to fine-tune cost efficiencies against more useful and targeted client prospects. An important research focus of recent years involves adding a communication component to the CPM mix. Rather than just measuring the number of prospects who are potential readers or viewers of our advertising, we now add some measure of communication impact and audience awareness to the mix.

Among the primary communication considerations that are generally considered by media planners are the following:

1. *Creative predispositions of the audience.* For example, teens are predisposed to radio in a different way than print.
2. *Qualitative environment for the message. Car and Driver* magazine reaches readers who are in the proper frame of mind for advertisements for automobiles and accessories.
3. *The synergistic effect.* Advertisers seek a combination of media that results in a communicative effect that is greater than the sum of each one. For example, cell phone manufacturers use outdoor advertising to gain brand recognition, magazines for detailed product information, newspapers for dealer location and price, and television for demonstration and image. The net effect is greater than any single medium used alone.
4. *The creative approach.* Does the need for long copy or quality reproduction require print, even if other media might be more cost efficient?

Intuitively, we can understand that these and other communication components should not be ignored in developing a media plan. However, the conversion of intuition into hard data is not an easy process. In recent years, a great deal of attention has been given to quantifying the value of communication in the media plan. Without going into the complex methodology involved, let's examine a few of the possible weighted CPM adjustments that might be made to take into account communication factors:

■ *Probability of exposure to a medium.* Should a magazine reader and a person who passes an outdoor sign be given equal exposure weight?

■ *Advertising exposure weights to equalize the probability of an ad being seen.* Are the readers of *Time* more likely to see the average message for your product than the viewers of *60 Minutes*?

■ *Communication weights to equalize the probability of an advertising message communicating.* What is the communication impact of a four-color magazine advertisement compared to a television commercial or a Web site banner?

■ *Frequency of exposure weights in the same medium.* Does the first exposure in a medium have the same or greater value than subsequent exposures?[9]

In some cases, we see the notation CPMI, which refers to cost per thousand involved, which is another way of saying that some measure of audience communication is being used to weight the audience of specific media or media vehicles.

Regardless of how we weight the audience for a medium, the rationale is the same relative to the CPM formula. That is, we are giving the audience greater or lesser value as we plug in the denominator of the CPM formula.

To use a hypothetical example, let's assume that in evaluating the cost efficiency of a media schedule, research shows us that a four-color magazine advertisement should be given a weight of 1.2 (1.0 being the average of all media advertising). Using our earlier *Family Circle* example, the CPM for mothers with children under 2 years old is now:

$$\text{Weighted CPM} = \frac{223,410 \times 1,000}{1,104,000} = \$202.36$$

In this example, we have taken the 920,000 mothers and multiplied them by our magazine weighting factor (1.2) to give this audience more value (and lower CPM, $202.36 versus $242.84) because they are seeing our message in a magazine. Remember that this is only an example. An advertiser wanting to measure cost efficiencies against teenage boys might give radio a weight of 1.5 and magazines a weight of 0.8. However, the point is that advertisers are trying to find some way of factoring in a communication component to their audience delivery measures.

Research has shown that high levels of audience involvement with a medium are positively related to advertising response. These and other methods of audience communication weighting are attempts to address this relationship in the media-planning process as well as to give accurate estimates to the value of the audiences of various media.

Claritas' Potential Rating Index by ZIP Market (PRIZM)

A shortcoming of many audience analysis methods is that they consider only a single variable. In our earlier *Family Circle* example we designated women with children under age 2 as our target market for diapers. However, we know that within this broad category there are a number of differences. For example, a working woman might purchase diapers from a day care center without making a brand decision. Some women may use a diaper service rather than purchasing disposable diapers. Likewise, income, education, and other factors might change the purchase behavior of a woman in this general category. Media planners realize that a multivariable approach is often needed to correctly identify a particular target segment.

One of the most innovative methods of segmenting markets on a multivariable basis is the **Potential Rating Index by Zip Market (PRIZM)** system developed by the Claritas Inc. PRIZM $_{NE}$ divides the population into 14 social groups (see Exhibit 7.2 a)

Potential Rating Index by Zip Market (PRIZM)
A method of audience segmentation developed by the Claritas Corporation.

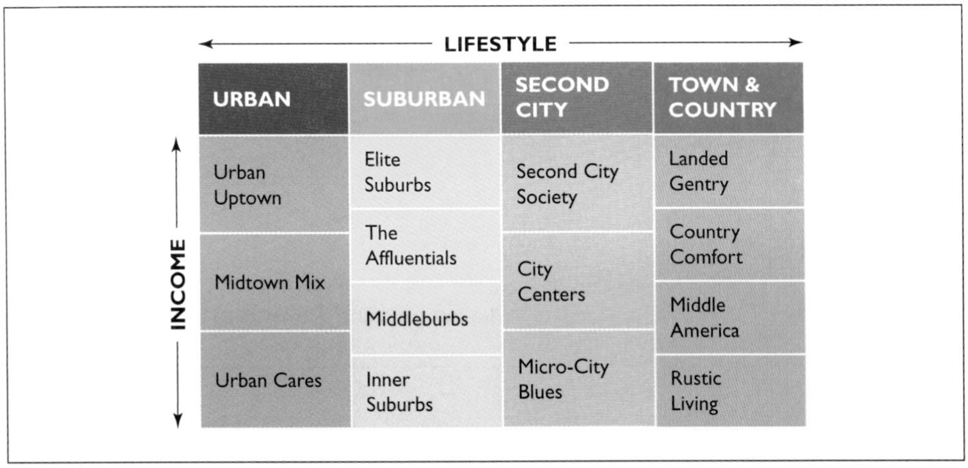

EXHIBIT 7.2 a

PRIZM Social Groups

Courtesy of www.claitas.com, accessed 25 January 2004.

LIFESTYLE			
URBAN	**SUBURBAN**	**SECOND CITY**	**TOWN & COUNTRY**
Urban Uptown	Elite Suburbs	Second City Society	Landed Gentry
Midtown Mix	The Affluentials	City Centers	Country Comfort
	Middleburbs		Middle America
Urban Cares	Inner Suburbs	Micro-City Blues	Rustic Living

INCOME

EXHIBIT **7.2 b**

PRIZM NE by Claritas Segmentation Groups

Courtesy of www.claitas.com, accessed 25 January 2004.

Urban Uptown		
04 Young Digerati	**U.S. Households:**	9,433,723
07 Money & Brains	**U.S. Population:**	24,637,282
16 Bohemian Mix		
26 The Cosmopolitans	**Median Income:**	$63,653
29 American Dreams		

Midtown Mix		
31 Urban Achievers	**U.S. Households:**	5,230,362
40 Close-in Couples	**U.S. Population:**	13,831,734
54 Multi-Culti Mosaic		
	Median Income:	$39,753

Urban Cores		
59 Urban Elders	**U.S. Households:**	5,462,433
61 City Roots	**U.S. Population:**	15,510,048
65 Big City Blues		
66 Low-Rise Living	**Median Income:**	$28,829

Elite Suburbs		
01 Upper Crust	**U.S. Households:**	6,053,928
02 Blue Blood Estates	**U.S. Population:**	17,428,670
03 Movers & Shakers		
06 Winners Circle	**Median Income:**	$98,983

The Affluentials		
08 Executive Suites	**U.S. Households:**	8,461,571
14 New Empty Nests	**U.S. Population:**	22,372,060
15 Pools & Patios		
17 Beltway Boomers	**Median Income:**	$66,913
18 Kids & Cul-de-Sacs		
19 Home Sweet Home		

Middle-burbs		
21 Gray Power	**U.S. Households:**	4,822,617
22 Young Influentials	**U.S. Population:**	11,895,083
30 Suburban Sprawl		
36 Blue-Chip Blues	**Median Income:**	$51,882
39 Domestic Duos		

Inner Suburbs		
44 New Beginnings	**U.S. Households:**	5,774,880
46 Old Glories	**U.S. Population:**	14,449,483
49 American Classics		
52 Suburban Pioneers	**Median Income:**	$36,798

Second City Society		
10 Second City Elite	**U.S. Households:**	4,029,214
12 Brite Lites, L'il City	**U.S. Population:**	11,297,780
13 Upward Bound		
	Median Income:	$75,249

City Centers		
24 Up-and Comers	**U.S. Households:**	8,186,692
27 Middleburg Managers	**U.S. Population:**	20,523,886
34 White Picket Fences		
35 Boomtown Singles	**Median Income:**	$46,631
41 Sunset City Blues		

Micro-City Blues			
47 City Startups	**U.S. Households:**	7,434,360	
53 Mobility Blues	**U.S. Population:**	19,646,849	
60 Park Bench Seniors			
62 Hometown Retired	**Median Income:**	$29,242	
63 Family Thrifts			

Landed Gentry			
05 Country Squires	**U.S. Households:**	9,637,425	
09 Big Fish, Small Pond	**U.S. Population:**	27,269,465	
11 God's Country			
20 Fast-Track Families	**Median Income:**	$71,639	
25 Country Casuals			

Country Comfort			
23 Greenbelt Sports	**U.S. Households:**	10,989,887	
28 Traditional Times	**U.S. Population:**	29,499,549	
32 New Homesteaders			
33 Big Sky Families	**Median Income:**	$47,629	
37 Mayberry-ville			

Middle America			
38 Simple Pleasures	**U.S. Households:**	11,144,896	
42 Red, White & Blues	**U.S. Population:**	29,607,110	
43 Heartlanders			
45 Blue Highways	**Median Income:**	$36,877	
50 Kid Country, USA			
51 Shotguns & Pickups			

Rustic Living			
48 Young & Rustic	**U.S. Households:**	11,086,657	
55 Golden Ponds	**U.S. Population:**	28,474,654	
56 Crossroads Villagers			
57 Old Milltowns	**Median Income:**	$28,294	
58 Back Country Folks			
64 Red Rock America			

and further subdivides these large segments into 66 subcategories (see Exhibit 7.2 b). The primary variables for determining these social groups are lifestyle and income.

The PRIZM segments are arranged in descending order of affluence from the "Upper Crust," who reside in the Elite Suburbs social group, to "Low-Rise Living," whose residents live in the most urban and lowest socio-economic areas of the country. The value of PRIZM groups is that these general segments can be matched with those products and media that members of a particular group are most likely to use. For example, inhabitants of the "Upper Crust" are likely to drive a Lexus E5300, read *Architectural Digest*, and watch *Wall Street Week* on television. By identifying these groups geographically, companies can develop efficient marketing and advertising plans without the wasted circulation of a less targeted campaign.[10]

COMMUNICATION REQUIREMENTS AND CREATIVE ELEMENTS

As discussed earlier, media planners are interested increasingly in the differential value of various media and the value they add or subtract to specific advertising messages. Another dimension of this process is the manner in which art directors, copywriters, and media planners have begun to engage in the process at the strategic level rather than simply seeing their role as executing someone else's advertising plan.

value-added opportunities
Extra things a medium will do for or provide to an advertiser that adds value to the purchase of time or space in their medium.

This is not to suggest that it is customary for the media and/or creative team to sit at the table when fundamental decisions are being made about the overall promotion strategy for a brand. However, there is growing recognition by both account supervisors and clients that the earlier in the process these functions are brought on board, the greater the opportunity for creative input into unique ways to position and advertise a brand. This early involvement also allows a more thoughtful approach to the various problems that will have to be addressed inevitably as the campaign goes from strategy to tactics to execution. Particularly now that **value-added opportunities** are usually an important part of the media buying and planning process, it is necessary for both the creative and media teams to know what opportunities are most desirable for a brand to pursue (see the accompanying Kleppner's Viewpoint 7.2).

As we have discussed, there is a wide gap between advertising exposure and advertising communication. The greater the input from the account team to both media and creative, the better the communication and coordination. Often the creative and media teams must make compromises among those media with the best cost efficiencies and those with the best creative attributes to properly communicate the brand's core message. The earlier that these decisions can be made, the better it is for media buyers who must negotiate prices and determine availabilities of space and time.

In the past, a major criticism of advertising execution was that media and creative functions did not have enough knowledge of what each area was doing within the campaign strategy. The result, according to critics, was advertising that did not fully utilize the communicative strengths of the various media vehicles. Fortunately, the separation between the creative and media functions seems to have diminished in recent years. Among major advertising agencies there seems to be a heightened sensitivity that creative/media cooperation is necessary for effective advertising.

In part, this cooperation has been necessitated by the convergence of media outlets, new media technology, and greater opportunities for interactive approaches to audiences. For example, when businesses experiment with Internet advertising, the integration of message, medium, and audience requires different approaches than in traditional media advertising. The process of planning advertising in new technologies and interactive media demand that all the advertising functions work in concert to make the greatest impact with an audience that is very much in control of the communications process.

GEOGRAPHY—WHERE IS THE PRODUCT DISTRIBUTED?

Geographical considerations are among the oldest factors in buying media. Long before advertisers were knowledgeable about the importance of demographics and target markets, they knew the areas in which their products were distributed and bought and those promotional vehicles that best reached those regions. Even in an era of narrowly defined audiences, geography remains a primary consideration of the planner.

Today, the geographic media-planning boundaries are often much smaller than in previous years. Instead of states or regions, the planner may be dealing in ZIP codes and block units or even individuals, especially in direct mail and Internet advertising. Geographical considerations also are becoming more important as advertisers find that consumers in different parts of the country demonstrate markedly different attitudes and opinions concerning various product categories. Sometimes these geographic differences are obvious—food preferences in the South are distinctly different from the Northeast, just as the demand for snow tires is different in Los Angeles than in Chicago. Other reasons for differences in brand demand are less apparent.

Account Executive,
Comcast, **Atlanta, GA**

Value-added is a trend in advertising that has taken place over the last 10 to 15 years. Due to increased competition, inventory constraints, and increased accountability, added value has become a way to entice advertisers to spend more dollars than they normally would by leveraging various additional advertising channels.

Added value can take on any form as long as it is seen to have a tangible worth in the eyes of the advertising purchaser. Contesting, remote broadcasts, mixed media promotions, the Internet, tickets, product placement, event marketing—all of these things can be added to a typical advertiser's purchase of television, radio, cable and so on to increase the value of the media buy. If the added-value item or items hold no value in the eyes of the purchaser, then they cannot be leveraged.

For example, during recent reality television programming, advertisers such as Coke, Pizza Hut, Reebok, Pontiac, and Visa all purchased inventory in the program. Then as an incentive to purchase advertising in every show once or twice, they were offered product placement within the actual program. So they were getting an added advertising message to drink Coke, eat Pizza Hut pizza, wear Reebok shoes, drive Pontiac automobiles, and use Visa credit cards in addition to the ads they were running in commercial break. This is added value.

For the past few years Home Depot has purchased a College Football schedule on CBS, and CBS throws in naming rights as added value. It is called the "Home Depot" half-time report. Home Depot sees a value to having its name associated with the half-time report. So the

Chris Oberholtzer

rate for the spots in games and the frequency of those spots (how many spots per game) are then leveraged along with the naming rights. CBS could sell the naming rights alone if it wanted to. But tying something like this into a spot schedule adds continuity to the on-air look. If Home Depot thought no one watched half-time reports, then that is added value that cannot work.

Added value, simply put, is free advertising leveraged on top of paid advertising. ■ ■ ■

Adding to the complexity of the media planner's job is the fact that media distribution demonstrates some of the same unpredictable distribution patterns as products. Some but not all of these differences can be explained when you look at the age or ethnic makeup of a particular market. For example, according to Nielsen data, Atlanta tends to have different television viewing patterns than the country as a whole. The larger concentration of younger adults and African Americans can account for some of the differences. These varying patterns of product usage and media preferences must be considered by planners as they develop a media schedule that will reach prime prospects. Planners must begin with the location of buyers and prospective buyers and their concentration in specific areas. Exhibit 7.3 demonstrates the dual nature of geographical areas and the concentration of prospects.

Obviously, Cell 1—with concentrated prospects in a local area—is the easiest to deal with. At the other extreme, an efficient plan for Cell 9 demands a great deal of

EXHIBIT 7.3

Location and Concentration of Prime Prospects

Prime Prospects	Local	Regional	National
Concentrated	1	2	3
	4	5	6
Dispersed	7	8	9

creativity to appeal to prospects with special interests—say, antiques or fine jewelry—who are not concentrated in any geographical area. These dispersed groups might be reached through specialized magazines, direct mail, or the Internet.

Media planners not only need to know where prospects are located but also how consumers in different areas rate in terms of current and future sales potential. A common method of relating sales, advertising budgets, and geography is the **brand development index (BDI).** An example of the BDI is shown in Exhibit 7.4.

Regional differences in product usage require many firms to develop a secondary, localized media plan to supplement their national media schedule. National advertisers are increasingly using regional advertising options such as local cable and specialized product-specific publications such as restaurant guides. As research data that allow advertisers to define their markets and media technology more narrowly to reach these segments become more readily available, we will see an even greater use of localized media. In some cases, this localization will be a supplement to national campaigns; in other instances, we will see national brands adopt an area-by-area media schedule as their primary strategy.

brand development index (BDI)

A method of allocating advertising budgets to those geographic areas that have the greatest sales potential.

MEDIA TACTICS: REACH, FREQUENCY, CONTINUITY, AND BUDGET

The media planner deals with four primary elements in developing the final media schedule:

1. *Reach (also called coverage).* Reach is the number of different people exposed to a single medium or, in the case of a multimedia campaign, the entire media schedule. It may be expressed as the number of prospects or as a percentage of the target audience, but in either case, it represents a nonduplicated audience. For example, if the target audience is 500,000 18- to 24-year-old males and 200,000 are exposed to the advertising, it may be expressed as a reach of 40 percent.

EXHIBIT 7.4

The Brand Development Index Emphasizes Prime Sales Areas

Computing the Brand Development Index

ACME Appliance has a media budget of $2 million and sells in 20 markets. The media planner wants to allocate the budget in the 20 markets according to the sales potential of each market.

Market	Population (%)	ACME Sales (%)	Budget by Population (000)	BDI (Sales/ Population)	Budget by BDI
1	8	12	$ 160	150	$ 240,000
2	12	8	240	67	160,800
3	6	6	120	100	120,000
etc.					
20	100%	100%	$2,000		$2,000,000

Example: Market 2, based on its population, should have an advertising allocation of $240,000 (0.12 × $2,000,000). However, the sales potential of market 2 is only 67 percent as great as its population would indicate (sales/population or 8/12). Therefore, the media planner reduces the allocation to market to 2 to $160,800 ($240,000 × 0.67) and reallocates funds to markets with greater potential such as market 1.

2. *Frequency.* **Frequency** is the number of times that each person in the audience is exposed to the media schedule. In our earlier example, if the 200,000 men reached in the campaign generated 1 million exposures, the frequency would be 5.0:

$$1,000,000/200,000 = 5.0$$

3. *Continuity.* Continuity is the length of time over which a campaign will run or the length of time that reach and frequency will be measured. In other words, a 20 percent reach and 5.0 frequency might be accumulated over one week, one month (which is most typical), or one year. In evaluating reach and frequency, it is important that the continuity over which these elements are measured be clearly stated.

4. *Budget.* The budget is the major constraint of any advertising plan. The core consideration in all media planning is the budget. Although the relative weight given reach and frequency can be adjusted, the overriding constraint on the total weight of the advertising schedule is the budget.

As the media-planning process progresses, the planner moves from general strategy considerations to specific tactics. The planner must determine the most efficient and effective media to achieve already determined marketing and advertising objectives.

The value of each media vehicle should be measured according to three criteria:[11]

1. the cost of the vehicle
2. the number of target market members or the weighted target market quality of the audience reached by the vehicle
3. the effectiveness of the advertising exposures the vehicles deliver (e.g., the communications or qualitative component)

These considerations can be combined in a concept known as frequency value planning (FVP). FVP evaluates media vehicles in terms of their frequency distribution—the proportion of the target market that receives different levels of advertising exposure. The important distinction between unweighted frequency and FVP is that FVP estimates the relative value of exposures rather than simply measuring the number of times a person comes into contact with a medium or an advertising message.

From a practical standpoint, the media planner has control over reach and frequency. The budget is a strategic decision largely determined by the client. Likewise, the length of most campaigns is one year, but regardless of the continuity of any campaign, it will not be the decision of the media department.

Reach, frequency, and continuity must be balanced against the demands of a fixed budget. However, the media planner must also consider the balance between the least expensive media (efficiency) and those most able to communicate the core message and reach the best prospects (effectiveness). Exhibit 7.5 shows the relationship among the three elements in some typical media strategies.

The tactics associated with reach and frequency are a direct result of the previously agreed to marketing and advertising objectives and strategies. The decision to emphasize reach or frequency in the communication strategy will most definitely influence the media tactics. A number of tactics can be used when reach or frequency is desired.[12] For example:

Reach Tactics

■ Prime-time television reaches a large mass audience but is very expensive, so the budget may be quickly expended.

---

frequency
In media exposure the number of times an individual or household is exposed to a medium within a given period of time.

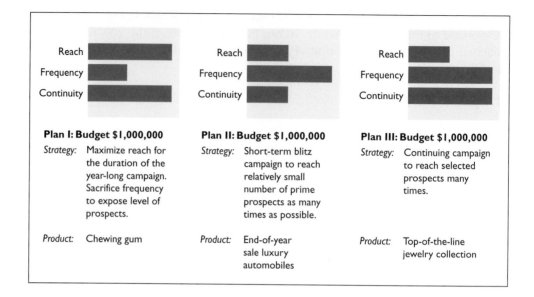

Plan I: Budget $1,000,000

Strategy: Maximize reach for the duration of the year-long campaign. Sacrifice frequency to expose level of prospects.

Product: Chewing gum

Plan II: Budget $1,000,000

Strategy: Short-term blitz campaign to reach relatively small number of prime prospects as many times as possible.

Product: End-of-year sale luxury automobiles

Plan III: Budget $1,000,000

Strategy: Continuing campaign to reach selected prospects many times.

Product: Top-of-the-line jewelry collection

■ Daily newspapers reach 60 million homes and cover from 30 percent to 50 percent of most markets.

■ Large circulation magazines such as *TV Guide* or *National Geographic* serve similar functions as network television but with smaller overall audiences.

Frequency Tactics

■ Cable television, particularly specialized outlets such as The History Channel or The Discovery Channel, can be purchased at relatively low cost and tend to build frequency by reaching the same core viewers over a long period.

■ Special interest magazines, as opposed to mass circulation publications, are able to reach the same audience over several issues.

■ Radio listeners tend to have one or two favorite stations and listen up to several hours daily.

Regardless of the specific techniques used by media planners to determine proper levels of reach and frequency, the overriding motive remains the same—to achieve cost efficiency with media dollars. However, a medium is not efficient if it is not first effective at communicating the message to the target audience. One of the most significant changes in media planning in recent years is a move from the goal of audience accumulation to one of measuring the effectiveness of the audience reached. In other words, advertisers realize that every member of a medium is not equal to every other member, even those with similar demographic characteristics.

The measurement of effective audiences takes various forms. Planners use a number of techniques to exclude waste circulation. For example, they develop estimates of communication impact versus exposure and they add qualitative variables such as media/message compatibility to their equations. Regardless of how they approach the issue, the overriding motive is to more precisely gauge the value of a particular prospect, medium, or message to the overall measure of advertising effectiveness.

media schedule
The detailed plan or calendar showing when ads and commercials will be distributed and in what media vehicles they will appear.

THE MEDIA SCHEDULE

One of the final steps in the media-planning process is the development of a detailed **media schedule.** The media schedule is the calendar or blueprint for the media portion of the campaign. It also is the guide for media buyers to execute the media strategy developed by the planner. The schedule must offer in specific detail exactly what media will be bought, when they will be purchased, and how much time or space will be used for each advertisement or commercial. For example, if we decide to purchase *Sports Illustrated*, will we use four-color or black-and-white advertisements? Will we use the entire circulation of the publication or one of the numerous geographic editions offered? Which weekly editions will we buy?

The advertising schedule for a national brand may entail dozens or even hundreds of similar decisions. If the local broadcast is a primary medium, there may be separate groups of media buyers who negotiate and purchase hundreds of radio and television stations. If cable or broadcast networks are a primary building block of the schedule, senior media executives with extensive television buying experience will negotiate buys that may run into the millions of dollars. Such advertising giants as General Motors and Procter & Gamble may spend over $1 million daily on network television alone. Television media budgets at this level are executed in close coordination among senior marketing executives on the client side, their counterparts at agency or independent media-buying firms, and, of course, the networks.

Another concern at all levels of broadcast buys, but especially among networks and major affiliates, is time availability. As will be discussed in Chapter 8, just because you want to buy spots on the Super Bowl or *Law and Order* doesn't mean they will be available. It is not unusual for a media-buying group to spend several days negotiating for time on a single network program.

The process of broadcast buying has improved in recent years through the introduction of electronic data interchange (EDI). Basically, EDI is a means of connecting the agencies, clients, and media involved in the buying process in a paperless system that allows the exchange of insertion orders and electronic invoicing. Not only is the system more efficient than former approaches to media buying, but also it significantly reduces errors by decreasing the number of people involved in the buying and billing process.

Another electronic media-buying process is available on the Internet. In the last two years, several companies have offered brokering services between advertisers and stations. These services not only list inventories of broadcast spots but also act as a central clearinghouse where media buyers can bid on available time. To this point, such services are a minor part of the total television time buying process, but they are becoming more important as the process of linking stations with agencies and clients becomes more complex.

Flighting   One of the most used advertising scheduling techniques is **flighting.** Flighting consists of relatively short bursts of advertising followed by periods of total or relative inactivity. For example, a company might run a heavy schedule of advertising for six weeks and then run only an occasional advertisement to its best prospects over the next six weeks. The idea is to build audience perception for the product so that brand awareness carries over those periods of inactivity. Done correctly, the advertiser achieves the same brand awareness at a greatly reduced cost compared to a steady advertising schedule.

The concept is obviously appealing to advertisers that rarely think they have enough funds to reach all their prospects with a consistent advertising program. The problem facing the advertiser is that available research on flighting cannot predict precisely the awareness levels needed to achieve any particular flighting strategy. One thing is certain, advertisers must guard against significant erosion of brand awareness during breaks between flights. Exhibit 7.6 demonstrates the ideal outcome of a properly executed flighting strategy compared to a steady schedule both using the same advertising budget.

In the steady schedule audience awareness peaks fairly quickly (after about 20 weeks) and afterward shows little if any increase. The flighting schedule grows much more slowly, but because of budget savings it is able to reach more prospects

flighting
Flight is the length of time a broadcaster's campaign runs. Can be days, weeks, or months—but does not refer to a year. A flighting schedule alternates periods of activity with periods of inactivity.

EXHIBIT 7.6

Steady Versus Flighting Media Schedules

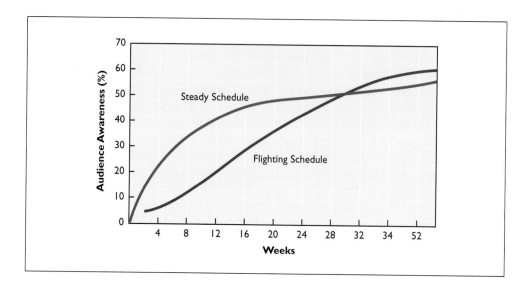

and, therefore, actually achieve higher levels of brand awareness in the long term. As we cautioned earlier, an advertiser must be careful to consider the communication component of the media plan. Some media planners think that a flighting plan may sacrifice depth of communication even though minimal awareness may be achieved.

Regardless of the flighting schedule used, the following factors should be considered before using the strategy:

1. *Competitive spending.* How does your plan coincide with primary competitors? Are you vulnerable to competition between flights?
2. *Timing of flights.* Does the schedule go contrary to any seasonal features found in the product purchase cycle?
3. *Advertising decay.* Are you spending enough in peak periods to remain visible between flights?
4. *Secondary media.* Should secondary or trade media be used between flights to maintain minimal visibility?

A less extreme form of flighting is called *pulsing.* Pulsing schedules use advertising more or less continuously throughout the year but with peaks during certain periods. These peaks coincide with primary sales periods or a special promotion during contests or sweepstakes.

The Pressure of Competition

Advertising operates in a competitive environment, usually with a number of companies vying for the same consumers. Advertisers must be constantly aware of competitors' advertising strategy, product development, pricing tactics, and other marketing and promotional maneuvers. The media planner must not only develop an effective campaign for a product but also must do so in a way that distinguishes his or her client's brand from the competition.

The media planner also must walk a tightrope between a healthy respect for competitors' actions and blindly reacting to every competitive twist and turn. Rather than operating from a defensive mentality, advertisers should take a practical stance in determining what their marketing and advertising plans can reasonably accomplish and how they meet the inroads of competing brands.

Many advertisers find it extremely difficult to analyze the market environment objectively. One of the primary functions of an advertising agency is to bring an objective voice to the table. Companies sometimes unrealistically judge the value and quality of their products. However, a key to successful marketing is an objective appraisal of both your products and those of the competition from the consumer's perspective.

For example, consumers who are aware of your brand but have never used it are probably satisfied with the product they are currently buying. Both the creative and media plans will have to work hard to give these consumers a reason to switch. In fact, we may have to recognize that some market segments cannot be captured regardless of the quality of our advertising. In such a case, brand switching would be an inappropriate strategy and instead we might target another market segment with new advertising appeals, creatively positioned products, or both.

A competitive analysis must also consider various media alternatives and how they might be used to accomplish specific marketing goals. For example, a smaller company in a product category may find that television is impractical if it is dominated by advertisers with budgets that are beyond its reach. Likewise, we might find that certain media are so saturated with competitors' advertising that it will be difficult to gain attention for our message in the midst of high levels of competitive advertising. Media buyers must be aware of a number of marketing conditions in preparing the plan. The key point is that advertisers should undertake a thorough and candid appraisal of all aspects of the competitive situation. In doing so, a media buyer becomes an integral member of the campaign team.

The Budget

If there is any advertising axiom, it is that no budget is ever large enough to accomplish the task. With the spiraling cost of media over the last several years, media planners view the budget with a growing sense of frustration. In addition, media planners are constantly caught between large media (especially the major television networks) demanding higher and higher advertising rates and clients demanding more efficiency for their advertising dollars. Because the allocation of dollars to media is by far the largest portion of the advertising budget, it is the media planner who is expected to gain the greatest cost efficiencies.

Advertisers and their agencies have reacted to this cost squeeze by instituting more stringent cost controls and accountability for their advertising dollars. In addition to these stricter controls on media costs, advertisers are constantly looking for alternative methods of promotion and advertising to hold down costs. Already, consumer sales promotion (sweepstakes, coupons, price-off sales, etc.) has passed advertising in terms of total share of promotional dollars. Advertisers also are using media such as cable and first-run syndicated programming to circumvent the high cost of network television. In addition, media planners and buyers will continue to put pressure on the media to provide them with a variety of value-added options. As media continue to fragment, we will see advertisers experiment with nontraditional media vehicles, some that did not exist only a few years ago.

If there is any encouraging sign for advertisers, it is that the increases in media costs of past years seem to have moderated. Instead of double-digit increases, overall media costs are being held to levels more in line with the general rate of inflation. In response to these increases, advertisers are more precisely defining their prospects to cut down on waste circulation and are negotiating more aggressively with media for time and space. The fragmentation of media and audiences is driving up the CPM levels to a point that it is costing more and more to reach selected target audiences.

The media schedule is normally summarized in a flowchart that presents the overall media to be included as well as their audience estimates and costs. Exhibit 7.7 presents a media schedule for a company that makes women's athletic shoes. The focus of this plan is largely on vehicles that reach young, active women.

	January				February					March				April				May					June				July				August					September				October					November				December			
	4	11	18	25	1	8	15	22	29	7	14	21	28	4	#	#	#	2	9	16	23	30	6	13	20	27	4	11	18	25	1	8	15	22	29	5	12	19	26	3	#	17	#	#	7	14	21	28	5	12	19	26
NETWORK TV																																																				
(30 sec)																																																				
Primetime																																																				
Late Night																																																				
SYNDICATION																																																				
(30 sec)																																																				
CABLE TV																																																				
(30 sec)																																																				
M–S Primetime																																																				
CABLE TV																																																				
(60 sec)																																																				
M–F Primetime																																																				
MAGAZINES																																																				
1-page 4-color																																																				
Prevention																																																				
Shape																																																				
Fitness																																																				
Health																																																				
In-Style																																																				
Lucky																																																				
NETWORK RADIO																																																				
(30 sec)																																																				
Morning drive																																																				

EXHIBIT 7.7

Media Flowchart 2004 Women's Athletic Shoe Brand

Courtesy of Susan Kahrs.

SUMMARY

The media function is undergoing rapid and significant changes at all levels. The competition for media dollars has never been greater and the growing importance of new media technology promises to add even more options to the media mix. The trend toward localized media strategies accompanied by the expansion of global markets places even greater strains on the research, planning, and execution of media buys. As clients, agencies, and media attempt to make sense out of the mix of traditional and new media opportunities, the role of the media planner takes on even more importance.

While dealing in an unpredictable environment, a number of trends are certain to occupy the media community in coming years:

1. *Developing media/creative strategies to fully utilize interactive media.* After 200 years of the media controlling the communication process, advertisers must quickly adjust to greater audience feedback and control.

2. *Measuring media synergism.* Research technology must account for a complex mix of communication techniques vying for consumer time. The era of fiber optics, the Internet, and online versions of traditional media will require creative planning by media planners.

3. *Controlling media costs and accountability will become driving forces in the media process.* As the costs of reaching narrowly defined audience segments or even individual consumers increase so does the demand for accountability

from clients. What were acceptable levels of waste circulation in a period of mass media and low CPMs are no longer tolerable in a stage of individual marketing.

4. *Evaluating the value and impact of value-added options.*

These are only some of the many complex issues facing the media executive of tomorrow. Regardless of what the future brings, it is clear that the media-planning function will occupy an even more important role in an era of targeted advertising. The tension between increased media costs and a search for cost efficiencies by clients will result in planners becoming more willing to try new media or spin-offs of existing media. If there is one sure trend in an otherwise unpredictable area, it is that the advertising media function will continue to look for narrowly defined markets and, with few exceptions, disregard those media vehicles that promise substantial but largely undefined or unmeasured audiences.

REVIEW

1. How has the fragmentation of media audiences affected media planning?

2. In what significant ways has the responsibility of media planners changed during the last decade?

3. Briefly define reach, frequency, and continuity.

4. Discuss the applications of the brand development index.

5. Discuss the role of media synergy in advertising planning.

6. What effect has audience fragmentation had on media cost?

7. Discuss cost-media buying from the perspective of the media and the advertiser.

8. Why is direct response growing at its current rate?

TAKE IT TO THE WEB

Media research is an integral part of media planning. Henderson Advertising is a relatively small firm located in Greenville, South Carolina, that uses both qualitative and quantitative methods of research. Visit the Henderson Advertising Web site (**www.hendersonadv.com**) and review how research is used to obtain the best results for clients.

Nielsen Media Research is a national ratings service for television and radio ratings. Review the data collection methods used by Nielsen as found at **www.nielsen media.com**. What are the strengths and weaknesses of this research approach? What kinds of improvements can be made?

The Television Bureau of Advertising (**www.tvb.org**) lists comparisons of the top U.S., Hispanic, and African American markets. Describe how this information might be of value to advertisers.

CHAPTER 8

Using Television

With ownership consolidations, blending of technology, and coproduced programming, television is truly a multidimensional medium. As the future penetration of digital television makes interactivity a reality, both advertisers and programmers will have to adapt to significant changes in the role of audiences with the medium. From a marketing standpoint, television is not a single medium; rather it is comprised of a number of related broadcast and cable entities that exhibit significant diversity as both advertising and programming sources. From large broadcast events such as the Super Bowl to local cable programming, each of the segments of the television industry has its special characteristics. After reading this chapter, you will understand:

1. the diversified nature of the television industry
2. the multiple roles of television as an advertising medium
3. the changing position of network television
4. syndicated rating services and television research methodologies
5. the various segments of television viewing

PROS

1. Television reaches 98 percent of all U.S. households weekly and is particularly popular with many market segments that are primary target markets for advertisers.
2. Television's combination of color, sound, and motion offers creative flexibility for virtually any product message.
3. Despite recent audience declines, television remains extremely efficient for large advertisers needing to reach a mass audience. By utilizing selected cable outlets and local broadcast stations, advertisers are able to provide a local or regional component to national television schedules.
4. Government-mandated moves to digital television will open more opportunities for advertising and programming by 2006.

CONS

1. The television message is short-lived and easily forgotten without expensive repetition.

2. The television audience is fragmented and skewed toward lower-income consumers. Daily viewing time declines significantly as income increases.

3. Shorter spots, some as short as 15 seconds, have contributed to confusing commercial clutter.

4. With the introduction of the remote control, channel surfing by viewers, and the VCR and DVR (digital video recorder), the amount of time spent viewing commercials by the average television user has greatly reduced.

Television, so ubiquitous and pervasive in our everyday lives, had very humble beginnings. In the 1920s when Philo Farnsworth, an Idaho teenager, envisioned the transmission of pictures over radio waves, he could not have imagined the medium that he was helping to launch. Unlike many scientists of the time who were experimenting with spinning disks similar to early film technology, Farnsworth was working on an all-electronic system. On September 7, 1927, Farnsworth and his team transmitted a line from one room to another. In his journal entry for the day, he stated:

> The received line picture was evident this time. Lines of various widths could be transmitted and any movement at right angles to the line was easily recognized. This was experiment #12.[1]

And so the age of television began.

In 1998, television marked its fiftieth anniversary as a major advertising medium. However, at an age when most institutions are maturing, television continues to exhibit dramatic change and innovations. Television-viewing levels and advertising dollars have never been higher and government-mandated introduction of digital technology by 2006 will bring even more innovations in both advertising and programming. Because television has long been the most influential medium for most of the population, even people who do not watch television are strongly influenced by it. Television news sets the political agenda, entertainment programming creates fads from hairstyles to the end zone antics of professional football players, and TV advertising slogans become part of our everyday vocabulary.

In May 2004, 52.5 million people in the U.S. tuned into the final episode of *Friends.* Many of the viewers had come to identify with Rachel, Ross, Monica, Chandler, Joey, and Phoebe as their friends and wanted to see what the future held for the group. Such is the power of television. It is more than a simple channel of communication. In a real sense, it connects on an emotional basis with the viewing audience and makes them part of the event they are watching.

The numbers for television are stunning. More than 98 percent of households have at least one set and average household viewing is more than seven hours daily. In fact, Americans spend about twice as much time with television than with radio, the second most used medium, and seven to eight times more than with newspapers.[2] As impressive as the sheer numbers are, it is the qualitative dimensions of television as a source of news, entertainment, and advertising that are even more significant.

According to the Television Bureau of Advertising (TVB), television is regarded as the primary source of news by 71 percent of respondents, with newspapers second at 12 percent. Obviously, advertisers want to be associated with a medium that not only reaches all segments of the population but also is highly regarded. TvB research found that television's credibility as a news source carries over to positive attitudes toward television advertising. For example, when asked about the image of media advertising, television ranked first as the most authoritative (48%), most exciting (79%), most influential (81%), and most persuasive (66%).[3]

Over the years, the complexion of television has changed dramatically. Television is moving from a mass medium to a niche medium similar in many respects to radio and magazines. Beginning with the VCR and moving toward the inevitable introduction of a number of interactive formats, audiences have become active participants in the communication process rather than passive receivers. A major catalyst for the introduction of two-way television communication is the Internet. Studies show that viewing levels among households using the Internet demonstrate lower levels of television viewing. Internet household penetration will likely continue to increase in the next several years. Consequently, it will be imperative for television to continue to move toward interactivity to combat the appeal of the Internet. Television's concerns are all the more warranted because research indicates that most adopters of new technology are concentrated among upscale consumers—prime targets for television advertisers.

TELEVISION AS AN ADVERTISING MEDIUM

The business of television, and advertising is a major part of that business, is to function as an audience delivery system. Commercial television programming decisions are rarely made on the basis of aesthetics, entertainment value, or which news personality is most credible. Instead, "These are merely the vehicles for pricing and delivering the real product in the television business: eyeballs. . . . television is a business for the mass manufacture, collection, and distribution of viewers to advertisers. . . . Not stars and stories, eyeballs and households."[4]

With an annual investment of more than $58 million in all forms of television advertising, it is difficult to imagine the medium without commercials. However, in the earliest days of experimental television, commercials were actually illegal. It wasn't until May 2, 1941 that the **Federal Communications Commission (FCC)** granted 10 commercial television licenses and allowed the sale of commercial time. The first commercial aired on July 1, 1941, during a Dodgers–Phillies baseball game. It was sponsored by Bulova watches and cost $4 for airtime and $5 for station charges. It is estimated that it was seen by 4,000 people.[5]

Federal Communications Commission (FCC) The federal authority empowered to license radio and TV stations and to assign wavelengths to stations "in the public interest."

Television commercial time is perishable inventory. If TV spots are not sold by air time, the opportunity for this revenue is lost by the station.

For a number of years, television has added program options at a growing rate. In the 1970s, a few independent stations offered sports and off-network reruns as an alternative to network affiliate programming. By the 1980s, cable was extending the number of stations available to the average household and a limited number of superstations such as TBS and WGN were accessible to most cable homes. However, although the number of channels increased, the variety of programming—most network retreads—remained relatively stagnant except for sports, which proliferated at a quickening pace. However, by the 1990s, this situation took a dramatic turn as cable networks realized that in order to sustain their audiences and compete with the major broadcast networks for advertisers, they had to develop original programming.

Led by premium cable services such as Showtime and HBO, cable began to produce a number of original movies and even an occasional series. During the 1990s, the premium channels were joined by major cable outlets such as TNT and USA in producing a number of made-for-TV films. In addition, basic cable networks were producing highly acclaimed programs such as A&E's *Biography*. More importantly, they were beginning to compete for the prime-time audience long dominated by the broadcast networks. Because both advertisers and audiences were attracted to these new programs, televison fragmentation accelerated and became the order of the day.

In 25 years, television has moved from basically three program and advertising options to a point where the average household receives more than 50 channels. As Clarence Page, noted columnist and television commentator, stated, "In my youth, Americans were united by watching the three network channels. Today, the audience is fragmented over dozens of channels and thousands of other new media choices, including video games, CD-ROMs, and the Internet. With broadcast audiences now fragmenting, we have to ask what happens to that common culture, those common reference points."[6]

The same television fragmentation that creates this lack of a common political culture also is making it more and more difficult for advertisers to reach large audiences with a unified selling message. By the end of the decade, most observers believe that television (or whatever convergence of cable/computer/telephone technology is the standard) will offer 10 times the number of options we have today.

With digital capabilities, networks can deliver a number of services to a household over the same conduit. Not only will there be more options, but also they will be tailored to the entertainment, news, and buying preferences of individual viewers on an interactive basis. In this interactive environment viewers can participate in their favorite game shows and order merchandise directly from commercials. The vertical integration and capital resources of conglomerates, such as Disney and Time Warner, make this new media landscape closer to a reality than many believe. It also will change the traditional relationships between the television industry and its advertisers.

Another advantage of broadband, digital delivery is that it allows multiple uses (or even versions) of programming, reaching viewers at their convenience and depreciating program costs over multiple cycles. For example, with additional channel capabilities, "CBS could repeat its afternoon soap operas at night for viewers who missed them during the day. NBC could run 'Jay Leno' and 'Conan O'Brien' in the daytime on a second channel in hopes of finding a newer or larger audience. At the local level, TV stations could run their morning, mid-day, and early news programs a second time, perhaps in prime time, when their main digital channel was carrying network programs."[7]

The "new" television will be characterized by a move to the local level. Many predict that the mass era of television is quickly coming to an end. It is being replaced by a localized medium more in touch with its audience and soon will be communicating on a two-way basis. Obviously, the major networks have the brand equity to be future leaders regardless of the method of advertising and programming distribution.

While many of the technological changes are at least a few years in the future, television remains the primary medium for many advertisers. In addition to its high household penetration, television offers creative flexibility not found in any other medium. With its combination of sight, sound, color, and motion, television is equally adept at communicating humorous, serious, or tongue-in-cheek commercials. Television is a 24-hour medium with an ability to reach viewers of every lifestyle from homemakers to third-shift workers. Television also offers a number of advertising formats from the 10-second ID to the 30-minute, program-length infomercial.

Limitations of Television

Cost Advertising and promotion, regardless of the medium or methods of distribution, are expensive. In recent years, there has been a great deal of publicity about the cost of television and commercials—especially those carried in blockbuster programs such as the Super Bowl, *CSI,* or *E.R.* However, most people would be surprised to learn that even the most costly television commercials are much less expensive on a CPM basis than print media. For example, the average prime-time television commercial has a CPM of about $15 compared to a typical daily newspaper that delivers 1,000 readers for $50 to $60 or a national magazine's rate of $25 to $35. Even with the highest rating series charging close to $500,000 for a 30-second spot, television is still cost-efficient for businesses needing to reach huge numbers of people.

However, as household viewing hours remain constant, the growing number of options for television audiences has created an extremely fragmented audience and generally lower ratings for all segments of the industry. As discussed earlier, this trend and resulting CPM increases will probably accelerate in future years. Network advertisers, especially products depending on mass marketing such as packaged goods, automobiles, and fast-food franchises, are particularly concerned about these increases. They know that in spite of high CPM costs and continuing commercial rate increases, there is still no more efficient method of reaching a broadly based consumer market than through television.

However, with the competitive environment for viewers' time and attention, it also is imperative to make attention-getting commercials, which are often the most costly. Consequently, it is important to consider not only the cost of television time but also the production cost associated with commercials. Chapter 19 discusses in detail the process of commercial production. However, with some network television commercials budgeted for over $1 million, production expenses are another important cost consideration for any television advertiser.

Clutter Television **clutter** is defined as any nonprogram material carried during or between shows. Commercials account for more than 80 percent of this material with the other time devoted to public service announcements and program promotional spots. In the last two years, the issue of television commercial clutter has become a major topic among advertisers and their agencies. As summarized by the director of communication insights at Omnicrom Groups' OMD, "As ratings decline and demand for shows with higher ratings, in particular, remains strong, pressure is on networks to raise the number of ad minutes."[8]

The clutter controversy has become more heated with reports that 1999 saw a significant jump in commercial time compared to previous years. Studies showed that ABC, NBC, and UPN averaged more than 15 minutes of nonprogram content. CBS, FOX, and WB all had over 14½ minutes of nonprogram content per hour.[9] Advertisers are left to wonder if the commercials are as valuable now that there is so much clutter. Consumers may increase their avoidance of commercials if they are annoyed by all of the clutter. "Americans spend an average of four hours a day

clutter
Refers to a proliferation of commercials in a particular medium. This reduces the impact of any single message.

watching TV, an hour of that enduring commercials. That adds up to an astounding 10 percent of total leisure time; at current rates, a typical viewer fritters away three years of his life getting bombarded with commercials."[10]

Advertisers also point out that not only has the total nonprogram time increased, but the number of commercials has also grown with the use of shorter spots. Prior to the early 1970s, 60-second commercials were the norm. They were replaced by 30-second commercials, but now more than 10 percent of commercials are either 10- or 15-seconds spots. Research has shown that the number of commercials contributes to the perception of clutter even when overall commercial time remains constant.

THE RATING-POINT SYSTEM

TV advertisers evaluate the medium according to the delivery of certain target audiences. In the case of networks and large affiliates, advertisers tend to look for exposure to fairly broad audience segments, such as women aged 18 to 49. Cable networks and some independent stations are evaluated by their ability to deliver more narrowly defined audiences that are both smaller in size and more expensive to reach on a CPM basis but have less waste circulation.

rating point
The percentage of TV households in a market a TV station reaches with a program. The percentage varies with the time of day. A station may have a 10 rating between 6:00 and 6:30 P.M. and a 20 rating between 9:00 and 9:30 P.M.

The basic measure of television is the **rating point.** The rating, expressed as a percentage of some population (either TV households or a specific demographic group such as women 18–49), gives the advertiser a measure of coverage based on the potential of the market. The rating is usually calculated as follows:

Rating = program audience/total TV households

When ratings are expressed as percentages of individuals, the same formula is used, but the population is some target segment rather than households. For example, if we are interested only in 18- to 34-year-old males, the formula would be:

Rating = 18–34 males viewing program/total 18–34 males in population

A household rating of 12 for a program means that 12 percent of all households in a particular area tuned their sets in to that station. Prime-time network programs usually achieve a rating of between 7 and 16, with the average being around 9.

As we discuss later in this chapter, TV advertising is rarely bought on a program-by-program basis. Instead, advertisers schedule a package of spots that is placed in a number of programs and dayparts. The weight of a schedule is measured in terms of the total ratings for all commercial spots bought (the **gross rating points** or **GRPs**).

gross rating points (GRP)
Each rating point represents 1 percent of the universe being measured for the market. In TV it is 1 percent of the households having TV sets in that area.

GRPs were calculated by multiplying the insertions times the rating. In the case of *All My Children*, the rating was 5.5×20 (the number of insertions) = 110 *GRPs* (see Exhibit 8.1).

Advertisers also use *GRPs* as the basis for examining the relationship between reach and frequency. These relationships can be expressed mathematically:

$$R \times F = GRP$$

$$\frac{GRP}{R} = F \text{ and } \frac{GRP}{F} = R$$

where R = reach and F = frequency.

To use these relationships, you must know (or be able to estimate) the unduplicated audience. In the TV schedule in Exhibit 8.1, we estimate that we reached about 50% of the entire target market and that the average number of times we

Vehicle	Rating	Cost	Spots	GRPs
All My Children	5.5	$25,000	20	110.0
General Hospital	4.5	21,000	20	90.0
Guiding Light	3.3	19,000	11	33.0
One Life to Live	4.2	19,500	10	42.0
Total GRPs				275
Reach = 50.0				
Average Frequency = 5.5				

EXHIBIT 8.1

GRPs measure weight of an advertising broadcast schedule.

reached each person in the audience was 5.5. We can check the formulas using the solutions previously calculated:

$$R \times F = GRP \text{ or } 50 \times 5.5 = 275$$

$$\frac{GRP}{F} = R \text{ or } \frac{275}{5.5} = 50$$

$$\frac{GRP}{R} = F \text{ or } \frac{275}{50} = 5.5$$

One of the principal merits of the *GRP* system is that it provides a common base that proportionately accommodates markets of all sizes. One *GRP* in New York has exactly the same relative weight as one *GRP* in Salt Lake City. *GRP*s cannot be compared from one market to another unless the markets are of identical size. However, Exhibit 8.2 shows that the cost of TV commercial time varies by city size. Here is an idea of the use of *GRP*s in two markets, Los Angeles and Boston: The advertiser has to decide how much weight (how many *GRP*s) to place in his or her markets and for how long a period. This is a matter of experience and of watching what the competition is doing. Suppose the advertiser selects 100 to 150 per week as the *GRP* figure (considered a good working base). Within this figure, the advertiser has great discretion in each market. How shall the time be allocated: Put it all on one station? Divide it among all the stations? Use what yardstick to decide? The answers depend on whether the goal is reach or frequency.

Look again at the hypothetical pricing structure in Exhibit 8.2.

If we buy three prime-time spots in these markets, we would expect to receive 24 *GRP*s (3 spots × 8 average rating). However, it would be a serious mistake to equate a 24-*GRP* buy in Los Angeles with the same level in Boston. In Los Angeles, 24 *GRP*s would deliver 1,284,000 household impressions (0.24 × 5,350,000 HH, or households) at a cost of $37,560 (3 spots × $12,520 per spot). On the other hand, a 24-*GRP* buy in Boston would deliver 556,800 household impressions at a cost of $18,792. To estimate buys, advertisers often use the **cost per rating point** *(CPP)* calculation to estimate the cost of a particular schedule they are thinking of buying or a particular spot:

**cost per rating point
(CPP)**
The cost per rating point is used to estimate the cost of TV advertising on several shows.

$$CPP = \frac{\text{Cost of schedule or commercial}}{GRPs}$$

	TV Homes Market (000)	Average Cost per Spot	Average Prime-Time Rating
Los Angeles	5,350	$12,520	8
Boston	2,320	6,264	8

EXHIBIT 8.2

Television cost efficiency is measured on a cost of audience delivered basis.

In this case:

$$\text{Boston:} \qquad CPP = \frac{18{,}792}{24} = \$783$$

$$\text{Los Angeles:} \quad CPP = \frac{37{,}560}{24} = \$1{,}565$$

If we make the mistake of comparing *GRP*s from markets of different sizes, it would appear that a rating point costs almost 200 percent more in Los Angeles than in Boston. However, a rating point represents 53,500 households (1 percent of 5,350,000) in Los Angeles versus only 23,200 in Boston. A rating point in Boston costs $782 less than in Los Angeles. However, the advertiser is actually getting 231 percent more households for only a 200 percent higher cost in Los Angeles. So Boston is hardly a bargain.

In addition to the problem of intermarket comparisons, the *GRP* has other limitations. It does not tell us the number of *prospects* for the product who are being reached by a program. Still, the *GRP* concept does provide a unified dimension for making scheduling judgments.

It must also be remembered that *GRP*s alone cannot tell how effectively a broadcast schedule is performing. If an advertiser's target audience is women aged 18 to 49, for example, 5 household *GRP*s will often deliver more women in that group than 10 household *GRP*s will. This, as you would expect, is a function of where the *GRP*s are scheduled. Five *GRP*s during a Sunday night movie will almost always deliver many times more women aged 18 to 49 than will 10 *GRP*s scheduled on a Saturday morning.

SHARE OF AUDIENCE

share of audience
The percentage of households using TV tuned to a particular program.

Although the rating is the basic audience-measurement statistic for TV, another measure, the **share of audience** (or simply, share), is often used to determine the success of a show. The share is defined as the percentage of households using television that are watching a particular show. It is used by advertisers to determine how a show is doing against its direct competition.

Let us assume that the *Good Morning America* show has 5,000 households watching it in a market with 100,000 households. In this case we know that the rating for *Good Morning America* would be 5.

$$\text{Rating} = \frac{Good\ Morning\ America\ \text{viewers}}{\text{total TV Households}} \times 100 = \frac{5{,}000}{100{,}000} \times 100 = 5$$

The share calculates the percentage of *households using television (HUT)* that are tuned to the program. Let us assume that of the 100,000 households, 25,000 are watching television. In this case, the share for *Good Morning America* would be 25:

$$\text{Share} = \frac{Good\ Morning\ America\ \text{viewers}}{\text{HUT}} \times 100 = \frac{5{,}000}{25{,}000} \times 100 = 20$$

It is understood that both the ratings and share of audience are expressed as percentages (hence, the factor of 100 in the equations). Therefore, we do not use decimal points to refer to the measures in the example as "5 percent" and "20 percent." Instead, we say that the rating is 5 and the share is 20.

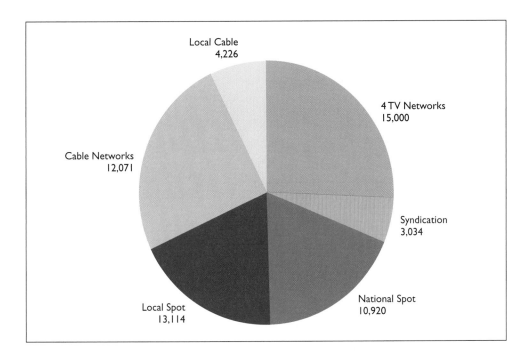

EXHIBIT **8.3**

Advertising Spending by Types of Television in 2002 (in million $)

Courtesy of McCann Erickson Worldwide. All rights reserved. www.mccann.com/insight/bobcoen.html.

THE MANY FACES OF TELEVISION

Although the average viewer probably makes little distinction among cable, premium cable, broadcast networks, syndicated programs, daytime, or any of the other permutations of television, they are in many respects unique marketing vehicles. Each of the various segments of the medium has its own advertising pricing structure, programming, target audience, and rating expectations. Exhibit 8.3 shows how advertising spending is distributed among the different types of television.

Except for the fact that they appear on the TV screen, there is little similarity between The Travel Channel and the Cartoon Channel or Home Shopping Network and MTV. Television has become primarily an individual-user medium with the majority of the audience viewing alone during most dayparts. The use of television as a personal medium is further demonstrated by the number of multi-set households.

In the near term, as television technology continues to evolve, the medium will demonstrate even more diverse advertising opportunities. To some viewers, it will be primarily a source of immediate information such as stock quotes, for others it will remain the primary entertainment outlet, and, as we enter a wireless society, for still others, an out-of-home companion serving multiple purposes.

The process of media planning and buying of television has become extremely complex. Besides the proliferation of programming options, you may recall from Chapter 7 that there is often a variety of value-added options for agency media experts to consider. This section examines the many aspects of this extremely complex medium, which occupies so much of our time and advertisers' dollars.

NETWORK TELEVISION

In the 1987–88 television season, *The Cosby Show* was the top-rated program with an average audience share of 44 percent. That same year, *Hunter*, a predictable police drama had a respectable 19 rating with an average share of 34. Now fast-forward 10 years to the top-rated, award-winning *Seinfeld*, a show that many people would

EXHIBIT **8.4**

Historical Ratings

Source: 1950–1998: Nielsen *2000 Report on Television*, Courtesy of Nielsen Media Research; 1999–2002: Nielsen Media Research as found on www.chez.com/fbibler/tvstats/recent_data.

**TOP RANKED REGULAR PROGRAM SERIES
BASED ON HOUSEHOLD RATINGS**

Year	Program	Network	Household Rating	Share
1950—51	Texaco Star Theatre	NBC	61.6	81
1951—52	Arthur Godfrey's Talent Scouts	CBS	53.8	78
1952—53	I Love Lucy	CBS	67.3	68
1953—54	I Love Lucy	CBS	58.8	67
1954—55	I Love Lucy	CBS	49.3	66
1955—56	$64,000 Question	CBS	47.5	65
1956—57	I Love Lucy	CBS	43.7	58
1957—58	Gunsmoke	CBS	43.1	51
1958—59	Gunsmoke	CBS	39.6	60
1959—60	Gunsmoke	CBS	40.3	65
1960—61	Gunsmoke	CBS	37.3	62
1961—62	Wagon Train	NBC	32.1	53
1962—63	Beverly Hillbillies	CBS	36.0	54
1963—64	Beverly Hillbillies	CBS	39.1	58
1964—65	Bonanza	NBC	36.3	54
1965—66	Bonanza	NBC	31.8	48
1966—67	Bonanza	NBC	29.1	45
1967—68	Andy Griffith	CBS	27.6	42
1968—69	Laugh-In	NBC	31.8	45
1969—70	Laugh-In	NBC	26.3	39
1970—71	Marcus Welby, MD	ABC	29.6	52
1971—72	All in the Family	CBS	34.0	54
1972—73	All in the Family	CBS	33.3	53
1973—74	All in the Family	CBS	31.2	51
1974—75	All in the Family	CBS	30.2	51
1975—76	All in the Family	CBS	30.1	44
1976—77	Happy Days	ABC	31.5	47
1977—78	Laverne & Shirley	ABC	31.6	49
1978—79	Laverne & Shirley	ABC	30.5	48
1979—80	60 Minutes	CBS	28.2	32
1980—81	Dallas	CBS	31.2	52
1981—82	Dallas	CBS	28.4	45
1982—83	60 Minutes	CBS	25.5	40
1983—84	Dallas	CBS	25.7	40
1984—85	Dynasty	ABC	25.0	37
1985—86	The Cosby Show	NBC	33.8	51
1986—87	The Cosby Show	NBC	34.9	53
1987—88	The Cosby Show	NBC	27.8	44
1988—89	The Cosby Show	NBC	25.5	41
1989—90	Roseanne	ABC	23.4	35
1990—91	Cheers	NBC	21.6	34
1991—92	60 Minutes	CBS	21.7	36
1992—93	60 Minutes	CBS	21.6	35
1993—94	Home Improvement	ABC	21.9	33
1994—95	Seinfeld	NBC	20.4	31
1995—96	E.R.	NBC	22.0	36
1996—97	E.R.	NBC	21.2	35
1997—98	Seinfeld	NBC	22.0	33
1998—99	E.R.	NBC	17.8	33
1999—00	Who Wants to Be a Millionaire?	ABC	18.6	29
2000—01	Survivor	CBS	16.9	27
2001—02	Friends	NBC	15.0	24

regard as a cult classic. In reality, *Seinfeld* finished behind the largely forgotten *Hunter* in average audience share for almost its entire run. Exhibit 8.4 shows the erosion of the audiences of top network shows over the years.

Although much has been written about the decline of network television numbers, why should anyone be surprised? Given the proliferation of television options, it would be an impossible task for **networks** to maintain earlier audience levels. As the television landscape is peppered with competition from The Discovery

networks

Interconnecting stations for the simultaneous transmission of TV or radio broadcasts.

Channel to The Disney Channel, it is amazing that the Big Four (ABC, CBS, FOX, and NBC) have sustained the share levels they currently enjoy. This section discusses some of the major elements necessary to understand television networks as an advertising medium.

Clearance and Affiliate Compensation Networks are comprised of local stations that contract to carry network programming. The exceptions are the so-called O&O (owned-and-operated) stations of the networks. These stations (e.g., KABC in Los Angeles and WNBC in New York City) are located in a few major markets and make up a small minority of any network's station lineup. The four major networks have affiliates in most television markets. The newest networks, The WB and UPN, have affiliation agreements with smaller stations in most markets. In fact, some of The WB and UPN affiliates are secondary affiliates, which means they belong to another network and air WB or UPN shows on a delayed basis, often during non-prime-time hours. There are interesting relationships. For example, Viacom, which owns CBS, also owns some UPN stations.

Networks sell national advertising on the basis of station **clearance.** Network clearance is expressed as the percentage of the network's lineup that has agreed to clear their schedules for network programming. In the case of the top four networks, clearances normally run close to 100 percent. The new networks often express their clearance rates as a percentage of the U.S. population that is potentially reached. Clearance rates are crucial to the economics of the smaller networks. For example, if a network fails to get clearance in New York City, it is shut out of 10 percent of the total national audience. Until a network reaches 70 percent potential coverage, it is usually not considered a national program by major advertisers.

Another primary factor in the relationship between networks and affiliates is network **compensation.** Compensation is a system whereby networks share advertising revenues with their affiliates in return for using local station time for their programs. At one time, station compensation was a major profit item for most stations. However, as the cost of network programming has increased and audience levels have fallen, the relationship between networks and stations over compensation has become contentious. Basically, networks have taken the position that the value of a station's local advertising spots is in large measure a result of the audience gained through popular network programming. Consequently, the networks are demanding that their affiliates share in the cost of this programming. For their part, the stations contend that without availability to stations, there would be no networks. In the future, stations may find that rather than a source of profit, affiliation may be an expense. Regardless of the form the compensation debate takes, the root causes of costly programming and falling revenues will make compensation a continuing issue for discussion between networks and their affiliates.

Network Ownership Despite the fact that the major television networks are very large companies with revenues in the billions of dollars, each of them is a relatively small part of a major conglomerate. They may not, even be the most profitable media holding of these corporations. For example, The Walt Disney Company owns the ABC Television Network and a number of local affiliated stations. It also owns, among many other holdings, ESPN's four networks and its magazine, Lifetime and A&E Networks, and, of course, The Disney Channel. In addition, the company owns theme parks as well as film studios and production facilities. A similar situation exists for each of the other networks.

The accelerated pace of acquisitions and mergers among media companies has raised some troubling questions in a number of quarters. For example, will the concentration of broadcast and cable ownership restrain the free flow of news and information especially in the case of stories that relate to their parent companies? Will a lack of competition among media affect the economic marketplace in setting

clearance
The percentage of network affiliates that carries a particular network program.

compensation
The payment of clearance fees by a TV network to local stations carrying its shows.

advertising rates? Will television content be restricted if networks are pressured to buy programming from production studios owned by the same parent company? Some have argued that Congress should prohibit companies from owning both the means of distribution (a station or network) and the production of content (a program production studio). It is unlikely to happen, but advertisers are very much concerned with the consequences of a marketing environment dominated by a few companies.

Network Commercial Pricing and Declining Audience Shares As we noted earlier, television is in the business of delivering prospects to advertisers. The networks find themselves in the difficult position of encountering higher and higher program costs at a time when audience levels do not justify significant commercial price increases. Prime-time spots vary according to ratings and audience demographics, but an average 30-second commercial will cost approximately $135,000 on the four major networks. At the high side, a spot on shows such as *E.R.* and *Will and Grace* will be over $400,000, while *Primetime* with its lower ratings and older audience will bring about $75,000.[11]

In the past few seasons, network advertising revenues have grown significantly. However, media buyers complain that these increases are a result of more commercials (the clutter problem) and unjustified rate increases that have resulted in higher CPMs. The networks are often in a dilemma, caught between advertisers clamoring for better cost efficiencies and stars of top-rated series demanding higher salaries. A further complication is that, as popular shows age, there is an inevitable slippage in ratings. However, each year the stars earn higher salaries and networks are reluctant to cancel even their more expensive series, fearing that the odds are slim that potential replacements would fare as well.

Block Programming Network executives not only have to choose programs that will appeal to a large segment of households and at least a handful of major advertisers, but also their work is made even more difficult by the fickle television audience. Research has consistently shown that shows do not stand on their own but instead are greatly influenced by the programs directly before, called the *lead-in,* and the total daypart schedule, called a *block*.

The importance of lead-ins can be seen in the investment local stations make to schedule the most popular programming they can buy prior to their early evening news shows. The demand for strong news lead-ins is in large measure responsible for the enormous prices paid for off-network syndicated programs. The same principle is at work in building a network schedule. Programmers strive to make sure that individual programs will attain high ratings, but just as importantly they want to ensure that the block will work together to attract consistently high audience levels.

Network programmers are very aware of the ebb and flow of audiences as they move from one program to another. The pricing of new network shows is dependent in large measure on their placement in the network schedule. Advertisers know that programs that follow proven hits have a high probability of success. An even better situation is the occasional new show that is scheduled between two popular returning programs. This is called a *hammock position*—the analogy being that the new program is placed between two trees (hit shows). Once a new show is on the air, it is judged by how it keeps the audience from its lead-in and sustains the strength of the block.

Network Television Advertising Criteria Clients and their advertising agencies apply a variety of criteria in determining if, and to what extent, they will use network television spots. However, buying decisions are largely determined by three factors: demographics (demos), CPM, and demand.[12]

- *Demos.* Whereas at one time households were the unit of measure, today television advertisers place major emphasis on the demographics of television audiences. This change in criteria has altered the manner in which networks choose shows and the pricing structure for advertisers. For most advertisers, the makeup of the audience of potential network buys has become more important than the size of the audience. Of course, both advertisers and the networks demand that a show attain a certain minimum rating, but the price for shows with favorable demographics usually exceeds what their ratings alone would bring.

For example, ABC has always been able to charge higher than normal prices for spots on *Monday Night Football* (MNF). MNF is highly rated, but it has especially strong appeal for younger men, a primary target audience for products such as beer and automobiles.

CPMs Although most advertisers are seeking favorable demographics and are willing to pay a premium to get them, other advertisers are driven primarily by cost considerations. Of course, no advertiser ignores the audience profile of its advertising buys. However, there are a number of advertisers who evaluate cost efficiencies and CPM levels on an equal basis with audience demographics. Advertisers of widely distributed packaged goods are more likely to take this approach than a product with more limited appeal. These companies take the position that, within certain broad audience criteria, they gain some benefit from virtually any audience because their product usage is so universal.

- *Demand.* The third criterion that determines the relationship between networks and advertisers is the demand for certain programs. Of course, demand is a function of both demographics and CPMs, but there are also qualitative factors, such as association with a special event such as the final episode of *Friends* or with a star who has unique appeal to a particular target market such as Oprah Winfrey, that create a pricing structure over and above the objective numbers.

Avails Next Thanksgiving, begin to take note of the number of pages in your favorite magazines. Some November and December issues of popular publications swell to catalog size as advertisers compete for holiday sales. After the first of the year, these same publications will be very thin, with many advertisers standing on the sidelines after spending a sizable percentage of their budgets during the previous two months.

The broadcast media do not have the advantage of flexible advertising inventory. Every day, 365 days a year, each local station and network must sell more than four hundred 30-second spots. Television advertisers, like their print counterparts, want to heavy-up in peak buying seasons and on the most popular shows. Combined with the problem of high demand and finite network commercial time there is the practical restraint that this amount of time cannot be sold on a spot-by-spot basis.

Networks must ration prime commercial spots among their major advertisers (see yield management in Chapter 2). The availability (called *avails* in network jargon) problem is solved, in part, by combining top-rated avails with less popular ones as advertisers buy packages of commercial time from each network. Whether an advertiser will gain availability to a top-rated show will depend largely on the company's total advertising investment on that network. Package plans allow the networks to work with agencies to place commercials across their entire schedule, with the understanding that each advertiser will have to accept some lower-rated (but demographically acceptable) spots in order to obtain some very desirable spots.

Up-Front and Scatter Buys Each May major advertisers begin the negotiation process to buy commercials on the network prime-time lineup for the coming fall season. This is the so-called **up-front buying** season in which most prime-time

up-front buying
Purchase of network TV time by national advertisers during the first offering by networks. The most expensive network advertising.

spots are bought. In a period of less than a month, advertisers will purchase prime-time commercials worth over $9 billion. The up-front period opens with each network previewing its shows, followed by the actual negotiation for time. There is a separate negotiating period for cable. At one time, the up-front period consisted primarily of negotiation between major agencies and the three major networks. Today, the up-front buying process has become much more complex with a number of new players and different approaches by advertisers. Among the major up-front trends are:

1. *Greater demand for time.* In recent years, a new category of advertisers, the prescription drug companies, have bought large amounts of television advertising as they compete for consumer attention in a very competitive marketplace (See Exhibit 8.5).

2. *Optimizers.* You will recall in Chapter 7, we discussed the role of computer models called optimizers, which sought to find the most efficient combination of television spots to reach specific target segments. Optimizers have provided additional data to major prime-time advertisers, which give them confidence to spread their budgets into other dayparts and television sectors such as cable. For example, one agency using optimizer modeling reduced its expenditures in the three major networks by 5 percent and increased cable and syndicated buys by 9 percent. Until recently, neither of these prime-time alternatives would have been considered in the up-front market. As one media planner who relies heavily on optimizers noted, "The old thinking that you had to use network prime-time to establish your reach goals is just not true."[13]

3. *Globalization.* If optimizer models began the process of extending the media options considered during up-front selling, globalization has taken it even further. Agencies are having to position their U.S. up-front buys in a context of global media for their multinational clients.

4. *Special events.* The up-front market also is affected by time demands made by special events. For example, every four years, demand for political advertising by presidential candidates places an inordinate strain on an already tight commercial inventory. Likewise, when the summer Olympics in Sydney coincided with the Bush/Gore election, advertisers were scrambling for television time, especially during the third and fourth quarters of 2000.

scatter plan
The use of announcements, over a variety of network programs and stations, to reach as many people as possible in a market.

The up-front season is followed by a second phase known as **scatter plan** buys.[14] Scatter plans are usually bought on a quarterly basis throughout the year. They are designed for larger advertisers that want to take advantage of changing marketing conditions or, more often, for smaller advertisers that are shut out of up-front buys. Generally, scatter plans will sell at a higher CPM than up-front spots because there is less time inventory and smaller advertisers don't have the leverage to negotiate the CPM levels of huge network advertisers.

There also are up-front markets for other dayparts, children's programming, and prime-time cable. In fact, many media buyers negotiate for cable and over-the-

EXHIBIT 8.5

Top 10 Network Television Advertisers, 2002 (in millions)

Source: Copyright Crain Communications. Reprinted with permission. *Advertising Age,* www.adage.com/page.cms?pageID =995.

1	General Motors Corp.	$777.8
2	Procter & Gamble Co.	723.7
3	Johnson & Johnson	508.5
4	Ford Motor Co.	437.9
5	Pfizer	380.7
6	PepsiCo	369.3
7	Time Warner	352.7
8	Walt Disney Co.	345.8
9	GlaxoSmithKline	316.2
10	Unilever	305.0

air networks simultaneously. Buyers interested in late night will fight for slots on shows such as *The Tonight Show with Jay Leno, The Late Show with David Letterman,* or *Conan O'Brien.* Similarly, early morning and midday programming each has its own up-front seasons, special advertising categories, and pricing structure. It is important to understand that network avails are largely filled through the up-front seasons in each daypart.

Negotiation   As mentioned in the last section, negotiation is the key to network buying. Because each advertising package is unique to a particular advertiser, there are no rate cards for network television advertising. Over the last several years, network rate negotiation has undergone a number of changes. First, the decline in network rating and share levels has created a more contentious atmosphere. But the fact is that network television, despite decreasing audiences, remains the best way to reach a mass market.

A second major change in the negotiation process is that advertisers are concurrently negotiating for time across a number of television options. As we mentioned, up-front negotiation still takes place among more or less discrete television formats (e.g., daytime, prime time, broadcast networks, cable networks, etc.). However, a number of media planners are looking to a diversity of options to reach a particular target market. As they negotiate network time, they are considering the cable, syndication, and even Internet markets that will be used as supplements to network or to keep overall costs down. With the billions of dollars at stake, agencies and their clients know that an extremely small difference in the cost of a rating point has great significance when a large national advertiser is involved.

Make-Goods   One of the major elements of network negotiation concerns **make-goods.** As the name implies, make-goods are concessions to advertisers for a failure to achieve some guaranteed rating level. Make-goods are normally offered on the basis of total GRPs for an advertiser's television advertising schedule. That is, when the advertiser fails to achieve a certain agreed upon cost per point the make-good provisions are initiated. At one time, make-goods were part of most advertising negotiations—they were always part of the up-front market. Make-goods usually take the form of future commercials to make up for a shortfall in ratings. Monetary refunds are virtually never given as part of a make-good plan.

make-goods
When a medium falls short of some audience guarantee, advertisers are provided concessions in the form of make-goods. Most commonly used in television and magazines.

It has only been in the last several years that make-goods have become a major point of contention between networks and agencies. Prior to that time, the networks were so dominant that it was rare for an advertiser to qualify for a make-good. Each network could reasonably expect to get a 25 to 35 share of the total prime-time schedule. Consequently, a make-good was a relatively risk-free incentive offered by networks to agencies and their clients.

The new competitive environment has changed the make-good situation dramatically. With several network shows achieving sub–10 ratings, the make-good has become a major negotiating point with agencies and a high-risk endeavor for networks. If a prime-time network schedule includes a number of low-rated or canceled shows, it may well mean the network will give up a significant portion of its inventory during the winter and spring to accommodate make-goods. In part because of make-goods, networks are very reluctant to support low-rated shows. Each season there are a few shows that are canceled after one or two airings to prevent a significant demand for make-goods.

SPOT TELEVISION

When national advertisers buy from local stations, the practice is known as **spot television** or spot buys. The term comes from the fact that advertisers are spotting their advertising in certain markets as contrasted to the blanket coverage offered by

spot television
Purchasing of time from a local station, in contrast to purchasing from a network.

network schedules. The primary disadvantages of spot television are that it requires a great deal more planning and paperwork than network because each market must be bought on a one-to-one basis and it is more costly on a CPM basis than network buys.

Spot advertising is an extremely competitive market. Not only are more than 1,000 local stations competing for spot dollars, but the several thousand local cable outlets are becoming important players with many spot advertisers. In the future, broadcast stations will probably face a number of new competitive options from Internet services and other forms of local, interactive media. Largely as a result of this environment, increases in spot dollars are projected to remain relatively flat for broadcast stations as advertisers divert budgets to other forms of local television.

representative (rep)
An individual or organization representing a medium selling time or space outside the city or origin.

Today, most spot advertising is placed through station **representatives** or **reps.** The rep is paid a commission by the station based on the time sold. The commission is negotiable, but it usually ranges from 5 to 10 percent depending on the size of the station. A good sales rep is both a salesperson and a marketing specialist for advertisers. The rep must be able to show a national advertiser how a schedule on WAWS-TV in Jacksonville or KDKA-TV in Pittsburgh will meet a national company's advertising objectives.

Rep firms may have 100 or more station clients on a noncompetitive basis. Reps go to agencies and advertisers to convince them that the markets in which their client stations broadcast are prime sales areas for their brands. To make the purchase of spot buys more efficient, a rep will allow advertisers to buy all or any number of stations it represents. Since the idea is to provide one order and one invoice, it offers similar advantages to a network buy. However, the stations sold through a rep are not linked in any way other than being a client of a particular rep firm.

non-wired networks
Groups of radio and TV stations whose advertising is sold simultaneously by station representatives.

These station groups are called **non-wired networks.** The commercials bought on a non-wired network, unlike a real network, are not necessarily broadcast at the same time or on the same programs. The non-wired concept is simply a means of providing buying efficiency and convenience for spot advertisers.

As in the case of much of the television industry, the rep's role in the spot market will probably undergo significant changes as the move to consolidation in the television industry accelerates. For example, at one time, a single owner could only hold seven television licenses. Today, the rules allow a person or corporation to control stations with total TV household coverage of up to 35 percent of the U.S. population. The FCC has recently considered a rule change that would allow networks to own stations that reach up to 45 percent of the population.[15] With this loosening of ownership rules, we have seen a significant growth in the number and size of station groups, some now owning dozens of stations. A number of these groups are large enough to support their own national sales force.

Group owners making direct deals with advertising agencies have created a potential conflict with their reps, since most rep firms have contracts with their station clients calling for a rep commission on all spot sales regardless of how the sale is made. In addition, a few advertising agencies have indicated their intention to deal directly with major stations and groups and bypass reps. These agencies think that they can negotiate more favorable buys directly than through a rep since it eliminates a rep commission. If this trend of direct station deals expands, there is a real question about the future of the station/rep relationship.

Regardless of changes in the manner in which spot advertising is bought and sold, the primary purposes for spot buys will remain the same:

1. To allow network advertisers to provide additional GRPs in those markets with the greatest sales potential.
2. To provide businesses with less than national or uneven distribution, a means of avoiding waste circulation incurred by network television.

Top 10 Prime-Time Broadcast TV Programs*

Rank*	Program	Network	Household Rating
1	*CSI*	CBS	18.1
2	*E.R.*	NBC	13.6
3	*Friends*	NBC	13.4
4	*CSI: Miami*	CBS	13.2
4	*CMA Awards* (S)	CBS	12.8
6	*8 Simple Rules*	ABC	12.7
7	*Survivor: Pearl Islands*	CBS	12.3
8	*Everybody Loves Raymond*	CBS	12.2
9	*Friends 11/6*(S)	NBC	12.0
9	*Without a Trace*	CBS	12.0

Top 10 Prime-Time TV Programs Among African Americans*

Rank*	Program	African American Network	Household Rating
1	*Girlfriends*	UPN	19.7
2	*Eve*	UPN	19.3
3	*My Wife and Kids*	ABC	19.1
4	*Half and Half*	UPN	18.7
5	*All of Us*	UPN	18.3
6	*The Parkers*	UPN	16.3
7	*One on One*	UPN	14.5
8	*CSI*	CBS	13.3
9	NFL *Monday Night Football*	ABC	13.0
9	*Rock Me Baby*	UPN	13.0

*During a week in November 2003.

EXHIBIT 8.6

TV ratings vary by ethnic group.

Courtesy of Nielsen Media Research, www.nielsenmedia. com/ratings/broadcast_ broadcast_programs.html.

3. Spot buys allow network advertisers to control for uneven network ratings on a market-by-market basis. For example, a network program with a 15 rating may demonstrate huge rating variances from one market to another. Ratings can vary widely due to demographic and viewing preferences of audiences within individual television markets. For example, one reason that ratings can vary widely between markets is the viewing patterns of different racial and ethnic groups. Exhibit 8.6 shows the ratings for the top 10 shows during a week in November. The first part of the chart shows the top 10 shows among total television households. The bottom half of the chart shows the top 10 shows during the same week among African American households. It is interesting to note that only one show, *CSI*, appears on both lists.

4. National advertisers can use spot advertising to support retailers and provide localization for special marketing circumstances. Automobile companies are the leaders in spot advertising. As shown in Exhibit 8.7, five of the top six spot television advertisers are automobile companies. Automobile companies have extensive local dealer networks that are supported through spot television advertising.

Defining the Television Coverage Area

Before the advent of television, companies generally established sales and advertising territories by state boundaries and arbitrary geographical areas within them. However, television transmissions go in many directions for varying distances. Television research uses three levels of signal coverage to designate potential station coverage of a market area.

1. *Total survey area* is the largest area over which a station's coverage extends.

2. *Designated market area (DMA)*, is a term used by the A. C. Nielsen Company to identify those counties in which home market stations receive a preponderance of viewers.

total survey area
The maximum coverage of a radio or television station's signal.

EXHIBIT **8.7**

Top 10 Spot Television Advertisers, 2002 (in millions)

Source: Copyright Crain Communications. Reprinted with permission. *Advertising Age*, www.adage.com/page.cms?pageID =995.

1	DaimlerChrysler	$557.3
2	General Motors Corp.	518.6
3	Ford Motor Co.	326.8
4	Honda Motor Co.	295.5
5	Nissan Motor Co.	235.6
6	Toyota Motor Corp.	211.0
7	Yum Brands	209.7
8	Verizon Communications	207.3
9	General Mills	200.9
10	Time Warner	173.8

3. *Metro rating area* corresponds to the standard metropolitan area served by a station.

Local television stations also provide advertisers with signal coverage maps to show the potential audience reach of the station. The signal coverage designations have become less important in recent years as cable has greatly extended the area over which a television station can be viewed.

Local Television Advertising

Television advertising is increasingly purchased by local advertisers. Businesses as diverse as record stores and banks place advertising on local stations. However, a significant portion of the dollars invested in local television is placed by local franchise outlets of national companies. For example, McDonald's is one of the largest local advertisers.

Currently, local television advertising expenditures are ahead of spot and could challenge network revenues by the end of the decade. Advertisers spend more than $28 billion on spot and local television combined (including cable), compared to $15 billion invested in network.[15]

Buying and Scheduling Spot and Local TV Time Because advertisers have shifted more of their budgets to local markets, media buyers must be familiar with the specifics of buying spot and local TV time.

The TV Day Spot and local TV advertising is often purchased by daypart rather than by specific program. Each daypart varies by audience size and demographic profile. Media planners must be familiar with the audience makeup of various dayparts. Some typical daypart designations for East and West Coast time zones are

1. morning: 7:00–9:00 A.M. Monday through Friday
2. daytime: 9:00 A.M.–4:30 P.M. Monday through Friday
3. early fringe: 4:30–7:30 P.M. Monday through Friday
4. prime-time access: 7:30–8:00 P.M. Monday through Saturday
5. prime time: 8:00–11:00 P.M. Monday through Saturday and 7:00–11:00 P.M. Sunday
6. late news: 11:00–11:30 P.M. Monday through Friday
7. late fringe: 11:30 P.M.–1:00 A.M. Monday through Friday

Preemption Rate A considerable portion of spot TV advertising time is sold on a preemptible (lower-rate) basis, whereby the advertiser gives the station the right to sell a time slot to another advertiser that may pay a better rate for it or that has a package deal for which that particular spot is needed. Whereas some stations offer only two choices, nonpreemptible and preemptible advertising, others allow advertisers to choose between two kinds of preemptible rates. When the station has the right to sell a spot to another advertiser any time up until the time of the telecast, the rate is called the *immediately preemptible* (IP) rate (the lowest rate). When the station can preempt only if it gives the original advertiser two weeks' notice, the rate is designated *preemptible with two weeks' notice* and is sold at a higher rate. The highest rate is charged for a nonpreemptible time slot, the two-week preemptible rate is the next highest, and the immediately preemptible rate is the lowest.

The following table is an excerpt from a rate card.

	I	II	III
Tues., 8–9 A.M.	$135	$125	$115

Column I is the nonpreemptible rate; column II, the rate for preemption with two weeks' notice; and column III, the rate for preemption without notice. Notice how the rate goes down.

Special Features

News telecasts, weather reports, sports news and commentary, stock market reports, and similar programming are called *special features*. Time in connection with special features is sold at a premium price.

Run of Schedule (ROS)

An advertiser can earn a lower rate by permitting a station to run commercials at its convenience whenever time is available rather than in a specified position. (This is comparable to run of paper in newspaper advertising; see Chapter 10.)

Package Rates

Every station sets up its own assortment of time slots at different periods of the day, which it sells as a package. The station creates its own name for such packages and charges less for them than for the same slots sold individually. The package rate is one of the elements in negotiation for time.

Product Protection

Every advertiser wants to keep the advertising of competitive products as far away from its commercials as possible. This brings up the question of what protection against competition an ad will get. Although some stations say that they will try to keep competing commercials 5 to 10 minutes apart, most say that although they will do everything possible to separate competing ads, they guarantee only that they will not run them back to back or in the same pod or group of commercials in a break.

Scheduling Spot and Local Time

Rotation of a schedule refers to the placement of commercials within a schedule to get the greatest possible showing. If you bought two spots a week for four weeks on a Monday-to-Friday basis, but all the spots were aired only on Monday and Tuesday, your rotation would be poor. You would miss all the people who turn to the station only on Wednesday, Thursday, or Friday. Your horizontal rotation should be increased. Vertical rotation assures there will be differences in the time at which a commercial is shown within the time bracket purchased. If you bought three spots on the *Tonight Show*, which runs from 11:30 P.M. to 12:30 A.M., but all your spots were shown at 12:15 A.M., you would be missing all the people who go to sleep earlier than that. To avoid this situation, you would schedule one spot in each half hour of the program, vertically rotating your commercial to reach the largest possible audience.

TELEVISION SYNDICATION

Television syndication is the sale of television programming on a station-by-station, market-by-market basis. Syndication companies have programming to sell and they seek to sell individual programs to at least one station in every market. Most major syndicated shows are sold on an advertiser-supported or barter basis. **Barter syndication** refers to the practice of offering the right to run a show to stations in return for a portion of the commercial time in the show, rather than selling the show to stations for cash. A majority of the commercial time on syndicated shows is packaged into national units and sold to national advertisers. The typical syndicated show comes with spots presold on a national basis and the station sells the remaining time to local and spot advertisers.

Syndication began when producers sold their canceled network shows to stations for inexpensive "fillers" during late afternoon or other time periods not programmed by the networks. During the early days of syndication no one thought that it was anything but a method for producers to pick up a few extra dollars by selling programs that had completed their network runs to local stations. During this period, syndication was a minor portion of television advertising.

Currently, syndication accounts for more than $3 billion in advertising revenues and major syndicated shows provide coverage comparable to the broadcast networks.[16] For example, leading syndicated shows such as *Wheel of Fortune* and *Home Improvement* have potential coverage in excess of 90 percent of television households, compared to network's 96 percent and significantly greater than the 51 percent provided by the average cable program. In addition, syndication is theoretically available in every television household, while cable programs can come only into the 70 percent of homes wired for cable.

Like any television format, the key to syndication's success is quality programming. Syndicated programs are either *first-run,* programs made for syndication, such as *Entertainment Tonight* and *The Oprah Winfrey Show,* or **off-network syndication** reruns such as *Friends* and *The X-Files.* Most long-running shows such as *Everybody Loves Raymond* and *Will & Grace* enter the syndication market during their original network runs. Less than 15 percent of syndicated programs are off-network. However, these shows are consistently the most popular and command the highest advertising rates.

barter syndication
Station obtains a program at no charge. The program has pre-sold national commercials and time is available for local station spots.

off-network syndication
Syndicated programs that have previously been aired by a major network.

New technology has made it possible for households to receive many more television signals than ever before. This created the need for more program content to be included in syndicated programs.

Off-network shows have built-in audiences and reach predictable demographic segments. Advertisers also feel more comfortable with the known content of a high-quality rerun versus the less predictable talk and entertainment first-run product. In fact, advertisers are willing to pay a significant premium for most off-network syndicated programs compared to first-run shows with comparable ratings. In fact, a 30-second spot on *Friends* or *Seinfeld* in syndication can cost more than many prime-time network shows.

Syndication advertising costs vary much more than other types of television programming. Essentially, there is a three-tier pricing structure for the top 50 syndicated shows:

1. The top 10 blockbusters include proven off-network reruns such as *Friends* and a handful of proven first-run winners such as *Entertainment Tonight* and *Jeopardy*. These shows will have 30-second spot prices of $68–180,000 with the network reruns invariably getting the top prices.
2. The second tier includes a small number of shows that fall short of the top 10 but still have a sizable, loyal audience. *Judge Judy* and *Access Hollywood* fall into this category and are priced in the $36–56,000 range for 30-second spots.
3. Finally, there is a large number of talk shows and less popular reruns that will charge from $12–31,000. [17]

The demand for syndicated shows is driven by television's insatiable demand for programming—any programming. For local stations and cable networks with 24 hours to fill, there is simply not enough programming for the thousands of hours required to fill their schedules. In addition, as more and more cable networks are added, the demand continues to increase. Nickelodeon, Lifetime, TNT, The Family Channel, and a host of other cable networks are competing with local stations for off-network programs and driving up the price of those that remain in the syndication market. Adding to the demand for syndicated time is a number of national advertisers that use syndicated programming as a means of extending reach on a demographic and/or geographic basis. Generally, broadcast syndication will surpass cable networks in achieving significant levels of audience reach because the average over-the-air station has higher audience levels than cable networks.

The demand for syndicated programming has moved some stations to sign long-term contracts with program producers to guarantee continued access to certain shows. For example, in 1988, ABC's O&O stations contracted with *Jeopardy* and *Wheel of Fortune* through 2004 and other stations extended these contracts until 2005.[18] With the relatively few shows that can generate high audience levels, the stations had to make long-term commitments to ensure having them on their schedule in future seasons.

The Audience for Syndicated Television

Syndication has some of the same characteristics as cable. For example, although syndication generates high aggregate audience levels, it does so over multiple programs and showings rather than delivering a mass audience in a single showing as in the case of broadcast networks. In fact, syndicators sell programs on the basis of multiple airings known as gross average audience ratings. For example, let's assume that an airing of *Friends* on NBC has a local market affiliate rating of 15.0 and a *Friends* syndicated version has a rating of 5.0. If ACME, Inc., runs one spot on the network version and three spots on the syndicated version, the total rating points would be 15 for both shows. However, it's very difficult to compare the two because on network you're achieving your audience all at once. The network audience exposures are unduplicated exposure. In syndication, your ratings are based on spots running within a week.[19]

The future of syndication is extremely bright because local stations find it very lucrative. In the typical network show, stations are allowed to sell 1 minute of commercial time. In a syndicated show the station can sell from 6 to 12 minutes of commercials depending on how the program was bartered to the station. Consequently, a syndicated program does not have to generate huge ratings to be a financial success for a station.

Because local stations find syndication profitable and the demand for new syndicated programming continues to grow, there is every reason to believe that syndication will be a major advertising vehicle for the foreseeable future. If anything, syndication will be an even stronger competitor to the traditional networks and the relationship between syndicators and stations may become more formal with long-term contracts and stations buying equity shares in syndicated programs to ensure continued access.

Stripping Most local stations schedule syndicated shows on a basis of five nights a week. That is, they will run *Jeopardy* or *Inside Edition* Monday through Friday in the same time slot. This practice is called **stripping** because the show is stripped across a time period. It is cost efficient to buy fewer shows for multishowings and allows a station to build a consistent audience for selling commercials to potential advertisers. Because most syndication is used as a lead-in either for early news or prime-time programs, stations don't want huge rating or audience composition swings from one day to another.

stripping
Scheduling a syndicated program on a five-day-per-week basis.

Cable Television

cable television
TV signals that are carried to households by cable. Programs originate with cable operators through high antennas, satellite disks, or operator-initiated programming.

Cable television has its roots in the small Pennsylvania town of Mahanoy City. In the 1940s, John Watson, an appliance store owner, was having difficulty selling television sets because of poor reception caused by a mountain range between Philadelphia stations and Mahanoy City. By placing an antenna on a surrounding peak combined with coaxial cable and amplifiers, cable television (then known as Community Antenna Television or CATV) had begun.

Soon cable systems were importing a variety of signals from different cities to rural households. By the 1970s, cable had become attractive to viewers throughout the country and it moved from remote areas to major cities. In 1972, pay television was launched when Home Box Office (HBO) began service. HBO initiated the era of original programming as opposed to simply extending the signals of over-the-air stations. Of equal importance, HBO's programming was delivered by satellite and provided universal availability for cable networks.[20]

From its humble beginnings, cable television has become a major medium in its own right with household penetration of more than 70 percent. In recent years, the cable advertising share of total dollars has shown double-digit increases. Both local and national cable advertising revenues continue to grow at a rate higher than many other forms of advertising.

The Contemporary Cable Television Industry

For the first two decades of its existence, cable customers were satisfied to get a wider option of over-the-air broadcast programs and cable operators were making satisfactory profits from cable subscription fees. However, cable industry executives realized that they were missing a major source of revenue by failing to open the medium to advertisers. For the last 25 years, cable has grown as it matured into a medium serving both viewers and advertisers.

The success of cable can be traced to two related elements:

1. Brand identification based on unique and selective networks and programs that appeal to targeted demographic audience segments.
2. The investment by cable networks in first-run programming.

Unlike broadcast networks that reach huge audiences for mass advertisers, cable provides advertisers with much smaller niche audiences that exhibit both common demographic characteristics and interests. Advertisers know that Lifetime, MTV, Cartoon Network, and The Discovery Channel will deliver predictable groups of viewers. Cable networks define their brands in the same way as product manufacturers. For both, brand identification and awareness create a consistent environment for the users of these brands.

It is favorable brand recognition that provides the major impetus to cable success in bringing large national advertisers to the medium. As shown in Exhibit 8.8, with leading advertisers such as Procter & Gamble, General Motors, and Time Warner, cable is competing for the same advertisers as the broadcast networks.

Cable networks know that it is original programming that will bring both viewers and advertisers to a particular network. Only a few years ago, the majority of cable network programming consisted of off-network reruns and theatrical films that had usually been run several times on both broadcast networks and local stations. Today, cable networks annually invest billions of dollars in original programming, some of which is among the most popular on television. From the irreverent Bravo's *Queer Eye for the Straight Guy* to ESPN's *Sunday NFL* games and A&E's *Investigative Reports* and *Biography*, cable networks are appealing to a larger share of the total viewing audience.

The Future of Cable Advertising

A number of factors make cable television an attractive medium for advertisers.

1. *Ability to target audiences.* When advertisers consider cable television, its ability to reach specific demographic and lifestyle segments is almost always the prime consideration.

2. *Low cost.* The cable industry is faced with a competitive environment that prevents significant increases in CPMs. With an abundance of cable channels, many trying to prove themselves to advertisers, it is very unlikely that we will see the type of advertising increases that have been so prevalent among the major broadcast networks in recent years.

3. *A strong summer season.* In recent years, cable has counterprogrammed the networks by presenting some of their strongest programs opposite network summer reruns. Many advertisers have taken advantage of the audience shifts inherent in this strategy to move dollars into cable during what is typically a down viewing time for networks.

4. *Opportunity for local and spot cable advertising.* The majority of cable advertising dollars are spent at the network level. However, local cable advertising is growing at a rate significantly higher than network advertising. Local cable spending comes from national spot buyers looking to enhance advertising weight in specific markets and a wide variety of local firms such as restaurants, video stores, and small retailers. Because of cable's low advertising rates, these retailers now have a chance to use television.

One interesting trend of the last few years has been for cable networks to branch out and begin their own magazines. ESPN launched its highly successful *ESPN The*

1	Procter & Gamble Co.	$386.3
2	General Motors Corp.	342.0
3	Time Warner	243.6
4	Altria Group	161.0
5	Johnson & Johnson	144.9
6	Viacom	134.9
7	Walt Disney Co.	129.8
8	Pfizer	126.6
9	U.S. government	125.0
10	AT&T Corp.	121.9

EXHIBIT **8.8**

Top 10 Cable Television Advertisers, 2002 (in millions)

Source: Copyright Crain Communications. Reprinted with permission. *Advertising Age,* www.adage.com/page.cms?pageID =995.

Magazine to sports fans in 1998. Since that time, other cable networks have launched magazines with much fanfare but with mixed success. Nickelodeon has two successful spin-offs with *Nickelodeon* and *Nick Jr.* magazines. A&E's *Biography* magazine, however, failed to make it as anything but a fan magazine.[21] In 2003, Lifetime launched a magazine of the same name that is targeted to the same female audience as is the network.[22] These types of magazines offer advertisers the opportunity to negotiate cross-media deals to potentially have more impact on their target audiences.

In the future, cable advertisers will have at least three readily available advertising options. The first is traditional advertising spots carried on regular analog cable. A second option is targeted advertising using digital technology. For example, advertisers will be able to reach cable homes in specific ZIP codes and neighborhoods or household members in specific demographic groups with tailored messages. A third option will be interactive advertising offered through special software added to cable boxes on viewers' television sets.

These interactive systems will allow consumers to shop directly from the screen during commercials. One company, RespondTV, has experimented with banners on commercials such as Domino's pizza. A viewer can click the yes key on a remote pad and order a pizza during the commercial. Television interactive selling (often called T-commerce) is already offered in selected homes.[23] Two innovations in local cable advertising have greatly enhanced the importance of this segment—cut-ins and interconnects.

Although some cable advertising options are not readily available, current technology offers advertisers some sophisticated coverage alternatives. The first innovation is the use of cut-ins on network cable programs. Cable networks, like their broadcast counterparts, provide some advertising spots to local system operators to sell to local advertisers. Rather than having a spot appear on a largely unwatched local channel, commercials for the local pizza shop now can air on CNN's *Larry King Show* or ESPN's *Sports Center*.

interconnects
A joint buying opportunity between two or more cable systems in the same market.

A further strengthening of local cable advertising comes from the use of **interconnects.** "An interconnect exists where two or more cable systems [in the same market] link themselves together to distribute a commercial advertising schedule simultaneously."[24] In larger markets, an advertiser can simultaneously air several different commercials in various areas of the city. The agency gets a single bill from all the systems, which facilitates individual client billing. The use of interconnects has helped some national brands such as Guinness back up their national televi-

Most cable operators can now insert commercials on their local systems.

sion plan in key markets. They have also been used with success by automotive dealers such as Ford to target spots to consumers in specific counties where various dealers do business.[25] The use of interconnects greatly enhances the prospects for bringing more spot advertisers to cable.

As cable has garnered more advertising dollars, research has improved to help advertisers measure the cable audience and plan the cable portions of their advertising campaign. In particular, Nielsen Media Research provides a number of services including overnight household ratings and local audience composition data. In addition, Mediamark Research, Inc., (MRI) offers national product and cable media usage information. Advertisers also are able to obtain customized data for local market commercials and information about optimum local commercial efficiencies.

VCRs and DVRs

Since its introduction in the 1970s, the VCR has become as commonplace as television itself. Approximately 95 percent of American homes have a VCR and many households having multiple VCRs. In some sense, the VCR is almost a medium in itself providing access to theatrical movies, made-for-VCR films, promotional and educational tapes, and, of course, recording television shows for later viewing (called **time-shift viewing**).

At one time, it was anticipated that the primary usage of VCRs would be for off-air recording. In the early days of the VCR, advertisers thought that the VCR would be a method of increasing the audience of a show for those too busy to watch it during its originally scheduled time. However, studies show that more than half of recorded shows are never watched, the audiences for time-shift viewing tend to be demographically different than original audiences, and the VCR allows viewers to fast-forward through commercials—hardly an advantage for advertisers!

The television industry is well aware that each hour spent watching these pre-recorded tapes is time not available for regular television viewing. Of particular concern to both broadcasters and advertisers is the demographic makeup of heavy VCR users. For example, young affluent adults, prime prospects for many television advertisers, are the most likely to rent videotapes. This audience is then unavailable for exposure to traditional broadcast and cable outlets and their advertisers.

Many industry observers think the VCR will soon be an outdated relic, replaced by digital technology that allows much greater flexibility than the VCR. The digital video recorder (DVR) allows viewers to take control of their viewing in a manner never before possible.

The DVR digitizes all incoming signals and stores up to 120 hours of programs. The viewer can then pause in a program to answer the telephone, provide instant replay or slow motion on demand, and record for later viewing any program just as with a VCR, but it can be done much more quickly and easily, and it doesn't require a tape. It also allows advertisers to customize commercials for individual viewers. For example, let's say your favorite show is *Monday Night Football,* but you are not a beer drinker. Therefore, instead of the network Coors commercial, you receive a commercial for Coca-Cola that is digitally stripped in the program. Furthermore, the commercial may be one that fits your age and interests known to Coke from information you previously provided the cable provider.

Obviously, a number of issues among network advertisers, secondary advertisers, program providers, and the networks would have to be addressed before the technology could be used to refit commercials. Advertisers also worry that the technology makes deleting commercials very easy. Of the people who purchased TiVo, one of the first personal video recorders (PVRs) with a computer-type hard-drive, 85 percent skip most commercials and can watch a half-hour program in 23 minutes.[26] However, one advantage of the system is that it can measure the households that are zapping commercials and measure actual commercial audience. This, in turn, brings up the issue of viewer privacy. Another concern of advertisers is that

time-shift viewing
Recording programs on a VCR for viewing at a later time.

the technology may make pay-for-view movies a more viable option for viewers, which would further decrease commercial viewing.

PVRs did not take off quite as quickly as predicted in the first couple of years. One of the reasons was the high cost of a unit. However, some satellite and cable television companies began offering PVRs in their set-top boxes in order to lure subscribers. Forrester Research estimates that in 2006, 27 percent of U.S. television households will have PVRs.[27] The PVR will provide technical convergence of computers, interactive communication, and multiple options for standard television. If PVRs achieve predicted levels of household penetration, advertisers will have to better target their commercials to audiences that are most likely to watch them and/or seek alternatives to the 30-second commercial. As stated by Chuck B. Fruit, a senior vice president at Coca-Cola, "It puts a great obligation on the part of the advertiser to be part of the viewing experience and to add to the experience" or otherwise "they will risk being ignored."[28]

Brand Integration or Product Placement

Fueled in part by advertisers' desire to increase the value of their television advertising and to recapture some of the audience lost to both network audience erosion and PVRs, advertisers have been more aggressive in seeking ways to integrate their brands into television programs. Brand integration can involve a range of activities from simply having the product appear in one episode of a television program to sponsorship of entire shows. The broadcast and cable networks have become very creative in the kinds of opportunities they offer advertisers. The following are some recent examples of brand integration:[29]

- On an episode of *Life with Bonnie,* Bonnie Hunt's husband gave her a diamond ring from Kay Jewelers.
- Florida Citrus worked with *Good Morning America* to sponsor a contest for Mother's Day called "Emeril's Breakfast in Bed."
- TNT integrated Kimberly-Clark's Kleenex brand into its rating system for sad movies called "Kleenex Tearjerker on TNT." A system of tissues (1 to 5) was used to rate the tearjerker quality of the movies.
- An unscripted original series was created for Lowe's Companies called *House Rules.* Lowe's products are featured throughout the show.
- Mountain Dew and Doritos were included in the reward program for the first *Survivor* show.

The value of such integration is debated among advertisers. Most industry experts seem to feel that the value of the integration depends on how well the brand fits into the program and how well it is integrated into the campaign.[30] Traditional CPM comparisons do not provide an adequate assessment. Some measurement services are beginning to look at ways to measure the effectiveness of product placements. More value is placed on characters using the brand and/or saying the product name than on simply showing the product. Product placements are not seen as something that will replace commercials. According to Steve Sternberg, director of research at MAGNA Global, "Product placement should not be the centerpiece of any strategy, but rather must still be seen as added value, until there is adequate research to place a 'value' on various levels of product placement."[31]

SYNDICATED RATING SERVICES

As mentioned earlier in this chapter, from an advertising perspective television is simply an audience delivery system. Needless to say, it is crucial for advertisers and their agencies to have reliable data on which to make buying decisions and to determine if they are paying a fair price. In recent years, the problems of accurately accounting for the fragmented television audience have become more and more difficult. At the same time, as audiences for each television outlet decrease, the magnitude of any error increases as a percentage of the total viewing audience. For example, a 1 rating-point error for a program with a 20 rating is 5 percent; the same error for a program with a 5 rating is 20 percent. Because advertising rates are determined directly by ratings, these errors are a cause for considerable concern among advertisers.

The Nielsen Ratings

The primary supplier of syndicated television ratings is Nielsen Media Research.[32] The company was founded in 1923 by A. C. Nielsen to collect radio audience information and it initiated television ratings in 1950. The Nielsen Television Index (NTI) provides network ratings on a national basis. Data are provided from 5,100 households. In these households, a **people meter** is attached to each television set. The people meter has buttons assigned to each person living in the home and additional buttons for visitors.

people meter
Device that measures TV set usage by individuals rather than by households.

 Many advertisers are interested in local viewing levels and Nielsen provides ratings for all markets through its Nielsen Station Index (NSI). In the 55 largest markets, Nielsen uses set meters (not people meters) to measure household television set usage on a continuous basis. In each of the 210 television markets, Nielsen provides diaries in which individuals record their viewing habits. These diaries are administered four times a year during February, May, July, and November. These four periods are known as *sweeps* and they are used to set the price of local commercials for the coming quarter. Each year, more than 1.6 million paper diaries are processed by Nielsen.

 In recent years, the ratings system has come under a great deal of scrutiny by both advertisers and broadcasters. Although a number of issues have been raised, we will discuss three major areas of concern:

1. *Sweep weeks.* In theory, **sweep weeks** (or simply sweeps) are an efficient and relatively inexpensive means of estimating quarterly local market ratings. In fact, local market stations have sometimes used the period to artificially distort their ratings by airing sensational news exposés, special promotions, and pressuring networks to program their best miniseries, movies, and specials to support their affiliates during sweeps.

   sweep weeks
   During these periods, ratings are taken for all television markets.

    The result is that the sweep period ratings of local stations may have little relation to the 36 "unrated" weeks. Advertisers are extremely frustrated by what they see as inflated ratings and the accompanying higher commercial rates they pay for them. The alleged abuses of sweep week programming have resulted in increasing calls for measuring of local audiences on a continuing basis.

2. *Diaries.* Everyone agrees that in an era of over 50-channel household reception and a trend toward individual viewing, the diary is an antiquated measurement tool. A number of major advertisers have called for people meters in at least the top 125 markets, which would include approximately 75 percent of television households. It also would largely eliminate the current sweeps problem by providing ongoing audience measurements for most of the country. The major obstacle to implementing local people meter ratings is cost. It is estimated that each metered market would require a minimum of 300 sampled households, or almost 40,000 homes, at a cost of several hundred million dollars—much more than either advertisers or broadcasters are currently willing to pay. By 2006, the company plans to replace dairies with people meters in the top 10 television markets.

3. *Exposure value.* Another area of ratings that has generated great interest is estimating exposure levels for television commercials versus set usage. Advertisers want to know who is watching, who is paying attention, and what level of attention is being given any particular show.

Recently Nielsen and Arbitron announced a joint research effort that holds promise in solving many of the problems facing broadcast audience measurement. They will be engaging in a study using a portable people meter (PPM). The PPM is a device about the size of a pager that measures inaudible signals from the audio portion of television, radio, cable, and the Internet. It eliminates the nuisance of keeping a diary and the PPM is particularly valuable in measuring the out-of-home audience of radio. The major barrier to its use is the cost associated with its introduction.[33]

Regardless of what form changes in syndicated ratings take in the future, it is clear that methods that served the television industry well in a period of three networks and a few stations in each market will not work in the fragmented landscape of the twenty-first century. A primary issue is how much are the major players—stations, networks, and advertisers—willing to pay to gather these elusive data.

Qualitative Ratings

As you will recall in our discussion of cable television, we commented on the need for cable networks to sell the quality and lifestyle of their audiences in contrast to the basic numbers reported by most major rating reports. Another type of qualitative audience measure seeks to offer insight into audience involvement or degree of preference for particular television shows or personalities. These measures can be used to determine if a person can be successfully used as a testimonial spokesperson or to see if a popular show is beginning to wear out.

The best-known qualitative research service is Marketing Evaluations, which compiles a number of "popularity" surveys called "Q" reports. The most familiar of these are **TvQ** and Performer Q.

TvQ
A service of Marketing Evaluations that measures the popularity (opinion of audience rather than size of audience) of shows and personalities.

Let us assume that a TV show, *Party Hardy*, is familiar to 50 percent of the population, and 30 percent of the people rank it as one of their favorite shows. The *Q* score would be calculated as follows:

$$Q = \frac{FAV}{FAM} \text{ or } \frac{30}{50} = 60$$

Interestingly enough, the fragmentation of television has taken its toll not only on average program ratings but also on the TvQ scores. Because the number of people watching any particular show is so much lower now than in past years, the general recognition level of television personalities has fallen significantly in recent years. A generation ago, Lucille Ball and Jackie Gleason were as well known as the president. Today, many television stars have a loyal following among their fans but are not necessarily household names. In 1990, the top 25 female television stars had a familiarity score of 68 percent, but by 1999 the average for the group had fallen to 50 percent.[34]

SUMMARY

The future of television is being written every day. In the near future, it will become more than a medium of information, entertainment, and advertising. Television, in its various permutations, will be an interactive system that will allow viewers to pay bills, make airline reservations, receive pay-per-view programming on demand, and even play computer games with other viewers. How long it will be before these systems are generally available and what their final form will take are still very much in question. However, programmers, advertisers, and the general public will all be dealing with a dramatically changed television medium in the not too distant future.

In addition to its functional options, television is becoming a gateway to a world of communication never before imagined. Every aspect of the media from audience research to news must be reevaluated in terms of viewer control and a changing economic base. Throughout most of the last century, it was understood that American mass media would be largely financed by advertisers using a business plan of reaching the largest audience possible at the lowest cost per person. The fragmentation of the television audience has changed programming, financing, and the criteria of what constitutes a "mass" medium.

Although television advertising faces an uncertain future, it is an uncertainty filled with opportunities for those who have the creativity and insight to operate in an era of an audience-driven medium. Nowhere will the customer-oriented notion of the marketing concept be more apparent than in interactive television. It appears certain that both advertisers and viewers will soon pay a higher price for access to the numerous options offered by television. In return, astute advertisers will be reaching customers and prospects on a one-to-one basis with some form of permission marketing being the rule rather than the exception.

 **REVIEW**

1. Discuss major changes in network television advertising during the last 20 years.

2. Define the following terms:

   a. rating

   b. share of audience

   c. people ratings

   d. TvQ ratings

   e. clutter

3. Compare and contrast syndication and spot television buying.

4. Discuss the relationship between networks and their affiliates.

5. Describe the up-front television buying market for prime time.

6. Compare and contrast cable networks with broadcast networks.

 **TAKE IT TO THE WEB**

The Television Bureau of Advertising (TVB) is a nonprofit trade association of the broadcast television industry in America. The TVB Web site provides valuable information about audience analysis, television ratings, ad revenue figures, and more. Visit **www.tvb.org** and compare weekly and monthly rating trends for both broadcast and cable.

Public information about the cable industry, including the history, research in the field, and technological developments of cable television, is provided by the Cable Center. Visit the Web site at **www.cablecenter.org** and review the history of cable television. Make predictions on what you think will be the next big thing for cable.

The mission of the Cable Television Advertising Bureau is to supply information to advertisers to assist in media planning. Visit **www.cabletvadbureau.com** and list three reasons why advertisers would choose to include cable in their media mix. While you are there, check out the special case study section profiling national companies that have chosen cable as a medium in which to advertise.

CHAPTER 9

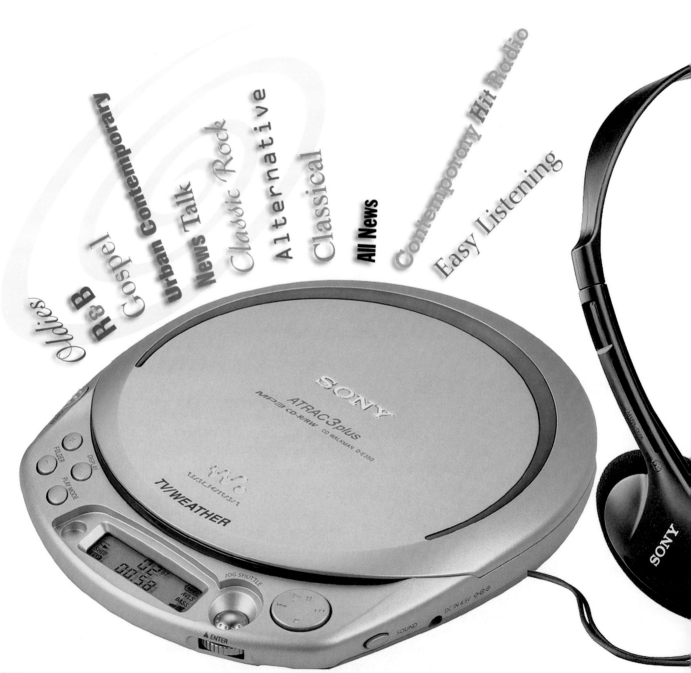

Oldies · R&B · Gospel · Urban Contemporary · News Talk · Classic Rock · Alternative · Classical · All News · Contemporary Hit Radio · Easy Listening

Using Radio

With a host of formats and numerous stations in even the smallest towns, radio provides advertisers with options to reach very narrowly defined niche prospects. Radio also is among the most popular media with high levels of listenership throughout the day. Radio offers the opportunity for advertisers to reach some audiences, such as teenagers, working women, and light television viewers, that are sometimes hard to reach with other media. After reading this chapter, you will understand:

1. the role of radio as a selective medium
2. radio's strength as a secondary medium
3. radio's ability to reach audiences at a low cost
4. attempts to overcome radio's lack of a visual dimension
5. different roles of AM and FM radio
6. the rating systems used in radio

PROS

1. Radio is a primary medium for targeting narrow audience segments, many of whom are not heavy users of other media.
2. Radio is a mobile medium going with listeners into the marketplace and giving advertisers proximity to the sale.
3. Radio, with its relatively low production costs and immediacy, can react quickly to changing market conditions.
4. Radio has a personal relationship with its audience unmatched by other media. This affinity with listeners carries over to the credibility it offers many of the products advertised on radio.
5. Radio, with its low cost and targeted formats, is an excellent supplemental medium for secondary building blocks to increase reach and frequency to specific target markets.

CONS

1. Without a visual component, radio often lacks the impact of other media. Also, many listeners use radio as "background" rather than giving it their full attention.
2. The small audiences of most radio stations require numerous buys to achieve acceptable reach and frequency.
3. Adequate audience research is not always available, especially among many small market stations.

In the early days radio listening was often a group activity.

During the week of March 6, 1949, the top-rated radio show was the *Lux Radio Theater,* which reached almost 30 percent of American households.[1] By contrast, the most popular television show of the 2003 season, *CSI,* achieved a 16.1 household rating. Until the 1950s when television became the major broadcast medium, radio was the primary national medium for both advertisers and audiences.

From 1926 when the first network (The National Broadcasting Company) was formed, until the mid-1950s, radio was the most prestigious of the national media. During those golden years of radio, the family gathered around the living room radio set to listen to Jack Benny, Fred Allen, and Bob Hope entertain them while news personalities such as Edward R. Murrow enlightened them. All of this programming was brought to the audience by the major advertisers of the day. By 1951, with the advent of coast-to-coast television broadcasts and the introduction of instant hits such as *I Love Lucy* and *The $64,000 Question,* radio quickly declined as a national medium.

Despite its minor position on the national scene, as a local medium, radio advertising revenues are over $18 billion and it demonstrates impressive reach (see Exhibit 9.1). Each week radio reaches about 94 percent of all adults and 93 percent of teenagers.[2] By reaching prospects with targeted formats from urban to all-talk, radio commercials can create an intimate, one-to-one relationship with prospects. In addition, radio can achieve effective creative effects at a lower production cost than virtually any other media.

THE CONTEMPORARY RADIO INDUSTRY

Like most media, radio is having to adapt to a new competitive environment and very different economic structure. Only a few years ago, the Federal Communications Commission (FCC) limited ownership of radio stations to seven FM and seven AM stations with only one of each in a single market. However, the FCC gradually loosened ownership restrictions and the Telecommunications Act of 1996 allowed corporations or individuals to control as much as 35 percent of the national market (with other rules governing local station ownership determined by the size of a

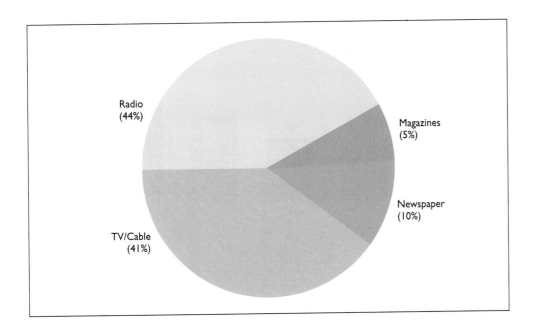

EXHIBIT **9.1**

Average Daily Share of Time Spent with Each Medium (average weekday 6 A.M. to 6 P.M.)

Courtesy of Arbitron/Radio Advertising Bureau (RAB)— Targeting 2000

market). The new ownership rules changed the radio industry from one of numerous small groups to one comprised of a few huge conglomerates.

Led by companies such as Clear Channel with over 1,200 stations and Infinity Broadcasting with over 180 stations, more and more radio stations belong to these mega-owners. Many radio stations are owned by large media companies that also own television stations or newspapers. Accompanying this new movement to large group ownership is a revival of radio as a preferred advertising medium for a number of major businesses. As many advertisers seek to reach more narrowly defined targets, radio offers them the opportunity to more efficiently reach a niche market.

Radio and New Technology

Some observers think that the audio platform of the next decade will be computers and satellites, not a radio dial. More and more radio executives see the future of radio as an Internet business with numerous options for reaching niche audiences and eventually individuals with tailored programming, music, and advertising. Web sites have become the new business model for radio. Broadcasters are facing new copyright regulations regarding the performance fees they must pay for streaming their on-air programming over the Internet.[3] Despite these challenges, Internet radio listening is continuing to grow.

To predict precisely the future of radio, even in the near term, is difficult. However, we can examine some of the major trends that will drive the medium during the coming years.

1. The size of the audience listening to radio stations over the Internet is growing rapidly. In Jaunary 2000, 11 percent of Americans said that they had listened to radio stations over the Internet. By January 2003, over one-third said they had listened (see Exhibit 9.2).
2. More listeners to Internet radio are becoming habitual listeners. As of 2003, almost 12 percent of Americans age 12 and older said they listened to radio stations online in the past month. About 6 percent said they listened to radio stations over the Internet in the past week.
3. Internet radio listeners report listening to local stations most often (46 percent), followed by stations from other parts of the country (40 percent). About 7 percent of online listeners say they listen most often to stations from other countries.[4]

EXHIBIT **9.2**

**One in Three Americans
Has Listened to Radio
Stations Online**

Courtesy of Arbitron/Edison Media
Research Internet and Multimedia
10—"The Emerging Digital
Consumer"

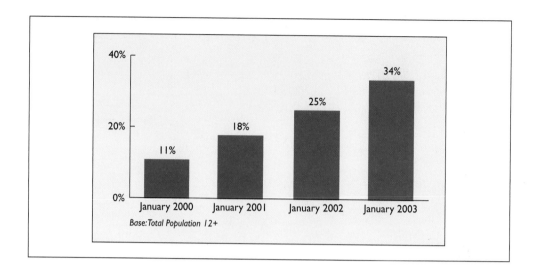

The future of radio as a medium for the delivery of more specialized and personalized programming is very bright. However, the form that this transmission will take, whether local stations can survive satellite and Internet systems, and how advertisers will utilize the new technological options fully are very much up in the air.

FEATURES AND ADVANTAGES OF RADIO

Radio is an ideal medium for the segmented marketing of the twenty-first century. In many respects, radio was the forerunner of many of the localized marketing and advertising strategies so much in use today. As the **Radio Advertising Bureau (RAB)** points out, "Radio gives you the opportunity to take advantage of the most powerful form of communication—the human voice. The right combination of words, voices, music, and effects on radio can help you establish a unique 'one-on-one' connection with your prospects that lets you grab their attention, evoke their emotions, and persuade them to respond. All this at a fraction of the production cost of other broadcast media."[5]

**Radio Advertising
Bureau (RAB)**

Association to promote the
use of radio as an
advertising medium.

According to the Radio Marketing Bureau, radio offers a number of advantages not found in most other media. Some of the primary elements of interest to advertisers are the following:

1. *Radio targets.* One of the greatest strengths of radio is its ability to deliver advertising to a very selective audience. It would be difficult to find a market segment whose needs, tastes, and preferences are not reached by some station's programming.

    Radio's combination of high overall reach and ability to provide numerous formats makes it a multifaceted medium. In some sense, each programming category, whether country, classical, all-talk, or rhythm and blues, can be treated as a distinct medium for marketing purposes. From a marketing perspective, radio has the ability to reach prospects by sex, age, or interest with a format that adds an even greater dimension to its already strong personal communication environment. For example, Exhibit 9.3 shows the age of the audience for three popular radio formats.

2. *Radio reaches a majority of the population several hours per day.* Radio can deliver higher income and educational segments that are of prime importance to many advertisers (see Exhibit 9.4).

3. *Radio advertising influences consumers closest to the time of purchase.* No major medium can compete with radio as a means of reaching prospects as they

Radio Format

	Alternative	Contemporary Hit Radio	Classical
Sex			
Male	63.3%	42.6%	47.4%
Female	36.7	57.4	52.6
Education			
High school or less	29.8%	41.9%	12.1%
Some college	39.2	39.5	26.6
College graduate	31.1	18.6	61.3
Age			
12–24	36.2	52.5	3.9%
25–44	50.9	37.7	19.1
45–54	9.8	6.8	20.1
55 +	3.2	3.0	56.9

EXHIBIT 9.3

There is a radio format for everyone.

Courtesy of Maximi$er Plus National Regional Database and Scarborough USA+ 2002. Courtesy of Arbitron Radio Today 2003.

approach a purchase decision. Although both outdoor and point-of-purchase ads also reach consumers in the marketplace, neither can deliver a sales message the way radio can.

4. *Radio reaches light users of other media.* Light television viewers spend more than twice as much time with radio as they do with television. In addition, radio can fill in gaps in both newspaper and magazine coverage of prime audiences. Teenagers, in particular, make extensive use of radio

5. *Radio works well with other media.* Radio can reach light users of other media and fill in gaps in a media schedule. For many years, a fundamental marketing strategy for radio has been to promote its ability to successfully work with other media to increase reach and frequency or to reach nonusers or light users of other media. The radio industry realizes that the majority of its revenues comes from advertisers that use radio as a secondary medium. Radio provides affordable repetition that delivers high levels of awareness—a key component in gaining market share.

6. *Much of radio listening takes place on an out-of-home basis.* This means that radio can reach consumers where they are and where other media are sometimes not readily available (see Exhibit 9.7).

7. *Radio delivers consistent listening patterns.* Unlike television, radio offers year-round coverage with little or no summer audience drop-off. Likewise, radio maintains high audience levels throughout the day. Even during television prime-time periods, radio reaches more than half the population.

8. *Radio delivers its messages at a very low CPM level.* Advertisers are increasingly giving more attention to cost efficiencies. Radio delivers its audience at a CPM level below that of virtually any other medium. Not only are the CPM levels low, but radio's recent increases also have been below that of major competitors.

Reach of Adults with Incomes $50,000 + 99.3% Each Week

Reach of College Graduates 97.0% Each Week

Reach of Professionals/Managers 96.3% Each Week

EXHIBIT 9.4

Radio Reaches Upscale Consumers

Courtesy of RADAR 71, Fall 2001, Copyright Arbitron. Courtesy of RAB Market Fact Book for Advertisers 2002–2003.

EXHIBIT **9.5**

Radio Is #1 Medium Close to Point of Purchase

Courtesy of Arbitron/Radio Advertising Bureau (RAB)— Targeting 2000.

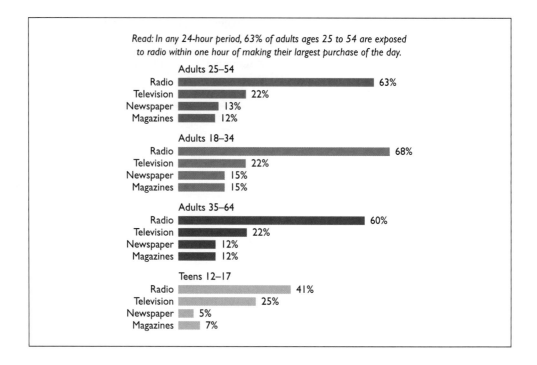

Read: In any 24-hour period, 63% of adults ages 25 to 54 are exposed to radio within one hour of making their largest purchase of the day.

Adults 25–54
Radio 63%
Television 22%
Newspaper 13%
Magazines 12%

Adults 18–34
Radio 68%
Television 22%
Newspaper 15%
Magazines 15%

Adults 35–64
Radio 60%
Television 22%
Newspaper 12%
Magazines 12%

Teens 12–17
Radio 41%
Television 25%
Newspaper 5%
Magazines 7%

9. *Radio provides advertisers with both immediacy and flexibility.* Radio advertising has the ability to react quickly to changing market conditions. With relatively short production deadlines and inexpensive creative techniques, radio is an excellent medium to take advantage of fast-breaking opportunities.

The ability to anticipate or react to changing conditions cannot be underestimated. For example, when the Indianapolis 500 ends on Memorial Day afternoon, radio commercials touting the winner's tire and oil brands begin running that evening. The simplicity of radio can be a major advantage in making tactical marketing decisions. Radio's sense of immediacy and flexibility, all at a cost within the budget of even the smallest advertiser, has made it an important part of the advertising strategy of many advertisers.

EXHIBIT **9.6**

People Spend More Time with Radio

Courtesy of Arbitron/RAB— Targeting 2000.

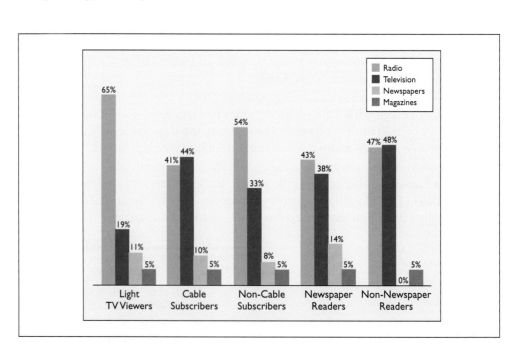

Legend: Radio, Television, Newspapers, Magazines

Light TV Viewers: 65%, 19%, 11%, 5%
Cable Subscribers: 41%, 44%, 10%, 5%
Non-Cable Subscribers: 54%, 33%, 8%, 5%
Newspaper Readers: 43%, 38%, 14%, 5%
Non-Newspaper Readers: 47%, 48%, 0%, 5%

LIMITATIONS AND CHALLENGES OF RADIO

No medium is suited for every marketing and advertising situation. Like all media, radio has special strengths and weaknesses that must be considered by advertisers considering placing radio in their media schedule. Radio has a number of characteristics that make it an ideal vehicle for numerous advertisers as either a primary or secondary medium. By the same token, advertisers need to be aware of some of the major disadvantages that must be considered before scheduling a radio buy. Two of the major problems facing advertisers using radio are (1) the sheer number of stations, which creates a very fragmented environment especially for those advertisers needing to reach a general audience, and (2) the medium's lack of a visual element.

Audience Fragmentation

One of the great strengths of radio is its ability to reach narrowly defined audience niches with formats of particular interest to specific listeners. However, some advertisers wonder if the extent of segmentation has resulted in an overly fragmented medium with audience levels for most stations so small that it is difficult to reach a brand's core prospects. For those product categories with broad appeal, it is difficult to gain effective reach and frequency without buying several radio stations or networks. Radio executives respond that although there are a few major markets where competition has forced stations into continually narrowing their program formats, for the most part, radio remains among the most effective means of achieving the target marketing desired by the majority of advertisers. However, to put the situation in perspective, in 2003, there were 10,754 commercial radio stations on the air in the United States. Exhibit 9.8 shows a breakdown of these stations by format.

audience fragmentation
The segmenting of mass-media audiences into smaller groups because of diversity of media outlets.

Clutter

As discussed in Chapter 8, clutter is a major concern to advertisers. The more commercials and other nonprogram content, the less likely it is that listeners will recall any particular advertising message. The number of radio commercials has always

EXHIBIT **9.8**

Radio Format Analysis

Source: M Street Corp., © 2003. Courtesy of Radio Advertising Bureau.

Rank	Format	Number of Stations
1	Country	2,088
2	News/Talk	1,224
3	Oldies	807
4	Adult Contemporary	692
5	Hispanic	628
6	Adult Standards	497
7	CHR (Top 40)	491
8	Sports	429
9	Classic Rock	425
10	Hot AC	399
11	Religion (Teaching, Variety)	347
12	Soft Adult Contemporary	336
13	Rock	273
14	Black Gospel	253
15T	Classic Hits	237
15T	Southern Gospel	237
17	R&B	207
18	Modern Rock	189
19	Contemporary Christian	167
20	Urban AC	128
21	Ethnic	102
22	Alternative Rock	99
23	Jazz	90
24	R&B Adult/Oldies	66
25	Gospel	64
26	Pre Teen	60
27	Modern AC	51
28	Variety	36
29	Classical	32
30	Easy Listening	18
31	Other/Format Not Available	1

been significantly greater than in television. However, with deregulation, the time devoted to commercials has steadily increased. In some cases, radio stations are running as much as 50 percent advertising during peak listening periods.

In yet another use of new technology, some radio stations have resorted to digital editing to add commercial minutes using time compression. For example, one station used sophisticated software known as Cash to take out the pauses between words on the *Rush Limbaugh Show*. Although these electronic snips were not noticed by the audience, they added as much as four commercial minutes per hour to the show. "While radio executives say the impact of Cash technology is often imperceptible to consumers, advertising executives complain that there is already too much clutter on the dial, making each commercial less effective."[6]

Lack of a Visual Element

A fundamental problem for advertisers is radio's lack of a visual component. At a time when advertisers are attempting to enhance brand image and build consumer awareness, many advertisers find radio's lack of visualization a difficult problem to overcome. With the growth of self-service retailing and competitive brand promotions, package identification is crucial for many advertisers.

Radio has long used a number of creative techniques to substitute the ear for the eye and attempt to overcome the lack of visuals. Sound effects, jingles, short and choppy copy, and vivid descriptions attempt to create a mental picture. In recent years, radio has attempted to show that images familiar to consumers from television commercials can be transferred to consumers through radio.

A look inside a radio studio.

TECHNICAL ASPECTS OF RADIO

The Signal

The electrical impulses that are broadcast by radio are called the *signal.* If a certain station has a good signal in a given territory, its programs and commercials come over clearly in that area.

Frequency

All signals are transmitted by electromagnetic waves, sometimes called *radio waves.* These waves differ from one another in frequency (the number of waves that pass a given point in a given period of time). Frequencies for AM stations are measured in kilohertz or KHz and FM stations' frequencies are measured in megahertz or MHz. The FCC has assigned the following frequencies to all radio stations.

AM = 540 to 1700 KHz

FM = 88.1 to 107.9 MHz

Amplitude

All electromagnetic waves have height, spoken of as *amplitude,* whose range resembles the difference between an ocean wave and a ripple in a pond, and speed, measured by the frequency with which a succession of waves passes a given point per minute. If, for example, a radio station operates on a frequency of 1,580 KHz, this means that 1,580,000 of its waves pass a given point per second.

On the basis of these two dimensions—amplitude and frequency—two separate systems have been developed for carrying radio waves. The first system carries the variations in a sound wave by corresponding variations in its amplitude; the frequency remains constant. This is the principle of **amplitude modulation (AM)** (see Exhibit 9.9a). The second system carries the variation in a sound wave by corresponding variations in its frequency; the amplitude remains constant. This is the principle of **frequency modulation (FM)** (see Exhibit 9.9b).

The technical structure of AM and FM radio has created, in effect, two distinct media, each offering different values to the listener and the advertiser. AM signals

amplitude modulation (AM)
Method of transmitting electromagnetic signals by varying the amplitude (size) of the electromagnetic wave, in contrast to varying its frequency. Quality is not as good as frequency modulation, but can be heard farther, especially at night.

frequency modulation (FM)
A radio transmission wave that transmits by the variation in the frequency of its wave, rather than its size (as in amplitude modulation [AM]). An FM wave is twenty times the width of an AM wave, which is the source of its fine tone. To transmit such a wave, it has to be placed high on the electromagnetic spectrum, far from AM waves with their interference and static, hence its outstanding tone.

EXHIBIT **9.9**

In amplitude modulation (a) waves vary in height (amplitude): frequency constant. Frequency modulation (b) varies the frequency but keeps the height constant. These drawings, however, are not made to scale, which would reveal that width is the significant difference between AM and FM. The FM wave is 20 times wider than the AM wave. This fact helps to explain how FM captures its fine tones.

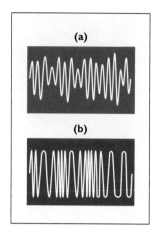

carry farther but are susceptible to interference. FM has a fine tonal quality, but its signal distances are limited. A particular station's quality of reception also is determined by atmospheric conditions and station power (broadcast frequency).

SELLING RADIO COMMERCIAL TIME

Radio advertising dollars are very much concentrated at the local level. Despite significant growth in both radio network and spot advertising, local advertising continues to dominate industry revenues.

Buying radio can be a difficult task because of the number of stations and formats available to advertisers. For example, there are over 70 stations in New York City alone. In addition, there are 90 distinct formats throughout the country from which to choose, from Adult Album Alternative to Eskimo. Even the most sparsely populated state, Wyoming, has over 50 commercial stations.[7]

Recent consolidation of radio ownership offers the potential for major changes in the radio rate structure and the way radio time is bought. From the outset of the move to group ownership, major radio group executives promised advertisers better service and more efficient buying procedures. Rather than dealing with many individual stations or independent rep companies, a media buyer in a streamlined environment could negotiate time availability and rates for hundreds of stations while dealing with a single person and submitting one insertion order.

Although ownership consolidation may have the potential to drive up local radio rates and give stations more leverage with advertisers, it does not eliminate the fierce competition that radio faces for local advertising dollars. Radio advertising continues to operate in a challenging environment as it competes for local advertisers. Radio must compete with traditional selective media, such as newspapers, Yellow Pages, and direct response, that also reach targeted audiences. In addition, radio is competing with new media such as the Internet and both broadcast and cable television, which see local advertising as major profit centers.

EXHIBIT **9.10**

Sources of Radio Revenue (percentage of the total)

Local	78.2 %
Spot	17.7
National	4.1

Network Radio

The demise of network radio as a major national medium and the beginning of local radio began in 1948 with the introduction of television. Average ratings for Bob Hope's radio show dropped from 23.8 in 1948 to 5.4 in 1953. Soap operas left radio for television throughout the 1950s until *Ma Perkins,* the last survivor, went off the air in 1960. The last major radio dramas, *Suspense* and *Have Gun Will Travel,* ended in 1962 and the era of network radio was essentially over. For the next decade, network programs were largely confined to news and occasional short features.

Network radio, while still a minor source of advertising dollars, has remained stable in the last few years. Media planners are looking increasingly to network radio as a means of extending reach to working women and light users of other media and building greater brand awareness through inexpensive additional frequency to prime target segments. Despite these gains, network radio advertising only accounts for $773 million of the $18.8 billion spent annually in radio. Leading advertisers on network radio include national retail chains, pharmaceutical companies, and packaged goods advertisers.

Radio networks are much different from those in television as is the relationship between radio networks and their affiliates. Radio networks are basically program providers, but unlike television, a single radio station may belong to several radio networks simultaneously. For example, a station might get sports reports from one network, personality profiles and news from another, and entertainment fare from yet another. Whereas in television local stations sell advertising time on the basis of the strength of the network programming, in radio the networks must depend on local ratings to garner national advertising support.

In contrast to television where each network such as NBC provides a single broadcast service (we will not consider cable-distributed services such as MSNBC or CNBC) and has a permanent lineup of affiliates, ABC Radio provides a number of targeted networks. For example, ABC has several full-service networks including the Prime Network directed at adults aged 25–54 with a news/talk format and

Network radio was huge in the late 1940s.

EXHIBIT **9.11**

Network Radio Top 10 Advertisers

Ranked by measured spending per medium in 2002.

Source: Reprinted with permission from *Advertising Age*. Copyright Crain Communications Inc. 2004. www.adage.com/pages. cms?pageID=995, 29 July 2003.

		Measured Ad Spending (in millions)	
Rank	Advertiser	2002	2001
1	AutoZone	$34.6	$18.8
2	Procter & Gamble Co.	24.8	19.9
3	J. C. Penney Co.	22.4	19.3
4	U.S. government	19.9	17.9
5	Sears, Roebuck & Co.	19.9	16.8
6	Pfizer	19.6	16.9
7	Hotwire	19.6	2.0
8	XM Satellite Radio	19.0	2.2
9	RadioShack Corp.	18.7	11.5
10	Mission Pharmacal Co.	18.7	13.2

Galaxy Networks with a number of 24-hour music formats for various demographic markets. In addition, ABC also provides individual programs such as *Paul Harvey News and Comment* and news breaks that are broadcast daily throughout the day.

Regardless of the way a radio station uses network programming and the many differences with television, radio networks do offer some of the same advantages as their television counterparts. For example, an advertiser prepares one insertion order for multiple stations, pays one invoice, and is guaranteed uniform production quality for the commercials scheduled on all stations. Radio networks also provide economical reach and, like all radio, target special audience segments who often are light users of other media.

The resurgence of radio networks has been largely a result of satellite technology. The availability of satellite links for national radio programmers offers a number of advantages for their local station affiliates:

1. Stations are guaranteed quality programming based on the latest audience research for a particular format.
2. Radio networks bring celebrities to the medium that local stations could not afford.
3. Even the smallest stations can obtain national advertising dollars as part of a network. Stations that would not be considered by national advertisers as part of a local spot buy may now be included in a network radio schedule.
4. The cost efficiencies of sharing programming with several hundred other affiliates keep both personnel and programming costs to a minimum.

Network radio will never return to its former status as a primary medium for national advertisers. However, as a source of program services, with its ability to target narrow audience segments, it will continue to play an important role for a number of national advertisers.

Spot Radio

spot radio
Buying radio time on local stations on a market-by-market basis by national advertisers.

As you will recall from our discussion in Chapter 8, spot advertising is the buying of local stations by national advertisers. Advertisers spend approximately $3.3 billion in **spot radio** advertising each year. It is almost always a second medium for national companies to build added reach and frequency against selected target markets. Spot radio offers these advertisers an opportunity to react quickly to changing competitive challenges and hit narrowly segmented markets with little waste circulation.

For example, Verizon Communications ranks among the top users of spot radio with expenditures of $71.5 million. However, this expenditure represents less than 7 percent of the company's annual advertising budget.

Satellite technology has helped radio networks become popular again.

Despite the relatively low percentage of total advertising dollars, spot radio serves important functions for a number of advertisers. To those companies with a national presence that have widely differentiated market potential it can provide added weight in selected regions or individual markets. A second group of heavy spot radio users are national companies with extensive retail outlets. Spot radio commercials allow these companies to build on their national brand awareness with localized spots directed at the local community. For example, Home Depot and Burger King are advertisers that depend on spot radio to augment their national advertising. As is the case in other categories of the medium, advertisers take advantage of the flexibility and low cost offered by spot radio.

Just as with television, most spot radio broadcast purchases, are made through reps. In principle, radio reps serve the same function as those in TV. The best reps are those who serve as marketing consultants for their client stations. They work with agencies to match target audiences with the appropriate stations in their client list. Sometimes this is done on a market-by-market basis. In other cases buys are made through nonwired networks in the same manner as TV nonwired networks, which we discussed in Chapter 8. It remains to be seen what effect consolidation within the radio industry will have on the relationship between reps and stations. As

	Measured Ad Spending (in Millions)		
Rank	Advertiser	2002	2001
1	SBC Communications	$108.6	$73.2
2	Verizon Communications	71.3	63.9
3	Home Depot	62.2	39.9
4	Time Warner	50.2	32.2
5	Viacom	47.0	35.0
6	AT&T Wireless	43.8	44.3
7	News Corp.	38.0	32.2
8	Signet Group	34.4	31.3
9	Walt Disney Co.	31.5	22.8
10	Burger King Corp.	30.8	19.8

EXHIBIT **9.12**

National Spot Radio Top 10 Advertisers

Ranked by measured spending per medium in 2002.

Source: Reprinted with permission from *Advertising Age*. Copyright Crain Communications Inc. 2004. www.adage.com/pages. cms?pageID=995,29 July 2003.

more and more local stations are bought by major groups, it may mean that a significant amount of spot advertising will be sold directly by group salespersons bypassing rep firms and that reps will be left primarily to sell smaller market stations through their nonwired networks. The rep/station relationship is just one more area of potential change in an industry where reorganization has become the rule.

AM Versus FM as an Advertising Medium

Of the more than 10,500 commercial radio stations, about 6,000 are FM and the remainder AM. However, despite the number of stations in each category, FM dominates the overall listening audience and is the clear leader in most formats. In some major markets, as much as 80 percent of the audience is normally listening to FM and, with the exception of several major all-talk stations, most AM stations are far down the list of stations in terms of ratings and audience share. In fact, AM stations tend to reach an older audience with talk, news, and specialty formats such as gospel and nostalgia.

The growth of FM radio audiences and advertising revenues during the last 30 years is the most important trend in the industry in recent years. FM technology was adapted for radio shortly before World War II. During the war, all broadcast station construction was halted, but a few stations that had gone on the air prior to the start of the war continued to operate. For almost three decades after the close of the war, FM was largely confined to noncommercial and classical stations with few listeners and little or no advertising. The exceptions were the jointly owned AM/FM stations, which usually duplicated programming on both stations. Because AM and FM radio sets were sold separately and there was little original programming, few incentives existed for listeners to purchase the more expensive FM sets.

In 1975, FM independent stations (those without an AM partner) reported a combined loss of almost $10 million. Just three years later, these same stations had profits of slightly less than $25 million. Obviously, this type of economic turnaround did not happen by accident. A number of factors contributed to the vitality of FM with both advertisers and audiences. Among the major elements are the following:

1. In 1972 the Federal Communication Commission ruled that joint owners of both AM and FM stations in the same market had to program different formats. This ruling opened the way for FM as a separate medium.
2. The sound quality of FM is markedly better than AM. Since music formats dominate radio, FM steadily gained audience share at the expense of AM.
3. The decline in the cost of FM sets coincided with the popularity of the medium. Thirty years ago radio sets with an FM band were much more expensive than AM-only sets. Also few cars were equipped with an FM radio. Currently, about nine out of ten car radios are AM/FM and virtually all radio sets are equipped with both AM and FM bands.
4. As radio audiences turned to FM for the most popular music formats, AM was left with an audience skewed to older listeners, a less than prime market segment for most advertisers. Therefore, the switch to FM by audiences was followed quickly by an increase in advertising dollars.

It is clear that FM will continue to be the dominant radio medium as AM stations search for those formats that will attract niche audiences. In fact, many observers say that it was only the popularity of talk radio in the last 15 years that saved AM from economic disaster.

Types of Programming   As we previously discussed, radio is a medium constantly searching for targeted audiences to deliver to advertisers. It also is a medium overwhelmingly devoted to music. The typical radio station depends on a music format and unique talent to appeal to the largest audience in a particular listener demographic. Unlike television, where viewers tune to a certain program for a half-hour or hour and then move to another station for another show, radio audiences tend to demonstrate loyalty to a station because of the type of music, sports, or information it programs.

For a number of years, the "country" format has been carried by more stations than any other. Approximately 2,000 stations report that they program some form of country music as their primary format. The number of country music stations can be attributed, in part, to the large quantity of small stations in rural and small-market areas where country music is most popular. Although many of the new country styles (e.g., Faith Hill and Shania Twain) have brought country into the mainstream and larger markets, it has its roots in small town America. While country format stations make up over nineteen percent of all stations in the United States, only about 8.2 percent of all radio listening is to country stations. In other words, the number of stations programming a format often has little to do with the size of the listenership.[8]

To advertisers, however, it is often the quality of the audience as much as its size that is of most importance. For example, those relatively few stations with "children," "public affairs," or "agriculture and farm" formats might be exactly the advertising vehicle for particular advertisers seeking to reach small but (for them) profitable prospects.

One of the problems for radio stations is that they function in an environment of economic Darwinism where only the strongest survive. Although every station would like to be the leader in a popular format, radio executives know that it is extremely difficult for more than one or two stations in a market to be financially successful in any particular format. Why would an advertiser buy a market's third- or fourth-rated country station?

Consequently, second- and third-tier stations are constantly searching for niche formats that will allow them to be the leader among some audience segment that is of value to advertisers. Specialty formats, such as classical or jazz, usually depend on an upscale audience that is difficult for advertisers to reach in other media. However, with as many as 50 stations in most large markets, developing niche formats is not only cutthroat but also often gets a little silly. For instance, stations without impressive total numbers may resort to calling themselves the number-one station in a particular daypart (e.g., midnight–6 A.M.) or developing subcategories of a format to differentiate themselves from other stations (easy listening country).

Radio should be considered a quasi-mass medium. Despite its high aggregate audiences, the number of people listening to any particular station at a given time is very small. Even the top stations in a market will be lucky to achieve ratings of 7 or 8, and a rating of 1 to 3 is more common. Consequently, an audience increase that would be insignificant in other media might make a major difference in the financial health of a radio station. For example, a change of one rating point for a station with an average rating of 3 is an increase of 33 percent, a figure that often will move a station significantly up the rankings among stations in a market.

RADIO RATINGS SERVICES

As discussed in Chapter 8, the growth of television has created some significant problems in determining accurate audience-rating data. However, the problems in television research pale in comparison to those facing radio. Not only are there more than 10 times the number of radio stations compared to television, but also the lack of specific programming on most stations makes respondent recall much more difficult than in television. As we have discussed, television recall is not a problem for the majority of viewers where meters are used. In addition, much of

Out-of-home radio
listening poses
measurement
challenges.

Courtesy of Ron Komball
Photography, www.ronkimballstock.
com.

The Arbitron Company
Syndicated radio ratings
company.

the radio audience listens out-of-home where it is impractical to keep a diary or reach respondents by telephone.

Dozens of companies provide research services for radio. However, most of these firms are engaged in program consulting or custom research for individual stations and advertisers. The major source of local syndicated radio ratings and the dominant company in radio research is **The Arbitron Company,** which provides audience data through its Arbitron Radio division.

Arbitron measures radio audiences in over 280 local markets through the use of listener diaries. All members of sampled households over the age of 12 have a personal diary in which they record listening behavior over a seven-day period. Rating periods in a specific market last for 12 weeks. The number of weeks that a market is sampled is determined by its size, with 90 of the largest metropolitan areas sampled on a continuous basis throughout the year. The smallest markets will be sampled for only one 12-week period and the ratings will be published in a condensed version of the larger ratings books. Overall, Arbitron collects and analyzes more than 1.5 million diaries each year.[8]

In 1999, Arbitron began a service to collect Webcast audience information. The service measures the audience of specific broadcast station Web sites. Arbitron estimates that the cumulative Internet radio audience is 20 million people who listen to the various Webcasts for an average of 5 hours per week.[9] Clearly, streamed audio has already become a major factor in radio, which only increases the complexity of collecting accurate rating information.

Because of the local nature of radio, station ratings are much more critical to most advertisers than those for networks. However, as we have discussed earlier, network radio is important to a number of national advertisers. As major businesses move into network radio advertising, the demand for accurate ratings will become even more important. The primary source of radio network ratings is the **Radio All Dimension Audience Research (RADAR)** reports, a service of Statistical Research, Inc. Research data for RADAR reports are collected through telephone recall interviews. Currently, over 35 networks are surveyed for RADAR reports.

**Radio All Dimension
Audience Research
(RADAR)**
Service of Statistical
Research, Inc., that is the
primary source of network
radio ratings.

Arbitron is testing the use of a portable people meter (PPM) for collecting radio listening data. The PPM device is worn by survey participants throughout the day. The listening data are collected automatically by the device and sent daily to Arbitron for analysis. The hope is that this device will eventually eliminate the need for diaries and permit more accurate data collection that is less intrusive for the respondents.

An overriding problem in dealing with radio ratings is money. The funds available to solve an advertising research problem are directly related to the level of advertising expenditures by major advertisers. For example, when General Motors and Procter & Gamble invest $1 billion annually in television, there is a major incentive to invest millions of dollars in research. On the other hand, even though the problems may be more difficult in media such as radio and outdoor, the overall advertising investment will simply not support a research expenditure comparable to television.

BUYING RADIO

Radio demonstrates a number of characteristics as an advertising medium:

- Advertising inventory is inflexible and when a spot goes unsold, revenue is permanently lost.
- Radio is normally used as a supplement to other media. Therefore, coordination with the total advertising plan is crucial for most radio sales.
- Every radio buy is unique. Almost all radio advertising is sold in packages of spots that are tailored, to some degree, to each advertiser.
- Because of the unique nature of each buy, a fixed rate card rarely exists for radio advertising. Pricing is largely the result of negotiation between media buyers and radio salespersons.

Despite the complexity of buying radio advertising, the fundamentals of buying radio are very similar to those of other media. For example, as with most advertising plans, we must examine a number of elements before we proceed to an advertising execution:

1. Review product characteristics and benefits and decide whether these benefits can be effectively communicated through radio.
2. Who is the target market and can they be reached effectively with radio and, if so, what formats, what dayparts? For example, Hispanics are more likely to spend time listening to radio than non-Hispanics, particularly to Spanish radio formats. According to Arbitron reports, African American audiences are more likely to spend their radio listening with urban, contemporary hit radio, or religious radio formats.[10] The ability to reach audience segments with this type of pinpoint precision remains radio's major strength.
3. Who is our competition? How are they using radio and other media? Will radio provide a unique differentiation for our product or will we be up against strong competing messages?
4. What is our basic advertising and marketing strategy and can it be effectively carried out with radio?

In virtually all advertising situations, we start with a clear delineation of our target market. This audience definition is particularly important in buying radio because of the narrowly defined formats that are offered by the medium. We then must look at the cost of alternative radio outlets and must compare the options available against the CPM/prospects or CPP. Radio, from both a marketing and creative standpoint, must be considered in terms of the advertising objectives we have set out for our advertising. For example, radio in general or a specific station may meet our objectives for reach and cost but fail in terms of the creative strategy.

Morning Drivetime	6:00 A.M. to 10:00 A.M.
Midday	10:00 A.M. to 3:00 P.M.
Afternoon Drivetime	3:00 P.M. to 7:00 P.M.
Evening	7:00 P.M. to 12:00 A.M.
Overnight	12:00 A.M. to 6:00 A.M.

EXHIBIT **9.13**

Radio Dayparts

Because radio advertising is often used as a secondary medium, it may be the case that we will evaluate radio in terms of how it complements other more primary media in our advertising schedule and what proportion of our budget should be devoted to radio in this complementary role.

Once we have decided that radio can play a role in our advertising plan, we must begin the task of selecting particular stations that both reach our target audience and also provide a program environment that fits our product image. As we have discussed, the number of radio stations provide advertisers, particularly those with national distribution, with many options from which to choose. For some advertisers, network radio is a better option, in terms of cost and guaranteed quality of editorial, than a spot or local schedule. Nevertheless, radio is one of the most challenging aspects of media planning.

The final step in radio buying is the actual scheduling of the spots. Because most advertisers use a great number of spots to achieve reach and/or frequency, the scheduling process can be difficult. Although most radio spots are 60 seconds, some advertisers use shorter messages to gain frequency while a few opt for longer-form commercials to achieve greater impact. In addition, decisions such as whether to use specific dayparts or use a combination of time periods and, in a few instances, whether to take advantage of program sponsorship or on-site event promotions must be considered. Regardless of the final determinations of these and other questions, radio can provide great flexibility and fit into the plans of virtually every advertiser.

Because of the complicated nature of radio, buyers must often rely on the expertise of radio sales personnel—at the station, network, or rep level. Given the nature of radio buys, it is imperative that both buyers and sellers understand the relationship involved in the process. This starts with credibility. One of the primary ways a radio salesperson gains trust is to position radio as a part of the marketing plan. This entails walking a fine line between aggressively selling the medium and your station, but, at the same time, acknowledging the strengths and contributions of other media.

Rather than trying to convince heavy newspaper advertisers to move out of the medium, it is more reasonable to show how radio can make newspaper advertising more effective. The key to successful selling is identifying with the problems of the clients. To do this, the salesperson needs to show advertisers that radio can solve their specific marketing problem. Remember, advertisers are not interested in buying time—they are interested in finding prospects and demonstrating major product benefits to these prospects.

One aspect of using spot radio for national advertisers was recently made easier. In October 2003, the radio industry announced the industry's first national system for electronic invoicing and commercial verification. This system, called RadioExchange, is designed to improve the speed and accuracy of spot radio buys.[11]

USING RADIO RATINGS

We defined both television ratings and share of audience in Chapter 8. Radio rating and share figures are calculated in the same way. However, the size of the radio audience and the highly fragmented nature of programming and formats have created a system in which ratings are used differently than in television. This section discusses some uses of ratings that are unique to radio.

Among the primary differences between the use of ratings in television and radio are the following:

1. Radio advertisers are interested in broad formats rather than programs or more narrowly defined television scatter plans.
2. Radio ratings tend to measure audience accumulation over relatively long periods of time or several dayparts. Most television ratings are calculated for individual programs.

3. The audiences for individual radio stations are much smaller than television, making radio ratings less reliable.

4. Because most radio stations reach only a small segment of the market at a given time, there is a need for much higher levels of advertising frequency compared to other media. Consequently, it is extremely difficult to track ratings information accurately for national radio plans that include a large number of stations.

Let's begin our discussion by examining several definitions used in radio-rating analyses.

Geographical Patterns of Radio Ratings

Radio audience ratings use two geographical boundaries to report audiences: Metro Survey Area (MSA) and Total Survey Area (TSA). Typically the majority of a station's audience comes from within the MSA.

Metro Survey Area An MSA always includes a city or cities whose population is specified as that of the central city together with the county (or counties) in which it is located.

Total Survey Area The TSA is a geographic area that encompasses the MSA and certain counties located outside the MSA, that meet certain minimum listening criteria.

Definitions of the Radio Audience

The basic audience measures for television are the rating and share of audience for a particular show. It would be a serious mistake to buy radio and television on the same basis without considering major differences in the way audience figures are considered between the two media. In radio, audience estimates are usually presented as either Average Quarter Hour (AQH) audiences or the cumulative or unduplicated audience (Cume) listening to a station over several quarter hours or dayparts.

Average Quarter Hour Estimates (AQHE)

1. *Average Quarter Hour Persons.* The AQH persons are the estimated number of people listening to a station for at least five minutes during a 15-minute period.
2. *Average Quarter Hour Rating.* Here we calculate the AQH persons as a percentage of the population being measured:

> AQH persons/population $\times$ 100 = AQH rating

3. *Average Quarter Hour Share.* The AQH Share determines what portion of the average radio audience is listening to our station:

> AQH persons to a station/AQH persons to all stations $\times$ 100 = Share

average quarter hour estimates (AQHE) Manner in which ratio ratings are presented. Estimates include average number of people listening, rating, and metro share of audience.

Cume Estimates

Cume estimates are used to determine the number or percentage of different people who listen to a station during several quarter hours or dayparts.

1. *Cume persons.* The number of different people who tuned to a radio station for at least five minutes.
2. *Cume rating.* The percentage of different people listening to a station during several quarter hours or dayparts.

> Cume persons/Population $\times$ 100 = Cume rating

Let's look at a typical station's audience and calculate these formulas.

Station XYYY,—Friday 10 A.M.–3 P.M., Adults 12 +

AQH persons = 20,000

Cume persons = 60,000

Metro Suvery Area population = 500,000

Metro Survey Area AQH persons = 200,000

For station XYYY:

The AQH rating = $(20,000/500,000) \times 100 = 4$

The Cume rating = $(60,000/500,000) \times 100 = 12$

Metro AQH share = $(20,000/200,000) \times 100 = 10$

Using our XYYY example, we can also calculate the following:

1. Gross Impressions (GI) = AQH persons × No. of commercials
If we buy six commercials on XYYY, we have purchased 120,000 impressions (20,000 AQH persons × 6 spots). Remember these are impressions, not people.

2. Gross Rating Points = AQH rating × No. of commercials
Again, six commercials would deliver 24 GRPs (4 AQH rating × 6 spots).

The media planner must be able to manipulate the various radio data to develop a plan most suited to a particular client. Although the computer makes these manipulations quickly, it doesn't substitute for a basic understanding of the process. The same budget, and even the same number of spots, used in different dayparts and across multiple stations, can deliver vastly different levels of cumes, reach, frequency, and demographics.

SUMMARY

Radio has never been more popular than it is now in terms of advertising revenues and listenership. Every day more Americans use radio than any other medium. With thousands of stations, multiple formats, inexpensive production, and low commercial cost, it can provide effective reach and frequency for a number of product categories.

Technology promises to take the already impressive immediacy and person-to-person nature of radio to another level. With satellite transmission and out-of-home capability, radio can reach individual customers with programs and commercials tailored to their demographics and lifestyle. However, this same technology, particularly computer-delivered programming and music services, represents a challenge to radio, especially small market stations.

Radio has a significant advantage in achieving high penetration among light or nonusers of other media. For example, many teens use radio almost exclusively as a means of entertainment and information. Given the current demand by advertisers for narrowly defined audience segments, radio is increasingly becoming at least a secondary option in more and more media plans.

Despite the opportunities for radio to become more important in the advertising plans of both large and small advertisers, the medium faces two major problems. First, the medium lacks the type of research data enjoyed by many other media. A mobile, out-of-home audience makes it very difficult to reach a large majority of radio listeners. In addition, the lack of traditional programming makes recall more complicated than similar audience research in television.

A second major problem with radio is the lack of a visual element. Many advertisers think that without strong visual brand identification the medium can play little or no role in their advertising plans. The industry has sponsored a number of research studies to show that radio can work effectively with television to remind consumers of the commercials they have seen previously. This concept, known as imagery transfer, offers radio advertisers a strong selling point to national advertisers seeking an inexpensive supplement to their television schedules. However, it fails to fully compensate for a lack of visuals.

Radio also is providing national advertisers with a number of opportunities through satellite-distributed, syndicated programming. Technological advances and decreases in the cost of satellite time and equipment have made it easier, cheaper, and less risky to launch nationally syndicated shows. When properly packaged, syndicated radio can deliver significant advertising impact to advertisers on both a local and national basis.

There is an irony that radio, once the major national medium, may be returning to its roots. Obviously, national syndication alone cannot bring radio back into the media spotlight. However, its newfound success coupled with advanced technology and radio's inherent strengths as a vehicle to deliver narrowly targeted audiences bodes well for the future.

 ## REVIEW

1. Define the following:

   a. drivetime

   b. run-of-station

   c. total audience plans

2. What is the major disadvantage of radio for most advertisers?

3. What are the primary advantages of radio to advertisers?

4. How do most national advertisers use radio?

5. What is the role of radio networks?

6. Who are the listeners of AM radio? What do they listen to?

7. Where do most advertisers obtain radio audience information?

8. What is the difference between an AQH rating and a Cume rating?

 ## TAKE IT TO THE WEB

At **www.arbitron.com** learn how the portable people meter device is used to measure media statistics such as traditional radio and television, Internet radio, and digital television. What benefits does the portable meter have over the traditional practice of manual measurement?

How does the Radio Advertising Bureau (**www.rab.com**) work to promote radio as the best alternative for advertisers?

Arbitron Internet Broadcast Service (**www.arbitron.com**) measures ratings for radio and video on the Internet. What are the key issues advertisers will need to address as Web Radio gains popularity?

CHAPTER 10

Daily News • Post • Citizen • Times • Sun

Morning News • Banner Herald • Daily Post

Observer • Times-Recorder • Journal

Sentinel • Gazette • Constitution • Herald

Using Newspapers

Newspapers trail only television in terms of total advertising revenues and they are the leader by a significant margin among local businesses. Each day approximately 55 million newspapers are distributed, providing a large segment of the population with news, entertainment, and advertising. Newspapers also enjoy a reputation for credibility that creates a positive advertising environment. After reading this chapter, you will understand:

1. the changing character and role of newspapers in the marketing mix
2. challenges to newspaper advertising from other media options
3. the marketing of newspapers to readers and advertisers
4. the many categories of newspaper advertising
5. the newspaper advertising planning and buying process
6. the role of weeklies and ethnic-oriented newspapers

PROS

1. Newspapers appeal primarily to an upscale audience, especially those adults age 35 and older.
2. Newspaper advertising is extremely flexible with opportunities for color, large and small space ads, timely insertion schedules, coupons, and some selectivity through special sections and targeted editions.
3. With coupons and sophisticated tracking methodology, it is much easier to measure newspaper response rates than most other media.
4. Newspapers have high credibility with their readers, which creates a positive environment for advertisers.

CONS

1. Most newspapers have about 60 percent advertising content. This high ratio of advertising, combined with average reading time of less than 30 minutes, means few ads are read.
2. Overall newspaper circulation has fallen far behind population and household growth. In many markets total newspaper penetration is below 30 percent. In addition, readership among a number of key demographics such as teens and young adults has not kept pace with population growth.
3. Advertising costs have risen much more sharply than circulation in recent years.

Each day some 55 million newspapers are distributed in large cities and small towns. These papers are read by almost 60 percent of the population and an even greater percentage of readers from households with higher than average income and education levels. Annual advertising revenues in these newspapers are almost $44 billion with approximately 85 percent coming from local advertisers. In addition, national advertisers are looking increasingly to local and regional advertising strategies to communicate with consumers in the most effective manner.

Newspaper advertising offers a number of advantages to businesses from large national corporations to the smallest retailer. Among the most important features of newspaper advertising are the following:

- Newspapers offer significant flexibility of advertising formats and audience coverage. Advertisers can buy space ranging from a full-page, four-color advertisement to a small classified notice. In addition, virtually every newspaper offers a variety of specialized advertising plans, including online options, to allow advertisers to reach selected portions of the newspaper's total circulation.

- Newspapers are especially useful in reaching upscale households and opinion leaders. However, compared to most other media, newspapers have significant reach in most major demographic segments.

- Newspapers offer advertisers a number of creative options including outstanding color reproduction and preprinted inserts.

- Finally, newspapers provide an environment of credibility and immediacy unmatched by most media. A number of surveys have shown that consumers regard newspaper advertising as an important and reliable source of both information and advertising—just the type of medium with which advertisers want to be associated.

With so much to offer both advertisers and readers, why is the newspaper industry so concerned about its future? The fact of the matter is that a number of trends cause concern for newspapers. Let's examine four areas that are keeping newspaper publishers awake at night.

1. *Circulation.* According to the Newspaper Association of America, in 1976 newspaper circulation was 77 million; by 2002 this figure was approximately 55 million in spite of significant increases in both population and households during that period. Throughout the 1990s, newspaper circulation dropped about 1 percent each year.

   The reasons given for the decline in newspaper circulation vary from not enough time in single-parent and two-income families to devote to newspaper reading, to younger demographic segments that don't like to read or that never developed the habit of reading newspapers, to other media, especially television and the Internet, that have encroached on the newspaper's position as the preferred method of getting news and information. All of these factors have probably played a role in the decline of newspaper readership.

   Different newspapers have attacked the readership problem with diverse approaches. In some cases, newspapers engage in aggressive subscription sales campaigns including telemarketing and setting up booths on college campuses. Other newspapers such as *The New York Times* have accepted the inevitability of circulation decreases but point to its upscale readership. For example, a *Times* executive said, "The quality of our journalism demands a premium price from readers. That, in turn, attracts the kind of audience that is very, very appealing to advertisers."[1] Of course, a formula that works for *The New York Times* is transferrable to few other papers.

2. *Advertising revenues.* Obviously, the advertising community has not ignored newspaper circulation problems. As recently as 1980, newspapers' share of total advertising revenue was 28 percent. Currently, the figure is around 19 percent.

Several problems have beleaguered newspapers in maintaining their share of advertising dollars. A number of retail chains have turned to direct mail and inserts to reach customers. Even the inserts that are distributed through newspapers provide lower profits for newspapers than traditional advertising. Second, newspapers have been unable to increase support from national advertisers. Even as national advertisers look to regional and local strategies, newspapers have had a difficult time gaining significant support from major national advertisers. Despite a number of newspaper initiatives to overcome national advertisers' reluctance to use the medium, dollars in the sector remain small. This hurt newspapers in the sluggish economy following the terrorist attacks of September 11, 2001, as local retail advertisers' dollars were slower to return than national advertising dollars.

Although newspapers have never enjoyed a large amount of revenue from national advertisers, currently their franchise with local advertisers is being threatened from a number of quarters. Local television; local cable cut-ins; free niche advertising books featuring real estate, automobiles, and so forth; regional and city editions of magazines; and, of course, radio continue to fight for local advertising dollars that 25 years ago would have gone automatically to newspapers. Later in this chapter we will discuss some of the ways that newspapers are countering these problems.

3. *Changing technology.* Newspapers, like all media, face challenges from new media technology. In fact, many believe that the newspaper as we know it will be dramatically changed by this technology—not the many functions it serves but the method of distribution. The argument is that the cost of paper, ink, postage, and physical distribution is simply not going to be viable in a world of electronic communication. Going back no further than 1990, virtually no one outside the scientific community had ever heard of the Internet.

Today, for many people the Internet is an indispensable, and preferred, form of communication. Research indicates that in 2000, 24 percent of adults used the Internet during a 24-hour period for news and information. Among 18- to 24-year-olds, the Internet and newspapers are used equally as a source of information with Internet usage growing.[2] Internet usage has grown at a rate of 20 percent per year since 1998 with well over half of the U.S. population over age 3 reporting having used the Internet.[3]

In light of the foothold already enjoyed by the Internet, imagine the improvements in instantaneous delivery, clarity and reliability of content, and portability of technology over the next 20 years—it is hard to imagine thick wads of paper being thrown in the driveways of the 2025 household! As one print executive predicted, "I believe that they [newspapers], and all forms of print, are dead. Finished. Over. Twenty, thirty, at the outside forty years from now, we will look back on the print media the way we look back on travel by horse and carriage, or by wind-powered ship."[4]

This gloomy prediction for newspapers does not mean the functions of newspapers will be dead or even the companies that provide these services will be gone. It certainly does not mean that there will not be reporters, advertising salespeople, and most of all businesses with dollars to spend to reach a literate audience. It does mean that the methods of reaching these customers and "readers" will change dramatically.

Currently, many newspapers provide Web sites for their readers and/or advertisers. But as we will discuss later in this chapter, the immediacy of newspapers is being replaced by electronic formats—many developed by newspapers themselves. In addition, newspaper classified advertising, which provides more than 36 percent of total revenues for the newspaper industry, is being challenged by dozens of online Web sites seeking a share of the lucrative employment (see monster.com) and real estate (see realtor.com) dollars.[5]

The continuing challenge for both newspaper publishers and newspaper advertising executives is to provide the audience with readers to look to the daily paper as a primary source of information, advertising, and entertainment. The task is becoming more difficult as newspapers try to serve a diverse audience of young and old, affluent and middle class, and numerous ethnic cultures. It is clear that newspapers will face growing competition from other media and information sources as they attempt to retain their position as a leading medium. The newspaper industry faces both problems and opportunities as we approach the next century. However, it is obvious that long-term trends will continue to endanger the basic foundation of newspaper readership and advertising. In the meantime, newspapers, despite declines in readership, remain one of the most effective means of reaching a broad, heterogeneous audience (see Exhibit 10.1).

As we will see throughout the remainder of this chapter, newspapers need innovative initiatives to function successfully in this competitive environment. As we discuss major aspects of contemporary newspaper advertising, we must keep in mind the evolving and dynamic nature of the industry.

EXHIBIT 10.1

Comparative Media Index

Source: Scarborough Research, Top 50 Market Report prepared by NAA Research Department. NAA Research Department. NAA Facts About Newspapers 2003, www.naa.org/info/facts03/18_facts2003.html, 11 September, 2003.

Note: Radio drive times reflect Monday–Friday average quarter hour.

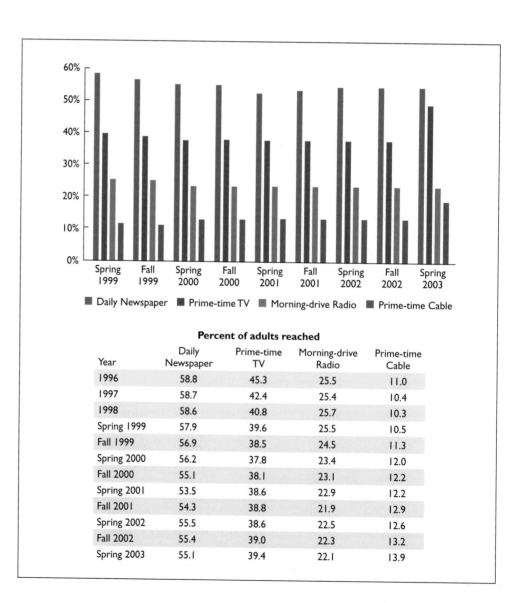

Percent of adults reached

Year	Daily Newspaper	Prime-time TV	Morning-drive Radio	Prime-time Cable
1996	58.8	45.3	25.5	11.0
1997	58.7	42.4	25.4	10.4
1998	58.6	40.8	25.7	10.3
Spring 1999	57.9	39.6	25.5	10.5
Fall 1999	56.9	38.5	24.5	11.3
Spring 2000	56.2	37.8	23.4	12.0
Fall 2000	55.1	38.1	23.1	12.2
Spring 2001	53.5	38.6	22.9	12.2
Fall 2001	54.3	38.8	21.9	12.9
Spring 2002	55.5	38.6	22.5	12.6
Fall 2002	55.4	39.0	22.3	13.2
Spring 2003	55.1	39.4	22.1	13.9

THE NATIONAL NEWSPAPER

Historically, the United States, unlike most other developed countries, did not have a national newspaper. When the first newspapers were founded, distances were too great and unique regional concerns made nationally distributed newspapers impractical. However, a number of newspapers now have national circulation, national stature, or both.

TNS Media Intelligence/CMR, a company that compiles data on advertising expenditures, defines a national newspaper as having the following characteristics:

- It publishes at least five days per week.
- It has no more than 67 percent of its circulation in a single area.
- More than 50 percent of its advertising revenue must come from national advertising (compared to 13 percent for all newspapers).

Based on these criteria, there are three national newspapers: *The Wall Street Journal, USA Today,* and *The New York Times. The Wall Street Journal* is an upscale, specialized paper with an emphasis on financial news but with great influence in politics and public policy issues. With a circulation of more than 1.7 million it is the second-highest circulation newspaper in the country. It also is among the most respected newspapers in the world and it reaches readers with the most elite audience demographics of any U.S. newspapers.

In 1998, *The Wall Street Journal* began a "Weekend Journal" lifestyle section in its Friday edition. The section allowed the newspaper to tap into advertising categories such as wine and liquor, entertainment, and other upscale brands that had never used the publication. The section proved so popular that online spin-offs such as wine.wsj.com have proved very popular.

All three of the leading national publications have extensive Web sites. However, *The Wall Street Journal* has one of the few profitable sites among all newspapers. Because of its reputation and specialized business content, it is able to charge an annual subscription fee of $79 (or $39 if a person subscribes to the print edition).[6] By comparison most other newspaper sites are free, advertising supported, and, at best, only marginally profitable.

In 1982, the Gannett Company made a commitment to develop *USA Today* as a general readership national newspaper. While newspaper purists often criticized the paper's lack of depth, *USA Today* was popular with readers from the beginning with a mix of bright colors, short articles, and extensive business and sports coverage. In a short time it gained wide distribution, especially bulk sales to hotels and airlines. After years of financial losses, Gannett has made *USA Today* profitable. However, few corporations would have had either the resources or management support to invest in such an endeavor. It is estimated that before *USA Today* had its first profitable year in 1993, it had lost over $250 million. This loss was not the result of a lack of readers. The paper has a circulation of over 2.2 million. Exhibit 10.2 shows the largest U.S. newspapers.

The problem facing all newspapers that aspire to national circulation is finding a profitable advertising niche. A national newspaper is a hybrid vehicle for most advertisers. Unlike other newspapers, national papers are unlikely to gain advertising from grocery stores, department stores, and other local product categories that have been traditionally major profit centers for newspapers. Instead, *USA Today* and other national newspapers depend on national automotive, computer, and communication companies and financial services for much of their revenue.

The New York Times has been classified only recently as a national newspaper. Most large metropolitan newspapers such as *The Washington Post* and *Chicago Tribune* are considered regional advertising media. They are bought much like spot broadcast to reach specific high-potential markets as a supplement to other primary media. Despite attempts by some newspapers to broaden their coverage,

EXHIBIT **10.2**

Top 20 U.S. Daily Newspapers by Circulation

Courtesy of Audit Bureau of Circulations, Editor & Publisher, www.mediainfocenter.org/newspaper/data/top_20_daily_news.asp.

Rank	Publication	Average Daily Circulation
1	*USA Today*	2,241,677
2	*The Wall Street Journal*	1,780,605
3	*The New York Times*	1,100,479
4	*Los Angeles Times*	972,957
5	*The Washington Post*	749,863
6	*Daily News*, New York	707,726
7	*Chicago Tribune*	613,162
8	*Houston Chronicle*	551,854
9	*Newsday*	552,848
10	*The Dallas Morning News*	514,665
11	*New York Post*	512,324
12	*San Francisco Chronicle*	482,389
13	*Boston Globe*	467,021
14	*Chicago Sun-Times*	454,452
15	*The Arizona Republic*	451,228
16	*Atlanta Constitution*	420,944
17	*Detroit Free Press*	402,524
18	*The Star-Ledger*, Newark	397,984
19	*Miami Herald/ElNuevo Herald*	386,473
20	*Rocky Mountain News*	382,642

most advertisers classify all newspapers other than *The Wall Street Journal* and *USA Today* as regional.

Newspapers will probably continue to have a difficult time reaching out to national advertising as a primary medium. Newspapers have a long tradition as a local vehicle, which is a difficult perception to change. The key to a move toward national newspapers is not how papers define themselves but how they are defined by readers and advertisers. Until a number of newspapers achieve widely dispersed, upscale audiences (not likely for any but a handful of papers), advertisers will continue to regard the medium as a local vehicle with occasional national advertising opportunities.

MARKETING THE NEWSPAPER

It is obvious from our discussion thus far that newspapers are a product in need of extensive marketing to both readers and advertisers. Like any product with declining sales, newspapers must make a number of strategic and tactical decisions to reverse the trends they are seeing. Despite being the second leading source of advertising dollars, the traditional retail base of newspaper revenues is being chal-

EXHIBIT **10.3**

Top 10 Advertisers in National Newspapers

Ranked by measured spending in 2002.

Source: Copyright Crain Communications. Reprinted with permission. *Advertising Age*, www.adage.com/page.cmspageID=995, 30 August 2003.

National Newspaper

		Measured Ad Spending	
		2002	**2001**
1	Time Warner	$71.0	$53.7
2	IBM Corp.	66.6	49.2
3	Ford Motor CO.	52.8	67.5
4	Hewlett-Packard Co.	48.9	43.3
5	General Motors Corp.	48.1	44.9
6	Walt Disney Co.	48.1	39.2
7	Federated Department Stores	42.6	40.9
8	Sony Corp.	41.8	30.1
9	Sprint Corp.	41.6	34.5
10	Dow Jones & Co.	38.7	23.0

lenged by a number of new and traditional media competitors. At the same time, newspapers are finding it more difficult to maintain the broad base of readership that has made them such a powerful medium for more than 200 years.

A positive trend among newspapers is the quality, as contrasted to the quantity, of readership enjoyed by newspapers. Newspapers are very strong among college graduates and households with incomes in excess of $100,000. Unfortunately, newspaper circulation also skews toward the oldest portion of the population. Newspaper readership is inversely related to age with those in the 18–34 age group (prime prospects for the majority of advertisers) the least likely to read newspapers on a regular basis. Newspapers must take strong steps to develop marketing strategies that will reverse the trend of declining readership and share of advertising revenues.

In the last 25 years newspapers have taken a number of steps to identify their customers and advertisers, as well as the preferences of both. This process starts with marketing research. It is rare for any newspaper not to conduct at least one readership or market survey each year. Large newspapers annually sponsor several studies of their markets. A number of concerns have become apparent as a result of these studies.

Among the most important is the fact that readers are obtaining their information from a number of sources including television, the Internet, and so forth. They no longer see the newspaper as an indispensable source of information. Although many advertisers regard newspapers as the most economical means of reaching a mass audience, especially at the local level, many are adopting strategies that replace newspaper advertising with direct mail and other forms of promotion such as product sampling. On the plus side, these same studies demonstrate that newspapers maintain their reputation for integrity and prestige as sources of both advertising and editorial information.

Although newspapers face some formidable challenges, there is no question that they will remain a major advertising medium in the foreseeable future as newspapers continue to offer unique advantages to both readers and advertisers. However, because newspapers dominated the local market for so long, they did not develop a marketing mentality. Unfortunately, the industry is now playing catch-up with its more aggressive media competitors. The next sections will discuss how newspaper publishers are marketing the medium to both readers and advertisers. We will examine some of the approaches that newspaper publishers are using to protect and extend their franchise with both readers and advertisers.

Marketing to Readers

Newspapers are fully aware that they cannot reverse the decline in advertising share unless they first address the problem of falling readership. Advertisers will only buy newspaper space when they are convinced that the medium will deliver prospects for their brands. Some elite newspapers may be able to survive decreasing readership by marketing the quality of their audience. However, most newspapers will continue to depend on a broadly based audience and high household penetration for their financial success.

It is obvious that the current problems facing newspaper advertising are caused by a number of factors. Consequently, publishers must address several issues if they are to compete with other media in the future. Among the primary steps that newspapers should take are the following:[7]

1. Make circulation growth the highest priority with constant tests of pricing, promotional and sales techniques, and new distribution methods. Newspapers should place renewed emphasis on getting newspapers into the hands of younger readers.

2. Editors and reporters should be free of control by marketing departments. The news staff should understand that the newspaper is a business enterprise and even they can make use of market research in the development of a more reader-friendly newspaper, but this does not mean that the editorial product should be directed by advertising or business concerns. To do so will undermine the newspaper's editorial credibility, which is one of its major strengths.

3. Go after the opportunities in national advertising. Newspapers should move aggressively to gain new national advertising dollars. Newspaper advertising departments must continue to explore creative approaches to demonstrate that newspapers can provide national advertisers with desirable audiences that cannot be reached effectively with other media. Too many newspapers simply accept the status quo that national advertising dollars cannot be diverted to newspapers, thus making it a self-fulfilling prophesy.

4. More newspapers should follow the lead of some innovative newspapers and consider their Web sites as a distinctive product rather than a mere spin-off from the printed paper. The Internet can offer profitable opportunities to exploit a fuller range of information than what is printed in the paper. The Internet can reach specific readers (and nonnewspaper readers) with selective news and advertising and, properly marketed, make it a profit center rather than a value added to both readers and advertisers.

5. Give readers a choice and market to new audience segments. For example, some newspapers have developed youth-oriented sections within the general newspaper. The marginal costs are often worth the expense, even if only relatively few new readers are added.

6. Take a long view toward profitability. Invest in research and new sections that will allow the newspaper to remain competitive over the long term even though it may not contribute to short-term profits.

These and many other areas are being considered as newspapers attempt to adapt to a changing media environment. To meet these changes, publishers are designing the newspaper with various sections that cater to a host of different tastes. The modern newspaper is more a cafeteria than a set meal. Most of the audience reads only certain sections of a paper and spends different amounts of time with those sections that they do read. For example, whereas the classified advertising and the main news sections are read almost equally by men and women, only 29 percent of women read the sport pages compared to 58 percent of men. Conversely, 45 and 30 percent of women read the food/cooking and fashion sections, respectively. This is in comparison to 21 percent of men reading the food section and 8 percent reading the fashion section.[8] Knowing readers' preferences among the different sections of a newspaper is a great advantage in selling advertisers that wish to reach specific prospects.

Finally, newspapers must face the problem of gaining young readers. Although maintaining overall readership remains the most important challenge for newspapers, publishers are particularly concerned about gaining younger readers. Newspaper publishers fear that once media habits that exclude newspapers are established, it will be very difficult to reach these people as older adults. Newspaper reading habits are formed by about age 30 and tend to change very little after that.

Despite the medium's many strengths, newspapers will continue to see a need to aggressively market the medium to readers. Most newspaper readers and potential readers see the value of a newspaper in local news and information with relevance to their lives. Readers want information about things to do and places to go, self-help articles, local news of personal interest, and national and international news that has an effect on their lives. In a diverse, multicultural society, appealing to diverse reader interests is extremely difficult. But newspapers will have to find ways to address this heterogeneous population if they are to maintain their position as a primary source of news and advertising.

Marketing to Advertisers

Advertising constitutes more than 70 percent of all newspaper revenues and more than 50 percent of total newspaper space is devoted to advertising. Clearly, newspapers must continue to attract a number of business categories if they are to remain financially viable. In a fragmented media market, newspapers are finding it more difficult to maintain their share of advertising. As shown in Exhibit 10.4, leading local advertisers include department stores and communication and entertainment companies.

Newspapers may take some solace in the fact that other media face similar problems. As shown in Exhibit 10.5, among major media categories, only cable television has increased its audience base consistently over the last several years, and that was from a relatively small base.

One of the problems facing newspapers is the dramatic increase in advertising rates and CPM caused by rising fixed costs. Obviously, other media have had significant advertising cost increases, but few were higher on a percentage basis than newspapers.

In order to justify this growth, it is imperative that newspapers continue to convince advertisers that they are an efficient means of meeting a variety of marketing and advertising objectives. In order to accomplish this goal, newspapers must develop a plan that shows a diverse group of current and potential advertisers that newspapers should be a part of their media plans.

The marketing task for newspapers is a twofold undertaking: (1) to deliver the audience and (2) to compete for advertisers. The newspaper industry must convince advertisers that it represents the best local medium and at the same time demonstrate to national advertisers that it should constitute an important element of their advertising strategy. To accomplish these goals, newspapers must retain local retailers that have traditionally comprised the bulk of newspaper revenues and must gain more support from national advertisers that have not used newspapers to any great extent. In the current media climate neither job will be easy. However, newspapers have a tremendous advantage in providing readers with localized, in-depth information concerning products and services in their community.

Newspapers have taken a number of steps to position themselves more favorably to advertisers. One approach has been to provide readership as well as paid circulation data. Virtually all media report readership or total viewers, whereas newspapers have traditionally reported only the number of newspapers distributed. Obviously,

Newspaper

Rank	Advertiser	Measured Ad Spending	
		2002	2001
1	Federated Department Stores	$478.2	$485.7
2	May Department Stores Co.	446.3	432.7
3	AT&T Wireless	382.7	328.4
4	Verizon Communications	340.4	322.2
5	SBC Communications	294.0	217.8
6	Time Warner	245.1	213.8
7	Sprint Corp.	230.0	182.8
8	Dillard's	218.6	204.3
9	Target Corp.	206.8	190.6
10	Walt Disney Co.	204.5	173.8

EXHIBIT 10.4

Top 10 Advertisers in Local Newspapers

Ranked by measured spending in 2002.

Source: Copyright Crain Communications. Reprinted with permission. *Advertising Age*, www.adage.com/page.cmspageID =995, 30 August 2003.

EXHIBIT 10.5

Top 50 Market Media Trends

Source: Scarborough Research Release 2, Top 50 Market Report prepared by NAA Research Department.

Note: Radio drive times reflect Monday-Friday average quarter hour.

Year	Daily Newspaper[1]	Prime-time TV[2]	Morning-drive Radio[3]	Prime-time Cable[4]
1996	58.8	45.3	25.5	11.0
1997	58.7	42.4	25.4	10.4
1998	58.6	40.8	25.7	10.3
Spring 1999	57.9	39.6	25.5	10.5
Fall 1999	56.9	38.5	24.5	11.3
Spring 2000	56.2	37.8	23.4	12.0
Fall 2000	55.1	38.1	23.1	12.2
Spring 2001	53.5	38.6	22.9	12.2
Fall 2001	54.3	38.8	21.9	12.9
Spring 2002	55.5	38.6	22.5	12.6
Fall 2002	55.4	39.0	22.3	13.2
Spring 2003	55.1	39.4	22.1	13.9

[1]Average day readership
[2]Average half hour
[3]Average quarter hour
[4]Average half hour

*Note: Radio drive times reflect Monday–Friday average quarter hour

Top 50 Market Media Trends

Daily Newspaper (average day readership): 58.8%, 58.7%, 58.6%, 57.9%, 56.9%, 56.2%, 55.1%, 53.5%, 54.3%, 55.5%, 55.4%, 55.1%

Prime-time TV (average half hour): 45.3%, 42.4%, 40.8%, 39.6%, 38.5%, 37.8%, 38.1%, 38.6%, 38.8%, 38.6%, 39.0%, 39.4%

Morning-drive Radio (average quarter hour*): 25.5%, 25.4%, 25.7%, 25.5%, 24.5%, 23.4%, 23.1%, 22.9%, 21.9%, 22.5%, 22.3%, 22.1%

Prime-time Cable (average half hour): 11.0%, 10.4%, 10.3%, 10.5%, 11.3%, 12.0%, 12.2%, 12.2%, 12.9%, 12.6%, 13.2%, 13.9%

Percentage of Adults Reached (y-axis); Years: 1996, 1997, 1998, Spring 1999, Fall 1999, Spring 2000, Fall 2000, Spring 2001, Fall 2001, Spring 2002, Fall 2002, Spring 2003

this difference in reporting standards relative to other media places newspapers at a significant disadvantage. As mentioned earlier, in 2002 daily newspaper circulation was approximately 55 million. However, when including pass-along readers, the newspaper audience was more than 141.6 million. Newspaper executives have long advocated readership as the circulation standard of the medium.[9]

Newspapers also have found that their marketing efforts are most successful when they develop a client-oriented perspective with their advertisers. Rather than attempting to sell an array of advertising options to their clients, many newspapers are training their salespeople in consumer relationship management, which is also known as **relationship marketing.** This concept, which has its roots in direct-response advertising, attempts to develop a team approach between the newspaper and its advertisers to work with them as partners to solve problems rather than operating on a salesperson/customer basis.

Newspapers are approaching major advertising agency media buyers on a personal basis to demonstrate the utility of newspaper advertising in national media schedules. Many of the complaints of media buyers center around the difficulty of making multipaper buys across a number of markets. This is a particular problem for media buyers who are accustomed to the relative ease of buying national broadcast spots and magazines.

To address the buying problem, newspapers have developed information centers to make it easier for national and regional advertisers to know what services

relationship marketing
A strategy that develops marketing plans from a consumer perspective.

and products are available for advertisers. The **Newspaper Association of America (NAA)** in cooperation with *Editor & Publisher* magazine provides advertisers with a database of which newspapers provide special editions, targeted inserts, and other advertising options to make it easier to plan multinewspaper media buys.

Despite the difficult competitive environment in which newspapers operate, there is little question that they are adapting quickly to this changing marketplace. As we will discuss in later sections, newspapers are developing advertising strategies that meet the demands of the smallest retailer as well as the largest national firms.

Newspaper Association of America (NAA)
The marketing and trade organization for the newspaper industry.

NEWSPAPER INSERTS, ZONING, AND TOTAL MARKET COVERAGE

Newspaper advertising executives must provide service to a number of advertisers, many with distinctly different marketing and advertising problems. Although there are a number of variations of newspaper advertising strategy, we will discuss four approaches here:

1. *Full coverage of a newspaper's circulation.* In the past, most newspapers simply sold advertising space in their pages and advertisers received whatever circulation the paper provided. Large department stores, grocery stores with a number of locations, and national businesses with widely distributed products could take advantage of the majority of a newspaper's readers while other advertisers had to accept some level of waste circulation.

2. *Zoned preprints.* By the early 1980s, targeted direct mail began to offer advertisers a viable alternative to newspaper advertising without its inherent waste circulation. Newspapers countered by offering advertisers the opportunity to have advertising circulars and preprinted inserts delivered with the paper. The first businesses to make significant use of inserts were grocery stores and major retailers. In recent years, newspaper preprints have become the major vehicle for the distribution of coupons for businesses such as fast-food franchises.

The next step in the evolution of newspaper preprints, again in reaction to direct-mail competition, was the zoned distribution preprints. Rather than simply being inserted in every issue of the newspaper, zoned preprints could be delivered to specific ZIP codes within a metropolitan area. Initially, most papers offered these so-called zoned preprints only in upscale ZIP codes, but in recent years advertisers have been able to buy any ZIP code within a newspaper's primary circulation area. In some instances, newspapers have begun to distribute preprints to even smaller, sub-ZIP-code circulation clusters called *microzones*.

Preprints have become so popular that they have replaced traditional advertising as the primary revenue source for newspapers. In 1997, preprinted inserts surpassed traditional newspaper advertising (or run-of-paper, ROP) for the first time. The growth of revenue produced by inserts continues to outstrip the growth in revenue provided by ROP. According to Gary Wilson, president of the Gannett Company's newspaper division, "The most striking trend we continue to see is the shift from ROP to preprint" as a source of newspaper revenue.[10] Today, the majority of newspapers provide ZIP-code zoning for advertising inserts.

Although preprinted inserts allow newspapers to compete with direct mail, they also create problems for the newspaper industry. Among the major issues are the following:

- Inserts are less profitable than ROP advertising.
- Although surveys show that newspaper inserts attain higher reach and are preferable to direct mail, the newspaper is no more than an advertising delivery system for these inserts.

zoning
Newspaper practice of offering advertisers partial coverage of a market, often accomplished with weekly inserts distributed to certain sections of that market.

■ As ROP advertising decreases, the space for news and editorial matter (the so-called *news hole*) shrinks and ultimately it may change the character of newspapers as both an advertising and information medium.

Despite any associated problems, **zoning** has offered newspapers a compelling weapon against direct mail and other forms of targeted media. It also holds the potential for bringing an increased number of national advertisers to newspapers. For example, Kmart recently announced that it would create "Urban Direct," an entertainment and lifestyle newspaper supplement for distribution within urban committees. According to Kmart spokesperson Susan Dennis, "We approach this as a 'Parade' type of concept that will allow us to reach the customers located in those markets with information that matters to them."[11]

1. *The zoned newspaper.* In addition to preprint zoning, many metropolitan newspapers are providing suburban weekly or even daily sections in the newspaper to serve both the reader and advertiser demand for information about particular suburbs of a city. In the past, many newspapers devoted limited resources to these sections. Today, most newspapers are making meaningful investments in their zoned editions and, in many cities, publishers have been rewarded with significant readership and advertising increases.

   The zoned newspaper has major advantages for both advertisers and publishers. Advertisers can gain the advantages of zoning but still run ROP advertising, which has greater prestige and credibility. The zoned newspaper also overcomes the problem of insert clutter. Some major newspapers, especially their Sunday editions, carry as many as 40 inserts, which drastically decreases their readership and impact.

2. *Total market coverage.* Ironically, while newspapers seek to serve those advertisers that are interested in a narrowly defined group of readers, they also find that a number of advertisers are seeking total penetration of a market. Because no newspaper has complete coverage of its market (in many markets it is as low as 30 percent), other means must be used to augment regular circulation and achieve **total market coverage (TMC).** Total market coverage may be accomplished in a number of ways:

■ Weekly delivery of a nonsubscriber supplement carrying mostly advertisements

■ Using newspaper-supported direct mail to nonsubscribers

■ Delivering the newspaper free to all households once a week

Regardless of the method used to achieve total market coverage, the aim is the same, that is, to reach all the households in a market whether or not they are newspaper subscribers. The objective is to combine the regular daily paper with a supplemental TMC product and, thus, allow advertisers to reach virtually 100 percent of the households in a market.

total market coverage (TMC)
Where newspapers augment their circulation with direct mail or shoppers to deliver all households in a market.

Categories of Newspaper Advertising

Newspapers derive approximately 70 percent of their revenues from advertising with the remainder coming from subscription and newsstand sales. Newspapers provide a number of categories and subcategories of advertising. This section discusses some of the primary types of newspaper advertising.

All newspaper advertising is divided into two categories: *display* and *classified.* **Classified advertising,** which is carried in a special section, is comprised of a variety of advertisements from a small notice announcing a yard sale to those for the largest automobile dealers and real estate firms. Display is all the nonclassified advertising in a newspaper. Within the display category, advertising is considered either *local* (also called *retail*) or *national.* According to the Newspaper Association of America, newspaper advertising revenues amount to more than $44 billion and come from the following sources:

classified advertising
Found in columns so labeled, published in sections of a newspaper or magazine set aside for certain classes of goods or services—for example, help wanted, positions.

	% of Total
Classified	36.0
Local	47.6
National	16.4

As we mentioned earlier, marketing research is an important element of newspaper advertising. Newspaper executives have sponsored a number of research studies showing that newspapers are equal to or better than their media competitors on a number of measures. Much of this research has been oriented toward audience delivery data, demonstrating the quality and/or the size of newspaper readership. However, advertisers also are interested in communication effectiveness and the Newspaper Association of America (NAA) has examined newspaper advertising from this perspective. Among the major findings were the following:

■ Newspaper color advertising works. It increases both attention and readership significantly compared to black-and-white advertisements. Furthermore, the more color the better as four-color advertising gains higher readership than two-color advertising.

- ■ Use pictures. Illustrations scored better than all text, and photographs are better than line art. Inclusion of a model also increases readership.

- ■ Showing the product in use will increase the reader's attention by as much as 25 percent.

- ■ Newspaper readers are driven by price and the prominent display of prices will increase readership.

- ■ Size is an important element in newspaper advertising. Full-page advertisements were noticed 39 percent more often than quarter-page advertisements.

- ■ Location is not important. The study showed that location of a newspaper advertisement had no effect on readership. Advertisements on the left-hand versus the right-hand page, below or above the fold, and placement within a section of the paper had the same level of readership.

- ■ Page clutter had no effect on readership. Advertisements on pages with as few as three advertisements scored the same as pages with as many as nine advertisements.

Classified Advertising

Classified advertising (the common "want ads") is often ignored unless you are looking for a car, house, or job. Newspapers also carry advertisements with illustrations in the classified section. These are known as *classified display* advertisements and normally are run in the automotive and real estate sections. All these notices are included under the heading of classified advertising, which has its own rate card and is usually operated as a separate department within the newspaper. Classified revenues account for almost $16 billion annually and they are the most profitable department of most newspapers.

In recent years, classified advertising has become a major competitive battleground for newspapers. Competition for classified advertising constitutes one of the most serious financial threats to the newspaper industry. The maintenance of classified advertising revenue is so important to newspapers that it has become a major preoccupation with most publishers. To understand the problem facing newspapers, we have to examine a number of factors that are rapidly changing the face of classified advertising. First, the classified advertising sector is very concentrated in three areas: employment, real estate, and automotive. These three categories account for about 75 percent of all classified dollars. This concentration among so few advertisers has allowed specialized online services to gain a foothold in competition with newspapers' more broadly defined classified sections. That is, a person wanting a car can look at Web sites that are dedicated to only automobiles.

The initial competition for newspaper classified advertising came from online services that introduced two concepts to the world of classifieds: *aggregation* and *vertical sites*. Newspapers regarded classified as local advertising and catered more or less exclusively to the local employment, and real estate markets, and so forth. However, new Web competitors offered vertical services, that is, a single category of classified advertising such as jobs and, perhaps more importantly, they compiled (or aggregated) classified advertising from across the country.

Prospective job seekers, particularly those looking to relocate from other areas, now could look at a single site and see employment opportunities anywhere in the country (or even internationally) without going to the trouble of subscribing to a number of out-of-town newspapers.

Newspapers have countered these incursions from independent online classified sites in two ways. First, the vast majority of newspapers have created their own Web sites, most with classified sections. Second, newspapers have established a number of aggregate sites such as www.careerpath.com, a consortium of six of the leading newspaper chains.[12]

Newspaper advertising executives know that significant dollars are going to be shifted to online classified services. For them, the key is to use their strong franchise in the classified market to capture the lion's share of the dollars being diverted from print classified advertising. As one newspaper consultant pointed out, "By now it's evident that classifieds work better online than they do in print—they are searchable, deep, interactive, and up to date, when done right. Help-wanted ads link job hunters with company websites. Car ads include photos and detailed specs. Homes for sale offer virtual tours. Best of all, classifieds can be distributed far more efficiently online than in print; no wonder it costs less to place classifieds on the Web than in a big-city paper."[13]

It is important to emphasize that despite the recent challenges to newspaper classified advertising, newspapers remain far and away the most used source of such notices. Nevertheless, in less than 10 years, the World Wide Web has brought dramatic changes to classified advertising. Some predict that in the near future, and we are already seeing this on a limited basis, print classified advertising will be devoted largely to a directory of Web sites—a starting place for further shopping and gathering detailed information. Regardless of where classified advertising moves, it seems that newspapers have positioned themselves to take advantage of future changes.

Display Advertising

Virtually all nonclassified newspaper advertising falls into the category of display advertising. The general segment of display advertising is divided into two subgroups: local and national.

Local Advertising Newspaper advertising has an overwhelming local focus. The financial structure of the newspaper industry is built on retailer support and, by any measure, newspapers are the most popular local advertising medium with both readers and advertisers. Local advertising refers to all nonclassified advertising placed by local businesses, organizations, and individuals. Traditionally, newspaper advertising revenues have been provided by major retailers and that continues to this day.

Because of their dependence on retail advertising, newspapers are acutely aware of any changes in the local advertising landscape that might impact advertising dollars. Some of the major retailing trends and the potential impact on newspaper advertising are the following:

- Consolidation of general merchandising and discount retailers will continue to reduce the number of retail advertisers and it has the potential to reduce the amount of total retail advertising dollars. In recent years, mergers and acquisitions have resulted in a greater concentration of sales among leading retailers. For example, the top 10 discount retailers accounted for 88 percent of all category sales in 1990; by 2000 it was 96 percent. Likewise, the top 10 specialty retailers held a 30 percent share of sales in 2000, up from 17 percent in 1990. Fewer retail outlets present two problems for newspapers. First, consolidation of retail ownership can result in a decrease in total retail advertising dollars. Second, because each of these retail conglomerates account for a greater share of dollars, the risk associated with the loss of any account is much greater than in past years when the number of retailers spread total newspaper advertising revenues among numerous businesses.

- In addition to a concentration of traditional retail outlets, they also have created a concentration of services not usually associated with these type of outlets. For example, rather than having separate outlets for automotive repairs, banking, home decorating, and eye care, many of the new mega-stores are housing all these services under one roof.

■ Retailers are moving to promote their store names as brands. Because price has traditionally been a key ingredient in newspaper advertising, this shift may have a significant effect on newspapers. As image, rather than price, becomes a core retail strategy for many of these chain retailers, we may see a diversion of dollars from newspapers to television or even upscale magazines.

■ Retailers will continue to add shopping options to cater to the changing preferences of consumers. Catalogs, online marketing, and other options will augment in-store selling and may result in a shift of advertising dollars to other media.

■ As retailers move to promote themselves as brands, we will see more emphasis on store brand and private-label merchandising. Traditionally, a private-brand marketing strategy has resulted in a reduction in advertising budgets and newspapers fear that this might happen if there is significant movement to house brands among national retailers.

Although predicting the future of retail advertising is difficult, newspaper advertising directors can anticipate continuing changes in the near term. As one newspaper marketing executive observed, "Newspaper marketers must keep up with changes taking place inside and outside markets. Reading trade publications,

EXHIBIT 10.7

A national display ad.

Courtesy of McRae
Communications and Snapper.

surfing retail World Wide Web sites and keeping close to local retailers can help publishers formulate strategies for future profitability."[14] Nowhere in advertising and marketing is the concept of relationship marketing more important than in the alliance between newspapers and their retail advertising customers.

National Advertising One of the recent success stories in newspaper advertising is the increase in national advertising. Despite these increases, national newspaper advertising remains a relatively small contributor to overall revenues. In 2002, national advertising represented almost 16 percent of all newspaper advertising revenue.[15]

Two elements have fueled the resurgence in national newspaper dollars. First, many national advertisers, particularly newer categories such as Internet services and telecommunications, are relying on newspapers to target high-potential markets. Many of these hi-tech companies also see newspapers as a highly credible source, just the environment needed for a new business with little consumer brand recognition.

A second factor in the growth of national newspaper advertising is the success of the Newspaper National Network (NNN). The NNN was formed in 1994 when 23 major U.S. newspaper chains gave funds to the NAA to provide an avenue for national advertisers to gain easy access to national newspaper buys. The NNN provides a network of participating newspapers, which could be bought using one insertion order and one invoice. The intent of the NNN was to duplicate for national media buyers the convenience they experience in buying network television.

Many national advertisers do not consider newspapers equal to other media. When they think of national media, media planners often think of network and cable television and magazines. If the NNN and other industry-wide efforts do no more than create a higher profile and greater consideration of newspapers among national advertisers, they will have served an important purpose.

The NNN also provides national advertisers with **Standard Advertising Units (SAU)** from one newspaper to another (see Exhibit 10.8). Standardization allows national advertisers to purchase space in virtually every major U.S. newspaper and prepare one advertisement that will be accepted by each of them. As you can see, NNN formats are flexible enough to provide virtually every advertiser a design that will fit any creative execution.

Overcoming some of the more cumbersome buying procedures has helped newspapers to market the medium more effectively on a national basis. However, these procedural changes have not addressed one of the most serious points of disagreement between national advertisers and newspapers—the continuing debate over the so-called local/national rate differential. Most newspapers charge a substantial premium to national advertisers. This differential generally ranges from 40 percent to 60 percent. Newspapers defend the difference on the basis that they must pay an agency commission for national advertising and many of these advertisers are only occasional users of their papers, unlike retailers from whom they enjoy continuing support.

In summary, newspapers must overcome several obstacles if they are to increase their national advertising share. Given the tight retail market and the potential for growth in the national sector, newspapers must continue to make it easier for national advertisers to buy the medium. An effective system of national newspaper advertising will take time. In addition, it seems clear that some accommodation must be made concerning the national/local rate issue. Perhaps the ultimate catalyst for finding solutions to the problems of national advertisers will be the mutual self-interest of both groups.

Standard Advertising Unit (SAU)
Allows national advertisers to purchase newspaper advertising in standard units from one paper to another.

Cooperative Advertising

One of the historical outgrowths of the newspaper local/national rate differential was the development of a relationship between national advertisers and their retail

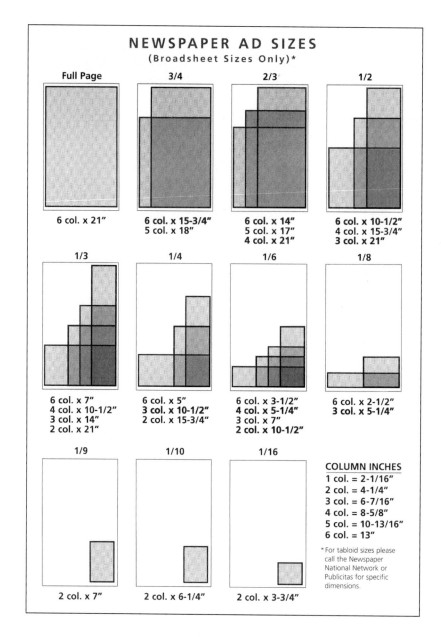

cooperative (co-op) advertising
Joint promotion of a national advertiser (manufacturer) and local retail outlet on behalf of the manufacturer's product on sale in the retail store.

distributors called **cooperative (co-op) advertising.** We will discuss cooperative advertising more fully in Chapter 14, but it is such an important part of newspaper advertising that we need to mention it here.

Co-op advertising is placed by a local advertiser but paid for, all or in part, by a national advertiser. The national manufacturer usually provides the advertisements, allowing space for each participating retailer's logo. The original reason for the development of co-op advertising was that it allowed national advertisers to place advertisements at local rates.

Today, co-op is a huge source of advertising funds. Co-op also is a source of building goodwill with distributors and retailers and exercising some creative control over local advertising as well as saving money for national advertisers.

Because national advertisers pay anywhere from 50 to 100 percent of the cost of locally placed co-op, it extends the budgets of local advertisers as it saves money for national firms. It is ironic that a system that was developed largely to circumvent the national/local newspaper rate differential is strongly supported by the newspaper industry. Because newspapers receive over half of all co-op dollars placed, their sales staffs are extremely aggressive in helping retail accounts find and use co-op money.

The Rate Structure

The local advertiser, dealing with one or two newspapers, has a fairly easy job buying newspaper space. The rate structure and discounts for any one newspaper are usually straightforward. However, as we have seen, the national advertiser has a much more difficult time. An advertiser buying space in a number of newspapers confronts an unlimited set of options and price structures, including discounts, premium charges for color, special sections, preferred positions, and zoned editions. In the following discussion, we look at some of the primary options and rate decisions that an advertiser must make.

Discounts Newspapers are divided into two categories: those with a uniform **flat rate** offering no discounts, and those with an **open rate** providing some discount structure. The open rate also refers to the highest rate against which all discounts are applied. The most common discounts are based on *frequency* or *bulk* purchases of space. A bulk discount means there is a sliding scale so that the advertiser is charged proportionally less as more advertising is purchased. A frequency discount usually requires some unit or pattern of purchase in addition to total amount of space.

flat rate
A uniform charge for space in a medium, without regard to the amount of space used or the frequency of insertion. When flat rates do not prevail, time discounts or quantity discounts are offered.

open rate
In print, the highest advertising rate at which all discounts are placed.

Frequency Within 52-Week Contract Period Full-Page Contract		Bulk Within 52-Week Contract Period	
Open Rate	$2.50/Column Inch	No. of Column Inches	Rate
10 insertions	2.10	500	2.40
15 insertions	2.20	1,500	2.30
20 insertions	2.10	3,000	2.20
30 insertions	2.00	5,000	2.10
40 insertions	1.90	10,000	2.00
50 insertions	1.80	15,000	1.90

ROP and Preferred-Position Rates The basic rates quoted by a newspaper entitle the ad to a run-of-paper (ROP) position anywhere in the paper that the publisher chooses to place it, although the paper will be mindful of the advertiser's request and interest in getting a good position. An advertiser may buy a choice position by paying a higher, preferred-position rate, which is similar to paying for a box seat in a stadium instead of general admission. An athletic shoe advertiser, for example, may elect to pay a preferred-position rate to ensure getting on the sports page. A cosmetic advertiser may buy a preferred position on the women's page. There are also preferred positions on individual pages. An advertiser may pay for the top of a column or the top of a column next to news reading matter (called *full position*).

Each newspaper specifies its preferred-position rates; there is no consistency in this practice. Preferred-position rates are not as common as they once were. Now many papers simply attempt to accommodate advertisers that request a position.

Combination Rates A number of combinations are available to advertisers. What they all have in common is the advantage of greatly reduced rates for purchasing several papers as a group. The most frequently seen combination rate occurs when the same publisher issues both a morning and an evening paper. By buying both papers, the advertiser can pay as little as one-third to one-half for the second paper. This type of combination may involve as few as two papers in a single metropolitan market or many papers bought on a national basis. In either case, the advertiser has to deal with only one group and pays a single bill.

The Rate Card

For most media, the advertising rate card, if it exists at all, is simply a starting point for negotiation. As discussed earlier, most radio and television stations don't publish formal rate cards because rates are determined by negotiated scatter plans that are unique to each advertiser. During the 1980s many consumer magazines also initiated a system of rate negotiation. Today, newspapers are one of the few media to maintain rate integrity by offering all advertisers the same rates and discounts. Many newpapers do offer frequent advertisers value-added options such as featured positions on their Web sites.

Unlike broadcast media with their fixed time inventory and magazines with their lengthy advertising production cycles, newspapers can adjust quickly to whatever advertising space is needed. We only have to look at the typical newspaper's bulky Sunday and Wednesday (best grocery day) editions compared to the lightweight Saturday edition to see the flexibility enjoyed by newspapers.

Despite a traditional rate card, we should not leave the impression that newspapers do not accommodate advertisers with flexible rates in the face of competitive pressure. For example:

- *Multiple rate cards.* Many newspapers offer a number of rate cards for different categories of advertisers. For example, packaged goods, travel, business, and retail stores may all qualify for different rates. Even the NNN provides buying opportunities for only seven categories of products such as automotive, drugs, and beverages. Some advertisers think that the array of different rates makes the buying process unnecessarily complex and, for national advertisers and other multiple-paper advertisers, it has the same effect as individual rate negotiation. Newspapers see the process as a type of yield management (see Chapter 2) where a premium is charged for high demand space.

- *Newspaper merchandising programs.* Many newspapers, while refusing to negotiate rates directly, are willing to make other types of merchandising concessions. These programs, also known as value-added programs, may include sharing of detailed audience research and providing free creative or copy assistance to advertisers.

- *Offer pick up rates.* An advertiser that agrees to rerun an ad may receive a lower rate. This encourages return business and passes along some of the savings that the newspaper enjoys from not having to deal with the production process involved with a new advertisement.

Because of the tradition of the newspaper rate card, it is unlikely that we will see the type of rate negotiation that has become so prevalent in other media. However, newspapers recognize that they will have to meet new competitive pressure. Consequently, we will see even more creative value-added programs offered by newspapers in the future.

Comparing Newspaper Advertising Costs

National advertisers, many of whom consider hundreds of newspapers in a single media plan, want to make cost comparisons among their potential newspaper buys. Advertisers use CPM for the purpose of making comparisons between advertising cost and audience delivery.

Using the CPM for newspaper rate comparisons has two advantages:

1. It reflects the move to page and fractional-page space buys. Media planners are much more comfortable using the standardized space units of the NNN than lines or column inches in space buys.

2. Comparisons among media are more easily calculated using a standard benchmark such as the CPM. Although qualitative differences among newspapers and other media must still be considered, the CPM does offer a consistent means of comparison:

Newspaper	Open-Rate Page Cost	Circulation	CPM
A	$5,400	165,000	$32.72
B	3,300	116,000	28.45

Example: $\dfrac{\$5,400 \times 10.00}{165,000} = \$32.72$

The Space Contract, the Short Rate

If a paper has a flat rate, obviously there is no problem with calculating costs—all space is billed at the same price regardless of how much is used. However, space contracts in open-rate papers must have flexibility to allow advertisers to use more or less space than originally contracted. Normally, an advertiser will sign a space contract estimating the amount of space to be used during the next 12 months. Such a space contract is not a guarantee of the amount of space an advertiser will run but rather an agreement on the rate the advertiser will pay for any space run during the year in question.

The space contract involves two steps: First, advertisers estimate the amount of space they think they will run and agree with the newspaper on how to handle any rate adjustments needed at the end of the year; they are then billed during the year at the selected rate. Second, at the end of the year, the total linage is added, and if advertisers ran the amount of space they had estimated, no adjustment is necessary; but if they failed to run enough space to earn that rate, they have to pay at the higher rate charged for the number of lines they actually ran. That amount is called the **short rate.**

As an example, let us assume that a national advertiser plans to run advertising in a paper with the following rates:

- Open rate, $5.00 per column inch
- 1,000 column inches, $4.50/column inch
- 5,000 column inches, $4.00/column inch
- 10,000 column inches, $3.50/column inch

The advertiser expects to run at least 5,000 column inches and signs the contract at the $4.00 (5,000 column-inch) rate (subject to end-of-year adjustment). At the end of 12 months, however, only 4,100 column inches have been run; therefore, the bill at the end of the contract year is as follows:

Earned rate: 4,100 column inches @ $4.50 per column inch = $18,450

Paid rate: 4,100 column inches @ $4.00 per column inch = $16,400

Short rate due = $ 2,050

or

Column inches run × difference in earned and billed rates

= 54,100 column inches × .50

=$ 2,050

short rate
The balance advertisers have to pay if they estimated that they would run more ads in a year than they did and entered a contract to pay at a favorable rate. The short rate is figured at the end of the year or sooner if advertisers fall behind schedule. It is calculated at a higher rate for the fewer insertions.

rebate
The amount owed to an advertiser by a medium when the advertiser qualifies for a higher space discount.

If the space purchased had qualified for the 10,000 column-inch rate ($3.50), the advertiser would have received a **rebate** of $5,000. The calculation then would be:

Paid rate: 10,000 column inches @ $4.00 per column inch = $40,000

Earned rate: 10,000 column inches @ $3.50 per column inch = $35,000

Rebate due = $ 5,000

Newspapers will credit a rebate against future advertising rather than actually paying the advertiser. Some papers charge the full rate and allow credit for a better rate when earned.

CIRCULATION ANALYSIS

The Audit Bureau of Circulations

Audit Bureau of Circulations (ABC)
The organization sponsored by publishers, agencies, and advertisers for securing accurate circulation statements.

Prior to the founding of the **Audit Bureau of Circulations (ABC)** in 1914, those newspaper publishers that bothered at all provided advertisers with self-reported circulation figures. Obviously, many publishers grossly inflated their circulation and created an adversarial relationship among newspapers, advertising agencies, and clients.[16]

The ABC serves advertisers, agencies, and publishers. It is a self-regulating and self-supporting cooperative body. Revenues for the ABC come from annual dues paid by all members and auditing fees paid by publishers.

The verification process involves three reports: two publisher's statements and the ABC audit. The publisher's statements are issued for six-month periods ending March 31 and September 30. The ABC audit is conducted annually for 12-month periods ending either March 31 or September 30. Exhibit 10.9 shows a portion of an ABC audit report. It should be noted that the information in ABC reports is constantly changing in response to subscribers' needs.

The ABC report includes the following primary information:

1. Total paid circulation.
2. Amount of circulation in the city zone, retail trading zone, and all other areas. (*Note:* The city zone is a market made up of the city of publication and contiguous built-up areas similar in character to the central city. The retail trading zone is a market area outside the city zone whose residents regularly trade with merchants doing business within the city zone.)
3. The number of papers sold at newsstands.

The ABC reports have nothing to do with a newspaper's rates. They deal with circulation statistics only. Publishers have always been glad to supply demographic data on their readers, but the ABC now has its own division for gathering demographic data for many of the markets in the United States. All data are computerized and quickly available.

Although the verification of newspaper circulation seems to be a relatively straightforward process, it has been surrounded by controversy in recent years. In particular, two areas are of primary concern to the newspaper industry:

1. *Discounted circulation and bulk sales.* ABC rules require that to qualify as paid circulation, copies must be sold for 50 percent or more of the standard subscription price. The rule was initiated to prevent newspapers from simply giving away unsold papers and counting them as normal circulation in determining advertising rates.

   Newspaper publishers, while admitting that strict controls must be applied to deep-discounted or free circulation, argue for greater flexibility.

EXHIBIT **10.9**

ABC reports provide valuable information regarding circulation.

Courtesy of Audit Bureau of Circulations.

AUDIT REPORT: Newspaper

ANYTOWN DAILY NEWS (Morning & Sunday)

Anytown (Blue County), Illinois

Audit Bureau of Circulations
900 N. Meacham Rd.
Schaumburg, IL
60173-4968
accessabc.com

12 months ended September 30, 2002

	Morning (Mon. to Sat.)	Sunday
1A. TOTAL AVERAGE PAID CIRCULATION	41,250	63,620
Estimated Average Issue Adult Readers		
(See Par. 6 for Readership Market Description)		
(See Separate Report for Details)	131,894	157,856
1B. AVERAGE PAID CIRCULATION:		
Paid for by Individual Recipients (Sold at 50% or more of basic price)		
Home Delivery and Mail	23,000	34,600
Single Copy Sales	14,140	24,840
Subtotal	37,140	59,440
Paid for by Individual Recipients (Sold at or more than 25% but less than 50% of basic price)		
Home Delivery and Mail	1,400	2,100
Single Copy Sales	940	1,240
Subtotal	2,340	3,340
Total Average Individually Paid Circulation	39,480	62,780
Other Paid Circulation:		
Single Copy Sales		
Hotel/Guest Copies	100	25
Event Sales	200	25
Car Rentals	50	10
Educational Programs		
Newspapers in Education	140	50
Newspapers in Education - Home Delivered	400	400
Registered College Student Copies	600	100
Employee Copies	200	190
Third Party Sales		
Airlines — Available for passengers	20	10
Clubs — Available for members	10	2
Hospitals and Nursing Homes — Available for patients	20	20
Retail/Business — Available for patrons	20	5
Other	10	3
Subtotal	1,770	840
Total Paid Circulation	41,250	63,620
Other Audited Distribution (Optional)	300	200
Total Distribution (Optional)	41,550	63,820
Days Omitted from Averages, See Par. 6	3	2

This publication also participates in the ABC Reader Profile Study:
May 2 - June 1, 2002
Latest Data Available
(See Separate Report for Details)

Estimate Average Issue Adult Readers	Morning (Mon. to Fri.)	Sunday
Anytown Daily News	131,894	157,856
Subscriber Readers	96,109	106,701
Single Copy Sales Readers	13,682	34,514
Pass-Along/Other Readers	22,103	16,641
Readers Per Copy	2.4	2.2

TMC Total Market Coverage

Audited TMC Distribution - Our Town News, published Wednesday   145,000
(See Supplemental Data Report for Details)

This publication also has Web Site Activity audited by ABCi. See Par. 6

www ABC Interactive®
July 2 - August 1, 2002
Latest Data Available

	Total	Daily	Mon. to Fri.	Sat. & Sun.
Page Impressions	816,775	27,226	30,828	17,319
Unique Users	3,906,226	130,208	147,417	82,882

3/26/03

They point out that newspapers delivered free to rooms in upscale hotels, made available on airplanes or at special events such as trade shows, or sold at greatly discounted prices to college students are reaching prime advertising prospects. Many advertisers take the position that the liberal interpretation of circulation advocated by some publishers would take the industry back to pre-ABC days when newspapers counted any distribution as quality circulation.

Ultimately, the debate will be settled by advertisers, not newspaper publishers. The basic ABC auditing process is the standard by which most media buyers judge newspapers. Advertisers may accept some changes in the requirements for audited circulation. However, it is doubtful that they will agree to the most liberal changes in bulk and discount circulation advocated by some in the industry.

2. *Readership versus paid circulation.* Newspapers are at a significant disadvantage in that they measure audiences by circulation or newspapers distributed rather than the total readers of these newspapers. Although magazine circulation is

audited by ABC, media buyers put great stock in readership of these publications. In 1998, the NAA enlisted the Competitive Media Index (CMI) to measure newspaper readership in the top 50 markets. That same year, the ABC agreed to a pilot study to audit readership studies conducted by independent research firms. Called the "Reader Profile Survey," the ABC certifies that a particular newspaper readership study was conducted according to accepted research methodology.

Most major papers routinely commission readership and market research from a number of companies. The Reader Profile Survey offers outside confirmation that these surveys have been done according to traditional research standards. Again, whether readership replaces or supplements circulation will be up to advertisers. Given the long history of circulation as the norm for measuring newspaper audiences, it may be a hard sell.

The ongoing debate over circulation simply emphasizes the competitive environment in which newspapers are operating. Regardless of how these issues are settled, the decline in paid circulation, the loss of household penetration, and the decrease in newspapers' share of total advertising dollars are all concerns that must be addressed by the industry.

Technology and the Future of Newspapers

As we discussed in an earlier section, the Internet has the potential to significantly change the way in which readers search and respond to classified advertising. Although we are still some years away from the fulfillment of the most optimistic predictions of the electronic superhighway, it is clear that new technology must be a factor in the marketing plans of any media company.

In the future, newspaper executives may come to view themselves as information providers, not newspaper editors and publishers. This distinction is not one of simple semantics. Rather, it allows people to think beyond the newspaper as a print-on-paper product and consider alternative delivery systems as well as the type of information that is provided.

Almost 1,500 daily newspapers have launched Internet Web sites.[17] Surveys by the NAA show that users of newspaper-sponsored Web sites read the print version with the same regularity as they did prior to introduction of the online version. According to NAA research, 62 percent of general interest Internet users look to newspaper sites to find online local news. This number increases to 86 percent for those who are users of online newspapers. That is, almost 9 out of every 10 users of online sites to get their local news say that they use online newspaper Web sites.[18] Complementary usage of online and print versions is encouraged by many newspapers that offer Web addresses at the end of some stories where readers can obtain more in-depth information than what is included in the printed newspaper.

Despite the relatively modest inroads into newspaper readership by the Internet, newspapers have reason for concern. Not only is serious erosion beginning to be seen in classified revenues, but also the newspaper's role as a news medium is being affected by the Web. Research shows that among people using the Internet for breaking news and current information, newspaper Web sites are far down their preference list.

The need to have an effective Web presence may be underscored by the fact that young adults are spending far less time with the printed newspaper than older adults. If these young adults can't be converted to readers of traditional newspapers, then newspapers must be in a position to capture their attention on the Internet. Young adults under the age of 23 are spending almost three-quarters of an hour per day on the Internet versus less than 15 minutes per day with the local newspaper (see Exhibit 10.11).

YOU ASK YOUR NEIGHBOR
WHEN THE BABY'S DUE.

SHE'S NOT PREGNANT.

Why do you need 40 acres of flowers?

🌹 Callaway Gardens

For reservations call 1.800.CALLAWAY or visit callawaygardens.com.

EXHIBIT 10.10

Newspaper ads can be a good way to deliver an advertiser's Web address to the target audience.

Courtesy of Sawyer Riley Compton and Callaway Gardens.

Despite its potential threat, it will be some time before the Internet is a viable competitor to the daily newspaper. The convenience, portability, and lack of Internet household penetration all will work against the so-called "electronic newspaper" as a substitute for traditional print. However, as technology and reading habits of younger generations become more mainstream, it may make some form of new media a decided threat to traditional newspapers. The fact that newspapers are moving aggressively into the world of new media is testimony to the changing world of both advertising and communication.

Minutes Per Day Spent With:	Age				
	Under 23	23–34	35–54	55–59	60+
Local daily newspaper	13.8	13.8	19.2	22.8	56.4
Any daily newspaper	18.0	17.4	24.0	30.0	57.6
Magazines	20.4	18.6	19.8	19.8	24.0
Internet	43.8	46.2	36.6	28.2	13.8
TV	192.6	163.8	168.0	188.4	246.6

EXHIBIT 10.11

A 23-year-old spends 25 percent less time reading a local paper than a 60-year-old.

Source: Copyright Crain Communications. Reprinted with permission. *Advertising Age*, www.adage.com.

NEWSPAPER-DISTRIBUTED MAGAZINE SUPPLEMENTS

One of the most enduring newspaper traditions is the Sunday magazine supplement. For years, most major dailies published a Sunday magazine with features on gardening, local lifestyles and fashion, and personalities. Today only a few survive. Most of these are concentrated in major newspaper markets such as New York City, Los Angeles, and Chicago where they attract national advertisers and the newspapers are large enough to invest millions of dollars annually in these upscale publications. From a marketing perspective, national supplements appeal to advertisers that gain network buying efficiency, a broad-based newspaper circulation, a magazine format, consistent quality reproduction, and a CPM lower than both newspapers and most magazines.

Individual newspapers view the expense of production combined with declining advertising support as the primary reasons to move to syndicated national publications. The two leaders in the category are *USA Today* and *Parade*. Both magazines deliver huge readership (at a cost to both newspapers and advertisers that is less than most independent supplements). *Parade* tends to be more popular at larger newspapers with a circulation of 35.7 million in 335 papers. In fact, *Parade* is the largest circulation consumer magazine by a wide margin. *USA Today* is distributed by more than 590 newspapers but has a lower circulation of 23.7 million. As is the case with most consumer magazines, both publications offer numerous opportunities for regional buys. Although a number of advertisers such as the Franklin Mint advertise on a national basis, some form of less-than-full-run buy is very common in Sunday supplements.

A number of other supplements reach ethnic markets in newspapers directed toward these readers. Among the most well known is *Vista*, a magazine carried in about two dozen newspapers with large Hispanic audiences. It is published on a monthly basis and has a circulation of 1 million.

In addition to these newspaper-distributed magazines, a number of newspapers have special sections that are carried throughout the week to reach a number of different prospects. These special issues cover topics as diverse as agriculture, boating, health, and senior citizen issues. The NAA provides a "Newspaper Advertising Capabilities Database," which allows advertisers to know which papers are offering particular special sections.

Comics

Any discussion of newspaper special features would have to include a mention of the comics. The newspaper comic traces its origins to 1889 when the *New York World* used newly installed color presses to build circulation with a comic section. The importance of comic strips became obvious in 1895 when two titans of journalism, Joseph Pulitzer and William Randolph Hearst, waged a fierce battle over ownership of the most popular cartoon of the day, "The Yellow Kid."

In 1897, "The Katenjammer Kids" was introduced as the first modern comic strip with separate panels and speech balloons. In 1912 Hearst's *New York Evening Journal* published the first full page of comics. From the 1920s on, comics became a major source of readership with the introduction of "Blondie," "The Phantom," "Beetle Bailey," and the only recently concluded 50-year original run of "Peanuts."

Although not a major advertising vehicle, comics are used by a number of advertisers to reach millions of readers. Editors constantly evaluate comics as they choose among the hundreds of available strips. Research indicates that about six out of every ten newspaper readers see the comics on weekdays and that number increases on Sundays.[19] For those advertisers that want to use the comic sections,

EXHIBIT **10.12**

Sunday Supplements Use Newspapers as a Delivery System.

Courtesy of *Parade, USA Weekend, NY Times*. Photographer: Amanda B. Kamen.

there are networks that sell the comic sections in a variety of combinations so that advertisers can place an advertisement simultaneously in a number of papers.

THE ETHNIC AND FOREIGN LANGUAGE PRESS

With the changing multicultural environment in the United States, it is not surprising that a number of media are being introduced to reach these audiences with information, entertainment, and advertising. The role played by newspapers varies among the major ethnic markets. The largest and fastest-growing group of ethnic newspapers is Spanish-language newspapers. This growth coincides with an Hispanic population that is outpacing all other segments in the United States. In 2000, there were approximately 515 Hispanic newspapers with a combined circulation of 12.7 million and advertising revenues approaching $500 million. Unlike other members of the ethnic press, many successful Hispanic-oriented newspapers are dailies. For example, in just five years the daily newspaper *Hoy* has become the second largest circulation Spanish-language newspaper in the country with a circulation of over 90,000 in New York and over 60,000 in Chicago.[20]

The best evidence of the importance of the Hispanic press is the support and investment in these publications by major newspaper companies. For example, the Tribune Company produces *Hoy,* the Tribune company is also part owner of the Los Angeles–based *La Opinion, The Dallas Star Telegram* publishes *Diario La Estrella,* and the *Miami Herald* began publishing *El Nuevo Herald* in 1976 as an insert, but it has been a stand-alone publication since 1998.

Despite healthy circulation growth, Hispanic newspapers face a number of problems reaching a very fragmented Spanish-language population with roots in a number of countries with different cultures and product preferences. In addition, surveys show a wide disparity in language preferences. Some would like their information in Spanish, some in English, and still others prefer a bilingual publication. Despite these problems, the Hispanic press is among the fastest-growing sectors of the newspaper industry in both readers and advertising revenues.

The African American press has not shown the same economic vitality as its Hispanic counterpart. The black press was at its height from the 1930s to the early 1960s with almost 300 papers and total circulation of 4 million. These newspapers were sources of news, political agitation, and advertising. They contributed to much of the social progress made during this period. Among their significant legacies was the drive for passage of the Voting Rights Act and other civil rights legislation during the term of President Lyndon Johnson.

Ironically, the black press has suffered financially as opportunities have opened to African American citizens. During the 1960s and 1970s, the majority press began to incorporate coverage of black readers into their papers. As time went on, it was less important to have separate newspapers to cover news of African American readers.

Today, there are still a number of newspapers directed primarily to the African American audience. Virtually every major metropolitan center has at least one newspaper published for these readers. With a few exceptions such as the *Chicago Daily Defender*, virtually all are weeklies or biweeklies. During the last two decades, most black-oriented newspapers have lost both circulation and advertising revenue.

The mergers and consolidations, so common in the media industry, have also influenced the black press. For example, in 2000 PublicMedia Works, Inc., a black-owned multimedia group, bought Sengstacke Enterprises, which published the *Chicago Defender*, the *Michigan Courier, New Pittsburgh Courier*, and the *Memphis Tri-State Defender*. With stronger financial backing and synergism from a more broadly based media company, it may be that these African American newspapers can be restored to their former vigor.

A continuing problem for traditionally black newspapers is the preference among African Americans for television and a few selected magazines. Given this trend, it is not surprising that advertisers, particularly major national companies, have shifted significant dollars from newspapers to television, radio, and magazines with high African American audiences.

The Asian press faces many of the problems of both the Hispanic and African American press—only more so. Like the Hispanic population, Asians come from dozens of different cultures from China to Korea. Lumping them into a single category makes the same mistake as considering all Hispanics to be alike. Added to the problem is that the Asian population is not nearly as large as the Hispanic population so the large population centers to support a national Asian press system are not as readily available.

Still, there are a number of newspapers that serve the Asian population. New York City's Chinese-language *Brooklyn Chinese Monthly* and Japanese-language *The Rafu Shimpo* and San Jose's *Viet Mercury* all have circulations of between 20,000 to 50,000. Interestingly enough, the foreign language press in the United States is not a new phenomenon. Beginning in 1732 when Benjamin Franklin published *Philadephische Zeitung* (*The Philadelphia Newspaper*), the foreign language press has played a major role in this country. The increasingly multicultural nature of the United States is reflected in a growing number of newspapers available in more than 40 languages. Virtually every language is represented by at least one newspaper. From French, Italian, and German to Vietnamese, Chinese, and Arabic, every part of the world is represented by a publication unique to an ethnic group.

Ultimately, the success of the ethnic press is largely determined by the same formula used by mainstream media—advertising support. As population diversity increases along with growing economic power among these groups, we should expect to see growth in advertising-supported media directed at these cultural and ethnic members. The degree to which newspapers will fill this communication gap remains to be seen.

WEEKLY NEWSPAPERS

Weekly newspapers fall into a number of categories: suburban papers covering events within some portion of a larger metropolitan area, traditional rural weeklies providing local coverage, specialty weeklies covering politics or the arts, and free shoppers with little editorial content. According to the NAA, there are almost 6,700 weekly newspapers in the United States with a total circulation over 50 million.[21] During the last 30 years, the complexion of the weekly newspaper field has changed dramatically. Far from its rural, small town roots, the typical weekly is more likely to be located in a growing suburb and, rather than covering weddings and family reunions, its major topics are probably zoning disputes, overcrowded schools, crime, and how to control future growth while increasing the county's tax base.

As important as their content is the marketing strategy employed by many weeklies. More and more weeklies are part of networks. These networks are sometimes owned by a single company, including the major local daily newspaper, or they may be independent weeklies that joined a consortium to sell their space through a single rep. These groups recognize that the core city trade zone is no longer as economically viable as in previous years. Today, many cities exist only as suburban clusters with one or two large malls anchoring the advertising base. Retailers in these malls depend on a narrowly defined suburban area or neighborhood for their customers rather than an entire metropolitan area.

In some cases, these suburban newspaper groups exist as a supplement to the daily metropolitan newspaper. "Suburban presses thrive on copy that metros can't squeeze in—crimes and fires, real-estate transactions, school news, township meetings. Many weekly publishers have tapped the efficiencies earned by technology to add newsroom slots, improving the quality of their local, local coverage and expanding news holes."[22]

From an advertising standpoint, the strength of suburban weekly newspaper networks is that they can serve equally well small, local advertisers that may buy a single member of the group and national advertisers or major retailers that want high penetration into most of the suburban market. Weekly growth will be concentrated in suburban and urban areas for the foreseeable future. Weeklies, once rarely considered by large metro retailers or national advertisers, now play a more important role in the localized marketing strategies of many advertisers.

 ## SUMMARY

With over $44 billion in annual advertising revenues, about 55 million daily circulation, it is hard to view the future of newspapers as anything but bright. However, newspaper publishers recognize that they face a number of challenges if they are to maintain their historical position as a major source of news and advertising.

Despite a number of industry-wide efforts, newspapers have had limited success in convincing national advertisers that newspapers should be a major part of their marketing plans. Newspapers must standardize all aspects of the buying and placing of ads. The NNN's attempt to build a national newspaper network is the latest hope for a move in that direction.

However, no amount of standardization will outweigh the perception by national advertisers that newspapers are unfairly priced. The huge local/national rate differentials are a primary impediment to increased national advertising investment. In addition, newspapers must be prepared to offer national discounts and value-added programs on an equal basis with their retail clients.

As newspapers attempt to increase national advertising, their local advertising franchise is coming under increasing attack from a number of quarters. For example, local cable companies provide advertisers opportunities to cut in to major cable networks that provide targeted opportunities to reach viewers interested in news, music, or sports, often at a CPM less than that of the newspaper. Metropolitan newspapers are competing with suburban weeklies and shoppers intent on exploiting the move to the suburbs by both consumers and retailers.

Added to the traditional advertising competitors is the potential for Internet and other new digital-based media formats to take away both readers and the lucrative classified advertising market. Finally, newspapers are continuing to deal with a declining reader base as younger market segments are increasingly finding alternative sources for information and entertainment.

Newspapers have a major advantage over most of their competitors in that they are perceived as among the most influential and credible communication vehicles. They have an established brand that most competitors look upon with envy. As we discussed in this chapter, newspapers must continue to experiment with alternative methods of reaching audiences to prepare for the electronic superhighway of the future. Larger newspapers have already made a number of strides in the area of technology. However, the major challenge for the future is how to make these alternative delivery systems widely accepted and profitable.

 **REVIEW**

1. What are some of the factors that have eroded the local newspaper advertising base?

2. What was the major hurdle *USA Today* faced in becoming an effective national newspaper?

3. Many newspapers are offering "value-added" merchandising to advertisers. Explain.

4. What does the term *relationship marketing* mean in newspaper advertising?

5. Contrast zoned editions and total market coverage programs.

6. What are three major categories of newspaper advertising and how much advertising revenue does each account for?

7. What are the two major problems in newspapers gaining national advertising?

8. In what area have newspapers been most successful in achieving standardization?

9. What is the difference between the short rate and rebate?

10. What are the primary advantages of newspaper magazine supplements?

 **TAKE IT TO THE WEB**

The Political Newspaper Advertising Web site (**www.naa.org/political/ads/**) produced by the Newspaper Association of America attempts to inform the political consulting community about the benefits of newspaper advertising. List three possible advantages of newspaper advertising for political campaigns.

The New York Times **www.nytimes.com** and The Washington Post both **www. washingtonpost.com** offer electronic editions of their newspapers. Compare "front-page" coverage of national issues. Decide which edition would fit your needs and why.

The *Amarillo Globe News Online* edition has a variety of online advertisements for viewing at **www.amarillo.com/ads**. Check out a few of the ads to get an idea of the different types of ads that can be created.

# CHAPTER 11

Using Magazines

CHAPTER OBJECTIVES   The successful magazines of today are those that appeal to niche readers, particularly those in categories with special value to advertisers. Virtually all magazines are targeted to the special interests, businesses, demographics, or lifestyles of their readers. Magazines have adopted Internet technology to provide Web versions of their publications as a way to reach new readers, increase loyalty among their readers, and offer as value-added resources for advertisers. After reading this chapter, you will understand:

1. the history and development of the American magazine
2. how magazine space is sold to advertisers
3. the characteristics of consumer and trade publications
4. the role of magazines as a targeted advertising medium
5. the usefulness of magazines in national media plans
6. the effect of new communications technology on magazines

PROS

1. The number and range of specialized magazines provide advertisers with an opportunity to reach narrowly targeted audiences that are otherwise hard to reach.
2. Magazines provide strong visuals to enhance brand awareness and they have the ability to deliver a memorable message to their niche audiences.
3. Most magazines offer some form of regional and/or demographic editions to provide even greater targeting and opportunities for less-than-national advertisers to use magazines.
4. Magazines are portable, they have a long life, and they are often passed along to several readers. Business publications are especially useful as reference tools and leading publications within various industries offer advertisers an important forum for their messages.

CONS

1. In recent years, magazine audience growth has not kept up with increases in advertising rates. Magazines are among the most expensive media per prospect.
2. Advertising clutter has become a concern of many magazine advertisers. Many magazines approach 50 percent advertising content and, consequently, time spent with any single advertisement is often minimal.

3. Most magazines have relatively long advertising deadlines creating a lack of immediacy of the message. This long lead time can reduce flexibility and the ability of advertisers to react to fast-changing market conditions.

4. Despite the obvious advantages of magazine specialization, it means that a single magazine rarely reaches the majority of a market segment. Therefore, several magazines must be used or alternative media must supplement magazine buys. With more than 2,400 consumer magazines, advertisers often have difficulty in choosing the correct vehicle.

ADVERTISING AND CONSUMER MAGAZINES

In 2002, approximately 4.6 percent of U.S. advertising dollars were spent in magazines. The top 10 advertisers in magazines include packaged goods companies, automobile manufacturers, and a media company. (See Exhibit 11.1.)

With the introduction of television as a national advertising medium in the 1950s, magazines began to market themselves as a specialized medium to reach targeted prospects within the more general population. Unable to duplicate the huge numbers that the three television networks at the time could deliver, magazines based their economic future on the quality of audience they could deliver rather than the quantity. The modern niche magazine evolved in much the same way as narrowly formatted radio stations and both did so as a reaction to the ultimate mass medium, television.[1]

Today, magazines find that they must continue to change and adapt to a marketplace that exhibits both competitive and economic pressures. The magazine industry is undergoing changes in all aspects of the way it does business. In fact, there is little in the way of magazine production, distribution, circulation, or advertising that is not undergoing some type of transition.

The contemporary magazine faces many opportunities and challenges in the twenty-first century. Some of these problems are also concerns in both the radio and newspaper industries. The segmented and fragmented nature of magazine publishing means that publications are constantly seeking to define their audiences in narrower ways. Like the radio industry, magazines find that marketers invest an overwhelming percentage of their advertising dollars in the two or three leaders in a category, leaving a small share of advertising dollars to the others. This has led magazines to attempt to create editorial differentiation directed to interest groups that are often too small to support them financially. More than two-thirds of magazine titles have a circulation of less than 500,000 readers.

Just as magazines are similar in some respects to radio, they also have characteristics in common with newspapers. The costs of paper, delivery, and marketing to readers and advertisers are creating profitability problems even as gross revenues increase. The Syndicated data source Standard Rates and Data (SRDS) lists

EXHIBIT **11.1**

Top 10 Magazine Advertisers

Source: Copyright Crain Communications. Reprinted with permission. www.adage.com/page.cmspageID=995, 30 August 2003.

Rank	Advertiser	Measured Ad 2002	Spending in 2001	Medium % chg
1	Procter & Gamble Co.	$495.0	$471.6	5.0
2	General Motors Corp.	395.5	388.5	2.3
3	Altria Group	382.0	436.7	−12.5
4	Time Warner	272.7	232.4	17.3
5	DaimlerChrysler	259.5	258.3	0.5
6	Johnson & Johnson	256.2	211.3	21.3
7	Ford Motor Co.	251.3	303.3	−17.1
8	L'Oréal	240.8	236.0	2.1
9	Toyota Motor Corp.	223.3	199.3	12.0
10	Unilever	176.8	121.8	45.1

more than 2,400 consumer magazines. In such a competitive marketplace, gaining and maintaining readership is a constant headache for publishers. One only has to look at the number of discounted subscriptions for even the most popular magazines to see the extent of the problem.

More than five magazines are introduced each week covering topics as diverse as shopping, aviation, and religion. Although consumer magazines have a number of attributes in common, in many respects each magazine or category of magazines has unique problems and opportunities. In this atmosphere simultaneous successes and failures exist among different categories of publications. Women's service magazines, long a leading consumer magazine category, have experienced a number of significant changes in recent years. Although most remain profitable, the 125-year-old *McCall's* ceased publication and several others have revamped their designs and installed new editors in an attempt to fend off competition from women's lifestyle magazines such as *O, The Oprah Winfrey Magazine*, and *Real Simple*.[2]

In order to understand the contemporary consumer magazine industry, we have to examine two primary factors: (1) selectivity and (2) cost versus revenue considerations.

SELECTIVITY

Although magazines represent an eclectic continuum of titles and interests, the success stories are almost universally confined to narrow editorial interests and audience segments. A sampling of the top magazines in terms of ad revenues and advertising pages demonstrates this range of interests. For example, *Maxim, O, Business Week, Vogue*, and *Good Housekeeping* are among the leaders in advertising revenue growth in recent years.[3] Virtually the only thing these publications have in common is that they have been able to find a distinctive niche among both readers and advertisers.

Magazines are searching for the right editorial formula in a market that is increasingly fragmented. Although there are very few large homogeneous groups, there are homogeneous segments within more general groups. For example, publishers have long tried to reach the valuable teen market effectively. However, they find that no market as such exists. Boys and girls differ markedly not only in what they read but also in the amount of reading they do, with teen girls reading significantly more than boys.

Some teen magazines such as *Seventeen* and *YM* reach a large percentage of teenage girls, but the magazines most often read by teenage boys are larger circulation publications such as *Sports Illustrated*.[4] Advertisers seeking to reach teenagers can't afford to waste money using this kind of adult-targeted publication. Consequently, advertisers must be content to reach narrow slivers of the teen market one publication at a time. Although *Swimming World, NYC*, and *Transworld Surf* all reach small but important parts of the teen segment, none gives the type of coverage needed by businesses trying to reach the broader teen market. At the same time, publishers continue to try to develop magazines that will reach teens and bridge the elusive gender gap. The readership of *Teen People*, launched in 1997, is over 1.5 million readers—hardly a huge number but still encouraging given the lack of past success in developing a general teen publication.[5]

The Evolution of the Modern Magazine

Although selectivity is one of the keys to contemporary magazine success, audience and editorial selectivity is actually rooted in the historical development of magazines. The magazines of the mid-nineteenth century were targeted to audiences of special interests, sold at a high cost, and carried little advertising. Most magazines were literary, political, or religious in content and depended on readers or special interest groups to provide most of their financial support.

In the latter years of the nineteenth century a rising middle class, mass production, and national transportation combined to provide the opportunity for nationally distributed branded goods. The opportunities offered by national brands could be exploited only with the efficiencies of mass promotion. During the 1890s, a number of publishers provided the foundation for today's ad-supported, mass circulation magazine. Frank Munsey (*Munsey's*) and S. S. McClure (*McClure's*) were among the most successful publishers of the period. However, it was Cyrus H. Curtis who "developed the magical possibilities of national advertising, and demonstrated more clearly than anyone else that you could lose millions of dollars on your circulation by selling at a low price yet make more millions out of your advertising. . . . "[6] The formula was so successful that by 1900 his *Ladies Home Journal*, under the editorship of Edward Bok, was the first magazine to achieve a circulation of 1 million.

Until the advent of radio in the 1920s, magazines remained the only national advertising medium. With the introduction of radio, they had to share the national advertising dollar. Still, magazines were the only visual medium available to national manufacturers. However, when television came on the scene in the 1950s, people's reading habits became viewing habits, and national magazines had to change to survive.

The change from a mass to a class medium, which began in the competitive turmoil of the 1950s, continues up to the present. Perhaps the most dramatic indication of this change was the March 2000 demise of the monthly version of *Life* after 64 years of publication. This was followed by the failure of the much-hyped *Talk* magazine in 2002.

Today, even the largest circulation publications tend to appeal to a fairly narrowly defined market segment. For example, *Sports Illustrated, Time, Better Homes & Gardens*, and *Modern Maturity*, all among the circulation leaders, would not be classified as general editorial magazines. Only newspaper-distributed *Parade* and *USA Weekend* have both huge circulations and general appeal. However, as we discussed in Chapter 10, they are hybrid publications that many advertisers consider more newspapers than magazines.

Costs and Revenues   Consumer magazine revenues are huge and publications are largely dependent on advertising for their existence. Typical consumer magazine content consists of just over 46 percent advertising pages. While the advertising industry as a whole was hit hard by advertising cancellations following the September 11, 2001, tragedy, many publications were dealt a further blow when tobacco advertisers substantially curtailed or eliminated their advertising in magazines. Publishers are increasingly concerned about profitability. In 2002, the average audited magazine had a 3.2 percent loss in the number of ad pages. Not all publications suffered, however. Some magazine categories, such as parenting titles, posted ad page gains ranging from 5 to 21 percent in the same time period.[7]

Magazine cost concerns can be summarized largely in four primary categories:

1. *Marketing costs.* With the number of publications and a sometimes fickle readership, publishers are seeing significant increases in the cost of gaining and maintaining readers. Currently, approximately 85 percent of all consumer magazines are sold through subscriptions as opposed to newsstand sales. Consequently, it is imperative for publishers to invest huge sums of money in gaining new readers and keeping current ones. Likewise, escalating printing and postage costs have made direct-mail campaigns increasingly expensive.

   The competitive environment of magazine publishing prevents many publishers from raising the cost of subscriptions to cover higher expenses. According to the Magazine Publishers of America (MPA), since 1990 the average cost of a one-year subscription has fallen 16 percent. Overall, publishers are

EXHIBIT 11.2

Circulations of Parenting Titles Have Grown

Courtesy of Meredith Corporation and Gruner & Jahr USA Publishing.

losing almost $15 on every new subscription they sell and are depending on advertising to make up the deficit. Only about 50 percent of magazine revenue comes from advertising.

2. *Postage and distribution costs.* Since 1995, the U.S. Postal Service (USPS) has imposed several rate increases on magazine publishers. These increases have been far greater than the rate of inflation and they have caused a major rift between publishers and the USPS. As the president of the MPA, the leading industry trade association, pointed out, "There is no doubt that increases of this magnitude are a significant bottom-line issue for publishers, and . . . they will have to be reflected in increased costs for readers and advertisers over the next few years."[8]

   At the same time publishers are facing hefty increases in postal charges, they are witnessing similar boosts in the cost of newsstand distribution. Consolidation at both the retail and wholesale levels has created a more streamlined—and limited—distribution channel. Retailers, concerned with profit margins, are insisting that wholesalers limit the number of titles sent to them. "As a result, magazines seem to be losing the distribution levels they once took for granted. More outlets are being controlled by a smaller group of companies, making it harder for new titles to get to the newsstand."[9] The result has been an even greater reliance on subscription sales and a continuing upward cost spiral for publishers. Wal-Mart, which accounts for 15 percent of all single-copy magazine sales, for example, has chosen not to carry several men's magazines such as *Maxim, Stuff,* and *FHM.* Wal-Mart executives reported that they received many complaints about the suggestive nature of the covers on these so-called "laddie" magazines.[10]

3. *Concentration of advertisers.* Although a primary strength of magazines is their selectivity, it works against them in terms of broadly based advertising appeal. Magazines receive a disproportionate percentage of their advertising revenues from a very few product categories. Twelve categories account for 86 percent of all magazine advertising (see Exhibit 11.3). Just 10 companies provide almost one-third of all magazine revenues. In fact, Procter & Gamble, the top magazine advertiser in 2002, accounted for about 3 percent of total advertising revenue in magazines.

   If even one of these major advertisers decreases its magazine spending, it can have a significant impact on a number of publications. Advertising cutbacks are even more damaging to magazines geared to a very narrow interest

EXHIBIT **11.3**

Top Categories Account for 86% of All Magazine Spending

Source: Publishers Information Bureau. Courtesy of Magazine Publishers of America.

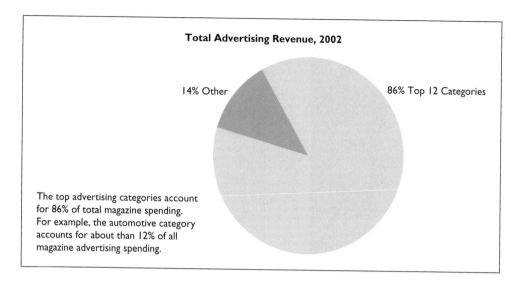

Total Advertising Revenue, 2002

14% Other

86% Top 12 Categories

The top advertising categories account for 86% of total magazine spending. For example, the automotive category accounts for about than 12% of all magazine advertising spending.

such as computing or golf. In these cases, a magazine has few practical alternatives to make up for the loss of even one large advertising client.

Over the past 20 years magazines have tried to insulate themselves from their dependence on advertising by shifting a disproportionate percentage of the cost of magazines to readers.

4. *Increases in discounting.* Growth in the amount magazines charge advertisers has slowed with the slowing of the economy. Many magazines are offering large discounts off of their regular rate card to regular advertisers. For example, advertisers who purchased as few as 4.8 pages in women's service magazines in 2003 received an average of 56.5 percent off of the rate card price. Discounts were much smaller in some categories, such as travel magazines, where 3.5 pages gave advertisers an average of 19 percent off of the rate card.[11] These discounts will likely decrease as the economy gets stronger and the number of ad pages increases.

Cross-Media Buys

In the twenty-first century, there are few magazine, television, or newspaper companies. They have been replaced by multimedia companies with interests in all traditional media as well as the Internet, interactive media, and various forms of direct response. Magazines are major players in many of these huge conglomerates and they form a symbiotic relationship with their media partners. From an advertising standpoint, it can be of great benefit for a magazine to be sold as part of a multimedia package—known as a **cross-media buy**.

cross-media buy
Several media or vehicles that are packaged to be sold to advertisers to gain a synergistic communication effect and efficiencies in purchasing time or space.

Because magazines reach niche audiences, they can often reach prime prospects who are light users of other media. Companies such as Time Warner, Disney, and News Corp. can offer advertisers hundreds of options for their advertising messages—often at a significant discount compared to buying the same properties on an individual basis. One of the most creative cross-media sellers is Disney, especially with its sports-oriented programming.

Because Disney is typical of many of the major media companies, let's look at how it handles some of its cross-media sales. One of Disney's most profitable franchises is *Monday Night Football* (MNF) through its ownership of the ABC Television Network. In order to gain synergism with some of its other media properties, Disney sold MNF as a package with ESPN's *Sunday Night Football* and the ESPN lead-in show to MNF. Because Disney is a major owner of ESPN, it was able to combine its ABC and ESPN football capital with both ABC and ESPN Web sites, *ESPN the Magazine*, and the ESPN radio show.

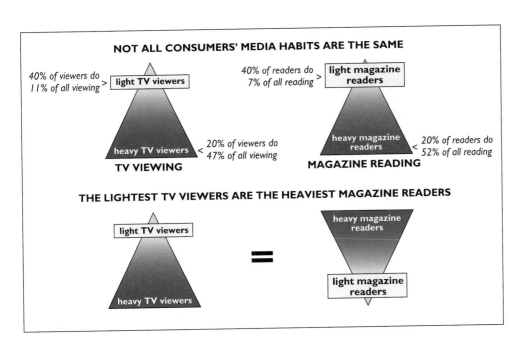

EXHIBIT **11.4**

Magazines' Role in the Media Mix

Source: MRI Media Quintiles. Courtesy of Magazine Publishers of America.

By combining the various Disney sports media and programs, an advertiser is able to reach a broad audience (e.g., the ESPN Web site audience is significantly younger than the audience of MNF), yet do so with only two basic media identities (ABC and ESPN). As the editor of *ESPN the Magazine* pointed out, "We (Disney) use all our brands to reinforce all the other brands. Personalities from the network write columns in the magazine. Linda Cohn is doing Linda Cohn's Hotline. At the end of an article we may say: 'For more on this, chat with the writer Wednesday at ESPN.com.'"[12]

One of the appealing features of cross-media buys for national advertisers is the complementary nature of magazines and television in reaching different segments of the general population. As Exhibit 11.4 demonstrates, television simply does not reach those prospects who are the heaviest users of magazines. There is such a strong inverse relationship between magazine readership and television viewing that mass advertisers are almost compelled to use both media. Not only does the combination of magazines and television extend reach, but it also provides a welcomed diversity of advertising themes and creative executions.

Despite some obvious advantages to advertisers in terms of lower media costs, they should be careful in analyzing cross-media buys. Marketers have to realize that a package of media owned by a single company is not necessarily the best choice in each category. For instance, even though we buy spots on MNF, are we sure that *ESPN the Magazine* is a better fit for our target audience than *Sports Illustrated*, or is ESPN.com a better Web choice than CNN/SI.com? There is nothing inherently wrong with cross-media buys as long as advertisers realize that they are put together largely for the benefit of the media companies. As single media companies come to control more and more media properties, the possibilities of building tailored media packages for individual advertisers increase.

MAGAZINES AS A NATIONAL ADVERTISING MEDIUM

Advantages of Magazines

Depending on the product and advertising objectives, magazines may offer a number of advantages as a primary or secondary media vehicle. This section will examine the primary considerations that determine whether or not magazines in general, or a particular title, will be included in a media plan.

1. *Does it work?* An advertiser is interested in the various advantages and characteristics of a medium only to the extent that these elements allow the medium to contribute to sales and profits. In recent years, the MPA has commissioned a series of studies conducted by independent research firms to determine the value of magazines as an advertising tool.

   In one study, results showed that for nine out of ten packaged goods measured, consumers exposed to magazine advertisements were more likely to purchase an advertised product than those who were not. In one case, the difference was 35 percent.[13] In another study, researchers found that magazines created high levels of brand awareness, especially when used in tandem with television. Advertising awareness increased 19 percent with magazines alone, compared to 16 percent with only television. However, when both magazines and television were used, advertising awareness was up 65 percent (see Exhibit 11.5).

2. *Audience selectivity.* Assuming that magazines can accomplish the required communication task, the next question is whether they can reach a specific target market. It is here that magazines excel. There is a magazine targeted for virtually every market segment and essentially everyone reads a magazine during a given month. There are magazines for almost every demographic and interest group. With magazines, total readership is often a secondary advertising consideration to how they reach target audiences. Approximately 70 percent of all consumer magazines have a circulation of less than 500,000.

3. *Long life and creative options.* Unlike a short-lived broadcast message or the daily newspaper, many magazines are kept and referred to over a long period of time, while some are passed along to other readers. In addition, magazines are portable with over three-fourths of magazine readers saying they sometimes read magazines in such places as doctors' offices, someone else's home, or at work. In this disposable media world, magazines are almost alone as a longterm medium. Magazines are often used as reference sources—articles are clipped, back issues are filed, and readers may go back to a favorite magazine numerous times before finally discarding it. Advertisers potentially benefit from each of these exposures.

   The magazine is also a visual medium with a number of creative options. Magazines offer advertisers a wide range of flexible formats such as double-page spreads, bright colors, and even product sampling. Magazines are particularly well suited to long copy. Discussions of detailed product attributes for automobiles and consumer electronics as well as advertising for financial services all lend themselves to magazines.

EXHIBIT 11.5

**Proving Magazine
Effectiveness**

Source: Millward Brown
International; Competitive Media
Reporting. Courtesy of Magazine
Publishers of America.

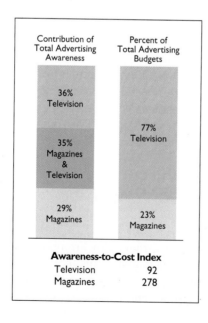

Don't hold your games back.

If you're not using an Intel® Pentium® 4 processor, it's game over. A Pentium 4 processor delivers split-second collision detection and blazing reaction time — the tools you need to stay in the game. To find out more go to intel.com/go/games.

intel inside pentium 4

EXHIBIT 11.6

This double-page spread takes advantage of magazines' ability to provide bright, high-quality color reproduction.

Courtesy of Euro RSCG MVBMS Partners and Jason Kreher.

4. *Availability of demographic and geographic editions.* In Chapter 10, we discussed newspaper zoning as a reaction to advertiser demand for selected segments of a publication's circulation. On a national scale, magazine demographic and geographic editions meet the same demands of large advertisers. It is very rare that a national magazine does not offer some type of regional or demographic breakout of its total circulation. These special editions are called **partial runs** and are so common and important to magazine advertising that they will be discussed separately in a later section of this chapter.

5. *Qualitative factors.* Advertisers are interested in the demographics of the audience, but they are also interested in how the audience thinks of themselves when they read a particular publication. The *Playboy* man and the *Cosmopolitan* woman are as much a matter of readers' perception as a reality. Unlike many other media, magazines offer advertisers relatively high levels of audience involvement. Consequently, magazine advertisers are more apt to use understated creative approaches as contrasted to the hard-sell advertising found in so many other media. Few media connect with their audiences to the degree that magazines do.

partial runs
When magazines offer less than their entire circulation to advertisers. Partial runs include demographic, geographic, and split-run editions.

In Chapter 7 we discussed the PRIZM system of categorizing people by their lifestyle characteristics. Increasingly, magazines use psychographic and lifestyle research to sell advertisers on the qualitative aspects of their audiences. Take a moment to review the various PRIZM categories in Exhibit 7.3a and try to match these audiences with the primary readers of some major magazines. Research indicates that magazines are preferred by a wide margin as a source of ideas and information on topics as diverse as automobiles, fashion, and fitness. This editorial connection with readers should carry over to a connection between readers and advertisers. When readers pick up *Fitness Swimmer, Money, Quarter Horse News,* or *PC Computing,* there is little doubt about their interests. These same readers also watch prime-time television, listen to the radio on the way home from work, and

I can go farther than anybody else out there.

I can stay out longer than anybody else out there.

Not that I'm competitive, or anything.

The 155-hp XL1200.

EXHIBIT 11.7

This ad for Yamaha watercraft uses an understated approach that works well in magazines.

Courtesy of VitroRobertson, Inc., Yamaha, and Marshall Harrington and Robert Holland, photographers.

see numerous billboards each day. However, it is difficult to anticipate what they are thinking about at these moments. On the other hand, specialized magazines can practically guarantee a synergism between reader and editorial content, which in many cases will carry over to advertising content.

Results of a study released by Knowledge Networks in June 2003 provide evidence that reader involvement is linked to advertising recall. They created an index of reader involvement that is calculated using reading frequency, amount of time spent reading, and preference for the magazine as measured by Mediamark Research, Inc. (MRI). Based on interviews with over 1,000 readers of five large circulation magazines (*Better Homes & Gardens, National Geographic, People, Reader's Digest,* and *TV Guide*), the results suggest that readers who are highly involved with a magazine are more likely to recall advertising in that magazine than low-involvement readers.[14]

Despite the recent attention given to the qualitative nature of magazines, the ultimate measure of magazines as an advertising vehicle will be determined by their ability to deliver prime prospects at a competitive cost. Media planners will continue to judge magazines on a cost-efficiency basis using criteria such as CPMs, and reach and frequency. The final evaluation of magazines, as with any medium, is whether they can deliver the right audience, at the right price, and in the right environment to help contribute to the achievement of the communication objectives.

Disadvantages of Magazine Advertising

Despite the many advantages that magazines offer advertisers, there are some important considerations for advertisers contemplating buying magazines.

1. *High cost.* As we have discussed, magazines generally are the most expensive medium on a CPM basis. It is not unusual for specialized magazines to have CPM levels of over $100 compared to $10 to $20 for even relatively low-rated television shows. However, in an era of niche marketing, the CPM is important only in relation to the prospects reached and the waste circulation of a medium. A related problem to overall cost is the fact that, as magazines have refined their audiences, many advertisers need to use several publications to achieve acceptable reach levels. As the number of magazines in a media schedule increases, so does the risk of duplicated audience levels, which often results in an unacceptable overlap in readership.

2. *Long **closing dates**.* Because of the printing process, most magazine advertisements must be prepared well ahead of publication. Unlike the spontaneity of radio and newspapers, magazines tend to be inflexible in reacting to changing market conditions. For example, a monthly magazine advertisement may run eight to ten weeks after an advertiser submits it. This long lead time makes it difficult for advertisers to react to current marketing conditions either in scheduling space or developing competitive copy. The long closing dates are one reason why most magazine copy is very general.

closing date
The date when all advertising material must be submitted to a publication.

Many magazines have one date for space reservations and a later date for when material must be submitted. Normally, the space contract cannot be canceled. It is not unusual for a magazine to require that space be reserved two months prior to publication and material sent six weeks before publication. Some publications require that material be submitted with the order.

Many magazines have sought to overcome the competitive disadvantage of long closing dates by providing **fast-close advertising**. As the name implies, fast-close allows advertisers to submit ads much closer to publication dates than standard closing dates allow. At one time, fast-close was very expensive, carrying a significant premium compared to other advertising. However, competitive pressure and improvements in print technology have seen many publications offer fast-close at little or no extra expense.

fast-close advertising
Some magazines offer short-notice ad deadlines, sometimes at a premium cost.

The remaining sections of this chapter will examine some specific features and techniques involved in buying advertising in magazines.

FEATURES OF MAGAZINE ADVERTISING

Partial-Run Magazine Editions

Partial-run editions refer to any magazine space buy that involves purchasing less than the entire circulation of a publication. The oldest and most common partial-run edition is the geographic edition, followed by demographic and vocational/special interest editions. Basically, the partial-run edition allows relatively large circulation magazines to compete with smaller niche publications for specialized advertisers.

As advertiser demand for more and more narrowly defined audiences has increased in recent years, magazines with fairly small circulations and/or specialized editorial formats have begun to offer some form of partial-run edition. Again, the smaller the circulation and the more specialized the content of a magazine, the more likely it is that the geographic edition will be the only partial run offered.

Of the more than 250 magazines that offer partial-run editions, many offer only geographic ones. On the other hand, major publications, especially large circulation weeklies such as *Time, Newsweek*, and *People*, offer dozens of options to advertisers. These publications combine both geographic and demographic editions so that an advertiser can reach *Time* readers who occupy positions in top management throughout the country or in selected locations. *Time*, for example, offers more than 400 ways to buy advertising in the magazine, including both demographic and regional editions.

As advertisers continue to demand that all media deliver narrowly targeted audiences and the techniques honed by direct mail and other direct-marketing media become more prevalent, we will see the majority of magazines offering some form of partial-run circulation. Computer technology and advances in high-speed printing also are allowing magazines to meet these advertiser requirements.

Split-Run Editions A special form of the partial-run edition is the split run. Whereas most partial-run editions are intended to meet special marketing requirements of advertisers, split-run editions normally are used by both advertisers and publishers for testing purposes. The simplest form of split-run test is when an advertiser buys a regional edition (a full run is usually not bought because of the expense) and runs different advertisements in every other issue.

Each advertisement is the same size and runs in the same position in the publication. The only difference between the advertisements is the element being tested. It may be a different headline, illustration, product benefit, or even price. A coupon is normally included and the advertiser, based on coupon response, can then determine the most productive version of the advertisement. This split-run technique is called an A/B split. Half of the audience gets version A and half version B.

As the competition for readers has grown, so has the use of split-run tests by magazines themselves. Magazines occasionally experiment with different covers for the same issue—either for testing purposes or to take advantage of some story of regional interest. The split-run technique has been instrumental in providing both publishers and advertisers with insight into how magazine advertising can be most effective. Partial-run and split-run editions offer a number of benefits to advertisers (and in some cases publishers).

1. Geographic editions allow advertisers to offer products only in areas where they are sold. For example, snow tires can be promoted in one area, regular tires in another.

2. Partial runs can localize advertising and support dealers or special offers from one region to another. As advertisers increasingly adopt local and regional strategies, the partial-run advantages will become even more apparent.

3. Split-run advertising allows advertisers to test various elements of a campaign in a realistic environment before embarking on a national rollout.

4. Regional editions allow national advertisers to develop closer ties with their retailers by listing regional outlets. This strategy also provides helpful information to consumers for products that lack widespread distribution.

Partial-run editions also have some disadvantages that make them less than ideal for all advertising situations.

1. CPM levels are usually much more expensive than full-run advertising in the same publication and close dates can be as much as a month earlier than other advertising.

2. In the case of demographic editions, the lack of newsstand distribution for these advertisements can be a major disadvantage if single-copy sales are significant for the publication.

3. Some publications bank their partial-run advertising in a special section set aside for such material. There also may be special restrictions placed on partial-run advertising. For example, such advertising often must be full page and only four color will be accepted by some publications.

selective binding
Binding different material directed to various reader segments in a single issue of a magazine.

Selective Binding Selective binding makes the customization of partial-run editions even more sophisticated. Although the concept of selective binding is essentially the same as that of partial-run advertising, it refers to different editorial material or large advertising sections that are placed in less than the full run of a publication. Using computer technology and sophisticated printing techniques, advertisers and publishers can develop advertising and editorial material specifically for one group or even for individual readers.

Selective binding first gained popularity among major farm publications in the early 1980s. Articles and advertisements were published only in editions delivered to farmers who raised certain types of crops or livestock. In recent years, selective binding has been offered to advertisers by consumer magazines on a limited basis.

Selective binding is most useful when there are significant subcategories of larger target markets within a publication's audience. Occasionally, a magazine will offer selective binding that is fully integrated into the editorial format of a magazine. More commonly, the technique is used with multipage advertising inserts distributed to a select audience segment identified by age, income, and so forth.

Selective binding is an example of a technology that, in order for it to be successful, must be advertiser driven. That is, advertisers must be convinced that it offers enough value to justify the additional expense. Many advertising executives think that the practical applications of selective binding are more apparent for business and farm publications than for consumer magazines where there are a number of selective publications.

Obviously, the widespread use of selective binding has major implications for direct mail. If the technique becomes widely used, advertisers could combine the individual characteristics of direct mail with the high-prestige environment of the magazine. Just as importantly, selective binding costs the advertiser about double what a normal magazine ad costs, but direct-mail CPMs generally run five times that of consumer magazines. Like most partial-run techniques, a major drawback of selective binding is that it can only be used for subscribers.

Because selective binding adopts some of the techniques of direct response, it also raises the same questions of readers' concerns with invasion of privacy. If subscribers are targeted by anything more than name and address, they may regard selective binding as inappropriate, with negative consequences to both the advertiser and magazine. Still, the idea that each reader can have a custom-made magazine, including both editorial and advertising material of specific interest to that individual, is an intriguing concept.

City Magazines Magazines directed to readers within a particular city are not a new idea. *Town Topics* was published in New York City in the late nineteenth century, but most observers credit *San Diego* magazine, first published in the 1940s, as the forerunner of the modern city magazine. Today, city magazines are available in virtually every major city.

At one time, city magazines were often regarded as nothing more than booster publications for a city. Many of them were published by a local business or tourism organization and they offered little in terms of hard news or in-depth reporting. Although most city magazines continue to feature lifestyle and entertainment stories, a growing number of publications report on local business, technology, and medical issues. Many publishers are combining the traditional strengths of the city magazines with specialized publication content and initiating such titles as *Chicago Bride, Atlanta Business Chronicle*, or the *Fulton County Reporter*, a publication devoted to the Atlanta legal scene.

Because of the generally upscale readership of city magazines, they are popular with upscale local and regional firms and even some national advertisers that want to target individual markets. Advertising revenues are very cyclical. A soft economy often leads to a decrease in ad pages because of the downturn in retailing and automobile sales, two prime categories of city magazine advertising. In addition, city magazines are normally a supplement to mainline advertising for many of these magazines' clients. Consequently, when the advertising market goes soft, they are often among the first media to be dropped. Whereas the city magazine was formerly a domain of large metropolitan centers, we now find successful publications in cities with populations of less than 100,000 (e.g., Macon, Georgia).

City publications are in some ways a hybrid between small circulation specialty publications and the partial-run editions of national magazines. However, they have an advantage over both in reaching upscale local audiences with editorial and advertising content specifically directed to the special, local interests of their prime prospects. Approximately 90 city and regional magazines have come together to sell their space to advertisers as a magazine network. Advertisers can buy space in groups of these magazines with one single insertion order at a cheaper price than if they were buying space in each separately. This allows the magazines to compete more effectively with national magazines. The combined total circulation of the magazines in the network is over 18 million.[15]

Custom Publishing

Another growing and specialized area of magazine publishing is custom publishing. It is one of the fastest-growing sectors of the magazine business and consists of advertiser-produced publications intended to reach prospects or current customers in a communication environment totally controlled by the marketer. These publications are a cross between direct mail and traditional magazine publishing. "Once a niche business dominated by specialty publishing houses with limited—if any—editorial credentials, custom publishing is now a mainstream discipline crowded with big-name publishers in search of new profit engines."[16]

Custom publishing is not a new concept. In 1949, General Motors commissioned its agency, Campbell-Ewald, to publish *Friends*, a magazine sent to Chevrolet car and truck owners. However, since those early days, custom magazines account for expenditures of $700 million with more and more companies seeing them as an extension of their direct-response marketing. Most mainline magazine publishers such as Time Inc., Meredith, and Hearst have customized publishing divisions.

The objectives of custom publishing vary from company to company. For Lincoln, *CitySource* was a way of introducing its Lincoln LS sport sedan. *Tomorrow* is published by DaimlerChrysler to reach its more than 75,000 United Auto Workers (UAW) employees. Sabre Group uses *VirtuallyThere* as a value-added guidebook for customers booking trips through its affiliated travel agencies.

Regardless of the specific use of custom publishing, to be successful it needs to function as part of a planned and integrated marketing program. Custom magazines can be a valuable tool for companies to speak directly to their customers and prospects. The current status of custom publishing is made possible by market research. "People and their buying patterns have never been segmented so precisely before. Most marketers today know a lot about the individual man, woman, or child buying their products, and custom media is considered the best way to talk to them."[17]

Some custom-published magazines are evolving to look much like traditional publications. One of the most obvious features of this transition is the acceptance of outside (albeit noncompetitive) advertising by some publications. It is sometimes hard to tell them from other magazines on the magazine racks. For example, *Crunch Magazine*, launched by Crunch Fitness Centers, contains advertising by many advertisers and sells at newsstands for $4.99.[18] Some of these magazines are less expensive than other magazines in their category. Walgreen's *Elite Teen* magazine, for example, is priced at just 99¢ at Walgreen's stores.

MAGAZINE ELEMENTS

Once an advertiser has made the hard choice of which magazine to select among the hundreds of options, the job is not over. Now the media planner must decide the size, color, placement, and format that will best serve the advertiser's marketing goals and the creative message.

Sizes

The page size of a magazine is the type area, not the size of the actual page. For convenience, the size of most magazines is characterized as standard size (about 8 by 10 inches, like *Time*) or small (about 4⅜ by 6½ inches, like *Reader's Digest*). There also are a few oversized publications such as *Rolling Stone*, but they are the exception. When you are ready to order advertising space and send creative materials to a publication, you must get the exact sizes from the publication because sizes may have changed.

Position, Color, and Size of Magazine Advertising

Space in magazines is generally sold in terms of full pages and fractions thereof (half pages, quarter pages, three columns or one column; see Exhibit 11.9). The small advertisements in the classified pages of many magazines are generally sold by the line. Magazine covers are the most expensive positions in most magazines, although some magazines offer deep discounts for large advertisers. The front cover of a magazine is called the first cover, which is seldom, if ever, sold in American consumer magazines (although it is sold in business publications). The inside of the front cover is called the second cover, the inside of the back cover is the third cover, and the back cover is the fourth cover.

Advertisers are trying constantly to determine the optimum combination of color, size, and placement that will achieve the highest readership. Exhibit 11.10 shows 21 different combinations of elements and the effect that they have on recall

EXHIBIT **11.9**

Various Ways of Using Magazine Space

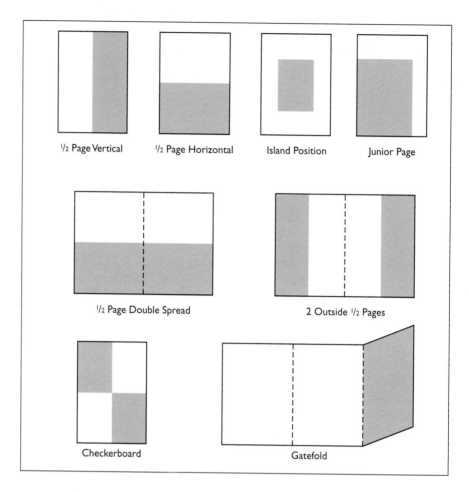

compared to a standard four-color advertisement. These findings are consistent with most research that has determined that four-color advertising is worth the additional cost in terms of added attention and readership. By the same token, this same research indicates that a two-color advertisement fails to add to reader attention levels and is usually not worth the additional expense.

EXHIBIT **11.10**

Readership by Advertising Unit Type

Source: Magazine Dimensions, 1999 Media Dynamics, Inc., based on Burke, Starch and Gallup & Robinson. Courtesy of Magazine Publishers of America.

Ad Type	Recall Index
Page 4C Ad	**100%**
4th Cover (4C)	120
2nd Cover (4C)	112
3rd Cover (4C)	90
Inside Spread (4C)	130
Inside Spread (2C)	110
Inside Spread (B&W)	95
Vertical 2/3 Page (4C)	81
Horizontal 1/2 Page (4C)	72
Vertical 1/3 Page (4C)	60
Horizontal 1/3 Page (4C)	60
Vertical 2/3 Page (2C)	60
Vertical 2/3 Page (B&W)	60
Horizontal 1/2 Page (2C)	56
Horizontal 1/2 Page (B&W)	56
Horizontal 1/3 Page (2C)	47
Horizontal 1/3 Page (B&W)	47
Vertical 1/3 Page (2C)	42
Vertical 1/3 Page (B&W)	42
Page 2C	78
Page (B&W)	74

Another concern of many advertisers is the placement of an advertisement within a magazine. Traditionally, many advertisers have regarded right-hand pages at the front of the book, preferably near related editorial matter, as the ideal ad placement. "FFRHPOE" or "far forward, right-hand page opposite editorial" is routinely stamped on many insertion orders delivered to magazines in spite of no evidence that these positions add any value to an advertisement.

As the size of an advertisement increases, the audience does not grow proportionately (nor does the cost). For example, in Exhibit 11.10, note that a half-page, four-color advertisement achieves 72 percent of the impact of a full-page unit. If we run a two-page spread, we increase readership by 30 percent (even though we have increased the space by 100 percent). The reason, of course, is that as size increases there are not enough nonexposed readers remaining to continue to increase readership at the same rate.

Although the increase in audience exposures is not proportionate to increases in magazine ad size, larger space allows more creative flexibility. Advertising objectives that require long copy can be much more effectively presented in a larger space. Larger advertisements have greater impact and recall over time, even though in the short term they don't score significantly higher than smaller space advertisements. It is important to remember that these studies held creative content constant while in reality the quality of the message is perhaps the most important variable in advertising readership and recall. These findings point out again that the specific objectives and creative approach must be considered in designing magazine advertising.

Bleed Pages

Magazine advertising is able to use a number of formats and designs unavailable or impractical in other media. A common technique is bleed advertising in which the ad

EXHIBIT 11.11

Two-Page Spread Bleed Advertisement

Courtesy of VitroRobertson, Inc., Taylor, and Stephanie Menvez, photographer.

bleed
Printed matter that runs over the edges of an outdoor board or of a page, leaving no margin.

runs all the way to the edge of the page with no border. **Bleed** ads are used to gain attention and use all the space available. Without a border, the advertisement does not have the appearance of being confined to a particular space. Typically, bleed advertising will be seen by 10 to 15 percent more readers than nonbleed advertising.

There is no standardization for premium charges for bleed advertising. In the competitive marketplace for magazine advertising, a number of publications offer bleed advertising at no charge as a value-added or extra incentive for advertisers. Even when a magazine has a standard charge for bleed advertising, large advertisers often make these charges a point of negotiation with publishers. With modern printing equipment, most advertisers contend that bleed charges are an unjustified anachronism and many resent even minimal charges for bleed.

INSERTS AND MULTIPLE-PAGE UNITS

Multiple-page advertising covers a broad spectrum of insertions. The most common form of multipage advertising is a facing, two-page spread. Among the most frequent users of multipage inserts and spreads are automobile manufacturers. They face an extremely competitive environment, they need to show their cars in the most favorable, bigger-than-life fashion, and they often have an in-depth story to tell about the features of their brands—all reasons to use large space advertising. A spread increases the impact of the message and eliminates any competition for the consumer's attention. Gatefold spreads come off the front cover and normally are either two or three pages.

Cost is a major consideration when planning inserts. Although the insert will be less expensive per page than run-of-publication advertising, the advertiser is still concentrating significant dollars in the publications that carry the inserts. This expense will reduce the number of media vehicles that can be included in a media schedule. Because an advertiser is putting a disproportionate share of advertising into one or a few vehicles, the likely result is a reduction in reach and frequency compared to a more traditional media plan.

Finally, one of the problems with the growing use of multiple-page advertising is that it has lost much of its novelty to consumers. When a reader can turn to practically any consumer magazine and find numerous examples of such advertising, they come to be taken for granted, even by serious prospects. It is important to work closely with the creative team to make sure that such expensive space is going to be fully utilized with a meaningful message. The most effective multiple-page units are for advertisers with an interesting product, a new story to tell, and an interested and involved group of prospects.

HOW SPACE IS SOLD

Advertising Rates, Negotiation, and Merchandising

In the competitive world of magazine advertising, it is not surprising that publishers are constantly seeking merchandising and value-added programs to differentiate their titles from others in a particular category. Unfortunately, many publishers find themselves in a situation in which advertising rates are the primary consideration for most advertisers.

Scheduling and buying full-run magazine advertising was at one time the easiest function for a media planner. Clients usually bought full-page advertisements, circulations were audited, discounts for frequent usage were obtainable from straightforward rate cards, and rates were consistent for every advertiser that qualified for available discounts. In addition, most advertisers would buy only a few high-circulation publications.

The rate situation underwent fundamental changes when magazine advertising experienced a downturn in revenues during the 1980s. Faced with flat advertising revenues and new publications continually coming into the market, magazines began to negotiate with individual advertisers for special rates. This practice of one-to-one negotiation is called going off the card. Starting as a short-term fix during a period of weak advertising spending, negotiation has become a common practice among magazines with many advertisers regarding the rate card as simply a point at which to start negotiation.

Obviously, publishers would like to maintain rate integrity and attempt to do so with a number of merchandising and value-added plans. One of the most common means of magazine merchandising is through brand extensions. The Good Housekeeping Seal is one of the oldest and most recognized merchandising tools. The publication sponsors test laboratories through which readers are offered a guarantee of the quality of the products and services advertised in the publication. The program is almost 100 years old and still going strong.

Magazine merchandising services take numerous forms and they are used by virtually every major magazine. *Better Homes & Gardens* produces greeting cards, provides real estate services, and franchises garden centers. Meanwhile, consumers can buy *Family Circle* classical CDs, *Field & Stream* bass lures, and *Popular Mechanics* work boots. In order to promote its *Parenting* magazine, Time Inc. bought a product sampling company, First Moments, that delivers products to new mothers in hospitals. Ownership of First Moments allows the delivery of *Parenting* magazine, subscription offers, and related samples to build relationships with both readers and advertisers.[19]

The key to merchandising programs is to coordinate a magazine's reputation and expertise with marketing techniques that help advertisers sell their products. Among the more traditional merchandising programs are trade shows, conferences, newsletters, database services, and copromotions such as point of purchase that highlights certain advertisers that are using a publication. For example, *Cooking Light* sponsored a series of *Cooking Light* Supper Club dinners in Manhattan to demonstrate the products of its advertisers. Attendees were charged about $50 for a value of $100 or more.[20] All of these techniques allow advertisers to extend the message of their advertising into related areas and provide an added value to their magazine advertising buy.

Magazine Merchandising and the Internet

Magazines were among the earliest media to utilize the Internet as part of their overall marketing and merchandising plans and they remain heavily involved in online endeavors. The most common use of the Internet by publishers is the online version of print publications. Hundreds of publications offer full or edited online versions of their magazines. These online vehicles may be advertiser supported, used as a value added for readers and advertisers, and/or intended to extend the audience reach of the core magazine to online users.

Magazines also have entered into numerous joint ventures with other businesses for various online objectives. Many of the online sites are established as part of cross-media programs as in the CNN/SI mentioned earlier. In other cases, magazines have coventured with established sites to create a synergy between the expertise of an online company and the visibility of a magazine. Hearst's purchase of an interest in Women.com allowed the company to promote its women's books (e.g., *Redbook, Country Living,* and *Good Housekeeping*) in a compatible environment. Interestingly, the relationship between magazines and online interests has moved in both directions. For example, Krause Publications published *eBay Magazine* and Ziff-Davis introduced *Yahoo! Internet Life* magazine. As a special offer to AOL subscribers, Time-Warner decided to make its popular online version of *People* magazine, People.com, available only to AOL subscribers.

In addition, a number of titles have begun to use the Internet as a traditional e-commerce business. For example, Meredith offers its *Better Homes & Gardens* books and a select group of other products on its Web site. Regardless of the objectives of a magazine's online presence, the selective, targeted audiences of magazines offer an ideal marriage for the one-to-one marketing of the Internet.

Magazine Rate Structure

In the examples that follow, we will assume the advertiser is making a full-run magazine buy. That is, the entire circulation of the publication is being purchased. An advertiser buying a partial-run edition will consider a number of other options. A typical rate card for a weekly publication might look like this:

Ebony's **Color Rates (4-color)**

Space	1 ti	3 ti	6 ti	12 ti
1 page	57,934	56,775	55,037	52,141
2/3 page	48,277	47,311	45,863	43,449
1/2 page	38,802	38,026	36,862	34,922
1/3 page	26,651	26,118	25,318	23,986

An advertiser buying this publication will pay $57,934 for a one-time, four-color, full-page insertion. The advertiser that buys at least 12 full-page insertions in the publication will pay only $52,141 per ad for the same space.

Before placing a magazine on its advertising schedule, the advertiser will compute the cost efficiency of that publication against others being considered. Let's assume that *Ebony* has an average circulation of 1,841,715. Using the CPM formula discussed earlier, we can calculate the efficiency of the publication as follows:

$$\text{CPM} = \frac{\text{cost per page}}{\text{circulation (000)}} = \frac{57,934}{1,841} = \$31.47$$

Discounts

Frequency and Volume Discounts　The one-time, full-page rate of a publication is referred to as its basic, or open rate. In the case of *Ebony*, its open rate is $57,934. All discounts are computed from that rate. Most publications present their discounts on a per-page basis in which rates vary according to frequency of insertion during a 12-month period, as we have done here. However, some publications use either **frequency** or volume discounts based on the number of pages run. For instance, *InStyle* magazine frequency discounts look like this:

frequency
In media exposure the number of times an individual or household is exposed to a medium within a given period of time.

Frequency	Discount %
3 times to 5 times	4
6 times to 8 times	6
9 times to 11 times	9
12 times to 17 times	12

In a similar fashion, the volume discount gives a larger percentage discount based on the total dollar volume spent for advertising during a year. The volume discount is convenient for advertisers that are combining a number of insertions of different space units or that are using a number of partial-run insertions. A volume discount might be offered as follows:

Volume, $	Discount %
83,000 or more	8
125,000 or more	11
180,000 or more	17
260,000 or more	20

Other Discounts In addition to discounts for volume and frequency, individual magazines offer a number of specialized discounts, usually for their largest advertisers. Among the more common discounts in this category is a lower per-page price for advertisers that combine buys with other publications or media owned by the same magazine group. We previously discussed these arrangements in the section on cross-media buys. As media companies become larger, the opportunities for these buys will be more numerous. Cross-media discounts operate similarly to volume discounts except advertisers accumulate credit across a number of media vehicles.

In addition, some magazines offer discounts called continuity discounts for advertisers that agree to advertise at a certain rate over a period of time, usually two years. These discounts are sometimes designed to guarantee the magazine a certain level of advertising pages even in normally slack months, such as January and July, in exchange for a lower cost to the advertiser. Continuity discounts might be compared to scatter plans in network television advertising in which advertisers buy lower-rated shows in order to gain commercials on the most popular programs. In magazine continuity discounts, advertisers accept "off periods" to get lower rates during peak advertising seasons. In both cases, the media are offering the discount to manage their time and space inventory.

The Magazine Short Rate

As we have seen, most magazine discounts are based on the amount of space bought within a year. However, the publisher normally requires that payment be made within 30 days of billing. Therefore, an advertiser and a publisher sign a space contract at the beginning of the year and agree to make adjustments at the end of the year if the space usage estimates are incorrect. If the advertiser uses less space than estimated, the publisher adjusts using a higher-than-contracted rate. If more space is used, the publisher adjusts using a lower rate.

Let's look at a typical short rate, using the rate card for *Ebony*. Acme hair care products contracted with *Ebony* to run six pages of advertising during the coming year. At the end of the year, Acme had only run five pages. Therefore, it was short the rate for which it had contracted and an adjustment had to be made, as follows:

Ran 5 times. Paid the 6-time rate of $55,037 per page $= (5 \times 55,037)$

$275,185

Earned only the 3-time rate of $56,775 per page $= (5 \times 56,775)$

$283,875

Short rate due $(\$283,875 - \$275,185) = \$8,690$

Some publishers charge the top (basic) rate throughout the year but state in the contract "rate credit when earned." If the advertiser earns a better rate, the publisher gives a refund. If the publisher sees that an advertiser is not running sufficient pages during the year to earn the low rate on which the contract was based, the publisher sends a bill at the short rate for space already used and bills further ads at the higher rate earned. Failure to keep short rates in mind when you are reducing your original schedule can lead to unwelcome surprises.

Magazine Dates

There are three sets of dates to be aware of in planning and buying magazine space:

1. *Cover date:* the date appearing on the cover
2. *On-sale date:* the date on which the magazine is issued (the January issue of a magazine may come out on December 5, which is important to know if you are planning a Christmas ad)
3. *Closing date:* the date when the print or plates needed to print the ad must be in the publisher's hands in order to make a particular issue

For example:

Latina
(published monthly)
- March issue
- On sale February 19
- Closes December 28

People
(published weekly)
- March 4 issue
- On sale February 22
- Closes January 14

Magazine Networks

The term *network*, of course, comes from broadcast when affiliated stations cooperated to bring audiences national programming as early as the 1920s. In recent years, a special adaptation of the network concept has been employed by virtually every medium as a means of offering advertisers a convenient and efficient means of buying multiple vehicles. There are newspaper networks, outdoor networks, and even networks for direct-mail inserts and comic strips. Magazines are no exception.

As we mentioned earlier, one of the problems of the growing specialization in magazines is that advertisers increasingly need to buy a number of titles to achieve reach and frequency goals. Another consequence of smaller circulations is that magazine CPM levels have increased. Many large national advertisers have complained about both the difficulty of buying numerous magazines and the higher CPMs. In order to accommodate these advertisers, a number of publishers have established **magazine networks.** As with networks in other media, their intent is to make it possible for an advertiser to purchase several publications simultaneously with one insertion order, one bill, and often significant savings compared to buying the same magazines individually.

magazine networks
Groups of magazines that can be purchased together using one insertion order and paying a single invoice.

Currently, there are more than 100 magazine networks, some representing dozens of different titles. The network concept allows several magazines to compete for advertisers by offering lower CPMs and delivering a larger audience than any single publication. Networks must be carefully tailored to reach a particular audience segment with as little waste circulation or audience duplication as possible. Although there are a number of magazine networks, they generally fall into two categories.

1. *Single publisher networks.* Here a network is offered by a single publisher that owns several magazines and will allow advertisers to buy all or any number of these publications as a group. For example, Hearst Magazine Group publishes over 20 magazines and allows advertisers that use multiple titles to build network discounts.

   The publisher network can be especially effective in encouraging a media buyer to choose among similar magazines. For example, let's assume a media buyer has decided to purchase space in *Cosmopolitan* and *Town and Country,* both Hearst magazines. A third option is to purchase either *Redbook,* another Hearst magazine, or *Ladies Home Journal.* Assuming both magazines meet the advertising criteria of a particular client, the discounts available from buying *Redbook* as part of the Hearst network may well sway the media buyer in that direction.

   To a degree, the single publisher network is being replaced by cross-media buying. As more and more magazines become part of media conglomerates, they no longer confine a "network" buy to magazines but broaden the concept to all media vehicles owned by a particular company.

2. *Independent networks.* The second type of magazine network is made up of different publishers that market magazines with similar audience appeals. A rep firm that contracts individually with each publisher and then sells advertising for magazines within the group usually offers these networks. The concept is similar to the space wholesaling that George Rowell began in the 1850s, discussed in Chapter 5. Media Networks, Inc., the largest independent network firm, offers several networks, each geared to a specific audience. For example, the Media Networks Executive Network consists of seven magazines including *Fortune* and *Business Week.* Even though different publishers own these magazines, they know that there are advantages to cooperating in selling space to large advertisers.

EXHIBIT 11.12

This magazine network is designed to reach business executives.

Courtesy of Amanda B. Kamen, photographer.

MAGAZINE CIRCULATION

As with any medium, accurate magazine readership measurement is extremely important to advertisers. Media planners don't buy magazines, television spots, or outdoor signs—they buy audiences. More specifically, they buy certain groups of people who are customers or prospects for their products. In the magazine industry there are two distinct methods of determining their audiences: *paid circulation and the rate base.*

The more commonly used and reliable method of audience measurement is paid circulation. Most major consumer magazines have their circulations audited by an outside company. Magazine rates are based on the circulation that a publisher promises to deliver to advertisers, referred to as the guaranteed circulation. Because the guaranteed circulation is the number of readers advertisers purchase, it also is referred to as the **rate base,** or the circulation on which advertising rates for a specific magazine are based.

rate base
The circulation that magazines guarantee advertisers in computing advertising costs.

You will recall from our earlier discussion that magazine publishers are finding it increasingly expensive to maintain high readership levels. As circulation for a magazine rises, the increases are sometimes created by marginally interested readers who subscribed because of special introductory deals, among other things. Publishers usually find it very expensive to keep these fringe readers when it is time to renew subscriptions. Added to the problem is the fact that major auditing organizations, such as the Audit Bureau of Circulations (ABC), require that a subscriber must pay at least 50 percent of the full subscription price to be counted as a reader. Consequently, magazines are limited in the marketing promotions they can use and still count readers as paid for auditing purposes.

In the last few years, a number of major magazines including *TV Guide* and *Reader's Digest* have lowered their rate bases substantially. Rate base management is fundamentally a financial consideration. As circulation rises, advertising rates also will increase. However, if publishers are spending more on marketing to keep circulation figures artificially higher than they can gain in increased advertising revenue, it doesn't make economic sense to continue to do it.

Magazine circulation figures can vary a great deal from month to month largely due to newsstand sales. In the past, many publishers have averaged their circulation over a six- or twelve-month period. According to *The Wall Street Journal,* ". . . magazines can finesse their monthly circulation figures to make it appear as though they are consistently delivering the rate base advertisers expect. Whether or not this fudging is deliberate, the monthly information provided by publishers—which is widely used to judge a magazine's success—is often inaccurate."[21] Many publishers argue that they should be judged by ABC on an average monthly circulation basis rather than on the circulation of individual issues.

Advertisers, on the other hand, are more interested in the audience delivered by particular issues of a magazine that contain their clients' advertising. As is typical for many advertising media decision makers, Robin Steinberg, a Vice President at the media-buying agency Carat North America, says she now demands compensation for her client if a magazine misses its circulation goal for an issue that contains her client's advertising.[22]

It is clear that advertisers would rather buy space in magazines with a quality readership, that is, those readers who are interested in both the magazine and its advertising. By the same token, advertisers generally will gravitate to those publications with the largest number of readers within their target audience. Common sense tells us that publishers, particularly of second-tier magazines, will continue to explore whatever steps necessary to keep circulation levels as high as possible within their profit constraints.

A magazine does not necessarily offer a guaranteed rate base to advertisers. In fact, a number of audited publications do not make a specific guaranteed circulation claim. These publishers provide advertisers with accurate circulation for past issues, but they don't take any risk for circulation shortfalls in the future. In the volatile world of magazine advertising, many smaller magazines do not want to deal with the financial problems of make-goods related to audience decreases.

Readership In magazine terminology *readership* usually combines paid circulation (subscribers and newsstand purchasers) with pass-along readers. For example, according to ABC, *Time* has a paid circulation of 4.1 million. According to Mediamark Research, Inc. *Time* has 23.1 million readers. This means that there are approximately 5.6 readers per copy (RPC).[23] The more general the publication's editorial, the more likely it is to have significant pass-along readership.

Many advertisers and even magazine publishers are concerned about the use of readership as a substitute for paid circulation. Historically, the use of readership is rooted in the magazine industry's competition with television. As we discussed in the last section, magazines are retrenching somewhat from a "numbers at any cost" circulation mentality and again selling quality of readership. Nevertheless, publishers want to keep readership surveys to take into account fairly their total readers.

It would seem that total readership, accurately measured, would be a reasonable approach to measuring magazine audiences. The problem arises from the fact that many media buyers regard pass-along readers of consumer magazines as inherently inferior to paid circulation. Between those advertisers that see no value in readership and those that view it as equal to paid circulation, there is probably a middle ground. As in most marketing and advertising questions, the real answer is determined by the specific objectives of the publication and its readers. However, regardless of the value that one placed on readership, most acknowledge that it is different from paid circulation.

MEASURING MAGAZINE AUDIENCES

We now turn to the issue of how publishers verify the circulation and readership of their magazines. Advertisers normally will not purchase a magazine unless its publisher can provide independent verification of the magazine's readership. In magazine terminology, readership has two distinct meanings. One refers to the time spent with a publication. The other, and the one we will discuss here, includes all readers of a magazine as contrasted to only those who buy a publication.

The Audit Bureau of Circulations The Audit Bureau of Circulations (ABC) is the largest of several auditing organizations that verify magazine circulation. The ABC provides two basic services: the Publisher's Statements or "pink sheets" (because of their color), which report six-month periods ending June 30 and December 31; and the ABC Audit, or "white sheets," which annually audits the data provided in the Publisher's Statements. The ABC reports total circulation, as well as circulation figures by state, by county size, and per issue during each six-month period. ABC reports also state the manner in which circulation was obtained—for example, by subscription or by newsstand sales—and any discounts or premiums provided to subscribers. Exhibit 11.13 is a sample of the ABC Publisher's Statement.

The ABC reports are matter-of-fact documents that deal only with primary readers. They do not offer information about product usage, demographic characteristics of readers, or pass-along readership. As we discussed in the previous section, the ABC continues to be embroiled in the debate over how to define paid circulation. The controversy is yet another indication of the importance that both publishers and advertisers place on the accuracy of audience data.

KLEPPNER VIEWPOINT

MARY BETH BURNER

Advertising Research Manager,
Southern Progress Corporation, a subsidiary of Time Inc.

R esearch. The mere word systematically invokes an immediate thought of pocket protectors, horn-rimmed glasses, and calculators. Bookish individuals who spend hours studying every minute detail of the inner workings then report these analyses in reams of charts, graphs, and tables of data. Well, you're right. As a manager of consumer magazine advertising research, I'm guilty as charged (minus the pocket protector). But there are countless more descriptors that should also be part of the stereotype for media researchers: strategist, creative mind, marketer, psychologist, brand developer, and armed competitor.

Magazine advertising researchers use strategic skills and creative analyses of data to demonstrate to advertising media decision makers that a magazine is the most efficient buy, has the most compatible editorial for a product's message, or can provide the best reach of a target market. Magazine selling in the ad industry is akin to brand marketing within the consumer marketplace. A sales representative from a consumer magazine seeks to have his or her product (the magazine ad space) included in the agency's media plan above other competitors considered. An integral part of the magazine selling process, research data are the "currency" with which comparisons of magazines are made. Who reads the magazine? What are the demographics of readers? How much time do they spend reading the magazine? How much do they spend on the client's product? What are desirable positions within the magazine editorial to place a particular ad? Did readers notice and absorb the advertisement after placement in an issue?

Mary Beth Burner

All of these questions can be answered with research: *Magazine X* has 15 million devoted readers nationwide—an educated, affluent, youthful readership that bought 12,879,534 packages of your product in the last six months, purportedly after noticing your ad next to their favorite column in the magazine, which they loyally spend an average of 90 minutes reading each month.

Prove it, you say? A plethora of research data reports all of these things and much, much more. Studies are conducted daily by magazines, by media research firms, or by magazine organizations like MPA. A variety of research

---

Simmons Market Research Bureau (SMRB)
Firm that provides audience data for several media. Best known for magazine research.

Syndicated Magazine Readership Research Advertisers are, of course, interested in the primary readers of magazines. But they are also interested in who these readers are and what they buy, as well as pass-along readers who are given the publications. Currently, there are two principal sources of syndicated magazine readership research: **Simmons Market Research Bureau (SMRB)** and Mediamark Research, Inc. (MRI).

MRI (www.mediamark.com) methodology consists of selecting a sample of approximately 26,000 people and eliciting media usage, demographic characteristics, lifestyle, and product purchase information. Using a combination of personal interviews and self-administered questionnaires, respondents report on magazine readership and product usage. SMRB (www.smrb.com) has a sample of approximately 20,000 adults. The data are collected via mailed questionnaires and measure

exists for marketing purposes: focus groups, online polls, reader panel surveys, advertising response measurement, third-party syndicated surveys (i.e., Mediamark Research, Inc.), magazine subscriber surveys, editorial readership surveys, ScanTron product purchase data, coupon redemption tracking, and circulation data, to name a few. Yet, all of these data are meaningless if you don't bring the presentation and interpretation to life using a little creativity in developing your "unique selling proposition" and strategy. This is where psychology, creativity, and brand marketing all play a key role in advertising research.

Consider this: An agency representing an athletic footwear client decides to run print advertising in consumer magazines, and the women's fitness magazine category is a top consideration. The agency, under heavy budget constraints, decides to put the majority of the print budget in one key fitness magazine to emphasize frequency. You must aid your sales rep in putting your magazine's best foot forward to prove why you are the athletic footwear client's ideal advertising and marketing partner. As *Magazine X*, your key competitor in this category is *Magazine* Y, another reputable fitness magazine. After running the numbers based on the footwear account's target audience of "women who purchased any athletic shoes in the last year," the data show the following:

	Page Rate	Audience	Composition	Index (US = 100)	CPM
Magazine X	$100,000	10,200,000	68%	144	$9.80
Magazine Y	$140,000	11,800,000	65%	141	$11.86

At a glance, it seems your competitor, *Magazine Y*, reaches more of the target audience and might be the better option. But consider that the agency's priority is frequency and readers' likelihood to purchase shoes. *Magazine X*'s strengths are cost efficiency (lower CPM) and a higher reader affinity (44 percent more likely than the average American to buy athletic shoes as shown in the index). Surely this will help your sales rep in negotiating against the competitor, but it's also important to bring it to life. It might sound impressive to say "over 10 million of *Magazine X* readers bought shoes in the last year," but without comparative data, how does that differentiate your magazine? If you did a little further digging to learn that your readers purchase an average of two pairs of athletic shoes a year, multiplied by 10.2 million, then extrapolate the data to something visible and tangible for the media decision maker. For instance, "If you were to line up toe-to-heel all of the shoes that *Magazine X* readers bought in the last year, it would cover the distance from Portland, Maine, to Los Angeles, California, *twice*." Or "The number of *Magazine X* readers who bought athletic shoes in the last year outnumber the population of the *largest* city in the United States—our group of 10.2 million readers sporting new shoes is larger in number than all of the residents of New York City combined!" Statements such as these illustrate just how viable a media partner your magazine can be for this athletic footwear company wishing to reach shoe fanatics.

Magazine researchers *are* guilty as charged with calculators and infinite graphs—necessary tools to depict data—but also wear the hats of *psychologist* for logic and reasoning and providing insight into the reader, *creative mind* to illustrate findings, *strategist* to discern the most competitive angle, and *brand developer* to uniquely market the magazine's identity.

Next time you spot an ad for a product in your favorite magazine, be aware of how much magazine researchers and sales reps reasoned and fought to get it there. ■ ■ ■

media usage, including data on several hundred magazines, with an emphasis on audience and product usage information.

CONSUMER MAGAZINES—SUMMING UP

The challenges and opportunities facing consumer magazines cover a wide range of concerns. From practical considerations of cost management in distribution and printing to the ways in which the Internet can be integrated into traditional magazine practices, publishers must deal with an ever-changing marketplace.

In spite of these challenges, magazines are well positioned to deal with the communication issues of the twenty-first century. Magazine readers are among the

EXHIBIT 11.13

ABC offers circulation analysis for publications.

Courtesy of Audit Bureau of Circulations.

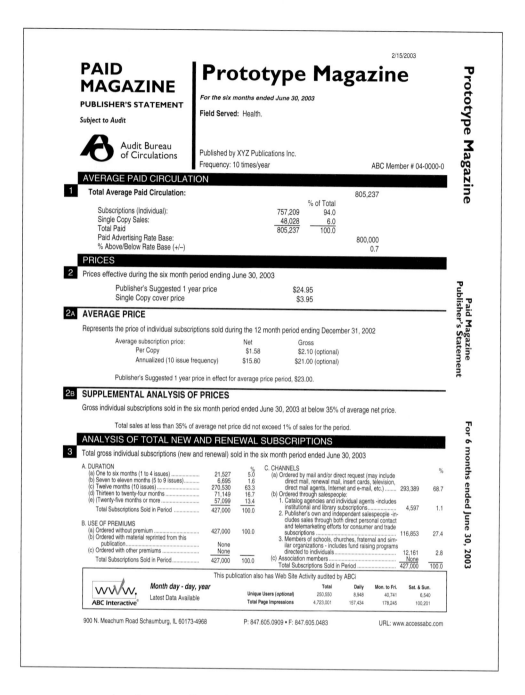

most upscale of any media audience. Ironically, they show great strength among Internet users that, combined with the selective nature of most publications, may offer a profitable convergence for many publishers. New technology aside, magazines are well positioned as a major marketing and advertising tool.

Magazines can play a role as either the primary medium for a national advertiser or as a niche medium to reach prime prospects. Magazines will continue to be a major source of news, information, and entertainment for millions of prime prospects. It is this combination of prestige and segmentation that gives magazines a major qualitative advantage over most other media. The fact that magazines are asking readers to carry a major share of the financial support of magazines also has enhanced their value to advertisers.

The combination of upscale readers, opportunities for targeted advertising, editorial involvement, and both reach and frequency among a number of qualitative and quantitative audience segments of importance to advertisers will work to the advantage of magazines in the future. Despite these positive characteristics, magazines will continue to face a number of economic problems. Some, like postage increases and newsstand distribution concerns, are beyond their immediate control. In the long term, it may be that financial elements will determine the future of the medium as much as readership.

THE BUSINESS PRESS AND BUSINESS-TO-BUSINESS ADVERTISING

Professional Candy Buyer, American Cemetery, The Science Teacher, Advertising Age, and *Journal of Knee Surgery* are only a handful of the more than 10,000 publications that make up the business press. In Chapter 2, we briefly discussed the business-to-business (B2B) media. It is a marketplace where million-dollar deals are commonplace and the methods for sales, marketing, and advertising are markedly different from those in consumer advertising. A number of media and promotions are used to reach business buyers. We will discuss them in this chapter because business magazines constitute the primary source of B2B expenditures.

Prospects for most business advertisers are fewer and more concentrated, they tend to be experts concerning the products they purchase, and audience selectivity is much more important than the CPMs or reach measures used in consumer media. Another feature of business publications is their efficient reach of major decision makers (see Exhibit 11.14). Given the specialized audience of these publications combined with moderate cost, the business magazine continues to be a bargain.

Both the tone and advertising of business publications differ significantly from consumer magazines. The business press is a medium of reference and commerce, whereas consumer magazines are vehicles of entertainment, news, and leisure reading. Many business publications are used on a regular basis to keep up with the latest industry trends, competitive activity, and product category marketing strategy.

Communicating the Business-to-Business Message

Business-to-business advertising has to consider a number of factors in addressing its specialized audiences. First and foremost, the message must be directed at the profitability of the customer. Whereas few consumer advertisements contain technical product specifications and details about equipment compatibility and delivery terms, these are the types of information commonly contained in business publications.

business-to-business advertising
Advertising that promotes goods through trade and industrial journals that are used in the manufacturing, distributing, or marketing of goods to the public.

EXHIBIT 11.14
Occupation of Readers of Specialized Business Magazines

Source: *Cahners Advertising Research Report* www.cahnerscarr. com.

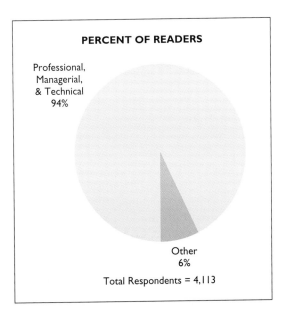

PERCENT OF READERS

Professional, Managerial, & Technical
94%

Other
6%

Total Respondents = 4,113

In communicating with the business community, there are a number of considerations. For example:

1. Appeal to prospects in terms of specific job interests and demands. The advertisement should address how a product or service can increase the productivity and enhance the job performance of a particular function.

2. Sell the benefits to the buyer, not the features of the product. Again, these benefits need to be couched in terms of sales and productivity. It is rare that cute or humorous business advertising is successful.

3. The job of business advertising, particularly for high-end products, is to support and facilitate the sales function. Business transactions, unlike their consumer counterparts, are rarely completed with a single advertisement or even solely through advertising. Most business advertising is a means of moving prospects into the personal sales channel. That is, advertising should function to make the job of personal selling or prospect follow-up easier.

4. Avoid product puffery. Remember the readers of your advertising are trained professionals with high levels of expertise in their fields. They expect to see product information, often with detailed diagrams, charts, and technical specifications. The type of appeals common in consumer media will not work in the business and trade press.

5. Business advertising, even more so than consumer advertising, needs to have clear objectives that are measurable in terms of specific target publics.

Corporate Branding

Although business-to-business selling is about buying products, it also is about buying the reputation of the companies with which other companies do business. A general consumer may take a chance with an unknown company for a product costing even several hundred dollars. The same is rarely true in the world of business marketing where the future of a business can be at stake when major purchases are made.

In recent years, more and more emphasis has been placed on corporate branding by companies. As companies grow and become more complex in terms of different divisions, products, and distribution channels, it becomes difficult to approach customers with a single message. Corporate branding attempts to integrate a company's total image through a coordinated marketing communications process.

Ideally, corporate branding allows a company to speak with its various customers through advertising, public relations, the Internet, and even product design and other identity programs such as logos and product trademarks. Effective corporate branding allows a company to establish its reputation and set brands apart from the competition. It also allows a company to provide a consistent message to prospects, customers, stockholders, and employees.[24]

The remainder of this section will examine some of the special features of the business-to-business sector and the differences and similarities with consumer advertising.

Audiences of the Business Press   There are both important qualitative and quantitative differences between readers of business publications and the typical audiences of consumer magazines. Most importantly, trade publications are for most readers part of the job. They are not read for entertainment but rather will be judged on the basis of how well they improve the readers' ability to do their jobs, market their products, and improve their profits. Consequently, business magazines must develop a depth of understanding of their readers that is not required typically in the consumer press.

In addition to the approach that readers take to the business press, there also are significant differences in the audience composition of business versus consumer magazines. In terms of age, income, job categories, education (see Exhibit 11.15), and

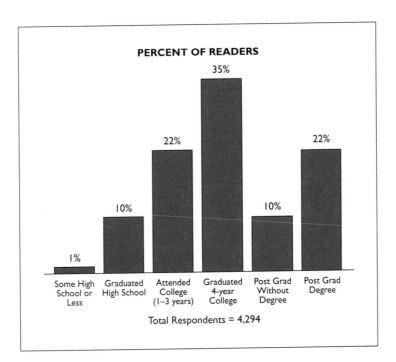

EXHIBIT **11.15**

The Maximum Level of Education Attained by Readers of Specialized Business Magazines

Over two-thirds of the readers have completed 16–20 years of schooling. Twenty-four percent of the general national population has four or more years of college and beyond.

Source: *Cahners Advertising Research Report* www.cahnerscarr.com.

other basic demographic data, business publications skew far higher than typical consumer magazines. Basically, the tone of a business magazine, both in editorial and advertising, is one of a problem solver. There is a special relationship between business magazines and the industries they serve.

Competition for Business-to-Business Advertising Television, newspapers, radio, and consumer magazines are the core of consumer advertising. On a national basis, television is in fierce competition for consumer dollars, whereas radio and newspapers serve local retailers in reaching these same buyers. However, business selling and marketing have devoted most of their dollars to personal sales, trade and business publications, direct mail, and telemarketing.

As discussed earlier, for most major accounts, marketing communication is used as a means of providing entry for personal selling. Studies show that, by an overwhelming margin, executives with purchasing authority will not make appointments with salespersons unless they have a thorough knowledge of the companies and products they represent. In many respects, the environment of business marketing was unchanged for the 50 years from the end of World War II to the mid–1990s. Then, you guessed it, the Internet became a major force in business marketing.

The Internet and Business-to-Business Marketing

The Internet gained acceptance faster in B2B marketing than in consumer marketing. For one thing, businesses were mostly computer savvy long before the Internet came along, so it represented just another phase in the development of computer integration into the business world. The Internet also was more functional for B2B marketing because the number of customers was infinitesimal compared to most consumer products. Both customers and their e-mail addresses could be identified easily and the Internet quickly became part of the integrated marketing communication plans of most companies.

Despite the greater utility of Internet B2B marketing, it was used in relatively traditional ways of reaching customers, providing Web sites with product information, and for less expensive products or regular customers it provided a method of order taking. However, the use of the Internet in B2B marketing and potentially the

EXHIBIT 11.16

This B2B e-mercial for CNN Newsource targets local television station executives.

Courtesy of Sawyer Riley Compton.

practices of business selling changed dramatically in the late 1990s with the introduction of the Internet auction.

The Internet Auction and Business-to-Business Marketing

When Ford Motor Company wants to purchase several million dollars' worth of rubber hoses or General Mills wants to buy 10 million cereal boxes, the procedure has been to send out product specifications to a network of suppliers or their wholesalers and typically, after a round of questions and negotiations, accept bids from qualified companies. In this process, however sometimes suppliers got the word about a buy, and purchasing agents were never sure that they were getting the best deal.

The coming of the Internet auction has promised to change many of the methods of marketing and selling goods in the business-to-business world. Basically, it allows buyers and sellers to make a connection, bid on parts and supplies, and make the final deal through a direct-marketing channel between buyer and seller. This process has even greater potential for change given the emphasis placed on price in the business-to-business environment. Once a supplier meets buyer specifications for steel, packaging cartons, or electrical wiring, it becomes a generic commodity.

It is a marketplace that closely resembles those envisioned in many economic models in which advertising, brand reputation, and company name have little relevance to how a product is purchased. These Internet auctions also provide a true global economy to the process. Sellers from around the world—even those where buyers and sellers have never heard of each other—theoretically have an equal chance to make a sale if the price is right.

Although a change of this magnitude in the business marketplace is no doubt interesting, why should advertisers care? If manufacturers have immediate and full communication with all potential suppliers and products become generic commodities with sales almost totally dependent on price, what role is there for advertising and promotion? If we review the section on corporate branding, we see that many of the advantages of such promotions assume the need for enhanced company reputation and product identity—roles largely unnecessary in a virtual auction marketplace.

Whether it is a household buying an airplane ticket from priceline.com or DuPont buying a million dollars' worth of chemicals from i2i.com, the concept is the same: Price, not advertising and promotion, sells. "The Internet is altering the rules on how companies manage their sales, service, and distribution operations. It is providing new opportunities for businesses of all stripes to reach new customers, as well as forge closer ties with existing customers. . . . [The Internet] enables companies that once relied on middlemen to begin selling directly to its retail customers. As a result, e-commerce can pit manufacturers against their wholesalers, retailers, and other traditional partners.[25]

Business Publication Expansion of Services   You will recall that we discussed the fact that many consumer magazines have introduced a number of merchandising and ancillary services. Because of the specialized nature of business-to-business publications, they are even better positioned to engage in ancillary services than their consumer counterparts. As the competition for B2B advertising and promotional dollars increases, business publications have increasingly engaged in a number of ventures to reach their core readers and at the same time increase the profitability of their companies.

1. *Subscriber list rentals.* Major business publications find that their subscriber list is one of the most valuable commodities they own. In fact, depending on the degree of specialization and the industry they service, business publications make as much as 10 percent of their total revenue from list rentals.
2. *Event-related publications.* Golf tournaments, car shows, and conventions from religious denominations to service organizations often provide an advertiser-supported program with the schedule of the event as well as information about the group. These publications are usually published by an independent trade publisher.
3. *Custom publications.* As we discussed in an earlier section, custom publishing is a very lucrative business. These custom magazines are a major source of revenue for many trade publishers.
4. *Trade shows.* In Chapter 14, we will discuss in detail the role of trade shows in the marketing channel. Major trade shows bring buyers and sellers from an entire industry together to view new products and methods of doing business. In some cases, business publications organize and sell sponsorship to these shows usually under the name of the publication. A named trade show demonstrates leadership in the field and can also be a profitable enterprise for the publication.

Entry into ancillary services usually is more successful for established magazines than their smaller competitors that are less well known. Magazines provide credibility and high visibility to these ancillary events, which would be lacking without the tie-in to a major publication. Seeing the growth of promotional techniques in business-to-business advertising, many magazine publishers employ ancillary vehicles to add to their overall profitability and decrease their dependence on advertising from their publications.

Regardless of their format, ancillary activities offer a number of advantages to a publisher. First, they utilize the publisher's knowledge of a particular industry to help clients develop a coordinated promotional and advertising campaign. Second, they gain revenue from companies that do not use advertising as a primary business-to-business marketing tool. Finally, they increase a magazine's credibility

EXHIBIT **11.17**

Some of the many business publications read by advertising media planners.

Copyright Crain Communications and © VNU Business Media, Inc. Reprinted with permission.

by demonstrating far-reaching expertise in a number of promotional areas. In the future, we will see publishers developing a variety of information services and promotional techniques in addition to their basic magazines.

Some Special Features of Business Publication Advertising

Business publications are different from consumer magazines in several ways. This section briefly discusses the more important ones.

Pass-Along Readership A significant number of business publications readers receive their magazines on a pass-along basis. We noted earlier that such readership among consumer magazines is generally regarded as inferior to paid circulation. However, one of the notable differences between business and consumer publications is the way advertisers view pass-along readership. The typical consumer medium has a relatively short life and low pass-along readership.

Occasionally, a recipe will be clipped or a magazine will be passed on to a neighbor, but consumer magazines are read largely for pleasure and tossed aside. In any case, advertisers view pass-along readership of consumer magazines as vastly inferior to primary readership.

Business publication advertisers, in contrast, view pass-along readership as quite valuable. For one thing, readers don't normally browse through *The Federal Health System Journal* or *Plastics Engineering*; they pay close attention to the copy. For another, some business publications limit their circulation in a way that forces pass-along readership.

Types of Business-to-Business Publications

Despite the wide array of business publications, they can generally be placed in one of four categories:

- Distributive trades (trade)
- Manufacturers and builders (industrial)
- Top officers of other corporations (management)
- Physicians, dentists, architects, and other professional people (professional)

Trade Papers Because most nationally advertised products depend on dealers for their sales, we discuss advertising in **trade papers** first. Usually, this advertising is prepared by the agency that handles the consumer advertising, and in any new campaign both are prepared at the same time. The term *trade papers* is applied particularly to business publications directed at those who buy products for resale, such as wholesalers, jobbers, and retailers. Typical trade papers are *Supermarket News, Chain Store Age, Hardware Retailer, Modern Tire Dealer, Women's Wear Daily*, and *Home Furnishings Retailer*.

trade paper
A business publication directed to those who buy products for resale (wholesalers, jobbers, retailers).

Almost every business engaged in distributing goods has a trade paper to discuss its problems. Trade papers are a great medium for reporting merchandising news about the products, packaging, prices, deals, and promotions of the manufacturers that cater to the particular industry. The chain-store field alone has more than 20 such publications. Druggists have a choice of over 30, and more than 60 different publications are issued for grocers. There are many localized journals, such as *Texas Retailer, Michigan Food News, Southern Jewelry News*, and *California Apparel News*.

Industrial Publications As we move into the world where a company in one industry sells its materials, machinery, tools, parts, and equipment to another company for use in making a product or conducting operations, we are in an altogether different ballpark—the industrial marketing arena.

There are fewer customers in this arena than in the consumer market, and they can be more easily identified. The amount of money involved in a sale may be large—hundreds of thousands of dollars, perhaps even millions—and nothing is bought on impulse. Many knowledgeable executives with technical skills often share in the buying decision. The sales representative has to have a high degree of professional competence to deal with the industrial market, in which personal selling is the biggest factor in making a sale. Advertising is only a collateral aid used to pave the way for or support the salesperson; hence, it receives a smaller share of the marketplace budget.

Advertising addressed to people responsible for buying goods needed to make products is called industrial advertising. It is designed to reach purchasing agents, plant managers, engineers, controllers, and others who have a voice in spending the firm's money.

Management Publications The most difficult group for a publication to reach is managers. After all, even the largest companies have only a relatively few decision makers.

When these decision makers are widely dispersed across a number of industries and job descriptions, publications find they must be extremely creative to reach them.

The management category is one that straddles a gray area between consumer and business-to-business publications. Magazines such as *Business Week, Fortune,* and *Nation's Business* have characteristics that would place them in either the business or the consumer category. Even magazines such as *Time* have at least some of their partial-run editions listed in the *Business Publications SRDS.*

Standard Rate and Data Service (SRDS)
SRDS publishes a number of directories giving media and production information.

Professional Publications The **Standard Rate and Data Service (SRDS),** in its special business publication edition, includes journals addressed to physicians, surgeons, dentists, lawyers, architects, and other professionals who depend on these publications to keep abreast of their professions. The editorial content of such journals ranges from reports about new technical developments to discussions on how to meet client or patient problems better and how to manage offices more efficiently and profitably. Professional people often recommend or specify the products their patients or clients should order. Therefore, much advertising of a high technical caliber is addressed to them.

controlled circulation magazines
Sent without cost to people responsible for making buying decisions. To get on such lists, people must state their positions in companies; to stay on it, they must request it annually. Also known as qualified-circulation publications.

Controlled Circulation Magazines are sometimes distributed free to selective readers. Free circulation is known as **controlled circulation.** The term *controlled* refers to the fact that publishers distribute only to a carefully selected list of people who are influential in making purchase decisions for their industry. They use the same database techniques that direct mailers use in building their mailing lists. Controlled circulation makes sense when dealing with an easily defined audience of decision makers. To some media planners, the logic of controlled circulation is not very different from that of direct mail except that the ad is delivered in an editorial environment. Despite the fact that controlled circulation is widely used in the trade press, it is not universally embraced. In the past, most research has indicated that a high percentage of both clients and media directors prefer the reader commitment inherent in paid circulation.

The number of controlled publications in the business field plays a major role in their share of advertising-to-circulation revenues compared to consumer magazines. On average, approximately two-thirds of trade publication circulation is controlled. A number of publications use a mix of controlled and paid circulations in which qualified readers receive the magazine free and others can buy it if they wish.

Controlled circulation creates a significant dependence on advertising support. Unlike consumer magazines, business publications have been largely unsuccessful in shifting to a reader-driven revenue stream. This dependency on advertising is another reason why business publications suffer so much during economic downturns.

vertical publication
Business publications dealing with the problems of a specific industry: for example, *Chain Store Age, National Petroleum News, Textile World.*

Vertical and Horizontal Publications Industrial publications are usually considered to be either horizontal or vertical. A **vertical publication** is one that covers an entire industry. An example is *Snack Food & Wholesale Bakery,* which contains information concerning research and development, manufacturing, product quality, marketing, warehousing, and distribution.

Horizontal publications are edited for people who are engaged in a single function that cuts across many industries. An example is *Purchasing* magazine, which is circulated to purchasing managers. It discusses trends and forecasts applicable to all industries.

Circulation Audits Business-to-business advertisers are keenly interested in the circulation of the publications in which they advertise. In some respects, the readership numbers are more important than those in general consumer magazines. The total audience is smaller, the CPM for most publications is significantly higher

EXHIBIT **11.18**

Two Major Magazine Auditing Services

a) Courtesy of Audit Bureau of Circulations.

b) Courtesy of Verified Audit Circulation.

than consumer magazines, and the competition makes it imperative that business-to-business marketers reach their target audience in a timely fashion.

Because of the number and diversity of audiences contacted by the trade and business press, a number of auditing organizations are used by business publishers and advertisers. More than 500 trade and industrial magazines are audited by the Business Publications Audit of Circulation International (BPA), the leading business auditor. Because many business publications are circulated to a general business audience, the ABC is used for publications such as *Business Week*, and a few publications use both auditing firms.

A third auditing organization is the Verified Audit Circulation (VAC). Founded in 1951, VAC provides circulation audits for a wide variety of newspapers, shoppers, magazines, and even Yellow Pages directories. There are a number of publications in the business area that are not audited. Although an unaudited publication can survive, there are a number of business-to-business advertisers and agencies that, as a matter of policy, will not consider an unaudited publication.

Agribusiness Advertising

At one time farm media, both print and broadcast, were geared largely to the millions of families who lived and worked on small farms. In recent years, the farm press has had to adapt to dramatic changes in the way agriculture is conducted in this country. Between 1940 and 1991, the number of farm workers declined by almost 70 percent. During that same period, the number of farm residents dropped from 31 million to 5 million.[26]

Contemporary agribusiness media and advertisers are tailoring their messages to a concentrated industry of huge farm cooperatives and farm managers with income and educational levels that rival those of the CEOs of any major business. Although weather and crop prices are still major topics of the farm press, these publications are just as likely to be discussing the weather in Russia and price controls and export policies as opposed to what is happening in a local community.

The farm press is facing many of the problems of the business press in general. A number of media competitors have come on the scene in recent years to take advertising dollars from the print media. Unlike business-to-business advertising in which television and radio have only recently been used by advertisers, farm broadcasting has a long history of serving the farm community.

There are a number of local and regional farm broadcasters, but on a national level the primary sources of agribusiness news and advertising are:

■ *AgDay*, a daily syndicated television show that reaches 130 markets, is carried by over 180 stations, and is supported by a number of national advertisers such as DuPont and Chevrolet, (www.agday.com).

- The weekly *U.S. Farm Report*, which is syndicated to about 90 percent of the nation's television households, is the nation's longest-running agricultural news program, (www.usfrontline.com).
- *National Farm Report*, which is syndicated to some 260 radio stations, (www.tribuneradio.com).
- *The Agri-Voice Network*, a network of 50 smaller midwestern radio stations broadcasting daily farm reports, (www.tribuneradio.com).

In addition, a number of Web sites have been established by the farm media and agribusiness advertisers.

Advertising products to the agribusiness community uses many of the same techniques demonstrated by other sectors of business marketing. However, agribusiness promotional techniques are even more specialized than those of traditional business-to-business selling. The relatively small agribusiness population makes sophisticated information readily available. Agribusiness advertising can target audiences and deliver a message that solves specific problems of the farm industry.

The business of farming has been hit hard during recent years with an uncertain farm economy, high prices for feed and other supplies, and unpredictable weather. These factors have combined to make it very difficult for farm magazines and agribusiness advertising in general. A continuing consolidation of farms has reduced the number of farmers and companies involved in agribusiness. This trend toward consolidation has been reflected in the farm press by lower circulation and fewer advertising dollars during the last two decades.

Ironically, as the number of farms and major agribusiness suppliers have decreased, the number and diversity of media competing for advertising dollars in the sector have grown dramatically. In order to compete in this environment, farm publications have utilized many of the techniques of the business press in expanding the means they use to reach their audiences. For example, these magazines have accumulated sophisticated databases to develop subscriber list rentals, do their own direct mail to nonsubscribers, and publish special catalogs and other material. Like the business press, farm magazines will probably see more revenue coming from nonpublishing sources as they become more successful in promoting these ventures.

EXHIBIT 11.19

Some of the Many Farm Publications

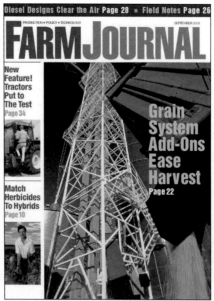
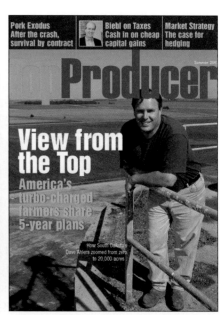

THE ORGANIZATION OF THE FARM PRESS

Farm magazines fall into three classifications: general farm magazines, regional farm magazines, and vocational farm magazines.

General Farm Magazines

The three major publications in the category are *Farm Journal, Successful Farming,* and *Progressive Farmer.* In recent years, each of these publications has experienced circulation decreases reflecting the consolidation of the farming industry. The general farm publications are designed to address all aspects of farm life but with a clear emphasis on business. For instance, the SRDS Publisher's Editorial Profile for *Successful Farming* reads as follows:

> *Successful Farming* editorial is published "for families that make farming and ranching their business." It serves the production, business and family needs of a divers. American agriculture. It provides ideas farm and ranch families can take right to the field, barn, shop, office, home, family or heart to add value to their lives, businesses and lifestyle.

Regional Farm Magazines A number of farm publications are directed to farmers in a particular region. These publications tend to be general in nature, but they contain little of the family-oriented topics found in the large circulation farm magazines. They address issues of crops, livestock, and government farm policy unique to a particular region. Among the publications in this category are the *Prairie Farmer,* the majority of whose readers live in Indiana and Illinois, the *Oregon Farmer-Stockman,* and the *Nebraska Farmer.*

Vocational Farm Magazines The last category of farm publications comprises those devoted to certain types of farming or livestock raising. Typical of these publications are *The Corn and Soybean Digest, The Dairyman, American Fruit Grower,* and *The Tomato Magazine.* Many of the vocational magazines combine elements of both regional and vocational publications—for instance, *The Kansas Stockman* and *Missouri Pork Producer.*

Whatever a farmer's interests may be, a number of publications are edited to cater to them. Many farm homes take several publications.

 **SUMMARY**

Summing Up—The Business Press

Business-to-business publications are facing a number of challenges now and in the future. Among the most obvious is the consolidation of many industries into fewer and fewer firms. This merging of firms has resulted in a decrease in both the number of potential advertisers to support the business press and in the number of companies that are being reached with advertising.

A second major trend in the business press has been the growth of competition for advertising dollars. At one time trade and business publications had a virtual monopoly in the business sector and the farm press had only radio as a major competitor. Today, that situation has changed dramatically. Business advertisers are putting their marketing communication dollars in numerous vehicles as well as the Internet and utilizing sophisticated database technology to demand immediate and measurable results from their advertising.

Because of the relatively low price of trade magazine advertising, it is possible to appeal to specialized job interests with different messages in a variety of publications. The messages of these publications are also specialized. Factual copy with product information is presented to a knowledgeable audience in a manner that would be impractical in most consumer magazines.

Business-to-business publications are an ideal medium for reaching the targeted audience segments that advertisers seek in an environment suited to the mood of that audience. Business magazines also provide audience involvement to a degree impossible in most other media formats and the affinity for these magazines carries over to the advertising messages.

With the ability of computers to track employment demographics and new technology to reach them through partial-run editions and selected binding, business magazines can compete in an increasingly competitive media environment. On the negative side, business magazines face the same problems of rising postage, printing, and marketing costs as their consumer counterparts. Quality, credibility, believability, and audience selectivity are the elements that will continue to make the business press a primary choice of business-to-business advertisers.

 **REVIEW**

1. Two of the major concerns of the magazine industry are costs and selectivity. Explain.

2. Why would an advertiser want to use both television and magazines?

3. What are some qualitative features of importance to magazine advertisers?

4. Contrast full-run and partial-run magazine editions.

5. What is selective binding?

6. What is the role of negotiation in setting magazine advertising rates?

7. Contrast circulation and readership in magazines.

8. What are the major competitors for business magazines?

9. What has been a primary method for business magazines to extend their services and increase profits?

10. What are vertical and horizontal publications?

 **TAKE IT TO THE WEB**

Several magazines have online extensions on the Web. Mediaweek.com (**www.mediaweek.com**) is the online version of *Mediaweek* magazine, which provides media professionals with the latest marketing profiles and indicators, directories for traditional media and national networks, and more. Visit Mediaweek.com as an example of an online magazine and discuss the advantages and disadvantages of having an online edition versus having a print edition only.

Visit either the online edition of *Lucky* magazine (**www.luckymag.com**) or the online edition of *Sports Illustrated* (**www.si.com**) and list ways in which the Web site encourages visitors to subscribe to the print version of the magazine. Were the tactics employed by the Web sites able to convince you to subscribe?

The Magazine Publishers of America (MPA) is the industry association for consumer magazines. Government Action is one of several topics addressed on the MPA Web site (**www.magazine.org**). Review the MPA's position on the topics addressed under this heading including marketing to children and the marketing of weight loss products and pharmaceuticals through direct-to-consumer advertising. What other issues facing the magazine industry will likely fall under government regulation?

CHAPTER 12

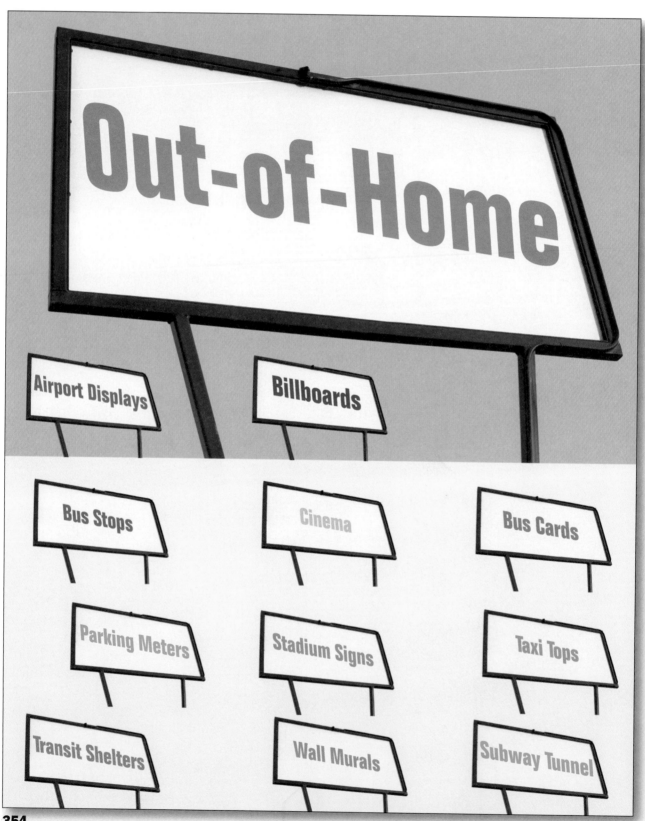

Out-of-Home

Airport Displays

Billboards

Bus Stops

Cinema

Bus Cards

Parking Meters

Stadium Signs

Taxi Tops

Transit Shelters

Wall Murals

Subway Tunnel

Out-of-Home Advertising

Outdoor advertising is an attention-getting medium without equal. With the current move to targeted formats in most advertising vehicles, outdoor is fast becoming the last of the truly mass media. In recent years, there has been a dramatic change in the definition of out-of-home media as the standard highway billboard is being joined by many innovative out-of-home approaches. After reading this chapter, you will understand:

1. basic marketing strategy of out-of-home advertising
2. the various types of out-of-home media
3. the legislative environment of outdoor advertising
4. out-of-home advertising's role in brand building
5. the complementary function of out-of-home media
6. measurement of the outdoor audience

PROS

1. Outdoor can provide advertising exposure to virtually every adult in a geographic market with high frequency and at a very low cost per exposure.
2. With 24-hour exposure, outdoor is an excellent means of supplementing other media advertising for product introduction or building brand-name recognition.
3. With the use of color and lighting, outdoor is a medium that gains immediate audience attention and can provide reminder messages in proximity to retail outlets such as fast-food franchises.
4. The outdoor industry has diversified the product categories using out-of-home in an attempt to lose its image as a "beer and cigarette" medium.

CONS

1. With a typical audience of high-speed drivers, outdoor is unable to communicate detailed sales messages. Copy is usually limited to headline length—seven to ten words.
2. Outdoor advertising is extremely difficult to measure, making audience comparisons with other media almost impossible.
3. Outdoor has been attacked in many communities as a visual pollutant, which has made it the topic of some controversy. It also faces a number of additional legal restrictions in selected jurisdictions. In a

few states (e.g., Alaska, Hawaii, and Vermont) some local governments have banned the medium altogether. This negative image may discourage some advertisers from using outdoor.

Outdoor is the oldest form of promotion. Evidence of outdoor messages can be found in prehistoric carvings on bronze and stone tablets in the Middle East. In ancient Egypt, outdoor was a popular means of posting public notices as well as sales messages. Placed on well-traveled roads, they became the forerunner of the modern highway billboard. Painted advertising dates to Pompeii where elaborately decorated walls promoted local businesses.

In this country, outdoor "broadsides" announced the Boston Tea Party and reported the Boston Massacre, and posters publicized the presidential campaign of Andrew Jackson. The first American commercial billboard was a poster by Jared Bell for the 1835 circus season. Throughout the 1800s, posters promoted a number of products and political causes. In 1850, signs were first used on streetcars in major cities and by 1870 some 300 bill-posting firms served advertisers throughout the East and Midwest.

In 1900, the first standardized outdoor sign format was introduced, and national advertisers such as Kellogg and Coca-Cola began to share the outdoor market with local advertisers. The modern era of outdoor advertising was introduced when the automobile created a mobile society early in this century. In addition to a population on the move, outdoor benefited from new printing techniques and a growing advertising industry that was always looking for effective means of reaching prospective customers. During this period, the industry adopted standardized signs; formed the forerunner of its national trade association, the **Outdoor Advertising Association of America (OAAA);** established what is now the **Traffic Audit Bureau for Media Measurement (TAB)** to authenticate audience data; and initiated a national marketing organization, OAAA Marketing.[1]

To most people, the contemporary image of the outdoor industry is far from the reality. An industry once known primarily as a medium for beer and cigarettes, outdoor is used increasingly by major advertisers. Fueled by advertisers' need to gain brand awareness and a number of new outdoor formats, the industry is growing at a rate surpassed by only cable television and Internet advertising (see Exhibit 12.1). The variety of outdoor advertising vehicles has even resulted in the term *out-of-home advertising* replacing the more familiar term *outdoor advertising* in recent years to more fully reflect the scope of this industry. Today, *outdoor* normally has a more narrow meaning, referring only to highway posters and large signs. The change is more than just semantic because it reflects the diversity of the industry and its marketing strategy.

Outdoor Advertising Association of America (OAAA)
Primary trade and lobbying organization for the outdoor industry.

Traffic Audit Bureau for Media Measurement (TAB)
An organization designed to investigate how many people pass and may see a given outdoor sign, to establish a method of evaluating traffic measuring a market.

EXHIBIT 12.1

Outdoor revenue growth.

Source: CMR and OAAA. Courtesy of Outdoor Advertising Association of America, www.oaaa.org.

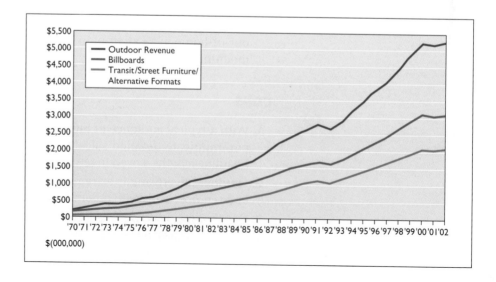

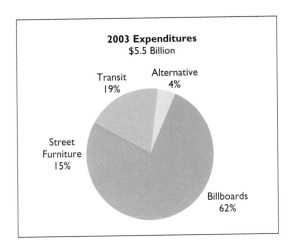

EXHIBIT **12.2**

Sources of Out-of-Home Advertising 2002

Courtesy of Outdoor Advertising Association of America, www.oaaa.org.

Although traditional billboards are still the primary source of industry revenues, they constitute only 60 percent of the industry's total income (see Exhibit 12.2). The growth of alternative advertising options offered by out-of-home is a major reason for the growth of the industry. Overall, the OAAA estimates that there are more than 30 types of out-of-home media, including everything from the largest outdoor signs, airport and shopping mall kiosks, stadium signs, and airplanes towing banners (see Exhibit 12.3).

Media executives predict that the future of the out-of-home industry will continue to be one of consistent growth. Among the contributing factors to out-of-home's popularity are the following:

1. *An increasingly mobile population.* Americans rarely stay in one place for long. Approximately 125 million people commute to work each day, placing them in the out-of-home market for a variety of messages. Consumers are spending more time traveling to their jobs. In 2002, average commute times were estimated to be 25.5 minutes.

2. *Cost of out-of-home advertising.* No major medium comes close to matching the inexpensive CPM levels of out-of-home advertising (see Exhibit 12.4). The relatively low cost of out-of-home means that advertisers can generate

EXHIBIT **12.3**

Types of Out-of-Home Media

Courtesy of Outdoor Advertising Association of America, www.oaaa.org.

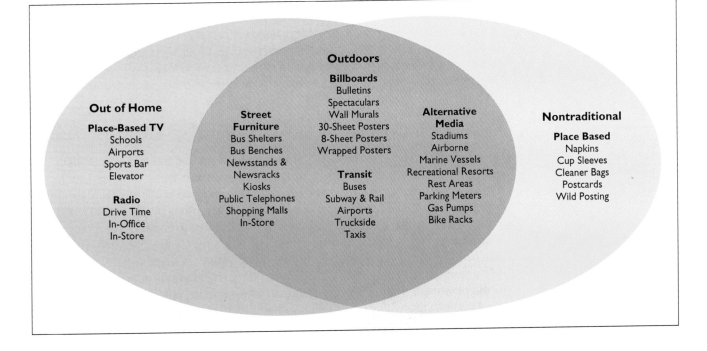

EXHIBIT **12.4**

Courtesy of Outdoor Advertising Association of America, www.oaa. org.

AVERAGE CPM ADULTS 181 (CALENDAR YEAR 2000)	
Outdoor (Top 100 Markets)	
8-Sheet posters #50 showing	0.98
30-sheet posters #50 showing	1.45
Rotary Bulletins #10 showing	3.76
Radio (Top 100 Markets)	
:60 drive-time	$5.92
Magazines	
4-color page	$9.62
Television	
:30 prime-time spot	$20.54
:30 prime-time network	$11.31
Newspapers	
Half page black & white	$23.32
Quarter page black & white	$11.66

extremely high levels of both reach and frequency at inexpensive levels. These affordable CPM figures mean that out-of-home is an ideal medium to fill in gaps among target segments missed or underexposed by other media.

3. *Media fragmentation.* Outdoor advertising is benefiting from the growing audience fragmentation witnessed in other media. In the last 35 years, the number of television channels per household has increased 800 percent and the number of magazines and radio stations has grown by some 200 percent during the same period. The result of this growth is a fragmented audience for most media. Although the ability to target prospects is a major benefit for many advertisers, widely distributed packaged goods and other mass-appeal brands need high levels of exposure to virtually everyone. Outdoor can inexpensively deliver massive audience exposures.

4. *Advertiser diversification.* The old saying that, "we are known by the company we keep" is very appropriate for outdoor. Even before the recent prohibition against outdoor tobacco advertising, the outdoor industry was appealing to a more diversified roster of advertisers. As shown in Exhibit 12.5, beer and wine rank ninth in outdoor advertising expenditures. When companies such as General Motors, Walt Disney, McDonald's, Procter & Gamble, Time Warner, and Verizon Wireless made major investments in outdoor, it encouraged other mainstream businesses to add outdoor to their media schedules. The result has been increased revenues and an improved public image for the outdoor industry.

STRATEGIC ADVERTISING AND OUT-OF-HOME

Out-of-home advertising is one of the most flexible and adaptive of all media. It provides one of the last opportunities to reach consumers prior to purchase. In this regard, it combines the best features of radio and point-of-purchase. Outdoor advertising has many characteristics that set it apart from other media vehicles. With its ability to command attention, outdoor also is well suited to enhance the effectiveness of other advertising media. It can function as an economical supplement to a media plan or it can stand alone as a primary medium. Although there are some opportunities to reach particular portions of a geographic or demographic market with outdoor, its major strength is its ability to reach broad population centers quickly and cheaply.

As is the case with other media, individual advertisers have specific marketing objectives when they select out-of-home. However, there are a number of primary

EXHIBIT **12.5**

Courtesy of Outdoor Advertising Association of America, www.oaaa. org.

Top 10 Outdoor Advertising Categories (based on 2002 year-end outdoor expenditures)

1. Local Services & Amusements
2. Public Trans., Hotels & Resorts
3. Retail
4. Media & Advertising
5. Restaurants
6. Automotive Dealers & Services
7. Financial
8. Insurance & Real Estate
9. Beer & Wine
10. Automotive, Automotive Accessories & Equipment

Top 20 Outdoor Brands (based on 2002 year-end outdoor expenditures)

1. McDonald's
2. Miller Beers
3. Anheuser-Busch Beers
4. Cracker Barrel
5. Verizon Wireless
6. Holiday Inns
7. Washington Mutual Bank
8. Dodge
9. Warner Brothers
10. AT&T Wireless
11. Chevrolet Auto & Trk Var
12. Nextel Wireless Service
13. Ford Auto & Trk Var
14. State Farm Insurance
15. Walt Disney Var Movies
16. Coca-Cola Soft Drinks
17. Nextel Cellular Service
18. Walt Disney World
19. Hampton Inns
20. AT&T Long Distance

marketing advantages that are common to most out-of-home buys. Among these are the following:

- Quickly builds awareness for new brands and maintains and reinforces brand identity for established products
- Creates continuity for a brand or message by extending basic advertising themes beyond traditional media
- Offers a localized approach for national advertising campaigns
- Is adaptable to virtually any advertising message or brand with multiple formats
- Provides local support by offering directions to retail outlets
- Serves as a point-of-purchase reminder to customers in the shopping and buying process
- Can enhance direct-response offers by providing Web addresses and telephone numbers

Despite the fact that a number of high-profile national advertisers are using out-of-home currently, the medium remains an essentially local vehicle. Less than 40 percent of outdoor advertising revenue comes from national advertisers. However, in recent years, a number of changes in the out-of-home industry have taken place that make it likely that more national advertisers will consider out-of-home as part of their future advertising schedule. For example:

1. *Consolidation of ownership.* Only a few years ago, the outdoor business was made up primarily of local companies that provided little audience research, had no national force, or had limited funds to upgrade their facilities. Today, the

industry is dominated by large conglomerates that control hundreds of sites throughout the country. These companies are in a position to deal effectively with large national and regional advertisers to gain a larger share of their advertising budgets.

2. *Research.* National advertisers routinely expect sophisticated audience and creative effectiveness research to justify their expenditures. In past years, out-of-home research fell far short of other major media. Even basic demographic data were unavailable in some markets. In recent years, the out-of-home industry has made major strides in providing meaningful research to prospective advertisers. As we will discuss later in this chapter, the industry provides audited audience information as well as eye movement research and demographic segmentation information in areas as small as ZIP codes. Obviously, the outdoor research investment does not compare to that of media with 10 times its advertising revenues, but marketers are being given reasonable information on which to base their media decisions.

3. *Creative improvements.* The quantity and quality of out-of-home production have improved dramatically in the last decade. Rather than simply printed or painted signs, advertisers have the choice of options such as backlit dioramas, vinyl surfaces for outdoor and transit, and a number of building-sized signs.

4. *Terminology.* Over the years, outdoor developed a terminology that was unique to the industry. Not only did media buyers feel uncomfortable dealing in a "foreign" language when buying outdoor, but also, more importantly, it made intermedia comparisons difficult. With the adoption of the gross rating point as the basic measure of outdoor audience reach, the industry has taken steps to address this issue.[2]

Although outdoor can achieve a number of advertising goals, it is not suitable for every advertiser or every advertising or marketing situation. Like other advertising medium, outdoor is most successful when it is used in accordance with narrowly defined marketing objectives that utilize the strengths of the medium. In some respects, outdoor presents special challenges since in almost every case it is used as a supplemental media in a more general campaign.

Since outdoor is rarely a primary campaign building block, it must be coordinated, both creatively and in terms of audience reach, with other media. It is important that the main advertising themes be translated properly to outdoor, so that the target audience is exposed to a seamless message. Outdoor is rarely effective as a stand-alone medium. Its major strength is the extension and reinforcement of the more detailed advertising messages carried in other media.

Of course, no amount of planning can overcome some of the inherent weakness in a medium. While analyzing the strengths of out-of-home, advertisers also must consider its shortcomings and how these may influence a particular marketing, media, or creative strategy. Because exposure to outdoor is both involuntary and brief, there is little depth of communication, even among a product's most loyal customers. It is estimated that the average person sees most signs for less than 10 seconds.

In addition, most out-of-home vehicles provide little audience selectivity. The major advantage of most out-of-home advertising is that it is more a shotgun than a rifle. Even though advertisers can tailor their messages to reach specific audiences by pinpointing certain neighborhoods or specific streets, such as roads that lead to stadiums or shopping malls, targeting specific audiences is not considered a primary attribute of the medium.

Finally, as the popularity of out-of-home advertising has grown, it has encountered availability problems. In major markets, demand for premium outdoor sites means some advertisers cannot have access to choice locations. Despite these disadvantages, properly executed outdoor advertising can be an inexpensive method of gaining immediate product visibility.

EXHIBIT 12.6

Outdoor advertising is most effective when the message takes advantage of the strengths of the medium.

Courtesy of Savannah Electric, A Southern Company.

OUTDOOR REGULATION AND PUBLIC OPINION

Outdoor advertising's major advantage—its size—is also a significant public relations problem. For years, a vocal minority of environmentalists and public activists have argued for strict limits or complete removal of all outdoor signs. However, a number of research studies conducted during the last decade indicate that a majority of the public sees value in outdoor advertising and think that its positive aspects outweigh any negatives. Given the controversies that surround outdoor, it might be well to examine some of the primary areas of criticisms and the reaction of the outdoor industry to them.

Federal Legislation

The most comprehensive attempt at regulating outdoor advertising dates to the **Highway Beautification Act of 1965** (known as the "Lady Bird Bill" since Mrs. Lyndon Johnson lobbied for the legislation). The act restricted the placement of outdoor signs along interstate highways and provided stiff penalties for states that failed to control signs within 660 feet of interstates. Since passage of the legislation, the number of signs has been reduced from 1.2 million to less than 400,000. Most of the remaining signs are concentrated in commercially zoned areas. Exhibit 12.7 outlines some of the major provisions of the act.

Highway Beautification Act of 1965
Federal law that controls outdoor signs in noncommercial, non-industrial areas.

Tobacco Advertising

Historically, one of the most criticized aspects of outdoor advertising was the promotion of tobacco. Critics charged that the uncontrolled exposure of cigarette messages encouraged usage by underaged smokers. In April 1999, the issue became moot when outdoor advertising of tobacco was banned as part of an agreement with 46 state attorneys general and the major tobacco companies.

In the 1980s, one-third of all billboards promoted tobacco products. This concentration of dollars not only made the outdoor industry too dependent on one product category, but the controversy surrounding outdoor also discouraged other product categories from buying the medium. "Conventional wisdom once dictated that the outdoor industry couldn't survive without the . . . dollars from U.S. tobacco marketers. Now it seems not only can the industry survive the loss of that revenue, it can thrive in a nicotine-free world . . . outdoor's day of reckoning is fast becoming its day in the sun."[3]

EXHIBIT **12.7**

Federal and State Controls

Source: The Highway Beautification Act of 1965 (23 USC 131).

Summary of Existing Outdoor Advertising Control Programs

- Billboards are allowed, by statute, in commercial and industrial areas consistent with size, lighting, and spacing provisions as agreed to by the state and federal governments.

- Billboard controls apply to Federal-Aid Primaries (FAPs) as of June 1, 1991; interstates, and other highways that are part of the National Highway System (NHS). The FAP routes were highways noted by state DOTs to be of significant service value and importance. Approximately 260,800 FAP Miles existed as of June 1, 1991 (226,440 rural miles and 34,360 urban miles). These roads have full HBA protections and controls are very important. Maps can be obtained from your state DOT or FHWA Division office or from the OAAA in Washington, D.C.

- States have the discretion to remove legal nonconforming signs along highways; however, the payment of just (monetary) compensation is required for the removal of any lawfully erected billboard along the Federal-Aid Primary, interstate, and other National Highway System roads.

- States not complying with the provisions of the HBA are subject to a 10 percent reduction in their highway allocations.

- States and localities may enact stricter laws than stipulated in the HBA.

- No new signs can be erected along the scenic portions of state-designated scenic byways of the interstate and federal-aid primary highways.

The OAAA Code of Advertising Practices for Children

The industry has moved on a number of fronts to improve its image and create positive public relations in the communities it serves. One step to counteract negative publicity toward the industry has been the enactment of a voluntary Code of Advertising Practice by the OAAA. As part of this code, outdoor companies are asked to limit the number of billboards in a market that carry messages about products that cannot be sold to minors. Specifically, the code asks that member companies "establish **exclusionary zones** which prohibit advertisements of all products illegal for sale to minors which are either intended to be read from, or within 500 feet of, established places of worship, primary and secondary schools and hospitals." Furthermore, such "off-limit" boards will carry a decal featuring the symbol of a child (see Exhibit 12.8 for a copy of the code and decal).

exclusionary zones (outdoor)
Industry code of conduct that prohibits the advertising of products within 500 feet of churches, schools, or hospitals of any products that cannot be used legally by children.

Outdoor Industry Public Service

Each year the outdoor industry contributes hundreds of millions of dollars worth of donated space to a number of charities and public service campaigns. Many of these messages are posted in connection with local service projects. However, the OAAA has formed a number of partnerships to coordinate national projects with organizations such as the Advertising Council, the National Center for Missing and Exploited Children, the American Red Cross, and Homeland Security. In 2002, the outdoor industry donated over $80 million worth of outdoor space to the Advertising Council alone.

The Outdoor Advertising Plan

Successful outdoor advertising depends on both a strategic marketing plan and effective execution of the creative, media, and research elements of this strategy. A number of strategic issues should be considered before we move ahead with the creation of outdoor messages. Among the most important are the following:

The OAAA Endorses this Code and Encourages its members to cooperate in conformance with the following principles.

The outdoor advertising medium delivers advertisers' messages to the consumer in a public arena necessitating a high sensitivity to community standards as well as a vigilant defense of commercial free speech.

We, the members of the Outdoor Advertising Association of America (OAAA), are careful to place outdoor advertisements for products illegal for sale to minors on advertising displays that are a reasonable distance from the public places where children most frequently congregate.

In our vigilant support of children and free speech, we recommend that each OAAA member company adopt standards that include the following code of advertising practices.

1. Establish exclusionary zones that prohibit outdoor advertisements of products illegal for sale to minors that are intended to be read from, or within 500 feet of, elementary and secondary schools, public playgrounds, and established places of worship.

2. Identify all outdoor advertising displays within the exclusionary zone(s) by attaching the international children's symbol in a clearly visible location.

3. Establish reasonable limits on the total number of outdoor displays in a market that may carry messages about products that are illegal for sale to minors.

4. Maintain broad diversification of customers that advertise in the outdoor medium.

EXHIBIT 12.8

Code of advertising practices for children

Courtsy of Outdoor Advertising Association of America, www.oaaa.org.

---

1. *Clearly stated objectives.* As we discussed earlier, most outdoor advertising is used as either an introduction for a new product or event (such as a sale) or as a reminder to keep consumers continually aware of a brand. With its headline format, outdoor is rarely suited to offer a complete sales message. Furthermore, national advertisers rarely use outdoor as their primary medium. Consequently, it is extremely important to plan the outdoor portion of the total advertising campaign in a manner that will assure maximum efficiency and support to other advertising and promotional vehicles.

2. *Define the target market.* Generally, outdoor media has broad coverage throughout a market. However, outdoor does offer some opportunities for geographic targeting. "Most products and brands have distinct regional and local-market purchase patterns. It is common to find that a large group of local markets [or areas within a single market] will index at or above 130 in per-capita brand purchases. Geo-targeting with outdoor is a fine complement to demo-targeting with television or print."[4] It is also a great way to put special emphasis in areas of cities or neighborhoods that contain a large number of residents who belong to specific ethnic groups that may be important to a brand.

3. *Specify measurable goals.* An outdoor plan needs to specify what objectives it hopes to accomplish and how these goals will be measured. For example, do we want outdoor to contribute to increases in brand awareness, increases in sales, or higher market share? Finally, what research methodology will be used to determine if these goals were met and what was the contribution of outdoor?

4. *Coordinating the buy.* Outdoor advertising is purchased from local outdoor companies known as **plants.** Increasingly, most local plants are part of large national outdoor companies that provide network buying options to national and regional advertisers. With today's tight marketplace, it is more important than ever for agencies and advertisers to work with plants well ahead of the starting date for a

plant
In outdoor advertising the local company that arranges to lease, erect, and maintain the outdoor sign and to sell the advertising space on it.

showing. Ideally, space should be purchased at least four months in advance; some markets require even more time. Like spot television and radio, out-of-home is a supply-and-demand business with site availability a recurring problem.

5. *Postbuy inspection (called riding the boards).* After the posters are up, an in-market check of poster locations should be made. This inspection determines that proper locations were used and that the signs were posted or painted properly. It also helps ensure that billboards containing the client's message are not obstructed by such things as trees or poles.

All this only emphasizes that successful outdoor advertising demands the use of the same fundamental principles of advertising planning that apply to other media. In some respects, planning in outdoor is even more complex than in other media. As a supplement to other media, planners must make certain that the characteristics and objectives of outdoor mesh properly with those of more dominant media. The complementary nature of outdoor is an overriding concern in most outdoor schedules. The planner must be certain that outdoor can, in fact, reinforce the media schedule in a cost-efficient manner.

FORMS OF OUTDOOR ADVERTISING

As we mentioned at the outset of this chapter, outdoor is only one of several categories of out-of-home advertising. However, in terms of revenues, public familiarity, and long-term usage, the two basic forms of outdoor are posters and painted bulletins (see Exhibit 12.9). In either case, the message is designed by the advertising agency. The creative design is then reproduced on paper or vinyl and posted on panels. The larger painted bulletins are prepared by outdoor company artists either in a studio or on-site. Even large posters that once were painted are now being reproduced in vinyl.

Poster Panels

The 30-sheet poster is the most widely used form of outdoor advertising. The most common type of poster is really two posters in one. Bleed and 30-sheet posters, which use the same frame, constitute the typical highway billboard with which we are so familiar. Poster buys can be made for a single location or total national coverage.

EXHIBIT 12.9

Posters and bulletins make up the standardized outdoor industry.

Courtesy of Outdoor Advertising Association of America, www.oaaa.org.

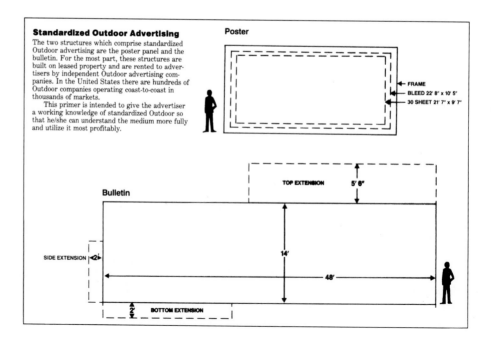

Standardized Outdoor Advertising
The two structures which comprise standardized Outdoor advertising are the poster panel and the bulletin. For the most part, these structures are built on leased property and are rented to advertisers by independent Outdoor advertising companies. In the United States there are hundreds of Outdoor companies operating coast-to-coast in thousands of markets.

This primer is intended to give the advertiser a working knowledge of standardized Outdoor so that he/she can understand the medium more fully and utilize it most profitably.

Poster

← FRAME
← BLEED 22' 8" x 10' 5"
← 30 SHEET 21' 7" x 9' 7"

Bulletin

TOP EXTENSION   5' 6"

SIDE EXTENSION |2|

14'

48'

BOTTOM EXTENSION   2'

The primary use of most posters is to reach the majority of a market quickly and inexpensively. However, with geomarketing, posters also can be used to reach more targeted prospects. For example, posters placed in financial districts or on routes to the airport reach more affluent customers and business travelers.

The standard poster panel measures 12 by 25 feet. The bleed poster either prints to the edge of the frame or uses blanking paper matching the background of the poster. The term *bleed* is, of course, borrowed from the bleed magazine advertisement that has no border. The term *sheet* originated in the days when presses were much smaller and it took many sheets to cover a poster panel.

Today, posters are often printed on vinyl instead of paper. The vinyl-wrapped poster uses the standard 30-sheet board, but by "wrapping" or covering the entire board, it expands the coverage area. Wrapped posters are usually available at any 30-sheet location. Although it lasts longer and retains color better than paper, vinyl is more expensive to produce so it is used at high-traffic locations and for longer contract periods than paper posters.

Poster displays are sold on the basis of **illuminated** and nonilluminated panels. Normally, poster contracts are for 30 days with discounts for longer periods. Those panels in locations with high-traffic volume are illuminated normally for 24-hour exposure. A typical poster showing will consist of 70 to 80 percent illuminated posters, but major advertisers often request full-illuminated postings. When buying an outdoor showing, the advertiser is provided information about the number of displays, the number that are illuminated and nonilluminated, the monthly and per-panel cost, and total circulation or exposure.

The Eight-Sheet Poster

Another important type of outdoor advertising is the eight-sheet poster. **Eight-sheet posters** measure 5 feet by 11 feet, slightly less than one-third the size of 30-sheet posters. Eight-sheet posters are bought by small, local businesses as well as by national companies. Often they are placed immediately adjacent to the point of sale as the last customer contact before a purchase decision. These compact posters add enormous reach and frequency to advertising plans at a modest cost.

Eight-sheet posters rapidly build brand awareness, announce new products and services, and provide reminder messages for a brand. In addition, eight-sheet space costs are much lower than traditional billboards and, because of their smaller size, production costs are significantly lower as well. The average CPM of eight-sheet posters is approximately half that of 30-sheets.

illuminated posters
Seventy to 80% of all outdoor posters are illuminated for 24-hour exposure.

eight-sheet poster
Outdoor poster used in urban areas, about one-fourth the size of the standard 30-sheet poster. Also called junior poster.

EXHIBIT **12.10**

This Korean billboard for high-speed Internet access offered by Korean Telecom contained only one word: "Bonus." It was in English and intended to support the television and print campaign as well as to drive consumer traffic to the Web site.

Courtesy of Korean Television, Chang Hwan Shin, and HyunJae Yu.

In most markets, zoning regulations are more favorable for the smaller eight-sheet posters than traditional billboards. Therefore, they can be used in a cost-effective way to reach various target audiences without expensive waste circulation. Like billboards, eight-sheet posters generally are bought to support a larger advertising campaign. Eight-sheet can enhance television by adding frequency and recall, and it adds a visual element to radio messages. It also can offer reminder messages to print media. Eight-sheet posters are handled by special poster plants but frequently appear concurrently with 30-sheet showings in a market.

Painted Bulletins

Painted bulletins are the largest and most prominent type of outdoor advertising. Painted bulletins are of two types: *permanent* and the more popular *rotary*. The permanent bulletin remains at a fixed location and can vary in size because it is never moved. The **rotary bulletin** is a standardized sign that is three times larger (14 feet by 48 feet) than the standard poster and it is placed at high-traffic locations for maximum visibility. Rotary bulletins can be moved from site to site to ensure maximum coverage of a market over a period of months. Both types of bulletins are almost always illuminated.

rotary bulletin (outdoor)
Movable painted bulletins that are moved from one fixed location to another one in the market at regular intervals. The locations are viewed and approved in advance by the advertiser.

Bulletins are approximately four times more expensive than posters. In recent years, the basic bulletin has been augmented with special embellishments, such as cutouts, freestanding letters, special lighting effects, fiber optics, and inflatables. Painted bulletin contracts usually are for a minimum of one year; however, short-term contracts are available at a higher monthly rate.

Rotary bulletins offer advertisers the advantages of the greater impact of the painted bulletin combined with more coverage and penetration than a single site could deliver. A rotary bulletin can be moved every 30, 60, or 90 days, so that during a 12-month period consumers throughout the market will have seen the advertiser's message.

Spectaculars

As the name implies, outdoor spectaculars are large, one-of-a-kind displays designed for maximum attention in urban centers. They may consist of special lighting or other types of ingenious material and innovations. In some cases they utilize a building as the canvas for the message. Spectaculars are very expensive and both production and space rentals are negotiated normally on a one-time basis with the minimum contract for most spectaculars being a year.

With the advent of new technology in outdoor advertising what was once a spectacular may soon be the norm. Currently the outdoor industry is using a variety of digital and laser technology for computerized painting/printing systems. More and more outdoor is being printed on flexible vinyl, which provides consistent, magazine-quality reproduction in all markets. In the future, outdoor planners envision the ability to provide satellite-distributed video images similar to giant television screens where computerized messages can be changed immediately. Regardless of what new technology comes to outdoor, it is obvious that the traditional paper poster soon may be history.

A growing segment of the spectacular category is the *wall mural* (also called *wallscapes*). Actually, it was ancient Roman wall paintings that gave outdoor advertising its start. Wall murals, done properly and in selected areas, can add a sense of urban art to an area. One of the largest examples of a wallscape was a series of four ads for Samsung electronics. The messages covered four New York City buildings and ranged in size from five to 12 stories. Most wall murals are printed on vinyl, which holds down production cost and makes installation much easier. Many building surfaces will not hold paint well and, from a practical standpoint, most building owners will not allow someone to paint their building.[5]

THE ELEMENTS OF OUTDOOR

Outdoor advertising is a visual medium with creative elements playing a much greater role than in most other advertising vehicles. The creative options available for outdoor and out-of-home advertisers are almost limitless with dozens of shapes and sizes offered to carry persuasive messages. As the OAAA points out, "Designing outdoor advertising is visual storytelling. The expression of an idea can surprise viewers with words or excite them with pictures. . . . Designing for the outdoor medium is a challenging communication task that requires the expression of a concept with clarity and austere focus."[6]

Outdoor Design

Designing an outdoor display is among the most difficult tasks for a creative team. Creating a picture and a few words to be seen by fast-moving traffic at distances of up to 500 feet is hard enough—to do so in a manner that moves customers to buy a product adds an obstacle not found in other media. However, outdoor also is one of the most enjoyable media to work with from a creative standpoint. Its size and color allow maximum creativity without the space constraints of other advertising vehicles. For example, in Tokyo, TBWA Worldwide took advantage of the unique qualities of billboards when it created human billboards for Adidas. These boards, designed to promote the beginning of soccer season, had a ball and two players suspended at a 90 degree angle on a giant vertical soccer field. The humans played 10- to 15-minute games five times per day attracting sizable audiences.[7]

Copy Outdoor only allows a headline, usually no more than seven words. Unlike copy in traditional media, there is no theme development and copy amplification. Conciseness is not only a virtue, but also a necessity. Advertisers have learned to work with these constraints to provide not only interesting but also motivating sales messages.

Color Color is one of the primary advantages of outdoor. However, colors must be chosen carefully to ensure readability. Outdoor designers use those colors that create high contrast in both hue (red, green, etc.) and value (a measure of lightness or darkness). For example, Exhibit 12.11 demonstrates 18 combinations of colors with 1 being the most visible and 18 the least visible.

EXHIBIT 12.11

Some color combinations are much more effective than others for outdoor advertising.

Courtesy of Outdoor Advertising Association of America, www.oaaa.org.

EXHIBIT **12.12**

Every outdoor ad has to attract attention and compete with distractions in the environment (Exhibit a). Some billboards send consumers to a Web site for more information (Exhibit b).

Courtesy of Bevil Advertising.

(a)

(b)

Outdoor Advertising and the Internet

One of the difficulties facing outdoor advertising is developing a way to have clients visualize creative concepts in a realistic environment. Most other media can demonstrate how an advertisement or commercial will look or sound in finished form. Translating an $8\frac{1}{2}'' \times 11''$ piece of paper to a 300-square-foot billboard is more difficult. However, a growing number of outdoor plants are providing Internet systems that allow advertisers and media planners to see how their posters will appear in actual locations. Exhibit 12.12a offers a driver's view of a poster location. Through computer scanning, any creative execution can be superimposed on the board. The system can also be used to make riding the boards a thing of the past as advertisers can now view posters from their office computers. Exhibit 12.12b offers a potential advertiser the address of the plant's Web site for further information and contacts about placing advertising.

Computer technology also offers the potential for a number of creative innovations in outdoor. Computers for some time have directed the design and painting process on vinyl, which is used in most of the larger bulletin displays. In addition, individual advertisers and plants are beginning to experiment with digital technology on billboards that offer changing messages such as days-to-Christmas and other current text. As we mentioned earlier, some outdoor executives envision a day when most high-traffic signs will consist of digital displays that are similar to large television screens and programmed from a central location.

BUYING OUTDOOR

Both the methods and terminology used in buying outdoor advertising are different in a number of ways from those used in other media. Poster advertising is purchased on the basis of *gross rating points (GRPs)*. You will recall from our earlier discussion of television that 1 *GRP* is equal to 1 percent of the population. Similarly, *GRPs* normally are bought in units of 50 or 100 and measure the duplicated audience reached by a poster allotment. An allotment is the number of posters used in an individual buy. To achieve a showing of 50 *GRPs* in a market means that an advertiser will have daily exposures to outdoor messages equivalent to 50 percent of the adult population of the market.

The audience for outdoor is called the *daily effective circulation (DEC)* and is calculated by using the following formula:

24-hour traffic count = 36,000

For nonilluminated posters the traffic cout is multiplied by .45; therefore,
.45 × 36,000 = 16,200 adult *DEC*

For illuminated posters the traffic count is multiplied by .64; therefore,
.65 × 36,000 = 23,040

Let's examine a market and work through these calculations:

Market: Anytown

Population: 800,000

Audience level purchased: 50 *GRPs*

Allotment: 26 posters (20 illuminated; 6 nonilluminated)

Explanation:

Our 20 poster allotment generated a *DEC* of 250,000. We calculate this by the following formula:

$$GRPs = \frac{\text{Daily effective circulation}}{\text{Market population}}$$

$$50 \ GRPs = \frac{400,000}{800,000}$$

You may not compare *GRP* levels in markets of different size, except as a measure of advertising weight and intensity. For example, 50 *GRPs* might require an allotment of 50 or 100 posters in a large market, whereas in a very small market 50 *GRPs* might be achieved with one or two posters. By the same token, in a market of 2 million population, a 50 *GRP* buy would generate a *DEC* of 1 million, whereas the same weight in a market of 50,000 would show a *DEC* of only 25,000.

VERIFYING

The success of outdoor advertising is dependent on providing advertisers and agencies with reliable research data on which they can base their media-buying decisions. The outdoor industry, dealing with an audience that is entirely out-of-home and on the move, faces significant challenges in developing audience research.

The Traffic Audit Bureau for Media Measurement (TAB)

The primary source of out-of-home audience information is the TAB. Founded in 1933, the organization audits the circulation of 30-sheet posters, bulletins, eight-sheet posters, shelter advertising displays, and, most recently, truck advertising. The TAB provides field auditors to check plant operators' adherence to TAB auditing standards and it also checks visibility of signs as well as traffic flow. A plant is audited every three years and a TAB Audit Circulation Report is issued after each audit.

Nielsen and Arbitron have both been working on new ratings systems for outdoor that can provide some of the demographic audience data desired by advertisers.[8] In the future, it is possible that a portable people meter, such as the one being tested for television and radio, will be available some day to track outdoor audiences. This would potentially allow the tracking of outdoor exposure in an affordable way.[9]

Communication Effectiveness

In addition to traffic audits, which are primarily measures of potential audiences, advertisers are interested in the communication effectiveness of outdoor advertising. In order to address this issue, Perception Research Services (PRS) was engaged by the OAAA to conduct eye-tracking studies to determine the levels of outdoor visibility and the impact of this visibility. Using a technique that recorded drivers' and passengers' eye movements, PRS found that 74 percent of subjects noticed outdoor signs and 73 percent of those read the copy. Results also showed that the size of boards and creative enhancements such as three-dimensional figures and board extensions increased attention levels. Overall the study showed that outdoor can be effective in building brand recognition and it is able to draw attention from all target groups.

EXHIBIT 12.13

Courtesy of Savannah Electric, A Southern Company.

Another approach to measuring outdoor communication uses personal computers to measure the potential audience exposed to an outdoor campaign. This system combines cost and audience information in order to determine if specific campaign objectives have been met with a particular outdoor campaign.

Marketing and Rate Data

■ The Simmons Market Research Bureau (SMRB) is a national consumer study conducted annually with over 27,000 respondents. SMRB reports the reach of target audiences, media usage habits, and outdoor delivery for over 8,000 consumer products and services.[10]

■ The *Buyer's Guide to Outdoor Advertising* contains rate guides for 30-and eight-sheet posters and bulletins. The *Buyer's Guide* provides information concerning costs, number of panels in a showing, and market population.

As the outdoor industry seeks to encourage more advertising from packaged goods and retail advertisers, it is adopting many of the buying practices used by other media. One of the potential benefits of consolidation within the outdoor industry is a movement toward more industry-wide support for a number of research and audience measurement studies. As outdoor continues to appeal to major national advertisers, it will become necessary to provide standardized audience data and research.

Trends in Outdoor Advertising

Out-of-home advertising is becoming a popular choice with a number of advertisers seeking increased brand awareness and a means of differentiating themselves from traditional media messages. In an environment where people are bombarded by hundreds of messages every day, outdoor is a means of gaining high attention levels to a mass audience.

Outdoor complements and enhances other media advertising by providing high levels of reach and frequency at a lower cost than other media. Research shows that outdoor creates a synergistic effect when combined with most other media. In particular, out-of-home offers advertisers a last chance to create brand awareness among potential prospects. The influx of product categories such as packaged goods, cellular companies, retailers, and high profile fashion brands have given the outdoor industry much needed diversification.

Research and reliable audience measurements continue to be a challenge to the industry. In recent years, outdoor has sponsored a number of new and innovative approaches to verifying the reach and communication effectiveness of the medium. Computer technology has permitted researchers to undertake a number of studies that would have been impossible only a few years ago.

Finally, the industry is able to provide even better creative approaches for advertisers. The use of computer design, vinyl and other new materials, and online visualization of final creative products combine to make outdoor even more appealing to advertisers. The many formats of out-of-home are motivating a number of advertisers to use the medium—even those who resist traditional outdoor posters. The remainder of this chapter will discuss some of the out-of-home formats beyond billboards.

TRANSIT ADVERTISING

Transit advertising is designed to accomplish many of the same tasks as traditional outdoor messages. It builds brand awareness and provides reminder messages to a mobile population. Transit provides extensive reach and high repetition at a fraction of the cost of other media. Because transit audiences demonstrate repetitive

EXHIBIT 12.14

Two of the most popular exterior transit formats.

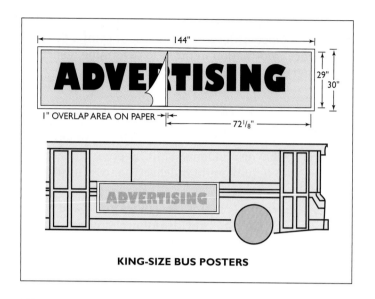

KING-SIZE BUS POSTERS

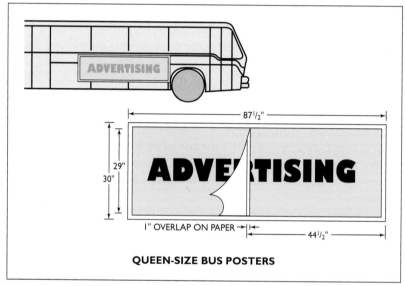

QUEEN-SIZE BUS POSTERS

travel patterns, it provides extremely high levels of frequency and consistent reach year-round.

The transit advertising category is defined by the OAAA as "advertising displays affixed to moving vehicles or positioned in the common areas of transit stations, terminals and airports."[11] The basic marketing strategy of transit advertising is that it reaches a mobile urban population on an out-of-home basis. Unlike billboards, exposure often takes place in an environment where there is more time to read a message and, in the case of interior displays, where the audience is exposed over a relatively long period of time during the average commute.

Exterior Displays

The majority of revenues for the transit industry come from exterior displays. These messages are carried on the outside of buses, subway cars, taxis, and, increasingly, on the sides of trucks. Whereas exterior signs are generally available on all sides of a bus, the basic units are the king-size bus posters and the queen-size posters (see Exhibit 12.14).

King-size posters are carried on both the curb and street sides of buses whereas queen-size posters are displayed on the curb. A relatively recent innovation is the full

EXHIBIT 12.15

Taxi toppers provide exposure to both pedestrians and vehicular traffic.

Courtesy of Howard, Merrell and Partners and ING Direct.

bus or subway wrap where an entire vehicle is covered by a single advertising display. Material is used to cover the windows so that passengers can see from the inside, but it maintains a continuous design when viewed from the outside. All exterior signs are printed on vinyl and either placed in frames or, more often, affixed with adhesive. In most markets, advertisers can choose from a number of bus routes to create all or only a portion of a market. The intent of exterior signs is to reach both pedestrian and vehicular traffic primarily during daylight hours.

Interior Displays

Interior signs, often referred to as *car-cards*, come in a number of sizes and they are fitted into racks inside buses and subway cars. The advantage of interior signs is that they can be seen over a relatively long period of time, especially compared to most other forms of outdoor. Interior signs are ideal for building high levels of frequency because most commuters travel the same routes on a daily basis. Occasionally, interior signs include cards or tear-off slips that can be taken by riders—thus combining features of both transit and direct-response advertising. Interior displays can also be found in some taxis.

Airport Displays

Although these messages are not "transit" in terms of being included in or on vehicles, airport displays are classified in the transit category because they reach the same audience as traditional transit advertising. Among familiar formats are back-lit panels, courtesy phone centers, wall wraps, baggage carousels, baggage carts, airport bus shelters, and kiosks in terminals and at the gates. Regardless of the specific format, airport displays are intended to reach pedestrian traffic in a captive environment. Transit costs are generally around $1 CPM. Its ability to generate significant audience levels and reach an upscale audience has resulted in a number of advertisers moving into the medium.

EXHIBIT **12.16**

Interior signs can build frequency.

Courtesy of Howard, Merrell and Partners and ING Direct.

STREET FURNITURE ADVERTISING

A specialized sector of the transit medium is street furniture advertising. This category of out-of-home advertising is defined as "advertising displays, many of which provide a public amenity, positioned at close proximity to pedestrians and shoppers for eye-level viewing, or at curbside to influence vehicular traffic."[12] In this category of out-of-home advertising are such options as bus benches, in-store displays, shopping mall displays, kiosks, bicycle racks, and bus shelter panels.

Shelter posters are a fast-growing medium in major metropolitan areas. Shelter displays are approximately 4 feet by 6 feet and provide attention-getting messages for both commuters and pedestrian traffic (see Exhibit 12.17). The back-lit panels provide 24-hour exposure with no clutter from competing media. Shelter operators offer full market coverage or geographic targeting in selected sections of a metropolitan area.

Like station posters and interior transit, shelter advertising generates extremely high frequency among commuters. The cost of individual panels varies with the population, the number of displays purchased, and the length of contracts (space contracts run from one to 12 months). The CPM for shelter is comparable to other forms of transit with CPMs running only a few cents. Even though the posters are small by outdoor standards, ". . . when you take into account that they're seen at eye level, they have every bit as much . . . impact as the big boards which obviously are viewed from a much greater distance."[13]

Shelter advertising is a large medium within the street furniture category. It is used by a number of major advertisers and it has been a leader in developing the type of diverse advertising support sought by other forms of out-of-home (see Exhibit 12.18). Shelter advertising, although accounting for a small portion of total

EXHIBIT **12.17**
A Typical Station Poster

EXHIBIT **12.18**

Shelter advertising is used to promote a variety of products.

advertising, will continue to grow at a faster rate than overall advertising expenditures. Finally, rather than facing the regulatory problems of outdoor, the revenues generated by shelter posters are often shared with municipal transit companies, making the medium a welcome revenue producer to many cities facing tight budgets.

ALTERNATIVE OUT-OF-HOME ADVERTISING

Alternative out-of-home advertising includes a variety of formats that reach audiences when they are engaged in specialized activities. This is the broadest form of out-of-home advertising and includes everything from parking meters, cinema, and stadium advertising to trash bins, health clubs, and subway tunnels. It also includes shopping bags, roadside logos, beach sand impressions or commercial restrooms.

There are many opportunities for advertisers within some of these alternative options. For example, cinema advertising can include ads in a slideshow or one to two minute commercials run before the movie, kiosks or posters in the theatres or product placements in the movies themselves. Stadium advertising can include scoreboard, restroom, trash can or concession stand signage.

Some of the media in the out-of-home category are more similar to promotions than to traditional advertising. For example, Procter & Gamble had the Pottypalooza created to bring to events such as festivals and fairs where consumers might be in need of a restroom. The Pottypolooza is a truck painted with signage for Charmin toilet tissue inside and out. It contains several extremely clean flush toilets and is stocked with Charmin, Safeguard soap, Pampers changing tables, and Bounty paper towels. It has been very popular with consumers. In addition, Procter & Gamble says that there is a 14 percent increase in Charmin usage among consumers who use the facilities.[14]

 **SUMMARY**

Out-of-home advertising is fast becoming part of mainstream media. Although it currently comprises less than 2.5 percent of total advertising revenues, this will likely grow in the next decade. Outdoor offers an opportunity for advertisers to provide brand reminders to current customers and introduce brands to prospective customers at a cost of less than virtually any other medium.

In many respects, out-of-home functions in the same way as point-of-purchase advertising to reach consumers immediately before purchase. With the many options available in out-of-home, there is a format for almost every advertising objective. As traditional media become more fragmented, outdoor remains a medium that can provide both reach and frequency to a mass audience. At a time when outdoor is appealing to national advertisers, industry consolidation is creating efficient means of buying multiple markets.

Out-of-home media also are enjoying the benefits of more sophisticated research addressing both audience measurement and communication effects of the medium. As more national advertisers begin to consider out-of-home advertising, it will be necessary for the industry to provide research similar to what is available from other media competitors.

REVIEW

1. Why is a diversity of product categories important to the outdoor industry?

2. Why has the term *out-of-home* replaced *outdoor*?

3. What are the primary categories of out-of-home advertising?

4. What is the function of the Traffic Audit Bureau for Media Measurement (TAB)?

5. Why has transit advertising grown significantly in recent years?

6. What are the primary uses of outdoor for most advertisers?

7. What are the major advantages of the eight-sheet posters?

8. What are the major disadvantages of outdoor posters?

TAKE IT TO THE WEB

The Outdoor Advertising Association of America (OAAA) is a trade association that represents the outdoor advertising industry. Visit its Web site (**www.oaaa.org**) and create a list of all the different kinds of creative outdoor advertising opportunities you see listed.

Lamar Transit Advertising is an extension of Lamar Advertising and provides transit shelters, bench advertising, and transit bus displays. View the product gallery on the Lamar Transit Web site (**www.lamartransit.com**) and list the advantages and disadvantages of these alternate forms of advertising.

The John W. Hartman Center for Sales, Advertising, and Marketing History is part of the Rare Book, Manuscript, and Special Collections Library at Duke University. Check out the Outdoor Advertising Archives (**http://scriptorium.lib.duke. edu/hartman/oa/outdoor.html**) and compare some of the earlier billboards with what you see on the roads today.

CHAPTER 13

Search Engines

Pop-ups

Banners

Web Sites

Direct Response
and
The Internet

Direct Mail

TV Shopping Networks

Catalogs

Telemarketing

Direct-Response and Internet Advertising

CHAPTER OBJECTIVES

Since the mid-1990s, every aspect of direct response from selling techniques to consumer information acquisition has undergone dramatic change. Today, virtually every advertiser is using the techniques of direct response as a key ingredient of marketing strategies. After reading this chapter, you will understand:

1. effects of new technology on direct-response advertising
2. the future growth of the Internet and direct response
3. planning for marketing on the Internet
4. the concept of consumer relationship management
5. the principles of integrated marketing and direct response
6. major components of direct-response marketing

DIRECT RESPONSE—PROS

1. Direct response has the potential to reach virtually any prospect on a geographical, product usage, or demographic basis.
2. Direct response is a measurable medium with opportunities for short-term, sales-related response.
3. Direct response allows advertisers to personalize their messages and build an ongoing relationship with prime target audiences that is often impossible in traditional mass media vehicles.

DIRECT RESPONSE—CONS

1. High cost per contact is a major problem with many forms of direct response, especially direct mail. Expenses for printing, production, and postage have all increased significantly in recent years.
2. To keep up with an increasingly mobile population, prospect lists must be updated constantly at considerable expense to advertisers.
3. Public and government concerns with privacy issues have become a major problem for the direct-response industry. Telemarketers and Internet marketers, in particular, are facing restrictive legislation and regulations at both the state and federal levels that have limited their ability to reach new prospects through certain types of contacts.

THE INTERNET—PROS

1. The Internet offers a relatively inexpensive, quick, and easily available interactive medium especially among niche markets such as the business-to-business market.

2. The Internet is the ultimate research tool with its ability to measure exactly how many people used the medium and/or purchased a product.

3. The Internet is among the most flexible media with an ability to change messages immediately in reaction to market and competitive conditions.

THE INTERNET—CONS

1. To this point, the Internet is just beginning to perform for advertisers. Early failures make it difficult to determine the effectiveness of the service because it is still looking for profitable executions.

2. Despite the growing popularity of the Internet as a means of informal communication, many consumers are still reluctant to use the service for purchasing products and services. In particular, consumers are reluctant to give their credit card numbers over the Internet even though secure sites are available.

3. The sheer number of commercial and noncommercial Web sites makes it difficult for consumers to know what is available or, once known, to have much time to spend with any single site.

There is nothing new about the concept of selling directly to consumers. Benjamin Franklin sold scientific books by mail in the 1740s and, more than 100 years ago, Montgomery Ward had a thriving mail-order business through its catalog (see Exhibit 13.1). For the last 25 years, marketers have moved toward a more personal relationship with their customers. They have progressed steadily:

- From mass marketing where prospects were reached relatively indiscriminately at the lowest possible cost per impression.

- To category marketing where prospects who belong to some broad demographic category such as women ages 18 to 34 were targeted.

- To niche marketing where these broad categories were more narrowly defined (e.g., women ages 18 to 34 with children).

- To group (or community) marketing where prospects who regard themselves as part of a group with common interests (e.g., tennis players, opera lovers, antique collectors) are reached with messages and product benefits that acknowledge these interests.

- To one-to-one marketing where products and messages are tailored to the expressed interest of the individual (e.g., Dell computers where every machine is made to order).

From the first direct-mail research of the 1920s to computer-driven technology of the Internet, direct-response marketers have been able to refine their identification and outreach more precisely to various customer groups. It was not that many years ago that people were amazed when direct-mail offers addressed customers by name in the body of letters.

At the same time this technological renaissance was taking place, the competitive environment was lessening the distinction among brands and resulting in (1) price competition with shrinking profit margins for sellers and/or (2) a reliance on trusted brands to provide customers with a perception of consistent quality. For example, the local Ford dealer faced with an informed customer armed with the latest dealer invoice information from edmunds.com is faced with a choice of lowering the profit margin or increasing after-sale service. In fact, the dealer probably will have to do some of both.

Marketers are increasingly asking their marketing communication programs to blend old and new communication strategies. On the one hand, television commercials and other traditional media messages are establishing or maintaining brand visibility and positioning. On the other hand, high brand identity makes contact through e-mail and Web sites much more effective. New technology can

EXHIBIT **13.1**

Mail order catalogs have been thriving for more than one hundred years.

Courtesy of Montgomery Ward & Co. Catalogue, (1895) 1969. Reprint, New York: Dover Publications.

rarely create brand image; it can reach consumers with interactive media at a time of the prospect's choosing and with messages crafted to meet the needs of each individual.[1]

DIRECT RESPONSE AND THE INTERNET

Throughout this text we offer examples of ways in which the Internet has dramatically changed the way marketers and the media do business. In this section, we will discuss not only how the Internet is being used directly by direct-response firms but also how the blending of the Internet and direct response is being used in both competitive and complementary ways to promote products and services. We also will examine some of the primary concerns facing direct response and its use of new technology.

It is estimated that in 2003 approximately 58 percent of United States households had Internet access. With over 140 million users in the United States, it is not surprising that advertisers are continuing to look for new and better ways to use the medium.[2] As you can see in Exhibit 13.2, the largest Internet advertisers still tend to be dot-coms. According to the research firm AdRelevance, almost 290 of the top 500 largest U.S. companies are spending money in online advertising. Seeing the potential of the Internet as an advertising medium, large advertisers such as

Measured Ad Spending		
Rank	Advertiser	2002
1	Time Warner	$292.3
2	Microsoft Corp.	126.3
3	Qwest Communications Int'l	117.3
4	Bank One Corp.	90.8
5	Netstock Investment Corp.	75.7
6	Ameritrade Holding Co.	75.6
7	eDiets.com	69.4
8	Yahoo!	67.9
9	Bertelsmann	61.0
10	USA Interactive	59.2

McDonald's, Estée Lauder, and General Motors are all beginning to use the Internet for branding campaigns as well as for a direct-marketing tool.[3]

Customer Relationship Management

customer relationship marketing (CRM)
A management concept that organizes a business according to the needs of the consumer.

Customer relationship management or **customer relationship marketing (CRM)** is a core principle of both direct-response and Internet marketing. The concept of CRM should be viewed from both the customer and marketer perspective. From the standpoint of the consumer, it is clear that the audience feels empowered by interactive media and they use this empowerment in a proactive manner. From a lifestyle standpoint, research shows that the online audience uses some traditional media less than they did before gaining Internet capability and less than those who are not online.

In addition to media usage, consumers also are embracing online couponing, entering sweepstakes online, and participating in other targeted sales promotion activities. It is not surprising that consumers would respond to targeted promotions tailored to their interests. Likewise, businesses are happy to avoid the expense of waste circulation by reaching this selective audience.

The CRM concept offers several other advantages to businesses. Although sacrificing some control to consumers, marketers are dealing with a much higher percentage of prospects than in mass advertising or even in the direct-response methods used only a few years ago. For example, the combination of sophisticated software and the Internet allows companies to achieve the following:

- More effective cross-selling and up-selling from current customers
- Higher customer retention and loyalty
- Higher customer profitability
- Higher response to marketing campaigns
- More effective investment of resources[4]

None of these benefits should be surprising. As a company develops a closer relationship with each of its customers, we would expect that it would use the greater understanding to approach consumers with offers that fit their interests and tastes. The use of interactive technology allows businesses to deal with the unique purchasing, lifestyle, and behavioral histories of each customer. Rather than dealing with statistical aggregations of groups of customer data, a business now has the capability of one-to-one marketing. Communication and product offers can be based on predetermined consumer needs and can be differentiated from similar competitive offers. The end result is that the consumer gains better value and the company engenders continued customer loyalty.[5]

Chapter 13 Direct-Response and Internet Advertising 383

THE INTERNET AND MARKETING RESEARCH

Clearly one of the primary benefits of Internet marketing is the ability to gain information about individual buying habits and product preferences. These data are, of course, collected as part of the consumer transaction process. However, one of the emerging advantages of Internet technology is the ability to collect market research quickly and inexpensively from a larger respondent base than might be possible with conventional research methodology. The Internet allows marketers to reach samples of specific consumers to determine a number of product, marketing, or advertising responses. Instead of being confined to a few locales, a marketer can now sample on a global basis. Even something as relatively simple as getting response data back from product testing is faster and demonstrates higher levels of cooperation than other methods.

The dangers of online testing involve a possible loss of competitive advantage by testing on the Web. In addition, there are questions about samples and perceptions in online testing. An important concern is that online respondents may be different than the general public. There are also troubling questions about whether concepts are graded differently during online surveys. As online transactions become more common and Internet household penetration continues to increase, the differences between online and off-line testing will likely diminish.

Privacy Concerns

The same technology that allows marketers to reach consumers on a one-to-one basis is creating major public relations problems over privacy concerns about the collection and use of personal information. The problem is so great that many observers think that the potential of new technology and online direct response will not be fulfilled until consumers are satisfied about the use and security of personal data.

Marketers are facing a number of concerns about how and under what circumstances they can contact a person online. The debate has created a new vocabulary for online marketers:

- **Spam** refers to unsolicited and usually unwanted online advertisements or promotional messages. Spammers are those companies that send these messages.

- *Opt-in* is a form of permission marketing in which online customers are sent messages only after they have established a relationship with a company. The customer may have purchased a product previously from the company or signed up on a company Web site giving the firm permission to send product announcements or promotional material. Ford Motor Company has an opt-in program known as "The Connection." The online system offers various promotions and discounts to Ford owners. However, only customers who have granted permission are contacted and Ford assures them that no information is shared with other companies.

- **Opt-out** is a mechanism by which customers can notify online promoters that they do not want to receive spam.

A study reported by *Advertising Age* shows that 40 percent of online users say that they are angry about e-mail spam and another 58 percent are furious.[6] Congress has considered and passed legislation to limit the use of spam. The direct-marketing industry has come out strongly against e-mail spam. According to H. Robert Wientzen, president and CEO of the Direct Marketing Association (DMA), "It recently occurred to me that spammers are to e-mail users what weeds are to gardeners."[7] In October 2003, the American Association of Advertising Agencies (AAAA), the Association of National Advertisers (ANA), and the DMA worked

spam
Online advertising messages that are usually unsolicited by the recipient.

opt-out
Procedures that recipients use to notify advertisers that they no longer wish to receive advertising messages. A term usually associated with online promotions.

together to establish a set of nine self-regulatory guidelines to help protect the use of legitimate e-mail marketing. These guidelines encourage members to:

1. Use an honest subject line.
2. Include a valid return e-mail address as well as a physical address for those who wish to contact the company.
3. Clearly identify the subject and the sender at the beginning of the e-mail.
4. Provide a clear and conspicuous e-mail option for consumers to remove themselves from the list.
5. Electronic name removal features must be prompt and reliable.
6. Each brand or product featured must offer options for removal of consumers from commercial e-mail lists.
7. Not acquire e-mail address through automated systems (i.e., spiders and robots) without the consent of the consumer.
8. Not provide e-mail lists to unrelated third parties for their use.
9. Provide the sender's privacy policy in the body of the e-mail or via a link.[8]

The idea of spam, opt-in, and opt-out seems relatively straightforward. However, specific implementation can be very difficult. For example, the first message in an online promotion is spam—it was unsolicited. Marketers, even the most ethical ones, are pushing to continue to allow mass online messages with the proviso that consumers can then opt-out of future communication. (For more Internet advertising terms visit the Ad Resource Web site at http://adres.internet.com/glossary.) Any regulation requiring that consumers give prior permission for every online promotional message could effectively kill many direct-response campaigns. It also is argued that stringent opt-in requirements would work against small companies and new brands by making it more difficult to get their messages to the public. However, consumers are often receptive to e-mail messages when they have opt-in to an e-mail list. A survey conducted by the e-mail firm Bigfoot Interactive found that when consumers have opted in to receive regular e-mail from a business, they derive more satisfaction from the relationship than those consumers who did not choose to receive the messages.[9]

In response to growing public concerns, the FTC has launched a number of inquiries about online policies and practices. The FTC advocates four elements for online privacy policies:

1. Disclosure of what information is collected
2. Choice for customers to opt out
3. Access by consumers to their personal information
4. Security standards for information use and access

Consumers have provided a wake-up call to the direct-response industry. As one consumer rights advocate commented, "Companies looking to keep their customers should pay attention to the privacy concerns that exist in the marketplace. Companies will find that having good privacy policies makes good business sense. Customers will feel comfortable buying products from companies that have privacy policies as opposed to those companies that don't."[10]

Online as a Complement to Other Media

Initial data indicate a decline in direct-mail investment as businesses take advantage of the efficiencies and lower cost of online promotion. However, for most media and direct-response categories such as telemarketing and direct-response television, online seems to serve a complementary rather than competitive role. As evidence of this, next time you flip through a magazine, take note of the number of advertisements that send readers to a company's Web site for more information or to place an order (see Exhibit 13.3).

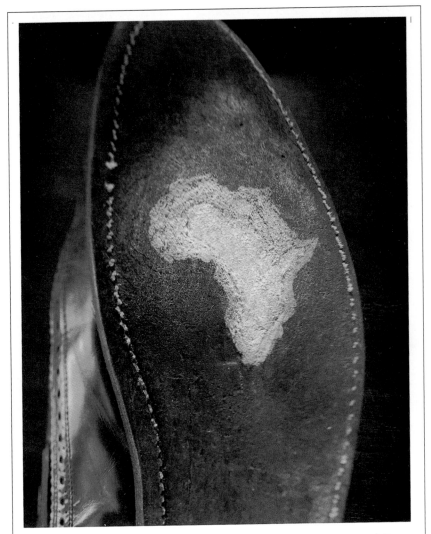

AFRICAN INFLUENCE ON AMERICAN DANCE.

When The Spirit Moves: The Africanization of American Movement. June 17–Nov. 7
at the Atlanta History Center. 404-814-4000 or www.atlantahistorycenter.com

⊛ ATLANTA HISTORY CENTER

EXHIBIT 13.3

A magazine ad can drive
customer traffic to a
Web site for more
information.

Courtesy of Huey/Paprocki, Inc.,
and Atlanta History Center.

Television seems to work well with online messages. The medium's high credibility can build brand equity among large groups of prospects very quickly. Television reaches a mass audience in a typical advertising environment of formal programming interspersed with 30-second commercials. During the same time that a person is viewing a television show, typical Internet users have visited five or six Web sites and the advertising they were exposed to was more like outdoor than traditional print or broadcast. That is, the Internet audience was exposed to a brief brand-oriented headline as they quickly pass the advertising.[11] Research suggests that many television audience members are surfing the Web at the same time they are "watching" television. This is particularly true of young adult and youth audiences.

Many online promotions must deal with two groups of prospects. The first, and by far the larger, group for most sites consists of surfers and casual users. For these consumers, Web advertising must gain attention quickly if they are going to click a banner or spend time with a commercial message. The other group of users consists of those who are actively in the market for a product or service. They are information seekers who may have seen the Web site in a media advertisement, run

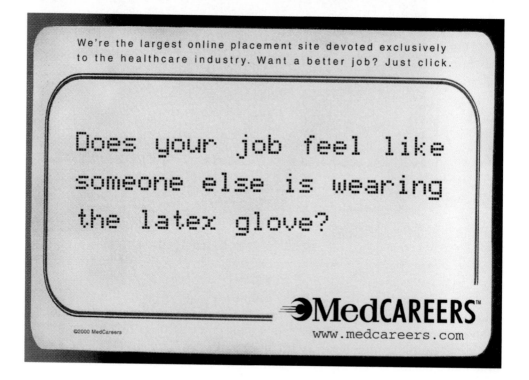

across the site on a search engine, or actively sought out a specific site because of familiarity with a brand. In any case, the site needs to provide up-to-date product information including price, purchase instructions, warranties, and so forth. If you think about it, the process is much the same for media advertising where advertisements and commercials first gain awareness and attention for a brand and retailers close the sale. The media/Internet relationship is, in some respects, the same as that of the media and retailers (see Exhibit 13.4 a and b).

Some research has shown that the average online user will not wait very long for a connection before moving to another site. The sheer number of online options has created a level of impatience unseen in other communication technology. The effect of this impatience is a heightened need by companies for brand awareness. Branding accomplishes two goals in the online world:

1. It gains awareness for the Web site itself. In the early years of online commerce, the Super Bowl might well have been named the "**dot-com**" Bowl given the number of commercials bought during the game by online companies. Some products such as prescription drugs send consumers to their Web sites to read a full disclosure of the possible negative side effects of their products in order to satisfy FDA requirements.

2. Branding is important for the companies that want high visibility on the Web. Online consumers, like their off-line counterparts, will gravitate to companies, products, and brands with which they are familiar. The difference is that the online attention span makes branding more important than ever before.

A number of companies have found that traditional advertising works better than online messages to encourage Web site visits. As long as this is the case, the complementary relationship between online and traditional media will continue. As one leading online executive pointed out, "At the end of the day, [interactive advertising] is just one more way to communicate with the consumer. It needs to be integrated in everything that an agency does for a brand or a business because treating it as a separate part of the mix ultimately doesn't work."[12]

dot-coms
A generic designation that refers to companies engaged in some type of online commerce.

Global Communication and Branding

The Internet is instant, intrusive, and international. It is a medium with no boundaries and, consequently, it presents a challenge to international advertisers. As we will discuss in Chapter 23, global companies realize they must adapt to local market conditions, but at the same time it is important for them to maintain a consistent presence and identification if they are to be truly worldwide companies.

Although the Internet presents problems for multinational companies attempting to execute localized strategies on a global basis, it does offer a number of major advantages to them. For example, companies can provide information about their products as well as receive orders from consumers in other countries without incurring additional expense. An example of a service that has benefited from being able to communicate to a broader international audience is higher education. Most college and universities in the United States provide information about themselves to an international audience on the Internet. In addition, most of these academic institutions put application materials and forms online, which saves them a great deal of money in materials and mailing costs.

Disintermediation

Disintermediation is a very fancy word referring to the potential of online technology eliminating most of the distribution channel by having manufacturers deal directly with consumers. In 1998, disintermediation was both the promise and the threat of the Internet. Local retailers saw the establishment of Amazon.com as the end of retailing as we know it.

A funny thing happened on the road to disintermediation—almost no one could make any money selling direct to customers for the first few years. One of the elements missing from many online transactions was customer service. As pointed out by the staff of internet.com, "The problems with dealing direct with the consumer is the customer: small orders, returns, complaints, shipping and all of the other issues that make up customer service . . . keeping a million people who have ordered a single pair of jeans happy is a lot harder than keeping a few big chains with huge orders satisfied."[13] In addition, consumers found that there were some products that they would rather see, try on, test-drive, or feel before they made a

disintermediation
The potential for online technology to eliminate all or part of the distribution channel by selling directly to customers.

purchase. In fact, online marketing has often benefited the traditional "bricks-and-mortar" retailers. Many marketers now feel that rather than replacing traditional retailing, the Internet will likely function as a complement to catalog selling, tele-marketing, and so-called "bricks-and-mortar" retailers.

Youth Audiences

The amount of time the Internet is used by audiences varies by age. Teens and young adult audiences who have grown up with the Internet—sometimes referred to as the Internet generation—now report spending more time using the Internet than watching television. According to research conducted by Harris Interactive and Teenage Research Unlimited, 13- to 24-year-olds spend 16.7 hours per week online (excluding e-mail) and 13.6 hours watching television. By contrast, they spend only about 12 hours per week listening to the radio, less than 7 hours talking on the phone, and 6 hours reading either books or magazines that are not related to their studies.[14]

Youth audiences report that the control over the content offered by the Internet is the primary reason that they prefer to use the Internet. Teens and young adults are better able than other demographic groups to use more than one form of media at a time and they often surf the Web while they are watching television.[15] As pointed out by Wendy Harris Millard, chief sales officer for Yahoo!, "Our industry needs to evaluate and change our communications approach to successfully reach this key target market. This generation is a revolutionary consumer group, actively in control and entrenched in their media experience, and their patterns will influence the future of media spending."[16]

Internet Dayparts

As with radio and television, there appear to be distinctive daypart usage patterns on the Internet. According to a study conducted by the Online Publishers Association, there are five distinct Internet dayparts:

1. Early morning (M–F 6 A.M.–8 A.M.)
2. Daytime (M–F 8 A.M.–5 P.M.)
3. Evening (M–F 5 P.M.–11 P.M.)

EXHIBIT 13.5

Teens and young adults now spend more time on the Internet than with other media.

4. Late night (M–F 11 P.M.–6 A.M.)

5. Weekends (Sat–Sun all day)

Although search engines and e-mail appear to have little variation in usage by time of day, content sites experience distinct differences in usage by daypart. Early morning and daytime dayparts have a larger concentration on news and information sites relative to other dayparts. Evening and weekend dayparts show an increased concentration in entertainment and sports sites relative to daytime. In contrast to television, Nielsen//NetRatings reports that daytime has the largest audience in terms of size and number of minutes of usage. However, evening and weekend dayparts are a better time to reach those under the age of 18.[17] Usage of the Internet at work peaks between 10:00 A.M. and noon. At home usage is the highest between 5:00 P.M. and 9:00 P.M.[18]

THE WIRELESS AND BROADBAND REVOLUTION

As exciting as the last decade's technological developments have been, most experts think that we have only scratched the surface of the potential for new communication systems. Their optimism is grounded in the possibilities afforded by wireless and broadband technology. As the name implies, wireless technology allows interactive communication without being wired to a computer. The first phase of the wireless revolution is the cell phone. Twenty years ago, with the exception of the military and public safety agencies, a "car phone" was a toy of the very rich. Today, your local mall is a sea of teens talking on their cell phones, and using cell phones on the highway is so common that it is part of a national debate about safe driving.

Cell phones are now also becoming an information tool with access to the Internet. Consumers can now check the weather, find movie schedules, and locate various retail categories in a particular location. Software already exists that will alert an individual about preprogrammed information. For example, if a particular stock dropped to a certain level, you can be alerted automatically so that you place a sale order with your broker—all from a fishing dock in the Bahamas! Some communication executives envision that the wireless communication revolution will usher in a period of **m-commerce** (mobile commerce). Rather than checking for the nearest Starbucks or a stock quote, we will be able to use a handheld device to receive and redeem coupons, make purchases, and comparison shop.

m-commerce
Mobile technology that allows consumers to receive information, make purchases, and conduct business anywhere they happen to be.

THE ROLE OF THE INTERNET IN ADVERTISING AND MARKETING

From an advertising and marketing perspective, there are a number of uses for the Internet and commercial Web sites:

1. *As a source of direct sales.* Internet direct sales may be accomplished as stand-alone e-businesses, such as Amazon.com, or as an ancillary to an established business, such as cataloger Lands' End (www.landsend.com), or as a traditional retailer, such as Home Depot, that augments walk-in traffic with a merchandising Web site.

2. *As a source of advertising-supported communication.* Virtually every magazine, newspaper, and major broadcast outlet has some Internet presence. Often newspapers give their Web site address at the end of news stories so that interested readers can obtain more in-depth information about a specific story. There also are a number of Internet-only media, such as Salon, that have only Internet audiences. Most of these communication outlets have attempted to be advertising supported, but few have been able to turn a profit from their Internet-only services.

EXHIBIT 13.6

A variety of businesses have established Web sites to provide product information.

Courtesy of Sawyer Riley Compton and James Hardie Siding Products.

3. *As a source of marketing and promotion information.* Thousands of businesses large and small have established Web sites to provide product information, enhance stockholder relations, and report current company news. Advertising agencies have scrambled to find a way to service clients' Internet demands effectively. Many major agencies such as Leo Burnett have established separate interactive divisions to offer interactive marketing to clients. Other agencies have integrated online and off-line advertising strategies within the traditional advertising agency account team (see Exhibit 13.6).

DIRECT-RESPONSE MARKETING: AN OVERVIEW

Although direct-response marketing has embraced many of the techniques and technologies of interactive media, it would be a mistake to think that traditional means of direct response from direct mail to telemarketing are going away in the near future. Direct marketing and advertising will continue to use a number of options to reach consumers and prospects. The next section will discuss some of the primary areas of direct response.

Objectives of Direct Response

Most direct-response campaigns have at least one of the following objectives:

1. *Direct orders* include all direct-response advertising that is designed to solicit and close a sale. All the information necessary for the prospective buyer to make a decision and complete a transaction is provided in the offer.

2. *Lead generation* includes all direct-response advertising that is designed to generate interest in a product and provide the prospective buyer with a means

EXHIBIT **13.7**

Business-to-business advertisers use direct-response ads to generate sales leads.

Courtesy of Huey/Paprocki, Inc., and YellowBrix.

to request additional information about the item or qualify as a sales lead for future follow-up (see Exhibit 13.7).

3. *Traffic generation* includes all direct-response advertising conducted to motivate buyers to visit a business to make a purchase. The advertisement provides detailed information about the product but usually no order form.[19]

Traditional advertising often works in concert with direct response. For example, direct-response advertisements and commercials offering a number of products and services are a major source of revenue for virtually every medium. In addition, direct-response offers, whether by mail, telephone, or media, are enhanced by brand advertising that gives consumers confidence to order goods directly.

Major Advantages of Direct Response

Regardless of the means of reaching consumers with direct-response offers, there are a number of characteristics that these approaches have in common:

1. *It is targeted communication.* With the exception of mass media direct response, the advertiser determines exactly who will be reached by the sales

message. The copy can be tailored to the demographic, psychographic, and consumption profile of the audience. In addition, both the timing and production of advertising are totally under the control of the advertiser.

2. *Direct response is measurable.* One of the disadvantages of most traditional advertising is that only the results can be estimated. However, in many forms of direct response the results can be computed to the penny. Furthermore, the advertiser is able to measure precisely various messages and other creative alternatives.

3. *The message of direct response is personal.* Whether by mail, media, or computer, the direct-response marketer is able to identify consumers more than ever and reach them with targeted, personalized messages. Many in the direct-response industry think it is only a matter of time before one-to-one advertising will be commonplace.

In part, the growth of direct response is directly attributable to a changing marketplace. We have moved from a manufacturer-driven economy to one that is dominated by huge retailers. In the twenty-first century, we are finding that consumers are increasingly in charge. Home computers and fiber optic technology are making it practical for consumers to avoid traditional media and make purchasing decisions on a one-to-one basis with sellers. Soon consumers will no longer be limited by traditional market channels, but rather, whether they live in a major city or a remote village, they will have immediate availability to goods and services. This is a marketing environment in which direct response will prosper.

In an environment of increasing accountability for marketing and advertising dollars, direct response can provide measured results. However, because of the expense of much direct response, it is imperative for most direct-response offers to reach a narrowly targeted audience. Many direct-response formats (e.g., mail catalogs, mail distributed product samples, etc.) can be extremely expensive if directed at nonprospects. On a CPM basis, any type of direct-mail solicitation is much more costly than traditional media exposure. However, a properly executed direct-response campaign will reach a significantly higher percentage of prospects with much less waste circulation than mass advertising. In addition, a major portion of the investment in direct response is intended to create an immediate sale whereas advertising investment is usually only one step in a process of building awareness and brand equity hoping to lead to a sale sometime in the future.

As we will see in this chapter, direct-response advertising takes many forms and is expected to accomplish a number of marketing objectives.

DATABASE MARKETING

The key to successful direct response is a thorough knowledge of each business's customers. This information includes not only consumers' demographic characteristics but also their purchase behavior and their interests and lifestyles. Not long ago, a consumer database consisted largely of basic information about the person, perhaps some information about recent purchases, and a lot of guesswork about what product might be bought next.

lifetime value
An estimate of the long-term revenue that can be expected from a particular prospect.

Today, database technology focuses on acquisition and retention of customers on a so-called **lifetime value** basis. That is, how can we attract those customers who will provide the greatest profitability over the coming years, not just for a single purchase? We discussed earlier the importance of customer relationship management and this concept of CRM is at the heart of database marketing.

Businesses are looking for methods of combining personal information with purchase behavior to predict future purchases and the type of offers and advertising messages that will move an individual to a future purchase. Seeking this information has required marketers to undertake much more sophisticated research and data cross-checking than in previous years. Many refer to this process as data mining. Using computer technology, businesses are "sifting through mountains of detailed customer transactional and demographic data to find concealed patterns, market segments and new customer insights. [Computers] are able to analyze enormous amounts of data to reveal undiscovered information."[20] Data mining attempts to find those characteristics of current customers that relate most meaningfully to prospects. It allows companies to enhance profitability by examining how they have been successful in the past and apply those lessons in the future.

The primary consideration of database marketing is how to use information to predict future purchases. A number of predictive models are being used by businesses. These models are referred to as *behavior maps* and they allow marketers to combine recent purchasing activity and consumer profiling to offer a relatively accurate picture of what will be purchased in the future and what offers will move that customer to make a purchase. For example, it is senseless for the local video store to offer a "Fifth Movie Free" promotion to a customer who usually rents five movies at a time. "When marketers understand individual purchase patterns, they learn what circumstances, if any, are necessary to spur sales. They also find out which offers may be exercises in futility—before they waste lots of time and money in the discovery process."[21]

In order to accomplish behavior mapping and other sophisticated consumer purchasing identification methods, consumer data must be managed centrally. This need for data management has led to the development of *data warehouses,* which are centralized company-wide data storage and retrieval systems.

The ACME Catalog Company has the following information on a customer:

Jane I. Buyer, married, 39, two children: boy 7, girl 9

Lives in an affluent ZIP code,

Address: 677 Brookhaven Dr., Evanston—June 1998–present

101 Sunny Lane, Chicago—April 1994–June 1998

44 Olive Blvd., Miami—May 1991–March 1994

777 Main St., St. Louis—Sept. 1989–May 1991

Purchases from ACME:			
	Crystal glasses	$210	5/12/01
	Man's leather jacket	340	9/22/01
	Woman's sweater	99	4/11/00
	Snow skis	233	3/25/00
	Desk set	49	12/10/99
	Dressing gown	98	12/10/99
	Perfume	124	10/4/98
	Diamond bracelet	750	8/3/98

From this very simple database example, you can tell several things about the customer. She comes from an upwardly mobile household and, judging by the items she purchases, she has reasonably high levels of discretionary income. From a marketing standpoint, she does not purchase children's items from ACME. (Is she a potential customer for these items?) The most troubling part of the data is that she has not made a purchase for some time. Should ACME make a special offer to renew the relationship, contact her by phone, by e-mail? We know that keeping her as a customer will be much less expensive than gaining a new customer with her profit potential.

The key to CRM and the benefits of database marketing are to provide information that allows a company to maintain the loyalty (and profitability) of its customers. The primary element in data mining is that the end result is a relationship that is beneficial to both the company and the consumer.

THE DIRECT-RESPONSE INDUSTRY

The direct-response advertising industry has grown dramatically in the last 20 years and this growth is likely to continue. According to eMarketer, online advertisers spent almost $7 billion on the Internet in 2003 and will reach over $8 billion by 2005. Advertising on search engines alone was estimated at over $2 billion in 2003.[22] However, there are many other forms of direct response including telemarketing, catalogs, inserts, coupons, direct television and radio, and direct and dimensional mail. This section will review some of the key forms of direct response and discuss some of the opportunities and challenges they present.

Telemarketing

Although we include telemarketing in our section on direct-response advertising, many practitioners view it as simply personal selling by phone. The advantage of telemarketing centers on the personal and flexible nature of a call. Unlike most other advertising and promotions, it can adapt in midmessage to repeat information, address customer concerns, and emphasize different product benefits. Although expensive on a cost-per-call basis, traditionally telemarketing has been very good at generating leads in both the consumer and the business-to-business sectors.

Following the "Do Not Call" registration, which took effect on October 1, 2003, telemarketers were greatly limited in terms of their ability to contact consumers. A company from which a consumer purchased a product is allowed to contact the consumer for up to 18 months following the purchase. A company representative may call a consumer up to three months after the consumer requests information from the company. Charities and political organizations are not covered by the "Do Not Call" list.

Outbound and Inbound Telemarketing

outbound telemarketing
A technique that involves a seller calling prospects.

Two forms of telemarketing are *outbound* and *inbound*. **Outbound telemarketing** occurs when the seller calls prospects to make a sale, to determine interest by offering catalogs or other sales material, or to pave the way for a personal sales call. Market research is another use of outbound telemarketing. Marketing research is not limited by the "Do Not Call" list.

Like most forms of direct response, the success of telemarketing depends on a targeted list of prospects, a quality product or service, and an interesting and informative script. The script is the "advertising copy" of telemarketing. However, unlike other forms of marketing, experienced telemarketing agents use the script as the framework of a more adaptable message. Coupled with database information about the prospects, callers are trained to up-sell and cross-sell as they develop the conversation. **Up-selling** is encouraging prospects to buy greater quantities or better quality of a product. Cross-selling is persuading buyers to purchase related merchandise. It is common to use the term *up-sell* for both techniques.

up-selling
A telemarketing technique designed to sell additional merchandise to callers.

Inbound telemarketing is used most often with some other medium and is usually an order-taking operation. The familiar mail-order catalog is the largest user of inbound telemarketing. Inbound telemarketing has been made possible largely through the creation of the toll-free 800 number. Since their introduction in 1967, toll-free 800 numbers have grown to the point that other 800-series numbers such as 888 have been added. (See Exhibit 13.8.)

In the last few years, a number of companies have replaced or supplemented personal inbound telemarketing with interactive voice response (IVR). IVR systems combine the technology of computers with telephones to provide a system that handles many more consumer calls at a fraction of the cost of operator exchanges.

EXHIBIT **13.8**

This ad directs consumers to a toll-free number as well as a Web site.

Courtesy of Huey/Paprocki, Inc., and Honda Engines.

When accessing the service, callers are asked a series of recorded questions and given an opportunity to use their push-button phone to respond until they get the automated answer they are seeking or in special cases a representative will come on the line. Companies using the system can greatly decrease the need (and expense) of online service personnel. Furthermore, information is available during nonbusiness hours.

If there is a downside to the service, it is the loss of personal contact between companies and their customers. Some consumers become frustrated when they can't seem to find a way to reach a real live human being with their questions. However, many customers seeking basic information, such as bank balances, prefer the speed and convenience of automated services. Virtually all companies provide service representatives for those customers wanting them, many on a 24-hour basis.

Television and Direct-Response Marketing

Television trails only telephone and direct mail as a source of direct-response marketing expenditures. Like all television advertising, direct response has the advantage of sight, sound, and motion, coupled with toll-free 800 numbers and/or

Internet ordering capability to make it a seamless sales process. Television direct response also has benefited from the growth of cable outlets, which offer firms a number of additional options to use the medium for direct selling.

Direct-response television (DRTV) comes in a variety of formats, but the most familiar are the short-form spot (30 seconds to 2 minutes) and the program-length infomercial. With the linkage of traditional television and the Internet or toll-free calling, television is becoming more and more a primary direct-response medium. The convergence of the Internet and television is moving us one step closer to interactive television, as discussed in Chapter 8. DRTV marketers are designing their messages with a twofold purpose: (1) immediate sales response and (2) bringing prospects to a company's Web site in order to have them bookmark the site and become regular customers. As one agency creative director commented, "Broadcast television and the Internet are a match made in heaven—both in terms of moving viewers to companies' Web sites and providing content materials to complement their e-commerce design."[23] The most used forms of DRTV are the following:

- *The traditional 30-second format with a tag line allowing consumers to order merchandise.* With DRTV being combined with Internet selling, this format is becoming increasingly popular, especially with well-known products and brands with established demand. This traditional advertising commercial format can be fairly expensive relative to the number of sales leads it generates.

- *The two- or three-minute commercial.* This longer spot usually has problems gaining clearance during peak periods and, consequently, most often is scheduled in fringe time programming such as late night movies. The format has the advantage of allowing more sales time and an opportunity for information about ordering the product.

- *The infomercial.* In the last decade, the **infomercial** has become a multibillion-dollar advertising format. Utilizing well-known personalities, slick production techniques, and blanket coverage during certain dayparts, the infomercial has created a number of legendary product success stories. However, with the advent of various forms of interactive and convergent technology, it remains to be seen whether infomercials will continue to be as prevalent in the future.

Regardless of its format, DRTV has certain inherent advantages as an advertising tool:[24]

1. It shows the product in use and provides opportunities for product demonstrations in realistic circumstances.
2. DRTV can create excitement for a product. For example, *Sports Illustrated* uses sports clips for what would otherwise be an advertisement for a static magazine.
3. DRTV offers immediate results. Within 15 minutes of a commercial spot, a company will receive 75 percent of its orders.
4. Because most DRTV spots are not time sensitive, they can be scheduled in fringe dayparts for significant discounts. In addition, production costs of most DRTV are less than traditional television commercials.
5. DRTV complements retail sales. For generally distributed products, businesses find that they sell as many as eight units at retail for every one ordered through direct response.
6. DRTV is a great technique for testing various product benefits and measuring sales response.

Direct-response advertising is sold both on a paid and **per inquiry (PI)** basis. In fact, with the competitive environment so prevalent in the broadcast area, PI is relatively common in television, especially in fringe time. Basically, PI advertisers share their risk with a television station or cable channel. There are no initial costs for time, but the television outlet will divide the profits (if any) when the orders

infomercial
Long form television advertising that promotes products within the context of a program-length commercial.

per inquiry (PI)
Advertising time or space where medium is paid on a per response received basis.

come in. PI advertising can be very beneficial, especially to companies with good products but little capital.

TV Shopping Networks

The logical extension of long-form infomercials is an entire network devoted to selling. Home shopping channels have been a major source of product sales for the past decade. It is not unusual to see name-brand merchandise being sold on QVC or the Home Shopping Network and celebrities as diverse as Marie Osmond, Pete Rose, or Joan Rivers appearing to sell products such as dolls, sports memorabilia, and jewelry. A number of major retailers and designers use home shopping networks to sell their products to this niche consumer market.

Although home shopping has grown significantly in recent years, the executives involved in these ventures see the full potential for home shopping being in interactive systems. The most optimistic proponents of shopping networks predict that they will change retailing fundamentally in the next two decades. Some experts estimate that sometime in the next 20 years traditional retailing will all but be replaced by interactive home shopping. Of course, we have seen similar predictions for the Internet in recent years. Nevertheless, there is little question that these networks will continue to grow and occupy a larger place in general retailing.

Radio and Direct Response

Radio, despite its targeted audiences and niche programming, has not been a major player in direct-response marketing. Traditional radio has suffered from its lack of visualization. Radio is deficient in many of the elements so familiar to direct response in other media. Radio cannot show a product, no coupons can be provided, and a toll-free number cannot be flashed on a screen.

As discussed in Chapter 9, all of this may change if so-called streaming audio becomes a major medium. With the introduction of computer-based audio programming, an advertiser can incorporate all the missing elements of traditional radio in this new convergent medium. As in the case with interactive television, electronic coupons can pop on the screen, offers can not only be seen along with the music but also downloaded at the request of the listener, and, with database technology, listeners can be prompted about products that fit their consumer profiles.

While the economic promise of "visual" radio is in the near future, for the present, radio can serve as a valuable supplement for a variety of direct-response marketers. The combination of low commercial rates and tightly targeted audience composition makes possible high frequency to saturate prime prospects. Even with the competition from other forms of direct response, radio can continue as a niche medium for direct-response marketing. For example, it can be fairly effective at delivering 800 numbers and Web addresses to potential customers.

Per inquiry also makes radio a bargain for many direct-response advertisers. Radio stations often find that PI advertising is a means of moving unsold commercial inventory. With the number of stations and commercial spots available, it is almost impossible for even the most prosperous station to sell all of its time. Unsold inventory can be especially acute during certain months such as the after-Christmas period. Rather than using this time for public service announcements or station promotions, the sales manager may be willing to run PI spots at significant discounts.

Magazines and Direct Response

Magazines provide a targeted medium for a number of direct-response advertisers. As discussed in Chapter 11, the success of most magazines depends on their ability to reach a targeted group of readers with common interests, demographics, or vocations. It is in the area of business and trade publications that direct response is especially important. Magazines with editorial objectives geared specifically toward some particular business or profession can be extremely beneficial for direct-response marketers. In the business press, the majority of direct-response messages are attempting to gain leads for personal salespersons and telemarketers or are being used as a means of follow-up.

Despite the importance placed on business-to-business magazine direct response, consumer magazines also can provide an important means of reaching prospects. You only have to look in the back of many major publications to find lengthy classified sections offering a number of direct-response products. In addition, the majority of regular magazine advertisements carry some form of direct response either to provide additional information to consumers or to provide opportunities for direct orders (see Exhibits 13.8 and 13.9).

Many of the magazine characteristics we discussed in Chapter 11 are of primary importance to direct-response advertisers. Audience selectivity combined with high reach among prospects who are not heavy users of other media (especially television) make it ideal for many direct marketers. Magazines also appeal to a number of major advertisers because of the prestige associated with national publications. Magazine direct response provides the intimacy of direct response with the traditional advertising virtues of magazines.

Catalogs

One of the oldest and one of the most popular forms of direct-response selling is the catalog. The use of catalogs dates at least to 1498 when Aldus Manutius published his book catalog containing 15 titles. Since its humble beginnings, the catalog has become a keystone of direct marketing. As early as 1830 New England companies were selling fishing and camping supplies by mail. By the end of the 1800s, both Sears, Roebuck and Co. and Montgomery Ward brought retail merchandise to every household in the country through their catalogs. By 1904, Montgomery Ward was mailing more than 3 million catalogs to potential customers in the United States. Consumers could even buy homes through catalogs. Sears, Roebuck and Company sold more than 100,000 homes by catalog from 1908 to 1940.[25]

Today, the catalog industry is facing many of the uncertainties and challenges of other forms of marketing and advertising. The role of the Internet has huge potential for the industry, and many in the industry see the need to make important long-term decisions regarding how interactive media will fit into their future. Whether the Internet is a curse or an opportunity is in the eye of the beholder.

The role of the Internet is a major question for cataloguers that mail billions of catalogs each year. However, it is only one of the several challenges facing traditional catalog sales companies. Another challenge is presented by the increasing number of companies, including mainline retailers such as Nordstom and Gap, that are going into either catalog sales or Internet sales, or, in many cases, both (see Exhibit 13.9). The growing number of catalogs has significantly increased the players in an already crowded field. Some like L. L. Bean, the longtime marketer of outdoor gear and clothing, have reacted to competition from mainline retailers by opening new retail stores themselves. Since 1998, Bean has expanded from one headquarters outlet in Freeport, Maine, to a number of retail sites.

At the same time, virtually every cataloguer has gone into Internet selling. Many traditional cataloguers such as Lands' End see a number of benefits in e-commerce. Online systems are able to adjust to changing trends in merchandising or weather. For example, if a particular winter proves milder than usual, a company may change its focus to lightweight outerwear. The Internet may offer catalog companies relief from catalog-related production and postage costs that account for a large percentage of their total operating costs. Catalog companies realize that the Internet, traditional brand advertising, and the core catalog are all part of multiple channels that must work together to reach consumers. Different customers prefer

EXHIBIT **13.9**

All of these popular catalogs are available online.

Courtesy of L.L. Bean, FrontGate, and The Territory Ahead.

different channels and the same customers will use various channels at different times. Earlier we discussed data warehouses. Cataloguers must embrace the concept of the data warehouse as they integrate information into a single transaction history regardless of what channels a customer uses.

As cataloguers move into online options, they are finding that their basic marketing techniques must adapt to these new channels. One of the primary challenges is to deal with the customer-controlled online environment and to find ways to encourage prospect visits to a cataloguer's Web site. Catalog companies find that there are fundamental differences between online and off-line selling. For example, "Paper catalogs are intrusive by nature, online catalogs are passive by nature. Once businesses understand this fundamental limitation of e-cataloging, they can become creative in the ways that generate more traffic and, importantly, more sales, through the Web."[26]

Regardless of the channel(s) used by a catalog seller to reach prospects and customers, there are a number of keys to the successful process of moving a person from a prospect to a buyer:

1. *The right product.* As with any product or service, the selling process must begin with merchandise that appeals to consumers. Quality, price, consumer benefits, and range of merchandise are all elements in successful selling.

However, cataloguers often find that an added consideration is uniqueness of products. Generally, catalog sellers have a difficult time moving merchandise that is easily obtainable at retail outlets. Product differentiation is always important, but doubly so for catalog products.

2. *Exciting creative execution.* Remember that the customer can't try on clothes, handle camping gear, or sample a food item. The sales story has to be conveyed in attention-getting messages that grab the imagination of the reader.

3. *Reach a targeted group of prospects.* No element of direct selling is more important than the prospect list. Waste circulation is even more expensive in direct marketing than in other forms of promotion and every effort has to be made to keep it to a minimum.

4. *Fulfillment and customer service.* Nothing will kill a catalog company faster than a reputation for faulty customer service. The process begins with knowledgeable customer representatives, then the right merchandise must be shipped promptly, and finally, when mistakes are made, they need to be dealt with fairly and quickly.

5. *The process of successful selling doesn't end with a single purchase.* Cataloguers must establish a means of database management that will allow product inventory management as well as a means of determining the quality of customers on a lifetime value basis.

Negative Option Direct Response

negative option
Technique used by record and book clubs whereby a customer receives merchandise unless the seller is notified not to send it.

Continuing relationships with loyal customers is a key to successful and efficient marketing. The **negative option** technique is designed to initiate and maintain just such an association. Rather than selling a single item, it provides consumers with an open-ended invitation for the purchase of future merchandise.

The Book-of-the-Month Club is credited with introducing this method of "one-package-a-month" selling. Today we see DVDs, CDs, as well as miniature cars, porcelain figurines, and a host of other merchandise offered on a negative option basis. The idea is that the buyers must notify the company in order not to have an item sent.

The consumer benefit of negative options is that companies make the initial offer ridiculously inexpensive in order to encourage consumers to sign up. For example, music distributors will offer 10 CDs for a dollar as an introductory offer. The advantage to sellers is that once customers join the plan, the company hopes to maintain them for some period of time. It is another example of the lifetime value concept we discussed earlier. Under negative option plans, sale costs are virtually nonexistent for continuing customers.

Fulfillment

fulfillment
The tasks of filling orders, shipping merchandise, and back in marketing.

One of the most important elements in the direct-marketing environment is the **fulfillment** function, that is, getting merchandise to customers after the order. Unfortunately, too many businesses view fulfillment as nothing more than a shipping service. In fact, the functions of a well-planned fulfillment operation include "telemarketing, order management, information management, order fulfillment, parcel distribution, returns processing, customer service, merchandise procurement, payment processing, and data mining."[27] If there is a breakdown in any of these functions, it affects the rest of the system.

Problems in fulfillment were especially acute during the Christmas seasons of 1998 and 1999 among Web-based retailers. After repeated customer complaints and news reports of poor service, the FTC announced that it was undertaking an investigation of a number of major online retailers to see if they were complying with federal mail-order rules. These rules require that merchandise be shipped within the time frame promised by sellers or that consumers be notified if the delivery date cannot be met. The FTC has levied fines of up to $900,000 for failure to comply with these rules.

The failure of so many businesses to manage their fulfillment operation has made it a major focus for companies seeking a competitive advantage. Customers are sensitive to the problems that a number of companies are having with fulfillment. Those companies that maintain a reputation for effective customer service have gained a significant competitive advantage in the race for online sales.

DIRECT-MAIL ADVERTISING

Despite recent competition from e-mail, telemarketing, and other direct-marketing options, direct mail remains a primary advertising vehicle. More than $45 billion is spent on direct mail advertising, which represents almost 20 percent of measured advertising expenditures in the United States.[28] Because of the rising expenses associated with direct mail, it is anticipated that direct mail's share of direct-response advertising will decrease in the future. However, it remains an important direct-response advertising tool.

One of the problems facing direct mail is that the sheer volume of mail coming to households makes gaining a competitive advantage very difficult. Clearly, the number of mailing pieces combined with the "junk mail" perception held by many people is a challenge for direct mailers. This challenge is all the more reason that direct mailers must take steps to reach targeted prospects with an interesting message and a worthwhile product. Assuming that a business has a quality product and a competitive offer, the success of direct mail usually hinges on the mailing list.

In direct mail, the advertiser determines the circulation. The list is the media plan of direct mail. Just as the media planner must carefully analyze the audiences of the various vehicles that will make up the final media schedule, the advertiser must carefully choose the list(s) that will provide the greatest number of prospects at the lowest cost. Most lists are compiled lists; that is, they are developed from a number of existing sources. The problem for the direct-mail advertiser is developing these names into a single list and then fine-tuning it for accuracy, nonduplication, and so forth.

There are a number of organizations that are involved in the direct-mail list process:

- *List brokers.* One of the key figures in direct mail are **list brokers.** Brokers function as liaisons between mailers who need lists of particular target prospects and those with lists to rent. The primary functions of list brokers include determining the availability of appropriate lists, negotiating with list owners on behalf of their clients, and offering general marketing advice. The list broker is generally paid a commission of approximately 20 percent by list owners.

- *List compilers.* The list compiler is usually a broker who obtains a number of lists from published sources and combines them into a single list and then rents them to advertisers. The first format list compiler is considered to be Charles Groves, superintendent of Michigan City schools. In the late 1800s, he compiled lists of teachers by writing to other school superintendents around the country. He then sold the lists to textbook publishers and other companies wanting to reach teachers.[29] Compilers tend to specialize in either consumer or business lists, although a few do both.

- *List managers.* The **list manager** represents the list owner just as the broker is the agency for the mailer. The primary job of the list manager is to maximize income for the list owner by promoting the list to as many advertisers as possible. List managers are usually outside consultants, but some large companies have in-house list managers. Most national magazines, DVD clubs, and other direct marketers offer their lists for rent. These lists are ideal direct-response vehicles because most have been accumulated through sales to narrowly defined, specialized audiences. They also have the benefit of providing prospects who are proven direct-mail buyers.

list broker
In direct-mail advertising an agent who rents the prospect lists of one advertiser to another advertiser. The broker receives a commission from the seller for this service.

list manager
Promotes client's lists to potential renters and buyers.

EXHIBIT 13.10

Retailers can use direct mail to help bring customers to their stores.

merge/purge

A system used to eliminate duplication by direct-response advertisers who use different mailing lists for the same mailing. Mailing lists are sent to a central merge/purge office that electronically picks out duplicate names. Saves mailing costs, especially important to firms that send out a million pieces in one mailing. Also avoids damage to the goodwill of the public.

lettershop

A firm that not only addresses the mailing envelope but also is mechanically equipped to insert material, seal and stamp envelopes, and deliver them to the post office according to mailing requirements.

■ *Service bureaus.* Service bureaus engage in a number of functions. One of the primary jobs of the service bureau is to improve the quality of lists. This function is called list enhancement, which includes a number of steps. One of the most important is known as **merge/purge.** Basically merge/purge systems eliminate duplicate names from a list. Such duplication is costly to the advertiser and annoying to the customer. For example, duplicate mailings offset any personal contact with the customer by portraying the message as a mass mailing—and one done with little care. Merge/purge is accomplished by computers that are so sophisticated that names are cross-checked against the same addresses and similar spellings.

■ *Lettershop.* The **lettershop** is in reality a mailing house. These companies coordinate the job of mailing millions of pieces of mail, from printing labels to keeping abreast of the latest postal regulations. Large lettershops even have a representative of the USPS on the premise to work with every aspect of the delivery of mail in a timely fashion.

■ *Response lists.* The majority of mailings are sent to people on existing lists. However, a number of mailing-list houses sell or rent lists of people who have responded previously to a direct mail offer or demonstrated some interest in doing so. People on **response lists** are those who are prone to order by mail; therefore, these lists are more productive than compiled lists and the rental charges are higher than for compiled lists. By combining response and compiled lists, a mailer can reach both previous customers and a larger pool of prospective customers.

Response lists are often obtained from previous customers of a company. These are called house lists and are among the most valuable commodities of a direct mailer. Owners of house lists rent their lists to noncompeting companies and they are often a major source of revenue. Advertisers can find an endless number of response lists of people who have gone on cruises, hunted specific animals, or have bought books on psychoanalysis in the past six months.

response lists
Prospects who have previously responded to direct mail offers.

List Protection

Because mailing lists are so valuable, companies go to great lengths to protect them from misuse. The most common list abuse is multiple mailings beyond an agreed upon limit. For example, one direct mailer reported that a company rented its list on a one-time basis and used it 13 times.

The traditional protection for such misuse is to include a number of fictitious names so that the list owner can trace the number of mailings. This is known as *list decoying.* In addition to protecting the list itself, list renters should also ask for a sample of the mailing material. Occasionally, a mailing may be in bad taste or contain a deceptive offer. However, the much greater problem is that the mailing offer may be too closely competitive with the list owner's products. Renting a list should provide additional profit, not additional competition!

Testing Direct-Mail Advertising

In 1926 Claude Hopkins published *Scientific Advertising,* which many advertisers credit with providing the foundation of formal advertising research. Hopkins based his findings on the results of direct mail and direct-response offers, and testing and research remain a core element of modern direct mail advertising. The key elements in testing direct mail are the list, the offer (or featured consumer benefit), and the creative presentation.

Let's look at some examples of the type of elements most commonly tested in direct mail:

1. List tests:
   Various list sources including response lists
   Demographic segments
   Geographic segments
2. Offer tests:
   Guarantee wording
   Free-trial, send-no-money-now offers
   Use of incentives
3. Format tests:
   Single mailing versus series
   Window versus closed envelope
   Live postage versus meter
   Envelope size

4. Copy tests:
Personalization
Letter length
Use of testimonial
Various opening paragraphs

5. Layout and design tests:
Photographs versus line art
Four color versus one or two color
Type size and font
Product alone or with models

Direct-mail testing can be expensive so it is important to concentrate on major elements that normally determine the success or failure of a mail campaign. It is extremely crucial to research validity to test only one element at a time. Too many mailers try to cut corners by testing several items in a single mailing. Obviously, if you change the format, the mailing list, and the offer, it is impossible to determine what factor created any changes in test results (see Exhibit 13.11).

Other Direct-Mail Techniques

Because of the expense of stand-alone direct mail, many advertisers are looking at alternative means of distribution of their sales pieces. Some of the primary print alternatives are the following:

- ■ *Package inserts.* A number of companies will allow the insertion of sales messages when they ship merchandise. These messages called bounce-back circulars are delivered to customers who are proven direct-marketing users. In addition, the cost is much less than solo mailings because the sales message is being delivered as part of another package. Generally, package inserts are limited to five offers.

ride-alongs
Direct-mail pieces that are sent with other mailings, such as bills.

- ■ *Ride-alongs.* A form of package inserts are ride-alongs, which are included in a company's own packages. **Ride-alongs** have many of the same advantages of package inserts except they are going to a company's loyal customers with whom a company has a proven and recent sales relationship. Depending on the product, ride-alongs can be extremely profitable because the overhead is so low.

EXHIBIT 13.11

Photos and artwork in direct-mail pieces can be tested.

Courtesy of Bright Ideas Group and Macon-Bibb County Convention & Visitors Bureau.

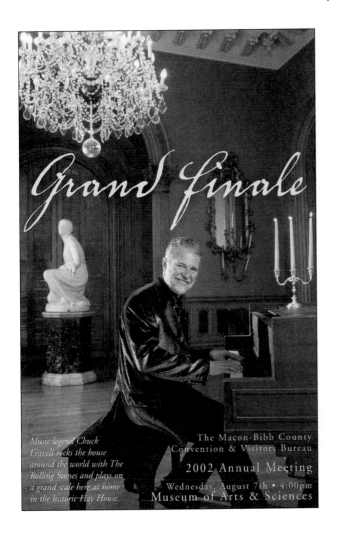

- *Statement stuffers.* Few companies miss an opportunity to include a message with your monthly bill. The idea behind statement stuffers is the same as ride-alongs and they have several advantages. First, they cost nothing to deliver since the mailing expense is going to be incurred in any case. Second, they are at least seen, because everyone eventually gets around to opening their bills. Finally, most recipients are credit qualified and have already dealt with the company before or they would not be getting a statement.

- *Ticket jackets.* A popular form of ride-alongs are promotions on airline, bus line, or train ticket jackets. Companies such as car rental firms find that they are an ideal way to reach their prime target audiences.

- *Cooperative (joint) mail advertising.* With the cost of postage continuing to increase, direct mailers often attempt to share expenses through cooperative mailings. A number of firms specialize in joint mailings. These mailings may include as many as 20 different advertising offers in one envelope. Each advertiser provides a coupon or other short message and the joint mailer handles the mailing and divides the cost among the advertisers.

Cooperative mailings have two major drawbacks. First, they are extremely impersonal because each advertiser's message must be very short. Second, it is difficult to reach specific customers through joint mailings with the same precision marketers would have with their own lists. The dilemma of joint mailings is that as the number of participating advertisers increases, the cost per advertiser goes down, but, likewise, the unique feature of the mailing decreases.

The use of inserts is big business and is growing as the cost of postage increases. It is estimated that as many as 25 billion inserts are distributed in various venues. Its position as an alternative "medium" can be demonstrated in the number of sources that are seeking to track the advertising options available to advertisers. For example, both SRDS and the DMA's Alternative Response Media Council have devoted resources to tracking the choices open to advertisers in placing inserts.

SUMMARY

Direct-response marketing is targeted, personal, and measurable. In an era of increasing accountability, these traits have moved it center stage as a means of reaching and selling to a diverse universe of consumers. In terms of sales produced and expenditures, it represents more dollars than all other forms of advertising combined. It is rare for a company not to include direct marketing and direct-response advertising as a major element in its marketing mix. Companies have come to realize that the ability to combine personal messages with highly selective audience segmentation gives direct response advantages seen in few other media. The tremendous strides in computer technology have made the future of direct response both exciting and uncertain.

The emergence of the Internet has given a new focus to many of the practices of direct marketing. The Internet and other forms of interactive media are changing the landscape of direct marketing dramatically. The challenge is to make the obvious advantages of e-commerce profitable for general selling. To date many companies have been successful in gaining online traffic but not necessarily in producing revenue.

Regardless of the channel that direct response uses, its flexibility makes it practical for virtually every advertiser. In addition, the ability to test and verify direct marketing is vitally important in the current era of accountability and measured results. Not only does measurement of direct response provide a major advantage to advertisers, but it also creates the type of audience databases so valuable to companies in all their advertising, marketing, and promotion endeavors.

There is little question that direct response will continue to outpace most other forms of media advertising. Not only will direct response become more important in the marketing plans of many companies, but also because of its influence even more sophisticated forms of audience segmentation will emerge in the future. History will probably mark the 1990s as the end of the era of mass media and mass audience delivery. In the future, even the one-to-one communication of today will slowly give way to some form of interactive media. There is little question that direct response will play a major role in this transition.

In addition to the technological advances of direct-response advertising, societal changes also are working in its favor. For example, the two-income family, working mothers, an aging population, and less leisure time are only a few of the factors leading people to favor in-home buying. Greater demand and customer acceptability of direct response are pushing more companies to enter the field.

Perhaps the greatest challenge facing direct marketing is public skepticism, especially concerns over privacy issues. However, industry-wide efforts sponsored by the Direct Marketing Association and other organizations have made great strides in improving the industry's image. The fact that most *Fortune* 500 companies routinely include some form of direct marketing in their promotional plans is testimony to its growing respectability among advertisers and improved credibility among consumers. Nevertheless, the industry is aware that legislation affecting its operation is constantly being introduced and presents a threat to future growth.

 ## REVIEW

1. What have been some of the major factors causing the growth of direct-response advertising?

2. What is direct marketing?

3. What steps have been taken to improve the image of direct-response advertising?

4. What role does database marketing play in direct-response advertising?

5. What is inbound telemarketing?

6. What is the key element in direct mail?

7. What is the function of a list compiler?

8. What is the fulfillment function?

9. What is the difference between a list broker and a list manager?

 ## TAKE IT TO THE WEB

Would you feel comfortable using your credit card to make an online purchase? Visit Amazon.com (**www.amazon.com**) and Barnes & Noble (**www.bn.com**) and review their privacy policies and terms of use agreements.

The J. Crew clothing company has traditionally been known for catalog sales. Visit the Web site (**www.jcrew.com**) to see how J. Crew has adapted to encourage online sales.

Almost every business you can think of has an Internet address. Visit Target at **www.target.com** and, from the generic to specific, list the benefits of an online store. Are there items you would never order online?

CHAPTER 14

Sales Promotion

When strategically planned and implemented, sales promotion and advertising should interact in a complementary fashion. In recent years, total investment in all forms of sales promotion has significantly outpaced spending in advertising. In particular, promotions directed to the trade channel have become extremely important as manufacturers compete for retail distribution for their products. The major challenge facing many sales promotion plans is achieving short-term sales motivation without diminishing brand equity. After reading this chapter, you will understand:

1. **the complementary roles of sales promotion and advertising**
2. **the various formats and executions of sales promotion**
3. **uses of sales promotion as consumer and trade incentives**
4. **current trends in sales promotion**
5. **the major reasons for the growth of sales promotion**

PROS

1. Sales promotion provides a means of encouraging consumer sales response.
2. Sales promotion is extremely flexible with a number of techniques to reach consumers across demographic and lifestyle categories. There are few product categories that cannot benefit from some form of sales promotion.
3. Promotion functions at both the consumer and trade levels to encourage high levels of distribution and goodwill with the distribution channel.

CONS

1. If not executed properly, sales promotion can damage brand equity by replacing the image of a product with price competition.
2. Because of the variety of formats and techniques of promotion, care must be taken to coordinate the various messages of advertising and sales promotion. High levels of promotion demand some form of integrated marketing communication if the company is to speak with a single "voice."
3. Some forms of promotion such as couponing have become so prevalent that they no longer provide a competitive differentiation for a

brand and, in fact, may become a consumer expectation rather than a temporary sales boost.

Traditionally, sales promotion has been considered an activity that offers customers, salespeople, or resellers a direct inducement for purchasing a product. And it still does. However, promotion may be more than a sales inducement today. As marketing communicators' tools have changed and the goal of integrated communications has evolved, the definition has broadened. Momentum, a global promotion company, says it moves "brand-in-mind" to "brand-in-hand" by using core disciplines such as event marketing, promotional and retail marketing, and sponsorships. WPP Group's classification of services lumps "direct, promotional and relationship marketing" together. Other companies also talk about adding brand value through promotion—about creating communications with a compelling sales stimulus and building promotional campaigns that build market share and executions that increase brand value. These ideas aren't really in conflict. They are actually holistic because integrated marketing is concerned with, to use Ogilvy's 360-degree branding model, every point of contact building the brand—including promotion. New technology is changing marketers' ability to communicate—from using in-store television networks to text messaging. We've talked about many of these technologies in the media chapters.

We all come into contact with numerous examples of **sales promotion** each day (see Exhibit 14.1). The various forms of sales promotion remind us of brands and persuade us to make purchases in subtle ways that often make little or no conscious impression. When you turn the page on the calendar from your insurance agent, the agency name is reinforced. When technical support managers tee up their golf balls given to them by their computer vendor, they are reminded of its services. And when doctors write prescriptions with the pen left behind by the pharmaceutical rep, a particular drug is being promoted. All of these items and thousands more are examples of sales promotion.

Many sales promotion techniques were well established by 1900, but they often consisted of gimmicks and trinket give-aways rather than the well-planned promotional campaigns we see today. However, many modern methods of sales promotion were initiated by retailers and manufacturers of the nineteenth century. In 1895, both Asa Candler and C.W. Post were offering coupons for free Coca-Colas and reduced prices on boxes of Grape Nuts cereal. At the same time, Adolphus Busch was promoting his beer with free samples, lithographs of "Custer's Last Stand," and red, blue, and gold pocket knives. By 1912, Kellogg was including rag dolls, cartoons, and spoons in its cereal boxes.

These and the other forerunners of modern sales promotion recognized that brands need attention and differentiation to gain sales and that customers react positively to extra incentives when making purchase decisions. Sales promotion provided both. What most sales promotion of the period failed to do was complement a company's overall marketing program and provide long-term strategies for brand building. In fact, on occasion the give-aways and promotions overshadowed the product. A classic example is Topps bubble gum baseball cards. After years of promoting the cards as an incentive to buy gum, in 1990 the company dropped the gum and simply began marketing the baseball cards as collectibles.

By the 1960s, promotion firms were offering marketing advice to complement their promotional programs. Promotion firms, in response to client demand, were transformed from companies developing stand-alone incentive programs to full-service marketing consultants. They began to offer expertise in consumer marketing, merchandising, and branding. During this period the full-service promotion shop took root and integration with advertising and marketing became the norm.[1]

Today, in order to provide better balance between advertising and sales promotion we are finding that a number of companies are consolidating overall responsi-

sales promotion
(1) Sales activities that supplement both personal selling and marketing, coordinate the two, and help to make them effective. For example, displays are sales promotions. (2) More loosely, the combination of personal selling, advertising, and all supplementary selling activites.

EXHIBIT 14.1

The Chiquita brand uses local grassroots marketing to gain attention.

Courtesy of The Botsford Group and Chiquita.

bility for both under a single corporate executive. Despite the fact that advertising and sales promotion are different in many respects, coordination between them is imperative. More and more sales promotion and advertising agencies are consolidating, or at the very least, coordinating their efforts to retain clients who demand a synergistic approach to their total advertising and promotional programs. "Ad agencies, promo shops, and even premium suppliers are feverishly buying or cultivating disciplines to complement their core expertise. Promo execs sitting at the pitch table with their sister ad agencies find themselves more central to the conversation as ad shops turn to promo types for their expertise at retail."[2] Despite the merging of advertising and sales promotion in terms of both management responsibility and creative execution, we should be aware that they differ in both execution and objectives. Yet, it is impossible to be successful as an advertiser, marketing executive, or promotion manager without a knowledge of the broad concepts involved in the total system of **marketing communication.**

This chapter discusses the primary types of sales promotion and how they complement media advertising. As with advertising, the opportunities for successful

marketing communication
The communication components of marketing, which include public relations, advertising, personal selling, and sales promotion.

execution of sales promotion programs depend on an understanding of the marketing objectives of a particular firm or individual brand. Both advertising and sales promotion failures are most often a direct result of poor planning and a lack of integration with the elements of the marketing mix.

PROMOTION AND ADVERTISING

Effective sales promotion has two basic functions: (1) to inform and (2) to motivate. Normally, sales promotion is most effective when its message is closely related to advertising themes. Point-of-sale displays may feature a testimonial spokesperson who is simultaneously appearing in television commercials, counter displays often use the same headlines and copy style as print advertisements, and product sampling will offer miniature packages to enhance brand identification promoted in the company's advertising. Although the means of communication may be different than in advertising, consistent information and formats are key ingredients in successful promotions.

The second aspect of promotions—motivation—differs in some major respects to advertising. Motivation, in a marketing sense, is the means used to move a customer to purchase a brand. This process usually moves across a continuum from awareness (initially hearing about a product) to purchase. In Exhibit 14.2 we can see that advertising and sales promotion have markedly different responsibilities in the communication and purchase process.

The key to successful marketing communication is determining the purposes and objectives of advertising, sales promotion, and other components and how best to coordinate and integrate these objectives. In the past, a major distinction between advertising and sales promotion was that sales promotion was viewed as a short-term sales incentive and advertising was intended to build brand equity over time. Today, most marketers recognize that it is counterproductive for sales promotion to gain short-term sales at the expense of long-term brand equity. One only has to look at a number of packaged good categories that have used coupons and other price-oriented deals to the point that consumers see little inherent value in the brands and simply purchase the one with the lowest cost at any given moment. In this environment where promotion must work with advertising and contribute to the overall marketing goals, objectives for promotion might include:

- To gain trial among nonusers of a brand or service
- To increase repeat purchase and/or multiple purchases
- To expand brand usage by encouraging product uses in addition to usual use
- To defend share against competitors
- To support and reinforce an advertising campaign/theme or specific image
- To increase distribution and/or retailer/dealer cooperation[4]

Note that none of these objectives advocates short-term sales increases except when these sales are part of a larger marketing strategy. For example, when we encourage product trial by nonusers or expansion of uses by present customers, the implication is that these trials will lead to long-term consumer relationships. In

EXHIBIT 14.2

Advertising and sales promotion should function in a complementary fashion.

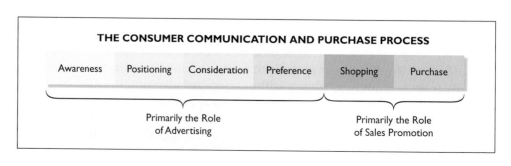

BUSINESS REPLY MAIL
FIRST-CLASS MAIL PERMIT NO. 87 MT. PROSPECT IL

POSTAGE WILL BE PAID BY ADDRESSEE

GEORGIA HIGHER EDUCATION SAVINGS PLAN
PO BOX 7610
MOUNT PROSPECT, IL 60056-9503

NO POSTAGE
NECESSARY
IF MAILED
IN THE
UNITED STATES

Ge✦rgia
Higher Education Savings Plan

Enroll by April 15ᵗʰ.
It's easy — you can even enroll online.

Prsrt STD
U.S. Postage
PAID
NEW YORK, NY
Permit #87

College dreams begin with HOPE.

But they soar when you have a plan.

Enroll by April 15ᵗʰ in the only 529 that can earn you
a Georgia income tax deduction.

Ge✦rgia
Higher Education Savings Plan

EXHIBIT 14.3

Is this direct-mail piece promotion or advertising?

Courtesy of the Georgia Higher Education Savings Plan.

turn, consumer relationships, initially gained through promotion, will be reinforced over time by advertising.

Promotion Strategy

An analysis of a product's performance takes into account both surface indications and underlying problems facing the brand. In-depth situation analyses and strategy development can help determine the incentive needed, the type of promotion likely to have the greatest appeal, and the media required to reach the desired audience. Partners & Levit suggests what to consider in establishing strategy:[5]

1. *Customer attitudes and buying behaviors.* Determine who your customers are demographically and psychographically. Establish what about your brand attracts them and how they make their buying decisions.
2. *Brand strategy.* Consider your level of dominance in the product category. How will sales promotion factor into performance? What are the strengths and time period before returns are realized?
3. *Competitive strategy.* Evaluate past performance, both yours and your competitors', and determine what activities, levels of spending, and time periods produced the best results.
4. *Advertising strategy.* How do you currently promote your product in your existing markets? Which media best suit your needs?
5. *Trade environment.* What are your distributors' attitudes toward the brand? What are your competitors' attitudes?
6. *Other external factors.* What resources are available and what unpredictable factors may influence a product's availability or pricing (e.g., weather, raw materials)?

Promotional expenditures are directed at a wide range of programs. *Promo* magazine lists some of the major categories of trade and sales promotions and the investment in each:

Event marketing	$132 billion
Premiums and incentives	$44.1 billion
Product sampling	$1.34 billion
Point-of-sale displays	$15.5 billion
Sponsorships	$9.4 billion
Licensing	$6.0 billion
Fullfillment	$3.6 billion
Sweepstakes, games, contests	$1.8 billion
In-store promotion	$867 million

Total promotion budgets are generally divided into three categories: consumer advertising, consumer promotion (usually referred to as either sales promotion or simply promotion), and trade promotion (known as dealer promotion or merchandising). Whereas coordination among these promotional classifications is important, they each serve a distinct purpose. Let's examine the role of each in the marketing mix and the share of promotional budgets spent in these promotional categories.

consumer advertising
Directed to people who will use the product themselves, in contrast to trade advertising, industrial advertising, or professional advertising.

1. *Consumer advertising.* The role of measured media advertising is to build long-term brand equity and promote basic product attributes, location of dealers, and/or comparisons with other products. The percentage of total promotional budgets spent on advertising has declined steadily over the last decade. Approximately 25 percent of promotional dollars are currently spent in advertising.

2. *Consumer sales promotion.* These are sales promotional incentives directed to the consumer. Cents-off coupons are the most common consumer promotion, but premiums, rebates, and sweepstakes also are frequently used. Driven primarily by a decrease in the use of coupons, consumer sales promotion has fallen slightly to 25 percent of spending.

3. *Trade promotions.* Accounting for about half of the promotional budget, trade incentives are designed to encourage a company's sales force or retail outlets to push its products more aggressively. These are the most expensive types of promotion on a per-person basis. Winning dealers or retailers may get a trip to Hawaii, a new car, or a cash bonus. Behind the significant increase in trade promotions is the fact that companies think they get more immediate payout for their spending in this sector and that they have more control over expenditures than in other forms of promotion.

Despite some movement of dollars among the three categories, the long-term trend seems to be a ratio of 75 percent of promotional dollars in trade and sales promotion and 25 percent in advertising. The relatively low figure for advertising might be even further depressed if we had an accurate measure of the advertising dollars that are allocated to support major promotions such as sweepstakes, rebates, or sales. For example, it is estimated that as much as 20 percent of total advertising expenditures are devoted to supporting some form of promotion. Most marketing executives predict minimal future increases in advertising's share of total promotion budgets.

FORMS OF SALES PROMOTION

The remainder of this chapter will discuss the primary types of sales promotion. Priority will be given to those techniques most associated with advertising, especially at the consumer level. However, we also will briefly discuss trade-oriented promotions. In all cases, we need to keep in mind the complementary purposes of advertising and promotion. The most frequently used forms of sales promotion are:

- Event marketing
- Premiums and incentives
- Point-of-sale displays
- Sponsorships
- Licensing
- Sweepstakes, games, and contests
- Product sampling
- In-store promotions
- Cooperative advertising

ADVANTAGE POINT

JACK AND HIS PROMOTIONS

Jack in the Box Inc. owns, operates, and franchises Jack in the Box quick-service hamburger restaurants. At fiscal year-end 2003, the Jack in the Box system included 1,947 restaurants, of which 1,553 were company operated, and 394 were franchise operated. Jack in the Box restaurants are located primarily in the western and southern United States. The Jack in the Box menu features a variety of hamburgers, salads, specialty sandwiches, tacos, drinks, and side items. Being a quick serve company, it integrates a number of promotions into its marketing mix. Let's take a quick look because these are typical of the service industry. First, a little more background on advertising and promotions follows.

Jack is the fictional founder, CEO, and ad spokesman for Jack in the Box. A former clown, Jack used to take customer orders from his position atop the company's drive-through speaker box until he was literally blown up in a 1980 television commercial that marked the company's strategy to cater to adult tastes. Since you can't keep a good clown down, Jack was brought back in 1995, not as a speaker box guardian but in his current role with the company. Jack, fluent in English and Spanish, has starred in more than 300 television and radio commercials, including more than 100 Spanish-language ads. Jack's linguistic talents also include Mandarin, which he spoke in the 1999 television ad "Titans." Jack often shares glimpses into his personal life through the chain's television commercials. Over the past seven years, viewers have met Jack's wife, Cricket, and his son, Jack Jr.

Jack is a vehicle to promote the company and is integrated into most marketing communication activities. Here are a few examples:

"Win Jack's Stuff"

From his private jet to his red-hot convertible, Jack, the ad spokesman for Jack in the Box restaurants, knows a thing or two about the good life. In 2004, Jack's customers had the chance to make their own champagne wishes and caviar dreams come true when Jack in the Box launched "Win Jack's Stuff" a new game that gave players a taste of life à la Jack.

The first game at Jack in the Box in 25 years, Win Jack's Stuff gave guests the opportunity to walk away with a variety of food and merchandise, from a small order of fries to two Kawasaki motorcycles. Customers could win two ways: An instant win provided opportunities to receive Game Boy Advance SP Systems, MP3 players, digital cameras, or one of 5 million food prizes. There is a 1-in-4 chance of winning. Or they could collect and win bigger prizes such as cars, toys, and trips. And even a ride in Jack's private jet.

Exclusive Muppet Figure with Jack's Kid's Meal® Purchase

The Jim Henson Company and Jack in the Box Inc. partnership gave away one of seven exclusive Muppet™ figures, specially designed for Jack in the Box restaurants, with the purchase of every Jack's Kid's Meal.

The promotion distributed exclusive Muppet figures including Kermit the Frog™, Miss Piggy™, Fozzie Bear™, The Great Gonzo™, Animal™, Pepe the King Prawn™, and the Swedish Chef™.

High Protein and Less Carbs

Jack introduced a new low-carb, bun-less option that Jack in the Box rolled out with plenty of in-store promotion, which allowed customers to eliminate the bun and sauce on any of the chain's burgers and sandwiches. Earlier the company introduced Jack's Ultimate Salads™. Available in three distinct styles—Asian Chicken, Chicken Club, and Southwest Chicken—the salads offered consumers a generous serving of fresh produce and nutrition. ■ ■ ■

- Trade shows and exhibits
- Directories and Yellow Pages
- Trade incentives

EVENT MARKETING/PRODUCT LICENSING

According to *Promo* magazine, event marketing is no longer a bit player in the promotion mix, as it moved to the top of the bill in 2003. At one time, marketers might have thought of events in terms of a stand-alone mobile unit parked at Wal-Mart to introduce new hair care products or a guerrilla team working the big city streets to pass out coupons for a cellular phone. Now, events are integral to the marketing mix—not necessarily always the centerpiece—but an element in an orchestrated promotional mix.[6]

What do Tide detergent, Home Depot, Hot Wheels, Coca-Cola, Viagra, and DuPont have in common? Besides being among the largest and most sophisticated brands in the world, they are primary sponsors of NASCAR racing teams. NASCAR television deals worth $2.8 billion with Fox, NBC, and TNT extend out to 2008, and recently NASCAR races were drawing the second-largest sports-viewing audience after the NFL. Thirteen million fans bought tickets to the 2,200 races in the different racing divisions in 2003, with a typical turnout of 186,000 for the big events—at an average ticket price of $75. Corporations spend more than $1 billion a year for NASCAR sponsorships and promotions and annual sales of NASCAR-licensed merchandise top $2 billion. It is estimated that there are 75 million fans with, more than half being hard core. For the 2004 season there were 36 *official sponsors,* from the Official Armed Services (the U.S. Army) to the Official Pizza Delivery company. Twenty-one other companies were promotional partners, from Ragu to Waste Management. Generally, each race car has a primary sponsor—putting up anywhere between from $9 million to $15 million per season—and a number of associate sponsors. In addition, drivers can make their own sponsorship deals.[7] This is a big deal for corporations.

U.S. marketers spent an estimated $132.3 billion on consumer event marketing in 2002, up a healthy 15 percent as the discipline gains favor with a broad range of marketers and brands adding event dates to their calendars. In 2003, event marketing spending grew at the rate of 15 to 20 percent.

One of the oldest types of advertising is the testimonial by which a brand gains from an association with a celebrity through a product endorsement. The idea, of course, is that the star power of famous sports or entertainment figures will rub off on the brand. It is this idea of benefit-by-association that has driven event market and product licensing deals to multibillion dollar levels.

There are three basic approaches to product association and tie-ins:

1. *Event marketing.* There is hardly a sporting event, musical concert, or art exhibit that does not enjoy some form of corporate sponsorship. From sponsored scoreboards at football stadiums to the Nike swoosh on players' uniforms, every aspect of public events is open to purchase by a business. We have even divided up parts of events for sponsorship. When a relief pitcher comes in from the Atlanta Braves bullpen, he gets a BellSouth call from the manager and each year the outstanding relief pitcher in major league baseball receives the Rolaids Award. The Olympics is among the most high-profile event marketing venues with companies making multimillion dollar investments in return for being named an official sponsor.

    Advertisers understand that sports fans and patrons of the arts are extremely loyal to their special favorites. Sponsors hope that an association with these events will increase brand visibility and foster goodwill for their products. Event marketing is most effective when it involves a long-term relationship that offers advertisers a chance to develop a continuing connection with a loyal audience.

EXHIBIT 14.4

Mentos Freshmaker
Tour concert
sponsorship.

Courtesy of The Botsford Group
and Perfetti/Van Melle's Mentos.

2. *Staged promotions.* A staged promotional event differs from event marketing in that the sponsor not only sponsors an event but also initiates it. For example, both *Mademoiselle* and *Glamour* magazines have for years sponsored college tours as an extension of the publications' efforts to reach young women and to enhance their image with this prime target market.

   Among the most sponsored events of this type are concerts. Each summer, companies with youth-oriented brands such as Coca-Cola, PepsiCo, and Levi Strauss hit the road with the band du jour for a cross-country tour (see the Mentos Freshmaker Tour, Exhibit 14.4). These events combine product sampling, couponing, interviews with local media, and in-store publicity to maximize brand identification with the band .

3. *Product licensing.* Related to event marketing is the concept of commercial relationships with movies, television shows, cartoon characters, and so forth to gain recognition for a brand. Examples of licensing agreements cover numerous opportunities. Sometimes it involves product placement in a film. Some of the best-known instances are when BMW introduced its roadster in a James Bond film and when Reeses's Pieces sales spiked after being showcased in *E.T.,* as did sales for Ray-Ban sunglasses when they were seen in two of Tom Cruise's movies, *Risky Business* and *Top Gun,* and later in *Men in Black.*

Movie licensing often involves a marketing tie-in between a fast-food company, a toy manufacturer, or some other children-related item. For example, Burger King has tied into movies in a number of its promotions: *Cat in the Hat, Men in Black II,* and *Lord of the Rings.* Yum Brands, Inc., Taco Bell tied into *Lara Croft: Tomb Raider.* It is common for fast-food companies to join in movies, television shows, or networks, using the popularity to bring customers into their restaurants for toys, books, cups, and so on.

The biggest beneficiaries of licensing agreements are toy manufacturers. It is estimated that nearly half of toy revenues come from licensed figures. From Charlie's Angels to the World Wrestling Federation, action toys have become a core income source for most toy manufacturers. These companies invest millions in these agreements and their success is largely dependent on the popularity of a particular entertainment project. Not all licensing agreements involve entertainment and some involve cross-licensing contracts between two brands. For example, the Lincoln Town Car Cartier model combined two prestigious brands and offers a number of cross-promotions.

As you can see from our discussion, the opportunities for event sponsorship and licensing agreements are endless. However, their success depends on a positive connection with a brand's target market. In order to accomplish this goal, it is imperative that the image of the event and that of the product are compatible and that there is a logical relationship between the product and the event (see Exhibit 14.5).

Virtual Advertising

EXHIBIT 14.5

Chiquita: The Official Banana of U.S. Soccer.

Courtesy of The Botsford Group and Chiquita.

Throughout the text, we have discussed advertising and marketing Internet and computer-based technology. Among the most interesting is the so-called virtual ads. Computer-generated ads, logos, and products are superimposed on a live video feed or inserted into a completed movie or television show. These computer-

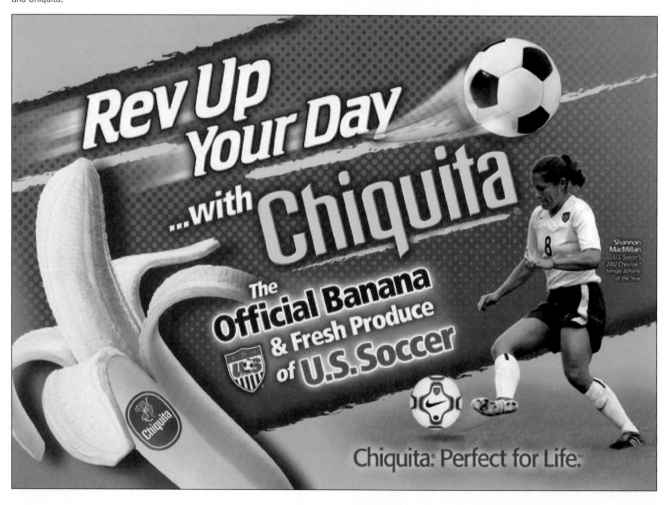

inserted brand messages are not seen and, in fact, don't exist at the actual event. By utilizing technology and creativity, it is now possible to seamlessly integrate an image into a live event or program after filming has taken place with the ability to target a specific demographic in any given market. You may have seen the yellow first down markers on your TV screen or the ads behind home plate that change. The fans at the games don't see these ads because they are electronic. And during the last summer Olympics, NBC virtually placed the national flags of swimmers into each lane—at the bottom of the pool.

The technique has been adapted for product placement in movies and television shows. Producers will be able to insert local or regional brands in films and television shows. As you might imagine, purists are not particularly happy about the intrusion of product promotions into entertainment content, but virtual advertising does open up interesting possibilities to reach target audiences. There are also potential legal ramifications to the use of this technique.

Deals

Deals are a catch-all category of promotional techniques designed to save the customer money. The most common deal is a temporary price reduction or "sale." The cents-off coupon is also a consumer deal because it lowers the price during some limited period. A deal also may involve merchandising. For example, a manufacturer may offer three bars of soap wrapped together and sold at a reduced price. Another deal possibility is attaching a new product to a package of another established product at little or no extra cost—an effective way of new product sampling. Among the most familiar deals are rebates toward the purchase of a product. Mail-in rebates are among the most common deals offered by manufacturers. Here consumers purchase a product and send away in order to receive the reward. Premium offers are offers that are free or discounted merchandise used as an incentive for the customer to purchase more.

The downside of offering frequent deals is that a promotion may start off as a temporary incentive and become, to some buyers, an expectation. Deals can be extremely effective in building sales at the trade level. Trade deals offered to retailers and wholesalers and others in the trade channel will be discussed later in the chapter as a type of trade incentive.

POINT-OF-PURCHASE ADVERTISING

With annual expenditures of almost $14 billion, **point-of-purchase** (P-O-P) displays are among the most prevalent and fastest growing segments of sales promotion. P-O-P is tailor-made for a retail environment in which almost 60 percent of consumer purchases are unplanned. In recent years, the industry has sponsored a number of studies to help retailers and manufacturers better utilize P-O-P. Findings of these studies demonstrate that P-O-P has several primary advantages as a sales promotion technique:

point-of-purchase
Displays prepared by the manufacturer for use where the product is sold.

1. *Motivate unplanned shopping.* One major study indicated that displays at the end of aisles and at the checkout counter were most conducive to promoting sales. The same study also found that factors such as the age of the shopper, predilection to influence by in-store deals, and time pressure all played a role in the influence of P-O-P. It also showed that retailers could influence impulse buying by encouraging shoppers to go down as many aisles as possible.[8]

2. *Brand and product reminders.* One of the major roles of P-O-P is to remind consumers about product categories and brands that they might overlook. The P-O-P industry is upgrading the creative options available for in-store selling. In addition to the familiar cardboard signage, more and more displays are utilizing

computer technology to change messages electronically and target selective demographic shopper segments. For example, AdMedia, Inc., is experimenting with in-store electronic billboards in which sound and images are rotated at one-minute intervals. Different messages can be downloaded from remote locations to respond to changing marketing conditions, different audiences in various day-parts, or in-store promotions.[9]

3. *Influence brand switching.* Consumers show remarkably low levels of brand loyalty in food categories. In a study by the Meyers Research Center, "more than half of grocery shoppers would switch brands if their preferred items were not available, compared to only a third of shoppers who would do the same if their favorite non-food items were unavailable."[10] This research not only shows the need for P-O-P but also indicates that the use of such displays will be an ongoing necessity to motivate unpredictable consumers.

The major industry trade association, Point of Purchase Advertising International (POPAI), in cooperation with the Advertising Research Foundation (ARF), is currently engaged in a multiyear study to provide reliable audience measures and place P-O-P on a level with other measured media such as print and broadcast. According to POPAI, the study seeks to measure:

1. *The amount of P-O-P advertising erected in stores.* The industry knows that all the signage that is purchased and distributed is not displayed.
2. *The estimated number of consumer impressions generated.* The study seeks to gather data concerning reach, frequency, and CPM in order to allow intermedia comparisons.
3. *The effectiveness of P-O-P advertising.* Ultimately, the industry hopes to provide information on sales increases that are attributable to P-O-P.

One of the historical problems facing P-O-P advertising has been guaranteeing that the displays were properly displayed or even displayed at all. In the past, manufacturers' salespersons were largely responsible for maintaining in-store displays. Particularly among small companies, signs were simply placed by manufacturers' reps in those stores that would give them space. Now marketing in-store displays is a much more sophisticated process and is highly coordinated at both the local and national levels. For huge retailers such as Home Depot and Wal-Mart, some P-O-P signs are made exclusively for their outlets.

To ensure better usage of in-store displays, a number of companies have hired independent firms called retail merchandising service companies to work with retailers to gain maximum P-O-P coverage on an outsourcing basis. Many companies find that "hiring merchandising companies may mean extra costs, but the expense is offset by the fact that crack sales forces don't need to waste valuable selling time setting up displays, doing store sets and out-of-stock correction, or updating merchandise."[11]

In the future, we will see even more innovations in the uses of P-O-P. The P-O-P industry will provide better research as well as utilize a number of electronic, interactive, and broadcast media. For example, the growing use of grocery store check-out computers will allow more accurate identification of local store customers, which, in turn, will allow targeted in-store messages. Video and audio displays will increase and provide immediacy in reacting to changing marketing conditions in local areas. In addition, new technology such as holograms will soon provide even more eye-catching store displays.

Increasingly, P-O-P will be dominated by retailers, and manufacturers will be required to meet rigid requirements to gain retail shelf and floor space. Retail space is the most valuable commodity that local merchants have, and they will allocate P-O-P spots only to those companies and brands that provide the highest-quality displays, greatest merchandising and advertising support, and, most importantly, the most significant profit potential.

ADVANTAGE POINT

THE CHIQUITA BANANA SUMMER FUN CLUB

Recently named the "Best Display Promotion in the World," Chiquita Fresh North America and its promotion agency, The Botsford Group, created the highly successful Chiquita Banana Summer Fun Club. Featuring Miss Chiquita, the 50-something brand icon, Chiquita leveraged its famous blue label, quality heritage, and warm brand personality for a summer-long continuity program targeting young families.

Chiquita wanted to boost banana sales in July and August when a plethora of summer fruits impact banana sales. A unique strategy motivated retailers to approve the promotion—Chiquita gave them a promotion that increased consumption of *all* produce, not just bananas.

EXHIBIT **14.6**

The Chiquita Summer Fun Club Life-Size P-O-P

Courtesy of The Botsford Group and Chiquita.

The Chiquita Summer Fun Club gave families a chart with ideas for fun things to do together and recipes for healthy snacks involving fruits and vegetables (especially Chiquita bananas). Families used stickers to track activities and eating. Once they completed their chart, it was mailed in to get club premiums. Each chart doubled as an entry to win a Disney Cruise Vacation for everyone in the family

Grocery stores could only get the program if they agreed to display the life-size Miss Chiquita P-O-P, run a circular ad featuring the promotion and Chiquita produce, and expand Chiquita displays by 15 percent or more. To speed up in-store execution, Chiquita offered Eddie Bauer gear to the first 100 produce managers in each of three regions who sent in photos of their displays. Ninety percent of Chiquita's U.S. retail stores signed up. The promotion was measured by the incremental sales it generated. The 90 percent retail participation and double-digit sales increases made it one of the most successful promotions in Chiquita history. As a result, Chiquita ran a Chiquita Summer Fun Club promotion every summer for the next five years, each one driving incremental volume and brand equity. ■ ■ ■

Not only are these innovations in point-of-purchase interesting in themselves, but also they point out once again that advertising, promotion, and marketing are increasingly becoming interrelated to the point that it is difficult to tell when one stops and the other begins. Rather than trying to decide in what category a promotion element belongs, managers are becoming more concerned with using whatever techniques work. Exhibit 14.7 shows an in-store marketing partnership (or cross-promotion) between Dasani brand water and Chiquita.

Premiums and Incentives

premium
An item, other than the product itself, given to purchasers of a product as an inducement to buy. Can be free with a purchase (for example, on the package, in the package, or the container itself) or available upon proof of purchase and a payment (self-liquidating premium).

Premiums are items given to customers in exchange for a purchase or some other action such as a store visit or test drive. In other words, they are rewards given with strings attached. Premiums are among the most common sales incentives, accounting for approximately $5 billion at the consumer level.

Premiums are not only one of the largest categories of sales promotion, but they also are among the oldest. Premiums date to the mid-1700s when calendars, wooden specialty items, and other promotional products were quite common. According to the industry's major trade association, Promotional Products Association International (PPAI), by the 1850s specialty printers had established a relatively formal business for premium items.

Premiums are comprised of a number of types of merchandise with writing instruments, calendars, and clothing being the most popular. The key to successful premium promotions is that the merchandise has some logical connection to the product and the target market. Remember that premiums are not traditional gifts, they are marketing gifts. Premium offers are generally categorized by either the purpose or the method of distribution. Among the major sectors of the premium industry are the following:

traffic-building premium
A sales incentive to encourage customers to come to a store where as a sale can be closed.

1. **Traffic-building premiums.** Most premiums are offered at the time of purchase. However, other premiums, particularly those associated with high-cost products and services, are given for merely visiting a retailer, real estate development, or automobile dealer.

2. *Continuity premiums.* Continuity premiums build in value as a consumer continues to buy a product. Slim Jims meat snacks awards points with each purchase for redemption in one of three catalogs. Developed in response to its target market demographics, the company provides merchandise related to wrestling, in-

EXHIBIT 14.7

A Chiquita marketing partnership example.

Courtesy of The Botsford Group and Chiquita.

line skating, and stock car racing. The key to successful continuity premiums is that "programs shouldn't neglect the brand. Points games are a great chance to build brand image by getting consumers actively involved with them for months, or even years. If prizes, too, are related to the brand, so much the better."[12]

In recent years, continuity premium programs have been widely adopted by e-commerce companies. Various incentive Web sites use continuity programs to encourage return visits and brand awareness. Consumers who visit these sites are offered points toward rewards for clicking on sponsoring merchant sites, searching for information, or making purchases. For example, MyPoints.com involves such companies as Target, Barnes and Noble, Toys "R" Us, Red Lobster, Blockbuster, Home Depot, Bloomingdale's, Carnival, and others.

3. *In- or on-pack premiums.* Also called **direct premiums,** these are among the most popular items with both advertisers and customers because they offer an immediate incentive and instant reward in return for a purchase. The direct premium has become so popular that advertisers are constantly searching for ways to differentiate their offers.

Many direct premiums are offered as a copromotion so that compatible brands can cooperate and extend promotional opportunities while at the same time reduce costs to the participating companies. General Mills' Cinnamon Graham cereal cosponsored a promotion with Old Navy. Cereal boxes included coupons for Old Navy stores and the stores provided samples of the cereal. Likewise, Diet Coke packs carried samples of excerpts from upcoming novels by major publishers such as Doubleday. The Diet Coke Story promotion was in response to research that showed Diet Coke drinkers were greater than average book readers.[13]

direct premium
A sales incentive given to customers at the time of purchase.

KLEPPNER VIEWPOINT 14.1

DAVID BOTSFORD

CEO, The Botsford Group

Getting the Retail Support You Want

No matter how much time and money a packaged goods manufacturer pours into its brands, what happens—or doesn't happen—on the sales floor can quickly turn dreams into nightmares on the market share front.

With 70 percent of all brand purchase decisions made at retail, according to the Point-of-Purchase Advertising Institute, the store is more than just a place to win a battle. It's an opportunity to win the war.

Increased display activity, more in-store merchandising, and additional retail ad support are three major avenues for influencing these purchase decisions.

Of course, the importance of your category to the retailer, as well as your brand's position in the category, determines the degree of retailer support possible. I've never met a manufacturer, however, whose retail support couldn't be increased. It comes down to three things: Motivate retailers to authorize incremental support for your brand; ensure the support you get builds the brand (all support is not created equal), and get the support promised implemented at the store level (which only happens 40 percent of the time).

The good news is you don't need a SWAT team to get this done. Just follow the five rules listed here and you'll see measurable results every time.

Rule 1: Collaborate. If you don't help the retailer build his business, he isn't going to be motivated to build yours. Don't take programs to your retailers that simply induce brand switching. Develop ideas that expand the category or increase profitability—or both if you can pull it off. Start by becoming familiar with each retailer's distinct needs, wants, and rules. Ditto for the retailer's brand personality and merchandising style.

Integrate with the retailer's brand and you'll earn the opportunity to talk about yours (don't, however, leave creative development in the retailer's hands!). Additionally, factor store employees, the gatekeepers of implementation, into your program. If your field force or agency doesn't know the lay of the land at the store level, get educated quickly. Talk to a representative sampling of key employees (two or three people per chain). Most appreciate being asked, plus you'll learn something.

David Botsford, CEO, the Botsford Group, an Atlanta-based promotion agency.

Rule 2: Differentiate. Retailers don't want the same program you gave their competitor down the street. They need promotions that set them apart from rivals. Differentiation doesn't have to be a budget buster. Lightly customized creative is one way to accomplish this in a cost-effective manner. For example, by using different photography for competing retailers in overlapping markets we were able to increase retailer support of a recent outdoor campaign. The return on investment for comarketing can also be very high, especially if you focus on high-volume retailers. We've seen clients use this avenue to achieve double-digit volume lifts, increases that resulted in the program paying for itself many times.

www.chiquita.com
www.chiquitakids.com

ENERGIZE YOUR CEREAL!

Chiquita. Quite Possibly, The World's Perfect Food.®

EXHIBIT 14.8

A Chiquita in-store cereal cross-promotion piece.

Courtesy of The Botsford Group and Chiquita.

Rule 3. Motivate. Even though some retailers will tell you it isn't necessary, find ways to tie store-level incentives to in-store implementation—it can make you look like a hero. Make sure the programs are flexible enough to meet retailer guidelines. For retailers that don't allow direct employee rewards, consider staging special events for top-performing associates, awarding the store's own gift certificates, or offering store-specific promotions (it's hard for a chain's headquarters to argue with this one).

Rule 4: Communicate. About a week before a program starts, make sure to check in with the folks who are physically responsible for getting displays and merchandising out of the back room and into the store. Clearly mark shipping containers with the program name, start date, and exact store location desired. Do the same thing with merchandising materials.

Rule 5: Participate. Let the retailer become part of your account-specific planning without relinquishing control of your creative, brand positioning, and marketing strategies. Most retailers not only have fun doing so, but also they'll be flattered at the offer and will begin to view you as a partner, not just a vendor.

At the close of a recent meeting of our agency and a client with marketers at one of the top 10 U.S. food chains, the retailer thanked us profusely for including it in the process, adding: "I wish other manufacturers approached account specific marketing this way."

That's a wake-up call to manufacturers and agencies if I've ever heard one.

Courtesy of David Botsford and The Botsford Group. ■ ■ ■

self-liquidating premium
A premium offered to consumers for a fee that covers its cost plus handling.

4. **Self-liquidating premiums.** Regardless of the method of distributing the premium, the most popular type of premium is self-liquidating offers (SLO). As the name implies, these premiums are designed to require that customers pay all or a major portion of their cost. On average, customers are required to pay approximately 75 percent of the premium. It is not surprising in this era of tight budgets, self-liquidating premiums are the most popular and the fastest growing category. During the last decade, self-liquidating offers have increased by more than 30 percent and the average cost to consumers has risen sharply.

At one time, it was thought that SLOs could only be marketed successfully for low-end merchandise, usually under five dollars. However, marketers are finding that consumers will pay considerably more for items that have high perceived value or interest.

In some cases, the premiums have become so popular that they have actually become major profit centers for a company. Coca-Cola and Harley-Davidson are but two of the many examples in which branded merchandise is so popular that it is sold as "stand-alone" stock. This merchandise is no longer a premium, but it shows the popularity that some brands (and their premiums) have achieved.

With the thousands of available items for premium markets, it is extremely important that great care be given to the selection of this merchandise. The primary concern is that any premium promotion is complementary to the overall marketing goals of a firm and that the relatively high investment in such an endeavor can be justified.

Fulfillment

fulfillment firm
Company that handles the couponing process including receiving, verification, and payment. It also handles contests and sweepstake responses. Full-run editions. An advertiser who buys the entire circulation of a publication is buying the full-run circulation.

As we discussed in Chapter 13, the physical work of handling, organizing, and responding to requests for merchandise is normally managed by **fulfillment firms.** The fulfillment function is extremely important to companies using mail-in premiums, especially self-liquidating offers. Fulfillment firms usually operate on a fee basis according to the number of requests. Their work is crucial to the success of any mail-in promotion. Sloppy fulfillment services can virtually guarantee an unsuccessful promotion as well as long-term damage to customer goodwill. Before contracting with a fulfillment firm, it is important to determine if the company is experienced in handling the type of promotion you are planning. Fulfillment is an extension of customer service and it is your company, not the fulfillment firm, that will be blamed if something goes wrong.

SPECIALTY ADVERTISING

The same items used in premium promotions—clothing, writing instruments, calendars—are among the most popular with specialty advertisers.[14] However, there are two major differences between premiums and specialties:

1. Advertising specialties are imprinted with the advertiser's name, logo, or short advertising message. Premiums are not normally imprinted because the customer is being given a reward for purchasing a product.

2. Unlike premiums, specialties are given with no obligation on the part of the recipient.

The uses and formats of advertising specialties are almost limitless with more than 15,000 items available to carry out virtually any marketing objective. Specialties also complement other media and can be targeted to prime prospects with little waste circulation. The ideal specialty is one that is used on a regular basis, thereby creating continuing frequency with no additional cost.

The disadvantages of specialties include their significant expense on a CPM basis and, like outdoor, they offer little opportunity for a sales message. In addition, there is no natural distribution system for specialties and, depending on the item selected, production time may take up to six weeks.

Specialty advertising has experienced significant growth in recent years as businesses attempt to establish brand identities in an increasingly competitive environment. Like so many areas of advertising, specialties have been influenced by e-commerce and the Internet. As one specialty executive pointed out, "With all the dot-com companies and e-commerce companies racing to create brands, people are looking for better, higher-end [specialty] products. Dot-coms are spending lavishly on promotional products to help their brand names stand out in the minds of consumers."[15]

The Web also has the potential to change many traditional sales approaches within the industry. Instead of carrying bulky catalogs from client to client, reps can show an array of targeted merchandise using portable computers. For low-end merchandise and small clients who don't warrant a personal sales call, the Web is a way for specialty suppliers to reach this market. In the future, direct selling by specialty manufacturers may become more important or even in some cases replace independent reps who have traditionally been the primary sales force in the industry.

Because a major role of specialty advertising is to provide long-term brand awareness, it is not surprising to find the heaviest users in markets with little perceived product differentiation and a number of competitive brands. Financial institutions, such as banks and stockbrokers, hospitals and health care providers, and telecommunication and Internet companies are examples of categories that spend heavily on specialty advertising.

Specialty advertising, like all forms of promotion, should be planned in terms of specific marketing goals and objectives. One survey of advertisers found that some of the primary reasons for using specialties are:[16]

1. to promote customer retention and appreciation
2. to use in connection with trade shows
3. to build goodwill and enhance company image
4. to create awareness for new products and services
5. to generate sales leads and responses

In choosing specialty items it is important to determine that the item has some logical relationship to both the target market and the product or service being promoted. The items need to have some useful function if the specialty is going to be kept as a reminder of a brand. Since the advertising message can be no more than a few words, a specialty needs to adapt the theme of a company's overall advertising campaign to offer an integrated communications approach to consumers.

Business Gifts A separate category of specialty advertising is business gifts (approximately 16 percent of specialty sales). Business gifts serve the same role as specialties, but they are given in a business-to-business setting. Because business gifts are usually given to a relatively small group of recipients, they can be more individualized than consumer items. Approximately half of businesses give gifts to either customers or employees and they suggest the following as primary reasons for offering gifts: to thank customers, to develop future business, and to recognize employee performance.

specialty advertising
A gift given to a consumer to encourage a purchase.

From a marketing perspective, specialties and business gifts serve many of the same functions; however, there are notable differences. The most significant contrast between business gifts and specialties is that business gifts often do not carry the advertiser's logo, although sometimes the items will be imprinted with the logo of the firm to whom the gift is given.

There are other factors that should be considered before a gift is given. For example, does the client company have policies that would prevent a person from accepting the gift? Normally, companies will allow executives to accept relatively inexpensive gifts—another reason to keep the price low. Be very careful to consider cultural, gender, and religious etiquette in choosing a gift. Finally, because the majority of business gifts are given at the end of the year, some companies choose other times for gift giving to gain a degree of exclusivity. The Fourth of July, Halloween, or some date of significance to the recipient such as the date of the founding of the company are typical alternatives to end-of-year giving.

COUPONS

coupon
Most popular type of sales-promotion technique.

Coupon promotions are among the oldest forms of sales promotion, and they are without question the most pervasive category within the promotion industry. Spending on coupons was $6.8 billion in 2002. The number of coupons printed and issued was 336 billion in 2002, after posting a drop for the first time in five years in 2001. Much of the growth was fueled by Procter & Gamble, which ran its own branded insert eight times in 2002 and issued coupons on such brands as Crest, Dawn, and Tide, not just those needing a boost. P&G in the late 1990s issued an edict to eliminate coupons entirely from its marketing lineup, but hasn't done so.

In 2002, 71 percent of consumers said coupons save them a lot of money, according to *Promo* magazine. However, redemption rates continue to fall to 3.7 billion. And while the number of consumers who say they sometimes use coupons increased to 37.6 percent (compared to 36.6 percent in 2001), the number of respondents who always use coupons fell from 21.3 percent to 18.5 percent. Those consumers who rarely use coupons increased from 17.9 percent to 23.3 percent. These figures give us clearly mixed consumer signals. Recently, the average expiration period was shortened to around four months, giving consumers less time to redeem coupons. *Promo* also reported that 65 percent of Hispanics use coupons. As a result, more manufacturers are producing double-sided coupons in both English and Spanish.[17]

free-standing inserts (FSI)
Preprinted inserts distributed to newspaper publishers, where they are inserted and delivered with the newspaper.

There are two basic approaches to coupon marketing and distribution. Traditionally, the primary marketing objectives for distributing coupons are to encourage product trial by prospective customers and to combat competitive encroachments against present customers. Both of these goals were normally addressed through mass coupon distribution. By far the most preferred method of coupon distribution is the **free-standing insert (FSI)** usually included in Sunday newspapers. FSIs are responsible for more than 86 percent of total coupon distribution, while handout co-op, handout off-store location, in-ad, in-pack, in-pack cross ruff, instant redeemable, Internet, and Sunday supplement coupons also increased. Electronic distribution accounted for 8.8 percent of total redemption, whereas Internet coupons measured 0.2 percent of total redemption. Folks' Southern Kitchen uses FSIs to distribute coupons on a quarterly basis (see Exhibit 14.9).

One of the recurring complaints about the number of coupon promotions is that they create price competition at the expense of building brand loyalty. In recent years, a number of major advertisers such as Kraft and Nestlé have taken steps to include coupon promotions within a traditional advertising environment. Such an approach serves to encourage product trial and build brand equity.

EXHIBIT **14.9**

The FSI is used to promote a number of coupon deals.

Courtesy of Bevil Advertising and Folks.

In addition to FSI and other blanket coupon distribution methods, we are starting to see a number of more targeted efforts. These more narrowly defined approaches to coupon promotions have one of two goals:

1. To reach targeted prospects based on lifestyle and demographic information
2. To build loyalty among current customers

In both cases, scanning checkout data and other computer-based data retrieval systems gives manufacturers insight into past purchase behavior of individual buyers. Using this information, retailers and manufacturers can provide offers that reflect specific consumer behavior and brand preferences. For example, CVS Pharmacy tracks purchases and, by using past transaction data, can customize future coupon offers to maintain or increase specific pharmaceutical purchases.[18]

Coupons and the Internet

Despite low numbers of coupons obtained online, the combination of consumer convenience and manufacturers' ability to build customer databases make the growth of Web couponing inevitable. Procter & Gamble's Web site typically tells consumers, "Don't forget to look for the P&G brandSAVER coupon insert in your home-delivered paper on Sunday, March 7—you could save more than $30 on some of your favorite P&G brands!" Online services such as Catalina Marketing's valupage.com and Val Pak Direct Marketing's valpak.com offer coupons in exchange for some consumer information. As online services continue to develop consumer databases, we will see a number providing services such as e-mail offers tailored to a person's past buying behavior. Although Internet-distributed coupons constitute a small percentage of total coupons, with increasing household Internet penetration online couponing offers significant potential for inexpensive, targeted coupon promotions.

Coupon Redemption Fraud

When we redeem our 50-cent coupons, we give little thought to the significant investment for manufacturers offering them. Unfortunately, those interested in defrauding manufacturers through the illegal redemption of coupons are very much aware of their value. The most common type of fraud occurs when a person sends in coupons for which no product purchase has been made. There have been instances in which criminals have obtained thousands of coupons and sent them to manufacturers using the name of supermarkets and other retailers. In some cases, manufacturers have spent millions of dollars on redemptions for fraudulent claims.

In 2003, federal law enforcement officials arrested a group of people participating in a clip-out coupon plan that generated more than $4 million. The investigation included 370 retailers in 15 states. The suspects posed as store owners (and in some cases used real store owners) to send the coupons to a clearinghouse for redemption.[19] With home computer–generated coupons, the potential for fraud entered a new arena. Manufacturers and retailers worry that altered coupons that change the amount or other redemption requirements will become more prevalent with scanning and graphic capabilities common on many computers. The industry is working with bar code technology and other techniques to address the problem. However, regardless of the distribution method, coupon fraud and misredemption remain a problem.

SAMPLING

We have emphasized throughout the text that, regardless of the quality of the advertising and promotion, ultimately the product must sell itself. This is the philosophy behind product **sampling.** Sampling is the free distribution of a product to a prospect. In recent years, product sampling has grown significantly and in many cases it has replaced coupons as a manufacturer's primary method of gaining product trial. The total cost of sampling, including products and distribution, is approximately $1.34 billion.

A new attitude is emerging as marketers offer samples to reward interaction or begin a conversation. It has always been a successful tactic for trial and conversion. Today there is a surge in mobile marketing events in which sampling seems less sterile (and goodies pique consumers' participation). The industry calls it "educated sampling," with a sample as a centerpiece of entertainment or education: It is considered sampling as event, not event sampling. Events afford longer brand interaction in a fun context: Unilever served Lipton Side Dishes after moms ran an obstacle course in its Dinner Games 2002 tour.

Direct mail is the most popular method of sample distribution, but it is not as strong today as in the past. Advertisers are increasingly utilizing creative approaches to getting samples in the hands of prospective buyers. One of the sig-

sampling
The method of introducing and promoting merchandise by distributing a miniature or full-size trial package of the product free or at a reduced price.

nificant changes in sampling is the move away from mass distribution campaigns and toward narrowly targeted dissemination. Targeting of prospects allows manufacturers to drastically decrease waste and obtain more accurate results from sampling tests. Some of the growing areas of sampling include the following:

1. *Newspaper distribution.* As newspapers define their delivery areas in smaller geographic areas (e.g., ZIP codes and block units), the medium has gained a share of sampling expenditures.

2. *Event/venues marketing.* Because events such as rock concerts and sporting events tend to appeal to specific demographic and/or lifestyle segments, they offer ideal venues for sampling. In many cases, venue sampling—suntan lotion at the beach—gives an immediate opportunity for product usage.

3. *In-store sampling.* Usually, in-store sampling is combined with a coupon incentive to encourage immediate purchases of the product. It is rare that a trip to the grocery store doesn't include at least one opportunity to sample some food product and receive a coupon.

4. *In-pack/co-op programs.* On-pack and in-pack distribution is popular when one product has a natural affinity to another. Washing machines often are delivered with a box of detergent, or shaving cream might come with a razor attached. In other cases, a multibrand manufacturer might want customers to inexpensively sample a new product by including it with one of its established brands.

5. *Internet sampling.* Many of the same characteristics that offer substantial advantages for Internet coupon distribution apply to sampling over the Internet. Samples woo consumers online, too, where they swap data for products. A study in March 2002 indicated 70 percent of consumers have completed a survey to get a sample. A major advantage of this approach is that by sending samples only on request, manufacturers drastically decrease waste distribution.

Because of the expense, sampling and couponing must be planned with a specific objective in mind. GlaxoSmithKline Consumer Healthcare and McNeil Consumer & Specialty Pharmaceuticals targeted boomers. They distributed samples and coupons to about a million adults over age 50 in independent-living retirement communities.[20] McNeil, a Johnson & Johnson company, promoted St. Joseph aspirin and Tylenol Arthritis Pain, whereas GlaxoSmithKline pushed Gaviscon, a heartburn remedy.

Campbell's Soup Co. traveled across the country to offer samples of its Campbell's Select soups. Its tour hit 24 malls in 18 cities where two free-standing "Soup Sanctuaries" furnished with tables and couches were set up so shoppers could drop in for a taste of hot soup. Shoppers also could pick up a $1-off coupon or a separate coupon for a 20 percent discount to be used at participating Bed Bath & Beyond stores. Campbell's goal was to have given out more than 192,000 three-ounce samples of soups. Campbell's Select soups are ready-to-serve soups that come in 25 flavors. The tour included stops in the Mall of America in Minneapolis, Spring Hill Mall in Chicago, and Discover Mills in Atlanta, among others.

SWEEPSTAKES AND CONTESTS

The primary goal of most promotions is to gain immediate sales and consumer involvement. Techniques often used to accomplish both of these goals is are sweepstakes and contests. Although the strategies of both are similar, there are significant differences in the two types of promotions. **Sweepstakes** are much more popular than contests, and are based solely on chance. **Contests,** on the other

sweepstakes
A promotion in which prize winners are determined on the basis of chance alone. Not legal if purchaser must risk money to enter.

contest
A promotion in which consumers complete for prizes and the winners are selected strictly on the basis of skill.

hand, must contain some element of skill, for example, writing a jingle or completing a puzzle. Annual expenditures for sweepstakes and contests are approximately $1.5 billion. Each year more than 70 percent of American businesses sponsor a game of some kind and it is estimated that almost 30 percent of the population will enter a commercially sponsored contest or sweepstakes. The major marketers of these games are soft drink companies, fast-food franchises, and movie studios. In the last few years, these traditional sponsors have been joined by the dot-com companies looking for new customers. A contest or sweepstakes is an ideal marketing strategy for these companies. They can involve customers with their Web sites at the same time they are entering the game.

In support of the Blimpie Carb-Counter Menu, Blimpie International, Inc., and the International Health, Racquet and Sportsclub Association (IHRSA) launched a promotion giving consumers a 15-day free guest membership with proof of purchase. The promotion ran in Florida, Michigan, Louisiana, Georgia, Utah, South Carolina, Indiana, New York, Connecticut, Iowa, and Nebraska markets. A consumer sweeps supporting the promotion features a three-month health club mem-

EXHIBIT 14.10

An Airheads' Equity-Building Promotion Partnership with Mattel

Courtesy of The Botsford Group, Mattel, and Perfetti/Van Melle's Airheads.

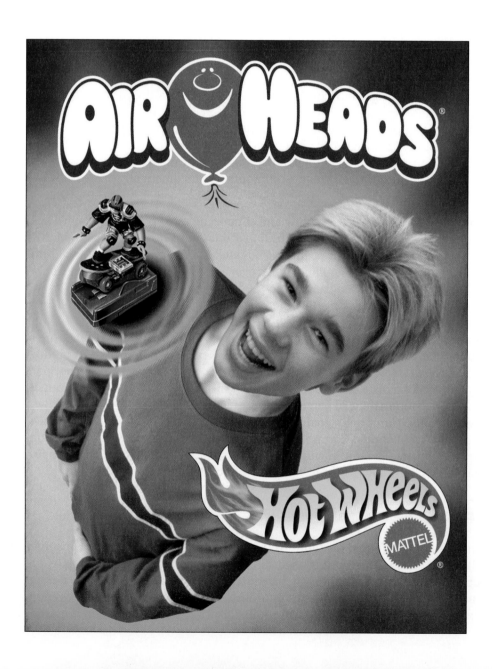

bership and free consultation with a personal trainer. The companies also used radio spots in support of the promotion.

Perfetti/Van Melle's Airheads brand partnered with Mattel in a sweepstakes to promote its chewy taffy brand. The sweepstakes offered a trip to visit Mattel and on-package coupons for savings on Mattel's new Hot Wheels line. Airheads' target is kids ages 6–12; The big idea strategy for this promotion: Candy sales are extremely impulse driven: thus, retail displays and merchandising are critical. At the time of the promotion, M&M Mars and Hershey brands were receiving more than their fair share of displays because they were perceived as bigger players in the category by the retail trade. The Botsford Group aligned Airheads with the toy category leader to help it look like the player it was quickly becoming (see Exhibit 14.10). A compelling consumer hook was also built into the promotion strategy: The Mattel $1 on-pack coupon and fantasy sweepstakes (a behind-the-scenes trip to Mattel toy headquarters) helped pull product off of the incremental displays generated. Airheads added a 10-second tag to its existing "Airheads: Out of Control" TV campaign developed by its ad agency. The spots ran on Nickelodeon and Fox Kids.

The Airheads AirDextron promotion is a great example of a promotion that increased sales while building the brand. Airheads' unique brand proposition is that kids like to play with the taffy-like candy—and make things out of it—before they eat it. It's all about invention and imagination. The brand's theme line was "Airheads. Out of Control." Cartoon Network's popular "Dexter's Laboratory" is about invention, imagination, and being out of control (Dexter—boy genius inventor—is always out of control). The Botsford Group negotiated the rights to use the Dexter property without a royalty (which is really unusual). Kids entered the sweepstakes to win the AirDextron, the ultimate control center for their room. The AirDextron featured a TV/DVD/CD system, laptop computer, Sony Playstation, Walkie Talkies, and a year's supply of Airheads. The promotion triggered double-digit to triple-digit sales increases at food, drug, and mass merchandise retailers across North America (see Exhibit 14.11).

Some company Web sites are established specifically for a particular game or contest. Procter & Gamble ran an online sweepstakes for Olay that awarded a grand-prize, two-night trip to the Miraval Resort and Spa in Tucson, Arizona. Consumers entered the contest at www.Olay.com. Web contests have become very popular with large segments of consumers. Some of the more creative Web games

EXHIBIT 14.11

An Airheads/AirDextron promotion and sweepstakes.

Courtesy of The Botsford Group, Mattel, and Perfetti/Van Melle's Airheads.

KLEPPNER VIEWPOINT

CRAIG McANSH

Senior Vice President
of *The Convex Group*

14.2

Effective Promotions Should Move More Than Sales Volume

Having been in the marketing business for over 15 years, I often get asked, "What makes an effective promotion?" Well, unfortunately, that's like asking someone what makes an effective song. Or asking what makes an effective sandwich. Without a generally agreed upon set of criteria, you cannot say what makes an effective anything.

Some may say that an effective promotion is one that works, one that achieves what it was designed to do. But promotions can work . . . and *not work* at the same time, just like other things. An effective painkiller stops you from feeling pain. But what if it also puts you to sleep for 30 hours or makes your stomach upset? Is that still an effective painkiller?

Effective is different than excellent.

So, I like to answer the question of promotion effectiveness by enlarging the topic slightly to address promotion excellence (which begins with effectiveness but goes so much further).

Excellent promotions are crafted toward achieving a specific result within the overall marketing of a product or service. Both parts of this sentence are important. To achieve an excellent promotion you must know the desired result *and* understand the marketing context within which this goal is being sought. For example, if Tiffany's has a goal of driving sales for Valentines Day, it could put $50.00 discount coupons into bags of Hershey Kisses . . . but that tactic would ignore the marketing strategy and exclusive brand positioning that Tiffany has cultivated since 1837.

This focus of this lesson will be to categorize, isolate, and explore the most common goals used within the promotion industry to achieve promotion excellence. In addition, I hope to introduce some new thinking about the power of promotions in building customer relationships.

Experience has shown that promotion is primarily used to accomplish results across two main categories. For our purposes here, let's classify these strategic categories as *Transactional* and *Relationship*. As the names imply, *transactional* promotional tactics are associated with the actual purchase of a product or service, or a visit to a distributor/retailer, whereas *relationship* tactics are focused on the customer's relationship with the product, service, or distributor/retailer. Understanding the differences between these two strategic uses of promotion is

significant as we work toward identifying what makes a promotion excellent.

Transactional

This is the territory most people still associate with the world of promotions. In the recent past, an effective promotion was only one that drove sales or customer traffic. This is why our industry was known for a long time as "sales promotion."

Companies that want to create an excellent promotion that sells more product or gets more customers in the door *right now* will have the best chance for success by selecting a tactic from one of the two following transactional promotion subgroups. They will (1) either provide a customer with an opportunity to obtain their product/service for less money, or they will (2) provide their customer with the opportunity to receive more than the customer pays for. The former is known as *Discounting* and the latter as *VALUE ADDED*. In my opinion, transactional promotions are as simple as that.

Loss leaders, money-off coupons, and price rollbacks are all effective ways to execute a discount promotion. These tactics become excellent when their implementation is well branded and simple, and meets the right customer motivation thresholds.

Value-added promotional tactics include, among many other tactics, gift with purchase, 2 for 1, percent more free, free delivery, and toys in cereal boxes. And, because even getting the *chance* to receive something free is an added value, sweepstakes and contests fall into this category as well. Promotion excellence occurs when the presentation of the value being added is simple, fits the brand image and target audience, and is the *perfect* amount to drive the sale without impacting long-term profitability of the business. And if the promotion tactic helps redefine an entire industry, that's good, too.

Little Caesars "Pizza Pizza" is an excellent example of a value-added transactional promotion. The idea of getting two pizzas for the price of one was not necessarily groundbreaking. However, the simplicity of the offer and the irreverence and downright fun of the message broke through the clutter and touched consumers. The result was huge business growth, a reinvigorated Little Caesars brand, and a new way of doing business in the pizza industry.

The McDonald's Happy Meal is another example of value-added promotional excellence in which the promotion became the product. It introduced (and, over time, perfected) the concept of immediate gratification, which changed the way quick service restaurants approach marketing to families. The Happy Meal, along with the free toy inside cereal boxes, has become one of the most enduring and iconic examples of value-added promotion.

To close out this section about transactional promotions, it is important to note one of the primary reasons for the consistent and pervasive use of discounting and value-added tactics: Their success or failure is immediate and measurable (and the success is often attributable directly and solely to the promotional tactic used). Old school marketers still feel that direct and immediate results are the only reason to use promotions. This belief is as old as box tops, and the more savvy marketing professionals are utilizing innovative promotional strategies to achieve a variety of amazing results that move beyond transactions.

Relational

I have labeled this category of promotional strategies as *relational,* and I have witnessed a surge in their usage in excellent promotions over the past decade. Relationship-building promotions are becoming more popular because traditional (i.e., one-way) communication has reached the point of over saturation and only uniquely crafted messages can achieve break throughs to make an impact on the consumer. Traditional marketing messaging from company to consumer has reached an apex by being applied to every possible (and many impossible) media vehicles from television to fruit to bathroom walls. And this invasion is continuing to proliferate. The Internet has been the most pervasive new weapon machine-gunning messages at consumers in all sorts of creative ways. E-mail spamming, adver-gaming, pop-up windows, banners, links, chat room infiltration, search engine optimization, and literally hundreds of other variations have been added to the message bombardment that exists in consumers' lives. Yet, despite the volume (or, more likely, because of it) emotional connections are only infrequently cultivated between customers and brands through this new medium.

As third-generation wireless technology spreads from Europe and Japan to America over the next few years, there will be a whole new way for marketers to wage message war on consumers.

The problem, of course, is not necessarily that the escalation of technology has made more communication possible—communication is basically good. The point is that even with all our advanced technology, very few companies have developed strategies that go beyond transactions and into connections. Connecting with the consumer is the goal of relationship promotional strategies. And it's a goal that has only relatively recently been accepted as valuable and achievable within the promotions industry.

There are four stages of connection within relationship-building promotional strategies, which are all gaining a more powerful role in the creation of excellent promotions. Each of these relationship stages is important at some point in the life cycle of a brand. And, because we are talking about relationships, I feel it is important to think about the four stages of connection in human terms.

Introductions are the first stage in building a relationship. This is when promotion is used to develop awareness for a product, service, or distributor/retailer. First impressions are very important in establishing company-to-consumer relationships because you don't often get a second chance. (Even if you do get a second chance, it's going to be more expensive the second time around.) Make sure your promotional introductions are infused with your product or service brand personality. Publicity, street marketing, and even cross-promotion are very simple promotional tactics employed to make introductions that are direct and personal. Remember, you *are* whom you associate with. Be smart; if you have a serious brand, don't use a troupe of singing clowns to intercept people on the street to make introductions. It's important to pick partners that accentuate what your brand represents, not just those who overlap a particular demographic audience segment. Make sure your first impression is powerful and representative of your brand.

Sharing is the next stage of relationship marketing and is the stage most conducive to promotional activation. Here promotion is used to educate and involve the customer. Extensive product knowledge and brand positioning (or repositioning) can be shared in a highly memorable way through experiential promotional tactics such as sampling, demonstrations, lifestyle infiltration, interactive mobile marketing, and events. In addition, companies can share with their customers via promotions that borrow interest from partners that appropriately accentuate their brands.

William Glasser, a noted educational researcher, published the theory that although we learn only 10 percent of what we read, 20 percent of what we hear, and 30 percent of what we see, *we learn fully 80 percent of what we experience.* Sharing an experience with your customers is the strategy that will help create promotional excellence.

Whether this means inviting thousands of children to the local park to watch a television network's animated programming on a 30-foot-tall inflatable screen while they win prizes, eat popcorn, and stay up late, or an apparel marketer's traveling fashion exhibit that invades crowded street fairs to give fans a free makeover, the experience of sharing with customers will result in a brand knowledge that is deeper and longer lasting.

The third stage of relationship building is *friendship*. Friendship is what you have (or should have) with your customers. Friendship is hard to build and harder to maintain, but promotional tactics can work effectively to win friends and keep them. Just don't forget to include your existing customers in your target audience for promotions. Companies that use promotions transactionally sometimes forget to include their existing customers in promotions in their search for new business growth. You need to reward existing customers for being loyal friends and give them special attention.

A great example of friendship is found at Saturn. The Saturn automobile company understood this strategy completely when it decided back in 1997 to throw a three-day party at company headquarters in Springhill, Tennessee, for all Saturn customers.

Fast Company magazine (one of the most successful new magazines today) understands the power of friendship in its promotion marketing efforts. It has cultivated a fan base called "Company of Friends" who meet in cities across the country to share and learn under the nurturing eye of the publishers.

The recent Pepsi-Stuff promotion was a way of rewarding existing friends as much as it was an exciting way to attract new ones.

Having a unique dialogue with your customers is another friendship tactic that has been executed with promotional excellence. In the early 1990s, 7-Eleven ran a promotion that turned its coffee cups into a vehicle for customers to communicate and feel connected to their community and the world. No, it didn't string cups together into a pre–Bell Telephone system. 7-Eleven turned each coffee purchase into a vote . . . a human connection . . . a position on a current affairs topic. Through integration with radio and TV advertising, 7-Eleven posed a question each day and friends of 7-Eleven could visit any of its convenience stores and purchase coffee in a "yes" or "no" cup. Tallies were made during the promotion and the results were reported back to their friends both on air and in-store. The human connection was established and friendship spread rapidly achieving one of the most excellent relationship-building promotions in recent history. It was so successful that the company repeated the promotion a second time gaining consumer feedback on the 2000 presidential election. (Interestingly, Bush won by a narrow margin in their vote as well.)

Of course, the best reason to nurture a relationship is that it can lead to *love*. And love is the all-important (non-transactional) goal in any relationship. Love is rare and can only ever really result when all four of the marketing "P's" are meshed in effortless unity. But, yes, love can be encouraged through promotion.

In the movie *Finding Forrester*, Sean Connery's character imparted a very noteworthy statement about love. In the movie, William Forrester told his young protégé that love is best communicated through an unexpected gift at an unexpected time. In the world of promotion marketing, we can take steps to build love among our best customers by offering extraordinary and unforgettable experiences at unexpected times. When an airline unexpectedly cancels a flight and it rewards frequent fliers with an unexpected $100 voucher in the mail within three days, that airline is building love.

A company that associates its brand with an event, an industry, or a movement that has a highly passionate fan base can tap into the love that already exists. The fanaticism of NASCAR racing and its continued surge in corporate alliances is one example of the power of love in relationship-building promotions.

Another is a recent trend toward cause marketing. Much love can be generated by companies that are able to tap into the growth in "doing good" for others. Nickelodeon's "Big Help" promotion has been an excellent relationship-building program and allows fans to get involved in something they believe in.

Despite these consumer-driven examples, it seems there are currently even more opportunities to impact love via business-to-business marketing channels. Extraordinary incentive travel experiences for top distributors or clients are examples of B2B promotions that go a long way toward building love. Also, elaborate and experiential meetings and presentations have become important relationship-building tactics for many companies' efforts to continue their strong bonds with key customers.

Remember that promotion is a powerful and versatile weapon in the marketing arsenal. Promotions can be successfully implemented to achieve both transactional and relationship goals. By understanding this and identifying the life-cycle stage through which a brand is passing (remember the spiral in Chapter 3), skillful marketers will maximize the effectiveness of promotions within the overall marketing mix.

To ensure an excellent promotion marketers must create an excellent connection between the brand and the consumer. The connection must be cognizant of the brand, the consumer, and the understanding that promotions can and will move more than sales volume.

Courtesy of Craig McAnsh and The Convex Group. ■ ■ ■

incorporate traditional gaming tactics such as scratch-and-win, only they use the mouse to "rub off" a game piece.

Because contests call for some element of skill, there must be a plan for judging and making certain all legal requirements have been met. The typical contest is much more expensive than a sweepstakes. When millions of entries are anticipated, even the smallest overlooked detail can be a nightmare for the contest sponsor. It is estimated that almost 30 percent of the public enters either a sweepstakes or contest each year. A major contest can place a tremendous burden on a company to properly administer and judge. Most games are handled by outside firms specializing in these promotions.

Another limitation of contests is the time (and skill) required of participants. The majority of consumers are not going to devote the time necessary to complete a contest. Therefore, if the intent of the promotion is to gain maximum interest and participation, a sweepstakes will probably be better suited to the objective. On the other hand, a cleverly devised contest that complements the product and appeals to the skills of prime prospects can be extremely beneficial and encourage greater involvement than a sweepstakes.

The Deceptive Mail Prevention and Enforcement Act

Sweepstakes that require a purchase (known as *consideration*) by an entrant are considered lotteries and, with the exception of state-sponsored lotteries, are usually illegal. The next time you receive a sweepstakes offer, notice that there is some language indicating that no purchase is necessary to enter. Despite these disclaimers, it has been alleged that a number of people, especially the elderly, have assumed that a purchase would enhance their chances of winning. In some cases, people bought thousands of dollars worth of merchandise as they entered one sweepstakes after another.

In 1999, Congress passed the Deceptive Mail Prevention and Enforcement Act, which addressed a number of these issues. Industry criticism of the bill has been directed largely at the provision for a national opt-out list in which recipients can remove their name from all sweepstakes solicitations. As one promotion executive commented, "It [the legislation] will have a chilling effect . . . . Some marketers who make occasional use of sweepstakes may not use them. I don't think you will see marketers abandoning sweepstakes, but they may proceed more cautiously."[21]

COOPERATIVE ADVERTISING

You will recall in Chapter 10 that we briefly discussed co-op advertising in the context of the local/national rate differential. Historically, co-op was initiated primarily as a means of overcoming the significant rate premiums charged to national advertisers by newspapers. Although that is still a purpose of co-op, it also has become a major category of trade promotion with annual expenditures of more than $30 billion. The marketing goals and objectives differ from one manufacturer or retailer to another, but some of the primary purposes of co-op include the following:

1. It benefits retailers by allowing them to stretch their advertising budgets. Most co-op is offered on a 50 percent basis; that is, the national firm pays half of the local advertising costs. However, a number of co-op plans will reimburse retailers at a rate of 100 percent. In other cases, a manufacturer will place some limit on the amount of reimbursement according to a formula based on sales of the product by the retailer. As we will discuss in Chapter 24, federal law requires that regardless of the formula of reimbursement, manufacturers must treat all retailers proportionately the same.

2. National manufacturers build goodwill with retailers, encourage local support of their brands, and, by having the retailer place the advertising, qualify for lower local rates, especially in newspapers. Manufacturers also gain a positive association between local retailers and their products, thus enhancing the brand equity among customers of specific retailers. Many co-op advertisements are prepared by national advertisers and require only that retailers add their logo.

3. The media are among the strongest supporters of co-op. Co-op allows current advertisers to place more advertising and at the same time brings new advertisers into the marketplace. Because co-op involves local advertising, it is not surprising that the majority of co-op dollars is spent in newspapers. However, in recent years co-op has reflected the diversity of local media. About 60 percent of co-op budgets are spent in newspapers, followed by direct mail, television, and radio, each with approximately 10 percent. In the future, we will see significant dollars going into local cable co-op programs and this will increase the share of television co-op.

EXHIBIT **14.12 b**

One of the surprising aspects of co-op advertising is the amount of money that is available but goes unspent. It is estimated that as much as one-fourth of co-op dollars goes unspent. The main reason for the failure to fully use co-op is primarily a result of a lack of knowledge on the part of retailers as to how to use co-op dollars or an unwillingness to meet the restrictions placed on their expenditure by manufacturers.

Special Forms of Co-Op

Vendor Programs A special form of co-op normally used by large retailers is the **vendor program.** The primary difference between vendor programs and other forms of co-op is that they are initiated by retailers. Vendor programs are custom programs designed by retailers (often in cooperation with local media). In vendor programs, manufacturers are approached by retailers to pay all or a share of the program.

vendor program
Special form of co-op advertising in which a retailer designs the program and approaches advertisers for support.

For example, a department store might plan a summer "Beach Party" promotion. The store would then approach manufacturers of swim wear, sunglasses, suntan preparations, and so forth and request funds to support the advertising and promotion of the event. Often manufacturers fund vendor programs from their unspent co-op money.

Ingredient Manufacturer Co-Op   Most co-op programs are set up between manufacturers and retailers. However, as discussed in Chapter 2, many companies make ingredients that they sell to other manufacturers for inclusion in finished products. This strategy is called end-product advertising and represents another opportunity for co-op. Often the ingredient manufacturer will contract with finished product manufacturers to co-op with retail outlets or even to co-op in the manufacturer's national advertising to promote the ingredient.

Manufacturer to Wholesaler Co-Op   Occasionally, distribution in an industry is dominated by a relatively few wholesale outlets and manufacturers have little direct relationship with retailers. In this situation, it often is more worthwhile for manufacturers to allocate co-op dollars to wholesalers that then make co-op arrangements with individual retailers. Most manufacturers avoid going through wholesalers because they lose both the goodwill and control achieved by direct allocation of co-op dollars by the national company.

CONTROLLING CO-OP DOLLARS

Retailers are paid for advertising when they submit documentation or proof of performance. For print inserts, the validation process involves having newspapers send tear sheets giving the name of the publication and the date an advertisement ran.[22] These advertisements can be matched with the media invoice. For radio and television cooperative ads, proof of performance was once a perennial problem until the Association of National Advertisers, the RAB, and the TvB developed an affidavit of performance that documents in detail the content, cost, and timing of commercials. The adoption of stricter controls in broadcast co-op has been a contributing factor in the growth of co-op dollars for both radio and television. In the near future, CD-ROM technology will probably be commonplace for broadcast co-op verification. Stations will be able to provide manufacturers with the actual on-air commercial and the context in which it ran.

Despite attempts to improve the process, expenditures of co-op dollars still are allocated improperly out of neglect or inexperience by retailers. In a few cases, there is evidence of outright fraud. Co-op fraud usually takes one of two forms. In the first, retailers bill manufacturers for ads that never ran, using fake invoices and tear sheets. The second type of fraud, called double billing, occurs when manufacturers are overcharged for the cost of advertising. Basically, retailers pay one price to the medium and bill the manufacturer for a higher price by using a phony (double) bill. It should be noted that double billing is regarded as an unethical (in most circumstances illegal) practice, and only a small minority of retailers and media engage in it.

Trade Shows and Exhibits

It is estimated that almost 100 million people will attend more than 5,000 trade and consumer shows this year. Products as diverse as boats and cosmetics will be promoted through these shows. In some cases, a show will be open to both the trade and the public and might be visited by 100,000 prospects. In other cases, the shows are extremely selective and open by invitation only to a few dozen prospects.

Trade shows are one of the best examples of integrated promotion. They combine a number of media and other forms of marketing communication. Trade show sponsorship is almost never used as a stand-alone marketing tool. A trade show can fulfill a number of objectives including product introduction, lead getting, and direct selling. Research shows that trade shows are most successful for those sponsors with high brand recognition. The use of trade magazines and other forms of promotion and communication, including e-commerce, work both before and after the show to encourage the final sale.

The higher the level of brand recognition created before a show, the less time sales reps have to spend creating a product image and the more time they can devote to selling. By the same token, trade shows create opportunities for on-site market research as well as follow-ups by personal or online selling.

Overall, trade shows are a major component in the marketing strategy of many firms. However, trade shows are normally only one piece in a total marketing program rather than an end in themselves. Trade shows provide a number of advantages for both buyers and sellers. They allow face-to-face selling at a cost much lower than traditional personal sales calls. In addition, trade shows are a self-selecting process with only serious prospects attending. Although some sales take place at these exhibits, they are more likely to provide leads for future sales calls or introduce new product lines to prospective customers.

Directories and Yellow Pages

Although often given little attention, one of the most important advertising vehicles for local businesses is the Yellow Pages and other business and consumer directories. Directories are a cost-efficient medium that reaches serious prospects who are in the mood to purchase. It is estimated that there are more than 10,000 directories aimed at both consumers and trade buyers. Because directory advertising is available when the purchase decision is being made, there are few companies that do not include at least some directory advertising in their marketing plans. Many retailers, particularly service businesses such as plumbers, rely on directories as their only type of promotion.

Eighty-nine percent of Yellow Pages users will make a purchase. Combine that with a 14-to-1 return on investment and the fact that Yellow Pages users spend an average of 25 percent more than the average consumer and the message is clear.

According to Knowledge Networks/Statistical Research Inc. (KN/SRI), 76 percent of all U.S. adults refer to the Yellow Pages monthly, and 88 percent of those who use the Yellow Pages ultimately make or are likely to make a purchase. Research also shows the average Yellow Pages user looks at more than five ads when scanning the directory, so it's even more important to make your brand stand out. As part of the integrated marketing media mix, the Yellow Pages research claims to extend the reach of other media, extending Internet, radio, and television by 22 percent, newspapers by 19 percent, and magazines by 23 percent.[23]

The evolution of the marketplace can be witnessed through Yellow Pages subject headings that trace changes in consumer lifestyles. For instance, the increases in listings for day care centers, elder care, divorce lawyers, moving companies, and truck rentals indicate a society that is increasingly mobile while pursuing careers and ending marriages. Without much thought, we make tremendous use of the Yellow Pages on a daily basis.

Directory advertising has many of the characteristics of the more expensive direct-response media with none of their intrusiveness. It also offers advertisers a continuing presence and high frequency without continuing advertising expenditures. Specialized directories are a major medium for business-to-business advertising and frequent reference sources for business buyers.

The Yellow Pages Industry   There are two types of Yellow Pages publishers: utility publishers and independent publishers. Utility publishers provide a directory in connection with their telephone service whereas independent publishers are not associated with a telephone company. In both categories, consumers might be provided with a number of directories from a core directory with general reach throughout the market to foreign language, special interest and age groups, or specialized business directories.

The Yellow Pages industry is not a unified medium. Instead it is comprised of some 250 publishers that produce more than 6,000 separate directories. Annual expenditures for Yellow Pages are about $13 billion and rank the medium as a major source of advertising dollars. Approximately 86 percent of these dollars are placed by local advertisers with the remaining 14 percent in the national category, which is a figure larger than expenditures for all consumer magazines. The Yellow Pages are an important complement to other forms of advertising and promotion. In many cases, the medium is the last chance to reach the prospect at the time a purchase decision is being made. In fact, more than half of Yellow Pages users have not made a purchase decision when they turn to the Yellow Pages.

Consumer usage of the Yellow Pages varies significantly from one product or service category to another. For many business categories, The Yellow Pages directories are a prime source of communication with prospects. For categories such as "Auto Repair," "Attorneys," and "Florists," Yellow Pages directories are the leading medium used by purchasers.

More important than the size of the Yellow Pages audience is the quality. Research shows that heaviest users of Yellow Pages directories are concentrated among higher income and educational groups. More importantly, because Yellow Pages users are already in the market for the products and services advertised, this finding is of particular significance. Yellow Pages directories are rarely intended to work alone. Rather than a competitor to traditional advertising media, Yellow Pages directories are designed to increase the effectiveness of other advertising vehicles.

Yellow Pages and New Technology Like most promotion and advertising, the Yellow Pages directories face the potential of new technology as both a complement and competitor to traditional Yellow Pages. For example, we are starting to see more and more directory advertising that includes a Web address so that customers can obtain detailed information that would be impractical to include in a directory listing. On the other hand, the Web presents a competitor if it is used instead of Yellow Pages and other directories. For some time publishers have made available Internet-based Electronic Yellow Pages, which provides information such as directions to a business, restaurant menus, and even the capability of making online reservations. In addition, these electronic directories provide businesses with the option of making copy changes and promoting specific merchandise on a seasonal basis.

In a number of locations, customers have access to interactive voice services called *audiotex*. Telephone numbers included in directory listings allow callers to access prerecorded information about a specific business. Sometimes audiotex services provide information such as local weather reports or information about upcoming civic events. These services are usually free to callers and sponsored by local businesses. Both online and audiotex services provide similar advantages to both customers and advertisers and they show the way in which new technology is continuing to change the advertising and promotion environment. In the near future, we will see more integration of directory advertising and online services.

Trade Incentives

Although the average consumer is not familiar with trade promotions, businesses will spend some $25 billion in promotions to reach wholesalers, retailers, and company sales personnel. These promotions are referred to as sales incentives or simply **incentives.** Incentives include everything from cash bonuses to travel, with

incentives
Sales promotion directed at wholesalers, retailers, or a company's salesforce. Independent delivery companies. Private companies that contract with magazine publishers to deliver their publications.

various types of merchandise (clothing leads the list) being the most popular type of incentive.

Sales promotions directed to the trade channel are called incentives. There are two types of incentives: *dealer incentives*, which are directed to retailers and wholesalers and *sales incentives*, which are directed to a company's sales force. Almost 80 percent of incentives are offered to direct salespeople. The most common incentives to wholesalers or retailers are price reductions in the form of promotional allowances. In effect, these incentives are comparable to cents-off promotions at the consumer level. In addition, sweepstakes, contests, and continuity promotions (some with prize catalogs) based on sales volume are all used at the trade level.

Employee motivation remains the backbone of the industry, and employers have broadened programs to recognize key personnel beyond the top sales earners. "We're seeing a higher proportion of incentive items that cost less than $100," says Mike Hadlow, president of USMotivation, Atlanta. "Managers are saying, 'OK, we've recognized the top 20 percent of our company, now what are we doing to motivate the middle 60 percent?.'" The types of incentives are changing as well. There is a rise in products that enhance life at home, like big-screen TVs and electronic equipment. In 2003, there was a strong desire for 'lifestyle' programs, and more programs that recognize the sacrifices of the family when it comes to work. Online fulfillment has created programs that are cheaper, faster and more efficient than distributing printed catalogs. Many companies are moving their incentive program online, enabling employees to check their status and the types of products to choose from."[24]

Regardless of the type of incentive used, primary objectives are to motivate either members of the distribution channel or company reps to achieve higher sales and profitability. Dealer and trade incentives are becoming more and more crucial as retailers take greater control of the distribution channel. Most dealers have the option of selling a number of brands from different manufacturers. Manufacturers have to compete for retail distribution and, once achieved, for dealer support for their brand (e.g., premium shelf space, co-op advertising agreements, and in-store recommendations to customers). As one incentive consultant pointed out, the relationship between a manufacturer and a dealer is similar to that of a tenant and a landlord. "The dealer actually owns the distribution channel. The manufacturer is really just a tenant in the channel. Just like anything else in life, the power lies with the owner."[25]

The key to successful incentive programs is to have them complement overall business strategy. The goals that the incentive program are intended to address should be very specific. For example, a company may use incentives to gain support for a new product line, to motivate salespersons to increase sales to current retailers, or to expand distribution to new retailers or in new territories.

There is no question that trade incentives can be extremely effective in increasing sales, productivity, and morale. However, increasingly regulatory agencies are questioning the ethics of some trade incentives that do not provide full disclosure to customers. For example, in a retail store consumers may seek objective information from a salesperson about one brand over another. How objective can retailers be if they are receiving significant rewards for promoting a particular brand? Currently, there is no effective system of providing consumer disclosure for trade incentives. However, as competition in many industries grows more intense and the financial value of incentives increases, we may see both state and federal regulators take a new look at the entire system of trade incentives.

SUMMARY

It is clear that distinctions among the various elements of marketing communication are becoming less clear and less important to both marketers and their customers. Businesses are increasingly demanding accountability for the dollars invested in promotion. Whether a customer is reached through traditional media, e-commerce, or one-to-one selling is less important than the contribution to profits that these elements contribute.

Another notable change in recent years in sales promotion is the concept that promotion, like advertising, must contribute to brand image and brand equity. Astute marketers reject the idea that sales promotion is intended only for a quick fix or immediate sale at any cost. Today, promotion and advertising have a complementary relationship that works to develop a seamless relationship with consumers. Not only must advertising and promotion be coordinated, but it also is crucial that promotion is used in a manner that will enhance, rather than erode, brand equity.

In addition to consumer sales promotion, companies normally use some combination of trade and retail promotions to carry out overall marketing objectives. In fact, by far the largest segment of marketing communication involves trade promotions. To a significant degree, the increase in trade promotions reflects the growth of large retail chains that require national manufacturers to compete for shelf space and divert funds from promotions and advertising that encourage consumer loyalty. The consequence of this emphasis on trade promotion is an erosion of brand equity in some product categories and an emphasis on price as the primary factor in consumer purchases.

Finally, we are only beginning to see the impact of the Internet on sales promotion. Technological convergence has created new ways to reach and cultivate prospects. It also has created concerns about privacy, the practicality of permission marketing, and how to deal with growing trends toward consumer opt-out programs. We may not be able to predict the twists and turns of new and old media, but as we see the growth in online couponing, sweepstakes and games accessed through the computer, and electronic versions of the Yellow Pages, it is certain that advertising and promotion will never be the same.

REVIEW

1. Contrast sales promotion and advertising.

2. What is the primary disadvantage of sales promotion?

3. What are the major advantages and disadvantages of event marketing?

4. What are the primary purposes of co-op advertising?

5. What is the primary regulation of co-op?

6. Why is point-of-purchase advertising so important to many advertisers?

TAKE IT TO THE WEB

Visit **www.origins.com** and notice how Origins encourages online purchases with free samples shipped with every order. What are the advantages of this business practice?

Daily e Deals (**www.dailyedeals.com**) is a Web site offering coupons from companies including L.L. Bean, Gap, Old Navy, Amazon.com, and more. What are some of the benefits of obtaining online coupons?

In 1944 Chiquita (**www.chiquita.com**) became the first company to brand a banana. Take a look at the distinctive stickers that have been used over the years to market Chiquita bananas. What are some advantages to having such a unique label?

LidRock, created by the Convex Group, has turned an ordinary fountain drink lid into a way to deliver mini CD and DVD disks to consumers anywhere fountain drinks are sold. How can LidRock (**www.lidrock.com**) change the ways in which music and movies are previewed? What are some of the advantages and disadvantages of this approach?

Creating the Advertising

PART FIVE

CHAPTER 15

CANDYSTAND.com

ms.**popularity**

always the first one picked,
cherry has taste and beauty.
and she knows it. tends to
act innocent. she isn't.

LIFESAVERS for everyone

Research in Advertising

I n order to create effective advertising, advertisers need to understand what motivates consumers in the marketplace. Research is a critical informational tool that can help advertisers understand how consumers react to their messages. After reading this chapter, you will understand:

1. how advertisers use research
2. the role of the account planner
3. anthropology, sociology, and psychology, in relation to advertising
4. values, lifestyle, and life-stage research
5. research steps in advertising
6. types of advertising research

As we discussed in earlier chapters, there are many questions to be answered before the advertising is developed. What consumer need does our product or service satisfy? How does it satisfy differently and/or better than competitors' product or service? How can we reach consumers? In this chapter, we look at various types of research available—product, market, consumer, advertising strategy, and message research—to answer the advertiser's questions. We also examine ways to judge whether an ad will communicate effectively before we spend the money to run it in the media.

You cannot build strong campaigns without knowing the motivations, attitudes, and perceptions behind consumers' choices. Failure to understand the consumer will likely result in failure for the product or service. If it were easy to be successful, new products wouldn't have such a high failure rate, and established brands might not get into trouble. Advertisers would simply plug in the magic formulas. But there are no formulas to guarantee success. Was the failure of the many upstart dot-coms a lack of money or strategy, or was it a lack of understanding of how consumers used (or would use) the Internet? Or was the medium so new that even consumers didn't understand it? Did the pioneering advertising not work?

Think about how you buy products or services. Why do you choose your toothpaste or laundry detergent? Why do you buy the products you put in your shopping cart—either in the store or online? Is it the brand? Is it the price? Quality? Package? Do you really know? It is not always rational. It is like asking someone, "Why did you fall in love?" The person likely would respond, "I just did." Could you explain your reasons for your preferences to a marketing researcher? Apply the same thought pattern to items you buy at the supermarket or drugstore. For that matter, why do you choose the supermarket where you usually shop? Location? Image? Layout of the

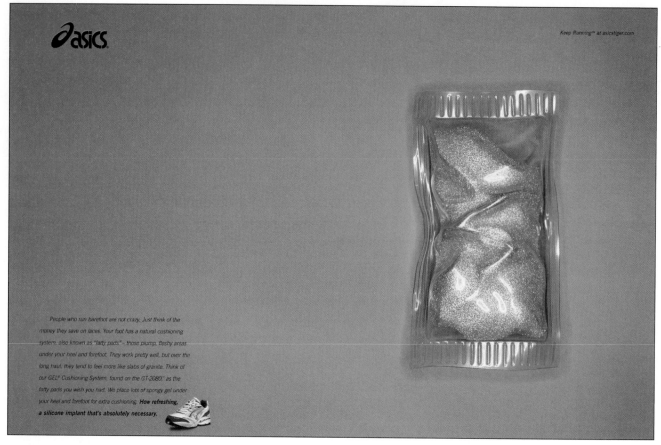

EXHIBIT 15.1

What a great visual. What do you take away from this advertisement?

Courtesy of VitroRobertson, Inc., Asics, and Craig Cutler, photographer.

store? Prices? Service? Fresh vegetables? Chances are you may consider as many as three options. Those options make up your competitive set. These brands immediately come to mind when you think about buying a product or service. How did they get to be the top-of-mind brands in your brain? Marketing guru, Sergio Zyman, says, "In marketing, understanding the why is the crucial step, because when you understand why, it's a lot easier to figure out how to produce what you want."[1]

What kind of advertising motivates you to buy something? As a marketer, how do I reach you? What was the last ad that made you go out and buy anything? And what message do consumers take away from viewing, hearing, or reading an ad message (see Exhibit 15.1)?

RESEARCH IS AN INFORMATIONAL TOOL

Research is and should be used to help improve an advertiser's effectiveness and profitability by staying in touch with the consumer. More specifically, research is used most often in the following ways:

- to help identify consumers
- to help look for new ideas in products or services
- to help improve what is offered in product or services
- to help pinpoint causes of possible problems
- to monitor activities
- to help in communications development
- to study promotional tools

THE RIGHT KIND OF RESEARCH

The kind of research and how much research is needed are always legitimate questions. And there are dangers. Former chairman of Roper Starch Worldwide's Roper division commented on a classic failure—Ford's Edsel—and the misuse of research. In the case of the Edsel automobile, the research was used to make people believe something that wasn't true, not to design a product to meet consumers' tastes. Ford designed a powerful, flashy car with a horse-collar grille before doing any consumer research. After the car was designed, research found consumers wanted a quietly styled, conservative, American-made, Mercedes-Benz–like vehicle. Ford then tried to make consumers fit the car by marketing Edsel as a conservatively styled automobile. It generated interest, but when consumers saw the car they were disappointed.

On the other hand, Roper cited the launch of new Coke in the 1980s as an example of research overreliance and overkill. In several taste tests, new Coke beat Pepsi, but other studies showed that sweeter products often are preferred initially. In-house and outside research for Coca-Cola failed because it didn't run normal usage taste tests on consumers. If the researchers had given consumers a case of new Coke and asked them what they thought two or three weeks later, more accurate responses would have been generated. Roper concluded that people shouldn't always follow the findings of a research study, whether it be a consumer products study or a political campaign. There are dangers despite the potential rewards.

PUBLIC ATTITUDE TOWARD SURVEY RESEARCH

Research shows that refusals to cooperate in survey research are on the rise as are negative attitudes toward survey research. The Council for Marketing and Opinion Research (CMOR) Respondent Cooperative Study conducted in 2003 shows that surveys are receiving record high refusal rates. The CMOR attributes this trend in part to the growth in answering machine ownership and call-screening devises used by consumers. Perhaps even more troublesome is the fact that fewer respondents see the value of participating in survey research. The study confirmed that shorter interviews can help increase the response rate.[2]

If consumers refuse to participate in consumer survey research, it will become more difficult for advertisers to gauge consumer attitudes and opinions. Refusal rates are often higher among African Americans and Hispanics, making it even more difficult to assess attitudes and opinions among these important segments of the population.

ACCOUNT PLANNERS AND CONSUMER INSIGHTS

A British concept of research has become fundamental for many worldwide agencies. In the 1980s, some U.S. agencies moved toward copying the British restructuring of the research department. British agencies found clients doing much of their own research, yet the agency research function remained necessary to understand the information on consumers and the marketplace. The agencies restructured or reduced the size of their research departments and added **account planners.** Their task was to discern not just who buys specific brands but also why. The account planners are usually responsible for all research including quantitative research (usage and attitude studies, tracking studies, ad testing, and sales data) as well as qualitative research (talking face-to-face with their target audiences).

Account planning is based on a simple premise. A client hires an advertising agency to interpret its brand to its target audience. The account planner is charged

account planner
An outgrowth of British agency structure where a planner initiates and reviews research and participates in the creative process. In some agencies, the planner is considered a spokesperson for the consumer.

with understanding the target audience and then representing it throughout the entire advertising development process, thereby ensuring that the advertising is both strategically and executionally relevant to the defined target. Planners provide the insight and clarity that move discussion from I think to I know. It sorts through the multilayers that develop around marketing a brand, eliminating the irrelevant and highlighting the relevant. According to British account planning guru Chris Crowpe, "Account Planning is the discipline that brings the consumer into the process of developing advertising. To be truly effective, advertising must be both distinctive and relevant, *and* planning helps on both counts."[3]

Jon Steel says, "If the agency has a true planning philosophy, it is interested in only one thing, and that is getting it right for its clients."[4] Account planning plays a crucial role during strategy development, driving it from the consumer's point of view. During creative development, account planners act as sounding boards for the creative team. They are responsible for researching the advertising before production to make sure it is as relevant as it can be, and finally, once the work runs, they monitor its effect in depth with a view to improving it the next time around.

The key benefit to the creative teams is usable research—information that explains and communicates, giving them useful insights. The key benefit to clients is a consumer-focused advertising strategy that speaks directly to the target audience in a persuasive way.

Because many marketers direct much of the needed research themselves, the agency is not necessarily a partner in planning the type and direction of research studies conducted for a specific brand or company. However, agency researchers or planners are available to the account groups to help them get the needed information and may be involved in all kinds of advertising research.

The planner works with both account management and creative, covering most research functions. The planner is more a partner to the account and creative teams than a traditional researcher. The planner is considered the team's spokesperson for the consumer and an interpreter of available research (see Exhibit 15.2). To work, advertising must deeply understand, empathize with, and speak the same language as the consumer.

AGENCY FUTURISTS

Clients are saying to agencies, "Tell me something I don't already know." More than ever before marketers want to know what comes next in trends, consumers, the market, and so forth. As a result many agencies hire futurists to help them think out of the box and bring a new perspective to marketing. Young & Rubicam launched its Brand Futures Group as the Intelligence Factory with its horizon-gazing services for clients. GSD&M established its Futures Lab to help clients with "brand visioning, repositioning and future mapping." OgilvyOne put in place a director of scenario planning as its internal forecaster. Saatchi & Saatchi established a director of knowledge management as its visionary. DDW Worldwide employs a cultural anthropologist as its resident prognosticator. The boom in forecasting has several antecedents, but experts agree that one overriding force has been today's fast-paced environment.

A futurist function at the agency appears similar to that of an account planner. Faith Popcorn, author of *EVEolution*, says, "Unfortunately, strategic planners don't do enough looking forward."[5]

WHAT KIND OF RESEARCH IS NEEDED?

Now that we have a better understanding of the research structure, let us look at the kinds of research available and some specific examples. Keep in mind that market-

CLOSES ANY GAP.

Use Great Stuff household foam sealant to close almost any gap imaginable.   ◆DOW▶

EXHIBIT **15.2**

Who do you think is the target audience for this message?

Courtesy of Sawyer Riley Compton and Dow.

ing has become far more complex than in the past because of the tremendous increase in new products, the high cost of shelf space, the expansion of retailer control over the distribution system, changing media habits, overload of information, and the bewildering array of communication choices.

Marketing research—up-front research—tells us about the product, the market, the consumer, and the competition. There are four basic considerations in any market research undertaking: (1) maintaining a consumer-behavior perspective, (2) being sure the right questions are being asked, (3) using appropriate research techniques and controls, and (4) presenting the research findings in a clear, comprehensible format that leads to action. After completing market research, we do advertising research—principally pretesting of ads and campaign evaluation—to get the data we need to develop and refine an advertising strategy and message.

The behavioral sciences—anthropology, sociology, and psychology—have had a strong influence on up-front research.

Anthropology and Advertising

Today, marketers employ anthropologists and ethnographers who use direct observation to understand consumer behavior. They study the emotional connection between products and consumer values. When Warner-Lambert wanted to find out what consumers thought of Fresh Burst Listerine, a mint-flavored product designed to compete with Scope, they paid families to set up cameras in their bathrooms and film their routines around the sink. Users of both brands said they used mouthwash to make their breath smell good, but they treated their products differently. Users of Scope typically swished and spat it out. Devotees of the new Listerine felt obliged to keep the mouthwash in their mouths longer; one went so far as to keep it in his mouth until he got to his car. (See the accompanying Kleppner's Viewpoint 15.1 for another example of observing consumers.)

Ogilvy & Mather's Discovery Group also uses cameras. They send researchers into homes with handheld cameras to get up-close pictures of how people behave in various aspects of their lives. Hours of footage then are condensed into a documentary-like 30-minute video that gives marketers and agency staff the chance to see how people really communicate and interact in certain situations. The videos may give marketers a clearer sense of how people use their products and their motivation, which can influence marketing decisions and help craft creative strategy.[6]

Whirlpool appliances enlisted an anthropologist to tap into consumers' feelings about, and interactions with, their appliances. They visited people's homes to observe how they used their appliances and talked to all the household members. Usage patterns and behavior emerged that helped Whirlpool gain insight into the flow of household activities and how tasks got accomplished. For instance, after finding that in busy families women aren't the only ones doing the laundry, Whirlpool came up with color-coded laundry controls that children and husbands can understand.[7]

Anthropologists have found that certain needs and activities are common to people the world over. Bodily adornment, cooking, courtship, food taboos, gift giving, language, marriage, status, sex, and superstition are present in all societies, although each society attaches its own values and traditions to them. Anthropologists see the United States as a pluralistic society made up of an array of subcultures. In each subculture lives a different group of people who share its values, customs, and traditions. Think about the cultural differences among Italians, Poles, African Americans, and Hispanics, as a starting point.

We are all aware of regional differences in the American language. For example, a sandwich made of several ingredients in a small loaf of bread is a "poor boy" in New Orleans, a "submarine" in Boston, a "hoagie" in Philadelphia, and a "grinder" in upstate New York. Geomarketing allows advertisers to use these cultural differences in food preferences, terminology, and subgroup identities when they advertise their products.

Sociology and Advertising

Sociology examines the structure and function of organized behavior systems. The sociologist studies groups and their influence on, and interaction with, the individual. Advertisers recognize group influences on the adoption of new ideas, media use, and consumer purchase behavior. They use sociological research to predict the profitability of a product purchase by various consumer groups.

Social Class and Stratification We are a society that is clustered into classes determined by such criteria as wealth, income, occupation, education, achievement, and seniority. We sense where we fit into this pattern. We identify with others in our

KLEPPNER VIEWPOINT

BRAD MAJORS

CEO, *Socoh Marketing*

15.1

Lessons in Brand Loyalty at the Point of Sale

I confess—I'm a stalker. Not the kind that makes women nervous. The kind that bothers store managers.

I stalk people shopping for goods and services. And when watching them doesn't answer my questions about their purchase decision process, I ask questions. Generally speaking, I only question friends and acquaintances, so don't worry about being accosted in a store when all you want to do is buy shampoo in peace.

Are people brand loyal and, if so, why? How much more will they pay for a brand before they select another? What would make them try another brand? Unfortunately, we marketers are learning that buyers are much less loyal than we would like.

Here's an example. Traditional marketing wisdom holds that brand preferences are formed early in life, when consumers are young and willing to experiment. As consumers age, they become more loyal to brands that perform according to expectation. Thus, if anyone in a brand's franchise is loyal, it's seniors.

The Roper Report's Public Pulse (April 2002) explored "The Myth of Brand Loyalty and the Reality." Roper looked for loyalty patterns among categories and age groups and found some behavior worth noting. One of the key findings was that "categories themselves drive brand loyalty a lot more than age does." In fact, Roper makes the point that older consumers have a certain savvy gained by their many life experiences, making them more inquisitive and adventurous regarding brand choices. The double whammy is that many seniors now have enormous disposable income. Losing them when they have all that money to spend hurts twice as much.

That brings me to Gloria, my neighbor. She's a senior and as savvy as the Roper folks say she is. We went shopping together Friday night, as we do from time to time. As I pushed my cart around the store to cover my stalking behavior, I watched different people read packaging copy, examine in-store displays, and make their brand choices. I kept an eye on Gloria as she considered the various brands of ice cream, studying flavors and ingredient information on the package. After she made her decision, I asked what had influenced her choice. "Well, I knew I wanted peach ice cream and usually get Breyers," she said. "But I've heard that Mayfield was very good and wanted to try their peach flavor." Sorry, Breyers, but don't take Gloria and her money

for granted. She's enjoyed your product for years but not without a regular assessment of its value.

In addition to that new brand trial, the Raspberry Vinaigrette flavor offered by Ken's Steakhouse intrigued Gloria enough for her to ignore her usual Wishbone and Kraft salad dressings. And recently Gloria tried an alternative cleaning product, OxiClean, because of its multipurpose flexibility and its advertised stain-removing claims. This is particularly interesting since Roper says that household cleaning products have traditionally had high brand loyalty among seniors. Well, they better not depend on Gloria to stick with those brands when something new just might work better.

Quantitative studies can tell us a lot about brand loyalty. They are a valuable tool for marketers. However, nothing beats observing real shoppers in the selling environment. This adds a human face to the insights of that research. You can take this a step further—instead of critiquing the ads you see on TV or in magazines, try withholding your own assessment and, instead, just watch the reactions of others as they review the advertisement. You might be surprised at what you see and hear.

Courtesy of Brad Majors and Socoh Marketing. L.L.C. ■ ■ ■

class ("these are my kind of people"), and we generally conform to the standards of our class. Experienced advertisers have recognized that people's aspirations usually take on the flavor of the social class immediately above their own.

Social-class structure helps explain why demographic categories sometimes fail to provide helpful information about consumers. A professional person and a factory worker may have the same income, but that doesn't mean their interests in products will coincide. In today's marketing environment, research has shown that no single variable, such as age, income, or sex, will accurately predict consumer purchases. We have discovered that using several variables gives a more accurate prediction of consumer behavior. Think of the differences between homemakers and working women of the same age, income, and education in their food preferences for themselves and their families, usage of convenience goods, childcare, and media habits.

Trend Watching Quantitative research is as important as ever, but there seems to be a premium on nuggets of more attitudinal, psychographic market smarts with which marketers hope to base the creative approach to their communication.

Trends come from all forms of media and advertising. They come from music, from politics, from travel, and from the Internet. They develop everywhere. Fads, on the other hand, are like crushes; they burn fast and hot but die quickly and often leave a bitter taste. The macarena and Beanie Babies came and went quickly. Trends are a product of society. They reflect our changing attitudes, behaviors, and values. They are the most obvious and most concrete signs of the times. Trends can be two sizes: macro and micro.

Macro trends are about the "big issues"—our definitions of happiness, success, fulfillment. Macro trends come from the way people think. They emerge when people feel a dissatisfaction with the status quo, in their own lives and in society. They announce our new definitions of happiness. Some of the neotraditionalism is reflected in the return to traditions—people setting new priorities in the balance among work, family, and friends.

Micro trends are the details in the bigger picture. They are the tangible manifestations of the macro trends in fashion, music, and sports activities. For example, the macro trend of neotraditionalism will foster micro trends such as cooking schools cropping up as the microwave generation tries to behave like their grandparents and throw dinner parties. In 2001, retro nostalgia was big. Chrysler's PT Cruiser became *Motor Trend*'s Car of the Year replacing the Lincoln LS.

Generally, young people set trends, but not every young person is a trendsetter. Those most comfortable on the cutting edge are the ones called *early adopters, alphas, trendsetters, leading edgers,* and *innovators*—all these terms mean the same thing. These are the people who are willing to experiment. Not all trends will work for a brand. Yet, look at what Mountain Dew did by using extreme sports and over-the-top imagery to become the extreme brand despite being around for over 30 years. Many companies spend a lot of money trying to track trends. Coffeehouses and teahouses—are they fads or trends?

Cohort Analysis Using a research technique called cohort analysis, marketers can access consumers' lifelong values and preferences, and develop strategies now for products they will use later in life. Cohorts are generations of people with the same birth years and core values. According to advertising executive Natalie Perkins, these values are formed by significant events between the ages of 13 and 20 and endure throughout one's life. For example, such events as the Great Depression, the Korean War, McCarthyism, the Vietnam War, the sexual revolution, the Gulf War, and the War in Iraq or the influence of Martin Luther King, Jr., television, computers, divorced and single families, and environmental crisis can form a value system.

Generally, we study consumers using demographics, psychographics, lifestyles, and behaviors. Cohort analysis combines these data and adds to the consumer profile by examining the past as well as the present. Four cohort groups exist: traditionalists, transitioners, challengers, and space-agers. Each group is unique, evolving, and maturing. The following is an example of challengers: In their thirties and forties, many challengers are in nontraditional households: single parents, working women. They have high incomes, high debt, and have started later than their cohorts before them to raise a family. They idolize youth but are becoming middle-aged, and they don't like it. Highly educated, they are concerned about retirement but are financially unable to plan for it. They are obsessed with reducing stress and guilt. They still believe in having it all. They seek information before they buy. They are caught between reality and their black-and-white morality and have difficulty dealing with the gray areas in life. They are still concerned with what others think, but they haven't abandoned the self-indulgent lifestyle.

By identifying a generation's collective hot buttons, mores, and memories, advertisers can hone messages and create persuasive icons to better attract them.[8] This kind of research can aid in developing a product marketing plan that follows the lifetime of a consumer.

Life-Stage Research   Advertisers have traditionally considered the family as the basic unit of buying behavior. Most traditional households pass through an orderly progression of stages, and each stage has special significance for buying behavior.

Knowledge of the **family life cycle** allows a company to segment the market and the advertising appeal according to specific consumption patterns and groups. Of course, the concept of the family has significantly changed over the past decades. Yet there are still crucial points in the lives of consumers—they leave home, get married or stay unmarried, bear children, raise children, and send adult children into lives of their own. As a result of these life transitions, people suddenly or gradually go from one stage of life to another.

family life cycle
Concept that demostrates changing purchasing behavior as a person or a family matures.

According to census data, the nature of the traditional family life cycle has changed in the past 30 years. For example, people are waiting longer to get married, women are postponing childbearing, the incidence of divorce has almost tripled, the proportion of single-parent households has significantly increased, and more young adults are living with their parents than in the past. As a result, some advertisers have reevaluated the way they look at the family life cycle. By examining these segments' subgroups, advertisers begin to get a clearer picture of buying behavior and lifestyles. Researchers refer to these subgroup studies as life-stage research. As with the family life cycle, life-stage research looks at the crucial points in consumers' lives. Advertisers can find syndicated research services that analyze young singles, newlyweds, young couples, mature couples, and teenage households. Advertisers need knowledge of the life stages to help them develop and understand the changes taking place today in the twenty-first century so they can create more effective integrated marketing communications (see Exhibit 15.3).

Psychology and Advertising

Psychology is the study of human behavior and its causes. Three psychological concepts of importance to consumer behavior are motivation, cognition, and learning. Motivation refers to the drives, urges, wishes, or desires that initiate the sequence of events known as "behavior." Cognition is the area in which all the mental phenomena (perception, memory, judging, thinking, and so on) are grouped. Learning refers to those changes in behavior relative to external stimulus conditions that occur over time.[9] These three factors, working within the framework of the societal environment, create the psychological basis for consumer behavior. Advertising research is interested in cognitive elements to learn how consumers react to different stimuli,

FOR SOME REASON, WE JUST DON'T SEE YOU IN A PONTOON BOAT.

You seem more like the 270-horsepower, twin jet-powered engine type. The type that wants breathtaking acceleration and nimble, precise turning. All while enjoying such niceties as a 160-watt JVC® stereo, Berber carpeting under your feet, a Bimini top over your head, pop-up ski pylon, even a matching trailer. It's all here in the LX2000™ Sport Boat. Get on board, and see if we guessed right about you. Call 1-800-6-YAMAHA or visit yamaha-motor.com.

©2002 Yamaha Motor Corporation, USA. Call 1-800-6-YAMAHA or visit yamaha-motor.com to find a dealer. Follow instructional materials and obey all laws. Drive responsibly, wearing protective apparel. Drive within your capabilities, allowing time and distance for maneuvers, and respect others around you. Don't drink and drive. Call the Yamaha WaterCraft Education & Training Center at 1-800-635-2232, and visit yamaha-motor.com to learn how we're helping protect the environment.

EXHIBIT 15.3

An advertiser may test the power of this lifestyle appeal.

Courtesy of VitroRobertson, Inc., Yamaha, and Aaron Chang, photographer.

and research finds learning especially important in determining factors such as advertising frequency. However, in recent years, the major application of psychology to advertising has been the attempt to understand the underlying motives that initiate consumer behavior. Companies are also interested in studying emotions. For example, Kellogg hired a cognitive psychologist to explore women's feelings about food. As a result of insights gained, Special K was not pitched as simply a low-fat breakfast food. Ads for Special K were developed that featured average women caught between polar passions for doughnuts and great-looking legs.[10]

Values and Lifestyles The research company that popularized psychographic segmentation developed Values and Life Style (VALS™). SRI Consulting Business Intelligence's VALS is designed to predict consumer behavior by profiling the psychology and demographics of American consumers. It segments respondents into eight clusters of consumers, each with distinct behavioral and decision-making patterns that reflect different primary motivations and available psychological and material resources (see Exhibit 15.4).

VALS classifies consumers along two key dimensions: primary motivation (what in particular about the person or the world governs his or her actions and activities) and resources (the range of psychological and material resources available to sustain that self-concept).[11]

This classification takes into account an individual's primary motivation such as ideals, achievement, or self-expression. Resources, on the other hand, include both material and acquired attributes (e.g., money, position, education) and psychological qualities (e.g., inventiveness, interpersonal skills, intelligence, energy).

According to VALS, an individual purchases certain products and services because he or she is a specific type of person. VALS is a network of interconnected

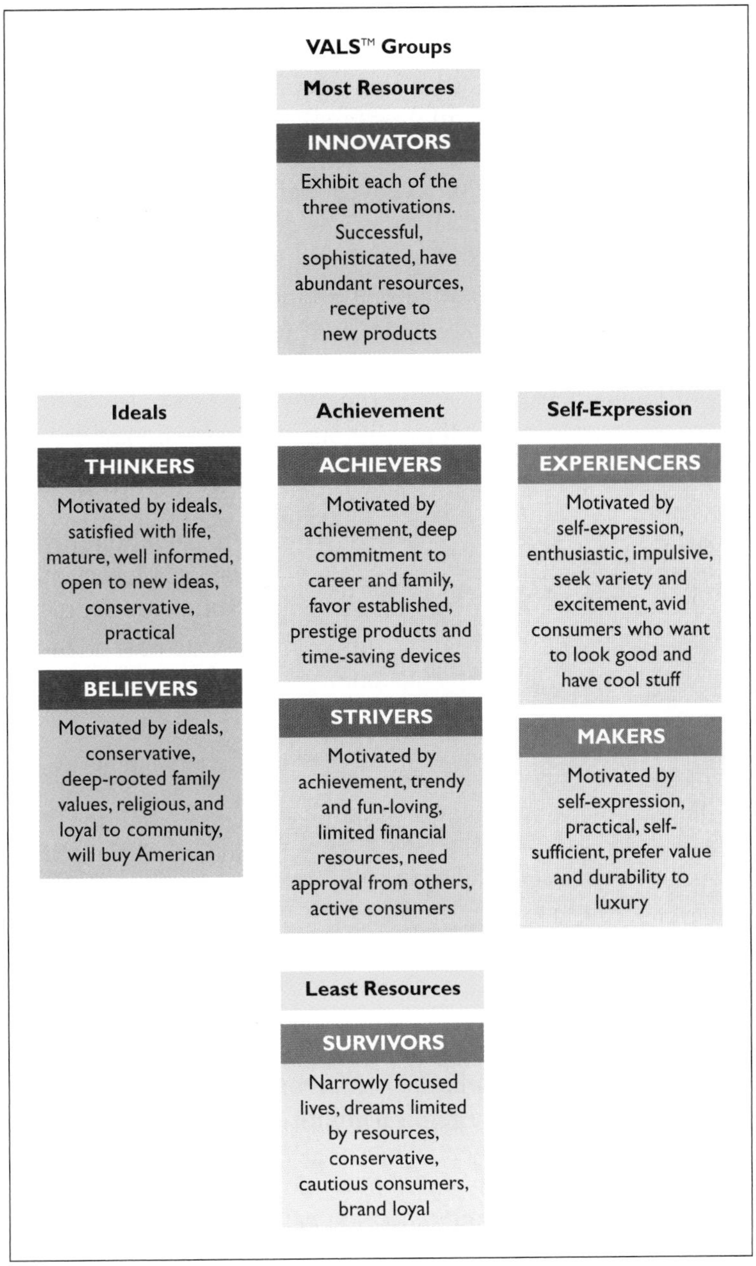

EXHIBIT **15.4**

VALS Lifestyle Categories

Courtesy of SRI Business Intelligence.

VALS™ Groups

Most Resources

INNOVATORS

Exhibit each of the three motivations. Successful, sophisticated, have abundant resources, receptive to new products

Ideals

THINKERS

Motivated by ideals, satisfied with life, mature, well informed, open to new ideas, conservative, practical

BELIEVERS

Motivated by ideals, conservative, deep-rooted family values, religious, and loyal to community, will buy American

Achievement

ACHIEVERS

Motivated by achievement, deep commitment to career and family, favor established, prestige products and time-saving devices

STRIVERS

Motivated by achievement, trendy and fun-loving, limited financial resources, need approval from others, active consumers

Self-Expression

EXPERIENCERS

Motivated by self-expression, enthusiastic, impulsive, seek variety and excitement, avid consumers who want to look good and have cool stuff

MAKERS

Motivated by self-expression, practical, self-sufficient, prefer value and durability to luxury

Least Resources

SURVIVORS

Narrowly focused lives, dreams limited by resources, conservative, cautious consumers, brand loyal

segments. Neighboring types have similar characteristics and can be combined in varying ways to suit particular marketing purposes.

Advertisers can use the VALS typology to segment particular markets, develop marketing strategies, refine product concepts, position products and services, develop advertising and media campaigns, and guide long-range planning.

Yankelovich's Mindbase, a segmenting tool, identified eight major consumer groups with shared life attitudes and motivations. These eight groups were further divided into 32 distinct subsegments for greater differentiation and clarification. Here is a brief summary of the eight major Mindbase segments.[12]

- *Up and Comers.* Young singles and couples without children who have a positive, upwardly mobile perspective and expect to benefit from their own skills and abilities. Up and Comers are gregarious and socially conscious, and they lead active lifestyles.

- *Aspiring Achievers.* Younger, self-driven individuals who are skeptical about institutions and feel the need to look out for themselves. Aspiring Achievers believe that money is the measure of success and will give them power to control their world.

■ *Realists.* Individuals who are resource constrained and strive to balance their needs with the needs of their family. The Realist group is ethnically diverse and concentrated in urban areas.

■ *New Traditionalists.* Innovative American families who are creating a new paradigm for parenting. New Traditionalists are upscale, involved in community, and interested in creating the "right" values environment for their children.

■ *Family Centereds.* Family-focused individuals who are not interested in social issues or self-exploration and have few interests or activities outside of family. Family Centereds are skeptical about institutions and view the family as a safe haven in the world.

■ *Individualists.* Individuals without children who are driven by technology and success at work. Individualists find little time for social interests and prefer to focus on climbing the career ladder.

■ *Renaissance Masters.* Mature, financially successful individuals who are vitally connected to community and to life. Renaissance Masters are upbeat about their future and remain interested in personal development.

■ *Maintainers.* Mature individuals who use the past as their point of reference. The Maintainer group is sedentary and resource constrained.

Brain Wave Research

Marketers are exploring the use of brain wave research to try to better understand consumers. Although this research may sound Orwellian at first blush, according to Harvard Professor Gerald Zaltman, brain wave research is trying to understand consumer motivation, not "insert ideas into people's thinking."[13] The theory behind this type of research is that it can provide marketers with an honest consumer reaction to a product or an advertisement.

With the help of neuroscientists, marketers can use an electroencephalograph to pick up activity in 12 regions of the brain that might be stimulated by exposure to an advertisement or a product. Different parts of the brain show attraction, revulsion, recall, and level of attention, for instance. They can be used to assess reactions to all or parts of a commercial message. Also in use are special magnetic resonance imaging machines (MRIs) to monitor blood flow in the brain. Different colors show up on the scan depending on which part of the brain is stimulated with thought. These tests can be very costly. For example, one facility in Atlanta that performs these MRI tests, BrightHouse Institute, charges an average of $250,000 to perform one of these studies on a group of consumers (see the accompanying Kleppner's Viewpoint 15.2.)[14]

Marketing Environment

Companies and agencies want to accumulate as much information about their markets as possible before making crucial integrated marketing decisions. Technology has been assisting marketers in getting more information faster.

Universal Product Code Universal product code (UPC) information has greatly enhanced the process of tracking product sales. When the grocer scans a price into the register at checkout, that information is instantly available to the retailer. Scanner reporting systems have allowed marketers to track their performance quickly, rather than monthly or bimonthly, and at local levels. UPC information allows marketers to determine what their share of market is, if one kind of packaging or in-store advertising sells better, and which retailers sell the most units. Cash-checking cards can be scanned into the system to keep a record of what kind of products consumers buy. This offers the retailer and manufacturer the opportunity to target promotions directly to people who have used the product in the past. This information can contribute to any database marketing effort by the retailer.

Single-Source Data For single-source data, retail tracking scanner data are integrated with household panel data on purchase patterns and ad exposure. The information comes from one supplier and is extracted from a single group of consumers. These data can be combined with other research sources to supply micromarketers with a wealth of information on who, what, and how. Despite these new micromarketing capabilities, research firms are far more adept at generating data than most clients are at using the information.

Database Marketers Database marketers use sweepstakes entries, rebate information, merchandise orders, free product offers, requests for new-product information, and purchase information to build consumer databases telling them a great deal about how consumers live. This information offers many opportunities for database marketing (see Exhibit 15.5).

EXHIBIT 15.5

One way to test the success of this ad is by the number of calls to the phone number provided.

Courtesy of Young & Rubicam San Francisco and Sausalito.

KLEPPNER

BRUCE F. HALL, PH.D.

Howard, Merrell and Partners

VIEWPOINT 15.2

Why Advertisers Do It

Does "traditional advertising" still work? It has been declared ill, dying, or already dead for years by analysts who predicted its demise at the hands of scanner-information-driven promotional marketing (1990), Interactive media (1998), or TiVo (2002). In 2003, it was media fragmentation, proliferation, and consolidation combined with the erosion of mass markets that were spelling the end of traditional advertising as we know it, according to Coca-Cola's chief marketing officer.

But this burgeoning and tendentious debate about the merits of traditional advertising in a world of product placement, guerilla marketing, and media proliferation is, in the end, not about media strategy, or tactics, or trends. At bottom it is not even about advertising. It is about how you build and maintain a brand. It is about how you balance strategy against tactics and brand sell against product sell.

We would like to propose a way to resolve this debate, an approach that we believe leads to consensus rather than rancor. That is, to develop a framework for understanding how advertising, in whatever form, really *should* build and maintain brands, when it is doing its job correctly. Because we believe beneath the disagreements on how the disciplines of advertising have been applied is a fundamental misunderstanding of its basic principles.

How Should Advertising Work?

In the absence of deep consensus about how advertising should work, there is a bias toward easily observable, short-term sales effects. Even though long-term effects get lip service, it is the short-term effects that get measured.

The problem is, this doesn't fit well with the reality of how traditional advertising is used in the real world. The vast majority of advertising dollars are not spent to drive short-term trial on new brands and products. Most of the dollars are spent on mature brands in mature categories that are already very well known to consumers. Assuming that advertisers are rational, profit-maximizing businesspeople, who have shown that they are willing to spend billions of dollars to advertise their products, what can we infer about the effects of advertising by looking at the behavior of advertisers?

To begin, we can certainly infer that since most advertising dollars are going to support established brands, not

Dr. Bruce F. Hall

drive trial on new brands, most of the time advertisers are trying to manipulate perceptions of known brands. Yet consumers, we are told, have become highly sophisticated connoisseurs of brands, too smart to be fooled by advertising. "It might have worked in the '50's, but it doesn't work any more."

An easy conclusion, but a wrong one. The human brain that was the product of 70,000 generations of evolution in 1950 hasn't changed a lot now that it has evolved through 70,002 generations. So let's see what psychology and brain science can tell us about how traditional advertising works.

Key Learnings from Psychology and Brain Science

1. Most neuroscientists now agree that the neurons and synapses of the brain are highly malleable in response to experience. This "neuroplasticity" is fundamental to learning and memory. As we experience the world, our brain is constantly reshaping itself as an efficient instrument of perception and learning and a repository of learned motor skills.

2. Psychology has also rediscovered the importance of the nonconscious mind. We now know that the nonconscious mind plays a much greater role in behavior than twentieth century psychology would have had us

believe—as much as 95 percent of our behavior is controlled nonconsciously. Yet, because we are so present in our own (conscious) minds, we tend to dismiss the critical role of emotions and the unconscious.

3. Finally, the field of memory research has exploded. Not only are children's memories of events extremely unreliable in response to questioning, but eyewitness reports by adults are also highly filtered through complex memory processes. For advertising, the *piece de resistance* is academic research demonstrating that consumers' memories of taste and flavor can be manipulated, simply by exposing them to relevant print advertising, *after they experience the product.*

What Is Branding?

Let's apply this knowledge from the academic laboratory to the question we raised earlier: Why do established brands, rather than new brands, spend the most on advertising? Everyone talks about something called "branding," but what is it really? Underlying that idea are some clearly defined physical and psychological processes that operate to shape and manipulate consumer perceptions of brands and, therefore, their behavior. Here they are.

Cueing and Neuroplasticity   The first process is "cueing." It is no more or less than the mechanism by which we create space, literally, in the consumer's head for our brands. This is why consistency of visual and auditory imagery in brand campaigns is so crucial for success.

Recent research on neuroplasticity has shown that experience hard-wires the brain to an extent previously unimagined. Two examples illustrate the point: Indians raised in tepees have greater visual acuity for diagonal lines than non-Indians; musicians playing repetitive patterns can experience dramatic physical dysfunction due to radical rewiring of the relevant neuronal space.

If these physical changes take place in the brain in response to experienced stimuli, it is logical to extend those findings to advertising. Advertising is an experienced stimulus, usually repeated over many exposures. Physical changes in the brain may be a key to the fundamental cueing function of advertising.

With the right research design we should be able to demonstrate that the visual acuity of American adults for the shape of the Nike "swoosh" is greater than for a naive population that had never been exposed to it. Similarly for other icons that we call "brands," from the Harley-Davidson sound to the voluptuous shape of the classic Coke bottle, from the NBC chimes to the emerging iconic treatment of the color brown for UPS.

All these visual and auditory symbols have carved out some neuronal space for themselves in the heads of consumers. Based on the findings of brain science, it seems likely that this is a literal, not a figurative space. Yes, Virginia, Coca-Cola does own some real estate in your head—and they're not paying rent. No wonder consumer activists object to advertising.

What does this tell us about advertising an established brand? The wiring for Nike's "swoosh" is not indelible—if advertising for Nike lapses, that space in the brain may lapse as well and be occupied by some other intrusive visual or auditory image. That may be a good thing for society (or not), but it's certainly not a good thing for Nike.

Anticipation and the Nonconscious Mind   Traditional advertising's role in stimulating actual purchases is not to trigger a rational purchase decision. It is to create a sense of anticipation, the emotional heat between the consumer and the brand that drives positive affect. That affect is nonconscious to a much larger degree than consumers, and most marketers, really understand.

When a potential customer stands in the Mercedes showroom lusting after a $100,000 automobile that will get him to his destination in exactly the same amount of time, with exactly the same number of passengers, as a $15,000 Toyota Corolla, the lust he feels in his heart is not because of great German engineering. It is a lust for the smell of the leather, the feeling of the wheel in his hand, the sense of privilege he will get as people's heads turn to see the great man go by. Traditional advertising feeds that lust, building the sense of anticipation that potential customer feels, with lush photography on fine paper, and video images of leaves swiring in the wake of this fabulous automobile as it powers down a country road.

Food advertising has the same function. It should make you hungry, or make you feel you will be loved and honored as a mother, or create some other warmth of anticipation that wells up from the archetypal depths of your limbic system. Beer advertising is about masculine camaraderie, not beer. Do frogs and lizards sell beer? Yes—if they bond a group of unrelated young men into an artificial tribe that shares the joke, and buys the brand that forms the common thread of that joke.

Remembering   Advertising also operates on the consumer's memory. When you access a memory, you are not hitting the "play" button on a videotape machine in your head. You access a memory of an event by recreating it in your head; what memory research has shown is that a researcher, by supplying additional, new information about an event at the time you access your memories of that event, can significantly change your memory of that event.

That is exactly what advertisers do with advertising for known brands. They augment their limited ability to control the consumer's experience with their products by supplying new information about that experience, after the fact. By lifting your experience to a higher emotional level, Coca-Cola becomes a remembered experience that was something more than black water with a little sugar and a lot of fizz—it's Coke, the Real Thing.

So now we can explain why Coca-Cola continues to spend heavily to advertise a brand that is already well known to virtually every human being on the planet. Without advertising to reshape that remembered experience, sales would undoubtedly fall. No one would forget about "Coca-Cola," but they *would* forget what it's supposed to taste like.

Similarly, the role of product advertising is not to keep McDonald's top-of-mind. Most of its customer base already eats there multiple times a week. Why would they need an ad to tell them about McDonald's? The value of the advertising is its ability to lift the remembered taste experience from their last visit, so they will come back for more.

Interpretation Finally, there is the consumer's cognitive interpretation of his or her reasons for making the purchase. One of the powerful new paradigms emerging from neuroscience research is the idea that the cognitive functions of our brains function to a large extent as "Interpreters" of the relevant bits of our life story. This interpreter is always active, and in response to the positive affect toward the brand the consumer is experiencing as a result of advertising, word of mouth, or any other source, it will supply a "story" that makes sense of those desires.

These stories are important, because consumers write stories for themselves only if the brand has become relevant emotionally. Once the brand becomes relevant emotionally, consumers will come up with fully articulated cognitive explanations for why it is relevant rationally.

What we must understand is that we cannot expect consumers to be rational—but we should expect them to be logical. Whether their stated reasons for purchase are the reasons stated or implied by the brand's communications or reasons they have made up for themselves doesn't really matter. What matters is that the story they tell is consistent with what the marketer wants the brand to stand for.

How Does Branding Really Work?

What we call "branding" is really the end result of a series of psychological and physical processes, based in the emotional system and the nonconscious mind, that drive consumer behavior. Traditional advertising is a key driver of those processes. It doesn't necessarily supply a purchase trigger—promotional marketing often does that. But without successful and effective branding, promotional marketing can't become a determinant of purchase behavior, because the consumer has no fundamental affect driving his or her decision process.

For established brands, traditional advertising performs four key functions. It maintains a consistent set of visual and auditory cues in the consumer's brain space. It manages the way consumers remember their experience with the brand and creates and emotional state of anticipation for the next purchase. And, finally, it supplies useful raw material for the consumer's personal, logical story, the story that supports his or her use of the brand.

Does traditional advertising always succeed in performing these functions? Of course not. Examples abound of iconic brands that have wandered from their roots and suffered the consequences. Every brand has its own unique balance of benefits, consumer need, and competition, which dictates a strategy for success. Over time that balance can shift, as the parameters shift, and finding a new balance can be tremendously challenging. Understanding why advertising works, when it does, is the key first step in regaining that balance.

Courtesy of Dr. Bruce Hall. ■ ■ ■

Internet Data Many major advertisers and research companies have embraced the Internet for online focus groups, surveys, and other marketing research, despite its flaws and problems (e.g., how representative Web users are of the overall population). Online research shouldn't replace traditional marketing research, but harnessing the Internet improves the research process. Web-based research should be part of the mix.

General Motors Corp. created real-time, online clinics to gather consumer reaction to upcoming products. Mark Hogan, president of GM's e-commerce unit, said, "The days (of bringing) 1,000 people over a weekend to look at our products will soon be a thing of the past." Nissan's development of the Xterra sport utility vehicle stemmed partly from cybersurfer input. After winning *Motor Trend* magazine's SUV of the year (1999), Nissan sent 1,500 e-mails to targeted buyers to find out the credibility of the awards among consumers.[15]

THE SERIES OF RESEARCH STEPS IN ADVERTISING

The term *advertising research* is broadly defined as including research that contributes to all four stages of the advertising process:

1. *Advertising strategy development.* Research tries to answer many questions: Who is the market and what do they want? What is the competition we are specifying? What communication do we want our selected market to get from our advertising? How will we reach the persons selected as our market?

2. *Advertising execution development.* There are two kinds of research used at the execution stage of advertising. The first is exploratory research to stimulate the creative people and to help them know and understand the language used by consumers. The other is research to study proposed creative concepts, ideas, roughs, visuals, headlines, words, presenters, and so forth, to see whether they can do what the creative strategy expects of them.

3. *Evaluating pretesting executions.* Pretesting is the stage of advertising research at which advertising ideas are tested. Partly because of the finality of much pretesting, it is the most controversial kind of advertising research.

4. *Campaign evaluation.* Campaign evaluation usually involves a tracking study to measure the performance of a campaign.

The primary goal of advertising research is to help in the process of creative development. Before we examine the research process advertisers would use in developing advertising strategy for campaigns, let us get a better perspective on using research information.

Translating Information into Strategy

Information isn't enough by itself to answer marketing problems. A few years ago the brilliant McCann Erickson researcher, Jack Dempsey, said, "By itself information has no value." It acquires value only when the strategist takes "a point of view" about what the information means—a point of view that is relevant to the marketing and advertising issues. You have to get involved in all the data at your disposal and, if necessary, fill in some gaps by acquiring more information. But then you have to step back from it. The secret of effective strategy formation lies in deciding which data are important and which are not. It is a process of organizing simplicity out of complexity, for the best strategic insights are usually the very simple ones.

Take the consumer's point of view. Ask yourself what the consumer is really buying. Is he or she buying the product because of its functional benefits? How important are the psychological benefits? The corporate landscape is littered with examples of companies and industries that failed to appreciate what their consumers were really purchasing. Because of this, they defined their markets inappropriately and often disastrously. Begin with an analysis of how people behave rather than an analysis of how they feel or what they believe. You will probably get into these issues, but behavior is the foundation from which you build. And above all, try to see the world with the consumers' eyes.

Think about the question, "How many pairs of shoes do you buy in a year?" Now, if you disregard such factors as style and fashion, the number of shoes bought in a year depends largely on how much walking is done, not on age, sex, or social class. These may be associated variables but less determinant than the amount of walking the individual does. You see, information by itself has no value (see the accompanying Kleppner's Viewpoint 15.3).

Market, Product, Competitive, and Consumer Research

Basic information is gathered and analyzed to determine the marketing strategy for a product or service, projected sales, the source of business, pricing and distribution factors, geographic information, and how to develop data to identify the size and nature of the product category. This kind of research includes data on competitors, sales trends, packaging, advertising expenditures, and future trends. Situation

KLEPPNER VIEWPOINT

AN INTERVIEW WITH STEVE WARNER

**VP/Account Management,
Sawyer Riley Compton**

*by Jason Boyd,
Graduate Student,
University of Georgia*

How much does research influence your marketing decisions?

We use research in a variety of ways—to assess a situation, to inform our thinking, and to document our results.

We use it first to get an accurate picture of the problem or issue we have to address. We use syndicated research for things like audience demographics, and we use clients' existing research. We get immersed in all available data to form a hypothesis about the situation and then use primary research to prove or disprove our hypothesis. Sometimes you need science to justify your hunch.

We quantify the issues and opportunities in the context of the competition and the marketplace. So research is used to benchmark the situation and to quantify attitudes, perceptions, and trends before we launch a campaign.

And we do postcampaign surveys to document results and make changes and course corrections for the future. So much of what we do is to prove that what we did worked. You have to prove your ROI [return-on-investment] somehow.

Steve Warner

What do you do if research contradicts your marketing decision?

If research contradicts your instincts, follow the research. But sometimes conventional research does not allow you to find the solution to the problem, and advertising alone isn't necessarily the solution to the problem. Sometimes a little fieldwork is in order, and it's usually informal "research." An account executive might go out to the stores or spend time with a salesperson to understand the sales and distribution issues.

Here's an example—we used to work with a client that made a glazing product for skyscraper windows. It was superior to the competitor's product, but still had trouble selling. The account executive on the business went to the job site and discovered that the product's container looked very similar to another chemical product. The workers couldn't read or speak English, so the companies they worked for were afraid the crew would mistakenly use the wrong product. So the account executive found out that all the client needed to do was change the packaging and they could sell the heck out of it—something that traditional research never would have discovered.

Courtesy of Sawyer Riley Compton, Steve Warner, and Jason Boyd. ■ ■ ■

Jason Boyd

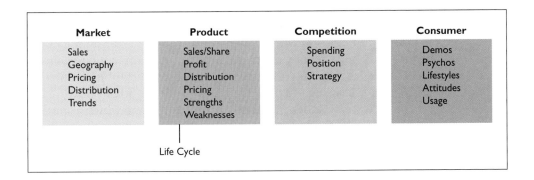

EXHIBIT **15.6**
Situation Analysis

analysis helps to define clearly the market in which the product or service competes (see Exhibit 15.6).

Prospect research is critical to define clearly who is expected to buy the product or service. Studies may identify users, attitudes, lifestyles, and consumption patterns—all of which identify the prime prospect.

The amounts and kinds of information required will vary according to the product category and marketing situation. Exhibit 15.7 outlines strategy choices indicated by different levels of brand trial and awareness. It is difficult to talk about strategy until you have information on awareness levels for each brand in the market. "Brand trial" will occur if what consumers know about the brand fits in with their needs and is sufficiently important or motivating. The relationship between a brand's level of awareness and its trials may be expressed as a ratio. A high ratio will suggest one strategy option, a low ratio another. For example, ratio of high awareness to low trial (lower left-hand box of Exhibit 15.7) clearly indicates that what people know about the brand is not sufficiently motivating or relevant, and the brand may need repositioning.

Research does not always tell us what we want to hear, which can create problems if we think an advertising idea is really strong. Take the classic "Avis. We try harder" campaign. It tested poorly in research. Consumers said the "We're number two" concept meant Avis was second rate. Research was against running it, but creative genius Bill Bernbach fervently believed in the idea and convinced Avis to take a chance with it. Today, the Avis campaign is considered one of the most powerful and most memorable ad campaigns in history.

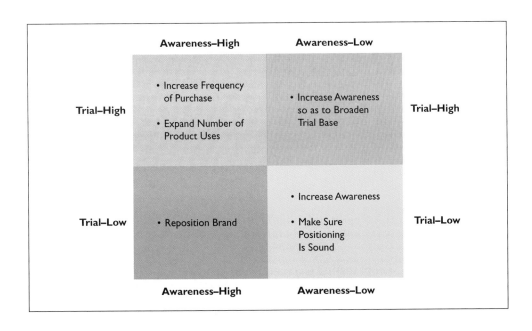

EXHIBIT **15.7**

Brand Trial/Awareness Ratios: Strategic Options

Advertising Strategy or Message Research

Most products have a number of positive appeals that could be successfully promoted, so how do we go about making the decision as to which direction to go with an ad or appeal? The idea is to choose the one that is most important to the majority of our target. Because selecting the primary appeal is the key to any advertising campaign, many research techniques have been developed to find which appeal to use. Message research is used to identify the most relevant and competitive advertising sales message. It may take many forms, but focus groups and concept testing are frequently used to evaluate creative ideas and strategies.

focus group
A qualitative research interviewing method using in-depth interviews with a group rather than with an individual.

qualitative research
This involves finding out what people say they think or feel. It is usually exploratory or diagnostic in nature.

Focus Group Research **Focus groups** became fashionable in the late 1960s as a **qualitative research** tool that was often used to provide a more in-depth way to explore creative ideas than through rigid quantitative tests. Later account planners saw it as a way of getting early consumer feedback to an idea without putting it through the artificiality of a formal test. Focus groups have also become an important qualitative tool used by marketers and account planners to find out why consumers behave as they do. The focus group offers a means of obtaining in-depth information through a discussion-group atmosphere. This process is designed to probe into the behavior and thinking of individual group members. The focus group can elicit spontaneous reactions to products or ads. A trained moderator leads a group of 8 to 12 consumers, usually prime prospects. The typical focus group interviews last one-and-a-half to two hours. The number of different group sessions vary from advertiser to advertiser based somewhat on expense, topic being discussed, and time considerations. The client usually watches the interview from behind a one-way mirror so as not to disrupt the normal function of the group.

An example of a client for whom focus groups provided much needed insight is Nikon. Nikon has long been considered the brand of choice of professional photographers and serious hobbyists. However, the company found a need to expand its message to consumers who shop at places such as Best Buy and Curcuit City to capture the average picture taker. In focus groups, Nikon heard things like, "Nikon is too much camera for me. I just need to take pictures of my kids." A new effort was aimed to broaden the consumer base, according to McCann-Erickson's creative director, Pete Jones, and give consumers the confidence to take a great picture.[16]

As we indicated earlier, researchers are using more online focus groups to gather consumers' responses to questions and products.

Videoconferencing links, television monitors, remote-control cameras, and digital transmission technology allow focus group research to be accomplished over long-distance lines. Many advertising agencies believe videoconferencing enriches the creative process because it gives more people input. This technique allows more agency and client people to watch groups from all over the country without having to travel.

There are critics of the overemphasis on focus groups. They point to the fact that many good ideas—whether a 30-second commercial or a new product or concept—often get killed prematurely because they did not do well with a focus group. One increasing criticism is the growing number of "professional" respondents who are savvy enough to go from focus group to focus group, speaking the marketers' language and picking up an easy $40 or $50 each time. Most account planners agree that focus groups should never be used as a replacement for quantitative research. But these groups are useful to determine consumer reaction to certain language in a TV commercial or in the development process for creative.

Concept Testing Concept testing is a method to determine the best of a number of possible appeals to use in your advertising. A creative concept is defined as a simple explanation or description of the advertising idea behind the product.

Response Criterion	Measurement
Cognitive (Think)	
Attention	Eye camera
Awareness	Day-after recall
Affective (Feel)	
Attitude	Persuasion
Feelings	Physiological response
Conative (Do)	
Purchase intent	Simulated shopping
Sales	Split cable/scanner

EXHIBIT 15.8

Effectiveness Measures by Type of Consumer Response for Copy Research

Source: Adopted from John D. Leckenby and Joseph T. Plummer, "Advertising stimulus measurement and assessment research: A review of advertising testing methods," *Current Issues and Research in Advertising*, 1983, 155.

A tourism association developed several appeals that might motivate prime prospects to drive two hours to the mountains from a large metro area in another state:

1. Only two hours to relaxation
2. Mountain fun in your own backyard
3. The family playground in the mountains
4. Escape to white-water rafting, fishing, and the great outdoors
5. Weekend vacation planner package

By using cards with the theme statement and/or rough layouts, the advertiser tries to obtain a rank order of consumer appeal of the various concepts and diagnostic data explaining why the concepts were ranked as they were. The tourism group found that targets had not realized they were so close to these mountain areas. As a result, mountain areas had not been considered in their vacation or recreation plans. In the case of a car rental company, a test of vacation travelers found that one benefit stood out: the lowest-priced full-size car. The second most important benefit was no hidden extras.

One drawback of concept testing is that consumers can react only to the themes presented to them. You may find that they have chosen the best of several bad concepts.

Pretest Research The client wants assurances that the advertising proposed will be effective. In pretesting, a particular ad passes or fails or is selected as being better than all the others. The only alternative is for the client to depend solely on the judgment of the agency or its own personnel.

In general, there are two levels of research aimed at helping advertisers determine how well an ad will perform. **Copy testing** is done in two stages:

1. Rough copy research is needed to determine if the copy is effectively achieving its goals in terms of both message communication and attitude effects.
2. Finished copy research is done on the final form of the copy to evaluate how well the production process has achieved communication and attitude effects (see Exhibit 15.8).

copy testing
Measuring the effectiveness of ads.

Pretesting is the stage of advertising research in which a complete ad or commercial is tested. It is important that the objectives of pretesting research relate back to the agreed advertising strategy. It would be wasted effort to test for some characteristic not related to the goal of the advertising.

A number of variables can be evaluated in pretesting, including the ability of the ad to attract attention, comprehension by the reader/viewer, playback of copy points (recall), persuasion (the probability that the consumer will buy the brand), attitude toward the brand, credibility, and irritation level.

Pretests should be used as guides and not as absolute predictors of winners or losers. In copy testing, a higher score for one ad over another does not guarantee a better ad. As Bill Bernbach once said, "Research is very important, but I think it is the beginning of the ad." Norm Grey, former creative director and now head of the Creative Circus, once commented on creative testing, "If you don't like the score an ad gets, demand another test. The only thing that's certain is that you'll get another score." These comments do not imply that creative testing is bad. They simply point to the fact that it is controversial and simply another tool for the advertiser.

There have been arguments about the value of testing ads for years. In general, clients demand them and agency creatives are suspect of the process. Australian social researcher Hugh Mackay says, "The best advertising research never, at any stage, mentions advertising. The pre-testing of rough executions puts a fence around what you can talk about with consumers. The real challenge is to establish what concepts exist in the consumer's mind."[17] Ed McCabe of McCabe & Company makes a distinction between research and testing: "Without great research, you can't make great advertising. However, testing is the idiocy that keeps greatness from happening. Testing is a crutch the one-eyed use to beat up the blind." He points to his Hebrew National hot dog campaign in which an actor portraying Uncle Sam is brought up short by the company's insistence on exceeding federal regulations because its products are kosher and must "answer to a higher authority." The ads did not test well, and the client was reluctant to run them. After much discussion, the ads ran. Some 20 years later, the ads are still running. The point is that testing can be useful, but it is not a foolproof science. If you were spending millions of dollars on a creative idea, wouldn't you do everything possible to reduce the risk or, to put it another way, "to better guarantee" a chance for success?

Campaign Evaluation Research In evaluating advertising, within the total marketing effort, an advertiser should analyze the market and competitive activity and look at advertising as a campaign—not as individual ads. This information can help determine whether changes in the advertising strategy are needed to accomplish the objectives established for the campaign or to deal with a changed situation (see Exhibit 15.8).

Advertisers frequently conduct tracking studies to measure trends, brand awareness, and interest in purchasing, as well as advertising factors. The research at the end of one campaign becomes part of the background research for selecting the next campaign strategy.

TESTING CREATIVE RESEARCH

Creative research takes place within the context of the preceding research stages. This kind of research aids in the development of what to say to the target audience and how to say it. Copy development research attempts to help advertisers decide how to execute approaches and elements. Copy testing is undertaken to aid them in determining whether to run the advertising in the marketplace.

1. A good copy-testing system provides measurements that are relevant to the objectives of the advertising. Of course, different advertisements have different objectives (for example, encouraging trial of a product).
2. A primary purpose of copy testing is to help advertisers decide whether to run the advertising in the marketplace. A useful approach is to specify action standards before the results are in. Examples of action standards are the following:
   - Significantly improves perceptions of the brands as measured by _____.

The future of your e-business is being decided right here.

Do you really know what goes on in the minds of your e-customers? What they might be thinking about buying? Or not buying? And why? That's where you need e-Intelligence from SAS. With e-Intelligence, you can quickly integrate bricks-and-mortar data with clicks-and-mortar data. To reveal insights that can help you optimize online merchandising, recognize cross-selling opportunities, build greater customer loyalty, and establish more profitable relationships with your very best e-customers. To learn more about e-Intelligence from SAS, and what it can do for your business, phone 1-800-727-0025 or stop by www.sas.com.

The power to know §sas

EXHIBIT 15.9

Research can test the power of this visual.

Courtesy of Howard, Merrell & Partners, Inc., and SAS.

- ■ Achieves an attention level no lower than _____ percent as measured by _____.

3. A good copy-testing system is based on the following model of human response to communications: the reception of a stimulus, the comprehension of the stimulus, and the response to the stimulus. In short, to succeed, an ad must have an effect.
   - ■ On the eye and the ear—that is, it must be received (reception)
   - ■ On the mind—that is, it must be understood (comprehension)
   - ■ On the heart—that is, it must make an impression (response)

4. Experience has shown that test results often vary according to how complete a test is. Thus, careful judgment should be exercised when using a less-than-finished version of a test. Sometimes what is lost is inconsequential; at other times it is critical.[18]

Forms of Testing

Each advertiser and agency use similar but modified steps in the testing of creative research. The following are examples of this process.

Concept Testing As mentioned earlier, **concept testing** may be an integral part of creative planning and is undertaken for most clients as a matter of course. Creative concept testing can be defined as the target audience evaluation of (alternative) creative strategy. Specifically, concept testing attempts to separate the "good" ideas from the "bad," to indicate differing degrees of acceptance, and to provide insight into factors motivating acceptance or rejection.

concept testing
The target audience evaluation of (alternative) creative strategey. Testing attempts to separate good and bad ideas and provide insight into factors motivating acceptance or rejection.

There are a number of possible concept tests:

1. *Card concept test.* Creative strategies are presented to respondents in the form of a headline, followed by a paragraph of body copy, on a plain white card. Each concept is on a separate card. Some concepts cannot be tested in card form (for example, those requiring a high degree of mood, such as concepts based on humor or personalities).

2. *Poster test.* This is similar to a card test except that small posters containing simplified illustrations and short copy are used rather than plain cards without illustrations.

3. *Layout test.* A layout test involves showing a rough copy of a print ad (or artwork of a TV commercial with accompanying copy) to respondents. Layout tests are more finished than poster tests in that they use the total copy and illustration as they will appear in the finished ad. Additionally, whereas a card or poster test measures the appeal of the basic concept, the purpose of the layout test may be to measure more subtle effects such as communication, understanding, and clarity.

Finished Print Tests This testing procedure can take many forms of measuring the finished ad as it would appear in print. One such testing procedure used for finished print ads goes something like this: Test ads, finished or unfinished, are inserted into a 20-page magazine-in-a-folder containing both editorial and control ads. Prospects preview the magazine in one-on-one interviews in high-traffic malls. Respondents are questioned regarding unaided, aided, and related recall of the test ad. Next they are asked to focus on the test ad only and are probed for reactions. Agencies are furnished with diagnostic data to improve the ad. The ads are measured for stopping power, communication, relevance, and persuasion. Likes and dislikes about the ad are also provided (see Exhibit 15.10).

Testing Unfinished Commercials Generally, commercial testing on film or videotape falls into one of four categories:

1. *Animatics.* This is artwork, either cartoons or realistic drawings. Some animatics show limited movement; those that do not are usually called video storyboards.

2. *Photomatics.* These are photographs shot in sequence on film. The photos may be stock (from a photo library) or shot on location.

3. *Liveamatics.* This involves filming or taping live talent and is very close to the finished commercial.

4. *Ripamatics.* The commercial is made of footage from other commercials, often taken from ad agency promotion reels. Ripamatics are used many times for experimentation on visual techniques.

Finished Commercial Testing TV testing techniques can generally be classified into two categories:

1. Those that attempt to evaluate a commercial's effectiveness in terms of viewers' recall of a certain aspect of the commercial

2. Those that attempt to evaluate a commercial's effectiveness in terms of what it motivates a viewer to say or do

Recent advances in production technology are helping the testing process. The more closely the test spot resembles the finished commercial, the more accurate the test results will be. Computer animation has become less expensive, and so there is more computer-generated artwork in commercial testing.

EXHIBIT **15.10**

Snapper measures what benefits this ad communicates to the target.

Courtesy of McRae Communications and Snapper.

Readership

Advertisers face mounting competition both in the market and on the printed page. It is important to have the ability to determine if an advertisement is being seen. One such readership service that supplies this kind of information is the Starch Readership Service from Roper Starch.

The Starch Readership Service is designed to measure the extent to which advertisements are being seen and read and the level of interest they arouse. Starch interviews more than 75,000 consumers each year to determine their responses to more than 50,000 print ads. Starch uses the recognition method of interviewing. With the publication open, the respondent explains the extent to which he or she has read each ad prior to the interview. For each ad, respondents are asked, "Did you see or read any part of this ad?" If yes, a prescribed questioning procedure is followed to determine the observation and reading of each component part of each ad—illustration, headline, signature, and copy blocks. After these questions are asked, each respondent is classified as follows:

■ *Noted reader.* A person who remembers having previously seen the advertisement in the issue being studied.

■ *Associated reader.* A reader who not only noted the advertisement but also saw or read some part of it that clearly indicated the brand or advertiser.

■ *Read most.* A person who read half or more of the written material in the ad.

Clients receive Adnorm data with the Starch Readership Reports. Adnorms enable advertisers to compare readership data of their ad in a given magazine issue to the norm for ads of the same size and color in the same product category. These data can help advertisers identify the types of layouts that attract and retain the highest readership. They can also compare current ads against those of competitors, compare the current campaign against previous campaigns, compare the current campaign against a competitor's previous campaign, and compare current ads against the Adnorm tables.

Criticisms of Copy Testing Research

Standard copy testing techniques have long been criticized by advertising agency personnel. They see many of these techniques as giving an unfair advantage to boring and/or irritating ads while penalizing more innovative approaches. According to John Kastenholz, vice president of consumer and market insights at Unilever, "There is a feeling, particularly among creative directors, that copy testing can undermine the ability to produce breakthrough creative ideas." [19] Many marketers and advertising agency executives recognize that most of the commonly used techniques do not adequately assess consumers' emotional response to advertising, and they don't feel as though there have been adequate advances in the methods used. The executive vice president director of research and insight for Interpublic Group of Companies, Joe Plummer, says that "there's been no fundamental advance in copy testing since the early 1980s. So much new information is available today on how the mind works and processes emotional responses to stories, metaphors and symbols."[20] Several companies have new techniques under development that hold promise for future copy testing research.

SUMMARY

Advertising is a people business. Successful advertisers know who their prospects are and—to whatever extent is practical—their needs and motives, which result in the purchase of one product or service and the rejection of another. Consumer behavior is usually the result of a complex network of influences based on the psychological, sociological, and anthropological makeup of the individual.

Advertising rarely, if ever, changes these influences but rather channels needs and wants of consumers toward specific products and brands. Advertising is a mirror of society. The advertiser influences people by offering solutions to their needs and problems, not by creating these needs. The role of the advertiser is to act as a monitor of the changing face of society.

Advertisers pay special attention to what we call up-front research or market research that reflects the market, the consumer, and the competition. Such information as cohort analysis, VALS, and Mindbase can help us understand consumer lifestyles and values, which aids in developing strategies.

Once all of this information is digested, it is used in the four stages of advertising development: strategy development, execution development, pretesting of executions, and campaign evaluation. By itself, information has no value. It aquires value only when we take a point of view about what the information means.

There are a number of stages of testing available in creative research ranging from concept testing and commercial testing techniques to finished print and commercial tests. It is much less expensive to test concepts and ads prior to buying expensive media schedules.

REVIEW

1. Why are sociology, psychology, and anthropology important to advertising?

2. What kind of research is used in advertising execution development?

3. What is the role of the animatic commercial?

4. How are focus groups used in advertising research?

TAKE IT TO THE WEB

Greenfield Online (**www.greenfieldonline.com**) is a survey center that gathers personal information about you in exchange for possible cash prizes and other rewards. How has the Internet changed the process of taking surveys? Are you more willing or less willing to participate in an online survey than a telephone or face-to-face interaction?

Stouffer's "Nothing comes closer to home" tagline emphasizes an emotional connection we have to home-cooked meals in order to entice consumers to buy the product. Visit **www.stouffers.com** to see how promotions such as the "real home cooking" contest further emphasize the familiar tagline.

How does Pepsi (**www.pepsi.com**) use Pepsi Promotions to attract consumers to its Web site? How could Pepsi use its Web site to gain both demographic and psychographic information about consumers?

CHAPTER 16

SAVANNAH'S AWARD WINNING
CHEFS NICK & TRACY MUELLER

WHEN THE RECIPE SAYS
COOK AT 425°
THEY MEAN THE TEMPERATURE
INSIDE THE OVEN

SAVANNAH ELECTRIC
A SOUTHERN COMPANY

You work hard enough in the kitchen, without having to endure a scorching environment. Thanks to electric cooking, that's no longer a problem. By eliminating the intense heat of open flames, your kitchen stays much cooler. Which, in turn, keeps chefs happier and air conditioning costs lower. Plus, electric cooking increases productivity with faster preheat and recovery, more even heating and a longer service life, to name a few. So your pastries will come out golden brown, yet you won't. More and more chefs are going electric, find out how it can benefit you at www.savannahelectric.com.

Creating the Copy

Great advertising copy is essential to great advertising. Understanding consumers and what appeals to them is part of the developmental process needed to create great copy. After reading this chapter, you will understand:

1. the nature and the use of appeals
2. elements of an ad
3. structure of an ad
4. copy styles
5. slogans
6. the creative work plan

> "At the heart of an effective creative philosophy is the belief that nothing is so powerful as an insight into human nature, what compulsions drive a man, what instincts dominate his action, even though his language so often can camouflage what really motivates him."
>
> Bill Bernbach

"The days are gone of left-brained reason-why messages; so insignificant and strained and boring and unbelievable they fall on deaf ears. The creative people who can get into the heart—not just the brain—and make people cry or laugh or silently say, 'yeah, that's how I really feel' will be the superstars," says Lou Centlivre, formerly of Foote Cone & Belding. "I believe in advertising," said John Pepper, former CEO of Procter & Gamble, "I have seen through 25 years that the correlation between profitable business growth on our brands and having great copy on our brands isn't 25 percent, it's not 50 percent. It is 100 percent. I have not seen a single P&G brand sustain profitable volume growth for more than a couple of years without having great advertising."[1]

Are there new rules for copy for today's ads? Since everything in the marketplace (and the world) appears to be changing, are there new rules for developing ads? Of course, the game has indeed changed. Earlier we said the long-held tenets sometimes distort our view of what might be and what should be. It has been asked, "What is going to replace the old rules? Anarchy?" In some ways new rules haven't been written. There is more scope for intuitive thinking, for experimentation, for innovation. Oh, once again I forgot to tell you, there are no rules. There have never been "rules." That said, we need to understand there are nonrules or guidelines that are generally accepted and sometimes draw on years of research results or accumulated wisdom of creative communicators. You might say they are similar to fashion rules—some things just work better. And it's your job to figure out which. This probably sounds like a contradiction, but it really isn't.

In this chapter we'll discuss "how to . . . " and the words will form what appear to be rules. It is a means of sharing and analyzing. Ken Roman, former CEO of Ogilvy & Mather Worldwide, says, "Recipes don't work for a very simple reason: This is a business of ideas. Ideas don't derive from rules; they derive from principles."[2] The real challenge is to use this knowledge in the context of your specific communication problem. Remember earlier in this text we talked about creative risk. Look at taking smart risks, where you know what the norm of thinking is and go from there—with caution. The goal is to communicate.

CREATIVE RISK TAKING

Many of the fundamental beliefs are under siege, but certain rules, beliefs, and methodologies have served the business well, and restraint is called for. At the same time, agencies owe their clients effective advertising and must find ways to accomplish this. "An idea that hasn't been done before might, on the surface, look really risky," argues Bob Isherwood of Saatchi & Saatchi. "It's an area where no one has gone before. There is no precedent. But usually the biggest risk lies in ideas that are predictable." Ideas that are predictable don't get noticed. As Oscar Wilde once said, *an idea that does not involve risk does not deserve to be an idea.* Risk is about breaking rules or guidelines. "A lot of creative people think creative risk taking means doing ads that scare the life out of you," says Singapore creative director Garry Abbott. "Good ads don't rely on borrowed ideas. Risk is about *freshness."* Finding out from consumers what it really is like being them so ads can respond to their needs is a risk many don't take. According to Hugh Mackay, one way to accomplish this is to "take a set of familiar elements and rearrange them in an unfamiliar so that the reader recognizes both the familiar and the unfamiliar. In other words, present something the readers recognize as themselves, their lives, their dreams, but with a twist, so they're a bit startled by it, or get an extra insight from it."[3] Is this a rule? No. It is a way of thinking about how to solve a problem. See how Sawyer Riley Compton uses a simple "slice of life" to get people to think about visiting Callaway Gardens' 40 acres of flowers (see Exhibit 16.1).

Creatives also have a responsibility. Erik Veruroegen, executive creative director, TBWA Paris, says: "I am against advertising where people just show crap and say 'but it works.' We have a mission to stop that. The consumer does not like advertising at all. It interrupts the film or magazine; it looks ugly on the poster. It is pretentious to believe that the consumer will give you a chance just because you're there. Advertising must earn the right to be paid attention to, but you can't be different for the sake of being different."[4]

A CHALLENGE AND CREATIVE VISION

Before we get to details about developing ads, let us put today's and tomorrow's advertising in perspective. Let us see what challenge lies ahead for us in creating effective concepts and ads.

We know we are living in an explosive information age. It is also true to say that knowledge is power, and the speed with which marketers utilize that knowledge in the future will determine success or failure. Because advertising is, in its most basic form, a conveyor of information, it will be at the center of this revolution. But there are a number of factors working against that happening.

According to global creative director John Hegarty, we are already having to deal with a major communication problem. It's called time famine. How do consumers assimilate this ever-growing mass of messages that is being directed at them? How do they cope with the volume of traffic going through their brains? How

SHE SAID, "DON'T GET ME
ANYTHING FOR MY BIRTHDAY."

YOU DIDN'T.

Why do you need 40 acres of flowers?

🌹 Callaway Gardens

For reservations call 1.800.CALLAWAY or visit callawaygardens.com.

EXHIBIT 16.1

Instead of showing
acres of flowers,
Callaway Gardens used
human insights to make
a connection with the
consumer.

Courtesy of Sawyer Riley Compton
and Callaway Gardens.

do they process this valuable information as opposed to allowing it to pass straight through unnoticed? Another related issue that has been debated for years is media clutter. Are consumers reaching the point of "overchoice," as futurist Alvin Toffler predicted? "We are racing against overchoice—the point at which the advantages of choice and individualization are canceled by the complexity of the buyer's decision-making process."[5]

Yet another issue is our audience's ability to turn us off. Advertisers interrupt viewing and listening, or we sit alongside printed material shouting for attention. As electronic media take a greater hold on the distribution of information, our audience will have great control over turning us off, unless we are compelling and necessary. This is totally true with the Internet or TiVo—the user controls the information. Unless we recognize the change in the balance of power and take into account our consumers' aspirations, we will be cut out of the loop and become irrelevant. What can we do as communicators?

Strategy and Great Writing

Earlier we discussed developing integrated marketing communication strategic plans. It has been said that strategy is everything. British creative director Tony Cox likened creative development to a dance: "Sometimes creative leads, sometimes strategy leads, but both have to remain close and in harmony for a great ending." So don't forget the importance of strategy as you read about "how to create. Often there are dangers in our decision process." Frederick Smith, founder of Federal Express, said, "We thought we were selling the transportation of goods; in fact, we were selling peace of mind. When we finally figured that out, we pursued our goal with vengence."[6] A few years ago, The Ritz-Carlton found its traditional market suddenly getting younger and looking at the hotel as old-fashioned. Sawyer Riley Compton helped the hotel change its focus to the next generation by telling its brand story in a more relevant and contemporary way (see Exhibit 16.2) meshing strategy and strong creative.

Another brilliantly simple idea was created for *The Economist*. The typical ad for *The Economist* (a British publication read in more than 140 countries) has been three columns of copy. The ads talked about the benefits of reading the publication—much information aimed at a sophisticated, well-educated target. Yet a simple poster says,

I've never read *The Economist*.

Signed, Management Trainee, Aged 42

The concept was even integrated in a longer T-shirt messages:

My dad reads *The Economist* and all I got was this lousy tee shirt, a penthouse apartment in New York, two Ferraris, an eighty foot yacht, my own private jet, and an island retreat in the Caribbean.

There is a valuable message in these examples for those creating advertising: The faster ideas get across, the more powerful they become. As you reduce the idea down, as you hone it to its essential structure, its power increases. The faster it pen-

EXHIBIT 16.2

Sawyer Riley Compton created a new focus and meshed strategy and creative to connect with a younger market.

Courtesy of Sawyer Riley Compton and The Ritz Carlton.

Its hard to believe only three wars have been fought over this island.

For reservations, call 1-800-241-3333 or visit www.ritzcarlton.com.   THE RITZ-CARLTON®

etrates the mind, the longer it stays there. You aren't trying to buy newspaper, magazine, or Web space or time in a commercial break. The space you are trying to buy is in the consumer's head. That is the most valuable space. That is what you are trying to influence.

Luke Sullivan, executive creative director at WestWayne, speaking of creating ad ideas, says it is simple: simplicity, simplicity, simplicity. Tony Cox says, "Inside every fat ad is a thinner and better one trying to get out." Maurice Saatchi on simplicity says: "Simplicity is all. Simple logic, simple arguments, simple visual images. If you can't reduce your arguments to a few crisp words and phrases, there's something wrong with your argument."[7]

Fallon Worldwide's self-promotion says, "The crucial part of the creative process is what we call relentless reductionism. It means having the discipline and will to drive for focus. A focus that results in a single-mindedly compelling idea. Then Fallon expands the idea. This is where creativity takes over, as we take this single-minded idea and apply it to every step of the consumer's path to purchase." You're getting the idea.

Was it Oscar Wilde—it doesn't really matter—who understood that an idea got better as it got faster? How do we do that? The brilliance of our craft is to reduce, to distill messages down, not to elongate. Remember Abraham Lincoln's quote, "You can fool all the people some of the time, and some of the people all the time, but you cannot fool all the people all of the time." He captured the essence of modern politics in one sentence, and most of us remember it. Great writing is about using fewer words to be more compelling. When you do that, you liberate your ideas to become more powerful, more involving, and hopefully more memorable. Brevity not only allows us to become more powerful, it allows us to become more stimulating. If you are more stimulating, there is a good chance you are becoming more relevant. We have to change because our audience is demanding it.

The Greeks said that information is taken through the heart. As we have moved from the unique selling proposition (USP) to the *emotional selling proposition*, we need to understand that the way we talk to consumers must also change. Advertising still needs to be based on the foundation of product or corporate attributes. But we must remember that it may no longer be unique nor will it necessarily be obvious.

Creative Vision

Creativity isn't just about putting a strategy down on a piece of paper. It is also about capturing the essence of that strategy and giving it a creative vision that is both compelling and competitive. What worked yesterday isn't necessarily going to work today or tomorrow. The consumer has not only less time to listen to us but also less inclination.

HOW DO WE CREATE GREAT ADVERTISING?

Saatchi & Saatchi's Kevin Roberts has said: "Do you really want a great ad? If you want a quiet life—no highs, no lows, no struggle, no passion—forget great ads." The opposite of a great ad is not a bad ad but an average one. The response to good ads? "Let's analyze." The response to great ads? "I want more."

We've already heard this, but we need to hear another viewpoint. Ron Huey, award-winning creative director of Huey/Paprocki, says, "Simplicity is the key to great advertising. Take the single most salient feature of your product or service and communicate that in a simple, thought provoking or entertaining way. Good copy speaks to the common man. It should be smart, entertaining and conversational, not fancy or frilly. Today's best creative people are resilient. Great ideas are killed every day for sometimes stupid reasons. The best creatives accept that and come

BRINGING THE POWER OF NASCAR HOME.   AT&T Broadband
Atlanta

EXHIBIT 16.3

The idea is imbedded in the visual solution. The copy line: "Bringing the power of NASCAR home."

Courtesy of Huey/Paprocki, Ltd. Advertising and AT&T Broadband.

back with something even better," (see Exhibit 16.3). Huey's thoughts on advertising through the years: "The great ads from Bernbach in the '60s, Fallon McElligott in the '80s, Wieden [Wieden & Kennedy], Goodby [Goodby, Silverstein & Partners] and The Martin Agency today, all have a common thread—The headline, visual and logo communicate the idea immediately." He also believes, "Three quarters of today's best ads use humor. But it's wry humor. Not a bathroom joke or humor that's intended to shock people."[8] Huey says, "One path we always investigate when concepting print is a 'visual solution.' By that, I mean an ad where the idea is really imbedded in the visual and usually communicates 90% of what you're trying to say. In this approach, the headline is more of straight payoff to complete, or bullet-proof, the communication. That was the approach we took with this AT&T ad, which was meant to illustrate how they bring the power of NASCAR racing to life."

THE NATURE AND USE OF APPEALS

Advertising motivates people by appealing to their problems, desires, and goals, and by offering a means of solving their problems. Let us look at the value of using a psychological **appeal** in advertising. David Martin, founder of The Martin Agency, points to decades of research indicating the relative strengths of motives and appeals in advertising. He believes human desires are woven into our basic nature. They do not change with lifestyles or external environmental stimuli. Consumers will always have a desire for food and drink; for rest, comfort, and security; and for a sense of social worth, independence, power, and success. Parental feelings to protect and provide are basic. Human nature is a constant. Humans are born with cer-

appeal

The motive to which an ad is directed, it is designed to stir a person toward a goal the advertiser has set.

KLEPPNER VIEWPOINT 16.1

RON HUEY

Partner,
Huey/Paprocki, Ltd. Advertising

Getting Your Message Through? It's Simple.

The average person is blindsided by over 3,000 messages a day. Not just television commercials, magazine and newspaper ads, but also outdoor boards, radio spots, Internet pop-ups, signs on trucks, signs on trees, signs on just about anything that will stand still. It's a deafening roar for the consumer's attention to say the least. So how do you create communication that can actually communicate in this environment? The key, for me at least, has always been simplicity. Make a simple point in a very compelling and simple way and, chances are, people may actually pay attention. The tendency, however, is to try and say everything. Put forth every conceivable product benefit. That's okay, it's a natural inclination. After all, they're probably all things worth saying. It's a fast car, a luxurious car, a safe car, a well-engineered car, a stylish car, a car that fits your needs. The problem is that now no one knows what kind of car you're offering. You've made a lot of pertinent points, but no one point has penetrated with any meaning. So the first step is to put a single strategic stake in the ground. Stand for something rather than trying to stand for everything. Now you must bring your simple strategy to creative life in an arresting, impactful way. Remember, consumers aren't eagerly awaiting the next advertisement from you or from anyone else, for that matter. (They've already been hit by 3,000

today.) In fact, you will be an uninvited guest, you will be interrupting their day. So it's important that you intrigue them and invite them in. Make your point and do so in a way that entertains them and rewards for spending time with your message. It's that simple.

Courtesy of Huey/Paprocki, Ltd. Advertising. ■ ■ ■

---

tain instincts: fear (self-preservation), hunger (need for food and drink), sex (love), and rage (anger). People also have five senses: sight, touch, smell, hearing, and taste. The instincts and senses are often a starting point for advertising appeals.[9]

The creative genius of the late 1960s, the late Bill Bernbach, put it this way:

> There may be changes in our society. But learning about those changes is not the answer. For you are not appealing to society. You are appealing to individuals, each with an ego, each with the dignity of his or her being, each like no one else in the world, each a separate miracle. The societal appeals are merely fashionable, current, cultural appeals, which make nice garments for the real motivations that stem from the unchanging instincts and emotions of people—from nature's indomitable programming in their genes. It is the unchanging person that is the proper study of the communicator.[10]

John Hegarty says, "There was always one word that came through [when defining great advertising]: irreverence. Because what you are doing is changing the rules. You are trying to do something in an incredibly different way which captures the imagination." Jeff Goodby of Goodby, Silverstein & Partners adds, "Great advertising scrabbles logic a little bit, it jumps beyond that by being likable and watchable and captivating. It surprises you." Someone once said that great advertising is great ideas simply executed.[11]

Most products have a number of positive appeals that could be successfully promoted, so how do we go about making the decision as to which direction to go with an ad or appeal? The idea is to choose the one that is most important to the majority of our target. Because selecting the primary appeal is the key to any advertising campaign, many research techniques have been developed to find which appeal to use, as discussed in Chapter 15.

Whether created by research or in other ways, the appeal provides the basis of the advertising structure. This appeal can be expressed in many ways. Here we discuss how to make use of words, called copy, in presenting the appeal.[12]

GREAT ADVERTISING ELEMENTS

The Creative Council of Ogilvy & Mather Worldwide found that examples of great advertising have certain elements in common (the same fundamental principles apply to direct-response and sales promotion):[13]

- *Potent strategy.* The strategy is the heart of advertising. It is impossible to do great advertising if the strategy is weak or does not exist at all.
- *Strong selling idea.* Great advertising promises a benefit to the consumer. The idea must be simple, and it must be clear. The brand must be integrated into the selling idea.
- *Stands out.* A great ad is memorable, even when competing for attention with news and entertainment.
- *Always relevant.* Prospects can easily relate the advertising to their experience and to the role of the product in their lives.
- *Can be built into campaigns.* No matter how clever one idea may be, if you cannot make it into a campaign, it is not a great idea.

STRUCTURE OF AN ADVERTISEMENT

In some instances, the promise is the whole advertisement.

Surf Removes Dirt and Odor

Usually, however, a fuller exposition is required, in which case the promise can act as the headline—the first step in the structure of the advertisement. Most ads are presented in this order:

- Promise of benefit (the headline)
- Spelling out of promise (the subheadline, optional)
- Amplification of story (as needed)
- Proof of claim (as needed)
- Action to take (if not obvious)

People tend to scan print ads in the following manner: illustration first, followed by the headline, first line of the body copy, and then the logo. If they are still interested, they will go back and read the rest of the copy. Yes, you can get people to read the copy, but the first sentence and first paragraph are extremely important in keeping readers. As a matter of fact, the drop-off rate of readers is pretty significant during the first 50 words, but not so great between 50 and 500 words.

The Headline

The headline is the most important part of an ad. It is the first thing read, and it should arouse interest so the consumer wants to keep on reading and get to know more about the product being sold. If the headline does not excite the interest of the particular group of prime prospects the advertiser wants to reach, the rest of the ad will probably go unread.

Gary Knutson's creative team at HM&P repositioned a typical weight-reducing spa as a world-class spa brand for stressed-out female executives. The series of ads increased inquiries 350 percent, which was no small feat, and sales increased 25 percent (see Exhibit 16.4). The head reads: "The spa for those who place more value on what they gain than what they lose." The body copy says, "Mind you, there's nothing inherently wrong with visiting a spa in hopes of returning home a few pounds lighter. We merely suggest that with the right spa you have so much more to gain. At Palm-Aire, you will enter a sanctuary in which the greatest ambition of those surrounding you is to provide a respite from the pressures of everyday life. . . . What you gain in self-awareness simply can't be measured on any scale."

No formula can be given for writing a good headline. However, several factors should be considered in evaluating an effective headline:

- It should use short, simple words, usually no more than 10.
- It should include an invitation to the prospect, primary product benefits, name of the brand, and an interest-provoking idea to gain readership of the rest of the ad.
- The words should be selective, appealing only to prime prospects.
- It should contain an action verb.
- It should give enough information so that the consumer who reads only the headline learns something about the product and its benefit.

EXHIBIT 16.4

This headline offers hope and emotional satisfaction.

Courtesy of Howard, Merrell & Partners and Palme Aire.

THE SPA FOR THOSE WHO PLACE MORE VALUE ON WHAT THEY GAIN THAN WHAT THEY LOSE.

PALM-AIRE

ADVANTAGE POINT

GARY KNUDSON'S MEMO (Howard, Merrell & Partners)

To: The creative department
From: Knutson
Re: wordplay
Date: 15 May

If this is what we want to say,
why can't we just say it?

How many times have you heard this from a client?

The answer is that if that was all there was to this business, we wouldn't need all you high-paid employees. It would be more like a civil service job, sort of like working at the post office.

You'd do what you're told, do it on time, and everyone would be happy. We wouldn't need fancy writers or art directors, certainly not for those clients who know exactly what they want to say and probably have a pretty good idea of how the ad should be laid out, too.

Imagine that Don Solomon's goal is to get all the single women in the agency to think that he's a wonderful, bright, handsome guy.

Now suppose that Don goes up to a girl and says, "I'm a wonderful, bright, handsome guy."

He has said what he wanted to say. Why wouldn't it work?

The reason, of course, is that there is a big difference between persuasion and flatulent braggadocio, and we're being paid to create the former.

Q: Who decides what is a good ad?
A: I do. There has to be a final say, one.

Not every headline is going to adhere to these guidelines. However, when you write a headline that excludes any of these points, ask yourself: Would this headline be more effective if it did adhere to the guidelines? You want to be sure you have thought through the process.

Many headlines fall into one of four categories:

1. *Headlines that present a new benefit.* The moment of peak interest in a product is when it offers a new benefit. That is why, in our innovative society, you often see headlines such as these:

**It's what you don't see that makes the biggest difference.
The new Microsoft wireless IntelliMouse Explorer.**

MICROSOFT

Announcing the world's first transatlantic B & B.

BRITISH AIRWAYS

Fruity, yet strong.

ALTOIDS

The world's first 4-blade razor.

WILKINSON SWORD QUATTRO

Nothing corners like a Mini.

MINI AUTOS

The new Lincoln LS.
0 to 60 in 6.2 seconds.

LINCOLN LS

We're about to take the minivan in a whole new direction.
Introducing the all-new Ford Freestar. Our most flexible minivan ever.

FORD FREESTAR

A revolution in purity.

WHIRLPOOL

2. *Headlines that directly promise an existing benefit.* Products cannot be offering new benefits all the time, of course, so headlines often remind consumers of a product's existing features:

Instant relief for every inch of itch.

EUCERIN LOTION

The ultimate weapon in the fight against gum disease.

ORAL-B

Heavy isn't healthy.

PURINA FIT & TRIM

Take clear control. Take Claritin.

CLARITIN

Every day, millions of cell phones die needlessly.

CELLBOOST

Soft on the outside.
Scented on the inside.

CHARMIN SCENTS

3. *Curiosity-invoking and provocative headlines.* By invoking curiosity, an advertiser may grab attention from an otherwise disinterested audience by challenging the curiosity of the readers, thereby prompting them to read further and leading them into the key message. David Ogilvy warned against using heads that don't communicate the benefits because of the large numbers of readers that don't read the body copy. It can work, but the writer must be careful to build a strong relationship between the curiosity point and the brand. "They just don't make testostrone the way they used to." That's an interesting statement. Readers want to find out what this means to them!, (see Exhibit 16.5). The copy ends with "Pinedale's Museum of the Mountain Man survives to tell the story of these men and the virgin West as they found it." Here are some more curiosity-invoking headlines:

Beware of interior decorators.

TIMBERLAND

When our sales pitch puts you to sleep.

MATTRESS MATTERS

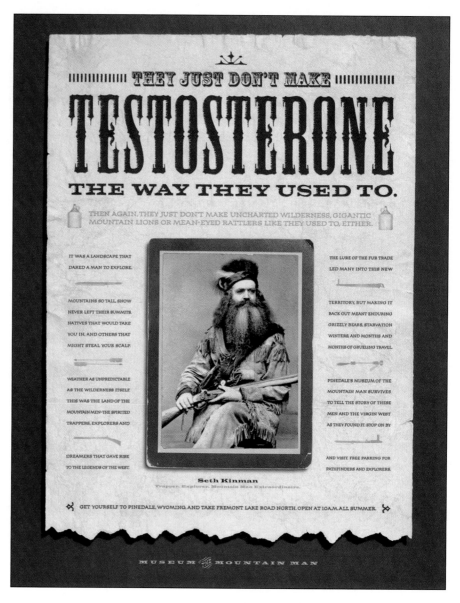

Every night you see a dirty film & don't even know it.

OLAY FACIAL EXPRESS

Live fast, die a senior citizen.

ROLLING STONE

Great Saturdays don't start with cartoons.

RAPALA

Use it as a concert hall—or a sanctuary.

BOSE

What the best dressed chickens will be wearing this year.

KRAFT FARM PLUS HERBS

The question headline that works best is the kind that arouses curiosity so the reader will read the body copy to find the answer. Readers do not like being tricked. They want a strong relationship between the curiosity and the product.

4. *Selective headlines.* Readers looking through a magazine or newspaper are more likely to read an ad they think concerns them personally than one that talks to a

broad audience. The selective headline aimed at a particular prime prospect who would be more interested in the product is often used. If the head says, "condominium owners," and you don't own a condominium, you probably won't pay attention; conversely, if you do own a condo, you might read it. A Pampers ad head reads, "Babies absorb everything around them. Wetness doesn't have to be one of them." Obviously, if you don't have a baby in your life, you probably aren't going to read this ad. However, if you do have a baby, you may be attracted to the copy. Four such headlines that specifically reach out to special groups are the following:

- To All Men and Women
- To All Young Men and Women
- To All College Men and Women
- To All College Seniors

The first headline is addressed to the greatest number of readers, but it would be of the least interest to any one of them. Each succeeding headline reduces the size of the audience it addresses and improves the chances of attracting that particular group. What about "All College Seniors Who Need Jobs"? You get the idea!

Besides addressing a particular group directly, headlines can appeal to people by mentioning a problem they have in common:

Designed by women for women to help even more women.

WILSON PRO STAFF INTRIQUE

Because older dogs don't commonly get dentures.

PEDIGREE

Most baby bottoms stink. (And their tops aren't great, either.)

HEALTHTEX

Children's seasonal medicines from the makers of Tylenol.

TYLENOL PLUS

Another vital quality in headlines is specificity. Remember, consumers are more interested in the specific than the general. Therefore, the more specific you can be in the headline, the better: "A Peppermint Peroxide Toothpaste That Will Help Kill Bacteria and Keep Tartar from Your Teeth" is better than "A Nice-Tasting Toothpaste That Cleans Your Teeth."

A headline must say something important to the reader. The actual number of words is not the deciding factor; long or short headlines may work well. But say what you need to say in as few words as possible (see Exhibit 16.6). Remember, simple is better, but it can be more than one sentence.

39.3 seconds
was the total time
needed by
Louise Cunningham
to fall in love with
her Taylor.
And that included 4.3 seconds to look
at the price tag
and wince.

TAYLOR

Commuting, every month:
$82
Health club, every month:
$54

39.3 seconds was the total time needed by Louise Cunningham to fall in love with her Taylor. And that included **4.3 seconds** to look at the price tag and wince.

EXHIBIT 16.6

The first sentence of this provocative head has 17 words. A headline may be as short as one word or as many as it takes to get the idea across.

Courtesy of VitroRobertson, Inc., Taylor Guitar, and Michael Eastman, photographer.

Insurance, every month:
$62
Trading a checkbook for a storybook:
Priceless

MASTERCARD

The Subheadline

If the message is long, it can be conveyed with a main headline (with large type) and a subheadline (with smaller type but larger than the body copy). The subheadline can spell out the promise presented in the headline. It can be longer than the headline, it can invite further reading, and it serves as a transition to the opening paragraph of the copy.

Headline	**It's not your shoes.** **It's not your car.** **It's not your music.**
Subhead	**It's your watch that** **Tells the most about you.**

SEIKO

Headline	**Medical studies indicate most people suffer a 68% hearing loss when naked.**
Subhead	**Getting the most out of a visit to the doctor's office.**

UNITED HEALTH FOUNDATION

Amplification

The headline and, if used, the subheadline are followed by the body copy of the ad. It is here that you present your case for the product and explain how the promise in the headline will be fulfilled. In other words, the body copy amplifies what was announced in the headline or subheadline. What you say and how deep you go depend on the amount of information your prime prospect needs at this point in the buying process. A high-cost plasma television screen probably calls for more explanation than a low-cost product, such as a barbecue sauce with a new flavor. If a product has many technical advances, there probably is not sufficient room to detail all the features. In this case, the objective is to create enough interest to get the prime prospect to the store for a demonstration and more information.

Amplification should emphasize those product or service features that are of primary importance but cannot be included in the headline. Take, for example, the Yamaha LX2000 ad (see Exhibit 16.7):

We don't know why boats are referred to like they're women, we just know this one is full-featured.

And then the amplification:

Get a load of this. The 270-horsepower LX2000 from Yamaha. Lots of dramatic curves, but it's more than just another pretty face. It's got twin jet-powered engines, room for seven, plush Berber carpet, a great stereo and a whole lot more. Oh, so you're picky, huh? Well how about explosive acceleration, nimble handling, brushed aluminum dash and a matching trailer. . . . Call 1-800-6-YAMAHA or go to yamaha-motor.com.

EXHIBIT 16.7

Body copy can explain the details of product or service features that can't be explained in the headline.

Courtesy of VitroRobertson, Inc., Yamaha, and Aaron Chang, photographer.

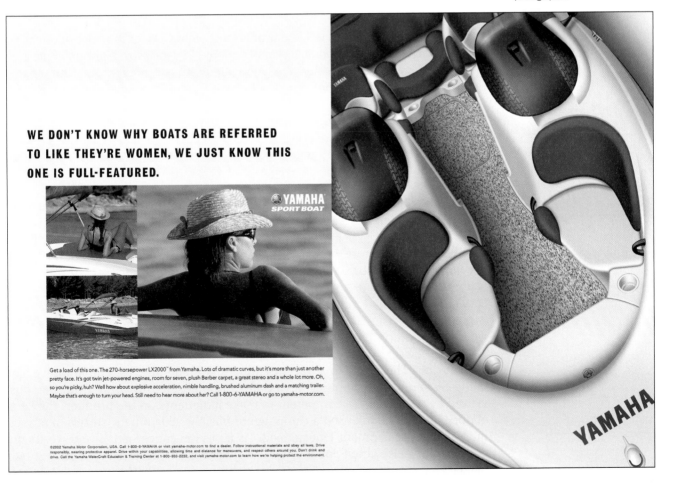

WE DON'T KNOW WHY BOATS ARE REFERRED TO LIKE THEY'RE WOMEN, WE JUST KNOW THIS ONE IS FULL-FEATURED.

Proof

The body copy does amplify what the headline promised. At times the process acts to reassure the consumer that the product will perform as promised. Consumers may look for proof in an ad, and proof is particularly important for high-priced products, health, and new products with special features. Here are a few ways in which proof can be offered to the reader.

Seals of Approval   Seals of approval from such accredited sources as *Good Housekeeping* and *Parents* magazines, the American Dental Association, the American Medical Association, and Underwriter's Laboratories allay consumers' fears about product quality. An Ayer senior vice president of planning says that it distinguishes a product and that a seal of approval can give a new product an edge of credibility in the market place. Phonak hearing systems advertises the Good Housekeeping seal. Added credibility may come from recognized awards; for instance, the headline read, "The GMC Yukon just got the J. D. Power and Associates Award for dependability."

Guarantees   Wendy's, Arby's, and Mrs. Winner's have offered consumers money-back guarantees for trying specific products to reduce the risk and get trial by consumers. Products such as Silent Floor systems guarantee their floors will be free from warping or defects. "Crest Whitestrips and Crest Whitestrips Premium provide you with a beautiful, visibly whiter smile—guaranteed. If you are not satisfied with your results, Crest Whitestrips will refund your purchase. Simply return your receipt and package UPC within 60 days of purchase. Call 1-800-395-8423 for more information." Pacific Coast Down Comforters suggests you "try one for 30 nights. If you're not completely comfortable, we'll give you a full refund."

Trial Offers and Samples   BMG Music offers any eight CDs for the price of one with its 10-day risk-free trial. Procter & Gamble offered free industrial-strength Spic and Span liquid samples to consumers who called a toll-free telephone number to reduce the risk and to get trial. Similar offers are made at www.pg.com.

Warranties   Pacific Coast Down Comforters also has a "100% allergy-free warranty." Sherwin-Williams SuperPaint is advertised with a 20-year warranty against peeling. James Hardie Building Products touts a 50-year warranty for its siding. Maytag water-heating appliances are covered by a 10-year tank warranty.

Reputation   Copy for Woolite says, "It's recommended by the makers of more than 350 million garments."

Demonstrations   "Before" and "after" demonstrations are used to show how a product works. Starch Research says showing models to demonstrate cosmetic products is powerful. In one ad, Almay showed a supermodel from the neck up, making it easy to see her facial imperfections—or lack thereof—after using Almay's line of hypoallergenic cosmetics. Find a way to tell consumers a benefit, and you will do well; find a way to show them, and you will fare even better.

Testimonials   The ability to attract attention to ads and offer a credible source has made testimonials a popular device. Testimonials should come from persons viewed by consumers as competent to make judgments on the products they are endorsing. BB&T bank used a campaign of business customers' stories to attract more business customers. One ad read: "As far as I'm concerned, if your word's no good, nothing else about you is good. . . . They're in the bank ready to answer our needs. That sets them apart." An Omega watch ad uses Pierce Brosnan's body to attract attention but only says, "Pierce Brosnan, Choices." It is a testimonial without words—the association of the person and product.

Dean Rieck, president of Direct Creative, promotes the use of testimonials and suggests that companies actively collect testimonials and success stories. He says they support advertisers' claims and build confidence. He also suggests:[14]

- Use testimonials from people who are similar and relevant to prospects. A teacher will believe other teachers, a business owner will believe other business owners, seniors will believe seniors. They are more effective if they are from experts or people with relevant experience.

- Don't try to rewrite or fabricate testimonials. The real words of real people are always more believable than anything a writer can come up with. Besides, making them up isn't ethical.

- Testimonials are a form of proof, so increase the credibility of that proof whenever you have a chance. Use full names when possible. Appropriate titles may be an indication of a person's experience or expertise.

COPY STYLE

As with a novel or a play, good ad copy has a beginning, a middle, and an ending. And, like a novel, the transition must be smooth from one part to another. Up to this point, we have discussed how the building blocks of copy are put together. Now we need to think about what it takes to create special attention and persuasion. It takes style—the ability to create fresh, charming, witty, human advertising that compels people to read. Remember what Ron Huey said: "Take the single most salient feature of your product or service and communicate it in a simple, thought provoking or entertaining way." See the product in a fresh way, explore its possible effects on the reader, or explain the product's advantages in a manner that causes the reader to view the product with a new understanding and appreciation.

Most ads end with a close by asking or suggesting that the reader buy the product. The difference between a lively ad and a dull one lies in the approach to the message at the outset.

The lens through which a writer sees a product may be the magnifying glass of the technician, who perceives every nut and bolt and can explain why each is important, or it may be the rose-colored glasses of the romanticist, who sees how a person's life may be affected by the product. That is why we speak of **copy approaches** rather than types of ads. The chief approaches in describing a product are the factual, the imaginative, and the emotional.

copy approach
The method of opening the text of an ad. Chief forms: factual approach, imaginative approach, emotional approach.

Factual Approach

In the factual approach, we deal with reality—that which actually exists. We talk about the product or service—what it is, how it is made, and what it does. Focusing on the facts about the product that are most important to the reader, we explain the product's advantages.

One of the interesting things about a fact, however, is that it can be interpreted in different ways, each accurate but each launching different lines of thinking. Remember the classic example of an 8-ounce glass holding 4 ounces of water, of which can be said: "This glass is half full" or "This glass is half empty." As you know, both are correct and factual. The difference is in the interpretation of reality, as the Mitsui O.S.K. ad headline for shipping seafood says, "We cater to the best schools." Their copy talks facts: "MOL takes a great deal of pride in catering to the needs of the world's most discriminating shippers. Salmon, shrimp, crabs, mussels and other gourmet seafood, for example, are delivered in 409 high-cube reefer containers so that they arrive fresh and delectable in Asian and American markets." Skill in presenting a fact consists of projecting it in a way that means the most to the reader.

The factual approach can be used to sell more than products or services. Facts about ideas, places—anything for which an ad can be written—can be presented with a fresh point of view.

Imaginative Approach

There is nothing wrong with presenting a fact imaginatively. The art of creating copy lies in saying a familiar thing in an unexpected way. Dow's Great Stuff household foam sealant doesn't sound like a fun product to market, but Sawyer Riley Compton thought otherwise. The headline for the campaign was "Closes any gap." Then they let the visuals (see Exhibit 16.8) do the attracting and talking. The copy line says, "Use Great Stuff household sealant to close any gap imaginable. Dow." Doesn't the creative approach get the message across for a product that has little consumer interest? When was the last time you thought about a foam sealant?

EXHIBIT 16.8

The visuals complete the story in a more interesting fashion than *reason why* copy.

Courtesy of Sawyer Riley Compton and Dow.

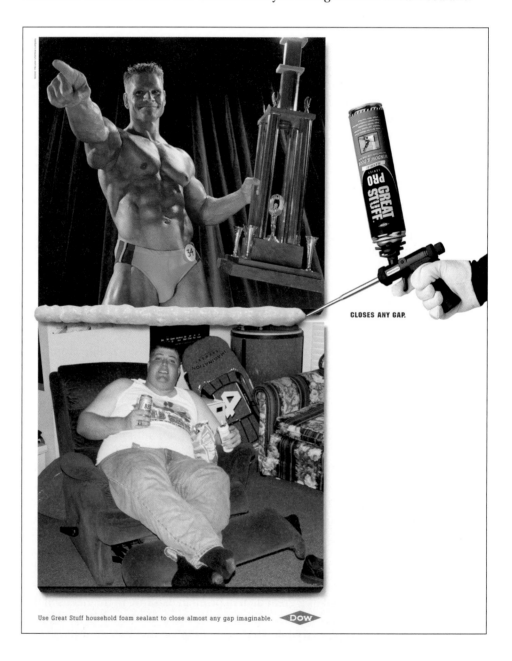

CLOSES ANY GAP.

Use Great Stuff household foam sealant to close almost any gap imaginable.   ◆ DOW ◆

Emotional Approach

Emotion can be a powerful communicator. The feelings about your product or company can be an important plus or minus. Copy using psychological appeals to love, hate, or fear has great impact. The illustration and headline in Exhibit 16.9 bring out not only warmth and maternal instincts but also emotion—every parent can identify with the photo. "The meaning of life has always been a mystery. For adults." Often the copy will continue the emotional appeal, although at times it will take a factual direction to inform the reader about specific features of the product to convince the reader of its value.

Research indicates that emotion can create positive feelings, such as warmth, happiness, and delight, which work best for low-involvement goods. For higher-involvement, higher-ticket items, such as CD players or automobiles, emotions must be unique and mesh with the brand. Kodak has produced ads that are so emotional they bring tears to your eyes.

What science can tell us about the brain and about "emotion" has grown exponentially over the last 20 years. Kevin Roberts, CEO Worldwide of Saatchi & Saatchi, talks about the use of emotion. Research tells us that human beings *think* with feeling and emotion. We just can't help it. Emotion is the *key* to every decision we make, every thought we have, whether it's to click on an attached file or reach for our usual brand of soap powder. Human beings tend to take everything personally and respond with feeling. Joseph Ledoux, one of the world's leading researchers into the emotional brain, had this to say: "Emotions are mostly processes at an unconscious level."

They are quick and focused on what really matters. They acknowledge that intuition, loyalty, and emotion can't be quantified, and then move on.

EXHIBIT 16.9

Every parent can identify with the emotional pull.

Courtesy of Sawyer Riley Compton and Carter's.

All the stuff we've been told about "think before you act" and "think it through" is rubbish. It doesn't happen. Rational man is a myth. Women, of course, have always been too smart to have gotten into the rationality arena because in reality it doesn't work. Humans have the ability to focus. People focus on new events, on changes in their environment. They disregard the everyday and the routine. They pay attention until a need is satisfied and then they move on. How do we attract attention? Kevin Roberts believes we can only do this with emotion.

Put emotion first. Pull them with emotion, touch them with emotion, compel them with emotion. It may make them laugh, make them cry, make them jump.[15]

However, using mixed emotions may have dangers. According to Williams and Aaker, our ability to assimilate mixed emotions is, to some extent, a function of age and culture. Older adults are more at ease with complex emotional issues. Cultural influences make an even larger difference. Americans are quite happy with mixed messages (such as images and word play), so long as they're not about emotions. In contrast, Asian cultures tend to be more comfortable with mixed emotions. Williams and Aaker found that Asian Americans were more at ease with appeals based on mixed emotions.

COMPARATIVE ADVERTISING

comparative advertising
It dierctly contrasts an advertiser's product with other named or identified products.

Comparing your product directly with one or more competitors is called **comparative advertising**. It is actually encouraged by the Federal Trade Commission, but it has risks. Some advertisers think it isn't smart to spend money to publicize your competition. Others think it creates a bad atmosphere for the company that demeans all advertising. Pepsi has frequently run ads in *Nation's Restaurant News* featuring "Coke and Pepsi View Your Business Two Different Ways," and the copy talks about how they do business differently.

Despite each comparative ad being different, there are certain rules of thumb that can be applied: (1) The leader in the field never starts a comparative campaign. (2) The most successful comparison ads are those comparing the product with products identical in every respect except for the special differential featured in the ad. The stronger the proof that the products are identical, the better. (3) The different features should be of importance to the consumer.

VitroRobertson, San Diego, developed a very competitive ad for King Cobra SS 350 (see Exhibit 16.10). The headline says, "Cobra out-drives Callaway on the front nine. The back nine. And the most important nine." The body copy compares, "We knew we had a long driver, but this is huge. An independent robotic test has proven that the new King Cobra SS 350 out-drives the Callaway VFT from nine different spots on the club face. We're not talking about a sweet spot, we're talking sweet zip code. Here's how it works. . . . "

SLOGANS

Originally derived from the Gaelic *slugh gairm*, meaning "battle cry," the word *slogan* has an appropriate background. A slogan sums up the theme for a product's benefits to deliver an easily remembered message in a few words—"It's the Real Thing."

There have been many very memorable slogans in advertising over the years for example: "Just Do It" (Nike); "Tastes Great, Less Filling" (Miller Lite); "Good to the Last Drop" (Maxwell House); "Does She . . . Or Doesn't She?" (Clairol); "When It Rains It Pours" (Morton Salt); "We Try Harder" (Avis). Even though not all effective slogans

are etched in every consumer's mind, many slogans do help communicate the essence of the product position: for example, "Pawleys Island. Arrogantly Shabby."

Used even more often on television and radio than in print, slogans may be combined with a catchy tune to make a jingle. Slogans are broadly classified as either institutional or hard sell.

Institutional Slogans

Institutional slogans are created to establish a prestigious image for a company. Relying on this image to enhance their products and services, many firms insist that their slogans appear in all of their advertising and on their letterheads. An entire ad may feature the slogan. Some institutional slogans are familiar:

The Document Company	XEROX
Inspire the Next	HITACHI
Easy as Dell	DELL
You're in Good Hands with Allstate	ALLSTATE INSURANCE
Global Network of Innovation	SIEMENS
Your Vision. Our Future.	OLYMPUS

Hard-Sell Slogans

These capsules of advertising change with campaigns. Hard-sell slogans epitomize the special or significant features of the product or service being advertised, and their claims are strongly competitive.

M&M's. The Milk Chocolate Melts in Your Mouth—Not in Your Hands.

M&M'S

Make Every Mile Count

KIA

Get Met. It Pays.

METLIFE

Don't Just Travel. Travel Right.

EXPEDIA.COM

In 2003, General Electric (GE) purged its 24-year old slogan "We Bring Good Things to Life" for "Imagination at Work." It is difficult to change a slogan in which you have invested millions of dollars to establish for one that isn't proven. The reason for the change was the old slogan no longer represented where the corporation was heading. Research about "Good Things" brought surprises. "Nearly everybody said it meant only two things: lighting and appliances," says GE's Judy Hu, general manager for corporate advertising and marketing communications. The company ranks as one of the world's largest and most diversified technology and service companies. Its holdings range from aircraft engines and power generators to financial services and a television network.

The U.S. Army took the risk in 2001 and dropped its 20-year-old slogan, "Be All You Can Be," in favor of "An Army of One." The change brought about cries from critics and Army traditionalists.

"Most companies want a really great tag line that can crystallize the brand across different audiences," says Tracey Riese, president of branding consulting firm TG Riese.[16]

Some marketing gurus argue that large marketers, such as Anheuser-Busch and Coca-Cola, should forget one-size-fits-all themes and come up with different slogans to reach different audiences. Most marketers haven't bought into this theory.

Slogans are widely used to advertise groceries, drugs, beauty aids, and liquor. These are products that are bought repeatedly at a comparatively low price. They are sold to consumers in direct competition on the shelves of supermarkets, drugstores, and department stores. If a slogan can remind a shopper in one of those stores of a special feature of the product, it certainly has served its purpose. Slogans can also remind shoppers of the name of a product from a company they respect. Not all advertising needs slogans. One-shot announcements—sale ads for which price is the overriding consideration—usually do not use slogans. Creating a slogan is one of the fine arts of copywriting.

Elements of a Good Slogan

A slogan differs from most other forms of writing because it is designed to be remembered and repeated word for word to impress a brand and its message on the consumer. Ideally, the slogan should be short, clear, and easy to remember.

Nobody Can Eat Just One.

LAY'S BAKED POTATO CHIPS

Nationwide Is On Your Side.

NATIONWIDE INSURANCE

Where Shopping Is a Pleasure

PUBLIX SUPERMARKET

Just Slightly Ahead of Our Time

PANASONIC

The Rules Are Changing.

DATEK ONLINE

Aptness helps:

Love the Skin You're In.

OLAY

Trusted by More Women Than Any Other Brand.

MASSENGILL

Choosy Moms Choose Jif.

JIF

It is an advantage to have the name of the product in the slogan:

Kroger. For Goodness Sake.

KROGER

Relax, It's FedEx . . .

FEDEX

It Pays to Discover.

DISCOVER CARD

THE CREATIVE WORK PLAN

Before most agencies start creating an ad, they develop a creative work plan to guide them in the right direction. The brief is the starting point for the creative process. You will recall from Chapter 3 that the creative brief consists of the following elements:

- Key observation
- Communication objective
- Consumer insight
- Promise
- Support
- Audience
- Mandatories

What does a brief accomplish? In simple factual terms, a good brief should accomplish three main objectives. First, it should give the creative team a realistic view of what the advertising really needs to do and is likely to achieve. Second, it should provide a clear understanding of the people that the advertising must address, and finally, it needs to give clear direction on the message to which the target audience seems most likely to be susceptible. In some agencies there is a creative briefing in which an account planner will outline the nature of the advertising problem for the creative team and suggest ways of solving it.[17]

The purpose of the work plan is to provide proper direction for the creative team prior to developing ideas, heads, and copy. Exhibit 16.11 shows a work plan format originally developed by Young & Rubicam that is widely used by a number of agencies. Note that the work plan emphasizes factual information and research data. The creative process is not a "shot in the dark" but rather depends on knowing as much as possible about the product, the consumer, and the expected benefits. The advertising professional is able to channel objective information into a creative and attention-getting sales message. Many agencies and clients have their own format and style for specific information they think necessary for creative strategy development.

TESTED GUIDELINES FOR CREATING AN AD

Philip W. Sawyer, editor, *Starch Tested Copy*, after years of studying Starch Advertisement Readership Studies, shares his findings with you. Following are some specific rules and thoughts on developing effective advertising:[18]

EXHIBIT **16.11**

A Creative Work Plan

CREATIVE WORK PLAN
PRODUCT: **NEW ORLEANS**

KEY FACT
Bevil Foods is a 30-year-old New Orleans– based frozen food company. In 1993, Bevil Foods will introduce a new line of premium frozen entreés to be distributed nationally.

PROBLEM THE ADVERTISING MUST SOLVE
Currently there is **NO awareness** of the New OrLeans product among potential consumers.

ADVERTISING OBJECTIVE
To achieve 70% awareness of the product at end of year 1. To communicate the taste and low-calorie/low-fat benefits of the product.

CREATIVE STRATEGY

PROSPECT DEFINITION
1. Women 25–54, professional/managerial, with household incomes of $25,000 plus.
2. Adults 25+ professional/managerial, with household incomes of $25,000 plus.

    Psychographically, these people tend to be active, concerned with their health, and "on the go" a lot.

PRINCIPAL COMPETITION
Lean Cuisine, Weight Watchers, Healthy Choice.

KEY PROMISE
New Orleans are lite entreés with the great taste of New Orleans.

REASON WHY
Less than 300 calories; low fat, great tasting, original New Orleans recipes, served in fine restaurants for 30 years.

MANDATORIES
Must use logo, calorie and fat information, and original New Orleans recipes in each ad.

What follows are 10 guidelines that we believe advertisers should keep in mind whenever they sit down to create an ad. As we offer these, we are well aware that any number of ads ignore these guidelines yet are very successful. That's fine. Mark Twain broke almost every rule of grammar when he wrote *The Adventures of Huckleberry Finn.* But he had to know the rules before he could break them effectively.

1. *Keep it simple, stupid.* The KISS principle, as this is called, has no better application than in advertising, yet it is probably the most abused principle of all. Here is the best argument for simplicity (see Exhibit 16.12): A great many magazine readers do not read magazines to look at the ads. Therefore, advertising needs to catch the eye quickly, deliver its message quickly, and allow the reader to leave as quickly as possible. Ads that clutter the page with multiple illustrations and varied sizes and styles of type offer no central focus for the eye, no resting place. Because of these visual disincentives for staying with "busy" ads, readers naturally move on, having spent little or no time with them.

2. *You're not selling the product; you're selling the benefits of the product.* An old *New Yorker* cartoon depicts a pompous-looking young man at a party, talking to a young woman. "Well, that's enough about me," he says. "Now, what do you think about me?" Most advertisements suffer from the same kind of egotism. They assume that the reader is as interested in the product as is the advertiser. In reality, most readers do not enter the advertiser's realm readily. They do so only when convinced that the product will do something for them. If an advertiser does not answer the reader's implicit question—What's in it for me?—the ad is unlikely to attract any real interest.

    Most ads are simply descriptive; they explain what the product or service is. The worst ads give you a long history about the company, its values, commitments, and size—as if anyone really cares. But the best ads directly address the

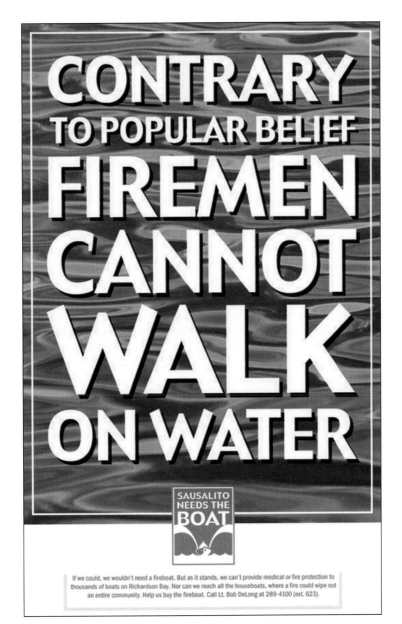

problems that the product or service solves and suggest how that solution makes life better for the potential consumer.

3. *When appropriate, spice it up with sex.* Psychologist Joyce Brothers once predicted that "the days of sexy advertising are numbered. The reason is that within five years, the number of marriageable women will be greater than the number of marriageable men. This will be the beginning of the 'she' generation, which will be a generation unimpressed with sex as a selling point."

Dr. Brothers makes the common (and, it could be argued, sexist) mistake of assuming that men are interested in sex and women are not. In truth, the publications that carry the sexiest advertising today are women's publications. And that kind of advertising attracts considerable notice and readership and will continue to do so until human beings reproduce exclusively by parthenogenesis.

At the same time, it should be emphasized that sexy ads tend to be simple ads—perfectly reasonable because clutter and salaciousness are not really compatible. The best ads of this type may feature nudity but are not explicitly erotic. To the politically correct, we say: Sex sells. Get used to it.

4. *Use celebrities.* Opinion surveys indicate that Americans do not believe an ad simply because it features a well-known person hawking the product. However, according to our data, ads with celebrities earn "noted" scores that are 13 percent higher than average. They are particularly effective with women readers, scoring 15 percent higher than average, compared with 10 percent higher for men. Overall, ads with testimonials from celebrities score 11 percent above the average, whereas testimonials from noncelebrities actually earn below-average scores. Celebrities may not be believable, but they are very effective at attracting reader attention, which is the first job of any advertisement.

5. *Exploit the potential of color.* Print advertising has the potential to contend with television. The moving image is a profoundly effective means of communication, and anyone who has ever tried to amuse a baby knows that the eye has an inherent attraction to motion. At the same time, the eye is also attracted to bold, bright, and beautiful color. Our data indicate that one-page color ads earn "noted" scores that are 45 percent higher on average than comparable black-and-white ads; two-page color ads earn scores that are 53 percent higher than similar black-and-white ads. Generally, the more colorful, the better (as long as the advertiser keeps in mind the other nine principles).

    Television has a lock on the moving image, but print's ability to generate astonishing, eye-catching colors is substantial, and publications should do everything possible to stay current with new advances in color technology.

6. *Go with the flow.* Every ad has flow to it, and the flow is determined by the positioning of the various creative elements. Ads with good flow send the reader's eye around the page to take in all the important elements: the illustration, headline, body copy, and brand name. Ads with bad flow may attract a fair amount of attention at first, but send the reader off the page. For example, a number of advertisers make the mistake of placing a flashy illustration toward the bottom of the page and the copy and headline at the top. In such cases, the most powerful element of an ad can turn out to be the most detrimental, because that alluring illustration steals attention away from the copy.

    For another example, consider the automobile industry and the way some advertisers position the automobile on the page. The eye, our data indicate, tends to follow the car from back to front. Thus, if the car is facing to the right on the page and is positioned above the body copy, the eye, moving back to front, ends up over the beginning of the copy, exactly the right place if you want to have your copy read. But consider how many advertisers position their cars facing left to right, thus "leading" the reader to the right side of the page, the point at which the reader is most likely to continue on to the next page without studying the rest of the ad.

7. *Avoid ambiguity.* Although it appears that Europeans accept, if not welcome, ambiguous themes and symbols, we have found that Americans have little tolerance for advertising that does not offer a clear and distinct message. Several years ago, Benson & Hedges attracted a great deal of attention with an ad featuring a man clad only in pajama bottoms and a bewildered expression, standing in a dining room in the middle of what appears to be a brunch party. The trade press evidently was far more attracted to the ad than were readers, who, our data indicated, were as nonplused by the ad as its star was by his predicament, and reacted with considerable hostility to the advertiser who dared to confuse them.

    Americans like it straight. They choose not to spend a great deal of time thinking about the messages in their advertising. If the point of the ad is not clear, the typical American reader will move on to the next page.

8. *Heighten the contrast.* We live in a visual culture, and one thing that delights the eye is contrast. So advertisers would do well to employ what might be called

"visual irony" in their advertising. One suggestion is to contrast the content of the ads.

American Express produced one of the best ads of 1988 by featuring the diminutive Willie Shoemaker standing back to back with the altitudinous Wilt Chamberlain. The contrast was humorous and eye-catching. Another way to fulfill this principle is to contrast the elements constituting the form of the ad—color, for example. Our data indicate that using black as a background makes elements in the foreground pop off the page. Stolichnaya earned average scores with a horizontal shot of the product against a white background. When the same layout was produced with a change only in the background, from white to black, the scores increased by 50 percent on average.

9. *Use children and animals.* Almost any advertising can succeed with an appeal to the emotions, and children and animals appeal to all but the most hard-hearted. It is logical, of course, to use a close-up of a child when selling toys. (Yet flip through an issue of a magazine for parents and notice how many products for children's clothing, for example, do not use children—a missed opportunity if there ever was one.) And pets, of course, are naturals for pet food.

The trick is to find an excuse to use a child or furry little beast when your product is not even remotely connected to those models. Hewlett-Packard pulled this off beautifully by featuring a Dalmatian and the headline, "Now the HP LaserJet IIP is even more irresistible." The ad won the highest scores in the computer and data equipment product category for a Starch Readership Award. Hitachi has used the double lure of celebrity Jamie Lee Curtis and various animals—cats and parrots primarily—to hawk the company's televisions in a campaign that has consistently garnered the highest "noted" scores for the category.

10. *When an ad has a good deal of copy, make it as inviting as possible.* A source of never-ending astonishment to us is the advertiser that insists on shrinking and squeezing copy into a tight corner of an ad in order to maximize "white space"—a triumph of style over common sense. Others present copy over a mottled background, making it almost impossible to read easily. Two other common problems are reverse print over a light background, offering too little contrast, and centered copy (i.e., unjustified right and left margins), which forces the reader to work too hard to find the beginning of each line. An advertiser that includes a fair amount of copy obviously hopes that it will be read. Relatively few readers choose to spend the time to read most of the copy of any advertisement; if you get 20 percent of magazine readers to delve into your copy, you are doing very well. So the challenge is to make the whole process as easy for the reader as possible. Good content alone will not attract readers. The best-written, wittiest, and most powerful copy will be overlooked unless it is well spaced and sufficiently large and clear to invite the reader.

Thoughts on Outdoor

The new production technologies offer the opportunity to create something bigger than life. Here you can create disruption from the ordinary. A giant peach sitting in a field will attract attention because it is a thousand times larger than a peach should be. The Richards Group in Dallas had cows painting an outdoor poster for its client Chick-Fil-A. We all know that cows don't paint or climb, but when they do, we look.

Just a few thoughts on outdoor. First, you have a responsibility to create something wonderful because most people dislike ads cluttering up the environment. You should ask, as with any medium, how the ad will be integrated into the other kinds of communications. In Chapter 12, an overview of creative was given.

JASON KREHER

Account Guy/Creative Guy
EURO RSCG MVBMS Partners/New York

How to Be an Account Person/How to Be a Creative Person

You know the steps to *becoming* either an account person or a creative person, but what do you need to know once you get there? This simple primer gets to the core of the most important aspects of your new career in advertising.

Word Choice

Account: This is very easy. You need only use these crucial seven phrases: synergies, value-add, testing results, out-of-the-box, closing the loop, holistic branding, client POV. Mix and match! All you need are a few linking verbs and you're ready to go.

Creative: If you are a writer, remember this rule of thumb: Copywriting is a showcase for your vocabulary, nothing more. A good tip is to write copy, and then use the thesaurus on your computer to change every word to its longer, more cumbersome synonym. Remember to sigh dramatically when the account people ask you to change it back.

Note: If you are an art director, don't worry about words. Just pick the prettiest colors and stay within the lines.

Wardrobe

Account:

Male: Variety is the order of the day for the well-dressed account man. Make sure to have a colorful spectrum of oxford button-ups, from off-white to bone to ecru and everything in between. Spice up your khaki collection with an occasional pleat. And never forget—the icon on your breast pocket makes the man. The little polo player or the tiny alligator? Choose carefully, young friends.

Female: Break out the Banana Republic credit cards, ladies! Your all-black, business-casual attire should exude confidence, style, and a willingness to compromise everything you believe in for a single nod of approval from the client. And remember—the higher the heel on your shoe, the more respect you will command. It's that simple.

Creative: Be you male, female, or "curious," tight, ironic t-shirts are crucial in communicating your status on the fringe of counterculture. "I'm no one's puppet," you'll

say, adjusting your clunky, black-frame glasses and sporting your brand-new "Don't Mess with Texas" ringer tee from Urban Outfitters. Spend 20 minutes making sure your hair looks like it's never been combed.

Desk/Office

Account: Fill your workspace with pictures of your family and children. If you are not married or do not have children, how about several framed pictures of your dog? Yeah, that's not pathetic at all.

Creative: Ensure your desk is completely free of impediments to creativity like folders, paper clips or Post-it Notes. Cover its surface in a chaotic jumble of action figures, magic 8 balls, snow globes, liquor bottles, obscure French design magazines, and unopened "Final Notice" bills. This will help you be creative.

Note: Jason Kreher spent his first two years at EuroRSCG MVBMS Partners as an account executive on the Intel business and then subsequently transitioned to a junior copywriter position on brands such as Intel, Volvo, Evian, and New Balance. He is currently considering another switch and wants to become either a high school principal or a caterpillar. ■ ■ ■

EXHIBIT 16.13

This creative not only included the message but also the pigeons.

Courtesy of Howard, Merrell & Partners and Auto Allies.

Generally, there should no more than seven words in the main head. No, we're not saying it won't communicate with more than seven, but the more you have the harder it is to grasp quickly. This is truly a medium where simple is better. Reduce all the elements, if possible. If you have a bottle of Sobe energy drink as your illustration, do you need to also have a logo? Maybe, but if the bottle is large enough you'll easily see the logo on it. The point is to reduce the visual and verbal elements down to their simplest form. But that offers a challenge to be creative (see Exhibit 16.13). The art director, Scott Ballew, designed fiberglass pigeons and had them manufactured (about three times normal size) to put on top of this outdoor board. That should not only attract attention but also entertain and be memorable.

The classic model of the conversational billboard was the long-lived Burma-Shave campaign. Throughout the 1920s, 1930s, and 1940s, the company put up signs at regular intervals along roads all over America, each carrying one line of a goofy poem:

> The bearded lady
> Tried a jar
> She's now
> A famous
> Movie star
> Burma-Shave

Instead of making lofty claims about the product, Burma-Shave admitted it was just selling a shaving cream and won affection by being playful. People went along looking for the next line. Today, Tide detergent has taken a leaf from Burma-Shave. Its copy seems irrelevant "Because paper cups weren't designed to be held between your knees." This technique has been called "referencing the environment of use." Tide knows you're stuck in traffic, unwrapping your burger, and balancing your Coke. The message says, "Go ahead. We'll clean it up if you spill anything." Within a week, the message changes: "Holy Guacamole." Then more: "For those who steer, shift, and eat jelly doughnuts." Molly Humbert, Tide spokeperson, says the idea behind the campaign is to make relevant connections with people at the point of dirt.[19]

 **SUMMARY**

Simplicity is the key to great advertising. Good copy speaks to all people. The great creative shops of today have a common thread running through their advertising—the headline, visual, and logo communicate the idea immediately.

Advertising motivates people by appealing to their problems, desires, and goals, and by offering them a solution to their problems, satisfactions of their desires, and a means of achieving their goals.

In general, ads have a definite structure consisting of a promise of benefit in the headline (and maybe the spelling out of the promise in a subheadline), amplification of the story or facts, proof of claim, and action to take. Effective heads can be long or short, but they need to clearly communicate the message. The subheadline can expand on the promise presented in the headline and can provide transition between the headline and the first sentence of the body copy. The body copy is where you build your case with consumers for the product and support the promise in the head or subhead. The details about the product or service are presented here, along with support for your claim.

The creative essence of copywriting is to see a product in a fresh, unique way. The chief approaches used to describe products are factual, imaginative, and emotional. A slogan sums up the theme for a product's benefits. It needs to be a memorable message with few words.

Slogans can be developed from several points of view; the institutional and hard-sell viewpoints are the most common.

The place to start planning an ad is the creative work plan or the creative brief. If written properly, the creative work plan will tell you what the message should be in the ad and what the ad is to accomplish. It tells you the ad's specific purpose. However, no work plan will tell you how to execute the copy—that's part of the creative process.

REVIEW

1. What is time famine?

2. How can advertisers use psychological appeals?

3. What are Ogilvy's great advertising elements?

4. What's the purpose of the headline?

5. What is the purpose of amplification?

6. What is meant by "copy style"?

7. What are the characteristics of an effective slogan?

8. What is the key to developing outdoor?

 **TAKE IT TO THE WEB**

Compare the Crest (**www.crest.com**) and Colgate (**www.colgate.com**) toothpaste Web sites. What type of approach is used to attract the consumer?

Think of a really memorable slogan, such as "Just do it" from Nike. What kind of claim does the slogan make about the product? Visit **www.nike.com** to see how closely the slogan is reflected in the online presentation of the brand. Does the feeling extend to Nike Soccer, Nike Running, etc.?

Compare the Pottery Barn Web site (**www.potterybarn.com**) to the Crate and Barrel Web site (**www.crateandbarrel.com**). What type of appeal does each company use to encourage sales? Is one more effective than the other? Why?

CHAPTER 17

The Ritz-Carlton. Now in New York City.

THE RITZ-CARLTON®
HOTELS OF NEW YORK

The Total Concept: Words and Visuals

CHAPTER OBJECTIVES

deas and ads. How does a creative team get from an idea to a finished ad? What kind of visuals are best? How do we generate fresh ideas? After reading this chapter, you will understand:

1. concepts and executional ideas
2. left- and right-brain ideas
3. how a creative team works
4. visualizing the idea
5. principles of design
6. kinds of visuals

We don't just create ad ideas and executions for the fun of it. Advertising is about motivating people to buy something. When we create advertising, we pray that consumers find it appealing and relevant and that it sells. According to John Butler, creative director of Butler, Shine, Stern & Partners, "Advertising is not art. It is a business masquerading as art." Butler claims to have told a good many art directors and writers when they balked at a layout comment or an editorial mandate and refused to budge, "Walk down to Pearl Paint (store) and buy yourself a canvas and some oils, my friend, because this is advertising, and it is not a spectator sport."[1] However, Jeff Goldsmit of Lowe & Partners says, "More and more clients are realizing creative ads work better, are more memorable and make their point effectively in the marketplace. You can run a good creative ad fewer times. People can remember it after seeing it three times rather than 30 times. Any USP advantage is gone in 15-minutes if you don't create an emotional bond with consumers." Grey Worldwide's chief creative officer says, "You should bring together art and commerce. But you can do some of the most engaging, funny work in the world and if it doesn't motivate the consumer to do something or stimulate some part of their brain, then it doesn't work."[2] So again we find that there isn't a simple set of rules that works for creating strong ads or other marketing communications. But all agree that strategic concepts and ideas are the foundation.

CREATE RELEVANT IDEAS

What are some of the great ads you remember from your growing-up years? Why do you remember them? There probably was an idea that was relevant or entertaining to you. Our minds work in mysterious ways. We have to learn to take the reader or viewer beyond the strategy. We also need to go beyond style into a magical dimension. Classic campaigns did this: Brylcream's Greasy Kid Stuff, Avis's When You're Only No.2, You Try Harder, Volkswagen's Lemon, Wendy's Where's the Beef, Nike's Just Do It, and AT&T's Reach Out and Touch Someone. Before we can create this kind of advertising, we have to learn to develop the idea behind the strategy.

George Lois, the outrageous art director, was once asked, "What is advertising?" He answered, "Advertising is poison gas. It should bring tears to your eyes, and it should unhinge your nervous system. It should knock you out." He admitted that his description is probably excessive but regards it as a forgivable hyperbole because it certainly describes the powerful possibilities of advertising. Great advertising should have the impact of a punch in the mouth. Great advertising should ask, without asking literally, "Do you get the message?" And the reader (viewer) should answer, without literally answering, "Yeah, I got it!" Lois says all of this can be accomplished with the "big idea." VitroRobertson appeals to the buyer of guitars by using a clean, simple design that plays to lifestyle: "It's a lot less stressful when your wife and your groupie are the same person." The name of the product is seen only on the guitar plus the Web address for Taylor guitars (see Exhibit 17.1).

Arthur Kiong, marketing director for the new Ritz-Carlton properties in New York, wanted to generate excitement for a grand opening in New York's "I've seen it all" market. "I did not want another ad featuring guys in black suits, white shirts and blue ties standing in the lobby," Kiong recalled. "The Ritz brand is strong enough to stand alone. We needed something mildly disruptive to make a significant splash in New York—even if it had to 'mildly' offend some of my colleagues, which it did." The campaign created by Sawyer Riley Compton began in June 2001 and featured Lady Liberty standing in New York Harbor, hands clenched and arms raised in triumph (see the chapter intro ad). The copy underneath read: "The Ritz-Carlton. Now in New York City." Beneath that, a lonely logo. After 9/11, the ad was almost pulled, but hundreds of letters came praising its patriotic spirit, which, of course, was unintentional.[3] The big idea represents the concepts of simplicity, clarity, and strength.

EXHIBIT 17.1

The headline, "It's a lot less stressful when your wife and your groupie are the same person," and the visual work well together.

IT'S A LOT LESS STRESSFUL WHEN YOUR WIFE AND YOUR GROUPIE ARE THE SAME PERSON.

WWW.TAYLORGUITARS.COM

The creative process can be broken down into four basic areas: concepts, words, pictures, and the medium or vehicle used to present them. The dictionary defines a concept as a general notion or idea, an idea of something formed by mentally combining all its characteristics or particulars. In advertising, the total concept is a fresh way of looking at something—a novel way of talking about a product or service, a dramatic new dimension that gives the observer a new perspective. A concept is an idea. Many in advertising, including Lois, call it the big idea—one that is expressed clearly and combines words and visuals. The words describe what the basic idea is, and the visuals repeat what the words say or, even better, reinforce what the words say or provide a setting that makes the words more powerful.

Your creative concept must not only grab attention, it must also get across the main selling point and the brand name. How often has someone seen a compelling ad only to later say, "I don't remember the brand name or product."

IDEAS COME FROM THE LEFT AND RIGHT BRAIN

The left hemisphere of the brain provides reasoning, controls verbal skills, and processes information (characteristics of copywriters). The right side provides intuition, processes information, controls the creative process, thinks nonverbally, responds to color, and is artistic (characteristics of art directors). So we are talking about a left-brain person and a right-brain person working together to develop a concept. Each comes to the table with a different point of view.

Having created a host of memorable campaigns—"Millertime," "Soup Is Good Food," "Things Go Better with Coke," "Tastes Great, Less Filling"—Bill Backer, in *The Care and Feeding of Ideas,* defines a basic idea or concept as an abstract answer to a perceived desire or need. And an **executional idea** is a rendering in words, symbols, sounds, colors, shapes, forms, or any combination thereof, of an abstract answer to a perceived desire or need. We use the word *execute* in ad development. It is a schizophrenic verb. It means to complete or put into effect or to use according to a pattern—as a work of art. Of course, it also means "to put to death."

John Hegarty believes it is the idea that drives things. He has a quote blown up on his wall from a dictionary and it says, "An idea is a thought or plan formed by mental effort." In other words, the color blue is not an idea. It's a means of making your idea more profound.

executional idea
It is a rendering in words, symbols, shapes, forms, or any combination thereof, of an abstract answer to a perceived desire or need.

THE CREATIVE TEAM

In general, the responsibility for the visual, layout, and graphics is that of the art director. The copywriter has the job of creating the words for the ad and maybe the ad concept. We say "maybe" because when creative teams are used it is the responsibility of the team to develop a concept. The copywriter needs to understand art direction and the art director needs to appreciate the impact of words. Together they need to have a rapport to be successful. Both are concept thinkers. Both think in terms of words and pictures, after the team arms themselves with all the information they need. When they have settled on a target audience and a creative strategy, these left- and right-brain people begin to create.

This relationship between copywriter and art director is almost like a marriage. You spend an average of 8 hours a day with your partner—that's 40 hours a week, or 2,080 hours a year. The truth is that better teams feed off each other. Each has their own method of developing big ideas. But there probably isn't a single method. Dick Lord, creative legend, says, "I get my biggest drawing pad and I'll draw little thumbnails and I'll just do headlines or visual ideas. I'll brainstorm myself. I'll sit by myself and do 60, 70—I don't edit them. And then you go over them a little later and you find maybe 10 or 12 that you could look at again. Then, you get with your art director

KLEPPNER VIEWPOINT

FRANK COMPTON

Chief Brand Storyteller (CEO),
Sawyer Riley Compton

The Quest for Great Advertising

The advertising agency world today covers a broad spectrum of businesses that, in some form or fashion, create perceptions of brands or awareness for products or services. These entities go about doing it in a variety of ways, some developing specialties and proprietary processes. But in the end, however, the goal is to sell something, and, ultimately, it's all about the business of creativity.

Yet, of the literally thousands of businesses called advertising agencies, a very small number of those actually become recognized for their creativity. These agencies stand out from the pack for their ability to consistently present relevant marketing messages in ways that are so unique and different they can't help but be noticed in the marketplace. So, if advertising agencies are in the business of creativity, what distinguishes those that seem to have this creative magic from those that simply do "good work?"

At Sawyer Riley Compton, we did "good work" for many years. We grew and we helped clients grow their businesses as well. But all the while, there was a yearning, a passion from within, to really create for our clients that cutting-edge work that truly stands out in an extraordinary way. And we simply set out to do it.

A decade later we're now included in a group of agencies known within the industry and among a certain genre of clients for our creative work. So, how did that happen? What does it take to consistently produce a level of creative thinking that is recognized as a cut above? These are some things we believe.

1. It begins at the top.

Unless it's a passion and a commitment by the people responsible for the vision and financial success of the agency, it simply can't happen. For a while, it's a huge investment with little return. Old clients leave because that's not why they hired you. New clients who expect great creative work won't come on board because you haven't proved you can do it yet. There's staff turnover because some don't share the vision. Others are simply not willing to make the commitment to go beyond where they've been. And others simply don't have the talent. So, for years, the agency is in transition resulting in inordinate emotional and financial stress, loss of identity and, in general, chaos.

Frank Compton

2. Great creative is just good business.

Louis Sawyer describes truly great creative work as "smart work." Not only is there a wonderful idea at the center but also you immediately recognize it as having true relevance and doing an extraordinary job for the client. The power of the idea multiplies the media budget. It finds its way into the streets. It shows up in conversations around water coolers. And ultimately, it works— something is sold! Then it becomes good business for the agency as well. The phone rings again with clients who want what we do.

3. It takes a very special group of clients.

They may be within a corporate giant or a rising, privately held organization. But you find each other. And when you meet, you know. The chemistry is there. You have big ideas and they have the courage to see the potential. They flatten their organizations to give you access to decision makers. They take you inside the tent to help them wrestle with all strategic issues relating to success in the marketplace. In turn, you become obsessed with their success. You challenge them; they challenge you. Trust grows. And so does substantial progress.

4. The whole agency is the creative department.

Sure, we have copywriters and art directors but one would have a hard time putting our people in traditional agency pigeonholes. The account managers are very creative. The copywriters and art directors think strategically. Media, PR, and interactive people contribute ideas that may very well become ads. Or vice versa. Production people are fanatical about the crafting of the idea in every tactical execution. And improvement to the idea never ends. Someone is constantly working to make it better. Even the financial staff realizes their importance in making ideas soar and brands successful. The passion to do better work becomes cult-like.

5. Find the talent.

I'm convinced creativity is like athleticism. Some people have an inordinate amount while others have less. We work hard to find the ones who have a lot. This means looking beyond a résumé to see the talent or the potential. As an agency's creative notoriety spreads, finding great talent becomes somewhat easier. The people who have it seek out places where they can use it. And they come to us.

6. No prima donnas.

No prima donnas and great creative talent—an oxymoron? Not so. It's a matter of confidence, I believe. When ad people are really good and they know it, they don't have to exhibit the stereotypical trappings ranging from "the look" to temper tantrums. There are nice people who possess amazing creative talent and we work hard to find them.

Peer selection and peer management are very important tools we use to avoid the prima donna trap. Interviews and portfolio reviews involve numerous team members from multiple disciplines. When someone becomes part of the SRC team, she or he has been thoroughly run through the proverbial ringer by a group of peers. This results in respect among the team that means accountability to the whole. Everyone not only wants to do their best for the others; they also readily solicit the critique of their ideas from their peers. Everyone makes everyone else's work better.

7. Respect the culture.

Yes, we have a culture. And so do our clients. Respecting both is essential to great work. Seldom do we have a fully developed idea summarily rejected by a client. If it's off strategy, the team detects it before it gets that far. But creating within each client's culture is equally important. The culture of The Ritz-Carlton is totally different from the culture of Dow. Thus, the approaches we'd take for each are totally different as well.

Internally, our own culture is based on respect. There is no distinction between how people are treated by "management" versus how people are treated by each other.

They are one and the same. There is no doubt about a passion for the work and an undying determination to constantly make it better. But beyond this, there's also a realization that we are also husbands and wives, fathers and mothers, girlfriends, golfers, runners, gardeners, and any number of descriptors that indicate there's a personal life outside of advertising. And it's often in real life where ideas begin anyway.

8. Unstructured structure.

This involves everything from office space to managing the clock. A total lack of structure means chaos but some amount of managed chaos is good. Within our office space, for example, there are no doors. So, it gets noisy. People aren't compartmentalized either. An art director is neighbor to a media planner. As a result, people overhear ideas for a brand's strategic direction or a campaign in the hallways. They come out and join in. Before you know it, a myriad of people is contributing. And the idea gets better.

There's also freedom to disagree, challenge, take charge, or even make mistakes. Certainly there are systems and procedures in place to manage the chaos. But the real accountability in a truly creative environment is to each other.

9. There's no substitute for hard work.

It begins long before a creative team ever starts to conceptualize. Observing. In homes. In stores. On sales calls. Great insights come from involvement with the brand and people who buy and use the brand. Research adds further clarification. Client and agency teams are meeting throughout. Pushing. Challenging. Progressing. Then it comes down to really smart creative people being prolific. Walls are plastered with good ideas. Then replaced by better ideas. Then more of the same. Ultimately, the idea gels. Is it smart? Does it surprise? Yes, but there's something better. Let's find it.

10. Celebrate the work.

Never get comfortable. We challenge ourselves by constantly reviewing what other agencies we admire are doing. We review award show reels and annuals. And we submit our work to the premier creative shows. When it's awarded, we unashamedly celebrate. When it's not, we try harder. Otherwise how do we know where our creative bar stands as compared to the work considered the best in the world?

So, as you can see, there is no magic. It's more about uncompromising vision and truly believing great work creates better value for clients. I'd have to say it's also about personal satisfaction in knowing we did our absolute best and we've been part of something pretty special. I can live with that.

Courtesy of Sawyer Riley Compton. ■ ■ ■

A MACHINE THAT TURNS ANY BODY OF WATER INTO THE FOUNTAIN OF YOUTH.

You're only as old as you feel. And, trust us, you'd feel a lot younger if you were spending your weekends with the family on a Yamaha FX140® WaveRunner. The FX140 features an energetic, 140 horsepower, four-stroke Yamaha marine engine that's ultra-quiet and clean. It's designed to provide non-stop playtime all weekend long. And, we might add, designed to make you feel like a kid again. In which case, your own kids will probably start wanting to hang out with you. Of course, the youth-enhancing FX140 is equipped with Yamaha features that your grown-up, practical side will appreciate, including 27 gallons of storage, tilt steering, reverse capability and a tow hook. Visit yamaha-motor.com or call 1-800-6-Yamaha

WAVERUNNER ©2003 Yamaha Motor Corporation, USA. If you're the kind of person who reads disclaimers like this, then you're obviously a person who likes to know the details. You can learn all the details about our whole line of WaveRunners – nine models in at – by calling 1-800-6-Yamaha and asking for a free WaveRunner brochure and video. We'll also help you find a dealer near you. And please remember, follow instructional materials and obey all laws. Ride responsibly, wearing protective apparel. Always ride within your capabilities, allowing time and distance for maneuvers, and respect others around you. Don't drink and ride. Call the Yamaha WaterCraft Education and Training Center at 1-800-830-2232 and visit yamaha-motor.com to learn how we're helping protect the environment. Now go have fun. **YAMAHA**

EXHIBIT 17.2

The art direction and the head work hard to communicate the ad's basic idea.

Courtesy of VitroRobertson, Inc., Yamaha Motor Corporation and Chris Wimpey, photographer.

partner, and say, 'Well, what have you got? I have this.'" Some art directors and copywriters like to work by themselves first.

We've all heard, "You're only as old as you feel." The ad in Exhibit 17.2 appeals to family men to spend their weekends with their families on the Yamaha WaveRunner. The head reads: "A machine that turns any body of water into the fountain of youth." How many headlines did it take to communicate this concept? And how many sketches before this appealing layout was finalized?

THE IDEA

Strong ideas may be difficult to develop but are worth fighting for when you find one. Strong ideas are simple ideas. People do not remember details as clearly as they recall concepts. In advertising, simple concepts become great ads through attention to detail—the words, type style, photography, and layout. A great advertising concept might survive poor execution, but the better crafted the ad, the better the chances that prospects will become customers.

We are not necessarily talking about hitting home runs with breakthrough advertising. We are not talking about Nike, Coke, or Pepsi, or glamorous products. We are talking about ideas that solve problems and communicate to consumers. Ogilvy & Mather took the declining Lever Brothers' Surf detergent brand and increased its sales by more than 20 percent by telling it like it is—doing laundry is a drag and there's no point in trying to deny it. Research showed that 45 percent of all laundry-doers do laundry only as a last resort. Lever's even has a name for them— the un-laundry people. The campaign's idea was to accentuate the negative by playing up the drudgery of doing laundry in a light-hearted way.

In 2003, BBDO presented a concept to KFC based on the old joke about the chicken crossing the road to illustrate customers' preference for KFC. But, in 1989, KFC had used a "Cross the Road" campaign from Young & Rubicam that franchises disliked. Also, rival Wendy's International was using a "Why People Cross the Road" campaign for chicken nuggets.[4] This is one of the reasons advertisers must do research and both agencies and clients maintain libraries of their work (and research the history of the category). At times, using an old idea may work but it could have risks. You could argue whether or not there are original ideas, but certainly we seek fresh executions.

In an ideal world, the idea needs to come alive, leap off the page, or grab your senses while you watch television. In addition, creative ideas do two important things: (1) They make the prime prospect consider your product first. (2) They implant your brand name indelibly in the prospect's mind and connect it to the positive attributes of your products.

Visualizing the Idea

It is time to execute the big idea. At this stage of the process, the creative team forms mental pictures of how the basic appeal can be translated into a selling message. Just as a good novel has various subplots that are brought together in a creative and interesting, cohesive story line, a good ad has a well-coordinated layout that flows freely to create a compelling message about the product and its benefits.[5] You might visualize a sports car as speeding on a mountain road and around hairpin curves. You might see a sedan of understated luxury in front of a country club. Or you might simply see a close-up of the grill.

These mental pictures can be shown in words or in the crudest form. The crucial thing is to imagine the kind of mental picture that best expresses your idea. While thinking in the visual form (remember a picture is worth a thousand words), find the words that work with the visual for the most powerful effect. Show, if you can. Make as many versions of the basic idea as you can. Tweak or stretch your idea to the limit. Remember, Dick Lord said he sketched 70 rough ideas with heads. And, yes, they could be done on the computer, but Fallon's Tom Lichtenheld believes in sketching on paper and tweaking on his Mac works best for him. There is no magic number of sketches. Try every possibility, but remember your end result must deliver the basic message and the brand name. Does the illustration and copy deliver the creative work plan promise?

Marketing Approach to Visualization

We know that ads are not created for the sake of creativity. Each ad is created for a specific marketing purpose. All ads for a product should conform to the same set of objectives, even though some ads may not appear to be related, and usually they use the same theme or slogan in each ad.

Using all the information you have about the product or service, write a statement of the one thing you need to say about the product to the prime prospect. This is your promise or the basic theme. A family restaurant might shift to low-fat menu items and promise, "We offer you all the things you like about family-style restaurants—convenience, great-tasting foods, and reasonable prices, with the added benefit of fitting into your lifestyle since you want food that is nutritious and good for you." The illustrations must reflect these marketing concepts.

The promise is a consumer benefit statement that tells the prospects what the product will do for them.

THE CREATIVE LEAP

Are we about ready to begin to create an ad? Yes, if we have done our homework. Joseph Wallas, a creative theorist, said creativity is the product of four developmental stages: preparation, incubation, illumination, and verification or evaluation. A Leo Burnett creative director has said, "The best creative comes from an understanding of what people are thinking and feeling. Creativity is a sensitivity to human nature and the ability to communicate it." Starch Research suggests that we have to evaluate the consumer, address the consumer's needs, and suggest the clear benefit of using the product: "Tell her how her life will change for the better if she uses the product, and she'll pay close attention."

Where does the inspiration come from? Some think brainstorming or free association is the answer to creative inspiration, but others say very few ideas come from these techniques. A crazy idea may be the spark for a great campaign. The idea usually comes when you are not looking.

Former Creative Director Jim Aitchison gives a few suggestions for the source of inspiration for an idea:[6]

- Is there an idea in the packaging—shape, color, label, or material the product is made of?
- How is the product made? Where is it made?
- How about the product's history?
- Can you show what happens with the product?
- Any new ideas from the product's old advertising?

The process is one part reason, one part heart, and one big part simple intuition, say others. So the creative leap is not necessarily the same for everyone. There may be truth that you spend more time on the logical process, and then the emotional part comes more easily. Once you get the idea—the concept and visual and words that work together—you've made the creative leap. Leonard Monahan developed a visual idea for North protective work gloves that got right to the point of product advantage by using a wet sponge cut out in the shape of a hand as the illustration. The headline read, "This is what your hand looks like to most toxic chemicals." The headline and visual spoke to the reader as one. A mundane product became the most talked-about ad in its industry.

Layout

The creative leap is only the first step in ad making. The ad itself has a variety of elements: headlines, illustration, copy, logotype, maybe a subheadline, several other illustrations of varying importance, a coupon—the number of components varies tremendously from ad to ad. Putting them all together in an orderly form is called making up the layout of the ad. **Layout** is another of those advertising terms that is used in two senses: It means the total appearance of the ad—its overall design, the composition of its elements; it also means the physical rendering of the design of the ad—a blueprint for production purposes. You will hear some say: "Here's the layout," while handing another person a typed or keyboarded copy and a drawing. Right now, we are talking about the layout as the overall design of the ad. See how the layout for Exhibit 17.3 is complex. The images and the copy must function as one. How did the creative team decide to present the "idea" in this manner?

Layout Person as Editor

Although the person who creates the visual idea may be the same as the one who makes the layout, the two functions are different. The visualizer translates an idea into visual form; a layout person uses that illustration and all the other elements to make an orderly, attractive arrangement.

layout
A working drawing (may be computer developed) showing how an ad is to look. A printer's layout is a set of instructions accompanying a piece of copy showing how it is to be set up. There are also rough layouts, finished layouts, and mechanical layouts, representing various degrees of finish. The term layout is used also for the total design of an ad.

EXHIBIT 17.3
How did the creative team decide on the style and computer image? The copy says, "You may think it's fun to use inhalants to get high. But your kidneys don't. Huffing will destroy them. Not to mention your heart and brain. Visit www.drugfreeamerica. org for more information.

Courtesy of Sawyer Riley Compton and Partnership for a Drug-Free America.

Before putting pencil to paper, however, the layout person—usually an art director—and the writer review all of the elements. The first task is to decide what is most important. Is it the headline? The picture? The copy? How important is the package? Should the product itself be shown, and if so, should it be shown in some special environment or in use? Is this ad to tell a fast story with a picture and headline, or is it a long-copy ad in which illustration is only an incidental feature? The importance of the element determines its size and placement within the ad.

The Need to Attract Attention

Disruption. Attracting attention. Getting noticed. High visibility. No matter how you say it, this is the primary creative objective of an ad. Today's advertising has to work very hard to get noticed. You cannot rely on strategy alone—the positioning, the product appeals, the demographic and psychographic data that tell you what wavelength the consumer is on—to sell the consumer. Obvious as it sounds, you cannot sell people until you attract their attention. Put another way, people are not going to read the ad if they do not see it. Remember, your ad is competing with all the advertising clutter and editorial matter in a publication. Unfortunately, most ads in most publications are invisible.

All the creative elements—the visual, the headline, the copy—must be strongly executed if the ad is to succeed. John Hegarty says, "You're using words and pictures. What you don't want to do is make the pictures do what the words are doing, and the words do what the picture is doing. So you've got to decide which is leading, which is taking you forward, and if it's the picture then you almost certainly will want a very simple headline. Or it's the other way around—a simple picture and an intriguing headline. So there is a kind of juxtaposition." If the idea is being carried by the headline, it will have a twist, a turn, maybe shock—or some sort of disruption. The visual will play a straight role. And vice versa if the message is being carried by the picture.[7] Research cannot tell us which creative techniques will work best because creative is not that scientific. Research generally tells us what has been successful, but there are no yardsticks to measure breakthrough advertising ideas. The basic guidelines for writing and designing ads are helpful, but there are not really any rules. How do you get an ad to stand out? The illustration is usually the key. Either an ad grabs people or it does not, and most often it is the illustration that gets them. Of course, many illustrations cannot tell the story alone—they require a headline to complete the communication. So the headline is extremely important to keep people's interest.

A picture is worth a thousand words, but we do not use illustrations solely to attract attention. They must have a strong relationship to the selling concept. Using a shock visual merely to gain attention is generally a mistake. If you are selling a hammer and your dominant visual is a woman in a bikini, you are using sexist imagery that has no relationship to the product. You are duping people. Now that we have your attention, buy our hammer. And because most people dislike being duped, they will resent your ad—and often your product as well. Yet, powerful images can demand your attention. The Carter's branding ad has powerful emotion built in. It tugs at the heart of every parent (see Exhibit 17.4). The powerful visual and copy function as a single thought. "Life's biggest events aren't necessarily the one's seen on the nightly news."

There are three basic means of attracting attention:

1. Using the visual alone
2. Using the headline alone
3. Using a combination of the visual and headline

Do not assume that because we listed the visual first that the art director is more important than the copywriter. Remember, they are a team working together on both visual and language ideas.

Basic Design Principles

There are some general principles that guide the design of advertising and promotional layouts. Some art directors may use different terminology from that used here, but the basic assumptions are the same.

The following design principles, properly employed, will attract the reader and enhance the chances that the message is read.

Unity All creative advertising has a unified design. The layout must be conceived in its entirety, with all its parts (copy, art, head, logo, and so forth) related to one another to give one overall, unified effect. If the ad does not have unity, it falls apart and becomes visual confusion. Perhaps unity is the most important design principle, but they are all necessary for an effective ad.

Life's biggest events aren't necessarily

the ones seen on the nightly news.

EXHIBIT **17.4**

Carter's uses a strong emotional visual that every parent can identify with in this branding ad. The copy makes the connection, "Life's biggest events aren't necessarily the ones seen on the nightly news."

Courtesy of Sawyer Riley Compton and Carter's.

Harmony Closely related to unity is the idea that all elements of the layout must be compatible. The art director achieves harmony by choosing elements that go together. This process is similar to dressing in the morning. Some items of clothing go together better than others—for example, stripes, plaids, or paisleys with solid colors. The layout needs harmonious elements to be effective; there should not be too many different type faces or sizes, illustrations, and so on.

Sequence The ad should be arranged in an orderly manner so it can be read from left to right and top to bottom. The sequence of elements can help direct the eye in a structural or gaze motion. Place the elements so that the eye starts where you want it to start and travels a desired path throughout the ad. "Z" and "S" arrangements are common.

Emphasis Emphasis is accenting or focusing on an element (or group of elements) to make it stand out. Decide whether you want to stress the illustration, the headline, the logo, or the copy. If you give all of these elements equal emphasis, your ad will end up with no emphasis at all.

Contrast You need differences in sizes, shapes, and tones to add sparkle so the ad will not be visually dull. Altering type to bold or italic or using extended typefaces brings attention to a word or phrase and creates contrast between type elements. Contrast makes the layout more interesting.

Balance By balance, we mean controlling the size, tone, weight, and position of the elements in the ad. Balanced elements look secure and natural to the eye. You test for balance by examining the relationship between the right and left halves of the ad. There are basically two forms of balance: formal and informal.

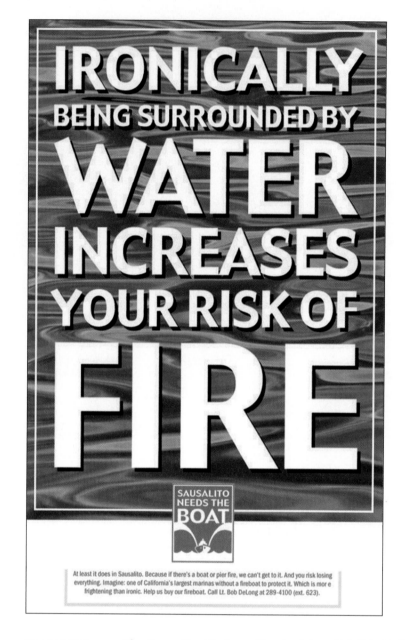

Formal Balance The Sausalito Fireboat Fund ad (see Exhibit 17.5) has elements of equal weight, size, and shape on the left and right sides of an imaginary vertical line drawn down the center of the ad. Such symmetrical ads give an impression of stability and conservatism. Keep in mind that not all formal layouts will have exactly equal weight. For instance, a logo may be on the lower right-hand corner and not have an equal element on the opposite side, but if all other elements are symmetrical, we would consider it a formal layout.

Informal Balance The optical center of a page, measured from top to bottom, is five-eighths of the way up the page; thus, it differs from the mathematical center. (To test this, take a blank piece of paper, close your eyes, then open them, and quickly place a dot at what you think is the center of the page. The chances are that it will be above the mathematical center.) Imagine that a seesaw is balanced on the optical center. We know that a lighter weight on the seesaw can easily balance a heavier one by being farther away from the fulcrum. (The "weight" of an element in an ad may be gauged by its size, its degree of blackness, its color, or its shape.) In informal balance, objects are placed seemingly at random on the page, but in such relation to one another that the page as a whole seems in balance. This type of layout arrangement

A. From the comfy rolled arms to the plush seating, the Sofa and Chair are as comfortable as they are stylish. The handsome Wall System is the perfect focal point with paneled doors that conceal a wealth of electronics.
B. An attic full of treasures awaits with Attic Heirlooms by Broyhill. Apothecary Chest, Splay Leg End Table, Round Dropleaf Table, Chairside Table, Door Dresser, China, Toy Box, Twin Panel Headboard, End Table, Library Cabinet and Chair.

Create memories of your own with these *vintage-chic treasures* from the original **ATTIC HEIRLOOMS**™
✸Broyhill®

¹ Queen bed shown. King and California King also available. ² Upholstery pieces available in other fabrics and/or leathers. ³ Unit accommodates most 36" televisions. Check the dimensions of the product and your individual TV for compatibility before purchasing. ⁴ Queen bed shown. Full, King and California King also available. ⁵ Twin bed shown. Full also available.

For a free copy of "Visions," our 26-page decorating guide, call Broyhill Consumer Assistance at 1-877-888-6006. Visit our web site at **www.broyhillfurn.com.** All items may not be available at all locations. Furniture items may be specially ordered. AD#XXX. ©2003 Broyhill Furniture Industries, Inc.

Construction features: In selecting materials for the Attic Heirlooms collection, designers and engineers at Broyhill create value by designing products that use a combination of oak solids, oak and other hardwood veneers, and wood products. Selected items may include panels of matching oak grain engraving.

EXHIBIT 17.6

This is an informal balanced layout for Broyhill Furniture.

Courtesy of Broyhill Furniture Industries.

requires more thought than the simple bisymmetric formal balance, but the effects can be imaginative and distinctive, as illustrated by Exhibit 17.6.

Other Composing Elements

Color One of the most versatile elements of an ad is color. It can attract attention and help create a mood. Depending on the product and the advertising appeal, color can be used for a number of reasons.

- ■ It is an attention-getting device. With few exceptions, people notice a color ad more readily than one in black and white. Roper Starch research studies indicated color newspaper ads were read 61 percent more often than black-and-white ads.

- ■ Some products can be presented realistically only in color. Household furnishings, food, many clothing and fashion accessories, and cosmetics would lose most of their appeal if advertised in black and white. Studies are done to find the best consumer colors and to spot color trends. For instance, the Pantone Color Institute asked consumers to select their current and future color preferences in specific product categories. In addition, a questionnaire collected data on demographics and placed the respondents into five lifestyle categories: prudent, impulsive, pessimistic, traditional, and confident.

■ Color can highlight specific elements within an ad but should be carefully built into the ad. Occasionally, an advertiser will use spot color for a product in an otherwise black-and-white ad. Any color needs to be an intregal part of the ad and not an afterthought. We'll discuss the technique of color production in Chapter 18 and packaging in Chapter 21.

A classic example of a product using color to differentiate itself was Nuprin analgesic tablets. It increased its share of the ibuprofen market by using a superficial product difference—the yellow tablet. Nuprin's ads that simply said research showed two Nuprins gave more headache relief than Extra Strength Tylenol did not advance its share. Grey Advertising's Herb Lieberman said, "You have to convince consumers that your product is different before they will believe the product is better." The color idea happened when their group creative director emptied a whole bunch of pain relievers on his desk and found Nuprin was the only yellow tablet there. Color was a way to dramatically and graphically show that Nuprin was different. Thus, the yellow-tablet campaign was born, showing a black-and-white photo of hands holding two yellow tablets. More recently, AstraZeneca's Nexium, a prescription pill that stops the stomach's acid producing mechanism, is known as the "little purple pill." Ads showed the purple pill and the copy said, "Get a free trial certificate and ask your doctor about the Purple Pill called NEXIUM." The ads sold $2.8 billion of the little purple things in 2002.

Color can be extremely important in everything from ad layouts, products, and packaging to the psychological messages consumers perceive. Starch Advertisement Readership Service also has consistently found that bold colors and contrast increase an ad's pulling power.

■ In creating for the Web, designers must deal with a smaller color palette than what is available in print. Advertisers are using bright colors to grab attention on the screen that they would never use in print. This use is making brighter hues more acceptable in our daily lives.

Predicting Popular Colors The Pantone Color Institute conducts color research on color psychology, preferences, and professional color applications. Another organization that predicts colors is the Color Association of America, which forecasts color trends for products and fashion. Another group, the Color Marketing Group (CMG), is a not-for-profit association of some 1,500 designers that forecasts trends one to three years in advance for all industries, manufactured products, and services. The Color Association of the United States forecasts are released 20 months in advance. Obviously, these predictions have an impact on advertisers. Usually color trends are evolutionary, but that has changed somewhat since 9/11. The stresses that beset our society are having a direct influence on the direction of the color palette. Leatrice Eiseman of the Pantone Color Institute indicates this continuing quest for harmony means colors should be pleasing and not disturbing. Margaret Walsh, director of the Color Association, sees soft, colorful hues coming to the rescue in an age of high anxiety. And for Color Marketing Group's Melanie Wood, today's consumer wants to feel safe and tranquil in an otherwise crazy world. Colors that refresh and rejuvenate will lead the way with innocent tones of pink and peach giving us a sense of freshness and a promise of tomorrow. Walsh predicts in 2005, with regard to interior/environmental design, "soft, colorful hues come to the rescue with yellowed greens, textured buff and brown earths, soft floral pinks and yellows used in combination with a soft aqua blue, or buff brown, pearl gray or white. The influence of global warming on colors for the home is very much about the red family but receives an unexpected bolt of electric blue, which is so much different from what was seen in the past."[8]

Most brands are so connected to one or two colors that the brand is evoked just by looking at two swatches side by side. Purple and orange? FedEx, of course. What about Home Depot? You get the idea. Would you brand a financial company with a pink and purple color scheme? These colors certainly have their place in communications but in this case probably would not create an image of a solid, savvy investment company.

Color Globalization and Regionalization With the global aspects of today's business and design environment, color is crossing borders and boundaries. Still, strong regional and cultural preferences remain. For example, the bright and sunny colors of tropical areas such as Costa Rica appear out of place and out of context when applied to a setting like New York City, and in Seattle where the weather is primarily gray all winter, people choose brighter colors such as yellow. Many of the same factors affecting the concerns and moods of Americans appear on a global basis, which is unusual. In 2003, indications from those that study global color trends found global turmoil a driving factor in color. People want their homes to be a haven for serenity. The cool, spalike shades of blue and blue-green are currently important. Spiritual purples also continue to be significant, to mention only a few color trends.

White Space Some layout people and designers become so preoccupied with the illustration that they forget that white space, or blank space, is a very significant design tool. The basic rule for using white space is to keep it to the outside of the ad. Too much white space in the middle of an ad can destroy unity by pushing the eye in several directions and confusing the reader. Exhibit 17.8 uses simple illustrations and lots of white space.

Preparing the Layout

The layout is the orderly arrangement of all the copy elements in a print ad. It is basically a blueprint that the production people will follow to complete the finished ad. An ad may go through different levels of roughness as it is developed. These different types of layouts represent different stages of conventional (not electronic) development of the ad.

- *Thumbnail sketches:* miniature drawings trying out different arrangements of the layout elements. The best of these will be selected for the next step.
- *Rough layouts:* drawings that are equivalent to the actual size of the ad. All elements are presented more clearly to simulate the way the ad is to look. The best

EXHIBIT 17.8

Lots of white space frames the illustrations in this ad.

Courtesy of Sawyer Riley Compton and The Ritz-Carlton.

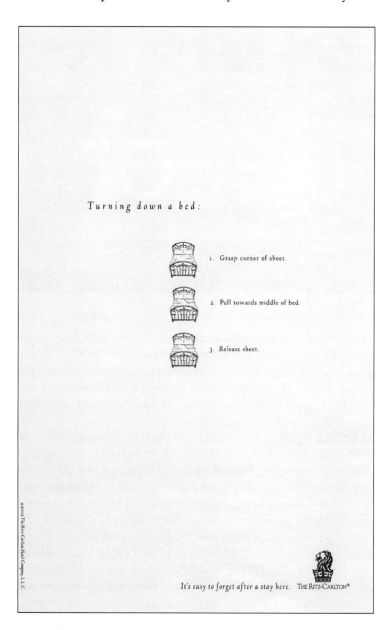

Turning down a bed:

1. Grasp corner of sheet.

2. Pull towards middle of bed.

3. Release sheet.

It's easy to forget after a stay here. THE RITZ-CARLTON®

of these will be chosen for the next step. Usually, a computer rough and a computer comprehensive will look very close to the finished piece (if there aren't any changes). You probably couldn't tell which was finished first. However, many times the rough is used for discussions and then any graphic or text changes are made.

■ *The **comprehensive**, or mechanical, layout (often just called the comp or the mechanical):* all the type set and placed exactly as it is to appear in the printed ad. Illustration are drawn or scanned into position. Most comps are computer comps but could be illustrated. Computer comps look very much like finished ads and are used for client approval.

The comprehensive layout in Exhibit 17.9 is computer generated (all elements were created on the computer). Exhibit 17.10 is the produced color piece. As you can see, they are different. Broyhill's advertising people made changes to the comp layout in an effort to make the piece better meet their objectives. It isn't unusual for a layout to be tweaked or changed.

Once the basic ad for a campaign has been approved, layouts for subsequent ads usually consist of just a rough and finished layout.

comprehensive
A layout accurate in size, color, scheme, and other necessary details to show how a final ad will look. For presentation only, never for reproduction.

EXHIBIT 17.9

An example of a computer comprehensive layout.

Courtesy of Broyhill Furniture Industries.

Computer Design

Today most agency ad layouts are created in-house on their own computers. However, there are independent graphic houses or freelance artists who may have a particular expertise in developing layouts from their computers. Both Exhibits 17.9 and 17.10 were created by Broyhill's in-house agency.

You know all about being able to do layouts and design on computers. However, let's be sure we're on the same page of information. We define *computer graphics* as the ability to draw or display visual information on a video terminal. Raster scan graphics is the most common computer display. Each spot on the screen, called a **pixel,** represents a location in the computer's memory. The number of individual pixels will determine the resolution of the image—this is the difference between poor-quality computer-set type or visuals and good reproduction-quality images. The more pixels, the higher the resolution and the smoother the image. The resolution of a screen controls its clarity and sharpness.

In the past, the creation and production processes have been separate and distinct. Because of today's computer hardware and software, it is possible for one per-

pixel
The smallest element of a computer image that can be separately addressed. It is an individual picture element.

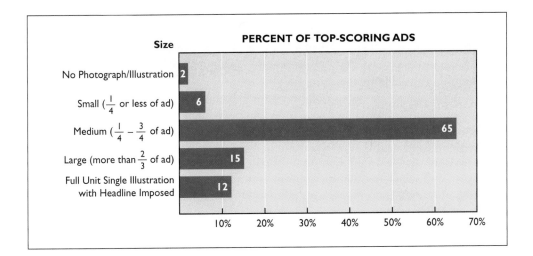

Size

PERCENT OF TOP-SCORING ADS

No Photograph/Illustration — 2

Small ($\frac{1}{4}$ or less of ad) — 6

Medium ($\frac{1}{4} - \frac{3}{4}$ of ad) — 65

Large (more than $\frac{2}{3}$ of ad) — 15

Full Unit Single Illustration with Headline Imposed — 12

10% 20% 30% 40% 50% 60% 70%

EXHIBIT 17.11

The majority of top-scoring ads contain a photograph or illustration.

son to do both layout and production, although software expertise may continue to keep these functions specialized. Today, mastery of layout demands a knowledge of art, type, design, and also photography, computers, and electronic imaging.

The Visual

Research indicates that 98 percent of the top-scoring ads contain a photograph or illustration, proving that human beings are highly visual creatures, according to Cahners Advertising Performance Studies. In most ads, the photograph or illustration takes between 25 and 67 percent of the layout space (see Exhibit 17.11).[9]

Art Directing and Photography

Art directing and photography are twin disciplines—each, in theory, raises the other up a notch. Having a great photo in the wrong layout makes for bad advertising. Betsy Zimmerman, art director at Goodby, Silverstein & Partners, says, "The layout's gotta come first. It might look great as a photo, but once you put it in its environment, it is totally different." Jeff Weiss, creative director, says every ad contains two things: what you want to say and how you want to say it. What art directing can do is deliver things emotionally, not intellectually. Great art direction takes the selling idea and furthers it without you even knowing it. Take Saks, for example. Its ads cannot just say that Saks is glamorous in words—they have to feel glamorous and sophisticated.[10]

Photography can be very expensive. A photo for use in an ad may cost between $700 and $10,000, depending on the photographer's reputation and the advertiser's willingness to pay. It costs money to go on location to take photos (see Exhibit 17.12).

The Artist's Medium

The tool or material used to render an illustration is called the artist's medium, the term *medium* being used in a different sense than it is in the phrase *advertising medium* (for example, television or magazines). The most popular artist's medium in advertising is photography. Britain's award-winning art director Neil Godfrey says, "I like to use something people can believe in. I rarely use illustration. Nine-tenths of the time, it just doesn't have the impact of photography." Tom Lichtenheld adds, "Even though people are savvy to retouching, they still believe that photographs don't lie." But sometimes there is the cost factor, "Photography, to be any good these days, costs the earth," says writer Malcolm Pryce, "but you can get brilliant illustration comparatively cheaply."[11] The food photo shoot in Exhibit 17.13 took over 8 hours to photograph three shots. Other popular tools are pen and ink,

EXHIBIT 17.12

Shooting photographs on location can be expensive.

Courtesy of SLRS Advertising, Inc.

pencil, and crayon. Perhaps a photograph will be used as the main illustration for an ad, but pen and ink will be used for the smaller, secondary illustration. The choice of the artist's medium depends on the effect desired, the paper on which the ad is to be printed, the printing process to be used, and, most important, the availability of an artist who is effective in the desired medium. Pepper/Seven Up, Inc. ran an ad promoting several of its diet brands, "Cut Calories, Not Choices," which used four illustrations of happy females drinking Diet 7 Up, Diet A&W, Diet Sunkist, and Diet Canada Dry. They chose art over photography.

Trade Practice in Buying Commercial Art

Creating an ad usually requires two types of artistic talent: the imaginative person, who thinks up the visual idea with a copywriter or alone and makes the master layout, and an artist, who does the finished art of the illustrations. Large agencies have staff art directors and layout people to visualize and create original layouts, as well as studios and artists to handle routine work.

In the largest advertising centers, a host of freelance artists and photographers specialize in certain fields for preparing the final art. In fact, agencies in some cities go to one of the major art centers to buy their graphic artwork for special assignments.

There are two important points to observe in buying artwork, especially photographs. First, you must have written permission or a legal release (see Exhibit 17.15) from anyone whose picture you will use, whether you took the picture or got it from a publication or an art file. (In the case of a child's picture, you must obtain a release from the parent or guardian.) Second, you should arrange all terms in

advance. A photographer may take a number of pictures, from which you select one. What will be the price if you wish to use more than one shot? What will be the price if you use the picture in several publications?

Freelance artists' and photographers' charges vary greatly, depending on their reputation, the nature of the work, in what medium the work is being used, and whether the ad is to run locally, regionally, or nationally. An art illustration for a magazine may cost $200 if by an unknown artist and up to about $5,000 if by an established artist. A photography session may cost $200 a day for an unknown photographer to about $2,500 for an established photographer. People charge what they think the art or photography is worth or what the client can or is willing to pay. As a result, the better the reputation of the artist or photographer, the more expensive the final product will likely be.

Other Sources of Art and Photography

Clients will not always be able to afford the money or time for original advertising art or photography. There are three basic sources of ready-made images: clip art, computer clip art, and stock photos.

Royalty-Free Stock Illustrations These illustrations are available from a multitude of services. The art may be available on CD-ROM (or on the Web), in which case the illustrations are ready to use. All you have to do is download to your computer. Almost any kind of image is available: families, men, women, children, business scenes, locations (e.g., farm, beach), and special events. The disadvantage to using these illustrations is that you have to match your idea to

EXHIBIT 17.14

Food ad in final form.

Courtesy of Bevil Advertising.

available images, and many of the illustrations are rather average. The advantages are the very reasonable costs and extensive choice of images. Some art services offer a monthly computer disk (or online service) with a wide variety of images; others offer specialized volumes—restaurant art, supermarket art, or medical art, for example. Once you purchase the service, the art is yours to use as you see fit.

EXHIBIT 17.15

Typical Model Release Used by Agencies

SLRS Advertising   MODEL/PERFORMANCE RELEASE

For value received and without further consideration, I HEREBY CONSENT that all pictures/photographs taken of me and/or recording made of my voice or musical or video performances, may be used for advertising purposes, by SLRS Advertising, Inc., and by advertisers SLRS Advertising, Inc., may authorize or represent, in any manner. I understand that illustrations/performances may be edited, changed or reproduced in any manner without by approval. I agree that all reproductiosn thereof andplates, films, and tapes shall remain the property of SLRS Advertising, Inc., or of advertisers represented by SLRS Advertising, Inc.

WITNESS_____   SIGNED_____

SOC. SEC. NO._____

IF SUBJECT IS A MINOR UNDER LAWS OF STATE OF PREFORMANCE

GUARDIAN_____

WITNESS_____   DATE_____

SLRS COMMUNICATIONS, INC./P.O. BOX 5488/ATHENS, GA 30604-5488/(706) 549-2665

Stock Photos There are hundreds of stock-photo libraries available to art directors and advertisers. Each maintains thousands of photographs classified according to the subject categories, including children, animals, lifestyle situations, city landscapes, sports, and models. A photographer submits photos to the stock company, which will publish some photos in its catalog (or on a CD-ROM). The photographer pays for the space occupied by the photos. Clients then browse through the stock company's catalog to research its files for a suitable photo. The art director or advertiser then leases or contracts for use of the selected photo to feature in an ad. The fee is based on the intended use of the photo. Some of these are royalty free.

More than 80 percent of graphic design professionals use stock imagery in their work when the situation calls for it. Graphic Design:USA found a number of reasons for deciding to use stock images. They include:[12]

- *time pressure:* deadlines and fast turnarounds
- *budget restraints:* stock is less expensive than assignment photography offering clients cost savings
- *quality, choice, variety:* stock collections have grown in quality, sophistication, and quantity
- *ease of accessibility:* lots of resources, royalty-free options, digital delivery, and e-commerce sites for easy access

SuperStock has a number of different product lines for art directors. Recently its catalog included five royalty-free disc volumes, which contained over 50,000 single images with thousands of exclusives. Also it has a royalty-free CD store on its e-commerce Web site with over 400 CD titles from a number of vendors. Another company, Comstock's online access service, which is a computer bulletin board, lets you access and preview images from one of its catalogs. It adds new images daily. Comstock says, "Stock photo pricing isn't based on the known cost of producing the photo: It's based on exactly how you will use it. The more modest your project, the less an image will cost." Its online service offers, "Your selection, hand picked from our library of more than 5 million images, will be fully digitized and accessible for you to download and review in 4 hours." The agency can select images and then instantly download low-resolution thumbnail images for inspection. The image may also be marketed and delivered by means of CD-ROM. Images are scanned, stored, digitized, and reproduced on a CD-ROM. It also has a series called Latino Lifestyles. AbleStock offers a one-year membership with unlimited access digital images for about $700. Here are a few of the Web sites:

www.digitalvisiononline.com
www.wonderfile.com
www.imagesource.com
www.photos.com
www.gettyimages.com
www.ablestock.com
www.picturequest.com
www.brandx.com
www.fStopimages.com
www.corbis.com

Other companies offer a whole disc of images—ranging from about 300 to 500 digitized picture files—on a CD-ROM for a single purchase price. The CD/DVD technology offers individual photographers the opportunity to market their images on their own CDs. When a user decides to order an image, the computer will notify the company and negotiate fees.

 **SUMMARY**

We have now made the transition from thinking of ideas to making ads. We have started with the primary consumer benefit, the most important thing we can say about the product.

In advertising, the total concept is a fresh way of looking at something. A concept is an idea. A big idea is one that expresses the message clearly and combines words and visuals. Another way of looking at it is that a basic idea is an abstract answer to a perceived desire or need.

The creative team consisting of an art director and a copywriter next develops the best approach to presenting the executional idea—a rendering in words, symbols, sounds, shapes, and so forth of an abstract answer to a perceived desire or need. Then comes layout preparation (usually done by an art director), in which the various elements of the ad are composed into a unified whole. Creating an ad that will attract attention is one of the art director's primary concerns. When arranging the elements of an ad, the layout artist has to consider the principles of design: unity, harmony, sequence, emphasis, contrast, and balance.

Ads usually begin as thumbnail sketches. Subsequent steps are rough layout, the finished layout, and the comps. The computer simplifies this process: In computer design, the roughs are no longer rough, and the comprehensives are better because the layout and typography are exact.

In most cases, art and photography are original executions of the art director's ideas, illustrated or shot according to his or her specifications by freelance artists or photographers. When time or money is short, clip-art or computer-art services or stock photography may be used.

REVIEW

1. What is the big idea?

2. What is the executional idea?

3. What do art directors and copywriters do?

4. What are the basic means of attracting attention?

5. What is a comp?

6. What are stock photos?

TAKE IT TO THE WEB

Visit the Coca Cola Web site at **www.coca-cola.com**. How does the Web site attract attention whil maintaining a corporate and professional appeal?

Check out the Clinique Web site (**www.clinique.com**) and compare the links to two different countries, for example, France and the United States. Notice the sites are visually similar while appealing to two very different cultures. Is visual continuity a plus? Why is continuity essential from a creative standpoint?

The Color Marketing Groups (**www.colormarketing.org**) is listed as the Premiere International Association for Color and Design Specialists. Check out the Web site to learn about the importance of color.

Look up Pantone at **www.pantone.com** to get an idea of how color can be used effectively. What is so important about a perfect match in terms of color?

CHAPTER 18

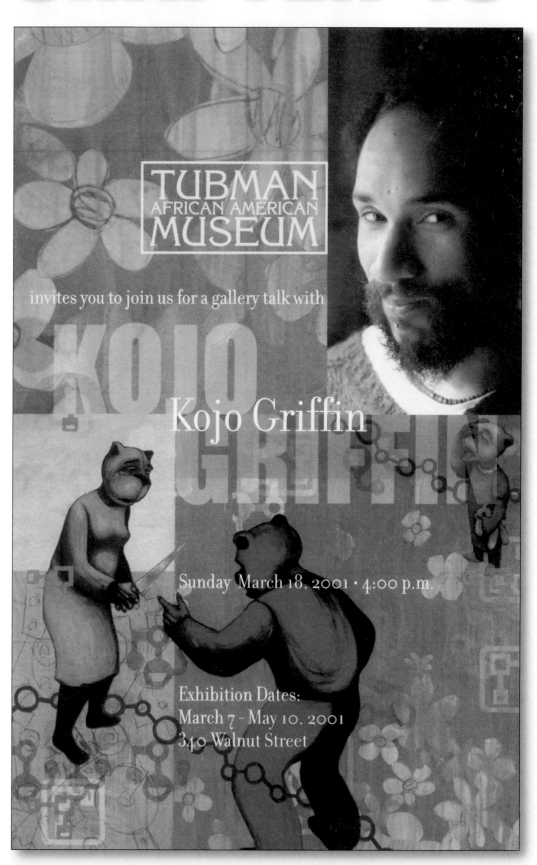

Print Production

O ver the past 10 or 12 years, computer-to-plate (CTP) and direct-to-press digital printing began to alter the print and publishing industries' production. Since then, the majority of printers and publishers have successfully completed the transition from film to digital file exchange. Advertisers were forced to join this journey. After reading this chapter, you will understand:

1. production department
2. digital and traditional production processes
3. mechanicals and artwork
4. proofing

At this point, we've come to the end of the creative process. All of our ideas have been developed and the client has approved everything. Now it is time for the print production people to take these ideas and create a finished ad. It is helpful if every advertising and marketing person involved in the process has a working knowledge of the basics of graphics and production processes because they involve quality, time, and cost factors: What do we need to send to the publication so it can print the piece? What are the preparation steps and printing procedures for the brochure or insert? How long will this take?

This conversion process, going from the original layout to the finished piece, is the responsibility of the advertiser or agency and is called *print production.* Production requirements differ from ad to ad. The staff may be producing magazine or newspaper ads, collateral brochures, or direct-response, outdoor, or transit ads. They need a working knowledge of all these production processes, as well as publication mechanical specifications. The planning process may involve a great deal of money and people. Before we get into the organization, let us look at some important issues.

ADVERTISING AND DIGITAL PRODUCTION

Although most ads are created on a computer, much of the production still involves converting the ad from the computer screen to film for the publication or printer according to specifications. To some extent, the advertising industry controls only a portion of its production efforts. If you have a print ad going into a publication, the publication sets its own specifications standards of how ads are to be produced and presented. Traditional production requires converting all of the ad elements to film and then to plates for printing. Total digital production is converting the computer images directly to plates, bypassing any film. The ad created digitally on your computer may have to be converted to a piece of film so that printing plates can be made. You have to understand the requirements.

The creation of an ad is primarily digital. A printer's or publication's prepress operation is probably a digital process. Once the press has a plate made from either technology, the printing process is generally traditional but changing. However, the actual printing changes are moving at a much slower pace than the prepress changes that we've seen over the past decade.

Technical Considerations

Problems with digital advertising are often attributed to technology issues, and there can be many of these. Not only must the printer be computer proficient, but also the computer artist must be knowledgeable in preparing files so they can output properly. The computer artist must have font and photo files in the proper resolution.

Compatibility File compatibility can also be an issue. The files should be saved in a version common to all parties involved in the process. Today's computer artists, writers, prepress service providers, and publishers work in a variety of computer environments that can lead to file compatibility problems. Often agencies will send a test file to determine whether or not their electronic files can be read correctly. This may avoid unnecessary lost time, frustration, and film costs. Some of the issues: On which types of digital files should the print workflow be based? Who should be responsible for creating these final exchange formats—the agency, a prepress vendor or service bureau, or the printer? And what tools and best practices should be put in place to ensure file integrity and a job's success? Software developers have created many of the sophisticated tools needed to verify digital file integrity regardless of the format.

Industry Standards Although we now have accredited file format standards such as PDF/X–1a and TIFF/IT-P1, industry-wide adoption has been slow. Many believe that the real issues aren't technological but instead are financial. The investment can be huge. Printers continue to accept, and even request, everything from native application files to nonstandard Adobe's PDFs (portable document format) to CT/LWs. CT/LW are RIPped files. Once a CT/LW is generated, depending on the components of your file, it may consist of two files (NLW and CT, or LW and CT) or one file (NLW or LW). All files must be present. All images and fonts are embedded in the files and do not need to accompany the CT/LW.

Some printers and publishers prefer their clients supply (digital) files that have been verified (RIP'd) for completeness and integrity before submission. Others prefer clients submit native application files, enabling the printer to control creation of the final RIP'd files and, of course, to pass processing costs on to the advertiser. It is the production director's job to understand what form or format(s) must be submitted.

Preflighting The term *preflight* has been adopted by the graphics arts community to generically refer to file verification at any stage in the print or multimedia work flow. The term was borrowed from the checklist procedures airplane pilots use before taking off. In print production it is used to make sure digital files will image correctly. But in today's digital work flow, it's common knowledge that the process of controlling digital content file quality occurs at various stages in the production chain. Some production people split the definition of file verification. They define preflighting as the process that happens at the creative stage during document creation in a native application file. This process thoroughly analyzes a design or electronic mechanical for output readiness, regardless of the intended output device. It is a way to discover incomplete or missing digital files or fonts.

Postflighting is defined as the verification that takes place at the prepress phase, when the final file format is created and used to drive digital contract proofing, platesetting, or digital printing. So just because you produce an ad or collateral material using accepted software, the process of verification of those images is still complex.

On any given job, agency production managers have to check who is responsible for preflighting, the prepress service provider/printer or the agency.

Color Calibration This is another issue of concern to everyone in the process. All monitors, proofing devices, and printers must be calibrated so that images and hard copy look the same no matter where the files are viewed. Otherwise, a client may output a digital proof on the other side of the country that doesn't match what the prepress or printer is producing.

Bidding When the advertiser or agency is producing collateral material, it must find a printer that can efficiently produce the job at a reasonable price. There are online services, such as printbid.com, that assist in getting the best cost. It should be remembered that not every printer can efficiently produce every job—or at the same quality. It becomes the production manager's job to ensure that the "right" printer is chosen. Usually, the advertiser or agency requests three bids from comparable printers.

PREPRESS PROCESS

What has to be done to the layout design before it can be printed involves the preparation for the act of printing. Here we outline the major steps for the traditional and digital methods. This Broyhill page is actually a comp used for discussion of concept, copy, layout, and illustration in Broyhill's in-house agency (see Exhibit 18.1). Then come executions and production.

Traditional:	Ad concept: copy, layout, and approvals
	Typesetting
	Electronic color separations
	Layout
	Film preparation
	Platemaking
	Printing
Digital:	Ad concept: copy, layout, and approvals
	Scanning
	Layout
	Proofing
	Preflight
	Proofing
	Film preparation (if not CTP)
	Platemaking
	Printing

Change to Digital

Here are a few of the changes that digital production has made to the production process:

Comprehensives, or Comps In the initial stages, a comp is created digitally by an art director or designer. Today there are very few "loose" comps (hand or marker

DISCOVERED
at an antique fair?
OR IN YOUR DREAMS

ATTIC HEIRLOOMS
Broyhill

drawn). The comp presented to the client appears to be finished. Costs for type, cellos, paper, and studio labor have all been eliminated, leaving only color-output charges for presentation comps.

Type Typography, photostats, and mechanicals rarely exist. These are subsumed in the digital studio under the heading of electronic type/mechanical. The material costs for typesetting, film, stats, mechanical boards, and studio labor have basically vanished.

Artwork The turnaround time for production has significantly decreased because of the digital process. For example, to produce a rush newspaper ad, once the idea is created, the agency sets it in the desktop (several hours), pulls stock photos off the Internet (several hours), and then digitally transmits the execution to six daily newspapers (one hour). The total cost of materials to the client is the stock-photo charge plus digital transmission: $550 to $1,200. The material costs are a fraction of what they were 10 years ago, and the turnaround time is slashed from days to hours.

Publication Material Photoengraving charges have been replaced by separation and composition, and the average turnaround time has been reduced from eight to one or two working days for the first submission. In addition, the average cost for separations and composition has been cut in half. The cost reductions are due to the advances in desktop publishing and telecommunications, which allow agencies to produce work more efficiently at a fraction of the cost.[1]

PRINT PRODUCTION

The agency's print production group performs the transformation process from the original creative concept to the client's printed communication. This may include magazines, newspapers, outdoor and transit, point-of-purchase, collateral brochures (see Exhibit 18.2), and direct response. This group must have a working knowledge of all these production processes, as well as publication mechanical specifications, budgetary considerations, and quality requirements. Last but not least, they must understand the time span available for the execution. All of these factors may be interrelated in a complicated manner.

Print production people are not merely technical people who are knowledgeable. They are also graphic arts consultants, production planners, and production liaison

EXHIBIT 18.2

The State of Georgia created a number of collateral pieces for its Higher Education 529 Savings Plan. This piece had 12 pages plus a fold for inserting smaller brochures, folders, and other printed information.

Courtesy of Georgia Higher Education Savings Plan.

people. They function both internally, with the creative, traffic, media, and account management areas, and externally, with graphic arts vendors and the print media.

The size of a print production group is related to the billing size of the agency. A very small agency may employ a single print production expert. In a very large agency, the print production staff, headed by a print production manager, may consist of a considerable number of people with very specialized expertise.

The print operations area encompasses the following:

- Illustration buyers are versed in various forms of photographic and illustrative techniques. They know the available talent and make all contracts with photographers, illustrators, digital artists, and others in coordination with art directors (see Exhibit 18.3).

- Typography experts are trained in the creative as well as technical aspects of typography. They select and specify type, working with the art directors. Of course, in some agencies the art director may create the final type on his or her computer. Or the type director may send the disk to a supplier for final output.

- Print producers coordinate all print production activities with the traffic, account management, and creative groups.

- Printing buyers specialize in the production planning and buying of outdoor and transit advertising, newspaper and magazine inserts, as well as collateral printed material from brochures to elaborately die-cut direct-mail pieces. A printing buyer's knowledge reaches into properties of paper and ink and into the capabilities of printing, binding, and finishing equipment.

In addition to those functions already mentioned, a large production department may include estimators and proofreaders. Generally, clients require an agency to submit a production budget on work to be done. As a rule, a total yearly campaign production budget is estimated to give the client an understanding of approximately how much ads and/or collateral will cost to produce. Clients must sign off on each project's production cost in advance of the work being prepared. It is important for the production department to supply accurate production cost estimates.

EXHIBIT 18.3

Buying the right photos or finding the right photographer is an important part of the creative process.

Courtesy of Sawyer Riley Compton and Callaway Gardens.

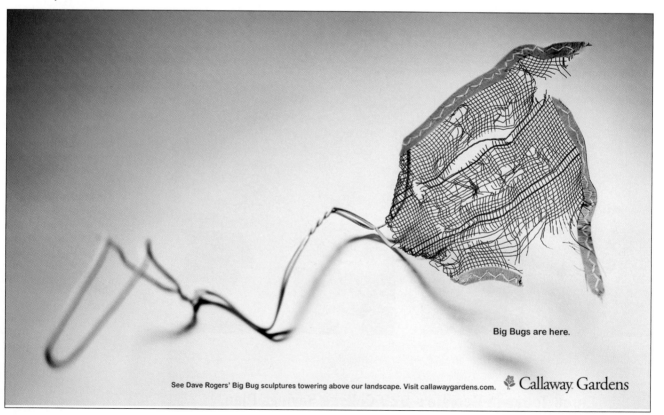

Big Bugs are here.

See Dave Rogers' Big Bug sculptures towering above our landscape. Visit callawaygardens.com.   🌹 Callaway Gardens

KLEPPNER VIEWPOINT 18.1

ALANA STEPHENSON

Print Production, *Luckie & Company*

Where Account Services is the liaison between client and agency, Print Production is the liaison between vendor and agency.

One of the hardest parts about production is meeting deadlines. Clients don't always understand the time it takes to turn around a quality piece. When I get approval to go ahead with a piece, the printer has to order paper from a paper mill. Then they have to print the piece, and then pieces are shipped to a mailhouse and customer data are lasered on. When customer data have been lasered, I receive samples to review and for client review for approval, and then the pieces are inserted and mailed. The time varies based on not only our demands, such as quantities and paper restraints, but also on the printer's schedule. If other jobs beat you to the printer, that could hold up your job.

Doing direct-mail pieces means having returned mail to deal with as well. We run our data through many checks by the post office, such as NCOA, and have data cleaning services to ensure accurate addresses, but there are still the occasional returned mail pieces. Most of our mailings come from addresses in our customer databases but if there are purchased lists, there are always returned pieces. It's very difficult to find an accurate list to purchase. ■ ■ ■

Alana Stephenson

The production department works closely with the traffic department, which sets and monitors schedules of the operation from creative through final production.

PRODUCTION DATA

Production people need to be well versed in the technical aspects of art and type processes, printing methods, and duplicate plates, which we discuss later in the chapter. Let us look first at sources of information for print media. The production person will usually reach for the Standard Rate and Data Service (SRDS) production source—SRDS Print Media Production Data—that carries essential production information for major national and regional publications. The SRDS publications for other media (e.g., newspapers, consumer, business) carry closing dates and basic mechanical production requirements but not in as complete detail as Print Media Production Data. Production people must directly contact publications that are not included in the SRDS publications to obtain their production requirements. Of course, each publication determines its own advertising due dates and mechanical specifications based on printing requirements. Exhibit 18.4 shows some of the digital ad specifications for a typical publication.

2005 MAGAZINE DIGITAL ADVERTISING SPECIFICATIONS

Desktop File Format
Quark XPress saved as Postscript (print to disk). Instructions for creating these files consistent with vendor specifications can be obtained from our production department or online.

High-End File Format
TIFF/IT-P1 (CT, LW/NLW, and/or HC and FP files required for each page; do not rename TIFF/IT/P1 files once they are created). CT Resolution 254 dpi (RES 10) or 304.8 dpi (RES 12). LW Resolution 2400 dpi. Supply one composite CT/LW, NLW per page. No offsets applied. Black text should be merged with LW/NLW file.

Media
- 100 or 250 MB Zip Disk
- ISO9660 CD-ROM
- Macintosh or Scitex formatted 5.25" 650 MB or 1.2 GB Optical Disks, (512 Bytes/sector). For Scitex disks, format must be RMX or UFS 2.0. Use native or extended handshake only.

Media Label Requirements
- Publication Name, Issue and Date
- Agency Name and Phone Number
- Contact Person and Phone Number
- Advertiser
- Vendor Name
- File Name/Number
- Print window of the directories on media

Electronic Transfer
Internet/FTP, WAM!NET, WAM!GATE, and Modem (e-mail not acceptable for transfer of ads). Instructions for electronic transfer are available from our production department.

Document Construction
- Build pages to trim and extend bleed 1/8" beyond page edge.
- All high-resolution images, artwork, and fonts must be included when the postscript file is written.
- Use only Type 1 fonts. Use stylized fonts only; DO NOT apply style attributes to fonts.
- All colors must be CMYK unless color will be printing as a spot color. Total area density should not exceed 300%. No RGB images allowed.
- DO NOT nest EPS files within other EPS files.
- All elements must be placed at 100% size. DO NOT rotate or crop images within Quark. This must be done in original application, (i.e., Illustrator, Photoshop, etc.) prior to placing.
- Place 6mm 5%, 25%, 50%, 75%, 100% CMYK patch strip on left side of document plate.
- Registration offset must be set to 30 pts.
- Bleed must be set to 0.125".
- Required trapping must be included in file.

Proofs
All off-press proofs must include a SWOP (Specifications for Web Offset Publications) approved color bar to be considered acceptable SWOP proofs. Proofs made using digital proofing systems should use a digital control bar having similar content to the hard-dot film control bar. Type of proof/manufacturer must be identified on proof.

This color control bar should have the following characteristics: Screened areas with rulings of 133 lines per inch with tint values of 25%, 50%, and 75% of each of the primary colors in physical proximity to a solid patch.

Two-color overprints of the same 25%, 50%, 75% and solids are also recommended. Additional areas, such as 1%, 2%, 3%, 5%, and 95%, 97%, 98%, 99%, may be useful, especially for digital output. A gray balance bar must be included on the proof, designed to match the neutral appearance and weight of black tints of three different values, under standard viewing conditions.

The three-color gray balance portion of the color bar should have the values below:

Black	Cyan	Magenta	Yellow
75%	75%	63%	63%
50%	50%	40%	40%
25%	25%	16%	16%

This color bar could take the form of a manufacturer's color control guide, a GCA/GATF Proof Comparator or a GATF/SWOP Proofing Bar or their digital equivalents. An exposure control element may also be included where appropriate.

A Digital Proofing Control Bar, provided by the manufacturer, obtained from SWOP, Inc. or created in-house, must be included on all proofs, in order for them to be considered acceptable SWOP proofs. This bar should contain all the elements as described above. Gray balance should appear neutral and similar to that of a SWOP press proof and the substrate should appear similar in hue and brightness to Textweb Proofing Paper.

Digital color bars should meet all requirements for color bars continued herein.

Supply a digital proof calibrated to SWOP specifications that represents the final digital file at 100%.

The following proofs are acceptable:
- Kodak Approval Digital Color
- Polaroid Pola-Proof
- Screen TrueRite
- Optronics Intelliproof
- Matchprint

Required SWOP color bars available as a free download at www.swop.org/downloads.html.

Note: If proper proof is not supplied, Publisher cannot be held responsible for faithful match and a Kodak Approval will be pulled at advertiser's expense of $100.

EXHIBIT 18.4

Mechanical Digital Requirements

PRODUCTION PLANNING AND SCHEDULING

To ensure that the creative and production work moves along with the necessary precision, a time schedule is planned at the outset. The closing date is the date or time when all material must arrive at the publication. Once this is known, the advertiser works backward along the calendar to determine when work must begin to meet the date.

Now that we better understand the production environment, let us take a look at the key considerations in a number of production steps.

Digital Studios

Before desktop computers became the staple for creating ads or promotional printed materials, most art directors had only to design, create accurate mechanicals, and specify color breaks or other information on paper tissues. The production managers were responsible for the remaining production steps and procedures. Today, many art directors and/or studio designers working on their computers perform many production steps.

Some agencies call their computer area an image studio or digital imaging studio, where art directors work on computers to develop the visuals and layout. In some agencies (especially in small- or medium-sized shops) art directors take on part of the production. They can design, typeset, do layouts, create tints, scan, separate, produce final film, and in some cases transmit the job directly to the press or service bureau. In general, many production jobs will require the services of outside vendors or service providers. Many agencies rely on outside services for image-setting, high-resolution scanning, and printing. Then there are electronic prepress shops that offer imagesetting verification for computer-generated files. If asked to do so, they will use their expertise in taking care of trapping and other operations necessary to prepare the files for film output. Suppliers can be found for almost every stage of the prepress operation.

Computer to Plate

As the printing industry moves from film to CTP (computer to plate), it means the production specifications are also changing. There has been a growing use of computer-to-plate printing, which eliminates the film traditionally required to make plates for the press. Now it is typical for the agency to give high-resolution PDF files to the printer. It may mean JPEGs can be used. But it should be remembered that the advertiser or agency doesn't control the specifications for publication. If it is an ad for a magazine, the magazine controls how the publication will be printed—digital or traditional or a mix. However, digital design is controlled by the agency. If the agency is producing collateral material (brochures, inserts, etc.), the agency controls more of the process. The agency selects the printers and can use those that match its production preferences.

Producing plates directly from computer files rather than film has its advantages. It may provide better registration and a crisper dot, which result in a sharper image on press. The digital work flow cuts both design and printing schedules.

Another advantage of computer-to-plate technology is the proofing and approval process. In traditional printing, if a problem was detected on the job, it could take as long as 16 hours to make corrections, shoot and strip new film, remake plates, and restart the presses. Digital technology allows a printer to pull the plate, correct the digital files, prepare a new plate, and mount the plate in approximately 30 minutes. Now let's look at the printing options.

SELECTING THE PRINTING PROCESS

In most cases, the printing process used depends on the medium in which the ad is running, not on the advertiser or the agency. However, in some areas, such as sales promotion, ad inserts, direct mail, and point-of-sale, the advertiser must make the final decision regarding print production. To deal effectively with printers, the advertiser must have some knowledge of the basic production techniques and which one is the most appropriate for the job at hand.

If the printing process is not predetermined, the first step in production is to decide which process is most suitable. There are three major printing processes:

- Letterpress printing (from a raised surface)
- Offset lithography (from a flat surface)
- Rotogravure (from an etched surface)

Each of these printing processes has certain advantages and disadvantages, and one process may be more efficient than another for a particular job. Once the printing process has been established, the production process has been dictated, for all production work depends on the type of printing used.

As we have indicated, the prepress operation is in transition from traditional to digital operations. Once the ad, collateral advertising, or promotion has been created and converted to a printing plate, the printing process is very similar to what it has been for many decades. The presses are more efficient now than ever before, but the printing concept is not new.

Letterpress Printing

Letterpress printing isn't as popular as it once was in printing publications; however, advertisers have many uses for this printing process, and you should know the basics. In its simplest form, think of the concept of **letterpress** as follows: If you have ever used a rubber ink stamp (with name, address, etc.), you've applied the principle of letterpress printing. You press the rubber stamp against an ink pad. Then, as you press the stamp against paper, the ink is transferred from the stamp to the paper, and the message is reproduced.

In letterpress printing, the area to be printed is raised and inked. The inked plate is pressed against the paper and the result is a printed impression (see Exhibit 18.5).

Your artwork, photographs, type, and so forth must be converted to a photoengraving (a process of making the plate a raised surface) before printing can occur. The advertiser or agency must supply the photoengraving or duplicates of such plates to the newspaper, magazine, or letterpress printer. In general, this process doesn't reproduce photos as well as offset or gravure. Each of the printing processes has advantages and disadvantages that the advertising person needs to learn over time. There are several types of letterpress presses. The "job press" platen can print many forms, but it can also die cut (cut shapes in paper), emboss (raise images on paper), perforate, and score (which creases so thicker paper can be folded).

letterpress
Printing from a relief, or raised, surface. The raised surface is linked and comes in direct contact with the paper, like a rubber stamp.

EXHIBIT 18.5

Letterpress Printing

The letterpress printing process involves a plate with a raised surface.

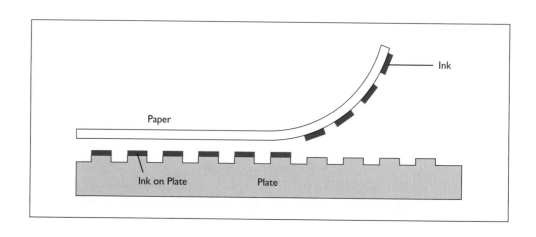

Offset Lithography

In its basic description, **offset lithography** is a photochemical process based on the principle that grease and water will not mix. In theory, offset can print anything that can be photographed. In reality, although there are some things that will not print very well by offset, it is the preferred process for most jobs, accounting for 80 to 90 percent of all printing jobs.

Offset lithography is a planographic (flat-surface) process using a thin, flat aluminum plate that is wrapped around a cylinder on a rotary press. The plate is coated with a continuous flow of liquid solution from dampening rollers that repel ink. The inked plate comes in contact with a rubber blanket on another cylinder. The inked impression goes from the plate to the rubber blanket. The inked blanket then transfers or offsets the inked image to the paper, which is on a delivery cylinder. The plate does not come in direct contact with the paper (see Exhibit 18.6).

Because offset is a photographic process, it is very efficient and is the most popular printing process in this country. It is used to reproduce books (including this text), catalogs, periodicals, direct-mail pieces, outdoor and transit posters, point-of-sale, and most newspapers.

Advertisers or their agencies must supply the artwork and electronic mechanicals or films from which offset plates can be made.

offset lithography
Lithography is a printing process by which originally an image was formed on special stone by a greasy material, the design then being transferred to the printing paper. Today the more frequently used process is offset lithography, in which a thin and flexible metal sheet replaces the stone. In this process the design is "offset" from the metal sheet to a rubber blanket, which then transfers the image to the printing paper.

Rotogravure

The image in **rotogravure** printing is etched below the surface of the copper printing plate—the direct opposite from letterpress printing—creating tiny ink wells (tiny depressed printing areas made by means of a screen). The gravure plate is inked on the press and wiped so that only the tiny ink wells contain ink. The plate is then pressed against the paper, causing suction that pulls the ink out of the wells and onto the paper (see Exhibit 18.7).

Gravure is used to print all or parts of many publications, including national and local Sunday newspaper supplements, mail-order catalogs, packaging, newspaper inserts, and large run magazines, for example, **National Geographic.** The gravure plate is capable of printing millions of copies very efficiently; however, it is not economical for short-run printing. Rotogravure becomes competitive with offset when printing exceeds 100,000 copies. When printing exceeds a million copies, gravure tends to be more efficient than offset. Rotogravure prints excellent color quality on relatively inexpensive paper, but the preparatory costs are comparatively high, and it is expensive to make major corrections on the press.

rotogravure
The method of printing in which the impression is produced by chemically etched cylinders and run on a rotary press; useful in long runs of pictorial effects.

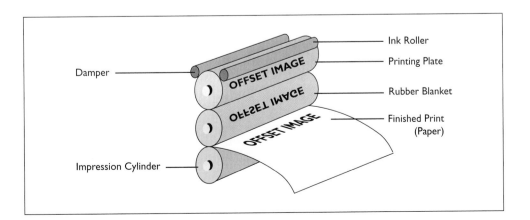

EXHIBIT 18.6

Offset printing press system, showing image coming off plate, onto rubber blanket, and offsetting to paper.

EXHIBIT **18.7**

Rotogravure

In the rotogravure process, ink wells fill with ink.

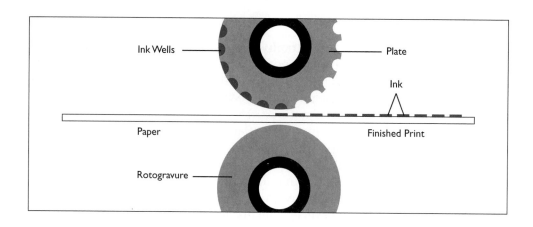

Sheet-Fed Versus Web-Fed Presses

Letterpress, offset, and gravure printing processes can all utilize sheet-fed or web-fed presses.

- Sheet-fed presses feed sheets of paper through the press one at a time. The conventional sheet-fed press prints about 6,000 to 7,000 "sheets" per hour.
- Web-fed presses feed paper from a continuous roll, and the printing is rapid—about 1,000 feet per minute. Most major promotional printing utilizes web-fed presses.

Screen Printing

screen printing
A simple printing process that uses a stencil. It is economical but is limited in reproduction quality.

Another printing process, **screen printing,** which is based on a different principle than letterpress, offset, and rotogravure, is especially good for short runs. This simple process uses a stencil. The stencil of a design (art, type, photograph) can be manually or photographically produced and then placed over a textile (usually silk) or metallic-mesh screen (it actually looks like a window screen). Ink or paint is spread over the stencil and, by means of a squeegee, is pushed through the stencil and screen onto the paper (or other surface), as illustrated in Exhibit 18.8.

Screen printing is economical, especially for work in broad, flat colors, as in car cards, posters, and point-of-sale displays. It can be done on almost any surface: wallpaper, bricks, bottles, T-shirts, and so on. Basically, screen printing is a slow, short-run process (from one copy to 100 or 1,000 or so copies), although sophisticated presses can print about 6,000 impressions per hour and in some cases accommodate billboard-sized applications. This expanding printing process is becoming more useful to advertisers.

EXHIBIT **18.8**

Screen Printing

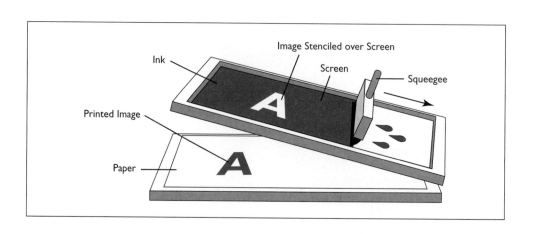

Printers and Agencies Interact

Digital technology is also changing how suppliers and advertisers or agencies interact. The digital environment has changed the way artwork is prepared; now it is changing the way jobs are designed. To speed communication, many computer artists post files on FTP (file transfer protocol) servers, which eliminates any incompatibility between designer-favored Macintoshes and client-favored PCs. Although some FTP servers are Web based, many are part of an intranet or extranet and may not require a Web browser for access. Some production houses have interactive Web sites, which allow the computer artist at the agency to access the job in progress across town or across country. As a virtual job jacket, it serves as a repository for all project-related correspondence and art files. Once everyone is satisfied with the artwork, the printer can use security codes to access and download files with all the specifications needed to print the job.[2]

UNDERSTANDING TYPOGRAPHY

Type has always been an important part of ad design. It creates moods, enhances or retards readability, and gives your communication an image (see Exhibit 18.9). Type inspires passion. Hermann Zapt's favorite typeface is Optima. George Bernard Shaw insisted all his works be set in Caslon.[3] Type is powerful. It is one of the most important design tools. Type creates communication that is friendly and inviting. It keenly focuses attention. It organizes the complex and creates a mood.

It is now more important than ever before for advertising people to understand how to use type because so much of it is being created in-house on the agency or client computer. Before the computer explosion, art directors would use specialists—typesetters or typographers—for type. Most agree that few art directors or designers have as good an understanding of type use as typesetters or typographers. Getting type up on the screen does not mean that it is typeset effectively. We talk about this again after we learn some of the fundamentals.

The art of using type effectively is called **typography.** It entails a number of issues: choosing the typeface and size of type; deciding on the amount of space between letters, words, and lines; determining hyphenation use; and preparing type specifications for all the ad copy. The Howard Merrell & Partners' ad for the Museum of the Mountain Man (see Exhibit 18.10) uses type that reflects the mood of the product. The treatment of the body copy also reflects the mood of the design.

typography
The art of using type effectively.

TYPE AND READING

The objective of text typography is to provide quick and easy communication. Display headlines are supposed to attract the reader's attention and encourage reading of the body copy. Using uppercase typography does not generally accomplish these objectives. Notice the difference in the typefaces in Exhibit 18.11. Which of these would not be good for body copy in a magazine?

This is Baskerville.

This is Century Gothic.

This is Helvetica.

This is Futura Condensed.

This is Gills Sans.

This is Times Text.

EXHIBIT 18.9

Although these examples of different typefaces are in the same size, they don't look the same size.

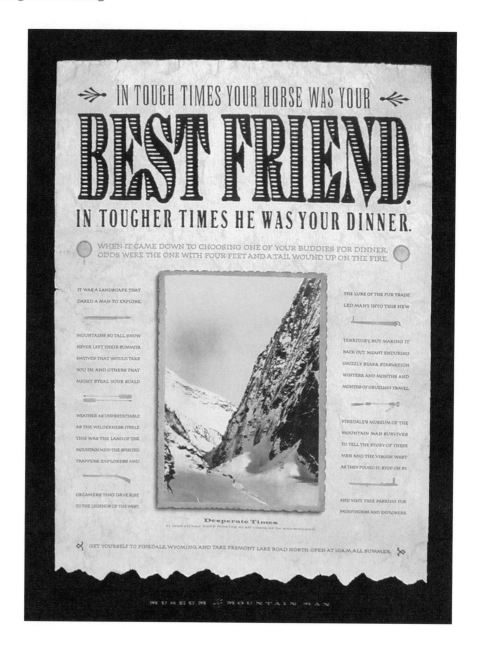

More than 95 percent of text is set in lowercase letters. Research has shown that readers are more comfortable reading lowercase letters than all caps. Studies have also proved that the varying heights of lowercase letters forming words create an outline shape that is stored in the reader's mind, which aids in recalling the words when they are seen. Words comprised of lowercase characters can be read faster than words set in all caps.

The ideal reading process occurs when the eye is able to scan across a line of copy, grasp groups of three or four words at a time, and then jump to another set of words, then another. The separate stops, or fixational pauses, take about one-quarter of a second each. Words in lowercase letters allow this process to take place. On the other hand, words set in all caps force the reader to read individual letters and mentally combine the letters into words, and the words into phrases and sentences. The result is a 10 to 25 percent slowdown in reading speed and comprehension.

There are times when all-cap headlines or subheadlines are, graphically, the right thing to use. Design may take precedence over the "rules of communication," or you may not be able to convince a client or art director that lowercase is a better

Optima DemiBold Advertising

Baskerville Semibold Advertising

Caslon Advertising

Copperplate gothic light Advertising

Gills Sans Advertising

Lucída Handwriting Advertising

Herculanum Advertising

EXHIBIT **18.11**

Examples of different typefaces, each representing a different mood or feeling.

idea. In these instances, words and lines should be held to a minimum. More than four or five words on a line and more than a couple of lines of all caps become difficult to read.[4]

TYPEFACES

The typeface selected for a particular ad is very important. Exhibit 18.12 illustrates the major classifications of type: text, old Roman, modern Roman, square serif, sans serif, and decorative.

TYPE FONTS AND FAMILIES

A type font is all the lowercase and capital characters, numbers, and punctuation marks in one size and face (see Exhibit 18.13). A font may be roman or italic. Roman (with a lowercase *r*) type refers to the upright letter form, as distinguished from the italic form, which is oblique. Roman (capital *R*) denotes a group of serifed typeface styles.

Type family is the name given to two or more series of types that are variants of one design (see Exhibit 18.14). Each one, however, retains the essential characteristics of the basic letter form. The series may include italic, thin, light, semibold, bold, medium, condensed, extended, outline, and so forth. Some type families have only a few of these options, whereas others offer a number of styles. The family of type may provide a harmonious variety of typefaces for use within an ad.

Text   Old English

Old Roman   Garamond

Modern Roman   Century

Square Serif   **Lubalin**

Sans Serif   **Avant Garde**

Decorative   Ransom

EXHIBIT **18.12**

Examples of Families of Type

Arial
abcdefghijklmnopqrstuvwxyz
ABCDEFGHIJKLMNOPQRSTU
1234567890$(&?!%',;)* VWXYZ

Arial Black
abcdefghijklmnopqrstuvwxyz
ABCDEFGHIJKLMNOPQRSTU
1234567890$(&?!%',;)*VWXYZ

Helvetica Thin
Helvetica Light
Helvetica Light Italic
Helvetica
Helvetica Italic
Helvetica Italic Outline
Helvetica Regular Condensed
Helvetica Regular Extended
Helvetica Medium
Helvetica Medium Italic
Helvetica Medium Outline
Helvetica Bold
Helvetica Bold Compact Italic
Helvetica Bold Outline
Helvetica Bold Condensed
Helvetica Bold Condensed Outline
Helvetica Bold Extended
Helvetica Extrabold Condensed
Helvetica Extrabold Condensed Outline
Helvetica Extrabold Ext.
Helvetica Compressed
Helvetica Extra Compressed
Helvetica Ultra Compressed

point (pt)
The unit of measurement of type, about 1/72 inch in depth. Type is specified by its point size, as 8 pt., 12 pt., 24 pt., 48 pt. The unit for measuring thickness of paper, 0.001 inch. Point-of-purchase advertising. Displays prepared by the manufacturer for use where the product is sold.

Measurement of Type

Typographers have unique units of measurement. It is essential to learn the fundamental units of measure if you are going to interact with production people. The point and pica are two units of measure used in print production in all English-speaking countries. Let us take a closer look at these two units of measure.

Point A **point (pt)** is used to measure the size of type (heights of letters). There are 72 points to an inch. It is useful to know that 36-point type is about 1/2 inch high and 18-point type is about 1/4 inch high. Exhibit 18.15 illustrates the major terms

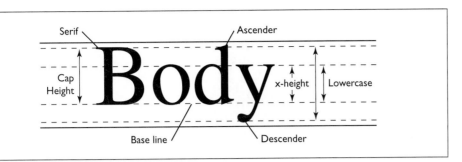

used in discussing the height of type. Type can be set from about 6 points to 120 points. Body copy is generally in the range of 6 to 14 points; most publications use type of 9, 10, or 11 points. Type sizes above 14 points are referred to as display or headline type. However, these ranges are simply labels—in many newspaper ads, the body copy is 18 points or so, and there have been ads in which the headline was in the body-copy size range. Exhibit 18.16 provides a visual perspective on basic type sizes.

Points also are used to measure the height of space between lines, rules, and borders, as well as the height of the type.

Pica A **pica** is a linear unit of measure. A pica equals 12 points of space, and there are 6 picas to an inch. Picas are used to indicate width or depth and length of line.

pica
The unit for measuring width in printing. There are 6 picas to an inch. A page of type 24 picas wide is 4 inches wide.

Em An em is a square of space of the type size and is commonly used for indentation of copy blocks and paragraphs. Traditionally, it is as wide as the height of the capital M in any type font.

Agate Line Most newspapers (and some small magazines) sell advertising space in column inches or by the agate line, a measure of the depth of space. There are 14 agate lines to a column inch, regardless of the width of the column. Newspaper space is referred to by depth (agate lines) and width (number of columns); for "100 × 2," read "one hundred lines deep by two columns wide."

Line Spacing Also called *leading,* line spacing is the vertical space between lines of type and is measured in points from baseline to baseline of type. Lines are said to be set solid when no additional line spacing has been added. Space is added to make type more readable. The rule of thumb is that the extra space should be no more than 20 percent of the type size. Thus, if you are using 10-point type, the maximum extra space between the lines is 2 points, for a 12-point leading.

EXHIBIT **18.16**

A Visual Perspective of Type Sizes

8 point Century Gothic Advertising Production
10 point Century Gothic Advertising Production
14 point Century Gothic Advertising Production
18 point Century Gothic Advertising

36 point Century Goth

48 point Century

Type specifications are usually determined by art directors, print production personnel, or specialized type directors. The following may be involved in the final decision:

■ Type set in lowercase letters is read 13.4 percent faster than type set in all caps.

■ Reverse copy—white or light type on a dark background—is read more slowly than black on white. As a result, you should be extra careful in choosing type size and a readable typeface when a reverse is desired. Exhibit 18.17 shows a number of different reverse copy treatments. For example, the stylized chalk effect under "Value Meals" is white on black; the "Southern Kitchen" is white on blue.

TYPESETTING

Earlier in this chapter we said that almost all typesetting is performed on a desktop computer. The typographer of the future is an art director or designer—maybe even a copywriter—for whom type is more a means than an end.

Guides for Using Type

- Use only original type. Don't assume the prepress service bureau or printer has the exact same font.

- Remember that as a buyer of a type package you only license the usage rights. You have to acquire a multilicense if the font is to be used on more than one computer.

- Computer artists need to keep a running list of both screen fonts and printer fonts (screen fonts are used by the computer for display on the screen; printer fonts are downloaded to the printer for output).

- Talk to your prepress service provider or printer about fonts being used in electronic mechanicals; otherwise, the ad or collateral piece may not look as intended.

- Avoid type smaller than 6 points, especially in serif typefaces (letters having "feet," such as Bodoni). The thin parts of small type characters can disappear when output is of high resolution, making text difficult to read.

- When using reverse type, avoid type that is too small (6 point) or delicate. Sans serif and bold typefaces are better choices. Large blocks of reverse type are difficult to read.

- When possible, convert type to a graphic (vector objects) in EPS files. Common problems for prepress service providers are font substitution or PostScript errors caused by type in imported EPS graphics.

ELECTRONIC MECHANICAL AND ARTWORK

After the copy has been approved and placed in the ad on the desktop system with the rest of the ad's material (e.g., illustrations, logos), the advertiser will approve the electronic comp or rough. After approval, the digital file is sent to prepress.

Art for Prepress Services

Discuss the types of art being used—transparencies (like 35-mm slides, reflective art), line drawings or illustrations, digital photography—with the prepress service or printer. Agency production people need to ask (or check publication mechanical requirements) about what kind of electronic files are preferred. You get the picture—the right files, fonts, and technical requirements are necessary for prepress production to run smoothly. You cannot assume the prepress service, printer, or publication can run your material just because it looks good on your computer.

There are several types of art that production people have to deal with, including line art and halftones in both black and white and color.

Line Art

Any art, type, or image that is made up of a solid color (and has no tonal value) is called *line art*. If you set type on your computer, it is line art (if it is in solid form). Artwork drawn in pen and ink is line art because the ink has no tonal value. Generally, such art is drawn larger than needed for the mechanical so as to minimize the art's imperfections when it is reduced and printed. Exhibit 18.18 contains an example of line art.

Linetint You can give line art some variation in shades by breaking up the solid color with screen tints or benday screens. Exhibit 18.19 uses a screen tint to give the illusion of gray and contrast. This may be done on the computer layout, or the platemaker adds the screens during the film-stripping stage just prior to platemaking.

Line Color Artwork does not need to be in color to produce line plates in two, three, or more flat colors. It can be added or changed on the computer. Remember, each color may require a separate plate. Line color provides a comparatively inexpensive

EXHIBIT **18.18**

This trade ad aimed at carpet retailers uses a pen drawing in black and white, which fits our definition of line art. The type also is considered line art.

Courtesy of SLRS Advertising, Inc.

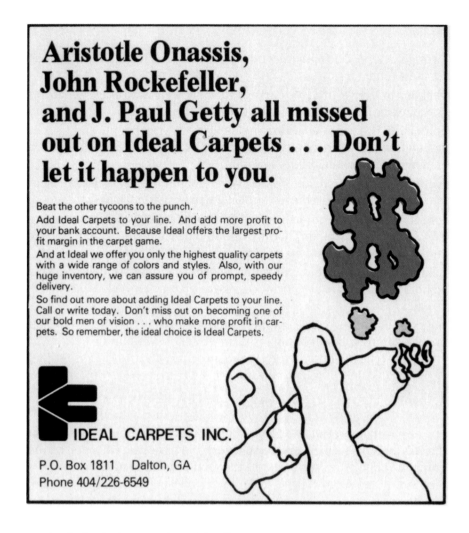

Aristotle Onassis, John Rockefeller, and J. Paul Getty all missed out on Ideal Carpets . . . Don't let it happen to you.

Beat the other tycoons to the punch.
Add Ideal Carpets to your line. And add more profit to your bank account. Because Ideal offers the largest profit margin in the carpet game.
And at Ideal we offer you only the highest quality carpets with a wide range of colors and styles. Also, with our huge inventory, we can assure you of prompt, speedy delivery.
So find out more about adding Ideal Carpets to your line. Call or write today. Don't miss out on becoming one of our bold men of vision . . . who make more profit in carpets. So remember, the ideal choice is Ideal Carpets.

IDEAL CARPETS INC.

P.O. Box 1811   Dalton, GA
Phone 404/226-6549

method of printing in color with effective results. For example, Exhibit 18.18 uses a black plate and another for the spot color green—one for each color.

A solid color (flat or match color) is printed with the actual color. The color is specified with a Pantone Matching System (PMS) color reference number, and the printer mixes an ink that is literally that color. It is like going into a paint store, choosing a color swatch, and having the clerk mix the paint to match your color. The ink is applied to the paper through printing, and the specified color is obtained.

Halftones

At the end of this chapter we discuss some of the new production technology (including stochastic screening), which may eventually change the way photos are reproduced.

EXHIBIT **18.19**

The top words are printed in solid (100%) cyan. The second line is screened at 50 percent cyan. The third line is screened at 20 percent cyan. The ink color is the same, but the screen gives it another shade. The background is at 20 percent black. Creating tints, as shown here, can change the look and feel of a shape, word, or color.

Advertising Production
Advertising Production
Advertising Production

If you look at black-and-white photographs, you will recognize they are different from line art—they have tonal value. Such photos have a range of tonal value between pure blacks and pure whites and are called **continuous-tone** artwork.

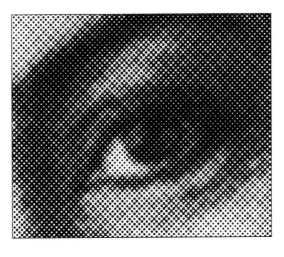

EXHIBIT **18.20**
Enlarged portion of halftone to show dots.

To reproduce the range of tones in continuous-tone art, the art (photo) must be broken up into dots or lines. The art is then called a halftone. Halftones may be reproduced either with a printer's camera (rarely these days) or digitally; either way breaks the image into dots. Remember that black ink is black ink and not shades of gray, so the production process must create an optical illusion by converting the tonal areas to different-size halftone dots on the printed paper that the eye perceives as gray. If you look at the printed halftone gray areas with a magnifying glass, you will see little black dots. Exhibit 18.20 shows a magnification. The more dots per inch, the greater the quality of detail reproduced from the original. The quality of the paper must also increase to accommodate the higher dot levels, which drives up paper costs. Again, you may need to check the printer/publisher's specifications on the number of dots or resolution that is required.

continuous tone
An unscreened photographic picture or image, on paper or film, that contains all gradations of tonal values from white to black.

The Halftone Finish   If you want to make a halftone of a photograph, the computer artist or the platemaker can treat the background in a number of ways; that treatment is called its *finish*. Several techniques that can be applied to halftones include the following:

- *Square halftone.* The halftone's background has been retained.
- *Silhouette.* The background in the photograph has been removed by the photo-platemaker or the computer operator.
- *Surprint.* This is a combination plate made by exposing line and halftone negatives in succession on the same plate.
- *Mortise.* An area of a halftone is cut out to permit the insertion of type or other matter.

Line Conversion   A line conversion transforms a continuous-tone original into a high-contrast image of only black-and-white tones similar to line art. The conversion transfers the image into a pattern of some kind: mezzotint, wavy line, straight line, or concentric circle. Most design software programs offer a number of line conversion choices.

Two-Color Halftone Plates   A two-color reproduction can be made from mono-chrome artwork in two ways. A screen tint in a second color can be printed over (or under) a black halftone. Or the artwork can be photographed twice, changing the screen angle the second time so that the dots of the second color plate fall between those of the first plate. This is called a *duotone*. It produces contrast in both colors of the one-color original halftone.

four-color process
The process for reproducing color illustrations by a set of plates, one that prints all the yellows, another the blues, a third the reds, and the fourth the blacks (sequence variable). The plates are referred to as process plates.

Four-Color Process Printing   Another printing system is needed when the job requires the reproduction of color photos. This system is called a **four-color process.** The four colors are cyan (blue), magenta (red), yellow, and black. (CMYK are the letters used to indicate these colors.) These are the least number of colors that can adequately reproduce the full spectrum of natural colors inherent in photography. The first three—cyan, magenta, and yellow—provide the range of colors; the black provides definition and contrast in the image.

Full-color or process color requires photographic or electronic scanner separation of the color in the photographs (or other continuous-tone copy) into four negatives, one for each of the process colors. This process of preparing plates of the various colors and black is called *color separation* (see Exhibit 18.21). If you examine any of the color ads in this text (or any other publication) with a magnifying glass, you will find the halftone dots in four colors.

Digital Scanners Transforming a photograph into a digital file is done by a device called a *scanner*. There are two basic types: flatbed and drum scanners. You probably have either seen or used a flatbed scanner. These require little training and their quality varies. Printers or agencies use professional scanners that are capable of creating high-quality images. In general, a drum scanner, in which the original photo or image wraps around a drum that rotates next to a light source, is capable of producing very high-quality results. It is the most expensive image-capturing device on the market. These machines digitally scan the photos to be used in ads. They create the dot pattern used in making a halftone by the traditional method. The important thing to remember is that photographs (whether color or black and white) must be broken up into a dot pattern to print.

Color Proofing

Achieving color reproduction that satisfies ad agencies and advertisers is one of the most crucial roles of the magazine production manager. Agencies generally demand to see a proof before the job is printed. In today's electronic color production, traditional proofing systems seem to have taken a back seat to digital color proofers, color printers, networked color copiers, and short-run color production devices.

EXHIBIT 18.21

Four-color process printing involves combining four plates—blue (cyan), red (magenta), yellow, and black—to produce the desired colors and contrasts.

Courtesy of Bevil Advertising.

red, yellow, blue, and black plates

yellow plate

red plate

yellow and red plates

blue plate

blue and yellow plates

blue, red, and yellow plates

black plate

For the most accurate contact proofs—those requiring the best match to jobs printed by conventional offset lithography—nothing beats a film-based laminated, or single-sheet, off-press proof. An off-press proof ensures the separator that color separations have been made according to customer expectations.[5]

Press Proofs

For years, press proofs, or progressives, usually made on special proofing presses, were the standard proofs sent to agencies for checking. Prior to the development of off-press proofs, color separators used press proofs. Making a press proof involved stripping the separations on film, making plates, mounting the plates on a proof press, and printing the desired number of proofs. Press proofs are made with ink on paper—often the same paper that will be used for the job—rather than with a photographic simulation process of off-press systems. Today press proofs are still used by many ad agencies that are willing to pay the steep price for what they believe is the most accurate proof. In theory, press proofs provide a virtually exact representation of the final project.

Progressive Proofs (Progs) These proofs give the advertiser a separate proof for each color (red, yellow, blue, and black), as indicated in Exhibit 18.21, as well as a proof for each color combination (red and yellow, red and blue, blue and yellow)—seven printings in all. After approval by the advertiser and agency, the proofs are sent to the printer to use as guides in duplicating the densities for each color.

Off-Press Proofs

These proofs are made from film negatives generated from the electronic file. The same films will be used to make printing plates. These proofs are less expensive and faster than press proofs, and they are adequate in most cases. Off-press proofs are the typical color proof today. No plate or printing is involved. There are numerous types of off-press (prepress) proofing systems. The most popular are overlay and adhesive proofs.

Overlay Proofs The development of overlay proofing enabled color proofs to be made from film without using a proof press. The overlay proofs consist of four exposed sheets containing the cyan (blue), magenta (red), yellow, and black process colors overlaid on a backing sheet. The four overlays (yellow, red, blue, and black) are then stacked to produce a composite image. Because they use multiple, separate, plastic layers, overlay proofs cannot be expected to accurately predict color on press, but they are still used today for checking color break or general color appearance and position.

Adhesive or Laminate Proof In 1972, DuPont introduced the first off-press proofing system that closely resembled printed images, known as the Cromalin system. Cromalin is a laminated or single-sheet proof, in which four (or more) layers are exposed separately and laminated together to reproduce the image of cyan, magenta, yellow, and black separations. Cromalins use dry pigments to produce images on photosensitive adhesive polymers or pretreated carrier sheets. Cromalin is generally considered the superior adhesive process. The proofs are keyed to SWOP (Specifications for Web Offset Publications)/GAA (Gravure Association of America) guidelines, which set standards for inks, density of tones, reverses, and other technical matters. Among the highest-fidelity four-color proofs are the **MatchPrint** and the Signature proof, both very similar but from different suppliers.

There are digital hard and soft copy systems that eliminate film to produce continuous-tone proofs. The soft proofing systems allow production and design people to call up a digitized color image and evaluate it before separations are made for an intermediate or position proof. The interactive proofing system gives the agency more flexibility with deadlines and saves time and money for clients.

MatchPrint
A high-quality color proof used for approvals prior to printing. Similar to a Signature print.

Types of Proofs The choices of types of proof are numerous. Production managers need to decide how accurate a proof is needed, or to put it another way, how much quality they need to pay for. Obviously, they don't want expensive proofs if they are not needed. Here are a number of proof types:

Proof Type	Color Accuracy	Cost
Black-and-white laser	Prints can show color breaks but no color. 300–600 dpi.	Inexpensive
Bluelines	Proofs made from exposing film to light-sensitive paper. They show only a single-color image. Uses halftone film.	Inexpensive
Velox	Simple black-and white proofs made from film on photographic paper. Uses halftone film.	Moderate
Digital high end	Proofs made from an electronic file. Made by Kodak, 3M, among others. Several processes all meet industry standards. 1800 dpi and higher. Cannot proof actual film.	Moderate
Desktop digital	Usually uses ink jet or thermal wax and gives fairly accurate approximation of color. 300 dpi. Needs color management system to give close approximation of color.	Inexpensive
Laminate/adhesive	Composite proofs are created by exposing the color separations in contact to proofing film and laminating the results. Uses halftone film. Very accurate in color match.	Moderate
Overlay	Made up of layers of acetate attached to a backing substrate. Each overlay film has an image from each separation color. Colors indicate color breaks; not very accurate. Uses halftone film.	Moderate
Press	Proof run on printing press. Uses halftone film. Uses actual printing inks to give most accurate proof.	Expensive

DUPLICATE ADS

How do we get this Ritz-Carlton (see Exhibit 18.22) out of our computer to 10 publications? Ten Zips? Maybe. Most print ads run in more than one publication. Frequently, advertisers have different publications on their schedules, or they need to issue reprints of their ads or send material to dealers for cooperative advertising. There are various means of producing duplicate material of magazine or newspaper ads. The most common means of sending ads to more than one publications is simply sending a digital file to the publication.

OTHER PRODUCTION ADVANCES

The changes in technology over the past decade have changed the prepress and printing processes. Future production managers and art directors will continue to have many new options for handling their projects. These new techniques will

Return flight:
last Wednesday.

For reservations, call 1·800·241·3333 or visit www.ritzcarlton.com   THE RITZ-CARLTON®

EXHIBIT 18.22

This great copy and visual appeared in numerous publications. Sawyer Riley Compton's production people had to send an electronic file to each publication (or as specified by the publication).

Courtesy of Sawyer Riley Compton and The Ritz-Carlton.

range from color separation, color management, proofing, and platemaking to printing. The following techniques are of particular interest.

Stochastic Screening and Color Separations

Stochastic screening, or frequency modulation screening, is a process for producing incredible tone and detail that approximates photographic quality. With conventional screens, the dots are spaced equally on a grid (e.g., 110 or 133 lines per inch) and the tonal value is achieved by increasing or decreasing the size of the dots. On the other hand, stochastic screening has very tiny dots all of the same size, and their numbers vary according to the tonal value. Used by a quality printer, the image appears to be continuous tone or photographic quality and much better than any traditional process. At this time, few companies produce this process. These companies offer an advertiser the ability to produce higher-quality color separations, which in turn allows them to print sharper color ads.

HiFi Color High-fidelity color is expanding what we know and can do with print reproduction techniques and processes. HiFi color was born out of the limitations of the conventional color printing gamut, which is only a fraction of what the human visual system can see. It is a group of emerging technologies that will expand this printing gamut and extend control by improving and increasing tone, dynamic range, detail, spatial frequency modulation, and other appearance factors of print and other visual media.

HiFi color comprises the technologies of stochastic, or frequency modulation screening, four-plus color process and waterless printing methods, specialty papers, films, coatings, and laminates, proofing systems, color management systems, software, and hardware.

Color Management Systems (CMS) The ideal—and we haven't yet gotten to this point in technology—is seeing an image on a screen and getting an exact printed image, or, as it is touted, what you see is what you get. This is very important in terms of quality control and design. As images go through the production process, the information is transformed in different ways; for example, as photographic data in the original; as pixels of red, green, and blue on the computer screen; as dots of cyan, magenta, yellow, and black on paper. Software color management systems can bring more consistency to this process, but designers need to know what they can and cannot control. It can be complex even with a color management system.

Waterless Printing The new technology of waterless printing is losing popularity. Most offset presses use a dampening system of water to cover the plate. Offset is based on the fact that water and grease (ink) don't mix. In waterless printing, a silicone-coated plate is used that rejects ink in the nonimage areas. The result is spectacular detail, high-line screens, richer densities, and consistent quality throughout the press run: in short, great quality. However, according to Doug Koke, principal of IP/Koke printing, "Waterless has not been widely accepted. The plates are far too sensitive, scratch easily, and are temperature sensitive."[6] Offset dominates printing today.

Digital Printing Today digital printing accounts for less than 2 percent globally of the $500 billion printing industry. It is an offshoot of offset technology. Indigo press, the first digital printing system, was created in the Netherlands in 1993. Presently, the resolutions and finish of the indigo' press's digitally printed materials rival offset. It requires a minimum of preflight production tweaking. However, the page size is relatively small to be competitive. Recently, the Indigo company merged into Hewett-Packard. In direct-digital printing, workstations send files to the press. Film is not used, and in some cases neither are plates. Today there are several digital printing systems. Basically, information is transferred onto electrophotographic cylinders, instead of plates, and these cylinders use toner to print process color instead of printing ink. There are also other presses that digitize pages onto special plates and are used for short printing runs. It is predicted that digital printing will eventually revolutionize the printing press. There is change in the air.

The computer and digitization are spawning most of this advancement in printing and production technology. The day is not far off when the printing and production industry will have a completely filmless, digital process.

The student of advertising production will have to learn these advances in the field, many of which will be both revolutionary and evolutionary, complicating the decision as to which system to use.

 **SUMMARY**

All advertising people need to understand the basics of production. The production terms, concepts, and processes are not easy to learn but are essential to know because they affect budgets, time, and efficiency issues.

Publishers set mechanical requirements for their publications. Advertising production people need to be familiar with sources of information pertaining to print production requirements.

Today most ads are created on the computer (digital). The comps presented to clients appear to be computer finished. The process from the computer screen to a finished ad in a publication may be completed digitally, or by using a mix of traditional processes. The future will involve more computer-to-plate digital production.

There are three basic kinds of printing processes: letterpress (printing from a raised surface), offset lithography (printing from a flat surface), and gravure (printing from a depressed surface). In addition, silk screen or screen printing offers advertisers additional production applications. The form of printing may affect the type of material sent to the publication to reproduce the ad.

Advertisers may use new prepress digital technology or traditional means to prepare ads for production. The publication tells the advertiser what type of material is required or accepted. Each method of prepress has advantages and disadvantages, depending on the degree of quality desired. Typography concerns the style (or face) of type and the way the copy is set. Typefaces come in styles called families. The size is specified in points (72 points per inch). The width of typeset lines is measured in picas (6 picas to an inch). The depth of newspaper space is measured in lines. The space between the lines of type is called leading or line spacing.

The graphics and production processes can be complex because what you see isn't always what really is. Continuous-tone art (a photograph) must be converted into halftone dots (may be scanned or use traditional printer's darkroom procedure) so that the tonal values of the original can be reproduced. Line art has no tonal value; it is drawn in black ink on white paper using lines and solid black areas.

Production technology is constantly changing to produce printed materials faster, more cheaply, and more efficiently. Achieving color reproduction that satisfies ad agencies and advertisers is one of the most crucial roles of the magazine production manager. There is a multitude of proofs for the production manager to choose from dictated by the need to match colors exactly and the expense involved. "How much quality do we need?" is an often-asked question in terms of which proof to use. Color management systems help advertisers get what you see.

 ## REVIEW

1. Differentiate among the three basic printing processes.

2. What is a digital file?

3. What is continuous-tone copy?

4. What is line art?

5. What are color separations?

6. What colors are used in four-color printing?

7. When is a laminate/adhesive proof used?

 ## TAKE IT TO THE WEB

Most magazines have ad specifications listed on their Web sites so advertisers will know the reproduction guidelines for their advertisements. Visit **www.quadarm. com/publisher_sites/conde/ny/guidelines.asp** to look over the ad specifications for The New Yorker.

Visit the Microsoft Web site to learn more about the importance of typography, and how fonts are used and developed. **www.microsoft.com/typography**

Look up Getty Images (**www.creative.gettyimages.com**) to learn what is available in terms of stock photography as well as review the process of reproduction of color photographs.

 # CHAPTER 19

The Television Commercial

CHAPTER OBJECTIVES

Despite TiVo, audience fragmentation, and the decline of influence of the traditional networks, television advertising remains a powerful medium. It is complicated by a number of factors, including the fact that every viewer is a television advertising expert. Everyone knows what he or she likes and dislikes about TV spots. This creates a challenge for advertisers. After reading this chapter, you will understand:

1. copy development
2. creating the commercial
3. producing the commercial
4. controlling the cost

Take the big idea; blend sight, sound, motion, and technology; and add the ability to impact emotions and you have a very powerful advertising tool. Maybe the Internet will rival TV as a marketing communications medium someday as an interactive person-to-person medium using sight, sound, motion, and emotion. But, for now, television still reaches multitudes of potential consumers with great impact. It has power.

THE POWER OF THE TV IDEA

Here are a few convincing examples of television's marketing and communication power.

As the last century ended, Subway found its sales to be flat promoting low-fat benefits. In January 2000 its agency developed two television spots featuring Jared Fogle, who lost 245 pounds on a strictly Subway diet, and Tae Bo master Billy Blanks. "We've been doing low-fat for 3 1/2 years and did well generating about 5 percent sales increases, but using those two spots drove the business 15 to 20 percent," said Chris Carroll, director of marketing. With this new approach some stores' sales were up as much as 40 percent. Initially, the client rejected the agency's commercial idea three times.[1] More recently, Subway has tied into the Atkins diet craze and developed products that are low in carbohydrates. Its commercials focused on the number of carbohydrates its low-carb line of sandwiches contained.

Whereas most top-tier banks sell products, BB&T preempts respect for the individual in its advertising. Consumer brand-switching intentions increased 300 percent after exposure to BB&T advertising. In Exhibit 19.1, a lady says, "I'm a great grandmother. Seventy-one and counting. I've danced to the swing. I've danced to the tango. I've seen money

EXHIBIT 19.1

BB&T focused on consumer dreams instead of pushing bank products in its advertising.

Courtesy of Howard, Merrell & Partners and BB&T.

EXHIBIT 19.1

BB&T focused on consumer dreams instead of pushing bank products in its advertising.

Courtesy of Howard, Merrell & Partners and BB&T.

wasted. Thrown away. I've seen, it used . . . to accomplish things . . . I never dreamed possible. I will teach my great grandchildren . . . to know the difference." The last frames says, "BB&T. You can tell we want your business."

Some of the characteristics of good television advertising cut through clutter, appealing to consumers with humor, intelligence, charm, and emotion. Good ads are like good people. They're smart, funny, and engaging. You tend to remember them long after they're gone. You shouldn't even think about getting into consumers' wallets unless you first get into their lives. If you knew how to do this, you wouldn't have to read the rest of this chapter. On the other hand, many people who are supposed to know this don't practice it.

THE PROBLEMS OF TV

The medium poses some problems discussed in earlier chapters: commercial clutter that leaves viewers confused about advertisers, loss of audiences, high production costs, zapping, and TiVo. For example, according to Roper Reports, 38 percent of viewers say they often switch to another channel when ads come on, up 24 percent from 1985.[2] These problems are constant reminders to advertisers of the need to plan their messages very carefully. But it is precisely this adversity that breeds creative innovation. Roper finds 31 percent of viewers say they are often amused by funny or clever commercials (up 5 percent from 1993); and about 70 percent agree that advertising is often fun or interesting to watch.

Artistic Fads

The creative teams are constantly looking for new ways to grab a viewer's attention. However, many of these techniques become popular and then soon fade from the scene. Remember the shaky camera, claymation, morphing one object into another object, and using the oldies film footage? There is a continuing search for some new way to wake up and shake up an audience. Simply having a sound strategy isn't enough to make a viewer watch. There must be a sound strategy wrapped in a strong creative idea. We're back to the big idea concept. We take the big idea and blend visuals, words, motion, and technology to create emotional reactions—done properly, this is what makes television the most powerful advertising medium. Recently, a Miller Lite's spot "DOMINOS," created by Young & Rubicam/Chicago, was highly discussed for its special effects. The spot had lines of people in train stations, offices, and restaurants fall in succession like dominos. One man in a bar stops the action by moving out of the way to reach for a bottle of Miller Lite. The voiceover says, "Because you can get in line and pick what they give you or you can make your own choice."

COPY DEVELOPMENT AND PRODUCTION TIMETABLE

The creative process is difficult to predict. It isn't always easy to develop new breakthrough copy within the planned timetable or guess the client's reaction to the copy. The agency may love it; the client may hate it. It may take time to develop the right ideas. However, it is important to develop a reasonable timetable for copy development and production. A typical copy development timetable sequence might include the following:

- Copy exploratory
- Present ideas to client
- Revisions to client for approval to produce
- Circulate copy for clearance (legal, R&D, management)
- On-air clearance (network/local stations)
- Prebid meeting (specifications/sets)
- Bid review/award job
- Preproduction meeting
- Shoot
- Postproduction
- Rough cut to client for approval
- Revisions
- Final to client
- Ship date

The responsibility for such a timetable is shared by the advertising agency and the client. How long does it take for a one- to five-day shoot with 2 to 10 actors to clear this process? Anywhere from 11 to 43 days. This range illustrates the complexity of the process. It isn't easy to generalize.

CREATING THE TELEVISION COMMERCIAL

Many creative people believe it is easier to create a good television commercial than it is to create a good print ad. After all, the TV creative person has motion to command more attention, sound, professional actors, producers, directors, and editors. They should be able to communicate with all that support if there is a grain of an idea.

The TV commercial has two basic segments: the video (the sight or visual part) and the audio (spoken words, music, or other sounds). The creation process begins with the video because television is generally better at showing than telling; however, the impact of the words and sounds must be considered.

Visual Techniques

Testimonials Testimonials can be delivered by known or unknown individuals. Viewers are fascinated with celebrities. Some celebrities (for example, Cindy Crawford and Michael Jordan) have staying power for years and years in their ability to grab a viewer's attention. And, of course, Tiger Wood keeps on successfully pitching for Buick. He's also pitched for American Express, Accenture, EA Sports, Nike, Rolex, Tag Heuer, and Titleist. About 20 percent of all TV commercials feature a celebrity. Athletes have outdistanced entertainers in the celebrity endorsement area since 1989.[3] James LeBron, Cleveland Cavaliers young basketball sensation, pitches for Sprite. He has a $100,000,000 endorsement deal. Even coaches get into the act; Dan Reeves, former coach of the Atlanta Falcons, has been spokesperson for Zocor cholesterol medication. And former Bear player and coach Mike Ditka pitched for Levitra. Beyonce Knowles was about the biggest pop star during the summer of 2003. Pepsi did a Carmen Miranda spot with her earlier in that year, and the spot "Directions" features Beyonce pulling up to a gas station, getting a Pepsi from the vending machine, and asking the attendant for directions. He's speechless when he realizes who she is. He's only able to squeak words, but she understands what he's saying.

There is always a risk with some celebrities getting into trouble or publicly saying the wrong thing or supporting the wrong cause, but it is worth it because of all the attention they get and the impact they have, says a vice president for Total Research Corp.[4] It costs an advertiser about $20,000 to research a celebrity to get diagnostic information of not only the personality but also whether the personality fits its product or service. Slim-Fast has used satisfied customers to show how much weight they have lost for credibility.

Serials Serials are commercials created in a series in which each commercial continues the previous story. The technique was made popular more than a decade ago by the Taster's Choice couple. People followed the life of the young Taster's Choice couple as they interacted with each other and described their relationship problems. Several beer companies have also tried the serial approach, as have Pacific Bell telephone, Ragu spaghetti sauce, and Energizer batteries.

Oldies Footage Classic television and film sequences are now easily manipulated to create ads that target media-savvy viewers. Audiences have seen John Wayne selling Coors beer, Ed Sullivan introducing the Mercedes M-class sport-utility vehicle, Fred Astaire sweeping with a Dirt Devil, and Lucy Ricardo and Fred Mertz pushing tickets for the California lottery.

Spokesperson Often this technique features a "presenter" who stands in front of the camera and delivers the copy directly to the viewer. The spokesperson may display and perhaps demonstrate the product. He or she may be in a set (a living room, kitchen, factory, office, or out of doors) appropriate to the product and product story or in limbo (plain background with no set). The product should be the hero. The spokesperson should be someone who is likable and believable but not so powerful as to overwhelm the product.

Demonstration This technique is popular for some types of products because television is the ideal medium for demonstrating to the consumer how the product works: how a bug spray kills, how to apply eye pencils in gorgeous silky colors, or how easy it is to use a microwave to cook a whole meal quickly. When making a demonstration commercial, use close shots so the viewer can see clearly what is happening. Try to make it unexpected, if possible. You may choose a subjective camera view (which shows a procedure as if the viewer were actually doing whatever the product does), using the camera as the viewer's eyes. Make the demonstration relevant and as involving as possible. Do not try to fool the viewer for two important reasons: (1) Your message must be believable; and (2) legally, the demonstration must correspond to actual usage—most agencies make participants in the commercial production sign affidavits signifying that the events took place as they appeared on the TV screen.

Close-Ups Television is basically a medium of close-ups. The largest TV screen is too small for extraneous details in the scenes of a commercial. A fast-food chain may use close-ups to show hamburgers cooking or the appetizing finished product ready to be consumed. With this technique, the audio is generally delivered off-screen (the voiceover costs less than a presentation by someone onscreen).

Story Line The story-line technique is similar to making a miniature movie (with a definite beginning, middle, and end in 30 seconds), except that the narration is done offscreen. A typical scene may show a family trying to paint their large house with typical paint and brush. The camera shifts to the house next door, where a teenage female is easily spray-painting the house, the garage, and the fence in rapid fashion. During the scenes, the announcer explains the advantages of the spray painter. In the James Hardie siding products spot, the story is told visually with suspense. It opens on a bright, enterprising young girl who appears to be drawing against the house. The shots show that she's intensely busy with her project. You then see her cutting and pasting. As the commercial begins to close, you see she has been trying to give her dollhouse the same quality siding that the house she lives in has—James Hardie siding (see Exhibit 19.2).

Comparisons Their soft drink has sodium. Our brand is sodium free. Their beer is loaded with carbs. Our beer has next to none. Comparing one product with another can answer questions for the viewer. Usually, the comparison is against the leader in the product category. You could do a user lifestyle comparison between your brand and a competitive brand. In direct product comparisons, you must be prepared to prove in court that your product is significantly superior, as stated, and you must be credible in the way you make your claim, or the commercial may induce sympathy for the competitor. BB&T has a commercial in which its customer tells what he expects from banks and is not getting from the competition.

Still Photographs and Artwork By using still photographs and/or artwork, including cartoon drawings and lettering, you can structure a well-placed commercial. The required material may already exist, to be supplied at modest cost, or it can be photographed or drawn specifically for your use. Skillful use of the TV camera can give static visual material a surprising amount of movement. Zoom lenses provide an inward or outward motion, and panning the camera across the photographs or artwork can give the commercial motion (*panning* means changing the viewpoint of the camera without moving the dolly it stands on).

Slice-of-Life Slice-of-life is a dramatic technique in which actors tell a story in an attempt to involve people with the brand. It is a short miniplay in which the brand is the hero. Most slice-of-life commercials open with a problem, and the brand becomes the solution.

The viewer must see the problem as real, and the reward must fit the problem. Because problem solving is a useful format in almost any commercial, slice-of-life is widely used. Brands selling largely emotional benefits (jeans, soft drinks, beer, greeting cards, athletic gear) have employed the format in great numbers. The humorous Budweiser "Whassup?" campaign promoted a new look at male bonding.

Customer Interview Most people who appear in TV commercials are professional actors, but customer interviews involve nonprofessionals. An interviewer or offscreen

EXHIBIT 19.2

The brand story is well told through a visual story. The little girl wants the same quality on her dollhouse as the house in which she lives.

Courtesy of Sawyer Riley Compton and James Hardie.

voice may ask a housewife, who is usually identified by name, to compare the advertised kitchen cleanser with her own brand by removing two identical spots in her sink. She finds that the advertised product does a better job.

Vignettes and Situations Advertisers of soft drinks, beer, candy, and other widely consumed products find this technique useful in creating excitement and motivation. The commercial usually consists of a series of fast-paced scenes showing people enjoying the product as they enjoy life. The audio over these scenes is often a jingle or song with lyrics based on the situation we see and the satisfaction the product offers. In many cases, it is the music that holds it all together. It can be used effectively to update a brand or sell a lifestyle. It is a challenge to link with the brand and can be costly to produce since you have to have shoot 15 or so vignettes.

Humor Humor has long been a popular technique with both copywriters and consumers because it makes the commercial more interesting. The dangers are that the humorous aspects of the commercial will get in the way of the sell and that the viewer will remember the humor rather than the product or the benefit. The challenge is to make the humorous copy relevant to the product or benefit.

Animation Originally, **animation** consisted of artists' inanimate drawings, which were photographed on motion-picture film one frame at a time and brought to life with movement as the film is projected. Historically, the most common form of animation was the cartoon. Certainly a favorite among children but also popular with all ages, the cartoon is capable of creating a warm, friendly atmosphere both for the product and for the message. Today, computer graphics can be extremely realistic and have changed the nature of animation. The cost of animation depends on its style: With limited movement, few characters, and few or no backgrounds, the price can be low. Many traditional animators have been replaced with digital artists.

animation (TV)
Making inanimate objects appear alive and moving by setting them before an animation camera and filming one frame at a time.

Stop Motion When a package or other object is photographed in a series of different positions, movement can be simulated as the single frames are projected in sequence. Stop motion is similar to artwork photographed in animation. With it, the package can "walk," "dance," and move as if it had come to life.

Rotoscope In the rotoscope technique, animated and live-action sequences are produced separately and then optically combined. A live boy may be eating breakfast food while a cartoon animal trademark character jumps up and down on his shoulder and speaks to him.

Problem Solution This technique has been around since the beginning of television. The purpose of many products is to solve the prime prospect's problem—a headache, poor communication, or plaque. You get the idea. The product is selling the solution. Problem solution is similar to slice-of-life but lacks the depth of story line or plot development. Be sure to let the visuals tell the story. Solve the problem with visuals.

Mood Imagery This technique is expensive and difficult. It often combines several techniques. The main objective is to set a certain mood and image for the product you are trying to sell. Strong imagery can sell ideas (see Exhibit 19.3). Savannah Electric sells the environment to viewers with strong visuals and copy. "One blade of grass is not small. Nor is it insignificant. Because one blade, after another, after another makes up something more amazing than anything we could create. In the grand design of nature, every seemingly little thing counts. And so the same goes for preserving it. If we all do our part, imagine what that could add up to. Savannah Electric, We live in the same world you do."

Split and Bookend Spots A variation on the serial commercial is the split spot: Two related (usually 15-second) spots run with a completely unrelated spot between them. For example, Post Grape-Nuts ran a split spot in which a woman asks a man how long the cereal stays crunchy in milk. The man does not want to find out, but she insists, and viewers are left hanging. Next is an unrelated 30-second commercial for another product. The couple then comes back, and she says, "After all this time it's still crunchy." The theory behind split and bookend commercials is that breaking out of the expected format will get your product remembered.

Infomercials As discussed in Chapter 8, the infomercial is a commercial that looks like a program. These commercials sell everything from woks to make-a-million-in-real-estate programs, and usually run for 30 minutes. The National Infomercial Marketing Association recommends that every infomercial begin and end with a "paid advertisement" announcement so that consumers understand what they are watching. The obvious advantage is that the advertiser has an entire program about its product.

EXHIBIT 19.3

Some ideas naturally lend themselves to mood imagery. Here Savannah Electric is showing the beauty of the natural environment that it wants you to protect.

Courtesy of Savannah Electric, A Southern Company, and Hauser Group.

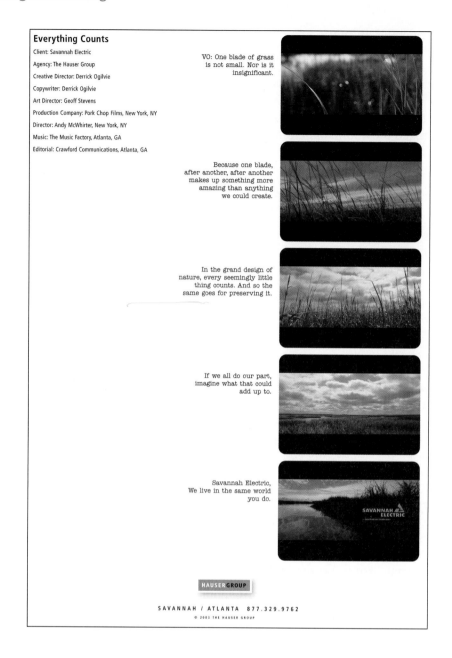

Everything Counts

Client: Savannah Electric

Agency: The Hauser Group

Creative Director: Derrick Ogilvie

Copywriter: Derrick Ogilvie

Art Director: Geoff Stevens

Production Company: Pork Chop Films, New York, NY

Director: Andy McWhirter, New York, NY

Music: The Music Factory, Atlanta, GA

Editorial: Crawford Communications, Atlanta, GA

VO: One blade of grass is not small. Nor is it insignificant.

Because one blade, after another, after another makes up something more amazing than anything we could create.

In the grand design of nature, every seemingly little thing counts. And so the same goes for preserving it.

If we all do our part, imagine what that could add up to.

Savannah Electric, We live in the same world you do.

SAVANNAH ELECTRIC

HAUSER GROUP

SAVANNAH / ATLANTA 877.329.9762
© 2001 THE HAUSER GROUP

Combination Most commercials combine techniques. A speaker may begin and conclude the message, but there will be close-ups in between. In fact, every commercial should contain at least one or two close-ups to show package and logo. Humor is adaptable to most techniques. Animation and live action make an effective mixture in many commercials, and side-by-side comparisons may be combined with almost any other technique.

Video Influence

Many visual techniques used in commercials have evolved from the music video industry. These include hyperkinetic imagery, visual speed, and sophistication; ironic, wise-guy attitudes; unexpected humor; quick, suggestive cuts rather than slow segues; narrative implications rather than whole stories; attitudes, not explanations; tightly cropped, partial images instead of whole ones; mixtures of live action, newsreel footage, animation, typography, film speeds, and film quality; and unexpected soundtrack/audio relationships to video.

Which Technique?

Over the years there have been a number of studies to help advertisers make up their minds as to what kind of commercials to run. None provides all the answers, however. Ogilvy & Mather found that people who liked a commercial were twice as likely to be persuaded by it compared to people who felt neutral toward the advertising. Perhaps the single most striking finding was the fact that commercial liking went far beyond mere entertainment. People like commercials they feel are relevant and worth remembering, which could have an impact on greater persuasion. Original or novel approaches alone seem to have little to do with how well a commercial is liked. Ogilvy & Mather also found that liking was a function of product category. A lively, energetic execution also contributed to liking but was less important than relevance. In other research findings, Video Storyboard tests reinforce that consumers like commercials with celebrities. In fact, consumer preference for this type of commercial has risen in the past 10 years. Such commercials are more persuasive than slice-of-life vignettes or product demonstrations. Exhibit 19.4 shows that celebrities are bested only by humor and kids as executional elements that characterize persuasive commercials.

Ideas generate production techniques and sometimes thinking of the technique choices generates "ideas." The technology allows you to create almost anything you can visualize. These are your communication tools.

Planning the Commercial

Let us review some of the basic principles of writing the commercial script. In planning the TV commercial, there are many considerations: cost, medium (videotape or film), casting of talent, use of music, special techniques, time, location, and the big idea and its relationship to the advertising and marketing objectives and, of course, to the entire campaign.

- You are dealing with sight, sound, and motion. Each of these elements has its own requirements and uses. There should be a relationship among them so that the viewer perceives the desired message. Make certain that when you are demonstrating a sales feature, the audio is talking about that same feature.

- Your audio should be relevant to your video, but there is no need to describe what is obvious in the picture. When possible, you should see that the words interpret the picture and advance the thought.

- Television generally is more effective at showing than telling; therefore, more than half of the success burden rests on the ability of the video to communicate.

	Women	Men	18–34	34–39	50+
Commercials with **humor**	57	**68**	58	63	64
Commercials with **children**	**61**	44	52	56	52
Commercials with **celebrities**	39	34	**44**	34	30
Real-life situations	34	30	**39**	33	24
Brand **comparisons**	32	23	**35**	31	20
Musical commercials	**29**	18	27	23	20
Product **demonstrations**	17	**26**	19	24	21
Endorsements from experts	**17**	13	16	16	14
Hidden-camera testimonials	12	10	**14**	10	9
Company **presidents**	6	**12**	**12**	9	7

EXHIBIT 19.4

Video Storyboard Persuasion Results

Source: *Adweek*, 15 August 1994, 17. VNU Business Media, Inc. Reprinted with permission.

- The number of scenes should be planned carefully. You do not want too many scenes (unless you are simply trying to give an overall impression) because this tends to confuse the viewer. Yet you do not want scenes to become static (unless planned so for a reason). Study TV commercials and time the scene changes to determine what you personally find effective. If you do this, you will discover the importance of pacing the message—if a scene is too long, you will find yourself impatiently waiting for the next one.

- It is important to conceive the commercial as a flowing progression so that the viewer will be able to follow it easily. You do not have time for a three-act play whose unrelated acts can be tied together at the end. A viewer who cannot follow your thought may well tune you out. The proper use of opticals or transitions can add motion and smoothness to scene transitions.

- Television is basically a medium of close-ups. The largest TV screen is too small for extraneous detail in the scenes of a commercial. Long shots can be effective in establishing a setting but not for showing product features.

- The action of the commercial takes more time than a straight announcer's reading of copy. A good rule is to purposely time the commercial a second or two short. Generally, the action will eat up this time, so do not just read your script. Act it out.

- You will want to consider the use of *supers* (words on the screen) of the basic theme so that the viewer can see, as well as hear, the important sales feature. Many times, the last scene will feature product identification and the theme line.

- If possible, show the brand name. If it is prominent, give a shot of the package; otherwise, flash its logotype. It is vital to establish brand identification.

- Generally, try to communicate one basic idea; avoid running in fringe benefits. Be certain that your words as well as your pictures emphasize your promise. State it, support it, and, if possible, demonstrate it. Repeat your basic promise near the end of the commercial; that is the story you want viewers to carry away with them.

- Read the audio aloud to catch tongue twisters.

- As in most other advertising writing, the sentences should usually be short and their structure uncomplicated. Use everyday words. It is not necessary to have something said every second. The copy should round out the thought conveyed by the picture.

- In writing your video description, describe the scene and action as completely as possible: "Open on husband and wife in living room" is not enough. Indicate where each is placed, whether they are standing or sitting, and generally how the room is furnished.

Writing the Script

It's probably obvious that writing a TV commercial is very different from writing print advertising. First, you must use simple, easy-to-pronounce, easy-to-remember words. And you must be brief. The 30-second commercial has only 28 seconds of audio. In 28 seconds, you must solve your prime prospect's problems by demonstrating your product's superiority. If the product is too big to show in use, be certain to show the logo or company name at least twice during the commercial. Think of words and pictures simultaneously. You usually divide your script paper into two columns. On the left, you describe the video action, and on the right you write the audio portion, including sound effects and music. Corresponding video and audio elements go right next to each other, panel by panel (see Exhibit 19.5).

Write copy in a friendly, conversational style. If you use an off-camera announcer, make certain that his or her dialogue is keyed to the scenes in your video portion. Although it is not always possible, matching the audio with the video makes a commercial cohesive and more effective. The audio—words, sound effects,

EXHIBIT **19.5**

**A TV Script with
Storyboard**

TV SCRIPT: Pawleys "Leave Us Alone"

VIDEO		AUDIO
1. MS: BEACH SCENE PEOPLE IN CHAIRS OUTSIDE OF HOUSE		MUSIC: IN AND UNDER (George Winston quiet jazz) ANNCR:Pawleys is a great
2. CU: CHILD DIGGING IN SAND WITH OCEAN BACKGROUND		family resort.
3. MS: PEOPLE WALK-ING ON ALMOST EMPTY BEACH		It is nature at its best....
4. LS: LADY ALONE WALKING INLET		a beautiful pristine...beach
5. WIDE SHOT OF EMPTY BEACH, FEW HOUSES		Don't come, we're having fun.
6. END FRAME	**Pawleys** *Don't Disturb Us!*	Pawleys is OUR beach.

VIDEO	AUDIO
	MUSIC: IN AND UNDER (George Winston quiet jazz)
1. MS: BEACH SCENE 3 PEOPLE IN CHAIRS SITTING OUTSIDE OF BEACH HOUSE. BEACH BLANKET IN SAND.	ANNCR: Pawleys is a great
2. CU: CHILD DIGGING IN SAND WITH OCEAN BACKGROUND.	family resort.
3. MS: PEOPLE WALKING ON ALMOST EMPTY BEACH. A FEW HOUSES ARE IN THE BACKGROUND.	It is nature at its best . . .
4. LS: LADY ALONE WALKING INLET WITH DISTANT HOUSE OR TWO.	a beautiful . . . pristine beach
5. WIDE SHOT OF EMPTY BEACH, FEW HOUSES.	Don't come, we're having fun.
6. END FRAME.	
	Pawleys is OUR beach.

EXHIBIT **19.6**

A Photoboard

Courtesy of Howard, Merrell & Partners and BB&T.

or music—in a script is as important as the video portion. They must work together to bring the viewer the message. You need strong copy and sound and strong visuals. All are vital for an effective commercial.

Some agencies add visuals to their scripts. They use specially designed sheets of paper, usually 8 by 11 inches, with boxes down the center for rough sketches of the video portion (see Exhibit 19.5) called photoscripts. For presentations, most agencies use full-size TV storyboards.

Developing the Storyboard

storyboard
Series of drawings used to present a proposed commercial. Consists of illustrations of key action (video), accompanied by the audio part. Used for getting advertiser approval and as a production guide.

Once the creative art and copy team has developed a script, the next step is to create a **storyboard,** which consists of a series of sketches showing key scenes developed in the script. It is a helpful tool for discussing the concept with other agency or client personnel, who may not know the background or who may not be able to visualize a script accurately. Without a storyboard, each individual may interpret the script's visuals differently.

Storyboard Versus Finished Look It is extremely difficult, if not impossible, to visualize the look of a finished commercial from the storyboard. Most clients are very literal minded and don't visualize storyboards very well. Storyboards are suppose to stimulate the imagination of someone's vision prior to shooting. Of course, the quality of the storyboards varies from virtual stick figures in limbo to full-color drawings or photos. Keep in mind, using this limited medium, it is a difficult task to show all the details that are necessary to understand for production purposes.

Storyboards consist of two frames for each scene. The top frame represents the TV screen (visual). The bottom frame carries a description of the video (as per script) and the audio for that sequence (some storyboards carry only the audio portion). The number of sets of frames varies from commercial to commercial and is not necessarily dictated by the length of the commercial. There may be 4 to 12 or more sets of frames, depending on the nature of the commercial and the demands of the client for detail.

The ratio of width to depth on the TV screen is 4 by 3. There is no standard-size storyboard frame, although a common size is 4 inches by 3 inches.

The storyboard is a practical step between the raw script and actual production. It gives the agency, client, and production house personnel a common visual starting point for their discussion. Upon client approval, the storyboard goes into production.

Assessing the storyboard requires answering a number of questions: Is there a campaign idea? Is it on strategy? Is the campaign idea meaningful? Credible? Provocative? Does the execution showcase the campaign idea? Is the benefit visualized? Does it tell a picture story? Is it clear, credible, and compelling? Does the board represent a commercial or a campaign? Are the ideas communicated clearly in visual-audio elements? Does it sell versus tell?

Exhibit 19.6 is an example of a photoboard. The photoboard is similar to the storyboard but shows the actual frames (photos) that were shot. It is frequently used by companies as a sales tool to show merchants and dealers exactly what kind of advertising support they will be given.

Other Elements of the Commercial

Opticals Most commercials contain more than a single scene. Optical devices or effects between scenes are necessary to provide smooth visual continuity from scene to scene. They are inserted during the final editing stage. The actual **opticals** may be one of the director's functions. However, these are used to aid in the transition of getting from one scene to the next scene or establishing a visual. Sometimes which technique depends on the importance of a particular scene or the detail that needs to be seen. Exhibit 19.7 illustrates some basic optical decisions. Among the most common are the following:

opticals
Visual effects that are put on a TV film in a laboratory, in contrast to those that are included as part of the original photography.

Cut

One scene simply cuts into the next. It is the fastest scene change because it indicates no time lapse whatsoever. A cut is used to indicate simultaneous action, to speed up action, and for variety. It keeps one scene from appearing on the screen too long.

Dissolve

An overlapping effect in which one scene fades out while the following scene simultaneously fades in. Dissolves are slower than cuts. There are fast dissolves and slow dissolves. Dissolves are used to indicate a short lapse of time in a given scene, or to move from one scene to another where the action is either simultaneous with the action in the first scene or occurring very soon after the preceding action.

Fade-in

An effect in which the scene actually "fades" into vision from total black (black screen).

Fade-out

This is opposite of a fade-in. The scene "fades" into total black. If days, months, or years elapse between one sequence of action and the next, indicate "fade out . . . fade in."

Matte

Part of one scene is placed over another so that the same narrator, for example, is shown in front of different backgrounds.

Super

The superimposition of one scene or object over another. The title or product can be "supered" over the scene.

EXHIBIT **19.7**

Examples of Camera Directions

ECU - An Extreme Close Up shows, for example, person's lips, nose, eyes.

CU - The Close Up is a tight shot, but showing face on entire package for emphasis.

MCU - The Medium Close Up cuts to person about chest, usually showing some background.

MS - The Medium Shot shows the person from the waist up. Commonly used shot. Shows much more detail of setting or background than MCU.

LS - The Long Shot shows the scene from a distance. Used to establish location.

Wipe

The new scene "wipes" off the previous scene from top or bottom or side to side with a geometric pattern (see Exhibit 19.8). A wipe is faster than a dissolve but not as fast as a cut. A wipe does not usually connote lapse of time, as a dissolve or fade-out does. There are several types of wipes: flip (the entire scene turns over like the front and back of a postcard), horizontal (left to right or right to left), vertical (top to bottom or bottom to top), diagonal, closing door (in from both sides), bombshell (a burst into the next scene), iris (a circle that grows bigger is an iris out), fan (fans out from center screen), circular (sweeps around the screen—also called clock wipe). Wipes are most effective when a rapid succession of short or quick scenes is desired or to separate impressionistic shots when these are grouped together to produce a montage effect.

Zoom

A smooth, sometimes rapid move from a long shot to a close-up or from a close-up to a long shot.

Sound Track The audio portion of the commercial may be recorded either during the film or videotape shooting or at an earlier or later time in a recording studio. When the sound track is recorded during the shooting, the actual voices of the people speaking on camera are used in the commercial. If the sound track is recorded

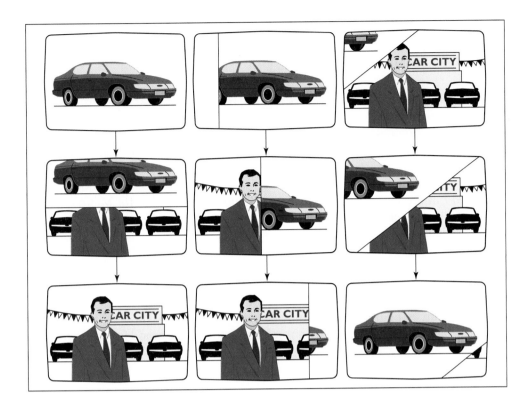

EXHIBIT **19.8**
Example of a Wipe

in advance, the film or videotape scenes can be shot to fit the copy points as they occur; or if music is part of the track, visual action can be matched to a specific beat. If shooting and editing take place before the sound track is recorded, the track can be tailored to synchronize with the various scenes.

Music Not all commercials need music. But think about it early in the process. Music has the ability to communicate feelings and moods in a unique way. As a result, the use of music can make or break a TV commercial. In some commercials, it is every bit as important as the copy or visuals. It is often used as background to the announcer's copy or as a song or jingle that is integral to the ad.

Nike created much controversy when it used the Beatles' "Revolution." At the time, purists screamed "Heresy!" Now it's no big deal. Respected artists, both famous and hoping to be famous, license their music to Madison Avenue all the time. "Music is the best means we have to automatically strike a chord," says Jeremy Miller, public relations director for TBWA/Chiat/Day L.A. "It's better than any amount of words or even images. When we used Rod Stewart's 'Forever Young' for an Apple Computer ad, we were positioning the product precisely where we wanted it. We'll cut one ad to a dozen different songs just to see which one works the best. It's that important."[5]

Here are some ways you can put music to work:[6]

■ *Backgrounds.* In many commercials, background music is used primarily to contribute to the mood. Appropriate music can be used to establish the setting; then it can fade and become soft in the background.

■ *Transitions.* Music can be an effective transition device to carry viewers from one setting to another. For example, the music may start out being sedate as the scene is peaceful. As it switches to the product being used, the music changes to rock and the tempo builds, marking the transition from place to place.

■ *Movement.* Sound effects (SFX), natural sounds, and music can contribute to movement. Music that moves up the scale, or down, supports something or someone moving up or down.

■ *Accents.* Music can punctuate points or actions. The "beat" of the music and visuals can match to hold viewers' attention and drive the commercial. Musical sounds—as little as a single note—can attract attention.

New or Old Music Some advertisers pay big money to professional musicians to develop a special tune or lyrics for a commercial or campaign. The previous wisdom was that original tunes could be cheaper. The cost of an original track ranges from $10,000 to $50,000 not factoring in residuals to singers and musicians. Licensing a hit song from an established act can range from $250,000 to more than $1 million. Of course, the superexpensive buys are what people talk about: Celine Dion's $14 million Chrysler deal, the $5 million "Start Me Up" for Microsoft, Bob Seger's "Like a Rock" for Chevy, Sting for Jaguar, or the Led Zeppelin association with Cadillac. There are countless smaller acts available for much less. "You have to have guts to buy songs no one has ever heard before," says Eric Hirschberg at Deutsch.[7]

A couple of years ago, General Mills successfully introduced Berry Burst Cheerios—in two versions, both flavored with freeze-dried fruit—by serving up to consumers an estimated $40 million campaign centered on the 1970 pop tune by the Partridge Family, "I Think I Love You." The song set the mood for the humorous television commercials, titled "Love Story," which showed a Cheerios truck and a farmer's truck loaded with fresh berries driving around together as if they were a loving human couple.

A year later when Berry Burst Cheerios added bananas to the mix it was introduced with an estimated $21 million campaign. Again, a vintage rock song was the vehicle for bringing to life the "romance" between the two trucks, which also return in a new commercial. The tune in the spot was the 1974 remake of B. J. Thomas's "Hooked on a Feeling" by the group Blue Swede. This kind of music in campaigns is indicative of the continuing popularity of well-known songs as the soundtracks for commercials rather than jingles written specifically for spots. The reason is the ability of such music to quickly capture the attention and interest of consumers, who can be targeted demographically by the song selection.[8] Berry Burst Cheerios are aimed at baby boomers old enough to remember the songs, along with their children, who may be familiar with the music from TV and radio.

Licensed music gains instant access to the listener's subconscious. It lets a brand such as Buick communicate trust and reliability when its "Stand by Me" had just done the same for Citibank. Or it lets McDonald's promote a folksiness with Randy Newman's "You've Got a Friend in Me," only months after it had gained fame in the popular family hit movie *Toy Story.*[9] Gap's khaki love fest, set to the tune of Donovan's "Mellow Yellow," unites baby boomers and Gen Xers in a nirvana of perceived coolness.

Whether you're using country, rock, or Latin, the tone of the music can help transfer drama, love, happiness, or other feelings to the viewer. It is a tool to cue the viewer's feelings. Original music can be written and scored for the commercial, or licensing of old or popular songs can be obtained, which can be very expensive. The least expensive music is stock music sold by stock music companies. It is cheap because it is not exclusive.

PRODUCING THE TV COMMERCIAL

The job of converting the approved storyboard is done by TV production. There are three distinct stages to this process:

■ Preproduction includes casting, wardrobing, designing sets or building props, finding a location or studio, and meeting with agency, client, and production house personnel.

EXHIBIT **19.9**

Instead of using computer graphics to show flowers and bugs walking through downtown, actors were cast by the director to disrupt and draw attention.

Courtesy of Sawyer Riley Compton and Callaway Gardens.

- ■ Shooting encompasses the work of filming or videotaping all scenes in the commercial. In fact, several takes are made of each scene.
- ■ Postproduction, also known as editing, completion, or finishing, includes selecting scenes from among those shots, arranging them in the proper order, inserting transitional effects, adding titles, combining sound with picture, and delivering the finished commercial.

Exhibit 19.9 shows how to attract attention by using something you don't normally see—flowers and bugs walking through a downtown area. The disruption of the norm attracts attention. In this case, the producer was able to attract attention by using actors instead of computer graphics, which could have showed real flowers and bugs walking. In this case, it also was less expensive.

In charge of production is the producer, who combines the talents of coordinator, diplomat, watchdog, and businessperson. Some producers are on the staffs of large agencies or advertisers. Many work on a freelance basis. The work of a producer is so all-embracing that the best way to describe it is to live through the entire production process. Let us do that first and pick up the details of the producer's job in the section headed "Role of the Producer."

Let us begin with the problems of shooting the spot, for which a director is appointed by the producer.

The Director's Function

As the key person in the shooting, the director takes part in casting and directing the talent, directs the cameraperson in composing each picture, assumes responsibility for the setting, and puts the whole show together. A director of a regional commercial will earn about $7,500 per day, and national commercial directors average about $13,000 per commercial; however, better-known directors may demand $25,000 to $35,000 per spot. The Source Maythenyi, an advertising/production database service, recently estimated that there are 4,000 specialized commercial directors and that doesn't include a growing number of feature film directors.[10]

The Bidding Process

There is only one way to provide specifications for a commercial shoot when you are seeking bids from production companies, and that is in writing. There is an industry-accepted form (AICP Bid and Specification Form). Information for this form is provided by the agency and client. The use of this form ensures that all production companies are provided with identical job specifications for estimating production costs. It ensures that all bids are based on the same information.

The Preproduction Process

A preproduction meeting must be held prior to every production. The agency producer is expected to chair this meeting. The following agency, client, and production company personnel usually attend:

Agency: producer, creative team, account supervisor
Client: brand manager or advertising manager
Production company: director, producer, others as needed

The following points should be covered at every preproduction meeting: direction, casting, locations and/or sets, wardrobe and props, product, special requirements, final script, legal claims/contingencies, and timetable update.

In addition to covering the points just listed, the creative team and the director will likely present shooting boards and the production thinking behind the commercial. The shooting boards should be used for the following purposes:

- to determine camera angles
- to determine best product angles
- to project camera and cast movement and help determine talent status (extra versus principal)
- to determine number of scenes to shoot
- to determine timing of each scene

ROLE OF THE PRODUCER

Agency Producer

The producer's role begins before the approval of the storyboard. Conferring with the copywriter and/or art director, the producer becomes thoroughly familiar with every frame of the storyboard.

1. The producer prepares the "specs," or specifications—the physical production requirements of the commercial—to provide the production studios with the precise information they require to compute realistic bids. Every agency prepares its own estimate form. In addition, many advertisers request a further breakdown of the cost of items such as preproduction, shooting, crew, labor, studio, location travel and expenses, equipment, film, props and wardrobe, payroll taxes, studio makeup, direction, insurance, and editing.

2. The producer contacts the studios that have been invited to submit bids based on their specialties, experience, and reputation; meets with them either separately or in one common "bid session"; and explains the storyboard and the specs in detail.

3. The production house estimates expenses after studying specs, production timetable, and storyboard. Generally, a 35 percent markup is added to the estimated out-of-pocket expenses to cover overhead and studio profit. Usually, the

production company adds a 10 percent contingency fee to the bid for unforeseen problems. The bids are submitted. The producer analyzes the bids and recommends the studio to the client.

4. The producer arranges for equipment. The studio may own equipment, such as cameras and lights, but more often it rents all equipment for a job. The crew is also freelance, hired by the day. Although the studio's primary job is to shoot the commercial, it can also take responsibility for editorial work. For videotape, a few studios own their own cameras and production units; others rent these facilities.

5. Working through a talent agency, the producer arranges, or has the production company arrange, auditions. Associates also attend auditions, at which they and the director make their final choices of performers. The client may also be asked to pass on the final selection.

6. The producer then participates in the preproduction meeting. At this meeting the producer, creative associates, account executive, and client, together with studio representatives and director, lay final plans for production.

7. During the shooting, the producer usually represents both the agency and the client as the communicator with the director. On the set or location, the creative people and client channel any comments and suggestions through the producer to avoid confusion.

8. It is the producer's responsibility to arrange for the recording session. Either before or after shooting and editing, he or she arranges for the soundtrack, which may call for an announcer, actors, singers, and musicians. If music is to be recorded, the producer will have had preliminary meetings with the music contractor.

9. The producer participates in the editing along with the creative team. Editing begins after viewing the dailies and selecting the best takes.

10. The producer arranges screenings for agency associates and clients to view and approve the commercials at various editing stages and after completion of the answer print.

11. Finally, the producer handles the billings and approves studio and other invoices for shooting, editing, and payment to talent.

The "Outside" Producer

An **outside producer** is the person representing a production company whose entire business is filmmaking. He or she is hired by the agency producer to create the TV commercial according to agency specifications.

outside producer
The production company person who is hired by the agency to create the commercial according to agency specifications.

Shooting

Most productions consist of the following steps:

1. *Prelight.* This is simply the day (or days) used to set the lighting for specific scenes. To do this exclusively on shoot days would tie up the entire crew.

2. *Shooting.* This phase of the production process is the filming (or taping) of the approved scenes for the commercial. These scenes are then "screened" the next day (dailies) to ensure that the scene was captured as planned.

3. *Wrap.* This signals the completion of production. It is at this stage that most of the crew is released.

4. *Editing.* This takes place after the shoot is completed. Scenes are screened and selected for use in the commercial. The scenes are then merged with a sound track, titles, and opticals, composing a completed or finished commercial.

The role of the client and account service at the shoot is one of advisor. It is really the creative's day and it is their responsibility to deliver the spot. In situations in which the client needs to provide input on the set, the prime contact is the account representative or agency producer. The producer is generally the liaison between the agency and the director. This chain of command is simple and direct and eliminates confusion on the set, which is an absolute necessity when shooting.

Postproduction Process

Postproduction begins after a production company exposes the film in the camera at the shoot. The film that comes out of the camera must be developed and then printed onto a new strip of positive film called the *dailies*. The editor then screens these dailies and selects the good takes from the day's shooting.

The editor then physically splices the takes selected from each scene together with the next to create a *rough cut*, which is a rough rendition of the finished commercial. Once the editor has cut this film and the agency and client approve the cut, the editor takes the original film that was shot and developed and pulls the takes from that film that match the selected workprint takes.

Today, virtually all final edits, effects, and opticals are done on videotape using computers. The original camera film takes (35 mm motion-picture film) are transferred electronically to 1-inch videotape. During this transfer of film to videotape, the color is corrected.

The editor then takes this material into a video edit, in which each take is run on videotape and the *cut-in* through *cut-out* points for each take are laid down in sequence, from the first frame of the first scene to the end frame of that scene (to match the workprint), until the entire commercial is laid down from the color-corrected videotape matter (called the *unedited tape master*). Titles and other special effects are added during this final unedited-tape-to-edited-tape session. The sound (which the editor and agency had worked on along with the picture) is then electronically relayed onto the video-edited master, and the spot is finished. Sound complicated? It is. Just think of the steps involved in Exhibit 19.10. They shot the young lady putting on makeup. There was the wide shot. They then shot close-ups of her putting lipstick on with a brush, powder in her hand, putting on powder with a brush, eye makeup, eye liner pencil, lip liner, and putting mascara on her eyelashes. They had to decide which parts of all the close-ups to use. Then they added classical music, which played the entire time she was applying her makeup. At the end of the commercial the camera shows the woman from the original wide shot, but this time she looks almost like a clown because the makeup is extremely overdone. The voiceover says, "Too much of anything makes you look like an idiot. Don't drink like one."

Postdirectors are independent contractors in the production mix. They are in the business of cutting film and creatively supervising videotape transfers from film; supervising video edits and special effects; recording narration, sound, music, and sound effects; mixing these sounds together; relaying them onto the picture; and delivering a finished product to the agency.

Computer Postproduction Technology

The computer has revolutionized some aspects of print production and prepress activities and is also active in revolutionizing TV postproduction. Advances in hardware and software are continuing to change the creation and production of TV commercials. Names such as Silicon Graphics, Avid, Inferno, Flame, and Quantel's Henry and Harry have been mainstays for a number of years. Terms such as *3-D animation, compositing, morphing, 2-D animation, nonlinear editing, live-action compositing,* and *real time* are common among the professionals who generate

visual images and special effects. The systems used for many special effects are still expensive. With any Mac iBook, producers can develop many of the same video effects at a lower costs but usually at a slower speed. When discussing computer hardware and software, each system has a plus and a minus. However, the availability offers creative and production people more options to create unique visuals and commercials.

It is safe to say that today's **computer-generated imagery (CGI)** offers creative minds great new opportunities in production and postproduction. This technology allows creative people to squash, squeeze, stretch, and morph objects in less time

computer-generated imagery (CGI)
Technology allowing computer operators to create multitudes of electronic effects for TV—to squash, stretch, or squeeze objects—much more quickly than earlier tools could. It can add layers of visuals simultaneously.

than ever before. Computers are turning live action into cartoon action. At production facilities, creative talents can use digital-graphics/animation-compositing systems to top four or five layers of live action with five or six layers of graphics, all simultaneously, allowing the finished visual composite to be seen as it develops. A Maybelline "Great Lash" spot created the blackest possible black for this 15-second commercial. Using an Avid suite, the individual computer layers were corrected to enrich the blacks around the model's eye's. The Avid allowed the operator to merge the layers with one image with three color corrections.[11]

CGI Wizardry   Remember the Budweiser Clydesdale who held the pigskin for the point-after attempt in the Super Bowl? Or the beer-slurpin' frogs? These are largely computer-generated (CG) or a mix of special techniques. The ability of animators and software engineers to imbue their characters with a greater sense of charm and warmth has made skeptics become computer converts. Now we have the ability to make photorealistic animals or monsters, for example. They look real, for the most part, only now they can do things no animal (or monster, for that matter) could be trained to do.

CGI and cel animation both play big roles in television commercial production. Costs of both are dropping, software is improving, and the proliferation of computer-generated graphics has created a growing reservoir of artists, techniques, and trends. The classic Coca-Cola polar bears could exist only in CGI. Cost, however, is still a major factor in using CGI and is considerably higher than live-action budgets. "National spots are rarely budgeted below $250,000 for a 30-second commercial; they can easily reach $1 to 2 million on the high end for clients like Coca-Cola, auto companies, and other large corporations," says executive producer Paul Golubovich.[12]

Recently, we have seen in television production an awareness that CGI can be used to help create things that couldn't otherwise be created. Taking different techniques and marrying them into one cohesive unit is difficult, but with developing software, and more skilled people, the process becomes easier and more creative.

The combination of elements from two or more photographic sources often produces a striking effect. With the advent of computers, the process of combining different layers became much easier, but at the same time it is more complex because the variety of combinations is now seemingly limitless. You may have heard of some of the following electronic production tools and techniques:

- *Compositing*. In the digital realm, *compositing* is the umbrella term for many processes required to technically accomplish image combination in the computer.
- *Matte*. Essentially a silhouette in black and white, matte is the necessary signal for the computer to cut out the part of the image intended to be visible. It can also exist in many other physical forms, such as a painting on glass or a masked-off camera composition.
- *Keying*. Keying is electronically composing one picture over another. The two types of keying are luminance and chroma-keying. This term came from the word *keyhole* and is interpreted by the computer as a signal enabling a hole to be cut in a clip layer.
- *Chroma-keying*. This is another matte derivation method in which the computer sources a specific color (usually green, blue, or red) to create a key signal. This is a way of performing automatic matte extraction, using the colored background. In a weather program that has a map and the weatherperson in front of the map, the map is an electronic image chroma-keyed off of a green screen. The weatherperson can't actually see the map without looking at a monitor. All that is actually behind them is a color screen. It is interpreted by the computer as a hole and is replaced with the layer behind, in this case a map.
- *Keyer*. A keyer is simply an electronic composer.

■ *Morphing.* **Morphing** is an industry term for metamorphosing, which means transforming from one object to another. For example, in a Schick shaving spot, a man's head is turned into a 3-D cube, and for Exxon a car turns into a tiger. This computer graphics technique allows its operator to move between the real world and computer graphics by electronically layering visual transitions between live action.

The cost of morphs varies. They can range from $5,000 for a "garage" job using a PC up to $70,000, depending on the complexity. But meticulous advance planning remains the key to a successful job. A Schick shaving heads commercial, which morphed a series of six talking shaving heads and upper torsos, required a two-day blue-screen shoot, composited over a bathroom background.[13]

morphing
An electronic technique that allows you to transform one object into another object.

■ *Harry.* The Quantel Henry/Harry online system is an editing device with an optical device tied to it. It allows computer composites to mix with live video. Ninety percent of Harry work can now be created on a Macintosh. The Harry is faster and much more expensive, but the Mac appears to be closing the gap.

■ *Flame.* On the other hand, Flame is an optical device with an editing device tied to it. It functions as a high-capacity, random-access, multilayer compositing system, with video editing/effects/digital-audio capacity. So you can see that you have to have the right technology for the right job. And, yes, it can be confusing to the nonproduction person in the advertising industry. A Bud Light commercial showed an invisible man breaking out of the "Secret Invisibility Lab" to get a six pack of Bud Light and astounds everyone he encounters. Aside from his floating six pack, the spot also featured hovering test tubes and another invisible character's bouncing paddle ball courtesy of some Harry and Flame effects.[14]

■ *In-house desktop.* Today agency Macintosh computers interface with video composers. This has made video editing, long the domain of highly trained specialists, a viable in-house option. This has allowed agency personnel to cut and paste video images just as desktop computers cut-and-paste print graphics. The quality isn't quite the level of the production houses' hardware/software, but it is getting closer and allows agencies to cut costs and use them for producing the storyboard, the animatic for testing, and rough cuts. The DVD is then sent to the production company, where the spot is polished into a final commercial of broadcast quality. Those clients that do not need top-quality images can complete the entire commercial postproduction process on the system.

CONTROLLING THE COST OF COMMERCIAL PRODUCTION

The cost of producing a TV commercial is of deep concern to both the agency and the advertiser. The chief reason that money is wasted in commercials is inadequate preplanning. In production, the two major cost items are labor and equipment. Labor—the production crew, director, and performers—is hired by the day, and equipment is rented by the day. If a particular demonstration was improperly rehearsed, if a particular prop was not delivered, or if the location site was not scouted ahead of time, the shooting planned for one day may be forced into expensive overtime or into a second day. These costly mistakes can be avoided by careful planning.

Cost Relationship

Several areas that can have a dramatic impact on TV production costs are the following:

■ *Location or studio.* Is the commercial planned for studio or location? Location shoots, outside geographic zones, mean travel time and overnight accommodations for the crew, adding a minimum average cost of $7,500 per away day.

■ *Talent.* The number of principals on the storyboard is important and can be expensive. The more people on-camera in your commercials, the higher the talent residual bill. The rates for talent are based on the Screen Actors Guild (SAG) union contract. For national commercials, you can roughly estimate your talent cost per on-camera principal as .0015 percent of your media budget for the spot, that is, $15,000 per person per $10 million in exposure. If 20 on-camera people are involved in your spot, expect a $300,000 bill. That chunk of your budget may exceed the entire net cost of production. So it is important to discuss how many on-camera principals are planned for the spot and how many are absolutely necessary.

■ *Residuals.* Another major expense is the residual, or reuse fee, paid to performers—announcers, narrators, actors, and singers—in addition to their initial session fees. Under union rules, performers are paid every time the commercial is aired on the networks, the amount of the fee depending on their scale and the number of cities involved. If a commercial is aired with great frequency, a national advertiser may end up paying more in residuals than for the production of the commercial itself. This problem is less severe for the local advertiser because local rates are cheaper than national rates. The moral is: Cast only the number of performers necessary to the commercial and not one performer more.

■ *Special effects.* If the board indicated the use of special effects or animation (either computer generated or cel), ask how the special effect will be achieved. It is not unusual for complicated computer-generated effects to cost $6,000 to $12,000 per second and more! To prevent surprises, ask questions. What may appear to be a simple execution on the surface may in fact contain extremely expensive elements. Neither the agency nor client should be satisfied until everyone understands the project. Anything short of this can result in surprise creative and expenditures.

■ *Estimate costs.* Given the potential complexity of shooting commercials due to a wide range of factors (location, special rigs, special effects, talent, set construction), it is not uncommon to believe a relatively "simple" looking spot presented in storyboard form will be "relatively" inexpensive. This is simply not the case. Both the client and the agency must always, always require a rough cost for each spot recommended. The number provided will help put the project into focus relative to the planned media support for the commercials. Generally, it is not uncommon for clients to spend 10 percent of their planned media budget in production. As this percentage escalates, the production decision becomes more difficult, particularly in today's economic climate.

■ *Editorial fee cost.* There is a creative labor fee for the editor's service. This charge is for the editor's and assistant editor's time. Depending on the editor and the difficulty of the edit, a creative fee can range from $400 to $500 (to supervise sound only, for example, on a single-scene commercial) to more than $9,000 to cut a multi-image, complex spot with special effects manipulations and music.

■ *The cost of film transfer and videotape conform or edit and finishing.* This cost can range from about $1,000 for this work, including tape stock and finished materials, to $7,500 for expensive and difficult treatments.

■ *Special effects and titling.* This cost can range from $100 to make a title art card and include it in the edit session to $10,000 to $30,000 for heavy design, frame-by-frame, picture manipulations.

■ *Recording and mixing.* The cost of recording and mixing a voiceover, music, and sound effects together can range from $450 to $4,000 or more.

If you total all of these possibilities, from the combined lowest to the combined highest, the cost can be $2,136 to $67,100 to edit a 30-second commercial!

Unions and Cost

In late 2003, the Joint National Boards of the Screen Actors Guild (SAG) and the American Federation of Television and Radio Artists (AFTRA) approved a new three-year contract negotiated with the Joint Policy Committee on Broadcast Talent Union Relations (JPC) of the Association of National Advertisers (ANA) and the American Association of Advertising Agencies (AAAA), ratified by the unions' 140,000 members. The contract expires October 29, 2006. It amounted to an up-front 5.5 percent increase in the industry's overall payment of wages and residuals, plus a 1 percent increase in employer contributions to the SAG and AFTRA pension and health plans. We mention this because the agreement affects production, residual payments, and total costs. It is also very complex and complicated. For example, the main session rate for on-camera principals is $535.00, the rate for on-camera groups of three to five is $391.65, and the rate for off camera groups is $226.90. Here is a snapshot of some of the areas covered, with rates and specifics:

> Program Class A Second use for On Camera Principals $122.70, On Camera Groups (3 to 5) $113.70, and Off Camera Groups (3 to 5) $226.90. The Third Use for On Camera Principals is $97.35.

> Program Class B/with New York market is $1,501.80 for On Camera Principal, $644.70 for the 3 to 5 On Camera Groups. However, without New York, On Camera Principals are paid $825.60. If it is a Spanish Language Program the On Camera principal rate is $1,932.00. The contract covers Stunt Adjustments, Ad LIB, Hazzard payments. It also states rates for casting and auditions, principals, general extras, hand models, body makeup/oil, costume fitting, interviews, location meal allowance, mileage allowances, meal period violations, travel time to and from location. There are also mileage fees based upon the vehicle: auto, trailer, motorcycle. It also includes skates, skateboard, bicycle, moped. It specifies Wet, Snow, Smoke, Dust work extra compensation. And, of course, the advertiser also has to pay an additional 14.3 percent toward Health and Retirement contributions.[15]

As you can see the union negotiated just about everything. It is one of the reasons that it is sometimes cheaper to shoot commercials in other countries. Because almost all the professional talent in this country are members of one of the appropriate unions, an advertiser/agency must abide by these contracts or be blacklisted from all the available talent.

AFTRA represents actors and other professional performers, and broadcasters in television, radio, sound recordings, nonbroadcast/industrial programming, and new technologies such as interactive programming and CD-ROMs.

A few other union advertisers are involved in one fashion or the other in the United States and Canada:

ACTRA—Alliance of Canadian Television and Radio Artists. A national organization of Canadian performers working in film, television, video and all other recorded media.

AFM—American Federation of Musicians. The largest union in the world representing the professional interests of musicians.

DGA—Director's Guild of America. Represents members in theatrical, industrial, educational, and documentary films, as well as live television, filmed and taped radio, videos, and commercials.

There is a host of other nonunion organizations that may be involved in creating and producing commercials.

ASCAP—American Society of Composers, Authors and Publishers. Allows creators and publishers to receive payment for the use of their musical property and provides users of that music with easy and inexpensive legal access to the world's largest and most varied catalog of copyrighted music.

BMI. Source for the song titles, writers, and publishers of the world's most popular music—the BMI repertoire—in a searchable database of millions of items, updated weekly, together with the Web's most complete fund of information for and about songwriting and music licensing.

TV Production Cost Averages

The average cost to produce national television commercials in 2000 declined 3 percent for 30-second spots and 1 percent for commercials regardless of length, according to the American Association of Advertising Agencies' (AAAA) 2000 Television Production Cost Survey. Only two times in the 14-year history of the annual report, in 1995 and 1997, was a decrease reported. In actual dollars, the 3 percent decrease represented $11,000—the difference between the national thirty average cost of $332,000 reported in 2000 and $343,000 reported in 1999. For national commercials of all lengths, production cost decreased to $306,000 in 2000.[16]

Lower Production Company Costs/Directors' Fees and Rise in Studio Shoots The survey showed that, among other factors related to decreased costs, the average total production company net cost was $228,000 in 2000.

Directors' fees per 30-second commercial averaged $21,000 in 2000. In 1999, they climbed 16 percent. Shooting commercials in the studio increased to 19 percent, while combination (in studio and location) shoots decreased to 17 percent when compared to the previous study. When shot in a studio, a national thirty took an average of 13 hours, compared to 14 hours when filmed on location. An average of 18 hours was required to shoot a 30-second commercial shot both in the studio and on location.

Commercial production days in Los Angeles rose slightly in 2003, according to numbers released by the Entertainment Industry Development Corporation (EIDC). For the year, the EIDC recorded 5,701 shooting days in 2003, compared with 5,615 in 2002. In 1999 commercial shooting in Los Angeles hit its peak with 6,569 shooting days recorded.[17]

DROP IN POSTPRODUCTION FEES

The 2001 survey found the average cost to edit and finish an original thirty decreased 2 percent to $42,000.

Creative/labor fees decreased by 8 percent, and music costs posted a 3 percent drop compared to a 35 percent increase in 1999. Video finishing remained the same whereas sound recording and mixing increased by 20 percent.[18]

Postproduction Management

The camera crew may be shooting in another country, your agency headquarters may be on the opposite coast from the production company, and creative directors may be in transit. Yet everyone needs to look at and approve the latest work (whether location, imagery, schedules, or treatments). There are several technology systems to allow consultation. For example, IOWA's WireDrive is used by many production companies/agencies to better manage projects online with all the cast of characters. It allows sharing of computer files and feedback of the commercial via a Web-based interface. Some of the production companies will put up location photos and storyboards as soon as they get a new job so clients and agency personnel can get involved from other locations. Clients only see their projects. Whenever new still images, QuickTime clips, or other materials are ready to be reviewed, a notification e-mail goes out. Since no one wants to download 10Mbs worth of data, people can view thumbnails, quickly accessible from any Internet dial-up or high-speed connection, and then click their computer for full details.[19] Clearly, times have changed as advertisers, production companies, directors, and agencies are all using different forms of digital links in the production process that save time, money, and travel.

ANA Guidelines for Achieving Cost Efficiencies in TV Production

Clients obviously have their say in the television production cost issue. The 340 members of the Association of National Advertisers (ANA) represent more than 8,000 brands that collectively spend over $100 billion in marketing communications and advertising. "Producing effective television commercials is one of the most important—and expensive—parts of the marketing process," said Soni Styrlund, Production Management Committee Chair and Manager, Advertising Production, General Mills, Inc. In 2003, the ANA issued new guidelines to its member companies for achieving cost efficiencies in TV commercial production. Created by the ANA's Production Management Committee, the 15 guidelines cover a wide range of issues: For example, preproduction planning, bidding procedures, location shooting, rights negotiations, digital asset storage, and talent reuse considerations.[20] Highlights of the guidelines include the following:

1. *Formalize TV production guidelines.* Prepare comprehensive guidelines that institutionalize best practices and establish expectations for all involved parties.
2. *Use a production expert.* Whether internal or external, project related or ongoing, tap the know-how of an experienced production person.
3. *Set production budgets prior to creative development.* Establish up-front budget parameters for producing commercials as well as for testing them. Don't discourage the agency from presenting ideas that exceed the parameters, but insist on options that stay within the budget estimate.
4. *Set a realistic time line prior to creative development.* Clarify the airdate at the start of creative development so that a realistic time line can be prepared.
5. *Determine whether multiple bidding or single bidding is more advantageous.* Potential cost considerations need to be balanced against deadline constraints, time input, and overall process efficiency.
6. *Consider building individual spots into pools.* Pooling the production of similar ads can reduce shooting days, resulting in significant cost savings.
7. *Consider shooting in secondary U.S. markets as well as off-shore.* Cities outside the major U.S. markets can provide a wealth of professional talent as well as other untapped resources.
8. *Evaluate the number of shoot days required.* Consider shaving a production day and extending overtime and/or using a prelight day for product shots.
9. *Use cost-plus on specific categories.* Within a firm bid, convert certain expenses (e.g., crew, film, pension, and welfare, and location) to a cost-plus basis.
10. *Break out color-corrected packaging for hero product.* Use your design resource or internal capabilities to produce color-corrected packaging and mock-ups rather than paying agency or production company markups.
11. *Leverage the overall buying power of your company and your agency/holding company.* Use your clout to negotiate reduced rates for such services as talent payment, commercial distribution, element storage, and insurance.
12. *Manage roles and responsibilities during the process.* Limit the number of people involved in the production process. Empower one key decision maker to call the shots during prep and production.

ADVANTAGE POINT

A typical complex production schedule for a finished computer commercial can cost more than $1.5 million and take 6 months to complete.

Production Schedule

Bidding Studio	*Stage or Location Shoot without Special Effects*	*Special Effects Shoot*
Includes:	2–3 Weeks	3–6 Weeks
• Screening directors' reels		
• Sending job specification		
• Bids (AICP form) returned		
• Bid comparison by agency		
• Estimating supplemental costs (music, travel, etc.)		

Preproduction	*Stage or Location Shoot without Special Effects*	*Special Effects Shoot*
Includes:	2–3 Weeks	3–6 Weeks
• Casting		
• Location search		
• Set design		
• Wardrobe fittings		

Shoot	*Stage or Location Shoot without Special Effects*	*Special Effects Shoot*
Roll camera	1–7 Days	1–7 Days

Postproduction	*Stage or Location Shoot without Special Effects*	*Special Effects Shoot*
Includes:	2–3 Weeks	4–10 Weeks
• Edit film		
• Film color correction		
• Post special effects		
• Casting voiceover talent		
• Recording voiceover talent		
• Demo music		
• Music recording		
• Final audio mix and masters		

13. *Establish a digital asset library to reuse and repurpose existing footage.* Create a centralized, Web-based storage facility for video, audio and logo assets. Before production begins, check this library to see what might be usable.

14. *Set up a profit center for music.* Actively claim and collect royalties for original music created for advertising. Be sure to negotiate retention of publishing royalties up front.

15. *Revisit talent payments and reuse often.* Considerable savings are possible via careful attention to talent use and rotation scheduling.

SUMMARY

Television remains the most powerful advertising medium because of its ability to blend sight, sound, and motion to create emotional reactions. The time to communicate is very short—usually 15 to 30 seconds—and creates a challenge for communicating the product story or position.

There are numerous creative techniques available to the creative team: testimonials, demonstrations, slice-of-life, interviews, humor, animation, serials, infomercials, and so forth. Research can aid the creative decision process in terms of which technique is appropriate for the strategy.

Storyboards are usually created to help communicate the idea to the advertiser and the production company. It is important that everyone clearly visualize the same commercial before time and money are invested in the idea.

Developing commercials requires some understanding of production terminology such as wipes, dissolves, and close-ups that help communicate the nature of a particular visual or transition from one scene to the next. Writing and visualizing the commercial in simple and easy-to-understand terms are essential to success—it is, after all, a visual medium. Because a good idea can be destroyed by bad production, producing the finished commercial is just as important as conceiving the big idea.

Producing the commercial involves three distinct stages: preproduction, shooting, and postproduction. Computer-generated imagery allows creative people to do almost anything they can imagine—but the cost may be high.

REVIEW

1. What is a bookend commercial?

2. What cost-relationship factors are involved in the making of a TV commercial?

3. What is the purpose of a storyboard?

4. Who attends the preproduction meeting?

5. What is a Harry?

TAKE IT TO THE WEB

Visit the Steak 'n Shake Web site (**www.steaknshake.com**) and view the television commercials posted. The ads often use humor to express the benefits of a 24-hour restaurant with fresh food and great service.

The Television Bureau of Advertising Online (**www.tvb.org**) provides information on selling ideas, media comparisons, and more.

AD-ID, which stands for Advertising Digital Identification, is a new identification system for advertising assets (including both broadcast and print) developed by the American Association of Advertising Agencies and the Association of National Advertisers. Visit **www.ad-id.org** for more information on this identification system.

CHAPTER 20

It's Thursday night. Usually, his favorite night of the week. But the drummer's out of town at a convention. Which means no band practice tonight. No offense, but that leaves a hole even "Friends" and "ER" can't fill.

The Radio Commercial

CHAPTER OBJECTIVES

I n print and television, visuals are an integral part of communication. Radio is a different medium, one for ears alone. After reading this chapter, you will understand:

1. the nature of the medium
2. how to create from a strategy
3. structuring the commercial
4. writing the commercial
5. musical commercials
6. producing radio commercials
7. unions and talent

Logic tells you radio advertising should be easy to create. All you have to do is talk to someone about the product. Right? Well, maybe. Great radio advertising is actually very difficult. Yet some advertisers get it right for years and years. They awaken images in the listener's mind by using sound, music, and voices. Some do simply talk to the listener.

Nobody talks one-to-one better than Tom Bodett in commercial after commercial. Bodett's voice is the voice of Motel 6. He was a regular commentator on National Public Radio's popular news program in the 1980s, *All Things Considered.* Someone at The Richards Group ad agency heard him and asked Bodett if he'd be willing to use his voice talents as a deadpan radio bullfrog to market a national chain of economy motels. He agreed. Ad-libbing the tag line, "We'll Leave the Light on for You," in the very first commercial session gained success for the chain and for Bodett. He remains the spokesperson for Motel 6 after more than 15 years. And the tag remains the same. The campaign is one of the longest-running advertising campaigns and continues to win awards for its creativity and effectiveness in the lodging industry. One of his commercials, "Business Talk," makes fun of today's business language. It is written by Christopher Smith and speaks to the business traveler:

> Hi. I'm Tom Bodett For Motel 6, With a word for business
> travelers. Seems business has its own language these days. Full
> of buzzwords, Like buzzwords. Or Net Net.

The commercial goes on to name a multitude of business speak sayings: *outsource* your accommodation needs, *deliverables, matrix* of *actionable* items, *cost-effective,* and so on.

> You'll get clean, comfortable rooms at the lowest price, Net Net,
> of Any national chain. . . .

Then he puts an unusual twist on the traditional Motel 6 ending, *"We'll leave the light on for you."*

> I'm Tom Bodett for Motel 6. We'll maintain the lighting device in its current state of illumination.

The agency uses a little "disruption of the norm" to hold your attention despite a formula that has worked and not tired. The concept is simple. The strategy and execution are superb.

If you awaken images in the listeners' minds, you have the opportunity to play with their imagination in what is referred to as "the theater of the mind."

THE NATURE OF THE MEDIUM

In print and television advertising, visual images can be powerful in attracting attention and full of emotion. Obviously radio is different. There is no visual image or color to attract people to the message. Yet, sound messages can be powerful. Some would argue that radio is the most visual medium, if you do your job right.

Copywriter Tom Monahan says, "In radio there's no place to hide anything. No place for the mistakes, the poor judgement, the weakness. Everything is right there in front for all 30 or 60 seconds. Everything must be good for the spot to be good. The concept, copy, casting, acting, production—everything. One of them goes wrong, sorry, but it's tune-out time."[1] Let us take a closer look at the nature of the medium.

Phil Cuttino, radio advertising expert, often refers to "watching radio—the most misunderstood medium." Before the beginning of widespread viewing of television in the mid–1950s, families used to "watch" the radio. We have all heard excerpts from radio's **theater of the mind**—*Superman, The Lone Ranger, Bulldog Drummon, Inner Sanctum,* and Orson Welles's fabulous spoof, *War of the Worlds.* People watched the radio because the mental imagery that came with every episode was breathtaking or scary or beautiful or just plain funny. However, television's combination of audio and visuals was very compelling and certainly effective as a storyteller and theater. TV also was, and is, a dynamic advertising medium. Unfortunately, radio was subordinated to the position of music, talk, and other audio-oriented programming.

theater of the mind
In radio, a writer paints pictures in the mind of the listener through the use of sound.

ANNCR:	Due to the highly technical nature of Hangers new dry cleaning process, the following commercial message is being translated.
KIRK:	Hi, I'm Kirk Kinsell, president and CEO of Hangers Cleaners.
ANNCR:	I'm Kirk and I'm da man at Hangers.
KIRK:	At Hangers, we've revolutionized dry cleaning by using liquid carbon dioxide instead of harsh chemicals.
ANNCR:	We've plowed a boatload of money into R&D so your clothes won't stink.
KIRK:	It's the same carbon dioxide that puts bubbles in soft drinks. Only now, we're using it to clean clothes.
ANNCR:	Our new dry cleaning process is kickin'.
KIRK:	Given the molecular properties of CO_2, only 74 BTUs are required to vaporize one pound of liquid.
ANNCR:	I don't have the foggiest idea what he just said.

KIRK:	As a result, there's no need to worry about heat-set stains, fading colors, or shrinkage.
ANNCR:	You'll look good. Really good.
KIRK:	Bring your dry cleaning to Hangers. We'll keep your clothes looking, smelling, and feeling like new.
ANNCR:	We can't wait to clean to your clothes.
TAG Morrisville up to 5/6:	Join us Saturday, May 6, for our Grand Opening in Morrisville. Cary Parkway and Highway Fifty-four.

Television remains the major means of developing impact in a campaign. It is also the fastest means for a creative team to get noticed. In major publications, there are commentaries on TV commercials, as well as objective and subjective ratings. TV is the closest that ad people come to "show biz." Another contributing factor to radio's lowly position in the creative pecking order is the fact that most creative teams consist of art directors, designers, and copywriters. Because radio has no material visuals, the visual arts people are out of business when it comes to radio. This tends to lead the creative team to either print or television advertising.

Over time, a new type of radio commercial has emerged, which Cuttino calls "print radio." When radio is needed, some copywriters, who are experienced in print advertising but know little about radio, tend to fall back on a familiar copy format. As a result, we hear "print radio" all the time. There is a headline, a subhead, body copy, a logo, and a slogan—an audio newspaper ad.

To understand the importance of radio, you need to understand the cynical nature of the American consumer.

No one believes anyone anymore. American consumers are searching for an excuse to disbelieve what you are saying. All they need is a cue that you are trying to sell them something and they will blank you out mentally. They may not change the dial; this is a case of "The lights are on, but nobody's home." Before you can tell consumers your story, you must disarm them, entertain them, amuse them, and get them on your side.

Radio, like magazines, is a very personal medium. Almost everyone has a favorite radio station. Many consumers listen to Net radio online where some stations use broadband and streaming video content. Consumers get to know the radio personalities; they attend events sponsored by their radio station. It is this kind of listener allegiance, this nonhostile environment, that makes it easier for marketers to approach the listenership. Remember, consumers are not waiting to hear your commercial. They are listening to the radio to be entertained, so entertain them and then sell them. Entertainment is your admission ticket to their consciousness.

The future is challenged for traditional radio. The Internet has challenged traditional radio in the home and office, but radio has maintained its dominance in the car. The prospects of direct-to-car digital satellite radio bring more challenges to local radio and advertisers.[2]

FLEXIBILITY, MARKETABILITY, AND PROMOTIONABILITY

Radio offers more than other advertising media. It has the flexibility, the marketability, the promotionability, and the price to fit advertisers' needs to reach their targets—if they choose the right stations and use the right message.

■ You have 60 seconds all to yourself. Print ads have to fight for attention with other ads on the page. TV has to contend with channel surfers because viewers have favorite TV programs, whereas radio listeners have favorite radio stations.

In the time span of a 60-second radio commercial, no other advertising can interfere with your message. The main equalizer in radio is the ability of a locally produced radio spot to be on a level playing field with any national spot. The power of a radio commercial is the idea, the imagery. Unlike TV, national-quality production can be easily created for a reasonable cost. Your advertiser can be as big as any other marketer for 60 seconds.

- Radio has the most captive audience of any media. The advent of mass transit has not changed the fact that in most cities, to get from point A to point B, you still have to get in your car and drive. The heaviest radio listenership occurs in the morning and afternoon drive times. During that time, listeners cannot go to the kitchen for a beer, answer the door, or pick up a magazine. They are trapped in their cars, listening to the traffic report, the news, and, of course, your radio commercial.

- Listeners and advertisers have many programming formats to choose from: country, adult contemporary, news/talk/sports/business, oldies, top 40, religion, classic rock, urban rhythm and blues, easy listening, alternative rock, variety, ethnic, classical, gospel, jazz, new age, and preteen. This makes radio a highly selective medium for the advertiser. Reflecting the ethnic multinational nature of our society, there also are foreign-language stations in many markets available to advertisers.

CREATING THE COMMERCIAL

Radio commercials are developed through a thought process similar to that used in other media despite requiring a different style of advertising. As with any advertising, you have to understand your target. As Tom Little, award-winning creative director, once said, "People don't buy products. They buy solutions to problems." Last year people bought about 350,000 quarter-inch drill bits in this country. People didn't want quarter-inch drill bits. They wanted quarter-inch holes.

The radio creative writer has to refer back to the objectives and strategy and describe the target in both demographic and psychographic terms before beginning the creative process. The writer needs to be sure the message is going to be believed—that it says the right things to the right people—and needs to ask if the copy strengthens the brand position, the place the advertiser wants to occupy in the consumer's mind. Is it credible? Does the writer have all the copy points that research indicates is needed? Is it human? Is it believable communication? Do people really talk like that? Or is it simply copy lingo? These are some of the things the radio copywriter must think about when sitting down to the blank page or the computer screen.

The writer for radio has the opportunity to develop an entire commercial alone (although in some agencies a creative team may work on a project). That means writing the script, picking the talent, and producing the commercial. In radio, the copywriter enjoys the freedom to create scenes in the theater of the listener's imagination by painting pictures in sound—a car starting or stopping, a phone ringing, water running, ice cubes falling into a glass, crowds roaring, a camera clicking. Remember, sound alone has an extraordinary ability to enter people's minds.

Spirit Mountain Casino enters the imagination in the beginning of this commercial:

GUY: As Sam left the house that morning, he tripped over his cat.

SFX: (Thud)

SAM: Hey, Kitty.

GUY: The jolt shook loose a giant blob of peanut butter from his toast, which landed on his shirt. The shirt his mom had given him on her

KLEPPNER VIEWPOINT 20.1

STEVEN H. LANG

Creative Director *Southern Broadcasting*

What makes a good radio commercial? It produces the desired results for the client. That is the only true measure of success. Not awards or compliments. Just results. Anything else is a failure. So how do you create a successful radio commercial? You observe the following methods as a template and build the rest of the ad around them.

Listening to people talk only about themselves can be extremely tedious. You try to get away as quickly as possible, don't you? So why do most radio commercials center on the client rather than on the listener? Radio can be such an engaging medium, yet most clients want to turn it into a brag fest. "We have the biggest this!!! We have the most that!!! We're number one in blah blah!!!" Yawn. Click. So what should you do? Change your focus.

Instead of making the client the subject of the ad, make the listener, or how the listener can benefit, the subject of the commercial. People, by nature, are self-interested. So by speaking about subjects of interest and importance to them, they'll naturally pay more attention. Talking to someone is always better than trying to talk at everyone. This doesn't mean just using the word *you* all the time but also fashioning a commercial the listener can identify with by showing both a problem and a solution. However, in our overcommunicated world, just getting the listener's attention and holding it can be an arduous task. So take them to the theater.

A runaway asteroid in deep space. High noon on the streets of the Old West. On a street corner during rush hour. With a few sound effects and a couple minutes in a studio, you can create any environment of sounds from the past, present, or future. Then you sit back and wait for your listeners' imagination to fill in the pictures. By using "theater of the mind" to involve the listeners in your commercial, they are more apt to follow your message and relate to your product or offer. Video and computer animation can also create these types of environments, but you lose the process of engaging the imagination and it is much more expensive and time consuming. However, it takes more than just "theater of the mind" to get your message across. You must also be sure that they'll hear it again and again and again.

Repetition plays a huge part in the success of a radio commercial. Even a poorly written ad can increase effectiveness to some degree by increasing repetition. Why? "Because sound is intrusive," says Roy H. Williams, a sales and marketing consultant. He notes, "While driving, how many times have you turned down the radio while trying to find a street or turn? How many songs do you know by heart, though you've never set out to learn them?" The intrusive nature of radio, combined with repetition, makes an extremely effective method of getting your message across.

With proper subject focus, "theater of the mind," and sufficient repetition, you can stand out from the clutter with radio commercials that get results. As radio programming and sales legend Dan O'Day noted, radio is mass salesmanship.

Courtesy of Steven H. Lang, Creative Director, and Southern Broadcasting. ▪ ▪ ▪

> deathbed. Just then he noticed the cat wasn't moving. Now he was late to work. And that was the day they gave out free trips to Hawaii.
>
> ANNC: Bad luck. . . Luck Happens. Spirit Mountain Casino.

Let us look at the three elements the copywriter uses to create mental pictures, memorability, and emotion: words, sound, and music.

Words

Words are the basic building blocks of effective radio commercials. They are used to describe the product, grab attention, create interest, build desire, and evoke a response from the listener. As with the success of Motel 6, the warmth of the human voice may be all that is needed to communicate your message.

Here Dow's Great Stuff tongue-in-cheek football commercial says,

> ANNC: (tongue-in-cheek delivery, background music) Every autumn Nate Turner embarks on a mission to explain football to women. Patiently he tries to clarify the West Coast offense. And why it is normal for one man to pat another's fanny. Maybe this year he'll break through.
>
> YOUNGER GUY: (more serious) Think that's a waste of energy? You should see what your home is doing! Get Great Stuff insulating foam sealant. It fills the cracks where heat and cold air escape. Look for Great Stuff in the red and yellow can anywhere home improvement products are sold.

Sound

Used properly, sound can unlock the listener's imagination and create feelings. Any sound effect used should be necessary and recognizable; you should never have to explain it for the audience.

The sound has to convey a special message or purpose; it has to attract attention and complement the words. Sound can be used to underscore a point; create feelings of suspense, excitement, or anger; and invoke almost any mood you desire.

There are three basic sources of sound effects: manual, recorded, and electronic. Manual effects are those that are produced live, either with live subjects or with studio props; opening doors, footsteps, and blowing horns are examples. Recorded effects are available from records, tapes, or professional sound libraries. They offer the copywriter almost every conceivable sound—dogs barking, cats meowing, leaves blowing, thunder crashing, cars racing. Electronic effects are sounds that are produced electronically on special studio equipment. Any sound created by using a device that generates an electrical impulse or other electronic sound is an electronic effect.

Music

Music can be very powerful in catching the listener's attention and evoking feelings. Thus, music has been called the "universal language." Different kinds of music appeal to different emotions: A minor key is sadder than a major key; an increased tempo creates a sense of anticipation.

jingle
A commercial or part of a commercial set to music, usually carrying the slogan or theme line of a campaign. May make a brand name and slogan more easily remembered.

Commercials are often set to music especially composed for them or adapted from a familiar song. A few bars of distinctive music played often enough may serve to identify the product instantly. Such a musical logotype usually lasts from 4 to 10 seconds. **Jingles** are a popular means of making a slogan memorable—think of the music for Coca-Cola, Pepsi, Chevrolet, and McDonald's over the years. Folk's Southern Cooking Cous Cous jingle version says:

"Now hold the capers and the sun dried tomatoes
Hold the Cous Cous and those tarragon potatoes
When I'm in the mood for some comfort food
Nobody knows me like my Folks."

Create from Strategy

What's brown, fuzzy, round on the outside, green on the inside, and tastes good? The California Kiwifruit Commission set an objective to increase awareness of its ugly little product. Its strategy was built around "Kiwifruit Is Fun." "The commission understands people's perception of the California kiwifruit and gave us permission to have fun with its outward appearance . . . knowing that it's what's inside that counts," says Christine Coyle. The spots humorously played out two situations: a recognizable school food pageant and a California Kiwifruit audition. The ads were able to convince consumers who were suspect of the funny-looking fruit to go ahead and give it a try. The vertical integrated program combined radio with some print and some in-store services that helped educate grocery produce managers. Unit sales the first year of the campaign went up 67 percent, or an increase of about 5 million new households purchasing the product. The strategy worked.

DEVELOPING THE RADIO SCRIPT

You will find some differences in the formats used in the script examples in this chapter. This is because most agencies have their own format sheets for copywriters. Formats also vary according to how the script will be used: If you are going to be in the studio with the producers and talents, you can verbally explain how the script is to be read or answer any questions that come up. If, however, you are going to mail the script to DJs to be read live, you need to be certain that anyone reading it will understand exactly what you want. The guidelines shown in Exhibit 20.1 illustrate explicit script directions.

EXHIBIT 20.1

Example of Radio Form Directions

Length: 60

Job No. 3364

LEFT SECTION OF PAGE IS FOR INFORMATION RELATING TO VOICES, ANNOUNCER, MUSIC, SOUND, USUALLY IN CAPS.	The right section of the script consists of copy and directions. It should be typed double-spaced. Pause is indicated by dots (. . .) or double dash (— —). Underline or use CAPS for emphasis.
MUSIC:	Music is usually indicated by all caps. WILLIAM TELL OVERTURE ESTABLISH AND FADE UNDER. In some cases, music is underlined. Directions may be indicated by parentheses ( ).
VOICE #1	(LAUGHING LOUDLY) Excuse me sir. . .
OLD MAN	Yes. . . (RAISING VOICE) What do you want?
SFX:	SUPERMARKET NOISES, CRASHING NOISES AS SHOPPING CARTS CRASH. Sound effects indicated by SFX: (:08) BUZZER
SINGERS:	He's bright-eyed and bushy-tailed. . .
ANNCR:	This indicates announcer talking.
VO:	Voice Over

Radio, Theater of the Mind

One of the biggest mistakes you can make in creating radio is the failure to recognize the fact that everyone has mental images of sounds that they hear. When no material images exist, sound creates an image in the mind's eye. It is the duty of the radio writer/producer to take control of the listener's imagery and guide it to a positive reaction that seeds the memory with the targeted message and leads to the proper response. For instance, a writer creates a commercial featuring a car dealer who is screaming about a sale, assuming that the tactic will get the listener's attention and will eventually lead the consumer to the dealership because of the "incredible savings." Unfortunately, the mind's eye of the listener doesn't see a sleek new car or the money he is saving; he sees a middle-aged man in a garish plaid suit yelling at him. In communications, it is important to be concerned about how people feel about your advertisement.

The late creative director Tom Little used to brag about radio's ability to paint pictures in the mind, "I had to spend $40,000 to build an airline set for our television ads, but I could build that same set in the minds of radio listeners for almost nothing."

Amy Lokken, copywriter at McRae Communications, used a little deadpan fantasy in this Snapper Lawn Tractor spot using an average Joe and the Snapper expert (see Exhibit 20. 2).

The Elements of a Good Radio Commercial

- *Be single-minded, focused.* Don't ask the consumer to take in too much information at one time. Prioritize your copy points. Think of your commercial as a model of our solar system. The major copy point is the sun and all the other copy points are planets of varying degrees of importance, but they all revolve around and support the central idea.

- *Research your product or service.* Many clients keep tabs on their competition, but they rarely relate their features and benefits to factual data. Meaningful statistics can give substantial support to your message.

EXHIBIT 20.2

Courtesy of McRae
Communications and Snapper.

Snapper :30 Radio	Copywriter: Amy Lokken
Ted and Henry/Lawn Tractor	McRae Communications
SFX:	Environmental sounds indicating we're at a Snapper dealer.
HENRY, THE SNAPPER EXPERT:	Hey Ted, check out the Snapper Lawn Tractors.
TED:	What about 'em?
HENRY:	Steel axles, convenient controls, up to a 48-inch deck and 18 horsepower.
TED:	Gee, that's big.
HENRY:	Big for a reason. Say an asteroid flies by.
TED:	Like that movie?
HENRY:	Sure. It messes up Earth's gravity, and your lawn stretches 10 times its size.
TED:	Can it do that?
HENRY:	Yeah. But with that wide deck and big engine, you handle those extra acres in no time.
TED:	Interesting.
VO:	Visit your Snapper dealer. Because a beautiful lawn is within your grass.

■ *Relate to the consumer.* When you tell consumers your story, always relate the brand to their wants and needs. Do not assume they will come to the right conclusion.

■ *Generate extension.* You can multiply the effect of your commercial many times over by achieving extension—consumers picking up phrases from the spot and using them. A clever phrase or execution can have consumers asking other people if they have heard the spot, people requesting the spot to be played on the radio, even getting mentions by DJs.

■ *Produce an immediate physical, emotional, or mental response.* Laughter, a tug on the heartstrings, or mental exercises of a consumer during a radio spot help seed the memory and aid message retention.

■ *Use plain, conversational English.* Be a clear communicator. Don't force your characters to make unnatural statements. This is not the boardroom—no "execubabble," just clear, plain, and simple English.

WRITING THE COMMERCIAL

Some agencies have a special creative director in charge of radio advertising. For years, the feeling has been that agencies have assigned junior talent to write radio commercials. It is now hoped that having a specific person in charge of radio will generate enthusiasm for doing great radio. Some agencies have special units that focus only on radio such as Hill Holiday Radio, a division of Hill Holiday Advertising.

There are radio boutiques that have been used for many years by clients and agencies to help create and produce radio commercials. Some of the most popular boutiques include The Famous Radio Ranch, Air Korman, BarzRadio, Radio in the Nude, World Wide Wadio, Oink Ink Radio, Atomic Radio, Radioland, Cat Paw Productions, Right Brain Visions, and Funny Farm Radio Hollywood. The Studio Center in Norfolk, Virginia (with several other offices and studios), produces some 14,000 spots a year.

The radio commercial, like the TV commercial, has as its basic ingredient the promise of a significant and distinctive benefit or position. Once the promise has been determined, you are ready to use the arsenal of words and sounds to communicate your product. Ways to vitalize the copy include the following:

■ *Simplicity.* The key to producing a good radio commercial is to build around one central idea. Avoid confusing the listener with too many copy points. Use known words, short phrases, and simple sentence structure. Keep in mind that the copy needs to be conversational. Write for the ear, not the eye. Get in the habit of reading your copy out loud.

■ *Clarity.* Keep the train of thought on one straight track. Avoid side issues. Delete unnecessary words. (Test: Would the commercial be hurt if the words were deleted? If not, take them out.) Write from draft to draft until your script becomes unmistakably clear and concise. At the end of the commercial, your audience should understand exactly what you have tried to say. Despite having several facts in your commercial, make sure you have the big idea.

■ *Coherence.* Be certain that your message flows in logical sequence from first word to last, using smooth transitional words and phrases for easier listening.

■ *Rapport.* Remember, as far as your listeners are concerned, you are speaking only to them. Try to use a warm, personal tone, as if you were talking to one or two people. Make frequent use of the word *you.* Address the listeners in terms they would use themselves.

■ *Pleasantness.* It is not necessary to entertain simply for the sake of entertaining, but there is no point in being dull or obnoxious. Strike a happy medium; talk as one friend to another about the product or service.

- *Believability.* Every product has its good points. Tell the truth about it. Avoid overstatements and obvious exaggerations; they are quickly spotted and defeat the whole purpose of the commercial. Be straightforward; you want to convey the impression of being a trusted friend.

- *Interest.* Nothing makes listeners indifferent faster than a boring commercial. Products and services are not fascinating in themselves; the way you present them makes them interesting. Try to give your customer some useful information as a reward for listening.

- *Distinctiveness.* Sound different from other commercials and set your product apart. Use every possible technique—a fresh approach, a musical phrase, a particular voice quality or sound effect—to give your commercial a distinct character.

Some Techniques

Basically a medium of words, radio—more than any other medium—relies heavily on the art of writing strong copy. However, just as print ads and TV commercials include pictures and graphics to add impact to the copy, radio creates mental pictures with other techniques. Radio copywriters can choose among many proven techniques to give more meaning to the copy, to help gain the attention of the busy target audience, and to hold that attention for the duration of the commercial. Some of these techniques parallel those used in television.

- *Humor.* Humor is an excellent technique for service and retail businesses. Consumers never relate an ad to the advertising agency that produced it; they only relate the spot to the advertiser. Therefore, humor can portray a company as friendly, likable, and easy when negotiating a sale. Each of the Hangers Cleaners and Snapper owner spots are not intended to break you up laughing. But each uses subtle "disruption" to raise a chuckle and make the commercial(s) memorable. Notice the similarity of writing style in these Snapper spots (see Exhibits 20.3 and 20.4).

Many award-winning radio spots use humor. Tom Little said humorous spots often won awards because they stood out from the hundreds that he had to listen to. If that's true, then the same probably works for consumers. Of course, humor may be part of any writing technique we have discussed. Humor is often appropriate for low-priced packaged products, products people buy for fun, products whose primary appeal is taste, or products or services in need of change-of-pace advertising because of strong competition. Be very careful about making fun of the product or the user or treating too lightly a situation that is not normally funny.

- *Emotion.* This is an effective method to use when the topic is indeed emotional. Family, health care, donations, mental care, security, and similar products and services use emotion to stimulate the targeted response.

- *Music/sound effects.* Music creates the mood and sound effects create the imagery in the consumer's mind. Jingles can be very memorable and effective when they relate directly to the product or service.

- *White space.* This is, of course, a term used in print advertising. However, white space in radio can be extremely compelling. A 60-second spot may start with music or sound effects with no copy for 45 seconds, bringing the consumers' curiosity into play and leaving them wide open to accept a provocative message.

- *Dialogue.* This is a great technique to use in many situations. Dialogue doesn't confront the consumer; it allows the listener to eavesdrop on the conversation. Dialogue is also very successful when the advertiser has a product that appeals to men and women. Dialogue between a man and a woman allows the commercial to play to both targets.

Snapper   :30 Radio

Ted and Henry/Walk Behinds

SFX:	Environmental sounds indicating we're at a Snapper dealer.
TED:	You got me to the dealer, but what's with you and these Snapper mowers?
HENRY, THE SNAPPER EXPERT:	Look at these walk behinds. Dura-Steel decks. 3-n–1 convertibility. 6-speed on-the-go shifting.
TED:	Why do I need six speeds?
HENRY:	Say aliens come down.
TED:	Aliens?
HENRY:	Yeah. They zap you to the prairie, tell you to cut the grass, or you have to go with them.
TED:	Why would they do that?
HENRY:	Who knows? But you downshift, cut the grass, and they zap you home.
TED:	Amazing.
VO:	Visit your Snapper dealer. Because a beautiful lawn is within your grass.

Copywriter: Amy Lokken

McRae Communications

EXHIBIT 20.3

This spot uses subtle humor and a similar writing format for all Snapper commercials. The type of voices and delivery of the lines are important in acquiring the intended mood and tone.

Courtesy of McRae Communications and Snapper.

Snapper   :30 Radio

Ted and Henry/Rear Engine Rider

SFX:	Environmental sounds indicating we're at a Snapper dealer.
HENRY, THE SNAPPER EXPERT:	My Snapper dealer here is gonna get you a real mower.
TED:	I've got a mower.
HENRY:	It's plastic. This is solid steel. It's America's number one selling Rear Engine Rider. And it's got quick-response steering.
TED:	Why do I need that?
HENRY:	Say you're mowing, and a giant badger jumps in front of you.
TED:	A badger?
HENRY:	Yeah, a big, snarling badger.
TED:	Why would he do that?
HENRY:	Doesn't matter. You easily turn out of the way. AND after one look at this extra tough mower, he won't be back.
TED:	Impressive.
VO:	Visit your Snapper dealer. Because a beautiful lawn is within your grass.

Copywriter: Amy Lokken

McRae Communications

EXHIBIT 20.4

Another spot in the series.

Courtesy of McRae Communications and Snapper.

- *Sex.* It can sell very well.

- *Straight announcer.* Sometimes the simplest approach works best. In this commonly used and most direct of all techniques, an announcer or personality delivers the entire script. Success depends both on the copy and on the warmth and believability of the person performing the commercial. Tom Bodett for Motel 6 is all of these things and one of the reasons the commercials are still so popular. This approach also works particularly well when a positive image has previously been established and a specific event is being promoted, such as a sale.

- *Combination.* Radio techniques may be mixed in countless ways combining music, sound effects, an announcer, and a person. You might notice that the advertisement uses the name of the product five times in interesting ways to gain brand recognition. To select the right technique for a particular assignment, follow the guidelines discussed in Chapter 19 for selecting TV techniques.

TIMING OF COMMERCIALS

Time is the major constraint in producing a radio commercial. Most radio stations accept these maximum word lengths for live commercial scripts:

- 10 seconds, 25 words
- 20 seconds, 45 words

In prerecorded commercials, of course, you may use any number of words you can fit within the time limit. However, if you use more than 125 words for a 60-second commercial, the commercial will have to be read so rapidly that it may sound unnatural or even unintelligible. Remember, if you insert sound effects, that will probably cut down on the number of words you can use. If you have footsteps running for 5 seconds, you are going to have to cut 10 to 12 words. You need to time the musical intros and endings or sound effects because each will affect the number of words allowable. It is not unusual to go into the recording studio with a script that is a couple of seconds short because the extra time allows the talents to sound more natural. Actors need some breathing room to sound sincere.

MUSICAL COMMERCIALS

Music can be a powerful tool for getting your product remembered. As musical writer Steve Karman has said, "People don't hum the announcer."[3]

In writing musical commercials, you have to start with an earthquake, then build to something really big. In other words, there is no room for subtlety. The thought process and strategy are different from those in regular songwriting.

There are three main elements to writing commercial music:

1. *Intro:* The beginning of the song. The tempo and lyrics may be established here.
2. *Verse:* The middle of the song. This is where the message is developed. There may be several verses.
3. *Theme or chorus:* May be the conclusion of the song.

Often you begin with the chorus to establish your theme, or you may repeat the theme throughout. The theme is what listeners remember. Some musical forms, such as blues, can be thought of as both verse and chorus. A theme may serve as a musical logotype for a product, lasting about 4 to 10 seconds.

Sheri Bevil of Bevil Advertising says, "Folks restaurants hired Jack Turner to do an original score and lyrics for a number of jingles. Usually the radio opens with one of the jingles. Then the promotional message goes over the bed of music (usually an announcer). Then it ends with another jingle. The jingle takes up 28 to 30 seconds leaving another 30 seconds for the specific message." In some cases, Bevil says, "The spot would also end with a 5- to 10-second tag."

> Southern Boy Version: Folks Southern Kitchen
> I've been a southern boy all my life
> Got a Southern drawl and a Southern wife
> When I'm in the mood for some comfort food
> Nobody knows me like my Folks.

Many commercials are composed especially for the advertiser or product. Others are simply adapted from a familiar song. A melody is in the public domain, available for use by anyone without cost, after its copyright has expired. Many old favorites and classics are in the public domain and have been used as advertising themes. That is one of their detriments: They may have been used by many others.

Popular tunes that are still protected by copyright are available only by (often costly) agreement with the copyright owner. An advertiser can also commission a composer to create an original tune, which becomes the advertiser's property and gives the product its own musical personality.

Do you have the talent to write a jingle? Does the typical copywriter have the ability to do so? In general, the job of writing such copy is left to the music experts.

Audio Technology

Since the mid–1980s there has been a radical change in the way music and sound are recorded. A little more than a decade ago, the world of high-fidelity multitrack recording (and sync-to-picture for TV) belonged solely to record companies, post-production houses, and commercial ventures.

In the early 1990s, software was created for the Macintosh that allowed true four-track recording and simultaneous MIDI (musical instrument digital interface) file playback. The simple interface was based on the integrated portable studio metaphor and required no sophisticated knowledge of the software. It looked and functioned like a four-track cassette mixer/recorder, but it turned any Macintosh into a CD-quality production environment.

You can record your basic ideas digitally from the very beginning, and add and edit digital audio tracks to your composition. You can then use the software to transfer the master digitally to a digital audiotape (DAT) or CD. Today every step in the multitrack production of digital audio is in the hands of the individual. Studio Center lists the typical technology options.

> Choose from real-time delivery via ISDN, distribution with DGS, digital delivery as a .wav, .aiff, or .mp3 file via e-mail or ftp posting. Digitally, we can send your audio via the internet as an .aiff file, .wav file, or .mp3 file. We can also upload your files to our ftp site for you to retrieve at your convenience. Fully produced spots may be transmitted for electronic distribution to radio stations via DGS. You have a format choice of audio CD, CD-ROM, DAT, Zip Disc, Beta, Reel or Cassette.

METHODS OF DELIVERY

There are three ways a radio commercial can be delivered: live, by station announcer, and prerecorded.

The Live Commercial

A live commercial is delivered in person by the studio announcer, disc jockey, newscaster, or other station personality, or perhaps by a sports reporter from another location. Although generally read from a script prepared by the advertiser, the commercial is sometimes revised to complement the announcer's style. If time allows, the revised script should be approved in advance by the advertiser. Ad-libbing (extemporizing) from a fact sheet should be discouraged because the announcer may inadvertently omit key selling phrases or, in the case of regulated products such as drugs, fail to include certain mandatory phrases.

Some commercials are delivered partly live and partly prerecorded. The prerecorded jingle, for example, can be played over and over with live-announcer copy added. Sometimes the live part (the dealer"tie-up") is left open for the tie-in ad of the local distributor.

One advantage of the live commercial is that the announcer may have a popular following, and listeners tend to accept advice from someone they like. For example, *The Steve and Vikki Morning Show* is the top-rated morning show in Atlanta. Vikki does endorsement commercials for Intimacy. "I'm Vikki Locke. Like most women I spent years wearing the wrong bra size until one day a friend told me about Intimacy. . . ." Steve McCoy talks about how his family breathes better because he installed a Pureatech air treatment system for his home. They both have a big following and bring credibility to their spots. Generally, the other big advantage is cost: Station announcers usually do your commercials free of extra talent costs, although some announcers may demand higher rates.

Station Announcer

For a campaign dealing with a retail offer that will change frequently, advertisers often use a station announcer reading copy written by the agency. This is recorded at the station at no charge to the client—sometimes even with the client's musical theme in the background. This type of delivery allows for frequent changes in copy at no cost.

The Prerecorded Commercial

Advertisers undertaking a regional or national campaign will not know local announcers' capabilities. In any case, it would be impractical to write a separate script to fit each one's particular style. Commercials for these campaigns are, therefore, usually prerecorded. Not only does this assure advertisers that the commercial will be identical each time it is aired, but it also allows them to take advantage of techniques that would be impractical in a live commercial. (Actually, in many instances, "live" commercials are recorded by the station so that they can run even when the announcer is not on duty.) Scott Crawford, creative director at HM&P, prerecorded the Hangers Commercials (see Exhibit 20.5).

Talent and Unions

As with television, the use of and payment to performers appearing in radio commercials are dictated by the AFTRA (American Federation of Television and Radio Artists) commercial contract. Talent is paid a session fee when the commercial is recorded. Other requirements for payment based on usage include spot, network, dealer, demo, and copy testing, and foreign use. It is another cost the advertiser must consider.

The complexity of the 2003 to 2006 union contract can be seen in the following list or in its entirety at AFTRA.org.

EXHIBIT **20.5**

This is an example of a prerecorded commercial script.

Courtesy of Howard, Merrell and Partners, Inc. and Hangers Cleaners.

:60 Jimspeak – AS RECORDED	Hangers Cleaners	Howard, Merrell & Partners
ANNCR:	Due to the highly technical nature of Hangers' new dry cleaning process, the following commercial message is being translated.	
JIM:	Hi, I'm Jim McLain, vice president technical development at Hangers Cleaners.	
ANNCR:	My name is Jim. But you can call me Jim.	
JIM:	My staff of engineers has spent the past four years developing a better way to dry clean clothes.	
ANNCR:	I lie awake at night thinking of dry cleaning.	
JIM:	The Hangers' process uses liquid carbon dioxide instead of harsh chemicals—the biggest innovation to hit dry cleaning in 50 years.	
ANNCR:	Our dry cleaning process will make you feel like a kid again.	
JIM:	With liquid carbon dioxide, there's no high heat required during the drying cycle.	
ANNCR:	I'm not just blowing a bunch of hot air up your slacks.	
JIM:	As a result, there's no need to worry about heat-set stains, fading colors, or shrinkage.	
ANNCR:	We won't ruin your clothes, your buttons, or your thongs.	
JIM:	Stop by Hangers Cleaners. We'll keep your clothes looking, smelling, and feeling like new. I promise.	
ANNCR:	You'll look great. And be transformed into a walking love machine. I promise.	
TAG – Morrisville up to 5/6:	Join us Saturday, May 6, for our Grand Opening in Morrisville. Cary Parkway and Highway Fifty-four.	

For example, minimum session fees:

Actor, announcer, sol, duo is	$235.40
Group singer/speaker	173.40

Then there are the use fees:	13 weeks
Network program commercial	$1,029.30
Regional network program	770.75
Outside New York, Chicago, or Los Angeles	235.40
New York alone	350.40
Chicago or Los Angeles alone	319.60
Any two of above	429.80
Demo/copy test	162.20
Additional hour	40.55

PRODUCING THE RADIO COMMERCIAL

Although there are certain broad similarities, producing radio commercials is far simpler and less costly than producing TV commercials. First, the agency or advertiser appoints a radio producer, who converts the script into a recording ready to go on the air. After preparing the cost estimate and getting budget approval, the producer selects a recording studio and a casting director, if necessary. If music is called for, the producer calls a music "house" that usually composes, arranges, and takes all steps necessary to get the finished music. If the music is not a big-budget item, the producer may call for "stock" music (prerecorded and used on a rental basis).

After the cast has been selected, it rehearses in a recording studio, which can be hired by the hour. However, because most commercials are made in short "takes" that are later joined in the editing, a formal rehearsal is usually unnecessary. When the producer feels the cast is ready, the commercial is acted out and recorded on tape. Music and sound are taped separately and then mixed with the vocal tape by the sound-recording studio. In fact, by double- and triple-tracking music and singers' voices, modern recording equipment can build small sounds into big ones. However, union rules require that musicians and singers be paid extra fees when their music is mechanically added to their original recording. After the last mix, the master tape of the commercial is prepared. When final approval has been obtained, duplicates are made for release to the list of stations.

Things to Remember During Production

Often the account executive or client will be at the recording session; however, Phil Cuttino has a bias against having either of them at a recording session. He feels their presence creates too many problems, which can inhibit great production. Among these are the talent and engineer tighten up, and everyone is concerned about time instead of producing an effective spot. He suggests that you use a phone patch from the studio to play the spot for the account executive first. Then, with his or her blessing, call the client for the final approval. The engineer and talent should remain in the studio until the final approval is achieved. Some other production thoughts:

- *Call ahead.* Have the studio pull the music and sound effects selections.
- *Studio.* Find a studio that has several talented engineers who will quickly learn your style. Make sure the studio has a good SFX and music library and the latest technology.
- *Brain power.* During production, use everyone's brain to make the spot better. Ask for input from your engineer and voice talent. Remember, they probably have been involved in more spots in a week than you have in months.
- *Take your time.* Don't push the talent or engineer. Lead them to what you want.
- *Keep up with the technology.* New technology will always broaden your creative envelope.
- *Casting.* Acting professionals usually have the best and most believable voices because they are visualizing the scene. This is particularly true with dialogue or group scenes. Go to plays often to find new talent. Do not look at the people who are auditioning for a part in the spot. They will try to sell you with facial expression, body language, and hand motions—all worthless on radio. At first, allow talent to give you their own interpretation of the scene. You may be inspired by their rendition.

Steps in Radio Production

We may summarize the steps in producing a commercial as follows:

1. An agency or advertiser appoints a producer.
2. The producer prepares cost estimates.
3. The producer selects a recording studio.
4. With the aid of the casting director, if one is needed, the producer casts the commercial.

EXHIBIT **20.6**

Finished Baskin-Robbins Spot

Courtesy of VitroRobertson, Inc. and Baskin-Robbins, Inc.

date: 1.8.01

client: Baskin-Robbins

job title: Generic Cake Radio :52/:08   radio script

spot title: "Pretend It's Your Birthday"

job no: BRO1–054

isci code: BROR–1010

As Produced on Air

MAN:	Hey, instead of getting just a quart, let's get an ice cream cake.
WOMAN:	A cake?
MAN:	Yeah, we can get that one. The one with the fluffy bunny on it. The Happy Birthday one. Come on, let's pretend it's my birthday.
WOMAN:	I don't wanna pretend it's your birthday.
MAN:	You don't have to give me anything. We'll have the cake. And that'll be enough.
WOMAN:	But what if I want it to be my birthday? Would we still get the cake?
MAN:	Uh, next time. Next time will be your birthday.
WOMAN:	I think I want a cone.
MAN:	What flavor?
WOMAN:	Mmmmm. . . Cookies 'n' Cream.
MAN:	Cookies 'n' Cream is exactly the flavor of that fluffy bunny cake. It'll be fantastic.
WOMAN:	No, it's not. It's chocolate.
MAN:	We'll put on hats!
WOMAN:	You are so weird.
MAN:	One cake, please.
ANCR:	Baskin-Robbins ice cream cake. Rich ice cream and moist cake. Try one today. Baskin-Robbins. What's your flavor?

5. If music is to be included, the producer selects a musical director and chooses the music or selects stock music.

6. If necessary, a rehearsal is held.

7. The studio tapes music and sound separately.

8. The studio mixes music and sound with voices.

9. The producer sees that the master tape is prepared for distribution on either tape or cassette and shipped to stations.

You are on the air!

SUMMARY

Radio can be visual, despite its lack of visuals. It paints a picture in the listener's imagination and truly becomes a theater of the mind. Words, sound effects, and music are the tools of the radio copywriter. The biggest limitation is that the radio copywriter is always working against the clock.

It is the duty of the radio writer/producer to take control of the listener's imagery and guide it to a positive reaction that seeds the listener's memory with the targeted message and leads to the proper response. The power of a radio commercial is the idea imagery.

When developing a commercial, it is important to keep it simple and concentrate on one main idea. Repetition of the main selling ideas is considered necessary, but the main thing is to get the listener's to remember the brand and message. Some of the writing techniques and formats include straight announcer, slice-of-life, jingle-announcer, customer interview, and humor.

As with television, all performers appearing in national commercials are subject to union compensation agreements.

REVIEW

1. Why is radio called the theater of the mind?

2. Briefly summarize the elements of good radio commercials.

3. What is white space in radio?

4. Name four radio station programming formats.

5. What are the three main elements to writing commercial music?

6. What are the steps in radio production?

 **TAKE IT TO THE WEB**

The Radio Advertising Bureau (RAB) is a service organization dedicated to the betterment of radio. Visit **www.rab.com** and take look at sample RAB Services as well as the workshops, research, and training available to those in the radio industry.

Radio @ Netscape Plus, powered by Spinner **(www.spinner.com),** offers Web Radio to consumers. What type of traditional radio commercial could encourage listeners to "tune in" to Web Radio?

TNS Media Intelligence/CMR provides tracking and advertising expenditure information for network, national spot, and local spot radio. Visit **www.tnsmi-cmr.com** to learn more about media analysis.

How does Web Radio differ from traditional radio? Will Web Radio users be easier to target than traditional listeners? What other factors will need to be considered? Visit Arbitron at **www.arbitron.com** to compare Internet broadcasting and National Radio. Also, visit **www.web-radio.fm** for a list of Web Radio stations.

CHAPTER 21

Trademarks and Packaging

Product names and trademarks are very important to brand equity, brand identity, and the marketing process. In today's market, advertising and packaging must support each other. After reading this chapter, you will understand:

1. **what a trademark is**
2. **protecting the trademark**
3. **forms of trademarks**
4. **general trademark rules**
5. **the process for developing memorable names**
6. **packaging and marketing**
7. **packaging and research**

The brand name is one of the most important assets of a company, and the trademark is the brand's asset. A name communicates the essence of a company, product, or service, forming the foundation of any brand. Today, naming presents a formidable challenge because legally available names that are clear, distinct, and memorable are in short supply. There are more than 2 million registered trademarks in the United States alone. If you attempt to come up with a corporate or product name, you may decide there are no appropriate new names left to claim. The wrong choice may lead to charges of trademark infringement if you pick a name owned by someone else. Once you have the right name, you must protect it.

Consider the financial investment in the name and trademark of Coca-Cola since 1886, when it was first developed. Think of the corporate and financial loss if Coca-Cola lost the exclusive right to its trademark. It is not impossible for companies to lose that right. It is for this reason they go to great lengths to protect their trademark with a special staff who monitor all use of the brand(s) to protect their investment. Companies such as Coca-Cola have become so concerned about their brand image, use, and reputation on the Web that they have taken steps to prevent, or at least monitor, what's going on in cyberspace. Coke has brand cop lawyers. Some spend their time surfing the Web, tracking repeat offenders, and writing cease and desist letters centered on Coke brand abuses, online and off. Many of these cases are first investigated by Coke's trade research department. The nature of such infractions is studied to determine the need for legal action by the corporate legal department. They ask interlopers to stop using the Coke brand or trademark. Among the most common types of online brand abuses are the following:[1]

■ Unauthorized use of logos and images
■ Use of a company's name on a competitor's site

- Unauthorized framing, in which a Web site appears within another site
- Domain abuse and parody sites
- Unauthorized use of a company's name or product in metatags
- Diverting users away from a Web site by hiding key words in background text

All companies face the same threat to their brand and trademark, which we talk about later in this chapter.

AN OVERVIEW

Today a brand name not only has to be memorable, distinctive, easy to pronounce, and durable, but also it may have to work globally. That takes more than a large vocabulary and a thesaurus. There are actually naming specialists who make a science of knowing the origin and esoteric meaning of words. In some cases, they also study the emotional reaction to certain sounds. They study naming trends and clichés, spelling and pronunciation ambiguities, and know expedient ways to conduct legal searches and acquire trademark protection. If it is to be a global name, they look at potential foreign language problems. Graphic experts may participate in the naming process because the graphic expression of the name often determines its success or failure in the marketplace. Although the ultimate reason for settling on a certain name may be purely subjective, it's usually tested to see the reactions of the target or users.

From Corporate Identity to Brand Identity

The first book dedicated to trademarks was published in 1924. A trademark established the character of a company and influenced the appearance of a product. Gordon Lippincott, founder of Lippincott & Margulies (now called Lippincott Mercer), coined the term *corporate identity* in 1943 to encompass all the ways a company identifies itself, from a new corporate name and logo to the color of its buildings. Today, the corporate mark is still the cornerstone of an identity program, but it involves much more. Partially due to technology and expanding avenues of communication, corporate identity has become an all-encompassing discipline that embodies the corporate personality, history, reputation, and vision. The best corporate programs closely associate the logo with what a company stands for. The Cobra name is long and sleek like a snake. It is strong and powerful. This association is strong for a company that makes golf clubs (see Exhibit 21.1).

Most people associate Volvo with safety, even though nothing in the logo or name (which means "rolling") directly conveys that attribute. A few years ago, research indicated that consumers thought Volvo cars were too boxy and staid. As a result, Volvo began to migrate its branded image by making sleeker cars and adding attributes such as high performance to safety. But the logo hasn't changed. Although logo can connect a company to its attributes and positioning in the marketplace, it can't do the job alone. A brand identity system can. It uses the elements of the corporate identity system but is wider and deeper. The building blocks of the system include a company's name, trademarks, tagline, and logo. It also focuses on the elements that come together in almost any communication: imagery, typography, design, color, and consistent message. It may include a system that maps different communication vehicles (e.g., brochure, Web site, direct mail, and CD-ROM) to audience content and production values. Education and training may play a part in the system.[2] Without a consistent and cohesive approach to brand identity, a company's communications may not generate the desired results.

There are also digital issues. Lippincott Mercer, a global identity company that currently helps manage identity (including Agrere Systems, Borders, ExxonMobil, medcohealth, NorskCanada, Agilyssys, and Zephyr), believes that globalization and

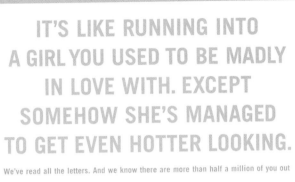

IT'S LIKE RUNNING INTO
A GIRL YOU USED TO BE MADLY
IN LOVE WITH. EXCEPT
SOMEHOW SHE'S MANAGED
TO GET EVEN HOTTER LOOKING.

We've read all the letters. And we know there are more than half a million of you out there that fell in love with the old King Cobra irons. And who can blame you, considering their incredible performance, feel and striking good looks. Well, today's your lucky day. The new King Cobra SS™ irons look, feel and play even better than the original, if that's possible. What have we been up to, you ask? Quite a lot, actually. We redesigned the new irons around a larger sweet spot, and in the process created the sweetest set of irons on the market. Here's how we did it. We added an oversized head and a thinner face reinforced with a "muscle arch." That gives you greater

With a huge new sweet spot, the King Cobra SS irons are a thing of beauty.

WWW.COBRAGOLF.COM

©2002 Acushnet Company. Acushnet Co. is an operating company of Fortune Brands, Inc. NYSE: FO.

wall thickness behind the strike zone for a more solid feel. And trust us, they feel better than ever. We moved more weight lower and to the back of the club head to promote greater carry distance and better accuracy. On the tough-to-hit lower irons, we strategically placed a Tungsten insert to help you get the ball up in the air for nice, long approach shots. Think about that for a second — a great approach shot can get you on the green in two on a par five. Do that consistently and you'll take every little side bet in the foursome. There's more. We also added a skid sole design to keep the club head moving forward post impact instead of digging into the ground. In other words, less thin and fat shots, more sweet shots. Add it all up and you've got perhaps the most accurate, forgiving irons out there. See? Some things get better the second time around. Just try to let your other irons down easy. cobra.

EXHIBIT 21.1

A Cobra is long, sleek, powerful, and accurate.

Courtesy of VitroRobertson, Inc., Cobra, and John Schultz, photographer.

consolidation will continue as major business trends for many years to come. As a result, advanced communications and information technologies, such as CD-ROM, the World Wide Web, and company intranets, will provide firms with bold new avenues for delineating and projecting their corporate and brand identities.[3]

A LITTLE HISTORY OF TRADEMARKS

Lanham Act

There were few trademarks used on general merchandise prior to the Civil War. In 1870, the rapid growth in trade identity gave rise to the first federal trademark law. Lacking sufficient legislative safeguards, concerned manufacturers met in 1878 and founded the United States Trademark Association. Its name was changed to the International Trademark Association (INTA) in 1993. This organization promoted the enactment of the Trade-Mark Act of 1881 and revisions in 1905 and 1920. In 1946, the Lanham Act was passed by Congress. It defined a trademark and expanded the concept of infringement, permitted the registration of service marks, provided incontestability status for marks in continuous use for five years, and provided that federal registration of a trademark would constitute "constructive notice of the registrant's claim of ownership thereof."

In 1996, President Clinton signed the Federal Trademark Dilution Act passed by Congress. It provided owners of famous trademarks with a federal cause of action against those who lessened the distinctiveness of such marks by the use of the same or similar trademarks on similar or dissimilar products or services. Unlike trademark infringement, a dilution action does not require proof or likelihood of consumer confusion. An amendment was added later that year in the form of the Anticounterfeiting Consumer Protection Act of 1996.[4]

Patent and Trademark Office and Technology

In 2000, the agency once known as the Patent and Trademark Office was renamed the United States Patent and Trademark Office (USPTO). The USPTO reviews all trademark applications for federal registration and determines whether an applicant meets the requirements for federal registration. Owning a federal trademark registration on the Principal Register provides several advantages, for example

- constructive notice to the public of the registrant's claim of ownership of the mark
- a legal presumption of the registrant's ownership of the mark and the registrant's exclusive right to use the mark nationwide on or in connection with the goods and services listed in the registration
- the ability to bring an action concerning the mark in federal court
- the use of U.S. registration as a basis to obtain registration in foreign countries
- the ability to file the U.S. registration with the U.S. Customs Service to prevent importation of infringing foreign goods

WHAT IS A TRADEMARK?

We have said that brands are among the most valuable assets a marketer has. When a product is manufactured and a brand is created, it must be distinctive from the competition.

There are several types of company and product identifications. The **trademark,** also called a brand name, is the name by which people can speak of the product. Very often a trademark will include some pictorial or design element. If it does, the combination is called a **logotype** (or simply a **logo**).

Trademarks are proper terms that identify the products and services of a business and distinguish them from products and services of others. Specifically, a trademark is a word, design, or combination used by a company to identify its brand and to distinguish it from others, and it may be registered and protected by law. Trademark formats can include letters, numbers, slogans, geometric shapes, pictures, labels, color combinations, product and container shapes, vehicles, clothing, and even sound.

Trademarks can also be termed *service marks* when used to identify a service. In general, a trademark for goods appears on the product or its packaging, and a service mark is used in advertising to identify the services.

The logo design is an extremely important element in the successful marketing of a product. It is difficult to sell a product until a reasonable level of name recognition is achieved among consumers. In fact, the creation of a logo is so important that a number of firms have been established whose primary function is the design of logos, packages, and corporate identity. Most designers attempt to forge a compatible relationship among the package design, logo, and advertising for the product. A strong logo on the package and in product advertising creates an environment of recognition. Exhibit 21.2 reflects a number of design options that were presented to Folks restaurants when it was searching for a new logo. Exhibit 21.3 shows a version as it is used today.

Logo designs come in several basic forms including abstract symbols (the apple used by Apple Computer) or logotypes, a stylized rendition of a company's name. You can also use a combination of both. Promoting an abstract symbol can prove very costly and isn't recommended for a small budget. Such logos are also harder to remember. Logotypes or word marks are generally easier to recall. If you use an abstract symbol, it should be used in connection with the business name. Some advertising agencies design logos for clients themselves. Some of the mega-agencies may have sister companies that specialize in this area of brand development. In many cases, the corporation takes responsibility for the process.

---

trademark
Any device or word that identifies the origin of a product, telling who made it or who sold it. Not to be confused with trade name.

logotype, or logo
A trademark or trade name embodied in the form of a distinctive lettering or design. Famous example: Coca-Cola.

EXHIBIT **21.2**

Design variations for possible ways to visually show the company's name.

Courtesy of Bevil Advertising and Folks.

Professional design firms will charge anywhere from $4,000 to $15,000 for a logo alone. Research and development of corporate identity programs may cost as much as $150,000. Keep in mind that there are thousands of independent designers around who charge from $20 to $150 per hour, based on their experience. As a rule of thumb, a good logo should last at least 10 years. If you look at the amortization of that cost over a 10-year period, it doesn't seem so bad.

Clearly, the most successful packages are those that combine an intriguing design scheme with a provocative logotype. What we mean is a logo that is distinctive enough to project the visual personality of the product even when not part of the packaging. After all, when pushing a shopping cart down a supermarket aisle, the consumer's first images will be recognizable brand names.

Trademarks should not be confused with trade names, which are corporate or business names. General Motors, for example, is the trade name of a company making automobiles whose trademark (not trade name) is Buick. The terms

EXHIBIT **21.3**

This is the current design scheme used by Folks.

Courtesy of Bevil Advertising and Folks.

trade name
A name that applies to a business as a whole, not to an individual product.

trademark and *trade name* are often confused. **Trade names** are proper nouns. Trade names can be used in the possessive form and do not require a generic form. Many companies, however, use their trade names as trademarks. For example, Reebok International Ltd. is the corporate name, and Reebok may be used as a trade name, as "Reebok's newest line of athletic shoes is for children." Reebok also is used as a trademark: "Are you wearing Reebok athletic shoes or another brand?"

If you're confused, think of yourself as a new product. Your surname is your trade name (e.g., Lane, Smith, Bevil). Your gender is the product classification (Female Lane, Female Smith, or Female Bevil). Your given name then is the brand (Lois Lane, Judy Smith, Sheri Bevil) because it distinguishes you from other family members (like Sarah Bevil).

Some personal names (as with product names) may sound the same but may have different spellings—Sherry, Sherri, or Sheri, or even Cheri (Kwik-Draw, Quick-Draw, Kwic, Kwik, Quick). Or they may simply be very familiar names—Jennifer, Jane, Jessica, Sarah, Hanna, Emily (or Jeff, Steven, Robert, Tom)—or clearly distinctive, like Ruhanna (or unusual like Hudson). Yet, distinctive names may appear difficult to read or pronounce. Companies and products have a similar problem. They want names that can easily become familiar to consumers, yet be easy to read and pronounce and be memorable.

General Electric's Naming Process

General Electric (GE) has a simple procedure for developing trademarks for its brands. GE's branding strategy has a number of steps:[5]

1. *Pick a name.* General Electric, for example.
2. *Create a memorable trademark.* The GE monogram is recognized the world over.
3. *Make a promise.* For 60 years, GE promised better living through electricity, which became better living through technology, for the past 30 years.
4. *Effectively communicate the promise.* GE has always had highly imaginative and memorable work produced by its agencies.
5. *Be consistent.* Even as GE grows and modifies its business, it carefully manages the use of its identity worldwide.
6. *Don't get bored.* GE kept the same strategic promise for 30 years before recently changing to "Imagination at Work."
   If you follow this basic strategy, your brand should thrive.

For a firm to qualify for an exclusive trademark, several requirements must be met. If these criteria are not satisfied, the trademark is not legally protected and will be lost to the firm.

The use of a design in an ad does not make it a trademark, nor does having it on a flag over the factory. The trademark must be used in connection with an actual product. It must be applied to the product itself or be on a label or container of that product. If that is not feasible, it must be affixed to the container or dispenser of the product, as on a gas pump at a service station.

The trademark must not be confusingly similar to trademarks on comparable goods. It must not be likely to cause buyers to be confused, mistaken, or deceived as to whose product they are purchasing. The trademark must be dissimilar in appearance, sound, and significance from others for similar goods. Of course, it is up to a court to decide these issues. The products involved need not be identical. For example, Air-O was held in conflict with Arrow shirts. The marks will be held in conflict if the products are sold through the same trade channels or if the public might assume that a product made by a second company is a new product line of the first company.

Trademarks must not be deceptive—that is, they must not indicate a quality the product does not possess. For instance, the word *Lemon* was barred from soap that contained no lemon, as was the word *Nylodon* for sleeping bags that contained no nylon.

Trademarks must not be merely descriptive. For example, when people ask for fresh bread, we cannot trademark our bread Fresh. When people ask for fresh bread, they are describing the kind of bread they want, not specifying the bread made by a particular baker. To prevent such misleading usage, the law does not protect trademarks that are merely descriptive and, thus, applicable to many other products.

Trademark Protection

Because a trademark is so valuable, companies go to great lengths to protect their brand names. In recent years, there have been a number of court cases involving allegations that one company has infringed on the trademark of another.

In deciding whether trademark infringement has taken place, several factors are considered by the courts:

1. distinctiveness of the complainant's mark
2. similarity of the marks
3. proximity of the parties' products
4. likelihood of the complainant's bridging the gap between noncompeting products
5. similarity of the parties' trade channels and advertising methods
6. quality of the alleged infringer's products
7. sophistication of the particular customers

Recently, a federal judge ruled that an Ohio-based Internet company infringed on copyrights held by BellSouth Corp. The judge held that the RealPages Web site owned by Don Madey did not have the right to use RealPages as its identification or as part of its Internet address. BellSouth has held a trademark on the phrase "Real Yellow Pages" since 1984. The Web site also used the phrase "let your mouse do the walking" but agreed to stop using that phrase. BellSouth also owns the copyright to the phrase "let your fingers do the walking." Bellsouth said it had no choice but to protect its marks, and it filed suit only after trying to discuss the issue with the Web site company.[6]

Beware if your trademark is based on a common word. It will be considered legally weak and difficult to protect. Monitor unpermitted use of your trademark vigorously, and don't let any competitor use your mark even briefly. If you want to start a trademark infringement suit, don't do it unless you have detailed records and can document lost profits accurately.

Trademark Loss

In short, if you don't use a trademark properly, you can lose the rights to it. What would happen to Pepsi if the courts ruled you or anyone could call a soft drink Pepsi? Some companies have seen the untimely demise of a trademark. That's right—untimely demise. Many familiar words today were once valid trademarks:

aspirin	cornflakes
yo-yo	nylon
escalator	thermos
lanolin	raisin bran
cellophane	linoleum

To protect a trademark, advertisers must use it with a generic classification so the trademark does not become the name of the product. Originally, Thermos was the trademark owned by the Aladdin Company, which introduced vacuum bottles. In time, people began asking, "What brand of thermos bottle do you carry?" The word *thermos* had come to represent all vacuum bottles, not just those made by Aladdin. The courts held that *Thermos* had become a descriptive word that any manufacturer of vacuum bottles could use because *thermos* (with a lowercase *t*) was no longer the exclusive trademark of the originator.

Selecting Brand Names

A strong brand name will aid marketing objectives by helping create and support the brand image. There are several considerations in the brand name selection.[7]

■ The name should differentiate the product from the competition. In some product categories, there is a limit to how different brand images can be. In fragrances there has traditionally been one basic image—romance. There is great similarity among the brand names: Caleche, Cacharel, and Chantilly. Consider more distinctive names such as Obsession, RED, Passion, Romance, Eternity, Fracas, and Tiffany. In either direction, creation and support of the brand image—abstract promise rather than actual benefit—are the dominant factors in name selection.

■ The name should describe the product, if possible. Brand names such as Post-it, Pudding Pops, Eraser Mate, and lastminutetravel.com are very descriptive. They communicate to consumers exactly what to expect.

■ The product should be compatible with the brand name. In other words, do not name a sleeping tablet "Awake."

■ The name should be memorable and easy to pronounce. One-word, one-syllable brand names are often considered ideal—Fab, Tide, Dash, Bold, Surf, Coke, and Tab. Even though short names may be more memorable, they may be limiting in identifying the type of product or its use.

Al and Laura Ries, brand consultants, recommend the following considerations in naming a brand:[8]

■ The name should be short, for instance, Jell-O, Nilla, TheraFlu. Shortness is an attribute that is even more important for an Internet brand.

■ The name should be simple. Simple is not the same as short. A simple word uses only a few letters of the alphabet and arranges them in combinations that repeat themselves. ThermaCare is simple and descriptive (see Exhibit 21.4). Schwab is a short name but not simple because it uses six letters of the alphabet. Coca-Cola is both a short and simple name. Autobytel.com suffers from being too complicated.

■ The name should be unique. Unique is a key characteristic that makes a name memorable. No name is totally unique unless you create it from scratch, such as Acura, Lexus, or Kodak. Remember, a common or generic name is not unique.

■ The name should be alliterative. If you want people to remember something, rhyme it for them. Alliteration is another way to improve your brand's memorability: Bed Bath & Beyond, Blockbuster, Volvo, and Weight Watchers.

■ The name should be speakable. Try Abercrombie & Fitch and Concierge.com.

Forms of Trademarks

Branding experts agree that although still very relevant, the overall value of a company's name has diminished. Convergence, globalization, and the dot-com influx have caused a shift in the branding strategy. The vast majority of the words in the *Oxford English Dictionary* have been registered and trademarked. A recent Interbrand corporate study revealed that 80 percent of the naming projects lasted three months or less. According to projected naming trends, 19 percent of those surveyed thought "coined" or fabricated names will remain popular because there

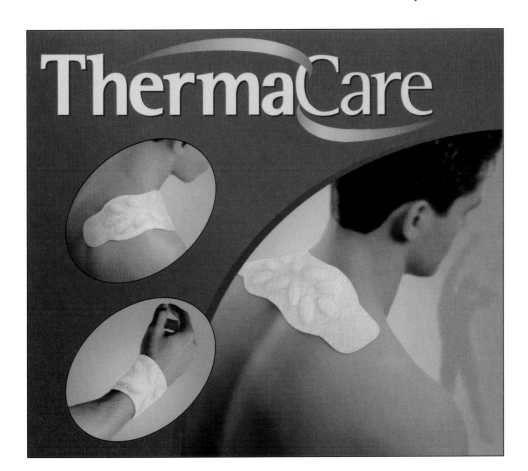

EXHIBIT 21.4

Although ThermaCare is not an extremely short name, it is simple, easy to understand, and descriptive.

Courtesy of The Procter & Gamble Company. Used by permission.

are not many good dictionary names left; 9 percent of respondents saw a trend toward adopting names that had been part of company heritage (e.g., a founder's name); and 57 percent saw a trend toward more "real" names—either a single or compound word (e.g., Apple, JetBlue, Tide).[9] Following, are examples of traditional trademark forms.

Dictionary Words Many trademarks consist of familiar dictionary words used in an arbitrary, innovative, or fanciful manner. Many common words have already been used, causing the advertiser to seek other methods to name a product: Apple computers, Verbatim data disks, Deer Park spring water, Nature Made vitamins, Ivory soap, Dial soap, Equal sweetener, Whopper burgers, Glad plastic bags, Coach leather, Target, Folks restaurant, and Pert shampoo. This type of trademark must be used in a merely descriptive sense to describe the nature, use, or virtue of the product: Look at the word *natural* and related names such as Natural Blend, Natural Brand, Natural Impressions, Natural Light, Natural Man, Natural Silk, Natural Smoothe, Natural Stretch, Natural Suede, Natural Sun, Natural Touch, Natural Woman, and Natural Wonder; or the prefix *opti* as used in Opti Fonts, Opti Free, Opti-Fry, Opti-Grip, Opti Heat, Opti Pure, Opti-Ray, Opti-Tears, and Opti Twist. A few years ago, OrangeGlo International created a new kind of cleaner using an oxygen booster to remove stains and odors and get laundry whiter. It was called OxiClean. In the beginning it was sold primarily on television directly to consumers, then in specialty stores like Bed Bath & Beyond, and later on grocery shelves. It cleaned and removed stains from clothes to carpets to outside decks. As it began moving more into the mainstream and taking away from established products, Clorox's chlorine and nonchlorine bleach sales declined 8.7 percent and 9.6 percent in a year, while Oxiclean's sales grew some 47.5 percent. As usual when you have a successful product, the competition takes note. In 2002 nine new products were introduced by competitors with their versions of "OXI" or "OXY" products.[10] Within the next six months, another 10 products had entered the market.

The possible advantage of using dictionary words is that consumers will easily recognize them. Of course, the task is to get people to associate the word(s) with the product. Just think what the following real product names using dictionary words are about: Healthy Choice, Skin Bracer, Budget Rent-A-Car, Wonder Bra, Big Mac, Action Plus, Hotmail, and AquaFresh.

At times, a name can be somewhat limiting. For instance, when Burger King moved into a breakfast menu, its name was a limitation because people do not think of burgers as breakfast.

Coined Words   When we run out of dictionary options, we sometimes make up words, such as Ticketron, Advil, Infiniti, Primerica, Kleenex, Xerox, NYNEX, UNUM, Norelco, Exxon, Delco, Keds, Kodak, Mazola, TransAir, Haagen-Dazs, and Tab. **Coined words** are made up of a new combination of consonants and vowels. The advantage of a coined word is that it is new, and it can be made phonetically pleasing, pronounceable, and short. Coined words have a good chance of being legally protectable. The challenge is to create a trademark that is distinctive. Ocean Spray took the ingredients of cranberries and apples and created the name Cranapple, which is distinctive, descriptive, and relatively easy to pronounce. There is, however, a Cranberry Apple herbal tea. Is this confusing? Probably not.

The simpler coined words are one syllable. It is common to coin trademark words that have a vowel next to a hard consonant or a vowel between two hard consonants, such as Keds. This structure can be expanded—Kodak, Crisco, or Tab.

coined word
An original and arbitrary combination of syllables forming a word. Extensively used for trademarks, such as PoFolks, Mazola, Gro-Pup, Zerone. (Opposite of a dictionary word.)

Personal Names   These may be the names of real people, such as Calvin Klein, Liz Claiborne, Anne Klein, Estée Lauder, Tommy Hilfiger, Perry Ellis, Pierre Cardin, Alexander Julian, Ralph Lauren, L.L. Bean, Jenny Craig, Forbes, and Sara Lee; fictional characters, such as Betty Crocker; historical characters, such as Lincoln cars; or mythological characters, such as Ajax cleanser. A surname alone is not valuable as a new trademark; others of that name may use it. Names such as Ford automobiles, Lipton teas, Heinz foods, and Campbell's soups have been in use for so long, however, that they have acquired what the law calls a "secondary" meaning—that is, through usage the public has recognized them as representing the product of one company only. However, a new trademark has no such secondary meaning.

There are a lot of names that use Mrs.—Mrs. Fields, Mrs. Winner's, Mrs. Richardson's, Mrs. Allison's, Mrs. Smith's, Mrs. Dash, Mrs. Baird's, Mrs. Butterworth's, Mrs. Lane's, and Mrs. Paul's.

Foreign names have been successfully used to endow a product with an exotic quality. Of course, because the market is now global, they are more and more common. The argument against creating foreign names may be the problem of pronunciation or remembering. However, foreign names are part of the global landscape: Toyota, Feni, Gianfranco Ferre, Corneliani, Lubiam, Bertolucci, Giorgia Brutini, Shiseido, Gucci, Volkswagen, Fila, Ferrari, and L'Aimant.

Geographical Names   A geographical name is really a place name: Nashua blankets, Utica sheets, Pittsburgh paints, and Newport cigarettes. These names are old trademarks and have acquired secondary meaning. Often the word *brand* is offered after the geographical name. The law does not look with favor on giving one person or company the exclusive right to use a geographical name in connection with a new product, excluding others making similar goods in that area. However, if the name was chosen because of a fanciful connotation of a geographical setting rather than to suggest that the product was made there, it may be eligible for protection, as with Bali bras and Klondike ice cream bars.

EXHIBIT 21.5

This catering service uses a geographical name.

Courtesy of Great South Catering and Bevil Advertising.

Geographical names can be combined with dictionary words to create trademark names such as Maryland Club coffee and Carolina Treat barbecue sauce. The options are many: Georgia Coffee, Texas Instruments, Texas Trails, New York Woman, Florida Queen, Newport Harbor, Georgia-Pacific, and Raleigh Community Hospital. Think of the number of businesses in your community using the city, county, or state name or a geographical region: mountains, coastal, piedmont, tidewater, lake, and so on—Piedmont Hospital, Mountain Man Museum, and Great South Catering (see Exhibit 21.5).

Initials and Numbers Many fortunes and years have been spent in establishing trademarks such as IBM, IKEA furniture, RCA, GE, AC spark plugs, A&W root beer, J&B whiskey, A.1. steak sauce, and V8 vegetable juice. Hence, these are familiar. In general, however, initials and numbers are the most difficult form of trademark to remember and the easiest to confuse and imitate. How many of these sound familiar: STP, DKNY, S.O.S., AMF, M.O.M.S., S.A.V.E., A.S.A., A&P, 6–12, or 666? There are also combinations of initials and numbers: WD–40 lubricant; numbers and words: 9-Lives cat food, 4 in 1, Formula 44, Formula 109, Formula 28, Formula 36, 4 Most; or dictionary words and initials: LA Gear. In 1949, Mr. Kihachiro Onitsuka began his athletic footwear company (Onitsuka Co., Ltd.) by manufacturing basketball shoes out of his living room in Kobe, Japan. He chose the name ASICS for his company in 1977, based on a famous Latin phrase *Anima Sana in Corpore Sano*, which when translated expresses the ancient ideal of "A Sound Mind in a Sound Body." Taking the acronym of this phrase, ASICS was founded on the belief that the best way to create a healthy and happy lifestyle is to promote total health and fitness (see Exhibit 21.6).

Pictorial Many advertisers use some artistic device, such as distinctive lettering style or a design, insignia, or picture. The combination, as mentioned before, is called a logotype or logo. As you can see, names can be categorized into a number of different types and functions. Some branding and naming experts include a few other categories and examples:

Connotative: Duracell
Bridge: DaimlerChrysler, Westin
Arbittrary: Apple, Yahoo!
Descriptive: Pizza Hut, General Motors

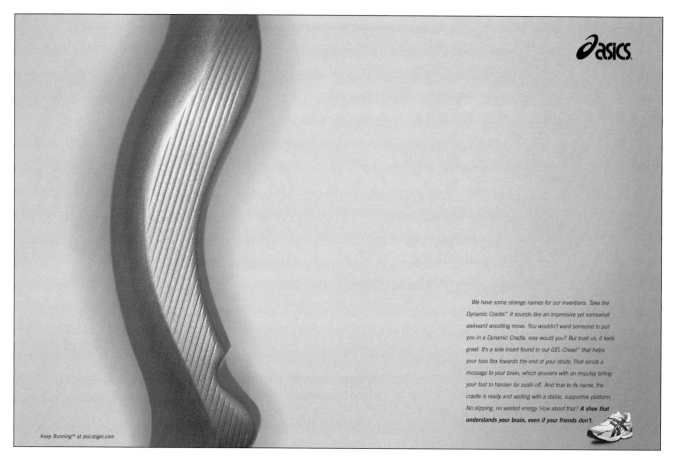

We have some strange names for our inventions. Take the
Dynamic Cradle.™ It sounds like an impressive yet somewhat
awkward wrestling move. You wouldn't want someone to put
you in a Dynamic Cradle, now would you? But trust us, it feels
great. It's a sole insert found in our GEL-Creed™ that helps
your toes flex towards the end of your stride. That sends a
message to your brain, which answers with an impulse telling
your foot to harden for push-off. And true to its name, the
cradle is ready and waiting with a stable, supportive platform.
No slipping, no wasted energy. How about that? **A shoe that
understands your brain, even if your friends don't.**

Keep Running™ at asicstiger.com

EXHIBIT 21.6

The company name
came from an acronym
based on a famous
Latin phrase *Anima
Sana in Corpore Sano*.
ASICS was founded on
the belief that the best
way to create a healthy
and happy lifestyle is to
promote total health
and fitness.

Courtesy of VitroRobertson, Inc.,
ASICS, and Craig Cutler,
photographer.

The Successful Trademark

Whatever the form of a specific trademark, it will be successful only if it is distinctive
and complements the manufacturer's product and image. As we mentioned earlier
in this chapter, the trademark cannot be considered an isolated creative unit. In most
cases, it must be adaptable to a package. It must also be adaptable to many different
advertising campaigns, often over a period of many years. The longer a trademark is
associated with a brand, the more people recognize it and the greater its value.

Global Trademarks

The federal registration of trademarks with the USPTO is not valid outside the
United States. However, if you are a qualified owner of a trademark application
pending before the USPTO or of a registration issued by the USPTO, you may seek
registration in any of the countries that have joined the Madrid Protocol by filing a
single application, called an "international application," with the International
Bureau of the World Property Intellectual Organization, through the USPTO. Also,
certain countries recognize a U.S. registration as the basis for filing an application
to register a mark in those countries under international treaties.

General Trademark Rules

Putting a lock on the ownership of a trademark requires taking the following steps:

1. Always be sure the trademark word is capitalized or set off in distinctive type.
   KLEENEX, *Kleenex*, **Kleenex.**
2. Always follow the trademark with the generic name of the product, or by using
   the word *brand* after the mark: Glad disposable trash bags, Kleenex tissues,
   Apple computers, Tabasco brand pepper sauce.

3. Do not speak of the trademark word in the plural, as "three Kleenexes," but rather, "three Kleenex tissues."

4. Do not use the trademark name in a possessive form, unless the trademark itself is possessive, such as Levi's jeans (not "Kleenex's new features," but "the new features of Kleenex tissues"), or as a verb (not "Kleenex your eyeglasses," but "Wipe your eyeglasses with Kleenex tissues").

It is the advertising person's responsibility to carry out these legal strictures in the ads, although most large advertisers will have each ad checked for legal requirements including trademark protection.

Companies should control how the trademark is used in writing ads and so forth. Many companies provide departments and units with written guidelines instructing the use of trademarks. For example, Kodak has a 10-page document for proper use, with examples of incorrect usage, of its trademarks. This document includes trademark printing instructions for black-and-white and color usage. Blockbuster Corporation warns its employees, "Always use the exact registration or trademark form." You should never change the word or design; never change the upper and lowercase letters; never change the colors; never change the plural or singular form; never add the word *the* to the word or design; never add a design to the word or vice versa; and never make the mark a possessive noun.

DuPont promotes the correct use of its Teflon trademark (see Exhibit 21.7). "Protecting the Teflon trademark is critical to the successful management of a very valuable asset. Improper use of the trademark, or allowing others to use it improperly, lowers its value and can ultimately turn a respected trademark into a common generic term."

Registration Notice

Legal departments at some companies go to great lengths to protect their valuable trademarks. Some common ways of indicating trademark registration follow:

■ The "®" symbol after the trademark as a superscript. Example: Mrs. Winner's®

■ A footnote referenced by an asterisk in the text.

>   Example: McDonald's*
>   *A registered trademark of McDonald's Corporation.
>   or
>   *Reg. U.S. Pat. Tm. Off.
>   or
>   Registered in the U.S. Patent and Trademark Office.

■ A notation of the registration in the text or as a footnote on the same page.

■ If a trademark is repeated frequently in an ad, some firms require the registration notice only on the first use.

Most companies require notice of unregistered but claimed words and/or symbols as their trademark by using the "TM" symbol.

HOUSE MARKS

As mentioned earlier in this chapter, trademarks are used to identify specific products. However, many companies sell a number of products under several different trademarks. These companies often identify themselves with a **house mark** to denote the firm that produces these products. Kraft is a house mark, and its brand Miracle Whip is a trademark.

house mark
A primary mark of a business concern, usually used with the trademark of its products. General Mills is a house mark; Betty Crocker is a trademark; DuPont is a house mark; Teflon II is a trademark.

EXHIBIT 21.7

Guidelines on the use of the Teflon trademark.

Courtesy of DuPont.

Rule 1: Show Registration.

Show registration status, by using the symbol "®" each and every time the trademark appears.

If there is no ® on a keyboard, as in some electronic mail systems, use parenthesis "R" parenthesis: (R). For countries where the registration symbol is not recognized, use an asterisk (*).

Acceptable	Unacceptable
Teflon® resin	No designation of registration status
Teflon(R) resin	
Teflon* resin	Teflon resin

IMPORTANT: Regardless of whether "®", (R), or (*) is used, a footnote must be used at least once in each document. Examples of acceptable footnotes:

*Teflon is a registered trademark of DuPont.

Teflon® is a registered trademark of DuPont for its fluoropolymer resins.

Rule 3: Use Correct Generics.

Use the correct generic (common name) for the trademark at least once per package. Generic is the term for the class of goods for which the mark is registered.

Acceptable	Unacceptable
Teflon® resins	*Teflon*® president, *Teflon*® gasket, *Teflon*® cookware, *Teflon*® business
Other acceptable generics: films, fibers, finishes, fabric protector, fluoropolymer, fluoroadditive, micropowder, coating solutions, PTFE, PFA, FEP, ETFE	

NOTE: Although not generics, it is acceptable to refer to the *Teflon*® trademark and the *Teflon*® brand.

Rule 2: Be Distinctive.

Make the trademark distinctive from the surrounding text each and every time.

Acceptable	Unacceptable
Initial Cap: Teflon® resin	Any instance where the trademark is not distinguished from surrounding text, such as: "gaskets with teflon"
All Caps: TEFLON® resin	
Bold: **Teflon**® resin	
Italics: *Teflon*® resin	
Color: Teflon® resin	

Rule 3: Use Correct Generics.

The trademark is the trademark. Don't embellish upon it!

Acceptable	Unacceptable
Wear resistance of *Teflon*®	**Possessives:** *Teflon*®'s wear resistance
Coatings of *Teflon*®	**Hyphens:** *Teflon*®-coated
Fabrics using *Teflon*® wear longer	**Line Breaks:** Fabrics using *Teflon*® wear longer
Coat pans with *Teflon*®	**Verbs:** Teflon® your pans
Teflon®	**Coined Words:** *Teflon*® ized

ADVANTAGE POINT

A FEW WORDS FROM USPTO'S WEB SITE

Any time you claim rights in a mark, you may use the "TM" (trademark) or "SM" (service mark) designation to alert the public to your claim, regardless of whether you have filed an application with the USPTO. However, you may use the federal registration symbol "®" *only* after the USPTO actually *registers a mark* and *not* while an application is pending. Also, you may use the registration symbol with the mark only on or in connection with the goods and services listed in the federal trademark registration.

What Is a Trademark or Service Mark?

- A *trademark* is a word, phrase, symbol, or design, or a combination of words, phrases, symbols, or designs, that identifies and distinguishes the source of the goods of one party from those of others.
- A *service mark* is the same as a trademark, except that it identifies and distinguishes the source of a service rather than a product. Throughout this booklet, the terms *trademark* and *mark* refer to both trademarks and service marks.

Do Trademarks, Copyrights, and Patents Protect the Same Things?

No: Trademarks, copyrights, and patents all differ. A copyright protects an original artistic or literary work; a patent protects an invention. For copyright information, go to http://lcweb.loc.gov/copyright. The United States Patent and Trademark Office (USPTO) reviews trademark applications for federal registration and determines whether an applicant meets the requirements for federal registration. The office does do not decide whether you have the right to *use* a mark (which differs from the right to register). Even without a registration, you may still *use* any mark adopted to identify the source of your goods or services. Once a registration is issued, it is up to the owner of a mark to enforce its rights in the mark based on ownership of a federal registration.

Form for Filing a Trademark Application

Using the Trademark Electronic Application System (TEAS) available at www.uspto.gov/teas/index.html, you can file your application directly over the Internet. Features of electronic filing include:

- *Online help.* Hyperlinks provide help sections for each of the application fields.
- *Validation function.* Helps avoid the possible omission of important information.
- *Immediate reply.* The USPTO immediately issues an initial filing receipt via e-mail containing the assigned application serial number and a summary of the submission.
- *24-Hour availability.* TEAS is available 24 hours a day, seven days a week (except 11 P.M. Saturday to 6 A.M. Sunday), so receipt of a filing date is possible up until midnight EST.

If you do not have Internet access, you can access TEAS at any **Patent and Trademark Depository Library (PTDL)** throughout the United States. Many public libraries also provide Internet access.

USPTO prefers you to file online but you may either mail or hand deliver a paper application to the USPTO. You can call the USPTO's automated telephone line at (703) 308–9000 or (800) 786–9199 to obtain a printed form. *You may Not submit an application by facsimile.*

SERVICE MARKS, CERTIFICATION MARKS

service mark
A word or name used in the sale of services, to identify the services of a firm and distinguish them from those of others, for example, Hertz Drive Yourself Service, Weight Watchers Diet Course. Comparable to trademarks for products.

A company that renders services, such as an insurance company, an airline, or even a weight-loss center, can protect its identification mark by registering it in Washington as a **service mark.** It is also possible to register certification marks, whereby a firm certifies that a user of its identifying device is doing so properly. Teflon is a material sold by DuPont to kitchenware makers for use in lining their pots and pans. Teflon is DuPont's registered trademark for its nonstick finish; Teflon II is DuPont's certification mark for cookware coated with Teflon that meets DuPont's standards. Advertisers of such products may use that mark. The Woolmark symbol (see Exhibit 21.8) is a registered trademark owned by The Woolmark Company. The Woolmark Company controls the use of its trademark by licensing manufacturers who are able to meet the strict performance criteria of the Woolmark program. The Woolmark is a symbol of quality which denotes that the products concerned meet the specifications laid down by The Woolmark Company and will give the consumer satisfaction for the life of the product, given average wear and usage conditions.

COMPANY AND PRODUCT NAMES

Corporate Name Changes

Over the years, thousands of companies have undergone corporate name and identity changes. Corporations can spend millions of dollars to complete the process. Costs include hiring consultants, advertising, and changing logos and designs on such items as stationery, uniforms, trucks, and planes.

Anderson Consulting, a global management and technology consulting company, spent $175 million to promote its new name—Accenture. To come up with the new name, it hired Landor brand identity company, owned by Young & Rubicam, which sifted through 5,500 potential options. The original list was pared down to 550, then to 50, and then to 10 names. The new name was then blitzed in January 2001 in college football bowl games, the Super Bowl, and in print (*The Wall Street Journal, Fortune, Forbes, Business Week,* etc.). Interestingly enough, the name didn't actually originate with the brand identity company. An employee from Oslo, Norway, combined *accent* and *future.* It also contains a "greater than" sign (>) hanging over the *t* like an accent mark, but the consonant isn't pronounced differently.[11]

Miles Laboratories ran an ad stating, "After all these years, we think it's time you call us by our first name: Bayer. Today Miles becomes Bayer." The copy started: "You know us as Miles, one of America's largest companies. But in nearly 150 countries, our name is Bayer. Bayer is one of the biggest health care, chemical and imaging technology companies in the world. . . . You already know Bayer for aspirin."

Corporate name changes and, accordingly, graphic identity programs have been on the rise since the mid–1990s, according to Interbrand, a subsidiary of the Omnicom Group, which looks at publicly traded companies on the New York, American, and NASDAQ stock exchanges. You'll recognize some of the new company names from the following:

Avaya	Lucent	PricewaterhouseCoopers
Spherion	Verizon	Aventis
Ventor	Cingular	Novartis

EXHIBIT 21.8
Certification mark.
Reproduced with the permission of The Woolmark Company.

The Process for Developing Memorable Names

There probably isn't a single procedure everyone accepts for selecting names. Ruffell Meyer of Landor Associates says, "The misconception is that you have a couple of people sitting around over a pizza lunch. The first step is to meet with senior management to talk about the direction of the company, its values and image. Does it want to be known for speedy service? Later employees and customers may be included in the discussion."[12]

Once the information is gathered, the brand identity staff begins the name-generation and image-making processes. The tools are likely to include software packages that can morph word combinations. Landor has a database with more than 50,000 names. A typical list of possibilities can exceed a thousand names. Cingular, the result of the merger of SBC Communications and BellSouth Mobility, was created from a list of 6,000 names.

A basic legal search should be made of each name to see if someone else owns the rights to it. Before investing too much time and energy in developing a total identity program around a name, find out if anyone else owns it. Naming consultants can refer you to patent attorneys who can conduct a preliminary screening of names registered in the United States. The cost is usually less than $100 per name. A more comprehensive U.S. trademark search typically costs more than $1,000 per name, so you may want to narrow your choice down to a couple of finalists before proceeding to that level.

Private trademark search firms will conduct searches for a fee. The USPTO cannot aid in the selection of a search firm. Search firms are often listed in the Yellow Pages section of telephone directories under the heading "Trademark Search Services" or "Patent and Trademark Search Services." This process reduces the possibilities by about 80 percent. You again analyze the remaining names against the objective and reduce them to a list of about a dozen or so. At this point, you would probably perform a linguistic analysis to determine what happens when the name is translated into foreign languages. Then you might test the names on consumers. You get the idea. Correctly done, the result is a memorable name that is adaptable to a number of advertising formats. Now let us look at the specific steps. First, pull together the basic information:

- *Describe what you are naming.* In your description, include key features and characteristics, competitive advantages, and anything else that differentiates your company, product, or service from the rest of the field.

- *Summarize what you want your name to do.* Should it suggest an important product characteristic (e.g., Blokrot for treated lumber) or convey a particular image (e.g., Pandora's Secrets for an expensive perfume)? Write down the characteristics and images you want your name to convey.

- *Describe whom you are targeting with the name.* Identify your targets and their demographic and lifestyle characteristics. Would they react more positively to a traditional, conservative name or to a liberal, flashy one? List the name qualities you think would appeal to them (name length, sound, and image). Newcastle Brown simply added "Ale" to its name (see Exhibit 21.9).

- *List names that you like and dislike.* Try to come up with a few dozen current names in both categories (include your competitors' names). Note words and roots that might work for your new name and jot them down.

- *Build a list of new name ideas.* Start with the list of names that you like and add to it by pulling ideas from a good thesaurus (e.g., *The Synonym Finder* by Jerome Rodale), a book of names (e.g., *The Trademark Register of the United States*), relevant trade journals, a book of root words (e.g., *Dictionary of English Word Roots* by Robert Smith), or other sources.

- *Combine name parts and words.* Take words, syllables, and existing name parts and recombine them to form new names.

EXHIBIT 21.9

Simply adding a product descriptor to the established name works.

Courtesy of VitroRobertson, Inc., Newcastle Brown Ale, and Greg Slater, photographer.

- *Pick your favorites.* Select several names that meet all your criteria (just in case your top choice is unavailable or tests poorly).

Next, verify the name's availability and test your favorites:

- *Conduct a trademark search.* As mentioned previously, before investing too much time and energy in developing a total identity program around a name, find out if anyone else owns it.

- *Test your name before using it.* Regardless of how fond you are of the new name, others may have different opinions. Solicit reactions to your name from prospective customers, stockholders, and industry experts.

Coca-Cola ran into a controversy with Fruitopia's name. In 1991, students at Miami University in Ohio came up with a total marketing plan, which included a product name, for a sparkling water and juice drink in development for the Minute Maid brand at Coca-Cola Foods Canada. When they presented it to Coca-Cola, Coca-Cola thought the name Fruitopia was very "iffy." The product rolled out in the United States in 1994 with the Fruitopia name; although there was no question about the legal rights of ownership—Coca-Cola had paid the university a fee for all of the students' work—there was a question of who developed the name. Coca-Cola said that a marketing group, working independently with its advertising agency, came up with the name. This is a reason most companies don't take unsolicited proposals for new products, ads, or product names. If Coca-Cola had not paid for the rights to the students' work, there could have been a legal battle for the name Fruitopia.

Name Assistance The naming of products may be developed by the advertiser or the advertising agency, working independently or together. There are companies and consultants that specialize in helping companies and agencies develop memorable names. The Namestormers uses software to help develop product and company names such as CarMax (used-car dealer network), Pyramis (medical systems), AutoSource (auto parts network), Spider's Silk (lingerie), CareStream (health care company), and Wavemaker (notebook computer). Goldman & Young, Inc. uses Linguistic Architecture to define image strategy and positioning, then creates names such as Polaroid Captiva, Nissan Pathfinder, Audi Avant, Clairol Whipsical, Honda Fourtrax atv, Pepboys PartsUSA, Pizza Hut QuickStix, Bristol-Myers Squibb Excedrin Migraine, Pfizer Zoloft, and GMC Yukon. Namelab, another company that

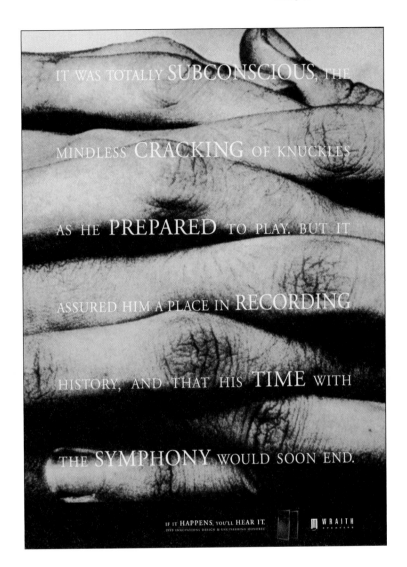

EXHIBIT **21.10**

The name for WRAITH speakers was created by a creative director at HM&P.

Courtesy of Howard, Merrell & Partners.

develops names, used constructional linguistics to create the names Acura, Compaq, Geo, Lumina, and Zapmail. Then there are the large global brand identity companies that also develop names (Landor Associates, Interbrand, Lippincott Mercer, etc.). Keep in mind that anyone in the process can create a name. Howard, Merrell & Partner's creative director coined the word *WRAITH* for WRAITH speakers (see Exhibit 21.10).

PACKAGING

Product packaging is the most important point-of-sale merchandising tool. The average package on the supermarket shelf has only about one-seventeenth of a second to attract our attention. After that, the design, color, words, and . . . oh yes . . . the product itself have to interest us enough to put it in our cart and take it home. With the thousands of food products on the shelves, products need to get noticed or else they become just another fallen casualty in the fickle supermarket arena.

How many times have you bought or almost bought a product simply because you liked the packaging? Some people will only buy milk in the clear plastic jugs instead of the opaque paper containers, even though the paper reduces the damage of nutrients from light. Packaging doesn't just focus on functional aspects such as versatility and food safety anymore. A great deal of the emphasis is directed purely to aesthetics. Revamping new products can be risky. If a product looks too different from before, companies may alienate loyal customers. For example, when

Nestlé decided to change the packaging of KitKat candy from foil wrap to plastic, emotionally attached consumers protested the change, even though the new package would keep the product fresh three times longer.

Holistic Approach

According to, designer Wendy Jedlicka, package design should be a holistic endeavor that requires looking at the entire environment the packaging is working within—the product's durability; manuals, instructions, and other printed materials that are stuffed into a package; and the package's ability to communicate on a retail shelf.[13]

The product package is much more than a container. The package must be designed to take several factors into account. First, it must protect the package contents (see Exhibit 21.11); every other consideration is secondary to the function of the package as a utilitarian container. Second, the package must meet reasonable cost standards. Because the product package is a major expense for most firms, steps must be taken to hold down costs as much as possible.

Once these two requirements of package protection and cost are satisfied, we move to the marketing issues involved in packaging. These include adopting a package that is conducive to getting shelf space at the retail level. A unique package with strange dimensions, protruding extensions, or nonflat surfaces is going to be rejected by many retailers. A package must be easy to handle, store, and stack. It should not take up more shelf room than any other product in that section, as a pyramid-shaped bottle might. Odd shapes are suspect: Will they break easily? Tall packages are suspect: Will they keep falling over? The package should be soil resistant. Does it have ample and convenient space for marking? The product should come in the full range of sizes and packaging common to the field.

For products bought upon inspection, such as men's shirts, the package needs transparent facing. The package can make the difference in whether a store stocks the item.

EXHIBIT 21.11

The TV commercial touts the milk jug's value of protecting flavor and vitamins.

Courtesy of Howard, Merrell & Partners.

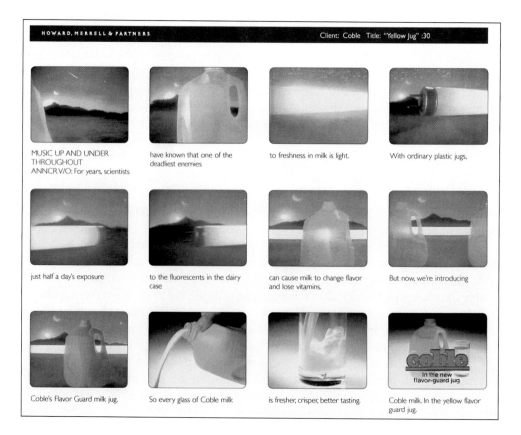

Small items are expected to be mounted on cards under plastic domes, called blister cards, to provide ease of handling and to prevent pilferage. Often these cards are mounted on a large board that can be hung on a wall, making profitable use of that space. Remember, the buyer working for the store judges how a product display will help the store, not the manufacturer.

Once we have considered the requirements of the retail trade, we can turn our attention to designing a container that is both practical and eye-catching. The package is, after all, the last chance to sell the consumer and the most practical form of point-of-purchasing advertising. Therefore, it should be designed to achieve a maximum impact on the store shelf. Striving for distinctiveness is particularly critical in retail establishments such as grocery stores, where the consumer is choosing from hundreds of competing brands.

Changing Package Design and Marketing Strategies

Design firms redesign packages to suit changing market strategies for existing consumer products and develop new packaging concepts for product introductions. In 1998, the Swiffer revolution began. Swiffer conveys speed and ease of cleaning, which translates into the same meaning around the globe. Today there are numerous Swiffer products: Swiffer Wet, WetJet, Max, and Dusters. Procter & Gamble took great care in designing the packaging. The packaging had to attract attention and hold the different content items (see Exhibit 21.12). Several trends in package design can be cited. One is the increasing tendency to use packaging to shore up

EXHIBIT 21.12

Here we see the Swiffer WetJet kit, package, and refill. Notice the similarity in design and colors.

Courtesy of The Procter & Gamble Company. Used by permission.

store brands. Another is the use of sophisticated design approaches or unique packaging to establish a high quality for upscale, private-label brands. There has also been a shift from packaging that suits the convenience of the manufacturer to packaging that is "consumer friendly" in terms of opening, using, and reclosing. In short, package design is responding to a more sophisticated, discerning consumer.

Problem-Solving Designs Old Spice Red Zone

Issue: Old Spice was ready to introduce a new, superior antiperspirant technology and needed a subbrand that embraced the positioning of "unapologetic masculinity."

Brand Response: Interbrand researched the target audience and competing products to understand how to clearly communicate the concepts of premium and masculine to men. Additionally, it examined language, color, and texture of traditional products purchased by men to create a visual vocabulary. Old Spice Red Zone is for guys who push limits. The strong, silver logotype includes a gauge built into the O of Zone. The background texture is reminiscent of texture found on power tools, and the metallic feel of the whole package communicates a masculine and premium message to men.

Tropicana Pure Orange

Issue: The Minute Maid Company introduced a new premium orange juice product named Simply Orange to compete directly with Tropicana in markets traditionally loyal to Tropicana. The product was completely branded as Simply Orange with no mention of the parent company. Tropicana hired Interbrand to develop a brand identity and package design for a new Tropicana Pure Premium to compete directly with Simply Orange.

Brand Response: Interbrand developed a range of package design concepts with a focus on the heritage of Tropicana and the naturalness of the brand. Following consumer testing, it selected a package design that featured an orange crate with the Tropicana Pure Premium logo embossed on the side. Contained in the crate is the familiar image of the orange with a straw in it, which has equity for the Pure Premium brand. As an added endorsement to build on the heritage of the brand, the character Tropic Ana is seen at the top of the label reinforcing the originality of the household chores.

Most brand identity firms not only assist in product or company names but also are product design and packaging experts.

Packaging and Marketing

At one time the role of product packages was generally confined to protecting the product. Only the package label was linked with promotional activities. The Uneeda Biscuit package introduced in 1899 is generally considered to be the first that was utilized for promotion. However, few companies followed Uneeda's lead.

During the depression of the 1930s, the role of packaging as a promotional tool changed dramatically. Most companies had limited advertising funds during this period, so they resorted to using the package as an in-store means of promotion. So successful were their efforts that the role of packaging in the marketing mix became routinely accepted by manufacturers.

The package design for most products is developed in much the same way as an advertising campaign. Although each package is developed, designed, and promoted in a unique fashion, there are some common approaches to the successful use of packaging as a marketing tool.

1. *The type of product and function of the package.* Is the product extremely fragile? Do consumers use the product directly from the package? Are there special storage or shipping problems associated with the product?

2. *The type of marketing channels to be used for the product.* If the product is sold in a variety of outlets, will this require some special packaging considerations? Will the package be displayed in some special way at the retail level? Are there special point-of-purchase opportunities for the product?

3. *The prime prospects for the product.* Are adults, children, upper-income families, or young singles most likely to buy the product? What package style would be most appealing to the target market?

4. *Promotion and advertising for the product and its package.* Will the package be used to complement other promotional efforts? Are on-pack coupons or premiums being considered? Can standard package-design ideas be adapted to any special promotional efforts being considered?

5. *The relationship to other packages in a product line.* Will the product be sold in different sizes? Is the product part of a product line that is promoted together? Does the product line use the same brand name and packaging style?

6. *The typical consumer use of the product.* Will the package be stored for long periods in the home? Does the product require refrigeration or freezing? Are only portions of the product from the package used?

Obviously, the answers to these and other questions can be obtained only through careful research. The package designer must strive for a balance between creativity and function.

Packaging and Color Influence

Advertisers are very much aware that colors work on people's subconscious mind and that each color produces a psychological reaction. Reactions to color can be pleasant or unpleasant. Color can inform consumers about the type of product inside the package and influence their perceptions of quality, value, and purity. Thus, color in packaging is an important tool in marketing communications.

What kind of consumer perceptions would you encounter if you brewed the same coffee in a blue coffeepot, a yellow pot, a brown pot, and a red pot? Would the perceptions of the coffee be the same? Probably not. Studies indicate that coffee from the blue pot would be perceived as having a mild aroma, coffee from the yellow pot would be thought a weaker blend, the brown pot's coffee would be judged too strong, and the red pot's coffee would be perceived as rich and full-bodied.

Kodak is yellow. Fuji is green. United Parcel Service is brown. Color has strong influence and should be considered carefully. Color is one of the main tools that package designers use to influence buying decisions. Consumer reactions to colors are emotional rather than intellectual. Because about 80 percent of consumer choices are made in stores and 60 percent of those are impulse purchases, marketers must consider that package colors can play a major role in the success or failure of a product.

On your next shopping trip, see if you react the way most shoppers do to packages that use these colors:

■ Red packaging (or a brand name that is bold and large) makes our hearts beat faster and increases our adrenalin flow. The color communicates power and vitality and stimulates a desire to conquer. Red also conveys a sense of structure, sensibility, practicality, and dependability. By retaining the red roof as an identifying symbol, Landor, branding consultants, helped reinforce the perception of Pizza Hut as a destination. To further differentiate the brand, a free-hand typography was used along with an entire palette of icons that symbolized the freshness of its ingredients and ultimately provided Pizza Hut with the brand relevance it desired. It followed through on all the boxes and promotional material.

- Yellow is the most visible of all colors (which is why it is used on road signs) and makes packages look larger. Kodak is yellow. Yellow is also used to convey a cut-rate price image and, if not used properly, can detract from the perceived quality of the product. The Swiffer Dusters package is a combination of yellow and green (see Exhibit 21.14).

- Blue implies cleanliness and purity and induces thoughts of sky and water. Often it conveys feelings of serenity, prestige, confidence, knowledge, and credibility. Think of how Tiffany's blue box has been burned into the consumer's mind. Repositioning Pepsi's brand identity worldwide in 1998,

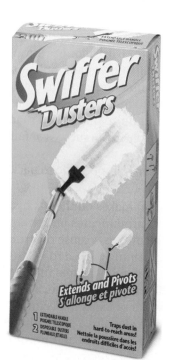

Landor, brand consultants, used blue as a conceptual platform and differentiating color to create distinctive new packaging. Pepsi moved toward a distinctively blue look to better compete against Coke's dominant red. The scope of the project included new designs for cans, bottles, vending machines, soda fountains, and vehicles, which in turn also triggered the need for graphic changes in collateral and signs. Pepsi changed to a heavier reliance on blue than in the past. The design supports this in several ways: the italicized logo, the use of a background with lots of depth and two blues, and an abstract ice background for the Pepsi logo that gives a "visceral representation of refreshment."

- White makes us feel fresh and light and is often used on lower-fat and diet foods. It is associated with dairy products (milk) and, hence, implies the ultimate in freshness and purity. Interestingly, in Germany white suggests premium quality, but in England white suggests budget quality.

- Black is always elegant and sophisticated, and manufacturers use this color to imply a sense of class and quality for their products.

Package Research

Today, effective packaging is a vital part of marketing a product. The only absolute in testing a package design is to sell it in a test-market setting. There are several aspects of assessing a package design, including recognition, imagery, structure, and behavior.

- *Recognition.* A package must attract attention to itself so that the consumer can easily identify it in the retail environment. The recognition properties of a package can be measured. Research can determine how long it takes a consumer to recognize the package and what elements are most memorable.

- *Imagery.* Although the package must be easily recognized, it must also project a brand image compatible with the corporate brand-imagery objectives. A package can reinforce advertising or it can negate it.

- *Structure.* The objective is to determine any structural problems consumers pinpoint that may inhibit repeat purchases. Is the package easy to open? Is it easy to close? Is it easy to handle? Is it easy to use?

- *Behavior.* This can be the most expensive means of researching packages. Often this approach presents simulated shelf settings to groups of people and monitors whether they pick up or purchase a product.

Package Differentiation

Twelve suburban women sit around a focus group table, psyching themselves up to talk about cat food for two hours. Through the course of the evening, only two things really perk them up: the chance to describe their cats and a vacuum-packed foil bag of cat food.

Even before they have examined the nuggets of cat food, most have said they would buy it, intrigued by the high-tech, bricklike bag they have come to expect to see in the coffee aisle, certainly, but never spotted before among the cans, boxes, and bags of pet food.

It is a point increasingly driven home to marketers of food, health and beauty product lines, and over-the-counter drugs: The package is the brand.

Marketers are paying more attention to package design because products are so much more at parity these days. When differentiation through taste, color, and other product elements has reached parity, packaging makes a critical difference.[15] A case in point is Pepsi-Cola's reaction to making its "plasticization" of the famous curved bottle. They couldn't duplicate the curved bottle, but they did create a stable

ADVANTAGE POINT

MINUTE MAID'S PACKAGING REDESIGNED FOR IMAGE CHANGE

The Minute Maid Company had long been a leader in the orange juice category, but by the mid–1990s, the category itself had gone flat. Juice alternative products, from fruit teas to flavored waters, had eroded the overall juice category. Young consumers looked on Minute Maid as "their mother's orange juice"—wholesome but not where they were at. Minute Maid's signature black carton had been "knocked off" by so many competitors that it was no longer distinctive.

Revitalizing the Minute Maid brand would encompass 160 SKUs (shopkeeping units) and packaging that ranged from paperboard cartons and shelf-stable plastic containers to aluminum cans, frozen juice canisters, and 16-ounce glass bottles. When you take on a brand that has a significant following, the last thing you should do is tear it apart and start over. Joe Duffy worked with the account planning group-shared with its advertising affiliate, Fallon, to analyze the equity in a brand. Consumer focus groups for Minute Maid associated the color black with Minute Maid, with some even reporting that they automatically picked up "the black carton" when shopping without reading the label. But people also admitted that they found the brand identity "boring and dormant" and felt it didn't speak to the quality of the product.

People also viewed the brand their mother used to serve them with nostalgic affection. "Consumers granted Minute Maid not only juice equity, but fruit equity," according to the research. The emotional connection to fruit was very strong, stronger than to the juice. These findings confirmed Minute Maid's goal of making the fruit the hero in the packaging to show that the product tasted like the fresh, ripe fruit.

Competitive research indicated photography might offer Minute Maid some advantages as well. Aside from appearing more real and natural, it's harder for competitors to knock off, if you do it in a distinctive way. That distinctive way was through a colorful and lavish photomontage of the fruit from which the juice is made, with brand information and a newly designed logotype contained in a black mortise. The production difficulty and cost of creating such graphics would give Minute Maid competitive distance from would-be copycats while maintaining the look and feel of the original packaging.

In arriving at the final brand image, the designers created different concept directions, soliciting feedback from consumers in three rounds of focus groups. They presented their initial solutions, got feedback, did modifications, and presented twice more.

One ongoing design issue was the amount of black that had to be used. Too much and it would look like the old identity, too little and the equity would be lost. In focus groups, consumers loved the fruit montage in the background and pushed to see as much of that as possible. At the same time, the more black was used, the more direct was the link to the Minute Maid heritage and where the brand had been. It was a continuous "real estate" struggle between the black mortise and the fruit montage.

Another consideration was the physical setting in which various containers would be viewed. First, there was the overall environment of the supermarket itself. It's a cluttered, chaotic environment. First and foremost, your brand is striving for attention among everything that comes into the consumer's view—not just within a category but everything going on in the aisle.

Then there were display issues:

- In many supermarkets, half gallon cartons are displayed in "coffin-style" coolers that shoppers look down upon, so the primary identity needs to be visible from the top.
- Shelf-stable products, heated and vacuum sealed in plastic containers, are in aisles that tend to have dimmer lighting than display cases. The products may be pushed back on the shelf, making them harder for customers to see. This means that the color palette must be very bright to stand out.
- Frozen juice canisters are often laid sideways in deep freezers. Information on the can also has to be large enough to read, which limits the photography.

Printing a detailed photographic image on aluminum cans was a challenge. Aluminum can printing is probably one of the crudest forms of printing because of the high-speed process. Needing white and black for the mortise, the designers had to use three colors to create the illusion of four-color printing in the photomontage. Nevertheless, placing an eye-catching photomontage on single-serve containers did pay off. Minute Maid experienced increases in all products after the new brand identity was introduced. Overall volume sales of single-serve bottles increased by more than 24 percent, and petroleum store sales, which account for nearly half of Minute Maid's total single-serve volume, increased by over 34 percent. Duffy says, "With a category like orange juice, consumer choice often comes down to brand personality, creating an identity that strikes an emotional chord with the target audience."[14]

of designs with monikers such as Fast Break or Big Slam. They found the bottles were a way to build excitement without changing the formula.

Brand Identity

Brand identity is a specific combination of visual and verbal elements that helps achieve the following attributes of a successful brand: create recognition; provide differentiation; shape the brand's imagery; link all brand communications to the brand; and—very important—be the proprietary, legal property of the company that owns the brand.

There are surprisingly few components that make up a brand identity. These include name logos, which are the designed versions of a name; symbols; other graphic devices; color; package configuration (the physical structure of a package—see Exhibit 21.15); and permanent support messages—slogans and jingles.[16]

Cotrends and Packaging

Cobranding, coadvertising, and copackaging are trends that enable companies with strong brand equities to team together to gain more market share at a lower cost. For example, Betty Crocker cobrands with Reese's Candy, Sunkist with Kraft, and Stayfree with Arm & Hammer. The challenge is to present the brand identities and brand communications in such a way that both brand names are strengthened by the visual association, while marketing costs are shared.

Package Design

A product's package is more than a necessary production expense. Therefore, much care needs to be given to the role of packaging in integrated marketing, relationship

marketing with its emphasis on quality, and interactive media. In its promotional function, the package does everything a medium should. At the point of purchase, it alone informs, attracts, and reminds the consumer. At the point of use, it reinforces the purchase decision. Quality and value are viewed as relatively new marketing concepts, yet some 18 years ago the Design and Market Research Laboratory showed that quality perception was one of the key criteria for packaging assessment. But quality and value have always been part of the marketing and packaging equation.

Because packaging is such an important weapon in the marketing arsenal, it should be approached as other marketing elements with marketing research, specifically user research with target consumers.

Frank Tobolski, president of JTF Marketing/Studios, says research techniques measure the communication strengths and weaknesses of package graphics. They answer such questions as: Do the graphics communicate well? Do the graphics reinforce and enhance the image positioning? Do the products and package sell? He reports on a case in which a toy company developed new packaging for a line of products. Perceptual and imagery evaluation in diagnostic laboratory tests was performed, indicating some problems and potential negative sales effects. To obtain behavioral sales data, test quantities of packages were produced for a balanced store test. For six weeks during the Christmas season, 18 stores stocked the new test design and 18 stocked the existing control design. Toy specialty, discount, department store, and mass merchandiser stores were used for the matched store pairings. The bottom line after six weeks found the existing control packages sold 63 percent more units than the test packages. Even after adjusting the test stores, the new designs sold 35 percent less.[17] A major loss in sales was diverted by testing. Imagine the loss if there had been a full new-package rollout.

Today's packaged-goods marketing managers constantly face the critical task of justifying expenditures in terms of the potential return on investment (ROI). Although most can instantly give you current sales figures, few know the yield on their latest shelf media or, specifically, packaging design.

Why? There is growing evidence that packaging design has a much stronger impact on sales than is realized.

As any brand manager will tell you, packaging represents a substantial portion of brand equity. When the word *Coke* is uttered, it is more than likely that an image of the trademarked, hourglass-shaped bottle comes to mind.

A Package Value survey suggests that marketers should benchmark new packaging proposals against their own brand equity. The study interviewed a total of 251 men and women, all primary grocery shoppers. Those polled were shown a card with a brand name printed on it and asked to rate the brand on a scale of 1 (agree strongly) to 5 (disagree strongly). Using "top box" methodology, only respondents who said they "agreed strongly" with all statements were included in the final results.

The subjects were then shown photos of actual packaging. The difference between the scores recorded when people were supplied with a brand name and when they were influenced by actual packaging is what makes the study intriguing. For example, when asked to rate the quality of Procter & Gamble's Tide, both the brand name and the packaging got scores of 61.[18]

Package Look-Alikes

Procter & Gamble sued the 124-store F & M drug chain over the chain's P&G look-alike packages. P&G said the look-alike products confused people and were a disservice to their customers. One of the products, for example, cloned P&G's Pantene, using the same color scheme with a swirl symbol in a small rectangle. Many private-label knockoff packages were displayed next to the brand-name products in the store. P&G's move was like a warning shot to everyone with look-alike packages. Of course, the burden of proof lies with P&G proving that knockoff packaging causes consumer confusion. Attorney Maxine Lans says, "You can't stop a competitor from bringing out a similar product, but you can prevent the consumer from buying another product by accident because it looks so much like yours."[19]

Brand Identity Firms

Corporate identity, brand identity, packaging systems, research, brand equity management, naming, branded environments, retail design, and event branding—all of these often require firms that specialize in packaging and brand identity programs for corporations. Landor Associates is one of the firms that does all of these. These companies work with the agency or the corporation or both in developing packaging and may be involved with the total design concept of a corporation or brand. For example, when you think of McDonald's Corporation—the hamburger people—what comes to mind? Golden arches? Employee uniforms? Cup designs? Paper or box designs? Logo? Paper bags? Premiums? Letterheads? Publications? There are many elements that help identify McDonald's, and every element has its name or logo for starters. The corporate design people help the marketer and sometimes the agency develop strong corporate visual communications. You have seen a lot of visual continuity among the Swiffer products—similar design, different colors to differentiate each product (see Exhibit 21.16).

Special Market Packaging

Welch Foods turned a patriotic packaging promotion for the Fourth of July into a dedicated program designed to spur sales of its sparkling juices throughout the year. In the past, 85 percent of Welch's sparkling juice sales were made during the holiday season. Promotional packaging has made juices relevant for other times of the year. Welch's has used a shrink-wrapped packaging process to wrap the entire bottle. The highly visible packaging generates awareness of sparkling juices, a small segment of the juice category. It is predicted to help increase sale by 40 percent. Traditionally such packaging is used during the holiday season.[20]

Future Predictions Although predictions are just that, one can usually make an intelligent and reasoned guess about the future by relying largely on the past and

EXHIBIT 21.16

This package is similar to other Swiffer packages that you have seen. However, each is differentiated by color.

Courtesy of The Procter & Gamble Company. Used by permission.

current trends that are evolving. With that caveat, Landor's brand identity expert, Allen Adamson, predicts five directions that may influence the future of branding.[21]

1. There may have been a time when the marketer called the shots, but that is certainly not true today. Consumer perception of a product's performance controls its success. Since a brand is a promise, one must insure that the promise is fulfilled at each and every point of contact.

2. Customers interacts with brands everywhere. 360-degree branding is here to stay. Purchase decisions are not made only at point-of-sale, so it is critical that you be in your customer's face with a consistent and coordinated expression of identity as often as is feasible.

3. Over-extending your brand is not much different. Brands can stretch too far and the result can be jarring: erosion of brand equity. Most brands can probably be stretched into a plethora of categories. But often, brands become stronger when their scope is narrowed.

4. Most brand alliances that are formed are driven more by short-term promotional tactics than by long-term strategy. All marketing tactics should be undertaken within the context of a brand being a long-term asset.

5. Branding is not solely the purview of the marketing organization. The brand is the soul of the organization, and understanding its core values becomes the responsibility of everyone within the organization. Every point of contact (not just advertising and promotion) must be on-brand, and every individual within the organization should be charged with the responsibility of knowing exactly what that means.

Once a trend has been assimilated into the culture, it no longer is a trend.

Brands are long-term assets. As such, they need to be managed that way. Considering the future, looking at trends that are currently evolving can help better position brands over the long term. Creating value in tomorrow's brands requires a look at what is changing today.

Change is often subtle. It is rarely an all-of-a-sudden epiphany. Brand stewards must respond as they see trends evolving; they must be cognizant of changes in consumer thinking and observant to even slight changes in consumer behavior because even small changes, over time, can accumulate to become major trends. The challenge is in identifying the change as it is happening and adjusting your branding in concert with that change.

Following are important evolutions that are taking place now and that will influence the way we create and manage brands in the future.

◼ There may have been a time when the marketer called the shots, but that is not true today. Today's consumer is self-reliant, demanding, and skeptical. There is less tolerance today for a product that doesn't deliver what it promises. Consumer perception of a product's performance controls its success. Because a brand is a promise, one must ensure that the promise is fulfilled at each and every point of contact.

◼ Customers interact with your brand everywhere: 360-degree branding is here to stay. Because purchase decisions are not made only at point of sale, it is also critical that you be in your customer's face with a consistent and coordinated expression of identity as often as is feasible. New distribution and communication channels allow you to be in the same place as your customer, whether that's in-store, online, in print, or on TV. Although budgets may dictate where and how often, it is essential to make sure your brand essence is delivered seamlessly across all points of touch.

◼ Brands can stretch too far and the result can be a jarring erosion of brand equity. Most brands can probably be stretched into a plethora of categories. But often brands become stronger when their scope is narrowed. The objective is not to "fit" your brand into as many categories as possible, but rather only market your brand in categories in which it can have the necessary leverage (relevant differentiation) to win in the marketplace. Remember that successful brands do not always beget successful offspring (who can forget New Coke, or rather, who can remember it?). Crest's whitener's line extension could get confusing, but distinctive names and packages keep them straight in the consumer's mind (see Exhibit 21.17).

EXHIBIT 21.17

Crest clearly differentiates each of its whitening system products.

Courtesy of The Procter & Gamble Company. Used by permission.

■ There are probably an infinite number of alliances that any one brand can form with any other. Most alliances that are formed are driven more by short-term promotional tactics than by long-term strategy. All marketing tactics should be undertaken within the context of a brand being a long-term asset. Partnering with competitors of nontraditional companies or products may enhance the brand's value, but choosing the wrong partner can cause substantial damage. Like people, brands are judged by the company they keep.[22]

 **SUMMARY**

Packaging is a very important part of the brand equity equation. It has been labeled as the only true method of international branding.

A product's trademark is like a person's name. It gives a product an identity and allows customers to be sure they are getting the same quality each time they purchase it. In addition, the trademark makes advertising and promotion activities possible. For established products, the trademark is one of the company's most valuable assets. It would be very difficult to estimate the value of trademarks such as Coca-Cola, Pepsi-Cola, IBM, and Mercedes. That is why companies take such pains to protect their trademarks.

The trademark can take the form of a word, a design, or a combination of both. Their formats can include letters, numbers, slogans, geometric shapes, color combinations, and so forth. When a trademark is a picture or other design, it is called a logotype. The same principle of trademark protection applies to logos as it does to brand names. Successful trademarks may take many forms; however, they should be easy to pronounce, have something in common with the product, and lend themselves to a variety of advertising and design formats.

The package design is developed in much the same way as an advertising campaign. Package research can help in assessing a number of factors, including recognition, imagery, structure, and behavior. Packaging is an important marketing tool and should be researched with target groups. Brand identity continues to be an important issue.

 **REVIEW**

1. What is a trademark?

2. What is a service mark?

3. How can you lose a trademark?

4. What are the steps to putting a lock on the ownership of a trademark?

5. Name several marketing issues involved in packaging.

 **TAKE IT TO THE WEB**

The International Trademark Association (INTA) Web site (**www.inta.org**) addresses many issues, one of which is Internet law. Review the INTA's position on these laws. Are there other issues that should be addressed relating to Internet law?

Consider a product with a recognizable trademark, such as the Delta Air Lines logo. What immediate associations do you make about the brand when you see the logo? Visit **www.delta.com** and see if your preception of the product reflects how Delta Air Lines is portrayed on the Web site.

When you think of Johnson & Johnson, what type of products come to mind? Review the Johnson & Johnson Web site (**www.jnj.com**) and you will see thousands of products trademarked by Johnson & Johnson, including products for diseases and conditions, dental care, skin and hair care, and more.

Capri Sun is an all-natural fruit drink packaged in a distinctive silver pouch. Visit the Web site (**www.kraftfoods.com/caprisun**) and see how Kraft uses the unique packaging as a selling point for the product.

CHAPTER 22

This promotion helped Mentos find and interact with new users.
If you need to engage new prospects, get in touch with us.

THE BOTSFORD GROUP
IDEAS THAT IGNITE

The Complete Campaign

CHAPTER OBJECTIVES

Advertisers usually create campaigns that fit into an integrated marketing communication program. They don't create just an ad by itself. After reading this chapter, you will understand:

1. **situation analysis**
2. **creative objectives and strategy**
3. **media objectives and strategy**
4. **sales promotion plans**
5. **research posttests**

Advertising may not be the first marketing tool used in creating an integrated marketing campaign. Certainly, it isn't the only tool used today. Most of today's advertisers and agencies attempt to view their marketing communications as "media neutral," so there won't be a bias toward using advertising or, for that matter, any other specific discipline as the main communication tool in order to receive maximum return on investment. This could mean that the priority would be developing a Web site or direct response before advertising or using public relations before starting advertising. Remember we said that in branding we're concerned about every consumer "touchpoint " or, as it has been called, the "whole egg."

Brands usually are not built overnight. Success may be measured in years or decades. Coca-Cola wasn't built in a year. BMW has been the ultimate driving machine for almost 30 years. We don't get there with a single ad. Maybe we get there with a strong campaign. More likely we depend on all of the integrated communications from the company or brand to dovetail all other messages or impressions about the brand. We build brand equity from everything we do. These messages may include public relations, direct response, events, packaging, Web sites, and promotion, among others.

In Chapter 3, we discussed a strategic marketing communication plan that could be applied to planning all marketing communications. Here we apply it specifically to advertising campaigns—*campaign*, as defined by Webster, being a "series of planned actions."

You've learned about the important components of the advertising process—development of strategy, media, research, print ads, and broadcast—all of which are extremely important. We don't generally think in terms of individual ads because most brand advertising depends on a series of ads run over a period of time—in other words, a campaign. We should always think in terms of campaigns.

A CAMPAIGN VERSUS ADS

As a general rule, campaigns are designed to run over a longer period of time than an individual ad, although there are exceptions. The average length of a regional or national campaign is about 17 months, although it is not uncommon for a campaign to last three or four years, and a few campaigns have lasted much longer.

For example, in 1929 DuPont started using the campaign theme "Better Things for Better Living Through Chemistry." Fifty-five years later it was changed—"Through Chemistry" was dropped. That is building a lot of brand equity. Basically, the messages remained true to their original campaign premise. On the other hand, some campaigns need to change. In 2001, Ford Truck Division dropped its year-old "Ford Country" for a back-to-basics return to its reliable "Built Ford Tough." The automaker's truck division decided that "Built Ford Tough" carried a punch similar to Chevy's "Like a Rock," that "Ford Country" hadn't been able to deliver. Ford hadn't totally stopped using "Tough", but it had faded somewhat during the "Ford Country" effort. The point is that advertisers must understand their product and consumers in a changing marketplace. There is no reason to change an advertising campaign for the sake of change.

CHANGING CAMPAIGNS

There is never a guarantee that the next campaign will be as strong, let alone stronger, than the original. And some companies grope for a better campaign over and over again with little success. For example, in the mid–1970s, Burger King had perhaps its most famous campaign, "Have It Your Way," but decided it was time to change. So it followed with 16 or so different campaigns, looking for success, from "Aren't You Hungry for Burger King Now?" to "We Do It Like You Do It When We Do It at Burger King" to "Get Your Burger's Worth." And it is still looking for success.

Ken Roman, former CEO of Ogilvy & Mather Worldwide, suggests that even the most successful campaigns need to be refreshed over time. People change, products change, markets change. There are times when campaigns simply wear out because market or competitive changes require a new message.[1]

Pepsi-Cola has been known for advertising to the "Pepsi Generation," but in the process different ad campaigns have been used to generate interest and success. Some are significantly different from previous ones, whereas others are simply tweaks in message or strategy:

> **Pepsi Generation Advertising Themes**
> 1979 Catch the Pepsi Spirit
> 1982 Pepsi's Got Your Taste for Life
> 1984 Pepsi. The Choice of a New Generation
> 1989 A Generation Ahead
> 1995 Nothing Else Is Pepsi
> 1997 GeneratioNext
> 1999 The Joy of Cola
> 2000 The Joy of Pepsi
> 2003 Pepsi. It's the Cola

Remember in the advertising spiral in Chapter 3 we said that sometimes companies will try to expand targets with different kinds of promotional efforts. In 2004, Volvo targeted under–35-year old buyers looking to trade in their VW Jettas, Honda Accords, and Toyota Camrys with a special Internet ad for its redesigned S40 sedan. Volvo ran ads on more than 30 youth-skewing lifestyle Web sites. The effort also included some TV and print, an Internet movie, grassroots marketing, direct mail dropped to some 5,000,000 prospects, and a cross-promotion with Virgin Megastores—all with a pop culture theme. A sweepstakes offered a chance to win an S40 and a dream vacation. This was one of the first Volvo efforts to reach the youth market.

Adding online advertising to a TV campaign boosts brand awareness, but the inclusion does little to impact sales, according to a study by Dynamic Logic. Although broadcast ads upped the linking of a brand to a message or value proposition by nearly 13 points, the Web added 7 points. TV spots increased the ability to influence purchase decisions by nearly 6 points, whereas the Web only contributed a mere 0.4 point incremental boost. The Web was stronger at raising awareness and association than influencing purchase decisions.[2]

DIVERSITY WITHIN THE CAMPAIGN TARGET

How would you as an advertiser handle diversity issues in a campaign? Separate campaigns for African Americans? Hispanics? Asians? What about for global products? This could become an issue.

In Chapter 4, we discussed targeting to different groups of people. In the 1980s and 1990s advertisers began to be very conscious of using multiracial faces in their ads, if not targeting exclusively to a specific group—Asian, African American, Hispanic and so on. Benetton, a global clothing chain, ads had a path-breaking campaign in the 1980s highlighting models of many races, each one very distinct. Today there are over 7 million Americans who identify themselves as members of more than one race—the look of America has indeed changed. Recently, *The New York Times* reported that among art directors and casting agents, there is a growing sense that the demand is weakening for P&G (Procter & Gamble), industry code for blond-haired, blue-eyed models. Ad campaigns for Louis Vuitton, YSL Beauty, and H&M stores have all purposely highlighted models with racially indeterminate features. *The New York Times*, calls this "Generation E.A.:Ethnically Ambiguous." Ron Berger, the chief executive of Euro RSCG MVBMS Partners, says, "Today what's ethnically neutral, diverse or ambiguous has tremendous appeal." He also states that in both the mainstream and high end of the marketplace, what is perceived as good, desirable, or successful is often a face whose heritage is hard to pin down. John Partilla, the chief executive of Brand Buzz, a marketing agency owned by the WPP group, states that some of us are just now beginning to recognize that many cultures and races are assimilating. He says, "If what we're seeing now is our focus on trying to reflect the blending of individuals, it reflects a societal trend, not a marketing trend."[3]

Any campaign needs to bring together all of the advertising elements we have discussed into a unified campaign. This calls for an advertising plan. As we have emphasized, good advertising starts with a clear understanding of both short- and long-term marketing goals. These goals are often expressed as sales or share-of-market objectives to be accomplished for a given budget and over a specific time period.

With our marketing goals in mind, we begin to build the advertising plan with a situation analysis.

SITUATION ANALYSIS

To plan and create future advertising, we need to establish a current benchmark or starting point—this is the role of the situation analysis. It has two time orientations: the past and the present. In other words, it asks two basic questions: Where are we today, and how did we get here? The rest of the advertising plan asks the third basic question: Where are we going in the future?

EXHIBIT **22.1**

Planning Cycle

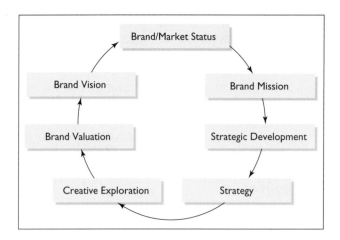

The situation analysis is the first step in developing a campaign. Exhibit 22.1 reminds us of the planning process discussed earlier in Chapter 3. There are strategic steps that must be taken in the planning process. Campaigns are planned; they don't just happen.

The Product

Successful advertising and marketing begin with a good product. At this point, we need to analyze our product's strengths and weaknesses objectively. Most product failures stem from an overly optimistic appraisal of a product. Among the questions usually asked are the following:

1. What are the unique consumer benefits the product will deliver?
2. What is the value of the product relative to the proposed price?
3. Are adequate distribution channels available?
4. Can quality control be maintained?

VitroRobertson's job is to help market Yamahas Watercraft products. Its task is not to sell one model but instead to sell a number of different products to different targets. Its campaign, as with retailer or a restaurant, must create ads that are product specific. Throughout this book, you've seen a number of Yamaha Watercraft ads. Now let's take a look at a sample of them side by side (see Exhibit 22.2).

Prime-Prospect Identification

The next step is to identify our prime prospects and determine if there are enough of them to market the product profitably. As discussed in Chapter 4, there are a number of ways to identify the primary consumers of our product.

Who buys our product and what are their significant demographic and psychographic characteristics? Can we get a mental picture of the average consumer? Who are the heavy users of the product—the prime prospects? Remember the 80/20 rule; do we need to find those market segments that consume a disproportionate share of our product and determine what distinguishes them from the general population? Finally, we need to examine the prime-prospects' problem. What are their needs and wants in the product or product type?

Competitive Atmosphere and Marketing Climate

We carefully review every aspect of the competition, including direct and indirect competitors. Which specific brand and products compete with our brand, and in what product categories or subcategories do they belong? Is Mountain Dew's com-

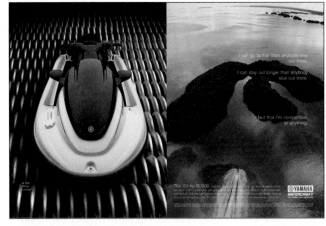

EXHIBIT 22.2

These Yamaha Watercraft ads are product specific, yet maintain a feel of the Yamaha brand essence.

Courtesy of VitroRobertson, Inc., Yamaha Watercraft, and Chris Wimpey, Marshall Harrington, Robert Holland, and Aaron Chang, photographers.

petition 7-Up or Sprite, Mellow-Yellow or Crush, or does it extend to colas, iced tea, and milk? If so, to what extent in each case?

With what does Neon directly compete? Indirectly? Neon's competitive subcompact set includes Honda Civic, Ford Focus, Saturn ION, Nissan Sentra, Toyota Corolla, Chevrolet Cavalier, Hyundai Elantra, Mazda 3, and Mitsubishi Lancer. When we examine the demographic competitive set, we find the typical subcompact buyers are 50 to 55 percent female, over half are married, 35 to 40 years of age, and less than half have a college degree. Honda Civic and Saturn ION models attract the most distinguishable buyer profiles—typically better educated, earning more income, and younger. The psychographic profile is the competitive set. The greatest fluctuations in psychographic profiles for this set exist between import and domestic buyers. Domestic buyers tend to be motivated by style over engineering; they prefer roomier cars and greater performance. Import buyers prefer engineering over style; they like compact cars and believe imports offer higher quality overall. Now we're beginning to scratch the surface. As you can see, there are numerous factors.

CREATIVE OBJECTIVES AND STRATEGY

At this point, we begin to select those advertising themes and selling appeals that are most likely to move our prime prospects to action. As discussed in Chapter 16, advertising motivates people by appealing to their problems, desires, and goals—it is not creative if it does not sell. Once we establish the overall objectives of the copy, we are ready to implement the copy strategy by outlining how this creative plan will contribute to accomplishing our predetermined marketing goals:

1. Determine the specific claim that will be used in advertising copy. If there is more than one, the claims should be listed in order of priority.
2. Consider various advertising executions.
3. In the final stage of the creative process, develop the copy and production of advertising.

Creative Criteria for Campaigns

Most advertising experts agree on the need for similarity between one advertisement and another in developing successful advertising campaigns. Another term, *continuity*, is used to describe the relationship of one ad to another ad throughout a campaign. This similarity or continuity may be visual, verbal, aural, or attitudinal.[4]

Visual Similarity All print ads in a campaign should use the same typeface or virtually the same layout format so that consumers will learn to recognize the advertiser just by glancing at the ads. This may entail making illustrations about the same size in ad after ad and/or the headline about the same length in each ad. A number of ads in campaigns have appeared throughout this book (e.g., Cobra, Yamaha Watercraft, Taylor guitars, The Ritz-Carlton, etc.). Each illustration in the The Ritz-Carlton campaign (see Exhibit 22.3) ads is the same size, copy is visually treated in the same manner, and there is a similar feel with the photograph in the same location, and so on. For a different kind of client and reader (see Exhibit 22.4), ads may use similar styles but there is still definite continuity. We have the same visual feel from ad to ad. We stress visual continuity—not sameness. These examples pertain to print, but the look could easily be carried over to television or direct marketing (see the BB&T television ad in Exhibit 22.5). Strong continuity from medium to medium can strengthen the communication. This also applies to all the elements of integrated communications (promotions, Web, etc.).

Another device is for all ads in a campaign to use the same spokesperson or continuing character in ad after ad. Still another way to achieve visual continuity is to use the same demonstration in ad after ad from one medium to the other.

Verbal Similarity It is not unusual for a campaign to use certain words or phrases in each ad to sum up the product's benefits. It is more than a catchy phrase. The proper objective is a set of words that illuminates the advertising and encapsulates the promise that can be associated with one brand only.

Here are a few campaign phrases that have worked:

Melts in your mouth, not in your hands.

M&M's

The ultimate driving machine.

BMW

Think different.

APPLE

Its hard to believe only three wars have been fought over this island.

EXHIBIT 22.3
The Ritz-Carlton ads are not only beautiful but also convey the same attitude of luxury and quality.

Courtesy of Sawyer Riley Compton and The Ritz-Carlton.

It all started when someone told you not to colour outside the lines.

Raises your expectations of the hereafter.

Love the skin you're in.

OLAY

No cavities.

CREST

Imagination at work.

GE

Pepsi used the words "You're in the Pepsi Generation" to help position it among a younger audience and make Coca-Cola appear to be an old-fashioned brand. But it didn't limit all the upbeat, self-assuring benefits of membership of being part of the Pepsi Generation to people between 13 and 24 years of age; it opened it up to everybody—everybody wanted to be in the Pepsi Generation. It wasn't a point of time in years, it was a point of view. No matter what your age, you could be part of the Pepsi Generation. Great words and great strategy make great campaigns. Here are a few other words and classic campaign strategies:

Aren't you glad you use Dial? Don't you wish everybody did?
You're in good hands with Allstate.
American Express. Don't leave home without it.
Have it your way at Burger King.
Is it true blondes have more fun? Be a Lady Clairol blonde and see!
You deserve a break today, at McDonald's.
Nike. Just do it.

EXHIBIT **22.4**

This campaign has great similarity from ad to ad.

Courtesy of McRae Communications and Humminbird.

EXHIBIT **22.5**

The same look and feel apply to television and all communications. The continuity between these ads is apparent.

Courtesy of Howard, Merrell & Partners and BB&T.

Repeating the benefits, theme, and key copy points in ad after ad bestows continuity across all media and helps to build brand personality.

We have shown a number of Cobra ads throughout this text to give you a real taste of its campaign. These ads use visual, verbal, and attitudinal similarity (see Exhibit 22.6).

Campaigns need to be flexible so they can carry from ad to ad. Baby Gap used a verbal concept that could be endless. Here are a few examples:

Baby Gap is gift.
Baby Gap is newborn.
Baby Gap is spring.
Baby Gap is jeans.

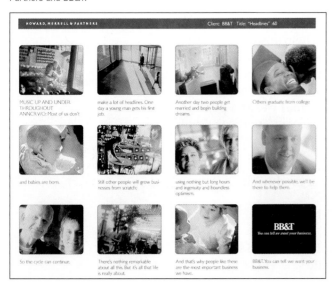

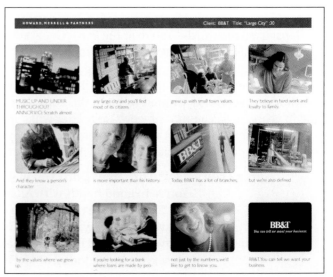

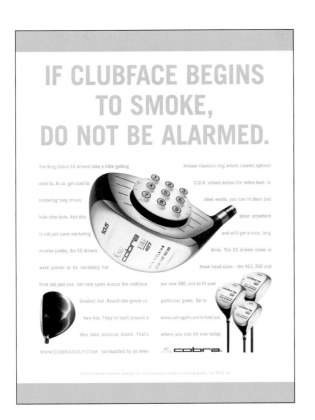

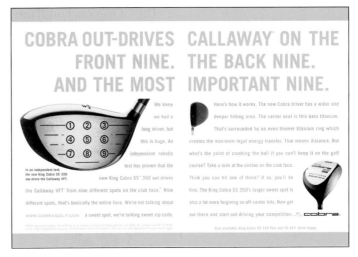

EXHIBIT 22.6

To be distinctive, Cobra uses color as a recognition device. The product treatment and type give the ads continuity. The copy speaks of attributes and benefits driving the reader to the Web address.

Courtesy of VitroRobertson, Inc., Cobra, and John Shultz, photographer.

The DOW Great Stuff ads' verbal continuity is the "Closes Almost Any Gap" (see Exhibit 22.7).

Aural Similarity You can create aural continuity in broadcast, if you desire. You may use the same music or jingle in commercial after commercial. Using the same announcer's voice in each ad also helps build continuity—a classic is "This is Tom

EXHIBIT 22.7

These Dow Great Stuff ads have visual continuity and they use the theme as the verbal continuity, "Closes Any Gap."

Courtesy of Sawyer Riley Compton and Dow.

Bodett for Motel 6." The same sound effect can make a campaign very distinctive. Avon used the sound of a doorbell for many years in its "Avon Calling" advertising. Maxwell House used the perking sound for its Master Blend commercials, giving an audible campaign signal.

Attitudinal Similarity Some campaigns have no theme line that continues from ad to ad. What they do have is an attitude that continues from ad to ad. Each ad expresses a consistent attitude toward the product and the people using it. The commercial's attitude is an expression of brand personality. The "Pepsi Generation" campaign was more than words. It communicated an attitude to younger consumers and older consumers. Of course, we cannot leave out the Nike shoe campaign, that said, "Just Do It"—or its swoosh campaign.

Everyone agrees that Nike is one of the strongest brand names in the world and not just because it sells great products. Its presence and identity are so strong that many people want to connect with the brand. It signifies status, glamour, competitive edge, and the myriad intricacies of cool. It is this description that is communicated in every message, no matter to whom it is directed. Nike's secret of success resides along a delicate and emotionally charged progression that connects the company, the consumers, and the abiding fantasies that are tethered to sports.[5] In true integrated marketing fashion, its personality is communicated to all—from employees, to stockholders, to consumers. It is conveyed through its corporate culture, as well as through its advertising.

Defining an attitude doesn't have to exclude visual or verbal continuity. Sawyer Riley Compton's campaign for The Ritz-Carlton has visual continuity. Each ad through the visual expresses the attitude of luxury and quality (see Exhibit 22.3).

MEDIA OBJECTIVES

Although we have chosen to discuss creative strategy before media objectives, both functions are considered simultaneously in an advertising campaign. In fact, creative planning and media planning has the same foundations—marketing strategy and prospect identification—and they cannot be isolated from each other. The media plan involves three primary areas.

Media Strategy

At the initial stages of media planning, the general approach and role of media in the finished campaign are determined:

1. *Prospect identification.* The prime prospect is of major importance in both the media and the creative strategy. However, the media planner has the additional burden of identifying prospects. The media strategy must match prospects for a product with users of specific media. This requires that prospects be identified in terms that are compatible with traditional media audience breakdowns. You will recall that this need for standardization has resulted in the 4A's standard demographic categories discussed in Chapter 4.
2. *Timing.* All media, with the possible exception of direct mail, operate on their own schedule, not that of advertisers. The media planner must consider many aspects of timing, including media closing dates, production time required for ads and commercials, campaign length, and the number of exposures desired during the product-purchase cycle.
3. *Creative considerations.* The media and creative teams must accommodate each other. They must compromise between using those media that allow the most creative execution and those that are most efficient in reaching prospects.

Media Tactics

At this point, the media planner decides on media vehicles and the advertising weight each is to receive. The question of reach versus frequency must be addressed and appropriate budget allocations made.

Media Scheduling

Finally, an actual media schedule and justification are developed, as described in the example in Chapter 7.

The Promotion Plan

As with any integrated communications planning, the promotion plan for consumers is discussed very early, and its relationship to the advertising plan (and other communications activities) is determined. Promotion activities may involve dealer displays, in-store promotions, premiums, cooperative advertising, and couponing offers.

Once a theme for communications has been established, creative work is begun on the promotion material, which is presented along with the consumer advertising material for final approval. Naturally, advertising and promotion materials reinforce each other. Once the promotion material is approved, the production is carefully planned so that all of the promotion material will be ready before the consumer advertising breaks.

OTHER INTEGRATED ELEMENTS

Don't forget the importance of every aspect of your integrated marketing communication (IMC) functioning as one voice. You need to keep focused on the brand or positioning throughout the marketing mix. "The brand is all about exhilaration and energy, and you see that in all that we do," says Scott Moffitt, director of marketing, Mountain Dew. "Whether it is advertising, events, endorsements, or simply premiums, conveying the 'Dew-x-perience' is paramount."[6] Not only does Dew have strong advertising, but it has grassroots marketing programs and a sports-minded focus. So the range of IMC is endless and should be seamless. With packaging, Remember Tiffany's blue box—a symbol of luxury. Or characters may become brand icons: Ronald McDonald, Wendy, Exxon Tiger, Jack of Jack-in-the-Box, Pillsbury Doughboy, and AFLAC's duck. Don't forget endorsers or spokespersons. You can even use color as *the purple pill* did. Every piece of marketing communication can be integrated including every piece of your Web effort.

Sawyer Riley Compton has used a number of different techniques to promote the Atlanta Film Festival: posters, giving away urinal bottles on "Opening Night," with a message that said, "Over 100 hours of film." Small signs appeared all over the city—on poles and cars—asking people to tune into the Film Festival's street radio and directing people to the Web site. Advertising included print, television, movie trailers, and posters (see Exhibit 22.8).

GETTING THE CAMPAIGN APPROVED

We now have a complete campaign: the ads, the media schedule, sales promotion material, and costs for everything spelled out, ready for management's final approval. For that approval, it is wise to present a statement of the company's marketing goals. The objectives may be to launch a new product, to increase sales by x percent, to raise the firm's share of the market by z percent, or to promote a specific service of a firm. Next, the philosophy and strategy of the advertising are described, together with the

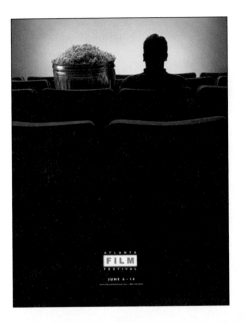

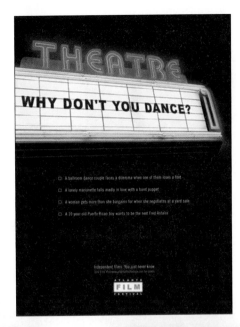

reasons for believing that the proposed plan will help attain those objectives. Not until then are the ads or the commercials presented, along with the media proposal and the plans for coordinating the entire effort with that of the sales department.

What are the reasons for each recommendation in the program? On what basis were these dollar figures calculated? On what research were any decisions based? What were the results of preliminary tests, if any? What is the competition doing? What alternatives were considered? What is the total cost? Finally, how may the entire program contribute to the company's return on its investment? Those people who control the corporate purse strings like to have definite answers to such questions before they approve a total advertising program.

RESEARCH—POSTTESTS

The final part of the campaign entails testing its success. Posttesting falls into two related stages. In the first, the expected results are defined in specific and measurable terms. What do we expect the advertising campaign to accomplish? Typical goals of a campaign are to increase brand awareness by 10 percent or improve advertising recall by 25 percent.

In the second stage, the actual research is conducted to see if these goals were met. Regardless of what research technique is used (e.g., test markets, consumer

EXHIBIT 22.8 b

More from the Atlanta Film Festival.

panels, etc.), the problem is separating the results of the advertising campaign from consumer behavior that would have occurred in any case. That is, if we find that 20 percent of the population recognizes our brand at the end of a campaign, the question arises as to what the recognition level would have been if no advertising took place. To answer this question, a research design is often used as a pretest. The pretest is intended not only to provide a benchmark for the campaign but also to determine reasonable goals for future advertising.

A 10-year study by Information Resources Inc.'s BehaviorScan showed that advertising produces long-term growth even after a campaign ends. The study emphasized TV campaigns and concluded the following:

- Increased ad weight alone will not boost sales.
- Typically, advertising for new brands, line extensions, or little-known brands produced the best incremental sales results.
- Campaigns in which the "message in the copy is new" or the media strategy had changed also produced good sales results.
- Results of copy recall and persuasion tests were unlikely to predict sales reliably.

The study also suggested that discounting results in "training customers to buy only on a deal," and the trade promotion actually worked against TV advertising. However, couponing often helped a brand message and spurred a sale.

The test was conducted in 10 markets with household panels of 3,000 respondents in each market. The commercials were transmitted to two equal groups of homes. This study compared purchase information obtained through scanners and a card encoded with demographic and other information that was presented at supermarket checkout stands.[7]

Campaign Portfolio

Savannah Electric Throughout the book you have seen examples from "There's a better way to cut electricity costs." Each headline/subhead runs three lines. The inset copy in each ad takes the reader in a different direction, for example, "Appliance Hints." Exhibit 22.9 shows three of the campaign ads.

EXHIBIT 22.9

These Savannah Electric ads focus on "There's a better way to cut electricity costs." The headline and subhead run three lines. The inset copy in each ad takes the reader in a different direction, for example, Appliance Hints. Obviously, there is great continuity in format. The colors make each ad distinctive in its own right.

Courtesy of Savannah Electric, A Southern Company.

Five long days at her in-law's cabin. Six people, one bathroom. No problem. But that's five long days she's gone without playing her Taylor. Sacrifice may be part of marriage, but this is ridiculous.

It's Thursday night. Usually his favorite night of the week. But this drummer's out of town at a convention. Which means no band practice tonight. No offense, but that leaves a hole even "Friends" and "ER" can't fill.

It was supposed to be a two-day trip. No need to pack his Taylor he thought. Then the snow came. Eleven inches overnight, no flights in or out. He called his wife. "I'm lonely," he said, "how's my guitar?"

Denver to Los Angeles. Two straight days in the car with his sister. And without his Taylor. That's 1,000 mile markers and not a single cord. He can't help but think, "If my guitar was riding shotgun, would I miss my sister this much?"

EXHIBIT 22.10

The circle contains stories about the people in the photo who play Taylor guitars. You might even call them Taylor fanatics.

Courtesy of VitroRobertson, Inc., Taylor, and Stephanie Menuez, photographer.

Taylor Guitars This series of ads is different from some shown in earlier chapters. The circle contains stories about the people in the pictures who play Taylor guitars. You might even call them Taylor fanatics. For example, "Five long days at her in-law's cabin. Six people, one bathroom. No problem. But that's five long days without playing her Taylor. Sacrifice may be part of marriage, but this is ridiculous." See Exhibit 22.10.

Pushing the Envelope of Taste: Shockvertising

In 2003, under pressure from conservative and religious groups, Abercrombie & Fitch, the marketer of preppie-wear, had to stop some of its half-naked marketing because of taste issues and young people. Another company on the edge is Pony, the athletic-shoe marketer, that seeks attention with shocking advertisements meant to generate discussion, coverage, and eventually sales. Its ads have featured personalities from Jenna Jameson and other stars of pornographic films to offbeat endorsers like former baseball star Pete Rose, who got into trouble for gambling while playing baseball. One of its recent campaigns was composed of print advertisements and posters with stark images aimed to draw the attention of boys and men ages 15 to 25. In one ad, an infant with a tough look on his face stands to show tattoos on his stomach and leg.

Stuart Elliott, the famous *New York Times* advertising columnist, says that pushing the envelope in terms of the taste and tone of ads is a time-honored tactic in fields like apparel, footwear, and fragrances, as smaller advertisers seek to appeal to consumers—particularly younger ones—by adopting the personas of risk-taking rule-breakers who defy the conventions of society. Some brands become known for such behavior whereas others fall short when they seek to imitate it.

Each image used for the Pony print ads and posters "is like a portrait with a point of view to generate strong debate," copywriter Farid Mokart says, because "when you speak in 120 countries, you have to find a language people everywhere understand. The icons, the strong pictures, are a universal language." Fred Raillard, a member of the Pony creative team, says he and Mr. Mokart "try not to use local cultural references" when creating campaigns, particularly when they are to run in so many regions around the world. As for that language being considered tasteless or even obscene by some consumers, Mr. Mokart says "It depends on who is speaking. Most of the time when it's controversial, it's not really the target complaining."[8]

The Diamond Trading Company

J. Walter Thompson (JWT) is the global agency for the Diamond Trading Company (DTC), known for decades as De Beers Consolidated Mines Ltd. It is the company that uses "A Diamond Is Forever" in its advertising. DTC's competition often comes not from another diamond company but instead from another luxury item such as a new sports car or a romantic, exotic vacation. One of the common misconceptions about the diamond market is that most diamonds are bought by nervous fiancés. Although this is true for a first diamond purchase, for those identified as diamond "addicts," this is merely the first of what will be many purchases. These consumers yearn for diamond jewelry, such as tennis bracelets and anniversary bands and in time they become real diamond enthusiasts. JWT research showed that even when women purchase a diamond themselves, many of them will say it is a gift.[9]

A diamond reflects and displays to the world the permanence of a romantic relationship and how much it means to the two people. This truth is the *branding idea* that informs every communication between DTC and diamond lovers. To express this, JWT developed the "Shadows" campaign. This campaign has been running since 1993. It captures the emotion of giving and receiving a diamond. The campaign has appeared in 23 countries. In addition to the advertising, the campaign is accompanied by a specially composed classical soundtrack, the recording of which has topped U.S. Classical charts for many weeks. Because of its ability to convey the allure and intrigue of the shadows as they contrast with the sparkle and brilliance of the diamonds, television has been the primary vehicle for this campaign, while print and other media are also extensively used.

Indeed, total branding (see Chapter 3) is a discipline that JWT uses to promote the DTC. Through the Diamond Information Center and Diamond Promotion Service, agency teams around the world supply an extensive range of public relations, point-of-sale, promotional, and educational materials covering the complete gamut of marketing activity.

DTC continues to work with JWT to keep "Shadows" advertising consistent over time, wherever in the world it appears. Perhaps the best evidence that a diamond is forever is a brand idea that connects with its audience is the fact that in 2002, hundreds of British brides called DTC to ask if they could play the music from this campaign as they walked down the aisle.

Sources: Paige Miller, Kaplan Thaler Group, "Bang," written by Linda Kaplan Thaler and Robin Koval, and press reports.

Background

In the past, AFLAC's supplemental insurance ads looked like other insurance ads—warm and fuzzy and focused on happy families. Although AFLAC had been advertisng for some 10 years, research indicated most people didn't know its name. The company asked Kaplan Thaler Group to create four ads to be tested against its current agency's work. AFLAC's product, supplemental insurance policies, may cover what standard insurance polices fail to cover—loss of income, deductibles, and nonmedical expenses, for example, and cancer insurance. Based in Columbus, Georgia, AFLAC's name is an acronym for American Family Life Assurance Company.

Objective

The assignment from AFLAC was to create awareness.

Creative Process

The creative teams at Kaplan Thaler Group (KTG) ad agency were having a hard time coming up with an idea for AFLAC. One of KTG's creative teams (Tom Amico and Eric David) kept saying to each other, "AFLAC! AFLAC! AFLAC! AFLAC! AFLAC!" One creative said to another, "'You sound like a darn duck quacking.' And a light bulb went off." Hence, the birth of the AFLAC duck "Park Bench" commercial:

Two businessmen sitting on a park bench during lunch hour, tossing leftover bread crumbs to a flock of nearby ducks. A guy rides by on a bike. Then you hear a resounding crash and see his bike upend in the distance.

First businessman:	Boy, when I got hurt and missed work, I'm glad I had supplemental insurance.
Second businessman:	Supplemental insurance? What's that?
One of the ducks:	AFLAC.
First man:	Well, even the best insurance doesn't give you cash to cover things like lost pay and other expenses. This does.
Second man:	What does?
Duck:	AFLAC.
First man:	You should ask about it at work.
Second man:	What's it called?
Duck:	AFLAC.

First man pauses and shrugs: I don't know.

Second man tosses a crumb to the duck. Duck groans, kicks the crumb back at the man, and walks away.

Linda Kaplan-Thaler, KTG's CEO, talked Dan Amos, AFLAC's chairman and CEO, into including the "Park Bench" commercial in the test between four KTG commercials and commercials AFLAC's current agency had created.

Testing

Preproduction testing, which included presenting storyboards to consumers in focus groups, was done by Ipos-ASI, Inc., a worldwide research company. The duck concept was tested against the other ads. Typically, insurance ads register a score of 12 percent. "Park Bench" scored 28 percent. "The fact that the duck is saying the name of the company over and over and over again, and it's humorous—and that's where the humor lies in the recall message—it is the perfect combination of entertainment and business strategy molded into one," said Linda Kaplan-Thaler.

Budget

AFLAC's media budget is about $40 million a year.

Initial Media

Spots originally aired on national television. The Airport spots running on CNN Airport closed-circuit news channel were lanched in 34 airports. A 30-second version of the airport spot ran on inflight television on American Airlines, Delta, United, and Continental.

Public Relations Benefits

The duck has been talked about on *Monday Night Football* and comments made in *People* magazine—the buzz has been worth millions of dollars of free advertising. AFLAC sells a stuffed toy duck and other duck-related merchandise through its Web site and in some department stores. Proceeds from the merchandise sales are donated to the AFLAC Cancer Center and Blood Disorder Center at Children's Healthcare of Atlanta.

Results

The campaign is still going strong after four years. Now part of popular culture, the duck has driven AFLAC to 91 percent name recognition with 55 percent sales growth. The AFLAC duck has become one of advertising's best-known icons. Dan Amos is smiling at AFLAC.

EXHIBIT 22.11

The AFLAC duck has become an advertising icon. The campaign not only entertains but also accomplishes the objective of creating awareness. These are screen grabs from some of the most effective commercials.

Courtesy of Kaplan Thaler Group and AFLAC.

Courtesy of Bevil Advertising and Folks.

Background

Folks Restaurant Management Group (FRMG) operates 20-plus restaurants in northern Georgia—primarily metropolitan Atlanta—known as Folks. Folks restaurant was reborn out of another restaurant concept in 1996. FRMG had operated as the largest fanchisee of PoFolks, Inc., a regional chain in the family restaurant category, for many years. It also operated another restaurant concept, County Seat Café. At times, it has also managed several fast-food operations in the market. Research indicated that PoFolks carried negative baggage of being a "fried food" restaurant and a staid concept. The ownership of the franchise (FRMG) decided it was time to update the concept. As a result it bought out its contract with PoFolks. After testing, FRMG decided the updated concept would be named "Folks." All of the stores were remodeled and a new menu was put into place. The new restaurant was in the "Casual Family" restaurant category—with a Southern Foods flavor. It moved from the original concept more toward the casual category. Retail or restaurant service marketing adjusts almost daily to sales and customer traffic. Not surprisingly, the biggest sales day of the year is Mother's Day.

Competition

The fast-growing Atlanta market is one of the most competitive restaurant markets in the country. Near every Folks restaurant, new concepts open almost weekly, keeping the competition fierce. Many of the competitors similar to the original PoFolks concept have closed or regrouped in the area—Black-Eyed-Pea and Shoney's, are examples. The Chili's, Longhorn's, and Applebee's of the world are generally near each of the Folk's sites.

Target

Historically, each store pulls a slightly different mix of consumers—some a little older, a little better educated, more ethnic, and so forth. Dinner attracts families—from young families to grandparents in the middle-income range. Research indicated the need to target women 25 to 49 years of age. This wasn't limited to advertising but encompassed the whole marketing mix including the menu and interiors.

Media

Folks primarily uses radio, direct marketing, newspaper, outdoor, and cable television. Television and radio have been used primarily for brand recognition and for promotions at specific times of the year. The Folks share of voice is low because of its small budget in comparison to the Outback and other national chains.

Creative

Bevil Advertising creates more than ads and promotions. The restaurant business demands a multitude of marketing communications including in-store material, table tents, menu designs, kids' coloring pieces, kids' menus, take-out menus, employee motivational programs, Web site promotions and public relations activities in addition to advertising. One plus is that the restaurant is positioned as a "Southern Kitchen," with the menu featuring many southern foods and vegetables. This is also problematic because the market migration is toward Hispanics and non-Southerners. Reaching consumers is a daily challenge against larger national competition.

Results

The restaurant continues to keep its core customer and is aggressively seeking a broader customer base. Despite the increase in competition, Folks continues to steadily grow.

EXHIBIT **22.12**

EXHIBIT **22.12** (continued)

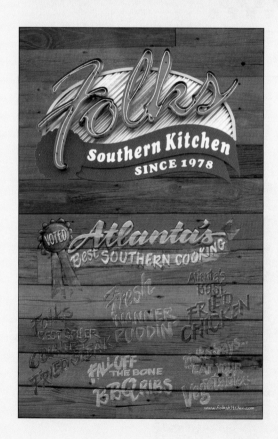

 **SUMMARY**

The steps in preparing a national campaign for a consumer product are the following:

1. Situation analysis
   a. Product analysis
   b. Prime-prospect identification
   c. Prime-prospects' problem analysis
   d. Competitive atmosphere and market climate
2. Creative objectives and strategy
   a. Determination of specific copy claims
   b. Consideration of various advertising executions
   c. Creation of ads and commercials (and other integrated communications)
3. Media objectives
   a. Media strategy—includes prospect identification, timing, and creative considerations
   b. Media tactics
   c. Media scheduling
4. Promotion plan (and/or other integrated programs)
5. Campaign approval
6. Research posttests

In general, advertising campaigns need to have similarity from ad to ad. It may be visual, verbal, aural, or attitudinal. Campaigns should be designed to last and not be changed simply because you are bored with them.

 **REVIEW**

1. What is the basic purpose of an ad campaign?

2. What is ad continuity?

3. What is involved in the situation analysis?

4. What are some of the means of guaranteeing continuity in a campaign?

 **TAKE IT TO THE WEB**

Visit the Land Rover Web site at **www.landrover.com**. Who are the typical Land Rover consumers? Who are the direct and indirect competitors for the brand?

Check out the ad gallery on the Altoids Web site (**www.altoids.com**). How do the print ads achieve visual continuity? How does continuity benefit a brand when new products are introduced?

How do the Got Milk? ads at **www.whymilk.com** express both attitudinal and visual similarity?

How can marketers use a Web site to assist in prospect identification? Visit M&M's Web site at **www.mms.com** for examples of how to get demographic information from consumers.

Other Environments of Advertising

PART SIX

CHAPTER 23

International Advertising

The idea of a "global village" was popularized by Marshall McLuhan some 40 years ago. Although there are many different and contradictory definitions of the term, the central theme of a world made smaller through instantaneous communication has become a reality. However, with globalization and the resulting confluence of culture, commerce, and politics, international companies must compete head-to-head with each in order to achieve success in the world marketplace. In this chapter, we will examine the challenges of companies that must increasingly compete for customers on a global scale. After reading this chapter, you will understand:

1. **the historical development of multinational marketing and advertising**
2. **the numerous approaches to global advertising strategy**
3. **changes in advertising agency organizations to serve multinational clients**
4. **effects of a diverse U.S. population on advertising**
5. **centralized versus localized marketing strategy and management**

The changing complexion of global advertising and marketing is readily apparent from an examination of how American businesses and advertising agencies are now competing with multinational companies from developed countries throughout the world. Whereas international business was once largely confined to the exportation of American products, management expertise, and marketing know-how to other countries, the United States is now a net importer of goods by a significant margin.

Although the United States remains the principal producer and consumer of advertising, the expansion of advertising abroad is growing rapidly. This expansion will be accelerated as more and more countries of the Far East, Middle East, and Latin America increase consumption of consumer goods and services. Another indicator of the worldwide reach of U.S. companies and their marketing efforts can be seen in the ratio of U.S. to global advertising spending. For example, traditional American businesses such as Coca-Cola, Procter & Gamble, and Colgate-Palmolive spend more than 50 percent of their advertising budgets abroad.

The advertising dollars allocated by these international companies to overseas markets are impressive. However, they don't tell the full story of the genesis of this economic expansion. It can be argued that the global business revolution of the last decade is fundamentally a communication revolution that, in country after country, has resulted in demands for more open political systems, which inevitably lead to demands for more economic choice. Without an expansion of communication, it is doubtful that the current political and economic environment would exist. As we discussed in Chapter 1, in the early days of this country, advertising grew as a part of the total economic and social fabric of the nation.

In nations around the world, we are seeing the same phenomenon take place as more open communication is leading one country after another to a freer political system, which leads directly to a more open economy. As *New York Times* columnist Thomas Friedman pointed out, "Countries that are globalizing sensibly but steadily are also the ones that are becoming politically more open, with more opportunities for their people, and with a young generation more interested in joining the world than blowing it up."[1]

The expansion of international marketing and advertising is occurring during a period of significant change in global relationships. These alliances cover a continuum from broadly based country and continental connections to aspirations of individual consumers for a better standard of living. Global marketers are faced with the question of how to deal with wide-ranging differences among people and at the same time find some commonality among diverse markets on which to base brand messages.

As we will discuss throughout this chapter, American companies face another set of obstacles in competing for global sales. Among the major challenges is overcoming significant anti-American opinions abroad. The roots of these attitudes are varied, but many are related to the marketing of American products. For example:

- *Exploitation*—the feeling that American companies take more than they give.
- *Corrupting influence*—the view that American brands enhance thinking and behavior that clash with local customs or cultural or religious norms.
- *Gross insensitivity and arrogance*—in many cultures there is a perception that Americans believe everyone wants to be like them.
- *Hyper-consumerism*—As we will see in this chapter, a continuing challenge for multinational marketers and their agencies is to find those shared feelings and attitudes that are consistent from country to country to give their brand messages continuity. At the same time it is imperative that these companies are sensitive to the distinct differences and pride that consumers feel toward their national and cultural heritages.

THE MULTINATIONAL CORPORATION

Since the end of World War II, the driving force behind the global economy has been the establishment and expansion of the multinational corporation. At the end of the war, American businesses were at the vanguard of the rebuilding process, first in Western Europe and later in Asia. During the early years of global expansion, multinational marketing was largely confined to American companies, with few competitors headquartered outside the United States. However, since the 1970s, American business has had to share the world market with a number of companies headquartered outside the United States.

In fact, in many product categories such as textiles and electronics there is virtually no U.S. manufacturing remaining. In other industries such as automobiles, the U.S. market share has shrunk by more than half in the last two decades. Likewise, advertising, long considered an American invention, is truly a global enterprise with many of the icons of U.S. advertising, such as J. Walter Thompson, now controlled by foreign holding companies.

The incentive for marketing, whether in the United States or abroad, is the pursuit of profits. As U.S. sales became saturated in a number of product categories, companies such as Coca-Cola and Procter & Gamble looked overseas to find new markets in which to expand. By the same token, giants as diverse as Nestlé based in Switzerland and Hyundai headquartered in South Korea obviously have had to move beyond the borders of those small countries to maximize sales potential.

A prime example of this search for profits is the Chinese automobile market. With sales of cars and trucks flat in most of the world, the Chinese market showed an annual increase of 36 percent in trucks and buses and 55 percent in passenger cars in 2002 compared to 2001. In that year, Volkswagen reported 15 percent of its profits from Chinese sales. A number of car makers including General Motors, Honda, and Toyota have announced plans to spend billions of dollars in manufacturing capacity in China.[2]

One of the primary features of global business during the last 10 years is the trend toward mergers, which has created larger and larger corporations. The scope of international business also means that these mergers are not confined to single countries. For example, DaimlerChrysler is an example of a huge cross-border buyout between German and American companies, which created the world's fifth largest corporation. As we will see later in this chapter, this trend has had profound effects on advertising agencies as they try to serve these clients.

Fortune magazine's review of global companies demonstrates a second trend of global marketing—volatility. When companies such as Unilever and General Motors operate in as many as 200 countries, it is not surprising that year-to-year sales will be affected by a number of factors, many of which are beyond management's control. For example, in 1995 Japanese companies held four of the top 10 positions among the world's largest firms. Last year, after a decade-long period of recession in Japan, only Toyota was in that elite group. Overall, the number of Japanese companies among the top 500 has declined from 149 in 1995 to 88 today. Currently, U.S. companies Wal-Mart, Exxon Mobil, and General Motors occupy the top three positions, and American companies account for 40 percent of the top 500 global corporations. On the other hand, reflecting the concentration of the global economy, Africa has no companies on the list and Russia has only two.[3]

A third trend is the emergence of countries that formerly had little economic clout in the world economic theater. China is a prime example of an emerging economic power. A widely held perception of China is that it is a market with vast potential in which advertising and marketing expenditures are an investment in future profits. In reality, China presently represents a prime market for many multinational companies. For example, firms such as Coca-Cola, Kodak, and Procter & Gamble all have profitable and growing operations in China. The CEO of Yum Brands, Inc., owner of KFC restaurants, characterized China as "an absolute gold mine for us."[4]

These emerging foreign markets offer not only new sales opportunities for established multinational firms but also, increasingly, sources of competition. For example, Haier, a leading Chinese appliance manufacturer, had sales of $500 million in air conditioners, refrigerators, and other household appliances in the United States in 2002 and has a goal of $1 billion by 2005. Likewise Chinese companies such as Tsingtao Brewery Co., Sanjiu Enterprise Group (pharmaceuticals), and Li-Ning Sports Goods Co. are all exporting their products and slowly beginning to build brand recognition in various markets. These companies hope to duplicate the success of Korean brands such as Samsung, Kia, and Hyundai, which have become major players in global marketing during the last two decades.[5]

Of course, global expansion is not without significant risk for both new and established companies. Multinational companies often find that many of the countries in which they do business lack the financial and political stability enjoyed by countries with long-established traditions of business and commerce. As an example, the bottom lines of multinational firms throughout the world were significantly hurt by the deep recession experienced by Argentina beginning in 2000. With unemployment at unprecedented levels and the peso at an all-time low, Argentine consumers cut back on all but essential purchases. Some major multinationals threatened to pull out of the country in spite of the risk of losing substantial investments in these markets. Overall, a number of international companies and advertising agencies cited Argentina as a primary reason for their profits and stocks underperforming expectations. Although Argentina is an extreme example, it serves to underscore the pitfalls faced by corporations attempting to take advantage of growth potential in economically volatile areas of the world.

Despite setbacks, the global economy will continue to grow, fueled by emergence of middle-class societies in an increasing number of countries. In addition, communication technology is permitting advertisers to reach prospective buyers never before available to them. A growing global demand and a rising standard of living will combine to make advertising even more prevalent throughout the world.

Another significant feature of global marketing and advertising is the paradox of a greater ability to communicate across international borders accompanied by growing nationalism and suspicion of outside influence in many countries. Clearly, communication technology, open trade movements such as the European Union (EU), and improved transportation are making international marketing and advertising more efficient. On the other hand, a growing sense of nationalism and an increasing protectionism are impeding foreign expansion into many markets. Perhaps people are reacting to a communication revolution that threatens to merge and blur the differences in cultures. Whatever the reason, a prevailing sense of isolationism is a factor that international marketers must consider with great care.

In some cases, isolationism can be overcome in part by greater sensitivity to other cultures, a willingness to learn local customs, and an openness to new ideas. A greater sense of local country traditions may be more important than business expertise. In the global arena, it is important to view differences in lifestyle and traditions, as well as consumer behavior, objectively rather than making judgments about customs or cultures in other parts of the world. Exhibit 23.1 shows how Home Depot recognized the Puerto Rico Olympic Committee in its advertising in this U.S. protectorate.

THE INTERNET AND INTERNATIONAL COMMUNICATION

International marketing has been fueled by a number of factors. However, a necessary element in the expansion of global business activity has been the growth of communication technology. We can expect an accelerated pace of the use of these innovations as the Internet and other new communication technologies become commonplace around the world. Even in countries with repressive governments and/or isolationist business policies, communication that crosses borders with little or no interference is a catalyst for change.

Two communication technologies that hold the greatest short-term potential for global marketing are the Internet and satellite television. The Internet, which began as a government-sponsored means of scientific exchange of defense information, has become a primary means of general communication and, increasingly, a means of commerce.

In the early days of the Internet, usage was overwhelmingly located in the United States, with an estimated 175 million users. America is still the leader per household by a wide margin. However, global Internet capability is increasing dramatically. Although projecting Internet usage is an inexact science, Exhibit 23.2 offers some insight into the relative penetration of the Internet.

The adoption of the Internet is moving at an accelerated pace throughout the world. As one Internet executive observed, "Don't expect. . . . American domination to last long . . . . Compared to a year ago, significantly more households in Europe and Asia Pacific now have a PC in the home and a greater proportion of homes are

EXHIBIT 23.1

Home Depot takes pride in being a good citizen in each of the local markets in which it does business.

Courtesy of Homer TLC, Inc., Copyright 2003.

making use of that PC to connect to the Internet."[6] In the very near future, projections are that the majority of Web users will be non–English speaking and the U.S. share of the worldwide online population will continue to drop. The advertisement for Megapass (see Exhibit 23.3) demonstrates the universality of Internet technology.

From an advertising perspective, satellite television holds great potential for the introduction of worldwide brands in a more traditional commercial venue than offered by the Internet. The dream of worldwide communication is as old as the early days of television. In 1945, Arthur C. Clarke, author of *2002; A Space Odyssey*,

Europe	185.8
Canada and United States	182.7
Asia/Pacific	167.9
Latin America	33.0
Africa	6.3
Middle East	5.1

EXHIBIT 23.2

Estimates of Worldwide Internet Users (millions)

Source: "How many online," Kadius, www.nua.ie/.survey.com, 9 September 2002.

EXHIBIT 23.3

The Internet has made worldwide communication a reality and, in many cases, heightened cultural understanding.

Courtesy of KT Agency and Megapass.

advanced the notion of worldwide communication from three space platforms orbiting 22,300 miles above the earth.[7] Barely 20 years later, in 1976, Home Box Office (HBO) initiated satellite delivery of television programming followed by Ted Turner's TBS "Superstation," which opened the potential for commercial satellite television on a regular basis. Today, the technological problems of global communications have been largely overcome. It is now a matter of country-by-country growth of the necessary hardware and television set ownership to achieve reasonable penetration for efficient advertising.

Although the Internet and satellite transmission can provide businesses with instantaneous worldwide communication and the potential for a truly integrated worldwide communication, there are numerous problems yet to be solved. For example, a single advertising theme can rarely overcome the distinct character and preferences within the global marketplace. Multinational firms realize that to be successful global marketing communication must relate to the interests of consumers in specific countries.

As we will discuss later in this chapter, the key to successful global marketing is finding those common appeals that will work on a universal basis (e.g., a mother's concern for her child's well-being). At the same time, marketers must understand the inherent differences in how these broad appeals may have to be adapted to various markets.

Unlike print or even traditional television advertising, the Internet, at a relatively low cost, can reach international market segments with messages adapted to both the language and local culture of these consumers. So-called "cultural Internet" is being developed in which a basic Web site may provide information and advertising in Spanish to a worldwide Hispanic market. However, within this larger service, there will be numerous opportunities for targeting with nuances of the language or specific brand appeals. In this country, a number of mainstream business sectors such as banks and automobile dealers have for some time offered Spanish-language versions of their Web sites.

In addition to basic differences in consumer language and cultures, multinational marketers also face the problem of country-by-country variances in matters such as privacy and legal and regulatory standards. The advantage of communication without borders can be a major problem when signals carrying illegal offers or advertising themes enter many countries. Often advertisers will carry a statement on their Web site that promotions are specific to a particular country or offers that are not permitted in particular countries should be considered void. In themselves, these steps may not eliminate the problem, but, at a minimum, they may show good faith on the part of the company and at least lessen any potential legal or regulatory problems.

THE DEVELOPMENT OF GLOBAL MARKETING AND ADVERTISING

Twenty years ago, entering the international market was an optional decision for most American firms. Today, becoming a player on the international scene is a given for most companies. Not only is the success of American businesses more and more dependent on exporting products abroad, but also even American companies that sell only domestically are finding major competition from imported goods in virtually every product category. Many American consumers are increasingly familiar with products from around the world and, as American car makers have witnessed, U.S. consumers have developed high levels of brand loyalty for many of these imported brands. As we will see throughout this chapter, the methods, organization, strategy, and execution of advertising are remarkably different because of the advent of international marketing.

During the years shortly after World War II, international business meant American products, marketing, and advertising carried abroad. American companies exported a variety of goods to Europe and Asia as these regions began the difficult recovery from the war. Today, America no longer dominates global commerce, and advertising and marketing are truly worldwide. As multinational companies compete on an international stage, we see the effects through the development of universal brands and even a similarity of product usage among people in diverse cultures and societies.

It is difficult to develop rigid guidelines for global commerce because each company faces unique issues and deals with them in different ways. However, we can gain perspective by examining the scope of how some selected international companies deal with these complex issues. Let's start by looking at some statistics relevant to multinational marketing. First, despite major increases in worldwide advertising, the United States still accounts for approximately 55 percent of the total spent on advertising. Early in this century, many experts predicted that U.S. advertising expenditures would make up less than half of the worldwide total. However, deep recessions in Japan and Latin America and a stronger than expected U.S. economy have contributed to a smaller than expected increase in non-U.S. advertising spending.

EXHIBIT **23.4**

Global Advertising Expenditures (in billions $)

Source: Table compiled from "100 Leading National Advertisers" and "Top 100 Global Marketers by Media Spending outside U.S.," www.adage.com, 15, September 2002.

Company and Origin	U.S.	Non-U.S.	Total	Non-U.S.%
General Motors (U.S.)	$3.4	$1.0	$4.4	22.7
Procter & Gamble (U.S.)	2.5	2.6	5.1	51.0
Ford (U.S.)	2.4	1.1	3.5	31.4
Unilever (Dutch)	1.5	2.9	4.4	66.0
Nestlé (Swiss)	1.5	1.0	2.5	39.0
Coke (U.S.)	0.9	1.2	2.1	57.1
McDonald's (U.S.)	1.2	0.7	1.9	36.8
Honda (Japan)	1.1	0.4	1.5	25.1
Toyota (Japan)	1.4	1.3	2.7	48.0

An examination of some of the major multinational corporations shows that while American companies are looking to global markets to increase sales and profits, the world is likewise coming to America for the same reason. In many cases, U.S. consumers probably don't know that brands such as Kit Kat candy bars are owned by foreign companies. In other instances, consumers have long voted with their dollars for foreign brands such as Honda and Toyota, which have been among the most popular cars in America for many years. Exhibit 23.4 shows the expenditures of several multinational companies headquartered in this country and abroad.

Using advertising expenditures as a rough gauge of sales potential, you can see that multinational corporations headquartered around the world, view the United States as a major market. Likewise, American companies, such as Coca-Cola, are spending the majority of their advertising budgets in a quest to capture a world market. In contrast, Swiss-based Nestlé and Japanese-headquartered Honda are spending 60 to 75 percent of their total budgets in the United States. There is little question that the huge domestic expenditures of both General Motors and Ford are a direct consequence of the successful inroads made by these overseas brands.

As American companies have had to adapt to the complexities of the global market, foreign companies have had the same challenge as they enter the U.S. arena. Toyota is a good case in point. A decade ago, Toyota, the world's third largest car maker, developed a global strategy to grow steadily in Japan, make modest gains in the United States, become profitable in Europe, and become dominant in Asia. However, currently Toyota is heavily dependent on American consumers. It derives two-thirds of its profits from U.S. sales and is a minor play in Japan and most of the rest of the world.

Rather than importing Japanese models to the United States, Toyota's biggest-selling U.S. models, the Camry and Tundra pickup, were designed specifically for the American consumer. In fact, Toyota is making more and more of its vehicles in the United States. We often think of international marketing as the exporting of goods and services from one country to another. In fact, global business has a significant influence on the companies that engage in it. As one Toyota executive stated, "The American market is our top priority, bar none. We'll do whatever it takes to succeed there."[8] Obviously, priorities will determine in large measure the management and marketing decisions involved in future planning.

As Toyota has found, the relationship between an international business and the countries it enters is a symbiotic one. That it, just as the products a company markets will change the perspective of consumers, so will a company change as it adapts to these new markets. Sometimes the change can be traumatic, as Coke discovered in the late 1990s. In the last 50 years, few companies have had as much success in the global market as coca-cola. It was a brand that was recognized and welcomed in the majority of the world. One of the primary foundations of Coke's prosperity was its reliance on local bottlers for insights into the various markets.

However, as the company expanded its global business in the 1980s, it began to centralize much of the decision making at its Atlanta headquarters. This change in management style allowed the company to take control of the decision-making process, but it also created a communication gap with local bottling partners. When Doug Daft became chairman of the company, he observed that "we [Coke] were operating as a big, slow, insulated, sometimes even insensitive 'global' company; and we were doing it in a new era when nimbleness, speed, transparency and local sensitivity had become absolutely essential to success . . . the very forces that were making the world more connected and homogeneous were simultaneously triggering a powerful desire for local autonomy and reservation of unique cultural identity."[9]

Under Chairman E. Nevill Isdell, we assume that Coke will continue a model that places more decision-making responsibility at the local level. It hopes that it can reinvent the "multilocal" heritage that accounted for much of its past success. However, as we will see later in this chapter, Coke is not alone in attempting to balance the need for efficient management with a system that permits two-way communication between top executives and the many global markets in which a company operates.

Traditionally, a major failing of American companies going abroad, especially those with little multinational experience, has been treating a foreign market as if consumers were homogeneous in terms of demography and product preference. Companies accept without question that domestic American markets demonstrate wide variance among different market segments. Yet, they sometimes don't translate this concept to foreign distribution. To a degree, this mind-set is based on a lack of research, but more often it shows an appalling insensitivity to local cultures and traditions.

As Coke discovered, a major challenge of international business is dealing with a world that is expanding in terms of marketing opportunity and simultaneously becoming more individualistic. As we view the various challenges facing international marketers, we will find that both companies and multinational advertising agencies are adopting management styles that stress a two-way flow of communication between headquarters and local markets. Marketing executives of the future will be valued as much for the information and insights they provide top management as for the sales and marketing skills they embrace.

International marketing involves many elements from organizational management to advertising execution. However, a common characteristic is the search for efficiencies when doing business on a worldwide basis. Indeed, as we examine the leading multinational marketers in various countries, many of the same companies and brands—Ford, Sony, Nestlé, Unilever, Coca-Cola—appear again and again. Even though a one-size-fits-all strategy for international marketing will rarely work, significant economies of scale do exist for these companies.

GLOBAL MARKETING AND ADVERTISING

The term **global marketing** was popularized in a classic article by Harvard professor Theodore Levitt entitled "The Globalization of Markets." At the heart of the concept is the assumption that consumer needs are basically alike all over the world and consumers will respond to similar appeals regardless of cultural differences. Among other things, Levitt argued that advances in communication technology and marketing efficiencies were making it possible to achieve unprecedented economies of scale by developing and marketing global brands. A fairer reading of Levitt would suggest that he advocated a global approach when it was appropriate, and he encouraged companies to look for such a viewpoint whenever possible.

The importance of branding and brand equity can't be overemphasized in global marketing. It is the identity and reputation of a specific brand that make the efficiencies of multinational marketing possible. However, experienced marketers such as Coke, Sony, McDonald's, and IBM know that they have to make significant local market adaptations to be successful. In fact, some marketing experts think that the move to common themes in global marketing may have gone too far. For example, Sir

global marketing
Term that denotes the use of advertising and marketing strategies on an international basis.

Martin Sorrel, chief executive of WPP Group, one of the world's largest advertising agency holding companies, said, "I think we're losing country focus, which is why we're creating country managers in Holland, Italy, and China. Our clients are doing the same thing. If you don't have someone leading the business [locally], you don't get government contacts, education contacts, and political contacts."[10]

In developing a successful multinational marketing organization a number of areas must be addressed:

Management

Regardless of the method of marketing strategy, it is invariably coordinated at top management levels. However, management coordination does not preclude significant latitude for decision making at the local level. It is unrealistic to think that a company such as Nestlé can effectively manage as many as 7,000 worldwide and local brands, including such disparate products as Polo clothing and Carnation milk products, from its Vevey, Switzerland, headquarters. However, Nestlé can create and maintain very sophisticated control centers to market its products according to consistent standards for product quality, advertising and promotion, and distribution. A commonly used management approach by multinational companies is to consolidate strategic management decisions at corporate headquarters and give local managers flexibility to develop specific tactics within general guidelines.

One of the major management challenges for multinational corporations is developing a strategic partnership with advertising agencies to execute corporate marketing communication strategy on a worldwide basis. Multinational advertisers find that they must develop partnerships with their agencies on both a strategic and tactical basis. For example, the "Priceless" campaign for MasterCard was strategically positioned to demonstrate that people don't buy products, they buy experiences. The idea was intended to be a simple, straightforward message easily adapted across cultures and languages.[11]

Not unexpectedly, management centralization has resulted in a consolidation of advertising agencies to handle these global accounts. Even the largest companies tend to have no more than four agencies—some only one—to create and manage their worldwide promotions (although it is common for local agencies to be retained for specific advertising projects). This trend in turn has led to the development of huge multinational advertising agencies, agency holding companies, and worldwide agency networks to service global accounts. As we will discuss later in this chapter, only a few of agencies have the personnel, offices, and expertise to fully service multinational clients. In fact, the top five agency holding companies now control more than 60 percent of global advertising.

Advertising Execution

It is important to remember that advertising agencies are judged by how well they achieve clients' objectives, not by how well they achieve maximum simplicity for the organization. For example, developing a global brand should not be an end in itself but, rather, part of an overall strategy that will gain greater product acceptance and, ultimately, higher profits. Regardless of the management approach used by a global company, the key marketing and advertising elements are the same as for domestic marketing, that is, to enhance brand identity, increase share-of-mind, and so on.

As various elements of the marketing program such as product quality, advertising themes, and marketing tactics become more decentralized, it becomes more difficult to establish a global brand. However, for many brands and product categories their success depends on a local approach with appeals that are focused on a particular country or even on a specific region of a country. Companies that try to force global brands on unreceptive consumers often pay a heavy price.

Procter & Gamble is a notable success story in finding a balance between the extremes of standardized global brands and total local marketing control, but its expertise has not been gained without some missteps. After some years of trying to develop truly global brands, the company found that each country and brand had to be evaluated on an individual basis. For example, Safeguard bar soap was marketed in Mexico under the Escuda brand. In order to accommodate a mandate for global branding, Escuda was dropped in favor of Safeguard. After a substantial dip in sales, the Escuda brand was reintroduced and sales returned to previous levels. A Procter & Gamble executive commented on the company's approach to global branding and product design, "There are hard points you want to keep consistent across geographies, like the kind of machine you use to make Bounty [towels]. But if you want to put different colors, patterns or brand names on the towels, that's a soft point. It doesn't cost us a lot extra. It meets local needs. I think we're getting better at deciding what are the hard points and what are the soft points."[12]

When considering global marketing and advertising managers normally consider three basic organizational options.[13] As we discuss these alternatives, it is important to realize that most companies will use some aspects of each in one or more countries or for particular products. There are few absolutes in the changing field of international business.

■ *Standardization.* Advertising strategy and execution are handled globally with changes in creative or other elements of a campaign kept to a minimum. Under this model, advertising agency account and creative teams interact with a centralized marketing vice president to determine overall global strategy. A major advantage of this approach is that it ensures consistent advertising execution and quality. More importantly, it allows the promotion for a company or brand to speak with a single voice throughout the world and establish global themes.

■ *Pattern standardization.* Under this plan, a global advertising agency controls overall strategy and general creative and media approaches while advertising execution is handled locally or regionally. Each country handles its own media selection and tailors campaigns to meet local needs. From a intuitive standpoint, this approach is the most reasonable one and, indeed, some version of **pattern standardization** is most popular with both companies and agencies.

Unilever markets its premium-quality detergent under a number of brand names including Wisk in the United States, Skip in parts of Europe, and Omo in its other global markets. While devising a campaign for the product, the company and its agency, Lowe & Partners, kept the established brand identities but developed a consistent campaign for them using the theme "Dirt is good." Advertising executions emphasized that part of being a child is getting dirty and that rather than having parents worry about it, they should use Unilever detergents to solve the problem. The commercials showed the fun that children have getting dirty and played up the fact that "Kids think differently about getting their clothes dirty" and invited parents to do the same.[14]

Problems that arise with pattern standardization tend not to be with the concept but instead in the execution and management of the various advertising plans. The question is how much country-to-country autonomy is practical and knowing when pattern standardization should shift to a fully localized approach. Obviously, there are no definitive answers, but companies and agencies undertaking this management philosophy will find that training and indoctrination into the foundation business and advertising and creative principles of the brand are the key to long-term success.

■ *Localization.* At the other end of the management spectrum from standardization is localization. Under this management philosophy, each country manages the strategy and execution of campaigns in that locale. Local advertising agencies tailor campaigns to each area's culture and needs. Tactical control is

patterns standardization
An advertising plan where overall strategy is controlled centrally, but local offices have flexibility in specific advertising executions.

EXHIBIT **23.5**

Multinational firms usually develop marketing plans that represent a compromise between the needs of consumers and the firm.

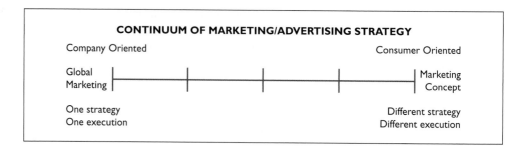

decentralized, but strategic planning at the corporate level provides an overall emphasis to local country marketing efforts.

Obviously, technology is becoming more readily available to make the *idea* of international advertising and global marketing a reality. However, it is impossible to accommodate all the cultural and national differences in any single marketing strategy. Global marketing is such an appealing concept from a cost and efficiency standpoint that companies are tempted to adopt it even when it has obvious pitfalls. It can be argued that the misapplication of global marketing places the well-being of the firm ahead of the consumer. Exhibit 23.5 demonstrates the continuum of a one-strategy, one-execution global marketing approach versus a consumer-oriented marketing concept with a different-strategy, different-execution approach in each country.

Sensitivity

In recent years, multinational businesses have had to deal with numerous complaints about their operations in developing countries. Even the corporations themselves acknowledge that there is a fine line between opening new markets for their products and exploitation. The problem is not a new one. In 1621, the charter of the Dutch West India Company gave it responsibility "for the preservation of the places, keeping good order, police and justice." Obviously, few companies are burdened with that level of responsibility. However, a primary consideration of globalization and effective management is the development of a sensitivity to the host countries. In a strict adherence to centralized management, it is sometimes difficult to envision either customers or employees from the same perspective as a local executive who shares a common culture and perspective with consumers. In recent years, there has been a heightened sensitivity to the responsibilities of companies operating as guests in host countries.

When Exxon Mobil began drilling operations in Chad, it encountered a number of unexpected problems. Nearby villagers complained that the company had cut down trees that brought rain and a fear that the holes drilled by the company would create earthquakes. In an earlier day, the company might have ignored the fears of these villagers. Instead, it hired a cultural anthropologist to work with the people and, in some cases, to cooperate in setting up cultural rituals to ward off evil spirits.[15]

On a more pragmatic basis, the company has established clinics and schools and dug wells for local communities. Granted, these actions were taken in part to ensure a smooth drilling operation. On the other hand, Exxon Mobil's actions demonstrate a far more enlightened attitude than one might have expected only a few years ago.

This same responsibility for sensitivity can take the form of an awareness of how advertising copy, themes, slogans, and brands should be displayed and promoted. Critics point out that major multinational corporations should not look to developing nations as only a source of cheap labor and additional sales and profits. Instead, international businesses should use their economic leverage to help raise economic standards in emerging countries where they operate. There is no expectation that companies should forgo the profit motive and stockholder equity as they go abroad. But, as many companies are demonstrating, there is an important balance to be reached between maximizing shareholder equity and being a responsible marketer.

The opinions of how to conduct multinational business cover a wide spectrum. However, it is clear that a growing debate over the conduct of global business is creating a changing environment for multinational businesses. Many people are questioning the benefit of globalization to developing countries. Clearly, the notion of global marketing has ethical and philosophical elements that cannot be ignored.

POLITICAL AND ECONOMIC MOVEMENT TOWARD A WORLD ECONOMY

As we discussed earlier in this chapter, communication technology has made traditional political borders irrelevant in terms of government control of communication. The availability of information in formerly closed societies has created demand for products and services that has put pressure on many repressive regimes to adopt more open trade policies.

This new openness has created the consumer demand that fosters international trade. Steps toward removing artificial barriers to commerce are in place or at the discussion stage throughout the world. The opening of China, Vietnam, and South Africa to trade with the United States is evidence of multinational business opportunities that would have been considered unthinkable only a few years ago. Even Cuba is being visited on a regular basis by U.S. companies and trade delegations in anticipation of lifting U.S. trade embargos with that communist country.

In addition, agreements such as the **North American Free Trade Agreement (NAFTA)** and the **General Agreement on Tariffs (GATT)** have moved to open overseas markets by lowering or eliminating tariffs and giving impetus to a free-trade environment among an increasing number of countries. Although member countries stand to benefit from a greater availability of goods, none of these agreements overcomes cultural, language, and product usage differences among nations. The job of the multinational advertiser is made easier but is hardly solved by these alliances.

The European Union

The most far-reaching and ambitious trade agreement to date involves the economic unification of Europe. Since 1992, Europe has moved toward a consolidated market consisting of most of the countries of the region. Called the **European Union (EU),** it has embarked on a plan that by 2007 will include as many as 27 countries with a population of approximately 500 million people, which is more than the United States, Mexico, and Canada combined.

A significant step toward a unified Europe was the 1998 introduction of a single currency called the *euro*. Consistent monetary policy offers consumers a means for price comparisons, gives products a universal value, and makes currency conversion much easier among the nations of the EU. When fully implemented, the EU will provide a common trade area stretching from former Soviet bloc countries such as Latvia and Estonia to the Western European nations of Spain and Portugal with a total market value greater than the United States.

Obviously, an undertaking of this magnitude is an enormous task. Countries that have been political and economic rivals for centuries are being asked to set aside their differences and make significant compromises for the common good. There are numerous elements to be negotiated to create a unified market, including issues as diverse as currency exchange and the regulation of advertising.

The French, in particular, have been extremely protective of what they see as encroachments on the French language in advertising and marketing. For example,

North American Free Trade Agreement (NAFTA)
A treaty designed to eliminate trade barriers among the United States, Mexico, and Canada.

General Agreement on Tariffs and Trade (GATT)
A treaty designed to lower trade barriers among 117 nations.

European Union (EU)
The developing economic integration of Europe. Potentially a single market of some 300 million consumers in 1991.

the EU has ruled that products sold across the EU should carry their original brands to save manufacturers the expense of creating separate labels for each of the 15 countries. On the other hand, a 1994 French law mandates that imported goods use French on labels and advertising. Hence, in French supermarkets Kellogg Corn Pops are "miel pops" and taco shells are "coquilles à tacos." In 2002, the European Court of Justice ruled that France was in violation of EU rules and threatened economic sanction. Despite one French newspaper carrying the headline, "It's going to be necessary to speak English to go shopping," it is expected that the French will drop their ban on foreign name brands.[16] The disagreement simply underscores the range of difficulties faced with any multinational trade initiative.

The detractors of the EU say that the concept will never be fully implemented because, in fact, there is no common European community. According to critics, to assume that geographic proximity alone can lead to economic cooperation on a scale suggested by the EU is impractical. Many economists cite differences in wage levels, taxes, and a variety of competitive factors as major impediments to cross-border cooperation. They point to statistics such as 70 percent home ownership in the Netherlands versus 40 percent in Germany to demonstrate major differences in local consumption patterns.[17]

Like global marketing itself, the EU concept will probably find its final place somewhere between the goals of its strongest supporters and its harshest critics. The EU does demonstrate the extent of the challenges facing the concept of pan-national economic agreements. If developed countries in relatively close proximity and with a number of common traditions and cultural heritages are having the difficulties demonstrated by the EU, it emphasizes the problems faced by all multinational marketers.

THE MULTINATIONAL ADVERTISING AGENCY

Advertising agencies are organized in a manner that best serves their clients. Therefore, it is not surprising that as marketing became a multinational enterprise dominated by huge companies, advertising agencies demonstrated similar growth and organizational patterns. The modern international agency is much different than in the 1940s and 1950s when McCann Erickson and J. Walter Thompson led American agencies into the international arena. They usually started foreign branches on a country-by-country basis with local branch agencies typically responsible for the advertising of a few large U.S. clients in a limited number of countries.

This approach to international advertising was extremely expensive and did not guarantee that the foreign branches would adequately service and coordinate the international marketing needs of their clients. During the 1970s, most U.S. agencies moved from full ownership of foreign offices to some form of joint venture or minority ownership of existing foreign agencies. This plan overcame the long start-up time involved in beginning a new agency and provided advertising plans that reflected local business practices and culture. Joint ventures also recognized the growing expertise of local advertising talent and the fact that around the world many overseas agencies were providing client services on a par with major American agencies.

In the last 20 years, there has been a number of significant changes in international advertising on the agency side. Some of the most significant developments follow.

Growth of Major Advertising Centers Outside the United States

Although America still leads the world in advertising expenditures, the development of global advertising is reflected in the advertising investment in a number of overseas markets. Exhibit 23.6 shows this international diversity of advertising markets.

1. New York	$61,264.4
2. Tokyo	36,618.5
3. London	23,448.1
4. Chicago	17,379.9
5. Paris	13,130.2
6. Los Angeles	10,545.6
7. Detroit	7,946.3
8. Frankfurt	7,389.3
9. Milan	6,150.7
10. Minneapolis	6,087.2

EXHIBIT 23.6

Major Advertising Centers by Capitalized Billings ($ in millions)

Source: "Top 15 U.S. Markets" and "Top 15 Cities Outside the U.S.," www.adage.com, 15, September 2002.

As we can see, half of the top 10 advertising markets are outside the United States. The list also demonstrates the highly concentrated nature of advertising with New York accounting for more billings than Tokyo and London, the number two and three markets, combined. In turn, the billings of these two markets are equal to the next six markets. The figures underscore once again the fact that advertising centers and individual agencies increasingly find that they must attain a size unheard of only a few years ago in order to compete for major multinational clients. For example, the three largest advertising holding companies account for approximately 44 percent of worldwide gross income.

Effects of Integrated Marketing Communication on Worldwide Agencies

It is obvious that in order to serve a client in dozens of countries, agencies must have a presence in each of these markets. Not so apparent is the diversification of agencies into many areas of marketing communication beyond advertising. For example, 2001 marked the first year that the big three advertising holding companies (Interpublic Group of Companies, Omnicom Group, and WPP Group) derived less than half their gross income from advertising services. The remaining income came from public relations, sales promotion, specialty shops, and research services.

The development of the diversified agency is largely in response to clients' shifting dollars out of traditional advertising into other areas of marketing communication. While the share of nonadvertising promotional dollars has grown significantly in the United States, these increases are even more apparent in foreign markets where reaching consumers often demands using a greater number of non-traditional communication channels than in the United States. Clients are increasingly demanding that their agencies be able to coordinate all phases of their marketing communication.

Although the move to provide clients with an array of communication services is understandable, the changes have had a number of ramifications for these agencies. For example, the need to provide more services has led to numerous mergers of advertising, public relations, and sales promotion agencies under a single management umbrella. The business model used in public relations and sales promotions is very different from advertising, and agencies have often demonstrated significant internal conflicts as they attempt to coordinate these functions. In addition, many agencies find that keeping consistent quality control across several promotional and marketing subsidiaries is a challenge, particularly on a worldwide basis.

Regardless of the challenges, international agencies realize that they must grow and diversify to serve global clients. International agencies must build parallel organizations to their largest clients. On the client side, marketing directors in countries around the world report to international brand management groups while their agency counterparts, local country account directors, report to agency international account teams. To be successful, agency organizations must operate in concert with their clients at both local and corporate levels.

The two-tier, local/centralized approach allows multinational marketers and their agencies to achieve beneficial efficiencies in building worldwide brands. The sharing of information and ideas from individual agency offices generates ideas and offers perspectives from a number of sources. Likewise, agencies gain valuable insights and develop a consistent approach to creativity and brand positioning by gathering information from individual markets rather than dictating strategy centrally. Finally, it allows a pooling of resources to face the challenges of operating on a global scale.

The Effect of Consolidation on Agency/Client Conflicts

One of the long-standing principles of advertising is that agencies do not accept clients that market competing brands to those they are currently servicing. It would not be permissible for the agency for Ford to simultaneously handle the Chevrolet account. Certainly, the noncompete principle is common sense for a number of reasons.

First, to be effective, an agency needs to be a partner with its clients. This partnership involves not only the preparation and execution of advertising but also, more importantly, a collaboration on basic marketing strategy and business goals, which includes sharing a great deal of proprietary information. Obviously, clients are reluctant to share this type of information with an agency that is simultaneously handling a competing account.

Noncompete clauses also have pragmatic considerations. For example, if an agency is servicing two competing brands, which brand is assigned to the more senior copywriter and art director? Which media planner handles which client? When media avails are scarce, which client has first priority on prime media spots? For a number of reasons, both agencies and clients have, from the beginning of the agency/client relationship, agreed that the client conflicts should be avoided.

The noncompete system worked well when there were hundreds of independent agencies and clients had little trouble finding an agency to handle their advertising. However, with the consolidation of both businesses and agencies, the fundamentals of the advertising relationship have changed dramatically over the last 25 years. Only a limited number of agencies have the resources to handle a top–50 multinational advertising account (or, more likely, a diversified marketing communication program).

In recent years, two major changes have taken place on the agency and client side to reflect the new reality of how agency conflicts might be handled. First, clients such as Procter & Gamble and Colgate-Palmolive have agreed that they will normally define agency clients by product category rather than on a corporate basis. That is, although an agency should not have Crest and Colgate toothpaste, a single agency might handle the Bounty paper towel account for Procter & Gamble and the Colgate toothpaste account for Colgate-Palmolive. The logic is sound because the marketing strategy, brand managers, and even the target markets are much different for the two brands, even though they are owned by competing corporations. That concession by major clients has alleviated many potential conflicts.

On the agency side, advertising holding companies have been established to create so-called *fire walls* among the agencies they own. The term indicates that there will be no cross-sharing of sensitive client information among agencies owned by the same corporate entity. In theory, this allows McCann Erickson Worldwide to simultaneously service accounts from competitors such as Johnson & Johnson, L'Oréal, and Unilever. For the clients, it gives them access to the best agencies to handle their globally distributed brands. The system is not perfect and there are still instances when even the best fire walls don't overcome client apprehensions. However, the combination of a liberalized view of what constitutes a conflict for the client with the emergence of the holding company concept by agencies addresses a serious issue in both domestic and international advertising.

Research and the Multinational Consumer

Marketers experienced only in U.S. markets find that multinational research presents unique challenges. Multinational research, especially studies attempting to discern common purchase behavior involving a number of countries, deals with issues that domestic marketing research rarely faces. In fact, research for multinational accounts is one of the primary areas in which centralization works far better than the locally oriented approach found in many creative or media executions.

Without centralized planning, research will not be comparable from country to country, making global strategy decisions all but impossible. As global marketing becomes more complex, there will be increasing reliance on research data. As a major multinational agency CEO commented, "I see more and more businesses asking for a global view of their customers' assets. When you are dealing with Ford Motor Company and IBM Corporation, you cannot have a country or region doing data on their side the way they want . . . [it requires] one person sitting on top of it aligning all the processes and tools."[18]

Although the reliability of global research data has improved immensely in recent years, it is the interpretation of the research that creates the major problems for international marketers. Even developing a logo that is both understood and effective across a number of countries can present major obstacles. At the heart of the research process is finding a means to effectively translate key advertising and marketing information into global advertising executions. Although traditional language translation is important, translation must also include an understanding of the subtle nuances of culture and traditions within a country.

In this sense, **marketing translation** refers to the execution of the basic marketing plan to a number of countries. This translation involves not only language and numerous shades of meaning but also accounting for differences in media usage and availability, legal restrictions on various types of promotion, and basic advertising practices. It is the unusual advertising plan that can be introduced worldwide without numerous adaptations.

marketing translation
The process of adapting a general marketing plan to multinational environments.

A vital element in the translation process is the brand audit. Brand audits are designed to gain consumer perspectives about a specific brand. The brand audit attempts to define what a brand means to consumers worldwide and then develop market strategies that will enhance the brand's future sales potential. Often a brand audit demonstrates that the general perceptions that a company has of its brands don't match those of its customers in specific countries.

Regardless of the function—creative, media, or research—agencies face two major problems in developing organizations that will meet the demands of clients:

1. First, they must accommodate the organizational structure of their clients. An agency with several multinational accounts often finds that the specific needs for account management will differ from one client to the other. In effect, some agencies find that they need different management organizations for each client.

2. The second major problem faced by multinational agencies is how to manage centrally and communicate locally. The adage "think globally, act locally" is a dilemma for every agency. Agencies must translate broad client marketing strategies to the level of the individual customer in each country they serve.

THE MULTINATIONAL ADVERTISING PLAN

Success in the international advertising environment requires a broader range of experience and an awareness of subtle nuances that domestic advertising rarely encounters. Having said that, it is still a fact that the basic functions of advertising remain the same regardless of the arena. All advertising begins with sound planning and an adherence to basic marketing strategy. Although consumer preferences may be more difficult to determine in overseas marketing, differentiated brand benefits still must constitute the central theme of most advertising messages. And like their domestic counterparts, all forms of marketing communication should be coordinated and integrated into a campaign rather than presented as a series of unrelated advertising and sales promotion messages.

Although advertising basics may be consistent, international advertisers deal with special problems in execution and practices from country to country. The multinational marketer will find that the use and receptivity of advertising as well as its objectives and basic goals demonstrate extraordinary diversity. As firms introduce products on a worldwide basis, their problems range from something as familiar as product category competition to the much more difficult problem of convincing buyers to change established habits or overcoming previously held cultural prohibitions.

Regardless of the objective of a particular international campaign, advertisers must deal with a host of situations unique to each country. In this section, we will discuss three areas of primary concern to international agencies and their clients: (1) creative considerations; (2) media planning and buying procedures; and (3) legal restrictions and regulations that affect both creative messages and media strategy.

Creative and Cultural Considerations

At one time, the creative process in international advertising for the most part entailed nothing more than a word-for-word translation of advertisements previously run in the United States. At the same time, broadcast advertising, especially television, was a minor component in the advertising plans for most companies. If advertisers simply avoided embarrassing translation pitfalls, they thought they had accomplished their task.

Today, the creative function has changed dramatically. Multinational advertisers are dealing with consumers who are increasingly sophisticated about the purpose of advertising. In addition, in more and more countries economies are improving and providing consumer options and meaningful competition among brands. It is no longer sufficient for advertisers to simply introduce new products and depend on latent demand for sales and profits. Finally, as we have mentioned earlier, there is a growing sense of worldwide nationalism where advertising must communicate a message of interest in a vernacular acceptable to local consumers. Even at the strategic level of global branding major companies have looked "to in-country natives who had their finger on the pulse of that culture to help develop statements that have visceral meaning to that culture and were not just literal translations of words developed in another country."[19]

Most international companies have moved through three phases in the last 30 years:

1. *Moving into foreign markets.* The first phase involved the decision by companies to move into international markets. Although many large companies had a limited international presence prior to World War II in the last half of the twentieth century companies began to routinely market their products on a worldwide basis.

2. *Local emphasis in marketing strategy.* Beginning in the 1980s, companies developed more pragmatic, locally oriented marketing and advertising plans. Companies realized that a one-plan-fits-all strategy would not work and began to view markets on a more individualized basis. Unfortunately, these efforts at localization were often based on little solid information and were too often more stereotypical than factual.

3. *Research-supported localization and segmentation.* Currently, we are seeing the start of consumer-based marketing guided by many of the same conceptual foundations found in the United States and other developed advertising economies.

For example, ACNielsen has conducted research in mainland China to determine the extent of consumer segmentation based on buying habits and brand preferences. The study found that Chinese consumers could be divided into five distinct groups based on shopping attitudes and price expectations:

- Adventurers
- Worker Bees
- Value Hunters
- Herds
- Laggards

The research showed that Chinese consumers in many ways are similar to consumers in other countries. Adventurers are innovators who buy new technology and new gadgets. Worker Bees will pay a premium for a product, but only if they are convinced that it is a high-quality item. Herds are status conscious and can be influenced by advertising whereas Value Hunters will postpone a purchase while waiting for a bargain.[20]

Mars, Inc.'s marketing strategy for its Mars candy bar demonstrated that a localized advertising strategy is valuable even within a single region. Mars's agency, Grey Worldwide, developed a core theme for the brand as a fun and pleasurable experience. However, the execution of this theme varies from country to country and even from medium to medium within a single country.

The campaign creative is so locally oriented that even the tag lines are unique to each country:

"Pleasure you can't measure" (United Kingdom)
"Mars—das hat was" [Mars—that's it] (Germany)
"Mars—Que du bonheur" [Mars—What happiness] (France)

The execution of the local campaigns included unique slogans for each country. In the United Kingdom it is "Saturday 3 P.M.," which refers to the weekend soccer kick-off time, a term totally without meaning in other countries. In France "August" refers to the traditional French holiday period and in Germany "the last parking place" has special meaning for harried urban drivers. Again, Grey took a core concept, a pleasurable experience, and creatively adapted it to the unique consumers of each country.[21] The type of research conducted in China and the Mars creative campaign are typical of the type of multinational consumer research becoming more common in the last decade.

In order to take advantage of the efficiencies of global creative themes, it is important to try to develop campaigns that are exportable. International campaigns increasingly seek to highlight similar consumer motivations based on an overarching "big idea," while developing messages that highlight local cultures and tastes among consumers. For example, Grey Advertising and Procter & Gamble successfully introduced Pantene Pro-V Shampoo as a global brand by positioning the brand with the signature line: "Pantene. For hair so healthy, it

EXHIBIT 23.7 a

Pantene developed a consistent global theme for its advertising with local variables in some markets.

Courtesy of Grey Advertising and Procter & Gamble.

shines." This common creative theme was then used to introduce the brand into markets throughout the world (see Exhibits 23.7 a & b).

Creative executions begin with an in-depth awareness of a country's culture, customs, and buying habits. Sometimes this analysis is as simple as being aware of local holidays, how they are celebrated, and if commercial tie-ins are appropriate. From worldwide holidays, such as Rosh Hashana to country-specific celebrations, such as German Unity Day and Health and Sports Day in Japan, advertisers need to know the local customs surrounding these events.

Much of the change in multinational advertising is a direct result of a better understanding of local cultures through personal contacts among business executives. An international marketer observed that success in a foreign market is often a matter of patience and learning another country's customers, "[Our customers] read the nonverbal signals of how respectful you are of their culture. So much of it depends on how comfortable they are with the partner."[22]

As we have seen, advertising creativity is no longer an American monopoly. Not only are ideas and advertising strategy routinely originated outside the United

EXHIBIT **23.7 b**

(continued)

States, but, more recently, television commercial production is increasingly shifting overseas. Many of these foreign-produced commercials are made for U.S. distribution. Part of the reason for the exodus is a growing number of talented actors and producers abroad. But the driving force for the change is economic.

The exchange rate of the dollar compared to many other currencies means that an agency can enjoy significant savings by shooting abroad. For example, commercials shot in Canada or South Africa are 30–40 percent cheaper than the same commercial produced in America. In addition, American actors receive residuals every time a commercial runs in this country, whereas their foreign counterparts receive a one-time fee. Los Angeles continues to be the hub of commercial production, but commercial shooting days fell more than 15 percent from 1999 to 2001. The growing importance of overseas commercial production is yet another indicator that advertising is indeed an international business.

MEDIA PLANNING: A GLOBAL PERSPECTIVE

The problems associated with media planning have improved dramatically in the last decade. Although global media planning still presents major challenges, two factors have dramatically improved the process:

1. *The rapid expansion of efficient global communication.* Cable and satellite television channels, combined with global distribution of movies and the introduction of the Internet, have created practical opportunities for millions of worldwide exposures.

2. *The expansion of global retailers.* For example, Wal-Mart provides customers with similar merchandise and shopping experiences on a worldwide basis. Although we have not fully achieved the goal of Theodore Levitt's global marketing, as customers become accustomed to similar goods and merchandise, both media and creative strategy can become more streamlined and universal.

In 2003, when Mattel, Inc., introduced the Rapunzel Barbie doll, it used similar promotions and advertising throughout the world. More importantly, contrary to earlier introductions, the doll was the same in all markets. Research showed that girls were interested in the Barbie fantasy and didn't care that the doll didn't necessarily look like them.[23] Obviously, the global introduction of a single model of Barbie with consistent promotions and marketing plans significantly reduced the costs to Mattel.

The Barbie example cannot necessarily be extended to other products or even to other toys. For example, action figures, which make up a large percentage of U.S. toy sales, are not popular in Germany. Likewise, European children want Formula One race car models rather than the NASCAR models so popular in America. However, the Barbie example does show that the world is shrinking and, at least, in some categories creative marketers can save significant dollars by introducing products and promotions that tap into commonly held global values.

Despite the rapid changes in global media, planners for multinational accounts encounter a number of problems—some unique to each brand. However, most of the challenges of media planning can be summed up in the following categories:

1. *Media availability and or/usage levels.* Even with the introduction of satellite television, higher worldwide household set penetration, and the distribution of a number of television networks on a global basis, media planning is still a complex problem for multinational companies. However, services such as CNN International, Disney Channels operating in more than 60 countries, and ESPN operating a number of international outlets have made uniform communication much easier for global marketers.

   International services such as these can be combined with local and regional services to offer advertisers a choice of general channels for global brands and more specialized coverage for brands unique to a single country or region. In addition, the introduction of global television opportunities allows similar brand-building strategies as those used in campaigns originating in more developed countries. Although satellite television is a significant improvement in media planning, numerous print vehicles, particularly news and business journals such as *Time* and *The Wall Street Journal*, have well-established international editions to reach targeted, upscale consumers.

   The growing availability of international vehicles should not ignore the fact that media usage varies greatly on a country-by-country basis. For example, cinema advertising, regarded as a very minor medium in America, is a primary vehicle in Asia and parts of Europe. Out-of-home advertising is also extremely important in many countries.

2. *Legal prohibitions.* As in this country, products such as alcohol and tobacco as well as other product categories may be limited or excluded from all or certain media. In addition, international media planning must be closely coordinated with creative executions because there are a number of restrictions on the messages that can be used in various media from country to country. Up until 2002, France did not allow retailers to advertise on television, which made outdoor a major retail medium in the country. Recently, the EU regulators told France that the prohibition violated EU rules and it will probably permit retailers on television in the near future. This change may cause a major shift in the media usage patterns of large retailers. For example, French advertisers presently invest 11.7 percent of their budgets in outdoor, compared to 5.9 percent worldwide and 4 percent in the United States.[24]

Space does not allow us to discuss the many advertising restrictions that are imposed by various countries. However, there are two areas that are so prevalent in terms of regulations that we should mention them here. The first is comparative advertising. In the United States, advertisers routinely demonstrate specific brand differentiation by direct comparisons with major competitors, often by name. However, the practice of comparison advertising is strictly regulated or banned outright in numerous other countries where it is considered a form of unfair competition. In fact, the prevalence of prohibitions concerning comparative advertising makes it ill-advised as a technique in most international advertising campaigns.

A second significant area of regulation is advertising to children. Again, the United States is among the most permissive countries in the world in terms of regulation of children's advertising. Many countries ban any advertising to children and exclude all advertising in children's programming. In other cases, the hours permitted for advertising to children are very limited. Outside the United States, a campaign directed to children would be very difficult to execute and, certainly, it would have to be conducted on a country-by-country basis.

We should not leave the subject of regulation without mentioning one of the newer challenges for multinational advertisers—the Internet. As more and more businesses turn to the Internet as a means of product information, promotion, and customer research, it becomes difficult to stay within the rules of international commerce. Because the Internet does not allow a marketer to limit geographic coverage, many advertisers include a statement that all product claims meet U.S. (or whatever countries the promotion is intended for) legal and regulatory standards and are intended for persons residing in those countries. This does not provide a foolproof solution, but it does provide the company with some defense if challenges are made in foreign jurisdictions.

In addition to legal requirements imposed on advertising by various nations, a number of self-regulatory rules are recommended in different countries or regions. Virtually every country with an established advertising industry has some self-regulatory mechanism in place and multinational advertisers should be well versed in such policies. Outside the United States, the most extensive organization is the European Advertising Standards Alliance (EASA), which reviews advertising practices of companies operating within the EU. The EASA and similar organizations throughout the world attempt to build consumer confidence in the truthfulness and honesty of advertising. In the next chapter, we will discuss the self-regulatory mechanism in the United States.

3. *Research.* Like all advertising executives, media planners must take a multinational perspective as clients and media move across borders to add market share and audiences. During the last two decades, the international media buying function has changed dramatically. Searching for cost efficiencies and recognizing the unique problems of international media buying, multinational

clients have demanded special expertise from their agencies. In this environment, the demands for cross-cultural media research have become crucial.

As we mentioned earlier, media and product usage data are just now becoming available in many countries. For example, Arbitron has begun gathering radio audience data in Mexico, the company's first move outside the United States. It is a fact that advertising research dollars follow advertising investments. As multinational advertisers increase their advertising presence in more and more countries, we should expect to see more reliable research become available.

However, for now, media planners must be extremely wary of using much of the research available in overseas markets because it often lacks the reliability and validity that are taken for granted in the United States. Also many foreign media offer little or no guarantees of their circulation or ratings data. Many advertisers simply have to take a calculated risk in buying media to reach potential markets.

Media planners must also deal with the special problems of developing and executing a plan on an international basis. Media buying is so complex for large multinational advertisers that the media function is increasingly concentrated in huge multinational media planning companies or brokers that buy for a number of agencies. These media specialists, such as London-based Zenith Optimedia Group, can afford to hire highly trained personnel, conduct multinational audience research, and establish databases that would be beyond the financial reach of most individual advertising agencies. These media planners also can gain significant media discounts by buying for groups of clients instead of on the basis of single companies or brands.

ADVERTISING AND ETHNIC DIVERSITY IN THE UNITED STATES

To this point, our discussion has emphasized the marketing practices of a relatively few global companies such as Sony, Nestlé, and Procter & Gamble. However, in a growing number of communities, even the smallest retailers are facing challenges in reaching out to a diverse American population. The three major ethnic minorities in the United States are Hispanics, Asian Americans, and African Americans with Native Americans comprising slightly less than 1 percent of the population.

At both the national and local levels, marketers cannot ignore the growing importance of this diverse population. For example, the Hispanic and African American share of the total U.S. population is about 13.4 and 12.7 percent, respectively. The Hispanic population passed the African American segment in 2001 and it will continue to outpace the population growth of all other segments in coming decades. Four percent of the U.S. population is Asian American, a group that increased by 30 percent during the decade of the 1990s. Moreover, it is estimated that by 2050 slightly more than 50 percent of the U.S. population will be comprised of this multinational population with Hispanics making up as much as one-third of the total.

Traditionally, the ethnic population has been concentrated in certain regions and urban centers of the United States. For example, Asian Americans comprise 12 percent of California's population. However, during the last decade this situation has changed dramatically with significant growth in the ethnic population taking place throughout the country. The assimilation of multicultural consumers into mainstream markets combined with their significant increase in buying power is one of the major developments in marketing in recent years.

Marketers in virtually every product category are taking note of the growing importance of these consumers. Not only is the multicultural market expanding, but its buying power is also increasing at a greater rate than the general population. For example, during the last decade, every major ethnic market demonstrated larger per-

	1990	2000	2002	2007	% Growth vs. 1990
White non-Hispanic	$3,739	$5,800	$6,252	$7,910	112
Hispanic	233	491	581	926	297
African American	317	559	646	853	169
Asian	118	255	296	455	286
American Indian	19	36	41	57	200
Other	85	198	234	379	346
Total	**4,511**	**7,339**	**8,050**	**10,580**	**135**

EXHIBIT 23.8

U.S. Buying Power on the Rise

Source: Copyright Crain Communications. Reprinted with permission. Laurel Wentz, "Cultural crossover," *Advertising Age,* 7 July 2003, S–2.

centage increases in buying power than whites. It is estimated that by 2007 these markets will constitute more than $1.7 billion in total sales with Hispanics soon passing the African American market in terms of total purchases (see Exhibit 23.8).[25] Their importance to advertisers is especially significant because many of these population segments are extremely loyal to companies and brands that reach out to them with products and advertising messages designed to meet their needs. For example, a survey of Hispanic female shoppers indicated that Colgate toothpaste was the favored brand by 78 percent and Tide was the preferred brand by 57 percent of respondents. Researchers concluded that these high preference levels were a result of both Tide and Colgate being global brands with extensive distribution in Latin American countries as well as the fact that both brands target U.S. Hispanic consumers.[26]

The diversity of the marketplace has not been lost on marketers, advertisers, or media. As population and wealth of the ethnic market have grown in recent years, many progressive companies have met the challenge of serving these communities. Companies as dissimilar as Bank of America and Burger King provide an array of services to their Latino customers, such as Spanish-language voice mail, fluent employees, and menus.

Diversity and U.S. Advertising

U.S. diversity has had major effects on advertising. Not only are companies reaching out to ethnic buyers as never before, but also they are increasingly depending on minority-owned advertising agencies to execute advertising campaigns directed to these markets. Most major advertising agencies either own minority-oriented subsidiaries such as Young & Rubicam's Hispanic shop, The Bravo Group, or have a partnership with such an agency. The income of virtually all of the major Hispanic agencies is growing at a far higher rate than mainstream agencies.

Each of the major ethnic groups presents special problems and opportunities for marketing and advertising. As we will discuss later in this chapter, there are many subcultures within each group. For example, an Asian American prospect of Japanese heritage may have much different product preferences than a person coming from Korea or Vietnam. In the following section, we will discuss some of the primary elements in marketing to various groups.

Media Media are an excellent barometer of the growth of the ethnic market in this country. The number of foreign-language and ethnic-oriented media outlets demonstrates both the size of these populations and also their potential for marketers. Ethnic newspapers are the largest medium in terms of numbers of vehicles (although they are far surpassed by the audiences of ethnic-oriented television). These publications provide a huge range of circulation, editorial quality, and advertising sophistication. Ethnic newspapers provide niches for reaching every imaginable target segment.

One can find newspapers aimed at Russian, Chinese, Korean, Filipino, Armenian, and African American readers, to name only a few. They include publications that are issued on a sporadic basis with circulations of a few hundred to major dailies with more than 100,000 readers. Most of the ethnic-targeted publications have demonstrated significant circulation and advertising increases during the last decade. The one exception is the African American press. With few exceptions, newspapers directed to the black community have shown severe drops in circulation compared to their peak during the 1940s.

The decline of the black press can be attributed to two primary causes:

1. The civil rights movement of the 1960s and 1970s pushed mainstream media, led by local newspapers, to begin more balanced coverage of the African American community. As major newspapers began to gain black readers, circulation and advertising revenue shifted from the African American press to traditional publications.

2. Another factor in the decline of the black press was the fact that it was much easier for major newspapers to assimilate black readers compared to other ethnic populations. There is no language barrier in reaching the African American community so advertisers don't have to make decisions concerning English versus indigenous languages. Also, although there are differences of media and product preferences among African Americans, just as among the white majority, they represent a much more homogeneous market than either Asian or Hispanic American consumers.

In the past, most ethnic newspapers were owned by small, independent publishers. However, major newspaper chains are aggressively marketing ethnic publications especially to the Hispanic market. Led by *La Opinion* in Los Angeles with a daily circulation of 125,000 and New York City's *Hoy* with more than 90,000 readers, both owned in part by the Tribune Company, national media companies are competing for the Hispanic market. For example, Knight-Ridder's *El Nuevo Herald* in Miami and *Diario La Estrella* in Dallas, and Belo Corporation's *Al Dia* in Fort Worth are just a few of the major Spanish-language papers in which mainstream corporations have an interest.[27]

Although print media, including magazines such as *People en Espanol* and *Essence,* have had some success in reaching the ethnic market, it is television that has attracted the majority of ethnic advertising dollars in the last decade. Reaching the ethnic market is not a new strategy. For almost three decades, syndicated television shows such as *Soul Train* have targeted African American audiences. Until the 1990s, ethnic programming was largely confined to syndicated shows and a few locally produced programs in major markets.

However, the coming of cable brought opportunities to reach segmented audiences that had never been possible through broadcast television. Just as satellites made it possible for history buffs, golfers, and chefs to have channels directed to their interests, the same technology made ethnic programming practical. Channels such as Black Entertainment Network (BET) furnished entertainment and information for the black audience that were not provided by mainstream networks.

The same model is now working for the Hispanic market. Most people would be surprised to learn that the Spanish-language channel, Univision, is the fifth largest network after CBS, NBC, ABC, and Fox. It has a potential reach of 97 percent of the U.S. Hispanic population and averages a 75 percent audience share among that population.[28] With NBC's recent purchase of the second leading Spanish-language network, Telemundo, the introduction of Azteca America, a U.S. version of Mexico's second leading network, and Black Entertainment Network (BET) coming under the ownership of Viacom's CBS, we will see even more quality programming for the African American and Hispanic markets.

Ethnic media face a problem very much like their larger counterparts—how to reach teens and younger adults. Radio has long been a primary medium of reaching younger African Americans. In recent years, radio has become a primary vehicle to target the teen and young adult Hispanic market. During the 1990s, Hispanic-oriented radio stations grew by 82 percent compared to an increase of only 10 percent in total commercial stations during the same period. Overall, Hispanic radio stations comprise almost 6 percent of all stations and account for 7.6 percent of total listeners.[29]

The traditional problems of reaching a multicultural audience are made even more complex by the introduction of the language variable. Most research indicates that younger Hispanics and Asian Americans are much more comfortable and accepting of bilingual communication than older Hispanics and Asian Americans. In addition, they watch traditional English-language programs such as *Friends* and *Monday Night Football* with greater frequency than their parents. Regardless of whether advertisers are using English-or foreign-language media, marketers must be sensitive to the messages and cultural connotations they communicate.

Recent examples demonstrate that advertisers are trying a number of approaches to address the problems inherent in reaching these audiences. For example, Spanish-language channel, Galavision, broke a long-established Spanish-only policy by broadcasting teen-oriented programs in English. At the same time, CBS and Nickelodeon changed their policies and accepted limited Spanish commercials.[30]

The Message As we have seen, advertisers are now able to communicate with ethnic buyers through a number of media outlets. However, reaching the U.S. ethnic markets presents challenges similar to the ones multinational advertisers have found overseas. Advertisers must develop messages that are both sensitive to local cultures and, at the same time, provide an effective sales point. Attempts by mainstream advertisers to do this have resulted in a huge growth in advertising agencies concentrated on various ethnic markets.

At a time when general-market advertising agency income was declining, agencies directed toward the Hispanic market were growing by more than 17 percent (see Exhibit 23.9).[31] The majority of this growth comes from major advertisers and agencies turning to Hispanic agencies for their expertise in reaching this market. Major advertisers such as Procter & Gamble, Ford, AT&T, Miller Brewing, and General Motors all have demonstrated significant increases in their advertising investments to the Hispanic market in recent years.

Dollars invested in ethnic advertising still lag behind the sales potential in these markets. However, marketers are beginning not only to invest more advertising in

EXHIBIT 23.9

Top 10 Hispanic Ad Agencies

Source: Copyright Crain Communications. Reprinted with permission. *Advertising Age*, 16 September 2002, S–15.

Rank				Gross Income		Billings
2001	2000	Agency	AD Organization(Network)	2001	%CHG	2001
1	1	Bravo Group	WPP Group (Young & Rubicam)	$26.1	12.0%	$246.3
2	3	GlobalHue*	Interpublic Group of Cos.	19.8	22.2	132.0
3	4	Dieste Harmel & Partners	Omnicom Group (BBDO)	17.2	24.5	145.1
4	2	Bromley Communications	Bcom3 Group (D'Arcy)	16.5	-5.7	161.0
5	6	Mendoza Dillon & Asociados	WPP	13.0	9.5	94.6
5	9	Zubl Advertising	Independent	13.0	20.9	106.0
7	7	La Agencia de Orci & Asociados**	Independent	12.3	9.8	82.0
8	8	Wing Latino	Grey Global Group (Grey Worldwide)	12.0	9.1	80.0
8	16	Publicis Sanchez & Levitan	Publicis Groupe (Publicis Worldwide)	12.0	199.8	84.7
10	10	Lapiz	Bcom3 (Leo Burnett Worldwide)	10.4	15.6	130.00

Notes: Dollars in millions. Ad organizations may own less than 100% of an agency. *GlobalHue is a merger of Don Coleman Advertising and Montemayor & Associates. The agency claims total U.S. gross income of $49.5 million, 40% from marketing to Hispanics and 60% from marketing to African-Americans.

**Figures are *Advertising Age* estimates. Source: *Ad Age* survey based on data supplied by agency

these markets but also to become more sensitive to a multicultural approach in their advertising messages. For example, Bank of America, rather than taking a single multicultural approach, developed different messages for the Hispanic, Asian, and African American markets. A bank executive, in announcing a quadruple increase in multicultural advertising, noted, "The company made a very strategic decision looking at [our] top three regions—Texas, Florida, and California. Instead of being part of the business in these regions, multicultural really is the business."[32]

The combination of higher ethnic advertising investments and an awareness by mainstream marketers of the importance of designing messages relevant to these markets will increase the importance of ethnic agencies in the future. For example, McDonald's, Burger King, and Wendy's spend a combined $60 million annually on Hispanic-oriented media, and each account is handled by a major Hispanic advertising agency.[33] In addition, companies in numerous product categories are incorporating ethnic events and holidays in their promotions. Cinco de Mayo, which promotes a Mexican victory over the French in 1862, is widely celebrated as is the Chinese New Year in major Chinese American population centers.

In coming years, multicultural advertising will become even more prevalent. The minority population of the United States will grow steadily during the next 50 years. By the end of this decade, the non-Hispanic white population will be less than 70 percent of the total U.S. population and by 2050, it will be less than half. Putting aside the fact that multicultural inclusiveness is the right thing to do, American businesses are finding that ethnic advertising and marketing are a necessity in the twenty-first century.

The Product It is clear that both media and advertising messages are being dramatically changed by increases in the U.S. multicultural population. However, communication can only go so far in building bridges with buyers. The most significant change in multicultural marketing, and the one of most importance, is the development of products and brands specifically for these segments. The marketing landscape shows numerous examples of how companies are adapting their product offerings to the ethnic markets.

Tropicana Products has changed all of its Dole brand packaging to include bilingual Spanish/English labels. It is now quite common for instructions that accompany household appliances to offer both Spanish and English versions.

The most meaningful recognition of multicultural markets is the offering of product categories that meet their needs. In the last decade, the food market in particular has seen tremendous growth in both domestic and imported brands directed at ethnic tastes. Most major grocery chains have aisles set aside for products aimed at various ethnic groups and major food makers routinely introduce new brands that cater to these markets.

Not only are ethnic food brands growing because of increases in the ethnic population, but they are entering the traditional American diet as well. Salsa sales have been higher than ketchup for a number of years and Mexican and Chinese restaurants have long been part of the mainstream. Imported beer accounts for 10 percent of total U.S. volume with brands such as Corona growing faster than most domestic beers.[34]

Testimony to the importance of the ethnic market is seen in the number of products and brands distributed by major manufacturers. Frito-Lay has been one of the most aggressive companies in developing products for the Hispanic market. Consumer research showed that Hispanics generally thought that American snacks were not spicy enough. Based on this information, Frito-Lay developed a line of products including items such as Cheetos Flaming Hot, Doritos Salsa Verde, and a lime-flavored potato chip called Lays Limon. Other marketers such as Pepsi have followed the trend with brands such as mango-flavored Xtremo sports drink."[35]

It is obvious that success in the ethnic market is based on relevant communication, delivered through credible media, and backed up with products that meet the needs of specific market segments. In other words, profits in the ethnic marketplace are based on the same formula found in any other sector. Success is also based on planning using insightful research. In the next section, we will discuss how marketers are trying to put the research part of the multicultural puzzle together.

Research For many years, marketers either ignored the ethnic market or based decisions on invalid research or stereotypes. The lack of reliable research was based on a number of factors including:

- often researchers had little or no experience in ethnic marketing
- respondents often were uncooperative with researchers because of language barriers and a lack of full explanation of the research process
- a lack of ethnic-oriented syndicated research
- weighting of research samples often did not fully take into acount the ethnic population especially in some major markets.

Regardless of the reasons, the result was a scarcity of information concerning the multicultural market. Today, that situation is changing, although information on the Asian market is not as available as data from the Hispanic and African American segments. Arbitron and Nielsen Media Research have been among the leaders in improving the quality and quantity of information concerning the ethnic marketplace. In large measure, this attention to the ethnic market has been fueled by its growth as demonstrated in the 2000 Census[36]. The combination of overall population increases and higher levels of buying power makes the ethnic market one that is hard to ignore.

Improved research in the ethnic markets also has resulted in a more realistic view of the significant differences exhibited within these groups. For example, the Asian American market is comprised of a number of subsets, each with its own cultural differences, language, and marketing preferences. The major categories of the Asian community are

Chinese Americans
Filipino Americans
Japanese Americans
Korean Americans
Vietnamese Americans

To assume that these diverse groups compose a single entity would be a major mistake and lead to major marketing blunders. The same situation would be true within the Hispanic market in which people of Spanish origin have roots in Latin America, Mexico, the Caribbean, and so on, each with their own distinct cultures. Multicultural research is beginning to examine the nuances of ethnic consumers in much the same way it has addressed regional and demographic categories among other consumers.

For the past 30 years, social scientists have been attempting to determine the degree to which immigrants have been assimilated into American society. An equally worthwhile question might be how American society is changing as a result of this multicultural environment. Multicultural research is underscoring the fact that investing dollars alone is not enough to successfully market to the ethnic population. These consumers have traditional purchase habits and customs that must be reflected in any advertising and promotion. However, research shows that when a brand gains acceptance in the minority community, there is a significant level of brand and company loyalty that makes the effort extremely profitable.

SUMMARY

Global and multinational advertising has moved from special niches to an integral part of the promotion plans of the majority of companies. In this country, even the smallest retailer engages in some form of international marketing—either in the goods it sells or those it buys. As more and more countries improve both their economic situation and their openness to trade with other nations, we will see even more business conducted on an international basis.

The driving force behind multinational marketing is the search for new markets by the mature economies of the United States, Japan, and Europe. In many respects, the search for overseas markets has been the motivation of foreign trade since the days of the early Dutch, English, and Spanish traders in the fifteenth and sixteenth centuries as well as the ancient of prehistoric times. When countries can no longer sustain economic growth within their own borders, they look to cross-border commerce for trading partners. Although the scope of contemporary international marketing is being conducted on an unprecedented scale, the basic foundations have remained the same for more than a thousand years.

Many of the recent innovations in international advertising have been driven by the introduction of new forms of technology. In the 1970s, major U.S. publications began worldwide distribution of foreign-language editions. Print was followed by satellite transmissions of television signals and, more recently, the emergence of the Internet. Each has contributed to a faster pace of advertising and marketing on a worldwide basis.

The potential rewards of marketing in emerging countries can be substantially greater than the same effort invested in domestic marketing. However, multinational companies have learned that overseas marketing and advertising are very different than traditional American advertising. Although the basic functions may be the same, the complexities of dealing in a global economy are testing the planning, research, and managerial abilities of both companies and their advertising agencies. The internal difficulties experienced by the European Union, a developed region with one of the highest standards of living in the world, reinforce the problems companies face as they introduce their products in emerging nations.

One thing is certain, advertising will play a major role as companies move into more and more overseas markets. The most successful brands usually will be those that establish the first beachhead in emerging markets by taking the pioneering risks. The common criteria for U.S. advertising—CPMs, cost-per-point, audited circulation and verified ratings, and even short-term return-on-investment—are simply not applicable in many foreign markets. Instead, experience, judgment, and calculated risk taking must be used to deal with the intricacies of international marketing.

Moreover, even those U.S. businesses that do not participate in multinational advertising will be faced with the challenges of ethnic diversity in this country. The growth in size and buying power of the African American, Hispanic, and Asian markets within American society will increasingly require the creative use of media, promotion, and sales messages to reach this eclectic marketplace. Not just business expertise but also a sensitivity to the culture, language, and values of other people will be a requirement in this new environment. However, for those willing to devote the time to learn how to operate in this diverse market, the rewards will be great. Clearly, multicultural advertising will continue to undergo a period of dramatic change throughout this decade.

 **REVIEW**

1. What are the primary reasons for companies entering the international market?

2. Discuss three primary developments in international marketing during the last 25 years.

3. What are the major advantages and disadvantages to a strict adherence to the concept of global marketing?

4. Multinational advertising agencies must be client driven. What are the challenges facing these agencies as they seek to serve their clients?

5. Discuss the importance of cultural considerations in executing international advertising.

6. What are the primary advantages of joint venturing as a method of agency expansion into international markets?

7. Discuss the role of product development to meet the demands of both international marketing and the U.S. ethnic population.

8. Discuss three ways that population diversity has changed U.S. advertising.

9. How has advertising research changed to accommodate a more diverse audience both domestically and abroad?

TAKE IT TO THE WEB

Grey Worldwide (**www.grey.net/flash.htm**) is an example of a global agency with advertising accounts throughout the world. How does the agency use its resources to create advertising and marketing programs for its worldwide clients?

Coca Cola (**www.coca-cola.com/flashIndex1.html**) represents an American company with customers throughout the world. How does the branding and marketing of its products meet the diverse requirements of this huge customer base?

Accentmarketing, Inc. (**www.accentmarketing.com/**) is one of a number of agencies established to provide advertising and marketing expertise directed to an ethnic market. How does their approach differ from other agencies which deal with traditional target markets?

CHAPTER 24

AFTER SOME DRINKING GAMES, WE LEFT THE PARTY TO HIT SOME BARS, WE STARTED BUYING

Economic, Social, and Legal Effects of Advertising

A dvertising is the most prominent element of the marketing process. Consequently, it receives more than its share of scrutiny from a number of government, legislative, and public policy organizations. However, it is the public's trust in its honesty and fairness that ultimately determines advertising's effectiveness as a sales tool. Because it is so pervasive, advertising has a special responsibility to adhere to high ethical and honest business standards as it serves to create economic expansion.

The basic goals of advertising have changed little over the last 150 years. Most advertising is intended to introduce consumers to products and brands and, once this is accomplished, to create brand loyalty and repeat purchases by establishing a unique position in the minds of consumers. Advertising is also used to advocate some social position, to sway public opinion concerning controversial issues, or to underscore a firm's corporate citizenship. This chapter will examine the diverse methods that advertisers employ as both economic and social communication tools.

After reading this chapter, you will understand:

1. **the societal and economic dimensions of advertising**
2. **advertising's legal, regulatory, and public policy environment**
3. **advertising and the First Amendment**
4. **corporate citizenship and advertising self-regulation**
5. **the Advertising Council's role as a social institution**

ADVERTISING CRITICISM: A HISTORICAL PERSPECTIVE

Advertising criticism is not a new phenomenon, but the public view of advertising and its expectations have changed markedly over the last 130 years. Before discussing some contemporary areas of advertising evaluation, let's begin by tracing the history of advertising criticism:

1. *The Era of Exaggerated Claims, l865–1900.* During this period most people accepted advertising as "buyer beware" communication in which virtually any claim for a product was allowed. Some advertising

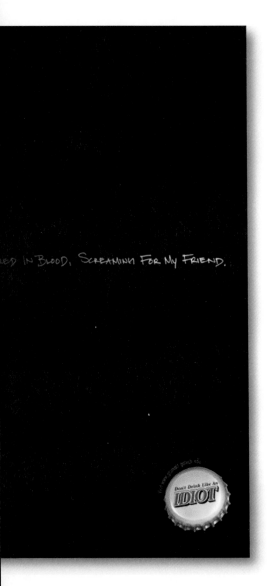

claims during this period, especially for patent medicine, were so outlandish that one wonders how anyone could have possibly believed them.

2. *The Era of Public Awareness, 1900–1965.* It was during this period that both the public and government regulators began to reject the notion of a laissez-faire, unregulated economic system. By the turn of the century, legislation such as the Pure Food and Drug Act of 1906 demonstrated Congress's recognition that the public was demanding protection from monopolies as well as the prevailing untruthful portrayal of products and services. Many responsible advertisers feared for the very existence of the industry as deceptive advertisements became more and more prevalent during the closing years of the nineteenth century.

3. *The Era of Social Responsibility, 1965–present.* During the last 40 years, advertisers have come to realize that truth alone is not sufficient to meet the demands of ethical advertising. Companies acknowledge that they must meet a higher standard of social responsibility than simply providing literally truthful advertising. Critics of advertising and, for that matter, advertisers themselves deal with a delicate philosophical balancing act. Without totally rejecting the classical economic concept of the rational buyer, both critics and enlightened marketers agree that some level of consumer protection is needed. It is this latter point of view, among others, that spawned the consumer movement of the 1960s, oversight of environmental safety, and a heightened awareness of various claims featured in modern advertising.

ADVERTISING AS AN ECONOMIC AND SOCIAL INSTITUTION

It is important to understand that the social and economic components of advertising are not mutually exclusive. Marketing executives are part of society and benefit from environmental awareness, better education, and other societal issues that are brought to the public's attention through advertising. By the same token, to the extent that advertising contributes to a stronger economy, advertisers and the public gain a higher standard of living.

The Economic Role of Advertising

In recent years, a great deal of attention has been given to advertising's relationship to the brands it promotes. Currently American advertising accounts for approximately 2.5 percent of the gross national product (GNP).[1] Although this figure is less than the comparable investment 50 years ago, it still represents a tremendous expenditure of resources. It is not surprising that those responsible for advertising are increasingly being asked to measure and justify the advertising effort.

In 1999, the American Association of Advertising Agencies (4As) announced its **Value of Advertising** initiative, which was intended to educate marketers about the role of advertising in building and protecting the brand franchise. The stated purpose of the initiative was to show "that diminishing the quantity and/or quality of advertising diminishes the value of the brand, and that the creative employment of media advertising is the only long-term means of achieving and retaining market dominance."[2]

The 4As' view of advertising is only one of a number of perspectives held by economists, social critics, advertisers, and regulators about the proper role of advertising. As expected, we find a wide variance among these groups as to the usefulness and proper role of advertising. However, these divergent perspectives tend to stem from one of two fundamental views of advertising and the economic benefits or liabilities that each fosters:

Value of Advertising
An initiative which was intended to educate marketers about the role of advertising in building and protecting the brand franchise.

■ *Advertising as a consumer information tool.* One view of advertising is that it is the most efficient and economical means of providing consumers with beneficial information about the availability of products and services.

■ *Advertising as a detriment to market entry.* A second, contrary position is that most advertising results in brand switching among major companies and prevents the introduction of new brands, especially by smaller firms.

Within these extreme positions are many specific pros and cons about the economic value of advertising. Let's review some of the major arguments for and against the economic role of advertising:

The Economic Arguments in Favor of Advertising

1. Advertising provides consumers with information to make informed decisions about new products, availability of products, price, and product benefits. "Brands and advertising are things people can see, touch and feel, and they know if a company's ads and brands are reliable and can be counted on. As is often said, the fastest way to kill a bad product is to advertise it—because consumers will try it and find out firsthand how bad it really is."[3]

2. Advertising supports free media that disseminate news and entertainment. In addition to the social benefits of an independent press, advertising provides employment for the thousands of editorial, production, and administrative workers in these media.

3. By promoting product differentiation, advertising encourages continuing product improvements and the introduction of new and innovative goods and services. Competing brands are forced to enhance the benefits of their products to maintain market share.

4. Mass advertising permits companies to achieve economies of scale in production that more than offset the per unit cost of advertising and, combined with competition among opposing brands, results in lower prices.

5. Advertising contributes to increases in the overall economy by increasing generic as well as brand consumption. For example, faced with a steady decline in consumption of cold cereals, a consortium of the big four cereal makers (i.e., Kellogg, General Mills, Post, and Quaker Foods) devised "The better breakfast" generic campaign to promote the nutrition and convenience of cereals.[4]

The Economic Arguments Against Advertising

1. The intent of advertising is to persuade, not inform. Critics dismiss the notion that advertising distributes information on which consumers can base informed decisions. They contend that advertising communicates extravagant product claims and, at best, is guilty of sins of omissions by providing only positive information about a brand.

2. On a macroeconomic basis, advertising spending is largely wasted because it primarily causes consumers to switch from one brand to another without any net economic gain to society.

3. Many economists challenge the notion that advertising lowers the price of products and services. To the contrary, they charge that one of the primary goals of advertising is to insulate a brand from price competition by emphasizing emotional appeals so that price comparisons become less important in purchase decisions.

4. The high rate of advertising expenditures in many product categories makes it difficult, if not impossible, for new products to enter the market. For examples in product categories such as cigarettes, beer, and laundry products in which two or three firms dominate each category, product introductions by other companies are extremely rare.

What conclusions can we draw after reviewing the pros and cons of these arguments concerning the economic role of advertising? The fact is that there is evidence to support each of these claims and counterclaims for advertising. One can find cases in which advertising was the catalyst for the introduction of a new and profitable brand or product category. On the other hand, there are numerous examples of product categories in which the objective of advertising is to maintain market share and encourage consumers to substitute one brand for another.

Even in product categories that seem to demonstrate evidence for one side or the other, there is often a middle ground. For instance, there is no question that market share in a number of food and household product segments is dominated by a handful of companies. However, although a few national firms hold dominant market share among these national brands, the emergence of store brands in outlets such as Wal-Mart and Kroger offer consumers many low-price options in products as varied as disposable diapers, batteries, garbage bags, and soft drinks.

It is difficult to deal in generalities when evaluating the economic value of advertising. Advertising's contribution to product sales depends on a host of circumstances unique to each product. The utility of advertising in a market for a relatively new product category, such as satellite radio, is much different than for beer or cigarettes, which are characterized by flat sales and brand switching. However, if sophisticated, multinational companies are spending billions of dollars on advertising, it is obvious that advertising must be contributing to their profitability.

THE SOCIAL ROLE OF ADVERTISING

Although the economic value of advertising is often debated, there is general agreement, even among its harshest critics, that advertising serves some role in the economic area. However, in recent years, the most frequent criticism has been associated with advertising's role in portraying and, to some observers, shaping and defining cultural values. Observations concerning advertising generally acknowledge that advertising functions in two distinct ways as a social force:

1. *Advertising's inadvertent social role.* In addition to its role promoting goods and services, advertising also conveys largely unintended messages that, nevertheless, impart information about society in general or some segment of the public. Rarely is it a goal of advertising to shape public opinion, mores, or social standards. The intent of most advertising is to mirror society by channeling the predispositions of consumers into purchases of particular brands. However, by the sheer weight of exposure, advertising sets a social agenda of what is expected, what is fashionable, and what is tasteful for a significant number of people. These influences are particularly true for the young, the undereducated, and the impressionable. Even more important than the influence advertising may have on individuals, some people claim, is the manner in which advertising portrays various segments of society—for example, the elderly, minority groups, and the young—because it determines in some measure how these people will be treated by others.

   In recent years, a number of research studies have been devoted to these "secondary consequences" of advertising. Advertisers realize that people react in a positive or negative way to the environment in which a product is presented and advertisers must be sensitive to these unintended cues.

EXHIBIT 24.1

Partnership for a Drug-Free America has been one of the major users of advertising to support the fight against drugs in the United States as a tool of public policy.

Courtesy of Sawyer Riley Compton and a Partnership for a Drug-free America.

As the public becomes more sophisticated about the social role of advertising, its indirect communication will become an even greater consideration for advertisers in the future. Increasingly, educated consumers are demanding more realistic and fairer presentations of society. Advertisers are seeking to make a realistic connection between their advertising and their customers.

2. *Advertising's overt social role.* As we mentioned in Chapter 2, advertising is increasingly being engaged to sell ideas as well as products. When advertising champions the fight against child abuse or drugs (see Exhibit 24.1), promotes adult literacy, or encourages higher levels of voter turnout, it becomes a tool of social activism. Given the efficiencies of advertising in selling products, it is not surprising that more and more special interest groups have recognized the value and effectiveness of advertising.

Some Specific Social Criticisms of Advertising

In recent years, social criticism of advertising has taken precedent over its economic effects. The range of criticism includes advertising strategies, its execution, the audience targeted, and even those groups making use of it. Everyone and everything in advertising's social realm are fair game. Some representative examples of social criticisms of advertising include:

■ *Advertising hard liquor (as contrasted to beer and wine).* In 2002, Diageo, maker of Smirnoff vodka and a number of other brands of spirits, reached an agreement with NBC to carry liquor advertising. The acceptance of Diageo advertising by NBC would have lifted the longtime voluntary ban on such advertising and, without question, would have given liquor commercials access to other stations and networks. However, NBC eventually reversed its decision after a coalition of public interest groups such as Mothers Against Drunk Driving, members of Congress, beer-advertisers, and others put pressure on NBC to continue the ban.

■ *Antidrug advertising campaigns.* One would think that advertising that encourages teens to abstain from using illegal drugs would be a "safe" topic. However, when the White House Office of National Drug Control Policy sponsored a campaign tying teen drug use to indirect financial support of terrorism, the campaign was met with criticism from a number of sources. Drug decriminalization advocates opposed the campaign on philosophical grounds and members of the Partnership for a Drug-Free America thought the ads were unrealistic and ineffective.

■ *Support of minority media and advertising agencies.* In the last several years, major national companies that don't employ minority-owned ad agencies and fail to place advertising in minority-oriented media have been threatened with various actions. The Federal Communications Commission (FCC) has undertaken an examination of the effects of media consolidation on minority-owned media. The NAACP, Rev. Al Sharpton's National Action Network's Madison Avenue Initiative, and the National Association of Black-Owned Broadcasters are just a few of the groups that have turned up the heat on the national advertising community.[5]

■ *Advertising's role in obesity.* A number of lawsuits have been filed against fast-food chains charging that their promotions of high-calorie, fatty menu items have led to various health problems. The suits are particularly critical of the chains' longtime emphasis on promotions to children.

We could cite other examples of social criticism of advertising's role. However, it is obvious that advertisers are being held accountable for both the products and services they provide and the advertising and promotion that support them. Although there are unique features to each of the social criticisms we have analyzed, they tend to focus on four areas:

1. *Advertising content.* The majority of socially related advertising criticism concerns the content of specific ads and commercials. Critics point to a spectrum of alleged abuses including the use of sexual themes, exaggerated product claims, debasement of language, the creation of stereotypes, and manipulating children with unrealistic promises. The majority of these objections are directed at alleged exaggerated claims in advertising. Many critics charge that advertising is more likely to provide misinformation, negative content, and in some cases, outright falsehoods rather than useful consumer information. As we will discuss later in this chapter, there are few business enterprises that undergo more governmental and regulatory scrutiny than advertising. But apart from these formal constraints, advertisers know that it is counterproductive to mislead consumers. Although false or misleading advertising may influence a consumer to make an initial purchase, it is rare that an unsatisfied consumer will return.

Another content-related advertising criticism is the exclusion or portrayal of various segments of society. Advertisers have increasingly come to realize that a realistic depiction of members of society is both morally correct and, just as importantly, good business. Great strides have been made in the treatment of the elderly, women, and ethnic groups in advertising. Most observers agree that advertising has made significant improvement from the time when ads were dominated by white male, 18 to 34-year-olds. However, critics still contend that many groups including women, minorities, and older consumers are not portrayed accurately in proportion to their importance in the marketplace.

For example, women buy 40 percent of new vehicles, 51 percent of consumer electronics, and share in 83 percent of household financial decisions.

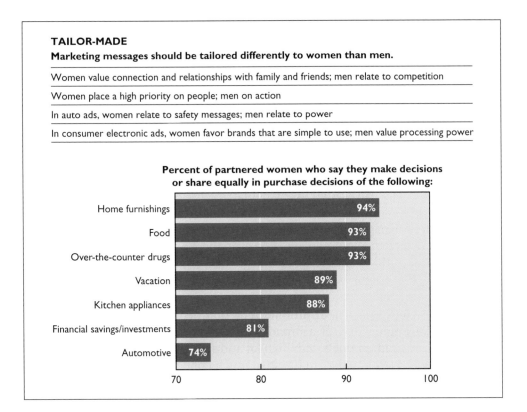

TAILOR-MADE
Marketing messages should be tailored differently to women than men.

Women value connection and relationships with family and friends; men relate to competition

Women place a high priority on people; men on action

In auto ads, women relate to safety messages; men relate to power

In consumer electronic ads, women favor brands that are simple to use; men value processing power

Percent of partnered women who say they make decisions or share equally in purchase decisions of the following:

Home furnishings	94%
Food	93%
Over-the-counter drugs	93%
Vacation	89%
Kitchen appliances	88%
Financial savings/investments	81%
Automotive	74%

EXHIBIT **24.2**

Advertising Age, 23, September 2002, 14.

However, their importance as consumers is not reflected in most advertising and marketing. As one executive pointed out, selling to women is different than connecting with them and marketing messages should be tailored to their needs (see Exhibit 24.2). "Instead of merely putting men's products in pretty pink boxes, marketers have begun to create differentiated products with obvious benefits aimed at women."[6] Recently marketed gender-specific products are:

- Quaker Nutrition for Women cereals with calcium supplement.
- Aquafina Essentials, a slightly sweetened, fruit-flavored water enhanced with vitamins and minerals.
- Crest Rejuvenating Effects, a toothpaste marketed to women.

As we discussed in the last chapter, similar efforts are being directed to ethnic markets, and older consumers are being approached with offers reflecting their higher levels of discretionary income, longer life spans, and diversified interests.

Astute advertisers regard cultural issues and ethics as constantly changing and they make every effort to implement steps to keep up with contemporary trends. However, sometimes the best intentions find advertisers caught between opposing factions on these issues. For example, as audiences have accepted gay characters on a number of television shows, some advertisers have tested the water by creating advertising targeted to the gay community.

Although many people see the trend as a progressive and realistic view of contemporary society, others view such advertising as unacceptable for general media. Despite the popularity of several gay characters in highly rated television shows, frequently advertisers have been slow to develop campaigns for the gay market, but, as we have seen, most companies lag behind the reality of society in their advertising messages. However, those companies that have advertised directly to gay consumers have generally been very successful, and they have encountered virtually no negative consequences.

Finally, there are many complaints about the manner in which advertisers direct their messages to children. For example, the "Joe Camel" campaign met with significant criticism from many quarters. Despite denials by the advertiser, critics contended that the cartoon figures had strong appeal to teens and children.

It is clear that advertisers must be extremely careful how they promote their products. Awareness of consumer sensitivity to a range of subjects is especially acute since the terrorist attacks of 9/11. The use of inappropriate humor, over commercialization of patriotic appeals, and the use of violent themes all must be avoided in the current environment. Clearly, consumers are in an unforgiving mood when it comes to what they regard as objectionable advertising.

2. *Advertising of certain product categories.* As we mentioned earlier, the most frequent criticism of advertising concerns the themes and appeals used in specific advertisements and commercials. However, there are some product categories that observers think should not be advertised regardless of how well the ads and commercials are executed. This category of criticism really involves two types of complaints:

   ■ Advertising a particular product type that people oppose is simply criticized as being part of a broader agenda. Tobacco, alcohol, and, more recently, food products with high fat and sugar content are included in this category. Here the debate is not so much concerned with advertising executions as it is with the appropriateness of the products themselves. For example, one study indicated that 74 percent of respondents thought that television liquor advertising would encourage teenagers to drink liquor.[7] Obviously, if an individual or group sees no value in a product category, the evaluation of the advertising for a particular brand is moot.

   ■ A second criticism related to product categories charges that advertising for particular products, although acceptable under certain circumstances, should be limited in some fashion. Some observers accept that tobacco may be legitimately advertised, but not on television or in media where a sizable portion of the audience is underage. There is also criticism about products such as condoms being advertised in mainstream media. Even in light of the current AIDS epidemic, most television outlets prohibit the advertising of condoms, a position that many in the public health community think is indefensible. Many advertisers argue that few, if any, limitations should be placed on the promotion of legitimate products, especially to adults.

3. *Excessive advertising.* Most of the criticism in this category is directed toward television because print ads are easily ignored by simply turning the page. Approximately 25 percent of television network time is devoted to commercials with far higher percentages on local stations and during late night and daytime periods. Both direct mail and telemarketing have for some time fought those who wish to impose legal restrictions on them. More recently, Internet spam (unwanted and unsolicited messages) has come under legislative scrutiny and may soon join telemarketing as an "invitation only" medium. In addition to the nuisance of unwanted and intrusive advertising, new technology, accompanied by sophisticated databases, has increased consumer concerns over privacy issues.

4. *Advertising's unwanted influences on society.* Criticism in this category covers a litany of alleged abuses. Charges that advertising *makes* people buy things they don't want or need, lowers morals, and generally exploits the most susceptible segments of society are among the most common indictments. However, most research shows that mass communication, especially overtly persuasive communication such as advertising, has a very difficult time making even small

changes in behavioral intentions or attitudes. The idea that consumers will take some action solely because of advertising is contrary to virtually every theory of communication.

ADVERTISING AND SOCIAL CAUSES— THE ADVERTISING COUNCIL

The most organized effort of social advocacy is the Advertising Council, which has for many years marshaled the advertising industry to support a number of causes. From its World War II beginnings as the War Advertising Council, the Advertising Council recently celebrated its sixtieth anniversary. During those six decades, the council has sponsored some of the most well-known public service campaigns and undertaken a number of projects, addressing issues such as racial tolerance, equal rights, job and fair housing opportunities, and education. The Ad Council continues to be a major means of disseminating social messages.

The council depends on volunteers from across the advertising spectrum. Most of the advertising is produced by major agencies on a pro bono basis and the media donate time and space to carry their advertisements and commercials. It is difficult to estimate the equivalent of paid advertising that the council has enjoyed since its founding, but it would certainly be in the billions of dollars.

The popularity of Ad Council initiatives is grounded in the simple fact that they work. Council campaigns not only have gained high recognition (Iron Eyes Cody ranked as the fiftieth top advertising icon in a survey by *Advertising Age*) but also, more importantly, they have contributed to significant changes in public attitudes and behavior.

Research findings underscore the success of Ad Council efforts:

- 80 percent of the general public were aware of "McGruff, the Crime Dog" campaign
- Awareness for colon cancer prevention resulted in a 43 percent increase in the number of people who consulted their doctors about the disease
- 70 percent of those who saw the "Friends Don't Let Friends Drive Drunk" campaign reported they had stopped someone from driving drunk
- Safety belt usage increased from 21 to 73 percent
- The United Negro College fund has raised more than $1.9 billion
- Some 6,000 children were paired with a mentor in the first 18 months of the Ad Council's mentoring campaign[8]

Despite the tremendous success of the Advertising Council over the last 60 years, the organization faces unique challenges as it enters the twenty-first century.[9] At one time, the council was the unchallenged focus for idea or public service advertising. However, based largely on its record of success, a number of other organizations have begun to use advertising as a primary tool to deliver social messages. In recent years, a number of organizations including the National Organization for Women (NOW), Mothers Against Drunk Drivers (MADD), and Planned Parenthood have all mounted campaigns that have competed with the Advertising council for creative services and donated time and space (seeExhibit 24.3). These private organizations have been joined by a number of companies placing paid advertising promoting some cause related to product marketing. We will discuss these marketing promotions in the next section, but they offer another type of alternative to Ad Council public service announcements.

A second challenge for the council is finding the type of galvanizing topics that were so prevalent in its early years. When the War Advertising Council was conceived, the war effort offered a number of campaigns that the public embraced without

EXHIBIT **24.3**

Colleges throughout the country are concerned about the epidemic of binge drinking among students. Georgia Tech sponsored an anti–binge drinking campaign that has been picked up by schools throughout the country.

Courtesy of Sawyer Riley Compton.

question. No one had to convince the public that it was a good idea to conserve tin and fat or not to discuss information about ship movements or factory output. Even after the war, campaigns directed at preventing forest fires and protecting the environment were overwhelmingly accepted by the majority of the public.

Today, the council must consider a much more fragmented public opinion and issues about which there is less than general agreement. The 1980s' council campaign advocating the use of condoms in the fight against AIDS marked a major departure for the council in taking on controversial topics.

Unlike the wartime efforts of the War Advertising Council and the early campaigns of the Ad Council, the environment, capitalism, the role of the family, and even the proper approach to the "war on terrorism" all are topics that engender significant controversy. When asking agencies to produce advertising and the media to carry it, the council often finds itself in the unenviable position of being asked to accept and promote causes for which there are more disagreement and controversy than the publicly held consensus, which was more the norm with earlier council efforts.

The Advertising Council continues to select, define, and address some of the nation's most pressing problems. Council programs will result in the donation of time and space in one year worth over $1.5 billion. In many respects, the council has created a new role for advertising in the promotion of ideas and opinions. Although some people have reservations about the role of advertising in promoting social institutions and issues, proponents argue that there is no more effective or inexpensive means of getting their messages to the public.

Advertising and Cause-Related Marketing

In 1983, American Express sponsored a campaign promising to make a donation to the renovation of the Statue of Liberty each time someone used an American Express credit card. This initiative is generally considered to be the introduction of *cause-related marketing* (also called *social marketing*). The days of companies supporting a number of charities with a check and a photo opportunity are nearly over. Today, large corporations are engaging in *strategic philanthropy* in which they market their good deeds in the same way they market their products. In 2004, cause-related marketed expenditures accounted for more than $1 billion.

Companies engaging in cause-related marketing strategically plan these campaigns around several concepts:

- Their charitable endeavors are likely to be those in which they can gain a unique association, for example, the Ronald McDonald Houses where parents and relatives of seriously ill children can stay near hospitals.

- The cause should be one that can be logically marketed with the core message of the product. Again, its previous association with children makes the Ronald McDonald House an excellent fit.

- The cause should be one that can be promoted and developed over a long period of time. Unfortunately, there will always be sick children and families in need of support, so the Ronald McDonald Houses serve an ongoing need. When a short-term, one-time cause is adopted, it should be one such as the Statue of Liberty renovation, which will be enthusiastically supported and probably gain public relations coverage in addition to the company's paid advertising. American Express's Statue of Liberty promotion gained a huge amount of free airtime on morning network news shows and other shows.

- Most importantly, the effort should be one that the public will view as important and link the purchase of particular brands to the charitable effort.

In the past, some companies have refrained from cause-related marketing efforts because they feared that consumers would view their efforts as exploitative. However, a number of research studies indicate that consumers welcome the opportunity to be part of a worthy cause with their purchases and they reward companies for their efforts. Exhibit 24.4 shows that many consumers have an expectation for companies to have a commitment to social causes. In addition, they indicate a willingness to reward those companies with their loyalty, even to the point of switching brands to show their support.

Cause marketing generally falls into one of the following tactical categories:[10]

1. *Transactional programs* in which a company contributes to a cause based on consumer purchase of a brand. Mars M&Ms gave 50 cents to the Special Olympics for every specially marked wrapper mailed to the company.

EXHIBIT 24.4

Research shows that a company that associates its marketing and advertising with a worthwhile cause can increase its image among consumers.

Courtesy of *American Demographics.*

Source: Cone/Roper ASW

Post–Sept. 11, almost 8 in 10 Americans (77 percent) say that a company's commitment to causes is an important consideration when making decisions about what to buy or where to shop, compared with just over half (52 percent) who said the same prior to Sept. 11.

	Percent Who Agree	
	Pre–Sept. 11 (March 2001)	Post–Sept. 11 (October 2001)
I believe that companies have a responsibility to support causes.	65%	79%
During an economic downturn and period of lighter consumer spending, it's important for companies to continue supporting causes.	71%	88%
I am likely to switch brands, when price and quality are equal, to support a cause.	54%	81%
A company's commitment to causes is important when I decide which businesses I want to see in my community.	58%	80%
A company's commitment to causes is important when I decide what to buy or where to shop.	52%	77%
A company's commitment to causes is important when I decide which stocks/mutual funds to invest in.	40%	63%
A company's commitment to causes is important when I decide where to work.	48%	76%
Companies should tell me how they are supporting causes.	73%	88%

2. *Message promotions* link a brand with information about some cause such as preventing skin cancer. Crest toothpaste supports dental hygiene programs through the Boys & Girls Clubs of America with its "Healthy Smiles 2010" campaign.

3. *Licensing programs* permit companies to use charities' logos in their advertising. For example, ConAgra Foods and America's Second Harvest partnered to focus on the "Feeding Children Better" campaign in many of the companies' promotions.

Advertising Influence on Editorial Decisions

For many years, a primary ethical principle of journalism was that media advertising and editorial departments would be separated by an impregnable wall so that editorial decisions were totally free of advertiser influence. A newspaper editor summed it up, "The philosophy is simple: You keep the news and the ads separate because otherwise readers can't trust you. Theoretically, readers look at a page and see clearly which parts of it are produced by . . . journalists and which parts are trying to sell you something."[11]

It would be naive to think that this wall was never breached but, nevertheless, that was the guiding principle. The first major change in the concept came in the early days of radio, and later in television, when sponsors produced and owned the shows carried by networks and local stations. Most of the audience considered this an acceptable arrangement because the shows were entertainment rather than news and information.

By the 1970s, it had become prohibitively expensive for single advertisers to bear the total cost of producing a show. This marked the end of "fully sponsored" shows. Programs such as *The Firestone Hour, The United States Steel Hour,* and *The Kraft Music Hall* were replaced by network-controlled programs in which advertisers participated by buying individual spots, but, in theory at least, had no control over program decisions. The move from single sponsorship to participating commercial buys was also motivated by quiz show scandals in which contestants had been given answers ahead of time. Congress and the public demanded that the networks take more control of content.

Today, the number of potential advertising outlets and the public's weariness with a constant bombardment of advertising have moved advertisers to experiment with a number of creative approaches to getting their brands before consumers in a context that complements their messages. Let's look at some of the ways in which relationships between advertisers and the media are changing:

1. *Attempts at direct control of editorial decisions.* There is no question that editors, publishers, and news directors are confronted by advertisers demanding that stories be changed or deleted from their news coverage. A survey by the Project for Excellence in Journalism reported that 20 percent of televisions news directors said that advertisers tried to prevent them from running unfavorable stories.[12] Nevertheless, major media don't cave into advertising pressure and major advertisers know that this heavy-handed approach will not work with respectable publications and broadcasters.

2. *Advertiser-financed productions.* When single sponsorship ended in prime-time network television, a few daytime soaps, such as *As the World Turns* and *The Guiding Light,* continued to have Procter & Gamble as their sole sponsor. In the last five years, we have seen limited attempts to return to more advertiser involvement in programming. One of the formal examples of such advertiser involvement is the Family Friendly Forum, a consortium of major advertisers, which underwrites the development of family-oriented shows. *The Gilmore Girls* on the WB network was one of the first shows supported by the Forum. Recently, Johnson & Johnson signed a contract with the TNT network for a

series of family-friendly movies. Under the terms of the contract, Johnson & Johnson will review and submit scripts for the movies that will air under the title *Johnson & Johnson Spotlight Presentations.*[13] Although few people question the motives of these companies to bring family entertainment to television, many critics see any involvement between advertising and programming as cause for concern.

3. *Product placement.* At one time, product placement was confined to the inclusion of a particular product in a television show or movie. Usually, the placements were no more intrusive than the occasional Coke machine in the background of a scene. However, with the growing antipathy toward advertising by viewers and the glut of commercials vying for prospects, product placement techniques have become more prominent and the relationship to programming more formal. For example, Revlon paid ABC a multimillion-dollar fee to have Revlon written into the story line for *All My Children.*

   Many companies see the introduction of advertising into program content as a means to overcome viewer fatigue with traditional advertising. However, according to a survey by *Advertising Age,* 62 percent of respondents found such product placements were distracting.[14] In addition, critics of the practice point out that any incursion by advertisers into the content of programming sets a dangerous precedent.

4. *The advertorial.* For many years, business firms and other organizations have used advertising to express their views about some issue or public policy concern, fights with labor unions, even potential legal problems faced by a company. These paid advertising messages promoting an opinion rather than a product are known as **advertorials,** that is, a combination of an advertisement and an editorial viewpoint. The expressions, when clearly identified as advertising, are an entirely acceptable means of expressing an opinion.

   advertorial
   The use of advertising to promote an idea rather than a product or service.

   However, since the early 1980s, the use of the advertorial has changed dramatically and its critics would say for the worst. Today, many advertorials are designed to look very much like editorial matter or television programming. Sometimes the advertorials are extended length sections of several pages liberally sprinkled with advertisements giving the section the look of the basic publication. Advertorial sections, rather than being written by the editorial staff, are produced by advertising copywriters or public relation specialists. The "editorial" matter is an extension of an advertising message and it is dictated by a sponsor.

   In the fall of 2002, Ace hardware sponsored spots on *Monday Night Football* that featured sportscaster John Madden with scenes similar to those used during the game telecast. The commercial had the potential of blurring the distinction between the commercial and the live broadcast of the game. The spot was characterized as a spoof by Madden's agent and, of course, it was approved by ABC's Standards and Practices Department. However, an executive at Commercial Alert, a public policy group, said that he was surprised that ABC would obscure the lines between programming and advertising in such a manner.[15]

   We will no doubt see more examples of product placement in the future. With the introduction of digital technology producers are able to place products in programs at any time. They can change brands for regional buyers and they can add a product to a program long after the original production of that show. For example, reruns of *Andy of Mayberry* might someday show the Taylor family sitting down to a meal with a box of Kellogg Corn Flakes or a bottle of Heinz 57 Sauce on the table.

5. *Withholding advertising.* Withholding advertising, or threatening to do so, is the oldest form of advertising interference in the editorial process. There is nothing

unusual about an advertiser choosing to refrain from advertising in a particular medium or program. Advertisers place their advertising in vehicles that not only reach a particular target market but also do so in an environment that is compatible with the consumer perceptions desired by the brand. However, a traditional media buying decision is much different than the situation in which an advertiser tries to coerce a medium into changing content that may be unfavorable to a company with a threat of withholding future ad dollars.

A much different circumstance of advertisers withholding advertising is when they refuse to buy spots in shows that they think may offend audience members or create controversy for their clients. When *The Shield* debuted on the FX cable network, a number of advertisers, including Burger King, Office Depot, and Pizza Hut, dropped their sponsorship due to concerns about the show's violence and language. However, when the show became an instant hit, a number of advertisers replaced those that had canceled their spots. Again, the advertisers' decision to opt out of the show was not unethical. However, it demonstrates the natural conservatism of many advertisers to avoid controversial content.

The relationship between advertisers and the media they support is often an uneasy truce. Critics point out that with 50–75 percent of the print media's revenues and virtually 100 percent of broadcast support coming from advertisers, it is unreasonable to expect that at least some publishers and station owners will not be influenced by those who pay the bills. The editorial and programming side wants total control over content with the ability to explore controversial and unpopular topics. Advertisers view the media as a means of reaching their target markets and, not unexpectedly, they often shy away from association with content they think will cause any negative connection to their brands. Fortunately, in the contemporary media mix with hundreds of outlets, there are ample options for virtually any company to have an opportunity to advertise its products and many outlets for even the most controversial programming.

ADVERTISING'S LEGAL AND REGULATORY ENVIRONMENT

To this point, we have dealt primarily with the philosophical and ethical dimensions of advertising. The value of advertising is rooted in the public's trust of its fairness and honesty. However, for the last 50 years, advertising has been controlled and monitored by a number of governmental, industry, and consumer advocacy groups. Today, advertising continues to operate in an environment of regulation and public scrutiny. Studies indicate that the majority of the public agrees that the government has a role in ensuring accurate product information because trustworthy advertising is an important ingredient in a free market economy. When untrue or misleading advertising is disseminated, the implied relationship between the consumer and the advertiser is violated, creating *market failure*.

Today, most advertisers agree that those companies that use illegal or unethical advertising tactics should be dealt with harshly. Not only is deceptive advertising wrong, but it also creates a lack of trust in all advertising, making it more difficult for honest businesses to effectively promote their products and services. There are three basic constraints on advertising used to prevent fraudulent practices:

1. Laws and regulations of legally constituted bodies such as Congress and the Federal Trade Commission.
2. Control by the media through advertising acceptability guidelines.
3. Self-regulation by advertisers and agencies using various trade practice recommendations and codes of conduct.

During the early days of exchange, businesses operated under the libertarian notion of **caveat emptor,** "let the buyer beware." This concept was based on the classical economic concept of a free marketplace of goods and ideas and assumed perfect knowledge on the part of the participants in that marketplace. That is, buyers and sellers were presumed to have equal information, and it was accepted that both groups, being rational, would make correct economic choices without government interference.

In this century, the complexities of the marketplace have led to the rejection of many of the principles of caveat emptor. Rather, we have substituted the principle that buyers have far less information than sellers and they must be protected by legal guarantees of the authenticity of advertising claims. To shield the public from false and misleading advertising, numerous laws have been passed. Chief among these is the Federal Trade Commission Act, which we discuss first.

caveat emptor
Latin for "Let the buyer beware," represents the notion that there should be no government interference in the marketplace.

THE FEDERAL TRADE COMMISSION (FTC)

As we briefly discussed in Chapter 1, the Federal Trade Act was passed in 1914 in reaction to public and congressional concerns over large firms driving out small competitors in a number of industries. Oil, railroads, steel, shipping, and several other core businesses were increasingly dominated by one or two companies. These corporations often introduced business practices that today would be considered restraint of trade but were often legal at the time.

The Federal Trade Commission Act, passed in 1914, declared that "unfair methods of competition are hereby declared unlawful." In its early years, the FTC regarded unfair methods of competition as those involving business-to-business transactions and did not have jurisdiction over consumer advertising and other consumer-related activities. A primary goal of the FTC during this period was to protect local retailers from unfair pricing practices by large national chains.

It was not until 1922, in *FTC* v. *Winsted Hosiery Company,* that the Supreme Court held that false advertising was an unfair trade practice. Then, in 1938, passage of the **Wheeler-Lea Amendments** broadened this mandate to include the principle that the FTC could protect consumers from deceptive advertising. Today, the FTC has sweeping power over advertising for virtually all products sold or advertised across state lines.

Wheeler-Lea Amendments
Broadended the scope of the FTC to include consumer advertising.

The Role of the FTC in Regulating Deceptive Advertising

Among the several objectives of the FTC is to create a free marketplace based on dissemination of complete, truthful, and nondeceptive advertising. In addition to advertising concerns, the FTC also investigates various sales practices and illegal pricing activities. One of the primary concerns of the FTC is to ensure that consumers are protected from deceptive advertising. At the heart of FTC enforcement is the notion that advertisers must be able to **substantiate** their claims. Failure to provide substantiation is the key finding when advertising claims are found to be deceptive. According to the FTC, the commission uses a three-part test to determine if an advertisement is deceptive or untruthful:

substantiation
The key to FTC enforcement is that advertisers must be able to prove the claims made in their advertising.

1. *There must be a representation, omission, or practice that is likely to mislead the consumer.* A statement does not have to be untrue to be deceptive. Sometimes advertisers will make a claim that is literally true but the total impression of the ad is misleading.
2. *The act or practice must be considered from the perspective of a consumer who is acting reasonably.* In other words, the advertiser is not responsible for every possible interpretation, no matter how unreasonable, that might be made by a consumer.

3. *The representation, omission, or practice must be material.* In other words, the claim, even if it is not true, must be judged to have had some influence over a consumer's decision. For example, the courts have ruled that using plastic ice cubes in a soft-drink commercial is not deceptive because no claims are being made about the ice cubes.

In most cases, when the FTC challenges an advertising claim, the company being investigated either provides substantiation or agrees to discontinue promoting the product benefit. For example, the FTC accused the maker of Wonder Bread of unsubstantiated claims that the bread not only built healthy bones but also helped children's memories because it contains extra calcium. The FTC challenged the claims, saying that they had no scientific support. The company, without admitting wrongdoing, agreed to stop the advertising.[16]

Methods of FTC Enforcement

The FTC has a number of means of addressing deceptive advertising. Unless there is evidence of fraud, the first step is for the FTC to work with advertisers to validate a claim or to have advertisers end deceptive practices. In the majority of cases, an advertiser and the FTC will reach a compromise concerning the advertising claims under review and the investigation will end. However, if an advertiser refuses to discontinue deceptive practices, there is further recourse for both parties. The following steps outline a typical model for FTC intervention in alleged deception:

1. *The first step in the process is a claim of deceptive practices to the FTC.* The complaint can come from the general public, special interest groups, competitors (by far the major source of complaints), or the FTC staff.
2. *The FTC begins its investigation with a request for substantiation from the advertiser.* At this point, many advertisers, rather than providing substantiation, voluntarily agree to delete the challenged claim from future advertising. However, if substantiation is provided, the FTC moves to the next step of evaluating the claims.
3. *If the Commission finds the practice to be unsubstantiated and, therefore, deceptive, a complaint is issued.* At this point, the advertiser is asked to sign a **consent decree** in which the firm agrees to end the deceptive practice or advertising. Most complaints are settled in this manner. An advertiser that continues the practice after signing a consent decree is liable for a fine of $10,000 per day.
4. *If an advertiser refuses to sign a consent decree, the Commission issues a* **cease and desist order**. Before such an order can become final, a hearing is held before an administrative law judge. The judge can dismiss the case and negate the cease and desist order. If it is upheld, the company may appeal the decision to the full commission.
5. *Even if an advertiser agrees to abide by a cease and desist order, the commission may find that simply stopping a particular practice does not repair past damage to consumers.* To counteract the residual effects of deceptive advertising, the FTC may require a firm to run **corrective advertisements** that are designed to "dissipate the effects of that deception."
6. *If a company cannot reach agreement with the commission, its next recourse is the federal courts* —first, to the Federal Court of Appeals and, finally, to the Supreme Court.

It is extremely rare that a case goes beyond the cease and desist stage. Companies know that they will incur significant legal costs even if they eventually prevail in the courts. More importantly, most companies don't want the continuing unfavorable

consent decree
Issued by the FTC. An advertiser signs the decree, stops the practice under investigation, but admits no guilt.

cease and desist orders
If an advertiser refuses to sign a consent decree, the FTC may issue a cease and desist order that can carry a $10,000-per-day fine.

corrective advertising
To counteract the past residual effect of previous deceptive advertising, the FTC may require the advertiser to devote future space and time to disclosure of previous deception. Began around the late 1960s.

publicity that invariably comes from extensive disputes with the FTC. In fact, because brand equity and brand reputation are so important to most firms, the threat of public embarrassment is a primary concern when an advertisement or sale is challenged.

FTC Rules

It is not the role of the FTC to harass legitimate advertisers. The commission is proactive in communicating its expectations and interpretations before advertisers inadvertently violate FTC rules. For example, the FTC is constantly developing and refining specific industry guidelines, known as *FTC Rules,* that describe exactly what a business can and cannot do in terms of advertising and other business practices with specific industries.

These rules and the means of enforcing them are quite specific. For example, the FTC's Funeral Rule, initiated in 1984 and revised in 1994, requires a number of steps that must be taken by funeral homes in dealing with customers. For example, according to the Funeral Rule:

- Consumers have the right to choose the funeral goods and services they want.
- The funeral provider must state this option in writing on the general price list.
- If state or local law requires consumers to buy any particular item, the funeral provider must disclose it on the price list with a reference to the specific law.
- The funeral provider may not refuse, or charge a fee, to handle a casket consumers bought elsewhere.
- A funeral provider that offers cremations must make alternative containers available.

Again, showing the efforts taken by the FTC to work with industries, when funeral homes are in violation of FTC disclosure rules, they can volunteer to enroll in a program sponsored by the National Funeral Directors Association to ensure that they will be in future compliance.[17]

The areas of FTC enforcement are extremely broad. However, no agency can provide complete oversight of all the consumer advertising and trade practices in the marketplace. Consequently, the FTC tends to concentrate its efforts on those areas that affect the most consumers and have demonstrated the highest percentage of buyer complaints. For example, weight-loss and fitness products have come under intense examination in recent years. The attention given such products is not surprising in light of an FTC study of 300 weight-loss promotions, which found that 40 percent contained at least one statement that was patently false and 55 percent of the ads contained at least one statement that was very likely to be false.[18] Obviously, an industry with this track record of consumer deception can expect continuing review of its advertising.

The Telemarketing Sales Rule is an example of the broad jurisdiction of the FTC. It was instituted in response to a host of consumer complaints concerning telephone sales calls. The rule addresses issues such as when calls can be placed and mandatory disclosures about the purpose of the call. In March 2003, President George Bush signed a bill authorizing the establishment of a national do-not-call list that is administered by the FTC. Modeled after several state laws, the registry went into effect in October 2003 and provided for fines of up to $11,000 per unauthorized call.

Some Basic FTC Guidelines

The FTC Rules normally apply to a single industry, but the FTC also continually reviews general advertising and marketing practices. As in the case of industry-specific rules, the FTC considers those practices that are most likely to create confusion among consumers as well as those that are clearly deceptive. Among the most common areas of FTC inquiry are:

The Term *Free* in Advertising The use of offers such as "buy one, get one free" or "two for one sale" and others has become so prevalent and abuses so widespread that the FTC issued a four-page guide for nondeceptive usage of the term *free*. The guide emphasizes that when the word *free* is used, a consumer has the right to believe that the merchant will not recoup any cost associated with the purchase of another item. A "two for one" deal requires that the first item is sold at regular price or the lowest price offered within the last 30 days. The commission also requires that any disclosure about the offer price must be made in a conspicuous manner in close conjunction with the offer. In other words, a fine print footnote in an advertisement is not acceptable disclosure.[19]

Advertising as a Contract One of the many gray areas of advertising is the degree to which an advertisement constitutes a binding, contractual agreement with consumers. For the most part, the courts and the FTC have ruled that it is unreasonable to expect an advertisement or commercial to contain all the details expected in a formal contract. The commission assumes that contractual details will be part of the final sales negotiation whereas advertising is normally the first step in the process of selling a product. To this end, the courts have been lenient on pricing errors in ads where no deception is intended. For example, a newspaper misprint offering a car for $2,000 would not place the dealer under a legal mandate to sell cars for that price. The courts have held that no reasonable buyer would expect that a sale would be made under those conditions.

However, under certain circumstances advertisements have been regarded as constituting binding offers. For example, when there is a specific commitment, no error in the ad, and the defendant has some control over potential liability, a court may find an obligation to provide a product or service at an advertised price. For example, retailers have been found liable for advertising claims when they offer a product at a certain price but have no intention of selling the product for that price. Instead sellers attempt to move potential buyers into a more expensive alternative. These so-called "bait-and-switch" tactics have been consistently held to be deceptive and heavy fines and other penalties have been levied against businesses found guilty of using such tactics. In general, advertisers would be well-advised to treat every advertisement as if it were potentially a contract.

Fact Versus Puffery "Puffery consists of exaggerated opinions, usually at the highest degree of exaggeration, which means superlatives, such as 'the best' or 'superior.' You puff your product. . . . It can be the best tasting, best looking, best lasting. . . . or just plain the best."[20] The use and boundaries of puffery are extremely controversial. Some critics categorize any statement that is not literally true as deceptive. However, the legal definition of **puffery** is that it is "an exaggeration or overstatement expressed in broad, vague, and commendatory language, and is *distinguishable* from misdescriptions or false representations of specific characteristics of a product and, as such, is not actionable." Advertisers must be wary of pushing the boundaries of puffery. For example, it is easy to cross the line between humor or hyperbole and misleading claims.

puffery
Advertiser's opinion of a product that is considered a legitimate expression of biased opinion.

Testimonials A long-held concept in both communication theory and advertising research is that people like to identify with role models and celebrities. This concept is at the heart of testimonial advertising, which seeks to enhance a brand's reputation by having a sports star, entertainment personality, or acknowledged expert endorse a brand. At one time testimonial advertising, especially celebrity endorsements, were viewed very liberally by regulators. However, in recent years, the commission has taken a much more literal approach to the role of product endorsements. Specifically the commission has ruled that:

- Endorsements must always reflect the honest opinions, findings, beliefs, or experience of the endorser.
- In particular, when the advertisement represents that the endorser uses the endorsed product, then the endorser must have been a bona fide user of it at the time the endorsement was given.[21]

In recent years, there has been a growing chorus of criticism concerning testimonial advertising for direct-to-consumer prescription drugs. Some critics view the choice of a prescription drug as too important to be based on a potential patient's favorite celebrity. However, regulators have taken the position that "credible endorsements with documented information from celebrities who actually use the drugs they pitch shouldn't fuel criticism."[22] This position is consistent with the position that testimonials are an acceptable advertising technique as long as spokespersons are legitimate users of the product. To put teeth into this opinion, the FTC and the courts have held that endorsers who willfully engage in deception can be held liable along with the advertiser for damages. This ruling gives many would-be endorsers pause before they jump into a commercial.

Lotteries The primary elements in a lottery are *consideration* (usually in the form of the purchase of a ticket or other payment to enter the lottery) and *chance* (prizes or cash is awarded at random through a drawing or other device in which no skill is required). In most local jurisdictions, lotteries, except those operated by states, are illegal. Advertising sweepstakes are not lotteries because they don't require consideration. Both the United States Postal Service and the FTC will move against illegal lotteries that use the mail or are advertised across state lines. Because of the restrictions against lotteries, any type of contest or sweepstakes promotion should be carefully reviewed by legal counsel to determine that a promotion is in compliance with state and federal laws.

The Robinson-Patman Act and Cooperative Advertising

The FTC, through its antitrust division, has responsibility for enforcing another law affecting marketing and advertising, the **Robinson-Patman Act.** The Robinson-Patman Act is part of a three-law "package" that evolved over a period of almost 50 years. These laws and their purposes are:

Robinson-Patman Act
A federal law, enforced by the FTC. Requires a manufacturer to give proportionate discounts and advertising allowances to all competing dealers in a market. Purpose: to protect smaller merchants from unfair competition of larger buyers.

1. *1890 Federal Sherman Antitrust Act.* It was designed to prevent alliances of firms conceived to restrict competition.
2. *1914 Clayton Antitrust Act.* This act amended the Sherman Act. It eliminated preferential price treatment when manufacturers sold merchandise to retailers.
3. *1936 Robinson-Patman Act.* In turn, this law amended the Clayton Act. It prevents manufacturers from providing a "promotional allowance" to one customer unless it is also offered to competitors on a proportionally equal basis. Prior to Robinson-Patman, some manufacturers were using a loophole in the Clayton Act to give money back to their bigger customers in the form of promotional allowances. For example, large retailers might be given co-op advertising allowances that were unavailable to small retailers that, in effect, lowered the price of the goods sold to favored customers. Thus, the promotional allowance was a device for under-the-table rebates.

The regulation of co-op allowances has evolved as the media environment has become more complex and the relationships between retailers and manufacturers have changed. At the time Robinson-Patman was passed, the vast majority of retail advertising dollars were placed in newspapers. Today, with a growing number of local advertising options, the FTC requires that retailers must be able to choose from various media and promotional alternatives. For example, a manufacturer may not limit co-op dollars to television, knowing that many retailers in smaller markets might not have practical access to television advertising. Such an offer is known as an *improperly structured program.*

The evolving relationship between retailers and manufacturers is another aspect of Robinson-Patman that has changed since the act was passed. As in the case of the FTC itself, the primary intent when the act was passed was to protect retailers from manufacturers. Today, many regulators are concerned with the leverage that is wielded by huge retail chains against these same manufacturers. Most large retailers charge **slotting fees,** which are payments to retailers by manufacturers to gain shelf space. Retailers argue that prime shelf space is their "product" and stores should receive payments to make this space available.

The FTC has a continuing review of the role of slotting fees if they prevent marketplace entry of new brands or prevent small comapanies from gaining access to established brands because of disproportionately high slotting fees. Again, slotting fees, as in the case of other promotional payments, are only illegal if they are administered with the intent to limit competition.

THE FEDERAL FOOD, DRUG, AND COSMETIC ACT

In 1938 Congress passed the Federal Food, Drug, and Cosmetic Act, which established the Food and Drug Administration (FDA). "No government body touches us where we live more than the FDA does. Whenever we eat, drink, take medicine, apply deodorant, fire up the microwave, feed the cat, take a pregnancy test . . . the FDA acts as our guardian and gatekeeper. It regulates products accounting for 25 cents of every dollar we spend."[23]

Although the agency's work does not deal directly with advertising, the agency has been given broad powers over the labeling and branding—as contrasted to the advertising—of foods, drugs, therapeutic devices, and cosmetics including food and drug product labeling. Because most advertising deals with branding issues and often contains information on product labels, the FDA's authority often overlaps with concerns of the FTC and other regulatory groups.

The jurisdiction of the FDA to control and regulate labeling was enhanced when Congress passed the Nutritional Labeling and Education Act of 1990. With its new authority, the FDA became much more aggressive in the enforcement of regulations dealing with health claims on labels and packaging, sometimes borrowing strategies from the FTC. For example, in August 2003 the agency required Bristol-Myers Squibb to run corrective advertising to counter claims for the cholesterol drug Pravachol that the FDA determined were exaggerated.[24]

The United States Postal Service

Benjamin Franklin created the forerunner of the United States Postal Service (USPS) in 1772. At the end of the Civil War there was a major outbreak of mail swindles and in 1872 Congress passed the Mail Fraud Statute, the nation's oldest federal consumer protection statute. Mail fraud is any scheme in which the USPS is used to obtain money by offering a deceptive product, service, or investment opportunity. To obtain a conviction, postal inspectors must prove (1) the offer was intentionally misrepresented, and (2) the U.S. mail was used to carry out the fraud. Postal inspectors investigate a number of criminal activities. In particular, the inspectors protect postal customers from mail advertising and promotion schemes involving the elderly and other susceptible groups.

For a number of years, the USPS has been empowered to obtain a mail stop order against a company sending false advertising. However, until recently there was no penalty attached to the stop order. In 1999, the Deceptive Mail Prevention and Enforcement Act (DMPEA) gave the USPS significantly more power to deal

slotting fees
Payments to retailers by manufacturers to gain shelf space. Social responsibility. The demand that advertising be aware of its responsibility to the public, i.e., it should do more than sell goods and services.

with mail fraud. The primary change brought about by DMPEA is that the USPS can impose civil penalities of up to $1 million for the first offense depending on the volume of mail involved.[25]

ADVERTISING AND THE FIRST AMENDMENT

The First Amendment makes no distinction between advertising or commercial speech and other forms of expression. However, until the 1970s the courts consistently ruled that advertising had virtually none of the rights guaranteed to other types of speech. The open "marketplace of ideas" was never considered a privilege of advertising and it was held to a much stricter standard than other forms of expression.

In addition to a variety of limitations, advertisers have been frustrated by what they regarded as changing and often contradictory decisions concerning commercial speech. Although advertising continues to function under regulations that would be unacceptable if applied to other speech, the trend of the last 60 years has been toward giving commercial speech greater constitutional protections. Nevertheless, despite a more open environment for commercial messages, judicial opinions supporting commercial speech still deny full First Amendment protection to advertising. In order to understand the legal protection afforded commercial speech, let's outline the major court opinions involving advertising.[26]

1942   The Supreme Court ruled that advertising was not entitled to First Amendment protection. The Court ruled that there were *no* restraints on government's right to prohibit commercial speech.

1964   The Court decided that advertising that expressed an opinion on a *public issue* was protected by the First Amendment, but only because it did not contain commercial speech.

1975   The Court gave advertising its first constitutional protection when it overturned a Virginia law making it a criminal offense to advertise out-of-state abortion clinics in Virginia newspapers. However, the ruling left open the question of protection for purely commercial speech that did not deal with opinions or controversial public issues.

1976   In what many advertisers regard as the major breakthrough for commercially protected speech, the Court held in the case of *Virginia State Board of Pharmacy* v. *Virginia Citizens Consumer Council* that the state of Virginia could not prohibit the advertising of prescription drug prices. It said, in effect, that society benefits from a free flow of commercial information just as it benefits from a free exchange of political ideas.

1979   Advertisers' optimism that they had finally achieved full constitutional protection was short-lived. In the case of *Friedman* v. *Rogers* the Court upheld the right of the state of Texas to prevent an optometrist from using an "assumed name, corporate name, trade name or any other than the name under which he is licensed to practice optometry in Texas." In its decision, the Court said that First Amendment protection for commercial speech is not absolute and that regulation of commercial speech can be allowed even when the restrictions would be unconstitutional "in the realm of noncommercial expression."

1980   Until this year, the Court seemingly ruled on each case involving commercial speech on a purely ad hoc basis. Advertisers were left with little if any guidance or precedents. However, in 1980 the Court articulated a set of guidelines concerning the limits of constitutional protection that would be afforded commercial speech.

These guidelines were set forth in the case of *Central Hudson Gas & Electric* v. *Public Service Commission of New York.*

This case concerned a prohibition by the New York Public Service Commission against utility advertising. The state's rationale was that the ban was compatible with public concerns over energy conservation. In overturning the prohibition, the Court established a four-part test to determine when commercial speech is constitutionally protected and when regulation is permissible. These guidelines known as the *Central Hudson Four-Part Test* are:

1. *Is the commercial expression eligible for First Amendment protection?* That is, is it neither deceptive nor promoting an illegal activity? Obviously, no constitutional protection can be provided for commercial speech that fails this test.

2. *Is the government interest asserted in regulating the expression substantial?* This test requires that the stated reason for regulating the advertisement must be of primary interest to the state rather than of a trivial, arbitrary, or capricious nature.

3. *If the first two tests are met, the Court then considers if the regulation of advertising imposed advances the cause of the governmental interest asserted.* That is, if we assume that an activity is of legitimate government concern, will the prohibition of commercial speech further the government's goals?

4. *If the first three tests are met, the Court must finally decide if the regulation is more extensive than necessary to serve the government's interest.*

In the *Central Hudson* case, the Court ruled that although the case met the first three guidelines, a total prohibition of utility advertising was more extensive than necessary. Thus, it failed the fourth part of the test and was ruled unconstitutional. The *Central Hudson* guidelines remain the foundation on which most commercial speech cases are considered.

1986 Most advertisers thought that *Central Hudson* had provided significant protection in limiting the right of states to ban legitimate advertising. However, in the case of *Posadas de Puerto Rico Associates* v. *Tourism Company of Puerto Rico* the Court seemed to once again strengthen the ability of states to regulate advertising. This case involved a Puerto Rican law banning advertising of gambling casinos to residents of Puerto Rico even though casino gambling is legal there. In a 5–4 decision, the Court ruled that the ban met all four standards of the *Central Hudson Four-Part Test.*

1988 Many legal scholars see this year as marking a significant change in the Court's attitude toward advertising and, just as importantly, a change in its interpretation of *Central Hudson. Board of Trustees of the State University of New York* v. *Fox* dealt with a college regulation that restricted "private commercial enterprises" on campus. Students challenged the regulation, arguing that at events such as "Tupperware parties" noncommercial subjects were discussed. Because the regulation had the effect of prohibiting both noncommercial and commercial speech, it was too broad and, therefore, did not meet the fourth part of the *Central Hudson* test.

In upholding the regulation, the Court ruled that regulations must be "narrowly tailored," but not necessarily the "least restrictive" option available. Critics of the decision point out that "narrowly tailored" is vague and may risk weakening the protections of *Central Hudson.*

1993 In *City of Cincinnati* v. *Discovery Network,* the Court seemed to offer a clear victory for proponents of First Amendment protection of commercial speech. In a 6–3 decision the Court held that the Cincinnati City Council violated the First Amendment by banning newsracks for free promotional publications but allowing them for traditional newspapers. The Court ruled that because the ban was based solely on the content of the publications in the racks, it did not meet the "narrowly tailored" test. The case was widely seen as a victory for commercial speech.

1996 Legal scholars predict that two cases heard in this year may provide a significant step in affording more complete constitutional protection to commercial speech. In *44 Liquormart, Inc.* v. *Rhode Island* the Court ruled that a Rhode Island ban on price advertising for alcoholic beverages was unconstitutional. The Court referred to the *Central Hudson* case and ruled that the Rhode Island law failed to prove that the ban on price promotions advanced the state's interest in promoting temperance (that is, it failed the third test of *Central Hudson*). Furthermore, the legislation was more extensive than necessary to accomplish the goals of the state (here it failed the fourth test of *Central Hudson*).

Writing for the majority of the Court, Justice John Paul Stevens said, "Bans that target truthful, nonmisleading commercial messages rarely protect consumers from such harms. Instead, such bans often serve only to obscure an 'underlying governmental policy' that could be implemented without regulating speech."[27] Commenting for the advertising industry, Wally Snyder, president of the American Advertising Federation, noted, "The Supreme Court ruling represented the strongest opinion to date protecting truthful advertising from government censorship."[28]

In a subsequent case that year, the Court underscored the *Rhode Island* decision by returning to the Fourth Circuit U.S. Court of Appeals a case involving a Baltimore ban on alcoholic billboard advertising. In *Anheuser-Busch, Inc.* v. *Schmoke* the beer maker challenged the city ordinance on constitutional grounds of denial of First Amendment right to free speech. However, demonstrating the unpredictability of advertising and the law, the appeals court upheld its original verdict, ruling that because alcoholic beverage companies had other avenues for their advertising, the ban was not as broad as the Rhode Island law and, therefore, constitutional.

1999 The Greater New Orleans Broadcasters Association sought to overturn a ban on broadcast advertising of gambling that dated to the Communications Act of 1934. Advocates of the ban argued that the government had a legitimate interest in protecting compulsive gamblers from the temptation that casino gambling fostered. In upholding the ban, the Fifth Circuit Court of Appeals commented that the restriction was appropriate because of the "powerful sensory appeal of gambling conveyed by television and radio."[29]

In June 1999, when the case reached the Supreme Court, the lower court decisions were overturned using the earlier *Central Hudson* guidelines. According to *Central Hudson*, any government restrictions on truthful commercial speech had to be shown to advance some government interest and be no more extensive than necessary. The Court ruled that the casino advertising ban does not sufficiently advance the government's stated interest to protect compulsive gamblers and does not do so in the least intrusive way.[30]

Some advertisers were encouraged that the *New Orleans Broadcasters* case might mean greater First Amendment protection for advertising, perhaps even lifting the prohibition against broadcast tobacco advertising. However, the Court was careful to write its decision narrowly. It "focused on the irrationality of making distinctions among advertisers, while at the same time suggesting that a more uniform and coherent policy of advertising restrictions might well have been upheld. . . . [It] left the door open for the Court to uphold, in future cases, restrictions on the advertising of other lawful products."[31]

2002 The turn of the century brought no precedent-setting cases concerning commercial speech. However, a number of decisions at the Supreme Court and district court levels continued the trend of conflicting decisions when applying First Amendment protection to advertising. On the one hand, a number of decisions seemed to offer even greater protection to commercial speech. For example, U.S.

District Court Judge Stephen Limbaugh ruled that portions of the Telephone Consumer Protection Act halting unsolicited faxes went too far in limiting commercial messages. He cited the fact that the government had not proved that it had a substantial interest in the matter or that such a ban was necessary to eliminate the problem. The case was particularly significant because the justification for limiting fax messages was similar to the arguments used to establish "do-not-call" lists for telemarketers.[32]

As another example, the Supreme Court ruled that the FDA's authority over the marketing communication of drugs and related products must meet certain First Amendment guidelines. Specifically, the Court ruled that the FDA did not have the authority to impose rules on tobacco marketers that would have prevented the use of certain types of imagery and colors in advertising and point-of-purchase material. As one industry lawyer commented, "The Supreme Court [has] told the FDA in no uncertain terms that its regulatory requirements must pass muster under the First Amendment. Hopefully . . . the FDA has finally gotten the message."[33]

However, other decisions since 2002 seem to be a step back for full First Amendment protection of commercial speech. Perhaps the most controversial decision was a ruling by the California Supreme Court in a case involving Nike. For a number of years, critics have charged Nike with poor working conditions in its overseas plants. In an effort to rebut its critics, Nike sent the news media information offering its side of the debate. Marc Kasky brought suit (*Nike* v. *Kasky*) and in a 4–3 decision, the California Court ruled that the comments by Nike constituted advertising and, therefore, the company was ordered to establish the truthfulness of its claims under the state unfair practices act. In June 2003, the Supreme Court returned the case to the California Court without comment. In September 2003, Nike and Kasky reached an out-of-court settlement, thereby leaving the legal position of corporate speech and related advertising in limbo. However, until the Supreme Court issues a definitive decision on commercial speech, companies will no doubt be more careful about their public positions on controversial topics.

An *Advertising Age* editorial commented that "in a society where free expression and freewheeling public debate is part of our hallowed constitutional tradition, applying false advertising laws to debates over corporate policy is strong medicine. . . . they impose legal duties and legal penalties on speakers, and allow government censorship, in ways we would never tolerate for other forms of speech."[34]

Despite the potential problems presented by the *Nike* case, the courts are affording advertising rights that it never enjoyed in the past. However, most of the decisions considered by the courts involve narrowly defined issues that often pertain to a single industry or product category. These decisions underscore the fact that each case has unique elements that don't necessarily provide precedents in other dissimilar circumstances. Still, there is no question that the Supreme Court will continue to demand that the government meets a high standard of public interest before agreeing to any prohibition of commercial speech.

Corporate Speech and Advertising

In recent years, we have seen a tremendous growth in corporate advertising espousing some idea or corporate philosophy as contrasted to selling a product or service. Like all other forms of commercial speech, corporate advertising falls into a gray area. Similar to its decisions regarding commercial speech, the Supreme Court has ruled that corporate advertising is protected under certain circumstances. In *First National Bank of Boston* v. *Bellotti* the Court overturned a state law that prohibited national banks from using corporate funds to advocate voting against a state constitutional amendment that would allow the legislature to impose a graduated income tax.

Over the years the Court has delineated several legal principles concerning corporate speech:

1. Spending money to speak does not, in itself, result in the loss of First Amendment rights.
2. Speaking on commercial subjects does not entail loss of First Amendment rights.
3. Speaking for economic interests does not entail loss of First Amendment rights.[35]

We should note that the Court is saying that a commercial aspect to speech does not *necessarily* remove that speech from the rights granted by the First Amendment. However, the converse of this view does not automatically grant these rights to either advertising or corporate speech. As discussed earlier, it remains to be seen what effect final disposition of the *Nike* case will have on the future use of corporate speech.

Advertising and the Right of Publicity

A private individual is protected by the right of privacy from having his or her likeness used in an advertisement without permission. Laws vary from state to state, but every state has some legislation that addresses the right of privacy of an individual. In many jurisdictions the use of a name or picture of a person without prior consent is a misdemeanor. However, civil liability, potentially involving significant monetary judgments, is a much greater concern to advertisers.

Generally, the courts have ruled that public figures have far less protection than the general public in terms of their right of privacy. However, in recent years the courts have made it clear that this distinction of public versus private persons is related to news, not advertising or other commercial use. Legal precedent makes it clear that public figures are protected from commercial use of their name or likeness by a doctrine of the right of *publicity* (as contrasted with a right of *privacy*).

In the past, most issues of privacy dealt only with living personalities. However, in recent years some states, notably California, have addressed the issue of deceased celebrities. John Wayne, Humphrey Bogart, and other stars from the past have been used in a number of commercials with the permission of their estates. Because state laws vary widely, advertisers should be extremely prudent in using a personality's name or likeness. The normal course of action is that an advertiser or agency will never use a model, personality, or likeness without legal permission. For example, the courts have ruled against a number of advertisers that used impersonators in commercials without permission.

ADVERTISING OF PROFESSIONAL SERVICES

One of the most controversial areas of commercial speech involves advertising by professionals, especially attorneys and health care providers. Until the mid–1970s virtually all forms of professional advertising were banned, often by trade associations such as state medical groups or bar associations. Critics of restrictions on professional advertising claim that one of the overriding concerns was to limit competition for established professionals and, in fact, constituted restraint of trade.

Supporting this claim, research indicates that among doctors, those most likely to use advertising are physicians who have been in practice the least time; those who have smaller practices; and females.[36] Due in part to concerns that the bans constituted barriers to market entry, absolute prohibition of attorney (and by extension most other professional) advertising was lifted in 1977 in the case of *Bates* v. *State Bar of Arizona.* The Supreme Court ruled that state laws forbidding advertising by attorneys were unconstitutional on First Amendment grounds. The fourth test of the *Central Hudson* case, not an issue in 1977, seems to reinforce the *Bates* decision. That is, most legal scholars think that the total prohibition of a class of advertising will generally not meet the fourth test because any such total ban will be considered broader than necessary. Professional associations still have regulatory powers over issues such as accuracy and presentation, but they cannot prohibit their members from advertising.

In 1988 the Supreme Court extended the right of attorneys to advertise professional services. A Kentucky lawyer, Richard Shapero, was cited for violating a Kentucky law prohibiting targeted mail solicitations to people who were facing foreclosure. The Court ruled that although personal contact by an attorney could be prohibited, a letter posed no threat of pressure to consumers who are under threat of legal action. The *Shapero* case had the immediate effect of lifting the ban on targeted letters in the 25 states that had previously prohibited them.

In 1993, the Court made an interesting distinction among various types of professional solicitations. The Florida board of accountancy banned personal solicitations for clients, either in person or by telephone. In *Edenfield* v. *Fane* the Court overturned the ban and, in doing so, made a clear distinction between lawyers and accountants. The Court held that, unlike lawyers, CPAs are not trained in the art of persuasion, they are dealing with clients who probably have had a previous professional relationship with an accountant, and the client of a CPA is probably not under the stress that a lawyer's potential client might be. The court found that it was unlikely that the potential clients of a CPA would be subject to "uninformed acquiescence" which might be the case with a lawyer's client.

A 1995 case demonstrated that the courts consider a number of circumstances in ruling on professional solicitations and they are not prepared to issue blanket denials of most state regulations. For example, the Court upheld a Florida Bar Association rule prohibiting lawyers from sending direct mail to accident victims. The Court took the position that an accident victim is in a more vulnerable state of mind than a person facing foreclosure—the circumstance of those solicited by Shapero. Again, referring to the *Central Hudson* guideline, "The state had a substantial interest in protecting the integrity of its legal system."[37]

STATE AND LOCAL LAWS RELATING TO ADVERTISING

For most of the twentieth century, advertising regulation was regarded as a function of federal laws and regulatory bodies with state laws largely confined to retail practices and companies operating within state borders. However, in recent years, the National Association of Attorneys General (NAAG) has become very aggressive in working in concert to address a number of national issues including advertising.

Most people probably believe that multibillion-dollar sanctions against major tobacco companies were the result of actions by the federal government. In reality, the 1998 Master Settlement Agreement (MSA) was between a consortium of 46 states and five territories. Obviously, the MSA, much of which addressed the manner in which tobacco could be advertised and promoted, was the most high-profile case brought by members of the NAAG. However, it is only one of a number of suits involving national companies that have been brought by individual or groups of state attorneys general. For example, attorneys general have negotiated a $100 million agreement with a major brokerage house concerning actions by some of its brokers, investigated pharmaceutical industry pricing tactics, and brought suit against major telecommunication companies and health insurance firms.

On the face of it, no one would question that companies and advertisers should be held accountable for their actions regardless of whether the oversight is conducted by state, local, or national authorities. However, many advertisers have raised questions about the extent that states will be allowed to go beyond or contradict national legislation. Formerly, it appeared the lines between state and federal enforcement were relatively clearly drawn. However, in the last decade there has been an obvious shift toward more state control, which creates potential problems for national advertising if it has to meet an array of local standards.

An example of the potential problems of state regulation of nationally distributed products was accented when a U.S. district court judge in California ruled that the maker of Paxil, an antidepressant drug, had to halt television advertising even though the commercials had previously been approved the FDA. His decision was based in part on California state law.[38] Without addressing the merits of the decision, advertisers are naturally concerned that a move to state-by-state regulation of advertising would make national advertising all but impossible and, when national advertisements are executed under such circumstances, costs will greatly increase for both advertisers and consumers.

COMPARISON ADVERTISING

One of the most controversial areas of advertising is the comparison of one brand with one or more of its competitors. J. Sterling Getchell is generally credited with the first major use of comparison advertising when the Getchell Agency introduced the Chrysler car in the 1930s by inviting customers to "Try all three."

Comparison advertising began to be widely used after the FTC pushed for more comparative advertising in 1972. The commission urged ABC and CBS to allow commercials that named competitors. Until then, only NBC had permitted such messages, whereas ABC and CBS would allow only "Brand X" comparisons in which competitors were implied but not directly named. The FTC continues to foster comparative advertising, even going so far as to warn trade associations against industry codes that prohibit such comparisons.

In recent years, comparison advertising has become more prevalent, especially in product categories where there are a number of competitors and where there is little obvious product differentiation (for example, paper towels and laundry products). Despite the widespread use of the technique, many advertisers worry that comparative advertising runs the risk of inadvertently promoting competitive brands and/or appearing to offer credibility to them by including their names in their advertising.

Beyond these conceptual problems, comparative advertising claims have precipitated a number of lawsuits by companies that think their brands have been disparaged. For example, Procter & Gamble was sued by Kimberly-Clark, maker of Huggies Pull-Ups, and Playtex, manufacturer of Playtex tampons, for P&G commercials that named their brands.[39] As we noted earlier in this chapter, product substantiation is important in any advertising but particularly in comparison advertising where, in effect, advertisers must substantiate both the qualities of their brand as well as those of any other brands to which they are making comparisons.

THE ADVERTISING CLEARANCE PROCESS

It would be a mistake to think that ethical and truthful advertising only takes place under the threat of legal or regulatory constraints. In fact, among the strongest advocates of honest advertising are advertisers themselves. The vast majority of advertisers not only want to produce truthful advertising but also are equally interested in making sure that their peers do likewise. When consumers are misled by dishonest advertising, all advertisers pay a price. Advertisers, advertising agencies, and the media that carry their advertising all play a part in the process of ensuring that advertising serves the public interest.

The media are a major element in the advertising clearance process because they represent an independent reviewer of advertising messages. There are numerous examples of specific media refusing to carry certain advertising messages.

advertising clearance process
The internal process of clearing ads for publication and broadcast, conducted primarily by ad agencies and clients.

Sometimes it is a magazine or newspaper that excludes an entire category of advertisers such as tobacco companies or NC–17 movies. In other cases, advertising is refused because it appears to be fraudulent or it may demean a competitor.

It is important to remember that in most cases the media review process is voluntary and it is up to each medium to set its own standards. It is important to remember that the standards, scope, and diligence exercised by the various media will vary a great deal.

> With the sole exception of broadcast advertising by a bona fide candidate for public office, no U.S. newspaper, magazine, radio, or television station or network must accept any advertising material it does not wish to publish or broadcast. Each vehicle imposes its own standards that advertisers must meet for the material to be acceptable: some vehicles accept virtually anything, many others limit their concerns to areas of potential legal liabilities. But each manager or owner is free to direct these standards based on his or her own assessments of the laws, the audience values and what is ethically right and proper.[40]

Sometimes it is difficult to predict when a commercial will be turned down. In one case, a network reportedly rejected a commercial because models were not wearing wedding rings even though it was obvious from the context of the commercial that they were living together. The voluntary nature of the media clearance process means that from time to time advertising that has been rejected by one outlet will be accepted by another. An example of this type of media disagreement occurred when the stockbroker, Charles Schwab, submitted a commercial to CBS. The commercial showed a meeting in which stockbrokers working on a commission basis are urged to persuade clients to buy a stock even though their boss thought it was a "pig." CBS rejected the commercial on the basis that it implied that stockbrokers at other firms act in an unethical manner. Other networks agreed to run the commercial and, in fact, CBS ran other commercials in the series.[41]

In other cases, however, the proliferation of media outlets and the resulting competitive pressure for advertising dollars have led to a lowering of review standards on the part of some media. FTC Commissioner Sheila Anthony has been especially critical of what she preceives as a failure by the media to adequately screen dubious advertising. Commenting on the rash of deceptive claims for dietary/weight-loss products, she said, "Our (FTC) recent law-enforcement experience suggests that some members of the media are, for the most part, not paying enough attention to the ads they publish."[42]

The importance of the media screening process was emphasized when the FTC issued a "Guide for the Media," which stressed the importance of the media in stopping dishonest advertising. In the prologue to the guidelines, the FTC wrote, "Government agencies and self-regulatory groups can step in once the law has been violated, but only the media can stop false ads before they disseminated."[43]

Media should carefully review advertising they accept as a matter of public trust, but careless acceptance of advertising also can carry legal liability for a medium. If a statement in an advertisement or commercial is false or defamatory, the media can be sued along with the advertiser. In 2002, FTC Chairman Timothy Muris introduced the notion that those media that ran clearly misleading advertising were leaving themselves open to legal action. In response a number of media trade organizations complained that the threatened action was unconstitutional under free speech protections. However, Chairman Muris responded that "there is no constitutional right to run false advertising."[44]

Despite threats of formal legal action, from a practical standpoint, unless a medium knowingly accepts deceptive or libelous advertising, its chances of liability are not great. However, a more practical concern of the media is the loss of goodwill with their audiences if a deceptive ad is cleared for publication or broadcast. No responsible agency or medium would argue that deceptive advertising should be created or run.

SELF-REGULATION BY INDUSTRY-WIDE GROUPS

Self-regulation by the advertising industry is not new. During the early 1900s, major advertisers realized that something had to be done to prevent the charlatans and frauds that were preying on an unsuspecting public and causing widespread mistrust of all advertising. However, most of their efforts were directed at the national level with local advertising abuses largely ignored. *Printers' Ink*, a leading trade magazine of the time, proposed state and local advertising regulations to address the growing problem of false advertising (see Exhibit 24.5). Basically, it sought to regulate "untrue, deceptive, or misleading advertising."

Today, there are a number of initiatives to ensure that advertising is truthful. Some of these efforts are undertaken by groups within specific industries and others are intended to review more general advertising. The advertising industry itself has a long history of promoting truthful advertising (see Exhibit 24.6). These efforts offer the public, competitors, and other interested parties a voluntary forum for negotiation without resorting to a formal legal or regulatory body for the adjudication of disagreements.

Industry self-regulation serves two important purposes beyond ensuring more informative and truthful advertising. First, it partially overcomes the relatively poor public perception of advertising by showing that there is a concerted attempt to foster responsible advertising. Second, strong self-regulation may ward off even stricter government control.

One of the ways in which the industry promotes better advertising is through various guidelines and codes of practice promoted by advertising agency groups and media associations as well as trade and professional associations. One of the leading advertising groups promoting truthful and ethical advertising is the American Advertising Federation (AAF). A primary aim of the AAF is to foster truthful and fair advertising through local advertising clubs.

Despite the best efforts of federal regulatory agencies, the media, and individual advertisers, the opinion persists among a large group of consumers that advertising is either basically deceptive or does not provide sufficient information. Given

THE *PRINTERS' INK* MODEL STATUTE FOR STATE LEGISLATION AGAINST FRAUDULENT ADVERTISING

Any person, firm, corporation, or association, who with intent to sell or in any wise dispose of merchandise, securities, service, or anything offered by such person, firm, corporation, or association, directly or indirectly to the public for sale or distribution, or with the intent to increase the consumption thereof, or to induce the public in any manner to enter into any obligation relating thereto, or to acquire title thereto, or an interest therein, makes, publishes, disseminates, circulates, or places before the public, or causes, directly or indirectly, to be made, published, disseminated, circulated, or placed before the public, in this state, in a newspaper or other publication, or in the form of a book, notice, handbill, poster, bill, circular, pamphlet, or letter, or in any other way, an advertisement of any sort regarding merchandise, securities, service, or anything so offered to the public, which advertisement contains assertions, representation, or statement of fact which is untrue, deceptive, or misleading shall be guilty of a misdemeanor.

EXHIBIT 24.5

Printers' Ink Was an Early Leader in the Fight for Truthful Advertising

EXHIBIT **24.6**

Advertising agencies take their responsibility for truthful advertising seriously.

Courtesy of the American Association of Advertising Agencies.

Creative Code of the American Association of Advertising Agencies

ADOPTED APRIL 26, 1962

The members of the American Association of Advertising Agencies recognize:

1. That advertising bears a dual responsibility in the American economic system and way of life.

To the public it is a primary way of knowing about the goods and services that are the products of American free enterprise—goods and services that can be freely chosen to suit the desires and needs of the individual. The public is entitled to expect that advertising will be reliable in content and honest in presentation.

To the advertiser it is a primary way of persuading people to buy his goods or services, within the framework of a highly competitive economic system. He is entitled to regard advertising as a dynamic means of building his business and his profits.

2. That advertising enjoys a particularly intimate relationship to the American family.

It enters the home as an integral part of television and radio programs, to speak to the individual and often to the entire family. It shares the pages of favorite newspapers and magazines. It presents itself to travelers and to readers of the daily mails. In all these forms, it bears a special responsibility to respect the tastes and self-interest of the public.

3. That advertising is directed to sizable groups or to the public at large, which is made up of many interests and many tastes.

As is the case with all public enterprises, ranging from sports to education and even to religion, it is almost impossible to speak without finding someone in disagreement. Nonetheless, advertising people recognize their obligation to operate within the traditional American limitations: to serve the interests of the majority and to respect the rights of the minority.

Therefore we, the members of the American Association of Advertising Agencies, in addition to supporting and obeying the laws and legal regulations pertaining to advertising, undertake to extend and broaden the application of high ethical standards. Specifically, we will not knowingly produce advertising that contains:

   a. False or misleading statements or exaggerations, visual or verbal.

   b. Testimonials that do not reflect the real choice of a competent witness.

   c. Price claims that are misleading.

   d. Comparisons that unfairly disparage a competitive product or service.

   e. Claims insufficiently supported, or which distort the true meaning or practicable application of statements made by professional or scientific authority.

   f. Statements, suggestions, or pictures offensive to public decency.

We recognize that there are areas subject to honestly different interpretations and judgment. Taste is subjective and may even vary from time to time as well as from individual to individual. Frequency of seeing or hearing advertising messages will necessarily vary greatly from person to person.

However, we agree not to recommend to an advertiser and to discourage the use of advertising that is in poor or questionable taste or is deliberately irritating through content, presentation, or excessive repetition.

Clear and willful violations of this Code shall be referred to the Board of Directors of the American Association of Advertising Agencies for appropriate action, including possible annulment of membership as provided in Article IV, Section 5, of the Constitution and By-Laws.

Conscientious adherence to the letter and the spirit of this Code will strengthen advertising and the free enterprise system of which it is a part.

---

the investment that companies are making in advertising, this perception is a major problem and one that needs to be addressed on a united front by all honest businesses. As we will see in this section, the advertising industry is making substantial investments in moving against deceptive advertising.

Better Business Bureaus

One of the best-known, aggressive, and successful organizations in the fight for honest and truthful advertising is the national network of Better Business Bureaus (BBBs) coordinated by the Council of Better Business Bureaus, Inc. (CBBB). The forerunners of the modern BBBs date to 1905, when various local advertising clubs formed a national association that today is known as the National Advertising Federation. In 1911, this association launched a campaign for truth in advertising coordinated by local vigilance committees. In 1916 these local committees adopted the name Better Business Bureaus and they became autonomous in 1926. Today, there are approximately 135 local bureaus in the United States and Canada.

The importance of advertising is demonstrated by the comprehensive two-volume *Do's and Don'ts in Advertising*. The volumes offer advertisers guidelines covering most of the basic questions encountered by companies. The "Basic Principles" outline an overview of the BBBs' philosophy of self-regulation:

■ The primary responsibility for truthful and nondeceptive advertising rests with the advertiser. Advertisers should be prepared to substantiate any claims or offers made before publication or broadcast and, upon request, present such substantiation promptly to the advertising medium or the Better Business Bureau.

■ Advertisements that are untrue, misleading, deceptive, fraudulent, falsely disparaging of competitors, or insincere offers to sell shall not be used.

■ An advertisement as a whole may be misleading although every sentence separately considered is literally true. Misrepresentation may result not only from direct statements but also by omitting or obscuring a material fact.[45]

Although the BBBs have no legal authority, they are a major influence on truth and accuracy in advertising. The BBBs are able to exert both the force of public opinion and peer pressure to set up voluntary efforts to address examples of potentially misleading or deceptive advertising.

THE NARC SELF-REGULATION PROGRAM

In 1971, in response to the many different consumer movements pushing for more stringent government regulation of advertising, the major advertising organizations—the American Advertising Federation, the American Association of Advertising Agencies, and the Association of National Advertisers—joined with the CBBB to form the National Advertising Review Council (NARC). NARC's primary purpose was to "develop a structure which would effectively apply the persuasive capacities of peers to seek the voluntary elimination of national advertising which professionals would consider deceptive." Its objective was to sustain high standards of truth and accuracy in national advertising through voluntary self-regulation.

NARC established a number of units that are administered by the CBBB (see Exhibit 24.7). The primary investigative unit is the **National Advertising Division (NAD)** of the Council of Better Business Bureaus. The NAD is staffed by full-time lawyers who respond to complaints from competitors and consumers and to referrals from local BBBs. They also monitor national advertising. The National Advertising Review Board (NARB) provides an advertiser with a jury of peers if it chooses to appeal a NAD decision. In 1974 the Children's Advertising Review Unit (CARU) was established to review the special advertising concerns of advertising directed to children. We will discuss the CARU in detail later in this section.

In recent years, many within the advertising industry have encouraged the NARC to further expand the scope of self-regulation. Specifically, it has been asked to consider guidelines for self-regulation of alcohol and tobacco advertising as well as advertising to teenagers. What form such self-regulation would take remains to be seen. However, the fact that a number of advertising executives look to the NARC emphasizes the important place that the organization occupies in the advertising industry.

National Advertising Division (NAD)
The primary investigative unit of the NARC self-regulation program.

EXHIBIT 24.7

The NARC review process is established to ensure fairness and provide an objective examination of advertising.

Reprinted with permission of the Council of Better Business Bureaus, Inc., copyright 2003. Council of Better Business Bureaus, Inc., 4200 Wilson Blvd., Arlington, VA 22203. World Wide Web:http//www.bbb.org.

After a complaint is received, the NAD determines the issues, collects and evaluates data, and makes an initial decision on whether the claims are substantiated. If the NAD finds that substantiation is satisfactory, it announces that fact. If the NAD finds that the substantiation is not adequate, it will recommend that the advertiser modify or discontinue the offending claims. If the advertiser does not agree, it may appeal to the NARB. NAD decisions are released to the press and also are published in its monthly publication *NAD Case Reports*.

The NARB is composed of 70 members—40 representing advertisers, 20 representing advertising agencies, and 10 from the public sector. Five members in the same proportion are assigned to hear an appeal. If the panel determines the NAD's decision is justified but the advertiser still refuses to correct the deceptive element, the NARB may refer the advertising to the appropriate government agency. For example, in September 2003, the NARB ruled that Sidney Frank Importing Company's Grey Goose brand vodka should end its claim that it was "Rated the No. 1 Tasting Vodka in the World." When the company refused to abide by the NARB ruling, the NARB's findings were turned over to the FTC and the Alcohol and Tobacco Tax and Trade Bureau, a government agency that oversees issues concerning alcohol advertising and marketing.[46]

Underscoring the competitive nature of advertising claims, competitor challenges are by far the largest source of NAD cases. According to the NAD, there are six primary areas that provide most of the challenges brought to the organization:

- product testing
- consumer perception studies
- taste/sensory claims
- pricing
- testimonial/anecdotal evidences
- demonstrations

In a number of cases, complaints involve comparative advertising. For example, a challenge is often made when product testing or product demonstrations involve other brands' alleged deficiencies in some area. In terms of complaints, the largest product category is health and health aids with more than 20 percent, followed by the food and beverage category with 15 percent. It is no coincidence that these are two of the most competitive product categories.

Among NAD cases, only a small minority is referred to a governmental agency. However, the number of cases turned over to the government has risen in recent years, a fact that is troublesome to some in the industry. Noting the increase in referred cases, one observer pointed out, "It might indicate some lack of respect for this organization [NAD] in the 1990s among members of the trade. However, the willingness of NAD/NARB to turn recalcitrant advertisers over to the government suggests a certain level of spine within the organization."[47]

In our examination of the NAD/NARB process, we should understand that it cannot

- order an advertiser to stop an ad
- impose a fine
- bar anyone from advertising
- boycott an advertiser or a product

What it can do is bring to bear the judgment of an advertiser's peers that the company has produced advertising that is not truthful and is harmful to the industry, to the public, and to the offender. This opinion has great moral weight. It is reinforced by the knowledge that, if the results of an appeal to the NARB are not accepted, the whole matter will be referred to the appropriate government agency and at the same time will be released to the public. This step, unique in business self-regulation machinery, avoids any problem of violating antitrust laws, presents the entire matter to public view, and still leaves the advertiser subject to an FTC ruling on the advertising.

The Children's Advertising Unit of the NAD

Children's advertising is one of the most controversial areas of marketing and promotion. The notion of marketing to children, regardless of its format or execution, has raised questions among a number of groups about the wisdom and ethics of advertising directed to this unsophisticated audience. Even among the proponents of such advertising, there is general agreement that advertising claims that would be perfectly suitable for adults might be unacceptable for children, especially preteens. Because of this concern with children's advertising, the NAD, in cooperation with the advertising community, founded the **Children's Advertising Review Unit (CARU)** in 1974.

The CARU's mission is similar to that of the NAD except it considers the special circumstances of the younger audience reached by children-oriented advertising. "CARU works with the industry to ensure that advertising directed to kids is truthful, and above all, fair. By promoting adherence to self-regulatory guidelines, CARU seeks to maintain a balance between regulating the messages children receive from advertising, and promoting the dissemination of important information to children through advertising."[48]

The key to CARU review is its *Self-Regulatory Guidelines for Children's Advertising*. The guidelines not only cover traditional advertising but also include a section on interactive and electronic media advertising to children. However, television remains by far the primary medium for reaching children and it is the most important focus for CARU. Children's television is not only a major concern of the CARU, but also recent legislative and regulatory actions indicate that advertisers will not be allowed the latitude in advertising to children that they have with adults. Beginning October 1, 1991, the FCC mandated limits on children's program advertising to 10½ minutes an hour on weekdays and 12 minutes on weekends. The action of the commission underscores the fact that children's television, both programming and advertising, is considered a separate category from that directed to general audiences.

Questions concerning children's advertising have few easy answers. To the critics that think that no advertising should be directed to children any guidelines are unsatisfactory. However, given the economic support of the media through advertising, it is unlikely that any such ban will ever be permitted. It is imperative that all parties involved (media, advertisers, parents, and special interest groups) work to ensure that children's advertising is appropriate for the audience to which it is intended. With public opinion running against them, advertisers must be extremely cautious about the content of all advertising messages directed to children.

Children's Advertising Review Unit (CARU)
The CARU functions much as the NAD to review complaints about advertising to children.

SUMMARY

As we have discussed in this chapter, advertising functions within an environment of legal, ethical, social, and economic considerations. It is obvious that legal and regulatory bodies are devoting increasing resources to review dishonest and misleading advertising. However, although these legal restraints on advertising are an important part of the advertising environment, major advertisers are rarely the target of these governmental agencies.

Advertisers, their agencies, and the mainstream media are much more interested in the ethical and social problems of content, presentation, and the acceptability of a host of product categories, claims, and advertising practices. As we saw in earlier chapters, the diversity of the marketplace, growing fragmentation of the media, and concerns with public policy issues such as the demand for consumer privacy are issues of primary concern to advertisers. A number of advertisers have inadvertently created major public relations problems for themselves by a failure to be sensitive to the feelings of consumers.

The future of advertising will be one of change and adaptation. The public interest will be an increasingly important part of the modern advertiser's agenda—much more important than formal legal restrictions. It is a given that the public will not tolerate untruthful, misleading, and deceptive advertising. But more than simply being truthful, contemporary advertising must incorporate the idea of social responsibility as routinely as it depends on a well thought out marketing plan for its success. As part of this social responsibility, advertising will be used more extensively as a tool for change in society. Rather than confined to selling products and services, advertising will play a larger role in presenting ideas and opinions concerning a host of social issues.

Among major advertisers, there is no disagreement that advertising should be fair and truthful and follow both the letter and the spirit of the law. In fact, advertisers are among the most aggressive groups in weeding out the charlatans who make it difficult for all advertisers by eroding public confidence. For the foreseeable future, it is clear that advertisers will have to contend with numerous, sometimes conflicting, and constantly changing advertising regulations.

 **REVIEW**

1. Discuss the three historical eras of advertising criticism.

2. From an economic perspective, what are three primary roles that advertising should play?

3. What is meant by "inadvertent" social roles of advertising? Give some examples.

4. Discuss the role of cause-related marketing as a sales tool. What do you see as its major advantages and disadvantages?

5. What role does substantiation play in FTC enforcement?

6. What are the primary methods used by the FTC to implement its ruling?

7. Briefly discuss the *Central Hudson Four-Part Test.*

8. How does the right of privacy differ from the right of publicity?

9. What are some of the pitfalls of comparison advertising from both a legal and practical perspective?

10. How does the FTC regard the advertising clearance process by media?

11. What is the primary role of the NARD, NARC, and the CARU in supporting advertising self-regulation?

 **TAKE IT TO THE WEB**

The Federal Trade Commission (**www.ftc.gov**) is the primary consumer protection agency at the national level. On which two primary issues is the agency currently concentrating its efforts?

Review how consumers can file complaints with the Better Business Bureau (**www.bbb.org**). What are some of the major categories of complaints?

How do the procedures and mission of the Children's Advertising Review Unit (**www.caru.org**) differ from self-regulation of advertising aimed at adults?

GLOSSARY

A

Above-the-line expenses. These usually include advertising in traditional media. In recent years, the development of the Internet and interactive media have blurred this line.

Account planner. An outgrowth of British agency structure where a planner initiates and reviews research and participates in the creative process. In some agencies, the planner is considered a spokesperson for the consumer.

Advertising. Advertising consists of paid notices from identified sponsors normally offered through communication media.

Advertising clearance process. The internal process of clearing ads for publication and broadcast, conducted primarily by ad agencies and clients.

Advertising Council. A non-profit network of agencies, media, and advertisers dedicated to promoting social programs through advertising.

Advertising goals. The communication objectives designed to accomplish certain tasks within the total marketing program.

Advertising objectives. Those specific outcomes that are to be accomplished through advertising.

Advertorial. The use of advertising to promote an idea rather than a product or service.

American Association of Advertising Agencies (AAAA, 4As). The national organization of advertising agencies.

Amplitude modulation (AM). Method of transmitting electromagnetic signals by varying the amplitude (size) of the electromagnetic wave, in contrast to varying its frequency. Quality is not as good as frequency modulation, but can be heard farther, especially at night. See Frequency modulation (FM).

Animation (TV). Making inanimate objects appear alive and moving by setting them before an animation camera and filming one frame at a time.

Appeal. The motive to which an ad is directed, it is designed to stir a person toward a goal the advertiser has set.

The Arbitron Company. Syndicated radio ratings company.

Audience fragmentation. The segmenting of mass-media audiences into smaller groups because of diversity of media outlets.

Audit Bureau of Circulations (ABC). The organization sponsored by publishers, agencies, and advertisers for securing accurate circulation statements.

Average quarter-hour estimates (AQHE). Manner in which ratio ratings are presented. Estimates include average number of people listening, rating, and metro share of audience.

B

Barter. Acquisition of broadcast time by an advertiser or an agency in exchange for operating capital or merchandise. No cash is involved.

Barter syndication. Station obtains a program at no charge. The program has pre-sold national commercials and time is available for local station spots.

Behavioral research. Market research that attempts to determine the underlying nature of purchase behavior.

Below-the-line expenses. These refer to promotions other than advertising such as public relations. Typically, they are more difficult to measure than above the line expenses.

Bleed. Printed matter that runs over the edges of an outdoor board or of a page, leaving no margin.

Block programming. A series of television shows that appeals to the same general audience.

Bounce-back circular. An enclosure in the package of a product that has been ordered by mail. It offers other products of the same company and is effective in getting more business.

Brand. A name, term, sign, design, or a unifying combination of them, intended to identify and distinguish the product or service from competing products or services.

Brand development index (BDI). A method of allocating advertising budgers to those geographic areas that have the greatest sales potential.

Brand equity. The value of how such people as consumers, distributors, and salespeople think and feel about a brand relative to its competition over a period of time.

Brand extensions. These are new product introductions under an existing brand to take advantage of existing brand equity.

Brand loyalty. Degree to which a consumer purchases a certain brand without considering alternatives.

Brand name. The written or spoken part of a trademark, in contrast to the pictorial mark; a trademark word.

Brand positioning. Consumers' perceptions of specific brands relative to the various brands of goods or services currently available to them.

Brand preference. When all marketing conditions are equal, a consumer will choose a preferred brand over another.

Building block strategy. A media concept that buys the medium that reaches the most prospects first and works down to those that reach the smallest number of prospects.

Business-to-business advertising. Advertising that promotes goods through trade and industrial journals that are used in the manufacturing, distributing, or marketing of goods to the public.

C

Cable networks. Networks available only to cable subscribers. They are transmitted via satellite to local cable operators for redistribution either as part of basic service or at an extra cost charged to subscribers.

Cable television. TV signals that are carried to households by cable. Programs originate with cable operators through high antennas, satellite disks, or operator-initiated programming.

Category manager. A relatively new corporate position, this manager is responsible for all aspects of the brands in a specific product category for a company including research, manufacturing, sales, and advertising. Each product's advertising manager reports to the category manager. Example: Procter & Gamble's Tide and Cheer detergent report to a single category manager.

Cause-related marketing. Marketing strategies that attempt to link a company to some social or charitable cause.

Caveat emptor. Latin for "Let the buyer beware." Represents the notion that there should be no government interference in the marketplace.

Cease and desist orders. If an advertiser refuses to sign a consent decree, the FTC may issue a cease and desist order that can carry a $10,000-per-day fine.

Central Hudson Four-Part Test. Supreme Court test to determine if specific commercial speech is protected under the Constitution.

Centralized exchange. A system of trade and marketing through specialized intermediaries rather than direct exchange of goods between buyers and producers.

Children's Advertising Review Unit (CARU). The CARU functions much as the NAD to review complaints about advertising to children.

Classified advertising. Found in columns so labeled, published in sections of a newspaper or magazine set aside for certain classes of goods or services—for example, Help Wanted, Positions Wanted, Houses for Sale, Cars for Sale. The ads are limited in size and generally are without illustration.

Clearance. The percentage of network affiliates that carries a particular network program.

Closing date. The date when all advertising material must be submitted to a publication.

Clutter. Refers to a proliferation of commercials in a particular medium. This reduces the impact of any single message.

Coined word. An original and arbitrary combination of syllables forming a word. Extensively used for trademarks, such as PoFolks, Mazola, Gro-Pup, Zerone. (Opposite of a dictionary word.)

Committee on Nationwide Television Audience Measurement (CONTAM). Industry-wide organization to improve the accuracy and reliability of television ratings.

Communications component. That portion of the media plan that considers the effectiveness of message delivery as contrasted to the efficiency of audience delivery.

Comparative advertising. It directly contrasts an advertiser's product with other named or identified products.

Compensation. The payment of clearance fees by a TV network to local stations carrying its shows.

Competitive stage. The advertising stage a product reaches when its general usefulness is recognized but its superiority over similar brands has to be established in order to gain preference. See Pioneering stage, Retentive stage.

Comprehensive. A layout accurate in size, color, scheme, and other necessary details to show how a final ad will look. For presentation only, never for reproduction.

Computer-generated imagery (CGI). Technology allowing computer operators to create multitudes of electronic effects for TV—to squash, stretch, or squeeze objects—much more quickly than earlier tools could. It can add layers of visuals simultaneously.

Concept testing. The target audience evaluation of (alternative) creative strategy. Testing attempts to separate good and bad ideas and provide insight into factors motivating acceptance or rejection.

Conjoint analysis. A research technique designed to determine what consumers perceive as a products most important benefits.

Consent decree. Issued by the FTC. An advertiser signs the decree, stops the practice under investigation, but admits no guilt.

Consumer advertising. Directed to people who will use the product themselves, in contrast to trade advertising, industrial advertising, or professional advertising.

Consumer Franchise Building. Creating promotional messages that allow consumers to differentiate one brand from others in the product category.

Consumer price index. Comparative index that charts what an urban family pays for a select group of goods including housing and transportation.

Contest. A promotion in which consumers compete for prizes and the winners are selected strictly on the basis of skill.

Continuity. A TV or radio script. Also refers to the length of time a given media schedule runs.

Continuous tone. An unscreened photographic picture or image, on paper or film, that contains all gradations of tonal values from white to black.

Controlled circulation magazines. Sent without cost to people responsible for making buying decisions. To get on such lists, people must state their positions in companies; to stay on it, they must request it annually. Also known as qualified-circulation publications.

Convergence. The blending of various facets of marketing functions and communication technology to create more efficient and expanded synergies.

Cooperative advertising. Joint promotion of a national advertiser (manufacturer) and local retail outlet on behalf of the manufacturer's product on sale in the retail store.

Copy approach. The method of opening the text of an ad. Chief forms: factual approach, imaginative approach, emotional approach.

Copy testing. Measuring the effectiveness of ads.

Corrective advertising. To counteract the past residual effect of previous deceptive advertising, the FTC may require the advertiser to devote future space and time to disclosure of previous deception. Began around the late 1960s.

Cost per rating point (CCP). The cost per rating point is used to estimate the cost of TV advertising on several shows.

Cost per thousand (CPM). A method of comparing the cost for media of different circulations. Also weighted or demographic cost per thousand calculates the CPM using only that portion of a medium's audience falling into a prime-prospect category.

Council of Better Business Bureaus. National organization that coordinates a number of local and national initiatives to protect consumers.

Coupon. Most popular type of sales-promotion technique.

Cross-media buy. Several media or vehicles that are packaged to be sold to advertisers to gain a synergistic communication effect and efficiencies in purchasing time or space.

Customer relationship marketing. A management concept that organizes a business according to the needs of the consumer.

D

Database marketing. A process of continually updating information about individual consumers. Popular techniques with direct-response sellers.

Direct houses. In specialty advertising, firms that combine the functions of supplier and distributor.

Direct marketing. Selling goods and services without the aid of wholesaler or retailer. Includes direct-response advertising and advertising for leads for sales people. Also direct door-to-door selling. Uses many media: direct mail, publications, TV, radio.

Direct Marketing Association (DMA). Organization to promote direct-mail and direct-response advertising.

Direct premium. A sales incentive given to customers at the time of purchase.

Direct-response advertising. Any form of advertising done in direct marketing. Uses all types of media: direct mail, TV, magazines, newspapers, radio. Term replaces mail-order advertising. See Direct marketing.

Disintermediation. The potential for online technology to eliminate all or part of the distribution channel by selling directly to customers.

Distribution channel. The various intermediaries, such as retailers, that control the flow of goods from manufacturers to consumers.

Dot-coms. A generic designation that refers to companies engaged in some type of online commerce.

Drive time (radio). A term used to designate the time of day when people are going to, or coming from, work. Usually 6 A.M. to 10 A.M. and 3 P.M. to 7 P.M., but this varies from one community to another. The most costly time on the rate card.

E

Effective reach. The percentage of an audience that is exposed to a certain number of messages or has achieved a specific level of awareness.

Eight-sheet poster. Outdoor poster used in urban areas, about one-fourth the size of the standard 30-sheet poster. Also called junior poster.

End-product advertising. Building consumer demand by promoting ingredients in a product. For example, Teflon and Nutrasweet.

European Union (EU). The developing economic integration of Europe. Potentially a single market of some 300 million consumers in 1991.

Event marketing. A promotion sponsored in connection with some special event such as a sports contest or musical concert.

Everyday low pricing (EDLP). A marketing strategy that uses permanent price reductions instead of occasional sales promotion incentives.

Exclusionary zones (outdoor). Industry code of conduct that prohibits the advertising of products within 500 feet of churches, schools, or hospitals of any products that cannot be used legally by children.

Executional idea. It is a rendering in words symbols, sounds, colors, shapes, forms, or any combination thereof, of an abstract answer to a perceived desire or need.

F

Family life cycle. Concept that demonstrates changing purchasing behavior as a person or a family matures.

Fast-close advertising. Some magazines offer short-notice ad deadlines, sometimes at a premium cost.

Federal Communications Commission (FCC). The federal authority empowered to license radio and TV stations and to assign wavelengths to stations "in the public interest."

Federal Trade Commission (FTC). The agency of the federal government empowered to prevent unfair competition and to prevent fraudulent, misleading, or deceptive advertising in interstate commerce.

Flat rate. A uniform charge for space in a medium, without regard to the amount of space used or the frequency of insertion. When flat rates do not prevail, time discounts or quantity discounts are offered.

Flighting. Flight is the length of time a broadcaster's campaign runs. Can be days, weeks, or months—but does not refer to a year. A flighting schedule alternates periods of activity with periods of inactivity.

Focus group. A qualitative research interviewing method using in-depth interviews with a group rather than with an individual.

Four-color process. The process for reproducing color illustrations by a set of plates, one that prints all the yellows, another the blues, a third the reds, and the fourth the blacks (sequence variable). The plates are referred to as process plates.

Free-standing inserts (FSI). Preprinted inserts distributed to newspaper publishers, where they are inserted and delivered with the newspaper.

Frequency. In media exposure the number of times an individual or household is exposed to a medium within a given period of time.

Frequency discounts. Discounts based on total time or space bought, usually within a year. Also called bulk discounts.

Frequency modulation (FM). A radio transmission wave that transmits by the variation in the frequency of its wave, rather than its size (as in amplitude modulation [AM]). An FM wave is twenty times the width of an AM wave, which is the source of its fine tone. To transmit such a wave, it has to be placed high on the electromagnetic spectrum, far from AM waves with their interference and static, hence its outstanding tone.

Fulfillment. The tasks of filling orders, shipping merchandise, and back in marketing.

Fulfillment firm. Company that handles the couponing process including receiving, verification, and payment. It also handles contests and sweepstake responses.

Full-run editions. An advertiser who buys the entire circulation of a publication is buying the full-run circulation.

Full-service agency. One that handles planning, creation, production, and placement of advertising for advertising clients. May also handle sales promotion and other related services as needed by client.

G

General Agreement on Tariffs and Trade (GATT). A treaty designed to lower trade barriers among 117 nations.

Generic demand. The demand demonstrated for a product class rather than a specific brand.

Global marketing. Term that denotes the use of advertising and marketing strategies on an international basis.

Gross rating points (GRP). Each rating point represents 1 percent of the universe being measured for the market. In TV it is 1 percent of the households having TV sets in that area.

H

Highway Beautification Act of 1965. Federal law that controls outdoor signs in noncommercial, non-industrial areas.

Hoarding. First printed outdoor signs—the forerunner of modern outdoor advertising.

House mark. A primary mark of a business concern, usually used with the trademark of its products. General Mills is a house mark; Betty Crocker is a trademark; DuPont is a house mark; Teflon II is a trademark.

I

Idea advertising. Advertising used to promote an idea or cause rather than to sell a product or service.

Illuminated posters. Seventy to 80% of all outdoor posters are illuminated for 24-hour exposure.

Imagery transfer research. A technique that measures the ability of radio listeners to correctly describe the primary visual elements of related television commercials.

Inadvertent social role of advertising. Advertising sometimes communicates social messages unintended by the advertiser. Stereotyping and less-than-flattering portrayals of individuals and ethnic or social audience segments can lead to negative perceptions of advertising.

Incentives. Sales promotion directed at wholesalers, retailers, or a company's salesforce.

Independent delivery companies. Private companies that contract with magazine publishers to deliver their publications.

Industrial advertising. Addressed to manufacturers who buy machinery, equipment, raw materials, and the components needed to produce goods they sell.

Infomercial. Long form television advertising that promotes products within the context of a program-length commercial.

In-house agency. An arrangement whereby the advertiser handles the total agency function by buying individually, on a fee basis, the needed, services (for example creative, media services, and placement, under the direction of an assigned advertising director.

Institutional advertising. Advertising done by an organization speaking of its work views, and problems as a whole, to gain public goodwill and support rather than to sell a specific product. Sometimes called public-relations advertising.

Integrated marketing communication (IMC). The joint planning, execution, and coordination of all areas of marketing communication.

Interactive era. Communication will increasingly be controlled by consumers who will determine when and where they can be reached with promotional messages.

Interconnects. A joint buying opportunity between two or more cable systems in the same market.

Internet. A worldwide system of computer links that provides instantaneous communication.

J

Jingle. A commercial or part of a commercial set to music, usually carrying the slogan or theme line of a campaign. May make a brand name and slogan more easily remembered.

Johann Gutenberg. Began the era of mass communication in 1438 with the invention of movable type.

L

Layout. A working drawing (may be computer developed) showing how an ad is to look. A printer's layout is a set of instructions accompanying a piece of copy showing how it is to be set up. There are also rough layouts, finished layouts, and mechanical layouts, representing various degrees of finish. The term layout is used also for the total design of an ad.

Letterpress. Printing from a relief, or raised, surface. The raised surface is inked and comes in direct contact with the paper, like a rubber stamp.

Lettershop. A firm that not only addresses the mailing envelope but also is mechanically equipped to insert material, seal and stamp envelopes, and deliver them to the post office according to mailing requirements.

Lifestyle segmentation. Identifying consumers by combining several demographics and lifestyles.

Lifetime value. An estimate of the long-term revenue that can be expected from a particular prospect.

List broker. In direct-mail advertising an agent who rents the prospect lists of one advertiser to another advertiser. The broker receives a commission from the seller for this service.

List manager. Promotes client's lists to potential renters and buyers.

Logotype, or logo. A trademark or trade name embodied in the form of a distinctive lettering or design. Famous example: Coca-Cola.

M

Magazine networks. Groups of magazines that can be purchased together using one insertion order and paying a single invoice.

Make-goods. When a medium falls short of some audience guarantee, advertisers are provided concessions in the form of make-goods. Most commonly used in television and magazines.

Market. A group of people who can be identified by some common characteristic, interest, or problem; use a certain product to advantage; afford to buy it; and be reached through some medium.

Marketing communication. The communication components of marketing, which include public relations, advertising, personal selling, and sales promotion.

Marketing concept. A management orientation that views the needs of consumers as primary to the success of a firm.

Marketing goals. The overall objectives that a company wishes to accomplish through its marketing program.

Marketing mix. Combination of marketing functions, including advertising, used to sell a product.

Marketing translation. The process of adapting a general marketing plan to multinational environments.

Market profile. A demographic and psychographic description of the people or the households of a product's market. It may also include economic and retailing information about a territory.

Market segmentation. The division of an entire market of consumers into groups whose similarity makes them a market for products serving their special needs.

Mass communication era. From the 1700s to the early decades of this century, advertisers were able to reach large segments of the population through the mass media.

Mass production. A manufacturing technique utilizing specialization and interchangeable parts to achieve production efficiencies.

MatchPrint. A high-quality color proof used for approvals prior to printing. Similar to a Signature print.

M-commerce. Mobile technology that allows consumers to receive information, make purchases, and conduct business anywhere they happen to be.

Media buyers. Execute and monitor the media schedule developed by media planners.

Media imperatives. Based on research by Simmons Media Studies, showed the importance of using both TV and magazines for full market coverage.

Media plan. The complete analysis and execution of the media component of a campaign.

Media planners. Media planners are responsible for the overall strategy of the media component of an advertising campaign.

Media schedule. The detailed plan or calendar showing when ads and commercials will be distributed and in what media vehicles they will appear.

Media strategy. Planning of ad media buys, including identification of audience, selection of media vehicles, and determination of timing of a media schedule.

Merge/purge (merge & purge). A system used to eliminate duplication by direct-response advertisers who use different mailing lists for the same mailing. Mailing lists are sent to a central merge/purge office that electronically picks out duplicate names. Saves mailing costs, especially important to firms that send out a million pieces in one mailing. Also avoids damage to the goodwill of the public.

Mergenthaler linotype. Ottmar Mergenthaler invented the linotype, which replaced hand-set type by automatically setting and distributing metal type.

Message management. Utilizes database information to offer different messages to various consumer categories.

Morphing. An electronic technique that allows you to transform one object into another object.

Multinational advertising. The coordination and execution of advertising campaigns that are directed to a number of countries.

N

National advertising. Advertising by a marketer of a trademarked product or service sold through different outlets, in contrast to local advertising.

National Advertising Division (NAD). The primary investigative unit of the NARC self-regulation program.

Negative option direct response. Technique used by record and book clubs whereby a customer receives merchandise unless the seller is notified not to send it.

Networks. Interconnecting stations for the simultaneous transmission of TV or radio broadcasts.

Newspaper Association of America (NAA). The marketing and trade organization for the newspaper industry.

Newspaper networks. Groups of newspapers that allow advertisers to buy several papers simultaneously with one insertion order and one invoice.

Niche marketing. A combination of product and target market strategy. It is a flanking strategy that focuses on niches or comparatively narrow windows of opportunity within a broad product market or industry. Its guiding principle is to pit your strength against their weakness.

Non-wired networks. Groups of radio and TV stations whose advertising is sold simultaneously by station representatives.

North American Free Trade Agreement (NAFTA). A treaty designed to eliminate trade barriers among the United States, Mexico, and Canada.

North American Industrial Classification System. System that uses six-digit identification numbers for classifying manufacturing firms.

O

Off-network syndication. Syndicated programs that have previously been aired by a major network.

Offset lithography. Lithography is a printing process by which originally an image was formed on special stone by a greasy material, the design then being transferred to the printing paper. Today the more frequently used process is offset lithography, in which a thin and flexible metal sheet replaces the stone. In this process the design is offset from the metal sheet to a rubber blanket, which then transfers the image to the printing paper.

On-line services. Refers to computer-accessed databases and information services for business and home use.

Open rate. In print, the highest advertising rate at which all discounts are placed.

Opticals. Visual effects that are put on a TV film in a laboratory, in contrast to those that are included as part of the original photography.

Optimizers. Computer model and software that allow media buyers to make decisions about the value of various audience segments in a media schedule.

Opt-out. Procedures that recipients to notify advertisers that they no longer wish to receive advertising messages. A term usually associated with online promotions.

Outbound telemarketing. A technique that involves a seller calling prospects.

Outdoor Advertising Association of America (OAAA). Primary trade and lobbying organization for the outdoor industry.

Out-of-home. Outdoor and transportation advertising.

Outside producer. The production company person who is hired by the agency to create the commercial according to agency specifications.

P

Partial runs. When magazines offer less than their entire circulation to advertisers. Partial runs include demographic, geographic, and split-run editions.

Pass-along readership. Readers who receive a publication from a primary buyer. In consumer publications, pass-along readers are considered inferior to the primary audience, but this is usually not the case with business publications.

Passive meters. Unobtrusive device that measures individual viewing habits through sensors keyed to household members.

Pattern standardization. An advertising plan where overall strategy is controlled centrally, but local offices have flexibility in specific advertising executions.

Penny press. Forerunner of the mass newspaper in the United States that first appeared in the 1830s.

People meter. Device that measures TV set usage by individuals rather than by households.

Per inquiry (PI). Advertising time or space where medium is paid on a per response received basis.

Personal drive analysis (PDA). A technique used to uncover a consumer's individual psychological drives.

Pica. The unit for measuring width in printing. There are 6 picas to an inch. A page of type 24 picas wide is 4 inches wide.

Pioneering stage. The advertising stage of a product in which the need for such a product is not recognized and must be established or in which the need has been established but the success of a commodity in filling those requirements has to be established. See Competitive stage, Retentive stage.

Pixel. The smallest element of a computer image that can be separately addressed. It is an individual picture element.

Plant. In outdoor advertising the local company that arranges to lease, erect, and maintain the outdoor sign and to sell the advertising space on it.

Point (pt). The unit of measurement of type, about 1/72 inch in depth. Type is specified by its point size, as 8 pt., 12 pt., 24 pt., 48 pt. The unit for measuring thickness of paper, 0.001 inch.

Point-of-purchase advertising. Displays prepared by the manufacturer for use where the product is sold.

Positioning. Segmenting a market by creating a product to meet the needs of a select group or by using a distinctive advertising appeal to meet the needs of a specialized group, without making changes in the physical product.

Poster panel. A standard surface on which outdoor posters are placed. The posting surface is of sheet metal. An ornamental molding of standard green forms the frame. The standard poster panel is 12 feet high and 25 feet long (outside dimensions).

Potential Rating Index by ZIP Market (PRIZM). A method of audience segmentation developed by the Claritas Corporation.

Pre-marketing era. The period from prehistoric times to the eighteenth century. During this time, buyers and sellers communicated in very primitive ways.

Premium. An item, other than the product itself, given to purchasers of a product as an inducement to buy. Can be free with a purchase (for example, on the package, in the package, or the container itself) or available upon proof of purchase and a payment (self-liquidating premium).

Printers' Ink Model Statute (1911). The act directed at fraudulent advertising, prepared and sponsored by Printers' Ink, which was the pioneer advertising magazine.

Product differentiation. Unique product attributes that set off one brand from another.

Product life cycle. The process of a brand moving from introductions, maturity, and, eventually, either adaptation or demise.

Product manager. In package goods, the person responsible for the profitability of a product (brand) or product line, including advertising decisions. Also called a brand manager.

Product user segmentation. Identifying consumers by the amount of product usage.

Professional advertising. Directed at those in professions such as medicine, law, or architecture, who are in a position to recommend the use of a particular product or service to their clients.

Psychographics. A description of a market based on factors such as attitudes, opinions, interests, perceptions, and lifestyles of consumers comprising that market.

Public relations. Communication with various internal and external publics to create an image for a product or corporation.

Puffery. Advertiser's opinion of a product that is considered a legitimate expression of biased opinion.

Pure Food and Drug Act. Passed in 1906 by Legislation, it was one of the earliest attempts by the federal government to protect consumers.

Q

Qualitative research. This involves finding out what people say they think or feel. It is usually exploratory or diagnostic in nature.

R

Radio Advertising Bureau (RAB). Association to promote the use of radio as an advertising medium.

Radio All Dimension Audience Research (RADAR). Service of Statistical Research, Inc., that is the primary source of network radio ratings.

Rate base. The circulation that magazines guarantee advertisers in computing advertising costs.

Rate differential. The controversial practice of newspapers charging significantly higher rates to national advertisers as compared to local accounts.

Rating point (TV). The percentage of TV households in a market a TV station reaches with a program. The percentage varies with the time of day. A station may have a 10 rating between 6:00 and 6:30 P.M. and a 20 rating between 9:00 and 9:30 P.M.

Rebate. The amount owed to an advertiser by a medium when the advertiser qualifies for a higher space discount.

Relationship marketing. A strategy that develops marketing plans from a consumer perspective.

Remnant space. Unsold advertising space in geographic or demographic editions. It is offered to advertisers at a significant discount.

Representative (rep). An individual or organization representing a medium selling time or space outside the city or origin.

Research era. In recent years advertisers increasingly have been able to identify narrowly defined audience segments through sophisticated research methods.

Residual. A sum paid to certain talent on a TV or radio commercial every time the commercial is run after 13 weeks, for the life of the commercial.

Response lists. Prospects who have previously responded to direct mail offers.

Retail advertising. Advertising by a merchant who sells directly to the consumer.

Retentive stage. The third advertising stage of a product, reached when its general usefulness is widely known, its individual qualities are thoroughly appreciated, and it is satisfied to retain its patronage merely on the strength of its past reputation. See Pioneering state, Competitive stage.

Return on investment (ROI). One measure of the efficiency of a company is the rate of return (profits) achieved by a certain level of investment on various business functions including advertising.

Reverse production timetable. Used in direct mail to schedule a job. The schedule starts with the date it is to reach customers and works backward to a starting date.

Ride-alongs. Direct-mail pieces that are sent with other mailings, such as bills.

Riding the boards. Inspecting an outdoor showing after posting.

Robinson-Patman Act. A federal law, enforced by the FTC. Requires a manufacturer to give proportionate discounts and advertising allowances to all competing dealers in a market. Purpose: to protect smaller merchants from unfair competition of larger buyers.

Rotary bulletins (outdoor). Movable painted bulletins that are moved from one fixed location to another one in the market at regular intervals. The locations are viewed and approved in advance by the advertiser.

Rotogravure. The method of printing in which the impression is produced by chemically etched cylinders and run on a rotary press; useful in long runs of pictorial effects.

S

Sales promotion. (1) Sales activities that supplement both personal selling and marketing, coordinate the two, and help to make them effective. For example, displays are sales promotions. (2) More loosely, the combination of personal selling, advertising, and all supplementary selling activities.

Sampling. The method of introducing and promoting merchandise by distributing a miniature or full-size trial package of the product free or at a reduced price.

Scatter plan. The use of announcements, over a variety of network programs and stations, to reach as many people as possible in a market.

Screen printing. A simple printing process that uses a stencil. It is economical but is limited in reproduction quality.

Secondary research. Research or data that is already gathered by someone else for another purpose.

Selective binding. Binding different material directed to various reader segments in a single issue of a magazine.

Self-liquidating premium. A premium offered to consumers for a fee that covers its cost plus handling.

Service advertising. Advertising that promotes a service rather than a product.

Service mark. A word or name used in the sale of services, to identify the services of a firm and distinguish them from those of others, for example, Hertz Drive Yourself Service, Weight Watchers Diet Course. Comparable to trademarks for products.

Share of audience. The percentage of households using TV tuned to a particular program.

Short rate. The balance advertisers have to pay if they estimated that they would run more ads in a year than they did and entered a contract to pay at a favorable rate. The short rate is figured at the end of the year or sooner if advertisers fall behind schedule. It is calculated at a higher rate for the fewer insertions.

Showing. Outdoor posters are bought by groups, referred to as showings. The size of a showing is referred to as a 100-GRP showing or a 75- or 50-GRP showing, depending on the gross rating points of the individual boards selected.

Simmons Market Research Bureau (SMRB). Firm that provides audience data for several media. Best known for magazine research.

Siquis. Handwritten posters in sixteenth- and seventeenth-century England—forerunners of modern advertising.

Situation analysis. The part of the advertising plan that answers the questions: Where are we today and how did we get here? It deals with the past and present.

Slotting fees. Payments to retailers by manufacturers to gain shelf space.

Social responsibility. The demand that advertising be aware of its responsibility to the public, i.e., it should do more than sell goods and services.

Spam. Online advertising messages that are usually unsolicited by the recipient.

Specialty advertising. A gift given to a consumer to encourage a purchase.

Spectacular. Outdoor sign built to order, designed to be conspicuous for its location, size, lights, motion, or action. The costliest form of outdoor advertising.

Spot radio. Buying radio time on local stations on a market-by-market basis by national advertisers.

Spot television. Purchase of time from a local station, in contrast to purchasing from a network.

Standard Advertising Unit (SAU). Allows national advertisers to purchase newspaper advertising in standard units from one paper to another.

Standard Rate and Data Service (SRDS). SRDS publishes a number of directories giving media and production information.

Stock music. Existing recorded music that may be purchased for use in a TV or radio commercial.

Storyboard. Series of drawings used to present a proposed commercial. Consists of illustrations of key action (video), accompanied by the audio part. Used for getting advertiser approval and as a production guide.

Stripping. Scheduling a syndicated program on a five-day-per-week basis.

Substantiation. The key to FTC enforcement is that advertisers must be able to prove the claims made in their advertising.

Sweepstakes. A promotion in which prize winners are determined on the basis of chance alone. Not legal if purchaser must risk money to enter.

Sweep weeks. During these periods, ratings are taken for all television markets.

Syndicated TV program. A program that is sold or distributed to more than one local station by an independent organization outside the national network standard.

Synergistic effect. In media buying, combining a number of complementary media that create advertising awareness greater than the sum of each.

T

Target audience. That group that composes the present and potential prospects for a product or service.

Target marketing. Identifying and communicating with groups of prime prospects.

Telemarketing. Contacting prospective buyers over the telephone. Major area of direct marketing.

Theater of the mind. In radio, a writer paints pictures in the mind of the listener through the use of sound.

Time-shift viewing. Recording programs on a VCR for viewing at a later time.

Total concept. The combining of all elements of an ad—copy, headline, and illustrations—into a single idea.

Total market coverage (TMC). Where newspapers augment their circulation with direct mail or shoppers to deliver all households in a market.

Total survey area. The maximum coverage of a radio or television station's signal.

Trade advertising. Advertising directed to the wholesale or retail merchants or sales agencies through whom the product is sold.

Trademark. Any device or word that identifies the origin of a product, telling who made it or who sold it. Not to be confused with trade name.

Trade name. A name that applies to a business as a whole, not to an individual product.

Trade paper. A business publication directed to those who buy products for resale (wholesalers, jobbers, retailers).

Traffic Audit Bureau for Media Measurement (TAB). An organization designed to investigate how many people pass and may see a given outdoor sign, to establish a method of evaluating traffic measuring a market.

Traffic-building premium. A sales incentive to encourage customers to come to a store whereas a sale can be closed.

Translation management. The process of translating advertising from one culture to another.

TV director. The person who casts and rehearses a commercial and is the key person in the shooting of the commercial.

TvQ. A service of Marketing Evaluations that measures the popularity (opinion of audience rather than size of audience) of shows and personalities.

Typography. The art of using type effectively.

U

Up-front buying. Purchase of network TV time by national advertisers during the first offering by networks. The most expensive network advertising.

Up-selling. A telemarketing technique designed to sell additional merchandise to callers.

V

Value added opportunities. Extra things a medium will do for or provide to an advertiser that adds value to the purchase of time or space in the medium.

Value of advertising. An initiative which was intended to educate marketers about the role of advertising in building and protecting the brand franchise.

Value gap. The perceived difference between the price of a product and the value ascribed to it by consumers.

Values and lifestyles system (VALS). Developed by SRI International to cluster consumers according to several variables in order to predict consumer behavior.

Vertical publication. Business publications dealing with the problems of a specific industry: for example, *Chain Store Age, National Petroleum News, Textile World.*

W

War Advertising Council. Founded in 1942 to promote World War II mobilization, it later evolved into the Advertising Council.

Wheeler-Lea Amendments. Broadened the scope of the FTC to include consumer advertising.

Y

Yield management. A product pricing strategy to control supply and demand.

Z

Zoning. Newspaper practice of offering advertisers partial coverage of a market, often accomplished with weekly inserts distributed to certain sections of that market.

ENDNOTES

Chapter 1

p. 2 © Digital Vision/PictureQuest

p. 4 Courtesy of Unilever. From John W. Hartman Center for Sales, Advertising & Marketing History; Duke University Rare Book, Manuscript, and Special Collections Library; http://scriptorium.lib.duke.edu/eaa/

1. J. Robert Moskin, *The Case for Advertising* (New York: American Association of Advertising Agencies, 1973), 7.

2. Roland Marchand, *Advertising the American Dream* (Berkeley: University of California Press, 1985), 76.

3. Randall Rothenberg, "The advertising century," *Advertising Age: Special Issue*, 1999, 12.

4. George Burton Hotchkiss, *An Outline of Advertising* (New York: Macmillan, 1957), 10.

5. James Playsted Wood, *Magazines in the United States* (New York: The Ronald Press, 1949), 99.

6. John McDonough, "From a birth in lower Manhattan to an unmatched global reach," *Advertising Age*, 18 March 2002, C8.

7. James Harvey Young, "The story of the laws behind the labels," www.cfsan.fda.gov, 3–4.

8. From the Federal Trade Commission Mission Statement.

9. Ralph M. Hower, *The History of an Advertising Agency* (Cambridge, MA: Harvard University Press, 1949), 180.

10. Edward Robinson, "Businessman of the century," *Fortune*, 6 September 1999, 227.

11. Lydia Boyd, "Brief history of the radio industry," John W. Hartman Center, Duke University, www.scriptorium.lib.duke.edu/radio, 2.

12. "Brief History of World War Two Advertising Campaigns: Conservation," John W. Hartman Center for Sales, Advertising and Marketing History, Duke University Library, http://scriptorium.l.b.duke.edu/adaccess/.

13. John McDonough, "Ad Council at 60—Facing a crossroads," *Advertising Age*, 29 April 2002, C–4.

14. Herbert Zeltner, "Proliferation, localization, specialization mark media trends in past fifty years," *Advertising Age*, 30 April 1980, 148.

15. This section is adapted from Cait Murphy, "Introduction: Wal-Mart rules," *Fortune*, April 15, 2002, www.fortune.com.

16. Cait Murphy, "Introduction: Wal-Mart Rules," www.fortune.com, April 15, 2002.

17. David Whelan, "Wrapped in the flag," *American Demographics*, December 2001, 37.

Chapter 2

p. 30 Courtesy of Huey/Paprocki, Inc.

1. Adapted from David W. Schropher, *What Every Account Executive Should Know About a Marketing Plan* (New York: American Association of Advertising Agencies, 1990).

2. This section is adapted from "Brand Awareness as a Tool for Profitability," *Cahners Advertising Research Report*, No. 2000.6.

3. A term coined in the early 1930s by Professor Neil H. Borden of the Harvard Business School to include in the marketing process such factors as distribution, advertising, personal selling, and pricing.

4. Jack Neff, "Ries' thesis: Ads don't build brands, PR does," *Advertising Age*, 15 July 2002, 14.

5. Leon Stafford, "More companies consider PR blitz a better tactic than ads," *The Atlanta Journal-Constitution*, 12 September 2002, E1.

6. Rance Crain, "Marketers look at new ideas, and PR becomes the closer," *Advertising Age*, 29 July 2002, 15.

7. Erin White, "Web, direct mail get larger share of marketers' pie," *The Wall Street Journal*, 18 December 2002, B2.

8. Pamela Paul, "Wake-up call," *American Demographics*, April 2002, 26.

9. Tobi Elkin, "Courting craftier consumers," *Advertising Age*, 1 July 2002, 28.

10. Christine Nuzum, "TV ads could get individual attention," *The Wall Street Journal*, 5 June 2002, B-11.

11. Kenneth Roman and Jane Mass, *How to Advertise* (New York: St. Martin's Press, 1976), 130.

12. Jamie Murphy and Edward J. Forrest, *The New York Times Guide to Marketing* (Cincinnati, OH: South-Western College Publishing, 2001), 59.

13. J. Robert Moskin, ed., *The Case for Advertising* (New York: American Association of Advertising Agencies, 1973), 15.

14. Benjamin Singer, *Advertising & Society* (Don Mills, Ontario: Addison-Wesley Publishers Limited, 1986), 143.

15. Gary F. Grates, "Working with the volume off," Newsletter (undated) of GCI BoxenbaumGrates, 4.

16. Kate MacArthur, "Red Lobster shifts creative to boost emotion quotient," *Advertising Age*, 2 September 2002, 8.

17. "Branded for life," *Food Processing*, September 2002, 20.

18. "Billion-dollar brands," *American Demographics*, January 2002, 23.

19. Scott Leith, "New sodas flood market," *The Atlanta Journal-Constitution*, 6 September 2002, F-1.

20. Sarah Ellison, "Is less risqué risky?" *The Wall Street Journal*, 3 September 2002, B1.

21. Jerry Flint, "A Mercedes in every garage," www.forbes.com, 25 March 2002.

22. Bill Britt and Dagmar Mussey, "VW's big bet," www.adageglobal.com, 23 April 2002.

23. Kevin Helliker, "In natural foods, a big name's no big help," *The Wall Street Journal*, 7 June 2002, p. B1.

24. Elliot Spagat, "Like, what's a spin cycle?" *The Wall Street Journal*, 4 June 2002, B1.

25. "Listening to customers in the electronic age," *Fortune*, 1 May 2000, 318.

26. Stephanie Thompson, "As fat fight rages, Frito battles back," *Advertising Age*, 2 September 2002, 1.

27. Kate MacArthur, "Food makers weigh in with ads," *Advertising Age*, 2 September 2002, 27.

28. Jonathan Fahey, "The lemon factor," www.forbes.com, 5 April 2002.

29. David J. Pike, "Product by design," *American Demographics*, February 2001, 38.

30. Shelly Branch, "At Kraft, making cheese 'fun' is serious business," *The Wall Street Journal*, 31 May 2002, 1.

31. Shirley Leung, "At McDonald's will 'extension' join the menu?" *The Wall Street Journal*, 29 May 2002, B1.

32. Jack Neff, "R&D marketing," *Advertising Age*, 25 March 2002, 4.

33. Arik Hesseldahl, "A flashlight that goes on forever," www.forbes.com, 17 May 2002.

34. Stephanie Thompson, "'To go' becoming the way to go," *Advertising Age*, 13 May 2002, 73.

35. Bernard Ryan, Jr., *It Works!* (New York: American Association of Advertising Agencies, 1991), 10.

36. John Diefenbach, "Survey finds most powerful brands," *Advertising Age*, 11 July 1988.
37. Elliot Spagat, "RadioShack's revamp runs on batteries," *The Wall Street Journal*, 25 June 2002, B5.
38. Peter Murane, "Low price no bargain as brand building tool," *Advertising Age*, 1 July 2002, 34.
39. Caroline Wilbert, "Hotels fight for control of Web bookings," *The Atlanta Journal-Constitution*, 15 September 2002, G1.
40. Schonfeld & Associates, "Advertising rates & budgets," www.rab.com.
41. "Advertising and promotion: How much should you spend?" *Cahners Advertising Research Report*, No. 2000.10.
42. Stephanie Thompson, "Ragu gets a robust boost in advertising," *Advertising Age*, 27 May 2002, 1.
43. Mark Schumann, "Mega brands," *Advertising Age*, 22 July 2002, S–1.
44. "Race you to the checkout," *American Demographics*, May 2000, 9.
45. Kathryn Kranhold, "Can GE make Lexan as famous as Teflon?" *The Wall Street Journal*, 7 March 2003, B1.
46. Karen Breen Vogel, "BTB requires new models, strategies," *DM News*, 6 March 2000, 26.

Chapter 3

p. 68 © Colin Anderson/Brand X Pictures/PictureQuest
p. 70 Courtesy of Euro RSCG MVBMS Partners and Intel.
1. Robert Berner, "P&G. New and improved," *Business Week*, 7 July 2003, pp. 52–63.
2. Bruce Tait, "A brand new idea," *Brand Marketing*, February 2002, 23.
3. Steven Rosenbush, "Verizon's gutsy bet," *Business Week*, 4 August 2003, 53.
4. Bruce Tait, "A brand new idea," *Brand Marketing*, February 2002, 23.
5. Charles Forelle, "Deodorant makers sniff out ways to sell a stagnant market," *The Wall Street Journal*, 16 June 2003, 1.
6. Jack Trout, *Differentiate or Die* (New York: John Wiley & Sons, 2000), 23.
7. "Royal Crown plotting a comeback with new owners' financial support," *The Atlanta Journal and Constitution*, 6 March 1994, C8.
8. Patricia Callahan, "Freeze-dried berries heat up cereal dual," *The Wall Street Journal*, 15 May 2003, B2.
9. Stephanie Thompson, "EZ being green: Kids line is latest Heinz innovation," *Advertising Age*, 10 July 2000, 3.
10. Charlotte Moore, "Glowing reports about the health benefits of inexpensive aspirin are still emerging," *The Atlanta Journal-Constitution, 13 May 2003 E1.*
11. Antonio Marraza, "The very tangible value of the brand," www.Landor.com, 2000.
12. *David Martin, Romancing the Brand* (New York: Amacon, 1989), xiv.
13. Norman Berry, "Revitalizing brands," *Viewpoint*, July–August 1987, 18.
14. Howard, Merrell & Partners, "Introduction," 2000.
15. J. Walker Smith and Ann Clurman, *Rocking the Ages* (New York: Harper Business, 1997), 276–286.
16. Diane Crispell and Kathleen Brandenburg, "What's in a brand?" *American Demographics*, May 1993, 26–28.
17. Charlie Wrench, "Brand integration: A tough nut to crack," www.Landor.com, May 2003.
18. Chip Walker, "How strong is your brand?" *Marketing Tools*, January/February 1995, 46–53.
19. Alan M. Webber, "What great brands do," *Fast Company*, August–September 1997, 96–100.

Chapter 4

p. 100 Courtesy of VitroRobertson, Inc., Asics, and James Schwartz, photographer.

1. Joe Marconi, "Targets big enough to miss," *American Demographics*, October 1996, 51–52.
2. John McManus, "Street wiser," *American Demographics*, July/August 2003, 32–35.
3. Alison Stein Wellner, "Generational divide," *American Demographics*, October 2000, 56.
4. Allison Stein Wellner, "The next 25 years," *American Demographics*, April 2003, 24–31.
5. Christine Bunish, "Multicultural guide," *Advertising Age*, 3 November 2003, M1.
6. William H. Frey, "Revival," *American Demographics*, October 2003, 26–31.
7. Christine Bunish, "Multicultural guide," *Advertising Age*, 3 November 2003, M1.
8. Ibid.
9. "Disney's Davila: Multicultural "not a fad," *Advertising Age*, 3 November 2003, M3.
10. Marcia Mogelonsky, "America's hottest markets," *American Demographics*, January 1996, 20–27.
11. Michelle Conlin, "The new gender gap," *Business Week*, 26 May 2003, 74–80.
12. Mary Lou Quinlan, *Just Ask a Woman* (Hoboken, NJ: John Wiley & Sons, 2003).
13. James Morrow, "A place for one," *American Demographics*, November 2003, 24–29.
14. "Ones add up fast," *American Demographics*, November 2003, 30–31.
15. Alison Stein Wellner, "Generational divide," *American Demographics*, October 2000, 52–58.
16. Stephen J. Kraus, "Gen Xers' reinvented traditionalism," *Brandweek*, 5 June 2000, 28–30.
17. Edna Gundersen, "Where will teen tastes land next?" *USA Today*, 22 September 2000, E1–E2.
18. Ellen Neuborne, "Generation Y," *Business Week*, 15 February 1999, 82.
19. Sholnn Freeman and Norihiko Shirouzu, "Toyota's Gen Y Gamble," *The Wall Street Journal*, 30 July 2003, B1.
20. David F. D'Alessandro, *Brand Warfare* (New York: McGraw-Hill, 2000), 38–39.
21. J. Walker Smith and Ann Clurman, *Rocking the Ages* (New York: HarperCollins, 1997), 16.
22. Philip Kotler, *Marketing Management*, 8th ed. (Upper Saddle River, NJ: Prentice Hall, 1994), 18–21.
23. Frederick E. Webster, Jr., "Defining the new marketing concept," *Marketing Management*, 2, no. 4, 23–31.
24. Frederick E. Webster, Jr., "Executing the new marketing concept," *Marketing Management*, 3, no. 1, 9–16.
25. Kevin Maney, "Tomorrow's super bar codes create today's nervous Nellies," *USA Today*, 8 October 2003, 3B.
26. Robert C. Blattberg, Thomas Buesing, and Subrata K. Sen, "Segmentation strategies for new national brands," *Journal of Marketing*, Fall 1980, 60.
27. Rebecca Piirto Heath, "The frontier of psychographics," *American Demographics*, July 1996, 40.
28. David J. Lipke, "Head trips," *American Demographics*, October 2000, 38.
29. Kevin J. Clancy and Robert S. Shulman, *The Marketing Revolution* (New York: Harper Business, 1991), 63.
30. Jack Trout, *Differentiate or Die* (New York: John Wiley & Sons, 2000), 185.
31. Alvin Achenbaum, "Understanding niche marketing," *Adweek*, 1 December 1986, 62.
32. Ira P. Scheiderman, "Niche marketers should follow old rules," *BrandMarketing*, August 2000, 6.
33. Jeff Neff, "Huggies little swimmers tests out a new niche," *Advertising Age*, 25 August 1997, 8.
34. Lisa Sanders, "Startup shop Amalgamated targets big-spending Bobos," *Advertising Age*, 9 September 2003, 89.

35. Kevin J. Clancy and Robert S. Shulman, *The Marketing Revolution* (New York: Harper Business, 1991), 84–87.

36. Jack Trout and Al Ries, *The Positioning Era* (New York: Ries Cappiello Colwell, 1973), 38–41.

37. David A. Aaker, *Managing Brand Equity* (New York: The Free Press, 1991), 114–115.

38. Philip Kotler, *Kotler on Marketing* (New York: The Free Press, 1999), 57–58.

39. David N. Martin, *Be the Brand* (Richmond: New Marketplace Books, 2000), 88–98.

40. Lewis Brosowsky, "Ad themes that last," *Advertising Age,* 28 February 1994, 26.

41. Scott Leith, "For a limited time," *The Atlanta Journal-Constitution,* 9 September 2003, C1.

42. Kenneth Hein, "The age of reason," *American Demographics,* 27 October 2003, 24–26.

Chapter 5

p. 134   © Ryan McVay.Photodisc/PictureQuest

p. 136   Courtesy of Savannah Electric, A Southern Company.

1. "We've been here before," *Graphic Design:USA,* September 2000, 70.

2. James Melvin Lee, *History of American Journalism,* rev. ed. (Boston: Houghton Mifflin, 1933), 74.

3. Ken Roman and Jane Maas, *How to Advertise* (New York: St. Martin Press, 2003), 216.

4. Ann Cooper, "Bernbach's children come of age," *Adweek,* 25 March 1996, 33–36.

5. Jeff Weiner, "Anxious ranks," *Agency,* Spring 1994, 42.

6. Suzanne Vranica, "Marketers shop for fresh creativity," *The Wall Street Journal,* 28 July 2003, B3.

7. Mark Gleason, "Agency nets puzzle over brand identity," *Advertising Age,* 6 May 1996, 15.

8. Jan Larson, "It's a small world, after all," *Marketing Tools,* September 1997, 47–51.

9. Ashish Banerjee, "Global campaigns don't work; multinationals do," *Advertising Age,* 18 April 1994, 23.

10. Ken Roman and Jane Maas, *How to Advertise* (New York: St. Martin Press, 2003), 43–44.

11. "How does global marketing benefit consumers?" *Adweek,* 17 November 2003, 96.

12. "Coke seeks Ad Formula with Global Appeal, *Atlanta Journal-Constitution,* 18 November 1991, A5.

13. Catharine P. Taylor, "Are holding companies obsolete?' *Adweek,* 9 June 2003, 30–31.

14. Claire Atkinson, "Publicis networks switch to client-based accounting," *Advertising Age,* 31 March 2003, 8.

15. Lisa Sanders and Jean Halliday, "GM hammers agency costs," *Advertising Age,* 17 November 2003, 1.

16. Noreen O'Leary, "The 30-second spot is dead long live the 30-second spot," *Adweek,* 17 November 2003, 12–14.

17. Interview with Kristen Kyle, 5 December 2000.

18. Scott Leith, "Coke names a huge winner," *Atlanta Journal-Constitution,* 24 November 2003, B1.

19. Terrence Poltrack, "Pay dirt," *Agency,* July/August 1991, 20–25.

20. Stan Beals, "Fresh approaches to agency compensation," *Advertising Age,* 29 August 1994, 20.

21. Leon Stafford, "Tourism officials barter to stretch tight advertising budgets," *The Atlanta Journal-Constitution,* 15 May 2003, D1.

22. David Aaker, "The agency as brand architect," *American Advertising Spring* 1996, 18–21.

Chapter 6

p. 170   Courtesy of McRae Communications, Techsonic Industries, Inc. and Humminbird.

1. Jack Neff,"P&G recategorizes marketing directors," *Advertising Age,* 31 March 2003, 6.

2. Scott Hume, "Integrated marketing: Who's in charge here?" *Advertising Age,* 23 March 1993, 3.

3. William N. Swain, "An exploratory assessment of the IMC PARADIGM: Where are we, and where do we go from here," *Integrated Marketing Communication Research Journal,* Vol 9, Spring 2003, 3–11.

4. Hy Haberman, "Why some agencies fail at integrated marketing," *Advertising Age,* 21 April 2003, 18.

5. Don E. Schultz, "Managers still face substantial IMC questions," *Marketing News,* 27 September 1993, 10.

6. Marian Burk Wood, "Clear IMC goals build strong relationships," *Marketing News,* 23 June 1997, 11.

7. Al Ries, "Why marketing people get it wrong," *AdAge.com,* 17 March 2003.

8. Matthew Boyle, "Brand killers," *Fortune,* 11 August 2003, 88–100.

9. Judann Pollack and Jack Neff, "Marketer decree: Be a top brand or begone," *Advertising Age,* 15 September 1997, 1.

10. Leslie H. Moeller, Sharat K. Mathur, and Randall Rothenberg, "The better half: The artful science of ROI marketing," *Strategy +Business,* Spring 2003, 32–45.

11. *26th Gallagher Report Consumer Advertising Survey.*

12. Speech Ad Age's Madison & Vine conference at Beverly Hills Hotel in Los Angeles, CA, 6 February 2003.

13. Robert M. Viney, "Solving the agency–client mismatch," *Advertising Age,* 24 May 1993, 20.

14. AnthonyBianco and Wendy Zellner, "Is Wal-Mart too powerful?" *Business Week,* 6 October 2003, 100–110.

15. Jack Neff, "Wal-Marketing:How to benefit in Bentonville," *Advertising Age,* 6 October, 1.

16. Andrew McMains, "Agency image a hot topic at 4A's summit," *Adweek,* 16 June 2003, 10.

17. Stefano Hat-field, "Testing on trial," *Creativity,* October 2003, 30.

18. Joe Mandee, "How far is too far?" *Agency,* May/June 1991, 9.

19. Eleftheria Parpis, "Moore to Come," *Adweek,* 18 September 2000, 28.

20. Lisa Sanders, "Ford ad chief hails content convergence," 18 April 2003, 3.

21. Normandy Madden, "Text messaging ads on fast track in Asia," Advertising Age, 2 December 2002, 12.

22. David Kaplan, "New survey shows where clients get no satisfaction," *Adweek,* 30 June 2003, 9.

23. Stuart Elliott, "Survey on client–agency relations," NYT.com, 21 October 2003.

24. Karen Benezra, "Sea change: Agencies diversify to regain client trust," *Adweek,* 19 April 1999, 42–43.

25. Jennifer Comiteau, "Power play," *Adweek,* 10 June 1996, 33–38.

26. Laura Petrecca, "The year in review: Is it a record pace?" *Advertising Age,* 2 June 1997, 1.

27. Suzanne Vranica, "Marketers shop for fresh creativity," *The Wall Street Journal,* 28 July 2003, B3.

28. Russell H. Colley, *Defining Advertising Goals for Measured Effectiveness* (New York: Association of National Advertisers, 1961).

Chapter 7

p. 200   © Jim Arbogast/Photodisc/PictureQuest

p. 202   Courtesy of VitroRobertson, Inc., Taylor Guitar, and Michael Eastman, photographer.

1. McCann Worldgroup, www.mccann.com/insight/bobcoen.html.

2. Stuart Elliot, "Forcasters expect end to ad industry's recession in 2004," *The New York Times,* 9 December 2003, C1, 6.

3. Brent Schlender, "Sony plays to win," *Fortune,* 1 May 2000, 144.

4. Rich Thomaselli, "Reebok's Terry Tate set to play dirty bass," *Advertising Age,* 21 April 2003, 4, 48.

5. "The state of the agency," *Adweek,* 17 November 2003, 70–71.

6. Jonathan Bond and Richard Kirshenbaum, "Using media to get under the radar," *Agency,* Winter 1998, 56.

7. Joe Mandese, "In the eye of the beholder," *American Demographics*, December 1999, 27.
8. Mickey Marks, "Millennial satiation," *Advertising Age*, 14 February 2000, S16.
9. Erwin Ephron, "A new media-mix strategy," *Advertising Age*, 28 February 2000, S10.
10. Claritas, www.claritas.com
11. Hugh Cannon, "Does traditional media planning apply to new media?" in *Proceedings of the 1999 Conference of the American Academy of Advertising*, Marilyn S. Roberts, ed., 279.
12. Allen Brivic, *What Every Account Executive Should Know About Media*, a publication of the American Association of Advertising Agencies, 1989, 14.

Chapter 8

p. 228   Courtesy of SuperStock, Inc.
1. David Fisher and Marshall Jon Fisher, *Tube: The Invention of Television* (Washington: Counterpoint, 1996), 22.
2. www.tvb.org/mediacomparisons, 31 August 2003.
3. Ibid.
4. Barry L. Sherman, *The Television Standard* (New York: Gerson Lehrman Group, 1999), 2.
5. Jane Dalzell, "Who's on first," *Advertising Age, 50 Years of TV Advertising*, Spring 1995, 8.
6. Clarence Page, "A bridge to the new media century," *The Park Distinguished Visitors Series*, Ithaca College, 2000, 6.
7. Sherman, *The Television Standard*, 161.
8. Andrew Green, "Clutter crisis countdown," *Advertising Age*, 21 April 2003, 22.
9. Ibid.
10. Scott Woolley, "Zap," *Forbes Magazine*, 29 September 2003, 77.
11. Richard Linnett, "*Friends* tops TV price chart," *Advertising Age*, 15 September 2003, 46.
12. "Mil-a-minute TV not all bad," *Advertising Age*, 23 September 1996, 28.
13. Chuck Ross, "Optimizers & TV upfront: How they affect ad buying," *Advertising Age*, 29 June 1999, 16.
14. The term *scatter plan* has two definitions. The first refers to buying a group of spots across a number of programs. The second meaning refers to those spots that are still available after the up-front buying season is completed.
15. Matthew Rose and Joe Flint, "Affiliates challenge power of networks," *The Charlotte Observer*, from www.montereyherald.com, 19 October 2003.
16. www.mccann.com/insight/bobcoen.html, 30 July 2003.
17. Wayne Friedman, "Familiar *Friends* tops syndie pricing," *Advertising Age*, 20 January 2003, 25.
18. Cynthia Littleton, "ABC inks long-term *Wheel/Jeopardy* deals," www.tvgen.com, 21 October 1998.
19. Joe Mandese, "Syndie stars easy to find," *Advertising Age*, 17 January 2000, S4.
20. "The history of cable," a service of the Pennsylvania Cable & Telecommunication Association, www.pcta.com.
21. "What is it About TV? Publishing makes the one magazine spin-off of a TV property suceed, while others fail miserably?" Real Media Riffs, Mediapost, 11 September 2003, www.mediapost.com.
22. Jon Fine, "Disney and Hearst extend Lifetime brand to newsstand," *Advertising Age*, 14 April 2003, 8.
23. Kalpana Srinivasan, "Interactive television allows for shopping by remote," *Athens Daily News*, 13 May 2000, 4B.
24. "1995 cable TV facts," a publication of the Cable Advertising Bureau, 72.
25. "A Guide to Cable Interconnects 2001/2002," *Advertising Age*, 1 October 2001, A3.
26. Woolley, "Zap," 77.
27. Frank Rose, "The fast-forward, on-demand, network-smashing future of television," *Wired*, October 2003, 160.
28. Scott Woolley, "Zap," 79.

29. "Map to entertainment marketing," *Advertising Age*, 15 September 2003, C1, C5.
30. Paul J. Gough, "Ad Execs debate value of plugs, sponsorships," *MediaPost's Media Daily News*, 11 September 2003, http://www.mediapost.com.
31. Paul J. Gough, "New TV ratings system tracks product placement, sponsorship," *MediaPost's Media Daily News*, 28 October 2003, www.mediapost.com.
32. Material in this section is from Nielsen Media Research.
33. Frank Saxe, "Nielsen expands partnership with Arbitron," www.mediapost.com, 6 March 2003.
34. Bill Carter, "Where have television's big stars gone?" www.nytimes.com, 14 June 1999.

Chapter 9

p. 258   Courtesy of Sony Electronics Inc.
1. Nielsen begins ratings; 'Lux,' 'Lone Ranger' lead," *Advertising Age*, 19 April 1999, 89.
2. http://www.arbotron.com, 16 June 2003.
3. http://www.rab.com, 28 September 2003.
4. Arbitron/Edison Media Research and Multimedia 10: "The emerging digital consumer," 28 September 2003, www.arbitron.com/webcast_ratings/home/htm.
5. How can I stand out from the competition," www.rab.com, 24 May 2000.
6. Alex Kuczynski, "Radio squeezes empty air space for profit," www.nytimes.com., 6 January 2000.
7. Station information from Broadcast and Cable Yearbook, 2002–2003 (New Providence, NJ: R.R. Bowker Publications, 2002).
8. Survey process," www.arbitron.com/ad_agencies/survprocess.htm 29 September 2003.
9. Arbitron/Edison Media Research and multimedia 10: "The emerging digital consumer," www.arbitron.com/webcast_ratings/home/htm, 28 September 2003.
10. Black radio today 2003 edition," www.Arbitron.com, 24 August 2003.
11. Radio indusry introduces EDI, new ad standards to facilitate buys," *MediaPost's MediaDailyNews*, www.mediapost.com/articleID=221105, 3 October 2003.

Chapter 10

p. 280   Courtesy of Corbis/Bettmann.
1. Marc Gunther, "Publish or perish?" *Fortune*, 10 January 2000, 148.
2. Rebecca Ross Albers, "Study reveals Internet gains," *Presstime*, November 2000, 25.
3. "A nation online: How Americans are expanding their use of the Internet," U.S. Department of Commerce, February 2002, 10.
4. Dan Okrent, "The death of print?" Hearst New Media Lecture, Columbia University, 14 December 1999.
5. www.naa.org/artpage.cfm?AID=1573&SID=1022, 1 October 2003.
6. Jon Fine, "New Web site in WSJ's plans for 'Weekend,'" *Advertising Age*, 14 August 2000, 1.
7. Adapted from Leo Bogart, "Newspapers," *Media Studies Journal*, Spring/Summer 1999, 68.
8. Facts about newspapers," www.naa.org, 10 September 2003.
9. How to reach 141.6 million people," *Advertising Age*, 13 October 2003, N3.
10. "The newest brand-building power tool: Targeted newspaper inserts," *Promo*, November 1999, 49.
11. John Gaffney, "Kmart insert grows up," *MediaPost's Media Daily News*, www.mediapost.com/dtls_dsp_news?newsID=194522, 4 February 2003.
12. Jake Finch, "Online classified ads: Branded for success," *Presstime*, May 1999, 32.
13. Gunther, "Publish or perish?" 152.
14. James Conaghan, "What's roiling retail," *Presstime*, January 2000, 2.
15. www.mccann.com/insight/bobcoen.html, 30 September 2003.

16. *Academic Casebook*, a publication of Audit Bureau of Circulations.
17. www.naa.org/info/facts03/20_facts2003.html, 8 October 2003.
18. www.naa.org/info/facts03/21_facts.html, 8 October 2003.
19. www.naa.prg/info/facts03/8_2003.html, 2 October 2003.
20. www.diversityinc.com/members/5534print.cfm, 9 September 2003.
21. www.naa.org/info/facts03/13_facts2003.html, 12 September 2003.
22. Nancy M. David, "Ring around the metros," *Presstime*, September 1999, 54.

Chapter 11

p. 312   Courtesy of Stockbyte.
1. Unless otherwise noted, the source of information in this chapter is the Magazine Publishers of America. www.magazine.org
2. Aimee Deeken, "Service upgrades," *Mediaweek*, 2 December 2002, 45–46.
3. www.mediaweek.com/mediaweek/magzine/top_title.jsp, 30 August 2003.
4. Cristina Merrill, "Keeping up with teens," *American Demographics*, October 1999, 29.
5. Medimark Research Inc. as found on www.teenpeople.com, 30 August 2003.
6. James Playsted Wood, *Magazines in the United States* (New York: The Ronald Press Company, 1949), 104.
7. Jon Fine, "Parenting titles see growth spurt," *Advertising Age*, 11 August 2003, 31.
8. Nina Link, "Postal rate plan is indefensible, must be fought," *Advertising Age*, 24 April 2000, 68.
9. "High circulation costs stymie magazine growth opportunities," *Advertising Age*, 14 February 2000, S14.
10. "Taking charge of America's newsstand," *Advertising Age*, 6 October 2003, 38.
11. Bradley Johnson, "Still a buyer's market, but turning," *Advertising Age*, 17 March 2003, S2.
12. Karla Nagy, "Print scores big for ESPN," *Media & Brand Marketing*, May 2000, 31.
13. www.mediapost.com/articleId=212870, 26 July 2003.
14. Jon Fine, "Regional titles form ad network," *Advertising Age*, 1 September 2003, 8.
15. Ann Marie Kerwin, "Are tailor-made publications the right fit for advertisers?" *Advertising Age*, 5 October 1998, 3.
16. Verne Gay, "Milk, the magazine," *American Demographics*, February 2000, 32.
17. HissanFattah, "Custom publishing grows up," *American Demographics*, 2002, July/August 2002 26.
18. Ann Marie Kerwin, "Time Inc. buys sampling biz to help bolster 'Parenting,'" *Advertising Age*, 2 November 1998, 6.
19. Kate Fitzgerald, "Food magazines rev up event marketing," 16 December 2002, www.adage.com QuikFIND ID:AAO28P, 29 July 2003.
20. Matthew Rose, "In fight for ads, publishers often overstate their sales," *The Wall Street Journal*, 6 August 2003, A1. 10.
21. Ibid.
22. www.time-planner.com, 2 September 2003.
23. "The value and role of corporate advertising for business-to-business marketers," *Cahners Advertising Research Report*, #2000.15.
24. "Setting up shop," *Fortune Tech Guide, 2000*, 44.
25. Marc Spiegler, "Hot media buy: The farm report," *American Demographics*, October 1995, 18.

Chapter 12

p. 354   © James Dawson/Image Farm/PictureQuest
1. Unless otherwise noted, material for this section was provided by the Outdoor Advertising Association of America.

2. Eugene Morris, "O-O-H—Media's plain Jane sister," *Inside Out of Home*, January 2000, 7.
3. Carol Krol, "Life after tobacco," *Advertising Age*, 19 April 1999, 48.
4. Erwin Ephron, "About the medium," Outdoor Advertising Association of America, www.oaaa.org, 11 November 2003.
5. "Wall to wall walls," *Inside Out of Home*, April 1999, 1.
6. "Creating award winning outdoor," www.oaaa.org, 11 November 2004.
7. Normandy Madden, "Adidas introduces human billboards," *Advertising Age*, 1 September 2003, 11.
8. Elizabeth Boston, "Outdoor tries ratings systems," *Advertising Age*, 16 June 2003, 8.
9. Erwin Ephron, "Arbitron's 'Star Trek' adventure," *MediaWeek*, 9 September 2002, 21.
10. www.smrb.com.
11. www.oaaa.org/outdoor/councils/transit.asp, 11 November 2003.
12. www.oaaa.org/outdoor/councils/furniture.asp, 11 November 2003.
13. "Eller goes whole hog to promote transit shelter O-O-H," *Inside Out of Home*, April 1998, 4.
14. "P&G brings potty to parties," *Advertising Age*, 17 February 2003, 22.

Chapter 13

p. 378   Courtesy of Getty Images Inc. - Image Bank.
1. Robert McKim, "Strengthen affinities with spiral branding," *DMNews*, 19 June 2000, 32.
2. Paul J. Gough, "News analysis: The year in online 2003," www.mediapost.com/articleID=232513, 5 January 2003.
3. Jane Black, "No complaints in the online ad biz," from www.businessweek.com:technology/content/jul2003/tc20030725_1182_tc055.htm?tc, 29 July 2003.
4. Bill Hopkins and Britton Manasco, "The new technologies of marketing," *DMNews*, 22 May 2000, 51.
5. Steve Diller, "Direct marketing's role in a new society," *DMNews*, 1 May 2000, 22.
6. Jeff Neff, "Spam research reveals disgust with pop-up ads," *Advertising Age*, 25 August 2003, 1, 21.
7. H. Robert Wientzen, "Tackling the spam issue," www.the-dma.org/memberguide/tacklingspam.shml, 6 January 2004.
8. Association of National Advertisers (ANA), www.ana.net, 14 October 2003.
9. Zachary Rodgers, "Financial services customers warmed by e-mail," http://cyberatlas.internet.com, 8 December 2003.
10. Jeanie Casion, "Prying eyes," *Incentive*, November 1999, 20.
11. Mark Grimes, "Online advertising boot camp: Take no prisoners," *iMarketing News*, 20 August 1999, 11.
12. "Interact & integrate," *Advertising Age*, 19 June 2000, S40.
13. "The dot-com bubble-burst and disintermediation," www.internetnews.com/bus-news/article.php/554641, 9 January 2001.
14. Rebecca Flass, "Web supplants TV as teen media hub," www.mediaweek.com, 30 August 2003.
15. Rebecca Gardyn, "Born to be wired," *American Demographics*, April 2003, 14.
16. Flass, "Web supplants TV as teen media hub."
17. "Targeting dayparts on the Internet," research @mediapost.com (online newsletter), 19 March 2003.
18. "Research brief—At work Internet use peaks between 10 A.M. and noon," research@mediapost.com (online newsletter), 24 September 2002.
19. *Direct Marketing Course Rationale*, a publication of the Direct Marketing Educational Foundation, Inc., 1.
20. Charles Berger, "Data mining key to unlocking sales," *DMNews*, 21 February 2000, 41.
21. Jeff Caplan, "Predictive data: It's the real-time thing," *DMNews*, 24 May 1999, 34.
22. Paul J. Gough, "News analysis: The year in online 2003."

23. Sandy Weiser, "TV, Net perfect match for DRTV marketers," *DMTV,* 20 March 2000, 53.
24. Denny Hatch, "Making DRTV work for you," *Target Marketing,* September 1999, 76.
25. National Trust for Historic Preservation, www.nationaltrust.org/help/mail_order_home.html, 5 January 2003.
26. Jack Schmid and Steve Trollinger, "Who's making the Net work?" *Target Marketing,* June 1999, 73.
27. John Buck, "What to look for in a fulfillment partner," *iMarketing News,* 24 September 1999, 22.
28. McCann Worldwide, www.mccann.com/insight/bobcoen.html, 8 September 2003.
29. Lewis Rashmir, "The first compiler was Charles Groves," *DMNews,* 15 February 1993, 35.

Chapter 14

p. 408   Courtesy of The Botsford Group.
1. David Vacek and Richard Sale, "100 years of promotion," *Promo,* August 1998, 142.
2. Betsy Spethmann, "Is advertising dead?" *Promo,* September 1998, 32.
3. Peter Breen, "Seeds of change," *Promo,* May 2000, A5.
4. Russell Bowman and Paul Theroux, "By the book," *Promo,* March 2000, 95.
5. www.partnerslevit.com/ConferenceRoom/Sales_ Promotions_and_Sweepstak/sales_promotions_and_ sweepstak.html.
6. Patricia Odell, "By the numbers," *Promo,* January 1 2004 promomagazine.com/ar/marketing_promo_exclusive_ numbers/index.htm.
7. Tom Lowry, "The prince of NASCAR," *BusinessWeek,* 23 February 2004, 90–98.
8. J. Jeffrey Inman and Russell S. Winer, "Where the rubber meets the road: A model of in-store consumer decision making," Working Paper, Marketing Science Institute, October 1998, 25.
9. "E-gads," *Promo,* August 1999, 59.
10. "Out of sight, out of mind," *Promo,* March 1996, 16.
11. Richard Sele, "The display police," *Promo,* March 1999, 80.
12. Kate Bertrand, "Premiums prime the market," *Advertising Age,* May 1998, S6.
13. David Vacek, "Getting in gear," *Promo,* May 1998, S5.
14. Unless otherwise noted, material in this section was provided by the Promotional Products Association International.
15. "The digital sales pitch," *Promo,* May 2000, A19.
16. Research by Louisiana State University and Glenrich Business Studies reported in www.ppai.org.
17. Matthew Kinsman, "The hard sell," *Promo,* April 1, 2003, http://promomagazine.com/ar/marketing_hard_sell/index.htm.
18. Richard Sale, "Not your mother's coupon," *Promo,* April 1999, 56.
19. Matthew Kinsman, "The hard sell."
20. Carol Angrisano, "Outside the boom box," *Brand Marketing,* May 2002, 16–17.
21. Ira Teinowitz, "Marketers yield to sweepstakes curbs," *Advertising Age,* 24 May 1999, 61.
22. The term tear sheets comes from the practice of a newspaper ad manager tearing a page from the paper and sending it to a manufacturer verifying that the ad ran in the paper.
23. Yellow Pages I.M.A., www.yellowpagesima.org/advertising/about.cfm, 30 October 2003.
24. Matthew Kinsman, "Signs of life," http://promomagazine.com/ar/marketing_signs_life/index.htm, February 4, 2004.
25. Paul Nolan and Vincent Alonzo, "Making the mark." *Incentive,* August 1999, 30.

Chapter 15

p. 447   © RubberBall Productions/Rubberball Productions/PictureQuest
p. 448   Life Savers® is a registered trademark of KF Holdings, Inc., and is used with permission. Courtesy of Foote Cone & Belding, New York.
1. Sergio Zyman, *The End of Marketing As We Know It* (New York: HarperCollins, 1999), 62.
2. CMOR, www.cmor.org/resp_coop_news1003_2.htm, 2 December 2003.
3. Jon Steel, *Truth, Lies & Advertising* (New York: John Wiley and Sons, Inc., 1998), 36.
4. Ibid., 43
5. Laura Petrecca, "The oracle workers," *Advertising Age,* 12 June 2000, 20.
6. David Goetzl, "O&M turns reality TV into research tool," *Advertising Age,* 10 July 2000, 6.
7. Tobi Elkin, "Product Pampering," *Brandweek,* 16 June 1997, 28–40.
8. Natalie Perkins, "Zeroing in on consumer values," *Advertising Age,* 22 March 1993, 23.
9. James A. Bayton, "Motivation, cognition, learning—Basic factors in consumer behavior," *Journal of Marketing,* January 1958, 282.
10. Melanie Wells, "In search of the buy button," *Forbes,* 1 September 2003, 62–66, 70.
11. SRI Consulting Business Intelligence, www.sric-bi.com/VALS, 14 January 2004.
12. Yankelovich, www.yankelovich.com, 10 December 2003.
13. Melanie Wells, "In search of the buy button," *Forbes,* 1 September 2003, 70.
14. Ibid., 66.
15. Jean Halliday, "Automakers involve consumers," *Advertising Age,* 31 January 2000, 82.
16. Kathleen Sampey, "Nikon widens target to capture casual shooters," *Adweek,* 26 May 2003, 9.
17. Jim Aitchison, *Cutting Edge Advertising* (Singapore: Prentice-Hall, 1999), 28–29.
18. PACT—Positioning Advertising Copy Testing, The PACT Agencies Report 1982, 6–25.
19. Lisa Sanders and Jack Neff, "Copy tests under fire from new set of critics," *Advertising Age,* 9 June 2003, 6.
20. Ibid.

Chapter 16

p. 476   Courtesy of Savannah Electric, A Southern Company.
1. "Great Advertising—it's simply a must," viewpoint, January 1999, pp 12–13.
2. Kenneth Roman and Jane Maas, *"How to Advertise,"* 3rd ed. (New York: St. Martin's Press, 2003), 215.
3. Jim Aitchison, *Cutting Edge Advertising* (Singapore: Prentice-Hall, 1999), 31–35.
4. Stefano Hatfield, "World's hot shop is in Paris, and it's Veruroegen's TBWA," *Advertising Age,* 4 August 2003, 16.
5. Luke Sullivan, *Hey Whipple, Squeeze This: A Guide to Creating Great Ads* (New York: John Wiley & Sons, 1998), 60–65.
6. John Hegarty, "My apologies for this letter being so long. Had I more time it would have been shorter," *Creativity,* March 1997, 12.
7. Jim Aitchison, Cutting Edge Advertising (Singapore: Prentice-Hall, 1999) pp.
8. Ron Huey, interviews by W. Ronald Lane, September 1994 , September 1997, August 2003.
9. David Martin, *Romancing the Brand* (New York: Amacom, 1989), 134–136.
10. From an American Association of Advertising Agencies speech, 17 May 1980.
11. Dick Costello, "The big picture," *Adweek,* 29 March 1999, 25.

12. The term *copy* is a carryover from the days in printing when a compositor, given a manuscript to set in type, was told to copy it. Before long, the manuscript itself became known as copy. In the creation of a printed ad, copy refers to all the reading matter in the ad. However, in the production of print ads, copy refers to the entire subject being reproduced—words and pictures alike. This is one of those instances in advertising when the same word is used in different senses, a practice that all professions and crafts seem to enjoy because it bewilders the uninitiated.

13. Luis Bassar, "Creative paths to great advertising," *Viewpoint*, September/October 1991, 23–24.

14. Dean Rieck, "Build consumer confidence with testimonials," *DM News*, 8 February 1999, 12.

15. Kevin Roberts, "Emotional rescue," speech, The AdTech Conference, San Francisco, May 2000.

16. Micahel McCarthy, "Imagination at work for GE," *USA Today*, 5 May 2003, 7B.

17. Jon Steel, *Truth, Lies, and Advertising* (New York: John Wiley & Sons, 1998), 141.

18. *Starch Tested Copy*, a publication of Roper Starch Worldwide.

19. Nancy Bernard, "Insight: Tide cleans up on the highway," *STEP*, May/June 2003, 30–34.

Chapter 17

p. 508   Courtesy of Sawyer Riley Compton and The Ritz-Carlton.

1. John Butler, "Want to make art?" *Adweek*, 26 May 2003, 20.

2. Noreen O'Leary, "Does creative count?" *Adweek*, 11 December 2000, 32.

3. Matthew Porter, "Sawyer Riley Compton, " *Communication Arts*, May/June 2002, 70–79.

4. Kate MaCarthur, "FCB's Taco Bell success might give it edge in KFC review," *Advertising Age*, 5 August 2003, 2.

5. Roper Starch Worldwide, Inc., *Starch Tested Copy*, Vol. 5, No. 3, 4.

6. Jim Aitchison, *Cutting Edge Advertising* (Singapore: Prentice-Hall, 1999), 112–165.

7. Jim Aitchison, *Cutting Edge Advertising* (Singapore: Prentice-Hall, 1999), 189.

8. Annual Color Forecast," *Graphic Design: USA*, June 2003, 61–80.

9. Cahners Publishing Co., CARR Report No. 118.5, 4.

10. "Art directing photography," *Art Direction*, March 1993, 42–54.

11. Jim Aitchison, *Cutting Edge Advertising* (Singapore: Prentice-Hall, 1999), 243–244.

12. "Stock visual decisions," *Graphic Design:USA*, 128.

Chapter 18

p. 534   Courtesy of Bright Ideas Group and the Tubman African American Museum.

1. Robert Hannan, "Better, faster, cheaper," *Agency*, Fall 1997, 42–43.

2. Halli Forcinio, "Let's get digital," *Brand Marketing*, October 2000, 46–48.

3. Allan Haley, "What's your type," *STEP*, May/June 2003, 83.

4. Allan Haley, "Using all capitals is a graphic oxymoron," *U & lc*, Fall 1991, 14–15.

5. Richard M. Adams II, "Color-proofing systems," *Pre*, March/April 1994, 55–59.

6. William Ryan and Theodore Conover, *Graphic Communications Today*, 4th ed. (Clifton Park, NY: Thomson, 2004), 308–309.

Chapter 19

p. 562   Courtesy of Howard, Merrell & Partners and BB&T.

1. Kate MacArthur, "Subway sales so strong marketer delays new ads," *Advertising Age*, 19 June 2000, 8.

2. "Entertained by commercials," *American Demographics*, November 1997, 41.

3. Colin Bessonette, "Q&A on the news," *The Atlanta Journal*, 1 January 1996, A2.

4. Cyndee Miller, "Celebrities hot despite scandals," *Marketing News*, 28 March 1994, 1–2.

5. Davin Seay, "The beat goes on as advertisers increase efforts to tag products with hip sound images," *Brandweek*, 22 May 2000, 3–10.

6. *Music—How to Use It for Commerical Production*, a publication of the Television Bureau of Advertising, New York.

7. Stefano Hatfield, "Music to watch sales by," *Creativity*, July 2003, 34–35.

8. Stuart Elliott, "Berry Burst Cheerios: A love story?" www.nyt.com, 13 January 2004.

9. Rick Lyon, "The circle game," *Creativity*, September 1997, 18.

10. Warren Burger, "Action fever," *Creativity*, June 2000, 47–49.

11. Trevor Boyer, "Hot spots," *Millimeter*, June 2003, 13.

12. Michael Spier, "Why CGI?" *Millimeter*, May 1997, 93–100.

13. Beth Jacques, "The do's and don'ts of mixing animation and live action," *Millimeter*, April 1994, 77–82.

14. Kristinha McCort, "Production review," *Millimeter*, April 1999, 27.

15. American Federation of Television & Radio Artists, www.aftra.org/member/irates.html, 15 January 2004.

16. American Association of Advertising Agencies, news release, 13 December 2003.

17. Adcritic.com from creativity magazine, www.adcritic.com, 12 Januay 2004.

18. "AAAA Survey Finds 3 Percent Drop in Cost to Produce 30-Second TV Commercials," American Association of Advertising Agencies, news release, December 2001.

19. Bootsie Battle, "Approval system speeds projects," *Millimeter*, August 2003, 61–62.

20. Association of National Advertisers, news release, 11 March 2003.

Chapter 20

p. 592   Courtesy of Howard, Merrell & Partners and Hangers Cleaners.

1. Tom Monahan, "Advertising," *Communication Arts*, July 1994, 198.

2. Erik Gruenwedel, "Net radio daze," *Adweek*, 1 May 2000, IQ26–27.

3. Bruce Bendinger, *The Copy Workshop Workbook* (Chicago: Bruce Bendinger Creative Communications, Inc., 1988), 214.

Chapter 21

p. 612   Courtesy of Bevil Advertising and Folks.

1. Beth Snyder Bulik, "The brand police," *Business 2.0*, 28 November 2000, 144–148.

2. Roger Sametz, "Moving from cooperate identity to brand identity: A great logo only gets you so far," www.sametz.com, 20 January 2004.

3. www.Lippincottmercer.com, 1 February 2004.

4. "The Lanham Act: Alive and well after 50 years," International Trademark Association, www.inta.org/lanham.htm, 20 June 2000.

5. Richard A. Costello, "Focus on the brand," *The Advertiser*, Spring 1993, 11–18.

6. Michael E. Kannell, "Judge sides with BellSouth on copyright," *Atlanta Journal-Constitution*, 10 September 1997, C2.

7. Daniel L. Doden, "Selecting a brand name that aids marketing objectives," *Advertising Age*, 5 November 1990, 34.

8. Al Ries and Laura Ries, *The Immutable Laws of Internet Branding* (New York: HarperBusiness, 2000), 59–70.

9. Julie Cottineau, Interbrand Special Report: "The 'Name Game,'" 2002.

10. Jack Neff, "OrangeGlo enters spray fray with Oxi," *Advertising Age*, 8 September 2003, 4.

11. Richard Linnett, "Anderson's accenture gets $175 mil ad blitz," *Advertising Age*, 4 December 2000, 20.
12. David Goetzl, "Delta flies toward $1 billion in Web sales," *Advertising Age*, 11 September 2000, 54–56.
13. Wendy Jedlicka, "Packaging," *Communication Arts*, March/April 2000, 111.
14. www.edf_org/edf/atissue/vol4–1 22 January 2004.
15. Betsy Spethmann, "The mystique of the brand: Jarred, bagged, boxed, canned," *Brandweek*, 27 June, 1994, 25.
16. Anita K. Hersh and John Lister, "Brand identity," *The Advertiser*, Spring 1993, 66–71.
17. Frank Tobolski, "Package design requires research," *Marketing News*, 6 June 1994, 4.
18. Terry Lofton, "If your brand's number two, get with the package program," *Brandweek*, 27 June 1994, 26.
19. Greg Erikson, "Seeing double," *Brandweek*, October 17 1994, 30–55.
20. Carol Angrisani, "The silent salesman," *Brand Marketing*, February 2002, 15–16.
21. Allen Adamson, "Future of branding based on current trends," *Landor.com*, 21 January 2004.
22. Allen Adamson. "Future of branding based on current trends," www.landor.com/index.cfm?fuseaction=cBranding. getArticle&storyid=264, 12 March 2004.

Chapter 22

p. 646   Courtesy of The Botsford Group and Mentos.
1. Kenneth Roman and Jane Maas, *How to Advertise*, (New York: St. Martin's Press, 2003), 48–49.
2. Ann M. Mack, "Web ads score on recognition factor," *Adweek*, 19 January 2004, 12.
3. Ruth La Ferla, "Generation E.A.: Ethnically ambiguous," *The New York Times*, 28 December 2003, Section 9, 1.
4. Kenneth Roman and Jane Maas, *The New How to Advertise* (New York: St. Martin's Press, 1992), 71–78.
5. Lisa Siracuse, "Looks aren't everything: An examination of brand personality," *Integrated Marketing Communications Research Journal*, Spring 1997, 38–39.
6. "Being true to Dew," *Brandweek*, 24 April 2000, 28–31.
7. Gary Levin, "Tracing ads' impact," *Advertising Age*, 4 November 1991, 49.
8. Stuart Elliott, "In advertising: The risky business of 'shockvertising'", *The New York Times Direct*, 9 February 2004,.
9. J. Walter Thompson, www.jwt.com/totalbranding, 14 December 2003.

Chapter 23

p. 670   © RubberBall Productions/Rubberball Productions/PictureQuest
p. 672   Courtesy of Homer TLC, Inc., Copyright 2003.
1. Thomas Friedman, "9/11 may save the day for globalization efforts," *The Atlanta Journal-Constitution*, 22 September 2002, F9.
2. Karby Leggett and Todd Zaun, "World's car makers race to keep up with China boom," *The Wall Street Journal*, 13, December 2002, A1.
3. Paola Hjelt, "The world's largest corporations," www.fortune.com, 14 September 2002.
4. Leslie Chang and Peter Wonacott, "Cracking China's market," *The Wall Street Journal*, 9 January 2003, B1.
5. Normandy Madden, "China's power brands eye global expansion," *Advertising Age*, 13 January 2003, 12.
6. Kim Allen, "Worldwide Internet usage near 430 million," www.digitrends.net, 9 September 2002.
7. "1945: Arthur C. Clarke's dream," www.orbitsat.com/AboutSat/history.com, 15 September 2002.
8. Chester Dawson, Larry Armstrong, Joann Muller, and Kathleen Kerwin, "The Americanization of a Japanese icon," www.businessweek.com, 15 April 2002.

9. Christopher Seward, "View from top: Coke wandered off its path," *The Atlanta Journal-Constitution*, 28 March 2000, D5.
10. Erin White and Jeffery A. Trachtenberg, "One size doesn't fit all," *The Wall Street Journal*, 1 October 2003, B1.
11. "Clients form strategic partnerships with the agency," *Advertising Age*, 18 March 2002, C12.
12. Jack Neff, "P&G flexes muscle for global branding," *Advertising Age*, 3 June 2002, 53.
13. "Three model approaches," *Target Marketing*, February 1996, 12.
14. Erin White and Sarah Ellison, "Unilever ads offer a tribute to dirt," *The Wall Street Journal*, 2 June 2003, B3.
15. Jerry Useem, "Exxon's African Adventure," www.fortune.com, 1 April 2002.
16. Keith B. Richburg, "French linguists lash out at EU's labeling rule," *The Atlanta Journal-Constitution*, 8 August 2002, A8.
17. Christopher Rhoads, "Europe is out of sync despite its common charter," *The Wall Street Journal*, 2 January 2002, A6.
18. Cara B. Dipasquale, "Making data more relevant at Wunderman, byte by byte," *Advertising Age*, 2 September 2002, 24.
19. From "Global Gate," newsletter of Direct Language Communications, Inc., September 1998.
20. Normandy Madden, "The faces of China," www.adageglobal.com, 31 May 2002.
21. Dagmar Mussey, "Mars goes local," www.adageglobal.com, 17 April 2002.
22. Sheila M. Poole, "U.S. executives, foreigners learn to negotiate a two-way street," *The Atlanta Journal-Constitution*, 3 April 2002, E1.
23. Lisa Bannon and Carlta Vitzhum, "One-toy-fits-all: How industry learned to love the global kid," *The Wall Street Journal*, 29 April 2003, A1.
24. Erin White, "Outdoor ads may get indoor rival," *The Wall Street Journal*, 17 July 2002, B10.
25. Leon Stafford, "Missing out on the trend," *Atlanta Journal-Constitution*, 27 October 2002, F1.
26. Felipe Korzenny, Betty Ann Korzenny, Rebecca Abravanel, and Adrien Lopen Lanusse, "Hispanic advertising effectiveness and loyalty," www.hamer.com, 22 September 2002.
27. Michael J. McCarthy, "Texas dailies battle for Hispanic readers," *The Wall Street Journal*, 4 August 2003, B1.
28. Joyce Howard Price, "Spanish joins U.S. culture," www.washingtontimes.com, 20, May 2002.
29. Sandra Yin, "Look who's tuned in," *American Demographics*, October 2002, 26.
30. Rebecca Gardyn, "Habla English?" *American Demographics*, April 2001, 54.
31. Laurel Wentz, "Doors opening wide," *Advertising Age*, 6 May 2002, 24.
32. Laurel Wentz, "Bank of America quadruples ethnic ad budget," www.adage.com, 15 April 2002.
33. Kate MacArthur, "Beefing up Hispanic," *Advertising Age*, 4 March 2002, 28.
34. Doreen Hemlock, "As U.S. broadens tastes, importers profit," *The Atlanta Journal-Constitution*, 4 May 2001, F7.
35. Eduardo Porter and Betsy McKay, "Frito-Lay adds Spanish accent to snacks," *The Wall Street Journal*, 22 May 2002, B4.

Chapter 24

p. 704   Courtesy of Sawyer Riley Compton.
1. GNP is the total market value of all goods and services produced in a country or other economic unit in one year.
2. Introduction of the 4As "Value of Advertising" statement, American Association of Advertising Agencies, Inc., www.aaaa.org, 16 June 1999.
3. Rance Crane, "Now here's a radical theory: Ads last bastion of honesty," *Advertising Age*, 1 July 2002, 32.
4. Stephanie Thompson, "Cereal consortium tests TV effort," *Advertising Age*, 15 July 2002, 6.

5. Ira Teinowitz, "Black leaders turn up heat," *Advertising Age*, 16 September 2002, 4.

6. Hillary Chura, "Marketing messages for women fall short," *Advertising Age*, 23 September 2002, 4.

7. Matthew Grimm, "A spirited debate," *American Demographics*, April 2002, 48.

8. "About the council," www.adcouncil.org, 25 September 2002.

9. The remainder of this section is adapted from John McDonough, "The Ad Council at 60," *Advertising Age*, 29 April 2002, Special Section.

10. "Cause market forum," a supplement to *Advertising Age*, 28 July 2003, 2.

11. Sharyn Vane, "Taking care of business," *American Journalism Review*, March 2002, 61.

12. "Gambling with the future," a study by the Project for Excellence in Journalism," www.journalism.org, 25 March 2002.

13. Matt Kempner, "TNT, advertiser reach TV film deal," *The Atlanta Journal-Constitution*, 23 April 2002, D3.

14. Claire Atkinson, "Ad intrusions up, say consumers," *Advertising Age*, 6 January 2003, 1.

15. Alice Z. Cuneo, "Ace ads on 'MNF' starring Madden blur content line," *Advertising Age*, 2 September 2002, 3.

16. Ira Teinowitz, "FTC Whacks Professor Wonder," www.adage.com, 17 April 2002.

17. "FTC announces results of inspection of New York metropolitan area funeral homes for compliance with consumer protection laws," www.ftc.gov/nerfuneral, 4 April 2002.

18. "Weight-loss ads under scrutiny," *Advertising Age*, 23 September 2002, 10.

19. Arthur Winston, "How to define the concept 'free' via the FTC," *DM News*, 24 June 1996, 15.

20. Ivan Preston, *The Tangled Web They Weave* (Madison, WI: University of Wisconsin Press, 1994), 103.

21. "FTC guides concerning use of endorsements and testimonials in advertising," www.ftc.gov, 16 April 2000.

22. Jack Neff, "Drugmakers up use of celebs in ads, risking an overdose of critics' ire," *Advertising Age*, 27 May 2002, S–4.

23. David Stipp, "The big gap at the FDA," www.fortune.com, 22 July 2002.

24. Otesa Middleton and Peter Landers, "Bristol-Myers ads For leading drug must be corrected," *The Wall Street Journal*, 11 August 2003, B4.

25. Andrew B. Lustigman, "DMPEA gives USPS sweeping powers," *DM News*, 6 December 1999, 14.

26. Stephen R. Bergerson, "Supreme Court strikes a blow for commercial speech," *American Advertising*, Summer 1993, 24.

27. "High court's hard line on ad bans," *Advertising Age*, 20 May 1996, 57.

28. "Advertising alcoholic beverages," *Advertising Topics*, a publication of the Council of Better Business Bureaus, May 1996, 2.

29. "High court overturns broadcasting ban on gambling advertising," *Advertising Topics*, 14 July 1999, 1.

30. Richard Carelli, "Supreme Court rejects ban on casino ads," www.nytimes.com, 14 June 1999.

31. Linda Greenhouse, "Justices strike down ban on casino gambling ads," www.nytimes.com, 15 June 1999.

32. Ira Teinowitz, "Court ruling supports fax ads," *Advertising Age*, 1, April 2002, 8.

33. Ira Teinowitz, "FDA reviews policies on ad regulation," *Advertising Age*, 20 May 2002, 1.

34. "Much at risk in Nike case," *Advertising Age*, 21 October 2002, 24.

35. Candiss Baksa Vibbert, "Freedom of speech and corporations: Supreme Court strategies for the extension of the First Amendment," *Communications*, Vol. 12, 1990, 26.

36. Boris Becker and Dennis O. Kaldenberg, "To advertise or not to advertise? Advertising expenditures by professionals," *Proceedings of the American Academy of Advertising, 1995*, Charles S. Madden, ed.

37. Rosalind C. Truitt, "The cases for commercial speech," *Presstime*, March 1996, 31.

38. "Paxil court order undercuts FDA," *Advertising Age*, 26 August 2002, 11.

39. Sarah Ellison, "Rivals take P&G to court to challenge ads," *The Wall Street Journal*, 17 June 2003, B1.

40. Herbert J. Rotfeld, "Media standards for acceptable advertising," *Proceedings of the American Academy of Advertising, 1995*, Charles S. Madden, ed., 238.

41. Randall Smith, "For CBS, a Schwab ad wasn't must-see, as network protects Wall Street's image," *The Wall Street Journal*, 6 June 2002, C1.

42. Sheila Anthony, "Let's clean up the diet-ad mess," *Advertising Age*, 3 February 2002, 18.

43. "Screen advertisement: A guide for the media," www.ftc.gov, issued September 1998.

44. John R. Wilke, "FTC asks media to reject false ads," *The Wall Street Journal*, 20 November 2002, A3.

45. "Basic Principles of the Better Business Bureau Code of Advertising," www.bbb.org, 19, June 2002.

46. Kate MacArthur, "Gov't to mediate vodka ad dispute," *Advertising Age*, 8 September 2003, 92.

47. Eric J. Zanot, "The evolution of advertising self-regulation at the National Advertising Division and National Advertising Review Board," *Proceeding of the American Academy of Advertising, 1995*, Charles S. Madden, ed., 237.

48. *Advertising, Nutrition and, Kids*, a publication of the Council of Better Business Bureaus, Inc.

INDEX